T0361426

Routledge Handbook of Energy Economics

Energy consumption and production have major influences on the economy, environment, and society, but in return they are also influenced by how the economy is structured, how the social institutions work, and how the society deals with environmental degradation. The need for integrated assessment of the relationship between energy, economy, environment, and society is clear, and this handbook offers an in-depth review of all four pillars of the energy-economy-environment-society nexus.

Bringing together contributions from all over the world, this handbook includes sections devoted to each of the four pillars. Moreover, as the financialization of commodity markets has made risk analysis more complicated and intriguing, the sections also cover energy commodity markets and their links to other financial and non-financial markets. In addition, econometric modeling and the forecasting of energy needs, as well as energy prices and volatilities, are also explored. Each part emphasizes the multidisciplinary nature of the energy economics field and from this perspective, chapters offer a review of models and methods used in the literature.

The *Routledge Handbook of Energy Economics* will be of great interest to all those studying and researching in the area of energy economics. It offers guideline suggestions for policy makers as well as for future research.

Uğur Soytaş is a Professor in the Department of Business Administration and the Earth System Science Graduate Program at the Middle East Technical University (METU), Turkey. He is the co-editor of the *Energy Economics* journal.

Ramazan Sarı is a Professor in the Department of Business Administration, Middle East Technical University (METU), Turkey. He is the Dean of Faculty of Economics and Administrative Sciences at METU.

"This is a comprehensive handbook of energy economics that covers a broad range of issues and debates in the space of energy modelling, climate change and environment. The book will constitute a valuable resource for students, academics and policy makers working in the area of energy."

Paresh Narayan, Alfred Deakin Professor,
Deakin Business School, Deakin University, Australia

Routledge Handbook of Energy Economics

Edited by Uğur Soytaş and Ramazan Sarı

LONDON AND NEW YORK

First published 2020
by Routledge
2 Park Square, Milton Park, Abingdon, Oxon OX14 4RN

and by Routledge
605 Third Avenue, New York, NY 10017

First issued in paperback 2021

Routledge is an imprint of the Taylor & Francis Group, an informa business

Publisher's Note
The publisher has gone to great lengths to ensure the quality of this reprint but points out that some imperfections in the original copies may be apparent.

British Library Cataloguing-in-Publication Data
A catalogue record for this book is available from the British Library

Library of Congress Cataloging-in-Publication Data
A catalog record for this book has been requested

ISBN 13: 978-1-03-208919-5 (pbk)
ISBN 13: 978-1-138-20825-4 (hbk)

Typeset in Bembo
by Apex CoVantage, LLC

Contents

Contents

Figures

Tables

Contributors

Guillermo Gil Aguirrebeitia, Fundación TECNALIA Research & Innovation, Parque Tecnológico de Bizkaia, Laida Bidea

Hassan Anjum, Department of Economics, Texas Tech University

B. W. Ang, Department of Industrial Systems Engineering and Management, National University of Singapore

Nicholas Apergis, Department of Banking & Financial Management, University of Pireaus

İzzet Arı, Middle East Technical University

M. Olcay Aydemir, Middle East Technical University

Adisa Azapagic, Sustainable Industrial Systems, School of Chemical Engineering and Analytical Science, The University of Manchester

Lance J. Bachmeier, Department of Economics, Kansas State University

Jozef Baruník, Institute of Economic Studies, Charles University

Syed Abdul Basher, Department of Economics, East West University

Nina Campbell, Energy Efficiency and Conservation Authority (EECA)

Cédric Clastres, University of Grenoble-Alpes, CNRS, INRA, Grenoble-INP, GAEL

Jasmin Cooper, Sustainable Gas Institute, Imperial College London

Lillian M. de Menezes, Cass Business School

Bradley T. Ewing, Center for Energy Commerce, Texas Tech University

Magda Fontana, Dipartimento di Economia e Statistica "Cognetti de Martiis", Università di Torino

Shinichiro Fujimori, Department Environmental Engineering, Kyoto University and Center for Social and Environmental Systems Research, National Institute for Environmental Studies, Japan

Patrice Geoffron, Université Paris-Dauphine, PSL Research University, Laboratoire d'Economie de Dauphine

Tian Goh, Department of Industrial Systems Engineering and Management, Systems Engineering & Management Laboratory, National University of Singapore

Alper Gormus, Department of Economics and Finance, Texas A&M University Commerce

Martina Iori, Dipartimento di Economia e Statistica "Cognetti de Martiis", Università di Torino

Kirsten Jenkins, School of Environment and Technology, University of Brighton

Aled Jones, Global Sustainability Institute, Faculty of Science and Engineering, Anglia Ruskin University

Nikki Kantelis, Center for Energy Commerce, Texas Tech University

Bora Kat, Graduate School of Natural and Applied Sciences, Middle East Technical University

Evžen Kočenda, Institute of Information Theory and Automation, The Czech Academy of Sciences

Erik Laes, E&IS/School of Innovation Sciences, Eindhoven University of Technology

Ulrike Lehr, Institute of Economic Structures Research (GWS mbH)

Janie Ling-Chin, Sir Joseph Swan Centre for Energy Research, Newcastle University

Lan-Cui Liu, Business School, Beijing Normal University

Christian Lutz, Institute of Economic Structures Research (GWS mbH)

Farooq Malik, College of Business, Zayed University

Ken'ichi Matsumoto, Graduate School of Fisheries and Environmental Sciences, Nagasaki University

Paul Munro, School of Humanities and Languages, University of New South Wales

Saban Nazlioğlu, Department of International Trade & Finance, Pamukkale University

Özlem Özdemir, Middle East Technical University, Department of Business Administration

Jyoti Prasad Painuly, Management Engineering, Technical University of Denmark

Anna Pellizzone, National Research Council of Italy, Institute of Geosciences and Earth Resources (CNR-IGG)

Michael D. Plante, Federal Reserve Bank of Dallas Research Department

Keerthi Rajendran, Sir Joseph Swan Centre for Energy Research, Newcastle University

Travis Roach, Department of Economics, University of Central Oklahoma

Anthony P. Roskilly, Sir Joseph Swan Centre for Energy Research, Newcastle University

Lisa Ryan, UCD Energy Institute, School of Economics, University College Dublin

Perry Sadorsky, Schulich School of Business, York University, Canada

Shanil Samarakoon, School of Humanities and Languages, University of New South Wales

Suwin Sandu, School of Information, Systems and Modelling, University of Technology Sydney

Ramazan Sarı, Middle East Technical University

Alessandro Sciullo, Department of Culture Politics and Society, Università di Torino

Deepak Sharma, Centre for Energy Policy, University of Technology Sydney

Benjamin K. Sovacool, Science Policy Research Unit, University of Sussex

Uğur Soytaş, Department of Business Administration, Middle East Technical University

Laurence Stamford, Sustainable Industrial Systems, School of Chemical Engineering and Analytical Science, The University of Manchester

David I. Stern, Crawford School of Public Policy, The Australian National University

Michael Tamvakis, Cass Business School

Govinda R. Timilsina, Senior Research Economist, Development Research Group, World Bank

Richard S. J. Tol, University of Sussex, Department of Economics

Burcin Atilgan Türkmen, Bilecik Şeyh Edebali University, Department of Chemical Engineering

Karen Turner, Centre for Energy Policy, School of Government and Public Policy, University of Strathclyde

Elena Vallino, Dipartimento di Economia e Statistica "Cognetti de Martiis", Università di Torino

Contributors

Daniela Velte, Fundación TECNALIA Research & Innovation, Parque Tecnológico de San Sebastián Mikeletegi Pasealekua

Yi-Ming Wei, Center for Energy and Environmental Policy Research, Beijing Institute of Technology

Rafał Weron, Department of Operations Research, Faculty of Computer Science and Management, Wroclaw University of Science and Technology

Norbert Wohlgemuth, Department of Economics, University of Klagenfurt

Muyi Yang, School of Information, Systems and Modelling, University of Technology Sydney

Florian Ziel, Universität Duisburg-Essen

Preface

Energy markets and businesses throughout the world are undergoing considerable transformation, and energy economics as a still relatively young subdiscipline of economics has made much progress over the years. Hence this new *Handbook of Energy Economics* is timely and most welcome. It offers academics, students and practitioners in government administration and industry ready access to, and a broad coverage of, the state of the art in the most relevant fields of the energy economics literature, and it also covers many different types of modeling approaches. Given that the number of textbooks and handbooks in energy economics (and policy) is still relatively small, this is particularly useful. This holds all the more true in light of the rapidly growing body of literature, both in number of publications but also in terms of the countries or regions or data covered, making it harder and harder to maintain good oversight.

The handbook is grouped into five distinct thematic areas. Part I is quite a mixed bowl on "Energy and Economy" (including the energy-economic growth nexus), covering topics such as decomposition analysis, multi-output production function modeling, energy-output cointegration analysis, economics and policy of renewable energy sources, rebound analysis, economic modeling of the sustainable energy transition (also referred to as *"Energiewende"*), electricity market integration, and energy security. Part II focuses on "Energy and Environment". It addresses, for instance, structural patterns and developments in energy intensity, population, income and carbon mitigation technology, and policy options, but also the energy-economy-environment nexus including life-cycle analysis (LCA) and energy systems modeling. Other chapters in this part of the book address renewable energy policy from an environmental perspective, the energy-food nexus, the water-energy nexus, digitalization of the energy sector, or market-based instruments for carbon mitigation in light of the Paris Agreement. Part III is dedicated to "Energy and Society", and contains chapters on the social cost of carbon (and the trade-offs between climate change mitigation and adaptation), social acceptance, ecological economics considerations on optimal socioeconomic-ecological use of energy, taking into account equity and fairness considerations, the concept of responsible investment in energy (tackling the economic, social, and environmental dimensions of energy supply and use), and concepts of energy justice explained to energy economists (illustrated for three very distinct country case studies). Part IV looks into "Energy and Other Markets", including those for financial assets (derivatives, etc.), commodities, and foreign currency issues, but also the topic of smart grids enabling exciting new business models and markets. Finally, Part V focuses on various approaches and the state of knowledge related to "Energy Modeling" in fields of interest to both energy economists, analysts, and energy policy-makers. Among these types of models are computable general equilibrium (CGE) models, top-down and bottom-up models, macroeconometric and structural models, decomposition models, forecasting models, behavioral economics models, and multi-criteria decision analysis

(MCDA) models, among others. Covering so many topics in 39 distinct and high-quality chapters renders this handbook a real treasure trove.

Many prominent scholars and young talents have contributed to this new handbook in light of the many remaining challenges towards truly sustainable energy transition pathways and the combat of anthropogenic climate change and its potentially dreadful consequences for mankind and other life on our planet. It presents a wide range of state-of-the-art literature reviews of topics, methodologies, and modeling approaches that will facilitate students and professionals to find their way in analyzing and better understand real-world energy markets, problems, issues, and phenomena. I am convinced that it has the potential to spread widely, educating people all over the world about the multi-faceted field of energy economics and related areas, such as environmental and behavioral sciences but also energy and climate policy.

Aachen, January 2019

Reinhard Madlener
Full Professor of Energy Economics and Management,
School of Business and Economics,
RWTH Aachen University, Aachen, Germany

Introduction

Uğur Soytaş and Ramazan Sarı

Energy consumption and production have major influences on the economy, environment, and society, but in return they are also influenced by how the economy is structured, how the social institutions work, and how the society deals with environmental degradation. Without environmental and social dimensions, economics of energy will not be complete. The need for integrated assessment of the relationship between energy, economy, environment, and society is apparent. Energy policy makers face the challenge of meeting a diverse set of criteria in these four dimensions. This handbook offers an in-depth review of all four pillars of the energy-economy-environment-society nexus. To that respect, a theme is reserved for each pillar. The handbook also attempts to provide a review of models and methods used in the literature from this multidisciplinary perspective.

Furthermore, this handbook also covers energy commodity markets and their links to other financial and non-financial markets. Energy commodity, energy derivatives, electricity, and carbon markets are receiving increased attention in both applied and academic work. The financialization of commodity markets have made the risk analysis more complicated and more intriguing. Hence, econometric modeling and forecasting of energy needs as well as energy prices and volatilities deserve a place in this handbook. The handbook also aims to cover studies incorporating advances in modeling, methodological frameworks, and forecasting methods.

In all parts of the handbook, the emphasis is on the multidisciplinary nature of the energy economics field. Each chapter also provides guidelines and suggestions for policy makers as well as for future research. This *Handbook of Energy Economics* aims to achieve a lot, and the collection of excellent contributions from all around the world ensures that they are met as best as possible.

Part 1: energy and economy

The first part of the handbook is allocated to the link between energy and economy. It purposefully includes a variety of chapters. While some of the chapters refer to historical developments and current trends in energy variables through statistical projections, others review the theoretical and empirical studies that investigate the link between energy and the macroeconomy.

In the first chapter, Timilsina starts with a very informative decompositions of energy demand by source, by country, and by industry. He explains what energy demand statistics reflect and discusses the drivers of energy demand. He provides a brief historical perspective and the role of IEA. Then concludes with projections and estimates for future energy demand, which is consistently rising over time. His projections show that energy demand will keep on rising with no definite saturation or turning point in the near future.

Following the energy demand chapter, Stern's chapter lays out the theoretical framework for the energy-output nexus. He lists and discusses factors that affect the link between energy and

1

GDP growth, from the perspective of a multi-output production function and explains how energy intensity declined while energy demand increased over time. Energy and economic growth link depend on factors such as substitutability between energy and other factors of production, shifts in energy and other inputs as well as in output composition, technological change and economies of scale. Stern explains the theoretical developments in ecological economics and classical economics regarding the energy-output link based on these factors. He also reviews the empirical literature that uses Granger causality and cointegration. Although there is no consensus in the literature, a stylized fact that growth leads energy use emerges when energy prices are taken into account. He points out that there are large gaps in scientific knowledge on the energy use and economic growth link. This chapter shows the importance of incorporating energy in economic models.

As Stern mentions in his chapter, energy prices play an important role in the energy-economic growth link. In addition to economic growth, there are other macroeconomic concerns such as inflation and unemployment that are affected by energy prices. Bachmeier and Plante build up their oil prices and the macroeconomy chapter on this fact. They lay out the important aspects of the broad literature on the economic consequences of oil price shocks and point out where more work is needed. Their chapter is composed of two parts. The first part deals with the empirical VAR literature, whereas the second part reviews the DSGE models. The discussions and evaluations of the two approaches are complementary rather than comparative. However, particularly, the presentation of the DSGE model development steps are very straightforward and educational in incorporating oil into the model.

Energy mix is an important factor in determining the link between energy and economy. As renewable energy shares in global energy mix increase, more attention is diverted to the economics of renewable energy. Painuly and Wohlgemuth discuss various renewable energy sources along with their investment prospects and costs over time. They discuss the efficiency and effectiveness issues in renewable energy policy and point out the importance of technical, social, political, and cultural factors that influence the diffusion of these energy sources. More information and appropriate policy support may be necessary to overcome the barriers and smoothly phase out fossil fuels globally.

Ryan, Turner, and Campbell's chapter focuses on energy efficiency, economic growth, and economy-wide rebound effect. They explain how we can minimize rebound effects of energy efficiency actions without hampering economic growth. In that respect, this chapter puts final touches on the picture painted by previous chapters on the energy and economy nexus.

The energy transition has been going on for a while. Although complete phasing out of fossil fuels is not expected to occur soon, the gradual transition process shows signs of increasing pace as technology advances rapidly and social barriers for renewable energy sources are resolved. This energy transition is by itself an important factor that influences economies worldwide. To account for the impacts of the energy transition, one must utilize appropriate models. Lutz and Lehr provide an excellent review of models on the economic impacts of energy transition. Various macroeconomic effects including price, income, trade relations, multiplier, learning, market, and productivity effects are considered. While this chapter reviews effects of energy transition estimated by various models, chapters in the energy modeling part discuss these models in more details. Lutz and Lehr conclude that to account for effects of mitigation and energy transition there is a need for integrating bottom-up and top-down models. Kat's chapter reviews this model integration issue in Part V of this handbook.

De Menezes and Tamvakis review the literature on electricity market integration. They point out the benefits from market integration but add that there are more expected benefits from integration of electricity markets. These benefits vary in magnitude depending on interconnectedness of markets among other things. The chapter summarizes the studies on American, Asia/Pacific, and European markets separately. Studies usually concentrate on price convergence due to the law of one price, but the methodologies vary a lot. Different methodologies used in energy economics literature are discussed in the relevant chapters of this handbook. The review also includes some studies on price convergence between electricity and other energy markets, which is explored in more detail in Part IV of this handbook. As Prasad and Wohlgemuth's chapter points out, the share of renewables in energy mixes of countries is increasing, and De Menezes and Tamvakis reserve an entire section for the role of renewables in market integration. In their conclusion, they provide an overview of the role of market integration in the energy policies of different countries.

Energy security is one of the most important aims of energy policy and countries can take different measures to ensure security, which in turn may influence the macroeconomy. Sharma, Sandu, and Yang discuss the macroeconomic impact of energy security improvements in seven Asian countries (China, India, Indonesia, Japan, Korea, Malaysia, and Thailand). They use the estimated impacts for Asia. The macroeconomic impacts of three scenarios are presented in this chapter: country policy, country aspiration, and sustainable development. There seems to be a trade-off between socioeconomic benefits and energy security policies. Hence a better understanding of the impact of energy security improvements is needed. The estimation methodology is presented in more detail in the relevant energy modeling chapter in this handbook.

Part 2: energy and environment

It is not possible to talk about energy and economy links without taking environmental issues into account. The major environmental problem associated with energy is climate change. Important mitigation and adaptation issues are covered by chapters included in this section.

The economics of climate change requires a special treatment, and Tol does a great job in doing so. Tol uses the Kaya identity to show patterns in energy intensity, population, and income under alternative scenarios. The scenarios are enriched by links to relevant literature including fertility and mortality, energy efficiency, rebound effect, and reserves. The chapter also includes a discussion of emission reduction technologies ranging from various renewables to carbon capture and storage and costs of emission mitigation options. Finally, the chapter reviews the climate policy literature, explains why models generate diverse results with varying cost estimates, and presents main determinants of climate policy costs. Tol argues that carbon tax is the most appropriate climate policy and may even generate benefits with appropriate fiscal reforms financed by this tax revenue.

While Tol's chapter covers scenarios in a global scale, Wei and Liu discuss carbon emissions and energy use in countries at different levels of economic development and emissions from different energy sources. They lay out the landscape for climate mitigation from the perspective of high-income, middle-income, and low-income country categories and show the similarities and differences in income, carbon intensity, and energy use statistics among these categories. They provide strategies that could be followed by countries in these three categories to meet absolute, incremental, and conditional emission reduction targets of the Paris Agreement, respectively.

The energy, economy, and environment chapter by Ling-Chi, Rajendran, and Roskilly provides a framework through which the dynamic links in this nexus can be viewed. They primarily focus on the interdisciplinary nature of energy systems modeling and cover topics such as economic and environmental costs and societal concerns. The chapter discusses techniques for measuring economic costs and environmental life cycle analysis. It also shows that economic, technological, environmental, and societal assessments have different spatial scales but are very interdependent in energy systems modeling, creating challenges for policy makers and researchers. The chapter paves the way for the energy modeling part of this handbook by providing a simple categorization of energy economic models (Markal, TIMES etc.) along with brief descriptions of models used in economic analysis ranging from input-output to multiagent models. Chin et al. conclude by emphasizing the need for a generic framework for model integration to facilitate more accurate analysis and appropriate policies.

Transition to renewables has a key role in climate change mitigation, but there are important policy challenges that need to be addressed appropriately. Roach provides a review of renewable energy policy. The chapter explains how renewable energy policy evolved and also takes up the efficacy of various renewable policies. The chapter distinguishes between standards set for the electricity and the transportation sectors and also discusses indirect effects of policies on emissions. While reviewing the impacts of various renewable energy policies, the chapter points out the doubt on the efficacy of ethanol standards and mentions possible adverse impacts on food prices especially in developing countries. The energy-food nexus is reviewed in more detail in Nazlioglu's chapter under the energy and other markets part of this handbook.

Climate change is not the only adverse environmental impact related to energy. Sovacool explains the interconnection between water, energy production, and conversion. The chapter includes one section on water and energy pollution and one section on other externalities related to water use. The reader will benefit from the detailed discussion of how water and energy are related. This chapter clearly shows that the water-energy nexus creates as big a challenge as climate change and there is an immediate need for more research into how water constraints may influence energy production.

Clastres and Geoffron point out that the energy transition towards renewables requires digitization of the energy sector. Effective management of the digitalized energy system needs a diverse set of smart-grid technologies, ranging from smart meters to electric vehicle charges, to be utilized at the production, transmission, and distribution stages. Smart grids create opportunities for all participants along the energy supply chain, but deployment is not free from problems. The chapter clearly shows that effective development, deployment, and diffusion of such technologies requires input from diverse disciplines across STEM and SSH. The regulatory framework for smart grids also creates overlapping areas for energy and communications authorities. The chapter includes a section on public acceptance of smart-grid technologies, a concept which is discussed in more detail in the relevant chapters under the social issues part of this handbook. Clastres and Geoffron conclude that although smart grids can help towards attaining climate targets, consumer behavior, among others, remains to be an important source of uncertainty and more research in this area is necessary.

Arı and Sarı state that the United Nations Framework Convention on Climate Change, the Kyoto Protocol, and the Paris Agreement encourage using market-based instruments. As a market-based instrument, carbon pricing such as carbon taxes and carbon trading ensures cost-effective emissions mitigation. Article 6 of the Paris Agreement promotes global carbon pricing and provides new opportunities to involve all countries' emissions reduction in line with their Nationally Determined Contributions. Their study analyzes Article 6 of the Agreement and negotiations on rules, procedures, and modalities about new global carbon pricing for reducing emissions and creating new financial resources.

Part 3: energy and society

Energy challenges require a transdisciplinary approach which is reflected throughout the entire handbook. This part of the handbook is particularly reserved for a dimension that gained track recently: social issues. The chapters in this part of the handbook deal with a variety of concepts that may be of interest to various social sciences and humanities disciplines, since they tap topics ranging from perceptions and attitudes to behavior.

Tol points out the policy dilemma: should we mitigate or adapt to climate change? The answer to this question depends heavily on the social cost of carbon. Tol first provides a conceptual discussion, starting with a distinction between "weather" and "climate", and then critically reviews the studies that estimate the social cost of carbon. The review shows that estimates vary a lot, partly due to a variety of models employed and assumptions made. The chapter includes an application with supplied MATLAB code that can be replicated by interested readers. The chapter shows that "a century of climate change is approximately equivalent to losing a decade of economic growth".

Scuillo and Pellizzone emphasize the need for engaging citizens and stakeholders for a smoother transition towards contemporary energy systems. They first examine the sociopolitical, community, and market dimensions of social acceptance to identify the determinants. They point out that these determinants can be used in a broader model of public engagement. They conclude by discussing the direct and indirect effects of an institutionalized public engagement policy.

Following the ideas developed on the theory of justice, Aydemir and Soytaş point out a need for reducing energy use, even if energy needs are completely met by renewables, and attempt to develop a new approach for measuring the appropriate cap for energy use. In line with ecological economics principles, they argue that the main goal of energy use should be quality of life and there exists a curvilinear link between energy use and well-being. They propose an approach to obtain the level of energy use after which contributions to well-being are negligible. They first select an appropriate functional form that allows for saturation. Then they use the "knee" concept mainly used in STEM disciplines to find the point of maximum curvature. Above this point, the marginal contribution of energy use on quality of life are very low. They call this point of maximum curvature the "fair energy use level", as the quality of life indicators account not only for ecological and economic concerns but also social concerns such as equity and fairness.

Jones explores the importance of responsible investment in energy during a large-scale transition from a fossil-fuel-based economy to one predominately supported by low carbon technologies. He points out that estimates for necessary investment to achieve energy transition targets reach $1 trillion per annum. He discusses both specific and general approaches in the search for responsible investment, tapping economic, environmental and societal dimensions underlying this concept. The scale of change is compared to a new industrial revolution, and responsible investment is an outcome of the need for change in investment structure.

Jenkins, Samarakoon, and Munro argue that energy transformations have economic and equity consequences and thus introduce the energy justice concept to those interested in energy economics. In this respect, theoretically discrete but practically interlinked procedural, distributional and recognition tenets of energy justice are introduced to the potentially new audience. Three case studies, from Malawi, Mexico and Germany – one for each tenet – illustrate the complexity of energy justice and difficulty with which it can be utilized in energy economics and energy transitions. They conclude that a system of redistribution and equitable access that is conscious of the competing visions of different social groups and achieved in a democratic way is true energy justice.

Part 4: energy and other markets

There is an immense literature exploring the price and risk transmission between energy and other markets. The "other" markets include various financial assets, commodities, and currencies. Since the literature is voluminous, most of the chapters in this part focus on the link between oil and other markets. The selected topics represent areas where more future research is needed and where new developments are observed. Furthermore, some chapters also cover the methodological intricacies and empirical aspects. In that respect, this part also complements the energy modeling part of this handbook.

This part of the handbook starts with a chapter on oil spot and futures prices. Kantelis and Ewing provide an excellent overview of historical development of these markets and point out major findings in the literature on the time series dynamics of these prices. The chapter includes an empirical application which confirms major findings in the literature and provides new insights. The chapter concludes by pointing out potential areas for future research.

Kantelis and Ewing's chapter shows the evolution of oil spot and futures prices. Partly due to structural changes and evolution in oil prices, the link between oil and financial asset markets has become richer. This extensive and rich literature is summarized by Sadorsky. He first lays out the conceptual framework by explaining the channels by which the two markets are linked. Then he summarizes the studies that employ various multivariable methods ranging from VARs and SVARs to copulas, wavelets, and switching models. The stylized findings of these studies are presented along with methodological intricacies. In the conclusions section, he points out practical, policy, and future research implications.

Oil market has an impact on the economy through not only prices but also volatilities. Apergis conducts an extensive review of the literature on how volatility in oil markets influence macroeconomic and financial variables. Separate sections are reserved for growth, stock markets, exchange rates, inflation, fiscal policy, and institutional variables. The chapter also covers econometric aspects of oil price volatility and empirical aspects of the asymmetric impact of volatility. Apergis concludes by stating the importance of oil volatility for real economic activity and financial asset markets and by suggesting interesting avenues for future research.

Gormus extends the energy discussion into mutual funds (MFs), a recently emerging field in the literature. He first shows how interest in MFs increased over time. Then he argues that both investors and fund managers need to closely follow energy markets, since a few studies that look into the interaction between the two markets show significant price and volatility spillovers. The chapter also focuses on specialized MFs, especially energy mutual funds (EMFs), and argues that as interest soars, more research will be needed in this area.

Oil is one of the major energy commodities and there is a vast literature on how fluctuations in oil prices influence other energy commodities. Basher effectively summarizes this extensive literature. The chapter starts with historical developments in coal, natural gas, and gasoline prices paralleling the oil price movements. Then empirical work on the linkages are presented. Complementing Kantelis and Ewing's chapter on oil spot and futures, Basher discusses how the spot and futures prices framework, market integration, and tail risks are handled by studies on energy commodity market interactions.

Although Nazlıoğlu's chapter seems to focus on energy and agricultural market linkages, he starts with a brief explanation of the general literature on all commodities. After this general introduction, he explains the main drivers of agricultural commodity prices from both the demand and supply sides. Then he sets up the framework via which energy and food markets are linked. An extensive review of the key studies in the empirical literature is provided. While summarizing the studies, Nazlıoğlu also provides some methodological comparisons and tips which may be useful for future researchers. The chapter concludes by providing an extensive list of implications for investors, policy makers, and researchers.

Anjum and Malik set out the theoretical framework and discuss the channels through which exchange rates and oil markets interact. Then they provide a comprehensive review of the studies on the link between the two markets. A simple Granger causality application, which shows a negative link between returns which increases in magnitude over time, is also included in the chapter.

The US dollar is the main currency used in world oil markets. It is only natural that the value of dollar and oil price is closely linked. In addition to correlated prices, as also mentioned by Anjum Malik in the previous chapter, there is also a risk transmission channel through which the two markets interact. Baruník and Kočenda discuss the volatility and frequency connectedness of oil and forex markets. The asymmetry of the dynamic links between the two markets are accounted for. They consider speculation and financialization of oil markets as possible sources of this asymmetry. They provide a connectedness analysis between the oil market and the Australian dollar, Canadian dollar, British pound, euro, Japanese yen, and Swiss franc using the volatility spillover index. They also present the methodology they used in a clear way that enables the reader to replicate.

Velte and Aguirrebeitia discuss role of smart grids (SG) in energy transition. They point out that digitization and decentralized production bring new opportunities and meet some economic and social challenges. Although digitization increases the complexity of energy systems, it also leads to a massive amount of data collection in real time, and hence SG is an excellent venue for big data analysis. The digitized channels established in a SG may benefit existing service providers in developing new services and reaching consumers but may also act as entry deterrents to new entrants. The chapter provides interesting examples of pilot projects across the EU. The chapter concludes that an essential factor in effective SG implementation is end-user motivation and behavior. Households for example are not willing to hand over the control of their appliances to third parties. The public acceptance/resistance issue is discussed further in the energy and society chapters in this handbook.

Part 5: energy modeling

In energy research various methodologies are employed. Depending on the research question, studies follow different frameworks even if the method is the same. The multidisciplinary nature of energy research more often than not calls for integrated frameworks. This part aims to provide a selective coverage of energy modeling tools taking this aspect into consideration.

Matsumoto and Fujimori start with an introduction to CGE models. They provide the intuition behind CGE models used in energy economics and also discuss strengths and weaknesses of these models. They distinguish between country versus global and static versus dynamic models. A full section is reserved for literature review of CGE applications in energy economics. This section shows the intricacies and complications in using CGE in the field of energy economics. The concluding section sheds light on the future of research in this area.

Sharma, Sandu, and Yang presented the macroeconomic impact of energy security improvements in Asia in their chapter in the first part of this handbook. Here, they provide a step by step guideline for the methodology they used in that chapter (see Figure 1.1 for a clear presentation of the entire methodology). This chapter starts with introducing impact attributes and integration of socioeconomic and energy security domains. Then scenario descriptions and model structure follow. The chapter also explains how to develop indices to facilitate the analysis. This chapter can be a very good starting point for developing a model for energy security impact assessment in other countries.

The previous two chapters on CGE models show the need for a more integrated approach to energy modeling. Kat's chapter does a perfect job in discussing developments in integration of top-down and bottom-up (also known as engineering or partial equilibrium) models. The chapter starts by laying out the foundation for the two modeling paradigms and discusses how this modeling literature evolved. The shortcomings of both paradigms lead to the idea of coming up with a model that integrates both approaches. The chapter presents a clear definition of two approaches of integration, soft (informal) links and hard (formal) links, with examples from the literature. Kat concludes the need for developing hybrid models that address recent technological improvements and environmental concerns.

The chapter by Lutz and Lehr is a very good follow-up to the previous chapters. They discuss the intricacies of macroeconometric (structural) models in the environment-economy-energy nexus. They provide excellent examples from Germany, the European Union and the United States and discuss the macroeconomic results of these applications. The chapter concludes by a brief discussion of opportunities and challenges for future macroeconometric modeling.

Goh and Ang discuss the latest developments in index decomposition analysis (IDA). Quantifying factors that determine energy demand is essential for designing appropriate policies. IDA is one of the most frequently used tools that breaks down energy use into several predetermined factors. The chapter talks about different indicator types and decomposition methods and procedures. There is a section that illustrates how emissions can be incorporated in IDA, and a case study that compares performances of OECD and non-OECD countries is also provided. The authors also discuss application areas for IDA, such as understanding drivers of energy use and emissions, tracking energy efficiency and cross-country comparisons among others. The chapter also presents intricacies and tips which are useful guidelines for using IDA. Future prospects are provided in the conclusion.

Another chapter that emphasizes the multidisciplinary nature of energy research is by Weron and Ziel. They argue that electricity price forecasting requires a mixture of econometrics and engineering. They provide an excellent summary of the literature by discussing different forecast horizons, forecast types, and forecast models. They also include a section on evaluation of forecasting performance. This chapter is a must read for both practitioners and scholars who are interested in forecasting electricity prices.

Sciullo, Vallino, Iori, and Fontana consider energy systems as complex adaptive systems. In order to reflect the complexity in energy systems modeling, processes such as technology diffusion and innovation as well as individual motives that drive behavior must be accounted for. The chapter presents agent-based modeling (ABM) as an increasingly relevant and multidisciplinary approach that can account for these factors. Compared to other tools, the authors argue that ABM is an appropriate tool in social science that addresses three challenges: heterogeneity, nonlinearity, and path dependence. The authors provide a clear, step-by-step description of how ABM can be designed and applied. ABM and network analysis allow integration of complex dynamic links between physical infrastructure, market actors, and the social environment whose interactions drive energy markets.

Although behavioral economics is a relatively new branch of economics to dive into energy research, the amount of research studies accumulated in the literature is impressive. Özdemir does an excellent job to condense and summarize this large literature in one chapter. She starts with why behavioral economics has received increasing interest in general, then points out key principles that are applied in energy market studies. The literature review has two parts. The first part summarizes the household behavior, while the second one concentrates on the workplace. The chapter has important implications for policy makers and future research.

Laes discusses the role of foresight in energy policy. The chapter presents the most important factors for scenario development. The chapter starts with a constructivist view of energy foresight and continues with different foresight methods. Following on the top-down and bottom-up approaches discussed in the previous chapters of this handbook, the role of scenarios is presented in the methodological process architecture. The conclusion stresses that there is no single best approach, and tailor-made scenarios are necessary to address specific problems and policy needs.

Since energy policy making taps into several aspects of economic and social life, sound and sustainable policy making depends on many and sometimes conflicting criteria. In this respect, this chapter fits perfectly to the multi-disciplinary focus of this handbook, and that is why we wanted to conclude the handbook with this chapter. The environmental, economic, and social criteria are so diverse in nature and measurement characteristics that Stamford, Atılgan Türkmen, Cooper, and Azapagic compare energy policy making to a game of chess, where each move has an impact on the outcome. The chapter does an excellent job in explaining the role of multi-criteria decision analysis (MCDA) in energy policy. Using illustrative examples, the chapter provides almost hands-on guidance for MCDA modelers. The authors also point out strengths, weaknesses, and caveats of MCDA. MCDA seems to be emerging as a promising tool that can treat various objective and subjective criteria simultaneously.

Energy economics is at the core of the solutions to many global challenges we face today. This handbook emphasizes this important role by showing the multidisciplinary nature of energy research and a diverse set of methodologies in the field. We hope that both scholars and graduate students find this handbook a valuable reference for understanding the energy economics field and a useful guideline for their research.

The contributors to this handbook are prominent figures or promising scholars in the field. We are grateful to all of them for their valuable chapters. We also would like to express our deepest thanks to people from Taylor & Francis: Andy Humphries for inviting us to work on the handbook, Anna Cuthbert and Marie L. Roberts for their support throughout the editorial process, and the production team for their efforts.

Part I
Energy and economy

Energy demand

Govinda R. Timilsina

1 Introduction

Energy is a vital input to economic development and human well-being (Goldstein et al. 1997; Csereklyei et al. 2016). In the absence of access to modern energy resources (electricity, petroleum), the economic development achieved today would not have occurred. Similarly, human life has become so dependent on energy – particularly electricity – that human survival would be extremely difficult if not impossible in the absence of energy, especially in developed countries. Being a basic need of the economic growth and social welfare, energy demand increases along with increasing economic growth and improved quality of life or living standards.

Energy demand has been ever increasing along with economic growth and its role in economic development has remained critical over the last two centuries (Goldstein et al. 1997; Stern and Kander 2012). Many economic historians believe that coal was one of the key drivers of industrial revolution in Britain (Church 1986). Since 1971, when the International Energy Agency (IEA), the energy wing of the Organisation of Economic Co-operation and Development (OECD), started to keep a systematic account of energy production, trade, and consumption, quantitative evidence suggests that energy demand is very closely following economic growth, measured in terms of gross domestic product (GDP). Based on a calculation later in this chapter using energy and economic data compiled by the OECD for more than 150 countries around the world, we have observed that each percentage change in GDP drives a 0.7% change in energy demand, on average, over the 45 years from 1971 to 2014.

Energy commodities are derived from various primary sources. Electricity is generated from hydro, nuclear, wind, and solar resources. Coal, crude oil, and natural gas are derived from energy mining or exploration/drilling. Biomass (e.g. fuelwood) is harvested from forest resources. Energy resources, thus derived directly from mother nature, are called 'primary energy' resources in the energy literature. Not all primary energy resources as such are useful to provide energy services; they require physical or chemical conversion from one form to another before being useful for energy services (e.g. heat, light). The conversion process is called 'energy transformation'. Generation of electricity from coal, refining of crude oil to produce various products (e.g. gasoline, diesel, kerosene, fuel oil), processing of raw natural gas, and conversion of wood to charcoal are some examples of energy transformation. The energy commodities derived through the transformation process are referred to as 'secondary energy' commodities. Electricity and heat could be both primary and secondary, depending on how they are derived. For example, electricity generated by using natural resources directly, such as from hydro, nuclear, solar, and wind, is primary electricity, whereas thermal electricity generated burning fossil fuels or biomass is secondary electricity.

Energy is used in various final demand sectors such as residential, industry, commercial/service, transport, and agriculture. The demand for energy for final consumption is referred to as 'final energy demand'. It does not account for energy consumption during the transformation process, such as consumption of coal for electricity generation. The difference between the primary energy consumption and final energy consumption is that the former accounts for all consumption of energy including at the transformation stage and at the final consumption stage, whereas the latter does not account for consumption for the transformation purpose. The definition of energy consuming sectors in the energy statistics are different from the economic statistics used in standard national accounts. For example, the household sector in the national accounts covers everything used by the households (e.g. fuel wood for cooking, gasoline for cars, electricity for televisions); the household or residential sector in the energy account does not include energy consumption for transportation. Energy consumption for transportation, no matter who uses the transportation services (household, governments, industry) is included in the transport sector. All energy consumption excluding those for transportation by commercial/service enterprises other than manufacturing, mining, and construction is included in the 'commercial/service' sector. Energy consumption in the mining, manufacturing, and construction activities is covered by the 'industrial sector'. Energy consumption in agricultural, forestry, and fishery activities is sometimes included in a separate 'agricultural' sector or in the industrial sector, depending on the convention practiced in a country.

Energy commodities are also used as raw materials in industry. For example, use of natural gas for fertilization production, or the use of petroleum products for production of chemicals and plastics. They are reported in energy statistics as 'non-energy' consumption. Energy consumed by international aviation and marine transportation is separately accounted as 'bunker fuels' and is excluded from transport sector energy consumption of a particular country.

Within a given sector, energy commodities are used for various purposes. For example, in the residential and commercial/service sectors, they are used for cooking, water heating, home heating, lighting, air conditioning and ventilation, refrigeration, and electrical/electronic devices such as television and computers. These energy services (heating, cooking, lighting, etc.) are referred to as 'end-use energy services'.

This chapter briefly discusses global energy demand from a historical perspective over the 45 years since 1971, when the IEA started a systematic reporting of energy statistics. This is followed by key drivers of energy demand, particularly in the long run. The chapter also discusses methodologies used and estimates made on future energy demand by well-known institutions, and finally it draws key conclusions.

2   Global energy demand – the historical trends

Global energy demand has increased at an average growth rate of 2% per year over the last 45 years (1970–2014). During this period, the highest annual average growth rate observed during the 1970s (3%) followed by the first decade of the 2000s (2.5%).

Figure 1.1 presents the fuel mix to supply global energy demand over the last 45 years. It is interesting to note that the mix of fuels to meet the primary energy demand has not changed significantly over the time period. In 1971, fossil fuels (coal, oil, and natural gas) accounted for 86% of the global energy demand; this has slightly decreased to 81% by 2014. The share of non-fossil fuels (i.e. biomass and waste, nuclear, hydro, and new and renewables such as solar, wind,

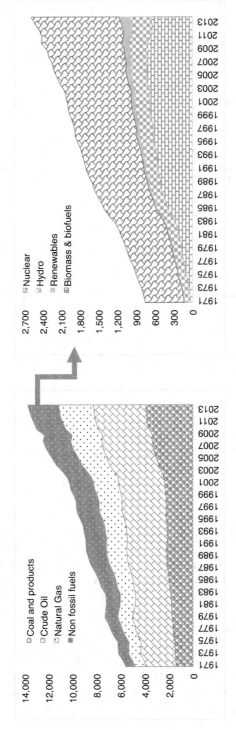

Figure 1.1 Global energy demand by fuel type (Mtoe)

Source: OECD (2017).

and geothermal) in the total primary energy demand has slightly increased from 14% in 1971 to 19% in 2014. It is worth noting that although the importance of new and renewable energy sources (i.e. solar, wind, and geothermal) has increased substantially to address global climate change, their contribution to the global energy supply is still insignificant, at 1% in 2014. This fact indicates the scale of the efforts that are needed to have significant substitution of fossil fuels with new and renewable energy sources.

Oil is one of the largest sources of energy supply, accounting for 32% of the global energy requirement. Its share was much bigger in the past. Until 1980, oil used to contribute more than 40% of the global primary energy demand. Despite the increasing pressure to cut coal use to address climate change, the share of coal in the total primary energy supply is increasing, from 24% in 1973 to 29% in 2014. The share of coal and oil would have been much higher in the absence of increased exploration and better economics of natural gas, whose share has continuously increased over the last 45 years, from 16% in 1971 to 21% in 2014. Natural gas has substituted for oil in industrial applications and coal for power generation.

Among the non-fossil fuel energy resources, the share of hydro and biomass and waste in total primary energy demand remained the same (2% and 10%, respectively) over the last 45 years. The share of nuclear peaked during the 1995–2002 period, with 7% of the global energy supply; however, it has decreased since then and stayed at 5% in 2014.

Figure 1.2 illustrates the evolution of energy demand growth of developed (OECD) and developing (non-OECD) countries. Until the year 2004, OECD countries used to consume more energy than non-OECD countries. However, their share of global energy consumption was continuously deceasing. It decreased from 61% in 1971 to 52% by 1990 and to 38% by 2014. On the other hand, the share of non-OECD countries continuously increased and surpassed the OECD countries in 2005, while non-OECD and OECD countries accounted for 36% and 61%, respectively, of the global energy demand in 1971. The situation has reversed by 2014, with non-OECD countries' share at 59% and OECD countries' share at 38%. Rapid economic growth in non-OECD countries driven by industrialization, along with urbanization and motorization, has played the role behind this. Among the non-OECD countries, China alone is responsible for almost 40% of the total non-OECD energy consumption. Other Asia (excluding China) is not far behind, with 22% of the total non-OECD energy consumption. On the other hand, the share of Africa in total non-OECD energy consumption remained almost the same over the last 45 years at around 10%. The same is true for non-OECD America (Latin America and the Caribbean, excluding Mexico which is an OECD member) with 8% to 10% share in the total non-OECD energy consumption during the last 45 years.

In the case of OECD countries, not a significant change in terms of energy consumption was observed over the last 45 years. The share of OECD America in total OECD energy consumption is almost the same (around 50%) over the time period. The share of OECD Europe in total OECD energy slightly decreased from 37% in 1971 to 32% in 2014. The share of other OECD increased due to inclusion of new countries (e.g. South Korea) in the group. It is, however, interesting to note that total energy consumption in OECD peaked in 2007 at 5,555 Mtoe and stabilized since then at a slightly lower level, at around 5,300 Mtoe.

Another interesting fact is that the sectoral mix of final energy demand has not changed over the last 45 years at the global level (see Figure 1.3). For example, the share of the residential sector in total final energy demand was 27% in 1971, whereas it slightly decreased to 25% in 2014. There does not exist any historical pattern (i.e. continuously increasing or decreasing over time) of final energy demand for a given sector; instead it increased in some years and decreased in others. The share of the industrial sector (which includes agriculture and forestry sectors) in the global final energy demand decreased from 39% in 1971 to 35% in 2014; on the other hand, the share of the

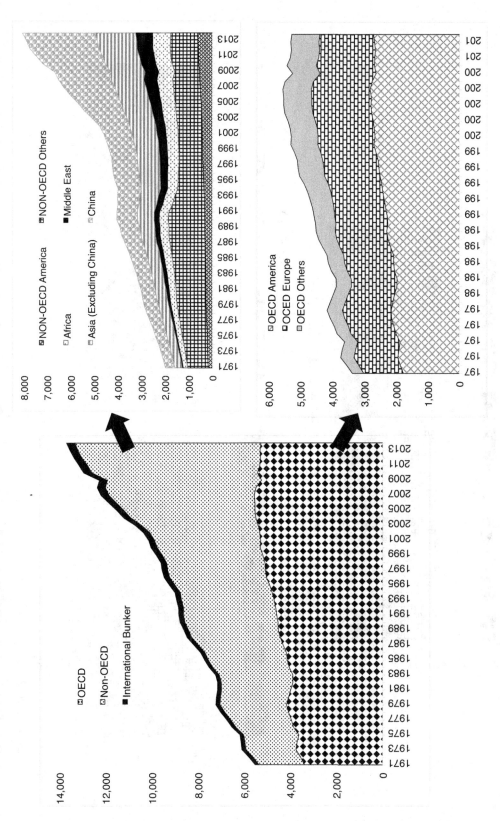

Figure 1.2 Global energy demand by economic blocks/geographical region or countries (Mtoe)

Source: OECD (2017).

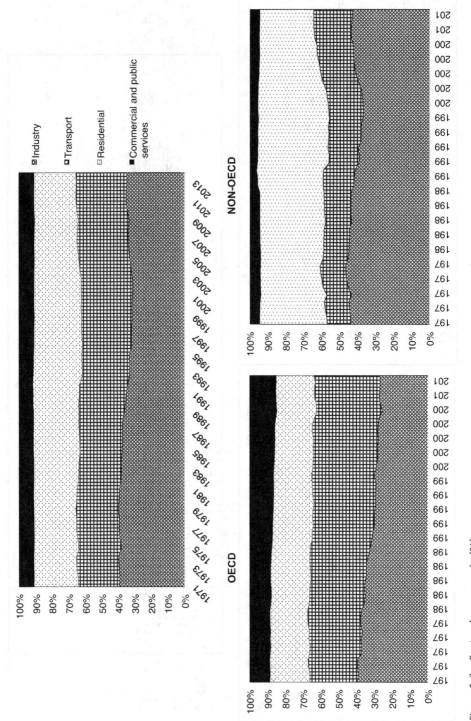

Figure 1.3   Sectoral energy mix (%)
Source: OECD (2017).

transport sector increased to 31% in 2014 from 25% in 1971. Note, however, that the transport sector share in the global final energy demand has remained flat at around 30% over the last 20 years.

In developed countries (i.e. OECD countries), significant changes have occurred in the sectoral energy mix. Increased motorization, especially during the 1975–1995 period, has substantially substituted energy consumption in the industrial sector with that in the transport sector. While the industry sector share in OECD countries' total final energy demand decreased from 40% in 1975 to 30% in 1995, the transport sector share increased from 29% in 1975 to 35% in 1995. The shares of residential and commercial sectors remained stagnant during the 1971–2014 period.

In the case of developing countries (non-OECD countries), the transport sector has played a greater role in driving total energy demand as its share has increased from 13% in 1971 to 22% in 2014. The increasing of the transport sector share started in the early 1990s. The shares of industrial sector went up and down, slightly increased during the 1970s, decreased during the 1980–2000 period and started to increase again. Interestingly, the share of the residential sector in developing countries total final energy demand has significantly decreased after 2000, from 40% in 2002 to 30% in 2014. This is contrary to several studies (e.g. Wolfram et al. 2012) which argued energy consumption in developing countries has increased due to rapid increase in use of energy, specifically electricity appliances caused by increased household income, thereby driving their total energy consumption and GHG emissions. However, as illustrated in Figure 1.3, this argument is untrue.

3 Drivers of energy demand

Energy demand is driven by different factors. In the long run, two factors (population growth and economic growth) are mainly responsible for changes in energy demand. The long-term factors are used to expand production capacity for energy generation, such as installed capacity of power generation and pipeline capacities for natural gas transportation. On the other hand, factors such as weather (e.g. heating or cooling degree days), energy prices, specific events (e.g. World Cup football matches) determine energy demand in the short run. Short-run factors basically affect the utilization of installed capacities to generate energy.

Figure 1.4 plots the indices of economic growth and population growth along with that of total primary energy demand at the global level over the last 45 years. The figure illustrates that

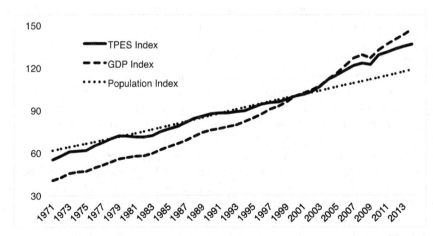

Figure 1.4 Key drivers for energy demand: economic growth and population growth

Note: Data to calculate these indices are from OECD online database. Indices for year 2000 are 100.

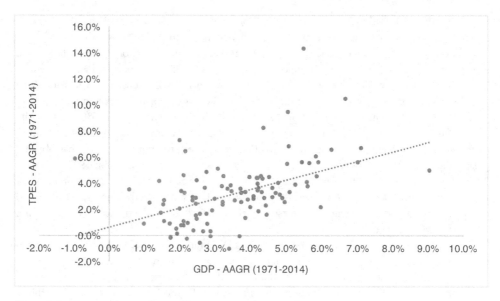

Figure 1.5　Energy demand growth vs. economic growth

Note: Data to calculate the energy-GDP elasticity are taken from OECD online database. Countries for which entire data series for the 1971–2014 period are not available (e.g. former Soviet republics, former Yugoslav republics, which exist as independent countries only after 1990) are not included.

growth of total energy demand follows economic growth and population growth. A closer look reveals that energy demand, in fact, follows GDP growth very closely. This fact is further illustrated in Figure 1.5 where average annual growth rates of energy demand in various countries over the last 45 years are plotted against corresponding economic growth (i.e. annual average growth rate of GDP over the last 45 years). The relationship is linear. At the global level, data for the last 45 years reveal that a 1% increase in economic growth has driven a 0.7% increase in energy demand. This energy-GDP elasticity (percentage change in energy demand with respect to the percentage change in GDP), varies between 0.3 and 2.0 for a majority of the countries for which data are available for all years during the 1971–2014 period.[1]

The power of economic growth to drive energy demand depends on the level of economic development. Figure 1.6 shows, based on data from more than 100 countries over 45 years, the inverse relationship between energy-GDP elasticity and level of economic development (proxied by per capita GDP). Similar observations were also made in some earlier studies (Gilland 1988). Developed or high-income (i.e. OECD) countries often have low economic growth in the long term. Energy demand also grows slowly in those countries because their basic energy needs have been already fulfilled. Therefore, their energy-GDP elasticity would be lower. On the other hand, developing (i.e. non-OECD) countries often have higher economic growth, which in turn drives energy demand faster to maintain economic growth as well as providing access to energy for an increasing population. Thus, their energy-GDP elasticity would be higher. During the last 45 years, the average annual growth rate of GDP of the OECD countries was 2.6%; their aggregated energy-GDP elasticity for the period (i.e. 1971–2014) was 0.41. On the other hand, non-OECD countries experienced annual economic growth rate of 4.3%, on average; consequently their energy-GDP elasticity for the period was 0.77 – almost double that of the OECD countries. Figure 1.6 also shows that a large cluster of countries which have GDP per capita less than USD

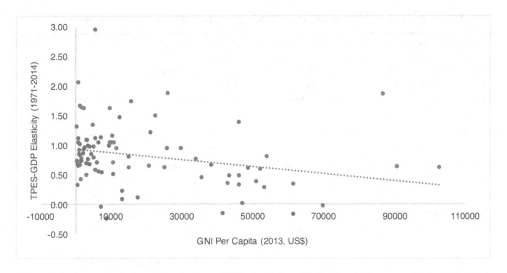

Figure 1.6 Inverse relationship of energy-GDP elasticity with the level of economic development

Note: Data to calculate the energy-GDP elasticity are taken from OECD online database and data for GNI per capita are from World Bank online database. Countries for which entire data series for the 1971–2014 period are not available (e.g. former Soviet republics, former Yugoslav republics, which exist as independent countries only after 1990) are not included. Middle Eastern countries, which are outliers due to very high energy-GDP elasticities, are also excluded.

10,000 have an energy-GDP elasticity around 1.0. Most countries with GDP per capita more than USD 30,000 have an energy-GDP elasticity less than 0.7.

4 Future energy demand

As discussed in Section 3, different approaches and techniques have been used for forecasting future energy demand.[2] The techniques are broadly divided into two categories: (1) econometric and (2) end-use accounting. Table 1.1 briefly illustrates the difference between the two approaches. The selection of techniques depends on a number of factors. For example, for forecasting of aggregate or total energy demand or demand for a particular fuel, the econometric approach would be preferable. For detailed demand forecasting, where forecasts of different energy commodities for different sectors and end-uses is needed, the econometric approach does not work because data for drivers for end-use or sectoral demand are often not available. Therefore, end-use accounting approaches, which are often based on scenario analysis and detailed data for a reference or base year, are preferred.

There exists a long list of literature utilizing both techniques. Examples of studies using econometric techniques are Gilland (1988 and 1995) for long-term global energy demand; Pindyck (1980) and Chan and Lee (1996) for residential energy demand; Limanond et al. (2011) for transport sector energy demand forecast in Thailand; and Semboja (1994) for industrial energy demand forecast in Kenya. Stinbuks (2017) compares various econometric models for forecasting electricity demand based on data from 106 countries around the world. The end-use accounting approach is being increasingly popular for energy demand forecasting because of its flexibility in incorporating scenarios and so-called expert judgments. Most commercially available energy models used by research institutions and consulting firms use this approach. Bhattacharyya and Timilsina (2010b) provides a comparison of these models. Organizations that regularly publish national and global energy demand projections mostly use the end-use accounting approach.

Table 1.1 End-use accounting vs. econometric approaches for energy demand forecasting

End-use Accounting Approach	Econometric Approach
Establish relationship between energy services and physical driving variables (e.g. hot water/person; lumens/sq. ft; no. of vehicles/persons; vehicle utilization rate; no. of refrigerators/household)	Establish relationship between final energy use and economic variables (e.g. gasoline consumption and household income or GDP; energy consumption and sectoral outputs)
Devices and process efficiency (MJ/liter of hot water; liter of gasoline per km of driving)	Project driving variables (e.g. GDP, household income, sectoral outputs)
Projection of driving variables (e.g. households, travel demand, commercial buildings, industrial output)	Project of energy demand based on above established relationship which is normally calibrated to historical observations
Project of energy demand based on above established relationship and efficiency, which are mostly static	Does not account technology specific features which are key determinants of fuel consumption
Does not account pricing effect on demand	Price is often the key driving variable for energy demand

Often, large and complex models are used that are capable to forecast future energy demand and generate supply plans to meet the demand; such models are referred to as energy system models.[3] These models use a hybrid approach combining econometric approach and end-use accounting (or algebraic) approaches. Econometric techniques are used to forecast demand for driving variables, such as stock of dwellings, stock of electrical appliances, manufacturing outputs, stock of vehicles, and passenger kilometers traveled, as these drivers are often closely linked with economic and demographic variables (GDP, household income, population). These drivers are then linked with energy commodities through technical coefficients such as unit energy consumption (e.g. kWh of electricity per square meter of floor space in a building; kilometer driven per liter of gasoline by a car) and utilization rate of energy consuming processes and devices to estimate energy demand for various activities (cooking, refrigeration, transportation, heating in a manufacturing plant, etc.) in different sectors (residential, commercial, industrial, transport).[4] The energy demand thus estimated across the end-uses and sectors is then aggregated to produce national and international energy demand forecasts. As discussed in Bhattacharyya and Timilsina (2010b), there exists a large number of energy system models to generate energy demand forecasts and to produce corresponding energy supply plans. In this chapter we present energy demand forecasts using three such complex energy system models to indicate how would global energy demand evolve over time in the next 20–25 years. These long-term global energy forecasts produced by three organizations: (1) the International Energy Agency (IEA), the energy wing of the OECD (OECD and IEA 2016); (2) the Energy Information Administration (EIA), the main organization responsible for official analysis of energy markets and policies including energy demand analysis and forecasting in the United States (EIA 2016); and (3) British Petroleum (BP), a major global energy company (BP 2017). These forecasts are selected for three reasons. First, these organizations have a long history of energy demand forecasting and they produce regular (annual) updates and publish their demand forecasts. Second, these forecasts are considered credible and are often used by most stakeholders including policy makers, researchers and the private sector. Third, these forecasts are free and publicly available, except for the World Energy Outlook of IEA (which contains the IEA energy forecast), which does come at a cost. These forecasts are generated by hybrid or integrated models discussed above, which use both econometric and end-use accounting approaches in their different modules.[5]

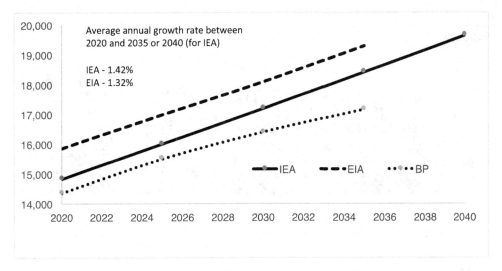

Figure 1.7 World energy demand forecasts by different organizations

Source: OCED and IEA (2016); EIA (2016) and BP (2017).

Figure 1.7 presents the latest forecasts of total energy demand for the next 20 to 25 years projected by IEA, EIA and BP. The trends are linear in all three forecasts, with small deviations in their average annual growth rate (1.42% IEA; 1.32% EIA and 1.2% BP). The difference in magnitude reflects the difference in assumptions and data used in the respective models utilized to generate these forecasts. The BP forecast has the smallest magnitude, as it already considers various policies including present and likely such energy efficiency standards, in its main forecasts. The baseline or reference case of other two forecasts (IEA and EIA), which we have considered here in this chapter, do not include future policies or scenarios; those are used in other scenarios, such as the 'New Policy' scenario and the 450 PPM scenario of the IEA forecast.

The breakdown of fuels (i.e. fuel mix) in these three forecasts are presented in Figure 1.8. There are two interesting observations here. First, there is no significant change in fuel mix over time; second, there is not much difference in the fuel mix between these three forecasts. For example, the share of coal is expected to remain between 24% and 27% in all years and in all three forecasts, implying that coal will continue to play a major role in meeting global energy demand unless there exists a significant policy shift due to global efforts on climate change mitigation.[6] The share of oil would vary between 28% and 32% during the next 20 years in the three forecasts. For natural gas, its share of the total energy supply will remain between 22% and 25% over the 2020–2035 period in all three forecasts. The share of renewable energy, including hydro and biomass, would remain between 12% and 16% throughout the forecast period in all three projections.[7]

Table 1.2 presents regional distribution of future energy consumption projected by IEA, EIA, and BP. All three projections concur that non-OECD countries' share in global energy demand would be more than 60% by 2020 and could reach almost 70% by 2040. China alone would account for one-quarter of global energy demand beyond 2020, whereas the US share would drop to 12%–14%. Non-OECD countries excluding China would account for more than 30% of the global energy demand after 2020. On the other hand, OECD countries' share in global energy demand is projected to drop significantly to around 30–35%. Note that their share was 61% in 1971, 52% in 1990, and 38% in 2014.

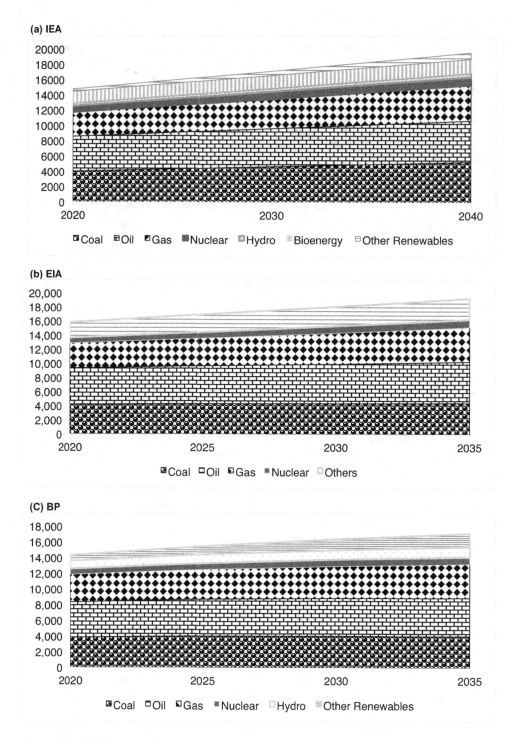

Figure 1.8 World energy demand forecasts by fuel type

Source: OCED and IEA (2016); EIA (2016) and BP (2017).

Table 1.2 Regional distribution of future energy consumption (%)

Forecasts	OECD				Non-OECD			
	2020	2025	2030	2035	2020	2025	2030	2035[a]
IEA	36%	n.a.	32%	28%	61%	n.a.	65%	68%
EIA	40%	39%	37%	36%	60%	61%	63%	64%
BP	40%	37%	34%	33%	60%	63%	66%	67%
	United States				China			
IEA	15%	n.a.	13%	12%	23%	n.a.	24%	23%
EIA	16%	15%	14%	14%	23%	24%	24%	24%
BP	17%	15%	14%	13%	24%	26%	26%	26%
	European Union				India			
IEA	11%	n.a.	9%	8%	7%	n.a.	9%	11%
EIA	13%	13%	13%	12%	5%	6%	6%	7%
BP	12%	10%	10%	9%	6%	7%	8%	9%
	Other OECD				Other Non-OECD			
IEA	10%	n.a.	10%	9%	31%	n.a.	32%	34%
EIA	11%	11%	10%	10%	31%	32%	33%	34%
BP	11%	11%	11%	10%	30%	31%	31%	32%

[a] IEA forecast is for year 2040.

Source: OECD and IEA (2016); EIA (2016) and BP (2017).

5 Conclusions

Being an essential input to economic growth and human well-being, energy demand increases along with population and per capita income, normally measured by GDP per person in a country. Historical data from more than 150 countries around the world reveals that energy demand has increased, on average, by 0.7% for each percent increase in GDP, on average, over the 45 years from 1971 to 2014. Historically, developed countries had a disproportionate share in global energy consumption. The trend has now reversed since 2005 due to rapid growth of energy demand in emerging economies along with their economic growth. Currently, China alone accounts for 40% of the total energy consumption of the non-OECD countries.

The current global climate change debate has put a strong pressure on the energy supply mix to meet the growing energy demand. This is important because the mix of fossil fuels and non-fossil fuels in meeting the global energy demand has not changed much over the last 45 years. In 1971, fossil fuels occupied 86% of the global energy demand; they still account for more than 80%. Despite the importance of new renewable energy sources (i.e. solar, wind, and geothermal) to combat global climate change, their current share in the global energy supply is negligible at around 1%, thereby indicating the scale of the efforts (e.g. public policies) needed to have significant substitution of fossil fuels with new renewable energy sources.

Although a large number of factors are identified in the literature that drive the energy demand, a careful look based on the historical data from more than 150 countries around the world suggests that economic (or GDP) growth is the primary driver of energy consumption in the long run, as income growth drives energy-consuming assets such as buildings, factories, and vehicles. In the short run, however, other factors such as energy prices, weather and special events affect the energy demand, as these factors influence utilization of energy consuming and producing facilities. Long-run energy projections made by reputed organizations, such as the International Energy Agency, the US Energy Information Administration, and a major oil company (British Petroleum) show that global energy demand would increase at an annual average rate of 1.2% to 1.4% over the next 20–25 years. Non-OECD countries will continue to occupy more than 60% of global energy consumption. Unless major policy shifts are made aiming to avoid global climate change, fossil fuels would still be predominant in the global energy supply mix, with a more than 75% share over the next two decades.

Notes

1 Ninety out of 110 countries for which data are available throughout the 1971–2014 period have energy demand elasticity with respect to GDP, in the range of 0.3 to 2.0. More than half of the countries (63) have energy-GDP elasticity between 0.6 and 1.5.
2 Please refer to existing studies such as Bhattacharya and Timilsina (2010a) for detailed discussions on energy demand modeling.
3 Bhattacharya and Timilsina (2010b) provides detailed comparisons of these models, their strengths and weaknesses, and their suitability.
4 Please see Malla and Timilsina (2016) for a simple account of energy demand estimations in different sectors for different end-uses.
5 The IEA uses its World Energy Model (WEM), which is an integrated model used by the IEA over the last 20 years to produce its world energy outlook each year. The energy outlook provides long-term energy demand forecasts by type of energy commodities and by major geographical regions or countries. The EIA uses its World Energy Projection System Plus (WEPS+) model. Like the WEM, it also has modular structure. Its end-use demand modules project demand for energy commodities in various sectors (i.e. residential, commercial, industrial, transport) and its transformation model produces energy mix to satisfy the demand (EIA 2016, Appendix L). It produces the energy demand and supplies for 16 regions/countries around the world. The BP energy demand forecasts are mainly based on secondary data on the key drivers of energy demand. It develops various scenarios based on current energy policies and uses experts' judgments over the evolution of various energy commodities in the future (BP 2017).
6 IEA projects that the share of coal in total primary energy supply falls to 13% by 2040 if policies are implemented to keep the global concentration of GHG emissions at 450 PPM level (IEA's 450 PPM scenario).
7 IEA projects that the share of renewable including hydro and biomass would increase from 16% in 2020 to 31% in 2040 under a scenario to keep the global GHG concentration at 450 PPM.

References

Bhattacharyya, S. and G. R. Timilsina (2010a). Modeling Energy Demand of Developing Countries: Are the Specific Features Adequately Captured? *Energy Policy*, Vol. 38, No. 6, pp. 1979–1990.
Bhattacharyya, S. and G. R. Timilsina (2010b). A Review of Energy System Models. *International Journal of Energy Sector Management*, Vol. 4, No. 4, pp. 494–518.
British Petroleum (BP). (2017). BP Energy Outlook 2017 Edition. BP, London.
Chan, H.L. and S.K. Lee (1996). Forecasting the Demand for Energy in China. *Energy Journal*, Vol. 17, No. 1, pp. 19–30.
Church, R. (1986). *The History of the British Coal Industry*, vol. 3, 1830–1913. Oxford: Clarendon Press.
Csereklyei Z., M.d.M. Rubio Varas, and D.I. Stern (2016). Energy and Economic Growth: The Stylized Facts. *Energy Journal*, Vol. 37, No. 2, pp. 223–255.
Energy Information Administration (EIA) (2016). International Energy Outlook 2016. EIA, Washington, DC.
Gilland, B. (1988). Population, Economic Growth, and Energy Demand, 1985–2020. *Population and Development Review*, Vol. 14, No. 2, pp. 233–244.
Gilland, B. (1995). World Population, Economic Growth, and Energy Demand, 1990–2100: A Review of Projections. *Population and Development Review*, Vol. 21, No. 3, pp. 507–539.
Goldstein, J. S., X. Huang and B. Akan (1997). Energy in the World Economy, 1950–1992. *International Studies Quarterly*, Vol. 41, No. 2, pp. 241–266.

Limanond, T., S. Jomnonkwao and A. Srikaew (2011). Projection of Future Transport Energy Demand of Thailand. *Energy Policy*, Vol. 39, No. 5, pp. 2754–2763.

Malla, S. and G. R. Timilsina (2016). Long-Term Energy Demand Forecasting in Romania, World Bank Policy Research Working Paper. No. 7697, World Bank, Washington, DC.

Organization of Economic Cooperation and Development (OECD) (2017). Online Database. http://stats.oecd.org.libproxy-wb.imf.org/

Organization of Economic Cooperation and Development (OECD) and International Energy Agency (IEA) (2016). World Energy Outlook, 2016, OECD/IEA, Paris.

Pindyck, R. S. (1980). International Comparison of the Residential Demand for Energy. *European Economic Review*, Vol. 13, pp. 1–24.

Semboja, H.H.H. (1994). A Dynamic Model of Industrial Energy Demand in Kenya. *Energy Journal*, Vol. 15, No. 4, pp. 203–224.

Stern, D.I. and A. Kander (2012). The Role of Energy in the Industrial Revolution and Modern Economic Growth. *Energy Journal*, Vol. 33, No. 3, pp. 127–154.

Stinbuks, J. (2017). Assessing the Accuracy of Electricity Demand Forecasts in Developing Countries. World Bank Policy Research Working Paper. No. 7974, World Bank, Washington, DC.

Wolfram, C., O. Shelef and P. Gertler (2012). How Will Energy Demand Develop in the Developing World? *The Journal of Economic Perspectives*, Vol. 26, No. 1, pp. 119–138.

2

Energy and economic growth

David I. Stern

1 Introduction

Figure 2.1 shows that energy use per capita increases with GDP per capita, so that richer countries typically use more energy per person than poorer countries. The slope of the logarithmic regression line implies that a 1% increase in income per capita is associated with a 0.7% increase in energy use per capita (Csereklyei et al., 2016). This means that energy intensity is on average lower in higher-income countries (Figure 2.2). These relationships have been very stable over the last several decades (Csereklyei et al., 2016). Energy intensity (energy used per dollar of GDP) in today's middle-income countries is similar to that in today's developed countries when they were at the same income level (van Benthem, 2015).

Mostly as a result of countries' energy intensity decreasing as they get richer, global energy intensity has decreased over time (Figure 2.3). However, global energy use per capita has increased over time, and when we also take population growth into account, total energy use has risen strongly. Between 1971 and 2010, total world energy use increased by about 140% while total GDP increased by 270%, and population by 80%.

Energy intensity has also converged across countries over time, so that countries that were more energy-intensive in the 1970s tended to reduce their energy intensity by more than less energy-intensive countries, and the least energy-intensive countries often increased in energy intensity (Figure 2.4). Though data are limited to fewer and fewer countries as we go back further in time, these relationships also appear to hold over the last two centuries: energy use increased, energy intensity declined globally, and countries converged in energy intensity (Csereklyei et al., 2016).

The next section of this chapter examines the factors that might lead to lower energy intensity with higher GDP and convergence in energy intensity, as seen in Figures 2.2 to 2.4. I then review the literature on the theoretical relationship between energy and economic growth. The penultimate section looks at the empirical evidence on the question of whether changes in energy use cause changes in GDP or vice versa. Concluding remarks point to the main gaps in our knowledge.

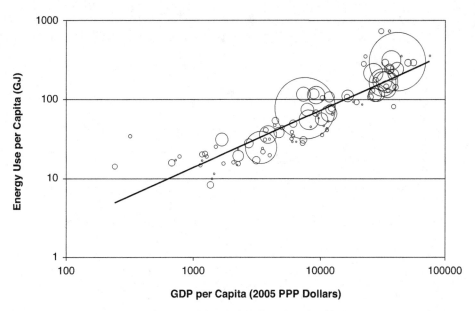

Figure 2.1 Energy consumption per capita and GDP per capita 2010

Note: Bubbles are proportional to total energy use. The two largest circles are the United States at upper right and China in the middle.

Source: International Energy Agency and Penn World Table 7.1.

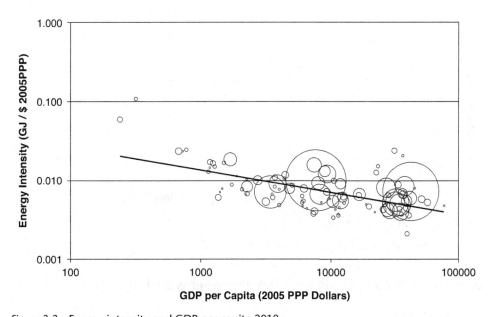

Figure 2.2 Energy intensity and GDP per capita 2010

Note: Bubbles are proportional to total energy use. The two largest circles are the United States at lower right and China in the middle.

Source: International Energy Agency and Penn World Table 7.1.

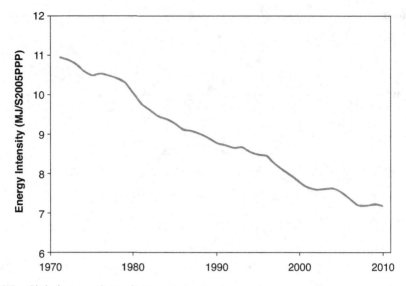

Figure 2.3   Global energy intensity

Source: International Energy Agency and Penn World Table 7.1.

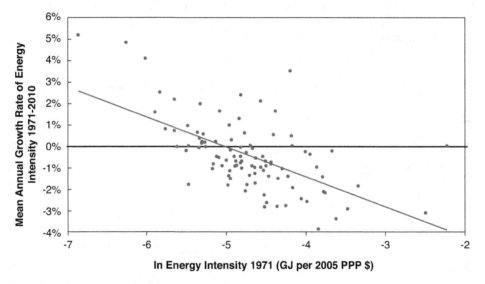

Figure 2.4   Convergence of energy intensity

Source: International Energy Agency and Penn World Table 7.1.

2   Factors affecting the linkage between energy and GDP

2.1 Introduction

Why is energy intensity lower in richer countries and declining globally over time? We can use a production frontier approach to examine the factors that could affect the relationship between energy use and economic activity. Assuming separability between inputs and outputs and factor-augmenting technological change, a production function for multiple outputs can be written as:

$$(Q_1, ..., Q_M)' = f(A_{X1}X_1, ..., A_{XN}X_N, A_{E1}E_1, ..., A_{EP}E_P) \tag{2.1}$$

where $Q_1, ..., Q_M$ are various outputs, such as manufactured goods and services, $X_1, ..., X_N$ are various non-energy inputs such as capital and labor, $E_1, ..., E_P$ are energy inputs such as coal and oil, and the A_i are indices of the state of factor-augmenting technology. The relationship between energy and an aggregate of output such as GDP is then affected by:

- Substitution between energy and other inputs
- Shifts in the composition of the energy input
- Shifts in the mix of the other inputs
- Shifts in the composition of output
- Technological change
- Economies of scale.

I discuss each of these in turn, apart from shifts in the mix of other inputs and economies of scale, as these have not been discussed much in the literature. An important factor offsetting the effects of technological change is the rebound effect, which I discuss separately.

2.2 Substitutability of energy and capital

Koetse et al. (2008) conduct a meta-analysis of the (Morishima) elasticity of substitution (MES) between capital and energy for an increase in the price of energy. Their base case finds that the MES between energy and capital is 0.216, so that capital and energy are poor substitutes. The MES estimated using panel or cross-section data is greater – 0.592 and 0.848, respectively. It is likely that these larger values reflect long-run elasticities and the lower values short-run elasticities (Stern, 2012a), so that in the long run substitution of capital for energy could reduce energy intensity substantially. Stern (2012b) found that capital deepening reduced energy intensity by 7% globally from 1971 to 2007. On the other hand, Wang (2011) found that capital accumulation was the main driver of reduced energy intensity in China.

2.3 Energy quality and shifts in mix of energy inputs

Not all energy sources and fuels are of equal economic productivity. These differences in productivity are termed energy quality. Some fuels can be used for a larger number of activities and/ or for more valuable activities. For example, coal cannot be used to directly power a computer, while electricity can. Some fuels, in particular electricity, can transform the workplace entirely and change work processes, thus contributing to productivity gains (Enflo et al., 2009). The productivity of a fuel is determined in part by a complex set of attributes unique to each fuel: physical scarcity, capacity to do useful work, energy density, cleanliness, amenability to storage, safety, flexibility of use, cost of conversion, and so forth. Fuel and energy quality are not necessarily fixed over time, as changes in technology in terms of both new techniques of production and new products and activities change the opportunities for using fuels. However, it is generally believed that electricity is the highest quality energy vector, followed by natural gas and oil, and then coal, wood, and other biomass in descending order of quality. This is supported by the typical prices of these fuels per unit of energy, which is one way of measuring relative energy quality (Stern, 2010).

The evolution of the energy mix over the course of economic development and over history in the technologically leading countries follows a typical pattern moderated by local energy endowments (Csereklyei et al., 2016). In the least developed economies, as in today's developed economies before the industrial revolution, the use of biomass and muscle power dominates. These energy sources decline in share with increasing income and over time. Direct use of coal tends to rise and then fall over time and with income. Increases in the share of oil and then natural gas follow. The share of electricity in total energy use tends to rise. Low-income countries tend to generate electricity from hydropower and oil, while high-income countries have more diverse power sources including nuclear power. Finally, electricity generated from solar and wind power are only now beginning to take off in more developed economies. Figure 2.5 illustrates this pattern for the United States.

Relatively few studies evaluate the role of the change in energy mix on energy intensity. Schurr and Netschert (1960), Berndt (1990), and Kaufmann (2004) argued that the shift in the composition of energy use towards higher quality energy inputs played a key role in reducing energy intensity in the United States. Other studies find, however, a much larger role for technological change than for changes in the composition of energy in the reductions in energy intensity seen around the world. For example, Ma and Stern (2008) find that interfuel substitution had negligible effects on the decline in energy intensity in China between 1994 and 2003. Stern (2012b) finds that between 1971 and 2007, changes in fuel mix within individual countries increased world energy use by 4% while global energy intensity declined by 40%. Shifts in the distribution of economic activity towards countries with lower quality energy mixes such as China and India contributed further to increasing energy intensity globally.

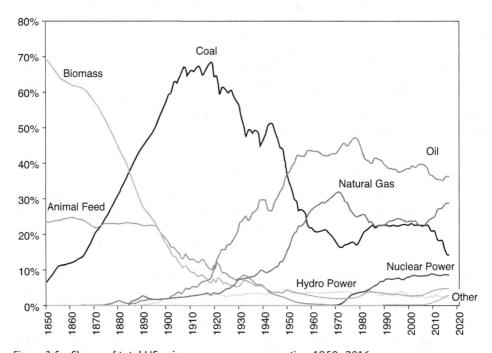

Figure 2.5 Shares of total US primary energy consumption 1850–2016

Source: US Energy Information Administration. Other includes solar, wind, and geothermal energy. Biomass includes wood, waste, and biofuels.

2.4 Shifts in the composition of output

Output mix also typically changes over the course of economic development. In the earlier phases of development, there is a shift away from agriculture towards heavy industry, while in the later stages of development there is a shift from the more resource-intensive extractive and heavy industrial sectors towards services and lighter manufacturing. It is often argued that this will result in an increase in energy used per unit of output in the early stages of economic development and a reduction in energy used per unit output in the later stages of economic development (Panayotou, 1993). However, the energy-saving effects of structural changes may be overstated (Henriques and Kander, 2010). The decline in the share of industry in GDP in developed countries is partly due to the decline in the relative price of industrial goods due to faster productivity increases in industry than in the service sector (Kander, 2005). Furthermore, when the indirect energy use embodied in manufactured products and services is taken into account, the service and household sectors are more energy-intensive than they first appear to be. Evidence also shows that trade does not result in significant reductions in energy use and pollution in developed countries through the offshoring of pollution-intensive industries (Levinson, 2010; Kander and Lindmark, 2006).

Kander (2002) and Stern (2012b) find a relatively small role for structural change in reducing energy intensity in Sweden (1800–2000) and the world (1971–2007), respectively. But, using a much finer disaggregation of industries, Sue Wing (2008) finds that structural change explained most of the decline in energy intensity in the United States (1958–2000), especially before 1980.

2.5 Energy efficiency and technological change

There are several ways of measuring changes in aggregate energy efficiency controlling for the other factors discussed above. The distance function approach measures the change in energy efficiency as the change in the minimum energy requirement to produce a given level of output. There are two main ways of measuring energy efficiency using this approach (Shen and Lin, 2017), neither of which obviously identifies a pure energy efficiency component. A second approach is to use an index of energy augmenting technical change. Based on Equation (2.1), the index of energy augmenting technical change can be constructed as:

$$A_E = \sum_{i=1}^{P} S_i A_{Ei} \tag{2.2}$$

where S_i are the shares of each type of energy in the total cost of energy. Change over time in this index can be computed using an index method such as Divisia aggregation. The actual energy augmentation indices need to be estimated econometrically. Bottom-up, engineering-based measurements of energy efficiency represent a third approach.

Estimates of trends in energy efficiency are mixed (Stern, 2011). The direction of change has not been constant and varies across different sectors of the economy. Judson et al. (1999) show that technical innovations tend to introduce more energy using appliances to households and energy saving techniques to industry. Stern (2012b) finds that energy efficiency improved from 1971 to 2007 in most developed economies, former communist countries including China, and India. But there was no improvement or a reduction in energy efficiency in many developing economies. Globally, such technological change resulted in a 40% greater reduction in energy use over the period than would otherwise have been the case and so was the most important driver of reduced energy intensity.

Changes in energy prices may induce endogenous technological changes, though only a fraction of historical improvements in energy efficiency have been due to increases in energy prices (Newell et al., 1999; Popp, 2002; Dechezleprêtre et al., 2011). According to the theory of directed technical change, it is the level of input prices rather than changes in input prices that determine the rate and direction of technical change (Acemoglu, 2008). New energy-using technologies initially diffuse slowly due to high costs of production that are typically lowered radically by a fairly predictable process of learning by doing (Grübler et al., 1999). Diffusion tends to follow a logistic curve with the speed of diffusion depending on among other things how well the innovation fits into the existing infrastructure. Energy-saving innovations such as LED lighting would be expected to diffuse rapidly once their price becomes competitive, while more radical innovations that require new support infrastructures diffuse much more slowly.

Research on the factors that affect the adoption of energy efficiency policies (Matisoff, 2008; Fredriksson et al., 2004) or on the actual adoption of specific technologies (Barreto and Kemp, 2008; Verdolini and Galeotti, 2011) has been limited, though more evidence is available from patent data (e.g. Verdolini and Galeotti, 2011; Dechezleprêtre et al., 2013). Differences in the adoption of energy efficiency technologies across countries and states, over time, and among individuals might be optimal due to differences in endowments, preferences, or the state of technology. But the rate of adoption may also be inefficient due to market failures and behavioral factors. Market failures include environmental externalities, information problems, liquidity constraints in capital markets, failures of innovation markets, and principal-agent problems such as between landlords and tenants (Gillingham et al., 2009; Linares and Labandeira, 2010). There is limited quantitative evidence on what role energy efficiency polices might play in reducing energy consumption compared to business as usual (Bosetti et al., 2011). Fredriksson et al. (2004) find that the greater the corruptibility of policy-makers, the less stringent is energy policy, and that the greater lobby group coordination costs are, the more stringent energy policy is. Matisoff (2008) finds that the most significant variable affecting the adoption of energy efficiency programs by US states is citizen ideology.

2.6 The rebound effect

Energy-saving innovations reduce the cost of providing energy services such as heating, lighting, and industrial power. This reduction in cost encourages consumers and firms to use more of the service in question. As a result, energy consumption usually does not decline by as much as energy efficiency increases. This difference between the improvement in energy efficiency and the reduction in energy consumption is known as the rebound effect. Rebound effects can be defined for energy-saving innovations in consumption and production. In both cases, the increase in energy use due to increased use of the energy service is called the direct rebound effect. For consumer use of energy, estimates of the direct rebound effect in developed countries are usually small – in the range of 10%–30% (Greening et al., 2000; Sorrell et al., 2009) – but are likely larger in developing countries (Roy, 2000). In the case of energy efficiency improvements in industry, the direct rebound effect is likely to be larger for export industries that have more opportunity to expand production than for industries serving the domestic market (Grepperud and Rasmussen, 2004; Allan et al., 2007; Linares and Labandeira, 2010).

Additionally, as a result of the reduction in the cost of the energy service, consumers will demand less of substitute goods and more of complementary goods, including other energy services. Firms will make similar changes in their demands for inputs. There will also be additional repercussions throughout the economy. Goods, whose demand has increased, require more energy for their production and vice versa; the fall in energy demand may lower the price of energy (Gillingham et al., 2013; Borenstein, 2015), increasing energy use, ceteris paribus; and the original energy efficiency improvement is a contribution to an increase in total factor productivity, which tends to increase capital accumulation and economic growth that results again in greater energy usage (Saunders, 1992). All these additional effects are called indirect rebound effects.[1] Direct and indirect rebound effects together sum to the economy-wide rebound effect.

It is usually assumed that the indirect rebound is positive, and so the economy-wide rebound is greater than the direct rebound effect and greater in the long run than in the short run (Saunders, 2008), but this might not be the case (Turner, 2013; Borenstein, 2015). At the economy-wide level, "backfire", where energy use increases as a result of an efficiency improvement, or "super-conservation" where the rebound is negative, are both theoretically possible (Saunders, 2008; Turner, 2009). Lemoine (2017) conducts a general equilibrium analysis of the rebound effect. Assuming that all sectors share the same technology, general equilibrium effects amplify the partial equilibrium rebound, as investigated by Saunders (1992). With heterogeneous technologies, general equilibrium effects amplify the rebound for low elasticities of substitution and reduce it for high elasticities of substitution between energy and non-energy inputs in production. Backfire is possible even for elasticities of substitution less than unity, especially for innovations in those sectors that are relatively energy inefficient or energy-intensive. In general, this analysis shows that the economy-wide rebound effect is likely to be large and backfire is likely.

There are few estimates of the economy-wide rebound effect, and these vary widely (Saunders, 2013; Turner, 2013). Evidence to date depends on computable general equilibrium models that have limited empirical validation or partial equilibrium econometric models that do not encompass all effects and mostly do not credibly identify the rebound effect. Turner (2009) finds that, depending on the assumed values of the parameters in a simulation model, the rebound effect for the UK can range from negative to more than 100%. Adetutu et al. (2016) use a stochastic frontier model to estimate energy efficiency and then use a dynamic panel model for 55 countries to estimate the effect of efficiency on energy use. This is the most credible empirical method proposed to date, however, as Adetutu et al. control for energy prices and output, it is a partial equilibrium approach. They find that in the short run rebound is 90%, while in the long run rebound is −36%.

3 The theory of the role of energy in economic growth

3.1 The ecological economics approach

Interdisciplinary ecological economists base their approach on the physical laws that describe the operating constraints of economic systems (Ayres and Kneese, 1969). In particular, production requires energy to carry out work to convert materials into desired products and to transport raw materials, goods, and people. The second law of thermodynamics (the entropy law) implies that energy cannot be reused and there are limits to how much energy efficiency can be improved. As a result, energy is always an essential factor of production (Stern, 1997), and continuous supplies of energy are needed to maintain existing levels of economic activity as well as to grow and develop the economy. Before being used in the production of goods and services, energy and matter must be captured from the environment, and energy must be invested in order to extract useful energy (Hall et al., 1986).

Ecological economists usually argue that substitution between capital and resources can only play a limited role in mitigating the scarcity of resources (Stern, 1997). Furthermore, some ecological economists downplay the role of technological change in productivity growth, arguing that growth is a result of either increased energy use or innovations allowing increased use of energy (Hall et al., 1986; Cleveland et al., 1984; Hall et al., 2003; Ayres and Warr, 2009). Therefore, in this view, increased energy use is the main or only cause of economic growth, and value is derived from the action of energy that is directed by capital and labor. Energy flows into the economy from fossil fuels and the sun. Capital and labor are considered intermediate inputs that are created and maintained by the primary input of energy and flows of matter. The level of these flows can be computed in terms of the embodied energy use associated with them.

However, because the quality of resources and the level of technology do affect the amount of energy needed to produce goods and services, this argument that energy is the sole factor of production is not so convincing. For example, the quality of resources such as oil reservoirs is critical in determining the energy required to extract and process fuels. As an oil reservoir is depleted, the energy needed to extract oil increases. On the positive side, improved geophysical knowledge and techniques can increase the extent to which oil can be extracted for a given energy cost. Odum's energy approach (Brown and Herendeen, 1996), which includes the solar and geological energy embodied in natural resource inputs in indicators of total embodied energy, is one attempt to address this issue. An alternative approach is to measure material and energy inputs on the common basis of their exergy (Ayres et al., 1998; Ukidwe and Bakshi, 2007). A third response is to measure energy inputs in terms of useful work (Ayres and Warr, 2009). However, Georgescu-Roegen (1971), Perrings (1987), and O'Connor (1993), among others, developed models that allow for a number of different factors of production while complying with the physical laws of the conservation of mass and thermodynamics to varying degrees. The ecological economics approach does not have to reduce to an energy-only model of the economy.

The effect of resource quality on the economy can be expressed using the concept of energy return on investment (EROI) – the ratio of useful energy produced by an energy supply system to the amount of energy invested in extracting that energy. Lower quality energy resources have lower EROIs. Ecological economists argue that the more energy that is required to extract energy, the less energy is available for other uses and the poorer an economy will be. In this view, the increase in EROI allowed by the switch from biomass to fossil fuels enabled the industrial revolution and the period of modern economic growth that followed it (Hall et al., 1986). Murphy and Hall (2010) document EROI for many energy sources, arguing that it has declined over time despite extensive innovation in the energy industry. Wind and direct solar energy have more favorable EROIs than biomass fuels, but worse than most fossil fuels. However, unlike fossil fuels, the EROI of these energy sources tends to improve over time due to innovation (Kubiszewski et al., 2010).

Substituting other inputs for energy or improving the efficiency with which energy is used could reduce the energy required in production. However, ecological economists argue that both these processes have limits. Technological change only allows us to get closer to the ultimate thermodynamic limits of energy efficiency; it cannot circumvent them. Substitution too is constrained by these thermodynamic limits.

Substitution can occur *within* a category of similar production inputs (e.g. between different fuels) and *between* different categories of inputs (e.g. between energy and machines) (Costanza and Daly, 1992). There is also a distinction to be made between substitution at the micro level (within a single engineering process or at a single firm) and at the macro level (in the economy as a whole) (Stern, 1997).

As shown in Figure 2.5, the long-run pattern of energy use in industrial economies, such as the United States, has been dominated by substitutions from biomass and animal power to coal, oil, natural gas, and primary electricity. Meta-analysis of existing studies of interfuel substitution suggests that the long-run substitution possibilities at the level of the industrial sector as a whole are good. But there seems to be less substitutability at the macro-economic level (Stern, 2012a).

Ecological economists emphasize the importance of limits to inter-category substitution; in particular, the substitution of manufactured capital for resources including energy (Costanza and Daly, 1992). Thermodynamic limits on substitution can be approximated by a production function with an elasticity of substitution significantly below 1 (Stern, 1997). As discussed earlier, a meta-analysis of the existing empirical literature finds that the elasticity of substitution between capital and energy is less than 1 but much greater than 0 (Koetse et al., 2008).

In addition to this micro-economic limit to substitution, there may also be macroeconomic limits to substitution. The construction, operation, and maintenance of tools, machines, and factories require a flow of materials and energy. Similarly, the humans that direct manufactured capital consume energy and materials. Thus, producing more of the "substitute" for energy – manufactured capital – requires more of the thing that it is supposed to substitute for. This again limits potential substitutability (Stern, 1997).

3.2 Neoclassical approaches

Despite the fact that energy must be an essential factor of production, the core mainstream economic growth models disregard energy or other resources. Aghion and Howitt's (2009) textbook on economic growth only discusses growth and the environment in a chapter near the end of the book. Acemoglu's (2008) textbook does not cover the topic at all. There has been some analysis of the potential for resources to constrain growth in the journal literature, but it has mostly been contained within the sub-field of environmental and resource economics, and the main focus has been on the implications of non-renewable resources for economic growth. Solow (1974) introduced non-renewable resources – which could represent fossil or nuclear fuels – into neoclassical growth models and showed that sustainability (or the ability of a nation to support a constant level of economic production indefinitely) is achievable under certain institutional and technical conditions. Stiglitz (1974) showed that if instead the economy is a free market economy with perfect competition but has the same technology as Solow's (1974) model, the resources are exhausted and consumption and social welfare eventually fall to zero. A large literature has developed in the wake of these and other classic papers (Stern, 2011). Recent examples of papers in this literature are André and Smulders (2014) and Peretto and Valente (2015). These models do not, however, usually specify whether the resources in question are energy or non-energy resources; André and Smulders (2014) is an exception in this regard. Neither do they mostly attempt to model a realistic historical economic development path (Tahvonen and Salo, 2001; Stern and Kander, 2012). Given the existence of renewable energy, it is not clear how relevant such an approach will be to the future, either. Shanker and Stern (2018) use a model with endogenous directed technical change and a constant price of energy – the price of energy usually rises in models with non-renewable resources – which does reproduce the stylized facts laid out in the first section of this chapter. Energy intensity falls due to energy-augmenting technical change but rebound means that energy use rises over time.

Economic historians have debated the importance of energy in the acceleration of economic growth known as the industrial revolution. Many researchers (e.g. Wilkinson, 1973; Wrigley, 2010; Pomeranz, 2001; Allen, 2009; Gutberlet, 2012; Kander et al., 2014; Fernihough and O'Rourke, 2014; Gars and Olovsson, 2015) argue that innovations in the use, and growth in the quantity consumed, of coal played a crucial role in driving the industrial revolution. But some economic historians and economists either argue that it was not necessary to expand the use of modern energy carriers such as coal (e.g. Clark and Jacks, 2007; Kunnas and Myllyntaus, 2009; Madsen et al., 2010) or do not give coal a central role (e.g. Harley and Crafts, 2000; Clark, 2014).

Before the industrial revolution, most energy was in the form of wood and animal and human muscle power – wind and water power contributed relatively little energy (Kander et al., 2014). The supply of this renewable energy was constrained by the availability of land, and so energy was scarce (Wrigley, 2010). Wrigley (2010) stresses that the shift from an economy that relied on land resources to one based on fossil fuels is the essence of the industrial revolution and can explain the differential development of the Dutch and British economies. Both countries had the necessary institutions for the industrial revolution to occur, but capital accumulation in the Netherlands faced a renewable energy resource constraint, while in Britain coal provided a way out of that constraint. This explanation emphasizes the low substitutability between the essential inputs of capital and energy. Allen (2009) focuses on innovations in the use of energy in his explanation of why the industrial revolution occurred in Britain. Many technological innovations were required in order to use coal effectively in new applications ranging from domestic heating and cooking to iron smelting. Like Wrigley, he compares Britain to other economies in Europe, but also to China. England stands out as an exception in two ways: coal was relatively cheap there and labor costs were higher than elsewhere. Therefore, it was profitable to substitute coal-fueled machines for labor in Britain, even when these machines were inefficient and consumed large amounts of coal, but not elsewhere. Continued innovation that improved energy efficiency and reductions in the cost of transporting coal eventually made coal-using technologies profitable in other countries too.

On the other hand, Clark and Jacks (2007) argue that an industrial revolution could still have happened in a coal-less Britain with only "modest costs to the productivity growth of the economy" (p. 68), because the value of coal was only a modest share of British GDP. They argue further that Britain's energy supply could have been greatly expanded, albeit at about twice the cost of coal, by importing wood from the Baltic. But Fernihough and O'Rourke (2014) and Gutberlet (2012) use geographical analysis to show the importance of access to local coal in driving industrialization and urban population growth in Europe, though Kelly et al. (2015) provide contradictory evidence from Britain on this point.

A number of researchers have attempted to model the role of energy in the acceleration of growth using mainstream economic growth models. Hansen and Prescott (2002) have two sectors, with a land input in the agricultural "Malthus" sector, no natural resource input to the industrial "Solow" sector, semi-endogenous population growth, and exogenous technical progress that is assumed, a priori, to be much faster in the Solow than in the Malthus sector. Once production using the Solow technology becomes more profitable, that sector quickly comes to dominate the economy and the growth rate accelerates. Though Hansen and Prescott (2002) do not explicitly model energy use in the Solow sector, they do mention that the reduction in the role of land in output can be seen as a transition to fossil fuels, which require less land area for production.

Tahvonen and Salo (2001), Fröling (2011), and Gars and Olovsson (2015) model fossil fuel use explicitly. However, like Hansen and Prescott (2002), these researchers all assume that productivity in the use of fossil fuels is higher or can increase faster than that in the use of renewable energy. Pezzey et al. (2017) instead assume that there is no a priori difference in the ease of developing new "machines" that use either biomass or coal. Instead, the supply of energy in the biomass-using sector is fixed while the supply of coal is infinitely elastic. Allen (2009) shows that the real price of coal was fairly constant over several centuries, which supports the latter assumption. Clark and Jacks (2007) explain that throughout the period of the industrial revolution innovation overcame the effects of depletion, resulting in the long-run supply of coal being highly elastic.

In Pezzey et al.'s (2017) model, each of the two intermediate goods sectors uses labor, an energy input (wood in one sector and coal in the other) and sector-specific machines. The output of these two sectors is combined into final output via a high-elasticity constant elasticity of substitution (CES) production function. Pezzey et al. show how the rising relative price of wood can cause the direction of technical change to shift increasingly towards the development of coal-using machines. As coal use can be expanded without limit, the rate of economic growth accelerates. However, they also show that with a high enough elasticity of substitution between the outputs of the two sectors in producing final output, an industrial revolution is not inevitable. Greater initial scarcity of wood relative to coal, greater initial knowledge of technologies for using coal relative to technologies for using wood, and/or higher population growth puts the economy on a path to an industrial revolution. The converse slows industrialization or even prevents it forever. The greater the elasticity of substitution and/or the smaller the output elasticity of energy, the more extensive is the set of initial conditions that lead to stagnation. Empirical calibration for Britain in the period 1560–1900 produces historically plausible results.

However, this study makes the simplifying assumption that the elasticity of substitution between machines and energy is unity. As discussed above, we should expect it to be less than 1 on both theoretical and empirical grounds. Stern and Kander (2012) add an energy input that has low substitutability with capital and labor to Solow's (1956) growth model. Otherwise, they make the same assumptions as Solow, including that technological change is exogenous. Using 200 years of Swedish data Stern and Kander estimate that the elasticity of substitution between energy and the other two inputs is 0.65.

When the elasticity of substitution is unity, cost shares in a single sector model must be constant. Assuming that the elasticity of substitution between energy and capital is less than 1 allows the share of energy in production costs to fall over time. The cost share of energy has fallen in the long run in both Britain and Sweden, countries for which we have data from 1800 till the present (Figure 2.6). An elasticity of substitution of less than unity also allows us to distinguish between labor-augmenting innovations and energy-augmenting innovations, which again is not possible using a Cobb-Douglas production function.

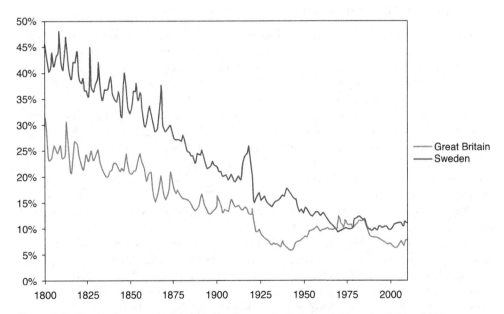

Figure 2.6 Share of energy in total production costs: Britain and Sweden 1800–2009

Source: Gentvilaite et al. (2015).

Stern and Kander's (2012) production function is given by:

$$Y = \left[(1 - \gamma) \left(A_L^\beta L^\beta K^{1-\beta} \right)^\phi + \gamma \left(A_E E \right)^\phi \right]^{\frac{1}{\phi}} \tag{2.3}$$

Equation (2.3) embeds a Cobb-Douglas function of capital, K, and labor, L, $L^\beta K^{1-\beta}$, in a constant elasticity of substitution production function of this combined input and energy, E, to produce gross output, Y. $\phi = \dfrac{\sigma - 1}{\sigma}$, where σ is the elasticity of substitution between energy and the capital-labor aggregate. A_L and A_E are the augmentation indices of labor and energy, respectively, which can be interpreted as reflecting both changes in technology that augment the effective supply of the factor in question and changes in the quality of the respective factors. $A_E E$ and $A_L L$ are called effective energy and effective labor, respectively.

In Solow's (1956) model, as long as there is technological change, the economy can grow in the long run. In Stern and Kander's model, depending on the availability of energy and the nature of technological change, energy can be either a constraint on growth or an enabler of growth. When effective energy, $A_E E$, is very abundant, the model behaves very similarly to Solow's original model and energy neither constrains nor drives growth. The more energy there is, the less important energy appears to be. But when effective energy is relatively scarce, the level of output depends on the level of energy supply and the level of energy-augmenting technology, and labor-augmenting technological change alone no longer results in economic growth. Stern and Kander (2012) find that increases in energy use and energy-augmenting technological change were the main contributors to economic growth in the 19th and early 20th centuries but in the second half of the 20th century labor-augmenting technological change became the main driver of growth in income per capita as it is in the Solow growth model.

4   Testing for Granger causality between energy and GDP

Two methods for testing for causality among time series variables are Granger causality tests (Granger, 1969) and cointegration analysis (Engle and Granger, 1987). These methods have been applied extensively to test for causality and cointegration between energy, GDP, and other variables from the late 1970s on (Kraft and Kraft, 1978; Ozturk, 2010). There are now hundreds of journal articles on this topic (Bruns et al., 2014).

Early studies relied on Granger causality tests on unrestricted vector autoregressions (VARs) in levels of the variables, while more recent studies often use cointegration methods. A vector autoregression model consists of one regression equation for each variable of interest in a system. Each variable is regressed on lagged values of itself and all other variables in the system. If the coefficients of the lagged values of variable X in the equation for dependent variable Y are jointly statistically significant, then X is said to Granger cause Y. Cointegration analysis tests whether variables that have stochastic trends – their trend is a random walk – share a common trend. If so, then at least one variable must Granger cause the other.[2]

Early studies also used bivariate models of energy and output while more recent research tends to employ multivariate models. Ignoring other relevant variables can generate spurious causality findings. The most common additional variables used are capital and labor or energy prices. A third way to differentiate among models is whether energy is measured in standard heat units or whether a method is used to account for differences in quality among fuels.

The results of early studies that tested for Granger causality using bivariate models were generally inconclusive (Stern, 1993). Using a multivariate vector autoregression (VAR) model of GDP, capital and labor inputs, and a Divisia index of quality-adjusted energy use for the United States, Stern (1993) found that energy use Granger caused GDP. Yu and Jin (1992) conducted the first cointegration study of the energy GDP relationship using the bivariate approach. Stern (2000) estimated a dynamic cointegration model for GDP, quality-weighted energy, labor, and capital. The analysis showed that there is a cointegrating relation between the four variables and, depending on the version of the model used, found that energy Granger causes GDP or that there is mutual causation between energy and GDP. Some subsequent research appeared to confirm these findings (Warr and Ayres, 2010; Oh and Lee, 2004; Ghali and El-Sakka, 2004; Lee and Chang, 2008; Lee et al., 2008).

Bruns et al. (2014) carry out a meta-analysis of 75 single-country Granger causality and cointegration studies comprising more than 500 tests of causality in each direction. They find that most seemingly statistically significant results in the literature are probably the result of statistical biases that occur in models that use short time series of data ("overfitting bias") or the result of the selection for publication of statistically significant results ("publication bias"). The most robust findings in the literature are that growth causes energy use when energy prices are controlled for in the underlying studies. However, Bruns et al. (2014) find that studies that control for capital do not find a genuine effect of energy on growth or vice versa. But they had too small a number of studies that used quality-adjusted energy to test whether there was a genuine relationship between energy and growth when this measure of energy use was employed. So, their findings do not necessarily contradict the previous research by Stern and others reviewed above.

5 Gaps in knowledge and policy implications

As this chapter has shown, the relationship between energy and GDP is one where there is remarkably little consensus and large gaps in knowledge remain. The field of energy economics has expanded rapidly in the last decade, but much research is repetitive and adds little to existing knowledge (Smyth and Narayan, 2015). In particular, there is a very large literature using reduced form time series models to test for causality and cointegration between energy and output. But this literature appears inconclusive with equal numbers of studies finding causation in each direction (Bruns et al., 2014), though Bruns et al. (2014) find that studies that control for the price of energy find a genuine effect of output on energy use but not vice versa. This could be because the effect of energy use on output is much smaller than that of output on energy use. Additionally, holding energy prices constant should measure the effect of an improvement in energy efficiency on output, which may be even smaller.

There is also a lack of consensus in research on the drivers of changes in energy intensity. In particular, energy intensity has risen in many developing countries. The reasons for this are little researched. There is also a lack of consensus on the size of the economy-wide rebound effect. Existing estimates derived from simulation models range from negative rebound to backfire, where energy efficiency improvements actually increase rather than reduce energy use. Empirical estimates are all partial equilibrium approaches that mostly do not credibly identify the economy-wide rebound effect. Therefore, there is little guidance on the potential for energy efficiency policies to actually conserve energy. However, historical evidence and theory suggest that rebound could be large.

Research is also hampered by inadequate data. With the exception of traditional biomass, energy use data are normally of good quality. But data on prices is much more fragmentary.[3] Most economic research is based on understanding the linkages between prices and quantities. So, this is an important area where comprehensive international datasets could be very useful.

Despite the lack of empirical clarity, we can draw some implications for policy from theory and the available evidence. Most countries need to plan on energy use continuing to increase. Increasing the availability of energy and improving energy efficiency is likely to be of more importance to development in developing than in developed countries. Policies that encourage innovation in energy efficiency will probably save much less energy than an engineering analysis or micro-level behavioral analysis would suggest. Climate mitigation policies need to mostly focus on switching to low or zero carbon energy sources rather than expecting gains from energy conservation or efficiency. On the other hand, if such policies to discourage energy use are implemented in developed economies, the effects on economic growth probably will not be that large.

Acknowledgment

I thank the Australian Research Council for funding under Discovery Projects DP120101088: "Energy Transitions: Past, Present and Future" and DP160100756 "Energy Efficiency Innovation, Diffusion and the Rebound Effect".

Notes

1 Some researchers (e.g. Azevedo, 2014; Gillingham et al., 2015) define changes in prices and growth effects as macro effects that they distinguish from indirect rebound effects.
2 The reverse is not the case. Variables may be causally related but not cointegrate because of relevant omitted variables. One of the most important of these may be the unobserved state of technology.
3 The International Energy Agency provides data on the prices of some fuels for a group of mostly developed economies. The World Bank provides data on the price of gasoline and, recently, electricity for a large number of countries.

References

Acemoglu, D. 2008. *Introduction to Modern Economic Growth*. Princeton, NJ: Princeton University Press.
Acemoglu, D., Aghion, P., Bursztyn, L., and Hemous, D. 2012. The environment and directed technical change. *American Economic Review* 102(1): 131–166.
Adetutu, M. O., Glass, A. J., and Weyman-Jones, T. G. 2016. Economy-wide estimates of rebound effects: evidence from panel data. *Energy Journal* 37(3): 251–269.
Aghion, P. and Howitt, P. 2009. *The Economics of Growth*. Cambridge, MA: MIT Press.
Allan, G., Hanley, N., McGregor, P., Swales, K., and Turner, K. 2007. The impact of increased efficiency in the industrial use of energy: A computable general equilibrium analysis for the United Kingdom. *Energy Economics* 29: 779–798.
Allen, R. C. 2009. *The British Industrial Revolution in Global Perspective*. Cambridge: Cambridge University Press.
André, F. J. and Smulders, S. 2014. Fueling growth when oil peaks: Directed technological change and the limits to efficiency. *European Economic Review* 69: 18–39.
Ayres, R. U., Ayres, L. W., and Martinás, K. 1998. Exergy, waste accounting, and life-cycle analysis. *Energy* 23(5): 355–363.
Ayres, R. U. and Kneese, A. V. 1969. Production, consumption and externalities. *American Economic Review* 59: 282–297.
Ayres, R. U. and Warr, B. 2009. *The Economic Growth Engine: How Energy and Work Drive Material Prosperity*. Cheltenham: Edward Elgar.
Azevedo, I.M.L. 2014. Consumer end-use energy efficiency and rebound effects. *Annual Review of Environment and Resources* 39: 393–418.
Barreto, L. and Kemp, R. 2008. Inclusion of technology diffusion in energy-system models: some gaps and needs. *Journal of Cleaner Production* 16S1: 95–101.
Berndt, E. R. 1990. Energy use, technical progress and productivity growth: A survey of economic issues. *The Journal of Productivity Analysis* 2: 67–83.

Borenstein, S. 2015. A microeconomic framework for evaluating energy efficiency rebound and some implications. *Energy Journal* 36(1): 1–21.

Bosetti, V., Carraro, C., Duval, R., and Tavoni, M. 2011. What should we expect from innovation? A model-based assessment of the environmental and mitigation cost implications of climate-related R&D. *Energy Economics* 33: 1313–1320.

Brown, M. T. and Herendeen, R. A. 1996. Embodied energy analysis and energy analysis: A comparative view. *Ecological Economics* 19: 219–236.

Bruns, S. B., Gross, C., and Stern, D. I. 2014. Is there really Granger causality between energy use and output? *Energy Journal* 35(4): 101–134.

Clark, G. 2014. The Industrial Revolution. In *Handbook of Economic Growth, Vol 2A*, edited by Philippe Aghion and Steven Durlauf, 217–262. Amsterdam: North Holland.

Clark, G., and Jacks, D. 2007. Coal and the industrial revolution 1700–1869. *European Review of Economic History* 11: 39–72.

Cleveland, C. J., Costanza, R., Hall, C.A.S., and Kaufmann, R. K. 1984. Energy and the U.S. economy: A biophysical perspective. *Science* 225: 890–897.

Costanza, R. and Daly, H. E. 1992. Natural capital and sustainable development. *Conservation Biology* 6: 37–46.

Csereklyei, Z., Rubio Varas, M. d. M., and Stern, D. I. 2016. Energy and economic growth: The stylized facts. *Energy Journal* 37(2): 223–255.

Dechezleprêtre, A., Glachant, M., Haščič, I., Johnstone, N., and Ménière, Y. 2011. Invention and transfer of climate change-mitigation technologies: A global analysis. *Review of Environmental Economics and Policy* 5(1): 109–130.

Dechezleprêtre, A., Glachant, M., and Ménière, Y. 2013. What drives the international transfer of climate change mitigation technologies? Empirical evidence from patent data. *Environmental and Resource Economics* 54: 161–178.

Enflo, K., Kander, A., and Schön, L. 2009. Electrification and energy productivity. *Ecological Economics* 68: 2808–2817.

Engle, R. E. and Granger, C. W. J. 1987. Cointegration and error-correction: Representation, estimation, and testing. *Econometrica* 55: 251–276.

Fredriksson, P. G., Vollebergh, H.R.J., and Dijkgraaf, E. 2004. Corruption and energy efficiency in OECD countries: Theory and evidence. *Journal of Environmental Economics and Management* 47: 207–231.

Fernihough, A. and O'Rourke, K. H. 2014. Coal and the European Industrial Revolution. *NBER Working Paper* 19802.

Fröling, M. 2011. Energy use, population and growth, 1800–1970. *Journal of Population Economics* 24(3): 1133–1163.

Gars, J. and Olovsson, C. 2015. Fuel for economic growth. *Sveriges Riksbank Working Paper Series* 299.

Gentvilaite, R., Kander, A., and Warde, P. 2015. The role of energy quality in shaping long-term energy intensity in Europe. *Energies* 8(1): 133–153.

Georgescu-Roegen, N. 1971. *The Entropy Law and the Economic Process*. Cambridge, MA: Harvard University Press.

Ghali, K. H. and El-Sakka, M.I.T. 2004. Energy use and output growth in Canada: A multivariate cointegration analysis. *Energy Economics* 26: 225–238.

Gillingham, K., Kotchen, M. J., Rapson, D. S., and Wagner, G. 2013. The rebound effect is overplayed. *Nature* 493: 475–476.

Gillingham, K., Newell, R. G., and Palmer, K. 2009. Energy efficiency economics and policy. *Annual Review of Resource Economics* 1: 597–620.

Gillingham, K., Rapson, D., and Wagner, G. 2015. The rebound effect and energy efficiency policy. *Review of Environmental Economics and Policy* 10(1): 68–88.

Granger, C.W.J. 1969. Investigating causal relations by econometric models and cross-spectral methods. *Econometrica* 37: 424–438.

Greening, L. A., Greene, D. L., and Difiglio, C. 2000. Energy efficiency and consumption: The rebound effect: A survey. *Energy Policy* 28: 389–401.

Grepperud, S. and Rasmussen, I. 2004. A general equilibrium assessment of rebound effects. *Energy Economics* 26: 261–282.

Grübler, A., Nakicenovic, N., and Victor, D. G. 1999. Dynamics of energy technologies and global change. *Energy Policy* 27: 247–280.

Gutberlet, T. 2012. *Cheap Coal, Market Access, and Industry Location in Germany 1846 to 1882*. Preliminary draft, Department of Economics, University of Arizona.

Hall, C. A. S., Cleveland, C. J., and Kaufmann, R. K. 1986. *Energy and Resource Quality: The Ecology of the Economic Process*. New York: Wiley Interscience.

Hall, C. A. S., Tharakan, P., Hallock, J., Cleveland, C. J., and Jefferson, M. 2003. Hydrocarbons and the evolution of human culture. *Nature* 426: 318–322.

Hansen, G. D. and Prescott, E. C. 2002. From Malthus to Solow. *American Economic Review* 92(4): 1205–1217.

Harley, C. K., and Crafts, N.F.R. 2000. Simulating the two views of the British Industrial Revolution. *Journal of Economic History* 60: 819–841.

Henriques, S. T. and Kander, A. 2010. The modest environmental relief resulting from the transition to a service economy. *Ecological Economics* 70: 271–282.

Judson, R. A., Schmalensee, R., and Stoker, T. M. 1999. Economic development and the structure of demand for commercial energy. *The Energy Journal* 20(2): 29–57.

Kander, A. 2002. *Economic Growth, Energy Consumption and CO2 Emissions in Sweden 1800–2000*, Lund Studies in Economic History No. 19, Lund.

Kander, A. 2005. Baumol's disease and dematerialization of the economy. *Ecological Economics* 55(1): 119–130.

Kander, A. and Lindmark, M. 2006. Foreign trade and declining pollution in Sweden: A decomposition analysis of long-term structural and technological effects. *Energy Policy* 34(13): 1590–1599.

Kander, A., Malanima, P., and Warde, P. 2014. *Power to the People: Energy and Economic Transformation of Europe over Four Centuries*. Princeton, NJ: Princeton University Press.

Kaufmann, R. K. 2004. The mechanisms for autonomous energy efficiency increases: A cointegration analysis of the US energy/GDP ratio. *Energy Journal* 25(1): 63–86.

Kelly, M., Mokyr, J., and Ó Gráda, C. 2015. Roots of the industrial revolution. *UCD Centre for Economic Research Working Paper* WP2015/24.

Koetse, M. J., de Groot, H.L.F., and Florax, R.J.G.M. 2008. Capital-energy substitution and shifts in factor demand: A meta-analysis. *Energy Economics* 30: 2236–2251.

Kraft, J. and Kraft, A. 1978. On the relationship between energy and GNP. *Journal of Energy and Development* 3: 401–403.

Kubiszewski, I., Cleveland, C. J., and Endres, P. K. 2010. Meta-analysis of net energy return for wind power systems. *Renewable Energy* 35: 218–225.

Kunnas, J. and T. Myllyntaus. 2009. Postponed leap in carbon dioxide emissions: Impacts of energy efficiency, fuel choices and industrial structure on the Finnish energy economy, 1800–2005. *Global Environment* 3: 154–189.

Lee, C.-C. and Chang, C.-P. 2008. Energy consumption and economic growth in Asian economies: A more comprehensive analysis using panel data. *Resource and Energy Economics* 30: 50–65.

Lee, C.-C., Chang, C.-P., and Chen, P.-F. 2008. Energy-income causality in OECD countries revisited: The key role of capital stock. *Energy Economics* 30: 2359–2373.

Lemoine, D. 2017. General equilibrium rebound from improved energy efficiency. *University of Arizona Working Paper* 14–02.

Levinson, A. 2010. Offshoring pollution: Is the United States increasingly importing polluting goods? *Review of Environmental Economics and Policy* 4(1): 63–83.

Linares, P. and Labandeira, X. 2010. Energy efficiency: Economics and policy. *Journal of Economic Surveys* 24(3): 583–592.

Ma, C. and Stern, D. I. 2008. China's changing energy intensity trend: A decomposition analysis. *Energy Economics* 30: 1037–1053.

Madsen, J. B., Ang, J. B., and Banerjee, R. 2010. Four centuries of British economic growth: The roles of technology and population. *Journal of Economic Growth* 15: 263–290.

Matisoff, D. C. 2008. The adoption of state climate change policies and renewable portfolio standards: Regional diffusion or internal determinants? *Review of Policy Research* 25(6): 527–546.

Murphy, D. J. and Hall, C.A.S. 2010. Year in review: EROI or energy return on (energy) invested. *Annals of the New York Academy of Sciences* 1185: 102–118.

Newell, R. G., Jaffe, A. B., and Stavins, R. N. 1999. The induced innovation hypothesis and energy-saving technological change. *Quarterly Journal of Economics* 114: 941–975.

O'Connor, M. P. 1993. Entropic irreversibility and uncontrolled technological change in the economy and environment. *Journal of Evolutionary Economics* 34: 285–315.

Oh, W. and Lee, K. 2004. Causal relationship between energy consumption and GDP revisited: the case of Korea 1970–1999. *Energy Economics* 26: 51–59.

Ozturk, I. 2010. A literature survey on energy-growth nexus. *Energy Policy* 38: 340–349.

Panayotou, T. 1993. Empirical tests and policy analysis of environmental degradation at different stages of economic development. *Technology and Employment Programme Working Paper* WP238, International Labour Office, Geneva.

Peretto, P. F. and Valente, S. 2015. Growth on a finite planet: Resources, technology and population in the long run. *Journal of Economic Growth* 20: 305–311.

Perrings, C. A. 1987. *Economy and Environment: A Theoretical Essay on the Interdependence of Economic and Environmental Systems.* Cambridge: Cambridge University Press.

Pezzey, J. C V., Stern, D. I., and Lu, Y. 2017. Directed technical change and the British industrial revolution. CAMA *Working Papers* 26/2017.

Pomeranz, K. L. 2001. *The Great Divergence: China, Europe and the Making of the Modern World Economy.* Princeton, NJ: Princeton University Press.

Popp, D. 2002. Induced innovation and energy prices. *American Economic Review* 92: 160–180.

Roy, J. 2000. The rebound effect: Some empirical evidence from India. *Energy Policy* 28: 433–438.

Saunders, H. D. 1992. The Khazzoom-Brookes postulate and neoclassical growth. *Energy Journal* 13(4): 131–148.

Saunders, H. D. 2008. Fuel conserving (and using) production functions. *Energy Economics* 30: 2184–2235.

Saunders, H. D. 2013. Historical evidence for energy efficiency rebound in 30 US sectors and a toolkit for rebound analysts. *Technological Forecasting & Social Change* 80: 1317–1330.

Schurr, S. and Netschert, B. 1960. *Energy and the American Economy, 1850–1975.* Baltimore: Johns Hopkins University Press.

Shanker, A. and Stern, D. I. 2018. Energy intensity, growth, and technical change. *CAMA Working Papers* 46/2018.

Shen, X. and Lin, B. 2017. Total factor energy efficiency of China's industrial sector: A stochastic frontier analysis. *Sustainability* 9(4): 646.

Smyth, R. and Narayan, P. K. 2015. Applied econometrics and implications for energy economics research. *Energy Economics* 50: 351–358.

Solow, R. M. 1956. A contribution to the theory of economic growth. *Quarterly Journal of Economics* 70: 65–94.

Solow, R. M. 1974. Intergenerational equity and exhaustible resources. *Review of Economic Studies* 41(5): 29–46.

Sorrell, S., Dimitropoulos, J., Sommerville, M. 2009. Empirical estimates of the direct rebound effect: A review. *Energy Policy* 37: 1356–1371.

Stern, D. I. 1993. Energy use and economic growth in the USA: A multivariate approach. *Energy Economics* 15: 137–150.

Stern, D. I. 1997. Limits to substitution and irreversibility in production and consumption: A neoclassical interpretation of ecological economics. *Ecological Economics* 21: 197–215.

Stern, D. I. 2000. A multivariate cointegration analysis of the role of energy in the US macroeconomy. *Energy Economics* 22: 267–283.

Stern, D. I. 2010. Energy quality. *Ecological Economics* 69(7): 1471–1478.

Stern, D. I. 2011. The role of energy in economic growth. *Annals of the New York Academy of Sciences* 1219: 26–51.

Stern, D. I. 2012a. Interfuel substitution: A meta-analysis. *Journal of Economic Surveys* 26: 307–331.

Stern, D. I. 2012b. Modeling international trends in energy efficiency. *Energy Economics* 34, 2200–2208.

Stern, D. I. and Kander, A. 2012. The role of energy in the industrial revolution and modern economic growth. *Energy Journal* 33(3): 125–152.

Stiglitz, J. E. 1974. Growth with exhaustible natural resources: The competitive economy. *Review of Economic Studies* 41: 139–152.

Sue Wing, I. 2008. Explaining the declining energy intensity of the U.S. economy. *Resource and Energy Economics* 30: 21–49.

Tahvonen, O. and Salo, S. 2001. Economic growth and transitions between renewable and nonrenewable energy resources. *European Economic Review* 45: 1379–1398.

Turner, K. 2009. Negative rebound and disinvestment effects in response to an improvement in energy efficiency in the UK economy. *Energy Economics* 31: 648–666.

Turner, K. 2013. "Rebound" effects from increased energy efficiency: A time to pause and reflect. *Energy Journal* 34(4): 25–43.

Ukidwe, N. U. and Bakshi, B. R. 2007. Industrial and ecological cumulative exergy consumption of the United States via the 1997 input-output benchmark model. *Energy* 32: 1560–1592.

van Benthem, A. A. 2015. Energy leapfrogging. *Journal of the Association of Environmental and Resource Economists* 2(1): 93–132.

Verdolini, E. and Galeotti, M. 2011. At home and abroad: An empirical analysis of innovation and diffusion in energy technologies. *Journal of Environmental Economics and Management* 61: 119–134.

Wang, C. 2011. Sources of energy productivity growth and its distribution dynamics in China. *Resource and Energy Economics* 33: 279–292.

Warr, B. and Ayres, R. U. 2010. Evidence of causality between the quantity and quality of energy consumption and economic growth. *Energy* 35: 1688–1693.

Wilkinson, R. G. 1973. *Poverty and Progress: An Ecological Model of Economic Development.* London: Methuen.

Wrigley, E. A. 2010. *Energy and the English Industrial Revolution.* Cambridge: Cambridge University Press.

Yu, E.S.H. and Jin, J. C. 1992. Cointegration tests of energy consumption, income, and employment. *Resources and Energy* 14: 259–266.

3

Oil prices and the macroeconomy

Lance J. Bachmeier and Michael D. Plante

1 Introduction

The combination of high inflation and high unemployment experienced in the 1970s and early 1980s has been one of the more important macroeconomic events since the Great Depression. Figure 3.1 shows that there were two spikes in the price of oil in this time period, and both were followed by large increases in inflation and unemployment. This was widely viewed as evidence that changes in the price of oil have large effects on the economy. Not surprisingly, this episode has been the subject of considerable research.[1]

More recently, as seen in Figure 3.2, the price of oil has been extremely volatile, but there has not been a corresponding increase in the volatility of either inflation or the unemployment rate. The post-1995 time period has witnessed the most stable inflation rate since the Great Depression, and the inflation rate fell to almost zero following the large increase in the price of oil in 2007 and 2008. Clearly something has changed since the 1970s and early 1980s. This has spurred renewed interest in oil prices, and as a result the literature has been growing at a fast pace.

There have been two main approaches to answering the question, 'What happens to the macroeconomy after an oil price shock?'[2] The first has been to estimate a vector autoregressive (VAR) model that includes a measure of energy prices and one or more macroeconomic variables. The motivation for using a VAR model is that it allows the researcher to estimate the effect of an oil shock without imposing strong assumptions about the structure of the economy, which reduces concerns about misspecification. Of course, there are costs associated with the use of a VAR model – efficiency may suffer when estimating many parameters, and there are some questions that simply cannot be answered with a VAR model.[3] In addition, reliable identification of causal relationships can sometimes be tricky in VAR models.

The other approach has been to specify a dynamic stochastic general equilibrium (DSGE) model. These models are structural in nature and require the modeler to make explicit assumptions about the nature of the economy. The primary advantage of DSGE models over VAR models is that they can answer a wider range of questions, whether that is because VAR models are not designed to answer the question of interest or because the VAR model would be too inefficient to provide a reliable answer. The downside of DSGE models is that one needs a considerable amount of information about the economy, including the process by which expectations are

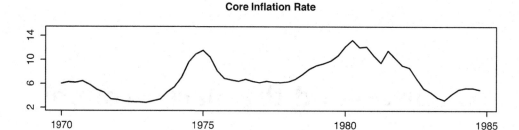

Core Inflation Rate

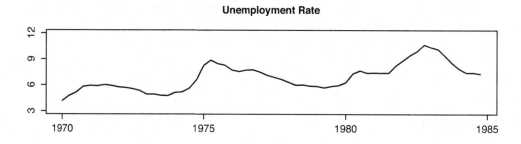

Unemployment Rate

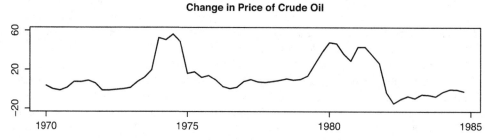

Change in Price of Crude Oil

Figure 3.1 The U.S. civilian unemployment rate, the U.S. CPI inflation rate, and the PPI for Crude Petroleum for the period 1970–1984.

Source: Bureau of Labor Statistics

formed, consumer preferences, and price-setting behavior. And as a result of the large number of assumptions that need to be made, the nature of the answer one gets from a DSGE model may be constrained by those very assumptions. Our view is that researchers should understand and be prepared to use both methodologies.

The primary goal of this chapter is to provide the reader with an introduction to the published literature on the response of output to oil shocks and to point out areas where work remains to be done. The chapter is organized into two broad parts, with the first focused on the empirical VAR literature and the second focused on DSGE models. Due to the large number of papers that have been published on this topic – some of which have been cited thousands of times – we focus on a small slice of the literature that we feel is most relevant for graduate students and other aspiring researchers. The review of the empirical literature focuses on works exploring the connection between oil prices and economic activity. We also provide a brief review of the empirical

Core Inflation Rate

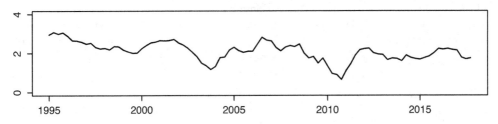

Unemployment Rate

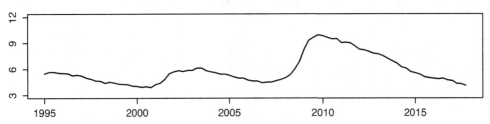

Change in Price of Crude Oil

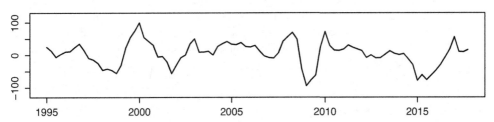

Figure 3.2 The U.S. civilian unemployment rate, the U.S. CPI inflation rate, and the PPI for Crude Petroleum for the period 1995–2017.

Source: Bureau of Labor Statistics

literature on the responses of inflation and consumption to energy price changes, but we do not discuss the response of financial variables such as stock prices, exchange rates, or measures of financial market volatility.

The DSGE section opens up by introducing an example of a simple DSGE model that incorporates oil. This provides some information about what those models look like and lets us discuss some issues related to calibration. We then use the example model to ask what happens to the economy when there is an unexpected increase in the price of oil due to some structural shock. The literature review focuses heavily on works exploring the connections between oil and economic activity, as well as papers on monetary policy responses to changes in oil prices. We briefly discuss other energy-related topics that have been looked at using DSGE models.

2   Early work

The modern empirical literature on the relationship between oil prices and the macroeconomy started with Hamilton (1983).[4] Hamilton motivated his investigation by noting that all but one recession after World War II was preceded by a large increase in the price of oil. The first row of Table 3.1 reports coefficients on the oil_{t-i} terms in the regression

$$y_t = \alpha + \sum_{i=1}^{4} \beta_i y_{t-i} + \sum_{i=1}^{4} \gamma_i oil_{t-i} + \varepsilon_t$$

where y_t is the percentage change in real GDP in quarter t and oil_t is the percentage change in the wholesale price index for crude oil.[5] For the time period 1960–1984, we reject the null hypothesis that the change in the price of oil does not Granger cause real GDP growth at any conventional significance level ($p = 0.007$). The coefficients on the lagged oil price changes are negative and large, with a 10% increase in the price of oil reducing the forecast of GDP growth by about 0.4 percentage points in the fourth quarter after the shock hits the economy.[6] Hamilton provided convincing evidence that the oil price changes in his sample could be treated as exogenous oil price fluctuations, which means the coefficients can be interpreted as the effect of an oil shock on the economy.

In contrast, the results for the 1985–2017 time period, also reported in Table 3.1, offer less support for the claim that changes in the price of oil are an important source of output fluctuations. The estimated coefficients are still negative, but they are close to zero. A Wald test of the null hypothesis that the coefficients on the change in the price of oil are jointly equal to zero fails to reject ($p = 0.52$). One possible explanation for this finding is that the price of oil no longer affects the economy. That does not seem plausible, because energy still accounts for a non-trivial share of marginal cost and consumption expenditures in many industries. Two alternative explanations, which we now discuss, are that a linear VAR model fails to properly capture the relationship between output growth and oil prices, and that failure to account for endogeneity of the price of oil leads to misleading results.

3   Deviations from linearity

Shortly after the publication of Hamilton (1983), evidence began to accumulate that a linear model might provide a poor approximation of the relationship between output and the price of oil. Mork (1989) found that only oil price increases had a statistically significant effect on GDP growth. This had little effect within Hamilton's sample, because there were very few oil price decreases, but by the late 1980s the United States had experienced large oil price decreases.[7]

Table 3.1 Estimated coefficients on the change in the price of oil

	$\hat{\gamma}_1$	$\hat{\gamma}_2$	$\hat{\gamma}_3$	$\hat{\gamma}_4$
		1960–84		
Coefficient	−0.025	−0.004	−0.039	−0.039
t-stat	(−1.20)	(−0.17)	(−1.77)	(−1.82)
		1985–2017		
Coefficient	−0.002	−0.001	−0.004	−0.001
t-stat	(−0.57)	(−0.20)	(−1.57)	(−0.41)

Hooker (1996) failed to find evidence of a relationship between US macroeconomic variables and the price of oil after 1973. Lee et al. (1995) and Ferderer (1996) found evidence that oil price volatility affected output. If oil price changes make it harder to predict the price of oil in the near future, there is an incentive for firms to delay investment and for consumers to delay major purchases, especially cars (see Bernanke 1983). Oil price decreases can even be contractionary if they increase uncertainty about future oil prices, and as emphasized by Hamilton (1988), it takes time for workers to transition from the oil sector to other sectors.

Responding to Hooker (1996), Hamilton (1996) introduced the "net oil price increase" (NOPI) measure of oil price shocks. The idea is to construct a measure of oil shocks such that the price of oil only affects the economy during periods that it is high relative to recent experience, because those are the oil shocks that cause firms and consumers to change their behavior in a meaningful way. Hamilton (1996) defined NOPI to be

$$NOPI_t = max(0, ln(oil_t) - oil_t^{max})$$

where oil_t^{max} is the natural log of the highest price of oil in quarters $t - 1$ through $t - 4$. Hamilton (2003) did a more rigorous investigation and concluded that it is best to compare the current price of oil against its highest price in the previous 12 quarters. Versions of the NOPI model have been estimated by Bernanke et al. (1997), Cuñado and de Gracia (2003), Davis and Haltiwanger (2001), Balke et al. (2002), and Lee and Ni (2002), among many others.

In Table 3.2 are the estimated coefficients on the NOPI terms in the regression

$$y_t = \alpha + \sum_{i=1}^{4} \beta_i y_{t-i} + \sum_{i=1}^{4} \gamma_i NOPI_{t-i} + \varepsilon_t$$

Although the coefficients estimated on the 1985–2017 subsample are smaller than those of the full 1960–2017 sample, the disappearance of the correlation between lagged oil price changes and real GDP growth does not carry through to the net oil price increase.

The hypothesis that oil price shocks have nonlinear effects on output has been challenged, most notably by Kilian and Vigfusson (2011a). Applying the simulation methodology proposed in Kilian and Vigfusson (2011b), they computed impulse response functions for real GDP growth for an oil shock that originated in the NOPI regime, and compared it with the impulse response function for the same shock originating in the non-NOPI regime.[8] They tested and failed to reject the null hypothesis that the two impulse response functions were equal at all horizons up to one year, and concluded that the NOPI model is not supported by the data. Other authors, including Herrera et al. (2011, 2015) and Herrera and Karaki (2015), applied the same test and

Table 3.2 Estimated coefficients on the net oil price increase

	$\hat{\gamma}_1$	$\hat{\gamma}_2$	$\hat{\gamma}_3$	$\hat{\gamma}_4$
		1960–2017		
Coefficient	−0.018	−0.010	−0.022	−0.027
t-stat	(−1.76)	(−0.98)	(−2.08)	(−2.51)
		1985–2017		
Coefficient	−0.010	−0.009	−0.012	−0.020
t-stat	(−1.11)	(−0.93)	(−1.26)	(−2.16)

also failed to reject the null hypothesis that the impulse response functions are the same across regimes.

Hamilton (2011) argued that there are several reasons to be skeptical of this conclusion. First, the failure to reject a null hypothesis is not evidence that the null hypothesis is true, and might instead be evidence that the test has low power. Second, Hamilton notes that Kilian and Vigfusson's test does reject linearity for large (two standard deviation) oil shocks. Moreover, using the local projections method for computing impulse response functions introduced by Jordà (2005), Hamilton rejects the null hypothesis of linearity for every model specification. Finally, working with just a prediction equation for GDP, which can be interpreted as one equation in a reduced form VAR model, Hamilton rejects the null hypothesis that all coefficients on the lagged NOPI terms are zero. It is difficult to reconcile these results with the claim that a linear VAR model provides the best representation of the data. Hamilton (2016) points out that all of the studies that fail to find evidence of nonlinearity rely on the Kilian and Vigfusson (2011b) test. Given the disagreements, and given this topic's importance, it is sure to continue to be the subject of research in the future.

An alternative to the NOPI model, which retains the property that the price of oil only affects the economy when it deviates substantially from its behavior in the recent past, is the net oil price change (NOPC) model proposed by Kilian and Vigfusson (2013). Define the net oil price decrease as

$$NOPD_t = min\,(0, ln(oil_t) - oil_t^{max})$$

where oil_t^{min} is the natural log of the lowest price of oil in the previous 12 quarters. We then have

$$NOPC_t = NOPI_t + NOPD_t$$

One of the advantages of the NOPC model over the NOPI model is that there are fewer censored observations of the oil price, which should result in more efficient parameter estimates, as well as less bias, if oil price decreases affect the economy. Similar to the NOPI model, the NOPC model allows for nonlinearity, but it rules out asymmetry. Kilian and Vigfusson considered a variety of alternative specifications, including those in which the NOPD and NOPI variables have different coefficients, but concluded that the NOPC model provides the best out-of-sample output forecasts out of all nonlinear models that they considered. Other out-of-sample forecast evaluations of nonlinear oil price models include Bachmeier et al. (2008), Ravazzolo and Rothman (2013), and Kilian and Vigfusson (2017).

4   Endogeneity of oil prices

One of the important findings of Hamilton (1983) was that changes in the price of oil could be interpreted as supply shocks. In the aftermath of the oil shocks of the 1970s, which were attributed to the OPEC oil embargo and the Iranian revolution, this was a reasonable conclusion. It should be noted, however, that it has long been recognized that the price of energy responds to changes in the economy. In a speech to Congress on 4 June 1971, President Nixon said,[9]

> During the last decade, the prices of oil, coal, natural gas and electricity have increased at a much slower rate than consumer prices as a whole. Energy has been an attractive bargain in this country – and demand has responded accordingly. In the years ahead, the needs of a growing economy will further stimulate this demand.

One cannot provide a useful answer to the question, 'What happens to output if the price of oil rises?' without knowing why the price of oil has risen. Macroeconomic theory predicts lower output if the price of oil has risen because of a shock to the supply of oil. On the other hand, output will obviously be higher if the price of oil has risen because the economy (and therefore the demand for oil) is growing faster than expected. A third possibility is that the demand for oil is rising because of higher foreign output, in which case the response of domestic output depends on whether the expansionary effect of increased exports is sufficient to offset the contractionary effect of the higher oil price. One cannot interpret an estimated relationship between output and the price of oil without first addressing the endogeneity of oil prices.

An important step toward solving this identification problem was made by Kilian (2009).[10] The key component in Kilian's analysis was the construction of an index of global economic activity based on shipping rates. In the short run, there is a ceiling on the quantity of goods that can be shipped due to lags in the production of new shipping capacity, causing periods of unexpectedly strong world economic growth to be accompanied by increases in shipping rates. Kilian estimated a VAR model with global crude oil production, real oil prices, and his constructed index of global economic activity, and identified three structural shocks, interpreted as "oil supply", "aggregate demand", and "precautionary demand" shocks. The oil supply and aggregate demand shocks have a straightforward interpretation. The precautionary demand shock represents an increase in purchases due to concerns about the future availability of oil, such as an airline purchasing additional jet fuel after news about a possible disruption of oil supplies, even if current oil production has not yet been affected.

Kilian concluded that the price of oil has historically been driven almost entirely by the aggregate demand and precautionary demand shocks, with oil supply shocks playing only a minor role. This should not be interpreted as a statement that the supply of oil is unimportant to the determination of oil prices, because the precautionary demand shock captures the effect of news about the supply of oil that has not yet affected global oil production.

Recent work has shown that decomposing oil price movements into the parts corresponding to oil supply shocks and oil demand shocks depends critically on assumptions about the short-run elasticity of oil supply. Caldara et al. (2019) propose an identification scheme that forces the elasticities implied by a VAR model to be consistent with the elasticities reported in published papers. They conclude that oil supply shocks explain 50% of the variation in the price of oil, while global economic activity shocks explain only 30%. Baumeister and Hamilton (2019) adopt a Bayesian approach to inference that is less restrictive than the traditional approach to VAR model identification.[11] The reported posterior distributions imply a non-zero short-run oil supply elasticity that they report is much larger than the upper bound of Kilian and Murphy (2012), for instance.[12] Baumeister and Peersman (2013) address a related problem by estimating a VAR model with time-varying parameters and stochastic volatility. They show that the assumption of constant VAR coefficients can make it difficult to properly identify the effects of oil supply and oil demand shocks on the economy.

An additional complication arises if one treats all oil price movements that are responses to the economy as a single shock. By construction, the price of oil and US real GDP growth will be positively correlated if the price of oil is changing as a response to US output. That will not necessarily be true when the price of oil is responding to foreign output shocks. In the extreme case in which the foreign economy does not trade with the United States, US output will respond in the same way as it responds to an oil supply shock.[13] Aastveit et al. (2015) found that most oil price fluctuations since the early 1990s could be attributed to changes in demand in emerging and developing economies. Thus, even if one adopts the view that the price of oil is largely driven by demand shocks, higher oil prices may still be a drag on US economic growth.

High-frequency data has been used to aid the identification of contemporaneous responses. Kilian and Vega (2011) study news about US macroeconomic data releases and conclude that energy prices can be treated as predetermined with respect to the US economy. Bachmeier (2013) is unable to reject the hypothesis that world oil prices are predetermined with respect to US gasoline prices. To the extent that gasoline price fluctuations reflect shocks to US economic activity, this is additional evidence that energy prices respond to macroeconomic shocks with a lag.

5   Gasoline prices and consumption

One mechanism by which oil shocks are transmitted to the economy is through retail gasoline prices. Higher gasoline expenditures have to be offset by reduced consumption of other goods. This effect has been verified by Edelstein and Kilian (2009), Farrell and Greig (2015), Gelman, et al. (2016), and Baumeister and Kilian (2016). One of the important outstanding research questions is how much this effect has changed over time. Edelstein and Kilian (2009), Ramey (2016) and Baumeister et al. (2017) have investigated this question. Sorting through these issues is a difficult task, but one of great importance, as it is impossible to accurately predict changes in consumption without doing so.

6   Monetary policy

VAR analysis, which most commonly takes the form of impulse response function analysis, does not provide any information about the mechanisms by which oil shocks are transmitted to the economy. In addition to the direct effect that oil shocks have on the economy through production and consumption, oil shocks will indirectly affect the economy through monetary policy if the Federal Reserve responds to them in an attempt to stabilize output and inflation. Bernanke et al. (1997) simulated the behavior of the US economy using an estimated VAR model combined with various choices of the monetary policy rule. They concluded that "the monetary policy response is the dominant source of the real effects of an oil price shock".

The conclusion drawn by Bernanke et al. (1997), that monetary policy is responsible for much of the response of the economy to an oil shock, has not been universally accepted. One problem, recognized by the authors, is that their analysis ignores the Lucas (1976) critique. Sims (Bernanke et al. 1997) questioned the choice of alternative monetary policy rule on the grounds that it is unsustainable. Hamilton and Herrera (2004) argue that implementing the alternative monetary policy rule would have required implausibly large changes in the federal funds rate. In addition, even if one assumes the Federal Reserve would have been capable of implementing such a policy, their conclusion is not robust to the use of longer VAR lag lengths. Kilian and Lewis (2011) provided additional evidence against the importance of monetary policy for the effects of oil shocks, most notably by demonstrating that the Federal Reserve has not responded to oil shocks at all since at least the mid-1980s. Other relevant papers that we will not discuss here include Bohi (1989), Barsky and Kilian (2001), Carlstrom and Fuerst (2005), Herrera and Pesavento (2009), and Bodenstein et al. (2012).

Due to the limitations of VAR models, we feel that DSGE models are better able to provide insights on the relative importance of the monetary policy rule. DSGE models are designed to address questions like this, and in fact, they have been used by many central banks for this purpose (Galí and Gertler 2007). We anticipate that most future research on the interaction of oil shocks and monetary policy will be done using DSGE models.

7 Oil shocks and inflation

Macroeconomic models imply that an increase in the price of oil will cause inflation to rise. A surprising finding highlighted by Hooker (2002) is that core inflation shows little or no response to oil price shocks. Clark and Terry (2010) estimated a time-varying parameter VAR model and found that the decline in the response of core inflation to oil shocks began in 1975, and that this was not affected by either the high volatility of oil prices in the early 2000s or changes in the Federal Reserve's monetary policy rule. de Gregorio, Landeretche, and Neilson (2007) and Chen (2009) looked at inflation in many different countries and found a similar decline.

Attempting to understand the reason for the decline, Blanchard and Galí (2009) found support for three potential explanations. First, wages have become more flexible through time, which allows the higher cost of production resulting from an oil shock to be partially offset by lower wages, which puts less pressure on inflation. Second, the credibility of monetary policy has improved, causing all inflationary shocks to have less effect on inflation. Third, energy is a smaller part of the economy today than it was in the 1970s. Bachmeier and Cha (2011) used disaggregate inflation data to sort through the relative importance of these explanations. They found that most of the decline in the response of inflation to oil shocks took place in sectors that saw large declines in energy intensity, and by itself, the change in energy intensity can predict most of the change in the response of aggregate inflation to an oil shock. Additionally, they found little correlation between the labor intensity of a sector and the change in response to oil shocks. See Blinder and Rudd (2012) and Castro et al. (2016) for additional analyses.

8 DSGE models

Dynamic stochastic general equilibrium (DSGE) models provide an internally consistent modeling framework for thinking about energy prices and the economy. Since the early works of Hamilton (1988) and Kim and Loungani (1992), a number of papers have been published that make use of DSGE models with energy. These have primarily considered oil, as opposed to other forms of energy, and have explored the importance of oil and oil prices for issues related to business cycles, monetary policy and many other topics.

In this chapter, we introduce a very simple DSGE model that incorporates oil and provide a review of the DSGE literature. One of our main goals in introducing the model is to provide a working example that goes through the model's equations and discusses several issues related to calibration. As an aide to the interested reader, an online appendix provides additional details regarding several variants of the model and further discussion on issues related to incorporating oil into DSGE models. The associated MATLAB code is also posted online.

Another goal is to use the model to investigate the theoretical relationship between oil prices and economic activity. To do this, we solve the model numerically and look at how oil prices and GDP respond to different structural shocks in the model. We highlight the importance of distinguishing between supply and demand shocks in the oil market as not every type of shock generates the same correlation between oil prices and economic activity. In particular, while oil supply shocks generate a negative correlation, other shocks need not do so.

Not surprisingly, a large literature exists that makes use of DSGE models to think about various issues related to oil and the economy. The literature review at the end of this section provides a number of references for those interested in learning more about specific topics. The review focuses primarily on works that discuss how oil can affect the economy (and vice versa), and works that explore monetary policy issues that arise because of oil and oil prices. We hope this review will be a useful starting point for those interested in learning more about the existing research.

8.1 Model

DSGE models require explicit assumptions about the structure of the economy.[14] When incorporating oil into a DSGE model this means that several questions must be answered in advance by the modeler. These include: Are oil prices exogenous or endogenous? Does the economy produce oil or not? If so, how much and how is that production modeled? What sectors of the economy use oil? How is that use modeled?

In our model, we make the following assumptions. First, since we are interested in discussing how different shocks affect oil prices and economic activity, we need endogenous oil prices. However, we do not need to go beyond the simple assumption that the supply of oil is exogenous. Second, we consider an economy that imports all of its oil from abroad, but we do not explicitly model the rest of the world except with regards to oil production. Finally, for simplicity we assume oil is used as an input into the production of a final good but abstract from household use of oil. These assumptions make the model very similar to the one used in Kim and Loungani (1992), except that the price of oil is endogenous in our setup.

We work with a decentralized model with a representative agent and a representative firm. The representative agent consumes a final good and earns income by providing labor to the private sector and from dividends it receives from the firm. The representative firm operates under perfect competition and produces the final good using labor and imported oil. Each period the economy in question trades some of its output of the final good for oil. The model assumes that trade balances each period.

The representative agent chooses consumption and labor to maximize the present discounted value of utility,

$$E_0 \sum_{t=0}^{\infty} \beta^t \left[\log(c_t) - \chi n_t^{1+\eta} / (1+\eta) \right] \tag{3.1}$$

where β is the discount factor, c_t is consumption, n_t is hours worked, η is the inverse Frisch elasticity of labor and χ is the weight on the dis-utility from working. Utility is maximized subject to a budget constraint,

$$c_t = w_t n_t + d_t \tag{3.2}$$

where w_t is the real wage and d_t are dividends from the firm. The household takes prices and wages as given when making its decisions.

Denoting λ_t as the multiplier on the budget constraint, the first-order conditions are given by

$$1/c_t = \lambda_t \tag{3.3}$$
$$w_t \lambda_t = \chi n_t^{\eta} \tag{3.4}$$

which can be combined into a single equation, $w_t = \chi n_t^{\eta} c_t$.

The representative firm maximizes profit by choosing the amount of labor and oil to be used in the production of the final good, y_t. The technology available to the firm is a CES production function of the form

$$y_t = \left[(1-\alpha_o)(n_t z_t^n)^{\frac{\sigma-1}{\sigma}} + \alpha_o (o_t z^o)^{\frac{\sigma-1}{\sigma}} \right]^{\frac{\sigma}{\sigma-1}} \tag{3.5}$$

where o_t is oil used by the firm and z_t^n is a labor-augmenting productivity shock. The term z^o is, in this case, a constant scaling factor but one can easily make it stochastic to represent exogenous shocks that affect the efficiency with which the private sector uses oil as an input.

Introducing oil into the production function adds two parameters that are not present in the basic real business cycle (RBC) model. The first is α_o, which controls the cost-share of oil in gross output, y_t. The second parameter is σ, which is the elasticity of substitution between oil and labor (or value-added). The exact nature of these parameters can vary across models. In Kim and Loungani (1992), for example, the elasticity parameter controls the degree of substitutability between capital and energy.

The first-order conditions for the firm are given by

$$w_t = \left(1-\alpha_o\right)\left(\frac{y_t}{n_t}\right)^{\frac{1}{\sigma}} z_t^{n\frac{\sigma-1}{\sigma}} \tag{3.6}$$

$$p_t^o = \alpha_o\left(\frac{y_t}{o_t}\right)^{\frac{1}{\sigma}} z^{o\frac{\sigma-1}{\sigma}} \tag{3.7}$$

For the oil market, we assume there is a stochastic endowment of oil whose ownership lies outside the domestic economy. The log supply of oil follows an autoregressive process,

$$\ln o_t^s = \left(1-\rho_s\right)\ln o^s + \rho_s \ln o_{t-1}^s + \sigma_s\varepsilon_{s,t} \tag{3.8}$$

The market clearing condition for the oil market is given by

$$o_t = o_t^s \tag{3.9}$$

One can derive a resource constraint for the economy using the household's budget constraint and the firm's first order conditions. The resource constraint for the economy is

$$c_t = y_t - p_t^o o_t \tag{3.10}$$

It is useful to note that in this model there is a difference between gross output and GDP/value-added and that there are several ways one can measure GDP. By the expenditure approach, real GDP is simply equal to c_t. Another way is to measure value-added from the final goods sector, which mathematically is equal to $y_t - p_t^o o_t$ and which is equivalent to c_t. Gross domestic income (GDI) could also be calculated as $w_t n_t$.

Finally, we need to specify a law of motion for productivity. We assume the log of labor-augmenting productivity follows an autoregressive process,

$$\ln z_t^n = \left(1-\rho_n\right)\ln z^n + \rho_n \ln z_{t-1}^n + \sigma_n\varepsilon_{n,t} \tag{3.11}$$

8.2 Calibrating the steady state

Typically, a DSGE model is linearized and solved using numerical methods. This requires calibrating or estimating the model's parameters and choosing steady state values for the variables. Our calibration approach here is illustrative and intended to provide a short discussion on some of the issues that arise because the model incorporates oil.

The model has nine parameters that need to be calibrated: β, α_o, η, χ, σ, z^o, ρ_s, ρ_n, σ_s and σ_n. Starting values also need to be chosen for w, y, c, p^o, z^n, o^s and o. We drop the time subscript to denote a steady state value.

The parameters β, η, and χ are not unique to models with oil, so we do not discuss their calibration in detail. We calibrate the model to be consistent with a quarterly frequency. We set the discount factor β to 0.99 and labor-supply elasticity η to 1, and determine the value of χ by using the household's first-order condition for labor. For simplicity, we set all persistence parameters for the shocks equal to 0.90 and all standard deviations to 0.001.[15]

The parameter σ is directly connected with the price-elasticity of demand for oil. Numerous estimates exist for this price-elasticity but a generally accepted finding is that short-run price elasticities for oil are low (i.e. well below unity). As a result, this parameter (or a related parameter) is also typically set well below 1. For illustrative purposes, we consider a value of 0.25.

One approach to calibrate α_o is to use data on the cost-share of oil or a related quantity, such as the GDP share of oil. For the United States, there is annual data available to help provide some guidance on what this number should be set to. Data on nominal spending on petroleum products is available from the US Energy Information Administration (EIA) from 1970 to 2015.[16] This covers spending by both firms and households. Another set of data from the Bureau of Economic Analysis (BEA) provides annual nominal spending by households on motor gasoline, heating oil, and other fuels.[17] This can be subtracted from the EIA data to produce an estimate of nominal spending by firms on petroleum products. Nominal GDP data comes from the BEA.

Figure 3.3 plots the time series for the ratio of nominal oil expenditures to nominal GDP for firms and households. One notable feature is that both shares vary over time. This variation is connected with the price of oil and has to do with the fact that the demand for oil is relatively inelastic. As a result, a large swing in oil prices can dramatically affect nominal expenditures. Another feature is that both shares have remained below the high values seen in the mid-1970s and early 1980s, even during recent period where oil prices were relatively high. This has to do with the fact that the economy has become less oil intensive.

It is important to point out that the series in the chart are GDP shares while in the model α_o determines a cost share in terms of gross output. It can be shown that if g is the GDP share, then

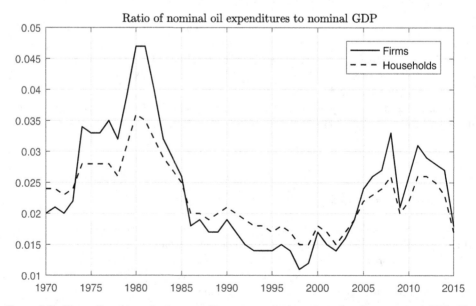

Figure 3.3 The ratio of nominal expenditures on petroleum products to nominal GDP. The dashed line is for household spending, the solid line for spending by firms.

$\alpha_o = g/(1 + g)$. For this exercise, we calculated the average GDP share for firm spending over the Great Moderation period (1986–2015), which turns out to be 0.02. The cost share is then equal to 0.0196.

Next we turn to the steady state values of the variables. There is some leeway in how to normalize the variables. A particularly convenient normalization for this model is to set y, n and z^n equal to 1. This ensures that α_o is equal to the cost share of oil and also allows the modeler to solve for the rest of the steady state by hand. The firm's first order condition for labor gives $w = 1 - \alpha_o$ while the first order condition for oil gives $p^o o = \alpha_o$. This implies that we can also normalize units for oil use, and we do so by setting $p^o = 1$. The value of o is then determined by our calibration of α_o. The market clearing conditions then imply trivially that $c = y - p^o o$ and $o^s = o$. Using the steady-state production function, one can then show that $z^o = 1/o$.

8.3 Impulse response functions (IRF)

We level linearize the model around the initial steady state and solve it using Dynare. MATLAB code can be found online. Our main goal is to show how GDP and the price of oil respond to the two shocks in the model. We consider a negative oil supply shock and a positive labor-augmenting productivity shock. The latter is an aggregate supply shock, but from the perspective of the oil market it acts as a demand shock. We standardize the size of the shocks so that in each case they boost the price of oil by 10%.

Figure 3.4 plots the percent deviations of the two variables from their steady states. The top row is the response of the price of oil while the bottom row is the response of GDP. The first

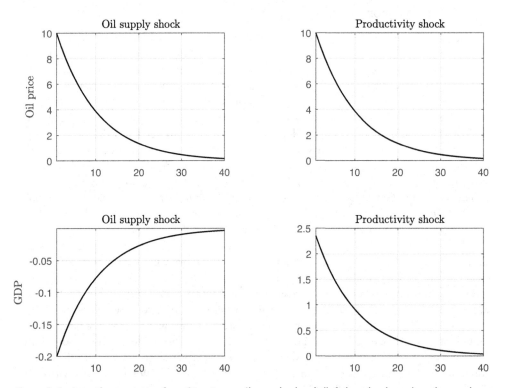

Figure 3.4 Impulse response functions to an oil supply shock (left-hand column) and a productivity shock (right-hand column). All figures show percent deviations from steady state values

column is for an oil supply shock while the second is the productivity shock. A negative oil supply shock reduces the supply of oil and drives up its relative price. As oil is an input into production, this raises costs for the firm, lowers the marginal product of labor, and leads to a decline in GDP. On the other hand, a positive technology shock boosts the marginal product of labor and also raises the demand for oil. In this case, the price of oil also rises, but so does GDP.

A direct implication of the IRFs is that in the model economy the correlation between oil prices and economic activity will depend a lot upon the nature of the shocks. If oil supply shocks are large relative to productivity shocks then a negative correlation could certainly occur, and vice versa. In small samples of time series the correlation could also depend upon the particular sequence of shocks. For example, if in a small window of time there were many large negative oil supply shocks, it would look like oil prices were negatively correlated with activity even if over longer periods of time the opposite correlation holds.

Obviously, these results are from a simple model with just two shocks. Other shocks could be introduced, each of which could potentially generate its own correlation between GDP and oil prices. Likewise, various extensions to the model could allow for a more richer analysis. For example, explicitly modeling the rest of the world would allow one to make statements about how different foreign shocks affect domestic GDP and oil prices. The literature review that follows provides many examples of papers with more complicated models that have extended the basic framework in numerous directions.

8.4 Literature review

Oil prices and economic activity

A large part of the DSGE literature has considered the potential importance of energy and energy prices for economic activity. The first work focused exclusively on this issue was Kim and Loungani (1992), which was aptly titled "The Role of Energy in Real Business Cycle Models". This work extended the RBC model of Hansen (1985) to include energy as an input to the production function. One of the major questions in Kim and Loungani (1992) was to what extent exogenous energy price shocks could generate volatility in output, thereby reducing the reliance of the RBC model on technology shocks. The main finding was that while energy price shocks could increase output volatility, price shocks alone could not be the main driver of fluctuations in output. Dhawan and Jeske (2008a) later extended Kim and Loungani (1992) by adding a consumer durable good and differentiating between firm and household demand for energy but reached a similar conclusion. Indeed, the results in Dhawan and Jeske (2008b) suggest that differentiating between household and firm energy use, while holding fixed the total amount of energy use, will actually reduce the ability of energy price shocks to generate volatility. A recent work, Balke and Brown (2018), estimates a DSGE model of the United States using data from 1991 to 2015 and finds a small elasticity of real GDP with respect to oil price shocks driven by foreign oil supply.

Rotemberg and Woodford (1996) present empirical evidence that oil price shocks generated large, persistent drops in US value-added during the period of 1948 to 1980. They show that a model of imperfect competition can match this empirical finding, while a model of perfect competition, such as the one in Kim and Loungani (1992), has trouble doing so. Finn (2000) shows that a model of perfect competition extended to include capital utilization, where the utilization rate is tied to energy usage, can match the empirical findings in Rotemberg and Woodford (1996). Aguiar-Conraria and Wen (2007) show that a model with increasing returns to scale in production can explain the impact the oil price shock of 1973–1974 on output and investment.

Oil prices and the Great Moderation

A related line of research has investigated the quantitative importance of oil prices in explaining the Great Moderation. Leduc and Sill (2007) found that much of the decline in US output volatility was due to a change in the behavior of TFP and oil supply shocks, rather than a change in monetary policy. Dhawan et al. (2010) showed that a negative statistical connection existed between energy prices and US TFP until 1982. Through the lens of a DSGE model, they find that disappearance of this negative connection after 1982 can explain a significant fraction of the moderation in US output. Nakov and Pescatori (2010) find that oil-related factors play an important role in reducing output volatility, although they are not the most important factor. On the other hand, Bjornland et al. (2018), using a Markov Switching Rational Expectations New-Keynesian model, find that oil price volatility does not play a major role in explaining the Great Moderation.

Changes in the effects of oil shocks

Another line of research has used DSGE models to try and explain why the oil price shocks of the 1970s had larger impacts on the economy relative to the effects in the 2000s. Blanchard and Riggi (2013), building on the work of Blanchard and Galí (2009), show that a lower degree of real wage rigidity, better monetary policy and smaller oil cost and consumption-expenditure shares are important factors that have reduced the ability of oil prices to impact the economy. Katayama (2013) shows that some of the weaker effects of the post-1970 period can be explained by deregulation of the US transportation sector in the early 1980s, improved energy efficiency and less persistent oil prices. In the model of Gavin et al. (2015), it is interactions between the tax code and inflation that led to the larger effects of the oil price increases in the 1970s. More specifically, they assume that during the 1970s oil prices boosted the Fed's inflation target, which increased the inflationary effects of an oil price shock and increased taxes on nominal capital gains. This created an additional, indirect negative impact on the economy as households reduced investment in the capital stock due to the higher taxes.

One finding from the recent empirical literature is that the oil price increases in the 2000s were driven primarily by global demand and not oil supply shocks.[18] Given this finding, it is less surprising that high oil prices were not associated with a slowdown in global activity: oil prices were high because the global economy was booming in the first place. A more subtle issue, though, is how that might have impacted the US economy. In Blanchard and Riggi (2013), it is assumed that a shock to oil prices due to foreign demand affects the US economy in a similar way to exogenous oil supply shocks. On the other hand, in the three-country DSGE model in Lippi and Nobili (2012), the impact on the US economy from an oil price increase due to the rest of the world can depend upon the exact nature of the shock. In some cases it is negative, in others the impact is ambiguous despite the fact that oil prices are higher.

Monetary policy and oil prices

Another branch of the literature has used DSGE models to consider monetary policy responses to oil prices. Motivated by the discussions in Bernanke et al. (1997) and Hamilton and Herrera (2004), Leduc and Sill (2004) considered how different specifications of monetary policy rules affect the responses of output and inflation to oil price shocks. They find that a pre-1979 specification of a monetary policy rule exacerbates the impacts of an oil shock on inflation and output, relative to a post-1979 rule. Later, Bodenstein et al. (2008) looked at the optimal monetary policy response to an oil supply shock in a DSGE model with an exogenous supply of oil and nominal price and wage rigidities. They find that the optimal policy calls for a rise in core inflation to help mitigate the impacts of sticky nominal wages. Numerous papers have considered extensions to the two works just cited. In Nakov and Pescatori (2010), optimal monetary policy is considered in a model with a dominant oil producer. Kormilitsina (2011) looks at optimal policy in a medium-scale estimated DSGE model of the US economy. Bodenstein et al. (2012) use a two-country DSGE model to discuss how policy responses can vary depending upon the underlying structural shock that has affected oil prices. Natal (2012) discuss the implications of a distorted steady state for optimal policy. Bodenstein et al. (2013) consider the interaction between oil supply shocks and the zero lower bound constraint. Plante (2014a) considers optimal policy in a model where oil supply and (aggregate) productivity shocks affect the price of oil.

Other topics

The literature review so far has focused on research looking at the economic impacts of oil prices or monetary policy issues related to oil. But DSGE models have also been used to explore a number of other topics, particularly in international macroeconomics but also in areas related to energy consumption and energy policy. Here, we provide a quick overview of some important works. For brevity's sake, we do not discuss the results of these papers in any detail. Backus and Crucini (2000) looked at how oil prices impact the terms of trade for a handful of OECD countries. Bodenstein et al. (2011) use a two-country DSGE model to consider how changes in oil prices affect trade balances, real exchange rates, and other macroeconomic variables. Lippi and Nobili (2012) use the model of Backus and Crucini (2000) to help motivate a VAR model of the oil market that is identified using sign restrictions. The role of fiscal policy in a small oil-exporting country is considered in Pieschacon (2012). Nakov and Nuno (2013) introduce a three-country DSGE model where Saudi Arabia is modeled as a dominant oil producer. Using the same model, Manescu and Nuno (2015) consider the impact of the shale oil boom on oil markets. Bergholt et al. (In press) consider the importance of oil prices for business cycles in a small oil-exporting country. Arezki et al. (2017) use discoveries of giant oil fields as an example of news shocks in a small open-economy setting.

Several papers have also looked at issues related to energy policy and energy use. Atkeson and Kehoe (1999) explore the ability of putty-putty and putty-clay models to match the low short-run and higher long-run price elasticities of demand for energy seen in the data. The long-term macroeconomic impacts of consumer subsidies on fossil fuels are investigated in Plante (2014b) using a small open-economy model. That work is extended in Balke et al. (2015), which uses a two-country DSGE model to consider the how those types of subsidies affect oil prices and the global economy. Atalla et al. (2017) show how prices and policies affect the energy mixes of several OECD countries through the lens of a DSGE model.

9   Conclusion

Despite over 30 years of research, the question 'What happens to the macroeconomy after an oil price shock?' continues to be asked to this day. This chapter has provided an introduction to the literature that, broadly speaking, has tried to answer that question, and related ones, using VAR or DSGE models. We hope that the literature review herein along with the accompanying code will be useful for those interested in learning more about the connections between oil and the macroeconomy.

While the literature is voluminous, in no way has it exhausted all of the possible avenues for research. One reason for this is that the tools available to researchers continue to evolve, as do the questions being asked. With more advanced tools, and new perspectives on old issues, comes the ability to answer new research questions. Another reason is that both the economy and the oil market are evolving over time, and as they change so do the questions people ask. While predicting the future path of research is likely to be as difficult as predicting the path of oil prices, several topics do seem likely to attract further attention. These include issues related to the asymmetric responses of the economy to oil price shocks, the importance (or not) of the US shale boom, and the ever-present question of how oil affects the macroeconomy. We also note the possibility of more interdisciplinary research on the broader impacts of oil price changes, with some obvious examples including integrated assessment models, energy poverty, and the effects of oil shocks on economic development and inequality.

Notes

1 The behavior of the macroeconomy following the oil shocks of the 1970s, and the inability of the macroeconomic models of the time to explain what was going on, led to a "major overhaul and reconstruction" of the field of macroeconomics (Blanchard 2006).
2 Although it is a valid question to ask about energy prices more generally, the literature has almost exclusively focused on oil prices due to its importance relative to other forms of energy. We follow suit with the literature.
3 An example of a question VAR models are not designed to answer is determining which of several potential monetary policy responses to oil shocks will deliver the best combination of inflation and unemployment.
4 Other early papers include Rasche and Tatum (1977, 1981), Burbidge and Harrison (1984), and Hamilton (1985).
5 This specification is taken from Hamilton (2003). The data used to estimate this regression can be found in the repository for this paper.
6 These results are similar to those reported by Hamilton (2003) for the period 1949–1980.
7 One reason for this is that US oil prices were regulated until the early 1980s (see e.g. Kilian 2014).
8 The impulse response functions in a nonlinear model will depend on the choice of the initial state of the economy and the size and sign of the shock. In a linear VAR model, the impulse response functions are constant.
9 https://www.presidency.ucsb.edu/node/240205.
10 Barsky and Kilian (2001) was an earlier paper that questioned the interpretation of oil price movements as oil supply shocks, but Kilian (2009) has been the foundation of much of the subsequent literature. See also Lippi and Nobili (2012), Peersman and Van Robays (2012), and Aastveit (2014).
11 The traditional approach imposes numerical values for some of the parameters and assumes no knowledge about the others, and can be represented as a special case of the approach used by Baumeister and Hamilton (2019).
12 Kilian and Zhou (2019) take issue with Baumeister and Hamilton's "highly unrealistic prior for the global impact price elasticity of oil supply".
13 Blanchard and Galí (2009) use a similar argument to justify their empirical methodology.
14 It is beyond the scope of this chapter to provide a detailed introduction to DSGE models. One nice introduction to both Real Business Cycle models and New Keynesian models is McCandless (2008).
15 An alternative approach is to jointly calibrate the shock parameters to match moments in the data, possible in conjunction with calibrating some other parameters. One could also estimate all of the parameters using maximum likelihood or Bayesian methods.
16 See Table ET1 of the US Energy Information Administration's 2015 State Energy Data report. Please note the data used here includes spending on natural gas liquids.
17 See specifically "Motor vehicle fuels, lubricants and fluids" and "Fuel oil and other fuels."
18 See, for example, Kilian (2009) and Lippi and Nobili (2012).

References

Aastveit, K. A. (2014): "Oil price shocks in a data-rich environment," *Energy Economics*, 45, 268–279.
Aastveit, K. A., H. C. Bjørnland, and L. A. Thorsrud (2015): "What drives oil prices? Emerging versus developed economies," *Journal of Applied Econometrics*, 30, 1013–1028.

Aguiar-Conraria, L. and Y. Wen (2007): "Understanding the large negative impact of oil shocks," *Journal of Money, Credit and Banking*, 39, 925–944.

Arezki, R., V. A. Ramey, and L. Sheng (2017): "News shocks in open economies: Evidence from giant oil discoveries," *The Quarterly Journal of Economics*, 131, 103–155.

Atalla, T., J. Blazquez, L. C. Hunt, and B. Manzano (2017): "Prices versus policy: An analysis of the drivers of the primary fossil fuel mix," *Energy Policy*, 106, 536–546.

Atkeson, A. and P. J. Kehoe (1999): "Models of energy use: Putty-putty versus putty-clay," *The American Economic Review*, 89, 1028–1043.

Bachmeier, L. J. (2013): "Identification in models of gasoline pricing," *Economics Letters*, 120, 71–73.

Bachmeier, L. J. and I. Cha (2011): "Why don't oil shocks cause inflation? Evidence from disaggregate inflation data," *Journal of Money, Credit and Banking*, 43, 1165–1183.

Bachmeier, L. J., Q. Li, and D. Liu (2008): "Should oil prices receive so much attention? An evaluation of the predictive power of oil prices for the US economy," *Economic Inquiry*, 46, 528–539.

Backus, D. K. and M. J. Crucini (2000): "Oil prices and the terms of trade," *Journal of International Economics*, 50, 185–213.

Balke, N. S. and S. P. Brown (2018): "Oil supply shocks and the U.S. economy: An estimated DSGE model," *Energy Policy*, 116, 357–372.

Balke, N. S., S. P. Brown, and M. K. Yücel (2002): "Oil price shocks and the US economy: Where does the asymmetry originate?" *The Energy Journal*, 27–52.

Balke, N. S., M. Plante, and M. K. Yucel (2015): "Fuel subsidies, the oil market and the world economy," *The Energy Journal*, 36.

Barsky, R. B. and L. Kilian (2001): "Do we really know that oil caused the great stagflation? A monetary alternative," *NBER Macroeconomics Annual*, 16, 137–183.

Baumeister, C. and J. D. Hamilton (2019): "Structural interpretation of vector autoregressions with incomplete identification: Revisiting the role of oil supply and demand shocks," *American Economic Review*, 109 (5), 1873–1910.

Baumeister, C. and L. Kilian (2016): "Lower oil prices and the US economy: Is this time different?" *Brookings Papers on Economic Activity*, 2016, 287–357.

Baumeister, C. and G. Peersman (2013): "Time-varying effects of oil supply shocks on the US economy," *American Economic Journal: Macroeconomics*, 5, 1–28.

Bergholt, D., V. H. Larsen, and M. Seneca (In press): "Business cycles in an oil economy," *Journal of International Money and Finance*.

Bernanke, B. S. (1983): "Irreversibility, uncertainty, and cyclical investment," *The Quarterly Journal of Economics*, 98, 85–106.

Bernanke, B. S., M. Gertler, and M. Watson (1997): "Systematic monetary policy and the effects of oil price shocks," *Brookings Papers on Economic Activity*, 1997, 91–157.

Bjornland, H. C., V. H. Larsen, and J. Maih (2018): "Oil and macroeconomic (in)stability," *American Economic Journal: Macroeconomics*, 10, 128–151.

Blanchard, O. J. (2008): "Neoclassical synthesis" *New Palgrave Dictionary of Economics*, 2nd edition, edited by Steven Durlauf and Lawrence Blume, Palgrave McMillan Ltd.

Blanchard, O. J. and J. Galí (2009): "The macroeconomic effects of oil shocks: Why are the in 2000s so different from the 1970s?" in *International Dimensions of Monetary Policy*, edited by J. Galí and M. Gertler, Chicago: University of Chicago Press.

Blanchard, O. J. and M. Riggi (2013): "Why are the 2000s so different from the 1970s? A structural interpretation of changes in the macroeconomic effects of oil prices," *Journal of the European Economic Association*, 11, 1032–1052.

Blinder, A. S. and J. B. Rudd (2012): "The supply-shock explanation of the great stagflation revisited," in *The Great Inflation: The Rebirth of Modern Central Banking*, Chicago: University of Chicago Press, 119–175.

Bodenstein, M., C. J. Erceg, and L. Guerrieri (2008): "Optimal monetary policy with distinct core and headline inflation rates," *Journal of Monetary Economics*, 55, S18–S33.

———— (2011): "Oil shocks and external adjustment," *Journal of International Economics*, 83, 168–184.

Bodenstein, M., L. Guerrieri, and C. J. Gust (2013): "Oil shocks and the zero lower bound on nominal interest rates," *Journal of International Money and Finance*, 32, 941–967.

Bodenstein, M., L. Guerrieri, and L. Kilian (2012): "Monetary policy responses to oil price fluctuations," *IMF Economic Review*, 60 (4), 471–504.

Bohi, D. R. (1989): *Energy price shocks and macroeconomic performance*, Washington, DC, Resources for the Future.

Burbidge, J. and A. Harrison (1984): "Testing for the effects of oil-price rises using vector autoregressions," *International Economic Review*, 25, 459–484.

Caldara, D., M. Cavallo, and M. Iacoviello. (2019): "Oil price elasticities and oil price fluctuations," *Journal of Monetary Economics*, 103, 1–20.

Carlstrom, C. T. and T. S. Fuerst. (2006): "Oil prices, monetary policy, and counterfactual experiments," *Journal of Money, Credit, and Banking*, 38 (7), 1945–1958.

Castro, C., M. Jerez, and A. Barge-Gil (2016): "The deflationary effect of oil prices in the euro area," *Energy Economics*, 56, 389–397.

Chen, S.-S. (2009): "Oil price pass-through into inflation," *Energy Economics*, 31, 126–133.

Clark, T. E. and S. J. Terry (2010): "Time variation in the inflation passthrough of energy prices," *Journal of Money, Credit and Banking*, 42, 1419–1433.

Cuñado, J. and F. P. de Gracia (2003): "Do oil price shocks matter? Evidence for some European countries," *Energy Economics*, 25, 137–154.

Davis, S. J. and J. Haltiwanger (2001): "Sectoral job creation and destruction responses to oil price changes," *Journal of Monetary Economics*, 48, 465–512.

de Gregorio, J., O. Landerretche, C. Neilson, C. Broda, and R. Rigobon (2007): "Another pass-through bites the dust? Oil prices and inflation [with comments]," *Economia*, 7, 155–208.

Dhawan, R. and K. Jeske (2008a): "Energy price shocks and the macroeconomy: The role of consumer durables," *Journal of Money, Credit and Banking*, 40 (7), 1357–1377.

——— (2008b): "What determines the output drop after an energy price increase: Household or firm energy share?" *Economics Letters*, 101, 202–205.

Dhawan, R., K. Jeske, and P. Silos (2010): "Productivity, energy prices and the great moderation: A new link," *Review of Economic Dynamics*, 13, 715–724.

Edelstein, P. and L. Kilian (2009): "How sensitive are consumer expenditures to retail energy prices?" *Journal of Monetary Economics*, 56, 766–779.

Farrell, D. and F. Greig (2015): "How falling gas prices fuel the consumer: Evidence from 25 million people," *Working Paper, JP Morgan Chase & Co Institute*, 28, 2016.

Ferderer, J. (1996): "Oil price volatility and macroeconomy: A solution to the asymmetry puzzle," *Journal of Macroeconomics*, 18, 1–26.

Finn, M. G. (2000): "Perfect competition and the effects of energy price increases on economic activity," *Journal of Money, Credit and Banking*, 32 (3), 400–416.

Galí, J. and M. Gertler (2007): "Macroeconomic modeling for monetary policy evaluation," *Journal of Economic Perspectives*, 21, 25–46.

Gavin, W. T., B. D. Keen, and F. E. Kydland (2015): "Monetary policy, the tax code, and the real effects of energy shocks," *Review of Economic Dynamics*, 18, 694–707.

Gelman, M., Y. Gorodnichenko, S. Kariv, D. Koustas, M. D. Shapiro, D. Silverman, and S. Tadelis (2016): "The response of consumer spending to changes in gasoline prices," Tech. rep., National Bureau of Economic Research.

Hamilton, J. D. (1983): "Oil and the macroeconomy since World War II," *Journal of Political Economy*, 228–248.

——— (1985): "Historical causes of postwar oil shocks and recessions," *Energy Journal*, 97–116.

——— (1988): "A neoclassical model of unemployment and the business cycle," *Journal of Political Economy*, 96, 593–617.

——— (1996): "This is what happened to the oil price macroeconomy relation," *Journal of Monetary Economics*, 38, 215–220.

——— (2003): "What is an oil shock?" *Journal of Econometrics*, 113, 363–398.

——— (2011): "Nonlinearities and the macroeconomic effects of oil prices," *Macroeconomic Dynamics*, 15, 364–378.

——— (2016): "Comment on lower oil prices and the U.S. economy: Is this time different?" *Brookings Papers on Economic Activity*, 337–343.

Hamilton, J. D. and A. M. Herrera (2004): "Oil shocks and aggregate macroeconomic behavior: The role of monetary policy," *Journal of Money, Credit and Banking*, 36, 265–286.

Hansen, G. (1985): "Indivisible labor and the business cycle," *Journal of Monetary Economics*, 16, 309–327.

Herrera, A. M. and M. B. Karaki (2015): "The effects of oil price shocks on job reallocation," *Journal of Economic Dynamics and control*, 61, 95–113.

Herrera, A. M., L. G. Lagalo, and T. Wada (2011): "Oil price shocks and industrial production: Is the relationship linear?" *Macroeconomic Dynamics*, 15, 472–497.

——— (2015): "Asymmetries in the response of economic activity to oil price increases and decreases?" *Journal of International Money and Finance*, 50, 108–133.

Herrera, A. M. and E. Pesavento (2009): "Oil price shocks, systematic monetary policy, and the great moderation," *Macroeconomic Dynamics*, 13, 107–137.

Hooker, M. A. (1996): "What happened to the oil price-macroeconomy relationship?" *Journal of Monetary Economics*, 38, 195–213.

——— (2002): "Are oil shocks inflationary?: Asymmetric and nonlinear specifications versus changes in regime," *Journal of Money, Credit, and Banking*, 34, 540–561.

Jordà, Ò. (2005): "Estimation and inference of impulse responses by local projections," *American Economic Review*, 95, 161–182.

Katayama, M. (2013): "Understanding the large negative impact of oil shocks," *Journal of Money, Credit and Banking*, 39, 925–944.

Kilian, L. (2009): "Not all oil price shocks are alike: Disentangling demand and supply shocks in the crude oil market," *American Economic Review*, 99, 1053–1069.

Kilian and Lewis (2011): "Does the Fed respond to oil price shocks?" *The Economic Journal* 121.555 (2011): 1047–1072.

Kilian, L. and D. P. Murphy (2012): "Why agnostic sign restrictions are not enough: Understanding the dynamics of oil market VAR models," *Journal of the European Economic Association*, 10, 1166–1188.

Kilian, L. and C. Vega (2011): "Do energy prices respond to US macroeconomic news? A test of the hypothesis of predetermined energy prices," *Review of Economics and Statistics*, 93, 660–671.

Kilian and Lewis (2011): Kilian, Lutz, and Logan T. Lewis. "Does the Fed respond to oil price shocks?" *The Economic Journal*, 121 (555), 1047–1072.

Kilian, L. and R. J. Vigfusson (2011a): "Are the responses of the US economy asymmetric in energy price increases and decreases?" *Quantitative Economics*, 2, 419–453.

——— (2011b): "Nonlinearities in the oil price: Output relationship," *Macroeconomic Dynamics*, 15, 337–363.

——— (2013): "Do oil prices help forecast us real GDP? The role of nonlinearities and asymmetries," *Journal of Business & Economic Statistics*, 31, 78–93.

——— (2017): "The role of oil price shocks in causing US recessions," *Journal of Money, Credit and Banking*, 49, 1747–1776.

Kilian, L. and X. Zhou (2019): "Structural interpretation of vector autoregressions with incomplete information: Revisiting the role of oil supply and demand shocks: Comment," Working paper, University of Michigan.

Kim, I.-M. and P. Loungani (1992): "The role of energy in real business cycle models," *Journal of Monetary Economics*, 29, 173–189.

Kormilitsina, A. (2011): "Oil price shocks and the optimality of monetary policy," *Review of Economic Dynamics*, 14, 199–223.

Leduc, S. and K. Sill (2004): "A quantitative analysis of oil-price shocks, systematic monetary policy, and economic downturns," *Journal of Monetary Economics*, 51, 781–808.

——— (2007): "Monetary policy, oil shocks and TFP: Accounting for the decline in US volatility," *Review of Economic Dynamics*, 10, 595–614.

Lee, K. and S. Ni (2002): "On the dynamic effects of oil price shocks: A study using industry level data," *Journal of Monetary Economics*, 49, 823–852.

Lee, K., S. Ni, and R. Ratti (1995): "Oil shocks and the macroeconomy: The role of price variability," *Energy Journal*, 16, 39–56.

Lippi, F. and A. Nobili (2012): "Oil and the macroeconomy: A quantitative structural analysis," *Journal of the European Economic Association*, 10 (5), 1059–1083.

Lucas Jr, R. E. (1976): "Econometric policy evaluation: A critique," *Carnegie-Rochester Conference Series on Public Policy*, Elsevier, 1, 19–46.

Manescu, C. B. and G. Nuno (2015): "Quantitative effects of the shale oil revolution," *Energy Policy*, 86, 855–866.

Mccandless, G. (2008): *The ABCs of RBCs*, Cambridge, MA, London: Harvard.

Mork, Knut Anton. "Oil and the macroeconomy when prices go up and down: an extension of Hamilton's results." *Journal of Political Economy*, 97.3 (1989): 740–744.

Nakov, A. and G. Nuno (2013): "Saudi Arabia and the oil market," *The Economic Journal*, 123, 1333–1362.

Nakov, A. and A. Pescatori (2010): "Oil and the great moderation," *The Economic Journal*, 120, 131–156.

Natal, J.-M. (2012): "Monetary policy response to oil price shocks," *Journal of Money, Credit and Banking*, 44 (1), 53–101.

Peersman, G. and I. van Robays (2012): "Cross-country differences in the effects of oil shocks," *Energy Economics*, 34, 1532–1547.

Pieschacon, A. (2012): "The value of fiscal discipline for oil-exporting countries," *Journal of Monetary Economics*, 59, 250–268.

Plante, M. (2014a): "How should monetary policy respond to changes in the relative price of oil? Considering supply and demand shocks," *Journal of Economic Dynamics and Control*, 44, 1–19.

——— (2014b): "The long-run macroeconomic impacts of fuel subsidies," *Journal of Development Economics*, 107, 129–143.

Ramey, V. A. (2016): "Comment on lower oil prices and the U.S. economy: Is this time different?" *Brookings Papers on Economic Activity*, 343–351.

Rasche, R. H. and J. A. Tatum (1977): "Energy resources and potential GNP," *Federal Reserve Bank of St. Louis Review*, 59, 10–24.

——— (1981): "Energy price shocks, aggregate supply, and monetary policy: The theory and international evidence," *Supply Shocks, Incentives, and National Wealth, Carnegie-Rochester Conference Series on Public Policy*, edited by K. Brunner and A. Meltzer, Amsterdam: North-Holland, vol. 14.

Ravazzolo, F. and P. Rothman (2013): "Oil and US GDP: A real-time out-of-sample examination," *Journal of Money, Credit and Banking*, 45, 449–463.

Rotemberg, J. J. and M. Woodford (1996): "Imperfect competition and the effects of energy price increases on economic activity," *Journal of Money, Credit and Banking*, 28 (4), 549–577.

4

Economics of renewable energy

Jyoti Prasad Painuly and Norbert Wohlgemuth

1 Types of renewable energy and their applications

Renewable energy refers to the energy that is generated from natural resources that are continuously replenished. This includes solar, wind, hydro, biomass, geothermal, and ocean (tidal) energy. Renewable energy has been in use since ages, as early as humans started using it for heating and lighting purposes. It is currently being used prominently in four areas: power generation (centralized), decentralized generation (off-grid energy services in rural areas), space and water heating/cooling, and transportation. A variety of technologies have been developed to generate and use energy from the renewable resources. Renewables supplied 23.8% of the global power generation in 2016 (IEA, 2018c). Renewables represented almost two-thirds of new net electricity capacity additions in 2016, with almost 165 gigawatts (GW) coming online (IEA, 2017b) Overall renewable power capacity, including hydro, had reached 2,195 GW by 2017, of which hydropower contributed 1,081 GW (REN21, 2018). Prominent renewable energy technologies and their shares in the total renewable energy are briefly described below.

1.1 Wind power

Wind turbines are used to convert wind energy into electricity with utility scale single turbines crossing 9 MW, though most of commercially used turbines are up to 5 MW. The power available from the wind depends on the wind speed and duration of the wind. Therefore, wind turbines are put up at high altitudes, and offshore of late, where wind speeds are higher. The wind speed and duration of wind determine the amount of power generated and variability of the generation. Whereas hydro energy has been used for power generation for a long time, wind grew fastest in the early stage of focus on renewable power to address the issue of climate change and installed wind power capacity increased from 47 GW in 2004 to 539 GW by the end 2017 (WWEA, 2018). Wind-generated electricity met nearly 4% of global electricity demand in 2015. WWEA (2014) also estimated total worldwide potential for wind at 94.9 TW, excluding offshore in most cases, indicating that the identified wind potential was almost double of the whole world's energy demand assuming on average 2,000 full load hours.

Top five wind power countries at the end of 2017 were China, the United States, Germany, India, and Spain.

1.2   Hydropower

Hydropower is electricity generated using the energy of moving water. This source of energy has been used for centuries – to grind wheat into flour using water wheel for example – but its major use is as source for generating electricity. In 2016 hydropower generated more than 15% of the world's total electricity and 65% of all renewable electricity (IEA, 2018c). The largest among renewable power, hydropower capacity (including pump hydro) had reached 1,114 GW by 2017 (REN21, 2018).

There are three types of hydropower plants:

- Large hydroelectric dams and reservoirs: Historically, hydroelectric power was generated by constructing large reservoirs, which is still popular in many developing countries. With an installed capacity of 22,500 MW, the Three Gorges Dam in China is the biggest such plant.
- Small hydropower plants: Typically plants not exceeding 50 MW capacity, built on small rivers or a series of plants on a big river to manage impacts on the local community.
- Run-of-river plants: As the title indicates, these plants have little or no water storage, minimizing the impact on the local community.

1.3   Solar energy

A number of technologies have evolved to use solar energy; these include already commercially viable technologies such as photovoltaics and solar heating, and other technologies under different stages of development such as concentrated solar power (CSP), concentrator photovoltaics (CPV), and artificial photosynthesis. In addition to this, in buildings, active and passive solar architecture helps harness solar energy.

A photovoltaic (PV) system uses the scientific phenomenon known as photoelectric effect to convert sunlight into electrical energy. PV is the most popular and widely used solar energy technology to produce electricity. Concentrated solar power (CSP) systems use lenses or mirrors and tracking systems and convert a large area of sunlight into a small beam.

The third-largest among renewable power (behind hydro and wind), global solar PV capacity and CSP systems capacity in 2017 were 402 GW and 4.9 GW, respectively.

1.4   Geothermal energy

Geothermal energy is thermal energy from the Earth. Originating from processes during earth formation and subsequent radioactive decay of minerals below the surface of earth, it is extracted for a variety of uses, including for electricity generation, water and space heating, and space cooling, depending on temperature gradation. Temperature at the core of earth can be very high (over 5,000°C), from where it conducts to the surrounding rocks and upwards. Thus, below the surface of earth, water gets heated to high temperatures, converting it to steam, which is used for generating electricity. Hot springs, used for bathing and cooking, are also examples of low grade geothermal energy.

Low temperature geothermal energy is also used for heating and cooling buildings, and in other refrigeration and industrial uses. Geothermal heat pumps (GHP) are used for this purpose. GHP helps reduce electricity demand for heating and cooling from buildings, which otherwise contribute to the peak in the system.

Worldwide geothermal power capacity was 12.8 GW in 2017.

1.5   Bioenergy

Bioenergy is primarily derived from biomass, which often refers to plants or plant-derived materials. Biomass is used directly through combustion to produce heat as well as indirectly through conversion to biofuels. Biomass resources include wood and wood waste, crops and crop residues, dung and all other type of organic waste from plants and animals (IEA, 2018a).

Biomass can be converted to other usable forms of energy; into gaseous fuels like methane or transportation fuels like ethanol and biodiesel. Methane is generated by landfills and also from agricultural and human waste. Some crops like corn and sugarcane are used to produce ethanol, and biodiesel is produced from a variety of agricultural produce that contain fats/oils. Second-generation biofuels that use plants and other organic material, which is not used for human consumption, are under advanced stage of research and development. Biomass is also used for electricity generation – wood residues, agricultural waste (sugar cane residue, rice husks), and animal husbandry residues are used as feedstock in boilers that produce steam for electricity generation.

Conversion of biomass to biofuel is achieved using *thermal, chemical,* and *biochemical* methods. Biofuels include bioethanol, biodiesel, biogas, landfill gas, and synthetic gas. Bioenergy production and use from renewable biomass resources, though carbon neutral, is associated with other harmful pollutants.

Modern bioenergy refers to the relatively efficient use of biomass heat in industry processes, space and water heating, district heating, electricity and transport. More than 50% of biomass energy relates to the traditional use of biomass in developing countries for cooking and heating, using inefficient open fires or simple cookstoves.

Bioenergy power capacity was estimated at 122 GW in 2017.

Existing technologies are getting better and new technologies are emerging. Some of the emerging technologies are indicated in Box 4.1.

Box 4.1   Emerging technologies

Several other renewable energy technologies are under development, and include the following:

Enhanced geothermal system (EGS): Generates energy without the need for natural convective hydrothermal resources. EGS technologies enhance and/or create geothermal resources in the hot dry rock (HDR) through "hydraulic stimulation".

Cellulosic ethanol: Also referred as one of the second-generation biofuel, ethanol is produced from plant cellulose instead from the oil seed, which has alternate uses.

Ocean energy (or marine energy): This refers to the energy from ocean waves, tides, and ocean thermal (due to temperature differences across water layers).

Other technologies under different stage of development: These include concentrated photovoltaics (CPV) systems, that employ concentrated sunlight onto photovoltaic surfaces to generate electricity; floating solar arrays in which PV systems float on the surface of water reservoirs, lakes, or canals; artificial photosynthesis in which solar electromagnetic energy is stored in chemical bonds by splitting water to produce hydrogen and then using carbon dioxide to make methanol; algae fuels that produce liquid fuels from oil-rich varieties of algae.

Modern forms of renewable energy are primarily displacing conventional energy in the areas of electricity generation, water and space heating and cooling, transport, and off-grid energy services, especially in rural areas. The major applications of renewable energy are briefly described below.

1.6   Electricity generation

Renewable power commissioned in 2017 reached a record 157 gigawatts (GW), far exceeding the 70 GW of net fossil fuel generating capacity. Of this solar alone at 98 GW crossed total fossil fuel capacity added, balance coming from other renewables, namely, wind, solar, biomass and waste-to-energy, geothermal, marine and small hydro. Installed capacity for solar PV and wind reached 402 GW and 539 GW, respectively, by the end 2017. Total renewable power capacity reached 2,195 GW (1,081 GW excluding hydro) and share of renewable electricity rose to 12% of total electricity generated in 2017, avoiding around 1.8 gigatonnes of carbon dioxide emissions (Frankfurt School-UNEP Centre, 2018). Overall, renewables accounted for an estimated 70% of net additions to global power generation capacity, up from 63% in 2016.

Renewables-based stand-alone and off-grid single home or mini-grid systems represented about 6% of new electricity connections worldwide between 2012 and 2016 (REN21, 2018).

1.7   Heating

Renewables' contribution to heating is currently limited but developments in some countries indicate that increased use of renewables is possible. Renewable energy share in heating and cooling in 2016 was 68.6% in Sweden, primarily from use of biomass, and the share of renewable energy (including recycled heat) in district heating reached 90% in 2017. Denmark has recently incorporated solar thermal also into its district heating systems. Bioenergy was used in Brazil to meet around 50% of its industrial heat demand in 2017. Geothermal energy directly for heating and geothermal heat pumps, which provide both heating and cooling, has also been introduced in this area.

Global solar water heating capacity reached 472 GW in 2017, with more than 70% of the capacity in China. Besides modern renewables that provided 10.3% of total global energy consumption for heat in 2015, another 16.4% was supplied by traditional biomass, predominantly for cooking and heating in the developing world (REN21, 2018).

1.8   Transportation

Production of bioethanol and biodiesel, used as fuel for vehicles as a substitute for gasoline and diesel, reached 106 and 31 and billion liters, respectively, in 2017. Growth was moderate in case of ethanol, and there was no growth in case of biodiesel over 2016 on account of concerns related to impact on agriculture and environment from increased use of these two fuels in transport (food-feed-fuel issue).

Electric vehicles (EV) are however gaining momentum in the transport, which also helps integration of variable production of electricity from renewables into the grid, as variable production can be absorbed through battery banks that vehicles and charging stations use. Fully electric passenger cars, scooters, and bicycles are becoming common place in countries such as Norway and China. More than 200 million two- and three-wheeled EVs were on the world's roads in 2016, and more than 30 million are being added each year. Electric passenger cars passed the three million mark in 2017 (REN21, 2018). Electricity use in other transport mediums is also planned in many countries, which may further increase renewables' contribution to transport.

1.9 Distributed Renewables for Energy Access (DREA)

More than one billion people do not have access to electricity, and about 2.8 billion people do not have clean cooking facilities. The majority of these are in rural areas in Asia and Africa. DREA systems, including off-grid solar systems and renewable-based mini-grids, are increasingly being supported to provide energy access along with support to diffusion of clean cook stoves. There are several support programs for decentralized renewables in Africa; African Development Bank (AfDB), for example, has recently initiated a USD 12 billion plan under its new electrification program that aims to provide decentralized solar technologies to 75 million households and businesses between 2017 and 2022 in Africa (Ford, 2017). A variety of business models are being tested and used to provide energy access – the pay-as-you-go (PAYG) business model for example has been used widely. Off-grid solar systems, and in particular those commercialized through the pay-as-you-go (PAYG) business model, were the most significant technology in the sector, providing electricity access to more than 360 million people worldwide (REN21, 2018).

2 Cost of renewable energy and trends

The cost of renewable energy has fallen substantially over the last two decades. Still the contribution of renewables to the world's energy mix is a rather modest one. According to IEA statistics (IEA, 2018c), all forms of renewable energy account for a mere 13.7% of total primary energy supply. Biofuels and waste (which is classified as renewable) dominate the renewables segment (69.5% of total renewables), solar and wind energy are still hardly noticeable on a global scale. In electricity production, however, renewables account for 23.8%, largely as a result of hydropower generation.

Between 1990 and 2016, total worldwide energy demand increased at an average annual rate of 1.7%, hardly outpaced by renewables which increased by 2% annually on average. Solar PV and wind energy were the fastest growing forms of renewable energy, with average annual growth rates of 37.3% and 23.6%, respectively (Figure 4.1). The use of solid biofuels and charcoal increased by just 1.1%, dragging the average growth of all renewables to 2.0%.

In 2016, the regional shares of renewables in total primary energy demand ranged from 0.4% in the Middle East to 49.5% in Africa. In OECD countries renewables provided 9.9% to total energy demand (IEA, 2018c). Between 1973 and 2016, the share of renewables in global energy demand increased by 1%, however total energy demand more than doubled over that time span. According to IEA projections, global energy demand over the period to 2040 is projected to increase under all scenarios considered, with fossil fuel shares ranging from 79% under the "Current Policies" scenario to 61% in the "Sustainable Development" scenario (IEA, 2017c).

The market penetration of any (new) technology depends on its economic competitiveness. In the case of renewable energy this competitiveness is largely driven by (generation) cost and the regulatory environment. In many cases, the cost of renewables have fallen dramatically and are likely to continue their decline over the coming decades. In Germany, for example, onshore wind power at good locations is already cost competitive with new coal and gas combined cycle power plants (Kost et al., 2018).

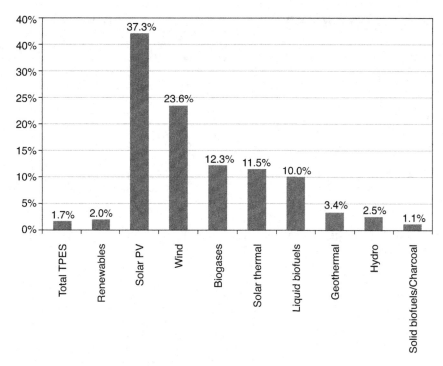

Figure 4.1 Average annual growth rates of world renewables supply, 1990–2016
Source: IEA (2018c).

In order to express the competitiveness of different generating technologies, the concept of levelized cost of electricity (LCOE) is usually adopted. It represents the cost in discounted real monetary units of building and operating a generating plant over an assumed financial life cycle. Capital costs, fuel costs, operation and maintenance costs, financing costs, and an assumed utilization rate are key inputs in the calculation. Incentives such as feed in tariffs and tax breaks also affect the calculation of LCOE. An alternative indicator of economic competitiveness is that of levelized avoided cost of electricity (LACE). It considers avoided cost – "a measure of what it would cost the grid to generate the electricity that would be displaced by a new generation project" (EIA, 2018, p 3).

Global LCOE from utility-scale solar PV projects (weighted by deployment) declined by 70% from 2010 to 2016. By 2040 an additional decline of 60% is expected by the IEA, and the learning curve is quite steep: "The assumed rate at which costs decline for solar PV in the future also varies slightly depending on local conditions, but in general it is around 20% for each doubling of cumulative installed capacity" (IEA, 2017c). Figure 4.2 show past and projected evolution of global average generation cost for utility-scale solar PV and EV battery technologies, and Figure 4.3 provides information on levelized cost of electricity generation for selected technologies in the European Union and India. Figures 4.4 and 4.5 show levelized cost for solar PV and wind technologies and conventional baseload technologies, depending on the cost of capital. The numbers clearly show that – without taking into account external costs of conventional technologies – most forms of renewables are still at a competitive disadvantage.

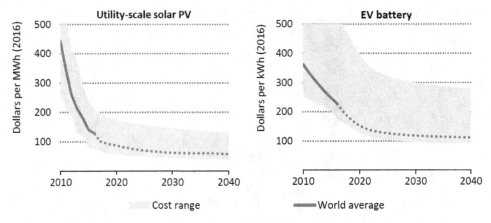

Figure 4.2 Global average costs for utility-scale solar PV and EV battery

Source: IEA (2017c).

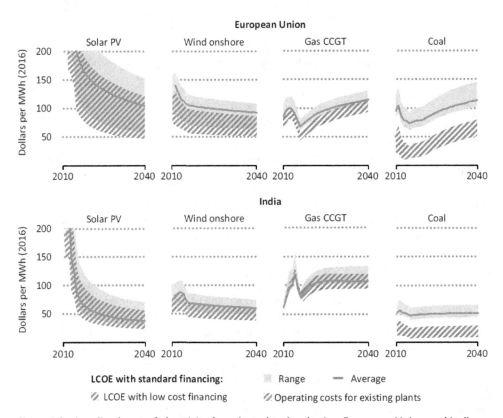

Figure 4.3 Levelized cost of electricity for selected technologies, European Union and India

Source: IEA (2017c).

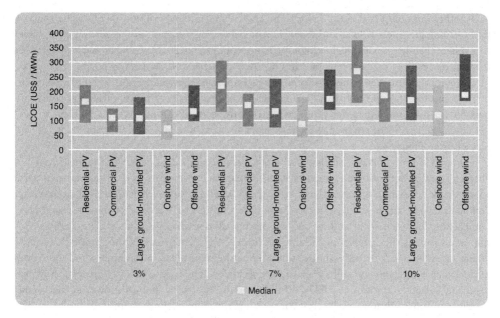

Figure 4.4   Levelized cost of electricity (LCOE) for solar PV and wind technologies
Source: IEA (2015).

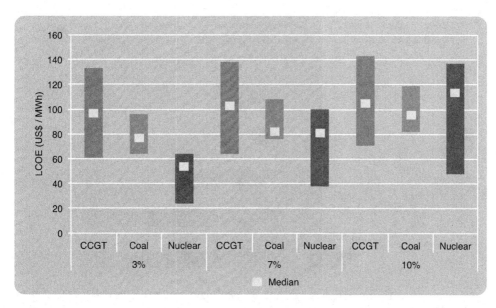

Figure 4.5   Levelized cost of electricity (LCOE) range for baseload technologies
Source: IEA (2015).

Another important cost component is the cost of intermittency of non-dispatchable generation technologies such as solar and wind. Dispatchable technologies have in general more value to a system than less flexible technologies (Khatib and Difiglio, 2016). A dispatchable generation technology refers to that can generate and dispatch electricity on demand of power grid operators, according to market needs. Dispatchable technologies allow generators to be turned on or off, or adjust their power output. When including costs (essentially capacity and energy costs) and benefits (such as avoided capacity and avoided energy costs according to the LACE principle), net costs and benefits of renewables are less favorable than those of gas, nuclear and hydro, as can be seen from Figure 4.6.

Comparing costs and benefits is a tricky task because individual generating technologies are characterized by very different impacts at the systems (i.e. the grid) level. These impacts vary substantially, depending on numerous factors. Even when performing LCOE calculations, many factors have to be taken into account to properly account for the "true" (generating) cost. Many comparisons between fossil and renewables are biased as result of an incomplete analysis. An important issue is the removal of subsidies. Critics of the "energy transition" argue that subsidizing renewables is too costly, and subsidies should be removed. On the other hand, fossil and nuclear fuels have been and still are massively subsidized. The IEA (2017c) estimates that global fossil fuel subsidies amount to USD 260 billion, with electricity and oil industries the largest recipient of those subsidies. Even though fossil fuel subsidies declined from their peak of USD 500 billion in 2012, they still provide an incentive for their use. Environmental externalities are another important factor that biases the comparison between fossil/nuclear technologies and renewables. Efforts to internalize those external costs (e.g. the costs of global warming), have so far not been sufficient in promoting renewables. Carbon pricing schemes, as those implemented

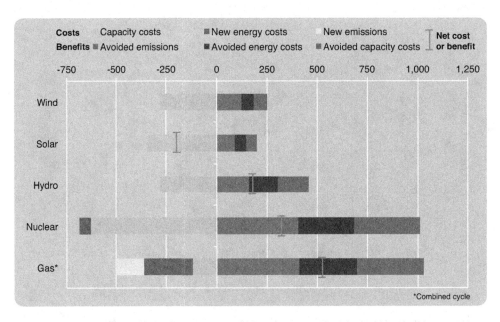

Figure 4.6 Net costs and benefits per year per MW compared with coal baseload generation, United States, $1000 (2014)

Source: Economist, 29 July 2014.

by the European Union, are largely flawed and provide too little incentive for a large scale switch to renewables (Agora Energiewende and Sandbag, 2018). Non-dispatchable renewables can contribute to fuel supply security, especially when fuels have to be imported. Largely as result of lower energy density, the use of renewables also can have significant impact on a region's economy (Jenniches, 2018).

Edenhofer et al. (2013) provide a comprehensive analytical framework for the assessment of renewable energy from a societal perspective. They point to numerous cases of market failure. A social welfare function must include aspects such as climate change mitigation, green jobs, energy security, green growth, poverty reduction, and regional impacts of energy use. Multiple public policy objectives, multiple instances of externalities and the availability of multiple policy instruments constitute a significant challenge for energy policy.

Expenditure on energy research and development (R&D) is important to assure further cost reductions. Composition of public energy-related R&D expenditure changed substantially over time. In 1974 it accounted for more than 70% of all public energy-related R&D expenditure, by 2015 this share has fallen slightly more than 20%. Renewable energy and energy efficiency increased, as can be seen from Figure 4.7. This figure shows quite impressively the focus on nuclear energy research in 1974. Had this amount been spent on renewables, they would probably already have achieved full cost competitiveness.

The ultimate goal of mechanisms to promote renewables must be their full competitiveness even without subsidization. Therefore, energy policy should always provide a "sunset clause" which defines a clear date for phase out of subsidies. Criteria for the assessment of mechanisms to financially support renewables are typically efficiency (least cost) and effectivity (extent to which a goal is achieved). Experience shows that there tends to be a trade-off between these two criteria. Highly effective mechanisms such as feed-in tariffs (FITs) are not cost-effective, at least not in the short run. On the other hand, theoretically superior instruments, such as auction-based mechanism, often fail due their lack of effectivity, which in many cases is result of investment

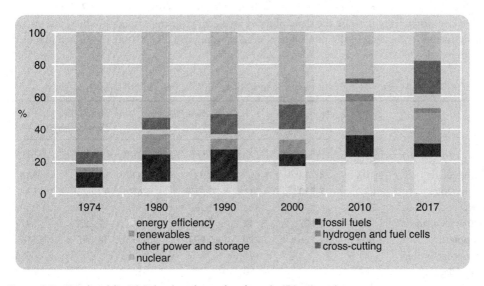

Figure 4.7 Total public R&D budget by technology in IEA countries

Source: IEA (2018b).

insecurity. Mechanisms can either focus on price (feed in tariffs, competitive bidding) or quantity (mandated market share). They can also target the supply or the demand side.

As a result of the financial burden they constitute, feed in tariffs are being phased out, especially in China. The country's alternative, "top runner", a reverse auction, is gaining popularity internationally. Power purchase agreements based on reversed auction have already resulted in unexpected low bids in sunny and windy places (see e.g. Dobrotkova et al., 2018; Rego and de Oliveira Ribeiro, 2018). Haufe and Ehrhart (2018) provide an overview of recent experience with auction-based mechanisms. They conclude that auctions are the instrument of choice globally and that success of renewable energy auctions is outstanding. Even though a high degree of competition may put project developers under pressure, high realization rates (i.e. effectiveness) can be achieved. The competitive environment also provides innovation incentives which can be expected to result in further cost declines.

The market penetration of renewables depends on investment decisions taken today. The IEA (2017c) estimates that even under the assumptions of the Sustainable Development Scenario, fossil fuel investment will dominate investment decisions in the world's energy sector over the simulation horizon 2017–2040.

Concerning investment in power plants,

> renewables capture two-thirds of global investment in power plants as they become, for many countries, the least-cost source of new generation. Rapid deployment of solar photovoltaics, led by China and India, helps solar become the largest source of low-carbon capacity by 2040, by which time the share of all renewables in total power generation reaches 40%. In the European Union, renewables account for 80% of new capacity and wind power becomes the leading source of electricity soon after 2030, due to strong growth both onshore and offshore.
>
> *(IEA, 2017c)*

Table 4.1 shows annual and cumulative global investment by type and scenario over the simulation horizon to 2014.

European Union energy policy wants to achieve a renewables share of 32% by 2030. In light of objectives to globally increase the share of renewable energy, current trends in renewable energy investment are pointing in the other direction. According to IEA (2018d), global investment in

Table 4.1 Global energy investment by type and scenario, 2017–2040 ($2016 billion)

	2010–16	New Policies		Current Policies		Sustainable Development	
	Per year	Cumulative	Per year	Cumulative	Per year	Cumulative	Per year
Fossil fuels	1,103	24,713	1,007	29,932	1,247	15,496	646
Renewables	297	7,950	331	6,350	265	12,828	534
T&D	236	8,025	334	8,524	355	8,145	339
Other low-carbon	14	1,127	47	1,095	46	2,325	97
Supply	**1,650**	**41,276**	**1,720**	**45,901**	**1,913**	**38,795**	**1,616**
Power sector share	41%		47%		41%		63%
Oil and gas share	54%		50%		55%		35%
End-use	**295**	**18,809**	**784**	**11,912**	**496**	**30,340**	**1,264**

Source: IEA (2017c).

renewable power generation fell by 7%, and fossil fuels increased their share in energy supply investment in 2017 – for the first time since 2014. Large part of the growth in fossil energy can be attributed to the fracking of oil and gas in the United States. Globally, energy investment fell by 2% in 2017, with electricity taking a bigger share than oil and gas for the second year in a row. The only exception is solar energy where a record investment could be achieved. China attracts most investment in solar energy, ahead of the United States and Europe. For the first time renewable energy investment dominates investment in fossil fuels in India. Bloomberg NEF (2018) provides a detailed overview of latest clean energy investment trends.

In regions with little growth in electricity demand, such as Europe, increasing generation by renewables depresses wholesale electricity prices, making renewables somehow victims of their own success, indicating the limits of marginal cost pricing (Edenhofer et al., 2013). Wholesale electricity prices slumped from about EUR 80/MWh in 2008 to EUR 30–40. In an industry where marginal costs are of great importance to the overall economics (merit order), the economics of renewables affects electricity markets to an extreme extent, leading electric utilities to separate their renewables (and grid) businesses from (loss making) conventional generation. Blazquez et al. (2018) claim that the world is caught in a vicious circle: renewable energy subsidies increase their deployment, which depresses prices, thereby further increasing the need for financial support. In the extreme case of 100% (non-dispatchable) renewables, the marginal cost-driven market price would fall to zero, deterring any investment that is not fully subsidized. Therefore, the more successfully policies to support renewables are, the more expensive and less effective policies become. The utility model of generating electricity is in many cases broken, as are markets. The "zero marginal cost society" (Jeremy Rifkin) may not be as easy to achieve as commonly thought.

Views on how expensive the transition to an energy (electricity) system fully based on renewables diverge substantially. For the United States there are estimates ranging from lower costs than fossil fuels, even when excluding nuclear, bioenergy, and combustion of fossil fuels with carbon capture and storage (Jacobson et al., 2015) to extremely high costs as result of the "vicious cycle" and the non-utilization of other carbon free options such as nuclear and energy storage (Clack et al., 2017).

The transition to a new energy (electricity) system is accompanied by a fundamental restructuring of the institutional setting of this industry. There is a trend towards a substitution of incumbent utilities by independent power producers in the European Union and the United States. Small-scale electricity producers at the household level ("prosumers") also contribute to this restructuring, by fundamentally changing the industrial organization towards a quite decentralized structure which makes grid operation more challenging. These changes produce winners and losers (Kelsey and Meckling, 2018). For example, between 2008 and 2013 the top 20 European utilities lost more than half of their stock market valuation. Transition pathways towards a sustainable energy future are characterized by different and still largely unexplored, distributional dynamics. New technologies, including blockchain, provide opportunities for new business models based on decentralized electricity generation.

3   Renewable energy policies, challenges, and barriers

3.1 Policies

REN21 (2018) provide an overview of the status of various renewable policies at the global level. Renewable energy targets, feed-in tariffs, renewable purchase obligation (RPS)/quota, renewable projects tendering/auctions, and financial incentives including tax rebates are well-known renewables support policies. In 2017, 179 countries had overall renewable energy targets, of which 57 had 100% renewable electricity targets. Feed-in policies, the most popular mechanism, was in use in 113 countries, and RPS/quota policy in 33 countries. For biofuels, 70 countries had mandates. A review of renewables policies in the REN21 based on inputs from a large number of stakeholders had the following observations:

- Renewable energy policies and targets remain focused on the power sector, with support for heating and cooling and transport still lagging;
- Policies aligning renewables and energy efficiency are common in the buildings sector, but not in industry;
- Cities lead in "greening" public transport fleets, but policy attention is lacking for rail, aviation and shipping;
- Use of tendering continues to spread, yet feed-in policies remain vital in support schemes for renewables;
- New cross-sectoral integrated policies are emerging to support integration of variable renewables.

3.2   Challenges

Energy systems integration: Energy from wind and solar is referred to as variable renewable energy (VRE) due to their intermittent nature of availability, leading to challenges to integrate it into the existing energy systems. The problem gets compounded in cases where electricity grid is primarily supplied from coal and nuclear, since backing them down creates problem for the system. At part loads, efficiency is low, and shutting down and re-starting a unit can take several hours, if not days. In case of grids that have hydro and gas-based electricity, integration is relatively manageable. For example, Denmark is able to dispatch its surplus production from wind to Nordic grid, which has a good proportion of hydro (from Norway). Depending on mix of power plants in a grid, or its access to flexible grids (with hydro and gas plants), the issue of integration puts a limit on percentage of renewable energy a grid can absorb. This is an area where a lot of research is going on, including on electrical storage systems, load management and load shifting, smart grids to manage supply and demand better, pump storage, new technologies and uses, such as heat pumps and electric vehicles.

Energy efficiency: The other challenge is to create awareness and take policy measures to integrate energy efficiency and renewable energy. Energy efficiency currently offers cheapest and huge opportunity to reduce GHG emissions and energy intensity of the output. Reduced energy use for same level of output along with shift to renewable energy can therefore bring synergy in addressing climate change problem (IEA, 2014).

100% Renewable: Several countries have targets to produce 100% renewable power by 2050. Challenges related to that are indicated in Box 4.2.

Box 4.2 100% Renewable energy

Advances in technologies, falling costs and increases in investment have led to faster growth than anticipated a few years back. As a result, renewable energy contributes to more than 20% of energy supply in more than 30 countries around the world (REN21, 2018).

A study by Jacobson and Delucchi (2011) indicated that producing all new energy with wind power, solar power, and hydropower by 2030 is feasible and existing energy supplied by non-renewables can also be replaced by renewables by 2050. The study concluded that it is

---

economically and technically feasible and barriers are primarily social and political. Wiseman et al. (2013) also confirmed these findings.

In the course of preparation of Global Status Report 2018, REN21 carried out a survey of experts and stakeholders in several countries to come out with barriers for 100% renewable by 2050. The results were mixed but on expected lines. African experts found it too ambitious and identified inconsistent and uncoordinated energy policies as a serious political barrier, in addition to the lack of knowledge and information. Chinese experts pointed to the variability of wind and solar as a major barrier, and a lack of appropriate technologies for industry and transport sector a significant barrier. European experts opined that it was feasible but requires political commitment. Experts in India were divided in their opinion on this, but overarching view was the need for consistent and long-term policies and availability of technical know-how. Cost competitiveness, financing, and a lack of political and institutional support were identified as barriers in Latin America. Experts in the United States were skeptical about the prospects of achieving 100% renewables as early as 2050. Application in transportation was identified as a major problem, followed by a lack of know-how on energy and technology issues and insufficient political will. Overall, a majority of the energy experts interviewed agreed (35%) or strongly agreed (36%) that 100% renewables on a global level is feasible and realistic, 17% disagreed, and 12% were neutral (IRENA, 2018).

3.3   Barriers

A number of studies have gone into the issue if barriers to renewable energy, including the IEA (Muller, 2011), REN21 (2018), IRENA (2018), IPCC (2012), Wiseman et al. (2013), UCS (2017), Kariuki (2018), Reddy and Painuly (2004). In the early years of the first decade, most of the barriers were common across countries and many, even across various type of renewables. The list of barriers included awareness, economic and financial, technical, political and regulatory, institutional, capacity, market, and social and cultural. However, over a period of time, many of these barriers have been addressed, particularly in developed countries and emerging economies, which the scale of investment in the renewables reflects. In many developing countries, most or all of these barriers still remain, but the nature of barriers in countries that are leaders in renewables has changed.

Technology specific barriers have emerged that impede large-scale deployment. Increased use of bioenergy requires a sustainable framework that also considers environmental issues. For geothermal, economic viability and sustainability of the enhanced geothermal systems (EGS) on a large scale is a challenge (IPCC, 2012). Ecological and social impacts in case of new hydropower projects can have ecological and social issues while ocean energy development may require testing infrastructure, enabling policies, and regulations. Environmental concerns and public acceptance in case of wind energy can be an issue. In many countries, issues include complicated licensing procedures and difficulty with land acquisition and permissions.

In case of some technologies, primarily solar and wind, the focus is now on large-scale deployment. It requires a level playing field through removal of subsidies to fossil fuels and accounting for their social and environmental costs. An infrastructure barrier has also emerged, which relates to capacity of the power grid to absorb variable renewable energy. With increase in deployment of renewable power, grid infrastructure may need to be upgraded to ensure adequate transmission and distribution infrastructure. In the case of Germany, for example, wind energy is produced in the north of the country, while demand is located in the south. Lack of transmission capacities result in severe problems in grid operation – problems that spill over to neighboring countries. Excess supply on windy days can drive wholesale electricity prices even into negative territory.

Policy ambiguity due to political uncertainty can also create problems. Unfavorable policies, a lack of transparency, and inconsistency in policies undermine investor confidence. A big dilemma facing policy makers is balance between competitive prices that are consumer friendly versus renewable power procurement by utilities through long-term power purchase agreements (PPAs) that creates certainty for investors but makes power expensive for consumers. With falling prices, many utilities in some countries are looking at heavy losses with long-term contracts through feed-in policies. Policies that ensure healthy growth of the sector and yet safeguard consumer interest are important

Some other recommendations include focus on end-use sectors in addition to power generation (current focus area), enabling policies for renewables use in heating and cooling, enabling policies for use of renewables in transport sector, and promoting measures to support integration of variable renewable energy (IRENA, 2018).

4 Conclusions

Advances in technology, falling costs and increases in investment have led to faster growth of renewables than anticipated only a few years ago. Renewable energy has come a long way with global investment in renewables reaching $279.8 billion in 2017, and renewable energy contributes to more than 20% of energy supply in more than 30 countries around the world (REN21, 2018). As of 2016, renewable energy accounted for an estimated 18.2% of global total final energy consumption, with modern renewables representing 10.4%. Maximum contribution from renewables came to power generation with renewables meeting 25% of the global power demand in 2017. Decentralized renewable power is being used to provide electricity access to those where grid is not available. Renewables also contributed marginally to heating and transportation sectors.

PV technology development coupled with supportive policies resulted in levelized cost of the electricity from utility-scale solar PV projects declining by 70% from 2010 to 2016, and this trend is continuing. There is some concern that subsidies to renewables through various mechanisms can be counterproductive. However, the support may be necessary until a level playing field has been provided by eliminating global fossil fuel subsidies and environmental externalities from use of fossil fuels are taken into consideration. Mechanisms such as feed-in tariffs, quotas, and auctions have been successfully used to promote renewables, but each one has its own limitations and inefficiencies. Reverse auctions are now being used successfully in several countries, including China.

Investment in renewable power plants was almost two-thirds of the global investment in power plants in 2017. With an increasing number of countries committing to renewables and 57 countries targeting 100% renewables power by 2050, overall trend in increase in investment in renewables can be expected to continue.

Renewable energy targets, feed-in tariffs, renewable purchase obligation (RPS)/quota, and renewable projects tendering/auctions have been popular mechanisms to promote renewables. However, these cater to only renewable use for power production. Renewable use for heating and cooling and transport holds a lot of potential and needs policy support.

As the renewable power production increases, it faces a challenge in integrating it into the existing energy systems due to its intermittent nature of production. Though a number of barriers have been addressed in developed countries and emerging economies, in developing countries, still a variety of barriers exist that include awareness, economic and financial, technical, political and regulatory, institutional, capacity, market, and social and cultural. They may need to be supported if their renewable energy targets are to be met.

Further research is urgently required on how to bring about – in a cost-efficient manner – the global "energy transition" towards an energy system (not only electricity) based to a large extent on renewables. Intermittency of some forms of renewable energy constitutes a very significant challenge, one that could be overcome as soon as feasible storage technologies become available.

References

Agora Energiewende and Sandbag (2018) The European Power Sector in 2017. State of Affairs and Review of Current Developments, available at https://sandbag.org.uk/wp-content/uploads/2018/01/EU-power-sector-report-2017.pdf.

Blazquez, J., Fuentes-Bracamontes, R., Bollino, C. A. and N. Nezamuddin (2018) "The renewable energy policy paradox", *Renewable and Sustainable Energy Reviews* 82, pp 1–5.

Bloomberg NEF (2018a) Clean Energy Investment Trends, 2Q 2018. Wind investment in the U.S. Spurs Global Clean Energy in First Half of Year, available at https://data.bloomberglp.com/bnef/sites/14/2018/07/BNEF-Clean-Energy-Investment-Trends-1H-2018.pdf.

Bloomberg NEO (2018b) New Energy Outlook 2018, available at https://about.bnef.com/new-energy-outlook/.

Clack, Ch. T. M., et al. (2017) "Evaluation of a proposal for reliable low-cost grid power with 100% wind, water, and solar", *Proceedings of the National Academy of Sciences* 114 (26), pp. 6722–6727, available at www.pnas.org/content/114/26/6722.

Dobrotkova, Z., Surana, K. and P. Audinet (2018) "The price of solar energy: Comparing competitive auctions for utility-scale solar PV in developing countries", *Energy Policy* 118, pp 133–148.

Edenhofer, O., et al. (2013) "On the economics of renewable energy sources", *Energy Economics* 40, pp. S12–S23.

EIA (2018) Levelized Cost and Levelized Avoided Cost of New Generation Resources in the Annual Energy Outlook 2017. U.S. Energy Information Administration, Washington, DC, available at www.eia.gov/outlooks/aeo/pdf/electricity_generation.pdf.

Ford, N. (2017) "AfDB unveils $12bn power plan for Africa", *African Business* 17 April, available at https://africanbusinessmagazine.com/sectors/energy/afdb-unveils-12bn-power-plan-africa/.

Frankfurt School-UNEP Centre/BNEF (2018). Global Trends in Renewable Energy Investment 2018. Frankfurt School of Finance & Management, Frankfurt, available at http://www.iberglobal.com/files/2018/renewable_trends.pdf .

Haufe, Marie-Christin and Karl-Martin Ehrhart (2018) "Auctions for renewable energy support: Suitability, design, and first lessons learned", *Energy Policy* 121, pp. 217–224.

IEA (2014) Capturing the Multiple Benefits of Energy Efficiency. International Energy Agency, Paris.

IEA (2015) Projected Costs of Generating Electricity. International Energy Agency, Paris.

IEA (2016) Next Generation Wind and Solar Power: From Cost to Value. International Energy Agency, Paris.

IEA (2017a) Energy Technology Perspectives 2017. International Energy Agency, Paris.

IEA (2017b) Renewables 2017: Analysis and Forecast to 2022. International Energy Agency, Paris.

IEA (2017c) World Energy Outlook 2017. International Energy Agency, Paris.

IEA (2018a) Bioenergy and Biofuels. International Energy Agency, Paris.

IEA (2018b) Key World Energy Statistics 2018. International Energy Agency, Paris.

IEA (2018c) Renewables Information 2018. International Energy Agency, Paris.

IEA (2018d) World Energy Investment 2018. International Energy Agency, Paris.

IPCC (2012) Renewable Energy Sources and Climate Change Mitigation: Special Report of the Intergovernmental Panel on Climate Change, available at www.ipcc.ch/pdf/presentations/Rio20/Rio20_puc_aivanova.pdf.

IRENA (2018) Renewable Energy Policies in a Time of Transition. International Renewable Energy Agency, available at www.irena.org/-/media/Files/IRENA/Agency/Publication/2018/Apr/IRENA_IEA_REN21_Policies_2018.pdf.

Jacobson, M. Z. and Delucchi, M. A. (2011) "Providing all global energy with wind, water, and solar power, part I: Technologies, energy resources, quantities and areas of infrastructure, and materials", *Energy Policy* 39(3), pp. 1154–1169.

Jacobson, M. Z., Delucchi, M. A., Cameron, M. A. and B. A. Frew (2015) "Low-cost solution to the grid reliability problem with 100% penetration of intermittent wind, water, and solar for all purposes", *Proceedings of the National Academy of Sciences* 112 (49), pp. 15060–15065, available at https://doi.org/10.1073/pnas.1510028112.

Jenniches, S. (2018) "Assessing the regional economic impacts of renewable energy sources: A literature review", *Renewable and Sustainable Energy Reviews* 93, pp. 35–51.

Kariuki, D. (2018) Barriers to Renewable Energy Technologies Development, available at www.energytoday.net/economics-policy/barriers-renewable-energy-technologies-development/.

Kelsey, N. and J. Meckling (2018) "Who wins in renewable energy? Evidence from Europe and the United States", *Energy Research & Social Science* 37, pp. 65–73.

Khatib, H. and C. Difiglio (2016) "Economics of nuclear and renewables", *Energy Policy* 96, pp. 740–750.

Kost, Ch., Shammugam, S., Jülch, V., Nguyen, H.-T. and T. Schlegl (2018) Stromgestehungskosten Erneuerbare Energien Fraunhofer ISE, available at www.ise.fraunhofer.de/content/dam/ise/de/documents/publications/studies/DE2018_ISE_Studie_Stromgestehungskosten_Erneuerbare_Energien.pdf.

Muller, S., A. Brown, and S. Olz (2011) Renewable Energy-Policy Considerations for Deploying Renewables. Information Paper, International Energy Agency, Paris, available at www.iea.org/publications/freepublications/publication/Renew_Policies.pdf.

Reddy, S. and J. P. Painuly (2004) "Diffusion of renewable energy technologies: Barriers and stakeholders' perspectives", *Renewable Energy* 29(9), pp. 1431–1447.

Rego, E. E. and C. de Oliveira Ribeiro (2018) "Successful Brazilian experience for promoting wind energy generation", *The Electricity Journal* 31, pp. 13–17.

REN21 (2018) Renewables 2018: Global Status Report, Renewable Energy Policy Network for the 21st Century, available at www.ren21.net/wp-content/uploads/2018/06/17-8652_GSR2018_FullReport_web_final_.pdf.

UCS (2017) Barriers to Renewable Energy Technologies, Union of Concerned Scientists, available at www.ucsusa.org/clean-energy/renewable-energy/barriers-to-renewable-energy#.W1tS9MInapo.

Wiseman J., Taegen, E. and K. Luckins (2013) Post Carbon Pathways Report: Towards a Just and Resilient Post Carbon Future. Discussion paper, Centre for Policy Development, available at https://cpd.org.au/wp-content/uploads/2013/04/Post-Carbon-Pathways-Report-2013_Revised.pdf.

Wiser, R. and M. Bollinger (2017) 2016 Wind Technologies Market Report, report for the US Department of Energy, Oak Ridge, available at www.energy.gov/sites/prod/files/2017/08/f35/2016_Wind_Technologies_Market_Report_0.pdf.

WWEA (2014) World Wind Resource Assessment Report, World Wind Energy Association, available at https://wwindea.org/wp-content/uploads/technology/WWEA_WWRAR_Dec2014_2.pdf

WWEA (2018) Wind Power Capacity Reaches 539 GW, 52.6 GW added in 2017. World Wind Energy Association, available at https://wwindea.org/information-2/information/.

5

Energy efficiency and economy-wide rebound

Realizing a net gain to society?

Lisa Ryan, Karen Turner, and Nina Campbell

1 Introduction

Improvements in energy efficiency have historically been promoted as a cost-effective and efficient way to reduce energy demand and greenhouse gas emissions (IEA, 2015; UNEP, 2014; European Council, 2014). Energy efficiency measures play a key role in many countries' strategies to mitigate climate change, while improving the security of energy supply by reducing pressure on the demand for energy. However, the benefits are not limited to energy and greenhouse gas emission savings. There is a wider set of potential benefits from improving energy efficiency that are now being coined 'the multiple benefits of energy efficiency' (IEA, 2014; ACEEE, 2015; Kerr et al., 2017). These benefits extend from individual level to national and regional level and across economic, social, and environmental contexts. Notwithstanding this, the merit of energy efficiency as a mitigation measure is regularly called into question in both academic and popular press with allusions to 'the rebound effect' (e.g. see Revkin, 2014; Gillingham et al., 2013; Shellenberger and Nordhaus, 2014). Rebound occurs when the realized reduction in energy demand is less than the engineering estimates would predict because of a range of economic responses triggered by the initial reduction in energy service price faced by the more efficient user.

There is an inherent tension in considering rebound as an indicator of the success, or not, of energy efficiency policy while adopting a multiple benefits prism. The measurement of rebound generally focuses on the ratio between actual and potential energy savings, where the latter is given by pure engineering savings that are technically possible. To have zero rebound in this setting would imply the absence of *any* economic response to a change in efficiency. This would seem to be a perspective peculiar to the energy efficiency rebound literature and not one that would enter consideration of increased efficiency in, for example, the use of capital or labor. The multiple benefits prism, on the other hand views the desired energy demand reduction as but one vector of many outcomes of energy efficiency policy measures (albeit the primary and thus potentially most heavily weighted objective).

In this chapter we examine the nature of economy-wide impacts of energy efficiency improvements more closely and the relationship with rebound effects. We argue that it is necessary to consider whether rebound in an economy-wide perspective reflects an outcome that delivers net socioeconomic gains from a societal perspective or whether rebound implies outcomes that are sufficiently negative (in terms of lost energy savings) to either deter from energy efficiency improvements or to warrant 'rebound mitigation' policy actions. However, we then go a step further, considering whether it might be possible to reduce economy-wide rebound effects (increasing energy savings) while retaining the socioeconomic gains of energy efficiency improvements, without resorting to mitigation tactics (such as additional tax burden associated with energy use) that may both constrain expansion and exacerbate inefficiencies/distortions in the economic system. We do so by considering the hypothesis that it may be possible to reduce rebound by focusing energy efficiency improvements on activities that are substitutes for more energy and/or carbon intensive competitors in delivering energy-using services such as transport, electricity generation, and heating. This introduces a different focus in terms of the types of substitution possibilities that have played such an important role in the rebound literature, traditionally with relatively high substitution possibilities between different types of fuel/energy uses and between energy and non-energy goods being associated with large rebound effects. Rather our argument relies on increasing substitution probabilities between different means of delivering the *services* produced to favor less energy and/or carbon intensive options.

This chapter is structured as follows. Section 2 considers the policy context for concerns over rebound effects. Section 3 then aims to clarify the different types of expansionary processes associated with energy efficiency improvements that give rise to economy-wide rebound and the traditional consideration of substitution possibilities in this respect. Section 4 then focuses on enhancing the relationship between economy-wide rebound effects and socioeconomic benefits delivered by increased energy efficiency. Finally, we conclude in Section 5 with some implications for policy makers and considerations for future research.

2   Why are we concerned about rebound effects from energy efficiency improvements?

A basic economic definition of an energy efficiency improvement would be enabling the use of less physical energy (e.g. gas) to provide the same service output (e.g. hours of heating at a given temperature) and, consequently, at a lower cost. This is the trigger for economic rebound at various (direct, indirect, and economy-wide) levels.

It is useful to begin by examining the objectives of energy efficiency policy and an overview of the recent academic literature on rebound in order to better understand how rebound effects impact the achievement of these objectives.

Many improvements in energy efficiency are designed as cost-effective measures to reduce energy consumption while addressing energy security, environmental, and economic challenges. Improvements in energy efficiency can also lead to a reduction in the need for investment in energy infrastructure and fuel costs as well as increased competitiveness and increased real household income and expenditure. Energy efficiency is widely considered a key tool and is promoted by many governments through policy measures, particularly in addressing climate change. This is illustrated, for example, in IEA models where it is estimated that energy efficiency would need to account for approximately 40% of the total emissions reductions needed to reduce CO_2 emissions by half by 2050 (IEA, 2015).

However, an academic literature on rebound effects in energy use that act to erode savings in energy and CO_2 emissions has been growing over the last 40 years. This was triggered by the contributions of Brookes (1978) and Khazzoom (1980) building on much earlier foundations laid by Jevons (1865). In recent years, perhaps prompted by policy attention to the potential implications of rebound (e.g. UK House of Lords, 2005; Maxwell et al., 2011) and well-known review works, such as the UKERC study edited by Sorrell (2007) and the Breakthrough report of Jenkins et al. (2011), the rebound debate seemed to explode for a decade or so. Attention has extended from basic direct rebound measures (the response of an energy user to the reduction in cost of an energy service when the efficiency of its delivery improves) to economy-wide rebound. The latter is broadly defined in terms of changes in all types of energy use across the whole economy triggered by the chain of economic reactions to a specific energy efficiency improvement in a given sector of the economy, set against the potential energy savings associated with that efficiency improvement.

The rebound literature can be divided into studies (1) reporting empirical measurements of mainly direct (e.g. Saunders, 2014, 2015; Small and van Dender, 2007) and more recently indirect (Zhang and Lawell, 2017; Lecca et al., 2014) rebound effects; (2) reviews of rebound effect estimates (Sorrell et al., 2009; Greening et al., 2000; Gillingham et al., 2014); (3) discussions of theoretical frameworks for rebound (e.g. Saunders, 2014; Howarth, 1997); and (4) categorizing different types of rebound effects (van den Bergh, 2011; Turner, 2013; Borenstein, 2015). However, one key problem for policy and wider understanding of the rebound issue is a lack of transparency in and common ground across many studies in how rebound is actually measured (at all levels, but particularly beyond the direct level).

While the basic definition of rebound as one minus the ratio of actual energy savings to potential energy savings (converted to percentage terms) is widely accepted, there is less clarity in terms of how actual and potential energy savings are actually measured in different studies. In particular, there is often a lack of clarity in terms of whether the focus is on impacts of the pure efficiency improvement alone or includes other 'baseline' scenario considerations, such as quantity adjustments in the energy supply chain directly serving more efficient users (see Guerra and Sancho, 2010; Turner, 2013).

However, a more fundamental problem may lie with the inherent perspective in the rebound literature – and, crucially, how it is interpreted – that anything less than a full realization of potential technical/engineering savings in energy use implicitly raises questions in terms of the effectiveness of energy efficiency enhancing instruments. This is a questionable perspective. For example, we do not expect or want labor efficiency improvements to lead to an erosion of employment. Rather, we expect economic responses to lead to an (efficient) expansion of (more productive) economic activity. Why then would we expect (or desire) economic actors to be unresponsive to the stimuli produced by an improvement in efficiency in energy use? The key difference in the context of the labor efficiency comparator would seem to be that public and politicians alike would welcome large rebound, ideally backfire[1] effects in employment. Indeed, this is likely to be a primary aim of economic policy built around labor efficiency improvements. On the other hand, any energy efficiency policy action that results in a net increase in energy use may be viewed as somewhat counterproductive (though empirical evidence suggesting likelihood of such a 'backfire' even at the economy-wide level in the case of energy efficiency is limited).

It may also be argued that the definition, measurement, and focus on of a single 'rebound' measure risk becoming a distraction from actually understanding and explaining how energy efficiency improvements work and impact on a full range of activities and agents in the wider economy in different case study and policy contexts (Turner, 2013). It would seem more important for policy purposes to clearly report and explain a full range of both increases and decreases in energy use in different sectors of the economy. Moreover, this should be considered in the context of both economic and social benefits (e.g. increased income in low-income households) and costs (including, as well as rebound, contractions in activity and employment in energy/fuel supply activities) that accompany (or are accompanied by) changes in energy use. Perhaps more crucially, analysis of different rebound pressures must be presented and explained in such a way as to permit policy makers to consider how/if they need to address 'the problem'. This perspective is aligned with the assertion by Gillingham et al. (2014, p. 26):

> Rather than consider the rebound effect as a deterrent from passing energy efficiency policies, policymakers should include [these] welfare gains in the tally of benefits of a policy. The mistake of designing policies to 'mitigate' the rebound effect stems from a focus on minimising energy use, rather than the broader objective of maximising economic efficiency.

Put simply, the success of energy efficiency improvements in delivering energy savings should be considered in the context of the full range of multiple benefits or indicators that are of interest to government as representing the interests of society. These include energy prices, security, and poverty, along with GHG emissions, a range of macroeconomic indicators such as GDP, employment and public budgets, as well as 'health and well-being'. The energy efficiency literature provides numerous examples where one or more of these parameters have been estimated and found to be positive and significant (ACEEE, 2014; Copenhagen Economics, 2012; Diefenbach et al., 2015; Howden-Chapman et al., 2009; Janssen and Staniaszek, 2012; Kuckshinrichs et al., 2013; Lehr et al., 2013; Liddell and Guiney, 2014; Worrell et al., 2003). Nonetheless, rarely are they comprehensively included in government policy evaluation.

The relatively narrow frame of assessment employed in evaluating policies in many countries can attribute undue importance to rebound effects in physical energy use and related emissions by underestimating the benefits of the energy efficiency measure (Ryan and Campbell, 2012; IEA, 2014). It is thus important to understand the wider non-energy impacts of an energy efficiency measure and the relationship with a consequent change in energy consumption (i.e. the rebound effect) in order to be able to assess the full value of energy efficiency measures. The rest of this chapter focuses on one category of these multiple benefits, namely the economy-wide or macroeconomic impacts of energy efficiency improvements. A key question from a policy standpoint is likely to be whether economic well-being can be further maximized while reducing (or at least not increasing) economy-wide rebound.

3 The macroeconomic impacts of improvements in energy efficiency

The multiple benefits of energy efficiency improvements include macroeconomic impacts as reflected in changes to key variables such as GDP, incomes, employment and trade.[2] The IEA (2014) identifies two distinct stages that trigger impacts at the macroeconomic levels: (1) investment in efficiency-enhancing technology and (2) the realization of efficiency improvements resulting in energy bill savings, although in practice the two steps may occur almost simultaneously with interacting effects.

Let's take these in turn. In many cases the first action taken as part of an energy efficiency measure is to invest in energy-efficient goods and/or services.[3] Investment spending, as well as enabling efficiency improvements, introduces additional demand along supply chains servicing this spending, which will lead to expansion involving energy use in different parts of the economy. However, as with any demand-led expansion, where there are constraints on supply this may impact prices and potentially 'crowd out' other activities. Moreover, given that the investment expenditure will take place in a given time frame only, the positive economic impacts are likely to erode after the initial demand boost delivered by investment spending. On the other hand, if a sustained program of investment in energy efficiency is put in place, this is likely to continue to deliver returns. Generally, there has been little work on the economy-wide impacts in enabling increased energy efficiency, with the literature tending to focus instead on the impacts of it being realized. See Figus et al. (2017) for one example of a study that considers the impacts over time of short-term government support to improve efficiency in household energy use.

The 'second step' arises in that when a more energy efficient technology is used, and the physical energy use required per unit of production of consumption activity falls, then more efficient users should enjoy reduced costs in delivery of the energy service in question. At this point, individuals or businesses will achieve real income increases and make decisions on real-locating savings from energy bills. However, as argued by Turner (2013) and Lecca et al. (2014), the nature of the subsequent wider economic expansion is likely to differ depending on the broad type of use where efficiency improves, of which we identify at least two cases.

First, where efficiency occurs in household energy use (i.e. the final consumption side of the economy), the increase in household disposable income is the source of a reallocation of demand away from energy spending towards spending on other goods and services. This translates to demand-driven expansion in economic activity. Again, the net direction and magnitude of the impact of this demand boost on macroeconomic indicators will depend on the nature of spending, supply and fiscal conditions and the impacts on prices and competitiveness. Similarly, the qualitative and quantitative nature of indirect or economy-wide rebound effects will vary, particularly where reduced energy demand leads to contraction in capacity and activity in energy supply chains (Turner, 2009, 2013).

In the second case, where an efficiency improvement takes place on the production side of the economy the successful implementation of energy efficiency enhancing technology will trigger a productivity-led, or cost-push expansion where a clearer path to net positive impacts on key macroeconomic indicators may be more unambiguously anticipated. While the extent and dynamics of expansion (and related energy use) will depend on the specific nature of the efficiency improvement and what type of activity it occurs in, as well as capacity and conditions particularly in labor and capital markets, the *net* impact on all components of GDP has a clearer potential to be positive. However, even where net positive impacts are likely to occur at a macro level, the *gross* impacts at the individual sectoral level may not all be positive. In particular, in energy supply sectors there may be a contraction in activity and capacity arising from a decrease in energy consumption. More generally, labor and capital supply conditions, as well as the strength of and demand response to positive competitiveness effects, will govern the extent to which different sectors are able to expand. The greatest pressure for expansion is likely to occur in sectors that are impacted (directly or indirectly) by the initial efficiency improvement (through supply chain linkages). However, these will not necessarily be sectors that produce the most value-added for the economy or employ the most people/provide the most income from employment, and may also be more or less energy and/or carbon intensive sectors. In short, the outcome of any energy efficiency enhancement cannot be predicted on a theoretical basis alone.

Rather, a review of applied case studies is required to answer the question of what magnitude of economy-wide rebound effects can be expected in either of these two (broad) cases. In the major UKERC review of rebound evidence reported in Sorrell (2007), economy-wide rebound estimates, mainly from studies using CGE modeling techniques, took on a wide range of values. A key conclusion was that economy-wide rebound is dependent on the nature and location of the energy efficiency improvement and the economic conditions prevailing in the economy under study. The findings of more recent CGE studies (e.g. Figus et al., 2017; Lecca et al., 2014; Broberg et al., 2015) continue to support this conclusion. Case-specific conditions include a range of factors, particularly the costs of introducing efficiency improvements, energy intensity of the sector where efficiency improves, and how the labor market functions.

However, Turner (2009) – and the sensitivity analyses of many CGE modeling studies – demonstrates that the assumed or estimated values assigned to key substitution elasticities play a key role in governing the extent of *both* economic expansion *and* economy-wide rebound. This is particularly (but not exclusively) in the production/consumption functions of sectors where energy efficiency improves and/or where more efficiency outputs are used. Rebound researchers (both CGE and more generally) have focused on the importance of the importance of (1) inter-fuel substitution elasticities; (2) elasticities of substitution between energy and materials/non-energy goods (in consumption and production), energy, capital and labor (just production); and (3) trade elasticities for energy and energy-using goods and services. All other things held constant, the higher these elasticities are, the greater will be both any expansion and the economy-wide rebound effects triggered by an efficiency improvement.

Consequently, rebound mitigation propositions have tended to focus on constraining substitution effects in favor of energy, in particular by countering the initial decrease in the effective price of a particular energy type following the efficiency improvement itself and/or the consequent energy demand reduction through economic instruments such as carbon taxes. However, such actions would be likely to also constrain the expansionary process itself, which will have wider implications in terms of lost economic opportunities from energy efficiency policies.

Moreover, to date the rebound literature has not addressed the question of whether economic expansion and economy-wide rebound need be so negatively tied following an energy efficiency improvement. This is an important gap. If it can be filled, well-informed policy analysts may look to target energy efficiency improvements so that they facilitate (rather than constrain) consequent expansionary processes in areas of the economy where such processes give rise to benefits (e.g. increased employment) and have lower carbon intensity. Moreover, where this may involve efficiency-induced stimuli favoring lower energy/carbon-intensive activities that are competitors for more energy/carbon-intensive ones in delivering services, well-aimed policy action may involve acting to enhance rather than constrain substitution possibilities.

4 Connecting economy-wide rebound effects and socioeconomic gains

A central question considered in this chapter is how to enhance the relationship between energy efficiency policy, economy-wide rebound effects and socioeconomic gains. More specifically, we focus on the question of whether it may be possible to consolidate economy-wide gains while limiting the energy rebound (or maximizing energy savings). In this context, we focus on economic prosperity but note that policy makers will also identify societal values associated with health and well-being, environment and climate change mitigation, employment, and social equality – that is, the basic interpretation of the term 'multiple benefits' proposed in IEA (2014). We consider this perspective by examining first the link between socioeconomic value at economy-wide level from energy efficiency measures and rebound, and then how the factors that determine the size of the resulting economy-wide rebound can be increased to enhance socioeconomic benefits.

4.1 Rebound and socioeconomic gains from increased energy efficiency

There has been limited analysis of the relationship between energy efficiency, socioeconomic gains, and rebound in the academic or policy literature. Linked to this, there are few examples of explicit estimations of the welfare impacts from rebound effects. Several papers acknowledge that the energy efficiency rebound effect is likely to have positive welfare implications (Gillingham et al., 2014; Borenstein, 2015), but this assertion has not yet been explicitly examined in the context of economy-wide analysis in any detail.

Chan and Gillingham (2015) provide the first welfare-focused treatment of the rebound at the *microeconomic* level. They use a theoretical model of consumer utility to derive conditions when rebound is likely to generate overall welfare gains. It does not include the costs of investment in energy efficiency, nor the dynamics or behavioral anomalies of the decision process. They show that, when there are external costs present, an 'exogenous costless increase' in energy efficiency and the consequent direct and indirect rebound may increase or decrease welfare. The determining factor in the Chan/Gillingham model is the external costs associated with increased energy consumption. If these are lower than the benefits from increased energy use through the rebound effect, then the rebound effect is welfare enhancing. This approach implicitly assumes that we do not consider the sole objective of energy efficiency policy to be energy savings but rather to be overall economic efficiency and societal welfare, as is true in other areas such as labor and health policy making.

How do we move from this to consideration of the societal well-being implications of economic expansion accompanied by rebound at the economy-wide level? If we were to apply a similar approach as Chan and Gillingham (2015), a detailed analysis and good comprehension of *societal* costs and benefits arising via the economy-wide response would be needed. If the primary objective of energy efficiency policy is to reduce energy use, then this should be weighted accordingly in policy assessment among the broad set of potential policy outcomes.

4.2 Boosting the energy rebound/socioeconomic well-being relationship

In Section 3 we discussed how improvements in energy efficiency will drive demand-led or productivity-led (cost-push) expansions in economic activity, but with supply conditions determining whether this will involve crowding out and/or reallocation of labor and capital between different sectors. Depending on the nature of production in the sectors that benefit most in the expansionary process, increased activity in any one sector is likely to be accompanied by some increase in energy use/energy rebound with associated external costs in that sector and potentially elsewhere. On the other hand, particularly in more labor and/or wage-intensive expanding sectors, these costs will occur alongside increases in employment and income from employment. These are two economic variables that are generally considered to be welfare-enhancing at a societal level (e.g. see Whelan et al., 2015).

Thus, a first point of interest in assessing whether costs associated with energy rebound are likely to dominate benefits from economic expansion may be whether the expansionary process favors more or less energy-intensive sectors as against (and/or combined with) other characteristics such as labor and/or wage intensity. That is, considering the likely *composition* of increased economic activity and the extent to which it will deliver social benefits that may be set against the costs associated with accompanying economy-wide rebound effects.

However, a second question is whether it is possible to design and target energy efficiency policy in such a way that the delivery of socioeconomic benefits can be decoupled from economy-wide rebound effects. We put forward the following hypothesis. If energy efficiency improvements can be targeted at a means of delivering an energy-using service (e.g. public transport or renewably sourced heat) that is a substitute for a more energy-intensive competitor in delivering a given service (e.g. private transport or oil-based heating), and it is possible to make the less energy-intensive option more attractive to service users, then such a decoupling may be possible. In other words, we propose that energy (and potentially other types of) efficiency improvements be targeted in a way that exploits substitution possibilities between different means of delivering energy-using services so as to favor relatively low energy/carbon options, and thereby limiting the extent of energy rebound accompanying economic expansion.

Exploring this hypothesis would require a broadening of our attention from one of the main-stays of rebound research, namely the focus on rebound occurring through substitution effects that favor increased but more efficient energy use. Rather, the focus would need to shift to consider not just energy use itself but the inputs to the production of energy services (which will be more or less directly *and* indirectly energy intensive). Crucially, it would also involve focusing on how service users respond to changes in price and other determinants of demand in the competing options they may choose between. For example, in choosing between electric rather than gas-powered heating systems (assuming that electricity is delivered in a low carbon way), or between different modes of public transport relative to fuel use in private cars to deliver mobility.

This service-focused argument may not be an immediately intuitive one for policy making, where the most energy-intensive production and consumption processes have generally been the first targets of energy efficiency policies (i.e. heavy manufacturing, inefficient lighting, driving private cars; see IEA, 2011). Moreover, it is one that requires considerable research effort. As discussed above, the economic channels for the economy-wide impacts of energy efficiency and resulting rebound are strongly case specific. Similarly, empirical analysis of different case studies for different types of service delivery in different economic conditions would be required in order to establish the conditions for which our hypothesis might hold and to determine how it might be exploited to further enhance the net socioeconomic gains of energy efficiency measures.

5 Conclusions: implications for policy makers and future research

Economy-wide rebound effects are generally symptomatic of increased economic activity triggered by improved energy efficiency. Here we have argued that, in a similar manner to any other policy, assessment of an energy efficiency policy should be considered from a societal cost-benefit perspective. In this light, the realized energy savings are unlikely to be the only measure of success or otherwise of the policy, rather the economic impacts and increased societal well-being and economic prosperity may be an equal or higher priority for many regional and national policy makers and members of the public.

We argue that a key question is not one of how to mitigate rebound. Rather it is one of recognizing the macroeconomic benefits that share the same trigger as rebound (the initial reduction in the relative price of energy services in the sector/activity where efficiency improves) and seeking to retain these, while identifying and understanding the distributional implications (across different industries and households). Where there is a binding constraint underlying the need to reduce energy use (e.g. climate change commitments) and therefore mitigate rebound, taking a perspective that focuses on maximizing socioeconomic gains implies that this should be treated in a similar way to any other macro-level constraints (on government budget, balance of payments etc.).

Through consideration of the channels through which economy-wide rebound occurs, we conclude that the level of substitution in demand between different energy-using *service* options may be a key parameter in decoupling rebound and societal gains from energy efficiency rather than reducing the demand for the service as a whole. We consider the implications of targeting energy efficiency measures at the less energy and/or carbon-intensive service options for delivering services that are commonly associated with relatively high energy use (e.g. mobility and using public rather than private transport option(s) for a given for journey). We hypothesize that this may involve improving the attractiveness of lower carbon/less energy-intensive options through price and/or other characteristics relative to more fuel-intensive competitors (e.g. using a private car for the same journey). Such developments may then lead to a decoupling the rebound from any economic expansion that may be triggered by improved efficiency.

Several policy implications arise. First, there should be more attention to identifying and considering service options that may be the target of energy (and possibly other) efficiency policies with a view to enhancing their competitiveness with higher energy/carbon alternatives. This involves a change away from the focus in current policy thinking that prioritizes energy efficiency improvements mainly in energy-intensive activities. In terms of the academic rebound debate, a shift of attention is required from focusing mainly on inter-fuel and energy/non-energy substitution possibilities in favor of considering how users substitute between competing means of delivering energy and energy-using services. This is also likely to require more attention to how various energy types and particularly durable/investment goods interact in both delivering different heating and transport services and in delivering efficiency improvements in these services and their underlying energy uses. Interdisciplinary research in energy use and diffusion of energy services would be useful that may involve combining behavioral models and societal issues with macroeconomic modeling.

However, as discussed above, and already accepted as the case in considering causal mechanisms that deliver economy-wide and macroeconomic effects of energy efficiency measures, this issue will ultimately need to be considered on a case-by-case basis. Initial research activity may involve theoretical analysis of the conditions under which more efficient and competitive low carbon energy service delivery is likely to translate to a decoupling of economic expansion and economy-wide rebound. However, as argued above, the outcome of any specific case study will be an applied question.

Acknowledgments

Ryan acknowledges the financial support of Science Foundation Ireland under the SFI Strategic Partnership Programme Grant Number SFI/15/SPP/E3125. Part of this work was conducted in the Electricity Research Centre, University College Dublin, Ireland, which is supported by the Electricity Research Centre's Industry Affiliates Programme, and received support from the Programme for Research in Third Level Institutions and the European Regional Development Fund (ERDF). Turner acknowledges support from the UK Engineering and Physical Sciences Research Council (EPSRC grant ref. EP/M00760X/1) through the EPSRC End-Use Energy Demand project titled 'Energy Savings Innovations and Economy-Wide Rebound Effects'.

Notes

1 Backfire occurs when the rebound effect is greater than 100%.
2 The term 'macroeconomic' in this paper is used to cover economy-wide effects that occur at national, regional and international level. It is concerned with the aggregate effects of energy efficiency measures which may be considered as comprising (1) the sum of the individual microeconomic effects and (2) the impacts of the whole economy resulting from non-linear complex interactions throughout the economy.
3 Energy efficiency improvements can also be undertaken without involving investment if we assume energy efficiency improvements are delivered as a public good, in which case only the energy cost reduction effects apply in this discussion. However, for large-scale improvements in energy efficiency globally, both behavioral change and investment – as well as financing systems that encourage behavioral change – will be needed. Therefore the investment effect will apply for most governments seeking to estimate the macroeconomic effects of energy efficiency measures.

93

References

ACEEE (2014). *How Does Energy Efficiency Create Jobs?* American Council for an Energy Efficient Economy Fact Sheet, Washington, DC.

ACEEE (2015). "Recognizing the value of energy efficiency's multiple benefits", *Report IE1502*, Washington, DC.

Borenstein, S. (2015). "A microeconomic framework for evaluating energy efficiency rebound and some implications", *The Energy Journal*, 36(1): 1–22.

Broberg, T., C. Berg, and E. Samakovlis (2015). "The economy-wide rebound effect from improved energy efficiency in Swedish industries: A general equilibrium analysis", *Energy Policy*, 83: 26–37.

Brookes, L. (1978). Energy policy, the energy price fallacy and the role of nuclear energy in the UK", *Energy Policy*, 6: 94–106.

Chan, N. and K.W. Gillingham (2015). "The microeconomic theory of the rebound effect and its welfare implications", *Journal of the Association of Environmental & Resource Economists*, 2(1): 133–159.

Copenhagen Economics (2012). *Multiple Benefits of Investing in Energy-Efficient Renovation of Buildings*, Report commissioned by Renovate Europe, Brussels.

Diefenbach, N, B. Stein, T. Loga, M. Rodenfels, J. Gabriel, and M. Fette (2015). *Monitoring der KfW-Programme „Energieeffizient Sanieren" und „Energieeffizient Bauen" 2014*, KfW, Frankfurt.

European Council (2014). Conclusions of the European Council, 23/24 October, EUCO 169/14, Brussels. www.consilium.europa.eu/uedocs/cms_data/docs/pressdata/en/ec/145397.pdf

Figus, G., K. Turner, P. McGregor, and A. Katris (2017). "Making the case for supporting broad energy efficiency programmes: Impacts on household incomes and other economic benefits", *Energy Policy*, 111: 157–165.

Gillingham, K., M. Kotchen, D. Rapson, and G. Wagner (2013). "Energy policy: The rebound effect is overplayed", *Nature*, 493: 475–476.

Gillingham, K., D. Rapson, and G. Wagner (2014) "The rebound effect and energy efficiency policy", *E2e Working Paper 013*.

Greening, L. A., D. L., Greene, and C. Difiglio (2000). "Energy efficiency and consumption: The rebound effect: A survey", *Energy Policy*, 28(6–7): 389–401.

Guerra, A. I. and F. Sancho (2010). "Rethinking economy-wide rebound measure: An unbiased proposal", *Energy Policy*, 38: 6684–6694.

Howarth, R. B. (1997). "Energy efficiency and economic growth", *Contemporary Economic Policy*, 15.

Howden-Chapman, P., N. Pierse, S. Nicholls, J. Gillespie-Bennett, H. Viggers, M. Cunningham, R.Phipps, M. Boulic, P. Fjällström, S. Free, R. Chapman, B. Lloyd, K. Wickens, D. Shields, M. Baker, C. Cunningham, A. Woodward, C. Bullen, and J. Crane (2009). "Effects of improved home heating on asthma in community dwelling children: Randomised controlled trial", *British Medical Journal*, 337: 852–855, British Medical Association, London.

International Energy Agency (IEA) (2011). *25 Energy Efficiency Policy Recommendations*, OECD/IEA, Paris. www.iea.org/publications/freepublications/publication/25-energy-efficiency-policy-recommendations-2011-update.html

IEA (2014). *Capturing the Multiple Benefits of Energy Efficiency*, OECD/IEA, Paris.

IEA (2015). *World Energy Outlook 2015*, OECD/IEA, Paris.

Janssen, R. and D. Staniaszek (2012). *How Many Jobs? A Survey of the Employment Effects of Investment in Energy Efficiency of Buildings*, The Energy Efficiency Industrial Forum.

Jenkins, J., T. Nordhaus, and M. Shellenberger (2011). *Energy Emergence: Rebound and Backfire as Emergent Phenomena*. Report by the Breakthrough Institute. http://thebreakthrough.org/blog/Energy_Emergence. pdf.

Jevons, W. S. (1865). *The Coal Question: Can Britain Survive?* First published in 1865, re-published by Macmillan, London, UK, 1906.

Kerr, N., A. Gouldson, and J. Barrett (2017). "The rationale for energy efficiency policy: Assessing the recognition of the multiple benefits of energy efficiency retrofit policy", *Energy Policy*, 106: 212–221.

Khazzoom, J. D. (1980). "Economic implications of mandated efficiency in standards for household appliances", *The Energy Journal*, 1: 21–39.

Kuckshinrichs, W., T. Kronenberg, and P. Hansen (2013). "Impact on public budgets of the KfW promotional programmes 'Energy-efficient construction', 'Energy-efficient refurbishment' and 'Energy-efficient infrastructure' in 2011", *STE Research Report*, Forschungszentrum Juelick, commissioned by KfW Bankengruppe, Frankfurt.

Lecca, P., McGregor, P. G., Swales, J. K., and Turner, K. (2014). "The added value from a general equilibrium analysis of increased efficiency in household energy use", *Ecological Economics*, 100: 51–62.

Lehr, U., C. Lutz, and M. Pehnt (2013). *Volkswirtschaftliche Effecte der Energiewende: Erneubare Energien und Energieeffizienz, GWS und Ifeu*, Osnabrueck und Heidelberg, Germany.

Liddell, C. and C. Guiney (2014). "Living in a cold and damp home: Frameworks for understanding impacts on mental well-being", *Public Health*, 26: 1–9.

Maxwell, D., P. Owen, L. McAndrew, K. Muehmel, and A. Neubauer (2011). *Addressing the Rebound Effect*. Report by Global View Sustainability Services. http://ec.europa.eu/environment/eussd/pdf/rebound_effect_report.pdf

Revkin, A. (2014). "Is there room for agreement on the merits and limits of efficient lighting", *New York Times*, 21 October. http://dotearth.blogs.nytimes.com/2014/10/21/is-there-room-for-agreement-on-the-merits-and-limts-of-efficient-lighting.

Ryan, L. and N. Campbell (2012). "Spreading the net: The multiple benefits of energy efficiency", *IEA Insights Paper*, OECD/IEA, Paris. www.iea.org/publications/insights/insightpublications/spreading-the-net-the-multiple-benefits-of-energy-efficiency-improvements.html.

Saunders, H. (2014). "Is what we think of as 'rebound' really just income effects in disguise?" *Energy Policy*, 57: 308–317.

Saunders, H. (2015). "Recent evidence for large rebound: Elucidating the drivers and their implications for climate change models", *The Energy Journal*, 36(1): 23–48.

Shellenberger, M. and T. Nordhaus (2014). "The problem with energy efficiency", Op-ed, *New York Times*, 8 October. www.nytimes.com/2014/10/09/opinion/the-problem-with-energy-efficiency.html.

Small, K. and K. Van Dender (2007). "Fuel efficiency and motor vehicle travel: The declining rebound effect", *The Energy Journal*, 28(1): 25–51.

Sorrell, S. (2007). "The rebound effect: An assessment of the evidence for economy-wide energy savings from improved energy efficiency", Report edited by S. Sorrell and produced by the *UK Energy Research Centre*. www.ukerc.ac.uk/Downloads/PDF/07/0710ReboundEffect.

Sorrell, S., J. Dimitropoulos, and M. Sommerville (2009). "Empirical estimates of the direct rebound effect: A review", *Energy Policy*, 27(4): 3115–3129.

Turner, K. (2009). "Negative rebound and disinvestment effects in response to an improvement in energy efficiency in the UK Economy", *Energy Economics*, 31: 648–666.

Turner, K. (2013). "'Rebound' effects from increased energy efficiency: A time to pause and reflect", *The Energy Journal*, 34(4): 25–42.

UK House of Lords (2005). Science and technology: Second report. Science and Technology Publications, 2nd report of session 2005–06.

UNEP (2014) Chapter 4, *The Emissions Gap Report 2014*, UNEP, Nairobi.

Van den Bergh, J.C.J.M. (2011). "Energy conservation more effective with rebound policy", *Environmental and Resource Economics*, 48: 43–58.

Whelan, R., T. Krebs, and T. Morgan (2015). *The Economic Impacts and Macroeconomic Benefits of Energy Efficiency Programs in Oregon*, ECONorthwest, OR, USA.

Worrell, E., J. A. Laitner, M. Ruth, and H. Finman (2003). "Productivity benefits of industrial energy efficiency measures", *Energy*, 28(11): 1081–1098.

Zhang, J. and C.-Y. Lin Lawell (2017), "The macroeconomic rebound effect in China", *Energy Economics*, 67: 202–212.

6

Economic impacts of the energy transition

Christian Lutz and Ulrike Lehr

1 Introduction and background

The Paris Agreement against climate change was decided in December 2015 and came into force on 4 November 2016. Its central aim is to keep global temperature rise below 2°C above pre-industrial levels and to pursue efforts to limit the temperature increase even further to 1.5°C. Climate change mitigation that will meet the targets of the Paris Agreement requires a fundamental transformation of the global energy system. Renewable energy sources and energy efficiency are the two main pillars of this energy transition (ET). The expected investment needed for the energy transition is huge. A recent OECD et al. (2017) study calculates additional investment of USD 29 trillion against a reference case between 2015 and 2050 just to meet the 2°C target. This sounds like a huge number, but it has to be put into context. With global GDP reaching USD 75.5 trillion in 2016 according to the World Bank, the additional investment will be well below 1% of economic activity for the next decades. One key result of OECD et al. (2017), supported by other research, is that

> transformation of the energy system in line with the "well below 2°C" objective of the Paris Agreement is technically possible but will require significant policy reforms, aggressive carbon pricing and additional technological innovation. Around 70% of the global energy supply mix in 2050 would need to be low-carbon.
>
> *(OECD et al. 2017, p. 13)*

Large investment, aggressive pricing, and policy reforms raise the question of the macroeconomic effects of the energy transition. The scientific debate is still on. While some research highlights the costs of the energy transition; others concentrate on the benefits.

The remainder of this contribution therefore wants to shed some light on the economic dimension of the energy transition. It starts with the methodology of measuring the different effects of the energy transition. This helps to better understand the sophisticated modeling studies that try to quantify macroeconomic impacts of the energy transition. Different models lead to different results; therefore, they have to be interpreted carefully and put into context. The results depend on modeling scale (global, national, regional), time horizon, bottom-up consistency, and the underlying assumption on economic framework conditions and instruments of the energy transition.

2 Economic effects in the literature

The energy transition has effects on all sectors in the economy. It changes household demand as well as industrial demand and supply and will lead to a global structural change. The demand for new energy technologies and efficient equipment causes direct and indirect effects. New wind farms require wind turbines produced by the respective industry and thermal insulation requires triple panes with special glazing, insulation material, and new building material. Direct effects comprise these additional turnovers from additional demand. Indirect effects are caused along the supply chain up- and downstream (e.g. in the steel industry for the tower of the wind turbines or in services for project planning).

The substitution of investment and use of fossil fuels by renewables and energy efficiency offsets the positive impacts of the latter. Operation and maintenance will shift from conventional sources to energy transition technologies. Conventional energy sources will be substituted by renewables or by capital in the case of energy efficiency investment. Additional to the direct and indirect effects various second-round or induced effects can be observed. These induced effects include

- Price and income effects
- Changes in trade relations
- Various dynamic effects such as multiplier, learning, market and productivity effects that are difficult to quantify.

(see IEA-RETD 2011 and 2012; Lehr et al. 2012; IEA 2014a,
Cambridge Econometrics et al. 2015; IRENA 2016).

Price effects result from economic instruments such as taxes, emission permits, or regulation. But the energy transition as such also changes relative prices: a more efficient use of energy leads to lower relative energy costs in production, consumption, or transport. Financing the additional costs for households or industry related to renewable energy or energy efficiency investment changes relative prices, too.

Private households as well as companies or the government have a certain budget to spend. For households, the disposable income reflects the budget constraint after the necessary expenditures for health care, taxes, and so forth are done. Higher prices for electricity will reduce consumption for other goods, as short-term price elasticity is low. Companies face similar constraints. However, reduced energy expenditures due to energy efficiency measures free additional budget for non-energy goods in both cases. In the long-term changes in relative prices play a decisive role for induced effects, especially regarding future behavior as they signal scarcity and drive technical change.

Income effects result from changes in income of households and companies. Additional demand, as described above, leads to additional employment and income in energy transition industries. Aggregate compensation of employees increases, who will spend the additional amount according to their marginal propensity to consume. This spending triggers effects for other producers of goods and services. Negative income effects are also possible, if conventional utility companies face reduced turnover, prices, and profits due to an increase in renewable power generation.

Foreign trade effects arise from the reduction of imports of fossil fuels and from trade in goods for renewables and energy efficiency. An example is mass production of solar panels in China, which are exported all over the world. The largest manufacturer for wind turbines is the Danish Vestas (WPM 2017), followed by the German-Spanish Siemens Gamesa and the wind sector of General Electric from the United States. Countries such as Denmark that have started the energy transition early, can hope for first-mover advantages in terms of additional exports for their goods and services on markets lagging behind. Discussing the effects from trade with energy transition goods leads to a discussion on who keeps the economic benefits from the energy transition. The largest physical potentials for electricity generation from renewable energy are found in developing countries in Africa and Asia where the establishment of own energy transition industries creates new paths for economic development.

In a long-term perspective, different dynamic effects play a role. Multiplier effects describe the relation between macroeconomic impulses such as higher demand for initially more expensive electric cars and various induced effects. Learning effects, often described as global learning curves for technologies such as solar PV, show the correlation between global capacity installed and cost reductions (learning by doing) or global research efforts and cost reductions (learning by searching). On the electricity markets, additional capacity with low variable costs such as wind or solar PV influences the wholesale price with impacts for all producers. The latter effects are very difficult to model endogenously in macroeconomic models. Typically, they will be treated in electricity market models that are soft linked to macroeconomic models. Table 6.1 summarizes the different effects.

An impact study can look at gross or net impacts (IEA-RETD 2012). Gross impact studies try to measure the relevance of the energy transition for the economy as a whole in terms of employment, production, or investment. They often only include direct investment but sometimes embrace indirect effects of investment as well as O&M and substitution effects. Net employment impact studies compare the effects from additional efforts towards the energy transition to the results in a world without these efforts.

The recent report by UN Environment, Frankfurt School-UNEP Collaborating Centre and Bloomberg New Energy Finance (2018) "finds that all investments in renewables totaled USD

Table 6.1 Overview of effects of the energy transition (ET)

	Effects	Additional	Reduced
Investment	Direct and indirect	Investment in ET	Reduced investment in conventional energy (CE)
Operation and maintenance (O&M)	Direct and indirect	O&M of ET technologies	Reduced O&M of CE technologies
Substitution/Savings	Indirect and induced	Additional use of ET sources	Reduced use of CE sources
Price	Direct, indirect and induced	Lower prices due to ET	Higher prices due to ET
Income	Induced	Higher income due to ET	Lower income due to ET
Foreign trade	Induced	Higher exports of ET technologies	Lower exports of energy/CE technologies
Dynamic	Induced	Multiplier, learning, market, productivity effects	

Source: IEA-RETD (2011, 2012); Lutz and Breitschopf (2016).

279.8 billion (excluding large hydro)" in 2017. These investments added 157 gigawatts to global power capacity in 2017, up 14% from the 138 gigawatts added the year before. According to that source, investment in renewables capacity was more than twice that in fossil fuel generation; the corresponding new capacity from renewables was equivalent to 69% of all new power, the highest to date. In 2016, global investment in energy efficiency increased by 9% to USD 231 billion (IEA 2017a). This increase coincided with a slowdown in investment on the supply side of the energy system. Energy efficiency investment now represents 13.6% of the USD 1.7 trillion invested across the entire energy market (IEA 2017b). Critics of the energy transition emphasize the cost side of financing this investment (e.g. Andor et al. 2017), if it is not market but policy driven.

IRENA (2018) informs in annual reports about global renewable energy employment, reaching 10.3 million jobs in 2017, up from 7.1 million jobs in 2012. These analyses are based upon a comprehensive annual desk research exercise and can be seen as gross effects. IRENA (2018) reports job losses in conventional energy industries, especially in the coal, oil, and gas industries due to substitution, as a first approach to net effect estimation. They summarize, however, that "project-level data indicates that, on average, renewable energy technologies create more jobs than fossil-fuel technologies".

More comprehensive analysis of the economic effects of the energy transition includes as much as possible the indirect and induced effects. To quantify the net effect of these counterbalancing tendencies, macroeconomic simulation models are used. This approach enables a closed framework for the analysis, in which no feedback effects and feedback loops are lost. A model-based analysis of net economic effects consists of the following steps.

Data on various possible courses of the future is collected in so-called scenarios. One scenario contains a future with no additional measures and investment and serves as a reference development against which all others compare. Bottom-up technology models, cost benefit analyses, feasibility calculations, and profitability analyses as well as future market analyses lead to the definition of scenarios for individual investment causes. The resulting information comprises monetary effects (e.g. energy prices) and/or energy related effects (e.g. energy savings) and serves as an input to the macroeconomic simulation model described in Chapter 33 on macro-econometric models in this handbook. The macroeconomic model calculates the future development of economic quantities such as GDP, employment, sector specific output, or value added, taking into account feedback effects. A comparison of these quantities under different scenario assumptions with a reference scenario provides information on overall (net) economic effects of the developments defined in the scenarios. The differences between the results are then attributed to the effect of different scenario specific measures since all other parameters in the model are kept constant in all model runs (so-called ceteris paribus method).

In Figure 6.1, a scenario with high investment in energy transition goods is compared to a reference scenario without such investment. The scenarios are translated into model variables such as total additional investment, total energy saved, energy saved by energy carrier, and so forth. These inputs are quantified in partial analyzes of different markets and fields of action.

Figure 6.1 summarizes the economic and environmental effects elaborated above. Firstly, investments directly increase final demand and if the demanded goods are produced domestically increase production. More production also requires additional staff and employment is higher. In a rather tight labor market such as currently the German market, wages will increase. In particular, wages can increase in sectors with no or low international competition. In sectors active on international markets, wage increases are somewhat capped by prices attainable on international markets. Profits, production, and the amount of additional employment will adjust accordingly. The additional employment yields more income, which in turn is spent. This increased consumption of goods leads to further production and income effects.

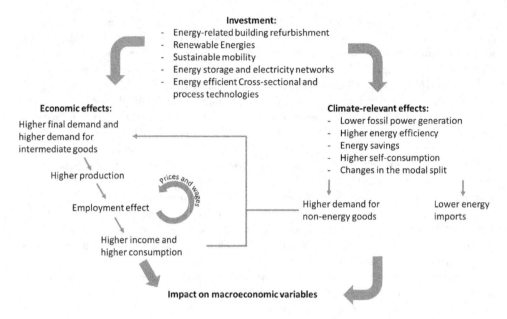

Figure 6.1   Economic and environmental effects of investment in energy transition
Source: GWS.

In addition to more labor, more intermediate goods are necessary for production, either domestic or imported. The production of intermediate goods itself increases the demand for these goods, and so on. These effects are taken into account in input-output tables using Leontief's approach, which link the production structure to the final demand. This makes it possible to determine the output of an industry as a whole. The input-output tables are at the center of some of the more complex macroeconomic models applied in Section 3.

Depending on the type of investment, environmental effects differ. Energy savings, increased self-consumption of energy and reduced fossil-fuel-based power generation are possible climate-relevant effects, which in turn lead to reduced energy imports. With the funds released, additional non-energy goods can be purchased, which leads to further economic reactions. Overall, investment affects the different macroeconomic variables such as gross domestic product and employment.

While most of the effects in Table 6.1 can be calculated directly, some of the discussed feedback and dynamic effects depend on assumptions about different circumstances such as business cycles or behavior of economic agents, which are to date not fully understood and difficult to model. These uncertainties include crowding out, the economic feasibility of investment partly due to uncertainties about future energy price developments, future technology cost development, the quantification of barriers and the cost of action, and behavioral changes such as rebound effects due to lower energy consumption. Rebound effects describe behavioral changes, which limit the energy savings of more energy-efficient technologies.

Crowding out refers to the possibility that the investments needed for the energy transition compete with and displace investments elsewhere in the economy. The likelihood of crowding out increases with the degree of capacity utilization. In an economy without unemployment and with fully functioning markets, crowding out will be (close to) 100%. After the economic and financial crisis starting in 2008, capacity utilization has been low in many countries and monetary policy extremely accommodative. Crowding out has been probably very low there.

Economic feasibility of investment is related to divergence of planned and realized investment. As future energy prices are uncertain, economic investment in energy transition can turn to not pay off for the investor. Different barriers such as the landlord-tenant problem can prevent investment. It is difficult to model them correctly. Technology cost development, especially for young technologies, is very difficult to project and model correctly. The modeling studies that are discussed next have to cope with all these effects.

3 Modeling studies

When comparing results of macroeconomic modeling studies of climate mitigation and energy transition, there is a striking difference between negative macroeconomic impacts reported by the IPCC (Clarke et al. 2014) and recently published positive results produced by or on behalf of international institutions (OECD 2017; Pollitt et al. 2017; IMF 2016). The fifth IPCC report shows cost for the idealized implementation scenarios of global consumption loss estimates for reaching levels of 430–480 ppm CO_2eq by 2100 ranging between 1% and 4% in 2030, 2% to 6% in 2050, and 3% to 11% in 2100 relative to consumption in the baseline (Clarke et al. 2014, p. 449). Similar deviations are reported for GDP. A comparison of different levels of ambition gives the robust result across studies "that aggregate global costs of mitigation tend to increase over time and with stringency of the concentration goal". The estimates are based on the assumption of a stylized implementation approach with a single global price for all GHG emissions. Carbon prices for reaching levels of 430–480 ppm CO_2eq by 2100 range from around 100 to almost 1000 USD2010/t CO_2eq in 2050 and between 100 and a few 1000 USD2010 in 2100. Carbon prices are estimated to be substantially smaller for lower ambition levels. The modeling studies make use of global integrated assessment models (IAMs) with low regional and sectoral resolution. Low-carbon or no-carbon technologies are specified on a high level. Assumptions about availability of mitigation technologies explain part of the variations of model results. Regional mitigation costs differ according to income levels. A unique carbon price is relatively higher in low-income countries. Therefore, impacts are about half of the average in OECD and highest in least developed countries.

A big caveat of these estimates is the assumption of idealized policy implementation with a single price instrument in perfectly functioning markets without any distortions, market failures, or institutional constraints. The authors of the IPCC conclude that "the reality that assumptions of idealized implementation will not be met in practice means that real-world aggregate mitigation costs could be very different from those reported here" (Clarke et al. 2014, p. 455). This does not devaluate these estimates, but they have to be interpreted accordingly.

The IEA has developed a scenario, which will reach the 2°C target with a probability of 66% and compares it to its new policies scenario as a reference (OECD et al. 2017). Carbon prices per t of CO_2eq will have to reach 190 USD in OECD countries in 2050, 170 USD for major emerging economies including China and 80 USD for other regions. The authors emphasize that carbon prices alone will not be sufficient to drive the energy transition. They assume the phase out of fossil fuel subsidies, additional fuel taxation, and the coordinated enforcement of command and control policies such as standards as well as energy market reforms, research, development, and deployment.

If this ambitious 66% scenario is combined with economic reforms in G20 countries, GDP on average across the G20 could be by 2.5% higher in 2050 compared to the reference (OECD 2017). Macroeconomic impacts will also be positive in the short term. According to the report,

the modelled growth effect is driven by a combination of investment in low-emission, climate-resilient infrastructure; an additional fiscal initiative to fund climate-consistent non-energy infrastructure; pro-growth reform policies to improve resource allocation; technology deployment; and green innovation. The benefits of combined growth and climate policies more than offset the impact of higher energy prices, tighter regulatory settings, and high-carbon assets that may become economically stranded before the end of their economic life.

Carbon tax revenues are used to lower public debt in most countries. Revenue recycling will also have economic impacts.

The OECD (2017) uses its Yoda model, which is a macroeconomic model with structural features such as hysteresis, which means that unemployment is possible. Parameters have been estimated econometrically using a panel of annual time series data as much as possible, especially for the growth and the Philipps curve functions. Other parameters are calibrated. Each country model comprises about 20 equations. The Yoda model is highly aggregated and does not differentiate any industry or technology detail.

Recent studies with the E3ME model show positive macroeconomic impacts of additional energy efficiency measures in the EU (Pollitt et al. 2017) and of an increased deployment of renewable energy at a global level (IRENA 2016). An increase in energy efficiency ambition in the EU to 40% in 2030 (against 27% in the reference) could boost GDP by 4% without crowding out. If partial crowding out is assumed, the positive GDP effect will reach 2.2% in 2030. For renewables, the ambitious deployment scenario REmap is compared to the new policies scenario of the IEA (2014b), which includes existing and expected policy measures from that date. REmap assumes a doubling of the renewable energy share in global energy consumption between 2010 and 2030 according to the IRENA roadmap. As a net effect, global GDP will be 0.6% higher compared to the reference in 2030. However, for some countries and industries impacts will be negative. Net employment effects are also positive in both studies. E3ME is a global, macroeconometric model designed to address major economic and economy-environment policy challenges (Cambridge Econometrics 2017). Behavioral parameters are estimated econometrically. A high level of disaggregation enables detailed analysis of sectoral and country-level effects from a wide range of scenarios. It is based on post-Keynesian principles with a focus on the demand side (IRENA 2016), while many other models as documented in Clarke et al. (2014) follow neo-classical economic thinking, which pronounces the supply side of the economy. In general, economic impacts of energy transition are reported to be negative in these models, if compared to an optimal state of the economy.

Therefore, the philosophy of the economic models is important for the sign of the effects, but Château et al. (2014) have calculated positive macroeconomic effects with a computable general equilibrium model as well, which is also based on neo-classical theory. They compare the efficient world scenario of the IEA (2012) with a new policies scenario. The efficient policy scenario includes energy efficiency investment, which pays off, but is prevented by various barriers. Simplified, it is assumed that the economic potential of energy efficiency is exhausted. Global GDP is 1.1% higher in the energy efficiency scenario in 2035. Some countries and industries, which are characterized by high shares of fossil fuels, will lose, however.

To model the economic impacts of the energy transition comprehensively, it is important to keep in mind that mitigating climate change is not the only target of the energy transition and there are wider socioeconomic benefits, which are often not correctly or not at all depicted in the national accounts. Accounting for the internalization of these external effects will reduce the economic costs of climate change. The energy transition can aim at increasing energy security as well as improving the health and well-being of the population and reducing local air pollution.

IEA (2014a) describes the multiple benefits of energy efficiency improvement. In many cases these additional benefits and other targets are the major drivers of energy transition policies.

China for example has announced its e-mobility quota for new passenger cars of 10% for 2019, not in the first place to mitigate climate chance, but to reduce local air pollution in large cities, thus improving health and well-being of the population. Some industrial policy ideas to foster domestic car production and strengthen the domestic car industry may have supported this regulation. Globally, deployment of electric cars is largely driven by the respective policies. Announcements of governments and cities around the world to prohibit fossil-fuel-driven vehicles from a certain year onwards will spur this development. This comes with other developments such as autonomous and connected driving and mobility as a service. All these trends have the potential to revolutionize the global car industry. Car manufacturers around the world plan massive investment in the new technologies to keep market shares and profits.

For the German government, the phase-out of nuclear energy in the light of the Fukushima accident has been the major trigger for starting the energy transition and is one of the key targets of the national energy transition concept, as the majority of the population is against nuclear power. In the United States, the shift from coal to gas in power generation is not mainly the result of climate mitigation policies but has been driven by technological progress and cost reduction in unconventional gas production. The resulting price decrease for domestic gas in the United States has been quite a game changer.

These examples show that understanding the economic dimension and effects of the energy transition in the short and medium term needs realistic models and a multi-target and multi-instrument perspective. Future models have to even better include the complexity of the different sectors and their interlinkage. Potential technical breakthroughs in battery technology for e-mobility will for example also open new options for power storage.

The simple assumption of a global carbon price, which has to induce all the changes to decarbonize the economies, cannot map this complexity. It is, however, a suitable proxy in long-term modeling, which has to abstract from concrete policies, technologies, and country specifics. Recognizing these different uses calls for a more elaborated portfolio of models to evaluate the various dimensions of the energy transition. No model is able to map all the effects on different regional and temporal levels. Therefore, authors have to clearly describe the scope and limits of their modeling exercises.

4   Conclusions and outlook

There are large differences in the results of macroeconomic modeling studies. While the last IPCC report shows negative effects of mitigating climate change during this century, recent studies of and on behalf of international organizations exhibit positive macroeconomic impacts of the energy transition at least until 2050. The devil lies in the details. IPCC reports the results of long-term global integrated assessment models with a global carbon price as major policy variable. While this is academically accepted, it has to be related to the benefits of mitigating climate change and it reflects reality only to a very limited extent. International institutions such as OECD, IRENA and the EU make use of models with more country and sector detail and focus on the next decades. In some cases, results of technology-based bottom-up models are used for scenario development in macroeconomic models. Compared to IPCC, the latter focus on energy transition rather than climate change mitigation. Though the two issues overlap, energy transition includes economic and fiscal aspects not necessarily covered by climate change mitigation studies. For instance, the IMF explicitly combines energy transition and macroeconomic reforms in its policy proposals.

But even the wider approach to energy transition falls short in covering some aspects. A first shortcoming of the models used is that effects such as learning are often not adequately included in the models. Here, the combination of bottom-up micro modeling and macro modeling needs to be improved. Other effects, such as crowding out, are very difficult to model, because they are not observable in the past and data are not available. Thus, modeling crowding out almost fully depends on assumptions.

Other differences in model results in the literature can be explained by the time horizon of the respective analysis, ambition levels to mitigate climate change and the industry or sector and spatial resolution of the models. In a long-term perspective until the end of the century, scenarios will be on a more aggregate spatial resolution and abstract from specific technologies, sectors and policies. The respective results inform about the cost side of a long-term transition, about key variables and the effects of acting immediately or later in the future. They should not, however, be misinterpreted as short-term policy advice.

Economic theory is struggling with the explanation of technological change. As Nobel Prize Laureate William Nordhaus wrote in 1969, "at the present time there is no compelling empirical evidence pointing toward technological change rather than associating increases in productivity with economies of scale, learning by doing, errors of measurement, or even sunspots". The empirical evidence has improved, but the difficulty of inclusion of endogenous technical change in many of the models remains. It calls for sensitivity analyses to better understand the implicit uncertainties. Economic theory and modeling fall short of explaining and guiding the whole energy transition. Diffusion of electric vehicles, societal acceptance of nuclear, windmills or grid extension, digitization, and storage all have behavioral and social aspects that have to be considered. Interdisciplinary approaches are needed in modeling energy transition.

The same holds for different economic uncertainties such as the probability and magnitude of crowding out of investment in the energy transition. More realistic scenarios have to be developed to take multi-targets and multiple policy measures into account. The macroeconomic benefits of mitigating climate change and of the transition to a more sustainable energy mix are highly relevant. In the future, more complex and realistic views will help to understand the macroeconomic impacts of the energy transition and relate them to wider socioeconomic effects to complete sustainable development. This is particularly important as mitigating climate change often needs additional talking points for governments and economic agents.

The recent perception of the globalization creating winners and losers also calls for more focus on the distributional effects of the energy transition. Costs and benefits for countries, industries, and groups of households have to be addressed to draw a more realistic picture of the energy transition and show possibilities and difficulties for policy making.

References

Andor, M., Frondel, M. & Vance, C. (2017): Germany's Energiewende: A tale of increasing costs and decreasing willingness-to-pay. *Energy Journal* 38, Special Issue #1: Renewables and Diversification in Heavily Energy Subsidized Economics, 211–228.

Cambridge Econometrics (2017): www.camecon.com/how/e3me-model/

Cambridge Econometrics, E3M-Lab, Warwick Institute for Employment Research IER & ICF International (2015): Assessing the Employment and Social Impact of Energy Efficiency, Final Report Volume 1: Main Report, Cambridge. https://ec.europa.eu/energy/sites/ener/files/documents/CE_EE_Jobs_main%20 18Nov2015.pdf

Château, J., Magné, B. & Cozzi, L. (2014): Economic Implications of the IEA Efficient World Scenario, *OECD Environment Working Papers*, No. 64, OECD Publishing. http://dx.doi.org/10.1787/5jz2qcn29lbw-en

Clarke, L, Jiang, K., Akimoto, K., Babiker, M., Blanford, G., Fisher-Vanden, K., Hourcade, J.-C., Krey, V., Kriegler, E., Löschel, A., McCollum, D., Paltsev, S., Rose, S., Shukla, P. R., Tavoni, M., van der Zwaan,

B.C.C. & van Vuuren, D. P. (2014): Assessing transformation pathways, in *Climate Change 2014: Mitigation of Climate Change*, contribution of Working Group III to the Fifth Assessment Report of the Intergovernmental Panel on Climate Change [Edenhofer, O., R. Pichs-Madruga, Y. Sokona, E. Farahani, S. Kadner, K. Seyboth, A. Adler, I. Baum, S. Brunner, P. Eickemeier, B. Kriemann, J. Savolainen, S. Schlömer, C. von Stechow, T. Zwickel and J. C. Minx (eds.)] (Cambridge, UK: Cambridge University Press and New York, NY, USA, 2014), p. 450. www.ipcc.ch/pdf/assessment-report/ar5/wg3/ipcc_wg3_ar5_chapter6.pdf

Frankfurt School-UNEP Centre & BNEF (2018): Global Trends in Renewable Energy Investment 2018, Frankfurt am Main. www.greengrowthknowledge.org/resource/global-trends-renewable-energy-investment-report-2018

IEA (2012): World Energy Outlook 2012, Paris.

IEA (2014a): Capturing the Multiple Benefits of Energy Efficiency, Paris.

IEA (2014b): World Energy Outlook 2014, Paris.

IEA (2017a): Energy Efficiency Indicators (database), Paris.

IEA (2017b): Energy efficiency 2017, Paris. www.iea.orgpublications/freepublications/publication/Energy_Efficiency_2017.pdf

IEA-RETD (2011): Review of Approaches for Employment Impact Assessment of Renewable Energy Deployment, by Breitschopf, B., Nathani, C., Resch, G. in "Economic and Industrial Development" EID: EMPLOY Final Report: Task 1. Study commissioned by IEA-RETD, November.

IEA-RETD (2012): Methodological Guidelines for Estimating the Employment Impacts of Renewable Energy Use in Electricity Generation, by Breitschopf, B. Nathani, C., Resch, G. Final Report of IEA-RETD in the Framework of "Economic and Industrial Development": EID: EMPLOY Project, November.

IMF (2016): After Paris: Fiscal, Macroeconomic, and Financial Implications of Climate Change. Prepared by Farid, M., Keen, M., Papaioannou, M., Parry, I., Pattillo, C., Ter-Martirosyan, A. & other IMF Staff, January. www.imf.org/external/pubs/ft/sdn/2016/sdn1601.pdf

IRENA (2016): Renewable Energy Benefits: Measuring the Economics, Abu Dhabi.

IRENA (2018): Renewable Energy and Jobs: Annual Review 2018, Abu Dhabi. http://irena.org/-/media/Files/IRENA/Agency/Publication/2018/May/IRENA_RE_Jobs_Annual_Review_2018.pdf

Lehr, U., Lutz, C. & Edler, D. (2012): Green jobs? Economic impacts of renewable energy in Germany. *Energy Policy* 47, 358–364. DOI: 10.1016/j.enpol.2012.04.076

Lutz, C. & Breitschopf, B. (2016): Systematisierung der gesamtwirtschaftlichen Effekte und Verteilungswirkungen der Energiewende, GWS Research Report 2016/1. Osnabrück.

Nordhaus, W. D. (1969): An economic theory of technological change. *The American Economic Review*, 2, 18–28. Papers and Proceedings of the Eighty-first Annual Meeting of the American Economic Association, May.

OECD (2017): Investing in Climate, Investing in Growth, OECD Publishing, Paris. http://dx.doi.org/10.1787/9789264273528-en

OECD, IEA & IRENA (2017): Perspectives of the Energy Transition: Investment Needs for a Low-Carbon Energy System. www.irena.org/DocumentDownloads/Publications/Perspectives_for_the_Energy_Transition_2017.pdf

Pollitt, H., Alexandri, E., Anagnostopoulos, F., De Rose, A., Farhangi, C., Hoste, T., Markkanen, S., Theillard, P., Vergez, C. & Boogt, M. (2017): The Macro-Level and Sectoral Impacts of Energy Efficiency Policies. Final report. European Union, July.

WPM (2017): Top ten turbine makers of 2017. *Wind Power Monthly*, 2 October.

7

Electricity market integration

Lilian M. de Menezes and Michael Tamvakis

Introduction

The benefits of market deregulation and subsequent market integration have long been advocated (Markusen, 1981; Joskow and Schmalensee, 1983). On the one hand, deregulation encourages competition, which may lead to more efficient allocation of scarce resources, reduction in production costs, lower wholesale prices, and ultimately, lower prices for final consumers. On the other hand, market integration results in joint operations and economies of scale which, at least in theory, make markets more efficient and improve social welfare. In the specific case of energy markets, greater competition should reduce market concentration and lead to lower wholesale prices, as expensive generation can be replaced by cheaper alternatives (Emerson et al., 1988; Turvey, 2006; Battle, 2013). From a policy maker's perspective, electricity market integration is a path to jointly address the objectives of higher security of supply and affordability (Boffa and Scarpa, 2009; Creti, Fumagalli and Fumagalli, 2010; de Menezes and Houllier, 2016), especially in a context of increasing generation from intermittent renewable sources. Electricity market integration would benefit consumers in high-cost energy markets and increase the profitability of lower-cost generation (Finon and Romano, 2009), since wholesale prices in integrated markets are expected to converge to the common marginal generation cost, which should fall between the lowest and the highest prices of generation in the individual coupled markets.

Market integration can decrease system operational costs because it allows for the possibility of dispatching modern and more efficient generation in a connected area rather than older local inefficient generation. Regional markets can take advantage of weather variations and diversity in hydro-regimes across the region, as well as of differences in electricity demand patterns that are due to distinct calendars and time zones. Most importantly, the system operational difficulties that can result from the uneven distribution of renewable generation sources across a region may be mitigated within the region. A larger market can accommodate expensive base-load and flexible backup generation that otherwise would not be profitable. By sharing resources, including reserves, the risk of shortages and price spikes can be minimized, and electricity prices are therefore expected to be more stable, which should increase market liquidity and facilitate planning and investment decisions. Not surprisingly, the last two decades have seen the creation of regional and supranational electricity markets, which comprise several states or countries.

In the European Union, the liberalization of energy markets has been strongly tied to the general principles of a single internal market rather than separate national markets for goods and services, which were introduced to the electricity sector with the Single Electricity Act of 1986 (Gebhardt and Höffler, 2007). Since then, a series of directives (e.g. 96/92/EC; 2003/54/EC; 2009/72/EC) has addressed not only how to improve competition in electricity markets but have also specified paths to the common objectives of decarbonization and energy security. The most important step of electricity market integration in Europe took place on 4 February 2014, with the day-ahead price coupling in North Western Europe (NWE). Since then, the coupled area has been extended and now encompasses 25 countries and 97% of electricity consumption in the EU. Nevertheless, recent empirical studies suggest that the degree of electricity market integration remains uneven across the region which faces several challenges, such as the lack of coordination between national policies and increasing decarbonization targets. The latter are laid out in the EU Renewable Energy Directive (2009), which sets the target of increasing renewable electricity generation to 20% (10% for transport fuels) and reducing carbon emission by 20% (in comparison to 1992) by 2020. On 30 November 2016, the EU Commission published a proposal for a revised Renewable Energy Directive (EC COM (2016) 860, European Commission, 2016), which raises the target of renewable energy sources (RES) to 30% by 2030, to be achieved in a cost-effective way across the three sectors of electricity (RES-E), heating and cooling (RES-H&C), and transport (RES-T). It also targets a minimum 40% cut in CO_2 emissions by 2030 and includes a set of measures to make sure the new targets are met. Among these measures are the easy access to consumption data that would enable individual consumers to change their demand pattern, the removal of obstacles to self-generation, and a new regulatory framework to ensure that renewables can fully participate in the electricity market, thus underlining the evolving process of electricity market integration. In the next sections, this chapter reviews studies of electricity market integration with a special focus on the liberalized European markets, reflects on policy implications, and ends by drawing conclusions for the future research agenda.

Studies on the integration of electricity markets

Most literature that addresses electricity market integration refers to the law of one price as the theoretical foundation to justify their assessment of price convergence. This law states that prices of a commodity offered in two markets should never differ by more than its transportation costs between the markets (after adjusting for the exchange rate, if the prices are denominated in different currencies). Violations of the law of one price are therefore indicative of barriers to trade (Marshall, 2000). In this context, several methodologies have been used to examine the extent of price convergence across regional markets, ranging from correlation analysis that presumes co-movement in prices; cointegration and fractional cointegration tests for long-run association; multivariate generalized autoregressive conditional heteroskedasticity (MGARCH) models that estimate the conditional correlation; vector error correction model (VECM) focusing on price differentials; Granger causality; impulse response functions; supply-demand models; and simulation and system dynamics, among others. Although interconnected electricity markets and the process of market integration are not unique to Europe, most studies have tended to focus on the EU or groups of neighboring countries within it, possibly due to the number of nations involved and the EU's aim to achieve an energy union.

On the American markets

Market integration has been addressed in different regional contexts outside Europe where there is some degree of interconnection between neighboring electricity markets, mostly in the Americas and Asia-Pacific. One of the earliest works on the performance of decentralized electricity markets in North America is by De Vany and Walls (1999), who looked for evidence of electricity market integration in the western United States. Their work covered 11 regional sub-markets during 1994–96 and used cointegration analysis and a VECM on daily spot electricity prices for both peak and off-peak periods. They found that all off-peak market pairs were cointegrated, with two-thirds of them being strongly integrated and half being perfectly integrated. Nearly 90% of peak market pairs were cointegrated, with one-third of them strongly integrated and just a few perfectly integrated. Overall, they concluded that deregulated western US markets priced power and transmission efficiently.

Park, Mjelde and Bessler (2006) considered firm peak spot prices for day-ahead trades between 1998 and 2002 in 11 spot markets and 23 different cities across the United States, including ERCOT in Texas, PJM in the Northeast and MAIN in the Midwest. The authors used a combination of VAR modeling, directed acyclic graphs and impulse response functions to investigate the relationships among the 11 markets. In most VAR equations, four or five markets had significant coefficients (i.e. they were integrated). While analyzing contemporaneous structures among markets, the authors found evidence that the United States was effectively split in three large areas, parallel to the three main power grids, or "interconnections": Western, which covers most of western United States from the Rocky Mountains to the Pacific Coast; Eastern, which covers most of the eastern United States and extends to the Atlantic Coast all the way from Maine to Florida; and Texas. Their analysis suggested that the Western interconnection had very few contemporaneous price information flows with the other two areas; Texas (ERCOT) had relatively little influence on any of the other two markets, possibly because at the time it used mostly gas as a generation fuel; and that PJM was dominant among other regional markets in the Eastern interconnection, most probably due to the fact that PJM real-time data provided a price discovery function not only to the Eastern Seaboard but also to markets further west due to the time zone difference.

Moving one step further, Mjelde and Bessler (2009) examined the interrelationships between wholesale electricity (base and peak) prices and four major fuel sources (natural gas, crude oil, coal, and uranium) in two regional US markets (PJM and mid-Columbia). The authors used cointegration and VECM methodology to model the long-run relationships between electricity and fuel prices in the two regions. Their study concluded that all price series examined were cointegrated in the long run, but not all series were fully integrated. They noted that "peak electricity prices move natural gas prices in contemporaneous time, which in turn influence oil prices. At longer horizons, fuel sources prices move electricity prices" Mjelde and Bessler (2009: p. 490).

Considering South America, Ochoa, Dyner and Franco (2013) looked at the integration of the electricity markets of Panama, Colombia, Ecuador, and Peru. They developed a system dynamics (SD) model to assess the likely effects of system expansion and security of supply. Their SD model outputs, such as generation capacities by technology and transmission capacities, were used as inputs in a dispatch algorithm which operated under market coupling conditions. The authors ran simulations under several scenarios, such as a base case of self-sufficiency and a free market scenario, where security of supply relied on interconnections and the generation capacity of neighboring countries. Their analysis concluded that a free market would bring more benefits in terms of supply costs, as it would allow a more efficient use of resources across all countries.

These benefits, however, were conditional on the absence of technical problems, political instability or any other issue that could interrupt cross-border electricity flows.

Following the same line of thought and methodology, Ochoa and van Ackere questioned the purported benefits of electricity market integration and developed a system dynamics model to examine the potential benefits and risks of market coupling. In Ochoa and van Ackere (2015a), Colombia and Ecuador were used as examples of countries with reliable interconnection and active cross-border electricity trading. Their model simulated how electricity prices would develop in the two countries under four different scenarios, three of which assumed capacity payments to incentivize investment in new electricity systems. Their simulation results showed that electricity market integration can bring benefits in terms of lower supply costs and better uses of resources, although these benefits are highly dependent on the degree of interconnection and the relative size of the countries. In some cases, there was a trade-off between lower prices and independence from the neighboring country, which highlighted the sensitivity to political relationships between the countries.

The issue of renewables integration into the electricity mix is increasingly drawing more attention, especially in the United States, where capacity expansion for both solar and wind generation have increased exponentially since 2000. The National Renewable Energy Laboratory has provided an impetus with their large-scale Renewable Electricity Futures (RE Futures) Study (Hand et al., 2012). The study provides an analysis of grid integration opportunities, challenges, and implications of high levels of renewable electricity generation for the US electric system. The focus is on the technical issues related to the operability of the US electricity grid and the integration of high penetrations of renewable electricity technologies. Building on this, Mai et al. (2014) revisited some of the analysis conducted in the RE Futures Study and modeled four scenarios where 80% of all electricity generation in 2050 is sourced from renewables, including wind, solar, geothermal, biomass, and hydropower. Their scenarios included a base scenario; a high-demand scenario; a constrained scenario, where RE capacity, transmission, and interconnection expansion is challenged; and an advanced technology improvement (ATI) scenario, which assumes greater future renewable technology improvement. Although the analysis remained focused on technical issues, the authors estimated the retail electricity price trajectory under the various scenarios. Of these trajectories, the highest (30% higher prices than the low-demand base scenario, by 2050) is associated with the constrained scenario, while the lowest (3% higher prices) is achieved by the ATI scenario. Among the authors' conclusions is the conviction that high renewables penetration is technically feasible, but would be more efficient with new transmission capacity, flexible conventional generation, grid storage, and changes in power system operations. Although this suggests a brave new future world with a high penetration of renewables in the electricity mix, the share of renewables in US electricity generation was actually 14.9% of approximately 4,000 TWh generated in 2016 (EIA, 2017), with hydro at 6.5%, wind at 5.6%, and solar at 0.9%. As renewable market shares are likely to increase in the coming years, so is the interest in assessing their impact on market prices.

Woo, Horowitz et al. (2011) used 15-minute price data from Texas' ERCOT and showed that rising wind generation is indeed likely to reduce spot prices, but it is also likely to enlarge the spot price volatility. In a further analysis of ERCOT data for wind-rich West Texas, Woo, Zarnikau et al. (2011) found that high wind generation and low demand in the West ERCOT zone led to congestion and zonal price differences. Gil and Lin (2013) analyzed the impact of wind generation on day-ahead PJM prices and concluded that even for low wind power penetration levels, the quantified expected benefit to wholesale market participants may be substantial. Hence, they advocated a benefit allocation mechanism to further encourage the development of wind power. A question that follows is whether these benefits remain substantial when a region already has alternative renewable generation. Woo et al. (2013) investigated this question in the context of the hydro-rich electricity system of the Pacific Northwest and found that increased wind generation decreased wholesale prices by a small but statistically significant amount. They also observed that a hydro-rich system can integrate wind generation at a lower cost than a thermal-dominated system, but the direct economic benefits to end users from greater investment in wind power may be negligible.

Woo et al. (2016) examined the possible merit-order effects of renewables on California electricity prices and the price divergence between day-ahead and real-time prices. Their study used hourly observations of CAISO (California ISO) market prices between December 2012 and April 2015, and applied a regression-based approach to evaluate (1) merit-order effects (i.e. displacement of conventional generation by renewables) and (2) why there is a divergence between day-ahead and real-time electricity prices. The authors used as explanatory variables fuel prices (Henry Hub natural gas); nuclear capacity availability; hydropower availability; and solar and wind generation. Their findings imply that merit-order effects from solar and wind generation are present in California's electricity markets, while the divergence between day-ahead and real-time prices was attributed to CAISO's renewable energy forecasting errors. The authors also concluded that while electricity prices may increase with nuclear capacity retirement and a reversal of low natural gas prices, this effect can be mitigated with higher renewables portfolio standards (higher renewables penetration), combined with increased energy efficiency and demand side management policies.

On the Asia-Pacific markets

The degree of interconnection among Asia-Pacific countries is not at the level seen in either the Americas or Europe. Except for the more developed Australian market, research tends to focus on the preconditions for a future integrated electricity market, such as investment in the necessary infrastructure, coordination among TSOs, increased renewable generation and concomitant policy implications.

Some of the earlier thinking of energy trade and energy market integration in the East Asia Summit Region (EAS)[1] were by Krishnaswamy (2007) and Bannister et al. (2008). Building on these, Wu (2013) reviewed electricity market integration in the EAS area and noted the heterogeneity of the various national markets. There are the more mature and integrated Australia, New Zealand, and Singapore, where generation, transmission, distribution, and retailing are unbundled and partly privatized. At the other end of the spectrum lies Brunei, whose electricity sector is vertically integrated and state-owned. In between are all other EAS countries, some of which have allowed unbundling of and private participation in generation, while others have also extended the process to transmission. The author suggests several progressive steps that need to be taken towards an integrated electricity market in the EAS region, or at least in its sub-regions. These include investment in infrastructure, especially in countries which have very low levels of electrification and need to move faster towards universal access to electricity; even before national markets are fully developed, it is important to increase bilateral and multilateral interconnections, sub-regional cooperation, and cross-border electricity trading, so that the foundation is laid for future market integration; EAS countries should work on harmonizing regulations and technical standards and follow best practice in preparation for market integration; and, finally, the aspiration of market integration should be reflected in national policies and planning in power sector investment and development.

The Association of Southeast Asian Nations (ASEAN), a subset of EAS which consists of ten member countries,[2] is integrating its power transmission infrastructure via the ASEAN power grid as part of the ASEAN Vision 2020. In this context, Ahmed et al. (2017) reviewed energy resources, their current utilization, and future projections. Given the potential for growth in renewables, export-import scenarios and renewable-generation-based transmission expansion, planning practices in ASEAN were analyzed. Major challenges for the establishment of an ASEAN grid that will require information sharing and coordination between different TSOs were identified. These included voltage and frequency deviation due to non-dispatchable production (intermittent power located in remote regions), congestion, blackouts, and demand-supply management for long distance power transmission network. They concluded that methods for efficiently allocating costs and revenues between different TSOs and inter-TSO compensation mechanisms will be needed, as well as coordinated investments in generation in order to avoid overestimation of reserve margins. Finally, they stressed that a lack of coordinated transmission and generation planning could limit the development and utilization of the interconnected transmission system, increase costs, and send negative signals to investors.

Considering Australia, Nepal and Foster (2016) argued that although its National Electricity Market (NEM) was established in 1998, the effects of integration had not been systematically examined. Thus, they analyzed daily electricity spot prices, which were obtained by averaging the publicly available real-time original and official half-hourly spot prices for electricity. The period from January 2000 to November 2013 was considered, except for Tasmania that joined NEM in May 2005, for which the sample was from 1 January 2006 to 1 November 2013. Pairwise unit root tests on the log-price differences indicated that an integrated market for electricity had not been universally achieved, price convergence seemed to be mainly driven by bilateral regional interconnections between separate markets. Cointegration analysis led to contradictory findings, and the authors concluded that they could not reject the existence of significant persistence in price differences (or the lack of long-run price equilibrium). Finally, a time-varying coefficient model that measured the strength of the relationship between prices in different markets, which was estimated using a Kalman filter, suggested price convergence in the two markets that had fully privatized generation. Overall, their results suggest that full market integration had not been achieved in NEM. More generally, they concluded that convergence in generation and network ownership plus a common regulatory approach would facilitate improvements in wholesale market integration, especially as these markets experience increasing shares of renewable energy.

Apergis, Fontini and Inchauspe (2017) questioned the appropriateness of cointegration analysis that is common to many studies and used a different method to assess market integration of the Australian regional markets. They argued that the methodology by Phillips and Sul (2007, 2009) is better suited to test for convergence in wholesale electricity prices, because it has three advantages over cointegration analysis. First, it allows for econometric testing of 'convergence clubs' and estimation of convergence paths relative to identified common trends. Second, it can be implemented on multivariate data comprising prices in the different markets rather than focusing on pairs of markets. Third, the methodology does not need to rely on assumptions of a presence of a trend or stationarity in the time series. Two types of price convergence were hypothesized. In the short run, price convergence is expected to be driven by arbitrage, for which opportunities reduce as markets become efficient, while in the long run price convergence should follow the exploitation of profits under free entry and exit conditions, and thus should depend on the structure and evolution of the power markets. Thus, the authors hypothesized that the more electricity markets are homogeneous with regard to technology and design, the more likely price convergence occurs, even with limited or absent interconnection capacity, and vice versa. Accordingly, "long-run price convergence is affected, by energy policies targeted at reducing externalities, and in particular, power production from carbon-intensive fuels" (Apergis, Fontini and Inchauspe, 2017, p. 412). Their data excluded the Northern Territories and consisted of weekly wholesale electricity prices for the remaining six states, spanning the period January 1999 to July 2014.[3] Three distinctive growth patterns in wholesale electricity prices across the six Australian states were identified. In all, their results confirmed that markets with limited physical interconnection can achieve price convergence over the long run, if there is some homogeneity in market structures. Tasmania and Western Australia, which have less competitive markets where a major role is played by state-owned companies, were found to share a separate, non-competitive convergence pattern, despite differences in how capacity is remunerated. In addition, the introduction of a carbon tax did not alter the price convergence process in the identified clubs of states, except South Australia, which would have converged to the club formed by the other NEM states (except Tasmania) had the carbon tax not been in place. The study highlighted that although interconnection is important, there is need to identify the features of market design that can foster integration.

In line with other electricity markets, the role of renewables and their impact on wholesale electricity prices and market integration is gaining momentum in the research agenda. In Australia, the government put in place a mandatory renewable energy target (MRET) in 2001, with the initial aim to source 2% of the nation's electricity generation from renewable sources. In 2009, the scheme was renamed renewable energy target (RET) and that target was raised to 20% of renewable electricity generation by 2020.[4] MacGill (2010) made a first attempt to evaluate the prospects of wind power integration in the Australian NEM by reviewing its decision-making framework in terms of governance, security, commercial, and technical regimes. The author concluded that Australia's National Electricity Market and renewable policy support arrangements both incorporate significant roles for commercial, competitively driven decision-making. He recommended that wind generation should be formally incorporated into the NEM's operational decision-making mechanism by requiring greater participation in data provision, scheduling, ancillary services, and security projection arrangements.

Cutler et al. (2011) explored wind power integration in the South Australian region, which has the highest wind penetration in NEM. They assessed the interaction of regional wind generation, electricity demand, and half-hourly spot prices over a two-year period from September 2008 to August 2010. They found that electricity demand was dominant in determining spot prices, with wind power having a significant secondary influence. There was a clear inverse relationship between wind generation and prices, but no clear relationship between wind generation and electricity demand. There were also several extreme events where prices were either very high or, conversely, negative. These were attributed to the relatively limited interconnection between South Australia and the other NEM regions. Bell et al. (2015) picked on the issue of wind speed and electricity demand correlation in an effort to determine the ability of wind generation to meet peak-load electricity demand on the Australian NEM without the need for energy storage. The authors used correlation analysis on half-hourly wind speed and electricity demand data, for the three calendar years 2010–2012 and for 50 regional nodes. Their analysis found low wind speed correlations in the peripheral states of Queensland, South Australia, and Tasmania, which could assist system balancing if adequate interconnection capacity is installed between these regions, via New South Wales and Victoria. They also found notable positive correlation between wind speed and electricity demand in Queensland, New South Wales, and South Australia, which pointed to the ability of wind generation to cover peak-load demand, once again under the proviso that interconnection capacity increases among the regions.

Worthington and Higgs (2017) studied the impact of generation mix, including fossil fuels (coal and gas) and renewables (hydropower and wind) on daily spot electricity prices across five regions of the Australian NEM. They used daily electricity prices between January 2006 and September 2012, alongside data on daily generation by type, available capacity for each generator and interconnection flows between regions. Their results indicated that electricity prices were lower with the use of coal and higher with the use of natural gas and renewables, suggesting the likelihood of higher wholesale prices as the electricity industry moves towards the announced RETs. The authors also concluded that the effect of price increases due to the introduction of renewables were mitigated in certain regions which had a comparative advantage: South Australia and Tasmania for wind, and Victoria and Tasmania for hydropower.

Turning their focus to Southeast Asia, Chang and Li (2015) used a linear dynamic programming model to assess the impact of energy market integration in the ASEAN region, taking into account renewable energy, feed-in-tariffs (FITs) and carbon pricing. Their study covered the ten ASEAN countries, included power generation from both conventional and renewable sources (coal, diesel, natural gas, hydro, small hydro, geothermal, wind, solar PV, and biomass), and covered the period 2012–2035. Based on the simulation results, the authors concluded that energy market integration in the ASEAN region would significantly promote the adoption of renewable energy. They also recommended the coordinated adoption of either renewable energy portfolio standards (i.e. renewable energy targets) or FITs. They concluded that energy market integration with policy coordination among the ten ASEAN countries would speed up the expansion of renewables and achieve carbon reduction targets while incurring only negligible increases in the total cost of electricity.

Not much has been written on the progress of energy market integration in other regions, especially developing ones. Before moving onto the European market, it is worth mentioning a comparison of three developing region power pools (SAPP, WAPP, and MER)[5] with Nord Pool by Oseni and Pollitt (2016). The authors initially embarked on a review of the benefits and disadvantages of opening electricity trade among countries in a region, including security of supply issues, price adjustments in low-cost and high-cost generators, impact on retail consumers, and possible reaction of large-scale industrial consumers. They then carried out a descriptive comparison of the four pools in terms of the nature of the trading platform used, the institutions developed to support it, the governance of those institutions, the practical steps to implementation, and the concrete evidence on the benefits of trade. Subsequently, they compared the extent of cross-border trading in the regions as a proportion of their respective total electricity consumption and interconnection capacity. The authors highlighted several common themes and lessons to be learned in electricity market integration: countries must be committed to free trade and have adequate transmission capacity for this trade to occur; there is a need for strong, independent institutions as well as appropriate market design, which make use of day-ahead and real-time markets; and timely development of regional power pools requires a timetable for reform, should start with a small number of countries, expanding over time, and can be facilitated by international organizations. Many of these conclusions emanated from the experiences of building a well-functioning Nord Pool, which brings us conveniently to focus on the European market.

On the European market

The prospect of a European single market for energy has led to a series of studies. The first stream of literature is focused on assessments of price convergence and the progress towards a pan-European market. These have identified enablers and deterrents of electricity market integration and led to at least three subsets of studies. Several authors have analyzed the role of inputs to electricity generation while others focused on interconnection and market coupling. More recently, as observed in other markets, a growing body of research addresses the impact of increasing renewable generation on interconnected electricity markets.

Studies of price convergence

One of the earliest attempts to assess European electricity market integration was by Bower (2002). His sample included mean daily prices, in 2001, for day-ahead trading in 15 different locations in eight countries: Norway, Sweden, Finland, Denmark, England and Wales, Spain, Germany, and the Netherlands. After an initial inspection of correlation coefficients, he proceeded to use cointegration analysis to assess the level of integration between markets. His results indicated that there were robust long-run equilibrium relationships between all pairs of locational spot prices within Nord Pool and between many Nord Pool locations and locations outside Scandinavia. Cointegration relationships between pairs of locations outside Nord Pool were weaker, but still statistically significant. The results of correlation and cointegration analyses between pairs of locations were used as evidence of price convergence (or lack of it). There was no effective arbitrage process connecting Spain and the rest of locations, while the remaining European locations exhibited strong price cointegration, but weak price change correlation. The latter was attributed to transmission constraints which prevented enough trade to occur in order to equilibrate prices between locations. Overall, the author concluded that, despite price co-movement and arbitrage trading between locations, the market was inefficient because generating firms exercised market power at some locations and mechanisms to allocate capacity on congested transmission lines were weak. From a policy perspective, he recommended that the European Commission should increase competition by breaking up dominant generating firms rather than subsidizing new transmission capacity.

Building on the analyses by Bower (2002), Galli and Armstrong (2003), and Boisseleau (2004), Zachmann (2008) performed a principal component analysis (PCA) of wholesale electricity prices between 2002–2006 for ten European countries: Austria, France, Germany, the Netherlands, the UK, Poland, the Czech Republic, Denmark (East and West regions), and Sweden. His results provided general evidence that a common European price pattern was increasingly able to explain national price developments. The author then tested for pairwise convergence of daily average electricity prices. Results were mixed, with convergence mostly occurring between directly linked markets. Further analysis confirmed the mixed results in terms of market integration, with nearly 60% of hourly pairs of national wholesale electricity prices converging. This convergence was evident primarily in off-peak prices, while three-quarters of peak prices were diverging. The author concluded that at the time the efforts for the creation of a single EU electricity market were only partially successful. In a subsequent study, Zachmann (2009) investigated the integration of the new member states, and observed that the trade of electricity across the German-Polish-Czech border did not lead to a convergence in wholesale prices. He concluded that buying electricity in the Polish and Czech markets was subject to high price uncertainty due to low levels of liquidity, market concentration, and difficulties in estimating the available transmission capacities. His observations highlighted a need for a common balancing market, which could manage transmission capacity and thus reduce transaction costs (improve liquidity).

Von Hirchhausen and Zachmann (2009) examined further the integration of new member states to the EU electricity market. They observed that the Eastern countries had implemented some reforms, but most market objectives were still to be achieved (e.g. competitive national markets, a functioning wholesale market, and efficient cross-border trade). For example, Poland had the largest power exchange among the new entrants, but market liquidity was insufficient to enable competitive wholesale prices. Slovenia was characterized by an unbundled electricity sector which was state controlled. Croatia had vertically integrated the state-owned electricity sector that was in place. Romania and Bulgaria had a small share of independent power producers in the almost completely state-owned generation and distribution sectors, while the Baltic countries (Lithuania, Latvia, and Estonia) were still part of the North-West Russian electricity system. In all, long-term power purchase agreements were in place and the new member states lagged considerably behind, with only Hungary and the Slovak Republic having achieved standards that were comparable to the remaining EU member states.

In the same spirit, Bunn and Gianfreda (2010) addressed the integration of the French, German, British, Dutch, and Spanish electricity markets at day-ahead, week-ahead, one-month-ahead, and two-month-ahead lead times. They tested several hypotheses on market integration, with regard to factors such as interconnection capacity, geographical proximity, level of cross-border electricity exports, demand seasonality, base versus peak price, and forward versus spot prices. They used diverse methods including causality tests, cointegration, and impulse-response techniques for both price levels and volatilities. In general, the authors found evidence of market integration increasing over time, despite an underlying inefficiency in each market with respect to the forward and spot price convergence. More specifically, integration was higher as the interconnection capacity of a market increased; integration was not a simple function of market proximity, with evidence that Germany was integrated with both the British and the Spanish markets; and a large exporter, such as France, did not always create price shock transmissions to the markets it exports to, possibly because its nuclear generation is normally low-cost. Finally, the authors did not find enough evidence that there is high integration between seasonal demand and peak periods and, surprisingly, neither did they find higher integration in the forward than in the spot market.

Moving away from cointegration studies, Autran (2012) developed a jump-diffusion model with time-varying estimates and concluded that, despite signs of regional convergence of electricity prices, market integration of the Belgian, Dutch, French, and German electricity spot and future markets had not been achieved in the period between 2006 and 2011. Differently from most of the literature thus far, the author noted that the convergence of electricity prices followed a *stepwise process*, which could be due to the implementation of market coupling.

Huisman and Kiliç (2013) examined the development of day-ahead prices in the Belgian, Dutch, French, German, and Nordic markets over the period from 2003 to 2010, which saw both increased liberalization in, and increased connectivity of, European electricity markets. Rather than looking at classic price convergence models, as in Bunn and Gianfreda (2010) above, the authors used a two-regime switching model to ascertain whether there were changes in the spike behavior of electricity prices. They defined two regimes: one where prices were normal; and one where prices were abnormal (i.e. more "spiky"). Their results for the first four markets indicated that the mean log price level in the normal regime increased, while the opposite happened in the abnormal regime. In the Belgian, Dutch, and French markets, the probability of price spikes decreased, while the same probability increased in the German and Nordic markets. The authors also noted a reduction in the speed of mean-reversion, implying more randomness in prices, which was interpreted as a sign of progressively more efficient electricity markets. Finally, they observed that the estimated parameters for the five markets converged over time, which could be explained by increased connectivity and market liquidity.

In contrast to studies that tested the integration of European electricity markets and assumed electricity prices to follow a trend, de Menezes and Houllier (2016) adopted a time-varying fractional cointegration analysis. Daily spot prices from February 2000 to March 2013 of nine European electricity spot markets (APX-UK, APX-NL, Belpex, EPEX-FR, EPEX-DE, IPEX, Nord Pool, Omel, and OTE) and month-ahead prices in four markets (French, British, German, and Dutch) from November 2007 to December 2012 were investigated. Their results showed that unit root tests are inadequate for assessing electricity spot market convergence, because spot prices were found to be fractionally integrated and mean-reverting time series. Geographically close or well-connected electricity spot markets were found to have longer periods of price convergence, and the authors concluded that market coupling initiatives were delivering a more robust electric system. However, overall electricity spot prices were not increasingly converging, and spot price dispersion could not be linked to market integration. Spot price behavior and their association with different markets were observed to change over time, reflecting changes in the EU electrical system. Their findings highlighted the relevance of extreme weather conditions, public holidays, reduced plant availability, and fuel price developments for changes in the speed of mean reversion and convergence of electricity spot prices. One-month-ahead prices, by contrast, were found to have become more resilient to shocks and to follow more stable trends.

Studies of interconnection and market integration

With several studies indicating only partial price convergence among EU countries, attention was given to the potentially detrimental effect of explicit auctions of interconnector capacity. Weber, Graeber and Semmig (2010) discussed the merits of utilizing implicit auctions to allocate transmission capacity on European cross-border interconnectors. The authors observed that the prevailing explicit auctions of such capacity often led to "adverse flows" (i.e. flows of electricity from a high-price to a low-price area), which highlighted market inefficiencies where the parties involved were not able to predict properly prices in the connected regions. The authors then juxtaposed the use of implicit auctions in coupled markets, where interconnector capacity simply forms part of the day-ahead auctioning of electricity in connected markets. They went on to show how market coupling results in "normal" flows of electricity from low-price to high-price markets, leading to prices converging (where interconnector capacity is restricted and may be congested) or even equalizing (where interconnector capacity is unrestricted) between these markets.

In the same spirit, Pellini (2012) evaluated the impact of replacing explicit auctions of interconnector capacity with market coupling, by looking at the case of Italy and its neighbors France, Switzerland, Austria, Slovenia, and Greece, with which it has interconnections. Using data from deterministic simulations of the Italian day-ahead market for 2012, which took account of all domestic generation sources, the author built two scenarios – a reference and a high scenario, with the latter assuming higher demand and fuel prices. She then proceeded to construct four alternative cases: (a) the baseline case of perfect competition, whereby generators are price-takers and offer their power output at marginal cost; (b) a business-as-usual case where generators compete and offer their power at above marginal cost prices; (c) case [b] with market coupling; and (d) case [a] with market coupling. After comparing the welfare results of cases [b–d] to the baseline case, the author concluded that welfare increases with market coupling and the welfare gain is maximized when market coupling is accompanied by perfect competition (case [d]).

Kiesel and Kusterman (2016) modeled the dynamics of neighboring European electricity markets which are implicitly or explicitly coupled. They focused on the NEW market coupling, which includes the 13 countries and TSOs involved in the power exchanges APX, Belpex, EPEX SPOT, and Nord Pool Spot; Spain and Portugal since May 2014; and Italy, France, Austria, and Slovenia since February 2015. They analyzed the effects of implicit market coupling on typical products traded on energy exchanges such as futures, options on futures, hourly power forward curves, and virtual power plants. They did this by constructing a supply-demand model for coupled electricity markets, where demand is inelastic (horizontal) and has to be satisfied at all times, supply is determined by the summation of capacity usage of the various generators according to their input fuel prices, and the markets are interconnected. They used their model to investigate the effects of market coupling for France and Germany. Although prices generated by the model followed the pattern of historical prices, the latter demonstrated higher variation, which highlights the challenges in modeling interconnected markets. The authors made two interesting conclusions first, introducing market coupling might lead to lower futures prices in all affected markets, with increasing interconnector capacity finally leading to price convergence; and second, introducing market coupling might lead to volatility spillover effects, with the low-volatility market likely to experience increased volatility. The latter is in line with observations by Zareipour, Bhattacharya, and Cañizares (2007) concerning interconnected North American electricity markets, as the authors showed volatility progressing in the direction of the smaller Canadian markets. Other studies of connected continental markets have also noted the role of the larger and more liquid German market in transmitting its price volatility in the region (e.g. de Menezes and Houllier, 2015).

The limitation of interconnection capacity between EU countries and its role in obstructing market integration is a recurring consideration in the literature. Gebhardt and Höffler (2013), for example, acknowledged that the integration of European electricity markets was still work in progress, and examined the question of whether price differences were caused by limited interconnector capacities or also by lack of cross-border competition. Their approach aimed to assess the extent to which price differences stem from limited participation in cross-border trade. Using the concept of a rational expectations equilibrium, they derived a theoretical integration benchmark, which they compared to data from European electricity markets. The market integration hypothesis was rejected and their findings indicate that well-informed traders were not engaging in cross-border trade.

Expanding their work on the benefits of electricity market integration in Latin American markets, Ochoa and van Ackere (2015b) used their system-dynamics model on the UK-France interconnection and found considerable differences from the Colombia-Ecuador case that they had studied earlier. They attributed these to differences in generation mix (nuclear and hydro in France, coal and gas in the UK, hydro predominant in both Colombia and Ecuador). In addition, UK and France are more mature markets, with slow demand growth and adequate capacity margins. Since then, of course, the UK energy mix has changed considerably, with nuclear, gas, wind, and even solar having displaced coal as a source of baseload generation, but with coal being maintained as a backup option with the help of capacity payments.

Regional interconnection was also at the center of work by Ciarreta and Zarraga (2015) who assessed electricity market integration between spot markets in Spain, Portugal, Austria, Germany, Switzerland, and France between 2007 and 2012. They used MGARCH models to estimate spillovers and price convergence, which were then used as indicators of market integration. They concluded that the target of achieving a single electricity market depends largely on increasing interconnections and efficient rules of market operation, since they found evidence of increasing price convergence and stronger price correlation between the market pairs of Spain-Portugal, Germany-Austria, and Switzerland-Austria.

Studies of common price dynamics with input fuels

Since it has been argued that in European electricity markets, common long-run price dynamics might reflect the cost of generation in the region, several authors assessed the association between fuel sources and electricity prices (e.g. Serletis and Herbert, 1999; Gjølberg and Johnsen, 2001; Emery and Liu, 2002; Asche, Osmundsen and Sandsmark, 2006; Bosco et al., 2006, 2010; Sensfuß, Ragwitz and Genoese, 2008; Roques, Newbery and Nuttall, 2008; Mjelde and Bessler, 2009; Mohammadi, 2009; Kalantzis and Milonas, 2010; Bollino, Ciferri and Polinori, 2013). In this spirit, a more recent study by Castagneto-Gissey (2014) analyzed electricity and carbon prices in the year-ahead energy markets during ETS Phase II. He observed that electricity prices in the EU can be driven by coal prices, but also that generators may excessively charge for the cost of carbon. According to his analysis, prices in the German market and Nord Pool increased 35% above the competitive threshold, given a unit increase in costs. Although prices could have reflected generation with greater emissions, he argued that generators might have pushed for higher electricity prices. Market power may, therefore, moderate the associations between fuel and electricity prices in European markets.

De Menezes, Houllier and Tamvakis (2016) also considered the potential impact of fuel inputs on the integration of European electricity markets. Using daily peak and base-load electricity spot prices from December 2005 to October 2013 from the British, French, and Nord Pool markets, the associations between electricity spot prices with neighboring electricity spot markets and fuel input prices were examined. The authors argued that the time-varying nature of the electricity price series were such that there were periods of mean reversion as well as periods of non-stationarity. Hence, the method to analyze co-movements should reflect these characteristics of the data. Indeed, estimates of localized autocorrelation functions confirmed that EU electricity spot prices were characterized by local non-stationarity, and illustrated that such periods could be linked with inputs to electricity generation. Moreover, British electricity spot prices were found to move with fuel prices and thus the British electricity market was mostly decoupled from the continental European markets, while in the French and Nord Pool day-ahead markets price movements were correlated with interconnected electricity markets. Overall, the electricity mix was shown to be linked to spot price behavior and, in turn, can impact market integration.

On the implications of renewables

As Renewable Energy Directives increased the pressure on EU nations to expand their renewable generation, the challenge to incorporate these new, often non-continuous energy sources increased as well. Several scholars turned their attention to the impact of RES-E on social welfare, price dynamics, and market integration. As Cochran et al. (2012) argued in their report on best practices based on the history of different countries integrating renewables to their power sector, there is no universal approach. Yet, critical factors for success could be identified, for example: public engagement, particularly new transmission; coordinated planning; the development of market rules that support system flexibility and access to diverse resources; and improvements in system operation. For example, Oggioni, Murphy, and Smeers (2014) and Neuhoff et al. (2013) investigated different wind integration policies by using simulation models of policies for dispatch and transmission capacity. Together, their findings suggest that, with high wind power penetration, priority dispatch is in detriment of electricity market integration. Although nodal pricing could make better use of existing transmission capacities, it was argued that this was unlikely to be sustainable under priority dispatch. Hence, their findings highlighted a need for wind power and solar generation to be subject to market signals.

A side-effect of increasing intermittent RES-E on wholesale electricity markets is an increase in day-ahead and intraday price volatility, since the merit-order curve changes significantly between high and low wind power scenarios. Different studies have therefore stressed the need for secure reserve capacity (e.g. Henriot and Glachant, 2013), especially since more expensive generators are more likely to face lower load factors (Cludius et al., 2014). As observed by de Menezes and Houllier (2015), Aatola, Ollikainen, and Toppinen (2013) might have been the first authors to consider RES-E policies in their assessment of electricity market convergence in Europe. Based on daily electricity and carbon forward price data from 2003 to 2011, they concluded that electricity market integration in Europe was increasing over time, and that carbon prices might have had a positive but uneven effect on integration.

Anaya and Pollitt (2014) explored trends in distributed generation across Germany, Denmark, and Sweden. They focused on the regulation of renewable energy generation, grid access, and connection mechanisms, and attributed the spread of distributed generation in these countries to the early support given to the expansion of renewable energy generation within their respective national policies. Germany and Denmark were countries with the most sophisticated and evolving support schemes, with Germany having the most favorable connection regime that prioritized connection and dispatch. Sweden, by contrast, treated equally different technologies. High connection costs were observed and, as network upgrade costs were shared across customers, policies that avoided unnecessary costs in expanding the distributed generation were needed. Accordingly, smart technologies, combined with new business models, should be considered in the context of interconnected markets in order to enable efficient use of the distribution infrastructure.

Tangerås (2015) developed a theoretical model of a multinational electricity market with transmission investment in order to analyze the effect of RES-E policies on market integration and national policy makers' incentives for implementing renewable policies. He concluded that goals of increased RES-E production and market integration can oppose one another when implementation is decentralized. He argued that, if national policy makers choose RES-E support schemes to maximize domestic welfare, a trade policy incentive operates independently of any direct benefit of renewable electricity. His model predicts electricity importing (exporting) countries to choose policies which reduce (increase) electricity prices, thus the pursuit of domestic objectives is inefficient as it distorts transmission investments and market integration. The added social benefit of additional transmission capacity may not be achieved. This inefficiency cannot be corrected by having national renewable targets, centralized subsidies to transmission investment as well as fewer and harmonized policy instruments, as for example an integrated certificates market for RES-E, are required to increase the efficiency in electricity markets and reduce the scope for local trade policy interference.

de Menezes and Houllier (2015) investigated electricity market integration before and after the closures of eight nuclear power plants that occurred within a period of a few months in Germany during 2011. Interrelationships of daily electricity spot prices, from November 2009 to October 2012, in APX-ENDEX, Belpex, EPEX-DE, EPEX-FR, Nord Pool, OMEL, and Swissix and wind power in the German system were examined with the use of MGARCH models with dynamic correlations and fractional cointegration analysis. Changes in short- and long-run behaviors were analyzed. Their results showed positive time-varying correlations between spot prices in markets with significant proportions of shared interconnector capacity and negative association between wind power penetration in Germany and electricity spot prices, not only in the German market but also in its neighboring markets. In addition, in most markets, a decreasing speed in mean reversion of spot prices was observed, which led the authors to conclude that electricity market integration in the EU might have been affected by an isolated national policy that changed its electricity mix.

Horst Keppler, Phan, and Le Pen (2016) assessed the impact of renewable production and market coupling on the spread between French and German electricity prices, with the use of panel data regression models. They observed that, since renewable electricity production is concentrated on periods with favorable meteorological conditions and interconnection capacity between France and Germany is limited, increases in production of wind and solar PV in Germany resulted in increasing price spreads between the two countries. Their estimates, based on a sample of French and German day-ahead hourly prices from November 2009 to June 2013, showed that RES-E production in Germany increased price divergence between the two markets, which however was mitigated by market coupling which has been in effect since 10 November 2010. Their findings, therefore, call for research on the optimal level of interconnection as well as further analysis that would include a larger number of countries.

Friesenbichler (2016) started from the principle that a single EU market for electricity does not exist and uses the fragmentation of the European electricity market as the background in order to examine cross-country variance in policy making. Germany showcases the promotion and diffusion of RES-E, which led to its exports increasingly causing difficulties in grid stability (i.e. imbalances between demand and supply and greater risk of outages). The author explored why other EU countries have not experienced such difficulties, by comparing German, Spanish, and Danish policies and institutional arrangements, and then linking the observed differences to differences in sectoral outcomes. These three countries were chosen because they financially promoted the diffusion of renewable technologies effectively leading to significant increases of RES-E in their electricity mix. His analysis underscores three cross-country differences. First, country size matters: Denmark successfully integrated volatile RES-E by compensating imbalances via the Nordic wholesale market, which is possible due to its size and open economy; by contrast, Germany and Spain have been less flexible in securing supply internationally. Second, the different designs of promotion instruments for RES-E: in Spain, the premium option required RES-E operators to meet predefined targets that mandated the management of systemic risks via balancing loads to RES-E generators, thus the system operator was exposed to less complexity which facilitated grid stability. Third, differences in institutional architectures might have contributed to a reduction in coordination problems and thereby led to different outcomes; while Spain implicitly imposed the prioritization of security of supply over other policy targets via its control agency, German policies are less centralized and their flexibility can lead to conflicting priorities. Hence, the author concluded that his findings indicate the relevance of energy policy coordination and a common hierarchy in objectives at EU and national levels.

Karanfil and Li (2017) used hourly data covering the period from January 2012 to May 2014 to investigate the causal relationships among the price differences between the intraday and day-ahead markets, the deviations of wind generation, conventional generation, and total demand from their committed day-ahead levels, as well as cross-border electricity trades in the Nordic electricity market. Their results, from VAR models and generalized impulse response (GIR) simulations, show that the wind and conventional generation forecast errors explain the price differentials between the two markets and that the relative intraday price decreases with the unexpected amount of wind generation. Zonal differences were also detected. The authors noted that the Nordic intraday electricity market can be regarded as effective because causality between the intraday price signals and the market fundamentals could be established. They noted that although their analysis highlighted the practicality of an intraday market, they could not conclude that the market is optimal, since balancing costs and other data would be needed in a more comprehensive analysis. Nonetheless, their study showed that cross-border exchanges are important in handling wind power forecast errors, as in the case of Denmark intermittent production deviations are effectively reduced, because the forecast errors are jointly handled through the responses from demand, conventional generation, and intraday international electricity trade. This management of forecast errors is important since wind power forecasts, rather than the actual levels of wind power, have been shown to be positively correlated with electricity spot price volatility (de Menezes and Houllier, 2015). Indeed, their conclusions underline observations by Woo et al. (2016) concerning the potentially positive impact of improvements in wind power forecasting on electricity markets.

As EU markets are looking for cost-efficient ways to maintain system reliability and price competitiveness, interconnection and market coupling will need to accommodate innovations to manage demand response. Feuerriegel and Neumann (2016) argued that when integrated into electricity markets, demand response can be used for load shifting and as a replacement for both control reserve and balancing energy. They compared these three usage scenarios using historic German data from 2011 and observed that load shifting provides the highest benefit: its annual financial savings was estimated to be 3.1 billion euros for the household and the service sectors and corresponded to savings of 2.83% compared to a scenario without load shifting. They concluded that reductions in bid sizes, delivery periods and the time-lag between transactions and delivery dates are needed to facilitate demand response, thus highlighting some design challenges and trade-offs that are faced by coupled EU electricity markets.

On the current status of market integration in Europe

The different streams of literature imply that full market integration is still work in progress. In fact, TenneT's Market Review 2016 (TenneT, 2016) reported that during the first month of the year, the CWE region had convergent prices, but subsequently prices diverged into two zones: a price region containing Germany and the Netherlands, and another including Belgium and France. According to the monthly average of day-ahead prices, in the first eight months of 2016, price differences between market areas in the CWE region were small, however in the last four months of 2016 the average price was approximately 54 €/MWh in Belgium and France, and 37 €/MWh in the Netherlands and Germany. Nevertheless, the report also underscored increases in hours of price convergence between many market areas in Europe from 2015 to 2016, which can be seen as a positive development for the integration of national electricity markets. In addition, the report shows that day-ahead electricity price volatilities in 2016 was on average comparable to 2015, which may suggest improvements in the management of renewable electricity generation. It is noteworthy that quarter-hourly products are traded in the intraday market and enable a better approximation of the real demand ramps and generation variability (e.g. from solar or wind power generation) than the hourly products at the more liquid day-ahead market. These products are especially important because imbalance settlement periods are on a quarter-hourly basis.

Comparatively higher electricity price volatility was observed in Great Britain. Possible explanations provided are a combination of heavy infrastructure maintenance, security of supply concerns following unplanned power plant closures, and the political turmoil of Brexit that devalued the British pound. The latter underscores the potential impact of isolated policies and the ongoing need for cooperation in connected markets, especially since the second- and third-highest volatilities were observed in the neighboring Belgian and French day-ahead markets. These observations reinforce the conclusions of many studies that relate to the need of coordinated policies in EU electricity markets.

Summary of findings and implications

Overall, studies of electricity market integration imply that transmission capacity, interconnection, and coordination between regions or countries can drive price convergence. However, price convergence is not always present, even within individual countries, such as Australia or the United States where there is one, or a small number of ISOs. In Europe, legislation, a common approach to regulation and market coupling has achieved some level of price convergence. Nonetheless, most studies imply that full market integration is yet to be achieved and that the extent of convergence is time-varying. Several studies highlighted the shortfalls of explicit auctions of interconnection capacity and strongly recommended implicit auctions, eventually leading to market coupling, as well as increased connectivity. Electricity prices appear to be responding to market coupling initiatives and increasing interconnector capacity, but studies also emphasize that short-run dynamics can be very volatile and generation fuel prices may be responsible for the mixed findings on market integration.

Government targets for energy efficiency, carbon reduction, and renewable generation have generated research interest into the various aspects of integrating increasing amounts of renewable sources, which are often interruptible and more difficult to predict. Although there seems to be consensus that renewables are the right pathway to controlling carbon emissions, high renewables penetration brings its own challenges. While the level of wholesale prices may be lower, volatility seems to increase. Increased interconnection is one way of dealing with the need to redirect increased amounts of renewable generation to neighboring regions or countries. Interconnection, however, is only one of the building blocks of a reliable electricity system. Given the increasing penetration of renewable energy, system flexibility is paramount. For example, Nord Pool Spot operates both the Elspot day-ahead and the Elbas intraday markets mainly in the Nordic (Denmark, Finland, Norway, and Sweden) and Baltic (Estonia, Latvia, and Lithuania) regions. In contrast to Elspot, where prices are settled through an hourly uniform-price auction after the day-ahead gate closure at 12:00 CET, Elbas is a continuous market where trading takes place from 14:00 CET on the day before the day of operation, and up to one hour before physical delivery. The intraday prices are set on a first-come, first-served basis, that is buyers and sellers choose directly the bids to be accepted in the market. A similar conclusion was reached for US regional markets, especially those which have set high renewable energy targets, such as California, or have high renewable generation, such as Texas. As a result, all US RTOs operate both day-ahead and real-time markets.

Even with increased interconnection capacity, market coupling, and competitive electricity trading, large-scale penetration of renewables still brings challenges to system operability, reliability, and security. Researchers increasingly point to the need for demand side management (or demand response) as a way of mitigating the weak predictability of renewable generation. Demand side response is also challenging, as much of the knowledge that has been acquired by system operators in forecasting load profiles that have led to very precise estimates of short-term aggregate demand may become less useful, especially in the context of interconnected markets.

While the jury may still be out on giving a verdict on the efficiency, effectiveness, and social benefits of the various electricity market structures, operations, and markets, we are faced with overhanging taxing issues and emerging fresh challenges. Of utmost urgency is the decarbonization of the energy and electricity supply chain, while at the same time maintaining security of supply. There is no panacea on how this can be achieved and most countries are pragmatic about future technology pathways. For some countries switching away from imported fossil fuels to domestic or regional renewables may be a no-brainer, assuming investment in generation capacity, transmission, and distribution is cost-efficient. Other countries will find it more difficult to adapt; existing thermal capacity offers reliability and security of supply, employment and the opportunity to generate profit (often from heavily depreciated assets) both in the domestic and cross-border markets.

Some countries have taken more definitive steps than others to tackle the issue of decarbonization. Great Britain has committed to a combination of increased wind and solar, a switch towards natural gas and away from coal (albeit with capacity payments made for backup generation during peak-load periods and winter months), and continuous commitment to nuclear generation with investment in new plants that have become too expensive given the decreasing costs of solar and even offshore wind power. Germany is continuing its path to energy transition (Energiewende), which has been expensive, but embraced by society and has led to local technological development. To do this, the country has had to rely on the rather odd combination of lignite, hard coal, and renewables, but in more recent months it seems committed to a switch to natural gas, despite the political ramification this may have in terms of security of supply. At the same time, the country has also reformed its Renewable Energy Act (EEG), initially in 2014 and again in 2017. EEG 2014 cast aside the FIT system and sought to control how much renewable capacity is installed every year, while at the same time it introduced auctions for solar PV. Voss and Madlener (2017) looked at bidding strategies for the pilot auction scheme and concluded that it was possible to successfully award funding authorizations for renewable energy plants via an auction process. EEG 2017 goes a step further with the extension of renewable capacity auctions to wind (both onshore and offshore) and biomass, in addition to solar.

Denmark is a good example of a country with very ambitious targets of 100% renewables in heat and power by 2035 and 100% in all sectors by 2050. Denmark currently has the highest wind penetration in the world and has benefited from monetizing its generation technology by selling it around the world. It relies, however, on its access to the interconnected Nordic market for its security of supply. Also, it is a relatively small market, approximately a tenth of the British electricity market and a twentieth of the German one.

As noted earlier, there is increased interest, and need, to harness a flexible demand side within the electricity system to match the uncertainty and, at the same time, inflexibility of renewables. In their discussion on how to integrate wind through changing the design of balancing and intraday market design, Borggrefe and Neuhoff (2011) suggest the use of six criteria: (1) facilitate system-wide intraday adjustments to respond to improving wind forecasts; (2) allow for the joint provision and adjustment of energy and balancing services; (3) manage the joint provision of power across multiple hours; (4) capture benefits from international integration of the power system; (5) integrate the demand side into intraday and balancing markets; and (6) effectively monitor market power. The authors point to the example of the market design for PJM (as well as the other US RTOs), where the system operator uses locational marginal pricing (LMP), centrally adjusts intraday dispatch close to real time, integrates demand side response and effectively monitors market power.

The dilution of market power could be one of the additional benefits brought by a higher participation of renewables in the energy mix. Renewables are to a large extent smaller scale projects, in comparison to conventional thermal generation assets. They, therefore, lend themselves to a more decentralized ownership by smaller financial units. For example, in Germany and Denmark distributed generation by smaller renewable units, such as wind, solar and biomass CHP, are positively encouraged. With an expanded portfolio of smaller renewable generation assets and a grid which is smart enough to handle both distributed and large-scale supply, demand response, and interconnections, new business models and entrepreneurial opportunities may arise. Examples include aggregators who can pool small-scale generation; demand response managers who can act on behalf of both large and small consumers, generate savings, and be remunerated for balancing services; energy storage managers who can absorb excess supply from poorly forecast renewables generation; electric vehicle (EV) fleet operators who not only offer transport services, but are effective managing "moving" batteries which could be used for small-scale demand response; and IT-based companies offering managerial and system-operation services.

The above examples of new business models and opportunities increased competition in electricity markets requires the implicit assumption of increased market liquidity, lower transaction costs, and the reduction of market power exercised by incumbent large-scale generators. In their study of the effects of the diversification of energy portfolios on the merit order effect in an oligopolistic energy market, Acemoglu, Kakhbod and Ozdaglar (2017) showed that when thermal generators have a diverse energy portfolio, which includes some or all of the renewable supplies, they offset the price declines due to the merit order effect because they strategically reduce their conventional energy supplies when renewable supply is high. In Great Britain, decreasing wholesale market liquidity alarmed the regulator (Ofgem), who instituted a system of license obligations, intended to help improve independent suppliers' access to the wholesale markets, and who also undertakes an annual review to assess the impact of the reforms and compliance of market participants (e.g. Ofgem, 2016). In Germany, the electricity market is also deemed to be liquid, but is this the case with other EU countries? The same could be said for many of the US RTOs, but is this the case for the entire US electricity grid, given the limitations in interconnections? As for Asia-Pacific markets, liquidity is for the time being an aspiration, linked to future plans for increased interconnection, renewable generation and more active cross-border trading.

Ultimately, electricity markets are an integral part of the broader energy markets and the lines separating the two are increasingly blurred with technological advance. For example, transportation has remained largely separate to electricity markets, as all modes have traditionally relied on some form of liquid fossil fuels, whether gasoline, diesel, fuel oil, or jet kerosene. Only electrified railways linked transportation with electricity. As car manufacturers are competing to bring more and more EVs to the average consumer, electricity (and how it is generated) is increasingly linked to transportation. This link has already started to have implications for the electricity sector, distribution through specialized battery-charging infrastructure, randomness of demand, increases in peak demand that may lead to new regulations, and the possibility that EVs could also be used for energy storage purposes. In fact, future energy scenarios, including those published by oil majors, imply that in order to address emission targets, greater diversity in energy sources and market integration are required. In this sense, there are technological, economic, social, and political challenges, which imply an interdisciplinary research and policy agenda.

The issues highlighted offer a glimpse to the complexity of integrating electricity markets, in the face of rapidly changing energy markets, technologies which are likely to create disruption and the unabated pursuit of energy which is secure, affordable and sustainable. As some scholars have observed "there is no 'one-size-fits-all' recipe for all markets and all countries" (Bollino et al., 2017, p. 2). With developments like those discussed above, common sense and good practice should point towards minimizing complexity of market design to reduce transaction costs, improve liquidity, ensure market depth to reduce investment risk and keep attracting investment. At the same time, continuous and integrated intraday trading can provide the right environment for maximizing the benefits from renewables integration, greater energy efficiency, and the resultant decarbonization of the world economy.

Notes

1 The East Asian Summit (EAS) is a forum of 18 nations in the East Asian, Southeast Asian, and South Asian regions. They are Australia, Brunei, Cambodia, China, India, Indonesia, Japan, Laos, Malaysia, Myanmar, New Zealand, the Philippines, Russia, Singapore, South Korea, Thailand, the United States, and Vietnam.
2 Brunei, Cambodia, Indonesia, Laos, Malaysia, Myanmar, the Philippines, Singapore, Thailand, and Vietnam.
3 Data for eastern Australian states (New South Wales, Victoria, Queensland, South Australia, and Tasmania) were obtained from the Australian Energy Regulator (AER, www.aer.gov.au). Data for Western Australia's SWIS market were obtained from the Independent Market Operator of Western Australia (IMOWA, www. imowa.com.au). For SWIS, they averaged half-hourly clearing prices of the short-term energy market.
4 In 2011, RET was further refined into a 'large-scale' section (looking at utility-scale renewables, such solar farms, wind farms, and hydropower plants) and a small-scale section (focusing on financial incentives for the installation of solar panels, wind, hydro systems, solar water heaters, and air source heat pumps) (Australian Government Clean Energy Regulator, 2016)
5 SAPP: South African Power Pool; WAPP: West African Power Pool; MER: Central American Power Market.

References

Aatola, P., Ollikainen, M. and Toppinen, A. (2013) 'Impact of the carbon price on the integrating European electricity market', *Energy Policy*, 61, pp. 1236–1251. doi: 10.1016/j.enpol.2013.06.036.

Acemoglu, D., Kakhbod, A. and Ozdaglar, A. (2017) 'Competition in electricity markets with renewable energy sources', *The Energy Journal*, 38(1). doi: 10.5547/01956574.38.SI1.dace.

Ahmed, T. et al. (2017) 'ASEAN power grid: A secure transmission infrastructure for clean and sustainable energy for South-East Asia', *Renewable and Sustainable Energy Reviews*, 67, pp. 1420–1435. doi: 10.1016/j. rser.2016.09.055.

Anaya, K. L. and Pollitt, M. (2014) *Integrating Distributed Generation: Regulation and Trends in Three Leading Countries*. EPRG Working Paper 1423, University of Cambridge, Cambridge, UK.

Apergis, N., Fontini, F. and Inchauspe, J. (2017) 'Integration of regional electricity markets in Australia: A price convergence assessment', *Energy Economics*, 62, pp. 411–418. doi: 10.1016/j.eneco.2016.06.022.

Asche, F., Osmundsen, P. and Sandsmark, M. (2006) 'The UK market for natural gas, oil and electricity: Are the prices decoupled?', *Energy Journal*, 27(2), pp. 27–40. Available at: http://0-search.ebscohost.com. wam.city.ac.uk/login.aspx?direct=true&db=bth&AN=20533606&site=ehost-live.

Australian Government Clean Energy Regulator (2016) *About the Renewable Energy Target*. Available at: www. cleanenergyregulator.gov.au/RET/About-the-Renewable-Energy-Target (Accessed: 11 July 2017).

Autran, L. (2012) *Convergence of Day-Ahead and Futures Prices in the Context of European Power Market Coupling*. Stockholm: KTH Royal Institute of Technology.

Bannister, H. et al. (2008) *Energy Market Integration in the East Asia Summit Region*. REPSF II Project No. 07/005. Jakarta: ASEAN Secretariat.

Battle, C. (2013) 'Towards a better integration of the EU electricity market (conference presentation online)', in *Berlin Conference on Electricity Economics: Modelling and Policy in Energy Transformation: Germany, Europe, and Beyond*. Berlin: DIW. Available at: https://youtu.be/Hrr8kqeC_Bs.

Bell, W. P. et al. (2015) 'Wind speed and electricity demand correlation analysis in the Australian National Electricity Market: Determining wind turbine generators' ability to meet electricity demand without energy storage', *Economic Analysis and Policy*, 48, pp. 182–191. doi: 10.1016/j.eap.2015.11.009.

Boffa, F. and Scarpa, C. (2009) 'An anticompetitive effect of eliminating transport barriers in network markets', *Review of Industrial Organization*. Springer US, 34(2), pp. 115–133. doi: 10.1007/s11151-008-9198-4.

Boisseleau, F. (2004) *The Role of Power Exchanges for the Creation of a Single European Electricity Market: Market Design and Market Regulation*. Delft University Press. Available at: https://inis.iaea.org/search/search. aspx?orig_q=RN:35039055 (Accessed: 3 July 2017).

Bollino, C. A. et al. (2017) 'Forward to the special issue on renewables and diversification in heavily energy subsidized economies', *The Energy Journal*. International Association for Energy Economics, 38(1). doi: 10.5547/01956574.38.SI1.cbol.

Bollino, C. A., Ciferri, D. and Polinori, P. (2013) *Integration and Convergence in European Electricity Markets*. Università di Perugia, Dipartimento Economia, Perugia, Italy.

Borggrefe, F. and Neuhoff, K. (2011) *Balancing and Intraday Market Design: Options for Wind Integration*. 1162. Berlin: DIW. Available at: www.diw.de/documents/publikationen/73/diw_01.c.387225.de/dp1162. pdf.

Bosco, B. et al. (2006) *Deregulated Wholesale Electricity Prices in Europe*. Università degli Studi di Milano-Bicocca, Dipartimento di Statistica, Milano, Italy.

Bosco, B. et al. (2010) 'Long-run relations in European electricity prices', *Journal of Applied Econometrics*. John Wiley & Sons, Ltd., 25(5), pp. 805–832. doi: 10.1002/jae.1095.

Bower, J. (2002) *Seeking the Single European Electricity Market: Evidence from an Empirical Analysis of Wholesale Market Prices*. Oxford. Available at: https://ora.ox.ac.uk/objects/uuid:b3aa59b6-4c86-4aef-8b0a-db4bb66173ae (Accessed: 3 July 2017).

Bunn, D. W. and Gianfreda, A. (2010) 'Integration and shock transmissions across European electricity forward markets', *Energy Economics*, 32(2), pp. 278–291. doi: 10.1016/j.eneco.2009.09.005.

Castagneto-Gissey, G. (2014) 'How competitive are EU electricity markets? An assessment of ETS Phase II', *Energy Policy*, 73, pp. 278–297. doi: 10.1016/j.enpol.2014.06.015.

Chang, Y. and Li, Y. (2015) 'Renewable energy and policy options in an integrated ASEAN electricity market: Quantitative assessments and policy implications', *Energy Policy*, 85, pp. 39–49. doi: 10.1016/j. enpol.2015.05.011.

Ciarreta, A. and Zarraga, A. (2015) 'Analysis of mean and volatility price transmissions in the MIBEL and ̀EPEX electricity spot markets', *Energy Journal*, 36(4), pp. 41–60. doi: 10.5547/01956574.36.4.acia.

Cludius, J. et al. (2014) 'The merit order effect of wind and photovoltaic electricity generation in Germany 2008–2016: Estimation and distributional implications', *Energy Economics*, 44, pp. 302–313. doi:10.1016/j.eneco.2014.04.020.

Cochran, J. et al. (2012) *Integrating Variable Renewable Energy in Electric Power Markets: Best Practices from International Experience*. NREL/TP-6A00-53732, National Renewable Energy Laboratory, U.S. Department of Energy.

Creti, A., Fumagalli, E. and Fumagalli, E. (2010) 'Integration of electricity markets in Europe: Relevant issues for Italy', *Energy Policy*, 38(11), pp. 6966–6976. doi: 10.1016/j.enpol.2010.07.013.

Cutler, N. J. et al. (2011) 'High penetration wind generation impacts on spot prices in the Australian national electricity market', *Energy Policy*, 39(10), pp. 5939–5949. doi: 10.1016/j.enpol.2011.06.053.

de Menezes, L. M. and Houllier, M. A. (2015) 'Germany's nuclear power plant closures and the integration of electricity markets in Europe', *Energy Policy*, 85, pp. 357–368. doi: 10.1016/j.enpol.2015.05.023.

de Menezes, L. M. and Houllier, M. A. (2016) 'Reassessing the integration of European electricity markets: A fractional cointegration analysis', *Energy Economics*, 53, pp. 132–150. doi: 10.1016/j.eneco.2014.10.021.

de Menezes, L. M., Houllier, M. A. and Tamvakis, M. (2016) 'Time-varying convergence in European electricity spot markets and their association with carbon and fuel prices', *Energy Policy*, 88, pp. 613–627. doi: 10.1016/j.enpol.2015.09.008.

De Vany, A. S. and Walls, W. D. (1999) 'Cointegration analysis of spot electricity prices: Insights on transmission efficiency in the western US', *Energy Economics*, 21(5), pp. 435–448. doi: 10.1016/S0140-9883(99)00019-5.

EIA (2017) *What Is US Electricity Generation by Energy Source?* Available at: www.eia.gov/tools/faqs/faq.php?id=427&t=3 (Accessed: 11 July 2017).

Emerson, M. et al. (1988) *The Economics of 1992: The EC Commission's Assessment of the Economic Effects of Completing the Internal Market*. Available at: http://ec.europa.eu/economy_finance/publications/pages/publication7412_en.pdf (Accessed: 10 July 2017).

Emery, G. W. and Liu, Q. (Wilson) (2002) 'An analysis of the relationship between electricity and natural-gas futures prices', *Journal of Futures Markets*. John Wiley & Sons, Inc., 22(2), p. 95. doi: 10.1002/fut.2209.

European Commission (2016) *Communication from the Commission to the European Parliament, the Council, the European Economic and Social Committee, the Committee of the Regions and the European Investment Bank: Clean Energy for All Europeans*. COM(2016) 860 Final. European Union: European Commission. Available at: http://eur-lex.europa.eu/resource.html?uri=cellar:fa6ea15b-b7b0-11e6-9e3c-01aa75ed71a1.0001.02/DOC_1&format=PDF (Accessed: 10 July 2017).

Feuerriegel, S. and Neumann, D. (2016) 'Integration scenarios of Demand Response into electricity markets: Load shifting, financial savings and policy implications', *Energy Policy*, 96, pp. 231–240. doi: 10.1016/j.enpol.2016.05.050.

Finon, D. and Romano, E. (2009) 'Electricity market integration: Redistribution effect versus resource reallocation', *Energy Policy*, 37(8), pp. 2977–2985. doi: 10.1016/j.enpol.2009.03.045.

Friesenbichler, K. S. (2016) 'Policy interaction and the integration of volatile renewable energy', *Environmental Economics and Policy Studies*, 18(2), pp. 193–211. doi: 10.1007/s10018-015-0130-5.

Galli, A. and Armstrong, M. (2003) *Comparing the Spot Prices from Powernext and EEX*. Available at: https://inis.iaea.org/search/search.aspx?orig_q=RN:37095431 (Accessed: 4 July 2017).

Gebhardt, G. and Höffler, F. (2007) 'How to determine whether regional markets are integrated? Theory and evidence from European electricity markets', *SSRN Electronic Journal*. doi: 10.2139/ssrn.1074983.

Gebhardt, G. and Höffler, F. (2013) 'How competitive is cross-border trade of electricity? Theory and evidence from European electricity markets', *The Energy Journal*, 34(1). doi: 10.5547/01956574.34.1.6.

Gil, H. A. and Lin, J. (2013) 'Wind power and electricity prices at the PJM market', *IEEE Transactions on Power Systems*, 28(4), pp. 3945–3953. doi: 10.1109/TPWRS.2013.2260773.

Gjølberg, O. and Johnsen, T. (2001) *Electricity Futures: Inventories and Price Relationships at Nord Pool*. Discussion paper, Norwegian School of Economics and Business, Bergen, Norway.

Hand, M. M. et al. (eds.) (2012) *Renewable Electricity Futures Study*. NREL/TP-6A. Golden, CO: National Renewable Energy Laboratory. Available at: www.nrel.gov/analysis/re_futures/.

Henriot, A. and Glachant, J.-M. (2013) 'Melting-pots and salad bowls: The current debate on electricity market design for integration of intermittent RES', *Utilities Policy*, 27, pp. 57–64. doi: 10.1016/j.jup.2013.09.001.

Horst Keppler, J., Phan, S. and Le Pen, Y. (2016) 'The impacts of variable renewable production and market coupling on the convergence of French and German electricity prices', *The Energy Journal*. International Association for Energy Economics, 37(3). doi: 10.5547/01956574.37.3.jkep.

Huisman, R. and Kiliç, M. (2013) 'A history of European electricity day-ahead prices', *Applied Economics*. Routledge, 45(18), pp. 2683–2693. doi: 10.1080/00036846.2012.665601.

Joskow, P. L. and Schmalensee, R. (1983) *Markets for Power: An Analysis of Electric Utility Deregulation*. Cambridge, MA: MIT Press.

Kalantzis, F. and Milonas, N. T. (2010) 'Market integration and price dispersion in the European electricity market', in *Energy Market (EEM), 2010 7th International Conference on the European IEEE*, pp. 1–6. Institute of Electrical and Electronic Engineers. ISBN 978-1-4244-6838-6.

Karanfil, F. and Li, Y. (2017) 'The role of continuous intraday electricity markets: The integration of large-share wind power generation in Denmark', *The Energy Journal*, 38(2). doi: 10.5547/01956574.38.2.fkar.

Kiesel, R. and Kusterman, M. (2016) 'Structural models for coupled electricity markets', *Journal of Commodity Markets*, 3(1), pp. 16–38. doi: 10.1016/j.jcomm.2016.07.007.

Krishnaswamy, V. (2007) *Potential and Prospects for Regional Energy Trade in the South Asia Region*. Washington, DC: World Bank. Available at: http://documents.worldbank.org/curated/en/985241468 170700557/Potential-and-prospects-for-regional-energy-trade-in-the-South-Asia-Region (Accessed: 6 July 2017).

MacGill, I. (2010) 'Electricity market design for facilitating the integration of wind energy: Experience and prospects with the Australian National Electricity Market', *Energy Policy*, 38(7), pp. 3180–3191. doi: 10.1016/j.enpol.2009.07.047.

Mai, T. et al. (2014) 'Envisioning a renewable electricity future for the United States', *Energy*, 65, pp. 374–386. doi: 10.1016/j.energy.2013.11.029.

Markusen, J. R. (1981) 'Trade and the gains from trade with imperfect competition', *Journal of International Economics*, 11(4), pp. 531–551. doi: 10.1016/0022-1996(81)90033-7.

Marshall, J. F. (2000) *Dictionary of Financial Engineering*. Toronto, Canada: Wiley.

Mjelde, J. W. and Bessler, D. A. (2009) 'Market integration among electricity markets and their major fuel source markets', *Energy Economics*, 31(3), pp. 482–491. doi: 10.1016/j.eneco.2009.02.002.

Mohammadi, H. (2009) 'Electricity prices and fuel costs: Long-run relations and short-run dynamics', *Energy Economics*, 31(3), pp. 503–509. doi: 10.1016/j.eneco.2009.02.001.

Nepal, R. and Foster, J. (2016) 'Testing for market integration in the Australian national electricity market', *Energy Journal*. Charles Darwin U, 37(4), pp. 215–237. Available at: www.iaee.org/en/publications/journal.aspx.

Neuhoff, K. et al. (2013) 'Renewable electric energy integration: Quantifying the value of design of markets for international transmission capacity', *Energy Economics*, 40, pp. 760–772. doi: 10.1016/j.eneco.2013.09.004.

Ochoa, C., Dyner, I. and Franco, C. J. (2013) 'Simulating power integration in Latin America to assess challenges, opportunities, and threats', *Energy Policy*, 61, pp. 267–273. doi: 10.1016/j.enpol.2013.07.029.

Ochoa, C. and van Ackere, A. (2015a) 'Does size matter? Simulating electricity market coupling between Colombia and Ecuador', *Renewable and Sustainable Energy Reviews*, 50, pp. 1108–1124. doi: 10.1016/j.rser.2015.05.054.

Ochoa, C. and van Ackere, A. (2015b) 'Winners and losers of market coupling', *Energy*, 80, pp. 522–534. doi: 10.1016/j.energy.2014.11.088.

Ofgem (2016) *Wholesale Power Market Liquidity: Annual Report 2016*. Available at: www.ofgem.gov.uk/system/files/docs/2016/08/wholesale_power_market_liquidity_annual_report_2016.pdf.

Oggioni, G., Murphy, F. H. and Smeers, Y. (2014) 'Evaluating the impacts of priority dispatch in the European electricity market', *Energy Economics*, 42, pp. 183–200. doi: 10.1016/j.eneco.2013.12.009.

Oseni, M. O. and Pollitt, M. (2016) 'The promotion of regional integration of electricity markets: Lessons for developing countries', *Energy Policy*, 88, pp. 628–638. doi: 10.1016/j.enpol.2015.09.007.

Park, H., Mjelde, J. W. and Bessler, D. A. (2006) 'Price dynamics among U.S. electricity spot markets', *Energy Economics*, 28(1), pp. 81–101. doi: 10.1016/j.eneco.2005.09.009.

Pellini, E. (2012) 'Measuring the impact of market coupling on the Italian electricity market', *Energy Policy*, 48, pp. 322–333. doi: 10.1016/j.enpol.2012.05.029.

Phillips, P.C.B. and Sul, D. (2007) 'Transition modeling and econometric convergence tests', *Econometrica*. Blackwell Publishing Ltd, 75(6), pp. 1771–1855. doi: 10.1111/j.1468-0262.2007.00811.x.

Phillips, P.C.B. and Sul, D. (2009) 'Economic transition and growth', *Journal of Applied Econometrics*. John Wiley & Sons, Ltd., 24(7), pp. 1153–1185. doi: 10.1002/jae.1080.

Roques, F. A., Newbery, D. M. and Nuttall, W. J. (2008) 'Fuel mix diversification incentives in liberalized electricity markets: A Mean-Variance Portfolio theory approach', *Energy Economics*, 30(4), pp. 1831–1849. doi: 10.1016/j.eneco.2007.11.008.

Sensfuß, F., Ragwitz, M. and Genoese, M. (2008) 'The merit-order effect: A detailed analysis of the price effect of renewable electricity generation on spot market prices in Germany', *Energy Policy*, 36(8), pp. 3086–3094. doi: 10.1016/j.enpol.2008.03.035.

Serletis, A. and Herbert, J. (1999) 'The message in North American energy prices', *Energy Economics*, 21(5), pp. 471–483. doi: 10.1016/S0140-9883(99)00015-8.

Tangerås, T. P. (2015) 'Renewable electricity policy and market integration', *The Energy Journal*, 36(4), pp. 331–353. doi: 10.5547/01956574.36.4.ttan.

TenneT (2016) *Market Review 2016: Electricity Market Insights*. Available at: www.tennet.eu/fileadmin/user_upload/Company/Publications/Technical_Publications/Dutch/2016_Market_Review_TenneT.pdf.

Turvey, R. (2006) 'Interconnector economics', *Energy Policy*, 34(13), pp. 1457–1472. doi: 10.1016/j.enpol.2004.11.009.

Von Hirchhausen, C. and Zachmann, G. (2009) 'Ensuring EU enlargement to new member states', in Glachant, J.-M. and Lévêque, F. (eds.) *Electricity Reform in Europe: Towards a Single Energy Market*. Cheltenham, UK & Northampton, USA: Edward Elgar Publishing Ltd, pp. 105–141.

Voss, A. and Madlener, R. (2017) 'Auction schemes, bidding strategies and the cost-optimal level of promoting renewable electricity in Germany', *The Energy Journal*, 38(1). doi: 10.5547/01956574.38.SI1.avos.

Weber, A., Graeber, D. and Semmig, A. (2010) 'Market coupling and the CWE project', *Zeitschrift für Energiewirtschaft*. Vieweg Verlag, 34(4), pp. 303–309. doi: 10.1007/s12398-010-0033-x.

Woo, C. K., Horowitz, I., et al. (2011) 'The impact of wind generation on the electricity spot-market price level and variance: The Texas experience', *Energy Policy*, 39(7), pp. 3939–3944. doi: 10.1016/j.enpol.2011.03.084.

Woo, C. K., Zarnikau, J., et al. (2011) 'Wind generation and zonal-market price divergence: Evidence from Texas', *Energy Policy*, 39(7), pp. 3928–3938. doi: 10.1016/j.enpol.2010.11.046.

Woo, C. K. et al. (2013) 'The impact of wind generation on wholesale electricity prices in the hydro-rich Pacific Northwest', *IEEE Transactions on Power Systems*, 28(4), pp. 4245–4253. doi: 10.1109/TPWRS.2013.2265238.

Woo, C. K. et al. (2016) 'Merit-order effects of renewable energy and price divergence in California's day-ahead and real-time electricity markets', *Energy Policy*, 92, pp. 299–312. doi: 10.1016/j.enpol.2016.02.023.

Worthington, A. C. and Higgs, H. (2017) 'The impact of generation mix on Australian wholesale electricity prices', *Energy Sources, Part B: Economics, Planning, and Policy*. Taylor & Francis, 12(3), pp. 223–230. doi: 10.1080/15567249.2015.1060548.

Wu, Y. (2013) 'Electricity market integration: Global trends and implications for the EAS region', *Energy Strategy Reviews*, 2(2), pp. 138–145. doi: 10.1016/j.esr.2012.12.002.

Zachmann, G. (2008) 'Electricity wholesale market prices in Europe: Convergence?', *Energy Economics*, 30(4), pp. 1659–1671. doi: 10.1016/j.eneco.2007.07.002.

Zachmann, G. (2009) 'The EU integration of the new member states' electricity markets: Testing for wholesale price convergence using the Kalman filter', in Glachant, J.-M. and Lévêque, F. (eds.) *Electricity Reform in Europe: Towards a Single Energy Market*. Cheltenham, UK & Northampton, USA: Edward Elgar Publishing Ltd, pp. 269–288.

Zareipour, H., Bhattacharya, K. and Cañizares, C. A. (2007) 'Electricity market price volatility: The case of Ontario', *Energy Policy*, 35(9), pp. 4739–4748. doi: 10.1016/j.enpol.2007.04.006.

8

Analysis of macroeconomic impacts of energy security improvements in Asia

Deepak Sharma, Suwin Sandu, and Muyi Yang

1 Introduction

This chapter analyzes the macroeconomic impacts of energy security improvements in Asia, with particular emphasis on the trade-offs that policy makers may like to consider while designing policies to redress the energy security challenge in the region. This analysis is based on estimates of impacts obtained from the application of the methodology described in Chapter 31. The cases in point for the analysis are provided by seven major Asian countries (China, India, Indonesia, Japan, Korea, Malaysia, and Thailand).

This chapter is organized as follows. Section 2 analyzes the macroeconomic impacts of energy security improvements for the three scenarios, namely, Country Policy (CP), Country Aspiration (CA), and Sustainable Development (SD), as described in Chapter 31. Section 3 further extends this analysis to identify major policy trade-offs. Section 4 presents some broad conclusions of the chapter.

2 Macroeconomic impacts

The macroeconomic impacts of energy security improvements are discussed in this section in terms of socioeconomic (Section 2.1) and energy security (Section 2.2) outcomes. The time-frames for analysis are short term (2015–2025), medium term (2025–2035), and long term (2035–2050).

2.1 Socioeconomic outcomes

Economic growth

Figure 8.1 presents the impact of energy security improvements on economic (GDP) growth.

The figure suggests that energy security improvements (CA and SD scenarios) would positively impact GDP for China, Japan, Korea, India, and Thailand over the entire study period (2015–2050). Further, this impact would be more pronounced in the SD scenario. For example, Korea's GDP, in the SD scenario, will increase by 0.71%, 0.88%, and 1.23%, in the short, medium, and long term, respectively. The corresponding figures for the CA scenario are 0.57%, 0.60%, and 0.63%.

For Indonesia, however, the CA scenario will result in a modest reduction (−0.08%) in GDP in the short-term, but appreciable gains of 0.13% and 0.60% in the medium and long term,

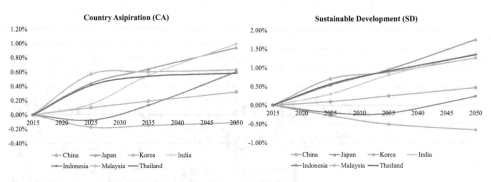

Figure 8.1 Changes in GDP (relative to CP scenario)

Source: Estimates – based on methodology described in Chapter 31.

respectively, in comparison with the CP scenario. The SD scenario would however lead to significant economic losses (–0.20% and –0.22%) in the short and medium term, and modest economic gains (0.24%) in the long term. Reduced GDP in the short term (in the CA and SD scenarios) and the medium term (in the SD scenario) is mainly due to reduced investments in developing indigenous energy resources, particularly oil and gas, and reduced royalty payments from these resources. In the long-term, however, reduced income from royalty payments is likely to be the only source of downward pressure on GDP, resulting in modest economic gains. This implies that the Indonesian economy has the capacity to adjust to the likely negative impact on its economy by shifting investment from energy resources sector to other productive sectors.

On the other hand, the Malaysian economy would be adversely affected by energy security improvements throughout the study period; these impacts would be more significant in the SD scenario. In the CA scenario, the short-, medium-, and long-term GDPs would decline by 0.17%, 0.15%, and 0.11%, respectively, as compared with the CP scenario. These declines will be 0.28%, 0.51%, and 0.66% in the SD scenario. Reduced investments in developing indigenous energy resources and reduced royalty payments from these resources will be the main reasons for reduced GDP for Malaysia.

These findings suggest that implementing aggressive policies to improve energy security in energy importing countries (China, Japan, Korea, India, and Thailand) are likely to result in improved GDP, but the opposite is likely to be the case for energy exporting countries (Malaysia and Indonesia). This implies that the policy makers of energy exporting countries should be particularly careful when implementing policies to improve energy security.

Total industry output

Total industry output, in the context of this chapter, represents the output of all economic sectors, grouped into four broad categories: agriculture, service, energy, and industry. Further, this output is made up of two components: intermediate output and final output. Intermediate output is output consumed by economic sectors for producing final products, whereas final output is output for satisfying final consumption. Figure 8.2 presents percentage changes in total, intermediate, and final outputs for the CA and SD scenarios, relative to the CP scenario. Main points are discussed as follows.

The *total output* of all countries (except Japan) will be adversely affected by the introduction of energy security improvement policies (CA and SD scenarios). This impact is relatively more pronounced for the SD scenario.

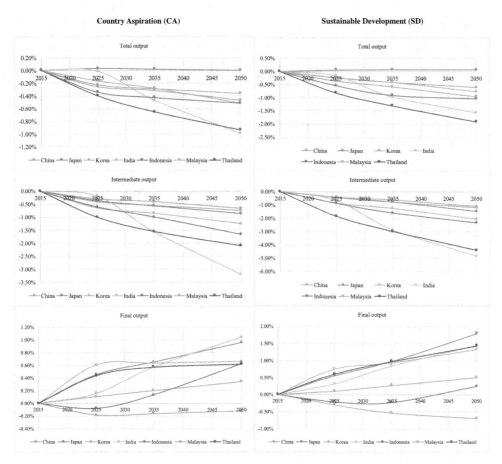

Figure 8.2 Changes in total, intermediate, and final output, compared with CP scenario

Source: Estimates – based on methodology described in Chapter 31.

For Japan, for example, the CA scenario would lead to a slight (0.02% to 0.08%) increase in total output throughout the study period, due probably to the small size of fossil fuel industry in the country. Further, this impact is more pronounced in the SD scenario. For example, the CA scenario would lead to a 0.03% increase in total output in the short term, decreasing to 0.02% in the medium term, and to less than 0.005% in the long term. In contrast, in the SD scenario, the total output impact will increase from 0.06% in the short term to 0.07% in the medium term and 0.08% in the long term.

Further, the adverse impact on total output (as noted above) would be mostly due to the impacts on the intermediate sectors of the economy. For example, in the CA scenario, China's short-, medium-, and long-term intermediate outputs would be 0.40%, 0.54%, and 0.73% less than in the CP scenario. The corresponding values for the SD scenario are 0.43%, 0.77%, and 1.18%.

The *final output* would however be positively affected in the CA and SD scenarios, especially in the medium and long term. Further, this impact would be greater in the SD scenario. Malaysia appears to be the exception, where energy security improvements would lead to significant reductions in the final output of the economy, as compared with the CP scenario.

Trade balance

Figure 8.3 presents the impacts of adopting energy security measures on trade balance. A review of the figure suggests that CA and SD scenarios would result in improved trade balance for most countries included in this chapter. For example, in the CA scenario, India's trade balance would improve, by the year 2050, by $6 billion in the short term, $42 billion in the medium term, and $150 billion in the long term, in comparison with the CP scenario. The corresponding increases in the SD scenario will be $13 billion, $62 billion, and $208 billion. Similar trends can be observed for Japan, Korea, China, and Thailand.

This improved trade balance in Asian countries is perhaps due to improved energy efficiency, and increased reliance on domestic renewable energy resources, which makes their products become more competitive vis-à-vis other trading countries. This is evident in the improved trade balance of all Asian countries considered in this chapter with respect to the rest of the world. For example, out of $85 billion increase in net exports from Japan in 2050 in the CA scenario, $65 billion will be due to trade with countries outside Asia.

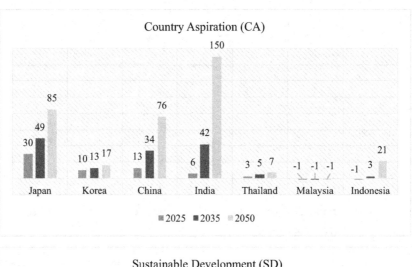

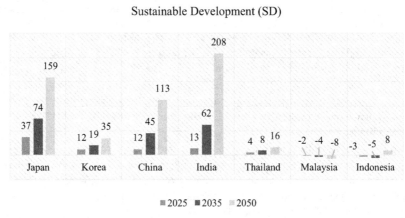

Figure 8.3 Changes in trade balance ($ billion), compared with CP scenario

Source: Estimates – based on methodology described in Chapter 31.

In contrast, for Malaysia, the CA scenario would result in worsened trade balance – by an average of $1 billion, compared with the CP scenario. In the SD scenario, the trade balance would be further reduced by $1 billion in the short term, $3 billion in the medium term, and $7 billion in the long term. While Malaysia would be able to export more of its products to countries outside Asia in the SD scenario, it would export less to countries within Asia. Similarly, for Indonesia, the short-term trade balance will reduce marginally in the CA scenario, but in the SD scenario these reductions will prevail in the short and medium terms.

Employment

The impacts of energy security improvements on total employment are shown in Figure 8.4. The figure suggests that the introduction of energy security measures will positively impact employment in Japan, Korea, and China, and this impact will be greater in the CA and SD scenarios. For example, for China, the CA scenario will lead to the creation of 1.68 million new jobs in the short term, 1.99 million in the medium term, and 2.06 million in the long term. The corresponding increase will be 2.33 million, 2.29 million, and 3.20 million, respectively, in the SD scenario.

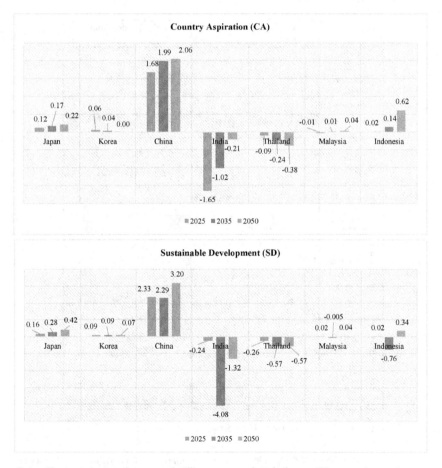

Figure 8.4 Changes in employment (million persons), relative to CP scenario

Source: Estimates – based on methodology described in Chapter 31.

In contrast, for India and Thailand, employment will be adversely affected by energy security improvements. This negative impact will be more severe in the SD scenario in Thailand. In India, stronger energy security improvements will reduce unemployment in the short term, but increase it in the medium to long term.

The employment impacts will be mixed for Malaysia and Indonesia. For Malaysia, introduction of ambitious energy security measures (CA scenario) will marginally increase short-term unemployment (by 0.01 million); however, in the medium to long term, there will be a modest decrease in unemployment. In the SD scenario, employment will slightly rise in the short and medium term; it will remain at the same level in the medium term as in the CP scenario. For Indonesia, the CA scenario shows modest employment gains (0.02 million) in the short term, 0.14 million in the medium term, and 0.62 million in the long term, compared to the CP scenario. In the SD scenario, there will be a modest rise in employment in the short and long term, whereas a rise in unemployment will be experienced in the medium term.

Summary of socioeconomic outcomes

Figure 8.5 summarizes the overall socioeconomic outcomes, as discussed.

Figure 8.5 Summary of socioeconomic outcomes

Notes:
1. This figure presents the effect of policies in CA and SD scenarios, compared with the CP scenario.
2. Dark gray (positive impact), dark (negative impact), and light gray (negligible impact).

Source: This table is developed based on details provided in Table 8A.1 (Appendix).

Main points, based on a review of the figure and discussion in the previous section, are presented below.

- The impact of energy security improvement on GDP would in general be positive in energy importing countries (India, Japan, Korea, and Thailand); it would be almost negligible (less than 0.5%) in China. In contrast, in energy exporting countries (Indonesia and Malaysia), strong energy security improvement measures (CA and SD scenarios) would negatively impact GDP; this impact would be more pronounced in the SD scenario, due mainly to a drastic reduction in energy demand of the region. Further, the Indonesian economy appears to have the capacity to absorb the negative impact on GDP over the long term. For example, in the CA scenario, the negative impact on GDP in the short term will be neutered in the medium term, and will turn positive in the long term. In the SD scenario, however, negative impact on GDP will last longer (until the medium term) before turning neutral in the long term.
- The total industry output for all countries (except, Japan) would be adversely affected by strong energy security improvements (CA and SD scenarios). This impact would be small (less than −0.5%) in the short term, but gradually increase over the medium to long terms. In contrast, energy security improvements are likely to positively impact total industry output for Japan, due probably to the small size of the country's fossil fuel industry. Further, it appears that while this positive impact for Japan is likely to persist throughout the study period (2015–2050) in the SD scenario, it will assume a neutral value in the long-term in the CA scenario.
- The CA and SD scenarios would result in improved trade balance for all countries except Indonesia and Malaysia. Further, this improvement would be more pronounced in the SD scenario. For Indonesia and Malaysia, energy security improvements are likely to worsen trade balance, primarily caused by lower energy exports to other Asian countries.
- The impact of energy security measures on employment would be mixed across the Asian countries. It will be mainly positive for China, Japan, and Korea; almost negligible (less than 0.3%) for Indonesia and Malaysia; and primarily negative for India and Thailand. These outcomes probably reflect the influence of a variety of employment determining factors, such as economic growth, economic structure, labor productivity, and so forth.

2.2 Energy security outcomes

Energy demand

As shown in Table 8.1, in the CP scenario, *primary energy demand* will increase in all countries, in order to support future economic growth. These increases will however be smaller, in the medium to long term (as compared with short term), as a result of energy productivity growth (as presented in Table 31.2, in the previous chapter). For example, primary energy demand for China will increase steadily from 2,864 million tons of oil equivalent (Mtoe) in 2015 to 4,700 Mtoe in 2050, representing an annual growth rate of 3.35% in the short term (2015–2025); it will reduce to 1.98% in the medium term and to 0.17% in the long term. Similarly, primary energy demand for India will increase more than twofold, from 849 Mtoe in 2015 to 2,176 Mtoe in 2050, while its annual growth rate will decrease from 5.91% in the short term to 4.13% in the medium term and 0.98% in the long term.

In the CA scenario, primary energy demand for Japan, Korea, Thailand, and Indonesia will continue to grow, but at much slower rates than in the CP scenario over the three time frames,

Table 8.1 Primary energy demand (million tons of oil equivalent)

	2015		2025	2035	2050	Annual growth rates (%)		
						2015–25	2015–35	2035–50
Japan	446	CP	529	607	727	1.85	1.47	1.32
		CA	484	521	563	0.84	0.77	0.54
		SD	472	476	453	0.59	0.07	−0.32
Korea	276	CP	354	414	475	2.85	1.70	0.98
		CA	324	372	413	1.78	1.48	0.72
		SD	319	357	413	1.78	1.48	0.72
China	2,864	CP	3,824	4,581	4,700	3.35	1.98	0.17
		CA	3,207	3,682	3,460	1.20	1.48	−0.40
		SD	3,082	3,219	2,176	0.76	0.44	−2.16
India	849	CP	1,351	1,908	2,187	5.91	4.13	0.98
		CA	1,347	1,716	1,397	5.86	2.74	−1.24
		SD	1,323	1,579	939	5.58	1.93	−2.70
Thailand	140	CP	187	241	302	3.37	2.86	1.69
		CA	177	225	259	2.62	2.69	1.02
		SD	165	192	200	1.74	1.66	0.29
Malaysia	96	CP	107	131	163	1.08	2.30	1.61
		CA	102	118	115	0.57	1.63	−0.22
		SD	91	95	73	−0.61	0.50	−1.52
Indonesia	199	CP	234	320	457	1.78	3.70	2.84
		CA	211	248	249	0.63	1.73	0.04
		SD	187	192	169	−0.56	0.23	−0.78

Notes: CP = Country Policy; CA = Country Aspiration; SD = Sustainable Development.

Source: Estimates – based on methodology described in Chapter 31.

suggesting that proposed energy security policies would lead to modest slowdowns in the growth in primary energy demand in these countries. For China, India, and Malaysia, modest reductions in primary energy demand will be experienced in the long term: 0.4%, 1.24%, and 0.22%, respectively.

In the SD scenario, a further deceleration of growth in primary energy demand would take place in Japan, Korea, China, India, and Thailand over the short to medium terms, as compared with the CA scenario. This deceleration would become more pronounced in the long term for Korea and Thailand. For Malaysia, primary energy demand would decrease in the short term, from 96 Mtoe in 2015 to 91 Mtoe in 2025. It would however increase slightly to 95 Mtoe in 2025 and then decrease to 73 Mtoe in 2050. Similar trends are also observed for Indonesia.

Greenhouse gas (GHG) emissions

In the absence of strong energy security measures (the CP scenario), increasing trends in GHG emissions would be observed in all countries over the period 2015 to 2050. These trends would slow down and even reverse, however, if ambitious energy security targets are to be met (Table 8.2). For example, GHG emissions for India will increase in the CP scenario at an average annual rate

Table 8.2 Greenhouse gas (GHG) emissions

	2015	2050			Annual growth rate (%)		
		CP	CA	SD	CP	CA	SD
Total GHG emissions (Mt CO₂eq)							
China	8,428	13,038	7,590	3,723	1.56	−0.28	−1.59
Japan	1,072	1,577	1,065	624	1.35	−0.02	−1.19
Korea	567	869	619	406	1.52	0.27	−0.81
India	2,220	5,386	2,334	928	4.07	0.15	−1.66
Indonesia	457	1,081	531	254	3.89	0.46	−1.27
Malaysia	228	324	232	108	1.43	0.05	−1.51
Thailand	276	501	389	215	2.33	1.18	−0.63
Emissions (t CO₂eq) per capita							
China	6.15	9.71	5.66	2.77	1.66	−0.23	−1.57
Japan	8.43	14.58	9.84	5.77	2.08	0.48	−0.90
Korea	11.11	17.06	12.16	7.98	1.53	0.27	−0.80
India	1.70	3.25	1.41	0.56	2.61	−0.49	−1.91
Indonesia	1.77	3.36	1.65	0.79	2.56	−0.19	−1.58
Malaysia	7.43	8.20	5.56	2.58	0.30	−0.72	−1.87
Thailand	4.02	7.66	5.96	3.29	2.59	1.38	−0.52

Notes: CP = Country Policy; CA = Country Aspiration; SD = Sustainable Development; Mt CO₂eq = million tons of carbon dioxide equivalent.

Source: Estimates – based on methodology described in Chapter 31.

of 4.07% over the study period. Annual emissions will increase at an average rate of just 0.15% in the CA scenario, and even decrease at the rate of 1.66% in the SD scenario. Similarly, for Indonesia, the GHG emissions will increase at an annual rate of 3.89% in the CP scenario, and at 0.46% in the CA scenario, but decrease at rate of 1.27% in the SD scenario. The large decrease in emissions in the CA and (particularly) SD scenarios will result from a significantly reduced reliance on fossil fuels, and a move towards nuclear (Korea) and renewable energy (all other countries).

Without strong energy security improvement measures, emissions per capita would increase in all countries over the period 2015–2050. This increase will however slow down, even reverse, with more ambitious energy security measures. From 2015 to 2050, for example, China's emissions per capita will increase at an average annual rate of 1.66% in the CP scenario, but decrease by 0.23% in the CA scenario and by 1.57% in the SD scenario.

Emissions intensity

In this chapter, emissions intensity is defined as kilograms of carbon dioxide equivalent per dollar of GDP at 2010 prices. It is a measure of the carbon intensiveness of an economy. The emission intensities for the seven Asian countries under the three scenarios are presented in Table 8.3. The table suggests that there are significant contrasts, in 2015, in emission intensities across the seven countries. The economies of China and India have relatively high emission intensities (more than 1 kg CO₂eq/$), and intensities are also quite high for Malaysia and Thailand (more than 0.6 kg CO₂eq/$). Korea and Indonesia have modest emission intensities (about 0.45 CO₂eq/$). Japan has the lowest emissions intensity among these countries (of 0.176 CO₂eq/$).

Table 8.3 Emissions intensity (kg CO_2eq/$)

	2015	2050			Annual growth rate (%)		
		CP	CA	SD	CP	CA	SD
China	1.005	0.545	0.316	0.155	−1.31	−1.96	−2.42
Japan	0.176	0.174	0.117	0.068	−0.02	−0.96	−1.75
Korea	0.438	0.312	0.221	0.144	−0.82	−1.41	−1.92
India	1.028	0.356	0.153	0.061	−1.87	−2.43	−2.69
Indonesia	0.479	0.307	0.150	0.072	−1.02	−1.96	−2.43
Malaysia	0.681	0.298	0.203	0.094	−1.61	−2.01	−2.46
Thailand	0.714	0.410	0.317	0.173	−1.22	−1.59	−2.16

Notes: CP = Country Policy; CA = Country Aspiration; SD = Sustainable Development; kg CO_2eq/$ = kilograms of carbon dioxide equivalent per dollar.

Source: Estimates – based on methodology described in Chapter 31.

Table 8.4 Energy-import dependency (%)

		Japan	Korea	China	India	Thailand	Malaysia	Indonesia
	2015	93	96	15	35	53	−57	−151
CP	2025	84	97	16	38	55	−68	−167
	2035	84	97	17	41	54	−70	−151
	2050	84	96	18	46	52	−76	−126
CA	2025	80	96	16	34	54	−67	−160
	2035	79	96	16	34	52	−76	−160
SD	2050	77	95	15	37	53	−107	−179
	2025	77	96	16	31	54	−75	−146
	2035	72	95	16	31	53	−90	−140
	2050	62	93	17	34	51	−129	−139

Notes: CP = Country Policy; CA = Country Aspiration; SD = Sustainable Development.

Source: Estimates – based on methodology described in Chapter 31.

The emission intensities would steadily decrease in all countries in all scenarios, with decreases considerably higher in the CA and SD scenarios, in comparison with the CP scenario. For example, from 2015 to 2050, India's emission intensity would decrease at an average annual rate of 1.87% in the CP scenario, 2.43% in the CA scenario, and 2.69% in the SD scenario.

Energy-import dependency

In this chapter, energy-import dependency is expressed in terms of the ratio of net energy imports to total primary energy consumption. Table 8.4 shows estimation of energy-import dependency under the CP, CA, and SD scenarios.

It is observed that energy-import dependency of Japan and Korea is extremely high, exceeding 90% in 2015. The introduction of strong energy security policies (CA and SD scenarios) will help reduce energy-import dependency for these countries. For example, energy-import dependence for Japan will decrease from 93% in 2015, to 77% in 2050 in the CA scenario and to 62%

in the SD scenario (it will decrease to 84% in the CP scenario). The prospects for any noticeable reduction in energy-import dependency for Korea are however rather low in all scenarios. This is mainly because Korea has limited renewable energy resources. In order to meet Paris Agreement, under the SD scenario, the only option is increased reliance on nuclear power. This will simply shift the energy imports from fossil fuels to uranium.

Energy-import dependency for Thailand is relatively (i.e. relative to Japan and Korea) modest (around 53%); it will not noticeably improve in the CP, CA, and SD scenarios, with dependency still staying above 50% in 2050.

China and India are comparatively less dependent on energy imports. The dependency for China will however increase, even though modestly, in the CA and SD scenarios – due probably to its growing reliance on imported oil. For India, energy-import dependency will increase from 35% in 2015 to 46% in 2050 in the CP scenario, but will stabilize in the CA (37%) and SD (34%) scenarios by 2050.

For energy-exporting Indonesia and Malaysia, introduction of ambitious energy security measures will contribute to significant enhancements of their export capacities, from 57% in 2015 to 76%, 107%, and 129% in the CP, CA, and SD scenarios, respectively (for Malaysia). The corresponding values for Indonesia are 151% (2015), and 126%, 179%, and 139% in 2050 in the CP, CA, and SD scenarios, respectively. Indonesia will therefore remain the largest energy exporter in the region.

Energy diversity

Energy diversity, in the context of this chapter, is measured by the Herfindahl index. Lower index values suggest greater diversity of a country's primary fuel supply. Estimates of Herfindahl indices for the seven Asian countries are presented in Figure 8.6.

It is observed that in the CP scenario, the Herfindahl indices will decrease in all countries (except Korea and Indonesia), especially in the medium and long term, suggesting greater diversity of fuel supply. For Korea and Indonesia, the Herfindahl indices will increase throughout the period. This probably reflects an overproportionate reliance on coal in Indonesia and nuclear in Korea. Further, noticeable improvements in energy diversity will be achieved in all countries in the long term in the CA scenario.

In contrast to the CP and CA scenarios, a worsening of energy diversity will be experienced for all countries (except China) in the SD scenario, especially in the medium to long term. This probably reflects growing reliance on renewable and nuclear for energy production in this scenario. For China, improvement in energy diversity will continue throughout the period.

Summary of energy security outcomes

Figure 8.7 presents the summary of overall energy security outcomes, as discussed.

Main points, based on a review of the figure and discussion in the previous section, are presented below.

• Policy measures to improve energy security (CP, CA and SD scenarios) will appreciably reduce (particularly in the medium to long term) GHG emissions in all seven Asian countries, and these impacts will be noticeably greater in the CA and SD scenarios. The emission intensities for these countries are also likely to be reduced, particularly in the long term in the CA scenario, and medium to long term in the SD scenario. These outcomes (i.e. reduced emissions) are mainly caused by reduced fossil fuel consumption in these countries, arising

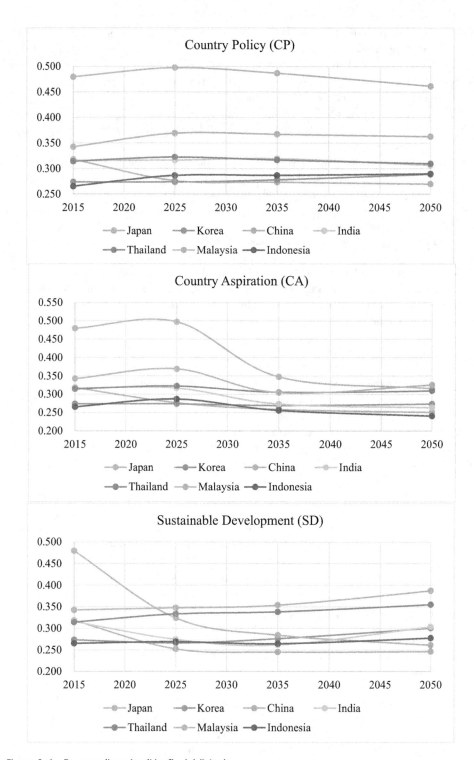

Figure 8.6 Energy diversity (Herfindahl) index

Source: Estimates – based on methodology described in Chapter 31.

from energy efficiency improvements and increased use of non-fossil fuels (particularly nuclear and renewables) for energy production.

• For energy-importing countries (China, India, Japan, Korea, and Thailand), the adoption of strong energy security measures (CA and SD scenarios) would help reduce their energy-import dependence, especially in the SD scenario. For energy-exporting Indonesia and Malaysia, introducing ambitious energy security measures would enhance their export capacities.

• In the CA scenario, energy security improvements would in general contribute to increased diversity of energy fuel mix for all countries. The fuel diversity will however reduce, in the SD scenario, for Korea, Malaysia, and Thailand, due to the growing reliance on non-fossil fuels for energy production: nuclear in Korea, and renewables in Malaysia and Thailand.

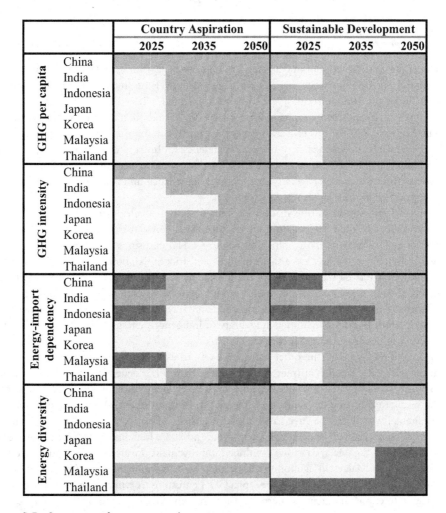

Figure 8.7 Summary of energy security outcomes

Notes:
1. This figure presents the effect of policies in CA and SD scenarios, compared with the CP scenario.
2. Dark Gray (positive impact), Dark (negative impact), and Light Gray (negligible impact).

Source: This table is developed based on details provided in Table 8A.2 (Appendix).

3 Policy trade-offs

The previous section presented an assessment of the impacts of the Country Policy (CP), Country Aspiration (CA), and Sustainable Development (SD) scenarios, in terms of socioeconomic and energy security outcomes, for seven Asian countries. This section synthesizes these assessments and extends the analyses to provide a more complete policy perspective. Specifically, it examines the trade-offs between energy security and socioeconomic outcomes that policy makers in the region may wish to consider while designing policies to improve energy security.

Figure 8.8 presents the overall socioeconomic and energy security trade-offs for all seven Asian countries.

This figure, read co-jointly with summarized version of socioeconomic (Figure 8.5) and energy security (Figure 8.7) outcomes, suggests the following.

3.1 CP scenario

- Under the existing set of policy measures to improve energy security (as reflected in the CP scenario), the overall energy security will deteriorate over the study period for most countries. India and Indonesia are likely to be most affected, where their respective composite energy security indices are estimated to reduce from 35 and 40 in 2015 to 8 and 11 in 2050. The major reasons for this increased energy insecurity are increased per capita emissions in both countries, increased energy-import dependency for India, and reduced energy diversity for Indonesia. Further, this increased energy insecurity reflects a continuation of their energy policies from the past, particularly their continuing reliance on primary fossil-based energy to support economic growth and job creation.
- A similar observation can be made for China and, to a smaller extent, Korea. Significant improvement in their socioeconomic conditions will come at the expense of a deterioration in energy security. For China, for example, GHG emissions will continue to increase drastically (albeit at lower rates than for India and Indonesia), both in total (55%) and per capita (58%) terms. China will also marginally increase its reliance on imported energy (from 15% to 18%) to fuel economic growth. Further, Korea will continue to rely on imported energy, with energy import-dependency staying well above 90% throughout the study period. Besides, the limited availability of indigenous energy sources will worsen the diversity of energy-mix in the country.
- Japan and Malaysia, on the other hand, are likely to experience improved energy security in this scenario. Japan is currently highly (more than 90%) dependent on energy imports to meet its energy needs. This dependency is likely to reduce modestly by 2025, after the restoration of nuclear generation. Despite this improvement, about 84% of its energy requirements will still be met from imported energy. Japan will not experience further improvements in the overall energy security beyond 2025. In contrast, the composite energy security index for Malaysia shows continued improvement throughout the study period. In particular, the Malaysian economy will become less emissions intensive (due to efficiency improvements) despite increased per capita GHG emissions. It will also be able to expand its capacity to export indigenous energy, further strengthening its economy.
- Thailand appears to be the only country that will experience a slowdown in overall socioeconomic outcomes beyond 2035; the composite socioeconomic index is estimated to increase from 35 in 2015 to 59 in 2035, then reduce to 50 in 2050. Increased trade deficits and reduced employment opportunities in the long term are the two main reasons for these negative outcomes. However, these reduced socioeconomic outcomes are likely to bring a

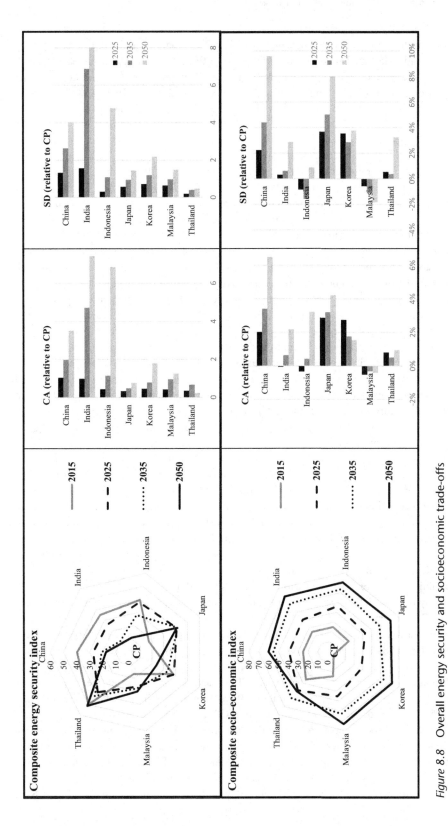

Figure 8.8 Overall energy security and socioeconomic trade-offs

Notes: Values of indicator closer to the origin represent worse outcomes. CP = Country Policy; CA = Country Aspiration; SD = Sustainable Development.
Source: Developed based on detailed socioeconomic and energy security outcomes provided in the Appendix.

reversal in the country's energy security condition in the long term, with the overall energy security index (50 in 2015) increasing from 40 in 2035 to 51 in 2050. Increased energy diversity and reduced emissions intensity for Thailand, supported by current biofuel policies (which emphasize replacement of relatively emission-intensive oil for transportation with biofuel) is the main reason for the reversal in energy security outcomes.

3.2   CA scenario

- The severity of overall energy security risks, especially for India, Indonesia, China, and Korea (where security will worsen in the CP scenario), could be reduced if these countries adopt aggressive energy security improvement measures (CA scenario). Compared with the CP scenario, composite energy security in this scenario is estimated to increase for all countries throughout the study period (Figure 8.8).
- This improved energy security is likely to come primarily from increased environmental sustainability (i.e. reduced per capita GHG emissions and reduced emission intensities) in all countries (Figure 8.7). These outcomes (i.e. reduced emissions and intensities) are mainly caused by reduced fossil fuel consumption as a result of energy efficiency improvements and increased use of non-fossil fuels, particularly nuclear and renewables. Improved energy diversity and reduced energy import-dependency are also likely to occur in most countries (Figure 8.7), thus contributing to improved overall energy security.
- While energy security would gradually improve over time for most countries, Thailand would experience improvement only until 2035 before energy security deteriorates again (Figure 8.8). This is because of a marginal worsening of energy-import dependency in 2050 (53%, compared with 51% in the CP scenario), as the country increases its reliance on imported coal to meet increased electricity demand. Notwithstanding such worsening, the overall energy security in 2050 will still be better than in 2015.
- Improved overall energy security in this scenario is likely to be associated with improved overall socioeconomic outcomes for most countries (Figure 8.8). The composite socio-economic index for China, for example, shows a consistent improvement throughout the study period, and could improve by almost 6% in 2050, in comparison with the composite socioeconomic index in the CP scenario. Most of the improvement is likely to come from improved trade balance (Figure 8.5); China would become a trade-surplus country under this scenario − a marked improvement from being a trade-deficit country in the CP scenario. China's economy is also likely to be $76 billion larger, and could create more than two million new jobs in this scenario, in comparison with the CP scenario. Japan and Korea are likely to have similar socioeconomic outcomes if they adopt energy policies embedded in the CA scenario.
- While Thailand and India are also likely to experience improved overall socioeconomic outcomes (Figure 8.8), employment would however be negatively affected in both countries (Figure 8.5). For example, the number of new jobs in Thailand, in 2050, would be 1.1% (0.4 million) less in this scenario than in the CP scenario. For India, the number of jobs in this scenario in 2025 will be almost two million (0.25%) lower than in the CP scenario in 2025. By 2050, however, the impact on employment in CA and CP scenarios would be insignificant.
- Unlike energy importing countries (China, Japan, Korea, Thailand, and India), where aggressive energy policy measures (CA scenario) will cause positive impacts, the impacts will be negative for energy exporting countries like Malaysia and Indonesia. The socioeconomic conditions in Malaysia, in particular, are likely to be adversely affected throughout the study period, while these effects will be observable only in the short term in Indonesia (Figure 8.8).

- The worsening socioeconomic conditions in Malaysia and Indonesia are likely to result from slower economic growth and worsening trade balance (Figure 8.5). For Malaysia, for example, the trade deficit would be higher by $2 billion in 2050, and GDP would be $1 billion lower, as compared with the CP scenario.
- Such declines in trade balance (and GDP) in energy exporting countries are due most likely to reduced fossil fuel exports, and exports of energy-intensive products, as a result of declining need for these products in the region. This implies that policymakers in energy exporting countries, while designing their energy policies, should take cognizance of the energy security measures adopted by their main trading partners.

3.3 SD scenario

- The severity of overall energy security risks could be further reduced if more drastic energy security measures are implemented (SD scenario). Figure 8.8 shows that energy security will significantly improve throughout the study period for all countries, in comparison with the CA scenario. This is because of the adoption of more aggressive policy measures to meet both the Paris Agreement and UN Sustainable Development Goals (SDGs).
- However, not all energy security attributes will improve consistently. For example, energy diversity will deteriorate for Korea, Thailand, and Malaysia (Figure 8.7), as these countries become increasing reliant on non-fossil fuels for domestic energy production (nuclear, in particular, in Korea, and renewable energy in Thailand and Malaysia). This implies that policy makers in these countries should also give priority, in the design of policy measures for improving energy security, to issues that may affect supply of non-fossil fuels. Some of these issues are: intermittency of non-combustible renewable energy (such as solar and wind), increased network requirements for integrating renewable energy, and nuclear waste treatment and disposal.
- Increased intensity of energy policy measures in the SD scenario (as compared with the CA scenario) will further accentuate the socioeconomic outcomes beyond those experienced in the CA scenario. For example, some energy importing countries (China, Japan, and Korea) are likely to experience even better overall socioeconomic conditions. Thailand and India, while experiencing better overall socioeconomic outcomes, are still likely to experience high unemployment. The number of jobs in Thailand in 2050, for example, would be 1.7% (0.6 million) less in this scenario, as compared with the CP scenario (where jobs will be 0.2 million less than in the CA scenario).
- This observation also applies to energy exporting countries: the socioeconomic conditions in Malaysia and Indonesia will be even worse in the SD scenario as compared with the CA scenario. Further, this worsening will be due to even slower economic growth and increasing trade deficit in the SD scenario. For example, the Malaysian economy in this scenario would be $7 billion lower in 2050 than in the CA scenario; the economy in the CA scenario will be $1 billion lower than in the CP scenario. This GDP loss is a result of increased trade deficit, particularly with other Asian countries whose demand for fossil fuel would be lower due to the adoption of aggressive measures to improve energy security.

4 Conclusions

This chapter analyses macroeconomic impacts of energy security improvements in Asia, with the view to identify trade-offs between energy security and socioeconomic outcomes that policy makers in the region may like to consider while designing policies to improve energy security.

The analysis is undertaken for seven major Asian countries (China, India, Indonesia, Japan, Korea, Malaysia, and Thailand), over the period 2015–2050. Three scenarios, reflecting a range of energy policy measures to improve energy security, are considered: Country Policy (CP), Country Aspiration (CA), and Sustainable Development (SD). Further, these policy measures aim to improve energy security through energy efficiency improvements (demand side) and fuel diversification (supply side). It is contended that analyses undertaken in this chapter complement, indeed augment, existing analyses on this topic.

The analyses suggest that despite ongoing efforts to improve energy security, as reflected in the CP scenario, energy demand would increase significantly in most countries over the study period. This is likely to pose significant energy security challenges for most countries. For example, China and India will become increasingly energy-import dependent, and Indonesia and Malaysia will increase reliance on cheap indigenous fossil fuels to meet their energy needs, thereby affecting their export incomes. Further, all countries will experience significant increase in greenhouse gas emissions, thus exacerbating the climate change processes.

The adoption of more drastic energy security measures (CA and SD scenarios) would significantly reduce energy demand and greenhouse gas emissions in all countries. The policy trade-offs between key socioeconomic and energy security outcomes will however vary across countries. For example, energy diversity will worsen for Korea, Malaysia, and Thailand, largely due to overreliance on non-fossil energy sources. This overreliance will also require the policy makers to find a satisfactory redress for a range of associated issues, for example, integration of intermittent renewable energy (Malaysia and Thailand), or to handle large-scale nuclear waste (Korea). Further, strong energy security measures (as in CA and SD scenarios) could bring significant socioeconomic benefits to energy importing countries, except Thailand and India where relatively weak employment opportunities will prevail. On the other hand, some economic losses could occur in energy exporting countries (Malaysia and Indonesia), due to reduced needs for fossil fuels in the region. This implies that policymakers in energy exporting countries, while designing their energy policies, should also take cognizance of the energy security measures of their major trading partners. The analyses in this chapter clearly demonstrates the need to exercise care while developing appropriate energy policy measures to achieve desired outcomes.

Appendix

Table 8A.1 Socioeconomic impacts (%)

		Country Aspiration			Sustainable Development		
		2025	2035	2050	2025	2035	2050
GDP	China	0.10	0.18	0.32	0.09	0.25	0.47
	India	0.14	0.56	0.99	0.31	0.81	1.38
	Indonesia	−0.06	0.13	0.63	−0.19	−0.21	0.26
	Japan	0.44	0.63	0.94	0.54	0.94	1.74
	Korea	0.59	0.61	0.65	0.70	0.89	1.26
	Malaysia	−0.18	−0.13	−0.09	−0.18	−0.51	−0.70
	Thailand	0.48	0.58	0.57	0.64	0.93	1.31
	China	−0.23	−0.29	−0.36	−0.24	−0.41	−0.60
Industry output	India	−0.01	−0.47	−0.99	−0.17	−0.96	−1.56
	Indonesia	−0.33	−0.44	−0.52	−0.53	−0.91	−1.03
	Japan	0.03	0.02	0.00	0.06	0.08	0.07
	Korea	−0.17	−0.28	−0.52	−0.24	−0.42	−0.77
	Malaysia	−0.27	−0.33	−0.48	−0.33	−0.56	−0.96
	Thailand	−0.43	−0.68	−0.96	−0.78	−1.30	−1.93
	China	9.38	21.25	245.16	9.38	28.13	361.29
Trade balance	India	1.27	3.71	5.85	2.53	5.48	8.11
	Indonesia	−1.54	2.01	7.72	−4.62	−3.36	2.94
	Japan	7.79	6.52	6.52	9.61	9.84	12.20
	Korea	6.29	4.53	3.68	7.55	6.62	7.36
	Malaysia	−2.70	−1.02	−1.08	−5.41	−4.08	−4.32
	Thailand	6.00	4.82	5.98	8.00	8.43	13.68
	China	0.22	0.23	0.29	0.30	0.27	0.45
Employment	India	−0.25	−0.11	−0.03	−0.04	−0.45	−0.16
	Indonesia	0.01	0.07	0.36	0.02	−0.42	0.20
	Japan	0.19	0.27	0.38	0.25	0.45	0.74
	Korea	0.20	0.13	0.01	0.30	0.30	0.27
	Malaysia	−0.07	0.03	0.19	0.08	−0.02	0.18
	Thailand	−0.18	−0.48	−1.12	−0.54	−1.16	−1.72

Note: Values in the table are percentage change in the socioeconomic attributes, relative to the CP scenario.

Source: Table 8A.3.

Table 8A.2 Energy security impacts (%)

		Country Aspiration			Sustainable Development		
		2025	2035	2050	2025	2035	2050
GHG per capita	China	−27.6	−32.6	−41.7	−35.3	−48.6	−71.5
	India	−9.6	−24.6	−56.6	−18.8	−41.6	−82.8
	Indonesia	−11.2	−25.0	−50.9	−25.0	−48.0	−76.5
	Japan	−12.2	−20.4	−32.5	−19.6	−38.8	−60.4
	Korea	−16.1	−20.8	−28.7	−24.0	−39.9	−53.2
	Malaysia	−0.3	−11.5	−32.2	−16.5	−34.5	−68.5
	Thailand	−9.0	−14.2	−22.2	−19.3	−33.7	−57.0
GHG intensity	China	−27.0	−33.3	−40.7	−34.8	−49.3	−72.2
	India	−12.5	−23.5	−29.4	−18.8	−41.2	−58.8
	Indonesia	−17.1	−18.9	−29.0	−24.4	−40.5	−54.8
	Japan	−10.2	−25.4	−58.3	−19.3	−41.8	−83.3
	Korea	−11.8	−25.0	−51.6	−23.5	−46.9	−77.4
	Malaysia	0.0	−11.1	−33.3	−16.3	−33.3	−70.0
	Thailand	−8.9	−14.0	−22.0	−19.6	−34.0	−58.5
Energy-import dependency	China	0.2	−4.7	−14.0	1.0	−3.6	−7.2
	India	−12.2	−17.3	−19.3	−18.0	−25.1	−25.2
	Indonesia	4.5	−6.0	−42.4	12.7	7.0	−10.8
	Japan	−4.4	−5.6	−8.2	−8.2	−14.7	−26.4
	Korea	−0.8	−0.9	−1.2	−1.3	−2.0	−3.2
	Malaysia	1.2	−8.5	−41.3	−10.7	−27.7	−70.0
	Thailand	−1.1	−4.3	0.6	−0.8	−2.4	−3.3
Energy diversity	China	−26.0	−28.6	−31.6	−34.8	−41.6	−43.4
	India	−8.1	−14.6	−14.1	−13.3	−18.1	−0.9
	Indonesia	−8.2	−10.9	−17.0	−6.1	−7.8	−4.2
	Japan	−5.2	−5.6	−7.1	−8.7	−10.3	−8.7
	Korea	−2.0	−3.3	−5.5	−2.7	−0.7	3.9
	Malaysia	−9.9	−17.1	−10.2	−5.9	−3.7	6.8
	Thailand	−3.0	−3.7	−0.1	3.4	6.7	14.6

Note: Values in the table are percentage change in the energy security attributes, relative to the CP scenario.

Source: Table 8A.4.

Table 8A.3 SOCIOECONOMIC OUTCOMES

		2015	Country Policy			Country Aspiration			Sustainable Development		
			2025	2035	2050	2025	2035	2050	2025	2035	2050
GDP ($ billion)	CN	8,385	12,724	17,901	23,926	12,737	17,934	24,002	12,736	17,946	24,039
	IN	2,161	4,154	7,692	15,112	4,160	7,735	15,261	4,167	7,754	15,320
	ID	955	1,570	2,338	3,514	1,569	2,341	3,536	1,536	2,333	3,523
	JP	6,110	6,896	7,737	9,055	6,926	7,786	9,140	6,933	7,810	9,213
	KR	1,294	1,705	2,128	2,782	1,715	2,141	2,800	1,717	2,147	2,817
	MY	335	547	782	1,146	546	781	1,145	546	778	1,138
	TH	386	624	861	1,222	627	866	1,229	628	869	1,238
Total industry output ($ billion)	CN	22,822	34,334	48,331	64,658	34,256	48,192	64,425	34,250	48,133	64,272
	IN	4,194	7,870	14,314	27,588	7,869	14,247	27,315	7,857	14,176	27,157
	ID	1,874	3,016	4,495	6,765	3,006	4,475	6,730	3,000	4,454	6,695
	JP	12,123	13,870	15,784	18,751	13,874	15,787	18,751	13,878	15,796	18,765
	KR	3,162	4,190	5,272	6,923	4,183	5,257	6,887	4,180	5,250	6,870
	MY	948	1,508	2,137	3,111	1,504	2,130	3,096	1,503	2,125	3,081
	TH	899	1,408	1,924	2,697	1,402	1,911	2,671	1,397	1,899	2,645
Trade balance($Bn.)	CN	365	128	−160	−31	140	−126	45	140	−115	81
	IN	−143	−474	−1131	−2566	−468	−1089	−2416	−462	−1069	−2358
	ID	−11	−65	−149	−272	−66	−146	−251	−68	−154	−264
	JP	103	385	752	1303	415	801	1388	422	826	1462
	KR	99	159	287	489	169	300	507	171	306	525
	MY	33	−37	−98	−185	−38	−99	−187	−39	−102	−193
	TH	27	−50	−83	−117	−47	−79	−110	−46	−76	−101
Employment (million persons)	CN	689	769	859	717	771	861	719	772	861	720
	IN	478	671	910	832	669	909	831	670	906	830
	ID	114	154	183	172	154	184	172	154	183	172
	JP	64	64	63	57	65	63	57	65	63	58
	KR	27	29	29	25	29	30	25	29	30	25
	MY	15	20	23	22	20	23	22	20	23	22
	TH	40	48	49	33	48	49	33	48	48	33

Note: CN = China, IN = India, ID = Indonesia, JP = Japan, KR = Korea, MY = Malaysia, TH = Thailand.

Source: Estimates – based on methodology described in Chapter 31.

Table 8A.4 Energy security outcomes

		2015	Country Policy			Country Aspiration			Sustainable Development		
			2025	2035	2050	2025	2035	2050	2025	2035	2050
Emissions (t CO$_2$eq) per capita	CN	6 15	8.04	9 47	9 71	5.82	6.38	5.66	5.2	4.87	2.77
	IN	1.7	2.5	3.29	3.25	2.26	2.48	1.41	2.03	1.92	0.56
	ID	1.77	1.88	2.44	3.36	1.67	1.83	1.65	1.41	1.27	0.79
	JP	8.43	9.18	11.11	14.58	8.06	8.84	9.84	7.38	6.8	5.77
	KR	11.11	13.31	14.97	17.06	11.17	11.85	12.16	10.12	9	7.98
	MY	7.43	6.73	7.4	8.2	6.71	6.55	5.56	5.62	4.85	2.58
	TH	4.02	5.02	6.26	7.66	4.57	5.37	5.96	4.05	4.15	3.29
Emissions intensity (kg CO$_2$/$)	CN	1 01	0.89	0.75	0.54	0.65	0.5	0.32	0.58	0.38	0.15
	IN	0.18	0.16	0.17	0.17	0.14	0.13	0.12	0.13	0.1	0.07
	ID	0.44	0.41	0.37	0.31	0.34	0.3	0.22	0.31	0.22	0.14
	JP	1.03	0.88	0.67	0.36	0.79	0.5	0.15	0.71	0.39	0.06
	KR	0.48	0.34	0.32	0.31	0.3	0.24	0.15	0.26	0.17	0.07
	MY	0.68	0.43	0.36	0.3	0.43	0.32	0.2	0.36	0.24	0.09
	TH	0.71	0.56	0.5	0.41	0.51	0.43	0.32	0.45	0.33	0.17
Energy-import dependency (%)	CN	15	16.2	16.8	18.0	16.2	16.1	15.5	16.4	16.2	16.7
	IN	35	38	41	46	34	34	37	31	31	34
	ID	−151	−167	−151	−126	−160	−160	−179	−146	−140	−139
	JP	93	84	84	84	80	79	77	77	72	62
	KR	96	97	97	96	96	96	95	96	95	93
	MY	−57	−68	−70	−76	−67	−76	−107	−75	−90	−129
	TH	53	55	54	52	54	52	53	54	53	51
Energy diversity	CN	0.479	0.497	0.487	0.461	0.368	0.347	0.316	0.324	0.284	0.261
	IN	0.316	0.317	0.319	0.306	0.291	0.273	0.263	0.274	0.262	0.304
	ID	0.265	0.287	0.287	0.290	0.263	0.256	0.241	0.269	0.265	0.278
	JP	0.318	0.276	0.273	0.270	0.262	0.258	0.251	0.252	0.245	0.246
	KR	0.274	0.273	0.278	0.289	0.268	0.269	0.273	0.266	0.276	0.300
	MY	0.343	0.369	0.367	0.362	0.333	0.304	0.325	0.347	0.353	0.387
	TH	0.314	0.323	0.317	0.310	0.313	0.305	0.309	0.333	0.338	0.355

Note: CN = China, IN = India, ID = Indonesia, JP = Japan, KR = Korea, MY = Malaysia, TH = Thailand.

Source: Estimates – based on methodology described in Chapter 31.

Part II
Energy and environment

9

Energy and climate

Richard S. J. Tol

1 Introduction

Energy market and energy policy are intricately linked with climate change and climate policy. Carbon dioxide is the main anthropogenic greenhouse gas causing climate change, and the burning of fossil fuels is the main source of carbon dioxide emissions. Fossil fuels are carbohydrates. Combustion breaks the chemical bond between the carbon and the hydrogen. They are oxidized to CO_2 and H_2O. More energy is released when new bonds are formed than when the old bonds are broken. Net energy is released. That is, CO_2 emissions are intrinsic to this process. You cannot get energy out of fossil fuel without forming CO_2. Unlike sulfur or particulates, which are externalities as well as nuisances to energy conversion, carbon dioxide is not a nuisance; it is a pure externality. You cannot solve, or even substantially reduce the climate problem without deeply affecting the energy sector, and you cannot understand climate change and policy without knowledge of energy markets and policies.

In this chapter, I do three things in a mixture of tutorial, review, commentary, and analysis. In Section 2, I discuss past trends in carbon dioxide emissions and scenarios of future emissions, placing these in the context of fuel resources and reserves. Section 3 treats technical options to reduce emissions and the costs of deploying these options in the first and second best. Section 4 surveys some of the issues around climate policy.[1] Section 5 concludes.

2 Trends and scenarios

2.1 Trends in carbon dioxide emissions

The *Kaya identity* is a useful tool to understand trends in emissions (Kaya, 1997). If applied to carbon dioxide from fossil fuel combustion, it looks as follows:

$$M = P \frac{Y}{P} \frac{E}{Y} \frac{M}{E} \tag{9.1}$$

where M denotes emissions, P population, Y Gross Domestic Product, and E primary energy use. Thus the Kaya identity has that emissions equal the number of people times per capita income times energy intensity (energy use per unit of economic activity) times carbon intensity (emissions per unit of energy use). This is an identity. On the right-hand side of Equation (9.1), P cancels P, Y Y and E E so that $M = M$.

Although an identity, it is useful, and perhaps more so if expressed in proportional growth rates. Take logs on both side of Equation (9.1) and the first partial derivative to time. Then

$$\frac{\partial \ln M}{\partial t} = \frac{\partial \ln P}{\partial t} + \frac{\partial \ln \frac{Y}{P}}{\partial t} + \frac{\partial \ln \frac{E}{Y}}{\partial t} + \frac{\partial \ln \frac{M}{E}}{\partial t} \tag{9.2}$$

As

$$\frac{\partial \ln X}{\partial t} = \frac{1}{X} \frac{\partial X}{\partial t} = \frac{\dot{X}}{X} \tag{9.3}$$

the growth rate of emissions equals the growth rate of the population plus the growth rate of per capita income plus the growth rate of energy intensity plus the growth rate of carbon intensity.

Fossil fuels come in a number of varieties. Peat emits the most CO_2 per unit of energy (99–117 tCO_2/TJ), followed by coal (98–109 tCO_2/TJ), oil (73–77 tCO_2/TJ), and natural gas (56–58 tCO_2/TJ).

Figure 9.1 shows global carbon dioxide emissions between 1971 and 2014.[2] CO_2 emissions rose by 2.0% per year. Why? The Kaya identity allows us to interpret past trends. Population growth was 1.5% per year over the same period. Emissions per capita thus rose by 0.5% per year. Per capita income rose by 1.8% per year, again slower than the emissions growth rate. Total income thus rose by 3.3% per year, considerably faster than emissions. This is primarily because the energy intensity of production fell by 1.4% per year. The carbon intensity of the energy system rose by 0.1% per year. In other words, population and income growth drove emissions up, with a bit of help from a switch to more carbon-intensive fuels. This was partly offset by improvements in energy efficiency.

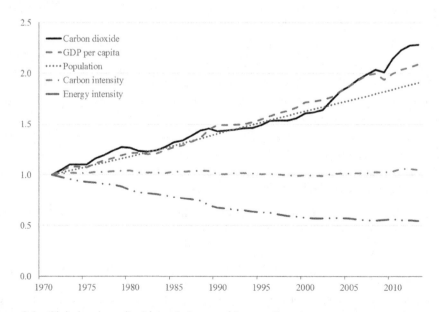

Figure 9.1 Global carbon dioxide emissions and its constituents

There was little climate policy for most of the period shown in Figure 9.1. Bell (2015) study the impact of the EU ETS on emissions, Murray and Maniloff (2015) the RGGI, and Aichele and Felbermayr (2012) and Aichele and Felbermayr (2013) the Kyoto Protocol. They find modest emission reductions, not surprisingly as carbon prices have been low and coverage incomplete.

2.2 Scenarios of future emissions

The Kaya identity shows that, in order to project emissions into the future, we need to build scenarios of population growth, economic activity, energy use, and energy supply. Although our understanding of the processes of long-term development has considerably improved in recent decades, it does not permit any confidence in forecasts over a century or longer. Therefore, scenarios are built instead. Scenarios are not (conditional) predictions. Scenarios are not implausible, internally consistent storylines of how the future might unfold.

Emission scenarios must include the number of people, but may also have their age structure, because that drives decisions on consumption and saving and hence economic growth and because people of different ages use energy differently (Dalton et al., 2008); their education, because that drives labor productivity and hence growth and because people with different skills use energy differently (Gebreegziabher et al., 2012; Buechs and Schnepf, 2013); and urbanization, because that drives travel and transport and hence energy use (Sadorsky, 2013). Emission scenarios must include per capita income, but may also have the structure of the economy, because certain sectors use more energy per unit value added than others (Hoekstra and Van Den Bergh, 2002); and expenditure patterns, because air-conditioning and long-distance holidays use a lot of energy (Reiss and White, 2005). Emission scenarios must include the energy intensity of economic production, and may include a range of primary and final energy sources and carriers, because emissions are more easily reduced in electrified transport than in liquid-fuel-based transport (Clarke et al., 2014). Emission scenarios must include the carbon intensity of the energy sector, and thus details of the supply of and demand for a range of different energy sources, their transformation and conversion, and transport of energy carriers.

There are two types of scenarios for climate change. In one, there is no climate policy. These are typically referred to as business-as-usual scenarios, although this is a bit of a misnomer as there has been climate policy in an increasing number of countries. In the other type of scenario, there is climate policy.

Figure 9.2 shows a key example of business-as-usual scenarios: the shared socioeconomic pathways (SSPs) (van Vuuren et al., 2011; Riahi et al., 2017). Values are for the world as whole. The scenarios are broken down according to the Kaya identity. The scenarios start in the year 2010. For comparison, the observed values for 1970–2010 are shown too. These scenarios were implemented with six alternative models. Figure 9.2 shows the mean plus or minus twice the standard deviation across these models.

There are five scenarios for each variable. However, two pairs of the population scenarios are really close together, while the income scenarios are more evenly spaced. The SSPs thus implicitly assume that population growth is independent of per capita income, an assumption at odds with everything we know about fertility and mortality (Galor and Weil, 1999; Herzer et al., 2012). All scenarios of per capita income show exponential growth, and most very rapid growth, even though some parts of the world have enjoyed little growth in the past. In the most pessimistic scenario, per capita income will roughly double. In 2100, the world average will be similar to the average income in Portugal in 2015. In the most optimistic scenario, per capita income will rise 14-fold. The world average in 2100 will be well above the 2015 average in Luxembourg. It is hard to imagine such riches, but then again people in 1940 would not be able to imagine 2020

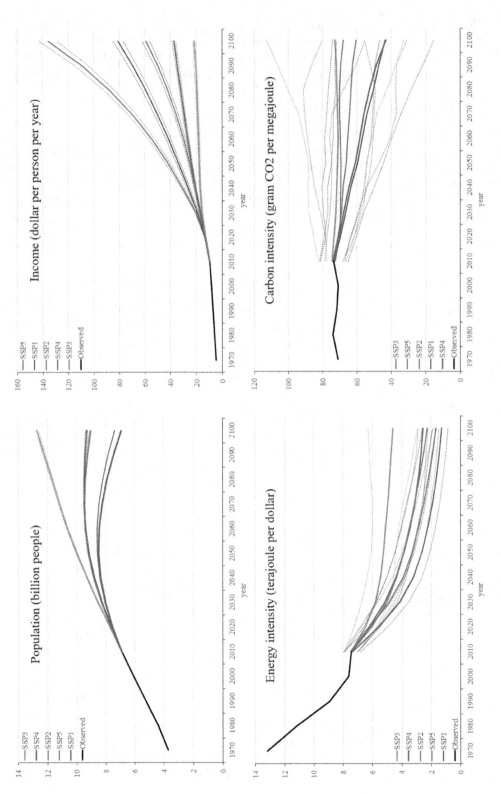

Figure 9.2   The SSP scenarios for the world broken down according to the Kaya identity

either. All scenarios show a steady improvement of energy efficiency, often at a rate that exceeds the experience of the last 40 years. Most scenarios show a steady fall in carbon intensity, even though recent history showed both decreases and increases. Although peculiar, the SSP scenarios form the basis of much research on climate change, its impacts, and policies to reduce greenhouse gas emissions.

The availability of fossil fuels is a crucial part of any scenario of future carbon dioxide emissions. Figure 9.3 shows estimates of the reserves and resources of fossil fuels by type (WEC, 2010).

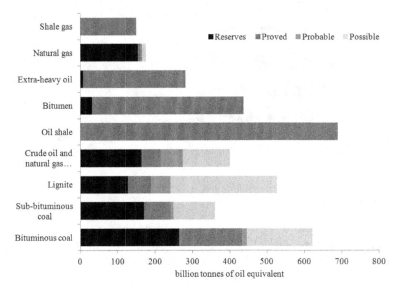

Energy

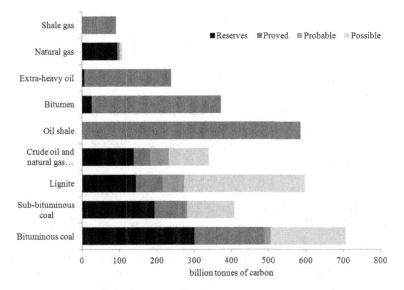

Emissions

Figure 9.3 Fossil fuel reserves and resources as estimated for 2010 (top panel), their carbon content (middle panel), and implied carbon dioxide concentrations (bottom panel)

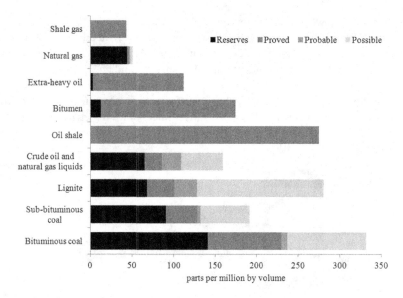

Concentrations

Figure 9.3 (Continued)

The estimates are from 2010, when the shale gas revolution was tentatively reaching beyond the United States and the shale oil revolution was in its infancy. Reserves can be profitably exploited with current technology at current prices and costs. Resources are known or suspected to be there, and may become commercial in the future. Figure 9.3 reveals that conventional oil and gas reserves are relatively small: 317 billion tonnes of oil equivalent. In 2009, total primary energy use was 11.6 billion metric tonnes of oil equivalent (GTOE). There is therefore enough conventional oil and gas to cover energy demand for another 27 years. Figure 9.3 also reveals, however, that there are plenty of other types of fossil fuels, including coal and (what used to be) unconventional liquids and gases.

The second panel of Figure 9.3 shows the carbon dioxide emissions that would result if these fossil fuels were burned. For comparison, global 2008 emissions were 30 billion tonnes of CO_2. We can keep up current emissions for 100 years or more. The third panel shows the impact on the atmospheric concentration, should all available fossil fuels be burned at once. Conventional oil and gas can contribute only about 100 ppm. Other fossil fuels, reserves and resources, are worth another 1,500 ppm.

This implies that the climate problem is not driven by conventional oil and gas, but rather by what will replace conventional oil and gas when they run out. The future energy sector will therefore be very different. Different companies and countries will dominate.

Technologies will be different too, and trillions of dollars will be invested in new equipment and infrastructure.

Table 9.1 further elaborates this. It compares cumulative emissions over the 21st century according to the five SSP scenarios to reserves and proven resources. In all scenarios, emissions exceed maximum emissions from gas and oil reserves, and from gas, oil and coal reserves. Two scenarios exceed gas, oil, and oil reserves plus proven resources of gas and oil. No scenario exceeds gas, oil, and coal reserves plus proven resources. As the scenarios project 80 years into the future, turning proven resources into reserves should be feasible.

Table 9.1 Cumulative emissions projected over the 21st century in levels and as a share of gaseous+liquid and all fossil fuel reserves and proved resources

Scenario	Level	Reserves		+ Resources	
	GtC	oil+gas	+coal	oil+gas	+coal
SSP1	1,002	375%	111%	64%	39%
SSP2	1,466	549%	162%	93%	58%
SSP3	1,758	621%	183%	106%	65%
SSP4	1,141	427%	126%	73%	45%
SSP5	2,056	770%	227%	131%	81%
6.0 Wm^{-2}	1,171	438%	129%	75%	46%
4.5 Wm^{-2}	820	307%	91%	52%	32%
3.4 Wm^{-2}	594	223%	66%	38%	23%
2.6 Wm^{-2}	373	139%	41%	24%	15%

Notes: Emissions are carbon dioxide emissions from fossil fuel combustion, cumulative over the period 2005–2100. Baseline scenarios are denoted by SSP*, policy scenarios by *Wm^{-1}. Results are averaged over models and, for the policy scenarios, baseline scenarios.

Feasible is not the same as realistic. Coal is primarily used for power generation, where non-fossil alternatives are (close to) competitive. Ritchie and Dowlatabadi (2017) point out that the majority of coal reserves are low grade. For all that coal to be burned, we need to assume that heat transport will be electrified and power generation coal-based, or that liquified or gasified coal will be cheaper than biofuel.

3 Emission reduction

3.1 Options for emission reduction

The Kaya identity allows us to assess how emissions can be cut. We would need to reduce population or income, or improve energy or carbon efficiency.

Fewer people is the first option (Bongaarts and O'Neill, 2018). Some murderous regimes in Africa and the Middle East actively seek to reduce the population of their countries. Few democratic countries would seek to emulate this in the name of climate policy. Indeed, population policy is controversial in most democracies. China, however, has often put forward its one-child policy as one of its major contributions to climate policy – although that policy dates back to a time when climate change was hardly recognized as a problem, and the policy has recently been relaxed.

Slower economic growth is the second option (Kallis, 2011). The collapse of the former Soviet Union and its aftermath has shown that reducing the level of per capita income is an effective way of cutting greenhouse gas emissions (Bashmakov, 1994). The Great Recession further demonstrated the power of economic growth over emissions growth: the fall in carbon dioxide emissions in Europe is primarily due to its lackluster economic performance (Bel and Joseph, 2015). However, promoting slower economic growth is not recommended to a politician seeking re-election.

That leaves us with just two of the four terms in the Kaya identity.

Energy efficiency improvements have kept the rise of carbon dioxide emissions in check. This is shown in Figure 9.1 for recent times, but has been true for much longer (Nordhaus, 1996;

Fouquet, 2008). Energy efficiency is likely to further improve in the future regardless of climate policy. This is because energy is a cost. A gadget that is identical to its competitor's but uses less energy is more appealing to customers. Companies therefore invest in improving the energy efficiency of their products.

Energy efficiency improvement does not necessarily imply reduced energy use (Schwarz and Taylor, 1995). For instance, the fuel efficiency of the US car fleet was roughly constant between 1980 and 2010. This is a remarkable feat of engineering as, over the same period, the size and weight of cars increased considerably.[3] The gains in fuel efficiency were used not to reduce energy use, but rather to increase comfort.

There is also the *rebound effect*, first formulated by Jevons (1865). Better energy efficiency means lower energy costs means higher energy use. Improving the insulation of homes, for instance, means that it is cheaper to heat the house. This often leads to higher indoor temperature at the expense of reduced energy use. Better fuel efficiency means it is cheaper to drive a long distance. This leads to longer drives. Estimates of the size of the rebound effect vary widely. This is no surprise, as energy is used for so many different things in so many different ways. Typical estimates have that the rebound effect is 10%–20% (Greening et al., 2000; Sorrell et al., 2009). That is, increased energy demand offsets one-tenth to one-fifth of the initial reduction in energy use.

Besides technical change, behavioral change can also reduce emissions (Kahn, 2007; Allcott, 2011). Engineers reckon that some 30% of energy used serves no purpose.[4] It is, however, easier to identify energy waste than to reduce it. People may boil a kettle full of water to make a single cup of tea. People may leave the light on in the bathroom. Most would agree they should not, but do it anyway. Government awareness campaigns are not particularly effective, and social pressure can be unpleasant.

Energy is also wasted because of misaligned incentives. A university lecturer is responsible for turning off teaching equipment at the end of class, but the money thus saved will disappear into the overall budget of the college. A landlord is responsible for building maintenance and retrofit, but the tenant often pays the energy bills. The costs of wall insulation cannot usually be recouped from increased rents, because running costs are not typically known to prospective renters (Fuerst and McAllister, 2011; Im et al., 2017).[5] If the rental market is tight, landlords have little reason to invest in maintenance. Solving these *principal-agent* problems – the principal pays the bills, the agent makes the decisions – make for nice exercises in industrial organization, but reality is more resistant (Laffont and Martimort, 2009).

Lower energy demand is another form of behavioral change. People can put on a sweater and turn down the thermostat. They can move closer to work and cycle instead of drive. They can shower less. They can go for a staycation rather than a holiday in the Kingdom of Far Far Away. Only a small minority is prepared to make these changes for a better climate.

The carbon intensity of the energy sector is the fourth component of the Kaya identity. The carbon intensity is improved by switching from high-carbon energy sources to low- or no-carbon energy. In recent years, power generation in the United States has switched from coal to gas, and carbon dioxide emissions fell as a result.[6] This was done because the shale gas revolution brought abundant and cheap natural gas. In Europe, the opposite has happened.[7] With a population wary of fracking, cheap American coal has replaced natural gas and emissions have gone up. Japan and Germany have taken it a step further, replacing carbon-free nuclear power by gas, coal, and even lignite.

There are several carbon-free energy sources. Hydropower and nuclear power are proven technologies (WEC, 2016d, 2016f). Both are controversial. Hydropower needs a reservoir, displacing people and valuable agricultural land. With nuclear power, people worry about nuclear waste and safety – problems of the past, if you ask me, but the resulting escalation of costs is a concern – and about proliferation of nuclear material and knowledge for military application. Because of this, there is limited scope for a large expansion on nuclear and hydropower.

Besides hydropower, there are many other renewable sources of energy. Some renewables are confined to small niches, such as geothermal energy and tidal power (WEC, 2016c, 2016e). Other renewables are more widely applicable (WEC, 2016h, 2016g). Wind power is a key part of the carbon dioxide emission reduction strategy in many countries. Onshore wind power is 25%–50% more expensive than coal- and gas-fired electricity – although it is approaching grid parity[8] in some areas. Offshore wind is more expensive still (IRENA, 2018). There has been some progress in reducing the costs, particularly through scale and material choice, but as wind is an established technology, breakthroughs are not expected. Cost savings come from scale economies. Besides the costs, wind power is intermittent and unpredictable. Backup generators are needed to prevent blackouts. On top of that, there is opposition to the visual intrusion of wind turbines, and turbines kill bats and birds.

Solar power is another key part of many a emission reduction policy. Apart from niche applications, solar power is expensive still, but costs have fallen faster and are likely to continue to fall rapidly (IRENA, 2018). This is because photovoltaic power piggybacks on technological progress in materials science and semiconductors. Intermittency is less than with wind, but photovoltaics do not work in the dark. Solar panels contain nasty chemicals and should be carefully disposed of at the end of their life time. Concentrated solar power, where sunlight is used to heat a material like water or salt, does have the momentum to be a reliable and dispatchable energy source, and it is at or near grid parity in sunny places with cheap land.

Biomass is the most widely used renewable source of energy, but primarily in its traditional forms – wood and dried dung (WEC, 2016a). Unlike wind and solar power, bioenergy can be used to substitute the liquid fuels that propel most vehicles, ships and aircraft. The first generation of modern biofuels is expensive, and the materials used are often edible. Bioenergy use thus drives up the price of food (Ciaian and Kancs, 2011; Lotze-Campen et al., 2014). There is much research into second- and third-generation process, but little commercial application. Second-generation bioenergy would use the same materials, thus directly competing with food production, but with improved processing. Fossil fuels are plant material nicely dried, compacted and converted by mother nature over millions of years. Biomass energy is recent plant material that needs to be gathered, dried, compacted, and converted by people and their machines. As this is relatively new, progress can be expected in bringing down the costs. Third-generation bioenergy uses different or modified source material. Over the last 10,000 years we have optimized plants for food, but we have never much bothered with optimizing plants for energy. Rapid progress can therefore be expected, particularly now that genetic engineering is routine. However, although there regularly is exciting news from the lab, there has yet to be successful commercialization (Guo et al., 2015; Enamala et al., 2018; Widjaya et al., 2018).

The Kaya identity is about the structural causes of emissions and structural solutions. There is also an end-of-pipe solution: carbon capture and storage (CCS). In CCS, carbon dioxide is separated before, during, or after burning. It is then captured and transported to be stored in a safe place (WEC, 2016b). Carbon capture requires capital and energy. In a conventional power plant, the investment cost of a power plant with capture is substantially higher than that of a similar plant without, and a large share of the energy output of the plant will be devoted to carbon capture (Davison, 2007; Rubin et al., 2007). The costs of carbon capture can be brought down with a radical redesign of power plants, for example the Allam Cycle (Allam et al., 2014), but that is as yet untested at scale. Transport of CO_2 is costly too. According to some estimates, if we want to capture all carbon dioxide from power generation, the transport network would be several times bigger than the network for oil and gas. The main issues with storage are permanence and safety. There is little point in storing carbon dioxide if it leaks out again. Sudden releases of carbon dioxide would endanger animal and human life.

3.2 The costs of emission reduction

Emission reduction costs money (Weyant, 1993; Clarke et al., 2014). There are various ways to look at this. Without climate policy, greenhouse gas emissions are free. With climate policy, emissions are not. Alternatively, climate policy imposes a new constraint on a maximization problem. If the constraint bites – that is, if emissions are lower than they otherwise would have been – the objective function must fall. Put yet another way, climate policy forces people and companies to use different technologies and different fuels than they would have without climate policy. Without climate policy, these technologies and fuels are available, but people choose not to use them, or not to the same extent. Climate policy gets people and companies to invest more in energy savings than they would of their own volition, and gets them to switch to more expensive energy sources.

It is difficult to estimate the costs of climate policy. Most climate policy analysis is done ex ante, comparing two hypothetical situations, with and without the policy. Ex post analysis compares observed history to a counterfactual. Cost estimates are only as good as the models used. Not all models are equally good, partly because there is little existing climate policy to calibrate models to, and partly because little attention is paid to model calibration (Tol, 2014).

Most studies agree that a complete decarbonization of the economy can be achieved at a reasonable cost if policies are smart, comprehensive, and gradual. Models disagree, however, on how much emission reduction would cost. This is illustrated in Figure 9.4: emission reduction costs vary by an order of magnitude or more.[9]

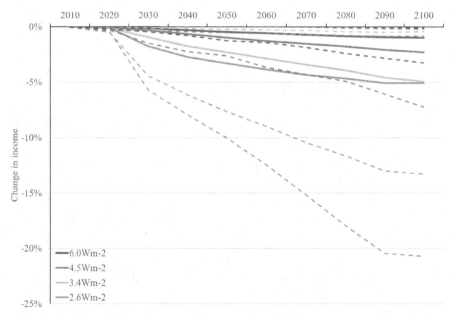

Figure 9.4 Total cost of emission reduction for the model average (solid line) and the most optimistic/pessimistic model (dashed lines) for four alternative atmospheric stabilization targets

There are various reasons for this. Modelers make different assumptions about what options are available to reduce greenhouse gas emissions, and at what cost. Obviously, if a model omits an option – say, hydrogen fuel cells for private transport – or assumes that its costs are high, then that model will find that emission reduction is more expensive. Vice versa, if a model assumes that an option exists – say, unlimited capacity for carbon storage – or puts its costs at a lower level than what is commonly believed, then that model will find that emission reduction is less expensive.

The rate of technological change is a key determinant of future emission reduction costs (Clarke et al., 2008). The difference in the costs between carbon-neutral energy (solar, wind, nuclear) and carbon-emitting energy (coal, oil, gas), for instance, is a key assumption: emission reduction would be cheap if solar is only slightly more expensive than coal. That cost difference is reasonably well known for the present and past, but has to be assumed for the future. If technology advances faster in carbon-neutral energy than in carbon-emitting energy – say, solar is getting cheaper faster than coal – abatement costs are lower. Different models make different assumptions about the rates of technological progress.

Some models assume that progress in carbon-saving technologies accelerates in response to climate policy. Other models do not have such a response. The latter models thus have slower technological progress in energy efficiency and renewables and higher costs of emission reduction. Some models assume that there is no opportunity cost to accelerating technological progress in energy; others do include an opportunity cost. Perhaps there are highly educated taxi drivers who would make a real contribution to the next generation of solar cells if only there were government support. But perhaps hiring clever people to work on solar power means that they will not work in materials science. These alternative assumptions further explain the wide range in cost estimates (Lans Bovenberg and Smulders, 1995; Goulder and Schneider, 1999; Goulder and Mathai, 2000; Smulders and de Nooij, 2003).

If a model assumes high price elasticities, high substitution elasticities, and rapid depreciation of capital, its cost estimates will be lower than of a model with low price elasticities, low substitution elasticities, and slow turnover of the capital stock. The latter model assumes that the world of energy use is set in its carbon-intensive ways, which makes it hard and expensive to change course.

Finally, some models assume that, in the scenario without climate policy, greenhouse gas emissions will not grow very fast. Consequently, emission targets (which are typically formulated as absolute targets) are within easy reach. Other models assume rapidly rising emissions, so that a large effort is needed to meet emissions targets.

The concentration target is the key policy variation in Figure 9.4. The more stringent the target, the higher the cost – and costs rise very rapidly from the more lenient to the more ambitious targets.

Participation of poorer countries in climate policy is another variation in policy scenarios (Clarke et al., 2009). This has a large impact on the estimated cost of emission reduction. If poorer countries are initially exempt from emission reduction, a fraction of emission is excluded from abatement, and the rest will have to be reduced more to meet the same target. As emission reduction costs are more than linear in emission reduction effort, this necessarily drives up the total costs. Furthermore, many of the cheaper emission reduction options can be found in poorer countries, partly because these economies tend to rely on older, less efficient technology, and partly because money buys more in poorer countries.

Wigley et al. (1996) and Manne and Richels (2004) provide insight into the allocation of emission reduction effort over time, contrasting emission trajectories that start with radical emission cuts to ones that begin with modest abatement that accelerates over time. Cost savings vary between 10% and 60% depending on the model.

There are four reasons why money is saved if emission reduction targets are lenient at first while becoming more stringent over time. Greenhouse gas emissions are to a large degree determined by things that change only slowly, such as machinery and buildings, technology blueprints, and location choice. Emission reduction requires changes in behavior and technology, but behavior and technology are constrained by durable consumption goods and invested capital. A carbon tax does not reduce the emissions of those households and companies that continue to use the same cars, live and work in the same place and in the same building, and operate the same machinery. In those cases, a carbon tax simply imposes a penalty on investment decisions made in earlier, pre-climate-policy times. In other words, rapid emission reduction implies capital destruction, particularly rapid emission reduction that was unexpected when investment decisions were made. This is a deadweight loss to the economy. This deadweight loss falls over time as capital turns over, so that the carbon tax can increase without inducing excessive costs.

Technological change is another reason why emission reduction is expensive in the short term but cheaper in the medium to long term. Carbon-neutral energy is still immature technology. Although fossil fuel technology continues to progress, it is well developed and all the easy improvements have been made. Although there has been rapid progress in oil and gas exploitation, this has been about unlocking relatively expensive reserves, such as shale oil and gas. In contrast, we can still expect major technological breakthroughs with solar power and bioenergy. Furthermore, the easily accessible sources of fossil fuels are getting exhausted. So, over time, we expect the costs of fossil fuels to rise and the costs of renewables to fall. As the costs of emission reduction are driven by the difference in costs between fossil and renewable energy, abatement costs should fall over time.

Third, emission reduction costs in the future are discounted. The discount rate makes that costs incurred in the future are less important than costs incurred today. Postponing emission reduction reduces the net present value of the costs.

Fourth, emissions are degraded in the atmosphere. Climate policy targets typically refer to the long term, say the year 2100. Emissions in 2090 are more important to concentrations in 2100 than emissions in 2020. Put differently, later emission reduction is more effective than earlier emission reduction. Atmospheric degradation thus functions as a discount rate, so that it is better to reduce emissions later.

Figure 9.5 complements Figure 9.4. It shows results for the same set of models and the same set of scenarios, but now for the marginal abatement costs. This is best thought of as the carbon tax imposed on all greenhouse gas emissions from all economic activities in all countries. Per policy scenario, the models again disagree by an order of magnitude or more. The initial carbon tax required for meeting the least stringent target is modest, but this escalates with increased stringency.

The most stringent target (2.6 Wm^{-2}, roughly equivalent to keeping global warming at 2.0°C above pre-industrial, as agreed in Paris 2015) requires a $14/$tCO_2$ carbon tax in 2020 (according to the average model). This is similar to the current carbon price in the EU and California, but the models assume that this carbon price applies to all greenhouse gas emissions from all sectors and in all countries. The carbon tax rises to $90/$tCO_2$ in 2030 and to $2,057/$tCO_2$ in 2100. The most pessimistic model has a global carbon tax of $41/$tCO_2$ in 2020, rising to $361/$tCO_2$ in 2030 and $8,321/$tCO_2$ in 2100.

Clarke et al. (2009) found that the 2°C target is infeasible for physical, technical, economic or political reasons, a result echoed by the Fourth Assessment Report (AR4) of the Intergovernmental Panel on Climate Change (IPCC) (Barker et al., 2007). Tavoni and Tol (2010) note that the aggregate results in the IPCC suffer from sample selection bias: only the models in which emission reduction is cheap, report costs for the most stringent policy targets. As the more

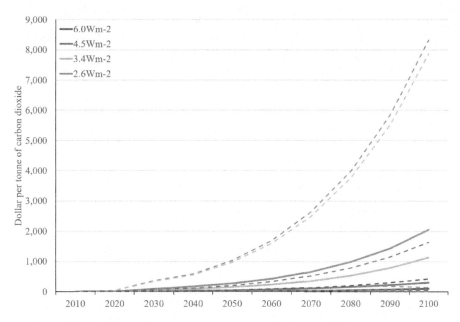

Figure 9.5 Carbon tax for the model average (solid line) and the most optimistic/pessimistic model (dashed lines) for four alternative atmospheric stabilization targets

stringent targets are more relevant for policy, there is attrition bias too. Some models were used in both AR4 and AR5 (Clarke et al., 2014). In AR4, these models reported on average a carbon tax of $13.83/tCO$_2$ needed in the near term to meet a 550 ppm CO$_2$eq target by 2100, with a standard error of 1.70. The models that were used in AR4 but not in AR5 reported an average carbon tax of $27.57/tCO$_2$ with a standard error of 2.24. The difference in means is close to significant ($p = 0.06$).

There is a political demand for the analysis of ambitious climate targets, initially focused on the 2.0°C target and more recently 1.5°C. Modelers have met that demand by expanding options for negative emissions. This includes negative carbon energy, biomass with carbon capture and storage (Wise et al., 2009); and direct air capture, artificial photosynthesis or some other chemical process to remove carbon dioxide from the atmosphere (House et al., 2011).

Figure 9.6 shows just how much emissions will need to be cut in order to meet the more ambitious targets. In one scenario, emissions will peak in 2050, in another in 2030. In the two remaining scenarios, emissions will peak in 2020. In the same two scenarios, emissions will be net negative by 2100. In 2010, carbon dioxide emissions were about 36 billion tonnes a year. Averaged across models, for the most ambitious policy target, in 2100, carbon dioxide emissions are a *negative* 10 billion tonnes per year.

As they grow, energy crops remove carbon dioxide from the atmosphere. This requires and deserves a carbon subsidy. If we take the above 10 GtCO$_2$ and a carbon tax of $2,000/tCO$_2$, the net carbon subsidy will thus be 20 trillion dollars per year – almost 4% of GDP. See Figure 9.7. This is the central estimate. In the worst case, this is almost 17%. Carbon subsidies may thus pose a very substantial burden on either the public finances or taxpayers. The central estimate is comparable to current spending on defense in the United States, the worst case to health care. Besides the cost, incidence is problematic too. Energy crops will be grown in monoculture on

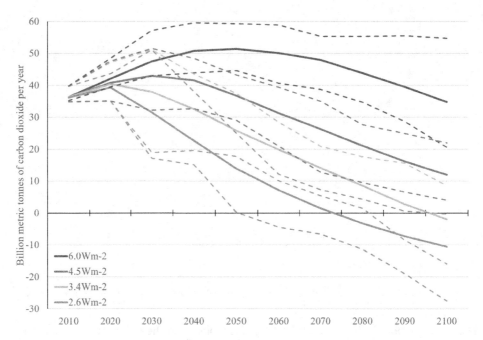

Figure 9.6 Carbon dioxide emission trajectories to stabilize the climate for the model average (solid line) and the most optimistic/pessimistic model (dashed lines) at four alternative levels of radiative forcing

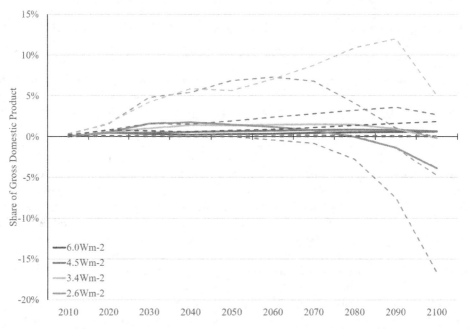

Figure 9.7 Carbon tax revenue for the model average (solid line) and the most optimistic/ pessimistic model (dashed lines) for four alternative atmospheric stabilization targets

large farms, probably corporate farms, and certainly heavily mechanized farms. Processing will similarly be done by large firms. It is hard to imagine an electoral strategy that would sustain a stream of large subsidies to agri-energy multinationals, particularly if negative carbon energy is successful and the threat of climate change recedes.

3.3 Double dividends

There are claims that the costs of emission reduction are negative – that is, that it would be possible to save emissions and save money at the same time. Some of the claims are the result of bad accounting. Two common mistakes are the following. First, people confuse the technological change that is part of the no-policy scenario with the accelerated technological change in the policy scenario. The no-policy scenario indeed contains a large number of actions that are both commercially viable and reduce emissions. Energy efficiency improves over time, also in the absence of climate policy. Because these investments are commercially viable, they do not need policy support – and it is thus wrong to attribute them to climate policy.

Another common mistake is to underestimate the costs of investment – this is often referred to as the *energy paradox* (Jaffe and Stavins, 1994; Metcalf and Hassett, 1999; van Soest and Bulte, 2001; Greene, 2011; Allcott and Wozny, 2014). Most greenhouse gas emission reduction requires an upfront investment (e.g. wall insulation, solar panel) in return for lower energy costs later. The discount rate is thus crucial in determining whether this investment is worthwhile. Some analysts assume that households and companies can borrow money at the same rate of interest as the government can. In fact, private rates of interest tend to be higher than public ones. That makes investment less attractive. As another example, well-established technologies have acquired a reputation and a dense network of mechanics for installation, maintenance and repair. New technologies lack those – a cost that is easily overlooked.

That said, there may be genuine reasons why the costs of emission abatement may be different than suggested above – perhaps smaller or even negative. The models in these tables are either optimization models or equilibrium models. A market equilibrium is a Pareto optimum. If the no policy scenario is an optimum, any policy intervention bears a cost.

In reality, however, the no-climate-policy case is characterized by many market imperfections and policy distortions. Climate policy may overcome some of these, and this would reduce its costs.

A carbon tax is one way to implement climate policy. A carbon tax raises energy prices, the *carbon tax effect*. Like any tax, a carbon tax is distortionary. In an undistorted market, rational actors find a Pareto optimum. A tax changes the choices people make, and leads that market to an equilibrium with lower welfare. The welfare loss is a measure for the degree of distortion of the tax.

However, a carbon tax brings revenue too, and that revenue could be used to reduce other, more distortionary taxes (Bovenberg and van der Ploeg, 1994; Goulder, 1995; Bovenberg and Goulder, 1996; Bovenberg, 1999; Parry and Bento, 2000). Taxes are distortionary because they distort behavior, moving people and companies away from the Pareto optimum, making them do things they would rather not. Taxes are more distortionary if they are higher, if price elasticities are higher (because behavior is more responsive), and if the tax base is narrower (as fewer people are affected, by definition, then, for the same revenue, the behavior of those people is further distorted). A carbon tax starts from a low level, price elasticities are low, and a carbon tax has a broad base. It is therefore not particularly distortionary (even though it is specifically designed to change behavior). If the carbon tax revenue is used to reduce another tax, there may well be a benefit – and that benefit may more than offset the initial cost of abatement. This is known as the *revenue-recycling effect*.

Let us assume that the revenue of the carbon tax is used to reduce the labor tax. A labor tax drives a wedge between the marginal productivity of the worker (the willingness to pay of the employer for the employee's efforts) and the marginal value of leisure (the willingness to accept compensation for the employee for giving up leisure). A labor tax thus reduces welfare and employment. Reducing the labor tax using the revenues of the carbon tax then increases welfare and employment.

Energy is a necessary good, so carbon taxes tend to be regressive, hurting the poor more than the rich. A reduction in labor taxes only helps the poor who are (potentially) in the labor market and who earn more than the personal exemption. A reduction in value-added tax disproportionally benefits all on the lower end of the income distribution. There may be a triple dividend: lower emissions, faster economic growth, and less inequality (Mayeres and Proost, 2001; van Heerden et al., 2006).

There is a third effect, however: the *tax-interaction effect*. A carbon tax increases the price of energy. As energy use is ubiquitous, all other prices increase too. The real wage falls – that is, the reward for labor falls. In other words, the revenue-recycling effect implies a smaller wedge between marginal productivity and marginal leisure but the tax-interaction effect leads to a large wedge. The carbon tax, through its effect on prices, increases the distortionarity of the labor tax. There are theoretical models in which the tax-interaction effect is necessarily larger, in absolute terms, than the revenue-recycling effect.

Applied models show mixed evidence (Bosquet, 2000). Results depend on the starting point. In Europe, labor taxes tend to be high and are thus a prime target for a beneficial reduction. In the United States, tax reform that stimulates savings and investment is more desirable. Results also depend on assumptions about market structure and elasticities. The revenue of a carbon tax may be used to reduce other taxes and this would bring benefits that at least partially offset the costs of emission reduction. If the tax reform is well-tailored to the specific circumstances of the fiscal system, then that benefit may be substantial. It is not the case that any use of the revenue is beneficial: it may be used to increase handouts to friends and allies of the government. It is also not the case that any tax reform is equally beneficial. The benefits that exist in theory are not necessarily realized in practice.

3.4 Suboptimal regulation

While there is a large literature on the double dividend, discussing whether regulatory and fiscal imperfections could be explored to reduce the costs of emission abatement, less attention has been paid to how imperfect climate policy might increase said costs.

Under ideal conditions, first-best regulation is straightforward: the costs of emission reduction should be equated, at the margin, for all sources of emissions (Baumol and Oates, 1971). Governments routinely violate this principle, with different implicit and even explicit carbon prices for different sectors and for differently sized companies within sectors. Although climate change is a single externality, emitters are often subject to multiple regulations on their greenhouse gas emissions (Boehringer et al., 2008; Boehringer and Rosendahl, 2010). Regulations are often aimed at a poor proxy for emissions rather than at emissions directly (Proost and Van Dender, 2001), and instrument choice may be suboptimal (Webster et al., 2010).

Conditions are not ideal. Optimal policy deviates from the principle of equal marginal costs to accommodate for market power (Baumol and Bradford, 1970), for multiple externalities (Rueb-belke, 2003; Parry and Small, 2005), and for prior tax distortions (Babiker et al., 2003). Such deviations are subtle and specific, and rarely observed in actual policy design.

All this makes that climate policy is far more expensive than what is assumed in models (Boehringer et al., 2009; Fowlie et al., 2018).

4 Climate policy

Greenhouse gas emissions can be reduced in a number of ways. More efficient energy use and a switch to alternative energy sources are the two main options. This is best stimulated by a carbon price. Incentive-based policy instruments are better suited for reducing emissions from diffuse and heterogeneous sources than rule-based instruments (Baumol and Oates, 1971). Taxes are more appropriate for stock pollutants than tradable permits (Weitzman, 1974; Pizer, 1999). A carbon tax, and only a carbon tax (Tinbergen, 1952) is therefore the cheapest way to reduce greenhouse gas emissions.

Net present abatement costs are lowest if all emissions from all sectors and all countries are taxed equally and if the carbon tax rises with roughly the interest rate (Lemoine and Rudik, 2017). Higher carbon taxes would lead to deeper emission cuts. Only a modest carbon tax is needed to keep atmospheric concentrations below a high target but the required tax rapidly increases with the stringency of the target.

4.1 The structure of the climate debate

The solution to climate change is simple: a carbon tax. I argue elsewhere that the optimal carbon tax is relatively small. A casual observer of climate policy and the media would have a different impression. Seven things stand in the way of simple solution.

First, there is a demand for an explanation of the world in terms of sin and a final reckoning. The story of climate change is often a religious one (Hulme, 2008; Bruckner, 2014). Emissions (sin) lead to climate change (eternal doom); we must reduce our emissions (atone for our sins). This sentiment is widespread. It is often referred to as millenarianism (Landes, 2011). It has led to an environmental movement (a priesthood) that thrives on preaching climate alarmism, often separated from its factual basis. In order to maximize their membership and income, environmental non-governmental organizations (NGOs) meet the demand for scaremongering and moral superiority (Bell, 2015), but the alt-green do little to win over the majority.

Second, climate policy is a godsend for politicians. Climate change is a problem that spans centuries. Substantial emission reduction requires decades and global cooperation. A politician can thus make grand promises about saving the world while shifting the burden of actually doing something (and so hurting constituents) to her successor and blaming some foreigner for current inaction. Climate change also provides an opportunity for politicians to distract attention (Kerry, 2009; Lagarde, 2013, 2015).

Third, climate policy allows bureaucrats to create new bureaucracies (Niskanen, 1971). Climate policy has been a political priority for about two decades. Emissions have hardly budged, but a vast number of civil servants and larger numbers of consultants and do-gooders have occupied themselves with creating a bureaucratic fiction that something is happening.

Fourth, besides expanded bureaucracies, climate policy can be used to create rents in the form of subsidies, grandfathered emission permits, mandated markets, and tax breaks. Climate policy thus serves the interests of rent seekers, as well as the interests of policy makers who use rent creation to reward allies (Pearce, 2006; Leahy and Tol, 2012; Brandt and Svendsen, 2014).

Fifth, climate policy requires government intervention at the global scale (Biermann et al., 2012). This antagonizes many, and feeds the fears of right-wing conspiracy theorists. This had led to a movement that attacks climate policy at any opportunity, and extends those attacks to the climate science that underpins that policy, and the scientists who conduct the research (Fisher et al., 2013). Alarmists have retaliated in kind, exaggerating wildly (Stern et al., 2007; Steffen et al., 2018) and playing nasty (Hauschild, 2011; Gleick, 2012). Political orientation is now a key predictor of attitudes towards climate science (McCright and Dunlap, 2011; Kahan, 2013, 2015; Krange et al., 2018). The result is polarization, which hampers reasoned discussion on climate policy (Hulme, 2009; Hoffman, 2011) and emission reduction (Steg, 2018).

Sixth, greenhouse gas emission reduction is a global public good (Barrett, 1990). The costs of emission abatement are borne by the country that reduces the emissions. The benefits of emission reduction are shared by all of humankind. It is thus individually rational to do very little, and hope that others will do a lot. As every country reasons the same way, nothing much happens. Providing public goods is difficult without a government (Bradford, 2008; Battaglini and Harstad, 2015). Any solution to the climate problem should start with acknowledging that we live in a world of many countries, the majority of which jealously guards their sovereignty. That means that climate policy should serve a domestic constituency. Opinion polls in democratic countries have consistently shown over a period of 25 years that a majority is in favor of greenhouse gas emission reduction, even if that means more expensive energy.

Unilateral climate policy is expensive, however. If a country raises its price of energy, but its trading partners do not, business will shift abroad. A country will be more ambitious if it is confident that its neighbors will adopt roughly the same climate policy. The United Nations Framework Convention on Climate Change (UNFCCC), reinforced in its Paris Agreement, foresees an annual meeting at which countries can indeed pledge their near-term abatement plans and review other countries progress against previous pledges. This is facilitated by internationally agreed standards on emissions monitoring and reporting. As the actions of trading partners matter most, regional trade organizations, such as the EU, NAFTA, MERCOSUR, and ASEAN, should play a bigger role in this process. The costs of emission reduction vary greatly. It therefore makes sense if countries were allowed to reduce emissions by investing in abatement in other countries. The Kyoto Protocol of the UNFCCC establishes exactly this. Unlike the emissions targets of the Kyoto Protocol, its flexibility mechanisms did not expire.

Seventh, global climate policy has been used as a tactical argument by those who desire a world government for other reasons. Because climate change is such a prominent issue, champions of other worthy causes too have joined the bandwagon. The ultimate goal of climate policy – decarbonization of the economy – is thus obscured, and the climate debate further complicated.

4.2 Misconceptions about climate policy

Employment

It is sometimes argued that switching to renewable energy would create jobs. Obviously, there is job displacement as renewables expand at the expense of fossil fuels. As the former are more labor-intensive than the latter, there would be net job creation, *all else equal*. Labor is expensive, so this is one of the reasons why renewables are more expensive than fossil fuels. Throughout history, productivity has increased, and wages with it, as capital and energy were used to complement labor. Needing more workers for the same output of energy – the very definition of an increase in the labor-intensity of energy supply – is thus a sign of *regress* rather than *progress*. Baumol's cost disease – a rise in wages without a concomitant rise in labor productivity (Baumol and Bowen, 1966) – affects energy.

But *all else is not equal.* Only a small fraction of the labor force is employed in the energy sector. Changes in the labor intensity of the energy sector therefore cannot have a substantial impact on overall employment. However, energy is used throughout the economy. More expensive energy has only a small, negative effect on employment in sectors other than energy, but this small proportional effect can, in absolute terms, outweigh the impact in the energy sector as it applies to so many more workers (Patuelli et al., 2005), unless the revenue of a carbon tax or permit auctions is used to stimulate the economy or reduce the cost of labor (Bovenberg and Goulder, 1996).

Grand plans

Some have called for a Manhattan program, an Apollo program, or a Marshall program for climate change (Yang and Oppenheimer, 2007; Layard et al., 2015; Courtney, 2016). The Manhattan program developed a new weapon of mass destruction. The Apollo program restored technological supremacy over an adversary. The Marshall program helped recover from devastation.

The misnomers aside, calls for a major public investment program are misguided. This is the wrong approach. The government should levy a carbon tax to incentivize private investment, and improve regulations to attract investment in natural monopolies such as transport networks and power grids. Greenhouse gas emission reduction does not require an expansion of the public sector.

Full decarbonization of the economy will take a long time. The costs of doing so depend on technological change. If the costs of renewable energy will continue to fall rapidly, relative to the costs of fossil fuels, then emission reduction policies will be cheap – and may even become redundant as renewables outcompete fossil fuels on merit. This is generally accepted. But there is some confusion about the nature of this technological progress, and the role of public policy. Technological progress comes in three stages: invention (a new blueprint), innovation (taking the blueprint to its first sell), and diffusion (taking a product from its first sell to market saturation). The public sector is best placed to provide invention and the precompetitive parts of innovation, but the private sector is better at competitive innovation and diffusion, with the government retreating to guaranteeing property rights and correcting externalities (Golosov et al., 2014). The bulk of the desired decarbonization of the economy can be done with proven technologies (Pacala and Socolow, 2004), so the government should take a back seat in directly stimulating technological progress (Newell et al., 1999).

Divestment

Some have called for divestment from fossil energy, with some success.[10] The intent is clear: fossil fuels will go out of business if starved of capital. Investors are free to choose their portfolio, of course, and while this approach should be commended for its bottom-up, grassroots spirit, it is unlikely to work.

Suppose that there are two types of investors – green and brown – where the former think that fossil fuels are bad and the latter do not care. If total green capital is relatively small, divestment would have a negligible effect on the market. Green investors, however, have denied themselves a profitable investment and an opportunity to diversify their investment portfolio. Green investors have thus made themselves worse off. They have also lost their vote as activist shareholders.

If total green capital is large enough to suppress the price of fossil capital when divesting, they create an opportunity for brown investors to purchase these assets at a discount as the price falls below the net present value of expected returns. Divestment makes green investors worse off and enriches brown investors.

However, in this case, divestment raises the cost of fossil capital, so that investment falls and emissions are reduced. These effects are probably minor. The gas, oil and coal industry are dominated by state-owned or state-controlled firms. The divestment campaign has had some effect in the Western Europe and North America, with some divestment from publicly owned companies. This does not really affect total investment.

The divestment movement is closely aligned with the "Keep It in the Ground" campaign.[11] It is clear from Section 2.2 that climate policy implies keeping fossil fuel reserves in the ground. What matters most is stopping the development of new coal mines, and the exploitation of unconventional oil and gas. The campaign, however, is concentrated in western countries and focuses on conventional oil and gas. The reserves and resources to be left in the ground are concentrated in other parts of the world (Cust et al., 2017; Manley et al.).

5   Conclusion

Over the last 45 years, emissions of carbon dioxide have grown, but considerably less fast than the economy. This is because of improvements in energy efficiency, rather than switching to less carbon-intensive fuels. Climate policy played a minor role. Future projections of emissions are optimistic about economic growth and energy efficiency. The higher emission scenarios assume an increase in coal exploitation that is at Trumpian odds with current trends in relative fuel prices and resource assessments.

The costs of climate policy are minimal if targets are moderate and implementation is (close to) first-best. If carbon tax revenue is used in fiscal policy reform, the costs may even be benefits. However, costs rapidly escalate for suboptimal policies and for the stringent targets favored by the Paris Agreement. Negative emissions would require subsidies, perhaps very large ones.

Actual climate policy and the debate about climate policy is beset by problems. Key players benefit from the rents created by inefficient policies, from creating confusion, and from mixing climate with other matters – and greenhouse gas emission reduction is a global public good that is hard to provide in the best of circumstances.

In sum, climate policy is likely to remain needlessly expensive and not very effective. Climate change will be curtailed by market forces that favor low-carbon gas and zero carbon renewables.

Future research in economics should focus on three things. For too long, economists working in this field have focused on an ideal future. Much greater attention should be paid to the impact of past efforts to reduce greenhouse gas emissions, the costs of these policies, and their effectiveness. This would automatically shift attention from the first-best to the crummy third-best. It would also highlight how climate policy has been used to create and seek rents. The lessons from actual climate policy should be used to project future policy.

The climate problem is much bigger than economics. The solution to climate change lies in innovation and diffusion of carbon-neutral energy. At the boundaries of our discipline, we should seek to better understand which technologies are likely to gain substantial market share, and what governments can do to steer this into the desirable direction.

Notes

1 I do not discuss the impact of climate change on energy use. See Auffhammer and Mansur (2014) for an excellent review.
2 Data from the World Bank.
3 See EPA.
4 This should be taken with a grain of salt. Experts also reckon that 30% of food is wasted, 30% of mobile data, and 30% of health spending.

5 If the landlord covers the energy bill, energy use increases (Levinson and Niemann, 2004).

6 See EIA.

7 See EuroStat.

8 A source of electricity is at grid parity if it can compete with other electricity supplies without government support.

9 The results are from the SSP database. These results are an update of a subsample of the results shown in Clarke et al. (2014). The older, larger sample shows an even greater variation of results.

10 See 350.org

11 See the Guardian: https://www.theguardian.com/environment/series/keep-it-in-the-ground

References

Aichele, R. and G. Felbermayr. Kyoto and the carbon footprint of nations. *Journal of Environmental Economics and Management*, 63(3):336–354, 2012. ISSN 0095-0696. https://doi.org/10.1016/j.jeem. 2011.10.005. URL www.sciencedirect.com/science/article/pii/S0095069611001422.

Aichele, R. and G. Felbermayr. The effect of the Kyoto protocol on carbon emissions. *Journal of Policy Analysis and Management*, 32(4):731–757, 2013. doi: 10.1002/pam.21720.

Allam, R., J. Fetvedt, B. Forrest, and D. Freed. The oxy-fuel, supercritical co2 allam cycle: New cycle developments to produce even lower-cost electricity from fossil fuels without atmospheric emissions. *ASME Turbo Expo 2014* 3B, 2014. doi: 10.1115/GT2014-26952.

Allcott, H. Social norms and energy conservation. *Journal of Public Economics*, 95(9–10):1082–1095, 2011. doi: 10.1016/j.jpubeco.2011.03.003.

Allcott, H. and N. Wozny. Gasoline prices, fuel economy, and the energy paradox. *Review of Economics and Statistics*, 96(5):779–795, 2014. doi: 10.1162/REST_a_00419.

Auffhammer, M. and E. T. Mansur. Measuring climatic impacts on energy consumption: A review of the empirical literature. *Energy Economics*, 46:522–530, 2014. ISSN 0140-9883. https://doi.org/10.1016/j. eneco.2014.04.017. URL www.sciencedirect.com/science/article/pii/S0140988314001017.

Babiker, M., G. Metcalf, and J. Reilly. Tax distortions and global climate policy. *Journal of Environmental Economics and Management*, 46(2):269–287, 2003. doi: 10.1016/S0095-0696(02)00039-6.

Barker, T., I. Bashmakov, A. Alharthi, M. Amann, L. Cifuentes, J. Drexhage, M. Duan, O. Edenhofer, B. P. Flannery, M. J. Grubb, M. Hoogwijk, F. I. Ibitoye, C. J. Jepma, W. A. Pizer, and K. Yamaji. *Mitigation from a Cross-Sectoral Perspective*, pages 619–690. Cambridge University Press, Cambridge, 2007.

Barrett, S. The problem of global environmental protection. *Oxford Review of Economic Policy*, 6(1):68–79, 1990.

Bashmakov, I. *Russia: Energy Related Greenhouse Gas Emissions: Present and Future*, pages 379–401. IIASA, Laxenburg, 1994. October 13–15.

Battaglini, M. and B. Harstad. Participation and duration of environmental agreements. *Journal of Political Economy*, 124(1):160–204, 2015. ISSN 0022-3808. 10.1086/684478. URL http://dx.doi. org/10.1086/684478.

Baumol, W. and W. Bowen. *Performing Arts, the Economic Dilemma: A Study of Problems Common to Theater, Opera, Music, and Dance*. Twentieth Century Fund, New York, 1966.

Baumol, W. J. and D. Bradford. Optimal departures from marginal cost pricing. *American Economic Review*, 60(3):265–83, 1970.

Baumol, W. J. and W. E. Oates. The use of standards and prices for the protection of the environment. *Scandinavian Journal of Economics*, 73(1):42–54, 1971.

Bel, G. and S. Joseph. Emission abatement: Untangling the impacts of the EU ETS and the economic crisis. *Energy Economics*, 49:531–539, 2015. ISSN 0140-9883. http://dx.doi.org/10.1016/j.eneco. 2015.03.014.

Bell, L. *Scared Witless: Prophets and Profits of Climate Doom*. Stairway Press, Las Vegas, 2015.

Biermann, F., K. Abbott, S. Andresen, K. Baeckstrand, S. Bernstein, M. M. Betsill, H. Bulkeley, B. Cashore, J. Clapp, C. Folke, A. Gupta, J. Gupta, P. M. Haas, A. Jordan, N. Kanie, T. Kluvankova-Oravska, L. Lebel, D. Liverman, J. Meadowcroft, R. B. Mitchell, P. Newell, S. Oberthr, L. Olsson, P. Pattberg, R. Sanchez-Rodriguez, H. Schroeder, A. Underdal, S. C. Vieira, C. Vogel, O. R. Young, A. Brock, and R. Zondervan. Navigating the Anthropocene: Improving earth system governance. *Science*, 335(6074):1306–1307, 2012.

Boehringer, C., H. Koschel, and U. Moslener. Efficiency losses from overlapping regulation of EU carbon emissions. *Journal of Regulatory Economics*, 33(3):299–317, 2008. doi: 10.1007/s11149-007-9054-8.

Boehringer, C. and K. Rosendahl. Green promotes the dirtiest: On the interaction between black and green quotas in energy markets. *Journal of Regulatory Economics*, 37(3):316–325, 2010. doi: 10.1007/s11149-010-9116-1.

Boehringer, C., T. Rutherford, and R. Tol. The EU 20/20/2020 targets: An overview of the emf22 assessment. *Energy Economics*, 31(Suppl. 2):S268–S273, 2009. doi: 10.1016/j.eneco.2009.10.010.

Bongaarts, J. and B. C. O'Neill. Global warming policy: Is population left out in the cold? *Science*, 361(6403):650–652, 2018. ISSN 0036–8075. doi: 10.1126/science.aat8680. URL http://science.sciencemag.org/content/361/6403/650.

Bosquet, B. Environmental tax reform: Does it work? a survey of the empirical evidence. *Ecological Economics*, 34(1):19–32, 2000. doi: 10.1016/S0921-8009(00)00173-7.

Bovenberg, A. Green tax reforms and the double dividend: An updated reader's guide. *International Tax and Public Finance*, 6(3):421–443, 1999. doi: 10.1023/A:1008715920337.

Bovenberg, A. L. and L. H. Goulder. Optimal environmental taxation in the presence of other taxes: General equilibrium analyses. *American Economic Review*, 86(4):985–1000, 1996.

Bovenberg, A. and F. van der Ploeg. Environmental policy, public finance and the labour market in a second-best world. *Journal of Public Economics*, 55(3):349–390, 1994. doi: 10.1016/0047-2727(93)01398-T.

Bradford, D. F. *Improving on Kyoto: Greenhouse Gas Control as the Purchase of a Global Public Good*, pages 13–36. MIT Press, Cambridge, 2008.

Brandt, U. and G. Svendsen. A blind eye to industry-level corruption? the risk of favouring domestic industries in the EU ETS. *Energy and Environment*, 25(2):263–280, 2014.

Bruckner, P. *The Fanaticism of the Apocalypse: Save the Earth, Punish Human Beings*. Polity Press, Cambridge, 2014.

Buechs, M. and S. Schnepf. Who emits most? Associations between socio-economic factors and UK households' home energy, transport, indirect and total co2 emissions. *Ecological Economics*, 90:114–123, 2013. doi: 10.1016/j.ecolecon.2013.03.007.

Ciaian, P. and D. Kancs. Interdependencies in the energy-bioenergy-food price systems: A cointegration analysis. *Resource and Energy Economics*, 33(1):326–348, 2011. doi: 10.1016/j.reseneeco.2010.07.004.

Clarke, L. E., J. Edmonds, V. Krey, R. Richels, S. Rose, and M. Tavoni. International climate policy architectures: Overview of the emf 22 international scenarios. *Energy Economics*, 31(S2):S64–S81, 2009. URL www.sciencedirect.com/science/article/B6V7G-4XHVH34-2/2/67f06e207a515adba42f7455a99f648e.

Clarke, L. E., K. Jiang, K. Akimoto, M. H. Babiker, G. J. Blanford, K. A. Fisher-Vanden, J. C. Hourcade, V. Krey, E. Kriegler, A. Loeschel, D. W. McCollum, S. Paltsev, S. Rose, P. R. Shukla, M. Tavoni, D. van Vuuren, and B. Van Der Zwaan. *Assessing Transformation Pathways*. Cambridge University Press, Cambridge, 2014.

Clarke, L. E., J. P. Weyant, and J. Edmonds. On the sources of technological change: What do the models assume. *Energy Economics*, 30(2):409–424, 2008. URL www.sciencedirect.com/science/article/B6V7G-4KHC38M-1/2/5aa43ec2fcfe3adeb997f61e896aea43.

Courtney, C. Marshall-style plan needed on carbon, 2016. URL www.concordmonitor.com/Successful-CO2-phase-out-requires-Marshall-style-plan-6983021.

Cust, J., D. Manley, and G. Cecchinato. Unburnable wealth of nations. *Finance and Development* (March):46–49, 2017.

Dalton, M., B. O'Neill, A. Prskawetz, L. Jiang, and J. Pitkin. Population aging and future carbon emissions in the united states. *Energy Economics*, 30(2):642–675, 2008. doi: 10.1016/j.eneco.2006.07.002.

Davison, J. Performance and costs of power plants with capture and storage of co_2. *Energy*, 32(7):1163–1176, 2007. doi: 10.1016/j.energy.2006.07.039.

Enamala, M., S. Enamala, M. Chavali, J. Donepudi, R. Yadavalli, B. Kolapalli, T. Aradhyula, J. Velpuri, and C. Kuppam. Production of biofuels from microalgae: A review on cultivation, harvesting, lipid extraction, and numerous applications of microalgae. *Renewable and Sustainable Energy Reviews*, 94:49–68, 2018. doi: 10.1016/j.rser.2018.05.012.

Fisher, D. R., J. Waggle, and P. Leifeld. Where does political polarization come from? locating polarization within the U.S. climate change debate. *American Behavioral Scientist*, 57(1):70–92, 2013.

Fouquet, R. *Heat, Power and Light: Revolutions in Energy Services*. Edward Elgar, Cheltenham, 2008.

Fowlie, M., M. Greenstone, and C. Wolfram. Do energy efficiency investments deliver? evidence from the weatherization assistance program. *The Quarterly Journal of Economics*, 133(3):1597–1644, 2018. doi: 10.1093/qje/qjy005. URL http://dx.doi.org/10.1093/qje/qjy005.

Fuerst, F. and P. McAllister. The impact of energy performance certificates on the rental and capital values of commercial property assets. *Energy Policy*, 39(10):6608–6614, 2011. doi: 10.1016/j.enpol.2011.08.005.

Galor, O. and D. N. Weil. From Malthusian stagnation to modern growth. *American Economic Review*, 89(2):150–154, 1999.

Gebreegziabher, Z., A. Mekonnen, M. Kassie, and G. Khlin. Urban energy transition and technology adoption: The case of Tigrai, northern Ethiopia. *Energy Economics*, 34(2):410–418, 2012. doi: 10.1016/j.eneco.2011.07.017.

Gleick, P. H. The origin of the heartland documents, 20 February 2012. URL www.huffingtonpost.com/peter-h-gleick/heartland-institute-documents_b_1289669.html.

Golosov, M., J. Hassler, P. Krusell, and A. Tsyvinski. Optimal taxes on fossil fuel in general equilibrium. *Econometrica*, 82(1):41–88, 2014. doi: 10.3982/ECTA10217. URL https://onlinelibrary.wiley.com/doi/abs/10.3982/ECTA10217.

Goulder, L. H. Environmental taxation and the double dividend: A reader's guide. *International Tax and Public Finance*, 2(2):157–183, 1995. doi: 10.1007/BF00877495.

Goulder, L. H. and K. Mathai. Optimal co 2 abatement in the presence of induced technological change. *Journal of Environmental Economics and Management*, 39:1–38, 2000.

Goulder, L. H. and S. H. Schneider. Induced technological change and the attractiveness of co 2 abatement policies. *Resource and Energy Economics*, 21:211–253, 1999.

Greene, D. Uncertainty, loss aversion, and markets for energy efficiency. *Energy Economics*, 33(4):608–616, 2011. doi: 10.1016/j.eneco.2010.08.009.

Greening, L., D. Greene, and C. Difiglio. Energy efficiency and consumption: The rebound effect: A survey. *Energy Policy*, 28(6–7):389–401, 2000. doi: 10.1016/S0301-4215(00)00021-5.

Guo, M., W. Song, and J. Buhain. Bioenergy and biofuels: History, status, and perspective. *Renewable and Sustainable Energy Reviews*, 42:712–725, 2015. doi: 10.1016/j.rser.2014.10.013.

Hauschild, J. Verurteilter forscher: Eklat um klimaberater der bundesregierung. *Spiegel*, 1 December 2011.

Herzer, D., H. Strulik, and S. Vollmer. The long-run determinants of fertility: One century of demographic change 1900–1999. *Journal of Economic Growth*, 17(4):357–385, 2012. doi: 10.1007/s10887-012-9085-6.

Hoekstra, R. and J. Van Den Bergh. Structural decomposition analysis of physical flows in the economy. *Environmental and Resource Economics*, 23(3):357–378, 2002. doi: 10.1023/A:1021234216845.

Hoffman, A. J. Talking past each other? Cultural framing of skeptical and convinced logics in the climate change debate. *Organization and Environment*, 24(1):3–33, 2011.

House, K., A. Baclig, M. Ranjan, E. Van Nierop, J. Wilcox, and H. Herzog. Economic and energetic analysis of capturing CO_2 from ambient air. *Proceedings of the National Academy of Sciences of the United States of America*, 108(51):20428–20433, 2011. doi: 10.1073/pnas.1012253108.

Hulme, M. The conquering of climate: Discourses of fear and their dissolution. *Geographical Journal*, 174(1):5–16, 2008.

Hulme, M. *Why We Disagree about Climate Change: Understanding Controversy, Inaction and Opportunity*. Cambridge University Press, Cambridge, 2009.

Im, J., Y. Seo, K. Cetin, and J. Singh. Energy efficiency in U.S. residential rental housing: Adoption rates and impact on rent. *Applied Energy*, 205:1021–1033, 2017. doi: 10.1016/j.apenergy.2017.08.047.

IRENA. *Renewable Power Generation Costs in 2017*. International Renewable Energy Agency, Abu Dhabi, 2018.

Jaffe, A. and R. Stavins. The energy paradox and the diffusion of conservation technology. *Resource and Energy Economics*, 16(2):91–122, 1994. doi: 10.1016/0928-7655(94)90001-9.

Jevons, W. S. *The Coal Question*. McMillan, London, 1865.

Kahan, D. M. Ideology, motivated reasoning, and cognitive reflection. *Judgment and Decision Making*, 8(4):407–424, 2013.

Kahan, D. M. Climate-science communication and the measurement problem. *Political Psychology*, 36(S1):1–43, 2015.

Kahn, M. Do greens drive hummers or hybrids? environmental ideology as a determinant of consumer choice. *Journal of Environmental Economics and Management*, 54(2):129–145, 2007. doi: 10.1016/j.jeem.2007.05.001.

Kallis, G. In defence of degrowth. *Ecological Economics*, 70(5):873–880, 2011. doi: 10.1016/j.ecolecon.2010.12.007.

Kaya, Y. *Environment, energy, and economy: Strategies for sustainability*. United Nations University Press, Tokyo, 1997.

Kerry, J. Climate change is our greatest long-term security threat, 2009. URL https://thinkprogress.org/john-kerry-climate-change-is-our-greatest-long-term-security-threat-f9c12e7d098f#.fe9h1xtyc.

Krange, O., B. P. Kaltenborn, and M. Hultman. Cool dudes in Norway: Climate change denial among conservative Norwegian men. *Environmental Sociology*, 5(1):1–11, 2018. doi: 10.1080/23251042.2018.1488516. URL https://doi.org/10.1080/23251042.2018.1488516.

Laffont, J.-J. and D. Martimort. The theory of incentives: The principal-agent model, 2009.

Lagarde, C. Transcript of a press roundtable with imf managing director, 1 August 2013. URL www.imf.org/external/np/tr/2013/tr080113a.htm.

Lagarde, C. Ten myths about climate change policy. *Finance and Investment* (1 December):64–67, 2015.

Landes, R. *Heaven on Earth: The Varieties of the Millennial Experience.* Oxford University Press, Oxford, 2011.

Lans Bovenberg, A. and S. Smulders. Environmental quality and pollution-augmenting technological change in a two-sector endogenous growth model. *Journal of Public Economics*, 57(3):369–391, 1995. doi: 10.1016/0047-2727(95)80002-Q.

Layard, R., G. O'Donnell, N. H. Stern, and A. Turner. The case for a global Apollo programme to limit climate change, 2015. URL http://voxeu.org/article/apollo-programme-conquer-climate-change.

Leahy, E. and R.S.J. Tol. Greener homes: An ex-post estimate of the cost of carbon dioxide emission reduction using administrative micro-data from the republic of Ireland. *Environmental Economics and Policy Studies*, 14(3):219–239, 2012.

Lemoine, D. and I. Rudik. Steering the climate system: Using inertia to lower the cost of policy. *American Economic Review*, 107(10):2947–57, October 2017. doi: 10.1257/aer.20150986. URL www.aeaweb.org/articles?id=10.1257/aer.20150986.

Levinson, A. and S. Niemann. Energy use by apartment tenants when landlords pay for utilities. *Resource and Energy Economics*, 26(1):51–75, 2004. doi: 10.1016/S0928-7655(03)00047-2.

Lotze-Campen, H., M. von Lampe, P. Kyle, S. Fujimori, P. Havlik, H. van Meijl, T. Hasegawa, A. Popp, C. Schmitz, A. Tabeau, H. Valin, D. Willenbockel, and M. Wise. Impacts of increased bioenergy demand on global food markets: An agmip economic model intercomparison. *Agricultural Economics (United Kingdom)*, 45(1):103–116, 2014. doi: 10.1111/agec.12092.

Manley, D., J. Cust, and G. Cecchinato. Stranded nations? The climate policy implications for fossil fuel rich developing countries. Technical report, Oxford Centre for the Analysis of Resource Rich Economies, University of Oxford, Oxford.

Manne, A. S. and R. G. Richels. The impact of learning-by-doing on the timing and costs of co 2 abatement. *Energy Economics*, 26:603–619, 2004.

Mayeres, I. and S. Proost. Marginal tax reform, externalities and income distribution. *Journal of Public Economics*, 79(2):343–363, 2001. doi: 10.1016/S0047-2727(99)00100-0.

McCright, A. M. and R. E. Dunlap. Cool dudes: The denial of climate change among conservative white males in the united states. *Global Environmental Change*, 21(4):1163–1172, 2011.

Metcalf, G. and K. Hassett. Measuring the energy savings from home improvement investments: Evidence from monthly billing data. *Review of Economics and Statistics*, 81(3):516–528, 1999. doi: 10.1162/003465399558274.

Murray, B. C. and P. T. Maniloff. Why have greenhouse emissions in RGGI states declined? An econometric attribution to economic, energy market, and policy factors. *Energy Economics*, 51:581–589, 2015. ISSN 0140-9883. https://doi.org/10.1016/j.eneco.2015.07.013. URL www.sciencedirect.com/science/article/pii/S0140988315002273.

Newell, R. G., A. B. Jaffe, and R. N. Stavins. The induced innovation hypothesis and energy-saving technological change. *Quarterly Journal of Economics*: 941–975, 1999.

Niskanen, W. A. *Bureaucracy and Public Economics.* Edward Elgar, Cheltenham, 1971.

Nordhaus, W. D. *Do Real-Output and Real-Wage Measures Capture Reality? The History of Lighting Suggests Not*, pages 27–70. National Bureau for Economic Research, Chicago, 1996.

Pacala, S. and R. Socolow. Stabilization wedges: Solving the climate problem for the next 50 years with current technologies. *Science*, 305(5686):968–972, 2004.

Parry, I.W.H. and A. Bento. Tax deductions, environmental policy, and the 'double dividend' hypothesis. *Journal of Environmental Economics and Management*, 39(1):67–96, 2000. doi: 10.1006/jeem.1999.1093.

Parry, I.W.H. and K. A. Small. Does Britain or the united states have the right gasoline tax? *American Economic Review*, 95(4):1276–1289, 2005.

Patuelli, R., P. Nijkamp, and E. Pels. Environmental tax reform and the double dividend: A meta-analytical performance assessment. *Ecological Economics*, 55(4):564–583, 2005.

Pearce, D. W. The political economy of an energy tax: The united kingdom's climate change levy. *Energy Economics*, 28:149–158, 2006.

Pizer, W. A. The optimal choice of climate change policy in the presence of uncertainty. *Resource and Energy Economics*, 21:255–287, 1999.

Proost, S. and K. Van Dender. The welfare impacts of alternative policies to address atmospheric pollution in urban road transport. *Regional Science and Urban Economics*, 31(4):383–411, 2001. doi: 10.1016/S0166-0462(00)00079-X.

Reiss, P. and M. White. Household electricity demand, revisited. *Review of Economic Studies*, 72(3):853–883, 2005. doi: 10.1111/0034-6527.00354.

Riahi, K., D. P. van Vuuren, E. Kriegler, J. Edmonds, B. C. ONeill, S. Fujimori, N. Bauer, K. Calvin, R. Dellink, O. Fricko, W. Lutz, A. Popp, J. C. Cuaresma, S. KC, M. Leimbach, L. Jiang, T. Kram, S. Rao, J. Emmerling, K. Ebi, T. Hasegawa, P. Havlik, F. Humpender, L.A.D. Silva, S. Smith, E. Stehfest, V. Bosetti, J. Eom, D. Gernaat, T. Masui, J. Rogelj, J. Strefler, L. Drouet, V. Krey, G. Luderer, M. Harmsen, K. Takahashi, L. Baumstark, J. C. Doelman, M. Kainuma, Z. Klimont, G. Marangoni, H. Lotze-Campen, M. Obersteiner, A. Tabeau, and M. Tavoni. The shared socioeconomic pathways and their energy, land use, and greenhouse gas emissions implications: An overview. *Global Environmental Change*, 42:153–168, 2017. ISSN 0959-3780. https://doi.org/10.1016/j.gloenvcha.2016.05.009. URL www.sciencedirect.com/science/article/pii/S0959378016300681.

Ritchie, J. and H. Dowlatabadi. The 1000 gtc coal question: Are cases of vastly expanded future coal combustion still plausible? *Energy Economics*, 65:16–31, 2017. doi: 10.1016/j.eneco.2017.04.015.

Rubin, E., C. Chen, and A. Rao. Cost and performance of fossil fuel power plants with CO_2 capture and storage. *Energy Policy*, 35(9):4444–4454, 2007. doi: 10.1016/j.enpol.2007.03.009.

Ruebbelke, D. An analysis of differing abatement incentives. *Resource and Energy Economics*, 25(3):269–294, 2003. doi: 10.1016/S0928-7655(03)00032-0.

Sadorsky, P. Do urbanization and industrialization affect energy intensity in developing countries? *Energy Economics*, 37:52–59, 2013. doi: 10.1016/j.eneco.2013.01.009.

Schwarz, P. M. and T. N. Taylor. Cold hands, warm hearth? Climate, net takeback, and household comfort. *Energy Journal*, 16(1):41–54, 1995. doi: 10.5547/ISSN0195-6574-EJ-Vol16-No1-3.

Smulders, S. and M. de Nooij. The impact of the energy conservation on technology and economic growth. *Resource and Energy Economics*, 25(1):59–79, 2003. doi: 10.1016/S0928-7655(02)00017-9.

Sorrell, S., J. Dimitropoulos, and M. Sommerville. Empirical estimates of the direct rebound effect: A review. *Energy Policy*, 37(4):1356–1371, 2009. doi: 10.1016/j.enpol.2008.11.026.

Steffen, W., J. Rockström, K. Richardson, T. M. Lenton, C. Folke, D. Liverman, C. P. Summerhayes, A. D. Barnosky, S. E. Cornell, M. Crucifix, J. F. Donges, I. Fetzer, S. J. Lade, M. Scheffer, R. Winkelmann, and H. J. Schellnhuber. Trajectories of the earth system in the Anthropocene. *Proceedings of the National Academy of Sciences*, 2018. ISSN 0027-8424. doi: 10.1073/pnas.1810141115. URL www.pnas.org/content/early/2018/08/07/1810141115.

Steg, L. Limiting climate change requires research on climate action. *Nature Climate Change*, 2018. ISSN 1758-6798. doi: 10.1038/s41558-018-0269-8. URL https://doi.org/10.1038/s41558-018-0269-8.

Stern, N. H., S. Peters, V. Bakhski, A. Bowen, C. Cameron, S. Catovsky, D. Crane, S. Cruickshank, S. Dietz, N. Edmondson, S.-L. Garbett, L. Hamid, G. Hoffman, D. Ingram, B. Jones, N. Patmore, H. Radcliffe, R. Sathiyarajah, M. Stock, C. Taylor, T. Vernon, H. Wanjie, and D. Zenghelis. *Stern Review: The Economics of Climate Change*. Cambridge University Press, Cambridge, 2007.

Tavoni, M. and R.S.J. Tol. Counting only the hits? The risk of underestimating the costs of stringent climate policy: A letter. *Climatic Change*, 100(3):769–778, 2010.

Tinbergen, J. *On the Theory of Economic Policy*. North Holland, Amsterdam, 1952.

Tol, R.S.J. Ambiguity reduction by objective model selection, with an application to the costs of the EU 2030 climate targets. *Energies*, 7(11):6886–6896, 2014. ISSN 1996-1073. doi: 10.3390/en7116886. URL www.mdpi.com/1996-1073/7/11/6886.

van Heerden, J. H., R. Gerlagh, J. N. Blignaut, M. Horridge, S. Hess, R. Mabugu, and M. Mabugu. Searching for triple dividends in South Africa: Fighting co2 pollution and poverty while promoting growth. *Energy Journal*, 27(2):113–141, 2006.

van Soest, D. and E. Bulte. Does the energy-efficiency paradox exist? Technological progress and uncertainty. *Environmental and Resource Economics*, 18(1):101–112, 2001. doi: 10.1023/A:1011112406964.

van Vuuren, D. P., J. Edmonds, M. Kainuma, K. Riahi, A. Thomson, K. Hibbard, G. C. Hurtt, T. Kram, V. Krey, J. F. Lamarque, T. Masui, M. Meinshausen, N. Nakicenovic, S. J. Smith, and S. K. Rose. The representative concentration pathways: An overview. *Climatic Change*, 109(1):5–31, 2011.

Webster, M., I. Sue Wing, and L. Jakobovits. Second-best instruments for near-term climate policy: Intensity targets vs. the safety valve. *Journal of Environmental Economics and Management*, 59(3):250–259, 2010. doi: 10.1016/j.jeem.2010.01.002.

WEC. *Survey of Energy Resources*. World Energy Council, London, 2010.

WEC. *World Energy Resources: Bioenergy*. World Energy Council, London, 2016a.

WEC. *World Energy Resources: Carbon capture & storage*. World Energy Council, London, 2016b.

WEC. *World Energy Resources: Geothermal*. World Energy Council, London, 2016c.

WEC. *World Energy Resources: Hydropower*. World Energy Council, London, 2016d.

WEC. *World Energy Resources: Marine resources*. World Energy Council, London, 2016e.

WEC. *World Energy Resources: Uranium & Nuclear power*. World Energy Council, London, 2016f.

WEC. *World Energy Resources: Solar*. World Energy Council, London, 2016g.

WEC. *World Energy Resources: Wind*. World Energy Council, London, 2016h.

Weitzman, M. L. Prices vs. quantities. *Review of Economic Studies*, 41(4):477–491, 1974.

Weyant, J. P. Costs of reducing global carbon emissions. *Journal of Economic Perspectives*, 7(4):27–46, 1993.

Widjaya, E., G. Chen, L. Bowtell, and C. Hills. Gasification of non-woody biomass: A literature review. *Renewable and Sustainable Energy Reviews*, 89:184–193, 2018. doi: 10.1016/j.rser.2018.03.023.

Wigley, T.M.L., R. Richels, and J. A. Edmonds. Economic and environmental choices in the stabilization of atmospheric CO_2 concentrations. *Nature*, 379:240, 1996. doi: 10.1038/379240a0. URL http://dx.doi.org/10.1038/379240a0.

Wise, M., K. Calvin, A. Thomson, L. Clarke, B. Bond-Lamberty, R. Sands, S. Smith, A. Janetos, and J. Edmonds. Implications of limiting CO_2 concentrations for land use and energy. *Science*, 324 (5931):1183–1186, 2009. doi: 10.1126/science.1168475.

Yang, C.-J. and M. Oppenheimer. A Manhattan project for climate Change? *Climatic Change*, 80(3):199–204, 2007. ISSN 1573–1480. doi: 10.1007/s10584-006-9202-7.

10

Carbon emissions and energy use

Yi-Ming Wei and Lan-Cui Liu

1 Introduction

Human-induced overgrowth of greenhouse gas (GHG) emissions is one of the main causes of global climate change (IPCC, 2014). Fossil fuel combustion, which contributes to more than 70% of all GHG emissions, directly affects global climate change. Dieter (2012) attributed the failure of the Kyoto Protocol to no consideration to coal consumption that entails carbon emissions, especially in China and India. Steckel et al. (2015) held that the carbon intensity of global energy supply increases with the coal consumption of China, India, and some less developed countries, and the ambitious emissions reduction targets will be hardly achievable if the future economic growth of less developed countries is driven by coal consumption. Reducing carbon emissions, especially those from fossil fuel combustion, has become a pivotal measure to mitigate climate change. Therefore, based on the data from IEA (2016a, 2016b), this chapter studies the relationship between carbon emissions and energy use in different countries from the perspective of income and identifies the driving factors of carbon emissions and energy use.

2 Global CO_2 emissions from fossil fuel combustion

The global energy consumption has significantly swelled from 1971 onwards, as shown in Figure 10.1. During 1971–2014, the total energy consumption increased by 1.48 times, from 5,523 Mtoe to 13,699 Mtoe, of which coal consumption multiplied by 1.73 times, oil 0.76 times, natural gas 2.25 times, nuclear 21.84 times, and renewable energy 1.67 times. The energy structure has also undergone great changes. The proportion of coal consumption exhibited a rise-fall-rise trend; the proportion of oil consumption as a whole showed a downward trend and natural gas, nuclear energy and renewable energy showed upward trends. More specifically, the proportion of coal and oil consumption dropped from 70.17% to 59.89%, while the proportion of natural gas, nuclear energy and renewable energy consumption grew from 29.83% to 40.11% – an increase of 10 percentage points.

However, the share of renewable energy just increased by 0.98%, which indicates that path dependence of current economic growth on conventional energy generates lock-in and rigidity. Especially, more and more coal is used to generate electricity. In 2014, coal to generate electricity

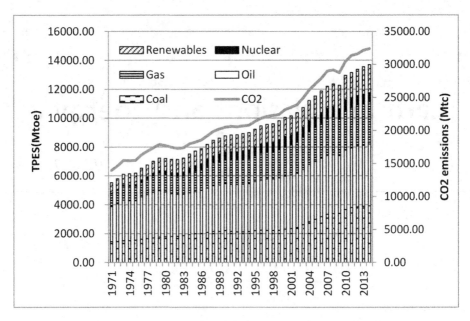

Figure 10.1 Global energy consumption and CO$_2$ emissions during 1971–2014

was 2,113 Mtoe, which can account for 53.92% of total coal supply and 15.42% of total primary energy supply, and increased by 18.66% from 1970 to 2014. Meanwhile, final coal use showed a declining trend, and the share decreased by 16.71% from 44.15% in 1971 to 27.44% in 2014. Thus, coal power generation is contributing to a larger share of CO$_2$ emissions.

2.1 CO$_2$ emissions from different energy use

The growth in energy consumption leads to an expansion in CO$_2$ emissions. As shown in Figure 10.1, carbon emissions became 1.32 times larger in 2014 compared with 1971. Carbon emissions increased by 2.9% per year in 2001–2010, but that growth has slowed dramatically over the past four years (Tollefson, 2015) to a surprisingly low growth of 1.0% per year in 2011–2014. However, it is unclear whether emissions are peaking (Jackson et al., 2016).

The carbon emissions from the consumption of coal, oil and natural gas increased by 1.84 times, 65.56% and 2.11 times, respectively, accounting for 52.29%, 23.35%, and 23.42% of the global incremental emissions, as shown in Figure 10.2. In 2003, coal consumption overtook oil consumption as the largest contributor to CO$_2$ emissions, and since then it has produced more emissions. As a result, the proportion of CO$_2$ emissions from oil consumption declined, in contrast to the increase from coal and natural gas consumption, which mirrors the changes in energy mix. In the total CO$_2$ emissions, electricity and heat production accounts for a higher share, and was 42.08% in 2014.

2.2 CO$_2$ emissions per unit of energy supply

The CO$_2$ emissions per unit of energy supply (i.e. carbon intensity) diminished with the change of energy mix from high-carbon coal and oil to low-carbon natural gas and zero-carbon nuclear energy and renewable energy, as shown in Figure 10.3. The carbon intensity of energy consumption first fell from 2.52 tC/toe to 2.28 tC/toe during 1971–1999 and then rebounded from

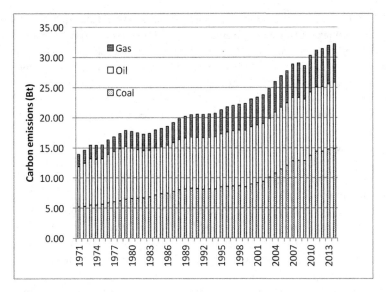

Figure 10.2 Global CO_2 emissions from fossil fuel use during 1971–2014

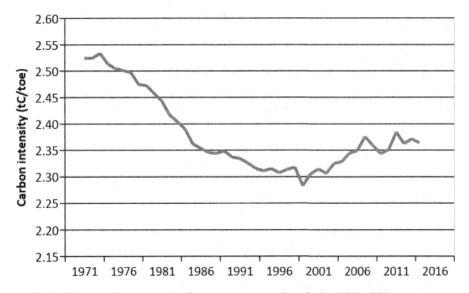

Figure 10.3 CO_2 emissions per unit of energy consumption during 1971–2014

2.31 tC/toe to 2.36 tC/toe after 2000, mainly due to the rapid increase in the total amount and proportion of coal consumption. Achieving the target of 1.5–2°C, a rapid and fundamental decarbonization of the global energy system is required (Rogelj et al., 2015).

3 CO_2 emissions from energy use in different countries

CO_2 emissions are not only directly correlated with energy consumption but are also closely related with economic growth and economic development stage (Wei. et al., 2011). As the disintegration of the Soviet Union in 1990 changed the pattern of countries in the world, the study focused on CO_2 emissions in different countries during 1990–2014 (World Bank, 2017a, 2017b, 2017c, 2017d).[1] In this chapter, CO_2 emissions from different countries come from the production, rather than the consumption, although a large number of studies have indicated that the higher consumer demand of high-income countries (HIC) largely drives the increase of carbon emissions in middle-income countries and low-income countries (LIC). In 2011, for EU-15 countries, Japan and the United States, CO_2 emissions based on consumption were respectively 22.07%, 21.09%, and 8.41% higher than those based on production; however, for China and India, 14.71% and 2.59% of emissions from production were caused by the export to meet the demand of other countries including the United States, EU-15, and Japan (Fernández-Amador et al., 2016).

There are many studies focusing on the driving forces of CO_2 emissions, but some of them divide the world into some geographic areas. Steckel et al. (2015) divided the world into OECD90, EIT (Economies in transition), Asia, LAM (Latin American countries), and MAF (countries of Middle East and Africa). IEA (2016b) decomposed CO_2 emissions of G20, OECD countries, and more than 100 individual countries. Jiang and Guan (2016) divided the world into developing countries and developed countries. Yao et al. (2015) focused on G20 countries. Although they tried to identity the effects of income on driving forces, it is still very difficult to compare the different influences.

High-income countries have produced huge emissions due to economic development. They accounted for more than half of the global total during 1990–2004, but the proportion fell below 50% after 2004 and down to 39.49% in 2014 as economic-driven carbon emissions expanded in upper-middle-income countries (UMC). In terms of total carbon emissions, they were also surpassed by upper-middle-income countries missions in 2009. The incremental carbon emissions from 1990 to 2014 reached 1,379.41 MtC in high-income countries, 8,143.32 MtC in upper-middle-income countries, 1,940.56 MtC in lower-middle-income (LMC) countries, and 35.09 MtC in low-income countries. They represented increases of 12.17%, 121.07%, 97.03%, and 18.25% in respective countries and global shares of 11.74%, 69.31%, 16.52%, and 0.30%, respectively.

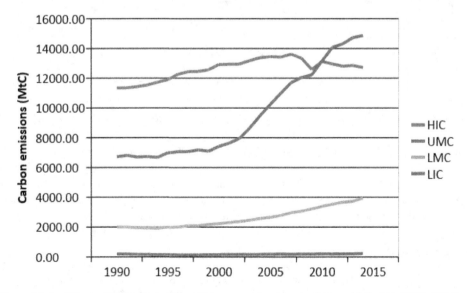

Figure 10.4 CO_2 emissions from different income countries in the world during 1990–2014

3.1 *CO₂ emissions from different energy consumption*

Figure 10.5 shows the energy-specific changes in CO_2 emissions in different countries from 1990 to 2014. In high-income countries, coal source emissions took up the lowest share, which was less than 36% and continued to decrease, while oil source emissions accounted for the highest, up to about 45%. The proportion of natural gas source emissions increased from 17.20% to 26.23% during this period. In upper-middle-income countries, the contribution of coal to carbon emissions ranged from 47.36 to 59.84% and exhibited a significant upward trend, which is different from high-income countries and low-income countries. The contribution of oil fell from 33.55% to 24.36% and natural gas from 19.10% to 15.80%. In lower-middle-income countries, the share of coal rose from 36.73% in 1990 to 49.53% in 2014. It was lower than that of upper-middle-income countries, but higher than that of high-income countries. There was also a decline in the proportions of oil and natural gas, with the former down from 41.92% to 35.69% and the latter down from 21.35% to 14.78% during this period. It should be noted that oil contributed more to carbon emissions compared with upper-middle-income countries. Low-income countries witnessed the highest share of coal in the contribution to carbon emissions. The proportion of coal tended to drop rapidly from 72.06% to 30.75%, while the proportion of oil and natural gas increased by 23 and 17 percentage points, respectively.

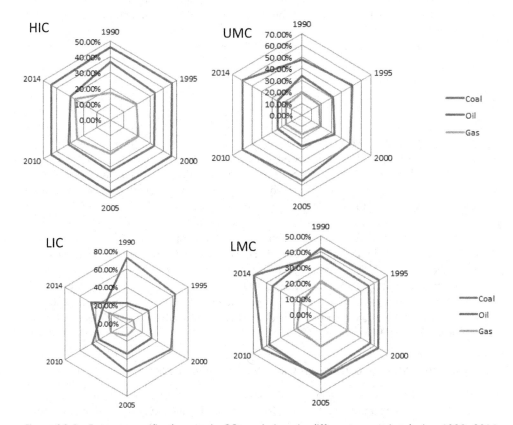

Figure 10.5 Energy-specific changes in CO_2 emissions in different countries during 1990–2014.

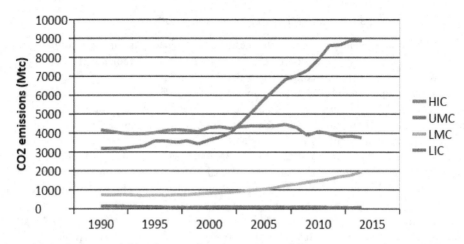

Figure 10.6 Carbon emissions from coal consumption in different countries during 1990–2014

Figure 10.6 shows the carbon emissions from coal consumption in different countries. The carbon emissions from coal consumption increased rapidly in middle-income countries, especially after 1999, but tended to decline in high-income countries due to adjustment of energy consumption structure. It can be said that carbon emissions from coal consumption have peaked in high-income countries. The growth in carbon emissions from coal consumption in upper- and lower-middle-income countries was mainly because of relatively abundant coal resources and lower coal prices.

3.2   Carbon intensity of fossil fuel use

In high-income countries, the carbon intensity showed a downward trend, and used to be significantly higher than that in the world, upper- and lower-middle-income countries and low-income countries. In 1995 and beyond, high-income countries managed to make carbon intensity lower than upper-middle-income countries as a result of carbon-intensive energy structure and in 2014, align with the global average. In upper-middle-income countries, carbon intensity was on the rise, mainly due to the expansion of coal consumption, and exceeded the level of the high-income countries and the global average in 1995. After peaking at 2.70 tons/toe in 2011, its carbon intensity started to drop in 2012, down to 2.66 tons/toe in 2014. In lower-middle-income countries, the carbon intensity also picked up markedly, but remained below the global average and levels of other country groups. It grew by 9.82% from 1.92 tons/toe to 2.11 tons/toe during 1990–2014. Low-income countries exhibited the lowest carbon intensity, which tended to decline over the years. It can be attributed to the dominance of renewable energy in a backward economy and the gradual decline in coal consumption from 1990 onwards.

3.3   Decomposition of carbon emissions from fossil fuel use

In order to further reveal the changes in carbon emissions from fossil fuel use in different countries, the decomposition method is used to study the drivers of carbon emissions from global energy consumption, including population, gross domestic product (GDP) per

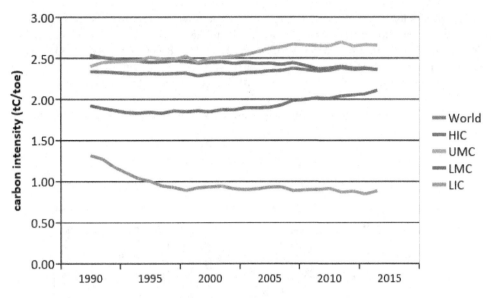

Figure 10.7 Carbon intensity in different countries and the world during 1990–2014

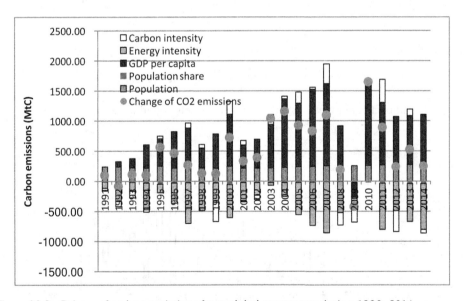

Figure 10.8 Drivers of carbon emissions from global energy use during 1990–2014

capita, population share, energy intensity, and carbon intensity. The results are as shown in Figure 10.8.

From 1990 to 2014, population growth and GDP per capita served as the major driver to the growth of carbon emissions, while energy intensity was the dominant factor in the decline in carbon emissions. The effect of carbon intensity was positive in some years and negative in other years. Population share also contributed slightly to the mitigation of carbon emissions. As a whole, carbon emissions from energy use increased by 11,498.38 MtC in these years. Specifically, the increments derived from population growth, GDP per capita growth, and carbon intensity attained 5,740.69 MtC, 15,810.70 MtC, and 210.80 MtC, respectively, of which carbon intensity contributed least. The reductions owing to energy intensity and population share reached 9,646.13 MtC and 617.68 MtC, respectively. However, the specific effects of these drivers vary in countries, as shown in Figures 10.9–10.13.

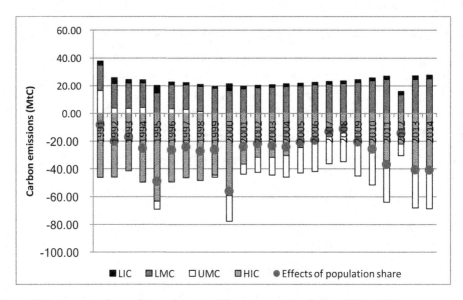

Figure 10.9 Impact of population share in different countries during 1990–2014

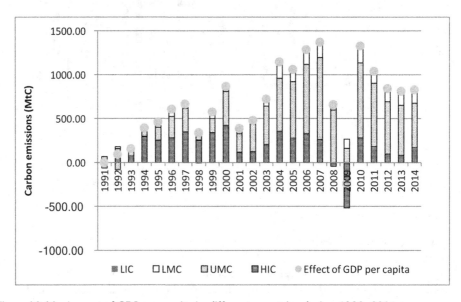

Figure 10.10 Impact of GDP per capita in different countries during 1990–2014

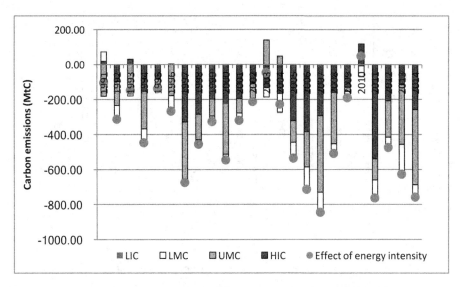

Figure 10.11   Impact of energy intensity in different countries during 1990–2014

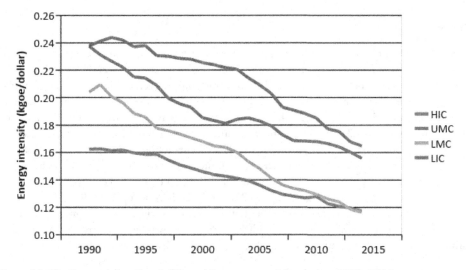

Figure 10.12   Energy intensity of different income countries during 1990–2014

Population share

The population share exerts different effects on carbon emissions in countries. More specifically, due to a reduction in the population share, carbon emissions shrank by 872.53 MtC in high-income countries and by 270.06 MtC in upper-middle-income countries. In contrast, carbon emissions grew by 465.96 MtC in lower-middle-income countries and 58.96 MtC in low-income countries as a result of increased population shares. Given an overall reduction of 617.68 MtC, the population share of different countries had a negative impact on carbon emissions. The annual emission reduction was less than 57MtC, so the impact was relatively small.

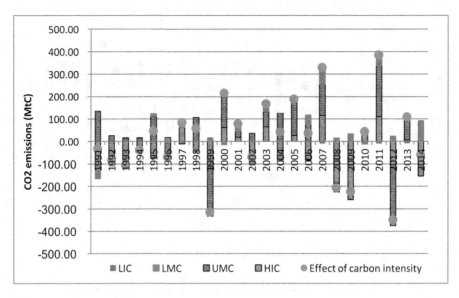

Figure 10.13 Impact of CO$_2$ emission intensity of different income countries during 1990–2014

GDP per capita

According to Figure 10.10, carbon emissions increased with GDP in different countries, except for GDP per capita reduction of high-income countries due to the 2008–2009 economic crisis. Prior to 2000, GDP per capita growth led to significantly larger carbon emissions in high-income countries than other countries. In 2000 and beyond, the case occurred in upper-middle-income countries. From 1990 to 2014, the incremental carbon emissions brought by GDP per capita growth reached 4,393.70 MtC in high-income countries, 9,317.16 MtC in upper-middle-income countries, 2,033.12 MtC in lower-middle-income countries, and only 66.72 MtC in low-income countries. At present, high-income countries embrace a significantly higher GDP per capita than other countries, but the growth rate is low, up by 41.75% compared with 1990. The GDP growth per capita registered 146.83% and 106.52% in upper- and lower-middle-income countries, respectively, and 41.57% in low-income countries. In the future, carbon emissions will mainly come from countries with lower incomes with income growth. To balance carbon emissions and economic growth in these countries will become the biggest challenge.

Energy intensity

Energy intensity is the most important factor to reduce carbon emissions. Except for 1991, 2003, 2004 and 2010, energy intensity mitigated carbon emissions to different degrees in countries. The sharpest decline in carbon emissions took place in high-income countries and the slightest in low-income countries, numbering 4,193.69 MtC and 66.10 MtC, respectively. The carbon emissions diminished by 3,905.29 MtC and 1,481.06 MtC in upper- and lower-middle-income countries, respectively. The annual emissions reductions were below 850 MtC, as shown in Figure 10.11.

Generally, the energy intensity shows a downward trend in different countries. It decreases while the income increases because of differences in energy efficiency and technology, as shown in Figure 10.12. In the future, with the change in global energy consumption and the progress of energy technology, the decline of energy intensity will offset more carbon emissions derived from economic growth, noticeably in upper-middle-income countries led by China and India.

Carbon intensity

From 1990 to 2014, the change in carbon intensity led to an increase of 210.80 MtC in carbon emissions. However, the impact on an annual basis varied in countries. In high-income countries, carbon emissions were reduced by 892.87 MtC with low carbonization of energy structure. In upper- and lower-middle-income countries, carbon emissions were increased by 838.50 MtC and 329.68 MtC, respectively, due to high carbon content of the energy structure (i.e. increased proportion of coal consumption), as in China and India. In low-income countries, carbon emissions decreased by 64.50 MtC with the proportion of coal consumption. The reduction in carbon intensity depends on the proportion of high-carbon energy, such as coal, and also on renewable energy. This means that more capital and technology support should be provided to low-income countries for the decarbonization of the energy system.

In the future, global carbon emissions will be driven by economic growth in the low-income countries, but with the further decline of energy intensity and decarbonization of energy supply in high-income countries and upper-middle-income countries, global carbon emissions are likely to maintain a lower growth rate.

4 The decarbonization transformation of energy system

No more than 2°C of warming above pre-industrial levels requires limiting the growth in global CO_2 emissions (Wei, et al., 2017), and eventually cutting these emissions to zero. Both the IEA and IPCC estimate that total anthropogenic CO_2 emissions are reduced to something less than 20 $GtCO_2$ per year by 2050, with further reductions to near zero or even net negative emissions by 2100 (Dowell et al., 2017; Rogelj et al., 2015). If taking into account CO_2 emissions prior to 2014, the remaining CO_2 emissions quota associated with a 66% probability of keeping warming below 2°C is estimated to be 1,200 (900–1,600) $GtCO_2$ (Friedlingstein et al., 2014).

As carbon emissions come from carbon-containing energy use, the mitigation depends to a large extent on low or zero carbon energy supply, which is too uncertain to meet the needs of economic growth. Therefore, more stringent policies concerning economic growth model, low-carbon energy structure, and emission reduction technologies are needed to ensure the achievement of the Paris Agreement target to control temperature rise below 2°C.

According to the intended nationally determined contributions submitted by 191 countries, the current policies of mitigating carbon emissions are characterized by "absolute emission reduction of high-income countries, incremental emission reduction of middle-income countries, and conditional emission reduction of low-income countries". High-income countries, represented by Japan and the European Union, have developed relatively complete mitigation targets, including in 2030, curtailing GHG emissions by 40% from the 1990 level and raising the proportion of renewable energy to 27%. Among middle-income countries, China pledged to peak CO_2 emissions in 2030, increase the proportion of renewable energy to 20% and cut carbon intensity by 60%–65% from the 1990 level. It has also placed caps on energy consumption considering the urgency of domestic environmental quality. Low-income countries proposed emission reduction targets that require the technical/financial support of the international community.

The differentiated climate change policies resulting from economic disparity will lead to further expansion of carbon emissions in lower-income countries that will partially offset the mitigation efforts in higher-income countries. If all submitted unconditional and conditional

INDCs are fully implemented, the emissions gap between their contribution to reductions and the least-cost emission level for a pathway to stay below 2°C is estimated to be 12 GtCO$_2$e (range: 10–15) in 2030 (UNEP, 2015), which is 37.06% of total CO$_2$ emissions in 2014. Therefore, the following efforts are recommended for global reduction of emissions, in addition to the mitigation efforts of high-income countries and middle-income countries.

1   All the countries should proactively promote global low carbon energy supply by 2050 and press ahead with the replacement of low-carbon energy for coal, oil, and natural gas based on key technological breakthroughs; at the same time, increase the transfer to and support for low-income countries and lower-middle-income countries in low-carbon energy utilization technologies to avoid the lock-in effect of high-carbon energy supply.
2   In addition to low-carbon transformation of energy supply system, it should pay great attention to the decarbonization of some industries with larger CO$_2$ emissions, such as thermal power plants, steel, and cement, and accelerate the development of carbon capture, utilization and storage technology to promote the large-scale commercial applications with low-cost.
3   High-income countries change their consumption patterns to avoid stimulation to carbon emissions in other countries and reduce high-carbon production and consumption to guide the low-carbon transformation of global economic growth in order to make global emission reductions match the 2°C target.

5   Conclusions

This chapter analyzes the relationship between global carbon emissions and energy use. From 1971 to 2014, the global energy consumption expanded markedly by 1.48 times and the energy consumption structure changed greatly. The proportion of coal and oil fell from 70.17% to 59.89%, while the proportion of natural gas, nuclear energy and renewable energy rose by 10 percentage points from 29.83% to 40.11%. Carbon emissions grew with energy consumption and multiplied by 1.32 times during these years. The carbon emissions from the consumption of coal, oil and natural gas tended to increase by 1.84 times, 1.66 and 2.11 times respectively, accounting for 52.29%, 23.35%, and 23.42% of the global incremental emissions. The carbon emissions per unit of energy consumption declined from 2.52 tC/toe to 2.28 tC/toe during 1972–1999 but rebounded from 2.31 tC/ toe to 2.36 tC/toe after 2000.

However, carbon emissions differ widely among countries due to income level. High-income countries accounted for more than half of the global emissions during 1990–2004, but the proportion fell below 50% after 2004 and down to 39.49% in 2014. In terms of total carbon emissions, they were also surpassed by upper-middle-income countries missions in 2009. Of global incremental carbon emissions, 69.31% came from upper-middle-income countries, 16.52% lower-middle-income countries, 11.74% high-income countries and 0.30% low-income countries. The decomposition results show that both GDP per capita and energy intensity are major factors for the growth of carbon emissions.

To achieve Paris Agreement targets, decarbonization of energy system and decoupling energy consumption and economic growth will be essential and urgent. However, it needs perfect combination of top-down policies with bottom-up technologies. In this reformative system, policies such as carbon pricing, investment and financing, industry development, energy supply technologies, energy storage technologies, process production technologies, and even socioeconomic effects of some policies and key technologies should also be addressed.

Acknowledgments

The authors gratefully acknowledge the financial support from the National Key R&D Program (grant No.2016YFA0602603), the National Natural Science Foundation of China (grant Nos. 71521002, 71642004, 71622012).

Note

1 The World Bank member countries are categorized by income and integrated with International Energy Agency (IEA) member countries, excluding other African countries.

Reference

Dieter, H., 2012. The Kyoto approach has failed. *Nature*, 491:663–665.
Dowell, N.M., Fennell, P.S., Shah, N., Maitland, G.C., 2017. The role of CO_2 capture and utilization in mitigating climate change. *Nature Climate Change*, 7:243–249.
Fernández-Amador, O., Francois, J.F., Tomberger, P., 2016. Carbon dioxide emissions and international trade at the turn of the millennium. *Ecological Economics*, 125:14–26.
IEA. 2016a. IEA Headline Energy Data. www.iea.org/search/?q=IEA+headline+energy+data.
IEA. 2016b. CO_2 Emissions from Fuel Combustion. www.iea.org/bookshop/729-CO2_Emissions_from_Fuel_Combustion.
IPCC. 2014. Climate Change 2014: Mitigation of Climate Change. Contribution of Working Group III to the Fifth Assessment Report of the Intergovernmental Panel on Climate Change. Cambridge: Cambridge University Press.
Jackson, R.B., Canadell, J.G., Quere, C.L., Andrew, R.M., Korsbakken, J.I., Peters, G.P., Nakicenovic, N. 2016. Reaching peak emissions. *Nature Climate Chang*, 6:7–10.
Jiang, X., Guan, D. 2016. Determinants of global CO_2 emissions growth. *Applied Energy*, 184:1132–1141.
Friedlingstein, P., Andrew, R.M., Rogelj, J., Peters, G.P., Canadell, J.G., Knutti, R., Luderer, G., Raupach, M.R., Schaeffer, M., van Vuuren, D.P., Quéré, C.L. 2014. Persistent growth of CO_2 emissions and implications for reaching climate targets. *Nature Geoscience*, 7:709–715.
Rogelj, J., Luderer, G., Pietzcker, R.C., Kriegler, E., Schaeffer, M., Krey, V., Riahi, K. 2015. Energy system transformations for limiting end-of-century warming to below 1.5°C. *Nature Climate Change*, 5(6):519–527.
Steckel, J., Edenhofer, O., Jakob, M. 2015. Drivers for the renaissance of coal. The Proceedings of the National Academy of Sciences, www.pnas.org/cgi/doi/10.1073/pnas.1422722112.
Tollefson, J., 2015. Global carbon emissions nearly stalled in 2014. *Nature*, doi:10.1038/nature.2015.18897.
UNEP, 2015. The Emissions Gap Report 2015. http://202.112.81.10/files/40880000006C112F/uneplive.unep.org/media/docs/theme/13/EGR_2015_Technical_Report_final_version.pdf.
Wei, Y., Liu, L., Liao, H., 2017. *CO_2 emissions and low carbon development in China.* China Science Publishing, Beijing (In Chinese).
Wei, Y., Liu, L., Wu, G., Zou, L., 2011. *Energy Economics: CO_2 Emissions in China.* Berlin Heidelberg: Springer.
World Bank. 2017a. High Income. http://data.worldbank.org/income-level/high-income
World Bank. 2017b. Upper Middle Income. http://data.worldbank.org/income-level/upper-middle-income
World Bank. 2017c. Lower Middle Income. http://data.worldbank.org/income-level/lower-middle-income
World Bank. 2017d. Low Income. http://data.worldbank.org/income-level/low-income
Yao, C., Feng, K., Hubacek, K. 2015. Driving forces of CO_2 emissions in the G20 countries: an index decomposition analysis from 1971 to 2010. *Ecological Informatics*, 26:93–100.

11

Energy economics and environment of energy systems

Janie Ling-Chin, Keerthi Rajendran, and Anthony P. Roskilly

1 Introduction

Growth in economy, population, and energy use remain the pillars of human development (Spataru, 2017). Even though the global economy faltered in 2015 due to various factors, including macro-economic uncertainties, declining trade, low commodity prices, and increasing volatility in capital flows and exchange rates (2016b), the world population grew to 7.3 billion (2015b). This growth required a primary energy supply of 13,647 millions of tonnes of oil equivalent (Mtoe) from oil (31.7%), coal (28.1%), natural gas (21.6%), biofuels and waste (9.7%), nuclear (4.9%), hydro (2.5%) and other sources including heat, solar, geothermal, wind, and tide (1.5%) (2017d). In total, the energy supply in 2015 caused an emission of 32,294 Mt of carbon dioxide (CO_2) due to fuel combustion (2017d). Development should embrace sustainability i.e. not only meeting the current needs but also safeguarding the "earth's life-support system" which affects the welfare of current and future generations (Griggs et al., 2013). Among the United Nations' sustainable development goals, universal clean energy, health and productive ecosystems, and thriving lives and livelihoods (Griggs et al., 2013) are particularly relevant to the research and development (R&D) in energy systems.

Energy systems, for instance buildings, urban cities, super grids, industrial plants, transport systems, and so forth cover energy production, conversion, distribution, consumption, and/or storage. They generally involve a range of components (demand, supply, transmission, storage, etc.), energy vectors (electricity, gas, sun, wind, hydrogen etc.) and technologies (thermodynamic power cycles, combined heat and power systems, waste heat recovery systems, distributed networks, heat storage etc.) at a particular spatial scale (i.e. unit, local, regional, national, continental or global) and level (micro versus macro). As such, they are of a multidisciplinary nature where energy economics is applied for demand and supply projections; engineering for technical application; economic appraisal for financial feasibility and environmental study for impact assessment. To better understand the interaction between energy economics and environment of energy systems, this chapter presents the fundamental concepts and methodologies of energy economics and systems modeling (Section 2), economic appraisal techniques and life cycle costing (LCC) (Section 3), environmental study (i.e. life cycle assessment (LCA)) in particular (Section 4), and policy implications of energy systems, research challenges and future directions in integrating energy economics, LCC and LCA (Section 5).

2   Energy economics and systems modeling

Energy systems models are used to generate a range of macro-economic and techno-economic analyses on energy demand and supply, from different perspectives ranging from impact analysis of specific technology to simulation that captures energy-economy interactions at the national and global levels. National energy security planning, climate policy analysis, and technology innovation assessment are all informed by energy systems models. These models underpin the decision-making process by providing insight into the potential impacts of changes to an energy system. They can be used to assess the success of existing initiatives, project future impacts of policy decisions or identify ideal options for given boundary conditions and constraints in an exploratory manner.

Research into energy systems modeling is a long-established field, which has resulted in a numerous variety of models and modeling frameworks (Nakata, 2004; Hall and Buckley, 2016; Allegrini et al., 2015), each with specific contexts and purposes as shown in Table 11.1.

The wide range of models indicate a variety of approaches, tools, and techniques for modeling. Figure 11.1 shows a categorization of energy economics models by approach and paradigm as in (Herbst et al., 2012) with examples. It is worth noting that attempts to categorize energy economics models have been made previously while models are developed and changed over time. As a result, some models show characteristics of more than one category where the boundaries of each category are not well defined. In addition, there are also several extensions and hybrid versions of models. For instance, the market allocation model (MARKAL), a generic, large scale bottom-up optimization model has been combined with energy flow optimization Model (EFOM) to become the integrated MARKAL EFOM system (TIMES) while TIMES integrated assessment model (TIAM) is a TIMES model which includes climate response modeling. The range of variations are referred to as the MARKAL/TIMES family of models. Nevertheless, categorization helps to show the basic approach and characteristic of the models. A brief explanation of different paradigms is shown in Table 11.2.

Table 11.1 Energy systems modeling research in various fields

Literature	Context
(Nakata, 2004)	• A review of existing energy-economic models. • Focus on national energy policies, renewable energy systems, and the global environment.
(Allegrini et al., 2015)	• A review of modeling approaches and associated software tools. • Focus on district energy systems.
(Bhattacharyya Subhes and Timilsina Govinda, 2010)	• A study of available models for their suitability to developing countries. • Results show that significant tailoring is required for the economic context.
(Huang et al., 2017)	• A review of current research into energy economics and climate policy modeling.
(Keirstead et al., 2012)	• An analysis of current modeling practice. • Identify opportunities for improvements in urban energy systems modeling.
(Lee, 2017)	• A review of econometric models. • Focus on development of bioenergy.
(Suganthi and Samuel, 2012)	• A review of energy models for demand forecasting. • Focus on soft computing techniques for forecasting.

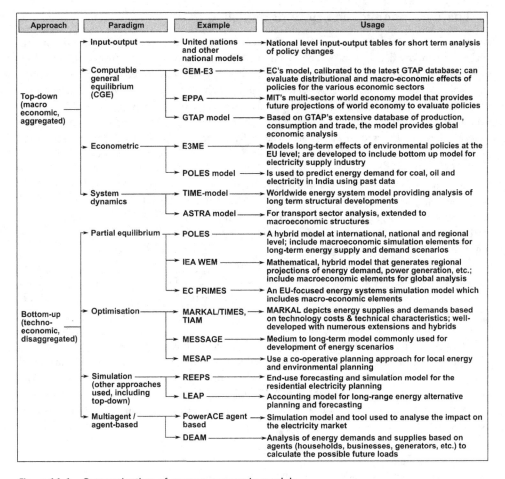

Figure 11.1 Categorization of energy economic models

Table 11.2 Paradigms which are commonly applied in energy economic models

Paradigm	Description
Input-output models	Input-output tables show goods or services in and out of particular sections of the economy, sector, or user base. These tables can be used to assess the output levels needed to satisfy demand. They are commonly developed at national levels for short-term analysis of policy changes, see (Pachauri and Srivastava, 1988; Suganthi and Samuel, 2012).
Computable general equilibrium (CGE) models	They simulate complex market interactions and are typically used for scenario analysis, to compare policies. The approach keeps the complex structure and simplifies the characterization of economic behavior and is numerically solved (not algebraically). The global trade analysis project (GTAP) model is widely referred to with many extensions (Hertel, 2012).
Econometric models	Probability, statistical, and economic theories are used to correlate variables such as energy demand with other macro-economic variables. Unlike CGE models, they can estimate future trajectory of variables. A review of application to bioenergy development analysis is presented in (Lee, 2017).

Paradigm	Description
System dynamics models	The models are a type of simulation model which analyze the long-term behaviors of social systems (e.g. large companies or cities). They model interactions, interdependencies and the dynamic changes over time using feedback loops. Computational analysis techniques are used to handle the complexity of the dynamic models (Mutingi et al., 2017).
Partial equilibrium models	The mechanism is similar to that of the CGE models. Unlike the CGE model, partial equilibrium models target only some parts of the economy, such as the energy market, and in doing so are able to include much more technical detail (Herbst et al., 2012).
Optimization models	Optimization models estimate technology capacity and utilization, marginal commodity prices, and emissions for a future energy system, given specific constraints and criteria. They provide "optimal" solutions to support decision-making (DeCarolis et al., 2017).
Simulation models	These models include logical descriptions of an energy system and reproduce its operation (Hall and Buckley, 2016). They can be applied to assess the uptake of technologies better than optimization models.
Multiagent models	The models are derived from the distributed artificial intelligence (DAI) concept. They represent a system in terms of components that have the ability to act autonomously and interact with other agents. This allows them to model and simulate macro-level complexities (Herbst et al., 2012).

To reduce complexity through granularity, energy systems models generally take one of the two approaches shown in Figure 11.1. Bottom-up models include detailed specifications of the technical components of an energy system. To assess the impact of a new technology or policy, detailed analysis of cost changes and market penetration, alongside in-depth technological and/ or process-oriented analysis, is valuable. However, they tend not to emphasize related macro-economic and societal implications. Top-down models take a macro-economic perspective and show the impact of energy supply and demand on issues like economic growth and national trade. They evaluate energy systems from aggregate economic variables and the terms "aggregated" and "disaggregated" may be used in place of "top" and "bottom", respectively (Nakata, 2004). Because they provide two different perspectives, with advantages and limitations, discussion about energy can be enhanced by improving awareness of both perspectives (Herbst et al., 2012). The need to integrate perspectives is well established in literature and research work has resulted in model-to-model linkages, integrations, and hybrids with several challenges presented for future research (Böhringer and Rutherford, 2008; Böhringer, 1998; Hourcade et al., 2006; Allegrini et al., 2015).

3 Economic analysis and life cycle costing (LCC) of energy systems engineering projects

From energy generation in power stations to utilization by end users, energy systems engineering projects involve multiple disciplines in evaluating the risk, cost, and environmental compliance in addition to the performance and efficiency of the systems as well as technologies. While economic competitiveness of innovative technology may be appraised during R&D, the financial benefits must be verified prior to investing in any energy systems projects. This is because

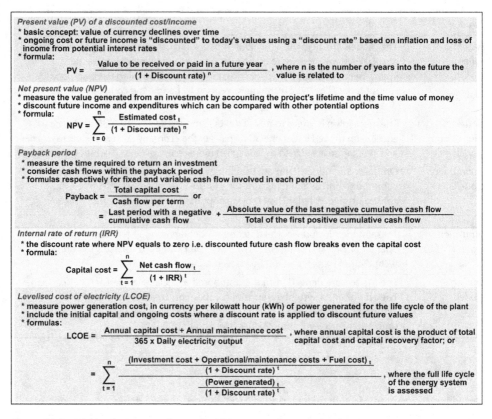

Figure 11.2 Methods commonly applied for economic analysis of energy systems engineering projects and their underpinning fundamental concepts

capital investment is a prerequisite to developing energy systems where financial feasibility affects decisions in design, construction and operation. A number of appraisal techniques, for instance, present value (PV) of discounted cost/income, net present value (NPV), payback period, internal rate of return (IRR) and levelized cost of electricity (LCOE) as depicted in Figure 11.2, are commonly applied in engineering projects.

Indeed, these appraisal techniques are the methodology applied in performing life cycle costing (LCC), as documented in the standards established for oil and gas (2006a), buildings and construction (2008b) as well as electrical and electronic industries (2017a). The establishment of industry-specific LCC standards is justifiable, as LCC should be tailored to suit the application and meet the needs and requirements – a common message conveyed in (2006a, 2008b, 2017a). Consequently, LCC steps vary with application process, as illustrated in Figure 11.3. In principle, a comprehensive economic analysis scrutinizes all tangible and intangible costs involved throughout the lifespan of the systems. Tangible costs encompass capital investment (e.g. material purchase, component acquisition and system installation) and operational costs (financing and interest rates, insurances, maintenance, disposal etc.). Intangible costs take account of any business loss and disruption (e.g. during installation and maintenance) and damage to the environment. During economic analysis, some data may not be readily available due to time and resource constraints. As such, assumptions are made in performing the analysis.

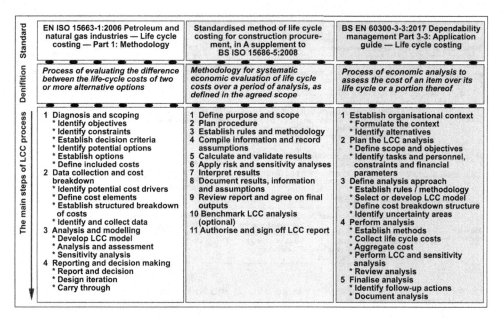

	EN ISO 15663-1:2006 Petroleum and natural gas industries — Life cycle costing — Part 1: Methodology	Standardised method of life cycle costing for construction procurement, in A supplement to BS ISO 15686-5:2008	BS EN 60300-3-3:2017 Dependability management Part 3-3: Application guide — Life cycle costing
Denifition Standard	Process of evaluating the difference between the life-cycle costs of two or more alternative options	Methodology for systematic economic evaluation of life cycle costs over a period of analysis, as defined in the agreed scope	Process of economic analysis to assess the cost of an item over its life cycle or a portion thereof

The main steps of LCC process	1 Diagnosis and scoping
	  * Identify objectives
	  * Identify constraints
	  * Establish decision criteria
	  * Identify potential options
	  * Establish options
	  * Define included costs
	2 Data collection and cost breakdown
	  * Identify potential cost drivers
	  * Define cost elements
	  * Establish structured breakdown of costs
	  * Identify and collect data
	3 Analysis and modelling
	  * Develop LCC model
	  * Analysis and assessment
	  * Sensitivity analysis
	4 Reporting and decision making
	  * Report and decision
	  * Design iteration
	  * Carry through
		1 Define purpose and scope
		2 Plan procedure
		3 Establish rules and methodology
		4 Compile information and record assumptions
		5 Calculate and validate results
		6 Apply risk and sensitivity analyses
		7 Interpret results
		8 Document results, information and assumptions
		9 Review report and agree on final outputs
		10 Benchmark LCC analysis (optional)
		11 Authorise and sign off LCC report
			1 Establish organisational context
			  * Formulate the context
			  * Identify alternatives
			2 Plan the LCC analysis
			  * Define scope and objectives
			  * Identify tasks and personnel, constraints and financial parameters
			3 Define analysis approach
			  * Establish rules / methodology
			  * Select or develop LCC model
			  * Define cost breakdown structure
			  * Identify uncertainty areas
			4 Perform analysis
			  * Establish methods
			  * Collect life cycle costs
			  * Aggregate cost
			  * Perform LCC and sensitivity analysis
			  * Review analysis
			5 Finalise analysis
			  * Identify follow-up actions
			  * Document analysis

Figure 11.3 LCC and its main steps as defined by Yao et al. (2006a, 2008b, 2017a)

4 Environment and environmental study

The International Organization for Standardization (ISO) has introduced ISO 14001 (2015a) and ISO 14004 (2010) to cover environmental management from an organizational perspective. The key attributes i.e. environmental aspects and environmental impacts are summarized in Figure 11.4. In brief, the environmental aspects of an organization (e.g. emissions and consumption of resources including energy and raw or intermediate materials) lead to environmental impacts (which are adverse or beneficial changes imposed on the environment). In "identifying environmental aspects and determining their significance", life cycle assessment (LCA) is an approach used to understand the environmental impacts of an organization or a product system (i.e. energy system in this context), as recommended by (2010). Four steps of LCA are established by ISO 14040 (2006b) and ISO 14044 (2006c), namely goal and scope definition, life cycle inventory analysis (LCI), life cycle impact assessment (LCIA) and life cycle interpretation, as summarized in (Ling-Chin and Roskilly, 2016b). According to (2006b, 2006c), the coverage of environmental impacts is not limited to natural environment but also resources and human health while impact categories are defined as "classes representing environmental issues of concern to which life cycle inventory analysis results may be assigned". As such, in scrutinizing the environmental compliance of energy systems, relevant environmental impacts should be appraised instead of only estimating greenhouse gas (GHG) emissions, in particular CO_2 (which is generally performed in carbon footprint calculation). More details about LCA methodology development of the four steps are available in (Ling-Chin et al., 2016).

As illustrated in Figure 11.5, LCIA involves three mandatory elements i.e. *selection, classification* and *characterization* in estimating the potential environmental impacts of a product system. During selection, characterization models, impact categories and indicators which are to be applied in the study are chosen. Common impact categories include but not limited to climate change, depletion of resources, ozone layer depletion, eutrophication, acidification, toxicity

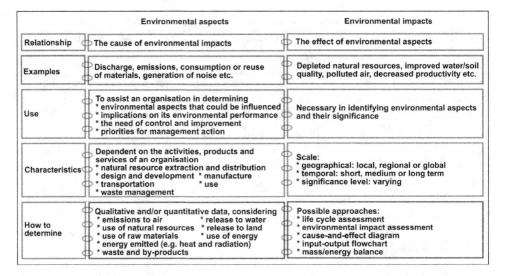

Figure 11.4 The concept of environmental aspects and environmental impacts as described in Yao et al. (2010, 2015a)

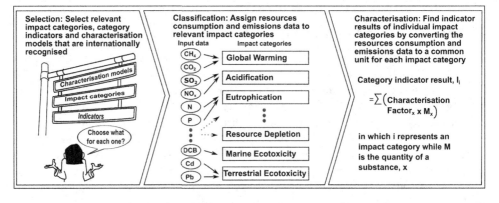

Figure 11.5 LCIA mandatory elements

Source: As adapted from Ling-Chin and Roskilly (2016a, 2016c).

covering human toxicity and (terrestrial, freshwater and marine aquatic or sediment) ecotoxicity, photochemical oxidant formation and impact of ionizing radiation, as depicted in Figure 11.6. As each characterization model has established its own impact categories, not any two single characterization models are exactly the same. Similar impact categories may be adopted but their underlying mathematic relationships, environmental mechanisms, reference substances and exposure routes are diverse.

During *classification*, the data of resources consumption and emissions are assigned to relevant impact categories. Based on predefined characterization factors, the data are converted into a common unit for each relevant impact category during *characterization*. The results are known as *category indicator results* or *indicator results*. *Normalization, grouping* and *weighting*, as illustrated in

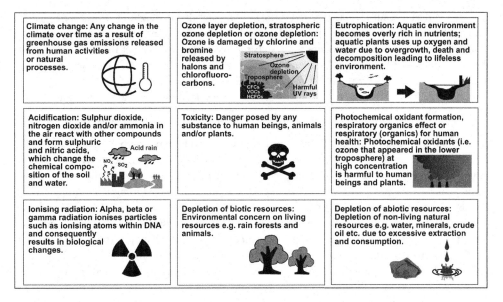

Figure 11.6   Some common impact categories

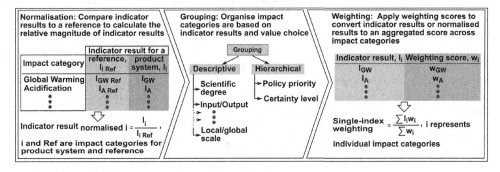

Figure 11.7   Optional LCIA elements

Source: Ling-Chin and Roskilly (2016c).

Figure 11.7, can be applied optionally, which take a reference system, value choice (e.g. policy priority and weighting scores) into account.

When commercial software (e.g. GaBi and SimaPro) is chosen for an application, the characterization models and individual impact categories readily adopted in the software will be selected while the underlying characterization methodologies are applied by default. Existing characterization models can be classified into (1) a midpoint-oriented approach (e.g. CML2001 and TRACI); (ii) an endpoint-oriented approach (e.g. Eco-Indicator99); or (3) a midpoint-endpoint approach (e.g. IMPACT2002+, Stepwise2006, ReCiPe, and ILCD). In applying a midpoint-oriented characterization model, the product of inputs/outputs (i.e. resources and emissions) and their corresponding characterization factors for each impact category is calculated one by one, summed up, and expressed as the category indicator results at an endpoint level. The category indicator results are aggregated to form a single index if weighting scores are assigned. An endpoint-oriented characterization model multiplies the mass and characterization factor of emissions one by one and aggregates the results to give an impact score at the level (or close to the level) of AoPs. A midpoint-endpoint characterization model is a mix of impact categories which are developed using midpoint or endpoint oriented approaches.

Alternatively, a new characterization model can be developed to estimate the indicator result, I, of an impact category, i, using the formula, $I_i = \sum_{xen} F_{xen}^i P_{xn}^i S_{xn}^i M_{xe}$ as explained in (Huijbregts et al., 2005; Bare and Gloria, 2006) by considering the fate and exposure pathways, F and effect (i.e. the potency or likelihood, P) of a substance, x, as well as damage (i.e. the severity, S) resulted in the impact when a quantity, M, is extracted from or released to an environmental compartment, e, such as air, water or soil along an exposure route, n. In the environment, substances are distributed through three stages of pathways (i.e. transport, dispersion and deposition) (Goedkoop et al., 2009). The distribution can be analyzed through fate analysis based on mass conversation principles where the concentration of the substance in a particular environmental compartment and the marginal change in resource availability or human intake following resources consumption and/or emissions are determined. If relevant, exposure factors are calculated from exposure analysis which considers the intake and absorption of substances (i.e. chemicals in particular) via various exposure routes including inhalation, liquid intake, food consumption, and dermal uptake by human beings. In some cases, intake factors which directly tell the exposure of a population are adopted by combining fate and exposure factors (Rosenbaum et al., 2008; van Zelm et al., 2009). Through effect analysis, the level of effects as a result of depleted resources and increased emissions, for instance atmospheric temperature rise, health issues of human beings, potentially disappeared fraction of living organisms, toxicity of ecology, and so forth is assessed in terms of potency and/or severity (Goedkoop et al., 2009). A dose-response relationship (Pizzol et al., 2011) – also known as exposure dose-effect response or concentration-response relationship (Van de Meent and Huijbregts, 2005) – derives linear and non-linear factors to estimate the potency or likelihood of a substance affecting the environment and human beings. The linear dose-response potency function predicts a low hazardous (or zero-effect) concentration baseline, y%, for impacts related to resources consumption or emissions and assumes a linear change in the response to a concentration below the baseline affecting y% of the population. In contrast, the non-linear dose-response potency function assesses responses to all changes in the concentration, regardless of the extent. The severity-based factors, also known as damage factors, quantify the damage or effect of resources consumption and/or emissions quantitatively or qualitatively using laboratory data, as reported by (Goedkoop et al., 2009). The severity-based factors are measured as years of life lived with a disability per affected person (YLDP), years of life lost per affected person (YLLP) or disability-adjusted life years per affected person (DALYP), in which DALYP are weighted YLDP against a reference (Rosenbaum et al., 2007). Should characterization factors, CF_x, of all substances attributable to individual impact categories be available, the formula can be simplified as $I_i = \sum_x CF_x M_x$, which is applicable to the development of a midpoint-oriented model (Ling-Chin and Roskilly, 2016a).

5 Implications of energy economics, LCC and LCA on policy making and future research directions

The development and application of technologies and energy systems (from energy demand to supply including production, distribution, and storage), economy, environment, policy, and society are mutually dependent, as illustrated in Figure 11.8. In addition to the economy and

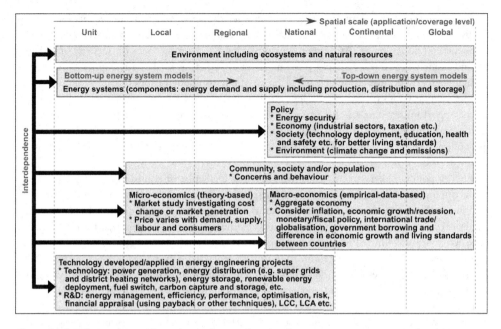

Figure 11.8 The scale and interdependence of technology, energy systems, society, economy, environment, and policy

environment (in terms of energy economics, economic analysis, LCC and LCA as presented in previous sections), the impact and implications of technology development, energy systems, policy and society are also of different spatial scale. The interdependence and diversified spatial scale can be explained by looking at the UK context, for instance. Following the international agreement on climate change (i.e. Kyoto Protocol), the UK has established the Climate Change Act 2008 for a 80% carbon emission reduction by 2050 compared to the 1990 level (2008a), leading to the development and enforcement of a series of national strategies, plans, and legislations which affect the local, regional and national industries as well as societies. A few recent examples include but are not limited to:

1   *The UK Industrial Strategy: Building a Britain Fit for the Future* (2017c), which invests in smart energy systems, clean and affordable energy, and advanced construction to boost individuals' earning power and productivity.
2   *The Clean Growth Strategy* (2017b), which targets for enhanced economic growth with declined carbon emissions through government leadership, green finance and energy efficiency improvement at homes, in transport and industry.
3   *The 25 Year Environment Plan* (2018), which sets action to restore landscapes, manage land, seas and ocean, reduce pollution and waste, improve resource efficiency, connect people with environment, and protect global environment during infrastructure development.
4   *The Energy Act* (2016a), which makes provision for offshore petroleum, wind power, and CO_2 storage.
5   *The Energy Saving Opportunity Scheme Regulations* (2014), which mandatorily requires organizations to measure energy consumption, perform energy audit, and identify energy saving opportunities in relevant industrial processes, buildings, and transport.

As the context varies from one country to another, the strategies, plans, and regulations would be diverse even though the interdependence of technology development, society, economy, environment, and policy exists. At present, policy making has a strong focus on security, affordability, and resilience of energy supply (Pfenninger et al., 2014) as well as environmental concerns (which currently do not consider a wider range of environmental issues but are more limited to climate change, GHG or CO_2 equivalent emissions). Policy is also concerned with making best use of opportunities: state-of-the-art technologies, emerging industries, distributed and sustainable energy production as well as new areas of rapid economic growth. Therefore, frameworks must allow models to be quickly adaptable to new requirements and able to reflect changes in policy decision-making.

Energy policy makers around the world face the challenge of considering the environmental, technological, and societal impact and their influence alongside economic models used for decision-making. However, due to computational constraints and practicalities of data availability, models tend to compromise with abstraction. Energy systems models, due to differences in perspective, are also limited to specific sectors instead of the whole energy system, and therefore dependencies and "interconnectedness" tend to be neglected (Crespo del Granado et al., 2018). Consequently, model results are not always accurate, showing different results in analyzing the same system (Böhringer, 1998; Herbst et al., 2012; Pfenninger et al., 2014; Crespo del Granado et al., 2018).

Two key areas have been identified for further development of energy systems modeling: the need for linking techno-economic, environmental, and macro-economic energy systems models for improved policy decisions, and filling gaps present in the application of existing modeling systems for different contexts. Examples of gaps in provision include applicability to developing countries (Bhattacharyya Subhes and Timilsina Govinda, 2010). This is an important area in mitigating climate change due to large-scale expansion of previously small economies (which results in high per capita emissions) (Huang et al., 2017). To date, energy systems technologies are primarily evaluated from techno-economic-environmental perspectives using engineering concepts, economic appraisal techniques, and LCA at a (unit or local) micro level. However, energy consumption is tied to economic development not only at a (unit or local) micro level but also at a (national, continental or global) macro level. Difficulties in attracting investment for sustainable energy development (as a result of uncertainty in the rates of return, which is prevalent in renewable energy systems) impede economic development (UNDP, 2000). Additionally, LCOE of renewable energy sources can be significantly higher than that of the less sustainable power sources (Aung, 2013). This is counteracted by policy to offer incentives and levies for less fossil fuels and more renewables usage (Aung, 2013, U.S.EIA(b), 2018). Policy elements have been included into established economic analysis methods for better decision-making, for example (Aung, 2013) presented economic analysis of two systems with and without policy interventions. To gain a better understanding of the impact, more research integrating energy technology with policy as well as macro-economics and society is required.

Future research should also address the current simplified treatment of specific industry sectors (for instance, agriculture) and the challenges in incorporating behavior analysis into the models (Gargiulo Maurizio, 2013). Behavior refers to modeling response to price signals and technology change (where a rational response is assumed by macro-economic models and techno-economic models are agnostic). This requires development of quantitative methods to incorporate behavioral scientific analysis into energy models (Gargiulo Maurizio, 2013). Incorporating behavior models into macro-economic models presents similar challenges of linking techno- and macro-economic models in general. Linkage efforts attempt to include spatial, technological and temporal dimensions into long-term, macro-level models used for policy decision-making. As mentioned before, the nature of linkage can be very much context and sector dependent. Different methodologies have been applied to link different systems; however, without application in a similar context, an evaluation of methodologies is difficult (Collins et al., 2017). Efforts at linking take a "hard-link" approach which completely integrates two different models into a new single model, or a "soft-link" approach in which models remain separate with a mechanism for information exchange. Examples include the soft-linked MESSAGE-macro and the hard-linked MARKAL-macro models.

Four challenges for energy systems modeling particularly relevant to national and international energy policy have been identified (Pfenninger et al., 2014). The challenges require research at the nexus of macro- and micro-economic models, as follows:

1   Including temporal fluctuations and spatial differences in macro-economic models for modern energy systems which involve issues such as distributed generation, renewable sources, intermittent supply, flexible demand, smart meters, and electrification. This is in contrast to the 20th-century energy systems which are based on centralized electricity production using fossil fuels.
2   Balancing uncertainty and transparency, which points to several wider areas of investigation (e.g. linking and designing models should take epistemic uncertainty into account). A lack of transparency in documentation impedes collaborations across the modeling community (Crespo del Granado et al., 2018).
3   Addressing the growing complexity of energy systems. Trade-offs need to be made between larger scale with less detail and lower scale with more detail. This in particular is relevant for integrated hybrid models where resulting uncertainty and potential hidden dependencies need to be resolved.
4   Integrating human behavior (typically micro-level analysis models) and social risks and opportunities (typically macro-level models with high abstraction).

Improvements in linking models can enhance policy decision-making and strategy analysis for the long term. To address many of the challenges in linking models, a framework of interconnected models, "Nexus", has been suggested (Crespo del Granado et al., 2018), with the intention of providing the underlying mechanism for linking different models. This would mean that less tailoring and development would be required to link individual models. It would also support experimentation with modeling methodology as well as evaluation and resolve transparency problems mentioned earlier.

Conclusions

Global economic development, population growth and subsequent energy use have brought about the need for sustainability: the production and consumption of energy in a way that meets current usage and protects the natural environment for future needs. The United Nations has set a number of goals for sustainable development and these underpin many of the policy motivations at national level. Policy decisions are based on information and forecasts presented by energy systems models. Energy systems modeling is a well-established field resulting in numerous techniques drawn from various disciplines and several large-scale models that underpin national and global policy. Due to the complex nature of energy systems, several challenges are inherent in the development of these models, including the multidisciplinary nature of a complete energy system. At micro-levels, economic analysis techniques are more involved in energy engineering projects where renewable energy sources, competitiveness, and policy implications are included. In connection to environmental management, LCA has been recommended by ISO as an approach to estimate the environmental impacts of an organization or product system. The LCA's impact assessment methodologies are mathematically based and knowledge about the product system (i.e. energy system in this context) is required for application. Energy systems, technology, economy, environment, policy, and society are mutually dependent despite their diverse spatial scale for application and coverage level. Research has shown that models are compromised by abstraction and simplification resulting in inaccurate analysis. Several challenges in integration are present and current research aims to better integrate models. In order to facilitate research and experimentation in this field, the need for a generic framework for integration is identified as a direction for future research.

Acknowledgments

The chapter was presented with financial support from the Research Councils UK Energy Program as research findings of the Thermal Energy Challenge Network (EP/P005667/1). The outcome was supported by the European Energy Research Alliance (EERA) Joint Programme on Economic, Environmental and Social Impacts (JP e3s).

References

2006a. EN ISO 15663–1:2006 petroleum and natural gas industries: Life cycle costing, Part 1: Methodology. UK: BSI Standards Limited.

2006b. Environmental management: Life cycle impact assessment: Principles and framework. British Standard.

2006c. Environmental management: Life cycle impact assessment: Requirements and guidelines. International Organization for Standardization (ISO).

2008a. *Climate Change Act*. UK: The Stationery Office Limited. Available: www.legislation.gov.uk/ukpga/2008/27/pdfs/ukpga_20080027_en.pdf [Accessed 8 May 2018].

2008b. Standardised method of life cycle costing for construction procurement: A supplement to BS ISO 15686–5:2008 Buildings and constructed assets: Service life planning, Part 5: Life cycle costing. UK: BSI Standards Limited.

2010. Environmental management system: General guidelines on principles, systems and support techniques. British Standard.

2014. *Energy Savings Opportunity Scheme*. UK: Environment Agency and Department for Business, Energy & Industrial Strategy. Available: www.gov.uk/guidance/energy-savings-opportunity-scheme-esos [Accessed 8 July 2018].

2015a. Environmental management systems: Requirements with guidance for use. British Standard.

2015b. *The World Population Prospects: 2015 Revision* [Online]. New York: Department of Economic and Social Affairs, United Nations. Available: www.un.org/en/development/desa/publications/world-population-prospects-2015-revision.html [Accessed 30 June 2018].

2016a. *Energy Act*. UK: The Stationery Office Ltd. Available: www.legislation.gov.uk/ukpga/2016/20/pdfs/ukpga_20160020_en.pdf [Accessed 8 July 2018].

2016b. *World Economic Situation and Prospects 2016: Global Economic Outlook* [Online]. Department of Economic & Social Affair, United Nations. Available: www.un.org/development/desa/dpad/publication/world-economic-situation-and-prospects-2016/ [Accessed 30 June 2018].

2017a. BS EN 60300–3–3:2017 dependability management, Part 3–3: Application guide: Life cycle costing. UK: BSI Standards Limited.

2017b. *Clean Growth Strategy*. UK: Department for Business, Energy & Industrial Strategy. Available: www.gov.uk/government/publications/clean-growth-strategy [Accessed 8 May 2018].

2017c. *Industrial Strategy: Building a Britain Fit for the Future*. UK: Department for Business, Energy & Industrial Strategy. Available: https://assets.publishing.service.gov.uk/government/uploads/system/uploads/attachment_data/file/664563/industrial-strategy-white-paper-web-ready-version.pdf [Accessed 8 May 2018].

2017d. Key world energy statistics. *International Energy Agency*. Available: www.iea.org/publications/freepublications/publication/KeyWorld2017.pdf [Accessed 29 June 2018].

2018. *A Green Future: Our 25 Year Plan to Improve the Environment*. UK: Department for Environment, Food & Rural Affairs. Available: www.gov.uk/government/publications/25-year-environment-plan [Accessed 8 May 2018].

Allegrini, J., Orehounig, K., Mavromatidis, G., Ruesch, F., Dorer, V. & Evins, R. 2015. A review of modelling approaches and tools for the simulation of district-scale energy systems. *Renewable and Sustainable Energy Reviews*, 52, 1391–1404.

Aung, K. T. 2013. Economic and life cycle analysis of renewable energy systems. *120th ASEE Annual Conference*. Atlanta: American Society for Engineering Education.

Bare, J. C. & Gloria, T. P. 2006. Critical analysis of the mathematical relationships and comprehensiveness of life cycle impact assessment approaches. *Environmental Science & Technology*, 40, 1104–1113.

Bhattacharyya Subhes, C. & Timilsina Govinda, R. 2010. A review of energy system models. *International Journal of Energy Sector Management*, 4, 494–518.

Böhringer, C. 1998. The synthesis of bottom-up and top-down in energy policy modeling. *Energy Economics*, 20, 233–248.

Böhringer, C. & Rutherford, T. F. 2008. Combining bottom-up and top-down. *Energy Economics*, 30, 574–596.

Collins, S., Deane, J. P., Poncelet, K., Panos, E., Pietzcker, R. C., Delarue, E. & Ó Gallachóir, B. P. 2017. Integrating short term variations of the power system into integrated energy system models: A methodological review. *Renewable and Sustainable Energy Reviews*, 76, 839–856.

Crespo del Granado, P., van Nieuwkoop, R. H., Kardakos, E. G. & Schaffner, C. 2018. Modelling the energy transition: A nexus of energy system and economic models. *Energy Strategy Reviews*, 20, 229–235.

Decarolis, J., Daly, H., Dodds, P., Keppo, I., Li, F., Mcdowall, W., Pye, S., Strachan, N., Trutnevyte, E., Usher, W., Winning, M., Yeh, S. & Zeyringer, M. 2017. Formalizing best practice for energy system optimization modelling. *Applied Energy*, 194, 184–198.

Gargiulo Maurizio, G.B.Ó. 2013. Long-term energy models: Principles, characteristics, focus, and limitations. *WIREs Energy and Environment*, 2, 158–177

Goedkoop, M., Heijungs, R., Huijbregts, M., DE Schryver, A., Struijs, J. & van Zelm, R. 2009. ReCiPe 2008: A life cycle impact assessment method which comprises harmonised category indicators at the midpoint and the endpoint level. First Edition: The Netherlands: Ministry of Housing, Spatial Planning and Environment Report.

Griggs, D., Stafford-Smith, M., Gaffney, O., Rockström, J., Öhman, M. C., Shyamsundar, P., Steffen, W., Glaser, G., Kanie, N. & Noble, I. 2013. Policy: Sustainable development goals for people and planet. *Nature*, 495, 305.

Hall, L.M.H. & Buckley, A. R. 2016. A review of energy systems models in the UK: Prevalent usage and categorisation. *Applied Energy*, 169, 607–628.

Herbst, A., Toro, F., Reitze, F. & Jochem, E. 2012. Introduction to energy systems modelling. *Swiss Journal of Economics and Statistics*, 148, 111–135.

Hertel, T. 2012. Applied general equilibrium analysis using the GTAP framework *In*: Peter Dixon, D. J. (ed.) *Handbook of computable general equilibrium modeling*, Volume 1B. North Holland: Elsevier.

Hourcade, J.-C., Jaccard, M., Bataille, C., Ghersi, F., Xe, X. & Ric. 2006. Hybrid modeling: New answers to old challenges introduction to the special issue of "the energy journal". *The Energy Journal*, 27, 1–11.

Huang, Z., Wei, Y.-M., Wang, K. & Liao, H. 2017. Energy economics and climate policy modeling. *Annals of Operations Research*, 255, 1–7.

Huijbregts, M.A.J., Rombouts, L.J.A., Ragas, A.M.J. & van de Meent, D. 2005. Human-toxicological effect and damage factors of carcinogenic and noncarcinogenic chemicals for life cycle impact assessment. *Integrated Environmental Assessment and Management*, 1, 181–244.

Keirstead, J., Jennings, M. & Sivakumar, A. 2012. A review of urban energy system models: Approaches, challenges and opportunities. *Renewable and Sustainable Energy Reviews*, 16, 3847–3866.

Lee, D.-H. 2017. Econometric assessment of bioenergy development. *International Journal of Hydrogen Energy*, 42, 27701–27717.

Ling-Chin, J., Heidrich, O. & Roskilly, A. P. 2016. Life cycle assessment (LCA): From analysing methodology development to introducing an LCA framework for marine photovoltaic (PV) systems. *Renewable and Sustainable Energy Reviews*, 59, 352–378.

Ling-Chin, J. & Roskilly, A. P. 2016a. A comparative life cycle assessment of marine power systems. *Energy Conversion and Management*, 127, 477–493.

Ling-Chin, J. & Roskilly, A. P. 2016b. Investigating a conventional and retrofit power plant on-board a Roll-on/Roll-off cargo ship from a sustainability perspective: A life cycle assessment case study. *Energy Conversion and Management*, 117, 305–318.

Ling-Chin, J. & Roskilly, A. P. 2016c. Investigating the implications of a new-build hybrid power system for Roll-on/Roll-off cargo ships from a sustainability perspective: A life cycle assessment case study. *Applied Energy*, 181, 416–434.

Mutingi, M., Mbohwa, C. & Kommula, V. P. 2017. System dynamics approaches to energy policy modelling and simulation. *Energy Procedia*, 141, 532–539.

Nakata, T. 2004. Energy-economic models and the environment. *Progress in Energy and Combustion Science*, 30, 417–475.

Pachauri, R. K. & Srivastava, L. 1988. Integrated energy planning in India: A modeling approach. *The Energy Journal*, 9, 35–48.

Pfenninger, S., Hawkes, A. & Keirstead, J. 2014. Energy systems modeling for twenty-first century energy challenges. *Renewable and Sustainable Energy Reviews*, 33, 74–86.

Pizzol, M., Christensen, P., Schmidt, J. & Thomsen, M. 2011. Impacts of "metals" on human health: a comparison between nine different methodologies for Life Cycle Impact Assessment (LCIA). *Journal of Cleaner Production*, 19, 646–656.

Rosenbaum, R. K., Bachmann, T. M., Gold, L. S., Huijbregts, M.A.J., Jolliet, O., Juraske, R., Koehler, A., Larsen, H. F., Macleod, M., Margni, M., Mckone, T. E., Payet, J., Schuhmacher, M., van de Meent, D. & Hauschild, M. Z. 2008. USEtox: The UNEP-SETAC toxicity model: Recommended characterisation factors for human toxicity and freshwater ecotoxicity in life cycle impact assessment. *International Journal of Life Cycle Assessment*, 13, 532–546.

Rosenbaum, R. K., Margni, M. & Jolliet, O. 2007. A flexible matrix algebra framework for the multimedia multipathway modeling of emission to impacts. *Environment International*, 33, 624–634.

Spataru, C. 2017. *Whole energy system dynamics: Theory, modelling and policy*. Taylor & Francis: London.

Suganthi, L. & Samuel, A. A. 2012. Energy models for demand forecasting: A review. *Renewable and Sustainable Energy Reviews*, 16, 1223–1240.

UNDP 2000. *World energy assessment: Energy and the challenge of sustainability*. New York: United Nations Development Programme, Bureau of Development Policy.

U.S. EIA(B) 2018. Levelized cost and levelized avoided cost of new generation resources in the annual energy outlook 2018.

van de Meent, D. & Huijbregts, M. A. 2005. Calculating life-cycle assessment effect factors from potentially affected fraction-based ecotoxicological response functions. *Environment Toxicology and Chemistry*, 24, 1573–1578.

van Zelm, R., Huijbregts, M.A.J. & van de Meent, D. 2009. USES-LCA 2.0: A global nested multi-media fate, exposure, and effects model. *International Journal of Life Cycle Assessment*, 14, 282–284.

12

Renewable energy policy

Travis Roach

1   Introduction

The growth in renewable energy capacity, production, and technological efficiency since the end of the 20th century has been staggering. In the United States alone, wind energy consumption and production is 83 times greater now than in 1990, and over 1,000 gigawatts (1 TW) of wind and solar capacity have been installed globally. This effort to incorporate nascent technologies into the energy mix has taken multiple forms, and policies intended to encourage this growth have been passed at all levels of governance. From the historic multinational Paris accord, to national-level policies like the renewable fuel standard or Germany's Energiewende, to state- and community-level efforts that drive rooftop solar development, the push to diversify the mix of energy technologies to include renewable forms of energy production and reduce carbon dioxide emissions has ultimately changed the energy landscape. This chapter discusses the policies and regulations that have been passed that incentivize renewable energy growth and assesses the efficacy of these policies.

This chapter separately discusses direct policy efforts that have sought to increase the usage of renewable energy in the electricity sector and spillover or "indirect" effects of renewable energy policies on emissions, and policies geared toward renewable fuels in the transportation sector. For the sake of this chapter, direct policies are those that specifically subsidize renewable energy consumption like the production tax credit (PTC) in the United States, or policies that quantify certain amounts of renewable energy consumption, for example ethanol fuel standards in transportation or renewable portfolio standards (RPS) in the electricity sector.

2   Renewable energy in the electricity sector

The second-best nature of most renewable energy policies was quickly noted in the literature, as Borenstein (2012) discussed the impetus for many of the existing policy frameworks that support renewable energy adoption.

> The most important market failure in energy markets is almost certainly environmental externalities, and the single most efficient policy would be to price those externalities

207

appropriately. Yet policymakers often find pricing externalities to be nearly impossible politically. Thus, the second-best discussion is over which, if any, alternative policy interventions are likely to do the most good, or at least to do more good than harm.

Policies intended to increase renewable generation in the electricity sector have largely taken the form of portfolio standards or generation quotas, or direct subsidies like the production tax credit in the United States or the feed-in tariff system in Europe.

2.1 Renewable portfolio standards

Renewable portfolio standards (RPS) are state-level policies that set a mandated amount of renewable generation that must be incorporated into the electricity supply. These policies vary in their stringency which impacts renewable energy certificate (REC) prices. RECs are essentially an accounting tool that allow electricity suppliers to show that they have satisfied their renewable portfolio requirements and, depending on the state's policy, these RECs may be traded to noncompliant entities if a utility has more than they are required. For example, the Texas RPS passed in 1999 required that (1) 5,880 MW of capacity be installed by 2015 and (2) set a goal for 10,000 MW by 2025. By the year 2009, only a decade into the RPS, the state had already passed their 2025 goal. Accordingly, REC prices are near zero in Texas. In other states that have more stringent RPS policies, REC prices have reached as high as $50–$60. In the United States, 29 states, Washington, DC, and three territories have an RPS, and eight states and one territory have a non-binding renewable goal. Vermont and Hawaii have the most ambitious policies, with 75% and 100% targets by 2032 and 2045 for each state, respectively.

2.2 Price-based mechanisms

The production tax credit was first established in the Energy Policy Act of 1992, but is a policy that has been as intermittent as the energy sources it is intended to support. The PTC offers a fixed subsidy per unit of renewable energy produced (e.g. 2.3 cents per kWh). This federal policy has been a political football, and extensions or cancellations of the policy have been passed under policies like the "Job Creation and Worker Assistance Act of 2002" and the "Working Families Tax Relief Act of 2004", among others. Since 1999, the first time the PTC expired, the PTC has been extended ten times, and in some cases the PTC was allowed to lapse before being retroactively extended. More recently, the PTC has been scheduled to expire, and this time the subsidy will gradually be phased out for wind facilities with a reduction of 20% in 2017, 40% in 2018, and 60% in 2019. The credit is not available for any systems whose construction began after 31 December 2017.

Feed-in-tariff (FIT) systems are a popular policy mechanism across European countries for incentivizing capacity building. FITs often take the form of a fixed price paid to renewable sources that is set above the market price for electricity. In many cases, FITs are coupled with a stipulation that guarantees dispatch that does not follow "merit order" (low to high price dispatch). FITs came to prominence in European countries in the early 1990s, beginning with Germany in 1990, moving to Switzerland in 1991, and with Italy, Denmark, and Spain adopting this system over the next three years (1992–1994). Germany continues to lead and set ambitious policy goals as the German Energiewende hopes to accomplish a 60% target of renewable generation by 2050.

2.3 Policy efficacy

It has taken time for data to accumulate on the efficacy of these policies with respect to capacity building or other outcome variables like carbon dioxide mitigation. Among the earliest empirical studies on the effect of renewable energy policies in incentivizing new renewable capacity additions is Hitaj (2013). In this analysis, the author finds that state and federal policies incentivize wind power development by providing financial support and improving access to the electricity grid, and that independent system operators (ISOs) and deregulated markets are correlated with greater wind energy development. Hitaj (2013) concludes by stating that "further deregulation of the electricity industry is likely to improve the ability of wind power to contribute to the US electricity generation portfolio". Nesta et al. (2014) and Nicolli and Vona (2016) support this by noting that deregulated systems that allow for independent power producers result in more renewable energy capacity. Roach (2015) also supports this by showing that the PTC led to more capacity building in deregulated electricity markets than regulated markets. With regard to RPS policies, Maguire (2016) finds that state-level portfolio standards have not had a significant influence on within state wind capacity additions. This null result may be due to the actual stringency in meeting RPS requirements and the endogenous process that is involved in setting these levels in the first place. Recall that Texas met its "lofty" 2025 goals with nearly two decades to spare. Evidence from Carley et al. (2018) suggests that RPS stringency may be the actual driver of capacity additions under an RPS. After developing a metric for how stringent a state's policy is, these authors find that "a one-point increase in RPS stringency leads to increases of 0.2%, 1% and 0.3% in renewable energy, solar generation and renewable energy capacity, respectively".

At local levels of governance, we also see an influence of RE policies changing capacity buildup. Crago and Chernyakhovskiy (2017) show that rebates are the financial instrument that have the most impact with each additional $1 per watt rebate yielding a 50% increase in residential PV capacity. These authors also find that there is a significant positive relationship between hybrid vehicle sales and residential PV capacity growth which shows the importance of environmental preferences as a predictor of solar PV demand. Matisoff and Johnson (2017) show that each additional dollar in incentives drives 500–1,000 watts of PV installations per thousand residential electric customers. Intuitively, they also note that policies that are facilitated by net metering and financing incentives drive capacity buildup. This finding is supported in Hittinger and Jawad (2017), which studies grid "defection" by residential customers. It is important to note that there are other factors than policies or price breaks that drive residential renewable energy demand. Rode and Weber (2016) show that imitative adoption behavior is important for explaining PV adoption. These authors find that households in Germany imitate one another in adopting PV. Similarly, Dastrup et al. (2012) show that homes in California with solar PV are able to command a price premium in areas with more Democratic and Green party registrations. Sexton and Sexton (2014) appropriately name this conspicuous conservation and note that "homeowners may overinvest in residential solar power because of its conspicuousness and under-invest in home insulation improvements".

2.4 Renewable energy policy and emissions reductions

Unfortunately, most renewable energy policies have been passed in lieu of a carbon-pricing policy as Borenstein (2012) noted. The effectiveness of any renewable policy on other outcome variables (e.g. other than capacity building or renewable penetration) must take account of the heterogeneous nature of different renewable technologies. For example, solar energy is only productive during daylight hours, and is (importantly) most productive at times of peak load demand. Wind energy, however, typically reaches peak output overnight when load demand is quite low. Moreover, heterogeneity in location and alternative generation sources affect the efficacy of renewable penetration because the shift to renewable sources must be considered against the generation that is replaced. To the end consumer, a kilowatt is a kilowatt. But, if that kilowatt was previously produced by hydroelectric sources, then the environmental impact of new renewable energy is, effectively, zero. Indeed, Metcalf (2009), Novan (2015), and Callaway et al. (2017) all note that renewable energy policies could potentially provide the exact same subsidy to producers that reduce very different amounts of pollution. Using hourly generation data in Texas, Novan (2015) shows that over a two-year period, wind turbines accounted for 4.7% of the total generation in the Texas electricity market and offset 3.5% of the CO_2 emissions, 4.5% of the NO_x emissions, and 2.6% of the SO_2 emissions. This shows the important step of identifying the actual set of generators which serve as substitutes to renewable output if environmental goals are a leading driver for new renewable energy policy making. Novan (2015) further shows that 37% of the total electricity supply came from coal-powered sources, and only accounts for 31% of the generation that was offset by wind turbines. Comparatively, 43% of the Texas electricity generation came from natural gas-powered sources, 68% of the total output that was offset by wind turbines. Thus, we cannot assume that a MWh of wind will reduce emissions by the same amount across different electrical markets. Or as Callaway et al. (2017) simply state, "Location, Location, Location".

Relative to a simple carbon tax, renewable energy incentives are not a cost-effective way to reduce carbon dioxide emissions.[1] Crago and Chernyakhovskiy (2017) find that financial support for residential solar PV installations are a costly way to reduce carbon emissions. They discuss some "back of the envelope" calculations which suggest that the cost of carbon mitigation through rebates is around $184 per ton of CO_2. Murray et al. (2014) make use of the Energy Information Administration's National Energy Modeling System to determine the effect on emissions from removing federal tax provisions for both electricity generation and renewable fuels. Concerning the PTC, these authors find that "although the renewable electricity tax credits lead to an appreciable increase in renewable power generation, the total contribution of these sources is still small relative to the entire fleet of electricity generating units. The emissions effects therefore turn out to be small". They further find that the existence of state-level renewable portfolio standards dampens the effect of this federal subsidy. These authors also comment on the cost-effectiveness of policies in reducing emissions from the vehicle fleet. As the next section shows, these policies are a very costly way to reduce emissions, and in some cases may actually lead to more life-cycle emissions.

3   Renewable fuels

Renewable fuel policies are among the most widespread and ubiquitous of any legislative effort to increase renewable energy consumption – more than 60 countries have some sort of renewable fuel policy. Accordingly, global ethanol production has increased by over 22 billion gallons per year since 2001. The majority of this production takes place in the United States and Brazil, though China has recently passed a new ethanol standard and boosted production.

Much like renewable energy in the electricity sector, renewable fuels policies have myriad rationales behind their implementation, including energy security and reduced reliance on foreign commodities, job creation, and environmental goals. Charles et al. (2007) note that because ethanol production and consumption can impact such a wide variety of policy goals and indus-tries, that it is a particularly popular policy vehicle. Despite widespread adoption of ethanol policies, many authors have found that the passing of an ethanol mandate has led to adverse or unintended consequences including higher land and food prices, increased use of water, and increased energy use from polluting sources to process plant materials into fuel (Pimentel 2003; Jaeger and Egelkraut 2011; Wu and Langpap 2015). Indeed, Charles et al. (2007) describe several potential drawbacks of developed countries championing a biofuels policy, including environmental drawbacks, and find the justification used by these countries' governments to be "questionable".

One measure of the energy intensity of a fuel type and its efficiency is the energy returned on energy invested (EROI),[2] which is a ratio of the amount of energy used to produce energy. For example, it takes energy to machine the separate parts of a generator in the nacelle of a wind turbine, gallons of gasoline or distillate fuel to ship the blades, energy to power the crane that raises the blades to the tower, and so forth, and in the end the wind turbine produces electricity for the next 25 years. Any number below one indicates that less energy is produced than the amount of energy that is used to produce that energy. In the case of ethanol, Murphy et al. (2011) find the EROI to be between 0.87 and 1.27. This clearly shows that there is very little return to the amount of energy invested. For comparison, Hall et al. (2014) find an EROI of 18 for wind power and between 27–80 for oil and gas. This metric is just one way to measure the relative efficacy of ethanol as a renewable fuel, and immediately casts doubt on the promise of any ben-eficial environmental effects when life cycle calculations are made. In fact, Murray et al. (2014) simulate future emissions amounts for the United States and find that removing ethanol-related provisions would actually decrease emissions. These authors even admit that "these results are, at first glance, counterintuitive".

Concerning the US Renewable Fuel Standard, Griffin (2013) concludes that it is time to reconsider ethanol mandates in the United States because the actual benefits have been minimal. Further, Griffin (2013) shows that the US ethanol mandate has had negative spillover effects in developing countries in the form of higher food prices. Similarly, Drabik and De Gorter (2013) show that there is a "leakage effect" from the US Renewable Fuel Standard because global emis-sions increase due to a drop in oil prices. Grafton et al. (2012) recognize this shift in equilibrium prices and the subsequent decrease in quantity demanded of non-ethanol (pure) gasoline demand as a green paradox. Greaker et al. (2014) use a numerical simulation to show that the introduc-tion of a renewable fuel standard slows the rate of oil depletion. The authors also find that even when biofuels are as emissions-intensive as oil, a renewable fuel standard may reduce climate costs. Grafton et al. (2012) finds that the opposite holds – that the adoption of new policies hurries the depletion rate of fossil fuels and causes more damage due to lower prices. It should be noted, though, that Grafton et al. (2012) do include the caveat that a green paradox is not a general result and that under certain specifications this effect ceases to hold. Given the very long half-life of CO_2 emissions, though, this discrepancy in the timing of emissions is less meaningful in the scope of greenhouse gas accumulation over time.

Beyond driving carbon emissions upwards through changes in fuel demand, or by emitting more life cycle emissions due to carbon-intensive inputs and a low EROI, conversion and loss of grassland may also lead to higher levels of CO_2 concentration. Brown et al. (2014) find that grassland conversion is positively correlated with the proximity to ethanol plants. Secchi et al. (2009) further find that farmers remove land from the US Department of Agriculture's Conser-vation Reserve Program, a subsidy program that incentivizes environmentally beneficial farming practices on fallow land, when the price of corn increases. An example of this occurrence is shown in Hellwinckel et al. (2016). In the six years following the passage of the 2007 Energy

Independence and Security Act (which further supported the renewable fuel standard), 56% of land in the Conservation Reserve Program did not re-enroll.

While there exists a number of simulation studies in the literature, few empirical studies have measured the exact amount of emissions that have been mitigated due to ethanol consumption. Szklo et al. (2005) find that 5.4 million metric tons of CO_2 emissions per year are avoided in Brazil due to ethanol consumption. Nguyen and Gheewala (2008) find that in Thailand the consumption of biofuels leads to a 4.3% life-cycle decrease in emissions compared to gasoline. Noel and Roach (2016) and (2017) discuss unintended consequences of an Australian state-level ethanol policy. These authors find that the switch to renewable fuels had the unintended effect of increasing (ethanol-free) premium fuel consumption at a major cost to consumers (Noel and Roach 2016) which resulted in the policy having nearly no effect on CO_2 emissions (Noel and Roach 2017). These authors estimate a cost per ton of CO_2 reduction at nearly $1,200.

Frankly, the near consensus of the literature is that the costs of a renewable fuel policy outweigh the realized benefits, especially if environmental goals are the focus. Indeed, the *Economist* may have summarized the literature on ethanol fuels most succinctly when they commented that the "biofuels that can best compete commercially are not, in fact, green", and that "those that are green cannot compete commercially" (*Economist*, 2015).

4   Conclusion

Renewable energy policies have been passed to expand the capacity of renewable energy and its ultimate consumption, but they have also been touted to meet myriad other goals from CO_2 mitigation to job creation and energy security. Although these various renewable goals and policy initiatives have been successful in terms of capacity buildup, future policy must take account of the intricacies of each technology and the location they will be utilized. A more granular look at the energy landscape reveals that in some cases these policies fell well short of their intended goals, and in some of the most dire cases these policies actually resulted in unintentionally increasing emissions. Certainly, mitigating CO_2 is a worthwhile endeavor to limit future global weather impacts, and renewable energy sources will necessarily play a role in achieving a low carbon society. The evidence presented here shows that, at least in the electric power sector, renewable energy policies must be complemented with other legislation to meet some of the more aspirational goals that are attached to passing these policies. Regarding ethanol policy, the evidence points to very limited positive impacts, if any, and in some cases there have been very harmful unintended consequences.

A ripe venue for future research is in the area of indirect effects from carbon legislation on renewable energy adoption and capacity building. Theoretical papers on the topic exist, but empirical applications will be able to be completed now that the few policies that exist have been passed and brought into force. The Regional Greenhouse Gas Initiative of 2009 is the oldest such policy in the United States, but it only covers emissions from the power sector, and only includes a few northeastern states. California passed carbon legislation in 2012, and Washington is due to vote on the topic soon. The European Emissions Trading System entered its first phase in 2005, yet recent factbooks from the system do not even include the words "wind" or "solar". Gauging the impact that new price signals and an internalized price of carbon have on renewable energy adoption will certainly be important to policy makers in the future as they reconsider subsidies like FITs or quota mandates like renewable portfolio standards. Moreover, the addition of grid-scale battery technology will certainly impact renewable energy market penetration, as well as the break-even costs of adopting new renewable energy capacity. All else equal, the intermittency issue wanes as more grid-scale batteries are brought online. These innovations could change the emissions profile of the electric grid by allowing wind energy to be sold during hot afternoon days – when wind speeds are typically at their lowest. However, early research indicates that the actual impact on emissions is critically dependent on the existing generation profile, and that emissions may in fact increase with more battery storage (Goteti et al. 2017; Fares and Webber 2017)

Renewable energy policy could also benefit from greater efforts regarding behavioral responses, and interdisciplinary collaboration in this area could be fruitful. For truly efficacious policy to be adopted, policies must be informed by research and economic models that account for "unexpected" psychological and social aspects.

Notes

1 For example, the price per emission allowance of CO_2 in Europe has stayed between EUR 5 and EUR 20 over the past few years.
2 EROI = Energy Produced Energy Invested.

References

Borenstein, Severin. 2012. The Private and Public Economics of Renewable Electricity Generation. *Journal of Economic Perspectives* 26 (1): 67–92. https://doi.org/10.1257/jep.26.1.67.

Brown, J. Christopher, Eric Hanley, Jason Bergtold, Marcelus Caldas, Vijay Barve, Dana Peterson, Ryan Callihan, et al. 2014. Ethanol Plant Location and Intensification vs. Extensification of Corn Cropping in Kansas. *Applied Geography* 53 (September): 141–148. https://doi.org/10.1016/j.apgeog.2014.05.021.

Callaway, Duncan S., Meredith Fowlie, and Gavin McCormick. 2017. Location, Location, Location: The Variable Value of Renewable Energy and Demand-Side Efficiency Resources. *Journal of the Association of Environmental and Resource Economists* 5 (1): 39–75. https://doi.org/10.1086/694179.

Carley, Sanya, Lincoln L. Davies, David B. Spence, and Nikolaos Zirogiannis. 2018. Empirical Evaluation of the Stringency and Design of Renewable Portfolio Standards. *Nature Energy*, 1 (July). https://doi.org/10.1038/s41560-018-0202-4.

Charles, Michael B., Rachel Ryan, Neal Ryan, and Richard Oloruntoba. 2007. Public Policy and Biofuels: The Way Forward? *Energy Policy* 35 (11): 573–746. https://doi.org/10.1016/j.enpol.2007.06.008.

Crago, Christine Lasco, and Ilya Chernyakhovskiy. 2017. Are Policy Incentives for Solar Power Effective? *Evidence from Residential Installations in the Northeast.* https://doi.org/10.1016/j.jeem.2016.09.008.

Dastrup, Samuel R., Joshua Graff Zivin, Dora L. Costa, and Matthew E. Kahn. 2012. Understanding the Solar Home Price Premium: Electricity Generation and Green Social Status. *European Economic Review* 56 (5): 96–173. https://doi.org/10.1016/j.euroecorev.2012.02.006.

Drabik, Duan, and Harry de Gorter. 2013. Emissions From Indirect Land Use Change: Do They Matter with Fuel Market Leakages? *Review of Agricultural and Applied Economics* 16 (02): 3–15. https://doi.org/10.15414/raae.2013.16.02.03-15.

TheEconomist. 2015. ThinHarvest, April 18, 2015. www.economist.com/science-andtechnology/2015/04/18/thin-harvest?Fsrc=Scn/Tw/Te/Pe/Ed/Thinharvest.

Fares, Robert L., and Michael E. Webber. 2017. The Impacts of Storing Solar Energy in the Home to Reduce Reliance on the Utility. *Nature Energy* 2.

Goteti, Naga Srujana, Eric Hittinger, and Eric Williams. 2017. How Much Wind and Solar Are Needed to Realize Emissions Benefits from Storage? *Energy Systems.* https://doi.org/10.1007/s12667-017-0266-4.

Grafton, R. Quentin, Tom Kompas, and Ngo Van Long. 2012. Substitution between Biofuels and Fossil Fuels: Is There a Green Paradox? *Journal of Environmental Economics and Management* 11 64 (3): 328–341. https://doi.org/10.1016/j.jeem.2012.07.008.

Greaker, Mads, Michael Hoel, and Knut Einar Rosendahl. 2014. Does a Renewable Fuel Standard for Biofuels Reduce Climate Costs? *Journal of the Association of Environmental and Resource Economists* 1 (3): 337–363. https://doi.org/10.1086/678189.

Griffin, James M. 2013. U.S. Ethanol Policy: Time to Reconsider? *The Energy Journal* 34 (4): 1–24.

Hall, Charles A. S., Jessica G. Lambert, and Stephen B. Balogh. 2014. EROI of Different Fuels and the Implications for Society. *Energy Policy* 64 (January): 141–152. https://doi.org/10.1016/j.enpol. 2013.05.049.

Hellwinckel, Chad, Christopher Clark, Matthew Langholtz, and Laurence Eaton. 2016. Simulated Impact of the Renewable Fuels Standard on US Conservation Reserve Program Enrollment and Conversion. *GCB Bioenergy* 8 (1): 245–256. https://doi.org/10.1111/gcbb.12281.

Hitaj, Claudia. 2013. Wind Power Development in the United States. *Journal of Environmental Economics and Management* 65 (3): 394–410. https://doi.org/10.1016/j.jeem.2012.10.003.

Hittinger, Eric, and Jawad Siddiqui. 2017. The Challenging Economics of US Residential Grid Defection. *Utilities Policy* 45 (April): 27–35. https://doi.org/10.1016/j.jup.2016.11.003.

Jaeger, William K., and Thorsten M. Egelkraut. 2011. Biofuel Economics in a Setting of Multiple Objectives and Unintended Consequences. *Renewable and Sustainable Energy Reviews* 15 (9): 4320–4333. https://doi.org/10.1016/j.rser.2011.07.118.

Maguire, Karen. 2016. What's Powering Wind? The Effect of the U.S. State Renewable Energy Policies on Wind Capacity (19942012). *Applied Economics* 48 (58): 571–730. https://doi.org/10.1080/00036846. 2016.1184375.

Matisoff, Daniel C., and Erik P. Johnson. 2017. The Comparative Effectiveness of Residential Solar Incentives. *Energy Policy* 108 (September): 44–54. https://doi.org/10.1016/j.enpol.2017.05.032.

Metcalf, Gilbert E. 2009. Market-Based Policy Options to Control U.S. Greenhouse Gas Emissions. *Journal of Economic Perspectives* 23 (2): 52–57. https://doi.org/10.1257/jep.23.2.5.

Murphy, David J., Charles A. S. Hall, and Bobby Powers. 2011. New Perspectives on the Energy Return on (Energy) Investment (EROI) of Corn Ethanol. *Environment, Development and Sustainability* 13 (1): 179–202. https://doi.org/10.1007/s10668-010-9255-7.

Murray, Brian C., Maureen L. Cropper, Francisco C. de la Chesnaye, and John M. Reilly. 2014. How Effective Are US Renewable Energy Subsidies in Cutting Greenhouse Gases? *The American 12 Economic Review* 104 (5): 569–574.

Nesta, Lionel, Francesco Vona, and Francesco Nicolli. 2014. Environmental Policies, Competition and Innovation in Renewable Energy. *Journal of Environmental Economics and Management* 67 (3): 396–411. https://doi.org/10.1016/j.jeem.2014.01.001.

Nguyen, Thu Lan T., and Shabbir H. Gheewala. 2008. Fuel Ethanol from Cane Molasses in Thailand: Environmental and Cost Performance. *Energy Policy* 36 (5): 1589–1599. https://doi.org/10.1016/j.enpol.2008.01.008.

Nicolli, Francesco, and Francesco Vona. 2016. Heterogeneous Policies, Heterogeneous Technologies: The Case of Renewable Energy. *Energy Economics* 56 (May): 190–204. https://doi.org/10.1016/j.eneco.2016.03.007.

Noel, Michael D., and Travis Roach. 2016. Regulated and Unregulated Substitutes: Aversion Effects of an Ethanol Mandate. *Economic Inquiry* 54 (2): 1150–1166. https://doi.org/10.1111/ecin.12258.

Noel, Michael D., and Travis Roach. 2017. Marginal Reductions in Vehicle Emissions under a Dual-Blend Ethanol Mandate: Evidence from a Natural Experiment. *Energy Economics* 64 (May): 45–54. https://doi.org/10.1016/j.eneco.2017.01.011.

Novan, Kevin. 2015. Valuing the Wind: Renewable Energy Policies and Air Pollution Avoided. *American Economic Journal: Economic Policy* 7 (3): 291–326. https://doi.org/10.1257/pol.20130268.

Pimentel, David. 2003. Ethanol Fuels: Energy Balance, Economics, and Environmental Impacts Are Negative. *Natural Resources Research* 12 (2): 127–134. https://doi.org/10.1023/A:1024214812527.

Roach, Travis. 2015. The Effect of the Production Tax Credit on Wind Energy Production in Deregulated Electricity Markets. *Economics Letters* 127 (February): 86–88. https://doi.org/10.1016/j.econlet.2014.12.017.

Rode, Johannes, and Alexander Weber. 2016. Does Localized Imitation Drive Technology Adoption? A Case Study on Rooftop Photovoltaic Systems in Germany. *Journal of Environmental Economics and Management* 78 (July): 38–48. https://doi.org/10.1016/j.jeem.2016.02.001.

Secchi, Silvia, Philip W. Gassman, Jimmy R. Williams, and Bruce A. Babcock. 2009. Corn Based Ethanol Production and Environmental Quality: A Case of Iowa and the Conservation Reserve Program. *Environmental Management* 44 (4): 732–744. https://doi.org/10.1007/s00267-009-9365-x.

Sexton, Steven E., and Alison L. Sexton. 2014. Conspicuous Conservation: The Prius Halo and Willingness to Pay for Environmental Bona Fides. *Journal of Environmental Economics and 13 Management* 67 (3): 30317. https://doi.org/10.1016/j.jeem.2013.11.004.

Szklo, Alexandre Salem, Roberto Schaeffer, Marcio Edgar Schuller, and William Chandler. 2005. Brazilian Energy Policies Side-Effects on CO2 Emissions Reduction. *Energy Policy* 33 (3): 349–364. https://doi.org/10.1016/j.enpol.2003.08.005.

Wu, JunJie, and Christian Langpap. 2015. The Price and Welfare Effects of Biofuel Mandates and Subsidies. *Environmental Resource Economics* 62 (1): 35–57. https://doi.org/10.1007/s10640-014-9814-8. 14.

13

The energy-water nexus

Benjamin K. Sovacool

1 Introduction

The hydrological cycle is the repeated process of the evaporation and redistribution of water in various forms around the earth. It highlights that water is truly a renewable resource, since the water that was here a million years ago is still here today, continuously moving back and forth between the earth's surface and atmosphere. Figure 13.1 shows that of the entire world's water, more than 97% is in the form of saltwater; 2% in the form of glaciers, ice caps, and snow; and less than 1%, or 200,000 cubic kilometers, easily accessible for human use.[1] The primary source of human freshwater is runoff from precipitation, naturally replenished through what scientists call the "hydrological cycle".

Prior to human interference, the hydrologic system was in long-term equilibrium. Discharges equaled recharges, and the volume of water remained constant. Groundwater levels did fluctuate over time, but only within a small natural range. Massive water use by the global energy sector has contributed significantly to altering this natural balance, a challenge made even starker by the cyclical and recurrent nature of drought. Furthermore, saltwater intrusion, due to rises in sea level that many scientists expect as a result of climate change, could cause a reduction of freshwater aquifers on both coasts of the United States by an additional 45% more than originally expected (U.S. Geological Survey 2003; Sovacool and Sovacool 2009). The US Government Accountability Office (2003) cautioned that water managers in 36 states anticipate freshwater shortages under normal conditions in the near future.

This chapter provides a broader overview of the energy water nexus in the United States and beyond – looking at how energy processes (coal mining, oil and gas production, uranium mining), sources of conversion/supply (power plants, dams, storage), and impacts (pollution, climate change) all effect water. It then discusses externalities and emerging impacts associated with this nexus, mainly increased water prices, water scarcity, subsidence, and negative impacts on agriculture, public health, and fisheries.

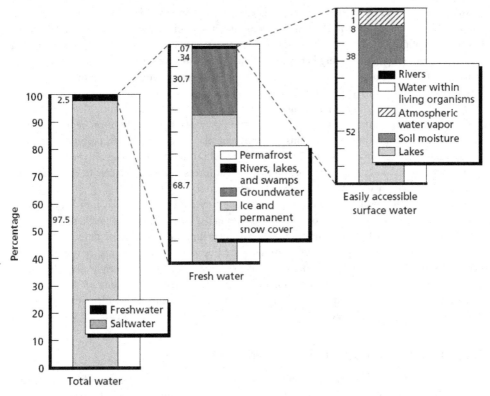

Figure 13.1 The earth's supply of water

Source: Boberg (2005: 16).

2 Water and energy production

2.1 Coal mining

The United States is home to roughly 2,100 coal mines currently operating in 27 states which mine about 1.131 trillion short tons of coal (Sovacool and Sovacool 2009). The Department of Energy (DOE) estimates that such mining activities use an additional 70 to 260 million gallons of water per day. Coal mining techniques naturally vary across the country based on geology and chemical composition of the rock and landscape, proximity to local water resources, mining methods, environmental regulations, types of coal, and extraction processes. Western coal is generally lower in sulfur content than eastern coal, but it also has a poorer heating value, meaning that more coal is needed to produce power. Due to the shallow nature of most western coal deposits, surface mining methods dominate coal mining in that region, making them less water intensive than their eastern counterparts, which rely on underground mining. In the western United States, 90% of mining is surface mining, whereas in Appalachia 65% is underground mining (Sovacool and Sovacool 2009).

In either case, water is needed to wash coal, remove sulfur, suppress dust, and reclaim vegetation for the surface. Depending on the mining techniques used, mines use between 10 and 150 gallons per ton of processed coal. The DOE estimated that, in 2000, overall water required for coal washing and mining was roughly between 4% and 12% of freshwater withdrawals for the entire mining sector. Coal mines also affect water quality and surrounding water resources. Underground and surface mines require the removal of material, topsoil, soil, and rocks in order to access coal. Western coals are often a significant part of a local aquifer, meaning that the removal of coal disrupts the natural recharge rate of the hydrological system. In addition, reclaimed areas in the West can be porous when it rains, allowing percolating water to leach pollutants through soil and into underground aquifers. Compressing the fill to reduce leaching only leads to lower recharge rates for the aquifer – a tenuous dilemma that forces mining managers to either directly pollute aquifers or greatly lower their natural recharge rates.

Mountaintop removal – a more recent technique for coal extraction that uses heavy explosives to blow apart the tops of mountains – has degraded streams and blighted landscapes, and reduced the water quality of communities. Coal slurry impoundments that fail, contaminated water, and occupational hazards (such as mine-related deaths and injuries) are among the social consequences of continued dependence on coal-fired power plants. In Pennsylvania, where 25% of the nation's historical coal production has occurred, drainage from abandoned coal mines has contaminated several thousand miles of surface streams and groundwater with acids, metals, and sediment (U.S. Geological Survey 2009).

2.2 Oil and natural gas production and refining

Fuel production facilities for oil need one to two billion gallons of water per day; those for natural gas use about 400 million gallons of water per day (Sovacool and Sovacool 2009). Again, however, the true water impacts from oil and gas production are not limited to water use. The USGS (2009) estimated that there are more than two million oil and natural gas wells in the domestic United States. The most intense areas of oil and gas production are off the shores of the Gulf of Mexico and along the northern coast of Alaska. The process of onshore oil production injects water into oil reserves to create extra pressure needed to push oil to the surface. As a result, offshore oil and natural gas exploration and production in the Gulf of Mexico leach chemicals into water sources by discharging drilling mud and cuttings, and also continually release low levels of hydrocarbons around production platforms (Peterson et al. 1996).

Liquefied natural gas (LNG) terminals bring their own assortment of water-related impacts, including the risk of harming local fish populations during routine operation, introducing invasive species from ballast water, and discharging toxic substances into the watershed. The construction of the proposed Broadwater Energy Project, an eight billion cubic feet large marine LNG terminal and underwater natural gas pipeline intended for Long Island Sound, would discharge approximately four million gallons of hydrostatic seawater treated with biocide (Sovacool and Sovacool 2009). The facility, once operating, would also utilize pollution control equipment that would discharge about 11 million gallons of brackish water every five years. During normal operation, Broadwater would withdraw about 28.2 million gallons per day of seawater, resulting in an estimated loss of 274 million fish eggs and larvae annually. The facility would also risk bringing invasive species to Long Island Sound from the ballast water of LNG tankers. The New York State Department of Environmental Conservation has warned that going ahead with Broadwater would create a "significant adverse impact to the aquatic environment and fishery of the Long Island Sound" (quoted in Sovacool and Sovacool 2009).

LNG re-gasification facilities typically release daily discharges of sodium hypochlorite (chlorine bleach) and wastewater during their operation. The lighting of LNG facilities can attract organisms, especially mollusks and marine invertebrates, from many miles away, only to suck them into intake structures where they are impinged and entrained. For these reasons, estimates of mortality rates for fish and marine species associated with LNG facilities may be underestimated by a factor of ten. The environmental impact assessment for the proposed Port Pelican Liquid Natural Gas processing facility on the coast of Louisiana, for instance, found that the entrainment from normal operation would effectively "sterilize" the entire water column around the facility (Thompson 2004).

2.3   Uranium mining and leeching

For nuclear power, uranium mining – the process of extracting uranium ore from the ground – is extremely water intensive. Since quantities of uranium are mostly prevalent at very low concentrations, uranium mining is volume intensive. Early mining techniques were very similar to other hard rock mining such as copper, gold, and silver, and involved the creation of underground mines. Open-pit mining – the most prevalent type of uranium extraction in the world today – ceased in the United States in 1992 due to concerns about environmental contamination and the quality of uranium, as most uranium ore found in the United States was lower grade from sandstone deposits. Currently, uranium miners use only one type of technique to extract uranium ore in Wyoming, Nebraska, and Texas – in-situ leaching.

Uranium miners perform in-situ leaching by pumping liquids into the area surrounding uranium deposits. These liquids often include acid or alkaline solutions to weaken the calcium or sandstone surrounding uranium ore. Operators then pump the uranium up into recovery wells at the surface, where it is collected. In-situ leaching was deemed more cost-effective than underground mining because it avoids the significant expense of excavating underground sites and often takes less time to implement. Nonetheless, it uses significantly more water – as much as seven to eight gallons for every kWh of nuclear power generated from US-based uranium.

3   Water and energy conversion and supply

3.1   Thermoelectric cooling cycles

Almost all conventional power plants employ one of two types of fuel cycles in their generation of electricity. Once-through cooling systems withdraw water from a source, circulate it, and return it to the surface body. Re-circulating, or closed-loop, systems withdraw water and then recycle it within the power system rather than discharge it.

Thermoelectric power plants – those relying on coal, oil, natural gas, and biomass/waste, or the use of uranium in nuclear reactors – withdraw water from rivers, lakes, and streams to cool equipment before returning it to its source, and they consume it through evaporative loss. The average power plant uses about 25 gallons (95 liters) of water for every kilowatt-hour (kWh) generated (see Table 13.1). Given that the world consumes about 17,000 terawatt-hours (TWh) of electricity annually, power plants ostensibly used 425 trillion gallons (1.61 quadrillion liters) of water that year. This means that, on average, thermoelectric generators use more water than the agricultural and horticultural industries combined. The water use of individual power plants is even more striking. A conventional 500 MW coal plant, for instance, consumes about

Table 13.1 Water use (consumption and withdrawals) for selected power plants, in gallons per kWh

	Withdrawals	Consumption	Withdrawals	Consumption	Total
	(Combustion/Downstream)		(Production/Upstream)		
Nuclear	43	0.4	0	0.11	43.5
Coal (mining)	35	0.3	0.17	0.045	35.5
Coal (slurry)	35	0.3	0	0.05	35.3
Biomass/waste	35	0.3	0.03	0.03	35.3
Natural gas	13.75	0.1	0	0.01	13.9
Solar thermal	4.5	4.6	0	0	9.1
Hydroelectric	0	0	0	4.5	4.5
Geothermal (steam)	2	1.4	0	0	3.4
Solar PV	0	0	0	0.3	0.3
Wind	0	0	0	0.2	0.2
Energy Efficiency	0	0	0	0	0

Source: Sovacool and Sovacool (2009).

7,000 gallons (26,498 liters) of water per minute, or the equivalent of 17 Olympic-sized swimming pools every day.

As their name implies, once-through cooling systems, or "open-loop" systems, only use water once, as it passes through a condenser to absorb heat. Plant operators commonly add chlorine intermittently to control microbes that corrode pipes and materials. Operators may also add several toxic and carcinogenic chemicals such as hexavalent chromium and hydrazine. After it passes through the plant, heated and treated water is then discharged downstream from its point of intake to a receiving body of water. Since such cooling systems release heated water back to the source, they can contribute to evaporative loss by raising the temperature of receiving water bodies. Once-through cooling systems are more common in the eastern United States. Once-through systems withdraw about 91% of the nation's water used for power plants, and 59 of the country's 103 nuclear reactors rely on this type of cooling, each drawing as much as one billion gallons of water into its cooling system per day (or more than 500,000 gallons a minute) (Gunter et al. 2001).

Re-circulating or closed-loop systems, by recycling water, withdraw much less of it but tend to consume more. Since it is being reused, the water also requires more chemical treatment to eliminate naturally occurring salts and solids that accumulate as water evaporates. To maintain plant performance, water is frequently discharged from the system at regular intervals into a reservoir or collection pond. Plant operators call this water cooling-tower blowdown. Once the plants release blowdown, operators treat freshwater with chlorine and biocides before it enters the cooling cycle. Closed-loop systems rely on greater amounts of water for cleaning and therefore return less water to the original source. Closed-loop systems are more common in the western United States.

At reactor sites, even when not generating a single kilowatt hour of electricity, nuclear plants must use water continuously. Nuclear plants need water to remove the decay heat produced by the reactor core and also to cool equipment and buildings used to provide the core's heat removal. Service water must lubricate oil coolers for the main turbine and chillers for air conditioning, in essence cooling the equipment that in turn cools the reactor. Even when plants are not producing electricity, service water needs can be quite high: 52,000 gallons of water are needed per minute in the summer at the Hope Creek plant in New Jersey; 30,000 gallons per minute for the Milestone Unit 2 in Connecticut; and 13,500 gallons per minute for the Pilgrim plant in Massachusetts (Sovacool and Sovacool 2009).

3.2 Nuclear accidents and spills

Electricity generation using nuclear technology can create wastewater contaminated with radioactive tritium and other toxic substances that can leak into nearby groundwater sources. Twenty-seven of the 104 nuclear reactors in the United States were recently found to have tainted groundwater with dangerous levels of tritium (Associated Press 2010). In December 2005, for example, Exelon Corporation reported to authorities that its Braidwood reactor in Illinois had since 1996 released millions of gallons of tritium-contaminated wastewater into the local watershed, prompting the company to distribute bottled water to surrounding communities while local drinking water wells were tested for the pollutant. Similarly, in New York, a faulty drain system at Entergy's Indian Point Nuclear Plant on the Hudson River caused thousands of gallons of radioactive waste to be leaked into underground lakes. The Nuclear Regulatory Commission (NRC) accused Entergy of not properly maintaining two spent fuel pools that leaked tritium and strontium-90 – cancer-causing radioactive isotopes – into underground watersheds, with as much as 50 gallons of radioactive waste seeping into water sources per day (Sovacool and Sovacool 2009).

3.3 Hydroelectricity

The act of building large hydroelectric dams with reservoirs degrades water quality in at least two ways: during construction when impoundment must occur, contributing to the diversion of water, flooding, and erosion; and during operation, when the dam acts as a physical barrier within rivers. For example, flooding reservoir areas converts all of the existing biomass there into carbon dioxide, methane, and nitrous oxide through decomposition, microbial methanogenesis, and denitrification. Dams thus change the hydrology of water sources near the reservoir and contribute to greenhouse gas emissions.

The physical structure of the dam, once built, alters water quality and flow. Often, hydroelectric dams negatively influence water quality through changes in the concentration of dissolved oxygen, nutrient loads, and suspended sediments, and that tidal encroachment could aggravate bank erosion. Table 13.2 provides an overview of these impacts, along with others, divided into the construction, impoundment, and operational phases.

For example, dams can trap sediment and most of the nutrients normally flowing through the river. This will alter downstream habitats because sediments are no longer able to provide organic and inorganic nutrients, and also change the acidification of the reservoir water. An additional problem is that tropical environments are prone to the proliferation of algae near the surfaces of nutrient-rich reservoirs, dramatically depleting the oxygen level of the water in concert with the decomposition of vegetation and soils. The rapid water fluctuations resulting from the operation of the spillway would also increase riverbank erosion downstream, wash away trees, and prevent the spawning of fish. Conversely, dams will negatively influence the population of freshwater fish which become easily disoriented in slow-moving waters, and fish living near the dam would be susceptible to pulverization from passing through the turbines or supersaturation and excess nitrogen from the water around the concrete face.

Table 13.2 Possible water impacts from large-scale hydroelectric projects

Stage	Environmental Impact
Clearing and construction	Increased turbidity
	Loss of pool nursery habitat
	Reduced organic input
	Impaired migration
Impoundment	Reduced river flow, turbidity, and organic input
	Loss of habitat due to reduced water depth
	Reduced reservoir turbidity
	Increased phytoplankton production
	Impaired fish migration
	Replacement of natural riverine habitat with artificial deep lake habitat
Operation	Reduced river turbidity
	Reduced river dissolved oxygen content
	Increased hydrogen sulfide
	Impaired fish migration
	Altered upstream species composition
	Replacement of native riverine species with lake-adapted species in reservoir

Source: Sovacool and Bulan (2011).

3.4 Power plant construction

Even constructing large fossil fuel and nuclear power plants can have significant water-related needs and impacts. Some of the largest power plant components, such as turbines, boilers, and reactor cooling towers, have special shipping requirements. In Georgia, billions of gallons of water had to be released from Lake Lanier to raise water levels on the lower Chattahoochee River so that replacement steam generators could be shipped to the Farley nuclear power plant near Dothan, Alabama. The Army Corps of Engineers even had to design and maintain a shipping channel from Savannah, Georgia, to August, Georgia, so that power plant equipment could be moved on the river. Since maintenance on the deepwater channel ended in 1979 and Lake Lanier is currently running low on water, power plant operators have warned that rivers in some parts of the South would have to be dredged to allow reactor upgrades and construction of new large power plants to occur.

3.5 Fuel storage and wastes

Thermoelectric power plants can degrade water resources in a number of other ways. At coal plants, coal pile runoff forms when water encounters coal storage piles. Coal pile runoff is usually acidic and contains high concentrations of copper, zinc, magnesium, aluminum, chloride, iron, sodium, and sulfate. When plant operators clean coal piles before combustion, the water used for coal cleaning transports pyrites such as suspended solids, sulfates, and metals into the surrounding ecosystem.

During the process of fossil fuel and nuclear electricity generation, impurities also build up over time in the boiler. To maintain quality, water is periodically purged from the boiler and replaced with clean water. The purged water, referred to as "boiler blowdown", is often alkaline and contains chemical additives (used for controlling corrosion) as well as trace elements of copper, iron, and nickel that leach from boiler parts.

Plant operators often withdraw and discharge small amounts of water to support the operation of air emissions controls. The combustion waste steam, a mixture of fly ash, bottom ash, boiler slag, and sludge from emissions controls, is typically drenched with water and placed in cooling ponds. Also,

> the country's 600 coal- and oil-fired power plants produce more than one hundred million tons of sludge waste every year. Seventy-six million tons of this waste is primarily disposed on-site at each power plant in unlined wastewater lagoons and landfills that are seldom monitored by the EPA. These wastes are highly toxic, containing concentrated levels of poisons such as arsenic, mercury, and cadmium that can severely damage the human nervous system.
> *(Sovacool and Sovacool 2009: 110–111)*

The Arizona Department of Environmental Quality, for example, documented that power stations in Arizona were contaminating ground and surface water with boron, sulfate, chloride, and sediments as a result of disposal of fly and bottom ash in unlined ponds with no leachate collection system to capture contaminants.

In addition to leaking into ground and surface water, lagoons and waste ponds can break and cause devastating spills. In 2000, water containing hundreds of millions of gallons of sludge busted through the bottom of an impoundment system in Kentucky and contaminated dozens of creeks and the Big Sandy River (Baum 2004). The sludge decimated local fish populations and buried some homes under seven feet of waste. In 2003, another coal impoundment in Virginia overflowed and spilled thousands of gallons of liquid coal wastes into surrounding rivers (Baum 2004). Following the disposal of coal combustion waste in Pines, Indiana, water from at least 40 residential wells and one business well became contaminated and undrinkable with levels of manganese, arsenic, lead, and boron that far exceeded safe drinking water standards in 2004. Another well near two power plants in Wyoming measured eight times the concentration of boron considered acceptable by the federal government. In late 2008, yet another incident occurred in Tennessee where more than one billion gallons of thick coal ash and sludge containing mercury and arsenic escaped from a Tennessee Valley Authority retention site at their Kingston power plant. The failing waste pond spilled enough toxic coal sludge to fill 1,660 Olympic-sized swimming pools into the Clinch River, contaminated 300 acres of land, destroyed 15 homes, and caused more than $1 billion in damages throughout an area bigger than the Exxon Valdez oil spill. Worryingly, of the 635 coal waste lagoons located nationwide, the Clean Air Task Force estimates that 240 have been constructed in areas atop abandoned underground mines at risk of collapsing.

Wastewater ponds and lagoons that do not leak can still cause serious environmental damage to migrating birds. Scientists have found that "ingesting water with large amounts of dissolved salts can make birds more susceptible to avian botulism" and can "pose chronic effects to aquatic birds" (Ramirez et al. 1992).

4 Water and energy pollution

4.1 Air pollution

Conventional electricity generation is by far the largest source of air pollutants that damages water supplies and contributes to global warming, including sulfur dioxide, nitrogen oxides, mercury, particulate matter, and carbon dioxide. Such pollution, which in some form is concentrated in almost every region of the country, can significantly degrade water quality. Furthermore, power plant emissions can completely shut off precipitation from clouds. One study utilized satellite data from space-borne and in situ aircraft and concluded that plumes of reduced cloud particle size and suppression of precipitation occurred near major urban areas and power plants (Rosenfeld 2000).

4.2 Climate change

Power plant emissions contribute directly to climate change, which negatively affects water resources by increasing temperatures, altering precipitation patterns, changing the availability of snowpack, and magnifying the risk of flooding and drought. Warmer temperatures resulting from global warming, for instance, will increase energy demands in urban areas and require more intensive air-conditioning loads, in turn raising the water needs for thermoelectric power generators (Nelson et al. 2007). Hotter weather also increases the evaporation rates for lakes, rivers, and streams, and thus accelerates the depletion of reservoirs. Hotter weather also causes more intense and longer-lasting droughts as well as more wildfires – which in turn need vast quantities of water to fight and control them.

The National Academies of Science projected (in three of four simulations) that continued climate change will result in winter decreases of available precipitation by 15% to 30%, with reductions of snowpack concentrated in the Central Valley and along the northern Pacific Coast (Hayhoe et al. 2004). Climatologists and atmospheric scientists already predict that continued rising temperatures will likely produce substantial reductions in snowpack in the Sierra Nevada Mountains, with significant reductions in Californian stream flow, water storage, and supply expected. Indeed, snowpack levels have been below average for 13 of the last 16 years in the Columbia River Basin, 11 of 16 years in the Colorado Basin, and 14 of 16 years in the Rio Grande. For the nation as a whole, warmer precipitation falling as rain instead of snow will likely reduce snowpack between 26% and 40% by 2049 and between 29% and 89% by 2099, resulting in less water available for power plants and other uses. Thus, by emitting carbon into the atmosphere, fossil-fueled power plants slowly but measurably contribute to climate change, rising temperatures, and drought, which in turn threaten to constrain future power production at those very power plants.

5 Externalities and emerging impacts of the energy-water nexus

5.1 Increased water prices

The first consequence of rising demand for water will be escalating prices for both water and electricity. As water demand increases while supplies decrease, water prices will escalate, and because of the immense costs of upgrading and building water infrastructure, water prices will rise even higher. For example, the American Water Works Association (2007) reported that water charges increased on average 7% for residential customers from 2004 to 2006 nationwide, due to a combination of constrained supply, infrastructure expenses, and water quality concerns. EPRI (2002) that the nation would need as much as $239 billion to properly maintain existing water treatment infrastructure. If demand for water continues to grow at current rates, one report estimated the need to invest more than $550 billion (Sustainable Water Res. Roundtable 2005), while other federal estimates project $1 trillion could be needed between 2000 and 2020 (Jehl 2003).

While calculating the effect of infrastructural investment on future prices is difficult, if the costs (at the low end of the estimate) are distributed equally over the next 17 years, the nation will need to spend $46.2 billion each year on water infrastructure, equal to roughly half the existing water industry's annual revenue. More worryingly, after assessing the global water infrastructure needs of 182 countries, Gleick (2003) found that most of these types of cost projections are "routinely and often substantially underestimated, even without accounting for hard-to-measure environmental and social costs". Perhaps because of these trends, one report concluded that "in the business as usual scenario . . . the cost of supplying water to domestic and industrial users will rise dramatically" (Rosegrant et al. 2002: 4–5).

5.2 Aggravated water shortages

Deficiencies in water supply and water quality already cause about 4,500 deaths throughout the world every day or 1.7 million deaths a year, 90% of these in young children. More than one billion people lack access to clean water, and 2.6 billion do not have access to improved sanitation facilities (Schaefer 2008). Some rivers, aquifers, lakes, and other water sources are so polluted that it is more profitable for residents to remove plastic bottles and trash from them for recycling than to fish. The US Central Intelligence Agency believes that more than three billion people will be living in water-stressed regions around the world by 2015 (with a majority concentrated in North Africa and China). Water tables for major grain producing areas in northern China are dropping at a rate of five feet per year, and per capita water availability in India is expected to drop 50% to 75% over the next decade (Pope 2005).

For example, in China the urban population grew from 300 million in 1990 to 550 million in 2005, creating a consequent increase in the demand for water. Surface and groundwater resources surrounding cities have diminished as a result and more than 100 million urban Chinese consume water contaminated with human and animal waste. The tension between providing water for drinking, manufacturing, and irrigation is especially acute in the Yellow River basin in Northern China, home to 13% of food production but only 3% of the nation's water (Schaefer 2008).

India, heavily dependent on groundwater for irrigation and drinking, has lost 15% of its aquifers due to contamination and overuse and is projected to lose 60% by 2030. Inefficient diesel water pumps provide most of the irrigation and well systems throughout India, but tend to leak (wasting water) and inject pollutants into water sources (Sovacool et al. 2014).

In the United States, sedimentation is reducing reservoir capacity by about 1.5 million acre feet (1.8 billion cubic meters) per year (Frederick 1995), and water managers in 36 states anticipate freshwater shortages under normal conditions in the near future (U.S. General Accounting Office 2003). Scientists looking at soil erosion and increased droughts in the past few years have warned about the likelihood of the western United Sates experiencing another "dustbowl" within the next 150 years (Dunham 2008).

5.3 Subsidence and deterioration of water quality

Rising electricity and water prices tell only part of the story. By using large amounts of water, power plants alter the flow of surface water and in some cases directly consume groundwater. Such intensive water practices alter the naturally balanced hydrological cycle by depleting water sources faster than they normally replenish. Ironically, the more water supplies are depleted, the more electricity is needed to help supply and convey water. Already, about 3% of the nation's electricity goes merely toward moving water. The most energy-intensive portion of water delivery is pumping, which varies with water depth: 540 kWh per million gallons from a depth of

120 feet, but as much as 2,000 kWh per million gallons at depth of 400 feet. In California, the state consumes 7% of its electricity just for pumping water (the amount of electricity required to transport water to Southern California is so significant because the water must be transported more than 1,000 kilometers via canal and pumped over the Tehachapi Mountains, a vertical lift of 610 meters). Greater use of thermoelectric power plants thus depletes available water, and then requires more electricity to pump water to existing plants, creating a feedback loop that worsens the problem.

In addition to creating a need to draw water from deeper and more distant places, sustained water pumping induces subsidence, the gradual settling or sudden sinking of the earth's surface. In the southwest, subsidence often occurs as deep fissures and cracks, while in the east it appears as sinkholes. More than 80% of subsidence in the United States is related to the withdrawal or pumping of groundwater. Subsidence significantly damages buildings, wells, highways, and water systems, as well as the operation of flood reservoirs and drainage facilities. If subsidence occurs over aquifers, it can compact the land and reduce permanent storage capacity by 30%. In some parts of Arizona, for example, water level declines have exceeded 300 feet and resulted in subsidence greater than 10 feet. When subsidence occurs near coastal aquifers, saltwater can migrate inland to completely contaminate water supplies.

5.4   Agriculture

In the agricultural sector, irrigation systems rely on electricity to convey water. For instance, three-fourths of irrigation systems in Colorado are electrical. Rising water prices could place great stress on cropland, livestock, and food production. Researchers at the University of Georgia calculated that for every $1 million decline in agricultural production, there is a resulting additional $700,000 decline in other sectors of the economy (U.S. General Accounting Office 2003).

5.5   Public health

In the health sector, degraded water quality and water shortages acutely affect chemotherapy patients, those living with HIV/AIDS, transplant patients, children and infants, the elderly, and pregnant women and their fetuses, in addition to others with special health needs (Sovacool and Sovacool 2009).

5.6   Aquaculture and fisheries

At the point of intake, thermoelectric plants bring water into their cooling cycles through specially designed structures. To minimize the entry of debris, water is often drawn through screens. Seals, sea lions, endangered manatees, American crocodiles, sea turtles, fish, larvae, shellfish, and other riparian or marine organisms are frequently killed as they are trapped against the screens in a process known as impingement. Organisms small enough to pass through the screens can be swept up in the water flow where they are subject to mechanical, thermal, and toxic stress in a process known as entrainment. Smaller fish, fish larvae, spawn, and a tremendous volume of other marine organisms are frequently pulverized by power plant cooling systems. One study estimated that more than 90% are scalded and discharged back into the water as lifeless sediment that clouds the water around the discharge area, blocking light from the ocean or river floor, which further kills plant and animal life by curtailing light and oxygen – a process known as "cultural eutrophication".

Impingement and entrainment consequently account for substantial losses of fish and exact severe environmental consequences. For example, US environmental studies of entrainment during the 1980s at five power plants on the Hudson River in New York (Indian Point, Bowline, Roseton, Lovett, and Danskammer) estimated grave year-class reductions in fish populations (the percent of fish killed within a given age class). Authorities noted that power plants were responsible for age reductions as high as 79% for some species, and an updated analysis of entrainment at three of these plants estimated year-class reductions of 20% for striped bass, 25% for bay anchovy, and 43% for Atlantic tom cod. Other researchers have evaluated entrainment and impingement impacts at nine facilities along a 500-mile (805 km) stretch of the Ohio River. The researchers estimated that approximately 11.6 million fish were killed annually through impingement and 24.5 million fish from entrainment. The study calculated recreational related losses at about USD 8.1 million per year (Sovacool and Sovacool 2009).

Thermoelectric power plants also alter the temperatures of lakes, rivers, and streams. The data on temperature intake and discharge points for 150 nuclear reactors in the United States, for example, revealed that they had summer or winter discharges with water temperature deltas (differences between intake and discharge water temperatures) greater than 25°F (3.9°C). In some cases, the thermal pollution from centralized power plants can induce eutrophication – a process whereby the warmer temperature alters the chemical composition of the water, resulting in a rapid increase of nutrients such as nitrogen and phosphorous and less oxygen. In riparian environments, the enhanced growth of algae can choke vegetation and collapse entire ecosystems, and this form of thermal pollution has been known to decrease the aesthetic and recreational value of rivers, lakes, and estuaries, and to complicate drinking water treatment (Baum et al. 2004).

6 Conclusion: tradeoffs and policy implications

These different impacts across water pricing, scarcity, subsidence, agriculture, health, and fisheries become compounded when they occur together, as part of an integrated electricity system rather than isolated, individual plants. One assessment of population growth, electricity use, and shortages of water during the summer in the United States found that 22 counties and 20 large metropolitan areas could experience severe water shortages by 2025. The study noted that the power plants could deplete the water available from Lake Lanier in Georgia and exacerbate interstate litigation between Tennessee, Alabama, and Florida. Biodiversity could perish along the Catawba-Wateree River Basin in North Carolina. Chicago could find itself embroiled in domestic and international legal disputes over the consumption and withdrawal of water from Lake Michigan. Households and businesses could run out of water from the South Platte River in Colorado. Rivers could stop recharging the groundwater needed for drinking and irrigation in Texas. Lake Mead and the Colorado River could continue to suffer drought, drastically affecting the state of Nevada, inducing an agricultural crisis in California and Mexico. Fisheries along the Hudson River in New York could collapse. The Delta smelt could become extinct in the San Joaquin River Basin in California. These impending but avertable risks serve an important reminder that climate change is not the only serious environmental issue facing the electricity industry (Sovacool and Sovacool 2009).

However, while growing electricity demand, more frequent and severe droughts, and changing precipitation patterns make an electric utility system predicated on thermoelectric power plants increasingly vulnerable to water constraints, vulnerabilities can be lessened by reducing the water intensity of thermoelectric generation, decreasing the electric grid's reliance on thermoelectric generation, and by improving data collection and dissemination on the link between electricity and water.

First, many technologies already exist to reduce the water intensity at thermal power plants. The most water intensive part of thermal plants, cooling cycles, can use commercially available recirculating and dry systems to reduce withdrawals. Alternative sources of water, including both wastewater and water capturable in power plant processes, can displace fresh water use. More efficient power plants also use less water. Reducing the water intensity of thermal power plants would reduce risks from water vulnerabilities while maintaining the current generation paradigm but faces challenges in cost and in retrofitting (Sovacool and Gilbert 2014).

Second, taking actions to shift our electric grid away from reliance on thermoelectric plants can reduce water related reliability concerns. These actions could include placing a moratorium on new thermoelectric generation while increasing energy efficiency, demand side management, and renewable energy production. Moratoriums have already been called for. Energy efficiency can reduce load growth to the point where additional generation is not needed. Increasingly cost competitive solar PV and wind can displace current water intensive generation.

Third, increasing and widening our understanding of how water constraints affect electricity and energy will better enable us to address the challenge. The average individual is unaware of this close connection and does not behave accordingly. Government agencies are collecting data about water use at thermal plants that is inconsistent and incomplete. Similarly, research efforts focusing on the energy water nexus are often fragmented by discipline or department. Inter-disciplinary teams that draw from the natural and physical sciences, social sciences, and arts and humanities are rare, as our transdisciplinary efforts that bridge the academic and non-academic divide. By improving data collection systems, and a broader range of researchers and stakeholders, we can better understand past and potential conflicts. Importantly this data can be used to inform policymakers who can then make better decisions about how to manage the electricity-water nexus.

Note

1 Freshwater is water that contains less than 1,000 milligrams per liter of dissolved solids; saltwater contains more than 1,000 mg/l, although generally more than 500 mg/l of dissolved solids is undesirable for drinking and for many industrial uses.

References

American Water Works Association. *2006 Water and Wastewater Rate Survey* (Washington, DC: AWWA, 2007).

Associated Press. "Leaks Spotlight Aging Nuclear Plants," February 1, 2010.

Baum, Ellen. *Wounded Waters: The Hidden Side of Power Plant Pollution* (Washington, DC: Clean Air Task Force, February, 2004).

Boberg, Jill. *Liquid Assets: How Demographic Changes and Water Management Policies Affect Freshwater Resources* (Santa Monica, CA: Rand Corporation, 2005).

Dunham, Will. "Fivefold Dust Increase Chokes the West," *Reuters*, February 24, 2008, available at www.reuters.com/article/environmentNews/idUSN2259224520080224.

EPRI. Water & Sustainability: An Assessment of Water Demand, Supply, and Quality in the U.S.: The Next Half Century 5.2–5.3(2002) [hereinafter EPRI, Water & Sustainability V.2].

Frederick, Kenneth D. "America's Water Supply: Status and Prospects for the Future," *Consequences* 1(1) (1995): 34–41.

Gleick, Peter H. "Water Use," *Annual Review of Environment & Resources* 28 (2003): 275, 303.

Gunter, Linda et al., Licensed to Kill: How the Nuclear Power Industry Destroys Endangered Marine Wildlife and Ocean Habitat to Save Money 1 (2001).

Hayhoe, Katharine et al., "Emissions Pathways, Climate Change, and Impacts on California," *Proceedings of the National Academy of Sciences*. 34 (2004): 12422, 12424.

Jehl, Douglas. "As Cities Move to Privatize Water, Atlanta Steps Back," *N.Y. Times*, February 18, 2003, available at http://query.nytimes.com/gst/fullpage.html?res=9D02E1DD113BF933A25751C0A9659C8B63

Nelson, Barry et al. Natural Res. Def. Council, in Hot Water: Water Management Strategies to Weather the Effects of Global Warming 16 (2007).

Peterson, Charles H. et al. "Ecological Consequences of Environmental Perturbations Associated with Offshore Hydrocarbon Production: A Perspective on the Long-Term Exposures in the Gulf of Mexico," *Canadian Journal of Fisheries and Aquaculture Science.* 53 (1996): 2637, 2637–2654.

Pope, Carl. "The State of Nature: Our Roof Is Caving in," *Foreign Policy*, 67 (2005).

Ramirez, Jr., Pedro U.S. Fish & Wildlife Serv., Trace Element Concentrations in Flue Gas Desulfurization Wastewater from the Jim Bridger Power Plant, Sweetwater County, Wyoming 7 (1992)

Rosegrant, Mark W. et al. Int'l Food Pol'y Research Inst., Global Water Outlook to 2025: Averting an Impending Crisis 4–5 (2002).

Rosenfeld, Daniel. "Suppression of Rain and Snow by Urban and Industrial Air Pollution," *Science* (March 10, 2000): 1793.

Schaefer, Mark. "Water Technologies and the Environment: Ramping up by Scaling Down," *Technology in Society* 30 (2008): 415–422.

Sovacool, Benjamin K. and L.C. Bulan. "Behind an Ambitious Megaproject in Asia: The History and Implications of the Bakun Hydroelectric Dam in Borneo," *Energy Policy* 39(9) (September, 2011): 4842–4859.

Sovacool, Benjamin K. and Alex Gilbert. "Developing Adaptive and Integrative Strategies for Managing the Electricity-Water Nexus," *University of Richmond Law Review* 48 (April, 2014): 997–1032.

Sovacool, Benjamin K., Sara Imperiale, Alex Gilbert, Jay Eidsness and Brian Thomson. "Troubled Waters: The Quest for Electricity in Water-Constrained China, France, India, and the United States," *New York University Environmental Law Journal* 21(3) (Fall, 2014): 409–450.

Sovacool, Benjamin K. and Kelly E. Sovacool. "Identifying Future Electricity Water Tradeoffs in the United States," *Energy Policy* 37(7) (2009): 2763–2773.

Sovacool, Benjamin K. and Kelly E. Sovacool. "Preventing National Electricity-Water Crisis Areas in the United States," *Columbia Journal of Environmental Law* 34(2) (July, 2009): 333–393.

Sustainable Water Res. Roundtable, Preliminary Report on Water Sustainability 36–37 tbl.4.5.1 (2005), available at http://acwi.gov/swrr/Rpt_Pubs/ prelim_rpt/Chapter_4_SWRRInd.pdf.

Thompson, Nancy B. Potential Impacts of Liquid Natural Gas Processing Facilities on Fishery Organisms in the Gulf of Mexico, at 7 (2004).

U.S. General Accounting Office. *Freshwater Supply: States' Views of How Federal Agencies Could Help Them Meet the Challenges of Expected Shortages* (Washington, DC: GAO-03-514, July, 2003).

U.S. Geological Survey, "Ground-Water Depletion across the Nation," *USGS Fact Sheet 103–03* (2003), available at http://pubs.usgs.gov/fs/fs-103-03/

USGS. *National Oil and Gas Assessment*, available at http://geology.usgs.gov/connections/blm/energy/o&g_assess.htm (last visited February 2, 2009).

14

Low carbon economy and smart grids

Cédric Clastres and Patrice Geoffron

1 Introduction

The transition towards a low carbon economy gives rise to scenarios based on dense deployment of renewable energy (RE) and greater energy efficiency (EE). By 2060 RE and EE are expected to respectively account for 35% and 40% of reductions in greenhouse gas (GHG) emissions, according to the 2°C scenario of the International Energy Agency (IEA, 2017a). The energy sector is contributing to this reduction by deploying intermittent and distributed RE technologies (primarily photovoltaic and wind). Changes of this nature necessarily impact the organization of the electricity sector, in particular balancing of supply and demand, and the security and reliability of electricity supply in the face of rising demand. It will consequently be necessary to "digitalize" the energy sector with a diverse portfolio of smart grid (SG) technologies, such as smart meters, sensors on electricity networks, data centers, software and appliances for demand-side management (DSM), and electric-vehicle chargers.

SG technologies have attracted considerable interest in fields as diverse as economics, sociology and electrical engineering for more than a decade (Coll-Mayor et al., 2007; Clastres, 2011). The European approach defines SG as "an electricity network that can cost efficiently integrate the behaviour and actions of all users connected to it – generators, consumers and those that do both – in order to ensure economically efficient, sustainable power system with low losses and high levels of quality and security of supply and safety".[1] In contrast the US Department of Energy focuses on safety. A smart grid should

> be self-healing from power disturbance events; enabling active participation by consumers in demand response; operating resiliently against physical and cyber-attack; providing power quality for 21st century needs; accommodating all generation and storage options; enabling new products, services, and markets; optimizing assets and operating efficiently.[2]

In Section 2 we briefly present the main issues regarding SG deployment, starting with the factors which prompted modernization of power grids. Section 3 outlines the mechanisms for financing smart grids, given that the majority of their assets are still in the regulated public sector. Some private investment, particularly to enable demand to be managed (software optimizing energy consumption, energy boxes), may also qualify for subsidies due to uncertainty as to the return on such investments (Clastres, 2011). After all, any reduction in demand depends on the consumer, not just on power-system instrumentation. The gains actually achieved may therefore not match investments. In Section 4 we analyze consumer acceptance of SG technologies. These new devices can lead to misunderstanding and hostility. Alternatively, they may optimize consumption and prompt virtuous shifts in behavior. Acceptance is crucial to promoting integration of renewable energies and the march towards a "low carbon" economy. Consumers are often seen as the main source of SG-related gains. Without their involvement it will be impossible to reap the full economic, social, and collective benefits of this innovation. Section 5 presents demand-side management, a means of integrating renewable energies (demand flexibility making allowance for the intermittent nature of renewable energy) and power-system flexibility (shifting or shedding consumption can compensate for the loss of an electricity power plant or reduce congestion on a transmission or distribution network).

2 Deploying smart grids on energy systems: key factors and strategies

A smart network comprises several technologies deployed along the supply chain, enabling the various players to exchange data: sensors on transmission and distribution lines, source stations, dispatch centers managing data flows, and smart meters in the premises of final consumers. Smart grids are being deployed in many areas. In 2016 alone EUR 47 billion was spent on "digital energy" (IEA, 2017c). There is broad consensus as to their usefulness: among others they integrate consumers as active players in the electricity system, reduce peaks in demand, manage the intermittency of renewable energies, and improve energy efficiency.

Whereas the overall aim is to encourage the energy transition, national strategies vary (Clastres, 2011), setting different priorities: integrating plug-in electric vehicles on a large scale (Denmark, Sweden); enhancing quality of supply (Spain); integrating renewables (Portugal); combating fraud (Italy); reducing GHG emissions (Netherlands); promoting dual-energy solutions (UK); and better informing the consumer (France).

Deploying smart grids would consequently bring new opportunities all the way down the electricity value chain, with improvements to the overall management of electrical systems (Nair and Zhang, 2009), and potential gains for all the players (Meeus et al., 2010). However, such gains may not be sufficient to cover investment costs. For instance, in France, with investment costs of EUR 250 per meter, it would make sense to equip no more than 60% of the consumer base. Above this level the marginal cost of meter deployment would exceed the surplus it generated (Léautier, 2014).

New offers are available to consumers in the deregulated sector, such as "energy boxes", various sensors, smart plugs and "in-home displays" (IHD) delivering various forms of data (consumption, temperature, tariff period). Widespread demand-management schemes could reduce investment in electricity infrastructure by $270 billion by 2040 (IEA, 2017b).

3 Finance and regulation

In most countries smart grids have been launched with demonstrators or experiments. These projects have been financed by a combination of private and public funds (Spain, France, the United States, the United Kingdom, Portugal) depending on how keen the authorities are to make allowance for the risk incurred by companies financing investments (in Australia for instance, private companies shoulder the full burden of risks related to SG projects). Other tools have also been used such as a monthly rent paid for the installation of a smart meter (Spain), and taxes on consumers to pay for infrastructure (New York State), preferential loans (Japan) or accounting facilities (France) for investors. Some energy companies have also issued green bonds to finance RE and EE investments.

Regulators have not yet defined specific schemes for the deployment of smart grids. Regulators have not yet defined specific regulatory schemes to supervise, regulate, and fund the roll-out of smart grids. Such investments are covered by regulatory mechanisms for the funding of technological innovation on power grids (Perez-Arriaga, 2010). Regulators appear to be waiting to see the outcome of demonstrator projects, which will give decision-makers a clear picture of the benefits of smart grids. However, price-cap or revenue-cap mechanisms (Kristiansen and Rosellon, 2006) do not seem suitable due to the uncertainty of both deployment costs and associated gains. Nor do regulatory contracts (Baron and Myerson, 1982; Crouch, 2006), which allow regulators to make allowance for the existing information asymmetry between regulators and regulated firms, seem appropriate either. Cost drift following the implementation of an innovation would cause a significant drop in revenue, or even losses, for the regulated company (Cossent and Gómez, 2013). So dual regulation seems the likely model for the future, with a cost-plus including "subsidized rates" for new investments, and incentive regulation for other transmission and distribution assets, to optimize system usage and efficiency (Littlechild and Skerk, 2008).

One initial step taken by regulatory authorities has been to make allowance for part of the risks incurred by the distribution system operators (DSO) by defining subsidized rates of return for "smart" investments (Italy, France, Portugal). Given the risks weighing on profits, these regulatory decisions are an attempt to "secure" some of the investments. Additional performance-related regulations (PBR) have been added to these relatively "classical" regulatory decisions. The latter measures generate additional revenue for DSOs, which maintain a quality of service in line with regulatory performance targets (Sappington, 2005). The regulator thus enjoys additional leverage for giving DSOs an incentive to invest, allowing them to keep part of the benefits generated by smart grids (reduced frequency and duration of failures, improved management of supply and demand). The threshold values for these efficiency targets is also an issue, in order to avoid "double financing" of smart infrastructure (involving the use of cost-benefit analysis). Despite regulation some costs may not be recovered, including stranded costs (Clastres, 2016). This question arose, for example, in New York State, where the cost of old, unamortized meters replaced by smart devices was not covered.

SG-related investment is not limited to power grids, the communications sector also being impacted by the large volume of data exchanged. Current debate focuses on the additional investments in bandwidth which Internet operators will have to make to enable this new batch of information to pass through their networks. Investment costs will have to be shared, as will data transmission rates, Internet operators being impacted in their investment strategies by these new data flows from the energy sector. Some authors (Heidell and Ware, 2010) consider that DSOs should make and manage part of these new investments. The increasingly close relations between the energy and telecommunications sectors will be reinforced with the development of the "energy Internet" (Huang and Baliga, 2009) and the "Internet of things". This degree of complementarity is also fueling research on links between the two regulatory authorities responsible for the data or energy markets: regulations decided by one authority, providing incentives and funding for certain investments, will impact the regulatory decisions and competitive structure managed by the other. For example, the share-out of broadband-network investment costs between the two sectors determines the access tariffs paid by users. Since tariffs for accessing the network can either be regulated or contractually fixed between Internet operators and energy players (aggregators, demand-response modes, load managers, or suppliers), the competitive structure in the Internet can impact the energy market. Expensive access to the Internet would certainly hamper the development of the load-management market by reducing access to data transmissions. The deployment of smart grids may consequently be delayed for lack of alternative data-transmission technologies. For this reason, online carrier current could be developed to compete with Internet service provider (ISP) transmissions. The advantage would be to keep data transmission in the energy sector – or even in the hands of a regulated body – enabling economies of scale and reducing the impact of the oligopolistic competitive structure of ISPs (few operators, few backbones). On the down side, data would certainly be lost during long-distance transmission over the power grid. To which must be added the cost of line reinforcement. Here we see a complex ecosystem combining regulatory authority, stakeholder strategies, and complementary or substitutable networks. With this in mind Fiocco and Scarpa (2014) studied the impacts on collective well-being of a business requiring intervention and coordination by two regulatory bodies. They concluded that it would be preferable for the two agencies to meet and come to terms. Exceptions to this rule arise when activities are substitutable or lobbying is intense: a single body can be "captured" more easily, thus reducing the benefits for competition of substitutable goods.

4 Acceptability and consumer willingness to pay

The behavior of consumers and their ability to control their demand for electricity is one of the key factors in successful deployment of smart grids. Kaufmann et al. (2013) indicate that consumers are more inclined to accept technology if it is of value to them. Pepermans (2014) calculated this willingness to pay (WTP) for smart meters and related devices. His results show that the WTP to switch from a conventional to a smart meter is about EUR 200. WTP for devices is ranked according to various criteria. The most important one seems to be protection of privacy with a high WTP for devices with no impact on privacy. Then comes comfort, with a preference for devices that are not visible. Consumers prefer to act on their own rather than letting an operator control their consumption. Direct load control (DLC) is thus perceived by consumers as being more "intrusive". Trust in the supplier or pilot operator is essential for users to accept DLC. Trust may take the form of actions carried out by the operator in the consumer's interest, such as only providing equipment that is strictly necessary and at the lowest cost, customer service, and follow-up (Kaufmann et al., 2013). The operator must also manage and use confidential personal data properly (Gerpott and Paukert, 2013), communicating regularly with consumers (explaining bills, for instance) in order to create trust (Krishnamurti et al., 2012). In the main consumers want to keep control over their own behavior with low preference for DLC (Leijten et al., 2014). However, given the heterogeneity of consumers, operators must diversify their offering, proposing different levels of technologies to suit individual preferences and reduce the risk of rejection (Darby, 2010).

These results also prompted the development of consumer profiles reflecting individual preferences for technology and the associated offering. The literature generally identifies four profiles reflecting consumer preferences (Kaufmann et al., 2013): technology; smart home services and not only energy supply; risk aversion (preference for homogeneous pricing); and price sensitivity (preference for well-differentiated pricing). These profiles are also borne out by the main motives cited by consumers to explain a change in behavior (Gangale et al., 2013). Consumers aim to reduce their energy bills, control consumption and use, improve comfort or reduce demand depending on their "environmental" preferences. For example, users in Great Britain equipped with smart devices and attaching great importance to information and the environment were satisfied with the services offered. In contrast, those wishing to reduce their energy bills were less happy because the gains achieved fell short of expectations.

Willingness to pay also depends on consumer beliefs regarding the benefits for other players in the electricity supply chain following adoption of smart meters (Verbong et al., 2013). So there is uncertainty as to the interests served by technological adoption and behavioral changes. Consumer WTP for smart technologies is low under these circumstances. They prefer a clear reward for their adaptation. Information provided to consumers is important because patterns of consumption and user expectations will determine the positive effects of demand-side management. It is generally advisable to combine several signals, leading to better results (Bergaentzlé et al., 2014). Raw and Ross (2011) concluded that smart meters could yield savings of about 10% at some times. To achieve this, information must be easily accessible and directly linked to the period of consumption (at least once a month) in order to optimize consumer attention (Carroll et al., 2014). In the long run there is less incentive to respond to information (through overload or lack of interest), so contact must be sustained frequently (Schleich et al., 2013; Faruqui and George, 2005). Kaufmann et al. (2013) note that WTP for real-time information is greater, so in-home displays are preferable to smart phone applications.

Hargreaves et al. (2010) note that information expressed in monetary terms is more effective than in terms of energy or CO_2 emissions. Incentives must be powerful (savings on bills, dynamic pricing, etc.) but of course depend on the distribution of consumer profiles. Efforts may also focus on incentives and hedging measures which allow consumers to choose more dynamic pricing, tailored to their consumption profile and convictions (Buryk et al., 2015). These incentives must be more powerful if electricity bills are low, consumers are poorly informed (particularly about pricing structures), or they choose a pricing system with higher incentives. This last point must make allowance for consumer risk aversion, with the threat of higher bills as a result of dynamic pricing (Clastres and Khalfallah, 2015; Park et al., 2014). Some consumers have suffered a loss of welfare after switching to dynamic pricing (Herter, 2007).

5   Demand response and value allocation

Demand response (DR) refers to reducing or shifting a load from peak to off-peak consumption, adding elasticity to electricity demand. DR is facilitated by smart grids because more information is available about demand and connected appliances managing consumption. Deploying smart grids and DSM programs should consequently reduce the last obstacle in the way of optimizing consumption: the inelasticity of demand by electricity consumers (Stoft, 2002; Haney et al., 2009). Many pilot schemes have been carried out to study DR in the United States and more recently in Europe (Coll-Mayor et al., 2007; Faruqui and Sergici, 2010; Faruqui et al., 2010a, 2010b). The initial conclusions suggest that peak load-shedding may be significant (Faruqui et al., 2007). According to the IEA (2017b), DR could concern as much as 40,000 TWh per year, or 15% of overall electricity consumption, mainly achieved by optimizing the building sector. In 2009 the FERC noted that smart grids and active consumer spending could be reduced by 20% in the United States by 2019, with a proportional decrease in users' electricity bills.

Information or tariff signals must reach consumers if they are to adapt their consumption. The literature has studied a variety of DR tools (Bergaentzlé et al., 2014; Buckley, 2018; Faruqui and Sergici, 2010; Horowitz and Lave, 2014). The simplest mechanism is time-of-use (TOU) or critical-peak pricing (CPP); the most complex systems involve real-time pricing (RTP). These dynamic tariffs are intended to send a signal to consumers about the state of the power grid. Thanks to SG infrastructure and smart applications, consumers can adapt their behavior, generally maintaining an equivalent level of comfort (Woo, 1990; Chao, 2010).

These signals may, however, lead to negative incentives because of the risk aversion of consumers. As dynamic pricing implies a price increase at times of high demand, some consumers may be worse off due to the increase (Horowitz and Lave, 2014; Clastres and Khalfallah, 2015).

Consumers, by reducing their consumption at certain times, are likely to reduce the size of their bills. However, such energy savings create value for the power system, which can be captured by other players in electricity value chain (suppliers, distributors). Some work has focused on how consumers are rewarded for this service, for they should receive a share of the gains a third party derives from DR (Crampes and Léautier, 2015). Several papers have studied the appropriate market design to compensate for load-shedding. Chao (2011) shows that, in a perfectly competitive market, the pricing of load-shedding equals to the difference between the retail rate and the real-time price should be optimal for welfare. Orans et al. (2010) show that a three-part rate, including time-of-use, a fixed fee, and compensation, provides an efficient means of giving consumers an incentive to adapt their behavior.

So deriving value from DR induces transfers between players giving rise to redistribution of rent (Chao, 2010; Crampes and Léautier, 2015). However, the issue of value allocation, between each of the economic agents involved, is particularly complex, because conflicting legitimacies clash:

- Consumers – who own their data – want to benefit from flexibility, over and above a cut in their energy bills.
- DR operators are used to aggregating various sources of flexibility and, in some cases, bear the risk and cost of investing in specific devices.
- Suppliers and balance managers may have to cope with imbalances following DR. As they are not responsible for such imbalances, it may be economically desirable for them to receive compensation (Crampes and Léautier, 2010).
- Network managers developing data-transmission infrastructures may also capture some of these benefits through the regulation scheme fixing their earnings.
- Producers see demand management measures as an additional source of risk for the return on investment in generating resources. The profitability of conventional production capacity (mainly used in advanced generation) is already jeopardized by incentive policies for the development of intermittent renewable energies. It becomes even more difficult to determine in a context of increasingly flexible demand. New payment schemes are needed to make allowance for some of these additional risks, such as the creation of capacity markets (Cramton and Stoft, 2005; Khalfallah, 2011) or the redistribution of benefits related to the valuation of DR (Crampes and Léautier, 2015).

The added value derived from DR and the redistribution of the resulting rent are still subject to debate. Uncertainty as to the level of these benefits discourages investors considering the deployment of new DR technology. The benefits of DR may not cover the cost of deploying smart technology which allows consumers to receive information signals that modify their behavior. This question was addressed in particular in the context of widespread deployment of smart meters (Léautier, 2014; Allcott, 2011). Such results confirm the intuitive assumption that, for deployment of smart technologies to be sustainable, they must benefit the entire electricity supply chain (especially network operators and producers who can achieve significant savings in terms of avoided investment). Analysis of the economic problem posed by DR must carry over into discussion of which market designs will maximize the associated added value. Consumers (or DR operators who aggregate them) resell their ability not to consume electricity for a given period. This resale raises the question of the purchase of an ex ante consumption profile by consumers. Consumers, having bought this profile, then benefit from the choice to consume the electricity on offer or give it up, thus allocating value to the DR achieved on the market (Crampes and Léautier, 2015). This solution, which is disputed by the DR operators and some consumers, makes it possible to take into account part of the risk incurred by suppliers and producers and boost the efficiency of DR (Chao, 2011). If DR, with the benefit of excess payment, takes the place of inexpensive production, then adaptation exceeds the collectively desirable level. Which in turn reduces collective welfare. The savings on production costs are offset here by the cost associated with the excess value of DR.

6 Conclusion

Deploying smart grids is one of the available means of achieving climate targets: greenhouse gas emissions can be reduced by improving the management of power grids and energy demand. However, these gains are tainted by uncertainty because they are observed over the long term and depend on many factors. The main factor is undoubtedly the behavior of consumers who must adopt these new technologies, thus contributing to better system management. The main gains expected from demand response are prompted by information and price signals. Recent studies have demonstrated that the use of nudges could also lead to interesting results in energy conservation (Buckley and Llerena, 2018). Consumers will be able to adapt their behavior in line with pressure on the power grid, while making direct and indirect financial gains (respectively through lower bills, and by deriving added value from flexible use of electricity markets or contractually with utilities). Similarly, utilities will benefit from this flexibility to reduce their investment costs, and better balance supply and demand, especially with increasingly intermittent supply. Reductions in consumption are therefore likely to take the place of infrastructure investments, both for centralized transmission, distribution and generation. Nykamp et al. (2012) has demonstrated the substitutability between traditional investments in expanding and reinforcing grids and "smart solutions".

The acceptability of smart technologies (see Chapter 17 in this handbook on acceptance and public engagement) obviously implies extended researches in psychology and sociology (Silvast et al. 2018). Il the economic field, this also goes hand in hand with an understanding of the signals sent to the various players along the electricity chain. To this end a certain allocative efficiency can be restored and improved thanks to dynamic pricing. In this respect the new approach to pricing would have a positive impact on collective welfare. The real price signal should be restored. However, the risk for consumers of manipulated prices cannot be ignored. To avoid price manipulation, we need electricity markets which optimize productive efficiency. The alternative would be unjustified surplus transfers between consumers and suppliers or producers. Similarly, although regulations are designed to reward risk, surplus profits for distributors must be avoided (otherwise SG would be deployed at the expense of consumers). Surplus skimming could reduce, perhaps reverse, the initial positive impact on welfare. Competition and regulatory authorities will therefore play an important part in the roll-out of smart grids, allocating profits all the way along the value chain.

Notes

1 http://s3platform.jrc.ec.europa.eu/smart-grids
2 See Kezunovic, McCalley, and Overbye (2012).

References

Allcott, H., 2011. Rethinking real-time electricity pricing. *Resource and energy Economics*, 33, 820–842.

Baron, D.P., Myerson, R.B., 1982. Regulating a monopolist with unknown costs. *Econometrica*, 50(4), July, 911–930.

Bergaentzlé, C., Clastres, C., Khalfallah, H., 2014. Demand-side management and European environmental and energy goals: An optimal complementary approach. *Energy Policy*, 67, April, 858–869.

Buckley, P., 2018. Incentivising households to reduce electricity consumption: A meta-analysis of recent experimental evidence. *Mimeo*, February 1, 30p.

Buckley, P., Llerena, D. 2018. Demand response as a common pool resource game: Nudges versus prices. Working papers GAEL. 35p.

Buryk, S., Mead, D., Mourato, S., Torriti, J., 2015. Investigating preferences for dynamic electricity tariffs: The effect of environmental and system benefit disclosure. *Energy Policy*, 80, May, 190–195.

Carroll, J., Lyons, S., Denny, E., 2014. Reducing household electricity demand through smart metering: The role of improved information about energy saving. *Energy Economics*, 45, 234–243.

Chao, H.-P., 2010. Price-responsive demand management for a smart grid world. *The Electricity Journal*, 23(1), 7–20.

Chao, H.-P., 2011. Demand response in wholesale electricity markets: The choice of customer baseline. *Journal of Regulatory Economics*, 39(1), 68–88.

Clastres, C., 2011. Smart grids: Another step towards competition, energy security and climate change objectives. *Energy Policy*, 39(9), 5399–5408.

Clastres, C., 2016. La régulation asymétrique: un mécanisme de financement des coûts échoués irrécupérables. *Revue d'Economie Politique*, 126(1), 89–126.

Clastres, C., Khalfallah, H., 2015. An analytical approach to activating demand elasticity with a demand response mechanism. *Energy Economics*, 52, Part A, December, 195–206.

Coll-Mayor, D., Paget, M., Lightner, E., 2007. Future intelligent power grids: Analysis of the vision in the European Union and the United States. *Energy Policy*, 35, 2453–2465.

Cossent, R., Gómez, T., 2013. Implementing incentive compatible menus of contracts to regulate electricity distribution investments. *Utilities Policy*, 27, December, 28–38.

Crampes, C., Léautier, T.O., 2010. *Dispatching, redispatching et effacement de demande*. Toulouse, Institut d'Economie Industrielle.

Crampes, C., Léautier, T.O., 2015. Demand response in adjustment markets for electricity. *Journal of Regulatory Economics*, 48(2), 169–193.

Cramton, P., Stoft, S., 2005. A capacity market that makes sense. *The Electricity Journal*, 18(7), 43–54.

Crouch, M., 2006. Investment under RPI-X: Practical experience with an incentive compatible approach in the GB electricity distribution sector. *Utilities Policy*, 14(4), December, 240–244.

Darby, S., 2010. Smart metering: what potential for householder engagement? *Building Research and Information*, 38(5), 442–457.

Faruqui, A., George, S., 2005. Quantifying customer response to dynamic pricing. *The Electricity Journal*, 18(4), 53–63.

Faruqui, A., Harris, D., Hledik, R., 2010a. Unlocking the €53 billion savings from smart meters in the EU: How increasing the adoption of dynamic tariffs could make or break the EU0s smart grid investment. *Energy Policy*, 38(10), 6222–6231.

Faruqui, A., Hledik, R., Newell, S., Pfeifenberger, H., 2007. The power of 5 percent. *The Electricity Journal*, 20(8), 68–77.

Faruqui, A., Sergici, S., 2010. Household response to dynamic pricing of electricity: A survey of 15 experiments. *Journal of Regulory Economics*, 38(2), 193–225.

Faruqui, A., Sergici, S., Sharif, A., 2010b. The impact of informational feedback on energy consumption: A survey of the experimental evidence. *Energy*, 35, 1598–1608.

FERC, 2009. A National Assessment of Demand Response. Federal Energy Regulatory Commission, June.

Fiocco, R., Scarpa, C., 2014. The regulation of markets with interdependent demands. *Information Economics and Policy*, 27(C), 1–12.

Gangale, F., Mengolini, A., Onyeji, I., 2013. Consumer engagement: An insight from smart grid projects in Europe. *Energy Policy*, 60, September, 621–628.

Gerpott, T. J., Paukert, M., 2013. Determinants of willingness to pay for smart meters: An empirical analysis of household customers in Germany. *Energy Policy*, 61, October, 483–495.

Haney, A.B., Jamasb, T., Pollitt, M.G., 2009. Smart metering and electricity demand: Technology, economics and international experience, Working Paper EPRG0903. Electricity Policy Research Group, Cambridge.

Hargreaves, T., Nye, M., Burgess, J., 2010. Making energy visible: A qualitative field study of how householders interact with feedback from smart energy monitors. *Energy Policy*, 38(10), 6111–6119.

Heidell, J., Ware, H., 2010. Is there a case for broadband utility communications networks? Valuing and pricing incremental communications capacity on electric utility Smart Grid networks. *The Electricity Journal*, 23(1), January–February, 21–33.

Herter, K., 2007. Residential implementation of critical-peak pricing of electricity. *Energy Policy*, 35, 2121–2130.

Horowitz, S., Lave, L., 2014. Equity in residential electricity pricing. *The Energy Journal*, 35(2), 1–23.

Huang, A., Baliga, J., 2009. Freedom system: Role of power electronics and power semiconductors in developing an energy internet. Proceedings of International Symposium on Power Semiconductor Devices, 9–12.

IEA, 2017a. *Energy technology perspectives, catalysing energy technology transformations.* Paris: OECD/IEA, 2017.

IEA, 2017b. *World energy outlook.* Paris: OECD/IEA.

IEA, 2017c. *World energy investment.* Paris: OECD/IEA.

Kaufmann, S., Künzel, K., Loock, M., 2013. Customer value of smart metering: Explorative evidence from a choice-based conjoint study in Switzerland. *Energy Policy*, 53, 229–239.

Khalfallah, M.H., 2011. A game theoretic model for generation capacity adequacy: Comparison between investment incentive mechanisms in electricity markets. *The Energy Journal*, 32(4), 117–157.

Kezunovic, M., McCalley, J. D. and Overbye, T. J. Smart grids and beyond: Achieving the full potentialof electricity systems. *Proceedings of the IEEE*, Vol. 100, May 13, 2012.

Krishnamurti, T., Schwartz, D., Davis, A., Fischoff, B., Bruine de Bruin, W., Lave, L., Wang, J., 2012. Preparing for smart grid technologies: A behavioral decision research approach to understanding consumer expectations about smart meters. *Energy Policy*, 41, February, 790–797.

Kristiansen, T., Rosellon, J., 2006. A merchant mechanism for electricity transmission expansion. *Journal of Regulatory Economics*, 29, 167–193.

Léautier, T.O., 2014. Is mandating smart meters smart? *The Energy Journal*, 35(4), 135–157.

Leijten, F., Bolderdijk, J., Keizer, K., Gorsira, M., van der Werff, E., Steg, L., 2014. Factors that influence consumers' acceptance of future energy systems: The effects of adjustment type, production level, and price. *Energy Efficiency*, 7(6), December, 973–985.

Littlechild, S.C., Skerk, C.J., 2008. Transmission expansion in Argentina: The origins of policy. *Energy Economics*, 30, 1367–1384.

Meeus, L., Saguan, M., Glachant, J.-M., and Belmans, R., 2010. Smart regulation for smart grids, *EUI Working Paper* no. 45.

Nair, N.K.C., Zhang, L., 2009. SmartGrid: Future networks for New Zealand power systems incorporating distributed generation. *Energy Policy*, 37, 3418–3427.

Nykamp, S., Andor, M., Hurink, J.L., 2012. Standard0 incentive regulation hinders the integration of renewable energy generation. *Energy Policy*, 47, 222–237.

Orans, R., Woo, C.-K., Horii, B., Chait, M., DeBenedictis, A., 2010. Electricity pricing for conservation and load shifting. *The Electricity Journal*, 23(3), April, 7–14.

Park, C.-K., Kim, H.-J., Kim, Y.-S., 2014. A study factor enhancing smart grid consumer engagement. *Energy Policy*, 72, September, 211–218.

Pepermans, G., 2014. Valuing smart meters. *Energy Economics*, 45, 280–294.

Perez-Arriaga, I.J., 2010. Regulatory Instruments for Deployment of Clean Energy Technologies. EUI RSCAS; 2010/25; Loyola de Palacio Programme on Energy Policy.

Raw, G., Ross, D., 2011. *Energy demand research project: Final analysis.* London: Office of Gas and Electricity Markets.

Sappington, D.E.M., 2005. Regulating service quality: A survey. *Journal of Regulatory Economics*, 27(2), 123–154.

Schleich, J., Klobasa, M., Gölz, S., Brunner, M., 2013. Effects of feedback on residential electricity demand: Findings from a field trial in Austria. *Energy Policy*, 61, 1097–1106.

Silvast, A., Williams, R., Hyysalo, S., Rommetveit, K., Raab, C., 2018. Who 'uses' smart grids? The evolving nature of user representations in layered infrastructures. *Sustainability*, 10, 3738.

Stoft, S., 2002. *Power system economics: Designing markets for electricity*. Piscataway: IEEE Press.

Verbong, G. P., Beemsterboer, S., Sengers, F., 2013. Smart grids or smart users? Involving users in developing a low carbon electricity economy. *Energy Policy*, 52, January, 117–125.

Woo, C.-K., 1990. Efficient electricity pricing with self-rationing. *Journal of Regulatory Economics*, 2(1), 69–81.

15

The role of carbon pricing in the Paris Agreement

İzzet Arı and Ramazan Sarı

1 Introduction

Anthropogenic activities, including greenhouse gas (GHG) emissions, are very likely to cause global climate change (IPCC, 2018). In response, tackling climate change will require global cooperation and partnerships for reducing GHG emissions cost-effectively (Nordhaus, 1991). Currently, there are three key emission reduction policies: behavioral change towards sustainable consumption and production, technological shifts from high carbon to low carbon alternatives, and carbon pricing (Stern, 2007). Both technological shifts and behavioral change policies can use carbon pricing instruments such as cap and trade, carbon taxes, or regulations in order to hinder market failure and correct negative externalities arising from global climate change (Ben-essaiah, 2012; Clarke, 2011; Nordhaus, 1991; Perdan & Azapagic, 2011). Accordingly, carbon pricing tools should be designed for minimizing the burden of externalities and eliminating unaffordable policies.

The United Nations Framework Convention on Climate Change (UNFCCC), the Kyoto Protocol, and the Paris Agreement are all well-known multilateral agreements on climate change. In 2015, the Paris Agreement was adopted by countries which have a collective responsibility for 97% of global emissions (Mehling, Metcalf, & Stavins, 2017).Even though implementation rules for combatting climate change are determined by these agreements, reducing GHG emissions in a cost-effective way at the global level still needs to be clarified. After exploring sufficient bottom-up development methods in carbon pricing for signatories of the Paris Agreement, the World Bank (2017) suggested continuing the development of aspects of carbon pricing such as scope, the amount of emissions reduction, standardized units and monitoring (World Bank, Eco-fys, & Vivid Economics, 2017). Although countries are familiar with carbon pricing initiatives such as cap and trade, the Clean Development Mechanism (CDM), and joint implementation in international climate agreements, the Paris Agreement contains unique emissions reduction commitments or contributions termed Nationally Determined Contributions (NDCs). A large number of NDCs include and are subject to carbon pricing.

Before the Paris Agreement was adopted in 2015, various countries had submitted and announced their NDCs. These submissions had been part of the complementary step for developing the Agreement before countries agreed on articles within the Paris Agreement itself (Ari

& Sari, 2017b, 2017a). Eighty-one countries announced the use of carbon pricing in their NDCs (UNFCCC, 2015b). This number shows that carbon pricing will be linked to countries' emission mitigation actions. However, this linkage will not be straightforward during the implementation period of the Paris Agreement, because NDCs were not submitted in a standardized common tabular format for the monitoring of actions related to carbon pricing.

Article 6 in the Paris Agreement will provide a new window for carbon pricing at the international level and this connects to a country's NDCs. Nevertheless, further discussions on Article 6 of the Paris Agreement are essential to ensure common understandings and methods until the beginning of the implementation period of the Paris Agreement. In this paper, the role of carbon pricing in the Paris Agreement and its linkages with NDCs will be addressed, specifically in the context of cost-effective emissions reduction. This reduction requires establishing a system of global cooperation among the committed countries, to support the overriding aims of the Agreement and to ensure the provision of climate finance through the operationalization of Article 6 of the Agreement. Section 2 focuses on the basics of carbon pricing, and Section 3 analyzes new regulatory frameworks for carbon pricing. Section 4 then presents carbon pricing for climate finance, and in Section 5, concluding remarks with recommendations are provided.

2 Principles of carbon pricing

Putting a price on carbon internalizes climate change externalities to the point where the marginal abatement costs of emissions mitigation is equal to the marginal damage of emissions (Clarke, 2011; Nordhaus, 1991; Perdan & Azapagic, 2011). In other words, a cost-benefit analysis of climate change can be conducted through carbon pricing (Bhattacharyya, 2011). There are two basic functions for this pricing: one is the emissions reduction abatement function as a cost function, and the second is a climate change damage function representing a clear benefit from preventing future damage (Bhattacharyya, 2011; Nordhaus, 1991). The aim is to maximize net benefit through determination of the optimum amount of total emissions reduction at the global level. In addition to minimizing the total cost of emissions reduction, carbon pricing provides a shift away from carbon intense technologies to low-carbon technologies (Bayon, Hawn, & Hamilton, 2009; Stern, 2007). Therefore, carbon pricing enables countries to achieve sustainable development at the very least (Benessaiah, 2012).

Carbon tax and carbon trade are the two main carbon pricing instruments. The former sets the price of carbon and the latter sets the quantity to be reduced. Since the main principle of carbon pricing is to reduce the total cost of emissions mitigation, cost functions including marginal control cost, damages by climate change and time dynamics (discount rate, time preferences) should be further explored (Nordhaus, 1991). However, both cost and damage functions and discount rates depend on various factors such as national circumstances, uncertainty around the exact impacts of global climate change, national inflation rates, and the speed and rate of technological change (Clarke, 2011; Stern, 2007). Accordingly, the marginal abatement cost might vary among countries and even sectors within an economy (Clarke, 2011; Nordhaus, 1991). Thus, a uniform price level of carbon might not be cost-effective, so it is essential that both the carbon tax level and trade caps should be determined according to each sector's marginal abatement costs. In an ideal case, in a competitive market, the marginal abatement cost, price of a carbon tax, and trade of one quantity of carbon allowance are expected to be equal.

Under the implementation of a carbon tax and trade system, there may be an increase in the cost of carbon intense production and the price of products which are purchased by consumers in the market (OECD, 2013). Therefore, producers and consumers might prefer to reduce their overall cost through changing production or consumption patterns. For example, consumers may prefer to buy more fuel-efficient vehicles or equipment, and producers use alternative materials rather than fossil fuels (OECD, 2013; Stern, 2007). While these preferences discourage production of emission intense products with a decreasing demand and additional price on carbon, producers will also encourage a transition to low carbon technologies and products which in turn is demanded by the market (OECD, 2013).

In a carbon tax system, an authority sets the price of carbon without any cap or allocation of allowances. There are four main advantages of carbon taxes (Bhattacharyya, 2011; Clarke, 2011; Stern, 2007). First, it minimizes total costs through converging and equalizing the marginal abatement cost of diverse sources at an upper bound price of carbon as a tax level. Second, it promotes innovation and seeks new technological change to reduce emissions in controlling part of the marginal cost curve. Third, it easily enables emissions to be monitored. Fourth, it overcomes market failure resulting in polluters paying for external costs, so carbon taxes then provide additional revenue for climate vulnerable groups while correcting market failures. The main disadvantage of the carbon tax is not to guarantee the attainment of a quantitative target for emissions reduction. Besides, a new tax might be a politically sensitive issue when applied by small and medium-sized entities (Bhattacharyya, 2011). This is because the introduction of a carbon tax requires an accountable and strong fiscal policy environment for collecting new and additional revenue from entities (Nordhaus, 2006). Therefore, the tax level should be well-monitored, due to fluctuations of inflation rates in an economy and the changing marginal abatement cost of various sectors over time.

The motivation for carbon trade is to minimize compliance costs of emissions reduction for avoiding market failure (Bayon, Hawn, & Hamilton, 2009; Perdan & Azapagic, 2011). There are three main advantages of carbon trading (Stern, 2007). First, it sets an emissions cap so that emissions targets or an explicit commitment to reduced emissions is guaranteed. Second, total cost is minimized through equalizing the carbon price to that of the marginal abatement cost in the market. Third, it provides a continuing incentive for polluters to seek ways to reduce emissions. The main disadvantage of carbon trading is that there is no fixed guarantee in the price of carbon. Thus, there might be fluctuations in the price of carbon in the market. In the case of free allocation of carbon credits or cap, it is not possible to raise revenue from trade.

The main difference between carbon taxes and carbon trading systems is that a carbon tax sets a fixed carbon price level but lets carbon emissions vary, whereas carbon trading fixes the quantity of emissions and lets the price vary (Pollitt, 2015). While the advantage of carbon trading is to reduce the risk of quantity, price volatility emerges as a disadvantage in the trade. On the other hand, carbon taxes guarantee the price of carbon but do not ensure any commitment to explicit emissions reduction by emitters (Stern, 2007). In market economies, measures should be taken for both tackling climate change and enabling better functioning market conditions. To this, price floors and ceilings, or a "price collar" can be implemented. A price floor which is equal to a carbon tax, can reduce the risk of quantity, and a ceiling which can fix the highest price via an authority, can eliminate the risks of speculative pricing. This combination of carbon taxes and carbon trading is a hybrid approach in carbon pricing (Mehling et al., 2017). The preferences for choosing better instruments for carbon pricing depends on variations among national circumstances (Stern, 2007). In the implementation of a hybrid approach, an authority should buy and retire carbon certificates to control price fluctuations, and the authority should provide additional and new certificates to eliminate price rises (Stavins & Stowe, 2017). An authority, which is responsible for monitoring carbon pricing, might suffer from either providing a benchmark for the price of carbon or allocating a fixed amount of carbon certificates among emitters. It is expected that this authority should provide both a standard price for one unit of carbon allowances and a fair allocation of carbon certificates. The former depends on the social cost of carbon, namely monetizing the damage of one unit of emissions, while the latter requires grandfathering of the individual emissions of each emitter.

3   Regulation framework of carbon pricing

For the first time, the Kyoto Protocol and its flexibility mechanisms recognized carbon pricing instruments at the global level. The Kyoto Protocol, which required emissions reduction commitments among developed countries, set rules and compliance measures for monitoring the quantified emissions reduction units of developed countries between 2008 and 2012 (UNFCCC, 1998). Although the Kyoto Protocol provided flexibility mechanisms such as the Clean Development Mechanism (CDM), Emissions Trading System (ETS) and Joint Implementation (JI) to reduce carbon emissions in a cost-effective manner, it was insufficient (as it covers only 14% of global emissions) for reducing carbon emissions with market mechanisms (Ari, 2013; Mehling & Görlach, 2016; Stavins & Stowe, 2017; UNFCCC, 1998). For example, major emitters such as the United States did not ratify the Protocol, and countries not listed in the Protocol did not show any willingness to reduce their emissions (Bhattacharyya, 2011). Therefore, these inactions led to the weakening of the development of international carbon markets.

In addition to international agreements for carbon pricing initiatives, national obligations to reduce carbon emissions called for states to incorporate carbon pricing within their national territories (Mehling et al., 2017; Stavins & Stowe, 2017). Over the Kyoto Protocol period, flexibility mechanisms such as the CDM, Joint Implementation, and International Emissions Trading were established to reduce emissions using market mechanisms (UNFCCC, 1998). These pricing tools were provided to reduce price volatility and ensure transparency through standardized emission reduction units including certified emissions reductions (CERs) and emissions reduction units (ERUs) in compliance with the Protocol (UNFCCC, 1998). In the first commitment period of the Protocol, more than 1.8 billion CERs were created by over 8,000 project activities (Stavins & Stowe, 2017). This period was also called "Carbon Markets 1.0" and signified a learning period for carbon pricing (ADB, 2018). The European Union Emissions Trading System (EU-ETS) which was a well-known regional initiative, was the largest cooperation among the EU countries (World Bank, Ecofys, & Vivid Economics, 2017). While EU-ETS seemed to be a successful cooperation among developed countries within the EU (Stern, 2007), other developed countries still had significant challenges to reduce their emissions in a cost-effective manner (Bhattacharyya, 2011). Besides, emerging economies and developing countries with large carbon emissions did not stabilize their emissions.

The Paris Agreement, which replaces the Kyoto Protocol, on the other hand, seems to be an opportunity to involve all countries for carbon pricing at the global level. The lessons learned from the Kyoto Protocol period, alongside associated regional and national initiatives that address mitigation outcomes, need to be subject to a common currency system, less price volatility, and strong institutional arrangements including monitoring, reporting, verification, and accountability mechanisms (Howard & Climate, 2018). Because the Paris Agreement has hybrid features, which includes top-down monitoring, reporting, and verification processes and bottom-up commitments in the form of NDCs, the Agreement requires better functioning carbon pricing systems globally. In addition, it is important to recognize that the Agreement targets 97% of global emissions while the Protocol accounted for only 14% of global emissions (Mehling et al., 2017). Table 15.1 compares the Kyoto Protocol and the Paris Agreements in terms of carbon pricing. While the Kyoto Protocol and its market-based initiatives focuses on more developed countries with their comparatively small amount of emissions, the framework of a new climate regime through NDCs and the Paris Agreement provide flexibilities, country-based unique solutions,

Table 15.1 Comparison of the Kyoto Protocol and the Paris Agreement

The Kyoto Protocol	The Paris Agreement
Developed countries had emissions reduction targets but the developing countries did not have emissions targets.	All countries submitted their NDCs but there is a variety of targets in the Agreement.
Strong and legally binding compliance system.	Transparency, country driven and global stock take based compliance system.
Three flexible mechanisms: 1 International Emissions Trading between countries with caps. 2 Joint Implementation project-based mechanism through ERUs between countries with caps. 3 Clean Development Mechanism based on CERs, which were created in countries without targets. Countries used CERs for their targets or carbon trading.	Article 6 of the Agreement states that any country can choose carbon pricing mechanism approaches, choosing either centralized (Article 6.4) or decentralized (Article 6.2) systems for pricing.

cooperation and partnerships for progressive emission reductions for all countries (ADB, 2018). In other words, the Paris Agreement provides cost-effective carbon emissions reduction for all countries for the first time (Stavins & Stowe, 2017). In contrast with the Kyoto Protocol, the Agreement defines comprehensive and inclusive approaches, namely the Sustainable Development Mechanism (SDM) and cooperative approaches (CA).

In the Paris Agreement, the NDCs of 81 countries announced the introduction of carbon pricing, including carbon taxes or trading systems, while meeting their commitments (Stavins & Stowe, 2017). Among these countries, top emitters such as China, Japan, and India will have plans to use carbon pricing for the first time, therefore, 55% of global carbon emissions will be explicitly subject to carbon pricing (World Bank, Ecofys, & Vivid Economics, 2017). This global tendency for cost-effectiveness in the mitigation of emissions will assist in supporting the establishment of global cooperation and partnerships among countries and public-private sectors as well (Howard & Climate, 2018). It is expected that, eventually, support for the progressive reduction of emissions through global carbon markets will lead to a global price of carbon (Stavins & Stowe, 2017).

Article 6 of the Paris Agreement outlines the scope of the new market mechanism. It detailed the linking of domestic actions with international cooperation and agreements and provides operational guidance for acquiring Internationally Transferable Mitigation Outcomes (ITMOs), which are defined under Article 6 (World Bank, Ecofys, & Vivid Economics, 2017). There are three approaches; namely cooperative approaches (Article 6.2), sustainable development mechanism (Articles 6.4–6.7), and non-market approaches (Articles 6.8–6.9) focusing on emissions limitation (Table 15.2). The main issues outlined under Article 6.2 are the promotion of sustainable development, ensuring environmental integrity and transparency, linking national emission trading systems, and avoiding double counting through robust accounting systems (Stavins & Stowe, 2017). Article 6.2 also provides guiding rules and principles to establish a carbon market at the global level. Article 6.4 is similar to international emissions trading which was established under the Kyoto Protocol.

Article 6 recognizes ITMOs for international cooperation through regional, national and local carbon pricing initiatives. Even though multilateral development banks recognize the types of

Table 15.2 Article 6 and its implications[1]

Article 6.	Further Explanations
Article 6.1	This paragraph highlights the importance of all kinds of voluntary cooperation to implement NDCs.
Articles 6.2 and 6.3	Article 6.2 recognizes and defines the objective of internationally transferred mitigation outcomes (ITMOs). This paragraph also generally mentions the role of the Conference of the Parties of the Paris Agreement (CMA).
	Articles 6.3 links to ITMOs with NDCs. However, this paragraph does not give any reference to the scope of the ITMOs, even the authorization process will be framed by countries in cooperation, through establishing a common understanding for decentralized approaches.
Articles 6.4, 6.5, 6.6, and 6.7	A new mechanism is established under the CMA. One country's ITMOs can be used another country's NDCs commitment. Double counting will be avoided through supervision of CMA. Priorities of the CMA while creating ITMOs will be defined in Article 6.6.
Articles 6.8 and 6.9	Non-market approaches are recognized in these two paragraphs. The priorities of the non-market approaches are listed, but there is no definition and scope of the approaches. The unfinished business of non-market approaches should be complemented until 2020.

ITMOs as emissions trading certificates, energy certificates, and so forth, the unit and standards of the ITMOs have not yet been defined (ADB, 2018; World Bank, Ecofys, & Vivid Economics, 2017). During the Kyoto Protocol commitments period, certain commodities for emission reductions were created such as Assigned Amount Units (AAU), Certified Emission Reductions (CER), Emission Reduction Units (ERU), but in the Paris Agreement, discussions continue to decide the standards and units of ITMOs. Unlike the Kyoto Protocol, where commodities for emissions reductions were inflexible and restricted, ITMOs are not restricted in the Paris Agreement.

Another difference between the Kyoto Protocol and the Paris Agreement concerns the categorization of activities in countries and whether they are eligible to be involved in global carbon initiatives or not. The Kyoto Protocol recognizes only Annex I countries of the UNFCCC that were eligible without hosting mitigation projects for the Clean Development Mechanism. Accordingly, non-Annex countries could host mitigation projects, but Annex I countries could not benefit from mitigation projects as a host partner in the Kyoto Protocol (UNFCCC, 1998). On the contrary, there is no classification or categorization of that kind of hosting criteria in the Paris Agreement. Therefore, any country will be eligible to participate in mitigation projects either as a host country or as a project developer in other countries. This flexibility in participation will enable a global price for carbon to be set.

4 Climate finance and carbon pricing

The motivation for putting a price on carbon is to decarbonize economies, including through encouraging low-carbon technologies, reducing energy demand, changing consumer behavior, and shifting to sustainable production patterns (Pollitt, 2015; Stavins & Stowe, 2017). While people face a social cost as a result of their actions, through putting a price on carbon as a tool to monetize the damage of carbon emissions (Stern, 2007), carbon pricing is also a revenue raising opportunity to finance and support further low-carbon development (World Bank, Ecofys,

& Vivid Economics, 2017). For example, in 2017, more than USD 33 billion revenue was raised in carbon pricing through carbon taxes, auctions allowances and payments to meet compliance (World Bank & Ecofys, 2018).

In 2017, the number of total carbon pricing initiatives stands at 51 with 11 GtCO2e, representing 20.0% of global GHG emissions (Carbon Pricing Leadership, 2018). The total value of this carbon pricing, including taxes and trades, reached US$ 81.68 billion in 2017, and price per unit of carbon was between USD 1 and USD 140/tCO2e (World Bank & Ecofys, 2018). Therefore, the provision of a carbon price signal, the use of carbon finance in cost calculations, and international agreements to regulate carbon reductions are all essential elements for increasing the share of emissions that are subject to carbon pricing.

The transition to low-carbon development requires USD 700 billion of investment by 2030 (World Bank, Ecofys, & Vivid Economics, 2017). This amount is an incremental part of the total climate investment required, so additional finance should be mobilized by innovative climate finance mechanisms such as carbon pricing (World Bank, Ecofys, & Vivid Economics, 2017). Domestic finance should be the main contributor of this investment, with carbon taxes and trading systems included as a part of the effective mobilization of domestic finance (World Bank, Ecofys, & Vivid Economics, 2017). This mobilization also reduces the marginal cost of emission reductions and the transaction cost of carbon certificates (World Bank, Ecofys, & Vivid Economics, 2017).

In addition to domestic finance, there are still some challenging issues and pressing questions, such as "who will provide the climate finance?" or "Which countries are eligible to use climate finance that is provided by developed countries for combating climate change ?" for accessing international finance such as grants, aid and concessionary funds. These questions originate from discussions on divergence and the definition of "developed/developing" countries and the classification of "Annex-I/non-Annex" countries in the UNFCCC. Similarly, this dichotomous approach in the climate negotiations has been continuing since the post-2012 climate negotiations (Aldy & Stavins, 2012; Bodansky, Chou, & Jorge-Tresolini, 2004). Since the negotiations did not clarify a developed and developing countries distinction in the context of climate finance, these challenges do not seem to be finalized. Though there is no clear definition and considerable divergence among countries commitments to contributing climate finance (Ari & Sari, 2017a, 2017b), Annex II countries in the UNFCCC will, however, routinely co-provide finance to developing countries (UNFCCC, 1992).

This challenging discussion so continues for accessing finance from the Green Climate Fund (GCF), which was established in 2010 in order to finance projects that combat climate change (UNFCCC, 2011). The GCF's priorities are to finance developing countries, in particularly, the least developed and most vulnerable countries. However, the Paris Agreement does not refer to any list of those countries. Although the developed and developing country division is clearly recognized within the operational articles of the Agreement, negotiations on the implementation phase of the Paris Agreement still rely on an Annex-based categorization of countries. Discussions on sources of climate finance and eligibility criteria for accessing to finance seem to continue until the beginning of the Paris Agreement. Unless this problem is solved during the implementation phase of the Paris Agreement, this challenge will negatively affect the performance of countries with regards to tackling climate change.

5 Conclusion

Climate change is one of the biggest global challenges and tackling climate change urgently requires emissions reduction. As mentioned in the introduction, there are three main actions that directly address emissions reduction. These are technological change in production, changing behavioral activities, and carbon pricing (Stern, 2007). The national and international commitments of countries to tackle climate change calls for the greater use of carbon pricing instruments. As a market instrument, carbon pricing provides cost-effective emissions reduction. Carbon pricing and its innovative approaches will also have opportunities to mobilize required finance for tackling climate change.

Carbon tax and trade are the main instruments widely used in countries. Both approaches are based on reducing carbon emissions in a cost-effective manner and monetizing the damage of carbon emissions (Stavins & Stowe, 2017).Carbon pricing not only reduces GHG emissions, but also encourages the development of climate friendly technologies and products in place of carbon intense ones, alongside discouraging emissions intense production and consumption styles (OECD, 2013).Both carbon tax and trade systems rely on national policy frameworks for climate change. Integrating climate change concerns into other sectoral polices and choosing a carbon tax, trade or hybrid approach will minimize the overall cost of emissions reduction within a country. This integration should be considered within all dimensions of sustainable development, namely economic, social, and environmental. Putting a price on carbon should not lead to rising poverty among low-income groups of societies, and it should not hinder competitiveness among entities. Therefore, both tax and trade are designed according to all aspects of national circumstances. In order to achieve an effective carbon tax level, the marginal abatement cost of entities, inflation rate of an economy, and the total required emissions reduction should all be taken into account. According to these dynamics, the tax level should be reviewed and updated accordingly. In addition, the revenues from carbon taxes should be used to finance climate change related projects.

Carbon trade is a market-based instrument so the price of carbon allowances are normally determined in the market. The cost of emissions reduction is reduced through maximizing benefit. In a competitive market carbon prices might not be easily volatile, so the marginal abatement cost might determine the price of carbon. Therefore, the marginal cost of emissions reduction can be equal to the marginal damage of emissions. This rule also provides transparency and predictability with regards to the price of carbon as a commodity. Policy makers, investors, and individuals might not hesitate to involve themselves in carbon pricing. This provides new ideas, such as personal carbon trading to widen participation of all of society in carbon markets (Fawcett & Parag, 2010). Providing that carbon trades are internationally possible without any discrimination, the global cost mitigation will be minimized (Clarke, 2011).

At the international level, carbon pricing has been applied since the Kyoto Protocol. However, the Kyoto Protocol was not a successful agreement for carbon pricing. The scope of projects, the number of participant countries and the various inactions of major emitters are some of the root causes of this failure to realize a global system of carbon pricing. Notwithstanding the established institutional framework of flexibility mechanisms within the Kyoto Protocol, flexibility mechanisms focused on only 14% of global emissions over the first commitment period of the Kyoto Protocol. Recently, the Paris Agreement has opened a new window to universalize a comprehensive and widespread carbon pricing system. It seems that the Paris Agreement and its Article 6 might provide this opportunity for all countries. However, there are many unclear issues on carbon pricing such as the linkages between NDCs, standards of carbon units for markets, scope and additionalities of emissions reduction projects. It is expected that these issues will be overcome by 2020. In addition, there is a significant deficiency for climate finance. The principle of common but differentiated responsibilities and respective capabilities (CBDR-RC) is the common guide for both the UNFCCC and the Agreement to fairly allocate responsibilities such as providing climate finance (UNFCCC, 1992, 2015a). Developed countries and the big emitters are mainly responsible for this deficiency problem. Thus, as a compensation, they should provide a significant part of the finance to the GCF.

In conclusion, carbon pricing in the Paris Agreement enables cost-effective emissions mitigation policy options and provides additional revenue raising for climate actions. In line with the spirit of the new climate agreements framed by the Agreement and the common objective of "no one left behind", all countries should be open to cooperation for global goals for climate change.

Future works can analyze and evaluate the benefits of carbon pricing on some sectors such as electricity generation, transportation, manufacturing industries, and agriculture. Further research and their associated results on these sectors can accelerate the usage of carbon pricing instruments. Future studies can focus on establishing global accounting system proposals for carbon credits and allowances, to monitor and verify global transactions of carbon pricing based commodities. In order to avoid double counting and determine the true price of carbon, a transparent system including a global dashboard for carbon trading is essential. Future researches can assist in developing linkages between total reduced GHG emissions via carbon pricing instruments, and through exploring the effectiveness of global climate funds including the GCF and initiatives of multilateral development banks. The results of this kind of research can the further quantify the impacts of relevant funds and market based instruments on the mitigation of GHG emissions.

Note

1 Further explanations in Table 15.2 are based on Article 6 of the Paris Agreement.

References

ADB. (2018). *Decoding Article 6 of the Paris Agreement*. Manila, Philippines: Asian Development Bank. https://doi.org/10.22617/TIM189218-2

Aldy, J. E., & Stavins, R. N. (2012). *Climate Negotiations Open a Window: Key Implications of the Durban Platform for Enhanced Action*. Harvard Kennedy School. Retrieved from http://belfercenter.ksg.harvard.edu/files/durban-brief_digital5.pdf

Ari, İ. (2013). Voluntary Emission Trading Potential of Turkey. *Energy Policy*, *62*, 910–919. https://doi.org/10.1016/j.enpol.2013.07.054

Ari, I., & Sari, R. (2017a). Developing CBDR-RC Indices for Fair Allocation of Emission Reduction Responsibilities and Capabilities across Countries Developing CBDR-RC Indices for Fair Allocation of Emission. *Cogent Environmental Science*, *3*(1). https://doi.org/https://doi.org/10.1080/23311843.2017.1420365

Ari, I., & Sari, R. (2017b). Differentiation of developed and developing countries for the Paris Agreement. *Energy Strategy Reviews*, *18*, 175–182. https://doi.org/10.1016/j.esr.2017.09.016

Bayon, R., Hawn, A., & Hamilton, K. (2009). *Voluntary Carbon Markets: An International Business Guide to What They Are and How They Work* (Second). London: Earthscan.

Benessaiah, K. (2012). Carbon and Livelihoods in Post-Kyoto: Assessing Voluntary Carbon Markets. *Ecological Economics*, *77*, 1–6. https://doi.org/10.1016/j.ecolecon.2012.02.022

Bhattacharyya, S. C. (2011). *Energy Economics*. London: Springer. https://doi.org/10.1007/978-0-85729-268-1

Bodansky, D., Chou, S., & Jorge-Tresolini, C. (2004). *International Climate Efforts Beyond 2012: A Survey of Approaches*. Pew Center on Global Climate Change. Retrieved from www.c2es.org/docUploads/2012new.pdf

Carbon Pricing Leadership. (2018). Carbon Pricing Dashboard. Retrieved July 23, 2018, from https://carbonpricingdashboard.worldbank.org/

Clarke, H. (2011). Some Basic Economics of Carbon Taxes. *Australian Economic Review*, *44*(2), 123–136. https://doi.org/10.1111/j.1467-8462.2011.00630.x

Fawcett, T., & Parag, Y. (2010). An Introduction to Personal Carbon Trading. *Climate Policy*, *10*(4), 329–338. https://doi.org/10.3763/cpol.2010.0649

Howard, A., & Climate, K. (2018). *Accounting for Bottom-Up Carbon Trading Under the Paris Agreement.* Retrieved from www.c2es.org/site/assets/uploads/2018/04/accounting-bottom-up-carbon-trading-paris-agreement.pdf

IPCC. (2018). *IPCC Special Report on the Impacts of Global Warming of 1.5 °C – Summary for Policy Makers.* Retrieved from www.ipcc.ch/report/sr15/

Mehling, M., & Görlach, B. (2016). Multilateral Linking of Emissions Trading Systems Systems (April).

Mehling, M. A., Metcalf, G. E., & Stavins, R. N. (2017). *Linking Heterogeneous Climate Policies* (CEEPR WP 2017–021 MASSA).

Nordhaus, W. D. (1991). To Slow or Not to Slow: The Economics of the Greenhouse Effect. *The Economic Journal*, *101*(407), 920–937.

Nordhaus, W. D. (2006). After Kyoto: Alternative Mechanisms to Control Global Warming. *American Economic Review*, *96*(2), 31–34. Retrieved from www.jstor.org/stable/30034609

OECD. (2013). *Effective Carbon Prices*. Paris Cedex: OECD Publishing.

Perdan, S., & Azapagic, A. (2011). Carbon Trading: Current Schemes and Future Developments. *Energy Policy*, *39*(10), 6040–6054. https://doi.org/10.1016/j.enpol.2011.07.003

Pollitt, M. G. (2015). *A Global Carbon Market?* Retrieved from http://ceepr.mit.edu/publications/working-papers/635

Stavins, R. N., & Stowe, R. C. (2017). *Market Mechanisms and the Paris Agreement.* (R. N. Stavins & R. C. Stowe, Eds.). Cambridge: Harvard Project on Climate Agreements.

Stern, N. (2007). Carbon Pricing and Emissions Markets in Practice. In *The Economics of Climate Change* (Vol. 32, pp. 368–392). Cambridge: Cambridge University Press. https://doi.org/10.1017/CBO9780511817434.025

UNFCCC. (1992). *UNFCCC.* Retrieved May 19, 2018, from http://unfccc.int/files/essential_background/background_publications_htmlpdf/application/pdf/conveng.pdf

UNFCCC. (1998). *Kyoto Protocol.* Retrieved May 11, 2018, from https://unfccc.int/process/the-kyoto-protocol

UNFCCC. (2011). *The Cancun Agreements.* UNFCCC. Retrieved from http://unfccc.int/resource/docs/2010/cop16/eng/07a01.pdf#page=2

UNFCCC. (2015a). *Adoption of the Paris Agreement.* Retrieved December 14, 2015, from http://unfccc.int/resource/docs/2015/cop21/eng/l09r01.pdf

UNFCCC. (2015b). *INDC Portal.* Retrieved May 18, 2015, from http://unfccc.int/2860.php

World Bank & Ecofys. (2018). *State and Trends of Carbon Pricing 2018: State and Trends of Carbon Pricing 2018.* World Bank. Washington, DC. https://doi.org/10.1596/978-1-4648-1292-7

World Bank, Ecofys, & Vivid Economics. (2017). *State and Trends of Carbon Pricing 2017.* Washington, DC. https://doi.org/10.1596/ 978-1-4648-1218-7

Part III
Energy and society

16

The impact of climate change and the social cost of carbon

Richard S. J. Tol

1   Introduction

The social cost of carbon is the incremental impact of emitting an additional tonne of carbon dioxide, or the benefit of slightly reducing emissions. When evaluated along an optimal emissions trajectory, the social cost of carbon is the Pigou tax (Pigou, 1920) – that is, the amount greenhouse gas emissions should be taxed in order to restore efficiency. The social cost of carbon is thus a key parameter in the discourse about climate change and what to do about it.

Carbon prices are increasingly used in climate policy (World Bank and Ecofys, 2018). Estimates of the social cost of carbon would be an important input into setting the price right. Unfortunately, as I argue below, it is difficult to put narrow bounds on the social cost of carbon. This is mostly because the social cost of carbon is inherently uncertain and controversial. Partly, however, the uncertainty about the social cost of carbon reflects gaps in knowledge and research.

There have been a number of reviews of the social cost of carbon (Pizer et al., 2014; Guivarch et al., 2016; Metcalf and Stock, 2017; Pindyck, 2017a, 2017b; Revesz et al., 2017) and its application (Rose, 2012; Greenstone et al., 2013; Heyes et al., 2013; Sunstein, 2014; Hahn and Ritz, 2015). Since my earlier surveys (Tol, 2005; Tol and Yohe, 2009; Tol, 2011, 2013, 2018), the volume of papers and estimates has increased further, but recent papers remap known territory without breaking new ground.

In this paper, I discuss conceptual issues around the social cost of carbon and review these new estimates, after assessing what we know about the total economic impact of climate change. Although estimates of the total cost of climate change have no immediate relevance for policy, estimates of the social cost of carbon derive from the total cost. Furthermore, total cost estimate reveal the Schelling Conjecture, which poses a policy dilemma: adapt or mitigate.

2   The total impact of climate change

Figure 16.1 shows the 27 published estimates of the total economic impact of climate change. See Howard and Sterner (2017) and Nordhaus and Moffat (2017) for markedly different assessments of the same literature. The horizontal axis has the change in the global annual mean surface air temperature, a key indicator of climate change. The vertical axis is the welfare equivalent income

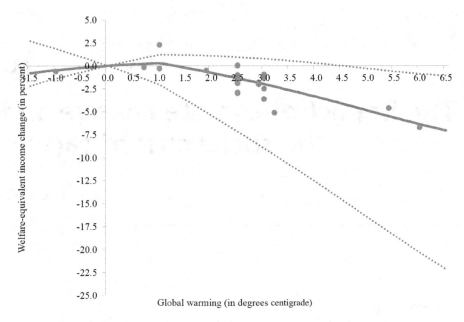

Figure 16.1 The global total annual impact of climate change

change. These numbers should be read as follows: A global warming of 2.5°C would make the average person feel as if she had lost 1.3% of her income (1.3% is the average of the 11 dots at 2.5°C).

2.1 Methods

These estimates were derived as follows. Researchers used models – of every description: process models, optimization models, equilibrium models, statistical models, spatial or temporal analogues – to estimate the many impacts of climate change for all parts of the world in their natural units, estimated the values of these impacts (using either market prices or monetary valuation methods), multiplied the quantities and prices, and added everything up (d'Arge, 1979; Nordhaus, 1982, 1991, 1994a; Fankhauser, 1995; Tol, 1995; Berz, 1996; Nordhaus and Yang, 1996; Plambeck and Hope, 1996; Tol, 2002; Nordhaus and Boyer, 2000; Hope, 2006; Nordhaus, 2008). This is the so-called enumerative method. The result is an estimate of the direct cost – price times quantity – of climate change. The direct cost is a poor approximation of the change in welfare, for instance because it ignores price changes, but it is an approximation nonetheless. The enumerative approach omits interactions between sectors, such as a change in water resources affecting agriculture.

Other studies use the same physical impact estimates that are used in the enumerative studies above, but use these to shock a computable general equilibrium model (Bosello et al., 2012; Roson and van der Mensbrugghe, 2012). These estimates thus include both price changes and interactions between economics sectors, be it through output, intermediate or input markets, and between economies through international trade and investment. The welfare measure used in these studies is typically the Hicksian Equivalent Variation, a proper welfare measure that is, within the model, measured exactly. Computable general equilibrium models are based on the national accounts, and thus misrepresent subsistence agriculture and omit direct impacts of welfare.

Other estimates involve regressions of an economic indicator on climate (Mendelsohn et al., 2000; Nordhaus, 2006). Agricultural land prices, for instance, reflect the productivity of the land and hence the value of the climate that allows plants to grow. You do not just buy the land, but also the sun that shines and the rain that falls on it (Ricardo, 1817). Price differences due to climate variation are used to estimate the direct cost of climate change. Household expenditure patterns (Maddison, 2003) and self-reported happiness (Rehdanz and Maddison, 2005; Maddison and Rehdanz, 2011) have also been used. The main advantage of the statistical method is that it is based on actual behavior (rather than modeled behavior as above). The main disadvantage is that climate variations over space are used to derive the impact of climate change over time. Space and time are different things, though. For instance, trade is much easier over space than over time; and technology and institutions differ more over space than over time.

One estimate elicits the views of *supposed* experts (Nordhaus, 1994b).[1] The question was about the impact of climate change on global output, which can alternatively be interpreted as a measure of economic activity (but not welfare) and a measure of income (and thus welfare).

2.2   Weather and climate

Climate varies only slowly over time – it is, after all, the 30-year average of weather. In empirical studies, the identification of the impact of climate therefore comes from cross-sectional variation. As the climate varies only slowly over space, the cross-section needs to be large. This is problematic as so many other things vary over space too. Ricardian and hedonic methods are therefore vulnerable to spurious associations because of confounding variables. This can be partly overcome with panel data, for confounders that vary over time as well as space – trade policy would be one example, if it has changed within sample, and if trade liberalization is preferentially between countries with similar climates. But panel data cannot help with confounders that do not change much over time – a cultural preference for pastoralism in dry areas would be one example.

In recent years, there have been a number of papers that estimate the impacts of weather on a range of economic indicators (Deschenes and Greenstone, 2007; Burke et al., 2015; Hsiang et al., 2017; Burke et al., 2018). The key advantage of weather impacts is that weather is, from an economic perspective, random. The impact of weather is therefore properly identified. Although the rhetoric in some of these papers would have you believe otherwise, the impact of a weather shock is not the same as the impact of climate change (Dell et al., 2014). See Deryugina and Hsiang (2017) for the conditions under which weather variability is informative about climate change.

Climate is what you expect, weather is what you get. Adaptation to weather shocks is therefore limited to immediate responses – put up an umbrella when it rains, close the flood doors when it pours. Adaptation to climate change extends to changes in the capital stock – buy an umbrella, invest in flood doors. In other words, weather studies estimate the short-run elasticity, whereas the interest is in the long-run elasticity. Extrapolating the impact of weather shocks will not lead to credible results for the impact of climate change.

2.3   Combining estimates

Besides the primary estimates, Figure 16.1 also shows a curve. Seven alternative impact functions were fitted to the data. See Table 16.1. Assuming normality of the residuals, the loglikelihood was computed for each model. The curve shown is the Bayesian average of the seven models. A piecewise linear model is the best fit to the data, and the average curve indeed looks

Table 16.1 Alternative models of the total impact of climate change

Name	Function	Weight
Golosov	$-4.16 \cdot 10^{-175} (e^{e^{T}} - e)$	0.0%
Ploeg	$-0.02 (e^{T} - 1)$	0.0%
Hope	$-0.71T$	0.2%
Nordhaus	$-0.19T^2$	8.7%
Tol (parabolic)	$-0.12T - 0.16T^2$	10.2%
Weitzman(7)	$-0.21T^2 - 5.79 \cdot 10^{-6}T^7$	13.6%
Weitzman(6)	$-0.22T^2 - 3.71 \cdot 10^{-5}T^6$	14.2%
Tol (piecewise linear)	$0.74T I_{T<1.01} + (0.74 \cdot 1.01 - 1.41\,T) I_{T \geq 1.01}$	53.2%

like that. The near-linearity of the impact function is driven by the two moderate estimates for high warming.

Only 7 of the 27 estimates have a reported standard deviation, or an upper and lower bound. I imputed upper and lower bounds from twice the reported standard deviations. I assume that the upper and lower bounds are linear functions of the temperature, with slopes 0.92% GDP/°C and 2.33% GDP/°C on the cold and hot side, respectively. I interpret this as a 90% confidence interval.

2.4 Results

Figure 16.1 contains many messages. There are only 27 estimates, a rather thin basis for any conclusion. Statements that climate change is the biggest (environmental) problem of humankind are not well-supported and, as argued below, probably false.

The 11 estimates for 2.5°C, which we may reach in 60–80 years' time, show that researchers disagree on the sign of the net impact. Climate change may lead to a welfare gain or loss. At the same time, researchers agree on the order of magnitude. The welfare change caused by climate change is equivalent to the welfare change caused by an income change of a few percent. The average of the estimates is negative. That is, a century of climate change is about as bad as losing a year of economic growth.

Considering all 27 estimates, it is suggested that initial warming is positive on net, while further warming would lead to net damages. The initial benefits are due to reduced costs of heating in winter, reduced cold-related mortality and morbidity, and carbon dioxide fertilization, which makes plants grow faster and more drought resistant. This does not imply that greenhouse gas emissions should be subsidized. The *incremental* impacts turn negative around 1.1°C global warming. Because of the slow workings of the climate system and the large inertia in the energy sector, a warming of 2°C can probably not be avoided and a warming of 1°C can certainly not be avoided – we may already have reached that point. That is, the initial net benefits of climate change are *sunk benefits*. We will reap these benefits no matter what we do to our emissions. For more pronounced warming, the negative impacts dominate, such as summer cooling costs, infectious diseases, and sea level rise.

The uncertainty is rather large, however. The error bars in Figure 16.1 depict the 90% confidence interval. This is probably an underestimate of the true uncertainty, as experts tend to be overconfident and as the 27 estimates were derived by a group of researchers who know each other and each other's work well.

The uncertainty is right-skewed. Negative surprises are more likely than positive surprises of similar magnitude. This is true for the greenhouse gas emissions: It is easier to imagine a world that burns a lot of coal than a world that rapidly switches to wind and solar power. It is true for climate itself: Feedbacks that accelerate climate change are more prevalent than feedbacks that dampen warming. The best estimate for the climate sensitivity, the eventual warming due to a doubling of atmospheric carbon dioxide, is 2.5°C, with a range of 1.5°C to 4.5°C. The impacts of climate change are more than linear: If climate change doubles, its impacts more than double. Many have painted dismal scenarios of climate change, but no one has credibly suggested that climate change will make us all blissfully happy. In that light, the above conclusion needs to be rephrased: a century of climate change is no worse than losing a decade of economic growth.

The right extreme of Figure 16.1 is interesting too. At 3.0°C of warming, impacts are negative, deteriorating, and (perhaps) accelerating. It is likely that the world will warm beyond 3.0°C. Yet, beyond that point, there are few estimates only. There is extrapolation and speculation.

2.5   Distribution of impacts

Thirteen of the 22 studies referred to above include estimates of the regional impacts of climate change and, in the studies involving David Maddison, national impact estimates. Regressing the estimated regional impact for 2.5°C warming on per capita income and average annual temperature, with dummies for the studies, I find that

$$I_c = -13.4(8.7) + 1.70(0.79)\ln y_c - 0.46(0.14)T_c \tag{16.1}$$

where I_c is the impact in country c (in % GDP), y_c is its average income (in 2010 market exchange dollars per person per year), and T_c is the average annual temperature (in degrees Celsius). Hotter countries have more negative impacts. Richer countries have more positive impacts. Of course, Equation (16.1) does not capture the special vulnerability of delta and island nations. I use this equation to impute national impacts, making sure that the regional or global totals match those in the original estimates.

Figure 16.1 shows the world average impact for 27 studies. Figure 16.2 shows results for individual countries for 2.5°C warming. Countries are ranked from low to high per capita income and low to high temperature. In Figure 16.1, the world total impact is roughly zero. In Figure 16.2, the majority of countries show a negative impact. However, the world economy is concentrated in a few, rich countries. The world average in Figure 16.1 counts dollars, rather than countries, let alone people.

Figure 16.2 suggests that poorer countries are more vulnerable to climate change than are richer countries. There are a few exceptions to this – such as Mongolia, which is poor but so cold that warming would bring benefits, and Singapore, which is rich but a low-lying island on the equator – but by and large the negative impacts of climate change are concentrated in the developing economies.

There are three reasons for this. First, poorer countries are more exposed. Richer countries have a larger share of their economic activities in manufacturing and services, which are typically shielded (to a degree) against the vagaries of weather and hence climate change. Agriculture and water resources are far more important, relative to the size of the economy, in poorer countries.

Second, poorer countries tend to be in hotter places. This means that ecosystems are closer to their biophysical upper limits, and that there are no analogues for human behavior and technology. Great Britain's future climate may become like Spain's current climate. The people of Britain would therefore adopt some of the habits of the people of Spain, and build their houses like the

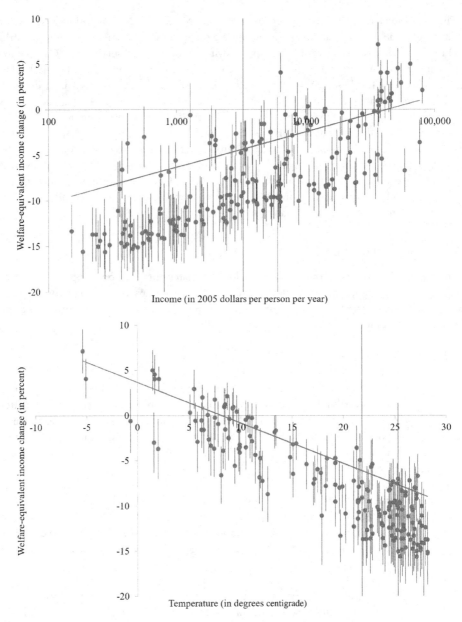

Figure 16.2   The economic impact of climate change for a 2.5°C warming for all countries as a function of their 2005 income (top panel) and temperature (bottom panel)

Spaniards do. Houses in Spain are designed to keep the heat out, whereas houses in the UK are built to keep the heat in. It makes sense to sleep through the heat of the day and, as digestion heats up the body, take the main meal in the cool of the night. If the hottest climate on the planet gets hotter still, there are no examples to copy from; new technologies will have to be invented, behavior will have to be adjusted by trial and error.

Third, poorer countries tend to have a limited *adaptive capacity* (Adger, 2006; Yohe and Tol, 2002). Adaptive capacity is the ability to adapt. It depends on a range of factors, such as the availability of technology and the ability to pay for those technologies. Sea level rise is a big problem if you do not know about dikes, or if you do but you cannot afford to build one. Flood protection has been known for thousands of years. Modern technology is at its summit in the Netherlands. Dutch engineers will happily share their expertise – for a fee. Adaptive capacity also depends on human and social capital. Coastal protection is both a natural monopoly and a public good, and so requires a competent government. An ounce of prevention is worth a pound of cure, but prevention requires that you are able to recognize problems before they manifest themselves (i.e. predict the future) and that you are able to act on that knowledge (i.e. analytical capacity is connected to policy implementation). Furthermore, the powers that be need to care about the potential victims. A country's elite may be aware of the dangers of climate change and have the wherewithal to prevent the worst impacts, but if those impacts would fall on the politically and economically marginalized, or if the victims think that floods are due to the wrath of God rather than the incompetence of politicians, the elite may choose to ignore the impacts.

Figure 16.2 shows that poorer countries are more vulnerable to climate change. Aggregating results by country hides information. Figure 16.3 again shows the impact of 2.5°C warming. The impacts are further downscaled, to income deciles, based on data from the University of Texas Inequality Project, using the same semi-elasticity used to downscale regional to national impact estimates; see Equation (16.1). Figure 16.3 shows three histograms, weighing the estimates by the share of the number of countries affected, by the share of the number of people affected, and by the share of total economic output affected.

Figure 16.3 reveals that focusing on countries overstates the impact of climate change, as small coastal and island states are heavily affected by sea level rise. Figure 16.3 highlights that the

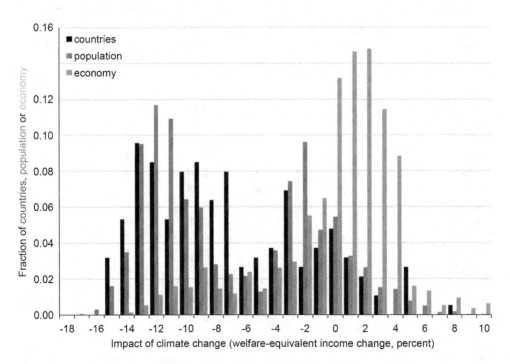

Figure 16.3 The distribution of the annual impact of 2.5°C global warming by country, people, and economy affected

majority of the world population will suffer large negative impacts while the larger share of the world economy will enjoy mild positive impacts.

2.6 Sectoral impacts

Four studies published estimates of the impact of 2.5°C warming by sector. See Table 16.2. Coverage varies between studies. The rightmost column has the average of the published estimates. Adding up these sectoral averages, the total impact is −2.0% of GDP, which is 28% higher than the average of the original studies. Using the sectoral averages to impute missing observations makes the original studies less incomplete. The estimate by Nordhaus and Boyer (2000) is the least complete.

Impacts are found across the economy. There is no sector or impact that dominates the total.

3 The social cost of carbon

3.1 Definition

The social cost of carbon is defined as the monetary value of the first partial derivative of global, net present welfare to current carbon dioxide emissions. It is sometimes calculated as a true marginal along a welfare-optimizing emissions trajectory, and so equals the Pigou (1920) tax on carbon dioxide. More often, the social cost of carbon is approximated as a normalized increment

Table 16.2 Sectoral estimates of the impact of climate change (in percentage of GDP)

	Fankhauser	Berz	Tol	Nordhaus	Average
Agriculture	**−0.20**	−0.19	**−0.13**	**−0.13**	−0.16
Forestry	**−0.01**	−0.02	−0.01	−0.01	−0.01
Energy	**−0.12**	−0.11	−0.12	−0.12	−0.12
Water	**−0.24**	−0.23	−0.24	−0.24	−0.24
Other market*	**−0.37**	−0.36	−0.26	**−0.05**	−0.26
Coastal defense	**0.00**	−0.01	**−0.08**	−0.03	−0.03
Dryland	**−0.07**	−0.07	**−0.09**	−0.08	−0.08
Wetland	**−0.16**	−0.16	**−0.17**	−0.16	−0.16
Coastal*	**−0.24**	−0.23	**−0.34**	**−0.32**	−0.28
Ecosystem	**−0.21**	−0.20	**−0.19**	−0.20	−0.20
Health	**−0.26**	**−0.40**	**−0.77**	**−0.10**	−0.38
Air pollution	**−0.08**	−0.08	−0.08	−0.08	−0.08
Time use	0.29	0.29	0.29	**0.29**	0.29
Settlements	−0.17	−0.17	−0.17	**−0.17**	−0.17
Extreme weather	**−0.01**	**−0.01**	**−0.01**	**−1.02**	−0.27
Migration	**−0.02**	−0.02	**−0.12**	−0.07	−0.06
Amenity	**−0.33**	−0.33	**−0.33**	−0.33	−0.33
Total	−1.61	−1.71	−2.24	−2.47	−2.01
Original	−1.4	−1.5	−1.9	−1.5	−1.6
Ratio	1.15	1.14	1.18	1.65	1.28

Bold face numbers are original estimates, normal face numbers are imputed from the average, italicized numbers are imputed by Berz from Fankhauser. * 'Coastal' and 'Other market' are the sum of the three sectors immediately above.

along an arbitrary emissions path. Essentially, you compute the impacts of climate change for a particular scenario; you slightly increase emissions in 2018 and compute the slightly different impacts; you take the difference between the two series of future impacts; discount them back to today; and normalize the net present value of the difference with the change in emissions.

Formally,

$$SCC = \left(\frac{\sum_c C_{c,0}}{\sum_c P_{c,0}}\right)^{-\eta-\omega+\eta\omega} \frac{\partial}{\partial E_0} \sum_s p_s \sum_t \frac{1}{(1+\rho)^t} \sum_c \frac{P_{c,t,s}}{1-\omega} \frac{1}{1-\eta}\left(\left(\frac{C_{c,t,s}}{P_{c,t,s}}\right)^{1-\eta}\right)^{1-\omega} \tag{16.2}$$

where SCC is the social cost of carbon at time 0, E_s denote emissions, $P_{c,t,s}$ population in country c at time t in state of the world s, and C consumption; ρ is a parameter, the pure rate of time preference, η is the rate of relative risk aversion and ω is the pure rate of inequity aversion; and p_s is the probability of obtaining state of the world s.

There is a lot going on in Equation (16.2). Climate change affects different countries differently. These effects need to be aggregated to a world total. This is the inner summation. The rate of risk aversion η reflects that a dollar to a poor woman is not the same as a dollar to a rich woman. We may follow Atkinson (1970) and care about the distribution of utility. If so, $\omega \neq 0$. Note that the consumption rate of inequality aversion is $\eta + \omega - \eta\omega$, so that we would still care about income differences (but not about utility differences) if $\omega = 0$; see Tol (2010). Carbon dioxide stays in the atmosphere for a long time, and the climate is a dynamic system. Therefore, an additional tonne of carbon dioxide emitted today will have a long-lasting impact, that needs to be discounted to today. This is the middle summation. While utility is discounted at rate ρ, consumption is discounted at rate $\rho + g_P + (\eta + \omega - \eta\omega)g_C$, where g_P is the growth rate of the population and g_C is the growth rate of consumption. The future is uncertain, so the outer summation aggregates across possible states of the world, with η and ω now reflecting risk aversion. Finally, the first partial derivative is welfare to emissions. The social cost of carbon is expressed in dollar per tonne of carbon. The first element in Equation (16.2) normalizes the marginal impact on expected net present welfare with the marginal utility of consumption at the time of emission.

Most estimates of the social cost of carbon are based on a parameterization of Equation (16.2). Alternatives are possible, of course. Constant rates of relative risk aversion are mathematically convenient, but not necessarily realistic (Donkers et al., 2001; Hartog et al., 2002; Cohen and Einav, 2007) and may be problematic under deep uncertainty (Millner, 2013). The rate of risk aversion triples in its role as inequity aversion and time preference (Saelen et al., 2009). Equation (16.2) assumes Knightian risk, but we may want to account for ambiguity aversion too (Lemoine and Traeger, 2016). Preferences are commonly assumed to be time-separable, but other assumptions are possible too (Cai et al., 2016). And we may not accept the Koopmans (1960) axioms of net present welfare (Llavador et al., 2011; Dietz and Asheim, 2012; Tol, 2013). Finally, the social cost of carbon is defined as the global social cost of carbon, implicitly assuming a global social planner, a benevolent philosopher-queen; Anthoff and Tol (2010) explore national attitudes towards global welfare.

The impact of climate change is implicit in Equation (16.2). The chain rule has that

$$\frac{\partial C_{c,t,s}}{\partial E_0} = \frac{\partial C_{c,t,s}}{\partial T_{t,s}}\left(\frac{\partial T_{t,s}}{\partial M_{t,s}}\frac{\partial M_{t,s}}{\partial E_0} + \frac{\partial T_{t,s}}{\partial T_{t-1,s}}\frac{\partial T_{t-1,s}}{\partial M_{t-1,s}}\frac{\partial M_{t-1,s}}{\partial E_0} + \cdots\right) \tag{16.3}$$

if we assume that impacts depend only on the global temperature $T_{t,s}$ and temperature only on its own past and the atmospheric concentration of carbon dioxide $M_{t,s}$. Reality is more complicated, but substituting (16.3) into (16.2) leads to an intractable result. Therefore, most estimates of the social cost of carbon rely on numerical models. Sample code in MATLAB is available.

Some of the controversy concerning the social cost of carbon arises from the complexity of its computation. Golosov et al. (2014) show that the social cost of carbon can be written as a function of total economic output, the pure rate of time preference, elasticity of damage with regard to the atmospheric concentration of carbon dioxide, and the rate of decay of carbon dioxide in the atmosphere. This result hinges on the assumptions that

1   *Utility is logarithmic in consumption.* As shown by Donkers et al. (2001), Hartog et al. (2002) and Cohen and Einav (2007), risk aversion is probably not constant, let alone equal to one.
2   *Time discounting is exponential.* Arrow et al. (2013, 2014) review the arguments against geometric discounting.
3   *The carbon cycle follows a linear difference equation.* Maier-Reimer and Hasselmann (1987) show that the removal of carbon dioxide from the atmosphere cannot be approximated by a linear difference equation.
4   *Climate change impacts are proportional to total output.* Figure 16.2 illustrates that poverty implies vulnerability to climate change – that is, impacts have a negative income elasticity, and so are less than proportional to output.
5   *Climate change impacts are proportional to the exponent of the atmospheric concentration of carbon dioxide.* The equilibrium temperature is logarithmic in the atmospheric concentration, so Golosov assumes that impact is proportional to the exponent of the exponent of temperature. Figure 16.1 suggests that the relationship between temperature and impact is close to linear.
6   *There are no catastrophic risks.* Keller et al. (2004) show that catastrophes break Golosov's smoothness, and hence their simple function for the social cost of carbon.

In sum, none of these assumptions is realistic. Stylized models are great for insight, but insight into irreality is worthless.

3.2   Simple model

I wrote MATLAB code to combine the impact models in Table 16.1 with the SRES (Nakicenovic and Swart, 2000) and SSP (Riahi et al., 2017) scenarios of population, income and emissions, the Maier-Reimer and Hasselmann (1987) carbon cycle model, and the Schneider and Thompson (1981) climate model. Readers are free to download, run, manipulate, and share the code.

Tables 16.3, 16.4, and 16.5 show selected results. Table 16.3 displays the social cost of carbon as a function of the pure rate of time and the rate of risk aversion. As there is no uncertainty in

Table 16.3 Estimates of the social cost of carbon (in 2010 dollars per tonne of carbon)

Time preference/risk aversion	0.5	1.0	1.5	2.0	2.5
0.001%	55.4	22.4	10.9	6.3	4.1
0.010%	35.4	15.6	8.2	5.1	3.5
0.020%	22.5	10.9	6.3	4.1	2.9
0.030%	15.1	8.0	4.9	3.4	2.5
0.040%	10.6	6.1	3.9	2.8	2.2
0.050%	7.7	4.7	3.3	2.4	1.9

Model = Tol (parabola); scenario = SRES A1; climate sensitivity = 3.0; income elasticity = –0.36.

the model, and one representative agent only, the rate of risk aversion only plays a role in trade-offs between current poverty and future richesse via the Ramsey (1928) rule of discounting. A higher rate of risk aversion thus implies a higher discount rate, as does a higher pure rate of time preference. The results are as expected: The lower the discount rate, the greater the care for the future, the more concern about climate change, and the higher the social cost of carbon.

Table 16.4 shows the social cost of carbon for different impact models and scenarios. Alternative scenarios do not affect the social cost of carbon that much, as the difference between scenarios only become really pronounced in the more distant (and more heavily discounted) future. Although the different impact models are calibrated to the same dataset, there are pronounced differences between models. Golosov's double exponential model advocates a zero carbon tax – it has essentially zero impacts below a temperature threshold, and infinitely large impacts above. Van der Ploeg's single exponential model shows the same behavior, but less extreme, and thus argues for a low social cost of carbon. Tol's piecewise linear model calls for a carbon subsidy – it emphasizes the positive impacts of modest climate change. The results for the remaining five models are relatively close to each other.

Table 16.5 has the social cost of carbon as a function of the two key parameters: The climate sensitivity and the income elasticity of impact. In the base calibration, the climate sensitivity is a warming of 3.0°C per doubling of the atmospheric concentration of carbon dioxide. Should the climate warm faster, the social cost of carbon increases. This relationship is more than linear. In the base calibration, the impact relative to income falls by 3.6% if income rises by 10%. The social cost of carbon falls (rises) if the income elasticity is higher (lower). Again, the relationship is nonlinear: A lower income elasticity has a greater effect than a higher one.

Table 16.4 Estimates of the social cost of carbon (in 2010 dollars per tonne of carbon)

Model/scenario	A1	A2	B1	B2	SSP1	SSP2	SSP3	SSP4	SSP5
Golosov	0.0	0.0	0.0	0.0	0.0	0.0	0.0	0.0	0.0
Ploeg	1.5	2.2	1.5	1.4	1.6	1.7	2.0	1.6	1.6
Hope	8.4	10.2	9.1	9.9	8.8	9.3	10.1	9.5	8.1
Nordhaus	7.7	10.0	8.3	8.7	7.8	8.6	9.6	8.5	7.5
Tol (parabola)	8.0	10.2	8.6	9.1	8.2	8.7	9.8	8.9	7.7
Weitzman (7)	8.8	11.3	9.4	9.9	8.9	9.7	10.9	9.7	8.5
Weitzman (6)	8.7	11.2	9.4	9.9	8.9	9.7	10.8	9.7	8.4
Tol (piecewise linear)	–3.8	–2.5	–4.1	–5.8	–4.6	–4.1	–3.2	–4.5	–3.7

Pure rate of time preference = 0.01%; rate of risk aversion = 1; climate sensitivity = 3.0; income elasticity = –0.36.

Table 16.5 Estimates of the social cost of carbon (in 2010 dollars per tonne of carbon)

Income elasticity/ climate sensitivity	1.5	2.5	3.0	4.5
–0.00	3.8	9.5	13.3	28.3
–0.18	3.0	7.3	10.2	21.6
–0.36	2.3	5.7	8.0	16.9
–0.72	1.5	3.7	5.2	11.0

Model = Tol (parabola); scenario = SRES A1; Pure rate of time preference = 0.01%; rate of risk aversion = 1.

Uncertainty and risk aversion

Table 16.5 shows that the social cost of carbon is more than linear in the climate sensitivity. For an income elasticity of -0.36, $SCC = 0.445CS + 0.736CS^2$ is an excellent fit, where CS denotes the climate sensitivity. This immediately implies that, if the uncertainty about the climate sensitivity is symmetric, the mode of the social cost of carbon, displayed in Table 16.5, is smaller than its mean. However, the probability density function of the climate sensitivity is right-skewed and may be fat-tailed. Roe and Baker (2007) argue that $CS = \dfrac{CS_{f=0}}{1-f}$ where $CS_{f=0} = 1.2K$ and total feedback f is normally distributed. They set its standard deviation to 0.13. If its mean is 0.6, the mode of the climate sensitivity is $3K$, as above.

The mode of the social cost of carbon is $\$8.0/tC$ for $3K$, the mode of the climate sensitivity. The expectation of the social cost of carbon is $\$50.6/tC$, if the uncertainty about the climate sensitivity follows the Roe-Baker distribution, as described above, and the social cost of carbon is a quadratic function of the climate sensitivity, as described above. Assuming a utility function with a constant rate of risk aversion equal to one, the certainty equivalent of paying the social cost of carbon as a tax is $\$51.1/tC$, if evaluated for the global average income of $\$9,500/person/year$ in 2010 and the average emissions of 1.3 metric tonnes of carbon per person per year. If the rate of risk aversion is two, the certainty equivalent social cost of carbon is $\$51.6/tC$.

This illustrates two things. First, as the uncertainty about climate change is large and skewed the wrong way, there is a large difference between the mode and the mean, the best guess and the expectation. The latter matters, of course, for decision analysis.

Second, because the carbon tax that would optimally be levied is small relative to income, the risk premium is relatively small. Uncertainty is more important than aversion to risk.

Combining this insight with the range of estimates in Table 16.4, suggests that ambiguity aversion is similarly of secondary importance – even though experts vigorously disagree. Similar conclusions are drawn by other studies (Welsch, 1995; Eismont and Welsch, 1996; Cameron, 2005; Traeger, 2014; Tol, 2015; Lemoine and Traeger, 2016; Heal, 2017).

3.3   Meta-analysis

Tol (2018) counts 111 studies of the social cost of carbon and 1,213 estimates. Since that survey was completed, 534 estimates have been published in 14 new studies (Ackerman and Munitz, 2016; Adler et al., 2017; Budolfson et al., 2017; Cai et al., 2016; Dayaratna et al., 2017; Dennig et al., 2015; Freeman and Groom, 2014; Freeman et al., 2015; Freeman and Groom, 2016; Hatase and Managi, 2015; Lemoine and Traeger, 2016; Nordhaus, 2017; van der Ploeg, 2015; Rose et al., 2017).

I construct a probability density of the social cost of carbon for all published estimates. The method follows Tol (2013), with the estimates weighted by study characteristics, as in Tol (2005). van den Bergh and Botzen (2014) argue that estimates below $\$125/tCO_2$ are not credible. Theirs is but one paper. Estimates are therefore weighted by $\dfrac{N-1}{2N-1} I_{SCC \leq \$422/tC} + \dfrac{N}{2N-1} I_{SCC > \$422/tC}$, where $N = 125$ is the number of studies, I is the indicator function, and $\$422/tC$ is their threshold in 2010 dollars. In addition, estimates in excess of $\$7,600/tC$ are excluded, as this would imply a carbon tax that exceeds 100% of GDP (at the global average of the carbon intensity of the economy). Estimates between $\$1,150/tC$ and $\$7,600/tC$ are discounted by a linear function that equals 1 for $\$1,150/tC$ and 0 for $\$7,600/tC$. If the carbon tax equals $\$1,150/tC$, 100% of government revenue is from the carbon tax (at the global average of the carbon intensity of the public economy). This assumes that the social cost of carbon is a tax that should be paid. If, on the other hand, the social cost of carbon is interpreted as a marginal welfare loss, then there is no upper bound.

The probability density function (PDF) is a kernel density. The kernel function is a Weibull distribution, a heavy-tailed PDF defined on the positive real line. The mode is set equal to the estimate, the bandwidth to the sample standard deviation. The models developed by Hope and Tol acknowledge the possibility that the impacts of modest climate change may be positive. For these estimates, the kernel function is a Gumbel distribution: defined on the real line, heavy-tailed, and right-skewed. The kernel functions for estimates by other authors are therefore knotted at zero.

Results from the meta-analysis

Figure 16.4 presents the probability density of the social cost of carbon for estimates based on selected pure rates of time preference (PRTP). The higher the discount rate, the lower the concern for the future, and the lower the social cost of carbon: The mode is $202/tC for a 0% PRTP, $100/tC for a 1% PRTP, and $28/tC for a 3% PRTP. Furthermore, as the uncertainty grows as we look further into the future, a lower discount rate implies a loss of confidence, with a standard deviation of $644/tC for a 0% PRTP, $471/tC for a 1% PRTP, and $35/tC for a 3% PRTP. The higher mode and standard deviation come together in the mean social cost of carbon, which is $686/tC for a 0% PRTP, $378/tC for a 1% PRTP, and $43/tC for a 3% PRTP. To provide some context, burning a barrel of oil emits 0.43 metric tonnes of carbon dioxide. A $28/tC carbon tax is thus equivalent to $3/barrel, while a $686/tC carbon tax is equivalent to $80/barrel. The former carbon tax is small (< 5%) relative to today's price of oil, while the latter tax is on the same order as the oil price. In early May 2018, the price of carbon permits in the European Union

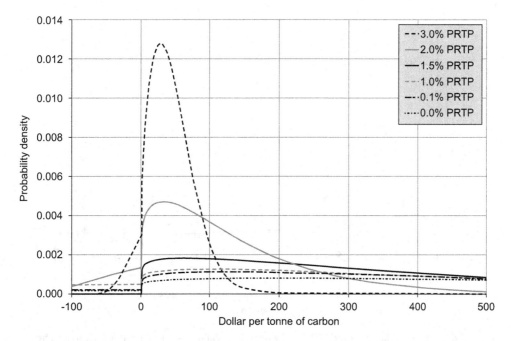

Figure 16.4 Probability density function of the social cost of carbon for alternative pure rates of time preference

Emission Trading System (EU ETS) was $59/tC. In February 2018, permits were auctioned by the California Air Resources Board at $55/tC. This suggests that current climate policy in the most progressive jurisdictions in the world can readily be justified by cost-benefit analysis, and may need to be tightened.

Publication bias

Havranek et al. (2015) argue that lower estimates of the social cost of carbon are less likely to be published than higher estimates. However, the literature on the social cost of carbon does not appear to suffer from confirmation bias. The received wisdom is regularly challenged, at least qualitatively (Tol, 2018). Figure 16.5 shows the median and the 90% confidence interval for estimates of the social cost of carbon published in a particular year and published in previous years. In 8 out of 14 years, new estimates fall outside the 90% confidence interval, 5.7 times more than expected. In this literature, people are not afraid to challenge each other.

Figure 16.5 suggests a gradual decline in the central estimate of the social cost of carbon and a modest tightening of its confidence interval. Downward revisions of the social cost of carbon are not support (because the trends are statistically insignificant) while upward revisions run against the balance of evidence.

3.4 Deep uncertainty

Weitzman (2011) argues that the uncertainty about climate change is so large that the expectation of the social cost of carbon is unbounded. Weitzman's argument is theoretic, but does not seem to be supported by evidence presented here. Moreover, Weitzman's result only holds in partial

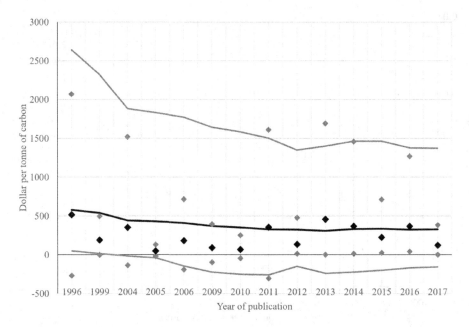

Figure 16.5 The median and the 90% confidence interval of the social cost of carbon as a function of the year of publication. The diamonds show the characteristics of estimates published in the year displayed on the horizontal axis, the lines show estimates for previous years.

equilibrium (Horowitz and Lange, 2014), for zero mitigation (Millner, 2013), and for constant relative risk aversion (Arrow, 2009), while alternative decision criteria do not lead to substantially different policy advice concerning optimal climate policy (Anthoff and Tol, 2014).

3.5   The social cost of carbon over time

Climate change is a dynamic problem, and so is climate policy. It is important to set a price of carbon today. It is at least as important to announce a carbon price for later, so that investors and inventors can anticipate the future demand for carbon-free energy. Figures 16.6 and 16.7 illustrate how the social cost of carbon should change over time.

Figure 16.6 uses the simple model discussed above to compute the social cost of carbon at the start of every decade from 1750 to 2100. Costs are discounted to the year of emission. The pure rate of time preference is 1%, the rate of risk aversion 1. The scenario is SRES A1. The impact model is parabolic; it only allows for negative impacts of climate change (see Table 16.1). The social cost of carbon starts low at \$0.26/tC in 1750[2] and rises to \$41.77/tC in 2060. Between 2010 and 2050, the social cost of carbon rises by 2%–3% per year.

After 2060, the social cost of carbon falls. This is because the model has its time horizon at 2100. Climate change will probably not stop then, but the model does. With a relatively low discount rate, for later years, an increasingly large share of the net present value is ignored in the estimation of the social cost of carbon. This highlights the interaction between the choice of time horizon and discount rate. Tol and Yohe (2009) show that a pure rate of time preference of 0.1% requires a time horizon of 10,000 years.

Figure 16.7 shows the kernel distribution of the growth rate of the social cost of carbon, using a Normal kernel function with 1.06 times the sample standard deviation over the quint root of the number of observations as bandwidth (Silverman, 1986). The sample is a subsample of the papers used above, restricted to those papers that published estimates of the social cost of carbon

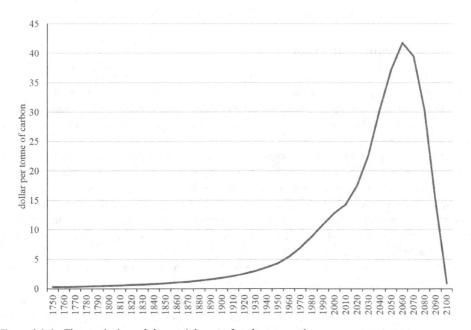

Figure 16.6   The evolution of the social cost of carbon over time

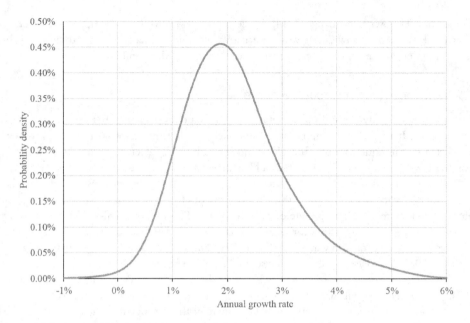

Figure 16.7 Probability density function of the growth rate of the social cost of carbon

at two or more points in time; if more than two time periods are reported, I used the earliest data and the latest at which the social cost of carbon was still rising.[3] The modal growth rate is 1.9% per year and the mean growth rate is 2.1%. The distribution is right-skewed. The probability that the social cost of carbon should fall over time is 0.6%. In other words, if you pick a carbon tax of $100/tC in 2018, you should pick a carbon tax of $102/tC in 2019.

4   Discussion and conclusion

Contrary to popular belief, the total economic impacts of climate change are modest. The best guess is that a century of climate is about as bad as losing a year of economic growth. The uncertainty is rather large, and negative surprises are more likely than positive ones. Poorer countries are more vulnerable. Taken that into account, a century of climate change is about as bad as losing a decade of growth.

There are many caveats. Valuing impacts is hard, and extrapolating values harder. Impact assessments are incomplete, but incompleteness only implies bias if the missing impacts are predominantly negative. Impacts are contingent on adaptation and development, but current models of adaptation are overly simplistic and typical estimates reflect the impact of a future climate on a society of the recent past. Impact estimates are comparative static, ignoring the dynamic effects. Impact assessments focus on the most likely outcomes at the expense of more salient but hard to quantify tail-risks.

As the economic impact of climate change is negative, there is a benefit to reducing greenhouse gas emissions. Indeed, a meta-analysis reveals that the vast majority of published estimates of the social cost of carbon is positive. That is, at the margin, emission reduction is beneficial. Greenhouse gas emissions should be taxed, at a rate that gradually increases over time. Estimates vary widely, because the social cost of carbon depends on many parameters that reasonable people can reasonably disagree about, including scenarios about how the future might unfold, the response of the climate system to emissions, and the impact of climate change and its valuation.

Estimates of the social cost of carbon are also determined by ethical parameters such as the rates of pure time preference, risk aversion, and inequality aversion (Anthoff et al., 2009). These parameters can be set with reference to the guidance provided by religious leaders (Augustine, Muhammad), philosophers (Socrates, Rawls), or other thought leaders (Johnny Rotten, Lady Gaga). But as the social cost of carbon is meant to guide the government in its choice of the ambition of climate policy in the near term, this is tantamount to paternalism. Alternatively, the government may decide to follow the will of the people. Unfortunately, measuring preferences is difficult (see e.g. Frederick et al., 2002) and preferences revealed through private transactions need not reflect preferences for public policy (for instance when that private transaction involves a public good; see Bergstrom et al., 1986).

Future research should lead to a better understanding of the social cost of carbon. Estimates for understudied impacts – transport, energy supply, tourism, ocean acidification, water, and air pollution – and the interactions between climate and development would complete the analysis, while further study of other impacts may narrow the uncertainties. Such research requires an understanding not only of economics, both for valuation and adaptation, but also of relevant academic discipline, be it ecology, hydrology, physiology, or agronomy. Part of the current uncertainty is irreducible, as the social cost of carbon measures the impact of future emissions on future societies. With regard to ethical parameters, the best we can do is a careful mapping of assumptions to conclusions, as it is not for us to decide what the right numbers or approaches are. We should nevertheless seek to estimate the relevant parameters, if only to highlight that certain ethical choices appear to have little support among the electorate.

Notes

1 This study was done at a time when no one could reasonably claim expertise on the economic impacts of climate change.
2 Linearization at the margin is the appropriate way to apportion liability for past emissions.
3 In the long run, the social cost of carbon may start falling as emissions approach zero and the climate starts to cool.

References

Ackerman, F. and C. Munitz. A critique of climate damage modeling: Carbon fertilization, adaptation, and the limits of fund. *Energy Research Social Science*, 12:62–67, 2016. URL www.sciencedirect.com/science/article/pii/S2214629615300773.

Adger, W. N. Vulnerability. *Global Environmental Change*, 16(3):268–281, 2006. ISSN 0959–3780. URL www.sciencedirect.com/science/article/pii/S0959378006000422. Resilience, Vulnerability, and Adaptation: A Cross-Cutting Theme of the International Human Dimensions Programme on Global Environmental Change.

Adler, M., D. Anthoff, V. Bosetti, G. Garner, K. Keller, and N. Treich. Priority for the worse-off and the social cost of carbon. *Nature Climate Change*, 7:443–449, 2017.

Anthoff, D. and R.S.J. Tol. Climate policy under fat-tailed risk: an application of FUND. *Annals of Operations Research*, 220(1):223–237, September 2014. URL https://ideas.repec.org/a/spr/annopr/v220y2014i1p223-23710.1007-s10479-013-1343-2.html.

Anthoff, D. and R.S.J. Tol. On international equity weights and national decision making on climate change. *Journal of Environmental Economics and Management*, 60(1):14–20, 2010. ISSN 0095-0696. doi: https://doi.org/10.1016/j.jeem.2010.04.002. URL www.sciencedirect.com/science/article/pii/S0095069610000422.

Anthoff, D., R.S.J. Tol and G. W. Yohe. Risk aversion, time preference, and the social cost of carbon. *Environmental Research Letters*, 4(2–2):1–7, 2009.

Arrow, K. A note on uncertainty and discounting in models of economic growth. *Journal of Risk and Uncertainty*, 38(2):87–94, April 2009. URL https://ideas.repec.org/a/kap/jrisku/v38y2009i2p87–94. html.

Arrow, K. J., M. L. Cropper, C. Gollier, B. Groom, G. M. Heal, R. G. Newell, W. D Nordhaus, R. S. Pindyck, W. A. Pizer, P. R. Portney, T. Sterner, R.S.J. Tol and M. L. Weitzman. Determining benefits and costs for future generations. *Science*, 341(6144):349–350, 2013. ISSN 0036-8075. doi: 10.1126/ science.1235665. URL http://science.sciencemag.org/content/341/6144/349.

Arrow, K. J., M. L. Cropper, C. Gollier, B. Groom, G. M. Heal, R. G. Newell, W. D. Nordhaus, R. S. Pindyck, W. A. Pizer, P. R. Portney, T. Sterner, R.S.J. Tol, and M. L. Weitzman. Should governments use a declining discount rate in project analysis? *Review of Environmental Economics and Policy*, 8(2):145–163, 2014. URL http://dx.doi.org/10.1093/reep/reu008.

Atkinson, A. B. On the measurement of inequality. *Journal of Economic Theory*, 2:244–263, 1970.

Bergstrom, T., L. Blume and H. Varian. On the private provision of public goods. *Journal of Public Economics*, 29(1):25–49, 1986.

Berz, G. Insuring against catastrophe. *Disasters*, 1996. URL www.ourplanet.com/imgversn/113/berz.html.

Bosello, F., F. Eboli and R. Pierfederici. Assessing the economic impacts of climate change. *Review of Environment Energy and Economics*: 1–9, 2012.

Budolfson, M., F. Dennig, M. Fleurbaey, A. Siebert and R. H. Socolow. The comparative importance for optimal climate policy of discounting, inequalities and catastrophes. *Climatic Change*, 145(3):481–494, December 2017. URL https://doi.org/10.1007/s10584-017-2094-x.

Burke, M., W. M. Davis and N. S. Diffenbaugh. Large potential reduction in economic damages under UN mitigation targets. *Nature*, 557(7706):549–553, 2018. URL https://doi.org/10.1038/s41586-018-0071-9.

Burke, M., S. M. Hsiang and E. Miguel. Global non-linear effect of temperature on economic production. *Nature*, 527(7577):235–239, 2015. doi: 10.1038/nature15725.

Cai, Y., T. M. Lenton and T. S. Lontzek. Risk of multiple interacting tipping points should encourage rapid co2 emission reduction. *Nature Climate Change*, 6:520–525, 2016.

Cameron, T. Updating subjective risks in the presence of conflicting information: An application to climate change. *Journal of Risk and Uncertainty*, 30(1):63–97, 2005. doi: 10.1007/s11166-005-5833-8.

Cohen, A. and L. Einav. Estimating risk preferences from deductible choice. *American Economic Review*, 97(3):745–788, 2007. doi: 10.1257/aer.97.3.745.

d'Arge, R. *Climate and economic activity*, pages 652–681. World Meteorological Organization, Geneva, 1979.

Dayaratna, K., R. McKitrick and D. Kreutzer. Empirically constrained climate sensitivity and the social cost of carbon. *Climate Change Economics*, 08(02):1750006, 2017. URL www.worldscientific.com/doi/ abs/10.1142/S2010007817500063.

Dell, M., B. F. Jones and B. A. Olken. What do we learn from the weather? the new climate-economy Literature. *Journal of Economic Literature*, 52(3):740–798, 2014.

Dennig, F., M. B. Budolfson, M. Fleurbaey, A. Siebert and R. H. Socolow. Inequality, climate impacts on the future poor, and carbon prices. *Proceedings of the National Academy of Sciences*, 112(52):15827–15832, 2015. doi: 10.1073/pnas.1513967112. URL www.pnas.org/content/112/52/15827.

Deryugina, T. and S. Hsiang. The marginal product of climate. Working Paper 24072, National Bureau of Economic Research, November 2017. URL www.nber.org/papers/w24072.

Deschenes, O. and M. Greenstone. The economic impacts of climate change: Evidence from agricultural output and random fluctuations in weather. *American Economic Review*, 97(1):354–385, 2007.

Dietz, S. and G. B. Asheim. Climate policy under sustainable discounted utilitarianism. *Journal of Environmental Economics and Management*, 63(3):321–335, 2012. ISSN 0095-0696. https://doi.org/10.1016/j. jeem.2012.01.003. URL www.sciencedirect.com/science/article/pii/S0095069612000058.

Donkers, B., B. Melenberg and A. Van Soest. Estimating risk attitudes using lotteries: A large sample approach. *Journal of Risk and Uncertainty*, 22(2):165–195, 2001. doi: 10.1023/A:1011109625844.

Eismont, O. and H. Welsch. Optimal greenhouse gas emissions under various assessments of climate change ambiguity. *Environmental and Resource Economics*, 8(2):129–140, 1996. doi: 10.1007/BF00357360.

Fankhauser, S. *Valuing Climate Change: The Economics of the Greenhouse*, volume 1. EarthScan, London, 1995. ISBN 1-85383-237-5.

Frederick, S., G. Loewenstein and T. O'Donoghue. Time discounting and time preference: A critical review. *Journal of Economic Literature*, 40(2):351–401, 2002.

Freeman, M. C. and B. Groom. How certain are we about the certainty-equivalent long term social discount rate? *Journal of Environmental Economics and Management*, 79:152–168, 2016. URL www.sciencedirect. com/science/article/pii/S0095069616300845.

Freeman, M. C. and B. Groom. Positively gamma discounting: Combining the opinions of experts on the social discount rate. *The Economic Journal*, 125(585):1015–1024, 2014. URL https://onlinelibrary.wiley.com/doi/abs/10.1111/ecoj.12129.

Freeman, M. C., B. Groom, E. Panopoulou and T. Pantelidis. Declining discount rates and the fisher effect: Inflated past, discounted future? *Journal of Environmental Economics and Management*, 73:32–49, 2015. URL www.sciencedirect.com/science/article/pii/S0095069615000492.

Golosov, M., J. Hassler, P. Krusell and A. Tsyvinski. Optimal taxes on fossil fuel in general equilibrium. *Econometrica*, 82(1):41–88, 2014. URL https://onlinelibrary.wiley.com/doi/abs/10.3982/ECTA10217.

Greenstone, M., E. Kopits, and A. Wolverton. Developing a social cost of carbon for us regulatory analysis: A methodology and interpretation. *Review of Environmental Economics and Policy*, 7(1):23–46, 2013.

Guivarch, C., A. Mjean, A. Pottier and M. Fleurbaey. Social cost of carbon: Global duty. *Science*, 351(6278):1160, 2016.

Hahn, R. W. and R. A. Ritz. Does the social cost of carbon matter? Evidence from us policy. *Journal of Legal Studies*, 44(1):229–248, 2015.

Hartog, J., A. Ferrer-i Carbonell, and N. Jonker. Linking measured risk aversion to individual characteristics. *Kyklos*, 55(1):3–26, 2002. doi: 10.1111/1467-6435.00175.

Hatase, K. and S. Managi. Increase in carbon prices: Analysis of energy-economy modeling. *Environmental Economics and Policy Studies*, 17(2):241–262, April 2015. URL https://doi.org/10.1007/s10018-014-0101-2.

Havranek, T., Z. Irsova, K. Janda and D. Zilberman. Selective reporting and the social cost of carbon. *Energy Economics*, 51:394–406, 2015. URL www.sciencedirect.com/science/article/pii/S0140988315002327.

Heal, G. The economics of the climate. *Journal of Economic Literature*, 55(3):1046–1063, 2017. doi: 10.1257/jel.20151335.

Heyes, A., D. Morgan and N. Rivers. The use of a social cost of carbon in Canadian cost-benefit analysis. *Canadian Public Policy*, 39(Suppl.2):S67–S79, 2013.

Hope, C. W. The marginal impact of co2 from page2002: An integrated assessment model incorporating the IPCC's five reasons for concern. *Integrated Assessment Journal*, 6(1):19–56, 2006.

Horowitz, J. and A. Lange. Cost benefit analysis under uncertainty a note on Weitzman's dismal theorem. *Energy Economics*, 42:201–203, 2014. URL www.sciencedirect.com/science/article/pii/S014098831300296X.

Howard, P. H. and T. Sterner. Few and not so far between: A meta-analysis of climate damage estimates. *Environmental and Resource Economics*, 68(1):197–225, September 2017. URL https://doi.org/10.1007/s10640-017-0166-z.

Hsiang, S., R. Kopp, A. Jina, J. Rising, M. Delgado, S. Mohan, D. J. Rasmussen, R. Muir-Wood, P. Wilson, M. Oppenheimer, K. Larsen, and T. Houser. Estimating economic damage from climate change in the united states. *Science*, 356(6345):1362, 2017.

Keller, K., B. M. Bolker, and D. F. Bradford. Uncertain climate thresholds and optimal economic growth. *Journal of Environmental Economics and Management*, 48:723–741, 2004.

Koopmans, T. C. Stationary ordinal utility and impatience. *Econometrica*, 28(2):287–309, 1960. ISSN 00129682, 14680262. URL www.jstor.org/stable/1907722.

Lemoine, D. and C. P. Traeger. Ambiguous tipping points. *Journal of Economic Behavior Organization*, 132:5–18, 2016. URL www.sciencedirect.com/science/article/pii/S0167268116300221. Thresholds, Tipping Points, and Random Events in Dynamic Economic Systems.

Llavador, H., J. E. Roemer and J. Silvestre. A dynamic analysis of human welfare in a warming planet. *Journal of Public Economics*, 95(11):1607–1620, 2011. ISSN 0047-2727. https://doi.org/10.1016/j.jpubeco.2011.05.017. URL www.sciencedirect.com/science/article/pii/S0047272711000922. Special Issue: International Seminar for Public Economics on Normative Tax Theory.

Maddison, D. J. The amenity value of the climate: The household production function approach. *Resource and Energy Economics*, 25(2):155–175, 2003.

Maddison, D. J. and K. Rehdanz. The impact of climate on life satisfaction. *Ecological Economics*, 70(12): 2437–2445, 2011. URL www.sciencedirect.com/science/article/pii/S0921800911003028.

Maier-Reimer, E. and K. Hasselmann. Transport and storage of co2 in the ocean: An inorganic ocean-circulation carbon cycle model. *Climate Dynamics*, 2(2):63–90, August 1987. URL https://doi.org/10.1007/BF01054491.

Mendelsohn, R. O., M. E. Schlesinger and L. J. Williams. Comparing impacts across climate models. *Integrated Assessment*, 1(1):37–48, 2000.

Metcalf, G. E. and J. H. Stock. Integrated assessment models and the social cost of carbon: A review and assessment of U.S. experience. *Review of Environmental Economics and Policy*, 11(1):80–99, 2017.

Millner, A. On welfare frameworks and catastrophic climate risks. *Journal of Environmental Economics and Management*,65(2):310–325,2013. URL www.sciencedirect.com/science/article/pii/S0095069612001209.

Nakicenovic, N. and R. Swart, editors. *Special Report on Emissions Scenarios: A special Report of Working Group III of the Intergovernmental Panel on Climate Change*. Cambridge University Press, Cambridge, 2000.

Nordhaus, W. D. Expert opinion on climate change. *American Scientist*, 82(1):45–51, 1994b.

Nordhaus, W. D. Geography and macroeconomics: New data and new findings. *Proceedings of the National Academy of Science*, 103(10):3510–3517, 2006. URL www.pnas.org/cgi/doi/10.1073/pnas.0509842103.

Nordhaus, W. D. How fast should we graze the global commons? *American Economic Review*, 72(2):242–246, 1982.

Nordhaus, W. D. *Managing the Global Commons: The Economics of Climate Change*. The MIT Press, Cambridge, 1994a.

Nordhaus, W. D. *A Question of Balance: Weighing the Options on Global Warming Policies*. Yale University Press, New Haven, 2008.

Nordhaus, W. D. Revisiting the social cost of carbon. *Proceedings of the National Academy of Sciences*, 114(7):1518–1523, 2017. URL www.pnas.org/content/114/7/1518.

Nordhaus, W. D. To slow or not to slow: The economics of the greenhouse effect. *Economic Journal*, 101(444):920–937, 1991.

Nordhaus, W. D. and J. G. Boyer. *Warming the World: Economic Models of Global Warming*. The MIT Press, Cambridge, MA and London, England, 2000. ISBN 0-262-14071-3.

Nordhaus, W. D. and A. Moffat. A survey of global impacts of climate change: Replication, survey methods, and a statistical analysis. Working Paper 23646, National Bureau of Economic Research, August 2017. URL www.nber.org/papers/w23646.

Nordhaus, W. D. and Z. Yang. Rice: A regional dynamic general equilibrium model of optimal climate-change policy. *American Economic Review*, 86(4):741–765, 1996.

Pigou, A. *The Economics of Welfare*. Macmillan, London, 1920.

Pindyck, R. S. Coase lecturetaxes, targets and the social cost of carbon. *Economica*, 84(335):345–364, 2017a.

Pindyck, R. S. The use and misuse of models for climate policy. *Review of Environmental Economics and Policy*, 11(1):110–114, 2017b. ISSN 21097.

Pizer, W., M. Adler, J. Aldy, D. Anthoff, M. Cropper, K. Gillingham, M. Greenstone, B. Murray, R. Newell, R. Richels, A. Rowell, S. Waldhoff and J. Wiener. Using and improving the social cost of carbon. *Science*, 346(6214):1189–1190, 2014.

Plambeck, E. L. and C. W. Hope. Page95: An updated valuation of the impacts of global warming. *Energy Policy*, 24(9):783–793, 1996.

Ramsey, F. P. A mathematical theory of saving. *The Economic Journal*, 38(152):543–559, 1928. URL www.jstor.org/stable/2224098.

Rehdanz, K. and D. J. Maddison. Climate and happiness. *Ecological Economics*, 52(1):111–125, 2005.

Revesz, R., M. Greenstone, M. Hanemann, M. Livermore, T. Sterner, D. Grab, P. Howard and J. Schwartz. Best cost estimate of greenhouse gases. *Science*, 357(6352):655, 2017. URL http://science.sciencemag.org/content/357/6352/655.abstracthttp://science.sciencemag.org/content/sci/357/6352/655.full.pdf.

Riahi, K., D. P. van Vuuren, E. Kriegler, J. Edmonds, B. C. ONeill, S. Fujimori, N. Bauer, K. Calvin, R. Dellink, O. Fricko, W. Lutz, A. Popp, J. C. Cuaresma, S. KC, M. Leimbach, L. Jiang, T. Kram, S. Rao, J. Emmerling, K. Ebi, T. Hasegawa, P. Havlik, F. Humpender, L.A.D. Silva, S. Smith, E. Stehfest, V. Bosetti, J. Eom, D. Gernaat, T. Masui, J. Rogelj, J. Strefler, L. Drouet, V. Krey, G. Luderer, M. Harmsen, K. Takahashi, L. Baumstark, J. C. Doelman, M. Kainuma, Z. Klimont, G. Marangoni, H. Lotze-Campen, M. Obersteiner, A. Tabeau and M. Tavoni. The shared socioeconomic pathways and their energy, land use, and greenhouse gas emissions implications: An overview. *Global Environmental Change*, 42:153–168, 2017. ISSN 0959-3780. https://doi.org/10.1016/j.gloenvcha.2016.05.009. URL www.sciencedirect.com/science/article/pii/S0959378016300681.

Ricardo, D. *On the Principles of Political Economy and Taxation*. John Murray, London, 1817.

Roe, G. H. and M. B. Baker. Why is climate sensitivity so unpredictable? *Science*, 318(5850):629–632, 2007. doi: 10.1126/science.1144735. URL http://science.sciencemag.org/content/318/5850/629.

Rose, S. K. The role of the social cost of carbon in policy. *WIREs Climate Change*, 3:195–212, 2012.

Rose, S. K., D. B. Diaz and G. J. Blanford. Understanding the social cost of carbon: A model diagnostic and inter-comparison study. *Climate Change Economics*, 08(02):1750009, 2017. URL www.worldscientific.com/doi/abs/10.1142/S2010007817500099.

Roson, R. and D. van der Mensbrugghe. Climate change and economic growth: Impacts and interactions. *International Journal of Sustainable Economy*, 4(3):270–285, 2012.

Saelen, H., S. Dietz, C. Hepburn, J. Helgeson and G. Atkinson. Siblings, not triplets: Social preferences for risk, inequality and time in discounting climate change. *Economics: The Open-Access, Open-Assessment E-Journal*, 3(26):1–28, 2009.

Schneider, S. H. and S. L. Thompson. Atmospheric co2 and climate: Importance of the transient response. *Journal of Geophysical Research*, 86(C4):3135–3147, 1981.

Silverman, B. *Density Estimation for Statistics and Data Analysis*. Chapman Hall, London, 1986.

Sunstein, C. R. On not revisiting official discount rates: Institutional inertia and the social cost of carbon. *American Economic Review*, 104(5):547–551, 2014.

Tol, R.S.J. Bootstraps for meta-analysis with an application to the impact of climate change. *Computational Economics*, 46(2):287–303, 2015. doi: 10.1007/s10614-014-9448-5.

Tol, R.S.J. The damage costs of climate change toward more comprehensive calculations. *Environmental and Resource Economics*, 5(4):353–374, 1995.

Tol, R.S.J. The economic impacts of climate change. *Review of Environmental Economics and Policy*, 12(1):4–25, 2018. URL http://dx.doi.org/10.1093/reep/rex027.

Tol, R.S.J. Estimates of the damage costs of climate change, part i: Benchmark estimates. *Environmental and Resource Economics*, 21(1):47–73, 2002.

Tol, R.S.J. International inequity aversion and the social cost of carbon. *Climate Change Economics*, 01(01): 21–32, 2010. URL www.worldscientific.com/doi/abs/10.1142/S2010007810000029.

Tol, R.S.J. The marginal damage costs of carbon dioxide emissions: An assessment of the uncertainties. *Energy Policy*, 33:2064–2074, 2005.

Tol, R.S.J. The social cost of carbon. *Annual Review of Resource Economics*, 3:419–443, 2011.

Tol, R.S.J. Targets for global climate policy: An overview. *Journal of Economic Dynamics Control*, 37(5):911–928, 2013.

Tol, R.S.J. and G. W. Yohe. The stern review: A deconstruction. *Energy Policy*, 37(3):1032–1040, 2009. ISSN 0301-4215. https://doi.org/10.1016/j.enpol.2008.11.008. URL www.sciencedirect.com/science/article/pii/S0301421508007076.

Traeger, C. Why uncertainty matters: Discounting under intertemporal risk aversion and ambiguity. *Economic Theory*, 56(3):627–664, 2014. doi: 10.1007/s00199-014-0800-8.

van den Bergh, J.C.J.M. and W.J.W. Botzen. A lower bound to the social cost of co2 emissions. *Nature Climate Change*, 4(4):253–258, 2014. URL http://dx.doi.org/10.1038/nclimate2135.

van der Ploeg, F. Untapped fossil fuel and the green paradox: A classroom calibration of the optimal carbon tax. *Environmental Economics and Policy Studies*, 17(2):185–210, April 2015. URL https://doi.org/10.1007/s10018-014-0097-7.

Weitzman, M. L. Fat-tailed uncertainty in the economics of catastrophic climate change. *Review of Environmental Economics and Policy*, 5(2):275–292, 2011.

Welsch, H. Greenhouse gas abatement under ambiguity. *Energy Economics*, 17(2):91–100, 1995. doi: 10.1016/0140-9883(95)00010-R.

WorldBank and Ecofys. State and trends of carbon pricing 2018. Technical report, World Bank, Washington, DC, 2018. URL https://openknowledge.worldbank.org/handle/10986/29687.

Yohe, G. W. and R.S.J. Tol. Indicators for social and economic coping capacity: Moving towards a working definition of adaptive capacity. *Global Environmental Change*, 12(1):25–40, 2002.

17

Energy and the public

The economic relevance of citizens' engagement

Alessandro Sciullo and Anna Pellizzone

Energy transitions have historically been a matter of innovating the incumbent energy systems by overcoming their implicit inertia in terms of technologies, infrastructures, resources, and processes (Smil 2010). Energy transitions thus are complex processes that produce the shift to a new regime of the energy socio-technical system as a result of interacting changes in a wider spectrum of technological and social elements, such as plants, conversion, and distribution devices, formal and informal rules, business models and market relationships, social actors, values and culture (Geels 2007). Given this complexity, engaging citizens and stakeholders in this process has been gaining attention in recent years among scientists and decision-makers as a crucial requirement for supporting the contemporary renewables transition (RES) (Sciullo and Padovan 2018). The relevance of this engagement lays primarily on the design of effective strategies for supporting the spread of new energy infrastructures and technologies by empowering the diffusion of new practices and behaviors, integrating different perspectives, knowledge and experiences in the debate around energy technologies, improving the innovation process, and lowering the potential conflicts often connected with new energy plants, also in the case of RES. In addition to these strategic aims, effective engagement of the wider public may have a direct economic impact at different level of the economic system from the micro-level of firms' R&D and market strategies through the meso-level of the processes connected to local development up to the macro-level of political economy.

In this chapter, we start from a general framing of engagement in energy transition (Section 1) with a particular focus on the crucial distinction between acceptance and engagement. Then, in Section 2, the Responsible Research and Innovation framework (RRI), a general approach to research and innovation processes adopted and promoted by European Commission in order to put society at the center of these processes both in theory and in practice, is outlined. Finally, in Section 3, some of the main economic impacts that engaging public, in the medium and long run, are addressed with specific attention to energy sector when applicable.

1   From acceptance to engagement

The involvement of citizens has been gaining in the recent decades a central role for the success or failure of innovation also in the energy field, particularly when dealing with the social aspects connected to new energy infrastructures. A variety of labels have been adopted to make reference to activities and processes aimed at spreading information, shifting awareness, and fostering inclusion of citizens in innovations development: public and/or stakeholder engagement, public and social acceptance, citizen and community involvement, and participatory and inclusive processes.

Even if they share a common focus, these labels refer to deeply diverse processes. The objective of this section is to clarify, from the theoretical as well from the practical perspective, the difference between involving people in terms of *engagement* and/or in terms of *acceptance*, concepts that are far to be synonymous.

1.1 Energy and society: framing the debate

As a growing number of researches show (see Sovacool 2014), if we want to succeed in moving towards a sustainable future, we have to alter both technologies and society, for instance, in terms of habits, behaviors, community organization, and institutional patterns. However, non-technical studies – meaning here social sciences and humanities (SSH) – are still neglected in the energy realm. As an example, in the United States, the rate between the dollars spent in behavioral and demand-side energy research and dollars spent in energy supply and infrastructure research is 1/35 (Gaffigan 2008). But this needs to change if we want to succeed in the development of a carbon-free society and reach two of the UN Sustainable Development Goals (SDGs): Affordable and Clean Energy (SDG7) and Climate Action (SDG13).

As governments from across the world have set ambitious goals in terms of reduction of the carbon emissions and increase of the share of renewables, a factor that has been increasingly recognized as a potential obstacle towards the energy transition is social acceptance. The concept has been described in the literature (Wüstenhagen et al. 2007) as a mix of three different components, namely (1) sociopolitical, (2) community, and (3) market acceptance (Figure 17.1).

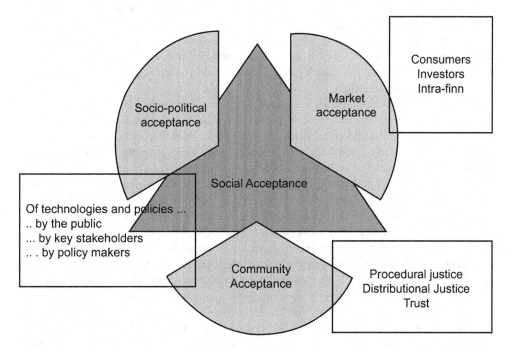

Figure 17.1 The triangle of social acceptance

Source: Adapted from Wüstenhagen et al. (2007).

The three dimensions of social acceptance are each other closely intertwined, but can be distinguished as follows. The sociopolitical acceptance regards both technologies (e.g. solar or wind energy) and policies (e.g. carbon tax or incentives) at a general level; the community acceptance is more site-specific and deals with issues such as procedural and distributional justice; the market-acceptance, as the process of market adoption of an innovation, has to do with consumers' and investors' choices.

In the past decades, policy makers highly underestimated the relevance of sociopolitical acceptance and for years didn't consider it as an issue to deal with. But they were wrong, for two main reasons. The first is that achieving a successful projects implementation requires more than being broadly accepted. As an example, if we consider the share of electricity from renewable energy sources, a great challenge comes from the fact that the energy sector is "locked" into a carbon-intensive system in terms of generation, transmission and distribution, as well as storage and demand (Unruh 2002). When electricity was massively introduced in our societies, human habits, market and infrastructure were organized around the needs of a fossil fuel-based system (centralized production, gas pipelines, distribution of grids, storage systems, international relationships, etc.). After decades, this is still resulting in a path dependence favoring fossil-fuel technologies over low-carbon alternatives. This means that in order to move beyond the way in which our societies are organized, we need to put in place some efforts in order to overcome the inertia of the current energy system.

Another important reason is that when moving from the global to the local the general support towards energy technologies and policies doesn't always correspond to the support of effective implementations of new plants and siting decisions.

This brings us to another component of social acceptance, which is community acceptance. The discrepancy between the general support and the resistance to specific projects, has been described trough the NIMBY (Not in My Back Yard) debate, arguing that people support new plants and infrastructures as long as they are not in their own backyard. However, some authors (see e.g. Wolsink 2006; Bell et al. 2005) have found evidence that NIMBYism represents an oversimplification of the issue (i.e. in a series of empirical studies on wind energy researches showed that opposition to new developments decreases rather than increases as the degree of being directly affected increases).

Furthermore, the studies around community acceptance in the energy realm are numerous and diverse, showing that there are a lot of factors influencing the levels of support or opposition to new technology and plants implementation. One of the most important factor in the field is undoubtedly trust, which has been described as a "dual" concept, composed by confidence, which is the competence and the technical ability to operate, and social trust or common values (Siegrist et al. 2003). Mutual trust among the different societal actors (developers, policy makers, citizens, civil society organization, investors, etc.) is a prerequisite for cooperation (Gambetta 2000) and socially sustainable developments. In fact, as many socio-scientific studies show, local communities can show high levels of openness towards new technologies implementations but nevertheless resist to new developments due to high degrees of distrust towards decision-makers (Pellizzone et al. 2017). Trust requires the lack of ambiguity in what people cooperate for and also strong, continuous efforts in communication; many authors indicate that trust and risk communication contributes to shaping perceptions, opinions and public attitudes (Renn and Levine, 1991; Poortinga and Pidgeon, 2003). Further interesting – and critical – hints around trust in techno-scientific experts can be found in Camporesi: "echoing Hardin, O'Neill argued that the relation of trustworthiness, and therefore not trust as a state of being, should be seen as the basis of accountability and responsibility in public life", meaning here that the final goal shouldn't be the increase of trust among societal actors, but "to secure and advance trustworthiness – that is, experts, institutions, and knowledge worthy of trust", focusing on the "qualities and conduct of experts, the practices of science, and to knowledge itself" (Camporesi et al. 2017).

Strictly connected to the issues of trust, cooperation and communication are also two other key factors, strongly impacting community acceptance: the distributional justice (How are costs and benefits distributed among the societal actors?) and the procedural justice (How fair is the decision-making process? Have all relevant stakeholders the opportunity to have a voice in the process?).

All the above mentioned issues – concepts such as the carbon lock-in theory, the mutual trust, the trustworthiness, the risk, the role of information, the fairness of the innovation process – can be framed also based on the different stages of research on science and society relationship (Bauer et al. 2007). In the early days of science literacy, the emphasis of researchers committed in the science-society field was mainly focused on public education. This approach, named "deficit model", is based on the assumption that if lay people would be informed about science and innovation as decided and defined by expert authorities, technological and research developments would run smoothly in the right direction. The focus of the scholars committed in the public understanding of science (PUS) shifted then from science literacy, with public communication as privileged approach, to research on attitudes and perceptions, leaving the stage to public consultation. In recent years (Owen et al. 2012; Stilgoe et al. 2013) the new trend in the field is to favor public engagement and deliberative initiatives. What is different among these three approaches is the type of flow of information between the public and the sponsors arranging the exercises. In the case of (1) public communication, the sponsor is the source of information and the public is the recipient; (2) public consultation, the information are gathered from the public to the sponsors; (3) public engagement, the information is exchanged among sponsors and the public in a dialogic way (Allansdottir et al. 2018, Rowe and Frewer 2005), where all participants play and active role in the debate. The reasons for involving the public are particularly relevant within the energy innovation realm, where citizens may play a pivotal function by moving from the passive role of acceptance (as consumers) into the active role of engagement (as prosumers).

1.2 Public engagement and public acceptance in the energy transition: the case of RES infrastructure

As mentioned above, *public engagement* and *public acceptance* must be considered as distinguished concepts. First of all because the former pertains to the realm of active participation, while the second to the realm of passive reception, and secondly because engagement could be intended as the process of involvement, while acceptance (both as merely lack of opposition or more convinced support) could be intended as the product of the involvement process. In other words, public engagement has to be considered as a complex and structured system of activities put in place in order to effectively involve people in the decision and implementation process while public acceptance (as well as lack of acceptance) may be a result of such activities (Batel et al. 2013).

In case of RES energy infrastructure, a successful process of public engagement is not inevitably connected with more acceptance since it may produce an actual support to the project and/or a convinced acceptance, or even neither of the two, when resulting in the so-called zero option of abandoning the project (Ravazzi and Pomatto 2014).

The main factors that seem to influence the level of acceptance for RES projects and that should be taken into account in designing engaging strategies can be grouped into three main categories. *Personal factors* refer to the socio-demographic characteristics (structural profile) of the public to be involved such as age, gender, and social class. *Sociocultural factors* refer to the perceptions of the project by the public (cognitive profile) by taking into account the degree of awareness and understanding about the proposed project, the political and environmental beliefs and concern, the place attachment and the perceived fairness and levels of trust in experts and institutions; *contextual factors* refer to the projects specificities and the context within which it should be developed (material profile) and relates technological factors (i.e. the scale of the project: micro-single building or household level, meso-local, community or town level, macro-'power station' level) and institutional factors (ownership structures, distribution of benefits, adoption of participatory approaches to public engagement). In addition to these *static* factors, attention should be paid to the process of implementation of the project in terms of strategies, actors and resources and the interaction among them at different levels of the energy system (Devine Wright 2007; Devine Wright et al. 2017).

RES infrastructures can determine undesirable land transformations, such as the consumption of soil, the micro-level deterioration of pre-existing ecosystems and the alteration of the landscape as well as various types of harmful or disturbing emissions (Puttilli 2014). Local negative externalities connected to infrastructures development can be objectively assessed only partially and often combine material aspects and symbolic aspects. As mentioned above among the factors for public acceptance (*place attachment*) the territory in fact does not simply correspond to an objectively given physical environment, as it regards also the articulated set of material and symbolic elements that are linked to the interaction of the social groups living in that area. This also means that these social groups are endowed with an emotional attachment to the territory and that part of their social identity is linked to it. A project can interfere with the sense of attachment and with the territorial identity of local communities and consequently with the awareness of local actors to be able to play an effective role in decision-making processes (Maggiolini and Pomatto 2016). Nevertheless, "place attachment need not inevitably be associated with negative attitudes or oppositional behavioral responses" (Devine Wright 2011), and "research on place attachment should be open to multiple possible relations between attachment and acceptance".

What is interesting to consider when dealing with public acceptance of RES is that even if it is a process mainly associated with positive images (energy sustainability, green economy and political autonomy from providing alternatives from fossil fuels), at the same time local conflicts on RES plants are a widespread phenomenon often driven by people in favor of RES. Large coalitions that opposed at local level against RES projects include citizens' committees and the same environmental associations, which also generally support the use of renewable energy (Puttilli 2014).[1]

Figure 17.1 offers a general scheme of the possible relationships among public engagement and public acceptance, taking into consideration these factors and their ontological differences. A number of different conditions (Institutional settings, social aspects, knowledge, and the peculiarity of the project) play the role of inputs and shape the development and results of a public engagement process. The process itself should be designed by taking into account these conditions in order to involve the relevant actors, through the most effective tools, towards the most relevant objectives, considering the existing processes and relationship in the public to be involved. The first effects (outputs) of the engagement process could be the modification of the initial inputs/conditions themselves so that a circular process of reinforcement may emerge. In other words, all along the engagement process the public may evolve (in terms of knowledge, awareness and motivation in participation) in such a way that the process itself could be reinforced. The final result of the process (outcome) may vary in a quite wide range of opportunities from a mere acceptance to a more convinced support and even to a reinforcement of the conflict or to a zero option, that is abandoning the project.

It is worth to underline that in order to effectively engage the public, properly designed and structured activities should be carried out, as ordinary citizens have in general very few opportunities to make their voices heard in the formulation of a public policy or intervention (i.e. RES project) and the forms of collective action may need social and institutional requirements (e.g. level of education, income, political and environmental awareness, competitive political system), which can't be considered as universally distributed (Maggiolini and Pomatto 2016). However, over the last decades, a series of tools that can be adopted by public administrations to allow citizens to take part directly in the formulation and implementation of policies and projects have been developed and implemented. *Participatory processes* that aim to enable citizens to press on public administrators to take care of their needs and *deliberative processes* that aim at promoting an open and in-depth discussion between citizens who have different or opposing ideas, points of view and interests, in order to develop solutions in a constructive way (Bobbio et al. 2017). Both these approaches, that can be operationalized by many different tools need some basic requirements to be effective: careful planning, public sharing of information, mediated respectful discussions, formal methods of recruiting participants (e.g. random selection or targeted selection), bringing together expert knowledge and profane knowledge; assistance of professionals experts in group dynamics (Ravazzi and Pomatto 2014).

2 Public Engagement as a tool towards responsible innovation

The importance of engaging the public in the innovation process has been increasingly recognized also within the institutional framework at different levels. Public engagement exercises are often being used as tools for the design of energy innovation path in several Countries across the world, from New Zealand to the Philippines, from the Netherlands to Canada (see for example, Manzella et al. 2019). In the European Union, the tradition of public participation within the research and innovation process – energy technologies included – has been institutionalized within the so-called Responsible Research and Innovation (RRI, Figure 17.2) framework, with the ultimate goal of aligning the techno-scientific developments to the needs and the expectations of society.

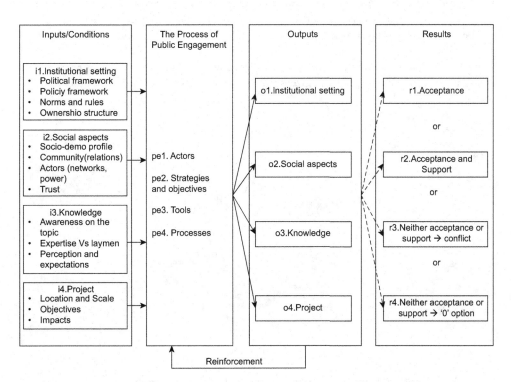

Figure 17.2 A scheme of the public engagement process: inputs, outputs, and results (our elaboration on the basis of Batel et al. 2013; Ravazzi and Pomatto 2014; Devine-Wright 2007[2])

Several definitions of RRI have been provided. According to von Schomberg (2013),

> Responsible Research and Innovation is a transparent, interactive process by which societal actors and innovators become mutually responsive to each other with a view to the (ethical) acceptability, sustainability and societal desirability of the innovation process and its marketable products in order to allow a proper embedding of scientific and technological advances in our society.

In order to "tak[e] care of the future through collective stewardship of science and innovation in the present" (Stilgoe et al. 2013), four key dimensions of responsibility to be considered in research and innovation processes are identified:

1 *Diversity and inclusion* means early involvement of a wide range of actors and publics in R&I practice, deliberation, and decision-making to yield more useful and higher quality knowledge. This strengthens democracy and broadens sources of expertise, disciplines, and perspectives.
2 *Anticipation and reflection* means to envision impacts and reflect on the underlying assumptions, values, and purposes to better understand how R&I shapes the future. This produces valuable insights and increases our capacity to act on what we know.
3 *Openness and transparency* means to communicate in a balanced, meaningful way methods, results, conclusions, and implications to enable public scrutiny and dialogue. This benefits the visibility and understanding of R&I.
4 *Responsiveness and adaptive change* means to be able to modify modes of thought and behavior, overarching organizational structures, in response to changing circumstances, knowledge, and perspectives. This aligns action with the needs expressed by stakeholders and publics (RRI tools).

Many more theoretical definitions could be provided, however it is clear that the upstream public engagement (i.e. the involvement of citizens from the first stages of the innovation process) plays

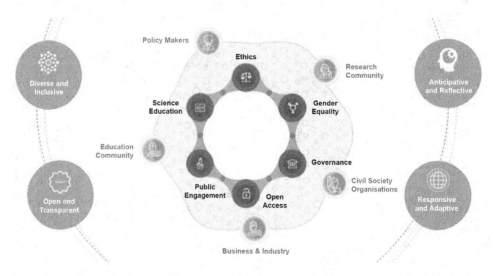

Figure 17.3 Responsible research and innovation: dimensions, actors, and key elements

Source: Adapted from www.rri-tools.eu.

a very important role in the game. Not by chance, public engagement is considered by the European Commission as one of the key elements of RRI, together with ethics, open access, gender equality, science education, sustainability, and social inclusion. Of course, public engagement is also adopted beyond the RRI framework, as it is crucial also for other approaches and methods (social innovation, inclusive business, shared value, B-corp, etc.).

The adoption of a participative and socially aligned approach is not only a matter of values, ethics or democracy. RRI approach has a lot of beneficial impacts on society as a whole, including the economic sphere. The next paragraph focuses on the economic relevance of engaging the public in research and innovation processes at different levels (i.e. individual company level, polling and community level and political economy level).

3   Economic relevance of public engagement

3.1   RRI and public engagement as firms' competitive strategy

As the growing literature and the increasing number of empirical case studies in the field show, RRI can help companies to address many challenges for their competitiveness: build and understand their community; identify new products and improve the existing ones; anticipate eventual ethical concerns and social perplexities; increase the trust of the end-users and their network; access new funding opportunities; building a critical mass in their sector (Van de Poel et al. 2017; Lees and Lees 2017; Flipse et al. 2015; Scholten et al. 2015). Furthermore, several project funded by the European Commission under the Horizon 2020 framework in order to support the implementation of RRI within the industrial realm (e.g. SMART-map,[3] PRISMA,[4] COMPASS[5]) provide concrete experiences and suggestion in the field. Here in the following some main contributions on this topic are presented that, even if not focused on energy field, provide useful insights on the potential of RRI approach applied at the micro level of individual firms.

As Van de Poel (2017) argues, RRI is gaining attention in the academic community, but it has not yet been systematically included in the innovation process of companies themselves. In order to put RRI in practice, the author proposes a conceptual model that is mainly composed of three elements: *the broader context* within which company operates that even if usually neglected is relevant to the extent to which RRI strategies depend on the resources and the market the company has to deal with; *the distinction* between the strategic and the operational level of RRI that is relevant in order to avoid to move too quickly to the formulation of RRI activities without a robust strategy aligned with the more general strategy of the company with specific identification of the area of impacts of the company on the society; *RRI outcomes* and the definition of key performance indicators (KPIs) to monitor them.

Talking about responsibility within the industrial realm often brings into play questions upon the commonalities and the differences between Responsible Research and Innovation and corporate social responsibility (CSR), the first usually considered more ambitious and forward looking for a series of reasons (e.g. RRI intervenes from the very first stages of the research and innovation process; focuses on the anticipation of R&I impacts on society and environment; aims at doing good to society and not only avoiding harm, etc.). Despite the differences between the two approaches, several experts in the field consider the CSR departments as key "places" for the implementation of RRI within companies. The main message of van de Pol's contribution is that companies don't need more tools for RRI, but a more comprehensive view that integrates RRI with company CSR strategy and activities and with company's general business strategy. In this framework, companies should focus, in particular, on selecting the specific societal dominions where they can profitably add value instead of generally considering the full spectrum of RRI activities.

More focused on the competitive potential of Responsible Innovation (RI), Lees and Lees (2017) present a case study on New Zealand sheep dairy (NZSD) starting from the consideration of the lack of practical model of implementing RRI at enterprise level. The author looks at RI as a powerful tool to support the competitiveness of a firm from the *resource based view* (RBV) perspective that focus on competitive advantage as the implementation of a value-creating strategy not simultaneously being implemented by any other current or potential competitor. RI can bring relevant contribute to face this challenge as it helps in shaping innovations with attention to their ethical acceptability, sustainability and social desirability thus resulting in a way for improving the willingness of stakeholders and consumers to collaborate. Through a comparative France-New Zealand case study, the author shows that the best option for the NZSD industry to pursue a differentiation strategy whereby it creates and sells a product that better satisfies customer needs over its rivals focused on customer responsiveness, innovation and quality products. These strategies also contain some aspects of RI as they are closely aligned with responsiveness and innovation that meets ethical, social and environmental issues. The differentiation strategy based on this approach allowed NZSD to attain a competitive advantage more than a low-cost strategy by focusing on RI outcomes as a distinctive competency that can support a competitive advantage. In this way, the industry can develop economically at the same time as achieving more responsible outcomes.

Instead of proposing theoretical and descriptive approach, Flipse et al. (2015) built an operational tool aimed at helping innovators to operationalize RRI in industry. The rationale behind this effort lays on the intimate nature of "wicked problems" that characterize research and innovation (R&D) practice in industry as there is usually no clear definition of the starting problem and innovators have to cope with technical, economic, and social levels that result in complex and uncertain decision-making. In practice, tool development started from the assessment of past successful innovation projects in light of RRI-relevant elements in order to clarify if and to what extent RRI may influence success of innovation. Key performance indicators (KPIs) and their interrelations may be identified which contain social and ethical components relevant from an RRI perspective, and a database of 72 completed projects evaluated on each of the eight KPIs was assembled. By using structural equation modeling (SEM) the authors assessed the relations between the KPIs and through an agent-based simulation model fed by SEM results, they replicate and validate the interaction detected among KPIs.

It is important to remark that the exploitation of RRI potential as a competitive advantage at company level requires the mobilization of a large number of societal actors (from citizens to decision-makers, including funding agencies, professional associations, research and academia, etc.), bringing into play the need to approach RRI as an ecosystem at the different levels of the innovation process and building communities of practice.[6]

3.2 Public engagement and energy market at the local scale: polling and communities

When moving from the individual level of the enterprises to the meso-level of a delimited geographical area (e.g. region/cities) the role of citizens in shaping and influencing the energy sector may gain relevance through diverse engagement solutions, within which the most promising are deliberative tools and energy communities.

A seminal contribution to explore the potential of public deliberation is provided by Luskin et al (1999) that carried out an experiment of deliberative polling in Texas as a way to collect and share knowledge among the people so that a more effective energy policy can be designed on the basis and with the aim of satisfying better informed public preferences. A win-win situation when the public raises in awareness and receives more targeted services and the administration is able to take informed decision. The initiative of polling was taken by the Public Utility Commission (PUC) that asked to all electric utility companies in the state of Texas to take customer preferences into account in the periodic integrated resource plan (IRP) aimed at meeting the territory's current need. The problem with collecting meaningful preferences lays in general on the fact that most people simply don't have enough knowledge about specific issues and in the electricity field public knows even less about them than about most other important policy issues. The polling involved eight utility companies and 800–1,500 customers per utility that were interviewed by telephone and invited to a deliberative weekend, an example of the deliberative processes mentioned in Section 1.2. Each deliberative mainly consisted in a structured presentation of the topic and of the rules of the event, a moderated discussion among people divided in small groups of around 15 participants and some plenary sessions, where the participants could put questions developed in the small groups to panels of experts. At the end, the same questionnaire submitted in the pre-deliberation telephone survey was administered to the participants.

The deliberative poll is in general a useful tool for eliciting more informed and thoughtful public opinion and may affect the course of public policy even if an indirect, hard to measure and presumably small way. But in Texas polling on energy market, policy making was directly affected. Deliberation leads to recognition that renewable technology cannot meet a very high proportion of electricity needs in the short term but strengthen support for including renewable energy as part of a long-term strategy. Large investments in wind energy have been made in West Texas, directly and consciously as a direct result of these deliberative polls.

Based on the direct and active engagement of citizens in the energy chain (production, distribution and consumption) Energy communities (ECs) have been gaining relevance as one of the most powerful tool to support energy transition. The EU Clean Energy Package recognizes the centrality of citizens that in the next future should have "a better choice of supply, access to reliable energy price comparison tools and the possibility to produce and sell their own electricity",[7] thus moving from being passive consumers to be active prosumers who also produce goods or services for sale in the energy market.

Energy communities are important for the transition towards a more sustainable and just energy system for at least two reasons: on the socio-technical side they allow the exploitation of RES that are implicitly more decentralized with respect to the fossil fuels; on the economic side they help in finding the needed resources to develop RES technologies (Bauwens 2016; Walker and Devine-Wright 2008) and influence energy prices and providing services with a direct impact on the justice of the energy sector in terms of inclusion of disadvantaged people, security, transparency.[8]

It has been estimated that the need of investments in renewables sources and technologies aimed at stabilizing greenhouse gas will range from USD 2,850 billion to USD 12,280 billion for the period 2011–2030.[9] Governments are unable to provide such a financial effort, and so it is necessary to include other resources from business, households, and civil society within which ECs seem promising (Bauwens 2016).

ECs are extremely heterogeneous. They can be aimed at managing energy production/distribution, demand response or energy storage and they can have many diverse practical implementations such as renewable energy generation, community hall refurbishments, collective behavior change programs but they share the nature of being citizen-led initiatives which propose collaborative solutions thus bringing public engagement to top-down policy initiatives (Seyfang et al. 2013).

An important distinction can be made between *communities of locality* and *communities of interest* with the former being particularly linked with local development processes while the latter refers to groups of dispersed people with a common interest such as investors in a cooperative project. As engagement may be defined and measured in terms of the volume of financial investment made and the degree of participation in the governance of organizations (Bauwens 2016).

From a strictly economic perspective, ECs are generally owned by their members and present different model of ownership than conventional business such as (cooperatives, development trusts, charity) that may be seen as more or less inclusive and collective (Walker 2008). Another relevant difference with the traditional private enterprise is that net earnings are usually divided among members not according to their shareholding but according to the volume of transactions they have conducted with the firm. Finally, as the profit distribution is formally constrained by ECs' statue and rules, maximization of return on capital may not be a key objective (Bauwens et al. 2016).

3.3 Public engagement as a perspective for political economy

Finally, public engagement may also play a relevant role as a component of a more general perspective in defining political economy strategies such as in the case of delivering of public services and in defining R&D policies.

Co-production as a way to delivery more targeted public services represents an approach to administration that, following and updating the tradition of new public management, NPM (Hood 1991), pushes the involvement of end-users as the main element for improving efficiency and efficacy of actions of public administration. Until the late 1980s, public services were considered as activities which professionals carried out to achieve results "in the public interest". This approach has been challenged by the idea, at the core of NPM, that public services should be designed "to bring about 'outcomes', not just 'results', and that these outcomes should, in large measure, correspond to those which service users and citizens see as valuable, not simply those which are valued by politicians and service managers" (Bovaird and Loeffler 2012). In line with the RRI philosophy, co-production of public services look at them not just as services produced *for* the public but *by/with* the public within the framework of a public sector, which continues to represent the public interest, not simply the interests of "consumers" of public services. In this framework, public sector and citizens should exploit the synergies between their diverse assets and resources to achieve better outcomes at improved efficiency rather than simply services (Bovaird and Loeffler 2012).

Involving end-users move service users from the traditional view of the public as "passive" to active components of service delivery as they are essential in defining service requirements, they have knowledge to be valorized, they can play the role of active contributor to their communities and promoter of the value of the public services they receive and can engage in collaborative rather relationships with staff and with other service users.

End-users (citizens) may be engaged in the coproduction of public services in many different not mutual exclusive) ways such as co-planning of policies (e.g. deliberative participation), co-design of product and services (e.g. user consultation, service design labs), co-prioritization of services (e.g. participatory budgeting), co-financing (e.g. fundraising), co-managing (e.g. community management of public assets), co-delivery (e.g. peer support groups), and co-assessment (including co-monitoring and co-evaluation).

Most of these different profiles can be detected in many of the public-private partnership (PPP) in delivering public services, but an actual co-production of services only occurs where they are both co-commissioned and co-provided (Table 17.1).

Public-value created by engaging citizens can be measured in terms of user value, value to wider groups, social value (social cohesion and interaction), environmental value and political

Table 17.1 Typology of co-commissioned and co-provided services (adapted from Bovaird and Loeffler 2012)

		Level of public engagement in Commissioning	
		Low	High
Level of engagement in Provisioning	Low	Traditional	Co-commissioned
	High	Co-provided	Fully co-produced

valued. The first two are traditionally taken into account by the private sector and in traditional procurement approach.

Some barriers that may hinder the development of this renewed public management approach are mainly funding and commissioning barriers, lack of professional skills, difficulties in generating evidence of value for people, risk aversion, and political and professional reluctance to lose status and control.

Adopting this approach is a matter of political economy as it is not cost-free. While user and community co-production can achieve major improvements in outcomes and service quality and can produce major cost savings, it is not resource free. Initiating such approaches can involve substantial setup costs and supporting them effectively will usually involve a flow of public sector resources. Co-production may be "value for money", but it usually cannot produce value without money. Furthermore, especially in the case of citizen science and innovation – a lively debate for the development of proper reward for the people engaged in co-design activities is also flourishing.

4 Conclusion

In research and in practice, commercial exploitation of scientific knowledge and public participation in policy making about science and technology are usually distinct. While the "capitalization" of knowledge is framed within innovation and management studies (Leydesdorff and Etzkowitz 1998), "participation" is one of the main focuses of science and technology studies (STS), where it is treated as a form of democratization of the policy making process and of socially nuanced coproduction of innovation. Bridging these two streams allow researchers and decision-makers to explore the interconnections between participation initiatives and economic policy, and the potential economic value of the public engagement in both shaping technological products for the market and preparing the market for the product.

Thorpe and Gregor (2010) consider this opportunity as "a novel situation in the public dimensions of science and technology" to be exploited through the explicit link between communication of science and national policy for investment and innovation in science and technology. At the systemic level of the general economic dynamics (that may be referred at the local as well as at the national or greater level, i.e. European Union) engaging people with R&D may bridge capitalization of knowledge and participatory models thus producing a confluence of knowledge transfer and social relations and in "wealth creation" (Thorpe and Gregory 2010).

Behind this proposal lays the convincement that science and technology are the main forces of production within advanced capitalism of knowledge economy and that the economic mobilization of science influence the institutional and policy context, including participation processes. Participation can be considered as a form of immaterial labor which has been gaining value in the recent decades of evolution of capitalistic model, closing the gap between production and consumption (i.e. presumption explored at Section 3.2), and between the economy and the communicative public sphere. If contemporary funding institutions wish to support innovation (Jessop 2002), in addition to fund research activities it should institutionalize and implement public engagement in order to take advantage and legitimize in a stable way the post-academic forms of responsible knowledge and innovation production.

Opening to the public and society the streams of scientific research, through the exploitation of the "third mission" of contemporary academies and the collection of diffused and tacit knowledge by the means of public engagement, pushes the encounter between parties from different backgrounds or with differing interests. These processes, as in the case of polling presented at Section 3.2, may be considered also as examples of "deliberative democracy" when applied, for example, in areas of service provision where the public is not able to make their preferences count via the simple choice of consumption. Participation, thus, should not be conceptualized and designed as an alternative to the market, but rather as a complement and a mean for articulating and valorize citizens choice and for driving research and innovation processes.

Notes

1 As an example, in Italy in 2016 there were 359 environmental local conflicts, with more than half in the energy sector (56.7%) followed by the waste management sector (37.4%). Within the energy sector, oppositions were mostly oriented against RES plants (75.4%) and in particular against biomass (43 plants), composting (20), and wind farms (13) (Nimby Forum 2017).
2 The scheme was discussed at Leibniz Institute Conference, Berlin, 16 June 2018.
3 http://projectsmartmap.eu/.
4 www.rri-prisma.eu/.
5 https://innovation-compass.eu/.
6 See also http://projectsmartmap.eu/wp-content/uploads/2018/08/SMART_Map_3Dmed.pdf.
7 http://europa.eu/rapid/press-release_IP-16-4009_en.htm
8 For a review of energy justice concepts, see Jenkins, K., Mc Cauley D., Heffron, R., Stephan, H., Rehne, R. (2016) Energy justice: A conceptual review. *Energy Research & Social Science*, 11, 2016, 174–182.
9 IPCC (2011) *Special Report on Renewable Energy Sources and Climate Change Mitigation*. Cambridge University Press, New York, USA.

References

Allansdottir, A., Pellizzone, A., Sciullo, A. (2018) Geothermal Energy and Public Engagement. In Manzella, A., Allansdottir, A., Pellizzone, A. (Eds.) *Geothermal Energy and Society*, Springer, Cham.

Batel, S., Devine-Wright, P., Tangeland, T. (2013) Social acceptance of low carbon energy and associated infrastructures: A critical discussion. *Energy Policy*, 58, 1–5.

Bauer, M.W., Allum, N., Miller, S. (2007) What can we learn from 25 years of PUS survey research? Liberating and expanding the agenda. *Public Understanding of Science.*, 16, 79–95.

Bauwens, T. (2016) Explaining the diversity of motivations behind community renewable energy. *Energy Policy*, 93, 278–290.

Bauwens, T., Gotchev, B., Holstenkamp, L. (2016) What drives the development of community energy in Europe? The case of wind power cooperatives. *Energy Research & Social Science*, 13, 136–147.

Bell, D., Gray, T., Haggett, C. (2005) The 'Social Gap' in wind farm siting decisions: explanations and policy responses. *Environmental Politics*, 14, 460–477.

Bobbio, L., Pomatto, G. (2007) Il coinvolgimento dei cittadini nelle scelte pubbliche. *Meridiana. Rivista di storia e scienze sociali*, 58, 45–67.

Bovaird, T., Loeffler, E. (2012) From engagement to co-production: The contribution of users and communities to outcomes and public value. *Voluntas: International Journal of Voluntary and Nonprofit Organizations*, 23, 4, 1119–1138.

Camporesi, S., Vaccarella, M., Davis, M. (2017) Investigating public trust in experts knowledge: Narrative, ethics, and engagement. *Bioethical Inquiry*, 14, 23, 23–30.

Devine-Wright, P. (2007) *Reconsidering Public Attitudes and Public Acceptance of Renewable Energy Technologies: A Critical Review*, School of Environment and Development, University of Manchester, Manchester.

Devine-Wright, P. (2011) Place attachment and public acceptance of renewable energy: A tidal energy case study. *Journal of Environmental Psychology*, 31, 366–343.

Devine-Wright, P., Batel, S., Aasc, O., Sovacool, B., Labelle, M.C., Ruud, A. (2017) A conceptual framework for understanding the social acceptance of energy infrastructure: Insights from energy storage. *Energy Policy*, 107. 27–31.

Leydesdorff, L., Etzkowitz, H. (1998) The Triple Helix as a model for innovation studies. *Science and Public Policy*, 25, 3, 195–203.

Flipse, S.M., et al. (2015) Operationalizing responsible research & innovation in industry through decision support in innovation practice. *Journal on Chain and Network Science*, 15, 2, 135–146.

Gaffigan, M.E. (2008) *Advanced Energy Technologies: Budget Trends and Challenges for DOE's Energy R&D Program*, US Government Accountability Office, Washington, DC.

Gambetta, D. (2000) Can we trust trust? In Gambetta, D. (Ed.), *Trust: Making and Breaking Cooperative Relations*, Department of Sociology, University of Oxford, Oxford, pp. 213–237, Chapter 13.

Geels, F.W., Schot, J. (2007) Typology of sociotechnical transition pathways. *Research Policy*, 36, 399–417.

Hood, C.(1991) A public management for all seasons. *Public Administration*, 69, 1, 3–19.

Jessop, B. (2002) *The Future of the Capitalist State*, Polity Press, Cambridge.

Lees, N., Lees, I. (2017) Competitive advantage through responsible innovation in the new zealand sheep dairyindustry. *International. Food and Agribusiness Managagement Review*, 21, 4, 505–524.

Luskin, R.C., Fishkin, J.S., Plane, D.L. (1999) *Deliberative Polling and Policy Outcomes: Electric Utility Issues in Texas*, Annual Meeting of the Association for Public Policy Analysis and Management, Washington, DC.

Maggiolini, M., Pomatto, G. (2016) Fonti nuove, conflitti vecchi: L'approccio topdown non paga: Due impianti fotovoltaici a confronto. *Rivista Italiana di Politiche Pubbliche*, 3, 399–426.

Manzella, A., Allansdottir, A., Pellizzone, A. (eds.) (2019) *Geothermal Energy and Society*. Springer, Cham.

Nimby Forum (2017) *IX Edizione Rapporto Nimby Forum, Comunicato Stampa*, www.nimbyforum.it/area-stampa/comunicati.

Owen, R., Macnaghten, P., Stilgoe, J. (2012) Responsible research and innovation: From science in society to science for society, with society. *Science and Public Policy*, 39, 751–760.

Pellizzone, A., Allansdottir, A., De Franco, R., Manzella, A., Muttoni, G. (2017) Geothermal energy and the public: A case study on deliberative citizens' engagement in central Italy. *Energy Policy* 101, 561–570

Poortinga, W., Pidgeon, N. (2003) Exploring the dimensionality of trust in risk regulation. *Risk Analysis*, 23, 961–972.

Puttilli, M. (2014) *Geografia delle fonti rinnovabili. Energia e territorio per un'eco-ristrutturazione della società*, FrancoAngeli, Milano.

Ravazzi, S., Pomatto, G. (2014) Flexibility, argumentation and confrontation: How deliberative minipublics can affect policies on controversial issues. *Journal of Public Deliberation*, 10, 2, 10.

Renn, O., Levine, D. (1991) Credibility and trust in risk communication. In Kasperson, R.E., Stallen, P.J.M. (Eds.), *Communicating Risks to the Public*, Kluwer Academic Publishers, The Hague, pp. 175–218.

Rowe, G., Frewer, L.J. (2005) A typology of public engagement mechanisms. *Sci.RRI Tools* website, accessed, 26th July 2018 www.rri-tools.eu/.

Scholten, V.E., Duin, P.A.V.D. (2015) Responsible innovation among academic spin-offs: How responsible practices help developing absorptive capacity. *Journal on Chain and Network Science*, 15, 2, 165–179.

Sciullo, A., Padovan, D. (2018) Public Engagement for Renewables Technologies development: a Socio-Technical Perspective. Culture della Sostenibilità (being published).

Seyfang, G., Park, J.J., Smith, A. (2013) A thousand flowers blooming? An examination of community energy in the UK. *Energy Policy*, 61, 977–989.

Siegrist, M., Earle, T., Gutscher, H. (2003). Test of trust and confidence model in the applied context of electromagnetic field (EMF) risks. *Risk Analysis*, 23, 705–715.

Smil, V. (2010) *Energy Transitions: History, Requirements, Prospects*. Library of congress, US.

Sovacool, B. (2014) What are we doing here? Analyzing fifteen years of energy scholarship and proposing a social science research agenda. *Energy Research & Social Science*, 1, 1–29.

Stilgoe, J., Owen, R., Macnaghten, P. (2013) Developing a framework for responsible innovation. *Research Policy*, 42, 1568–1580.

Thorpe, C., Gregory, J. (2010) Producing the post-fordist public: The political economy of public engagement with science. *Science as Culture*, 19, 3, 273–301.

Unruh, G.C. (2002) Escaping carbon lock-in. *Energy Policy*, 30, 317–325.

Van de Poel, I., et al. (2017) *Company strategies for responsible research and innovation. Sustainability 2017, 9, 11, 2045*

von Schomberg, R. (2013) A vision of responsible research and innovation. In Owen, R., Bessant, R., Heintz, M. (Eds.), *Responsible Innovation: Managing the Responsible Emergence of Science and Innovation in Society.* John Wiley&Sons, Chichester, UK, pp. 51–74.

Walker, G.P. (2008) What are the barriers and incentives for community-owned means of energy production. *Energy Policy*, 36, 12, 4401–4405.

Walker, G.P., Devine-Wright, P. (2008) Community renewable energy: What should it mean. *Energy Policy*, 36, 497–500.

Wolsink, M. (2006). Invalid theory impedes our understanding: A critique on the persistence of the language of NIMBY. *Transactions of the Institute of British Geographers* pp. 85-91, NS31.

Wüstenhagen, R., Wolsink, M., Bürer, M. J. (2007) Social acceptance of renewable energy innovation: an introduction to the concept. *Energy Policy* 35, 2683–2691.

18

Quality of life and energy use

Is there a fair energy use level?

M. Olcay Aydemir and Uğur Soytaş

1 Introduction: need for a cap

There are diverse views about how to sustain a safe and coherent relationship between humanity and nature. Main distinctions center around the two following connected questions of sustainability: "Is natural capital substitutable to human-made capital or not?" and – if substitutable – "What is the extent of this substitution?" One argument is that increasing income will eventually lead to a decline in human related ecological degradation (environmental Kuznets curve hypothesis) (Grossman and Krueger, 1991). Main basis for this idea is the assumption that technologic improvements will make us more efficient in using natural resources and human made capital will be able to replace natural capital in most cases (Grossman and Krueger, 1995). Proponents usually justify this idea by claiming that people will be more demanding about environmental quality with increased wealth and put pressure on politicians and adjust behavior in markets towards that demand (Beckerman, 1992). Although the theory may explain the success of high developed countries in curbing air pollution, as several empirical studies show, there has not been strong evidence of such a trend between CO_2 and GDP as is implied in the environmental Kuznets curve (Yandle et al., 2002; Stern, 2014). It may be possible to observe a decoupling between increasing income and carbon dioxide emissions in some highly developed countries; however, this does not necessarily mean that there is really a decoupling at the global level (see Chapter 10 for a discussion of the link between carbon emissions and energy use). What lies behind the carbon reduction success of some developed countries may be their ability to transfer the carbon-intensive production activities to other countries. Therefore, when a country is becoming more environmentally efficient on paper, it may be due to this shift in the structure of the economy. This does not guarantee a decline in total global emission budget.

The total impact of humans on ecosystems is often described by the formula called IPAT. In brief, the formula implies that the human impact (I) is the product of population (P), affluence (A) and technology (T) (Chertow, 2000). The median of world population projections estimates an increase from 7.3 billion in 2015 up to 9.7 billion for the year 2050 (United Nations, 2015). In most of the projections it is predicted that the world population will continue to increase in the second half of the century, but at a slower pace, and a UN (2015) report predicts a peak around 11 billion. Majority of this population will be consisting of developing country citizens. Total economy of the world is also projected to grow by more than double until 2050 (PWC Global, 2017). If developing countries follow the same path of development as their predecessors, there will be a very heavy pressure on the ecosystems. What counterbalances the negative impact of population and GDP growth is improvements in efficiency (which is represented by technology in the formula). However, the relationship between these parameters is not that straightforward due to strong interdependencies between population, affluence, and technology. Alcott (2010) presents a detailed analysis of possible interdependencies between the parameters of the IPAT equation which may offset the expected impact. Improving technological efficiency, for instance, may not guarantee a decline in environmental degradation in total. He offers direct impact caps as better tools for controlling ecological impact. This is consistent to what Jevons (1865) observed more than a century ago; efficiency does not always lead to a reduction in total resource consumption (Jevons paradox).

In particular, energy consumption, which is responsible for an important share of our contribution to the ecological degradation, is expected to keep increasing for a long time as the population and GDP grow (U.S. Energy Information Administration, 2016). Energy efficiency has been one of the most promising environmental policies towards fighting climate change and other ecological problems. Energy efficiency has received more attention among other environmental measures since it presents a win–win situation, at least in theory. Financial and environmental gains are possible at the same time. However, what seems like a win–win situation, may actually turn into a win-lose situation when long term impacts are considered. Most of the time when energy efficiency measures are applied, a rebound effect occurs in which consumption patterns offset the energy savings achieved by energy efficiency measures. Chapter 5 in this handbook discusses the economy-wide rebound effect in more detail. There is a vast number of empirical studies observing significant rebound effects after many diverse efficiency improvements (Greening, Greene and Difiglio, 2000). This may be the consequence of the belief that energy efficiency is an effective tool for economic growth. Furthermore, economic growth, driven also partly by efficiency improvements, is another factor that offsets some part of the environmental achievements of energy efficiency (Ayres and Warr, 2009). Energy efficiency programs that take financial concerns as the main targets may fail to consider the long-term aggregate energy savings and the corresponding ecological impact. This does not mean energy efficiency is totally useless but its impact and capacity to counterbalance degradation should be carefully examined and not exaggerated. Efficiency should not be the only concern.

Contrary to a mainstream (neoclassical) economic view that assumes natural and human-made capital as almost perfect substitutes, there is a considerable literature recognizing the limited extent of substitutability (they are complements with a very limited substitutability) due to ecological limitations (Daly, 2007; Stern, 2011; also see Chapter 2 on the energy-growth nexus). This idea suggests that there is a critical natural capital or irreversible nature which could not be replaced by human-made capital and needs to be preserved. Therefore, downward trends of per capita consumption should not be seen as an indicator of success where the total consumption continues to increase and drags us fast to the critical limits of the ecosystems beyond which irreversible damages to natural capital can occur. This is also part of the argument of ecological economics that sees the human social-economic system as an open subsystem of a larger system, the biosphere, which is finite, non-growing, and closed with respect to matter while open to a flow of solar energy that is also non-growing (Figure 18.1) (Gowdy and Erickson, 2005; Daly, 2007).

Therefore, a physically growing social-economic system carries the risk of hitting the boundaries of the ecosystem. In regard to the second law of thermodynamics (the entropy law), ecological economists and biophysical economists claim that there are limits to growth, limits to efficiency, and therefore total scale of the aggregate economy, and relatedly, aggregate material

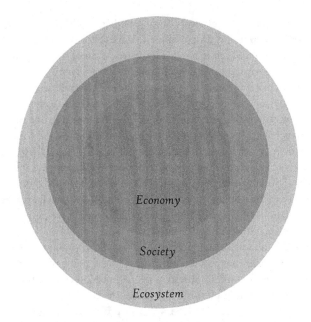

Economy

Society

Ecosystem

Figure 18.1 Ecological economist's vision of the earth system

and energy throughput should be taken in to account (Cleveland, 1999). In order not to hit the boundaries of biosphere, focus should be on limiting total energy consumption by energy conservation rather than only energy efficiency. Sachs (1999) states that "Efficiency without sufficiency is counterproductive, the latter must define the boundaries of the former". Without capping the total energy consumption, it is not guaranteed that we develop within safe ecological boundaries.

One may argue that an energy cap is not needed when fossil energy resources are completely replaced with renewable and carbon free resources. This may not be exactly true. Increasing the total energy supply with renewable resources will possibly lower the prices and will probably cause a further demand increase and encourage energy and therefore material intensive lifestyles (energy boomerang effect) (Zehner, 2012). This abundance signal may lead to a more consumerist behavior. For instance, cheaper and cleaner fuel for cars may encourage people to buy cars. The vehicle and related industries will grow. More roads will be built, and eventual ecological effects of a clean energy technology may outweigh the economic and environmental gains. Therefore, to prevent increasing pressure on ecosystems, we may need to constrain both non-renewable and renewable energy consumption to a certain level. Clean energy is less energy (Zehner, 2012). The relevant question is then, "What would be the fair boundary for our energy consumption?"

2 From ecological to social boundaries

As stated in Section 1, caps that directly limit material and energy throughputs are needed for an absolute lowering of pressures on ecosystems in order to prevent irreversible damages. In order to limit our impact and explore our safe playground, we have to determine the critical natural boundaries. Consuming energy resources could lead to pressures both on the source and sink capacities of the ecosystems. There are studies in ecological/biophysical economics literature which attempt to determine a critical level of impacts that would threaten the carrying (sink) capacities of ecosystems when (transgressed) exceeded. Rockström et al. (2009) made one of the most comprehensive studies in which they tried to define seven of the planetary boundaries that they suppose humanity can operate safely (atmosphere's sink capacity of GHG, ocean acidification, stratospheric ozone, biogeochemical nitrogen cycle and phosphorus cycle, global freshwater use, land system change, and the rate at which biological diversity is lost). These boundaries represent the maximum sustainable scales of ecosystems. Transgressing one of them may trigger abrupt, nonlinear irreversible changes in ecosystems. The studies on carrying capacities of the ecosystem provide only rough estimates of these boundaries which are subject to large uncertainties and knowledge gaps. Therefore, these boundaries are the levels that we should not risk being close to as the precautionary principle suggests. For instance, for non-renewable fossil energy resources, sink capacity of atmosphere may be a constraint for sustainability. However, climate change scientists' estimations of critical global average temperature range from 1.5 to 2 degrees. Presupposition of each has different implications.

Ecological economists also seek an optimal scale for the economy which operates within biosphere's limits. An optimal scale could be described as the point where marginal costs (both ecological and social) of the economic subsystem begin to become larger than its marginal benefits (Daly and Farley, 2004). Although it is a step taken towards the purpose of operating within safe ecological boundaries, it still features one important problem. Ecological costs are not always obvious, and some may be observed only in long run. Furthermore, climate change is not the only ecological impact of energy consumption. There are many others like land use and degradation, air and water pollution (see Chapter 13 on the energy-water nexus), and biodiversity loss, which are also partly (directly or indirectly) driven by energy consumption. Measuring the GHG emissions and air pollution caused by energy use may seem relatively feasible, but some other impacts may not be easily measured and predicted. For instance, considering the Deepwater Horizon oil spill disaster at 2010, it is not possible to completely assess the aggregate impact of the spill to the ecosystem or to exactly appraise the damage caused by a loss of endemic species in that ocean ecosystem. Further, assigning (monetary) values for some ecosystem services is not practical or realistic and needs ethical justification. Therefore, even the most careful calculation effort will inevitably involve uncertainties regarding option values and inherent values of ecosystems. In other words, if one would like to be more bio-centric, determining an optimal scale would be more complicated. For example, setting a critical limit to biodiversity loss may not be possible since we don't have enough information on the consequences. Loss of critical species may create a domino effect that we could not have predict before. Setting a cap for greenhouse gas emissions involves similar uncertainties. There are suggestions for caps to greenhouse gas emissions in the Contraction and Convergence framework (Meyers, 1999). While these caps may help lower the impacts, they may not be sufficient by themselves. As Daly (1974) states, capping the source is easier than capping the wastes, since the energy is in low entropy on the source side.

This may not be very relevant for non-renewable resources. What is depletable, cannot be sustainable in the long run. What seems as sustainable at first sight is to substitute all our fossil resources with renewable resources. However, it is not an easy task both politically, technically, and economically and it may take a long time to replace all resources and set up infrastructures for renewable and zero carbon energy resources. This does not mean that we should not undertake this transformation. As we cannot be sure how long this transition period will last, we can follow the precautionary principle to minimize the possible damage by decreasing energy use while phasing out fossil fuel consumption.

Daly (2007) states that the efforts to stabilize consumption do not have to wait for us to identify the exact ecological scales. Otherwise, knowing boundaries will only enable us to wave goodbye as we grew through them. It seems better to avoid using ecological measures for the sake of the ecosystem itself. This does not mean disregarding environmental concerns. Bearing in mind the difficulty and uncertainty in assessing the ecological degradation, this study attempts to search for a cautious social boundary for energy consumption which is (hopefully) distant enough from estimated maximum ecological scales.

Social boundaries for resource consumption have been suggested in a number of previous studies that discuss resource justice. Mostly, a lower social boundary that points the minimum level of resource use for a decent life has in the focus of these studies. Henry Shue's (1980) "moral minimum" was one of the earliest proposals of a subsistence level for resource use. More recently, Raworth (2012) proposed a "safe and just space" for sustainability. Lower boundary of this space is the social foundation line and the upper boundary is the environmental ceiling. True sustainability is possible through a lower social boundary guaranteeing basic rights and an environmental ceiling to prevent irreversible harms. It is also consistent with the ecological economics perspective, where social equity and ecological scales are joint concerns. Further, there is also a need for a social ceiling which will serve as a benchmark for detecting excessive use of resources, in particular, energy.

Costs of consuming energy resources are not precisely measurable but obviously approaching to a perturbing level. We change our focus from costs to benefits and inspect the relationship between our energy consumption and the benefits we get from using it. Hence, we seek a minimum level of energy use beyond which gains to quality of life sharply level off. We call this level the "fair energy use level".

3   In search of a social boundary: "fair use"

Before elaborating on how much energy we need, it is better to start with a simpler question: "why do we consume energy?" Energy is used to carry out activities in the need for survival and to reach a level of well-being. What we have to know is the quantity and quality of energy that is sufficient for an acceptable level of well-being. At this point another difficult task arises: defining and measuring well-being.

Well-being has no easy definition. In the literature, well-being and quality of life are used interchangeably in many instances. Well-being is often represented as only subjective, self-reported life satisfaction and quality of life mostly refers to objective measurements of human condition. There are others proposing the opposite or that one overlaps the other (Noll, 2004). Despite ambiguity in the definitions, it could be said that there is a consensus that well-being and quality of life are concepts broader than affluence and material wealth.

Various views from philosophy, psychology, and sociology have been developed during the 20th century on conceptualizing and measuring the human well-being. Most of these views were based on justice theories. On one side, there is the utilitarian view which basically discusses well-being over maximizing pleasure and satisfying preferences of an individual. On the other side, objectivist views mainly argue that well-being is related with realizing particular objective needs or capabilities (Crisp, 2017). Several attempts have been made for functionalizing these different understandings in purpose of measuring well-being.

Affluence, and GDP as an indicator of it, has been widely used as a measure of human development. On the other hand, it has long been a point of criticism to consider affluence as sole indicator of development. This is because affluence is just a means towards an end, the human well-being. Easterlin (1974) observes that within a country at a certain point of time more income could mean more satisfaction; however, increased income over time does not necessarily lead to more satisfaction. GDP remained popular also because it has the advantage of being available and measurable. However, GDP alone fails to draw the picture of human development due to many reasons. More comprehensive, multidimensional, and measurable indicators are needed for comparison and monitoring the development of nations. As Costanza et al. (2014) elegantly put it, "it is time to leave GDP behind".

Human well-being is a very complex concept and any attempt to measure it requires normative arguments which are open to dispute. However, this elusiveness has not discouraged scientists trying new formulas for measuring progress. Several attempts resulted in a number of indexes which aggregate many objective and subjective indicators of human well-being. The Human Development Index (HDI), which is used by the United Nations, could be seen as the most popular one among others. HDI is underpinned by Amartya Sen and Martha Nussbaum's "capabilities approach" on well-being (Sen, 1999). Objective well-being indicators like life expectancy, literacy rates, access to water, food, sanitation, and infant mortality rates have the advantage that they have been regularly measured and recorded worldwide for nearly half a century. Some claim that objective indicators are not alone enough for measuring well-being, how people experience their quality of life (subjective well-being) is also important (Constanza et al., 2008). Subjective well-being is measured through self-reported life satisfaction information gathered by public surveys. However, subjective well-being is also criticized from many points. Reliability of the answers of people to the questions in the surveys, cultural variations in the understanding of life satisfaction and happiness could lead to misleading and incomparable scores. Not any index or indicator alone proves perfect in describing and measuring human well-being; however; despite deficiencies they can be used to understand and measure progress. Acknowledging the critics on subjective well-being, in this study, we adopt the objectivists' approach.

In the search for a fair energy use level, we need to measure the current state of consumption and well-being. Then we need to assess how efficiently we utilize our total energy consumption in achieving the current level of quality of life. Efficiency then indicates increasing the average level of well-being in the society with minimum energy consumption per capita. This can be achieved by reducing energy use via technological efficiency and conservation. Eliminating inequity in the society also enhances efficiency. While a number of people are able to consume large amounts of energy, there are also people that do not have access to adequate energy resources for their basic needs. If the well-being improvements per energy use is low for some group, capping and/or conserving energy use by that group and making it available to the ones with higher marginal well-being gains would result in improved efficiency. We call the upper benchmark as "fair use" level, for the reason that it refers also to justice. Fair use indicates a consumption level which does not endanger others' basic rights to access sufficient energy resources. It also serves for the purpose of stabilizing the resource consumption in order not to hit the critical natural boundaries.

To be able to measure this fair use level, we need to understand the nature of the relationship between resource use and well-being. We inspect the extent which they are dependent to each other or in other words, we have to find out whether there is decoupling or not. When carefully examined, indication of a decoupling could inform us about the inefficiency of energy consumption in achieving well-being.

3.1 Literature

There are many studies analyzing the relationship between GDP and energy and material throughput. In general, ecological economists see GDP as tightly coupled to material and energy throughput and loosely coupled to welfare, while neoclassical economists believe that GDP is only loosely coupled to throughput but tightly coupled to welfare (Daly, 2007). On the other hand, there are a few empirical inspections on the relation between well-being and energy consumption. As can be seen from Table 18.1, HDI itself is used as an indicator of well-being in most of the studies, while others used HDI components separately. Life satisfaction is also integrated into the analysis in some studies. To measure energy use, primary energy consumption and electricity consumption are commonly used. The studies depicted in Table 18.1 also have some methodological differences. Despite all the differences, a correlation in lower levels of consumption and a saturation in higher consumption levels are observed. This indicates a non-linear relationship and a strong possibility of an existing decoupling between energy consumption and different measures of well-being. We propose that this saturation level is a strong candidate for an acceptable social upper boundary (fair use level) above which human well-being has low correlation with energy use.

Our study coincides with the concept of "sustainable consumption corridors" in which lower and upper boundaries of consumption are proposed to be determined via well-being concerns (Di Giulio and Fuchs, 2014). Authors suggest an upper boundary at levels of consumption at which no substantial further improvement in well-being is to be expected and the quality of life of others is being endangered. Our study could be considered as an attempt to determine that upper boundary for energy consumption.

Some authors use bottom-up methods to determine energy consumption levels for a decent living. Through some engineering calculations, Goldemberg et al. (1985) proposed a 1 KW/cap of energy consumption as a reasonable level for basic needs. Spreng (2005) proposed a target of global average per capita energy consumption as 2,000 W/cap. He chose the climate model's estimation of 1 ton CO_2/cap as a safe level of global average per capita emissions for the year 2050 as a reference point for reasonable energy consumption. He proposed a basic needs limit of 600 W as depending on estimations of the energy consumption of the poorest decile in 2050. Rao and Baer (2012) attempt to determine a level of emissions for a decent standard of living by appealing to the basic goods approach of Kenneth Reinert (2011). Dietz et al. (2009) conceptualized "environmental efficiency of well-being (EWEB)" as an indicator of sustainability. The concept indicates how efficient a nation is, in consuming natural resources for achieving well-being.

Table 18.1 Selected studies from literature (TPED: annual per capita total primary energy demand. EC: annual per capita electricity consumption. FEC: annual per capita final energy consumption) (Arto et al., 2016)

Study	Threshold	Well-being criteria
(Pasternak, 2000)	EC: 4000 kWh (14.4 GJ)	HDI > 0.9
(Goldemberg, 2001)	TPED: 42 GJ	"acceptable standard of living"
(Smil, 2003)	TPED: 110 GJ	Saturation level in well-being
(WBGU, 2003)	Average TPED : 35.4 GJ	0.7 < HDI < 0.8
(Dias et al. 2006)	TPED: 120 GJ	Lowest HDI of OECD countries
(Martínez and Ebenhack, 2008)	16.7 GJ < TPED < 33.5 GJ	"extremely low" < HDI < 0.7
	TPED: 121.4 GJ	HDI > 0.9
(Steinberger and Roberts, 2010)	TPED dynamic function: 60 GJ (2005)	HDI > 0.8
(Steckel et al., 2013)	FEC: 100 GJ	"very likely" HDI > 0.8
(Lambert et al. 2014)	TPED: 150 GJ	Saturation level in well-being
(Rao et al., 2014)	TPED: 30 GJ	90% of population living in "decent conditions"

While we use similar approaches with some previous researchers, what distinguishes our approach from the literature is that our empirical analysis formulates a different energy indicator which we think that is better for reflecting true energy-well-being performances of nations. We also tried different non-linear models and presented a few different alternatives for determining the saturation level. Furthermore, in the multidisciplinary spirit of this handbook, to estimate the fair energy use level we adopt the "knee" concept mostly used in STEM disciplines to identify the point on a function after which marginal improvements are relatively small.

3.2   Data

We first identify indicators that would best represent the energy consumption and human well-being. In our study, we preferred to use nation states as a unit of analysis like other studies in the literature did. It is because the data is available only at the national level for most countries. National level data and indicators, however, should be carefully chosen and analyzed. There could be different underlying factors that lead to the same level of consumption as well as quality of life. This may mislead us about the true nature of the relationship between energy use and well-being in a country. In the literature, primary energy consumption is commonly used as an energy use indicator. However, primary energy consumption does not inform us well about the true amount of the energy that is directly relevant for well-being. It can mask the true reason of the progress in efficiency. For example, a country can develop the citizens' well-being without increasing its primary energy consumption simply by importing energy intense products. This would bias our analysis since we are trying to determine what amount of energy is responsible of a certain level of well-being. The best indicator would be a kind of energy footprint indicator which also includes the amount transferred through international trade. There is only one recent study taking embodied energy into account in analyzing the relationship between energy use and well-being (Arto et al., 2016). The study proves how the true energy need figure of a nation changes when embodied energy in the products consumed is accounted for. However, this is not an easy task and requires massive calculations. Instead of trying to compile data for all countries, we use household energy consumption as an indicator of energy use since they are not transferable to another country. Another reason to use household energy consumption is that it can more directly be related to well-being. Energy used in industry, for instance, leads to economic development and economic development leads to an increase in well-being. Relationship seems to be more indirect and prone to inefficiencies between economic growth and well-being. On the other hand, energy used for heating the house, for cooking, for house appliances, and for mobility has a direct impact on the quality of life of a household. Decomposed energy consumption could also provide more specific information for understanding the relation considering the different nature of consumption in different areas of use. Last but not least, we think that results of the analysis with decomposed energy data would be more useful for policy making purposes.

We tried to eliminate as many factors as we can that could bias our analysis. Climate is one of them. Assume two identical countries with different climatic characteristics. They would end up with different energy consumption values for the same level of quality of life. Therefore, for better comparison, we corrected household energy consumption data for climate. Household energy consumption consists of space heating, space cooling, water heating, appliances, lighting, and cooking energy components. Energy used for space heating and cooling is affected by climate. The impact of climate on heating and cooling energy demand is generally quantified by using the indicators called heating degree days (HDD) and cooling degree days (CDD). Heating demand of a location is assumed to be linearly proportional to the number of HDD of that location. For our analysis, we choose not to correct cooling energy with CDD values since cooling energy still corresponds to a very small percentage of total domestic energy consumption. Moreover, estimating cooling demand is not as simple as estimating heating demand. Most of the people in the tropical regions cannot afford cooling equipment and the energy needed for running such devices. Therefore, for countries where theoretically a high cooling demand is expected, we do not observe cooling energy consumption. The space heating energy consumption data is not also readily available for many countries. We were able to collect data for about 40 countries out of 70 with a significant heating demand. We first removed actual space heating data from residential energy consumption figures, and then we added new space heating figures which are corrected for the same HDD value (1,000 HDD chosen arbitrarily). At the end, what we obtained is the residential energy consumption figures of countries as if all have the same HDD (in other words, heating demand). See Figure 18.2 to observe how correcting for

Country	HDD	REC/c (GJ/c)	Country	REC/c Corrected for 1000 HDD (GJ/c)
Finland	5212	41.87	USA	25.52
Canada	4493	40.18	Canada	20.81
Luxembourg	3467	37.15	Australia	19.01
Norway	4535	34.59	Finland	18.19
USA	2159	33.65	Luxembourg	17.59
Denmark	3621	32.81	Russia (2007)	17.10
Sweden	4375	32.53	Sweden	16.97
Austria	3446	32.44	Greece	16.86
Russia (2007)	5235	32.21	Norway	16.73
Belgium	3009	31.59	Belgium	16.40
Estonia	4605	30.69	Italy	16.25
Switzerland	3419	30.36	France	15.96
Germany	3252	29.60	UK	15.70
Latvia	4237	28.35	Estonia	15.66
France	2478	26.85	Austria	15.63
UK	2810	26.42	Germany	15.46
Netherlands	3035	25.72	Switzerland	15.32
Slovenia	3290	24.35	Cyprus	14.15
Italy	1838	24.19	Netherlands	13.82
Czech Republic	3569	24.11	Latvia	13.74
Ireland	2977	23.97	Japan	13.67
Poland	3719	22.06	Denmark	13.34
Hungary	3057	21.52	Ireland	13.14
Lithuania	4218	21.46	Uzbekistan (2011)	13.14
Uzbekistan	2251	20.94	Slovenia	12.81
Greece	1269	19.18	Korea	12.65
Australia	828	17.73	Czech Republic	12.48
Croatia	2289	17.69	New Zealand	12.17
Korea	2480	17.01	Hungary	12.11
Romania	3157	16.82	Spain	11.71
Slovak Republic	3498	16.02	Portugal	11.27
Japan	1901	15.51	Romania	11.09
Chile	1613	14.37	Chile	10.77
New Zealand	1609	13.72	Poland	10.77
Spain	1431	13.60	Lithuania	9.82
Bulgaria	2624	13.35	Slovak Republic	8.81
Cyprus	710	12.81	Croatia	8.18
Portugal	1367	11.94	Bulgaria	7.88
Turkey	2048	11.65	Turkey	7.48
China	2158	6.25	China	4.44

Figure 18.2 Climate corrected residential energy consumption figures

climate changes the energy consumption ranking of countries. We find the ranking with HDD corrected data as intuitively more appealing. Nevertheless, we also tabulated a residential energy consumption without space heating data, but which is also free of climate impacts and includes 117 countries. Now we have two datasets for our analysis each of which is expected to provide additional insights on the relation between energy and quality of life. Correcting energy use by HDD brings us one step closer to a fair comparison.

In addition to climate conditions, there are other factors that could bias our analysis if not accounted for. The level of resource endowment could have impacts on the relationship in concern. For instance, in our preliminary analysis of the data set, we noticed that energy rich countries tend to achieve the same quality of life levels with higher amounts of energy compared with an energy importing country. States could subsidize or manipulate prices with taxes and policy measures and control the access to energy. Nevertheless, a low energy price and accordingly what could be arguably an energy overconsumption is observed in most of the energy-rich countries. Therefore, excluding energy rich countries will provide us with a more homogeneous set of countries with similar conditions in terms of access to energy. For the purpose of estimating a fair energy use level, we first try to isolate our analysis from the influence of factors that could not be changed (climate, resource endowment). Second, we also account for factors over which countries have some control and that may have a misleading impact on our analysis of the relationship between energy and well-being.

Access to modern energy (electricity, natural gas) is an example of the second type of factors. Countries meeting most of their energy demand by traditional biomass showed a different trend in our preliminary analysis of model. This is likely due to the inefficiency of traditional biomass and its direct negative impacts on quality of life. Again, for fair comparison, we exclude countries using more than 60% of its energy demand with traditional biomass. We also excluded a few former Soviet states for a better model fit. In the end, for the empirical analysis, we are left with a group of countries having similar energy availability, normalized climate, and access to modern energy carriers. Limiting the set of countries decreases the generalizability of our results, but our main purpose here is to see if we can develop an approach for measuring the fair energy use level. Furthermore, our approach can be developed and applied to any group of countries as well as at the city level for individual countries provided that there is enough data.

We use non-income components of the Human Development Index. Average life expectancy and expected years of schooling are chosen as representatives of progress in health and education, respectively. Life expectancy and other well-being indicators lack a distributional dimension like GDP per capita. However, average well-being indicators are not mis informative as average GDP. For example, the wealth of a small privileged group of people may bias the average wealth of the society upwards. However, high life expectancy of a group of people could only have marginal impact on the average life expectancy in a country. This is due to a natural upper limit in life expectancy and a lack of an upper limit in wealth.

3.3 Methodology and results

As indicated in the previous section, we tabulated two sets of energy data: climate-corrected residential energy consumption (at 1,000 HDD) and residential energy consumption without space heating. We regressed each dataset with total life expectancy, expected years of schooling, and HDI (for comparison).

Since we omitted traditional biomass-dependent countries from the analysis, our datasets do not include underdeveloped countries. Especially climate corrected residential energy dataset consists mostly of developed countries. One reason is that developed countries are mostly in colder regions. Therefore, we won't be able to observe the trend in low development levels, however, our aim is to find the energy use level at which saturation in quality of life is expected. The scatter plots imply that there is a considerable increase in life expectancy following the increasing energy consumption at medium development levels and a saturation is visually apparent (Figures 18.3 and 18.4). Plots are similar for other quality of life indicators, but not presented here for brevity. We utilize some functional forms that follow a saturation behavior. In the literature, a few different models are fitted to energy and quality of life data. Most of the studies use primary energy consumption as energy indicator and HDI and its components separately as quality of life indicators. Some models employed in the previous literature are the semi-logarithmic model,

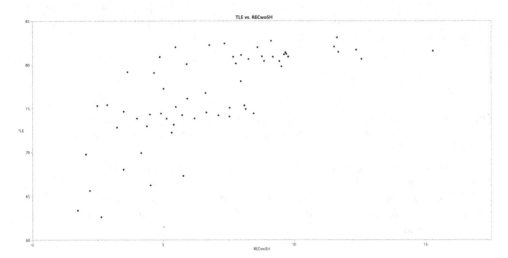

Figure 18.3 Total average life expectancy vs. residential energy consumption without space heating

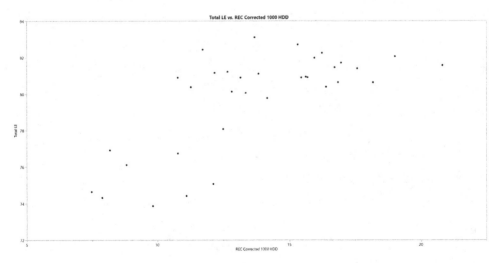

Figure 18.4 Total average life expectancy (years) vs. residential energy consumption corrected for climate (GJ/c)

logistic model, quadratic model, and hyperbolic model. Other non-linear models we think that will possibly explain the relationship well are the Brody model, general logistic model, Michaelis Menten model, Gompertz model, and log-logistic model. The most appropriate model for each pair of datasets is chosen according to AICc values, which are the small-sample-size corrected version of the Akaike Information Criterion (AIC).

What these fitted models tell us about the level of a fair use is still a question to be answered. We can observe an approximate level where the curve starts to level off. However, it is better to detect that level by using a certain methodology instead of arbitrarily choosing a point on the function. There are a few different ways to utilize this model for our purpose. A mathematical concept, knee, could be useful. Knee is simply defined as the point of maximum curvature of a function. The curve has a lower curvature on both sides of the knee point. This point therefore indicates a leveling off in quality of life indicators. For any continuous function f(x), curvature is expressed as Equation 18.1.

$$K_f(x) = \frac{f''(x)}{\left(1 + f'(x)^2\right)^{1.5}}$$

(18.1)

Knee point could be interpreted as a transition from high gain to low gain region. A small improvement in quality of life requires a considerably large increase in energy consumption after this knee point.

One other possible candidate for fair use level is the UNDP's country classification benchmarks. In the Human Development Report released in 2013 (which reports the figures of 2012), UNDP ranks countries according to their HDI values and puts them into four groups based on a fixed HDI cut-off points: the first quartile of total 187 countries as very high development (HDI > 0.800), the second quartile as high development (HDI between 0.700–0.799), the third quartile

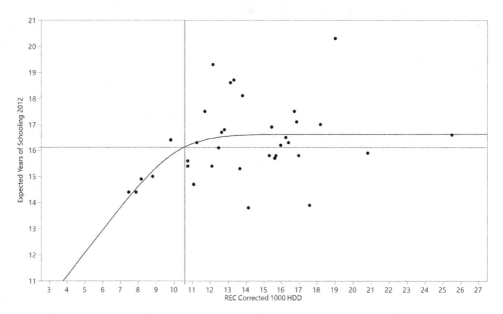

Figure 18.5 Expected years of schooling vs. residential energy consumption (corrected for 1,000 HDD)

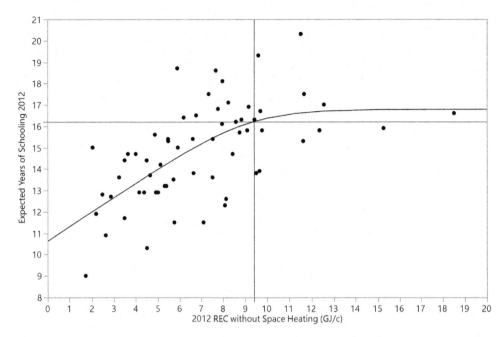

Figure 18.6 Expected years of schooling vs. residential energy consumption (without space heating)

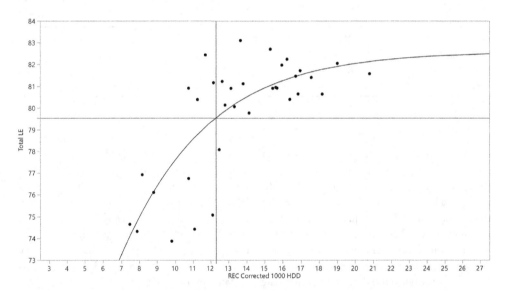

Figure 18.7 Life expectancy vs. residential energy consumption (corrected for 1,000 HDD)

as medium development (HDI between 0.550–0.699), and the last quartile as low development (HDI < 0.550) (UNDP, 2013). For each quartile, average values of HDI, life expectancy, mean and expected years of schooling and GDP/c are computed. We re-ranked countries according to life expectancy and expected years of schooling and grouped them similarly into quartiles. Then

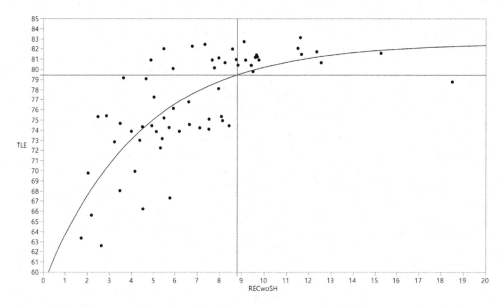

Figure 18.8 Life expectancy vs. residential energy consumption (without space heating)

Table 18.2 UNDP benchmarks of development derived from 2012 data

	HDI	Total Average Life Expectancy (Years)	Exp. Years of Schooling (Years)
Average of First Quintile	0.884	80.1	16.3
Lowest of First Quintile	0.814	76.92	15

we took the lowest of the first quartile as a benchmark for very high development and also noted the average of the first quartiles (Table 18.2). We used these values in our models to identify the corresponding energy consumption. We also calculated the corresponding energy consumption for very high development countries' HDI, life expectancy, and expected years of schooling averages given in the UNDP (2013) report. We highlighted the best performer among the countries that reach the benchmark quality of life level. Taking into consideration that the best performer may have a special advantage, so we took the average of the best performing quintile.

Based on UNDP benchmarks, we can say that around 6.25–6.69 GJ/cap (residential energy consumption without space heating) and around 8.52–9.49 GJ/cap (residential energy consumption at 1,000 HDD) levels are candidates for fair use. If we determine fair use based on our knee calculations, figures get a little higher: 8.8–9.4 GJ/cap (residential energy consumption without space heating) and 10.6–12.3 GJ/cap (residential energy consumption at 1,000 HDD) (Table 18.3). Note that the figures of residential energy consumption that include space heating energy are calculated for 1,000 HDD. If we want to know what is fair for another HDD level, all calculations should be repeated with the new HDD value.

Steinberger and Roberts (2010) points out that the saturation level changes over time. They observed a steady decline in energy threshold levels from 1975 to 2005. This trend is expected

Table 18.3 Fair energy use levels derived from four different data pairs (GJ/c)

	UNDP quartile	Best Performer	UNDP average	Best performer	KNEE	Best performer	20% best average
EDU vs RECwoSH	6.69	4.89	9.74	5.9	9.4	5.9	6.55
TLE vs RECwoSH	6.25	3.65	9.4	4.89	8.8	4.89	6.43
EDU vs RECwSH	8.52	8.17	11.16	9.82	10.6	9.82	11.71
TLE vs RECwSH	9.49	8.17	13.22	10.77	12.3	10.77	11.71

(EDU: Exp. Years of Schooling, TLE: Total Life Expectancy, RECwoSH: Residential Energy Consumption without Space Heating, RECwSH: Residential Energy Consumption with Space Heating)

as a result of technological improvements. We also admit that the fair energy use level should be dynamic and needs to be updated periodically. Fair use level informs us about the level of energy consumption that is just enough to achieve an average level of quality of life with the current available technology.

4 Discussion and conclusion

Neoclassical economics often ignore distributional equity as it fails to notice the ecological boundaries. Ecological/biophysical economics diverges from the neoclassical view in its emphasis on both. Our proposed fair use concept could serve both purposes if it is fine-tuned and utilized for policy making purposes.

The responsibility of the ecological costs of the historical energy use can be mostly attributed to the political north of the world. Today 45% of total energy consumption is in G8 countries. On the other side of this energy consumption continuum, there are nearly 1.2 billion people in less developed countries living without access to electricity (IEA, 2015). Fair use level will be a reference point for nations to see their position in this picture and share responsibilities fairly. The distance from fair energy use level will imply the inefficiency of a nation in achieving quality of life (efficiency gap).

When we determine a global fair use level, we would expect world average energy consumption to converge to a level much like the one in the Contraction and Convergence framework designed for GHG emissions. This convergence would certainly require high consuming countries to curb their excessive use and allow developing countries some space to meet their developmental needs. In total, it has the potential to stabilize the global energy consumption, and when updated for the current level of technology periodically, a reduction in global total in long term is possible. When implemented together with decarbonization, an energy cap could achieve a lot in terms of both just distribution and ecological health.

Maintaining well-being of an increasing number of people with increasing affluence is not only possible by increasing resource throughput or by improving the efficiency. Re-distributing the resources could be more reasonable since it enables us to achieve progress without extracting more. Fair use level contributes to both intragenerational and intergenerational justice. Stabilizing our average consumption is an attempt to keep the choices for the next generations and a step forward to maintain a fair distribution among generations. Without a fair distribution, we are sacrificing the survival needs of some to the prosperity needs of others.

While presenting the potential of our proposed level, we acknowledge the difficulty of implementing restrictive policies. It also requires a full global involvement in order to prevent leakages. This study is an attempt to develop an approach that can be used to set a fair energy use level by accounting for both environmental, economic, and social concerns.

Further research could be focused on urban areas which are responsible of most of the growing energy consumption. Comparing urban data will prevent us from ignoring the heterogeneities in consumption of energy between rural and urban areas and also between different geographical and climatic regions within a country. In our study, we analyzed only residential energy consumption. Urban passenger transport energy consumption has similar characteristics with residential energy consumption as both have direct impact on well-being and both figures reflect the true responsibility of the final user. A further analysis could be implemented with urban transport energy consumption data as to understand the relationship between our mobility needs and well-being.

There is also a need for a lower social boundary for guaranteeing the basic rights to a subsistence level of energy. This level could be considered as a lower boundary of energy consumption, a reference point indicating the amount of energy where each individual has a right to have access. A similar study could be implemented with a different set of well-being indicators as to understand the relationship in the lower development levels. Time series analysis would also be useful to get complementary insights and to understand how fair energy use level evolves over time.

References

Alcott, B., 2010. Impact caps: Why population, affluence and technology strategies should be abandoned. *Journal of Cleaner Production*, 18 (6), 552–560.

Arto, I., Capellán-Pérez, I., Lago, R., Bueno, G., and Bermejo, R., 2016. The energy requirements of a developed world. *Energy for Sustainable Development*, 33 (May), 1–13.

Ayres R.U., and Warr, B., 2009. Energy efficiency and economic growth: The 'rebound effect' as a driver. In: H. Herring and S. Sorrell, eds. 2009. *Energy Efficiency and Sustainable Consumption*. Energy, Climate and the Environment Series. London: Palgrave Macmillan, pp. 119–135.

Beckerman, W., 1992. Economic growth and the environment: Whose growth? Whose environment?. *World Development*, 20 (4), 481–496.

Chertow, M., 2000. The IPAT equation and its variants. *Journal of Industrial Ecology*, 4 (4), 13–29.

Cleveland, C.J., 1999. Biophysical economics: From physiocracy to ecological economics and industrial ecology. In: J. Gowdy and K. Mayumi, eds. 1999. *Bioeconomics and Sustainability: Essays in Honor of Nicholas Georgescu Roegen*. Cheltenham: Edward Elgar Publishing, pp. 125–154.

Costanza, R., Fisher, B., Ali, S., Beer, C., Bond, L., Boumans, R., Danigelis, N.L., Dickinson, J., Elliott, C., Farley, J., Elliott Gayer, D., MacDonald Glenn, L., Hudspeth, T.R., Mahoney, D.F., McCahill, L., McIntosh, B., Reed, B., Abu Turab Rizvi, S., Rizzo, D.M., Simpatico, T., and Snapp, R., 2008. An integrative approach to quality of life measurement, research, and policy. *Surveys and Perspectives Integrating Environment and Society*, 1 (1), 11–15.

Costanza, R., Kubiszevski, I., Giovannini, E., Lovins, H., McGlade, J., Pickett, K.E., Ragnarsdottir, K.V., Roberts, D., and De Vogli, R., 2014. Time to leave GDP behind. *Nature*, 505 (7483), 283–285.

Crisp, R., 2017. Well-being. In: Edward N. Zalta, ed. *The Stanford Encyclopedia of Philosophy* (Fall 2017 Edition). Stanford: Stanford University.

Daly, H.E, 1974. The economics of the steady state. *The American Economic Review*, 64 (2), 15–21. www.jstor.org/stable/1816010

Daly H.E., 2003. Ecological economics: The concept of scale and its relation to allocation, distribution, and uneconomic growth. In: H.E. Daly, ed. 2007. *Ecological Economics and Sustainable Development, Selected Essays of Herman Daly*. Cheltenham: Edward Elgar Publishing, Ch.8.

Daly, H.E., and Farley, J., 2004. *Ecological Economics: Principles and Applications*. Washington, DC: Island Press.

Dias, R., Mattos, C., and Balestieri, J.P., 2006. The limits of human development and the use of energy and natural resources. *Energy Policy*, 34 (9), 1026–1031.

Dietz, T., Rosa, E.A., and York, R., 2009. Environmentally efficient well-being: Rethinking sustainability as the relationship between human well-being and environmental impacts. *Human Ecology Review*, 16 (1), 114–123.

Di Giulio, A., and Fuchs, D., 2014. Sustainable consumption corridors: Concept, objections, and responses. *GAIA: Ecological Perspectives for Science and Society*, 23 (3), 184–192.

Easterlin, R.A., 1974. Does economic growth improve the human lot? Some empirical evidence. In P. David and M. Reder, ed. 1974. *Nations and Households in Economic Growth*. New York: Academic Press, pp. 89–125.

German Advisory Council on Global Change (WBGU), 2003. *World in Transition: Towards Sustainable Energy Systems*. Flagship Report. London: Earthscan, p. 123.

Goldemberg, J., 2001. Energy and human well being. Human Development Occasional Papers (1992–2007) HDOCPA-2001–02. New York: Human Development Report Office (HDRO), United Nations Development Programme (UNDP).

Goldemberg, J., Johansson, T., Reddy, A.K.N., and Williams, R., 1985. Basic needs and much more with one kilowatt per capita. *Ambio*, 14 (4/5), 190–200. www.jstor.org/stable/4313148

Gowdy, J., and Erickson, J.D., 2005. The approach of ecological economics. *Cambridge Journal of Economics*, 29, 207–222.

Greening, L.A., Greene, D., and Difiglio, C., 2000. Energy efficiency and consumption: The rebound effect: A survey. *Energy Policy*, 28 (6–7), 389–401.

Grossman, G.M., and Krueger, A.B., 1991. *Environmental Impacts of a North American Free Trade Agreement*. National Bureau of Economic Research Working Paper 3914, NBER, Cambridge, MA.

Grossman, G.M., and Krueger, A.B., 1995. Economic Growth and the Environment. *The Quarterly Journal of Economics*, 110 (2), 353–377.

IEA, 2015. *World Energy Outlook 2015*. Paris: OECD Publishing.

Jevons, W.S., 1865. *The Coal Question: An Enquiry Concerning the Progress of the Nation, and the Probable Exhaustion of Our Coal-Mines*. Macmillan, London.

Lambert, J., Hall, C., Balogh, S., Gupta, A., and Arnold, M., 2014. Energy, EROI and quality of life. *Energy Policy*, 64, 153–167.

Martínez, D., and Ebenhack, B., 2008. Understanding the role of energy consumption in human development through the use of saturation phenomena. *Energy Policy*, 36 (4), 1430–1435.

Meyer A., 1999. The Kyoto Protocol and the Emergence of "Contraction and Convergence" as a Framework for an International Political Solution to Greenhouse Gas Emissions Abatement. In: Hohmeyer O., Rennings K. (eds) *Man-Made Climate Change. ZEW Economic Studies, vol 1*. Heidelberg: Physica.

Noll, H., 2004. Social indicators and quality of life research: Background, achievements and current trends. In: N. Genov, ed. 2004. *Advances in Sociological Knowledge over Half a Century*. Wiesbaden: VS Verlag für Sozialwissenschaften, pp. 151–181.

Pasternak, A.D., 2000. *Global Energy Futures and Human Development: A Framework for Analysis*. Oak Ridge: US Department of Energy.

PWC Global, 2017. *The Long View How Will the Global Economic Order Change by 2050?*. London: PricewaterhouseCoopers LLP.

Rao, N., and Baer, P., 2012. "Decent living" emissions: A conceptual framework. *Sustainability*, 4 (4), 656–681.

Rao, N., Riahi, K., and Grubler, A., 2014. Climate impacts of poverty eradication. *Nature Climate Change*, 4 (9), 749–751.

Raworth, K., 2012. A safe and just space for humanity: Can we live within the doughnut? *Oxfam Discussion Papers*, 26.

Reinert, K., 2011. No small hope: The basic goods imperative. *Review of Social Economy*, 69 (1), 55–76.

Rockström, J., Steffen, W., Noone, K., Persson, A., Chapin, F.S., Lambin, E.F., Lenton, T.M., Scheffer, M., Folke, C., Schellnhuber, H.J., Nykvist, B., de Wit, C.A., Hughes, T., van der Leeuw, S., Rodhe, H., Sorlin, S., Snyder, P.K., Costanza, R., Svedin, U., Falkenmark, M., Karlberg, L., Corell, R.W., Fabry, V.J., Hansen, J., Walker, B., Liverman, D., Richardson, K., Crutzen, P., Foley, J.A., 2009. A safe operating space for humanity. *Nature*, 461, 472–475.

Sachs, W., 1999. *Planet Dialectics*. New York: Zed Books.

Sen, A., 1999. *Development as Freedom*. New York: Oxford University Press.

Shue, H., 1980. *Basic Rights: Subsistence, Affluence, and U.S. Foreign Policy*. Princeton: Princeton University Press.

Smil, V., 2003. *Energy at the Crossroads*. Cambridge: MIT Press.

Spreng, D., 2005. Distribution of energy consumption and the 2000W/capita target. *Energy Policy*, 33 (15), 1905–1911.

Steckel, J., Brecha, R., Jakob, M., Strefler, J., and Luderer, G., 2013. Development without energy? Assessing future scenarios of energy consumption in developing countries. *Ecological Economics*, 90, pp. 53–67.

Steinberger, J., and Roberts, J., 2010. From constraint to sufficiency: The decoupling of energy and carbon from human needs, 1975–2005. *Ecological Economics*, 70 (2), 425–433.

Stern, D.I., 2011. Economic growth and energy. *Encyclopedia of Energy*, 2, 35–51.

Stern, D.I., 2014. *The Environmental Kuznets Curve: A Primer*, CCEP Working Paper 1404, June. Canberra: Crawford School of Public Policy, The Australian National University.

United Nations Development Programme (UNDP), 2013. *Human Development Report 2013, the Rise of the South: Human Progress in a Diverse World.* NewYork, NY: United Nations Development Programme, pp. 144–147.

United Nations, Department of Economic and Social Affairs, Population Division, 2015. World Population Prospects: The 2015 Revision, Methodology of the United Nations Population Estimates and Projections. ESA/P/WP.242.

U.S. Energy Information Administration (EIA), 2016. *International Energy Outlook 2016.* Washington: U.S. EIA.

Yandle, B., Vijayaraghavan, M., and Bhattari, M., 2002. The Environmental Kuznets Curve: A primer. *PERC Research Study*, 2 (1), 1–24.

Zehner, O., 2012. *Green Illusions: The Dirty Secrets of Clean Energy and the Future of Environmentalism.* Lincoln: University of Nebraska Press.

19

Responsible investment

Aled Jones

1 Introduction

The investment needs within global energy markets over the next few decades are enormous. Estimates vary but broadly coalesce around the need for an additional $1 trillion per annum in investment required in energy infrastructure over the next 30 years. The need to target policy and business interventions to enable capital to flow into these investments is clear. Responsible investment, as a niche, potentially plays an important role in demonstrating markets for these types of investment. Further, responsible investment approaches could underpin future investment growth and provide tools, metrics, and processes that allow new investments to be as effective and efficient as possible. The use of economic theory and tools to better explore responsible investment should ensure that the capital flows are better managed and produce maximum impact when deployed.

This chapter first outlines the definition of responsible investment before going on to outline the investment needed for the anticipated energy transition. It then explores the sources of capital in current responsible investment vehicles before briefly discussing the role of energy economics and potential areas for future research.

2 Definitions of responsible investment

Responsible investment has its origins in religious groups who screened out investments, and became more mainstream when taken up through political campaigns such as the anti-Vietnam War and anti-apartheid movements (Sparkes, 2002; Renneboog et al., 2008a). This early phase of responsible investment activism focused on divestment from companies who supported or profited from activities that were not aligned with the beliefs and values of the investors.

The idea of bringing non-financial criteria into investment decision-making (Hiss, 2013) frames the approach to responsible investing, however, responsible investment is not a well-defined term (Sandberg et al., 2009). While generally speaking it covers any investment that includes non-financial information in the decision-making process it is often used to describe a niche market of particular firms and investment vehicles.

The perception of investment managers towards responsible investing depends on whether they view this as a particular investment product or a general approach to investing (Berry &

Junkus, 2013). Investment managers tend to view specific responsible investment products scep-tically (Berry & Junkus, 2013; Apostolakis et al., 2016). Using the formal socially responsible investing (SRI) definition, a survey of the American Association of Individual Investors (AAII) found that general investors prefer to reward positive practices while SRI investors focus more on excluding investments they deem to be not aligned with the responsible investing (Berry & Junkus, 2013). Therefore, formal responsible investment products may be seen as a way of pri-oritizing companies with good environmental or social policies whereas the ethos of respon-sible investment is more aligned with transitioning the economy towards an overall solution to environment and social challenges. Both approaches have their merits and challenges, and both require an informed engagement between all stakeholders.

If pension beneficiaries are asked about responsible investment, while there may be a prefer-ence towards the approach of responsible investment (Apostolakis et al., 2016), there is a lack of financial skills and acumen to be able to make such financial decisions (Borgers & Pownall, 2014), as well as a lack of non-financial technical knowledge (Gatzert & Kosub, 2016). Even where investors have experience of direct investing in projects such as local onshore wind (Gamel & Decker, 2016), they still require a positive environmental attitude to consider such investments.

Initiatives such as the United Nations Principles for Responsible Investment (PRI), while being voluntary, have strong backing within the investment community and therefore demon-strate some salience of the issues within responsible investing to that community (Majoch et al., 2017). Although there is no evidence that they view this as an urgent issue. Within the insurance sector, one of the most exposed sectors to the impacts of climate change, there is still limited evi-dence that an overall approach to responsible investment is being made (Jones & Phillips, 2016).

In this chapter an attempt to define responsible investment is therefore not made, rather both specific responsible investment products and the broad approaches to investing when environ-mental, social and governance issues are considered.

3 Investment requirements for energy transitions

The scale of opportunity to invest in solutions that address global sustainability challenges, such as climate change (see Chapter 9 of this book for an exploration of climate change economics), is often seen as a new technology revolution (Linnenluecke et al., 2016). For example, the require-ments for capital investment into energy infrastructure, both supply and consumption, over the next few decades are huge. USD 270 trillion is due to be invested into the energy system between 2007 and 2050 (IEA, 2009). To meet the climate change targets laid out in the United Nations Framework Convention on Climate Change (UNFCCC) agreements, USD 1 trillion per annum is required over that timescale.

Over the past few decades resource and energy efficiency have dominated environmental finance (Chapter 5 of this book discusses energy efficiency). Efficiency can be considered a part of a responsible investment approach. Often corporate investment into best practice was done for cost saving purposes rather than any external or specifically environmental driver. However, additional incentives, such as the creation of a trading scheme to put a price on carbon (Convery & Redmond, 2007), have driven more investment into efficiency than would otherwise have occurred.

The challenge of transforming the investment landscape from one based on fossil fuels to a low carbon economy has led many to explore the path dependent nature of those investments (Lovio et al., 2011). There needs to be a significant and active process of driving the required change in investment landscape to move away from this 'carbon lock in' (Kemp-Benedict, 2014). One aspect that is helping drive this change is the increased perception of risk that is now dem-onstrated by a lack of shift away from the high carbon pathway. Theoretical approaches, such as the social cost of carbon (see Chapter 16 of this book), also contribute to a better incorporation of future risks into current economic valuations. Impacts from climate change, biodiversity loss, resource depletion (Jones et al., 2013) that have already occurred have all contributed to an increase in the perception of material financial risk.

Globally, clean energy investment passed USD 200 billion in 2010 (Frankfurt School-UNEP Centre, 2013; PEW Charitable Trust, 2010; WEF, 2011) with investments in infrastructure accounting for over half. China saw the highest proportion of this investment at $54 billion. Investments reached almost $350 billion in 2015 although this fell 18% in 2016 (Bloomberg New Energy Finance, 2017) as shown in Figure 19.1. Investments in Asia still dominate and were just under half of the total investment in 2016. Renewable energy capacity investments in 2016 reached $227 billion with the vast majority being in wind and solar technologies (Bloomberg New Energy Finance, 2017). These investments represent a substantial market and a significant portion of all responsible investment.

Despite this large investment market there is clearly a gap between what is required and what is being delivered. In particular developing countries' requirement for investment is estimated to be in the region of $240–$640 billion per annum by 2030 with only 40% of that currently being invested by both public and private sources (Vivid Economics, 2014b). Private finance is relatively smaller in developing countries than in developed countries. Estimates put private investment at 88% of the total in developed countries and 57% in developing countries (Vivid Economics, 2014b). Additionally, the current global focus in investments is towards energy infrastructure while transport requirements are equally as challenging (see Figure 19.2). Many scenarios for

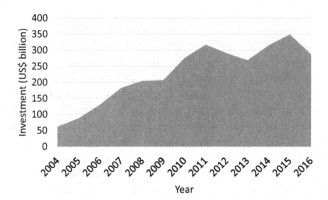

Figure 19.1 Investment in clean energy between 2004 and 2016 (Bloomberg New Energy Finance, 2017)

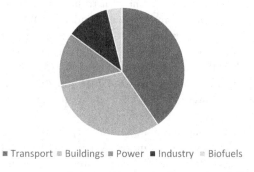

■ Transport ■ Buildings ■ Power ■ Industry ■ Biofuels

Figure 19.2 Share of investment needs, by sector, to meet international climate targets (IFC, 2011)

combating climate change also have a significant role for carbon capture and storage or biofuel (to enable biomass carbon capture and storage) and both of these solutions are also underinvested.

4 Sources of responsible investment

Over the past few years the level of capital flowing into responsible investment has increased dramatically with a six fold increase in SRI funds between 1995 and 2005 to over $3.5 trillion (Renneboog et al., 2008a). The majority of this investment is from institutional investors such as pension funds and insurance companies. Some of this growth has been enabled through the introduction of SRI related regulations (Renneboog et al., 2008a), such as the tax deductions available in the Netherlands for green investments or the 1995 Pensions Act in the UK, which requires pension trustees to disclose their engagement with social, environmental, and ethical issues. A particular advantage of including such risks into decision-making may be an increased portfolio diversification (Wustenhagen & Menichetti, 2012).

There is in addition a number of voluntary actions that have been set up by the finance sector. The UN Principles for Responsible Investment (PRI), for example, can be seen as an organization which facilitates and mobilises collective action (Gond & Piani, 2012). However, when examining the $216 billion (UNEP, 2018) of climate change–related investments globally in 2017, institutional investors (for example, pension funds) are found to be a negligible source of total investment. The majority of investments, over $120 billion, is on balance sheet investment by utilities and energy companies (UNEP, 2018), with a further $90 billion coming from project finance (mainly through equity from project developers such as Invenergy and Ørsted).

As part of the United Nations Climate Summit, led by the United Nations secretary-general, several private investment funds made commitments to increase their investments into low carbon sectors by 2020. Substantive progress was made in the first year (see Table 19.1).

The evidence for how SRI funds perform in comparison to other investments is mixed. Some studies show an outperformance (Mallin et al., 1995; Gregory et al., 1997; Sparkes, 2001), while others find that they perform no better than market norms (Bauer et al., 2005) or only outperform when dividend payments are taken into account (Brzeszczynski et al., 2016). There is also some evidence, from US and European SRI funds, that investors may be willing to invest in assets with lower returns if they also meet SRI criteria (Renneboog et al., 2008b). However, there is some degree of scepticism that current responsible investments (Scholtens, 2014) are in fact responsible. Therefore, there appears to be a move towards considering climate risk and other aspects of responsible investment into investment decisions but this has not directly translated into a substantive change in real investment into assets or infrastructure.

There are fiduciary duty–related arguments that trustees of institutional funds cannot take social or environmental considerations into account (Sandberg, 2011) other than in very specific cases although there are counter arguments that they are already legally required to do so (Sethi, 2005). Sixty percent of asset owners, representing $27 trillion in investment, now incorporate some level of climate risk in their decision-making processes (Asset Owners Disclosure Project, 2017). This represents a significant change between 2016 and 2017, with 45 asset owners adding climate risk considerations. However, within US asset owners only 0.5% of investment is in low carbon assets (Asset Owners Disclosure Project, 2017).

The private sector will continue to invest significant capital into energy projects over the next few decades and so the issue facing policy makers is how to influence strategic choices towards renewable energy investments and away from conventional energy investment (Wustenhagen & Menichetti, 2012). To really scale up investment into renewable infrastructure long term and

Table 19.1 Private sector commitments made during the UN Climate Summit in 2014 and their delivery during the first year (UN, 2015)

Organization	Original commitment/target	Progress over the last year	Assessment
International Cooperative and Mutual Insurance Federation (ICMIF)/ International Insurance Industry	Doubling of 'climate-smart' investments to reach $84 billion by COP21, and a tenfold increase by 2020	$109 billion by July 2015 expected to reach $130 billion by October	Reached initial target
Portfolio Decarbonization Coalition	To mobilize investors to commit to collectively carbon footprint $500 billion of AuMs and to decarbonize $100 billion	Decarbonization commitment of $63 billion reached, expected to increase to $75 billion by October Investors have committed via the UNPRI-organized Montréal Pledge to carbon footprint $3 trillion	On track
CalSTRS, APG, Pension Danmark	To allocate more than $31 billion to 'low-carbon' investments by 2020	Currently around $29 billion allocated, an increase of $11 billion over the year	On track
Swiss Re	Advise 50 sovereigns and sub-sovereigns on climate risk resilience and to have offered them protection of $10 billion against this risk	Advice to nine sovereigns and sub-sovereigns (seven from developing countries) and offered protection to more than $1.5 billion (of which $1.1 billion offered to developing countries)	On track
Bank of America	Catalytic Finance Initiative (CFI) – $10 billion of new investment in high-impact clean energy products by 2022	Closed around 10 deals totalling $1.5 billion (of which $250 million from its balance sheet). $400 million of deals in emerging markets.	On track

stable policy is required (IIGCC, 2011; UNEP & Partners, 2009) and this is seen as lacking by investors (Jones, 2015). Low carbon investments currently offer both opportunities and risks which require a different approach in policy development (Foxon, 2011; Hilden, 2011; Safarzynska et al., 2012). Policy design is critical (Wustenhagen & Menichetti, 2012) with many examples of energy policy to encourage investment in renewables resulting in badly designed markets which in turn leads to retrospective policy changes undermining trust in the investment climate (Jones, 2015).

An important policy request from investors has consistently been for a price to be put on carbon (IIGCC, 2011). As yet there has been no real move towards a global carbon price although various regions have adopted policies to create local markets for carbon. Emissions trading schemes have been set up in various regions and countries around the world. The largest is the European Emissions Trading Scheme (ETS) and, despite issues with allocation of emissions, demonstrates that it is possible to create a carbon market after being launched in 2005 (Convery & Redmond, 2007). However, some have questioned the effectiveness of trading schemes in either achieving the required emissions reductions or carbon price levels (Phelan et al., 2010) to enable a transition to an economy that would solve the climate change challenge. Indeed additional measures have been introduced into the European ETS to stabilize the carbon price (Grubb & Neuhoff, 2006) and proposals for floor prices and other stabilization mechanisms (Mo et al., 2016) are increasingly put forward for these types of markets.

In the absence of a carbon price, the private sector has expressed some hesitation in significantly increasing investments due to a perception of increased risk (Jones, 2015). To counter some of this perception the public and private sectors are working in partnership, creating public-private partnerships and opportunities for blended finance (Vivid Economics, 2014a). By investing alongside the public sector SRI funds should see lower risk and increased market opportunities. However, the majority of these public-private partnerships focus on institutional investors while the largest portion of current investments come from energy companies and project developers (Vivid Economics, 2014a).

5 Responsible investment and energy economics

Classical economic theory (Renneboog et al., 2008a) states that both shareholder value and social value would be maximized together – both financial return and social welfare is maximized. In equilibrium, with fully efficient financial markets, it is also not possible for responsible investments to outperform (or underperform) the market (Knoll, 2002). However, in real markets and modern economic theory, where assumptions on social welfare do not hold, profit maximization does not lead to social welfare maximization. Indeed, the use of 'popular' models that take into consideration issues including responsibility, as opposed to economic models, could provide some insights into company performance that would allow a degree of market outperformance (Winnett & Lewis, 2000).

Current financial markets operate in such a way that the majority of environmental and social challenges are external (not measured or monetized). While there are moves to monetize environmental capital (Costanza et al., 2014) and bring it into economic theory and financial markets, there are many problems with being able to accurately monetize ecosystem services (Kallis et al., 2013; Temel et al., 2018), in particular where they may be near, or at, a tipping point and thereby exhibit the properties of inelastic demand (Farley, 2008).

Energy economics, in particular econometric methods, is increasingly used to assess approaches to responsible investment. This ranges from understanding the requirements for full energy system transitions to more specific modeling of particular investment opportunities. For example, econometric tools have been used to explore individuals' willingness to invest in green shares in Austria (Getzner & Grabner-Kräuter, 2004). Econometrics is also used to explore the need for targeted investment alongside other policy interventions such as carbon prices (Kemp-Benedict, 2014).

However, as already discussed, the scale of change required to meet climate change targets represents a transition from a fossil fuel–based economy to one predominantly supported by low carbon technologies. This scale of change has been compared to another industrial revolution and as such it requires substantial interventions into policy as well as changes to investment structures. This may represent a challenge for standard economic theory. To counter this new techniques are being developed that can explore this transition. In particular, the study of this transition has incorporated economic understanding by building on evolutionary economics (Nelson & Winter, 1982) as a discipline.

6   Research areas for the future

There is an urgent need to better understand, model and capture lessons from the global shift in energy sources that is needed, and underway. The field of energy economics is of course an important part of developing this understanding. Other chapters in this book outline considerations across the field of energy economics, and so this chapter will reflect on the need for specific research that builds on the responsible investment community rather than the wider need for a holistic understanding of the whole energy transition. However, it is important when considering the whole energy transition that any research that really contributes to the necessary solution will, by its very nature, require an interdisciplinary approach. In particular, there is a need to bring together expertise from science and engineering to better understand the technological solutions together with knowledge from social sciences and humanities to better understand the actual mechanisms of transition. Energy economics can contribute to this interdisciplinary endeavor.

As already outlined, responsible investment is not a well-defined term although it often refers to a niche part of the investment community. This niche community has a parallel in the business sector – that of corporate social responsibility. Further research to explore the links between corporate approaches to responsibility and those of investors is required. Over the last few years while the responsible investment community has evolved, so too has the corporate social responsibility (CSR) field. The link between responsible investment and CSR is still emerging (Sparkes & Cowton, 2004), and it should be noted that both have had criticisms for their protective stance. As an approach to business or investment there should be many parallels and lessons to be drawn.

As the clean energy investment market grows we need to gather evidence on the various risks, either real or perceived, of these investments. A key area for research is whether marketing energy infrastructure projects for their 'green', or responsible investing credentials, increases or decreases the cost of capital for those projects (Knoll, 2002; Getzner & Grabner-Kräuter, 2004).

The use of responsible investment metrics is increasing. Occasionally these are driven by individual firms but often they form part of a wider community level approach. For example, several groups have been set up to facilitate access to data and metrics including the Global Reporting Initiative (GRI), the Asset Owners Disclosure Project (AODP) and the Carbon Disclosure Project (CDP). Such voluntary initiatives allow those within responsible investment to collaborate and form a coalition with a much larger voice than individual organizations. The Carbon Disclosure Project (CDP) represents investments of over $100 trillion. However, there is less evidence that these initiatives have driven real change (Kolk et al., 2008) although there is some evidence that there is a learning effect around how firms report on the greenhouse gas emissions by taking part (Matisoff et al., 2013). Much more research is required to investigate the effectiveness of such initiatives in creating both common standards of practice in responsible investment as well as a real change in energy investment.

Building on the common approach to responsible investment, it is also important to understand how real financial decisions are made. Economic theory and real financial decisions are very different, and it is important to understand this difference (Wustenhagen & Menichetti, 2012). While this is a growing field for research we need to explicitly examine responsible investment to expand on the additional aspects of decision-making that come to the fore in energy infrastructure investment including risk perceptions associated with new technology and different operational models for running renewable energy infrastructure projects.

The processes involved in responsible investment decisions operate within an ever-changing political landscape. A clear picture is needed of how this political landscape influences and interacts with investment and how this may change over the next few decades. For example, Kemp-Benedict (2014) concludes that targeted investment is also required above and beyond carbon prices in particular if investors hedge against the uncertainty of transitioning from 'brown' to 'green' investment.

Additionally an important area for further research is around the effectiveness and efficiency of public-private partnerships. As the scale of individual investments and capital flows reaches billions of dollars and becomes more globally exposed, particularly in developing countries, it is likely that governments will need to invest alongside private sector capital. There are now some examples of these types of partnerships being set up and operationalized and capturing the new knowledge created in this process to increase both effectiveness and efficiency of public sector funding in future is needed.

7 Conclusions

This chapter has explored responsible investment and the interrelationship between responsible investment and energy infrastructure. Responsible investment, as a term, is most used to indicate a niche part of the investment community which is engaged with a values led approach to investment. Often the responsible investment community is linked to voluntary networks or codes of practice. This type of responsible investment faces a significant challenge, and critique, in being able to scale up investment to meet the challenges of climate change and rising non-renewable energy costs.

However, responsible investment as an approach can be seen as a way to incorporate future risk and economic change into investment decisions. If the responsible investment community can share its learning, and embed its approaches, across all investments then the business as usual landscape looks very different and may support the changes demanded by the challenges that the physical world is now putting onto our financial systems.

New research within the field of energy economics is required to broaden our understanding of economic behaviors, interlinkages between policy, society, and business decisions, as well as the speed of change required to enable the energy transition to a zero carbon world within a few decades. As new investments are made and the sector for low carbon energy infrastructure starts to reach one trillion dollars per year the need to capture lessons, learn from mistakes and develop policy that will underpin and not undermine this shift, will be vital. Creating public-private partnerships for sharing risks, investments and, importantly, knowledge is a key requirement to unlock this future.

Acknowledgements

The author has received funding from the European Union's Horizon 2020 research and innovation program under grant agreement No. 691287: MEDEAS – Modelling the Renewable Energy Transition in Europe.

References

Apostolakis, G., Kraanen, F., van Dijk, G., 2016, Pension beneficiaries' and fund managers' perceptions of responsible investment: A focus group study, *Corporate Governance*, 16 (1), 1–20.

Asset Owners Disclosure Project, 2017, *Global Climate Index 2017*, Asset Owners Disclosure Project, Sydney, Australia.

Bauer, R., Koedijk, K., Otten, R., 2005, International evidence on ethical mutual fund performance and investment style, *Journal of Banking and Finance*, 29 (7), 1751–1767.

Berry, T.C., Junkus, J.C., 2013. Socially responsible investing: An investor perspective, *J Bus Ethics*, 112, 707–720.

Bloomberg New Energy Finance, 2017, *Global trends in clean energy investment*, Bloomberg New Energy Finance, London, UK.

Brzeszczynski, J., Ghimire, B., Jamasb, T., McIntosh, G., 2016, Socially responsible investment and market performance: The case of energy and resource firms, *Cambridge Working Paper in Economics 1609*, University of Cambridge, UK.

Borgers, A.C.T., Pownall, R.A.J., 2014, Attitudes towards socially and environmentally responsible investment, *Journal of Behavioural and Experimental Finance*, 1, 27–44.

Convery, F., Redmond, L., 2007, Market and Price Developments in the European Union Emissions Trading Scheme, *Review of Environmental Economics and Policy*, 1, (1), 88–111.

Costanza, R., de Groot, R., Sutton, P., van der Ploeg, S., Anderson, S.J., Kubiszewski, I., Farber, S., Turner, R.K., 2014, Changes in the global value of ecosystem services, *Global Environmental Change*, 26, 152–158.

Farley, J., 2008, The role of prices in conserving critical natural capital, *Conservation Biology*, 22 (6), 1399–1408.

Frankfurt School-UNEP Centre, 2013. Global Trends in Renewable Energy Investment 2013. *Frankfurt School-UNEP Centre & Bloomberg New Energy Finance.* Frankfurt, Germany

Foxon, T.J., 2011, A coevolutionary framework for analysing a transition to a sustainable low carbon economy, *Ecol. Econ.* 70 (12), 2258–2267.

Gamel, J., Menrad, K., Decker, T., 2016, Is it really all about the return on investment? Exploring private wind energy investors' preferences, *Energy Research & Social Science*, 14, 22–32.

Gatzert, N., Kosub, T., 2016, Risks and risk management of renewable energy projects: The case of onshore and offshore wind parks, *Renewable & Sustainable Energy Reviews*, 60, 982–998.

Getzner, M., Grabner Kräuter, S., 2004, Consumer preferences and marketing strategies for "green shares": Specifics of the Austrian market, *International Journal of Bank Marketing*, 22 (4), 260–278.

Gond, J-P., Piani, V., 2012, Enabling institutional investors' collection action: The role of the principles for responsible investment initiative, *Business & Society*, 52 (1), 64–104.

Gregory, A., Matako, J., Luther, R., 1997, Ethical unit trust financial performance: Small company effects and funds size effects, *Journal of Business Finance and Accounting*, 24 (5), 705–725.

Grubb, M., Neuhoff, K., 2006, Allocation and competitiveness in the EU emissions trading scheme: Policy overview, *Climate Policy*, 6 (1), 7–30.

Hilden, M., 2011, The evolution of climate policies e the role of learning and evaluations, *J. Clean. Prod.* 19, 1798–1811.

Hiss, S., 2013, Responsible investing as social innovation, in Osburg, T. and Schmidpeter, R. (Eds.), *Social Innovation, CSR, Sustainability, Ethics & Governance*, Springer, Berlin, Heidelberg, 229–237.

IEA, 2009, World Energy Outlook 2009, International Energy Agency, Paris, France.

IFC, 2011, Climate Finance: Engaging the Private Sector, International Finance Corporate, Washington, DC, USA.

IIGCC, 2011. Investment-Grade Climate Change Policy: Financing the Transition to the Low Carbon Economy. Institutional Investors Group on Climate Change (IIGCC), Investor Network on Climate Risk (INCR), Investor Group on Climate Change (IGCC), & United Nations Environment Programme Finance Initiative (UNEP FI).

Jones, A., 2015, Perceived barriers and policy solutions in clean energy infrastructure investment, *Journal of Cleaner Production*, 104, 297.

Jones, A., Allen, I., Silver, N., Howarth, C., Cameron, C., Caldecott, B., 2013, Resource constraints: Sharing a finite world: Implications of limits to growth for the actuarial profession, The Institute & Faculty of Actuaries, London, UK.

Jones, A., Phillips, A., 2016, Voluntary business engagement in climate change: A study of the ClimateWise principles, *J Cleaner Production*, 137, 131–143.

Kallis, G., Gomez-Baggethun, E., Zografos, C., 2013, To value of not to value? That is not the question, *Ecological Economics*, 94, 97–105.

Kemp-Benedict, E., 2014, Shifting to a Green Economy: Lock-In, Path Dependence, and Policy Options, *Stockholm Environment Institute Working Paper 2014–08*, Stockholm, Sweden.

Knoll, M.S., 2002, Ethical screening in modern financial markets: the conflicting claims underlying socially responsible investment, *Business Lawyer*, 57 (2), 681–726.

Kolk, A., Levy, D., Pinkse, J., 2008, Corporate responses in an emerging climate regime: The institutionalisation and commensuration of carbon disclosure, *European Accounting Review*, 17 (4), 719–745.

Linnenluecke, M.K., Smith, T., McKnight, B., 2016, Environmental finance: A research agenda for interdisciplinary finance research, *Economic Modelling*, 59, 124–130.

Lovio, R., Mickwitz, P., Heiskanen, E., 2011, Path dependence, path creation and creative destruction in the evolution of energy systems, in Wustenhagen, R., Wuebker, R. (Eds.), *Handbook of Research on Energy Entrepreneurship*. Edward Elgar Publishing, Cheltenham, UK and Lyme, US, 274–304.

Mallin, C., Sadoumi, B., Briston, R., 1995, The financial performance of ethical investment funds, *Journal of Business Finance and Accounting*, 22 (4), 483–496.

Majoch, A.A.A., Hoepner, A.G.F., Hebb, T., 2017, Sources of stakeholder salience in the responsible investment movement: Why do investors sign the principles for responsible investment?, *J Bus Ethics*, 140, 723–741.

Matisoff, D., Noonan, D., O'Brien, J., 2013, Convergence in environmental reporting: Assessing the carbon disclosure project, *Business Strategy and the Environment*, 22 (5), 285–305.

Mo, J., Agnolucci, P., Jiang, M., Fan, Y., 2016, The impact of Chinese carbon emission trading scheme on low carbon energy investment, *Energy Policy*, 89, 271–283.

Nelson, R. R., Winter, S. G., 1982, *An Evolutionary Theory of Economic Change*. Harvard University Press, Cambridge, USA.

PEW Charitable Trust, 2010. Who's Winning the Clean Energy Race?, 2010 ed. *G-20 Investment Powering Forward*, Philadelphia, USA.

Phelan, L., Henderson-Sellers, A., Taplin, R., 2010, Climate change, carbon prices and insurance systems, *International Journal of Sustainable Development & World Ecology*, 17 (2), 95–108.

Renneboog, L., Horst, J.T., Zhang, C., 2008a, Socially responsible investments: Institutional aspects, performance and investor behaviour, *Journal of Banking and Finance*, 32, 1723–1742.

Renneboog, L., Horst, J.T., Zhang, C., 2008b, The price of ethics and stakeholders governance: The performance of socially responsible mutual funds, *Journal of Corporate Finance*, 14 (3), 302–322.

Safarzynska, K., Frenken, K., van d.Bergh, J., 2012. Evolutionary theorizing and modeling of sustainability transitions, *Res. Policy*, 41 (6), 1011–1024.

Sandberg, J., 2011, Socially responsible investment and fiduciary duty: Putting the freshfields report into perspective, *Journal of Business Ethics*, 101 (1), 143–162.

Sandberg, J., Juravle, C., Hedesstrom, T. M., Hamilton, I., 2009, The heterogeneity of socially responsible investment, *Journal of Business Ethics*, 87 (4), 519–533.

Scholtens, B., 2014, Indicators of responsible investing, *Ecological Indicators*, 36, 382–285.

Sethi, S.P., 2005, Investing in socially responsible companies is a must for public pension funds: Because there is no better alternative, *Journal of Business Ethics*, 56, 99–129.

Sparkes, R., 2001, Ethical investment: Whose ethics, which investment, *Business Ethics*, 10 (3), 194–205.

Sparkes R., 2002, *Socially Responsible Investment: A Global Revolution*. Wiley, Chichester.

Sparkes, R., Cowton, C.J., 2004, The maturing of socially responsible investment: A review of the developing link with corporate social responsibility, *Journal of Business Ethics*, 52, 45–57.

Temel, J., Jones, A., Jones, N., Balint, L., 2018, Limits of monetisation in protecting ecosystem services?, *Conservation Biology*, 32 (5), 1048–1062.

UN, 2015, Trends in Private Sector Climate Finance, Report Prepared by the Climate Change Support Team of the United Nations Secretary-General on the Progress Made since the 2014 Climate Summit.

UNEP, 2018, Global Trends in Renewable Energy Investment 2018, United Nations Environment, Frankfurt School-UNEP Collaborating Centre & Bloomberg New Energy Finance. Available at: www.greengrowthknowledge.org/resource/global-trends-renewable-energy-investment-report-2018

UNEP and Partners, 2009. Catalysing Low-Carbon Growth in Developing Economies, Public Finance Mechanism to Scale up Private Sector Investment in Climate Solutions. United Nations Environment Programme (UNEP) and Partners.

Vivid Economics, 2014a, Delivery Vehicle Options for the International Climate Fund, Report Prepared for ICF Spending Departments, January, 2014, Vivid Economics, London, UK.

Vivid Economics, 2014b, Financing Green Growth, June, 2014, Vivid Economics, London, UK.

WEF, 2011, The Green Investing 2011: Reducing the Cost of Financing, World Economic Forum.

Winnett, A., Lewis, A., 2000, You'd have to be green to invest in this: Popular economic models, financial journalism, and ethical investment, *Journal of Economic Psychology*, 21 (3), 319–339.

Wustenhagen, R., Menichetti, E., 2012, Strategic choices for renewable energy investment: Conceptual framework and opportunities for further research, *Energy Policy*, 40, 1–10.

20

Energy economics as an energy justice dilemma

Case studies of normative trade-offs in Malawi, Mexico, and Germany

Kirsten Jenkins, Shanil Samarakoon, and Paul Munro

1   Introduction

The Paris Agreement has set ambitious goals that demand an average reduction of energy-related carbon dioxide emissions of about 2.6% per year (IEA 2017); an unprecedented challenge that will necessitate the transformation of our energy infrastructure and the societies that surround them. To this end, we must reduce our dependence on fossil fuels, increase energy efficiency, reduce energy demand (where possible), and increase our utilization of renewable energy sources, all while populations grow and lifestyles become more energy intensive. It is easy to frame this challenge as an economic one: complex energy systems and the actors behind them must grapple with the uncertainties of evolving energy provision and use, the prices of fossil fuels, non-fossil fuels, and carbon emissions trading, for instance. They must also factor in the economic advantages and challenges of new and emerging technologies, the impact of new emissions or resource dependencies, and how to incentivize various regulatory regimes around the "good" technologies, processes, and ownership models that reverse previous and often damaging trends (Huang et al. 2017). Yet we cannot forget that the implications of energy transitions also go beyond the issue of market-led material expenditure, financial benefit, or loss.

As energy infrastructures change, so do the social justice outcomes of energy provision and use. Transformations will carry implications for human health, economic advancement, and education (Labelle 2017) and will require large-scale behavioral change and alterations to social practices and cultural norms. Furthermore, transformations that are not mindful of justice process and outcomes carry the risks of providing insufficient services, insufficient access, underconsumption, poverty, health risks, shortened lives, gender bias, or non-participation, as well as the overburden risks of waste, overuse, and pollution (Sovacool et al. 2016). In this regard, each stage of the energy system carries implications for who "wins" and who "loses" on a global scale (Jenkins et al. 2016a). The argument here, then, is that energy transformations are both an economic *and* an equity concern, and that both are intimately linked.

While it seems somewhat obvious that energy economics *should* grapple with questions of justice and equity (and indeed, we must acknowledge that some modes of economics already aspire to or achieve this), this challenge can be forgotten or misunderstood. In a critical account,

Heffron et al. (2015) illustrate this through their exploration of an imbalance of the energy trilemma, a triangular model in which energy law and policy is in the center, and economics (e.g. energy finance), politics (e.g. energy security), and the environment (e.g. climate change mitigation) make up each of the points. They outline that while each competes to place different demands on law and policy outcomes, more often than not, economic arguments win out, often to the detriment of long-term resource sustainability and climate change goals. Indeed, Özden-Schilling (2015) notes that even if motivated by political or cultural concerns, economic frameworks often return to the efficient functioning of the system rather than transfers conscious of one or other social group. In this regard, Breslau (2013) establishes that economic practitioners and economic reports not only represent the economy, but go on to define economic markets, agents, and outcomes. This means that economic knowledge is "performative" (MacKenzie 2007) and defines social justice consequences and world states both positively, and without appropriate censorship and monitoring, negatively (Alvial-Palavicino and Ureta 2017). According to Heffron and McCauley (2017), a more just and reasonable focus for energy decision-making (i.e. one that balances the energy trilemma) would include other economic concerns such as energy finance (project finance); energy prices (e.g. oil and gas); electricity prices; insurance costs; subsidy support (in all its forms); tax incentives; and affordability alongside classical goals. In our argument, energy economics would seek to fully embed justice principles and outcomes in economic thought.

Beyond the fact that classical economic thinking often wins out, there is a further weakness in our approaches to such issues to date. While many authors have highlighted the necessity of applying the concepts from ethics and justice to energy economics, and vice versa, the reality is that very few articles have dealt with this subject in a great deal of depth (at least within the field of energy justice in particular). Indeed, what does exist are primarily conceptual reflections or single-case explorations that do not engage with economic tradeoffs. With this in mind, this chapter has two aims. First, it seeks to introduce concepts of energy justice to a potentially new audience – those interested in energy economics. For this reason, the first section of this short chapter outlines the core tenets of the energy justice approach; distributional justice, justice as recognition and procedural justice and briefly covers what work *has* been done. Second, it aims to introduce the complexity of this challenge through three empirical case studies, each of which focuses on a different tenet of energy justice, and therefore, a theoretically discrete but practically interlinking set of demands. Specifically, we present real-world energy dilemmas that illustrate the challenge of economic *and* ethical thinking in Malawi, Mexico, and Germany.

2　Energy justice and economic applications to date

It bears mentioning that there is an extensive literature that seeks to embed justice thinking into economics that will *not* be caught under the umbrella of "energy justice approaches". One such example is the work on intersectional justice, where financial exchanges are taken not only to represent commodity chains, but a variety of social exchanges with potential social justice interactions (Bies 1987; Symington 2004). This chapter does not seek to introduce these literatures in depth. Indeed, it is, by necessity, too short to do so. Instead, the aim is to introduce energy justice as one increasingly popular strand of literature that provides a framework through which to explore the relationship between justice challenges and economic thought.

The exact format of the energy justice concept is now well debated in the energy and social science literature. With acknowledgement of its roots in environmental and climate justice (Jenkins 2018), some authors introduce the core tenets of distributional justice, justice as recognition and procedural justice (see Schlosberg 2004, 2007; Walker 2009; McCauley et al. 2013). Others consider cosmopolitanism and restorative justice (Sovacool and Dworkin 2015; Heffron and McCauley 2017). In contrast, (and although the authors flip between different approaches in other works) Sovacool et al. (2016) speaks of eight core themes: (1) availability, (2) affordability, (3) due process, (4) intra-generational equity, (5) sustainability, (6) transparency and accountability, (7) equity, and (8) responsibility (see Table 20.1). Here, we take the approach of distributional justice, justice as recognition, and procedural justice and in the following paragraphs briefly introduce each in turn.

Table 20.1 Concepts discussed in relation to the energy justice approach

Tenet	Approach
Distributional justice	Distributional justice recognises both the physically unequal allocation of environmental benefits and ills, and the uneven distribution of their associated responsibilities (Jenkins et al. 2016b).
Justice as recognition	Recognition justice is more than mere tolerance and states that individuals must be fairly represented, that they must be free from physical threats and that they must be offered complete and equal political rights (Jenkins et al. 2016b).
Procedural justice	Procedural justice concerns access to decision-making processes that govern the distributions outlined above. It manifests as a call for equitable procedures that engage all stakeholders in a non-discriminatory way (Jenkins et al. 2016b).
Cosmopolitan justice	Acknowledges that all ethnic groups belong to a single community based on a collective morality (Sovacool et al. 2016).
Restorative justice	Restorative justice aims to repair the harm done to people (and/or society/nature), rather than solely focus on punishing the offender – as societies use the legal system for. Further, restorative justice can assist in pinpointing where prevention needs to occur (Heffron and McCauley 2017).
Availability	People deserve sufficient energy resources of high quality (Sovacool et al. 2016).
Affordability	The provision of energy services should not become a financial burden for consumers, especially the poor (Sovacool et al. 2016).
Due process	Countries should respect due process and human rights in their production and use of energy (Sovacool et al. 2016).
Intragenerational equity	All people have a right to fairly access energy services (Sovacool et al. 2016).
Intergenerational Equity	Future generations have a right to enjoy a good life undisturbed by the damage to our energy systems inflicted on the world today (Sovacool et al. 2016).
Sustainability	Energy resources should not be depleted too quickly (Sovacool et al. 2016).
Transparency and accountability	All people should have access to high-quality information about energy and the environmental and fair, transparent, and accountable forms of energy decision-making (Sovacool et al. 2016).
Responsibility	All nations have a responsibility to protect the natural environment and reduce energy-related environmental threats (Sovacool et al. 2016).

The first tenet of energy justice in the framework used throughout this piece is distributional justice. Energy justice is an inherently spatial concept that includes both the physically unequal allocation of environmental benefits and ills and the uneven distribution of their associated responsibilities (Walker 2009: 615). Thus, energy justice can appear as a situation where "questions about the desirability of technologies in principle become entangled with issues that relate to specific localities" (Owens and Driffill 2008: 4414), and represents a call for the distribution of benefits and ills on all members of society regardless of income, race and so forth (Bullard 2005; Heffron et al. 2015). This embodies, in essence, a concern over the inequitable distribution of energy facilities and infrastructure, as well as access to energy services – issues of "what" is in question and "where".

Throughout this chapter, justice as recognition – the second tenet – is taken to be a means of explicitly engaging with the questions of "who" is energy justice for, and, who is responsible for its provision (Jenkins et al. 2017). Justice as recognition appears as a concern for "how people are involved in environmental decision-making, or 'who (and what) is given respect'" (Eames 2011). Drawing on Fraser (1999), Schlosberg (2007: 18) conceptualizes the concerns around justice as recognition as three separate issues: (1) practices of cultural domination, (2) patterns of non-recognition (invisibility of people and their concerns), and (3) disrespect through stereotyping and disparaging language (misrecognition). Within this context, justice as recognition is more than tolerance, and requires that individuals are fairly represented, free from physical threats, and offered complete and equal political rights (Schlosberg 2003).

The last tenet in this tenet framework is procedural justice, or the "how" of energy justice. Procedural justice concerns access to decision-making processes that govern the distributions outlined above, and manifests as a call for equitable procedures that engage all stakeholders in a non-discriminatory way (Walker 2009; Bullard 2005). It states that all groups should be able to participate in decision-making, and that their contributions should be taken seriously throughout. It also requires participation, impartiality and full information disclosure by government and industry (Davies 2006), and the use of appropriate and sympathetic engagement mechanisms (Todd and Zografos 2005). It is concerned about the fairness of decision-making processes, or justice in "doing", and emerges as a claim for representational space and free speech (Sayer 2011; Sze and London 2008). To illustrate, procedural justice manifestations include questions arising around how and for whom community renewables projects are developed (Walker and Devine-Wright 2008), and the ethics of the emergent voluntarism debate, where communities volunteer to host facilities (Butler and Simmons 2013).

Within the energy justice literature (and commonly using the three tenet framework introduced directly above) several approaches have been made to engage with economic thought. Capaccioli et al. (2017) explore "participatory energy economics", for instance, where they describe that shifts towards decentralized renewable energy exposes new challenges and possibilities for communities to become economic actors (see also Schoor et al. 2016). They state too that participation in such initiatives can also mean that actors become engaged in direct public participation, allowing the establishment of effective civic participation and self-government – forms of justice as recognition and participatory justice (see also Hoffman and High-Pippert 2010). Alvial-Palavicino and Ureta (2017) consider how energy justice is economized – the process by which political and ethical claims about injustice can or may be turned into economic valuations. This approach is in line with Heffron et al. (2015), who suggest that the cost of energy justice can be included into economic model cost calculations when planning for the construction of different energy infrastructure – a process that may coincide with a cost-benefit analysis model. Liljenfeldt and Pettersson (2017) link the process of energy siting to the socioeconomic characteristics of consumers.

Two of the most prominent writers in this area are Heffron and McCauley, who have delivered a series of critiques of economic thought, arguing, in the first instance, that security and environmental goals are more important to the long-term future of a society than economic competition. Within Heffron et al. (2015), they write that the contribution of economics to policy formation on new energy infrastructure needs to be revised, and that we need to look past Chicago neoclassical economic perspectives. Indeed, they identify that current thinking has led to economic malaise in many sectors, including for all things energy, where, for instance, six companies in the UK have around a 90% market share. This includes a continued emphasis on delivering low-cost and/or efficient outcomes that often perpetuate fossil fuel–based status quo (Heffron and McCauley, 2017). Heffron and McCauley (2018) add, in this regard, that traditional economics has yet to deliver positive justice outcomes for society and that philosophical underpinnings of economic policy have yet to advance. Indeed, the injustice caused by energy systems can be framed as a set of pervasive negative externalities (Le Grand 1991; Alvial-Palavicino and Ureta 2017). The weakness of this and related works, however, is that it is largely conceptual and infrequently draws on comparative empirical material that considers difficult trade-offs. To illustrate the challenges involved as well as highlight alternative, arguably more socially just economic models, this chapter now draws on three empirical examples – Malawi, Mexico, and Germany – each of which coincides with one of the distributional, recognition, and procedure tenets.

3 Beyond economics: empirical cases of energy justice *and* economic trade-offs

Case 1: distributive justice – Zuwa Energy in Malawi

Power cuts in the sub-Saharan African nation of Malawi can last over 24 hours and most days, in the capital city of Lilongwe, are punctuated by the thrum of diesel generators as businesses, government departments, and affluent households attempt to navigate their way through an enduring energy crisis. Meanwhile, most urban low- and middle-income households are forced to revert to energy sources used by the rural majority, such as candlelight, kerosene lamps, and battery-powered torches. The combination of an unreliable supply, rising electricity tariffs, and the slow rate of grid expansion has resulted in acute energy poverty for most Malawians (*Guardian* 2017). Of its approximately 18 million people (World Bank 2018), only 11% of Malawians are estimated to have access to electricity through the national grid, the vast majority of whom are concentrated in a few urban centers (NSO 2018).

While some of the aforementioned challenges are acknowledged in Malawi's energy policy, there has been little in the form of investment to improve reliability and increase supply (Zalengera et al. 2014). In the context of energy justice, this is equivalent to a lack of distributive justice. The limited and unreliable supply of electricity in Malawi disproportionately impacts the livelihoods and well-being of Malawians across both income and geography, with the rural poor being the worst affected.

One response to the lack of access to electricity has been the adoption of off-grid solar technologies, often provisioned through a blend of philanthropic projects and entrepreneurial approaches (ODI 2016). Yet, while off-grid technologies like solar lanterns have helped further distributive justice in rural Malawi by displacing kerosene lamps and battery-powered torches, they are increasingly viewed as entry-level products. Growing demand for energy means that rural households and energy insecure urban households are increasingly looking for more capable energy solutions that can power multiple lights, charge mobile devices, and even household appliances. While larger solar household systems are available for purchase in urban centers, they are often prohibitively expensive and thus beyond the reach of most Malawian households (see also Batchelor et al. 2018; Monyei 2018). This is further complicated by an influx of cheap, substandard solar products that most Malawian households may have a limited ability to differentiate from more expensive, quality-certified products.

It was against this backdrop that social enterprise Zuwa Energy launched its operations in late 2016, aiming to provide affordable, quality-certified solar household systems to *both* rural and urban populations in Malawi. Following in the footsteps of the remarkable success of solar businesses like M-Kopa, Off-Grid Electric, and Mobisol in East Africa (Bloomberg New Energy Finance 2018), the company is addressing the issue of solar affordability by using pay-as-you-go (PAYG) technology. The company sells a range of quality-certified solar household systems that can charge mobile phones, power multiple LED lights, and appliances such as radios and flat-screen televisions. Zuwa Energy's efforts in furthering distributional justice are primarily through the use of financial innovation. PAYG technology allows Zuwa Energy's customers to purchase a solar household system with a 20% deposit. The 80% balance is then paid across an 18- to 24-month period through the use of mobile money or via cash installments to a local agent. This greatly reduces the up-front cost of a solar household system (typically between USD 250–1,000), making them more affordable to a wider range of rural and urban households. Further to addressing solar affordability, Zuwa Energy's model also has social and economic impacts through its commission-based distribution network. The company reaches its customers through a network of women entrepreneurs, youth groups, and cooperatives across several districts in Malawi, providing them with systems on loan and extensive training (both sales and technical) – here, overlaps with justice as recognition appear. The organization is illustrative of a market-based approach to furthering distributive energy justice, a model that has enjoyed considerable success in Eastern and Southern Africa, yet this is not the norm.

Case 2: recognition justice – Los Proyectos de Muerte: the case of unconventional gas in Mexico

In 2013, Mexico's energy policy was fundamentally changed, effectively opening the nation's energy industry to mass private and foreign investment for the first time in 75 years (Santiago 2015). Sparked by state-owned Petróleos Mexicanos' (PEMEX) decline in productivity in the 2000s and an increased reliance on imported oil from the United States, the notion of "energy security" emerged as a rationale for the Mexican government to liberalize the energy industry and pursue large-scale mining projects as a national priority (Castro-Alvarez et al. 2018; Silva Ontiveros et al. 2018). This ended PEMEX's monopoly over hydrocarbon production and distribution – a dramatic shift given that for much of Mexico's history, resource extraction was a state-led affair that was seen as an integral part of its national identity and sovereignty (Hyatt 2017). In striving for energy security, and in recognition that they possessed some of world's largest deposits of shale gas resources, the Mexican government has started to promote unconventional gas extraction in the country's northeast (García Chediak 2016; Silva Ontiveros et al. 2018).

Unconventional gas extraction often utilises controversial commercial practices such as horizontal drilling and hydraulic fracturing (i.e. "fracking"), and is commonly associated with a range of negative social and environmental impacts (de Rijke 2013). Therefore, in parallel to the Mexican government's prioritization of mega development projects (unconventional gas being one nascent type), rural social movements have coalesced in opposition to what they provocatively term as being *Los Proyectos de Muerte* – "The Projects of Death". While the drive to capitalise on the nation's endowment of gas resources is rationalized by the Mexican government as being in the national interest, the firm opposition from rural social movements present deeper questions of justice as recognition. Perhaps most pertinent is the question of whose vision of development counts (Silva Ontiveros et al. 2018).

A notable part of the 2013 energy reforms was the inclusion of the requirement of social impact assessments (SIAs) to determine potential project effects on communities, and develop mitigation strategies and approaches to community engagement (Silva Ontiveros et al. 2018). In practice, however, comments from affected rural and Indigenous communities suggest that these SIAs may not be providing the due recognition and participation they were intended to (Legarreta et al. 2016). Among the reasons cited are asymmetries in power that result in corporations being slow and selective with the release of vital information to affected communities (Silva Ontiveros et al. 2018). Another stated reason is that the government, despite the reality of its underresourced departments, guarantees project permits within three months to attract investors (Legarreta et al. 2016). The latter, in particular, is quoted as being a systemic impediment to conducting rigorous SIAs that feature meaningful consultations with communities. For instance, Indigenous communities claim that rushed SIAs fail to recognize traditional decision-making bodies and practices such as the *Asamblea* (Assembly), leading to the impression that the process is more a technocratic exercise than one aimed at genuinely furthering justice (Silva Ontiveros et al. 2018).

Underlying these conflicts between energy megaprojects and rural social movements are different "languages of valuation" (Martinez-Alier 2008, 2014). For the Mexican government, energy megaprojects are modernist, nation-building endeavors that are critical to furthering the well-being of Mexicans as they raise vital revenue, generate employment, reduce reliance on imported energy, and thereby provide energy security. Given these ambitions, populations that resist energy development projects might be branded as an inconvenience as they are seen as obstructing national progress. In contrast, the very phrase *"Proyectos de Muerte"* frames these projects in terms of their destructive impact on lives (human and more than human), heritage and livelihoods, and as such they are the antithesis of development: regressive and devastating (Silva Ontiveros et al. 2018). Thus, the social movements against energy megaprojects (among others) identify themselves as being anti-death rather than anti-development (Deckard 2016; Silva Ontiveros et al. 2018). As populations that disproportionately experience the burdens of such megaprojects, they seek to shift the discourse about what "development" means in the context of rural Mexico – complexifying projects pursued for economic and energy security gain (Silva Ontiveros et al., 2018). This case also highlights the challenges of implementing energy reforms given the diversity of perspectives gained through justice as recognition approaches – even for projects ostensibly tasked with addressing issues of justice.

Case 3: procedural justice – Energie-Genossenschaften (German energy cooperatives)

Introduced in 2000, *Erneuerbare Energien Gesetz* (EEG – *The Renewable Energy Act*) has been Germany's main legislative tool for promoting renewable energy power generation. A central feature of this legislation involves offering an above-market feed-in tariff rate to anyone generating renewable power for a 20-year period. This has served as an important incentive for German households to install solar panels on their roofs to generate power for their own consumption or sell to the national grid. Yet, further to this, citizens have also banded together to invest and operate larger scale renewable energy installations, allowing for projects that would be beyond the financial means of individual households. For more than a decade, this has led to a growing wave of *Energie-Genossenschaften* (energy cooperatives) that permits citizens to own solar parks and wind farms.

According to the German apex body for cooperatives, *Deutscher Genossenschafts- und Raiffeisenverband* (DGRV), Germany has 853 energy cooperatives (DGRV 2018), which are credited as being vital to the nation's clean energy transition (Klagge and Meister 2018). Renewable energy sources provided 33% of Germany's electricity in 2017, in comparison to just shy of 4% in 1990 (DESTATIS 2018). Most energy cooperatives are formed at the scale of towns and villages, though they have also been established at regional and interregional scales across Germany. In contrast to traditional centralized energy generation and distribution infrastructure (public or privately owned), energy cooperatives represent a prime example of procedural justice in that citizens, who are both owners and consumers, are able to make democratic decisions about all aspects of their energy system. The democratic governance of cooperatives is epitomized by the fact that all members have a single vote, regardless of the number of shares owned or their capital contributions. As such, cooperatives can be seen as an example of alternative economies, where users are equal owners and as such, the distribution of burdens and benefits tend to be more democratic and equitable when compared to firms, which are often guided by the interests of major shareholders (Sovacool and Dworkin 2014; Klagge and Meister 2018).

The success of energy cooperatives in Germany has been closely linked to the attractive feed-in tariff rates that were introduced in the EEG. The feed-in tariff rates created a low-risk environment in which energy cooperatives thrived. However, an amendment of the EEG in 2014 that led to the phase out of feed-in-tariffs has had negative financial implications for energy cooperatives. The lack of favorable feed-in-tariffs has resulted in energy cooperatives being forced to adopt market-based approaches, such as participating in tender and auction processes in order to compete with other energy providers. This has consequently raised transaction costs and increased financial risk, resulting in a slowdown of energy cooperative formation from 2014 onwards (Klagge and Meister 2018). This change in energy policy has shaped a context where cooperatives may need to pursue aggressive growth strategies to absorb costs and remain profitable, even if they tend to be value-driven, citizen-led action representing a less-carbon intensive and more just energy system.

While the role of cooperatives in shaping Germany's energy transition to renewable energy sources is widely acknowledged, the question of their part in Germany's energy future is a matter of ongoing debate. Some advocate for policies that better incentivize the formation of energy cooperatives as they are more localized and democratic, others contend that market forces should steer Germany's energy sector. Nonetheless, energy cooperatives remain an excellent example of a bottom-up economic approach to ensuring equitable participation.

4   Conclusion

Given its brevity, this chapter is certainly unable to meet the challenge of resolving socially just approaches to energy economics. First and foremost, though, we have argued that energy economics *should* seek to fully embed justice principles and outcomes in economic thought, and indeed, throughout this piece we have highlighted that there are numerous exciting empirical and conceptual instances through which to do so. It goes without saying that in order to achieve this, we need both a good understanding of the challenges involved and an ongoing and reflexive consciousness of their existence. Put simply, this chapter provides an early introduction to the former and advocates for the latter.

The solution to current social justice failings, as Alvial-Palavicino and Ureta (2017) point out, appears to be one of achieving a rebalancing or relocation of both systems costs and benefits in order to correct or prevent further negative externalities, and in so doing, alleviate underlying inequity. Simple? Definitely not. Such an outcome is unlikely to happen given that markets appear irrational rather than rational (Fourcade and Healy 2007: 299). This is especially true where complex and often conflicting normative frames appear (Fuller and McCauley, 2016). In this regard, we need new, innovative financial models and new ways of evaluating and tackling their impacts. As an illustration of distributive justice thinking, our chapter has introduced Zuwa Energy as one such example, where the challenge of solar affordability are met through a pay-as-you-go scheme in rural and urban areas distributed by women entrepreneurs, youth groups and cooperatives. Alongside such financial schemes, we must also question whose "vision" of justice they represent. Our case study of Mexico highlights dissatisfaction with the process of social impact assessments among rural and Indigenous communities. Further, we illustrate that you must not only consider what and who is at question, but also *how*, as our case study of German energy cooperatives has shown. As a sum of all three, you might suppose that a system of redistribution and equitable access that is conscious of the competing visions of different social groups and achieved in a democratic way is true "energy justice".

It is worth noting too that pursing social justice goals can make *good* economic sense. We can achieve co-benefits including the potential enhancement of energy security, reduction of emissions and the impacts of climate change, and reductions in poverty and the empowerment vulnerable groups among other social and environmental gains (Sovacool et al. 2017). Business opportunities may also arise from these co-benefits, "creating situations where justice principles go hand in hand with enhanced business revenue" through innovative business models for services, equipment and supply (Sovacool et al. 2017: 27; Hiteva and Sovacool 2017). Wishful thinking, some may say, but then at one point in time, climate change also wasn't on the agenda and look how far we have come there.

References

Alvial-Palavicino, C. and Ureta, S. (2017) 'Economizing justice: Turning equity claims into lower energy tariffs in Chile', *Energy Policy* 105(2017): 642–647.

Batchelor, S., Brown, E., Leary, J., Scott, N., Alsop, A. and Leach, M. (2018) 'Solar electric cooking in Africa: Where will the transition happen first', *Energy Research & Social Science* 40: 257–272.

Bies, R.J. (1987) 'The predicament of injustice: The management of moral-outrage', in Cummings, L.L. and Staw, B.M. (Eds.) *Research in Organizational Behaviour.* Vol. 9: 289–319. Greenwich, CT: JAI Press.

Bloomberg New Energy Finance (2018) 'Powering last-mile connectivity', 26th February, [Online]. Available at: https://data.bloomberglp.com/bnef/sites/14/2018/02/Powering-Last-Mile-Connectivity-BNEF-and-Facebook.pdf [Accessed 23rd March 2018]

Breslau, D. (2013) 'Designing a market-like entity: Economics in the politics of market formation', *Social Studies of Science* 43(6): 829–851.

Bullard, R.D. (2005) Environmental justice in the 21st century', in Dryzek, J. and Schlosberg, D. (Eds.) *Debating the Earth.* 3222–3356. New York: Oxford University Press.

Butler, C. and Simmons, P. (2013) 'Framing energy justice in the UK: The nuclear case', in Bickerstaff, K., Walker, G. and Bulkeley, H. (Eds.) *Energy Justice in a Changing Climate: Social Equity and Low-Carbon Energy.* London: Zed books.

Capaccioli, A., Poderi, G., Bettega, M. and D'Andrea, V. (2017) 'Exploring participatory energy budgeting as a policy instrument to foster energy justice', *Energy Policy* 107: 621–630.

Castro-Alvarez, F., Marsters, P., de León Barido, D. P. and Kammen, D. M. (2018) 'Sustainability lessons from shale development in the United States for Mexico and other emerging unconventional oil and gas developers', *Renewable and Sustainable Energy Reviews* 82(1): 1320–1332.

Davies, A. (2006) 'Environmental justice as subtext or omission: Examining discourses of anti-incineration campaigns in Ireland', *Geoforum* 37: 708–724.

Deckard, S. (2016) 'Latin America in the world-ecology: Origins and crisis', in Anderson, M. and Bora, Z. M. (Eds.) *Ecological Crisis and Cultural Representation in Latin America: Ecocritical Perspectives on Art, Film, and Literature* (2016): 3–20.

de Rijke, K. (2013) 'Hydraulically fractured: Unconventional gas and anthropology', *Anthropology Today* 29(2): 13–17.

DESTATIS (2018) 'Energy', [Online]. Available at: www.destatis.de/EN/FactsFigures/EconomicSectors/Energy/Energy.html [Accessed 2nd April 2018]

DGRV (2018) 'Cooperatives in Germany', [Online]. Available at: www.dgrv.de/en/cooperatives.html [Accessed on 2nd April 2018]

Eames, M. (2011) 'Energy, innovation, equity and justice: Energy justice in a changing climate: Defining an agenda', *InCluESEV Conference*, London.

Fourcade, M. and Healy, K. (2007) 'Moral views of market society', *Annual Review of Sociology* 33: 285–311.

Fraser, N. (1999) 'Social justice in the age of identity politics', in Henderson, G. and Waterstone, M. (Eds.) *Geographical Thought: A Praxis Perspective*. Routledge: London.

Fuller, S. and McCauley, D. (2016) 'Framing energy justice: Perspectives from activism and advocacy', *Energy Research and Social Science* 11: 1–8.

García Chediak, C. (2016) ¿Populismo petrolero? Experiencias recientes en México y Ecuador. *Revista Perspectivas de Políticas Públicas* 6(11): 121–146.

The Guardian (2017) 'The day the lights went out: the terrible toll of Malawi's power cuts', Vidal, John, 14th December, [Online]. Available at: www.theguardian.com/global-development/2017/dec/13/malawi-power-cuts-national-blackouts-poor-hungry [Accessed 23rd March 2018]

Heffron, R.J. and McCauley, D. (2017) 'The concept of energy justice across the disciplines', *Energy Policy* 105 658–667.

Heffron, R.J. and McCauley, D. (2018) 'Just transition: Integrating climate, energy and environmental justice', *Energy Policy* 199: 1–7.

Heffron, R.J., McCauley, D. and Sovacool, B.K. (2015) 'Resolving society's energy trilemma through the energy justice metric', *Energy Policy* 87: 168–176.

Hiteva, R. and Sovacool, B.K. (2017) 'Harnessing social innovation for energy justice: A business model perspective', *Energy Policy* 107: 631–639.

Hoffman, S.M. and High-Pippert, A. (2010) 'From private lives to collective action: Recruitment and participation incentives for a community energy program', *Energy Policy* 38: 7567–7574.

Huang, Z., Wei, T., Wang, K. and Liao, H. (2017) 'Energy economics and climate policy modeling', *Annals of Operations Research* 255: 1–7.

Hyatt, J. F. (2017) "The energy-water nexus: Water regulation in the wake of Mexico's hydrocarbon reform', *Houston Journal International Law* 39: 695–722.

IEA (2017) 'Perspectives for the energy transition: Investment needs for a low-carbon energy system', International Energy Agency, IEA Publications: 1–200.

Jenkins, K. (2018) 'Setting energy justice apart from the crowd: Conceptual insights from the environmental and climate justice movements', *Energy Research & Social Science* 39: 117–121.

Jenkins, K., Heffron, R., and McCauley, D. (2016a) 'The political economy of energy justice in Canada, the UK and Australia: A nuclear energy perspective', in Graaf Van de T., Sovacool, B.K., Ghosh, A., Kern, F. and Klare, M.T. (Eds.) *The Handbook of the International Political Economy of Energy*. Palgrave Macmillan: Basingstone.

Jenkins, K., McCauley, D., Heffron, R., Stephan, H. and Rehner, R. (2016b) 'Energy justice: A conceptual review', *Energy Research and Social Science* 11: 174–182.

Jenkins, K., McCauley, D. and Warren, C. (2017) 'Attributing responsibility for energy justice: A case study of the Hinkley Point Nuclear Complex', *Energy Policy* 108: 836–843.

Klagge, B. and Meister, T. (2018) "Energy cooperatives in Germany: An example of successful alternative economies?', *Local Environment*, DOI: 10.1080/13549839.2018.1436045

Labelle, M.C. (2017) 'In pursuit of energy justice', *Energy Policy* 615–620.

Le Grand, J. (1991) *Equity and Choice: An Essay in Economics and Applied Philosophy*. London: Routledge.

Legarreta, P., Letona, A., Hernández, M. (2016) 'Ética, política y trabajo en la antropología mexicana', del siglo XXI, *Avá* 28: 19–42.

Liljenfeldt, J. and Pettersson, O. (2017) 'Distributional justice in Swedish wind power development: An odds ration analysis of windmill localization and local residents socioeconomic characteristics', *Energy Policy* 105(2017): 648–657.

MacKenzie, D. (2007) *Do Economists Make Markets? On the Performativity of Economics*. Princeton: Princeton University Press.

Martinez-Alier, J. (2008) 'Languages of valuation', *Economic and Political Weekly*, 43(48) (Nov. 29–Dec. 5): 28–32.

Martinez-Alier, J. (2014) 'The environmentalism of the poor', *Geoforum* 54: 239–241.

McCauley, D., Heffron, R., Stephan, H. and Jenkins, K. (2013) 'Advancing energy justice: The Triumvirate of Tenets', *International Energy Law Review* 32(3): 107–110.

Monyei, C. G., Adewumi, A. O. and Jenkins, K. (2018) 'Energy (in)justice in off-grid rural electrification policy: South Africa in focus', *Energy Research & Social Science* 44: 152–171.

NSO (2018) 'Fourth integrated household survey', *National Statistics Office of Malawi*, [Online]. Available at: www.nsomalawi.mw/images/stories/data_on_line/economics/ihs/IHS4/IHS4%20REPORT.pdf [Accessed 25th February]

ODI (2016) 'Accelerating access to electricity in Africa with off-grid solar: The impact of solar household solutions', *Overseas Development Institute*, [Online]. Available at: www.odi.org/sites/odi.org.uk/files/odi-assets/publications-opinion-files/10229.pdf [Accessed 24th March 2018]

Owens, S. and Driffill, L. (2008) 'How to change attitudes and behaviours in the context of energy', *Energy Policy* 36(12): 4412–4418.

Özden-Schilling, C. (2015) 'Economy electric', *Cultural Anthropology* 30(4): 578–588.

Santiago, M.I. (2015) 'Mexico's energy reform: National coffers, local consequences', *ReVista the Harvard Review of Latin America* 15(1): 16–19.

Sayer, A. (2011) 'Habitus, work and contributive justice', *Sociology* 45(1): 7–21.

Schlosberg, D. (2003) 'The justice of environmental justice: Reconciling equity, recognition, and participation in a political movement', in Light, A. and de-Shalit, A. (Eds.) *Moral and Political Reasoning in Environmental Practice.* MIT Press: Cambridge.

Schlosberg, D. (2004) 'Reconceiving environmental justice: Global movements and political theories', *Environmental Politics* 13(3): 517–540.

Schlosberg, D. (2007) *Defining Environmental Justice: Theories, Movements and Nature.* Oxford: Oxford University Press.

Schoor, T., van der Lente, H., van Scholtens, B. and Scholtens, A. (2016) 'Challenging obduracy: How local communities transform the energy system', *Energy Research and Social Science* 13: 94–105.

Silva Ontiveros, L., Munro, P.G. and Melo Zurita, M., (2018) 'Proyectos de Muerte: Energy justice conflicts on Mexico's unconventional gas frontier', *The Extractive Industries and Society* 5:4: 481–489.

Sovacool, B.K., Burke, M., Baker, L., Kotikalapudi, C.K. and Wlokas, H. (2017) 'New frontiers and conceptual frameworks for energy justice', *Energy Policy* 105: 677–691.

Sovacool, B.K. and Dworkin, M. (2014) *Global Energy Justice: Problems, Principles and Practices.* Cambridge, MA: Cambridge University Press.

Sovacool, B.K. and Dworkin, M. (2015) 'Energy justice: Conceptual insights and practical applications', *Applied Energy* 142: 435–444.

Sovacool, B.K., Heffron, R.J., McCauley, D. and Goldthau, A. (2016) 'Energy decisions reframed as justice and ethical concerns', *Nature Energy* 1: 16024.

Symington, A. (2004, August). Women's rights and economic change: Intersectionality: A tool for gender and economic justice (No. 9). Available at: www.awid.org/publications/primers/intersectionality_en.pdf

Sze, J. and London, J.K. (2008) 'Environmental justice at a crossroads', *Sociology Compass* 2(4): 1331–1354.

Todd, H. and Zografos, C. (2005) 'Justice for the environment: Developing a set of indicators of environmental justice for Scotland', *Environmental Values* 14(4): 483–501.

Walker, G. (2009) 'Globalizing environmental justice', *Global Social Policy* 9(3): 355–382.

Walker, G. and Devine-Wright, P. (2008) 'Community renewable energy: What should it mean?', *Energy Policy* 36(2): 497–500.

World Bank (2018) 'Malawi: Overview', [Online]. Available at: www.worldbank.org/en/country/malawi/overview [Accessed 23rd March 2018]

Zalengera, C., Blanchard, R.E., Eames, P.C., Juma, A.M., Chitawo, M.L. and Gondwe, K.T. (2014) 'Overview of the Malawi energy situation and a PESTLE analysis for sustainable development of renewable energy', *Renewable and Sustainable Energy Reviews* Elsevier 38: 335–347.

Zuwa Energy 'Team Zuwa', [Online]. Available at: www.zuwaenergy.com/team-1/ [Accessed 20th April 2018]

Part IV

Energy and other markets

21

Oil spot and futures prices

Nikki Kantelis and Bradley T. Ewing

1 Introduction

This chapter provides an overview of oil spot and futures prices. We begin with an historical overview of how these prices developed and identify some of the major changes that occurred over time. Given the importance of oil in the domestic and global economies, a great deal of research has been conducted to understand the time series dynamics of oil spot and futures prices, particularly in real terms. We provide an empirical analysis that summarizes and confirms the major findings in the literature to date and we add some insight that ties these results to real-world observations. Along the way, we note the areas that have been the topic of recent research. We also extend the line of inquiry and add some new empirical evidence on the interaction between oil prices and upstream exploration and development activity. Finally, we close this chapter with a few concluding remarks that describe today's markets in general terms.

2 History and development of oil spot and futures prices

The first oil discovery in Pennsylvania, and later discoveries in Texas, Oklahoma, and California, were characterized by small wells, most producing less than 100 barrels per day. The Spindletop discovery near Beaumont, Texas, in 1901 was the first gigantic oil gusher and represented a significant portion of US domestic production at the time. Significant further production resulted in excess capacity both in the United States and following other discoveries in Russia, the Middle East and Indonesia. By 1928, the crude oil glut in the market continued to depress crude oil prices.

In 1928, the leaders of the largest oil companies in the world met in Scotland and agreed not to compete against one another outside the United States as a means to helping each other sustain profitability. The mechanism was known as the "as-is" agreement, since each company's relative market share outside the United States was kept at the 1928 ratios. Independent oil companies were not parties to the "as-is" arrangement and ultimately undercut the "as-is" member's price in order to grow their own market share.

Most of the crude oil produced outside the United States was priced on the basis of concession agreements. Concession agreements were specific agreements between an international oil company (IOC) and the host government (national oil company, or NOC) where the crude oil was produced. These agreements were typically negotiated on a 50/50 profit sharing scheme wherein the IOC set the posted price for the crude oil, taking into account a transportation cost from the producing country to the United States.

The concession agreement regime was not acceptable to NOCs generally, since the IOCs set the price, the profit sharing splits, the term of the agreements, and so forth. Problems developed in the concession agreement methodology as early as the 1950s with the nationalization of the Iranian oil industry. In response to this action, the British government imposed an embargo on Iranian oil, bringing Iran close to bankruptcy when refineries and other oil market participants were prevented from purchasing Iranian oil.

During the period (1930s until 1970), the Texas Railroad Commission (TRC) effectively controlled world oil prices as a result of its ability (by government mandate) to impose production restrictions or rations on oil production. However, once US domestic oil production reached its peak in 1970, the only spare production capacity resided in the hands of OPEC (Organization for Petroleum Exporting Countries), who were able to exert more control over oil production and prices. By early 1971, most of the oil companies were forced to negotiate a new round of concession agreements with OPEC, resulting in more attractive terms for the producing nations than the earlier rounds.

Thereafter, and up until the 1980s, most crude oil transacted was traded on a term supply, fixed price basis. Buyers and sellers typically agreed to specific quantities of crude oil at specified fixed prices for scheduled intervals in the future, usually a year in duration. By contrast, a small amount of crude oil was exchanged via spot supply contracts. These arrangements were mostly undertaken for "close-in" operational reasons. Barrels contracted in the spot market provided a good measure of the most current market supply and demand conditions since they represented barrels contracted for immediate or "prompt" delivery.

In the mid-1980s, the introduction of the New York Mercantile Exchange (NYMEX) futures contract for West Texas Intermediate (WTI – Cushing, OK delivery) and the subsequent launch of the Brent Futures (North Sea crude oil) on the Intercontinental Exchange (ICE) provided a new transparent price discovery mechanism. These futures contacts (along with the subsequent introduction of the Oman crude oil futures contract on the Dubai Mercantile Exchange founded in 2007) have evolved into benchmark prices, against which the vast majority of crude oil is currently traded. Benchmark prices are an important component of crude oil formula pricing mechanism, by which most crude oil is currently priced. For example, a cargo of West African crude oil may be priced as ICE Brent futures plus or minus a differential to account for differences in quality, location or timing (commonly referred to as basis). Similarly, US domestic crude oil prices are priced as a differential versus the NYMEX WTI futures contract price. US domestic posted prices (price bulletins published by refinery supply interests) are adjusted daily to reflected daily fluctuations in NYMEX WTI settlement prices. Trade journals such as Argus and Platts are also used as benchmarks in crude oil pricing.

Benchmarks have also emerged for finished petroleum products such as gasoline, heating oil, and gas oil with the introduction of a series of futures contracts for refined products on the various exchanges. Additionally, the trade journals previously mentioned also provide price data for various spot refined products in various trading regions, including the US Gulf Coast, northwest Europe, Mediterranean, and Singapore (to name just a few).

3 Empirical analysis of oil spot and futures prices

According to Hamilton (2009), oil spot and futures prices are linked for several reasons. In fact, Hamilton describes three economic restrictions on the time path of oil prices: storage arbitrage, futures contracts, and oil as a depletable resource. The latter of which is further complicated by heterogeneous geophysical properties and a wide variance in the geographic distribution of reservoirs, basins, and plays. Briefly, storage arbitrage dictates that in equilibrium the expectation of price made in period t for period $(t + 1)$ would equal the price in period t plus the net cost of carry. Future contracts may link the current spot price in t with the futures price in $(t + 1)$ given the latter must equal the expectation of price made in period t for period $(t + 1)$ plus a risk premium. Finally, oil is "mined" or extracted as opposed to manufactured or produced (in the traditional sense), and once "burned" is not reusable. Accordingly, price may exceed marginal cost even if the oil market is perfectly competitive. Hotelling's principle thus describes this scarcity rent as having important implications for commodity speculators.

For purposes of this analysis, we utilize a data set comprised of weekly observations of real West Texas Intermediate (WTI) and UK Brent spot prices and a set of four WTI futures prices. The sample period begins August 1987 and ends February 2018 for a total of 367 observations. We follow the convention used by the Energy Information Administration and compute real petroleum prices such that the latest (most current) observation is the base period and real prices are in current dollars. This convention facilitates the direct comparison of prices across time.

Petroleum prices, rig count, and production data are obtained from the Energy Information Administration (www.eia.gov). CPI data are from the Federal Reserve Economic Database (FRED; http://fred.stlouis.org) maintained at the St. Louis Federal Reserve Bank. According to the EIA, an oil futures price is the price quoted for delivery of a predetermined quantity of crude oil at a specified time and place in the future. Contract 1 is the futures contract that expires on the third business day prior to the 25th calendar day of the month preceding the delivery month. Adjustments are made for contracts that expire on non-business days. Once a contract has expired, Contract 1 for the remainder of the month is the second following month. Contract 2–4 are for delivery months following Contract 1 (www.eia.gov). We let RSW and RSB denote real spot price of WTI and Brent. Futures prices corresponding to Contract 1–4 are denoted RF1, RF2, RF3, and RF4, respectively. Oil rig count is denoted RIGS and is the number of oil producing rigs in the US (onshore and offshore). Total US oil production is denoted PROD.

A first step in traditional empirical analysis of time series, and commodity prices in particular, is to determine whether or not the series is stationary. The importance of this step cannot be overstated as econometric modeling may otherwise be subject to spurious regression problem (Stock and Watson 2007). In order to evaluate the univariate properties of RSW, RSB, RF1, RF2, RF3, and RF4 we employed several popular unit root tests including augmented Dickey-Fuller (Dickey and Fuller 1979, 1981), Dickey-Fuller GLS/ERS (Elliott et al. 1996), Phillips and Perron (1988), and the KPSS (1992). Since the tests are well known, we do not provide the empirical specifications here and instead simply report our conclusion. Our results are consistent with the vast literature on time series properties of real oil prices and indicate that both real spot and real futures prices are non-stationary and integrated of order one. However, we do not rule out time-varying volatility, the possibility of breaks in the data series, nor the possibility of periodically collapsing bubbles, which is the subject of more recent studies (Ewing and Malik 2017; Gronwald 2016).

Figure 21.1 plots real spot prices of oil over time. As expected, RSW and RSB generally follow similar patterns with some notable exceptions such as in 2011–2014 when the disparity was quite wide. Also, to a smaller degree, in periods of heightened volatility such as those experienced in the early 1990s and early 2000s and then again after the price drop in June 2014. Given the finding that these series appear to be non-stationary, we formally test for the property of cointegration. A great deal of prior research has focused on testing for the existence of cointegration among commodity prices as this has implications for econometric model specification and forecasting (Banerjee et al. 1993). The general finding is that oil prices are cointegrated such that

Figure 21.1 Real WTI (RSW) and Brent (RSB) spot prices

perturbations in one or more series die out over time and that the respective series are restricted from drifting "too far" apart from one another over time (Serletis and Banack, 1990). Of course, the notion of how long it takes for the disequilibrium to be erased and just how far is "too far" is still open to debate. Consequently, much research has incorporated error-correction modeling with emphasis on speed-of-adjustment coefficients and determining whether or not one variable "Granger causes" another variable (Bekiros and Diks 2008). Many new studies have incorporated a variety of methods to address these issues and with somewhat mixed results. We utilize the standard Johansen (1991) multivariate (system) method for testing for cointegration and find evidence that spot prices are cointegrated. The Johansen cointegration procedure determines if a long-run relationship exists among a set of time series variables. The vector autoregressive (VAR) model is given by:

$$\Delta X_t = \Gamma_1 X_{t-1} + \ldots + \Gamma_{k-1} \Delta X_{t-k-1} - \Pi X_{t-k} + \varepsilon_t$$

where X is the vector of variables under examination; k denotes the number of lags; ε is a vector of white noise error terms; $\Gamma_1 = -I + \Pi_1 + \ldots + \Pi_i$; and $\Pi = I - \Pi_1 - \ldots - \Pi_k$. The long-run relationship among the variables is contained in the p $\times$ p Π matrix. If the Π matrix has rank zero, r = 0, then the variables in X are nonstationary, implying the absence of cointegration. If r $<$ p, then there are r nonzero cointegrating vectors among the variables in X and p $-$ r common stochastic trends. We can factor the Π matrix into $\alpha\beta'$ where $\propto$ is a p $\times$ r matrix of the vector error correction parameters and β represents a p $\times$ r matrix of cointegrating vectors. The null hypothesis that the number of cointegrating vectors is r against the alternative r $+$ 1 is examined using the maximum eigenvalue test (λ_{max}). The null hypothesis that the number of cointegrating vectors is less than or equal to r against a general alternative is examined using the trace test (λ_{trace}). We find that there is a cointegrating relationship among RSW and real futures prices. In terms of the latter, when all five series are entered in the system we find evidence of up to four cointegrating vectors which is generally taken to mean that the long run relationship among these variables is particularly stable. Figure 21.2 provides a plot of RSW and the four futures prices. Rather than plotting these variables separately, the series are shown together to emphasize

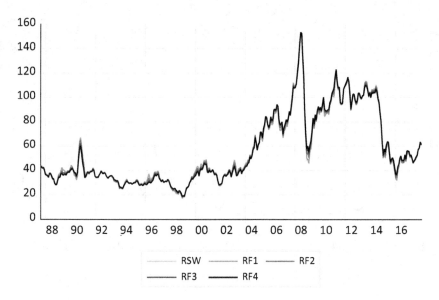

Figure 21.2   Real WTI spot and futures prices

the relative "closeness" of movements over time. In fact, the notion of a stable long-run relationship is strongly evident in the graph, as well. We interpret this finding as being consistent
with the notion Hamilton (2009) put forth, namely, that spot prices may help to predict futures
prices. As noted above, this allows for and may even encourage the development of commodity
futures speculation. In terms of energy policy, the notion of scarcity rent may be used for decisions pertaining to investment tax credits, production incentives, and/or determining appropriate
depletion allowances.

4   Oil prices and upstream activity

Following the oil price boom of 2012 to mid-2014 and the interest in unconventional oil exploration and development, there has been interest in studying the relationship between oil prices
and upstream activity (Apergis, Ewing and Payne 2017). Recent studies have documented the
increases in new well efficiency (Apergis, Ewing and Payne 2016a) and modeled relationships
among oil prices, interest rates, production, and even energy ratios such as reserve life (Ewing
2017; Apergis, Ewing and Payne 2016b). Given these findings, we turn our attention to real spot
and futures prices and traditional measures of upstream activity, namely, oil rig count and crude
oil production.

Figures 21.3 and 21.4 provide plots of RSW and RF4, with values shown on left axis, and
either RIGS (Figure 21.3) or PROD (Figure 21.4) shown on the right axis. A casual review
indicates that rig count follows real prices generally with a lag. Moreover, drops in rig counts
following oil price declines appear greater in magnitude than increases in rig counts following
oil price upswings. Clearly, this is consistent with the technical aspects of oil exploration and
production and capital requirements associated with drilling. Perhaps what is more interesting
is how this relationship may be changing or intensifying in recent years and cycles. Specifically,
as new rigs have become more efficient (as well as the introduction of many new and improved
production technologies), production has either rebounded more quickly or remained higher

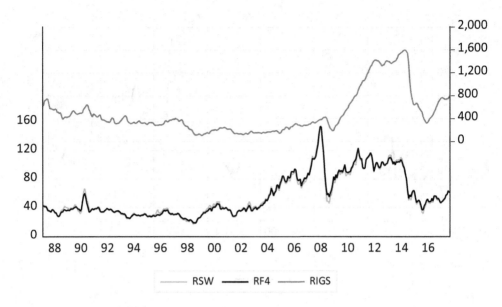

Figure 21.3 Oil rig count, real WTI spot and futures prices

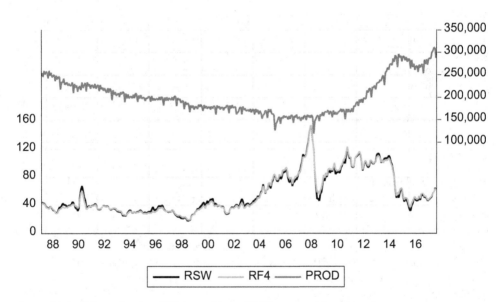

Figure 21.4 Oil production (BBL/month), real WTI spot and futures prices

(relative to the past), even with less price recovery. Some reasons associated with this phenomena are given in Ewing et al. (2015) and include a number of drilling/completion technology trends such as horizontal drilling, slick-water fracking, multiple well pads, and multi-zone completions, to name a few. Here, we repeat our empirical analysis and examine the univariate and multivariate properties concerning RSW, RF4 with RIGS and then with PROD. As before, unit root testing suggest that all series are nonstationary and require first-differencing to render the series stationary. There is some evidence that both rig count and production exhibit more dependency on past observations than prices. However, we proceed to test for long run stable relationship using the cointegration methodology of Johansen. We find strong evidence of a cointegrating relationship among spot, futures, and production but only weak evidence of this type of relationship among spot, futures, and rig count. The findings regarding price and upstream activity represent a relatively new but potentially important direction for future research and inquiry.

5 Concluding remarks

Pricing in today's market is very transparent compared to the past. The next development is likely to be a transparent pricing mechanism in Asia, particularly as the structure of liquefied natural gas (LNG) contracts change and the market develops for US crude and gas exports to that region. Recently, China debuted a crude oil futures contract on the Shanghai Futures Exchange (ShFE) denominated in yuan. The 25 March 2018 launch is viewed as an opportunity for China, the largest energy consuming nation, to have more control over crude oil pricing, especially as it exerts its influence in global trade.

Over time the oil market and the relevant benchmark prices have responded to structural changes in the industry. For example, beginning in early 2011, with increased US domestic crude oil, (via the shale revolution), and lack of adequate infra-structure to get crude oil to refining centers, the (monthly) real Brent/WTI spread widened significantly to a high of $29.97 per barrel by November 2011 (Figure 21.5). Since late 2015, when Congress lifted the 40-year old crude oil export ban, coupled with significant pipeline investment (particularly in the Permian Basin), the Brent/WTI price differential has narrowed. Going forward, the price gap between Brent/WTI will continue to fluctuate. A wider Brent/WTI differential makes US domestic crude oil attractive for export, but a narrowing of the price gap will act as a ceiling on US crude oil exports. Recent improvements to handle larger vessels at the Louisiana Offshore Oil Port (LOOP) and continued pipeline projects are likely to contribute to the continued appeal of domestic crude oil. Given these observations and the summary of price patterns described here, we expect a fruitful avenue of future research will be to explore oil prices with midstream and upstream operations.

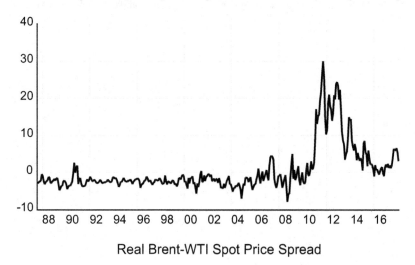

Real Brent-WTI Spot Price Spread

Figure 21.5   Spread between real Brent and real WTI prices (per BBL)

References

Apergis, N., B. Ewing and J. Payne (2016a) Persistence in New-Well Oil Production per Rig across U.S. Regions: Evidence from Modified Panel Ratio Tests. *Energy Sources, Part A: Recovery, Utilization, and Environmental Effects*, 38(14), 2058–2064.

Apergis, N., B. Ewing and J. Payne (2016b) Oil Reserve Life and the Influence of Crude Oil Prices: An Analysis of Texas Reserves. *Energy Economics*, 55, 266–271.

Apergis, N., B. Ewing and J. Payne (2017) Well Service Rigs, Operating Rigs, and Commodity Prices. *Energy Sources, Part B: Economics, Planning, and Policy*, 12(9), 800–807.

Banerjee, A., J. Dolado, J. Galbraith and D. Hendry (1993) *Co-Integration, Error-Correction, and the Econometric Analysis of Non-Stationary Data*. Oxford University Press. New York.

Bekiros, S. and C. Diks (2008) The Relationship between Crude Oil Spot and Futures Prices: Cointegration, Linear and Nonlinear Causality. *Energy Economics*, 30, 2673–2685.

Dickey, D. A. and W. A. Fuller (1979) Distribution of the Estimators for Autoregressive Time Series with a Unit Root. *Journal of the American Statistical Society*, 75, 427–431.

Dickey, D. A. and W. A. Fuller (1981) Likelihood Ratio Statistics for Autoregressive Time Series with a Unit Root. *Econometrica*, 49(4), 1057–1071.

Elliott, G., T. J. Rothenberg and J. H. Stock (1996) Efficient Tests for an Autoregressive Unit Root. *Econometrica*, 64, 813–836.

Ewing, B. (2017) Discoveries of Proved Reserves and the Influence of Oil Price and Interest Rate. *Energy Sources, Part B: Economics, Planning, and Policy*, 12(5), 452–459.

Ewing, B. and F. Malik (2017) Modelling Asymmetric Volatility in Oil Prices under Structural Breaks. *Energy Economics*, 63, 227–233.

Ewing, B., M. Watson, T. McInturff and R. McInturff (2015) The Economic Impact of the Permian Basin's Oil and Gas Industry. In Uddameri, V., Morse, A., and Tindle, K. J (Eds.) *Hydraulic Fracturing Impacts and Technologies: A Multidisciplinary Perspective*. Boca Raton: Taylor and Francis Group, CRC Press.

Gronwald, M. (2016) Explosive Oil Prices. *Energy Economics*, 60, 1–5.

Hamilton, J. (2009) Understanding Crude Oil Prices. *The Energy Journal*, 30(2), 179–206.

Johansen, S. (1991) Estimation and Hypothesis Testing of Cointegration Vectors in Gaussian Vector Autoregressive Models. *Econometrica*, 59, 1551–1580.

Kwiatkowski, D., P. Phillips, P. Schmidt and Y. Shin (1992) Testing the Null Hypothesis of Stationarity against the Alternative of a Unit Root: How Sure Are We That Economic Time Series Have a Unit Root? *Journal of Econometrics*, 54, 159–178.

Phillips, P. and P. Perron (1988) Testing for a Unit Root in Time Series Regression. *Biometrika*, 75, 335–346.

Serletis, A. and D. Banack (1990) Market Efficiency and Cointegration: An Application to Petroleum Market. *Review of Futures Markets*, 9, 372–385.

Stock, J. and M. Watson (2007) *Introduction to Econometrics*. 2nd edition. Pearson. Boston, MA.

22

Oil and stock prices

Perry Sadorsky

1 Introduction

Between December 1973 and January 1974, US spot oil prices rose from $4.31 per barrel to $10.11 per barrel.[1] This 135% increase was the result of an Arab embargo on oil flowing to Western countries. The United States and many other Western countries were major importers of Middle East oil, and any oil supply disruption was immediately transmitted to the price of oil. Before the decade was out, the oil market received another shock in 1979 when the Shah of Iran was overthrown. Oil prices increased 149% between April 1979 and April 1980. The 1970s are often characterized as a decade of stagflation: a term used to describe slow economic growth and high inflation. This created a whole new research area as researchers began to study the impact of oil prices on the macroeconomy. Hamilton (1983) is one of the first and most influential papers on this topic. Motivated by the oil price shocks of the 1970s and using recently developed vector autoregression (VAR) techniques, Hamilton investigated the relationship between oil prices and several important macroeconomic and financial variables. The focus was mostly on which variables have a Granger causal impact on oil prices, but there is one regression that tests whether stock prices as measured by the Dow Jones Industrial Average impact oil prices (they don't). Hamilton's paper became the basis for many empirical papers further investigating the impact of oil prices on the macroeconomy (Barsky and Kilian, 2004). Following the publication of Hamilton's paper, a new area of research developed that specifically looked at the relationship between oil prices and stock prices. Seminal papers include Chen et al. (1986), Huang et al. (1996), Jones and Kaul (1996), and Sadorsky (1999). The empirical approach used in these papers was either a multi-factor model or VARs.

Before 2000 there was a small number of papers published on the relationship between oil prices and stock prices. The literature on the relationship between oil prices and stock prices has exploded over the past 15 years. There are now thousands of papers published on this topic. Figure 22.1 shows the index of Google Scholar hits per year for the search terms "oil" and "stock prices" for the years 1997 to 2017.[2] The base year of 1997 is set to 100. The base year value for 1997 is 657. Patents and citations are excluded from the search. There has been a sevenfold increase in these search terms over the past 20 years, which demonstrates the popularity of the topic.

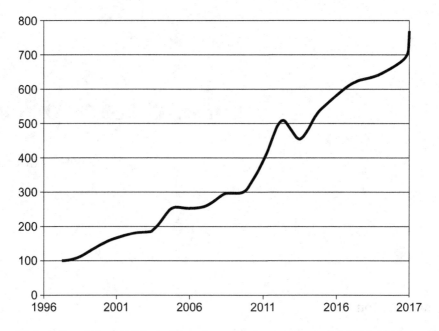

Figure 22.1 Index of Google Scholar hits per year for the search terms "oil" and "stock prices". The base year 1997 is set to 100. The base year value for 1997 is 657. Patents and citations are excluded from the search.

The purpose of this survey is to present the conceptual framework for how and why oil prices affect stock prices and stock markets and present examples of the main empirical approaches to the analysis. The survey is selective in the choice of papers discussed and not meant to be a comprehensive review of every paper published on this voluminous topic. Papers selected for inclusion were mostly based on their citations in Google Scholar keyword searches. This process of selecting papers tends to favor older papers with more citations. There is also a large literature looking at volatility spillovers between oil and equities, but this topic is covered in Chapter 23 in this handbook.

The chapter is organized as follows. The following section sets out the main conceptual framework and empirical approaches for measuring the relationship between stock prices and oil prices. These approaches include multi-factor models, VARs, SVARs, switching models, copulas, and wavelets. The chapter concludes with a summary and some important implications for researchers looking for new avenues of research.

2   Conceptual framework

Stock prices can be expressed as the expected present value of discounted future cash flows (Huang et al., 1996; Jones and Kaul, 1996). Oil prices can impact stock prices through the effect that oil prices have on cash flow and the discount rate. Energy along with capital, labor, and raw materials are the basic inputs into the production of most goods and services. Higher oil prices affect the costs of production because almost all consumer goods and services use oil or products refined from oil in the production, transportation, or distribution of goods. For non-oil producing companies higher oil prices, in the absence of complete substitution among the other factors of production, increase the costs of production and dampen cash flow. Higher oil prices can also impact the discount factor used in the present value calculation. Higher oil prices are often indicative of inflationary pressure and central banks respond to higher inflation by increasing interest rates. Higher interest rates increase the denominator in the stock price equation, pushing stock prices down. Interest rates affect the cost of financing, the cost of margin debt, and the risk return tradeoff between financial assets. Since stock prices are inversely correlated with interest rates, higher interest rates reduce stock prices. For oil producing companies, higher oil prices are expected to lead to higher stock prices because higher oil prices increase the cash flows of oil producers. At the stock market country level, higher oil prices reduce stock prices provided there are more oil consuming companies than oil producing companies.

In the early literature the changes in oil prices were often associated with an oil shock and many papers refer to changes in oil prices as oil shocks. This is not technically correct, because a change in oil prices need not be large enough in magnitude to be labeled a shock. More recently, however, Hamilton (2003, 1996) has offered some constructive insights on how to actually measure an oil shock. For example, one approach to measuring an oil price shock is to compare the current price to the maximum value over the past year. This approach is particularly useful when working with monthly or quarterly data sets. This distinction between changes in oil prices and oil shocks is now becoming more apparent in the literature.

3   The multi-factor model approach

Multi-factor models relate stock returns to the returns of other important factors that may influence stock returns (Chen et al., 1986). For example, a two-factor model relating stock returns to market returns and oil price returns can be written as follows (Faff and Brailsford, 1999):

$$r_t = \beta_0 + \beta_1 R_t + \beta_2 o_t + e_t \tag{22.1}$$

Where r_t is the return on an asset, R_t is the return on the market index, and o_t is the return on oil prices. A statistically significant estimated coefficient on the oil price return variable provides evidence for oil returns impacting stock returns. Notice that if there are no oil returns and stock returns are expressed as excess returns, then Equation (22.1) is the capital asset pricing model (CAPM). The multi-factor model is related to arbitrage pricing theory (APT) (Hamao, 1988) and in some specifications the market return may be omitted. The model in Equation (22.1) can be estimated for company stock returns, industry stock returns, or country stock returns using daily, weekly, or monthly data. Regression specification tests can be carried out to check the adequacy of the model fit. In some cases, it is desirable to include GARCH terms in the error term. Equation (22.1) can be extended to include asymmetric oil prices, time varying parameters, or quantile effects. The multi-factor model approach is widely used in studying the relationship between oil prices and stock returns. The remaining paragraphs of this section provide examples of using multi-factor models to investigate the impact of oil price changes on stock returns. Results are presented for analysis at the national level, industry level, and company level.

Chen et al. (1986), in a seminal paper, use US monthly data from 1953 to 1983 to estimate several multi-factor models for US stock returns. They find the oil factor is not statistically significant. Hamao (1988) following the approach of Chen et al. (1986) finds that oil returns are not a priced risk factor for Japanese equities. Kaneko and Lee (1995), however, use more recent data and find that oil price returns are a priced factor for Japanese equities. Jones and Kaul (1996) use quarterly data to test whether oil is a priced risk factor for equities in Canada, Japan, the United Kingdom, and the United States. Several different econometric specifications are estimated where real stock returns are related to current and lag values of oil price changes and future changes in industrial production. In simple specifications that relate stock returns to current and lagged oil price changes, they find that oil price changes have a negative impact on real stock returns in all four countries and the impact varies considerably across the countries. These simple specifications do not, however, control for other important market effects like future expected cash flows and a deeper analysis is conducted. Granger causality tests are used to determine whether stock markets are rational or they overreact to new information. Canadian and US stock markets are rational in their reaction to oil shocks because the impact of oil shocks on stock markets in these countries can be accounted for through the impact of current and expected future real cash flows. For Japan and the United Kingdom, however, the effect of oil prices on stock markets cannot be explained using changes in future cash flows or other financial variables. Basher and Sadorsky (2006) study the impact of oil prices on stock returns in 21 emerging market economies. They use a multi-factor model that incorporates conditional and unconditional risk factors. Additional risk factors like total risk, skewness, and kurtosis are also studied. In most countries an increase in oil price returns has a negative impact on stock returns. There is also some evidence of nonlinear effects. Nandha and Hammoudeh (2007) study the relationship between oil risk and stock returns in 15 Asia-Pacific countries. The Philippines and South Korea are the only countries with significant oil price risk when stock returns are measured in local currency. No countries exhibit significant oil price risk when stock returns are measured in US dollars. Asteriou and Bashmakova (2013) examine the impact of oil prices on the stock markets of ten Central and Eastern European countries. Using multi-factor models and daily data from 1999 to 2007, they find that oil beta is negative and statistically significant. There is some evidence of asymmetric oil price effects. Narayan and Gupta (2015) use predictive regressions to explore the relationship between stock prices and oil prices over the past 150 years and find that oil prices do help to predict stock prices in a statistically significant manner.

A number of papers have investigated the impact of oil prices on stock prices using industry sector data. Faff and Brailsford (1999) study the impact of oil prices on Australian equity industry sectors. They estimate a two-factor model (market returns, oil prices) over the period 1983 to 1996. They find a significant positive relationship between an oil factor and oil and gas industry stock returns. They find a significant negative relationship between an oil factor and stock returns in the paper and packaging and the transport industries. Sadorsky (2001) uses a multi-factor model to investigate the impact of oil prices, exchange rates, and interest rates on the stock prices of Canadian oil and gas companies over the period April 1983 to April 1999. He finds that increases in oil prices increase the stock returns of Canadian oil and natural gas stocks. Building on Sadorsky (2001) and Boyer and Filion (2007) add company specific factors to the multi-factor model and also find that oil price appreciation increases the stock returns of Canadian oil and gas stocks. El-Sharif et al. (2005) investigate the impact of oil price returns on UK equity returns. They find that oil price increases increase the return to UK oil and gas stocks. For other industries like banking, transportation, and computers, the relationship is weak. Nandha and Faff (2008) investigate the impact of oil price changes on the stock returns of 35 global industry indices over the period April 1983 to September 2005. They find that oil price increases have a negative impact on equity returns for all of the industries studied except mining and oil and gas. Arouri and Nguyen (2010) model the relationship between the stock returns of European industry sectors and oil prices using weekly data for the period January 1998 to November 2008. They find that European industry stock returns and oil prices are weakly correlated and the reaction of stock returns to oil prices varies considerably by industry. There is also some evidence of asymmetric interactions between oil changes and stock returns. Gogineni (2010) uses daily data spanning 1986 to 2007 to investigate the impact of oil price changes on

US stock returns using a multi-factor model. Using a large data set, he finds that oil price changes do impact daily stock returns (as measured by the value-weighted NYSE/Nasdaq/AMEX index) for the full sample and the first sub-sample (1986 to 1997) but not over the second sub-sample (1997 to 2007). Further investigation at the industry level reveals that oil intensive industries like petroleum and manufacturing and some other industries like financial services and insurance are impacted by oil price changes. Industry estimates of cost side and demand side dependence on oil are provided. Arouri (2011) uses GARCH models estimated on weekly data covering 1998 to 2010 to investigate the impact of oil price returns on stock returns for 12 European sectors. Results are presented showing the strength of the relationship varies across sectors and in addition there is evidence of asymmetries. Elyasiani et al. (2011) used daily data from December 1998 to December 2006 to analyze the impact of oil price changes on the stock returns of US sector stock returns. Empirical models are estimated using Fama-French factor models augmented with either oil price returns or oil price volatility. Nine of the 13 industry sectors studied are affected by either oil price changes or oil price volatility. The impact of oil prices on Gulf stock markets is investigated by Mohanty et al. (2011). They estimate multi-factor models for Bahrain, Kuwait, Qatar, Oman, Saudi Arabia, and the United Arab Emirates (UAE) using weekly data spanning June 2005 to December 2009. In addition to analysis at the country level, analysis is also conducted at the industry level. At the country level, oil price changes affect stock prices for all countries except Kuwait. At the industry level, oil price changes have a statistically significant impact on 12 of the 20 industries studied. Ramos and Veiga (2011) study the impact of oil price changes on oil and gas industry stock return in 34 countries. They find that oil is a priced risk factor and the impact is greatest in developed countries. Aloui et al. (2012) find that for a sample of 25 emerging economies, oil beta is significant and positive for moderately oil-dependent countries during bull markets and negative during bear markets. The largest net oil importing countries are not sensitive to oil beta regardless of the market phase. Broadstock et al. (2012) uses multi-factor models to explore the impact of oil prices on Chinese energy industry stock prices. Weekly data is used covering the period January 2000 to May 2011. A number of different multi-factor models are estimated over different sub-samples. They find the relationship between oil prices and stock prices is stronger after the 2008–2009 financial crises. They suggest that this result is because investors in the Chinese stock market are more sensitive to shocks in the world oil market. Ramos and Veiga (2013) find that oil price increases lead to increases in the stock markets of oil exporting countries. Asymmetric oil price effects are found for oil importing countries. Inchauspe et al. (2015) model renewable energy stock price returns using a multi-factor model. They allow for time variation in the estimated coefficients. The market return and technology stock prices exert a greater influence on renewable energy stock prices than do oil prices.

There are fewer studies that study the impact of oil prices on stock prices using company data. Al-Mudhaf and Goodwin (1993) use a two-factor model to investigate the impact of the oil risk factor on 29 NYSE oil companies. They find the oil price risk premium was very unstable. Sadorsky (2008) follows a large panel of US stocks over a 17-year period to study the impact that firm size has on the relationship between oil prices and stock prices. The relationship between oil prices and stock prices varies with firm size. The relationship is strongest for medium-sized firms. One possible explanation for this result is that medium-sized firms do not have the production efficiency and financial leverage of large firms, nor do medium-sized firms have the flexibility and responsiveness of small-sized firms. Demirer et al. (2015) use multi-factor models and firm level data from the Arab Gulf stock markets over the period March 2004 to March 2013 to test the significance of an oil price factor. The Fama-French size and book-to-market factors are included in the analysis. Stocks that are more sensitive to oil price changes yield higher returns.

Cross-sectional tests, however, do not reveal a significant oil price risk premium suggesting that other firm factors may adequately capture oil price effects. Gupta (2016) uses a large data set of company level data on oil and gas companies from 70 countries to investigate the impact of oil price shocks on these companies. He finds that oil price increases positively impact oil and gas stock returns. Firms located in oil producing countries are more sensitive to macroeconomic events and oil prices shocks. Firms in non-competitive industries are less affected by oil price shocks.

In summary, many of the existing studies that use a multi-factor model to study the impact of oil prices on stock prices find evidence supporting a statistically significant relationship between the two variables. For most countries or industries, higher oil prices dampen stock prices. Higher oil prices are beneficial for oil industry stock prices. Some research has investigated the asymmetric relationship between stock prices and oil prices, but so far the results are inconclusive. Recent developments in panel quantile regression techniques should be useful for further examining the relationship between stock prices and oil prices.

4   The VAR approach

Vector autoregressions (VARs) which date back to the 1970s are a natural extension of univariate autoregressive models. VARs are useful for modeling the dynamic interaction between variables. A VAR is a system of equations where each variable in the system is endogenous. Consider the following VAR.

$$y_t = c + A(L) y_{t-1} + \varepsilon_t, \tag{22.2}$$

In Equation (22.2), $\mathbf{y}$ is a vector with p variables, L is the maximum lag length and ε is a serially uncorrelated error term. VARs are useful for testing Granger causality, calculating impulse response functions and forecast error decomposition. The dynamic relationship between stock returns and oil price returns can be studied by using a VAR with these two variables. If omitted variables are a concern or a deeper analysis with other variables is needed than additional variables can be added. A good fitting VAR has serially uncorrelated errors and polynomial roots less than unity. A VAR model can be extended to a vector error correction model (VECM) when investigating specific cointegration relationships.

Most of the studies that use VAR to investigate the relationship between stock prices and oil prices use national stock market data. Sadorsky (1999) uses monthly data for the period 1947 to 1996 and VARs to determine the impact that oil prices have on real US stock returns. The basic model includes real stock returns and changes in industrial production, interest rates, and oil prices. There is evidence that oil prices and oil price volatility impact stock returns. There is also evidence that after 1986 oil prices movements explain a larger fraction of stock return forecast error variance than do interest rates. As US monetary policy has become more transparent and predictable, its impact on stock prices has diminished in relationship to sudden changes in oil prices. Papapetrou (2001) uses a VAR to investigate the dynamic relationship between stock prices, oil prices, interest rates, economic activity, and employment in Greece over the period 1989 to 1999. There is evidence that oil prices affect real economic activity, employment and stock prices. Hammoudeh and Li (2005) use vector-error correction models (VECMs) and multi-factor models to explore the dynamic relationship between oil prices and stock prices in Mexico, Norway, and US oil and transportation industries. They find that increases in oil price changes increase stock returns for the countries and industries studied. In other words, stock markets comprised of oil producing companies increase with increases in oil prices. Systematic risk has a larger impact on stock returns than does oil price risk. Hammoudeh and Choi (2006) estimate VECMs using weekly data to investigate the impact of oil prices, US interest rates, and the S&P 500 on Gulf Cooperation Council (GCC) member stock returns. US oil prices and stock prices have no direct impact on GCC stock prices. Impulse response functions do reveal that oil prices impact GCC stock prices. Maghyereh and Al-Kandari (2007) use nonlinear cointegration techniques to test the relationship between oil prices and stock prices in Gulf stock markets. There is evidence of non-linear cointegration between stock prices and oil prices in Gulf countries. Park and Ratti (2008) investigate the impact of oil prices on stock prices in the United States and Europe over the period 1986 to 2005. They find that oil prices have a statistically significant impact on stock returns either contemporaneously or within the following month. For oil exporter Norway, an increase in oil prices leads to an increase in stock returns. For European countries, increases in oil price volatility have a negative impact on stock returns. Cong et al. (2008) study the impact of oil prices on stock returns in China. They find that oil prices do have statistically significant impacts on stock returns in manufacturing and oil companies but do not have a statistically significant impact on stock returns in other industries. Oil price shocks have a larger impact on manufacturing stock returns than interest rates. Miller and Ratti (2009) study the long-run relationship between the world oil price and OECD stock markets over the period January 1971 to March 2008. Using VECMs that allow for structural breaks, they find evidence of a cointegrating relationship between oil prices and stock markets. Evidence of a negative relationship between oil prices and stock markets is found in the early part of the data set but after 1999 this relationship weakens considerably. Filis (2010) studies the dynamic relationship between consumer prices, industrial production, stock prices, and oil prices in Greece using VECMs to study the data in levels and VARS to study the cyclical components. Cyclical components are extracted using the Hodrick-Prescott filter. The cyclical analysis shows that oil prices have a significant negative impact on stock prices. Arouri et al. (2011) use VAR-GARCH models to study the relationship between oil prices and the stock prices of Gulf Cooperation Council countries over the period 2005 to 2010. They find that oil price returns have a strong positive impact on the stock returns of Bahrain, Oman, and Qatar. The impact of oil prices and oil price volatility on stock prices in South Korea are studied by Masih et al. (2011). They use a VECM with real stock returns, real oil prices, oil price volatility, interest rates, and economic activity (measured using industrial production). They find that oil prices and oil price volatility both have an impact on stock returns with oil price volatility having the largest impact. A linear VECM is preferred over a two state Markov-switching model. Arouri and Rault (2012) study the impact of oil prices on Gulf stock markets using bootstrap cointegration techniques and seemingly unrelated regression (SUR). There is evidence of cointegration between stock prices and oil prices. The results from SUR indicate that oil price increases have a positive impact on stock prices for all countries except Saudi Arabia. Using VARs, Lee et al. (2012) do not find much evidence that oil prices impact composite stock indexes in the G7 countries. At the sectoral level, however, there is evidence that oil prices impact stock prices in the information and technology, consumer staples, financials, utilities and transportation sectors. Cunado and Perez de Gracia (2014) analyze the impact of oil shocks on 12 European stock markets. Several different specifications for oil shocks are used. Evidence shows that oil shocks impact stock prices and this result is robust to different measures of oil price shocks.

There are several studies that use VARs to analyze the stock price–oil price relationship at the sector level. Huang et al. (1996) use VARs to investigate the dynamic relationship between oil futures prices and US stock prices. They find that oil futures prices do lead petroleum stock prices, but there is little evidence to support the hypothesis that oil prices lead stock prices in other industries. Ciner (2001) revisits the Huang et al. (1996) paper and suggests that their failure to find a strong relationship between oil price changes and stock returns is because they only considered linear tests for causality. Using daily data he finds evidence of nonlinear causality between oil prices and the S&P 500. The relationship is strongest in the 1990s. Henriques and Sadorsky (2008) explore the relationship between the stock prices of alternative energy companies, technology companies, and oil prices. Alternative energy companies are those that are mostly focused on renewable energy generation. They find that technology stock prices have a greater impact on alternative energy stock prices than do oil prices. This result is plausible because the success of alternative energy companies is often closely aligned with the success of technology to reduce the cost of producing alternative energy. Kumar et al. (2012) uses VARs to study the relationship between the stock prices of clean energy companies, technology stock prices, oil prices, and carbon dioxide prices. They find that oil prices and technology stock prices impact the stock prices of clean energy companies. They do not, however, find much support for carbon dioxide prices impacting clean energy stock prices.

Most of the literature that uses VARs to study the dynamic relationship between oil prices and stock prices finds evidence that oil prices impact stock prices. The standard VAR model can be extended in many ways including a structural interpretation (the topic of the next section), time varying parameters, and a Bayesian approach. Some of these newer approaches to modeling the oil price–stock price relationship are now just entering the literature.

5 The structural VAR (SVAR) approach

Structural VARs (SVARs) build on the VAR framework by incorporating structural relationships between the variables. $\mathbf{A}_0$ is the contemporaneous matrix, $\mathbf{A}(L)$ is the sequence of autoregressive coefficient matrices and ε is the uncorrelated structural error term.

$$A_0 y_t = \alpha + A(L) y_{t-1} + \varepsilon_t \tag{22.3}$$

The reduced form of the structural model can be obtained by pre-multiplying Equation (22.3) through by A_0^{-1}.

$$y_t = \beta + B(L) y_{t-1} + e_t \tag{22.4}$$

For example, $e_t = A_0^{-1} \varepsilon_t$. The structural disturbances ε_t can be obtained by imposing identifying restrictions on $\mathbf{A}_0$.

The SVAR approach to modeling the impact of oil shocks on stock prices is mostly derived from the work of Kilian (2009) who models oil shocks as originating from oil supply, global economic demand, or oil specific. In this framework oil shocks can have different impacts on economic activity depending upon their origin. This approach is a considerable improvement over previous literature that uses changes in oil prices to measure oil price shocks. Using this approach, Kilian and Park (2009) investigate the impact of oil shocks on US stock returns. They find that the impact of oil shocks on stock returns depends upon whether the shocks are demand or supply shocks. Demand and supply shocks account for 22% of the long run variation in US real stock returns. Impulse responses show that oil specific demand shocks have a negative and statistically significant impact on US stock returns. The Kilian and Park (2009) approach is very unique, innovative, and useful in that it allows for oil shocks to be characterized as originating from either the demand side or supply side. This facilitates a much more detailed analysis of the impact of oil shocks on stock returns than what would be obtained by only looking at oil prices.

Apergis and Miller (2009) uses the Kilian (2009) and Kilian and Park (2009) approach to identifying oil shocks to explore the impact of oil shocks on stock returns in eight countries (Australia, Canada, France, Germany, Italy, Japan, the United Kingdom, and the United States). The analysis uses a two-step procedure. In the first step, the structural oil shocks are estimated from a three-variable SVAR. In the second stage, the structural oil shocks are combined with stock returns to investigate the impact of oil shocks on stock returns using a VAR. They find that structural oil shocks do have a significant impact on stock returns but the magnitude is small.

Bjornland (2009) analyzes the impact of oil price shocks on stock returns in Norway using a SVAR model. A 10% increase in oil prices increases stock returns by 2.5%. The results are robust to different specifications of the oil price shock (linear or non-linear). For Norway, higher oil prices increase demand and wealth. Basher et al. (2012) use a SVAR to examine the dynamic relationship between the oil market, exchange rates, and emerging economy stock returns over the period 1988 to 2008. Impulse response functions are calculated using standard methods as well as orthogonal projections. They find that oil price shocks dampen emerging market stock prices and US dollar exchange rates in the short run. In addition, evidence is presented showing that an increase in emerging market stock prices increase oil prices. Wang et al. (2013) use SVAR to explore the impact of oil price shocks on oil importing countries (China, France, Germany, India, Italy, Japan, Korea, the United Kingdom, and the United States) and oil exporting countries (Canada, Saudi Arabia, Kuwait, Mexico, Norway, Russia, and Venezuela). The stock market response to oil shocks depends upon whether the country is an oil importer or oil exporter. The impact of oil shocks on stock markets also depends upon whether the shock is a demand or supply shock. Oil price shocks explain approximately 20% to 30% of stock returns. Positive demand and precautionary demand shocks have a higher degree of co-movement among the stock markets in oil exporting countries. Kang et al. (2015) use a time-varying parameter VAR to study the impact of structural oil price shocks on US stock market returns. Structural oil shocks account for 25.7% of the long-run variation in stock returns. The contribution of oil supply shocks has decreased across time while oil market shocks increased across time. Global economic activity shocks have increased across time.

SVARs add structure to VARs by imposing zero restrictions on the contemporaneous relationship between the variables of interest. The Kilian and Park (2009) approach is useful for analyzing the impact of oil supply, global economic demand, and oil specific shocks on stock prices. Another approach to imposing structure on VARs is to use sign restrictions. Gupta and Modise (2013) use this approach to analyze the impact of oil shocks on stock returns in South Africa. They find that oil supply shocks contribute more to real stock return variability than oil demand shocks.

6 Switching approaches

The relationship between oil prices and stock prices may be characterized by distinct periods of high or low returns or high or low volatility. Stock markets, for example, are often characterized by bull and bear regimes. Threshold autoregression, smooth transition, and Markov-switching models are popular ways of modeling regime switching in economics and finance.

Huang et al. (2005) use multivariate threshold models to study the impact of oil price changes and oil price volatility on real stock returns for Canada, Japan, and the United States. Many studies characterize asymmetric oil price changes as either non-negative or negative. This is rather arbitrary and does not allow for deeper nonlinear relationships or threshold values that vary by country. This paper finds oil price change threshold values between 2.58% and 2.70%. Oil price changes have greater explanatory power on stock returns than oil price volatility.

Aloui and Jammazi (2009) use a Markov-switching EGARCH model to investigate the relationship between equity returns in France, Japan, and the United Kingdom and oil shocks. They find that oil price shocks affect the volatility of stock returns and the probability of transition between regimes. Chen (2010) uses a Markov-switching model to determine the impact that oil price shocks have on the probability of being in a bear stock market. Oil price shocks are measured in several different ways including: changes in oil prices, oil price increases, net oil price increases, and scaled oil price increases. Evidence is presented showing that higher oil prices increase the probability of switching from a bull market to a bear market. Narayan and Sharma (2011) investigate the impact of oil price changes on the stock returns of 560 US companies. They find the impact of oil price changes varies across industries. There is also evidence that oil prices impact stock returns with a lag effect. Further analysis using a threshold model shows that oil price effects vary by regime for 5 of the 14 industries studied. Similar to Sadorsky (2008) evidence is presented showing that the impact of oil prices on stock prices varies with firm size. Zhu et al. (2011) use a panel threshold cointegration approach to examine the relationship between oil shocks and stock markets for OECD and non-OECD panels over the period January 1995 to December 2009. Evidence of threshold cointegration is found and threshold error correction models are used to understand the asymmetric dynamic adjustment. Granger causality tests find evidence of bidirectional long-run causality between oil prices and stock prices. Naifar and Al Dohaiman (2013) use Markov switching techniques to investigate the nonlinear relationship between GCC stock returns oil volatility. Evidence is presented showing that for most countries the relationship between GCC stock market returns and OPEC oil market volatility is regime dependent. Mensi et al. (2014) use quantile regression techniques to study the impact of global macroeconomic factors on BRICS stock returns for the period September 1997 to September 2013. Evidence from quantile regressions is presented showing that US stock prices, oil prices and gold prices do have an impact on BRICS stock returns. Angelidis et al. (2015) use Markov-switching models to investigate the impact of oil shocks on US stock market returns and stock market volatility. Oil shocks are modeled as in Kilian (2009) using a SVAR. Probit models are used to relate the probability of being in the low volatility state in relationship to a set of explanatory variables that include oil shocks (supply, demand, and oil price), interest rates, dividend yields, unemployment, inflation rates, and default spreads. There is some evidence that oil shocks affect the transition from a low volatility state to a high volatility state.

Balcilar et al. (2015) use a Markov-switching vector error correction model and monthly data from 1859 to 2013 to investigate the impact of oil prices on stock prices. They find that the high volatility regime was more frequent before the Great Depression and after the 1973 oil price shock. The high volatility regime tends to occur more frequently when the economy is in a recession.

Switching approaches are useful ways to model the regime dependent relationship between stock prices and oil prices because stock prices are often characterized by bull market and bear market regimes. Most of this literature finds evidence for a regime dependent relationship between stock prices and oil prices.

7 Copula approaches

Copulas are used to model the dependence structure between random variables by coupling univariate marginal distributions into a joint multivariate distribution. More precisely, copulas separate the modeling of the dependence between assets from the modeling of their univariate marginal distributions. The main advantage of using copulas is that copulas can model many different types of correlations while standard measures of linear correlation like the widely used

Pearson correlation coefficient cannot. Copulas are useful in finance for modeling tail risk. Some examples of using copulas to model dependence between oil prices and stock prices are included below.

Nguyen and Bhatti (2012) use copulas to study the dynamic relationship between oil prices and stock prices in China and Vietnam. They find evidence of left tail dependence between oil prices and stock prices in Vietnam and evidence of right tail dependence between oil prices and stock prices in China. Aloui et al. (2013) use time-varying copulas to investigate the dynamic relationship between oil prices and stock prices in six Central and Eastern European countries (Bulgaria, Czech Republic, Hungary, Poland, Romania, and Slovenia). The daily data covers the period 1 December 2005 to 20 August 2012. There is evidence of dependence between oil and these stock markets implying a lack of diversification between these assets. The survival Gumbel copula is the best. There is strong lower tail dependence during financial crises. Zhu et al. (2014) use copulas to study the relationship between oil prices and stock prices for Asia-Pacific countries over the period 4 January 2000 to 30 March 2012. Overall, they find the dependence between oil prices and stock prices is weak but has increased after the 2008–2009 financial crisis. In the post-crisis period, the lower tail dependence is larger than the upper tail dependence except in Japan and Singapore. Sukcharoen et al. (2014) use copulas to study the dynamic relationship between oil prices and stock prices for a large number of countries. They create country specific stock market indices by removing the oil and gas sector. They find a weak dependence between oil prices and stock markets. In the case of Canada and the United States the dependence is larger. The dependence structure between oil prices and stock prices changed considerably after the introduction of the euro in 1999.

Most of the papers that use copulas to model the oil price–stock price relationship find evidence of tail risk. This is in itself not surprising because copulas are more sophisticated ways of conducting correlation analysis. There is a need to move beyond the establishment of tail risk to incorporate more practical implications of these results.

8 Wavelet approaches

Wavelet analysis is a frequency and time domain approach which traces its origins from Fourier analysis and spectral density analysis. Fourier analysis and spectral filtering methods impose strong restrictions on the data structure and in doing so lose information about the time dimension. By comparison, wavelets combine information from the time dimension and frequency dimension. Wavelet analysis facilitates studying data relationships at different time scales (typically categorized as short run to long run). Wavelets do not make strong assumptions about the data generating process. The wavelet approach has been used to investigate the relationship between oil prices and stock prices. Here are some examples of using wavelets to explore the relationship between oil prices and stock prices.

Jammazi and Aloui (2010) use wavelets to decompose stock prices and oil prices. Markov-switching models are then estimated using the decomposed data. Changes in crude oil prices have temporary impacts on the stock market volatility of France and the UK. The effects are stronger for Japan. Akoum et al. (2012) use wavelet coherence to study the relationship between oil prices and the stock prices of Bahrain, Kuwait, Oman, Qatar, Saudi Arabia, the UAE, Egypt, and Jordan over the period 2002–2011. Weekly data is used in the analysis. There is a lack of dependence between oil price changes and stock price returns in the short term. In the long term there is evidence of co-movement between oil price returns and stock returns. Market dependencies increased after 2007. Reboredo and Rivera-Castro (2014) use wavelet analysis to examine the relationship between oil prices and stock prices in Europe and the United States.

Results for the period 2000 to July 2008 indicate the oil price changes had no impact on stock returns. After July 2008, however, there is evidence of contagion and co-movement between oil prices and stock prices. Boubaker and Raza (2017) use wavelets to decompose the relationship between oil prices and stock prices for the BRICS countries. They find the co-movement between oil and stock prices increases with time scales. Over a time scale of less than two weeks the co-movement is weak. The strongest co-movement if found for longer time scales of 16 to 32 days. At these longer time scales, Brazil and South Africa show the greatest co-movement. Reboredo et al. (2017) use wavelets to study the relationship between oil prices and six different renewable energy stock indices. They find that the relationship is strongest in the long run. Non-linear causality was present at the higher frequencies while linear causality was present at the lower frequencies. Non-linear causality tests show causality running from renewable energy stock prices to oil prices.

Wavelet analysis shows that the relationship between oil prices and stock prices can depend upon the frequency. Wavelet techniques like copulas are incorporated into popular software like MATLAB and R and this has resulted in a proliferation of papers using these techniques to analyze the relationship between stock prices and oil prices. The next step is to use the results from these techniques to provide practical implications. For example, Khalfaoui et al. (2015) combine wavelets with GARCH models to estimate hedge ratios between oil prices and stock prices in the G7 countries.

9 Summary

This chapter provides a selective survey of the oil price and stock price literature. Growth in this topic has been substantial over the past 20 years with Google Scholar citations increasing some sevenfold between 1997 and 2018. Research investigating the impact that oil prices have on stock prices has used a number of different empirical approaches. The most common approaches are multi-factor models and VARs. Multi-factor models are easy to justify on a theoretical basis because they fit well within finance theory like APT. Multi-factor models are easy to estimate and can be extended to include asymmetric effects, time varying parameters and GARCH effects in the error term. VARs are attractive because they impose little or no structure on the dynamic relationship between the variables being investigated. Specific structure can be imposed though SVARs or sign restrictions. Switching models are useful in that they allow estimation of the transition from one state to another. Data-driven approaches like copulas and wavelets have increased in popularity. These approaches can be used to look at specifics of tail risk (copulas) or how the dynamics between stock prices and oil prices change in the time-frequency domain (wavelets). Copulas and wavelets are statistical techniques that can be used on their own or as a filtering tool whereby the filtered data can then be estimated using more conventional econometric techniques. Overall, there is a large literature showing that changes in oil prices affect stock returns. For oil consuming companies, positive oil price changes leads to lower stock returns. For oil producing companies, positive oil price changes leads to higher stock returns.

Looking forward there are several important factors to consider when conducting research on the topic of oil and stock prices. First, world energy intensity has been decreasing since 1990. Over this time period energy intensity in non-OECD countries, the world average, and OECD countries declined by 40%, 32%, and 28%, respectively.[3] Declining energy intensity implies that oil price changes will most likely have a lesser impact on economic activity and stock prices in the future. Second, countries that are currently heavily oriented towards manufacturing (like emerging markets) are the ones that are most likely to be affected by oil price changes. Third, the impact of oil prices on national stock markets depends upon whether a country is an oil exporter or oil importer. Fourth, new empirical techniques and combinations of existing techniques should help to further our understanding of this important topic. Analyzing data at different frequencies is also useful as is mixed frequency analysis. Fifth, the literature needs to move beyond testing relationships between oil prices and stock prices and instead focus more on practical implications like portfolio analysis, risk management, and hedging.

Acknowledgments

Thanks to an anonymous reviewer for helpful comments.

Notes

1 https://fred.stlouisfed.org/series/WTISPLC.
2 This search was conducted on 24 October 2018. The total number of citations from 1997 to 2017 is 53,329.
3 www.eia.gov/todayinenergy/detail.php?id=27032.

References

Akoum, I., Graham, M., Kivihaho, J., Nikkinen, J., Omran, M., 2012. Co-movement of oil and stock prices in the GCC region: A wavelet analysis. *Quarterly Review of Economics and Finance* 52, 385–394. doi:10.1016/j.qref.2012.07.005

Al-Mudhaf, A., Goodwin, T.H., 1993. Oil shocks and oil stocks: Evidence from the 1970s. *Applied Economics* 25, 181–190. doi:10.1080/00036849300000023

Aloui, C., Jammazi, R., 2009. The effects of crude oil shocks on stock market shifts behaviour: A regime switching approach. *Energy Economics* 31, 789–799. doi:10.1016/j.eneco.2009.03.009

Aloui, C., Nguyen, D.K., Njeh, H., 2012. Assessing the impacts of oil price fluctuations on stock returns in emerging markets. *Economic Modelling* 29, 2686–2695. doi:10.1016/j.econmod.2012.08.010

Aloui, R., Hammoudeh, S., Nguyen, D.K., 2013. A time-varying copula approach to oil and stock market dependence: The case of transition economies. *Energy Economics* 39, 208–221. doi:10.1016/j.eneco.2013.04.012

Angelidis, T., Degiannakis, S., Filis, G., 2015. US stock market regimes and oil price shocks. *Global Finance Journal* 28, 132–146. doi:10.1016/j.gfj.2015.01.006

Apergis, N., Miller, S.M., 2009. Do structural oil-market shocks affect stock prices? *Energy Economics* 31, 569–575. doi:10.1016/j.eneco.2009.03.001

Arouri, M.E.H., 2011. Does crude oil move stock markets in Europe? A sector investigation. *Economic Modelling* 28, 1716–1725. doi:10.1016/J.ECONMOD.2011.02.039

Arouri, M.E.H., Lahiani, A., Nguyen, D.K., 2011. Return and volatility transmission between world oil prices and stock markets of the GCC countries. *Economic Modelling* 28, 1815–1825. doi:10.1016/j.econmod.2011.03.012

Arouri, M.E.H., Nguyen, D.K., 2010. Oil prices, stock markets and portfolio investment: Evidence from sector analysis in Europe over the last decade. *Energy Policy* 38, 4528–4539. doi:10.1016/j.enpol.2010.04.007

Arouri, M.E.H., Rault, C., 2012. Oil prices and stock markets in GCC countries: Empirical evidence from panel analysis. *International Journal of Finance and Economics* 17, 242–253. doi:10.1002/ijfe.443

Asteriou, D., Bashmakova, Y., 2013. Assessing the impact of oil returns on emerging stock markets: A panel data approach for ten Central and Eastern European Countries. *Energy Economics* 38, 204–211. doi:10.1016/j.eneco.2013.02.011

Balcilar, M., Gupta, R., Miller, S.M., 2015. Regime switching model of US crude oil and stock market prices: 1859 to 2013. *Energy Economics* 49, 317–327. doi:10.1016/j.eneco.2015.01.026

Barsky, R.B., Kilian, L., 2004. Oil and the Macroeconomy Since the 1970s. *Journal of Economic Perspectives* 18, 115–134. doi:10.1257/0895330042632708

Basher, S.A., Haug, A.A., Sadorsky, P., 2012. Oil prices, exchange rates and emerging stock markets. *Energy Economics* 34, 227–240. doi:10.1016/j.eneco.2011.10.005

Basher, S.A., Sadorsky, P., 2006. Oil price risk and emerging stock markets. *Global Finance Journal* 17, 224–251. doi:10.1016/j.gfj.2006.04.001

Bjornland, H.C., 2009. Oil price shocks and stock market booms in an oil exporting country. *Scottish. Journal of Political Economy* 56, 232–254. doi:10.1111/j.1467-9485.2009.00482.x

Boubaker, H., Raza, S.A., 2017. A wavelet analysis of mean and volatility spillovers between oil and BRICS stock markets. *Energy Economics* 64, 105–117. doi:10.1016/j.eneco.2017.01.026

Boyer, M.M., Filion, D., 2007. Common and fundamental factors in stock returns of Canadian oil and gas companies. *Energy Economics* 29, 428–453. doi:10.1016/j.eneco.2005.12.003

Broadstock, D.C., Cao, H., Zhang, D., 2012. Oil shocks and their impact on energy related stocks in China. *Energy Economics* 34, 1888–1895. doi:10.1016/j.eneco.2012.08.008

Chen, N.-F., Roll, R., Ross, S.A., 1986. Economic Forces and the Stock Market. *Journal of Business.* 59, 383–403.

Chen, S.-S., 2010. Do higher oil prices push the stock market into bear territory? *Energy Economics* 32, 490–495. doi:10.1016/j.eneco.2009.08.018

Ciner, C., 2001. Energy shocks and financial markets: Nonlinear linkages. *Studies in Nonlinear Dynamics and Econometrics* 5, 203–212.

Cong, R.-G., Wei, Y.-M., Jiao, J.-L., Fan, Y., 2008. Relationships between oil price shocks and stock market: An empirical analysis from China. *Energy Policy* 36, 3544–3553. doi:10.1016/j.enpol.2008.06.006

Cunado, J., Perez de Gracia, F., 2014. Oil price shocks and stock market returns: Evidence for some European countries. *Energy Economics* 42, 365–377. doi:10.1016/j.eneco.2013.10.017

Demirer, R., Jategaonkar, S.P., Khalifa, A.A.A., 2015. Oil price risk exposure and the cross-section of stock returns: The case of net exporting countries. *Energy Economics* 49, 132–140. doi:10.1016/j.eneco.2015.02.010

El-Sharif, I., Brown, D., Burton, B., Nixon, B., Russell, A., 2005. Evidence on the nature and extent of the relationship between oil prices and equity values in the UK. *Energy Economics* 27, 819–830. doi:10.1016/j.eneco.2005.09.002

Elyasiani, E., Mansur, I., Odusami, B., 2011. Oil price shocks and industry stock returns. *Energy Economics* 33, 966–974. doi:10.1016/j.eneco.2011.03.013

Faff, R.W., Brailsford, T.J., 1999. Oil price risk and the Australian stock market. *Journal of. Energy Finance & Development* 4, 69–87. doi:10.1016/S1085-7443(99)00005-8

Filis, G., 2010. Macro economy, stock market and oil prices: Do meaningful relationships exist among their cyclical fluctuations? *Energy Economics* 32, 877–886. doi:10.1016/j.eneco.2010.03.010

Gogineni, S., 2010. Oil and the stock market: An industry level analysis. *Financial Review* 45, 995–1010. doi:10.1111/j.1540-6288.2010.00282.x

Gupta, K., 2016. Oil price shocks, competition, and oil & gas stock returns: Global evidence. *Energy Economics* 57, 140–153. doi:10.1016/j.eneco.2016.04.019

Gupta, R., Modise, M.P., 2013. Does the source of oil price shocks matter for South African stock returns? A structural VAR approach. *Energy Economics* 40, 825–831. doi:10.1016/J.ENECO.2013.10.005

Hamao, Y., 1988. An empirical examination of the Arbitrage Pricing Theory. *Japan and the World Economy* 1, 45–61. doi:10.1016/0922-1425(88)90005-9

Hamilton, J.D., 2003. What is an oil shock? *Journal of Econometrics* 113, 363–398. doi:10.1016/S0304-4076(02)00207-5

Hamilton, J.D., 1996. This is what happened to the oil price-macroeconomy relationship. *Journal of Monetary Economics* 38, 215–220. doi:10.1016/S0304-3932(96)01282-2

Hamilton, J.D., 1983. Oil and the macroeconomy since World War II. *Journal of Political Economy* 91, 228–248.

Hammoudeh, S., Choi, K., 2006. Behavior of GCC stock markets and impacts of US oil and financial markets. *Research in International Business and Finance* 20, 22–44. doi:10.1016/j.ribaf.2005.05.008

Hammoudeh, S., Li, H., 2005. Oil sensitivity and systematic risk in oil-sensitive stock indices. *Journal of Economics and Business* 57, 1–21. doi:10.1016/j.jeconbus.2004.08.002

Henriques, I., Sadorsky, P., 2008. Oil prices and the stock prices of alternative energy companies. *Energy Economics* 30, 998–1010. doi:10.1016/j.eneco.2007.11.001

Huang, B.-N., Hwang, M.J., Peng, H.-P., 2005. The asymmetry of the impact of oil price shocks on economic activities: An application of the multivariate threshold model. *Energy Economics* 27, 455–476. doi:10.1016/j.eneco.2005.03.001

Huang, R.D., Masulis, R.W., Stoll, H.R., 1996. Energy shocks and financial markets. *Journal of Futures Markets.* 16, 1–27. doi:10.1002/(SICI)1096-9934(199602)16:1<1::AID-FUT1>3.0.CO;2-Q

Inchauspe, J., Ripple, R.D., Trück, S., 2015. The dynamics of returns on renewable energy companies: A state-space approach. *Energy Economics* 48, 325–335. doi:10.1016/j.eneco.2014.11.013

Jammazi, R., Aloui, C., 2010. Wavelet decomposition and regime shifts: Assessing the effects of crude oil shocks on stock market returns. *Energy Policy* 38, 1415–1435. doi:10.1016/j.enpol.2009.11.023

Jones, C.M., Kaul, G., 1996. Oil and the Stock Markets. *Journal of Finance* 51, 463–491. doi:10.2307/2329368

Kaneko, T., Lee, B.-S., 1995. Relative importance of economic factors in the U.S. and Japanese Stock Markets. *Journal of the Japanese and International Economies* 9, 290–307. doi:10.1006/jjie.1995.1015

Kang, W., Ratti, R.A., Yoon, K.H., 2015. Time-varying effect of oil market shocks on the stock market. *Journal of Banking and Finance* 61, S150–S163. doi:10.1016/j.jbankfin.2015.08.027

Khalfaoui, R., Boutahar, M., Boubaker, H., 2015. Analyzing volatility spillovers and hedging between oil and stock markets: Evidence from wavelet analysis. *Energy Economics* 49, 540–549. doi:10.1016/j.eneco.2015.03.023

Kilian, L., 2009. Not all oil price shocks are alike : Disentangling supply shocks in the crude oil market. *American Economic Review* 99, 1053–1069. doi:10.1257/aer.99.3.1053

Kilian, L., Park, C., 2009. The impact of oil price shocks on the U.S. stock market. *International Economic Review. (Philadelphia)* 50, 1267–1287. doi:10.1111/j.1468-2354.2009.00568.x

Kumar, S., Managi, S., Matsuda, A., 2012. Stock prices of clean energy firms, oil and carbon markets: A vector autoregressive analysis. *Energy Economics* 34, 215–226. doi:10.1016/j.eneco.2011.03.002

Lee, B.-J., Yang, C.W., Huang, B.-N., 2012. Oil price movements and stock markets revisited: A case of sector stock price indexes in the G-7 countries. *Energy Economics* 34, 1284–1300. doi:10.1016/j.eneco.2012.06.004

Maghyereh, A., Al-Kandari, A., 2007. Oil prices and stock markets in GCC countries: New evidence from nonlinear cointegration analysis. *Managerial Finance* 33, 449–460. doi:10.1108/03074350710753735

Masih, R., Peters, S., De Mello, L., 2011. Oil price volatility and stock price fluctuations in an emerging market: Evidence from South Korea. *Energy Economics* 33, 975–986. doi:10.1016/j.eneco.2011.03.015

Mensi, W., Hammoudeh, S., Reboredo, J.C., Nguyen, D.K., 2014. Do global factors impact BRICS stock markets? A quantile regression approach. *Emerging Markets Review* 19, 1–17. doi:10.1016/j.ememar.2014.04.002

Miller, J.I., Ratti, R.A., 2009. Crude oil and stock markets: Stability, instability, and bubbles. *Energy Economics* 31, 559–568. doi:10.1016/j.eneco.2009.01.009

Mohanty, S.K., Nandha, M., Turkistani, A.Q., Alaitani, M.Y., 2011. Oil price movements and stock market returns: Evidence from Gulf Cooperation Council (GCC) countries. *Global Finance Journal* 22, 42–55. doi:10.1016/j.gfj.2011.05.004

Naifar, N., Al Dohaiman, M.S., 2013. Nonlinear analysis among crude oil prices, stock markets' return and macroeconomic variables. *International Review of Economics and Finance* 27, 416–431. doi:10.1016/j.iref.2013.01.001

Nandha, M., Faff, R., 2008. Does oil move equity prices? A global view. *Energy Economics* 30, 986–997. doi:10.1016/j.eneco.2007.09.003

Nandha, M., Hammoudeh, S., 2007. Systematic risk, and oil price and exchange rate sensitivities in Asia-Pacific stock markets. *Research in International Business and Finance* 21, 326–341. doi:10.1016/j.ribaf.2006.09.001

Narayan, P.K., Gupta, R., 2015. Has oil price predicted stock returns for over a century? *Energy Economics* 48, 18–23. doi:10.1016/J.ENECO.2014.11.018

Narayan, P.K., Sharma, S.S., 2011. New evidence on oil price and firm returns. *Journal of Banking and Finance* 35, 3253–3262. doi:10.1016/j.jbankfin.2011.05.010

Nguyen, C.C., Bhatti, M.I., 2012. Copula model dependency between oil prices and stock markets: Evidence from China and Vietnam. *Journal of International Financial Markets, Institutions and Money* 22, 758–773. doi:10.1016/j.intfin.2012.03.004

Papapetrou, E., 2001. Oil price shocks, stock market, economic activity and employment in Greece. *Energy Economics* 23, 511–532. doi:10.1016/S0140-9883(01)00078-0

Park, J., Ratti, R.A., 2008. Oil price shocks and stock markets in the U.S. and 13 European countries. *Energy Economics* 30, 2587–2608. doi:10.1016/j.eneco.2008.04.003

Ramos, S.B., Veiga, H., 2013. Oil price asymmetric effects: Answering the puzzle in international stock markets. *Energy Economics* 38, 136–145. doi:10.1016/j.eneco.2013.03.011

Ramos, S.B., Veiga, H., 2011. Risk factors in oil and gas industry returns: International evidence. *Energy Economics* 33, 525–542. doi:10.1016/j.eneco.2010.10.005

Reboredo, J.C., Rivera-Castro, M.A., 2014. Wavelet-based evidence of the impact of oil prices on stock returns. *International Review of Economics and Finance* 29, 145–176. doi:10.1016/j.iref.2013.05.014

Reboredo, J.C., Rivera-Castro, M.A., Ugolini, A., 2017. Wavelet-based test of co-movement and causality between oil and renewable energy stock prices. *Energy Economics* 61, 241–252. doi:10.1016/j.eneco. 2016.10.015

Sadorsky, P., 2008. Assessing the impact of oil prices on firms of different sizes: Its tough being in the middle. *Energy Policy* 36, 3854–3861. doi:10.1016/j.enpol.2008.07.019

Sadorsky, P., 2001. Risk factors in stock returns of Canadian oil and gas companies. *Energy Economics* 23, 17–28. doi:10.1016/S0140-9883(00)00072-4

Sadorsky, P., 1999. Oil price shocks and stock market activity. *Energy Economics* 21, 449–469. doi:10.1016/ S0140-9883(99)00020-1

Sukcharoen, K., Zohrabyan, T., Leatham, D., Wu, X., 2014. Interdependence of oil prices and stock market indices: A copula approach. *Energy Economics* 44, 331–339. doi:10.1016/j.eneco.2014.04.012

Wang, Y., Wu, C., Yang, L., 2013. Oil price shocks and stock market activities: Evidence from oil-importing and oil-exporting countries. *Journal of Comparative Economics* 41, 1220–1239. doi:10.1016/j. jce.2012.12.004

Zhu, H.-M., Li, R., Li, S., 2014. Modelling dynamic dependence between crude oil prices and Asia-Pacific stock market returns. *International Review of Economics and Finance* 29, 208–223. doi:10.1016/j. iref.2013.05.015

Zhu, H.-M., Li, S.-F., Yu, K., 2011. Crude oil shocks and stock markets: A panel threshold cointegration approach. *Energy Economics* 33, 987–994. doi:10.1016/j.eneco.2011.07.002

23

The role of oil price volatility in the real and financial economy

A survey review

Nicholas Apergis

1 Introduction

Volatility has turned out to be a substantial issue in the energy markets and especially in relevance to oil prices, since oil-based energy consumption still dominates the portfolios of such energy consumption across the globe. Oil prices are the most volatile among all the commodity prices. More specifically, crude oil exhibits significant price fluctuations, which in turn contribute to higher uncertainty in the minds of consumers and producers. Bernanke (1983) and Pindyck (1991) assert that investors and market participants delay investment projects because of the presence of such uncertainty, with this delay in investments resulting in inefficient resource allocation in the long run.

The goal of this chapter is to present as many studies as possible in relevance to how oil price uncertainty/volatility affects various components of real economic activity. Since oil is a salient factor for both households' consumption and firms' production decisions, it is conceivable that changes in oil price uncertainty could have effects on economic fluctuations. In other words, it is plausible that the variability of oil prices could have a significant impact on economic agents' decision-making process.

A great number of empirical studies have demonstrated the significance of oil price uncertainty in various perspectives. In particular, Lee et al. (1995) emphasize the importance of the second moment of oil prices in forecasting economic activity. In that case, oil price shocks reflect both the size and the variability of oil shocks forecast errors, and explain GDP growth with great accuracy. Kellogg (2010) tests for the responsiveness of firms' investment decisions to changes in uncertainty using Texas oil well drilling data and expectations of future oil price volatility. His results provide supportive evidence that oil firms reduce their drilling activity when expected volatility rises. Moreover, Elder and Serletis (2010) and Bredin et al. (2010) use a two-variable Generalized Autoregressive Conditional Heteroskedasticity (GARCH)-in-Mean VAR with oil price and economic activity for the United States and the G7 countries. Their findings document that increases in oil price uncertainty decrease real economic activity, measured by output, investment, and consumption in the United States and four of the G7 countries. Moreover, they illustrate that the 2003–2008 oil price surge has been rather steady and continuous, keeping oil price uncertainty at a very low level. Hence, the overall change in oil price was less disruptive than previous oil price episodes and did not lead to an immediate economic recession. Given the importance of oil price uncertainty, this survey paper will explore how oil price volatility affects not only a number of macroeconomic drivers, but also financial drivers of the economy. Therefore, the structural pattern of this paper will individually report those impacts per category of macroeconomic and financial variables. The paper is organized as follows. Section 2 describes the literature of the nexus between oil price volatility and economic growth, while Section 3 illustrates the relevant literature that links oil price volatility and stock markets. Section 4 reviews the literature between this volatility and exchanges rates, with Section 5 documenting the literature on the empirical aspects in relevance to the econometric modeling of oil price volatility. Section 6 considers the literature on the presence of asymmetric effects of oil price volatility from an empirical perspective, while Section 7 reviews the literature on the impact of oil price volatility on specific economic and institutional variables. Finally, concluding remarks are offered in Section 8.

2   Oil price volatility and economic growth

Due to many potential exogenous supply shocks, oil prices are subject to uncertainty. Even when prices remain relatively stable over an extended period of time, a sudden exogenous event could disrupt the balance, independently of previous events and cause significant upward or downward price changes. When prices are stable, economic agents (i.e. households, firms, and governments) usually overlook the ubiquitous, permanent underlying uncertainty, when making economic decisions. However, in an environment of volatile prices, agents are more likely to take future price uncertainty into account when making investment decisions. Overall, oil price volatility typically results in an increased sense of economic uncertainty, whereas the absence of volatility may instill a false sense of stability. In order to hedge against negative effects of oil price volatility, it is of utmost importance for policy makers to understand how significant the potential dimensions of negative effects are, and which factors determine the level of vulnerability.

The literature exploring the link between oil price volatility and economic activity strongly suggests that such volatility negatively affects economic output in the short to medium term (Sadorsky, 1999; Kuper and Soest, 2006, Rahman and Serletis, 2012). Adverse short-term economic impacts largely reflect the deterioration of aggregate demand as volatility intensifies. While industrial production has been found to decline in the short run (Lorde et al., 2009), production declines are more likely to be a response to downward trends in aggregate demand than to production cost uncertainty. This is because industrial producers respond to production/input cost uncertainty by raising product prices to incorporate an uncertainty premium, rather than by reducing production levels. In the medium term, aggregate supply is more responsive than aggregate demand to the effects of volatility. This is foremost the product of decreasing investment in the short term, which results in constrained production capacity and increased supply-side inelasticity in the medium term. Other negative economic effects of oil price volatility in the medium-term such as inflation (Lorde et al., 2009), are also likely to stem from supply-side responses to volatility changes.

Guo and Kliesen (2005) construct the 'realized volatility' (RV) variable suggested by Andersen et al. (2004), rather than employing the standard method of considering oil price shocks directly, while Rafiq et al. (2009) extend Cunado and Gracia's (2005) study by analyzing the effects of oil price volatility for various macro-indicators in the Thai economy. In a vector auto-regression (VAR) and vector error correction model, they show that the realized volatility of oil prices Granger causes GDP growth, investment, unemployment, and inflation. Their results support Bernanke's (1983) theoretical explanation of postponed investments due to expected oil price volatility and the associated uncertainty.

The literature has first identified the linear/symmetric relationship theory of growth which postulates that GDP volatility can be driven by oil price volatility. These authors base their theory on what happened in the oil market between 1948 and 1972 and its impact on the economies of oil-exporting and importing countries, respectively. Hooker (1996) documents that between 1948 and 1972, oil prices and its changes exerted a substantial influence on GDP growth. Mork et al. (1994) confirm the asymmetry in effect of oil price volatility on economic growth. Ferderer (1996) explains the asymmetric mechanism between the influence of oil price volatility and economic growth by focusing on three potential channels: counter-inflationary monetary policy, sectoral shocks, and uncertainty. He finds a significant relationship between oil price increases and counter-inflationary policy responses. Balke et al. (2002) supports Federer's position/submission by positing that monetary policy alone cannot sufficiently explain real effects of oil price volatility on real GDP. The renaissance growth theory is considered as an offshoot of the symmetric and asymmetry in effect theoretical approaches. Lee (1998) focuses on attempting to distinguish between oil price changes and oil price volatility, while he defines volatility as the standard deviation in a given period. She provides evidence that both have a negative impact on economic growth, but in different ways: in particular, volatility has a negative and significant impact on economic growth immediately, while the impact of oil price changes delays until after a year.

Various empirical studies illustrate that oil price increases have a clear negative impact on economic growth, while oil price declines do not affect economic activity significantly. Mork et al. (1994) confirms the asymmetry in effects for a number of OECD countries. Oil price increases seem to slow down economic growth in the United States to a great extent, even if this country is less dependent on imported oil than countries such as Germany, France, and Japan. Lee et al. (1995) also reveal the stability of asymmetric effects in the period before and after 1985. In order to explain the presence of the 'asymmetry puzzle', the asymmetric mechanism between oil price changes and economic activity, Ferderer (1996) focuses on three possible mechanisms: counter-inflationary monetary policy, sectoral shocks, and uncertainty and establishes that oil price falls increase oil price volatility.

Jiménez-Rodríguez and Marcelo Sánchez (2004) assess empirically the effects of oil price uncertainty on the real economic activity for the case of the main industrialized OECD countries, i.e. individual G7 countries, Norway and the euro area as a whole. Their analysis carries out multivariate vector autoregressions by considering both linear and nonlinear models. The consideration of non-linear transformations re-establishes the negative relationship between increases in oil prices and economic downturns. Their findings show that Granger causality tests allow to conclude that the interaction between oil prices and macroeconomic variables is found to be significant, with the direction of causality going in at least one direction in all countries, and in both directions in most countries. The effects of oil price increases on real GDP growth are found to differ substantially from those of an oil price decrease, providing evidence against the linear approach that assumes that oil prices have symmetric effects on the real economy.

The effect of oil price uncertainty on real economic activity depends on the impact of the oil price on investments, but also on how firms face the uncertainty regarding their investment decision plans. Indeed, depending on the sectors, the delay from the investment decision to the beginning of the production can differ, and short-run uncertainty can thus have no impact on long-run investment strategies. All in all, accounting for the effect of maturity when investigating the impact of uncertainty is thus of crucial importance.

3 Oil price volatility and stock markets

Although numerous studies have explored the effect of oil price shocks on real economic activity, only a few have focused on investigating how oil price volatility has influenced stock market returns. The most known works in this field remain those of Kilian (2009), Kilian and Park

(2009) and Güntner (2013). Sadorsky (1999), Malik and Ewing (2009) and Oberndorfer (2009) also argue that apart from oil prices, oil price volatility also can impact on stock market returns. They provide evidence that higher oil price volatility causes a negative effect on stock market returns. Chiou and Lee (2009) document that oil price volatility exerts a negative impact on the S&P 500 index.

Park and Ratti (2008) examine the effects of oil price shocks and oil price volatility on US real stock returns and 13 European countries, spanning the period January 1986 to December 2005. Using a multivariate VAR model, they find that oil price shocks exert a statistically significant impact on real stock returns in the same month or within one month. Their findings remain robust to changes in the VAR model in terms of the variable order and the inclusion of additional variables. Naifar and Al Dohaiman (2013) investigate the nature of the relationship between crude oil prices, stock market return, and macroeconomic variables. Their analysis first examines the impact of oil price changes and volatility on stock market returns under regime shifts using a sample from the Gulf Cooperation Council (GCC) countries. To generate regime probabilities for oil market variables they employ a Markov regime-switching model. Moreover, they investigate the non-linear connections between oil price, interest rates, and inflation rates before and during the subprime crisis. They consider various Archimedean copula models with different tail dependence structures. Their findings document a regime dependent relationship between GCC stock market returns and OPEC oil market volatility, with exception to the case of Oman. Their results also illustrate the presence of an asymmetric dependence structure between inflation rates and crude oil prices, with this structure orienting toward the upper side during the financial crisis. Moreover, they find a significant symmetric dependence between crude oil prices and short-term interest rates during the same crisis.

The negative reaction of real stock prices to the increase in oil price is primarily attributed to the direct effects of such changes on cash flows and inflation. In fact, oil price can corporate cash flows, since oil prices constitute a substantial input in production. Moreover, oil price changes can significantly influence the supply and the demand for output across industrial sectors, as well as the entire economy. Therefore, oil price changes can impact firms' performance through their effect on the discount rate for cash flows, as well as through the direct effect that may exert on both the expected inflation and the expected real interest rate. These direct and indirect effects of the high volatility in oil prices seem likely to increase uncertainty for firms and for the economy as well. In this line, Bernanke (1983) and Pindyck (1991) document that higher volatility in energy prices leads to higher uncertainty about future energy prices and incites firms to postpone irreversible investment decisions in reaction to their profit prospects. Other studies provide important evidence on the association between oil prices and stock returns. The analysis of the relationship between oil price risks and stock returns has been also the subject of the study by El-Sharif et al. (2005) for a sample composed of the UK-listed oil and gas firms. They find that changes in oil prices enhance stock market and exchange rate risks which in turn exert a significant impact on both oil and gas stock returns. Agren (2006) employs weekly stock market data for Germany, Japan, Sweden, the United Kingdom, and the United States from 1989 to 2005 and finds strong evidence in favor of volatility spillovers running from oil price volatility to the equity markets in Germany, Japan, and the United Kingdom. Both German and UK equity markets seem to display an asymmetric volatility-response to oil shocks, implying that positive shocks affect stock market volatility more than negative ones do. Evidence of volatility spillovers running from oil prices to US stocks is detected, but is considered rather weak since it does not hold under some intuitively appealing parameter restrictions. No support for oil price volatility spillovers in the Swedish stock market is observed. Furthermore, empirical evidence is found that oil price changes have an impact on US stock returns, while some evidence is provided that supports the presence of asymmetric oil price volatility. Aloui and Jammazi (2009) develop a two-regime Markov-switching EGARCH model to explore the interdependence between oil shocks and stock returns. Using data for France, the United Kingdom, and Japan spanning the period January 1987 to December 2007, they illustrate that net oil prices play a pivotal role in determining not only the volatility of real returns, but also the probability of transition across regimes. Ramos and Veiga (2013) examine 43 stock markets and find that for the case of developed countries' stock markets, the volatility of oil prices has a negative impact on international stock market returns. In the case of emerging market returns, they appear not to be sensitive to oil price variations. In addition, the asymmetry of oil price changes impacts oil volatility: when oil prices soar, oil volatility also increases, while negative oil price changes dampen that volatility. Hammaa et al. (2014) the interaction between oil and stock markets in Tunisia in terms of volatility at the sector level, as well as they determine the best hedging strategy for oil-stock portfolios against the risk of negative variation in stock market prices. Through a bivariate GARCH model their empirical results indicate that the majority of relationships are unidirectional running from the oil market to the Tunisian stock market, while the conditional variance of stock sector returns is affected not only by the volatility surprises of the stock market, but also by those of the oil market.

4 Oil price volatility and exchange rates

Only a few empirical studies have focused on the impact of oil price volatility on exchange rates. Rickne (2009) documents that the co-movements between oil price and real exchange rates in a sample of 33 oil-exporting countries are conditional on political and legal institutions. Specifically, currencies in countries with strong bureaucracies are less affected by oil price variation. Englama et al. (2010) examine the relationship between oil price and exchange rate volatility in Nigeria. Their findings illustrate that exchange rate volatility is positively influenced by oil price volatility. Ghosh (2011) also indicates that positive and negative shocks have similar effects on exchange rate volatility.

5 Empirical volatility methodologies for oil prices

In general, a number of studies (Sadorsky, 2006; Narayan and Narayan, 2007 for a survey of literature) impose a particular structure of volatility models to analyze oil price volatility. In particular, in the case of linear modeling, these studies make use of the Engle (1982) approach to determine the choice of volatility model and also to validate the choice of the preferred model over other competing models. In addition, the volatility could be time varying and therefore, the choice of appropriate model for oil price volatility may change over time based on the significance of variations over time. Thus, generalizing with a particular model over the entire available data may be misleading.

Overall, the studies in oil price volatility cover a number of different areas and issues and examine the characteristics of these markets in various respects. More specifically, certain studies document that oil prices are characterized by fat-tail distribution, volatility clustering, asymmetry and mean reversion (Morana, 2001; Bina and Vo, 2007). Oil price dynamics during 2002–2006 have been characterized by high volatility, high intensity jumps, and strong upward drift and was concomitant with underlying fundamentals of oil markets and world economy (Askari and Krichene, 2008). Standard GARCH modeling is used by Yang et al. (2002) for the US oil market and by Oberndorfer (2009) for the case of the oil market of the Eurozone, and by Hwang et al. (2004) for the case of major industrialized countries. Fong and See (2002) make use of a Markov regime-switching approach allowing for GARCH dynamics, and sudden changes in both mean and variance to model the conditional volatility of daily returns on crude oil futures prices. They document that the regime-switching model performs better non-switching models, regardless of evaluation criteria in out-of-sample forecast analysis. A similar approach has been followed by Vo (2009), who explains the behavior of crude oil prices of the WTI market. Duffie and Gray (1995) construct in-sample and out-of-sample forecasts for volatility in the crude oil, heating oil, and natural gas markets. Their forecasts from GARCH, EGARCH, bi-variate GARCH, regime switching, implied volatility, and historical volatility modeling are compared with the realized volatility to compute the criterion RMSE for forecast accuracy. Their findings highlight that implied volatility yields the best forecasts in both the in-sample and out-of-sample cases. Sadorsky (2006) has also modeled and forecasted the oil volatility by using a five-year rolling window. The daily ex post variance is measured by squared daily return which is consistent with the approach of Brailsford and Faff (1996) and Brooks and Persand (2002). He applies the random walk, historical mean, moving average, exponentially smoothing, linear regression, autoregressive, GARCH, threshold GARCH, GARCH in mean, and bivariate GARCH modeling approaches. The out-of-sample forecasts are evaluated using forecast accuracy tests and market timing tests. No one model fits the best for each series considered. Most models outperform the random walk model, while parametric and nonparametric value at risk measures are calculated and compared. Non-parametric models outperform the parametric models in terms of number of exceedances in back tests. Narayan and Narayan (2007) use the Exponential Generalized Conditional Heteroskedasticity (EGARCH) model with the intention of checking for evidence of asymmetry and persistence of shocks. They document an inconsistent evidence of asymmetry and persistence of shocks, indicating the presence of strong permanent and asymmetric effects on volatility. Their findings imply that oil prices change over short periods of time. Kang et al. (2009) focus on investigating the efficacy of a volatility model for three crude oil markets (Brent, Dubai and West Texas Intermediate (WTI)). They used different competitive GARCH volatility (CGARCH, FIGARCH, GARCH and IGARCH) to assess the persistence in the volatility of the three oil prices. They document that the estimated value of the persistence coefficient is quite close to one in the standard GARCH model, a fact that favors the IGARCH specification. Arouri et al. (2010) investigate whether structural breaks and long memory are relevant features in modeling and forecasting the conditional volatility of oil spot and futures prices using three GARCH-type models (i.e. linear GARCH, GARCH with structural breaks and FIGARCH). They provide evidence of parameter instability in 5 out of 12 GARCH-based conditional volatility processes, while long memory is effectively present across all series considered and a FIGARCH model seems to better fit the data, but the degree of volatility persistence diminishes significantly after adjusting for structural breaks. Finally, out-of-sample forecasting findings indicate that forecasting models accommodating for structural break characteristics of the data often outperform the commonly used short-memory linear volatility models. Yaziz et al. (2011) use the Box-Jenkins methodology and Generalized Autoregressive Conditional Heteroscedasticity (GARCH) approach in analyzing the crude oil prices. GARCH modeling is found to be the appropriate model under model identification, parameter estimation, diagnostic checking, and forecasting future prices. Hou and Suardi (2012) consider an alternative approach in relevance to nonparametric methodologies to model and forecast oil price volatility. They focus on two crude oil markets, Brents and West Texas Intermediate (WTI), and they show that the out-of-sample volatility forecast of the nonparametric GARCH model yields superior performance relative to an extensive class of parametric GARCH models.

6   Asymmetric effects of oil price volatility: an empirical perspective

The presence of potential asymmetries in oil price volatility documents that positive and negative news have a different impact on the future volatility of oil prices. Acknowledging and explicitly considering the presence of asymmetries in oil price volatility seems to be imperative for correctly estimating the volatility of oil prices, forecasting future oil price volatility, and understanding the broader financial markets and the overall economy. Nevertheless, there have been a few empirical attempts in explicitly considering the presence of asymmetries in relevance to oil price volatility. In particular, oil price volatility implies that this volatility seems to react more to positive shocks than to negative shocks. Narayan and Narayan (2007) employs an exponential GARCH modeling approach to evaluate time-varying effects of positive and negative shocks on oil price volatility, while Cheong (2009) illustrates the asymmetric effects on two crude oil prices: WTI and Brent crude oil. The findings clearly document that volatility seems to react more to negative shocks than to positive shocks. However, such results are evident only for the case of Brent crude prices and not for the case of WTI crude oil prices. Furthermore, Hasan et al. (2013) estimate and compare the presence of asymmetry in relevance to the volatility of crude oil prices. Their methodological approach evaluates the effect of the recent global financial crisis on the returns and volatility of such oil prices. Both threshold GARCH (TGARCH) and fractionally integrated GARCH (FIGARCH) models are employed to facilitate the empirical analysis. The results confirm that the volatility of crude oil prices increases after positive shocks in these prices.

In terms of the oil price volatility and economic growth link, Huang et al. (2005) apply a multivariate threshold model to explore the impact of oil price changes and their volatility on economic activity. Using monthly data of the United States, Canada, and Japan spanning the period 1970 to 2002, their findings show that changes in oil prices, along with their volatility only above a threshold level can help explain output changes. Moreover, Cologni and Manera (2009) use a Markov-switching analysis for the case of the G7 countries and highlight that positive oil price changes, net oil price increases, and oil price volatility tend to have a greater impact on output growth. In addition, their analysis suggests that the role of oil shocks in explaining recessionary episodes have decreased over time. Finally, they conclude that oil shocks tend to be asymmetric.

With respect to the volatility type of the oil price–stock returns nexus, Dhaoui and Khraief (2014) investigate the effect of oil price shocks on stock market returns for eight developed countries, over the period 1991–2013. Their findings indicate that there is a strong negative relationship across all countries under consideration, except in the case of Singapore. Moreover, on the volatility front, changes in oil prices turn out to be significant in the case of six markets. Their results receive statistical support by a study for the case of developed countries (i.e. the G7 countries) carried out by Diaz and Gracia (2016) who confirm the negative reaction of these G7 stock markets to an increase in oil price volatility. In the case of emerging economies, the study by Masih and Mello (2010) for South Korea represents a good example on the role of the volatility of oil prices. In particular, it investigates the impact of oil price fluctuations and their associated oil price volatility on equity stock market returns, using a vector error correction model which includes interest rates, economic activity, real stock returns, real oil prices and oil prices volatility. They provide robust evidence in support of the dominance of oil price volatility on real stock returns, which increases over time. Finally, Gomez and Chaibi (2014) provide further evidence on the volatility transmission mechanism across frontier markets (i.e. 21 stock markets). A bivariate BEKK-GARCH (1,1) model has been employed using data for the period 2008–2013. Their results suggest significant transmissions of shocks and volatility between oil prices and some of the markets under examination. They also find that the second highest coefficient measuring the volatility spillover from oil prices to stock markets is that of Jordan, following Qatar, Nigeria, and the United Arab Emirates.

7 Oil price volatility and other variables

7.1 Oil price volatility and inflation

The final section of this survey reviews the studies that have explored how oil price volatility can affect inflation, as well as inflationary expectations. Given that in many incidents in the past oil price shocks had different implications on both the economic activity and inflation, while if we further explore the link between oil price volatility and both average inflation and output, the findings indicate that larger oil price volatility has been associated with high inflation rates. Such statistical evidence poses questions regarding the link between oil price volatility and inflation. The literature has attempted to address questions like whether oil price volatility does matter for inflation or what is the associated role of monetary policy. Blanchard and Gali (2008) address the above questions using a log-linear New Keynesian model that includes the role of oil as both a production factor and a component of the consumer price index. The authors document that a monetary policy improvement, more flexible labor markets and smaller shares of oil in production have all had an important role in explaining the different macroeconomic performance of the global economy in the past and especially between the 1970s and 2000s. However, their approach has received certain negative critical points on the grounds that their log-linear solution misses crucial channels through which oil prices can affect inflation, such as its own volatility, the precautionary behavior of price setters and the convexity of the Phillips curve.

7.2 Oil price volatility and fiscal policy

According to Alley (2016), oil price volatility could be transmitted to the economy event rough the fiscal channel. In particular, this may happen because oil revenues accrue to governments, while such revenues can affect the economy mainly through government spending decisions. However, optimal decisions on current government expenditures take explicitly into account information about current and future revenues (Collier et al., 2009). However, very few studies have paid attention onto the implications of oil price volatility on fiscal policies. Anshashy and Bradley (2012) focus on the responses of government expenditure to oil price volatility. Fiscal policies are can be characterized as the transmission channel through which oil price movements and their volatility can affect the entire economy. As oil revenues are usually large and accrue to governments, the volatility in oil prices often poses serious challenges to macroeconomic stabilization policies, especially in the short run. It undermines intergenerational equity and fiscal sustainability in the long run (Sturm et al., 2009), especially in economies which lack appropriate countercyclical fiscal measures to deal with oil revenue fluctuations (Frankel, 2010). Whether or not appropriate fiscal policies would be deployed to contain the effects of oil price volatility on the economy depends on the quality of the institutions in effect (Collier et al., 2009). Moreover, Mehlum et al. (2006) document that countries with good institutions have had oil price booms positively affect the economy, while those with poor institutions have experienced a resource curse (Collier et al., 2009). The countries with weak fiscal institutions would have their fiscal instruments or strategies rendered ineffective (IMF, 2008), as resources allocation and government expenditures on projects would be inefficient (Budina and Wijnbergen, 2008). Finally, unexpected increases in oil price volatility adversely affects government budgets (Rutten, 2001).

7.3   Oil price volatility and institutions

Finally, according to the resource curse hypothesis, abundance of oil resources tends to be an important determinant of economic failure. This section reviews the literature that has explicitly documented whether the poor performance of resource-rich countries comes from the abundance of oil or whether it is associated with price volatility in global oil markets. This literature explores whether there is a role for institutions and the government in offsetting certain parts of the negative growth effects due to the curse.

The relevant literature provides different explanations for why resource-rich economies might be subject to a curse. Dutch disease (Neary and van Wijnbergen, 1986; Krugman, 1987) is one of the channels: increases in natural resource revenues lead to an appreciation of the real exchange rate, which raises the cost of exports, making them less competitive with possible negative effects on economic activity. Economic growth might also be adversely affected by the resulting real-location of resources from the high-tech and high-skill manufacturing sector to the low-tech and low-skill natural resource sector. Another explanation for the resource curse paradox focuses on the political economy considerations and argues that large windfalls from oil and other resources create incentives for the rent-seeking activities that involve corruption (Mauro, 1995; Leite and Weidmann, 1999), voracity (Lane and Tornell, 1996; Tornell and Lane, 1999), and possibly civil conflicts (Collier and Hoeffler, 2004). A number of empirical works have also focused explicitly on the role of institutions. More specifically, Mehlum et al. (2006) and Beland and Tiagi (2009) use a cross-sectional approach and illustrate that the impact of natural resources on growth and development depends primarily on institutions, while Boschini et al. (2007) illustrate that the type of natural resources possessed is also an important factor. They also argue that when we control for institutional quality and include an interaction term between institutional quality and resource abundance, a threshold effect arises, implying that there are levels of institutional quality above of which resource abundance becomes growth enhancing.

The empirical support for the resource curse hypothesis has been provided by Sachs and Warner (1995), who show the presence of a negative relationship between real GDP growth per capita. However, the empirical evidence on the resource curse paradox is rather mixed. The majority of papers follow Sachs and Warner's cross-sectional specification, while others derive theoretical models that are loosely related to their empirical specification (Rodriguez and Sachs, 1999; Gylfason et al., 1999; Bulte et al., 2005). An important drawback of these studies is in relevance to the measure of resource abundance. Brunnschweiler and Bulte (2008) argue that the so-called resource curse does not exist when one uses the correct measure of resource abundance, while they confirm that resource dependence, when instrumented in growth regressions, does not affect growth.

Moreover, the literature has provided alternative mechanisms through which institutions can mitigate the effect of oil rent volatility on economic growth. These mechanisms are associated with the types of institutions which are likely to dampen such an effect. According to economic theory, the most relevant and key institutions that mitigate the effects of volatility on an economy are the institutions of finance. This is due to the well-known role of finance in risk diversification (Levine, 1997; Leong and Mohaddes, 2011) may be driven by financial depth. The empirical findings do confirm that the financial measures do mitigate the effects of oil price volatility, since these measures reduce or completely eliminate the negative effects of oil volatility on growth.

8   Final remarks

Given that the role of oil price volatility seems to be very important for both the real economy and financial markets, this survey paper intended to contribute to the relevant literature by shedding more light on the arguments, notions, and definitions underlying the existing literature on the issue.

This review documented the general consensus among economists that the economic significance of oil price volatility can affect both the real economy and the financial markets. Stock prices are shown to be very sensitive to oil price volatility, while methodological challenges, such as causality and endogeneity, can affect the validity of the empirical findings. The results provided in the relevant literature call for further empirical analysis, based on more advanced econometric techniques some of which are introduced in Chapter 22 of this handbook. However, the rise of shale gas and substantial progress on renewable energy technologies could signify the mitigating impact of such volatility on the economy, as well as on financial markets. Furthermore, carbon markets, such as the European Union Emission Trading Scheme (EU ETS) could also contribute to such diminishing role (Chevallier, 2011). In terms of the empirical approach, the studies reviewed in this paper documented a lack of consensus on the role of the forecasting capability of the modeling approaches for clarifying the role of oil price volatility in an economy, indicating an inherent need for alternative approaches, such as artificial intelligence, which has not been thoroughly explored for oil price volatility. It is expected that this area of research will form the core of a new future research agenda on this issue.

References

Agren, M. 2006. Does oil price uncertainty transmit to stock markets? Department of Economics, Uppsala University, Working Paper, No. 2006-23.

Alley, I. 2016. Oil price volatility and fiscal policies in oil-exporting countries. *OPEC Energy Review* 40, 211.

Aloui, C., Jammazi, R. 2009. The effects of crude oil shocks on stock market shifts behaviour: A regime switching approach. *Energy Economics* 31, 789–799.

Andersen, T.G., Bollerslev, T., Meddahi, N. 2004. Analytical evaluation of volatility forecasts. *International Economic Review* 45, 1079–1110.

Anshashy, A.A., Bradley, M.D. 2012. Oil prices and the fiscal policy response in oil-exporting countries. *Journal of Policy Modelling* 34, 605–620.

Arouri, M., Amine, L., Nguyen, D. 2010. Forecasting the conditional volatility of oil spot and futures prices with structural breaks and long memory models. Development and Policies Research Center (DEPOCEN), Vietnam, Working Paper, No. 13.

Askari, H., Krichene, N. 2008. Oil price dynamics, 2002–2006. *Energy Economics* 30, 2134–2153.

Balke, N.S., Brown, S.P.A., Yücel, M.K. 2002. Oil price shocks and the U.S. economy: Where does the asymmetry originate? *The Energy Journal* 23, 27–52.

Beland, L.P., Tiagi, R. 2009. *Economic freedom and the "resource curse": An empirical analysis*. Studies in Mining Policy, Fraser Institute, Toronto.

Bernanke, B.S. 1983. Irreversibility, uncertainty, and cyclical investment. *Quarterly Journal of Economics* 98, 85–106.

Bina, C., Vo, M. 2007. OPEC in the epoch of globalization: An event study of global oil prices. *Global Economy Journal* 7, 1–49.

Blanchard, O., Gali, J. 2008. *The macroeconomic effect of oil price shocks: Why are the 2000s so different from the 1970s?* NBER, International Dimensions of Monetary Policy, Massachusetts.

Boschini, A., Pettersson, J., Roine, J. 2007. Resource curse or not: A question of appropriability. *Scandinavian Journal of Economics* 109, 593–617.

Brailsford, T., Faff, R. 1996. An evaluation of volatility forecasting techniques. *Journal of Banking and Finance* 20, 419–438.

Bredin, D., Elder, J., Fountas, S. 2010. Oil volatility and the option value of waiting: An analysis of the G7. *Journal of Futures Markets* 31, 679–702.

Brooks, C., Persand, G. 2002. Model choice and value-at-risk performance. *Financial Analysts Journal* 58, 87–97.

Brunnschweiler, C.N., Bulte, E.H. 2008. The resource curse revisited and revised: A tale of paradoxes and red herrings. *Journal of Environmental Economics and Management* 55, 248–264.

Budina, N., Wijnbergen, S. 2008. Managing oil revenue volatility in Nigeria: The role of fiscal policy. URL: http://siteresources.worldbank.org/INTDEBTDEPT/Resources/468980120758863500/4864698 1207588597197/AFRI427460Ch10.pdf.

Bulte, E.H., Damania, R., Deacon, R.T. 2005. Resource intensity, institutions, and development. *World Development* 33, 1029–1044.

Cheong, C.W. 2009. Modelling and forecasting crude oil markets using ARCH-type models. *Energy Policy* 37, 2346–2355.

Chevallier, J. 2011. Evaluating the carbon-macroeconomy relationship: Evidence from threshold vector error-correction and Markov-switching VAR models. *Economic Modelling* 28, 2634–2656.

Chiou, J.S., Lee, Y.H. 2009. Jump dynamics and volatility: Oil and the stock markets. *Energy* 34, 788–796.

Collier, P., der van Ploeg, F., Spence, M., Venables, A. J. 2009. Managing resource revenues in developing economies. OxcCarre Research Paper, No. 15.

Collier, P., Hoeffler, A. 2004. Greed and grievance in civil war. *Oxford Economic Papers* 56, 563–595.

Cologni, A., Manera, M. 2009. The asymmetric effects of oil shocks on output growth: A Markov-Switching analysis for the G7 countries. *Economic Modelling* 26, 1–29.

Cunado, J., de Gracia, F.P. 2005. Oil prices, economic activity and inflation: Evidence for some Asian countries. *Quarterly Review of Economics and Finance* 45, 65–83.

Dhaoui, A., Khraief, N. 2014. Empirical linkages between oil price and stock market returns and volatility: Evidence from international developed markets. Kiel Institute for the World Economy, Economics Discussion Paper, No 2014-12.

Diaz, E., Molero, J., Gracia, F. 2016. Oil price volatility and stock returns in the G7 economies. *Energy Economics* 54, 417–430.

Duffie, D., Gray, S. 1995. Volatility in energy prices. In *Managing energy price risk*. Risk Publications, London, 39–55.

Elder, J., Serletis, A. 2010. Oil price uncertainty. *Journal of Money, Credit and Banking* 42, 1137–1159.

El-Sharif, I., Brown, D., Burton, B., Nixon, B., Russell, A. 2005. Evidence on the nature and extent of the relationship between oil prices and equity values in the UK. *Energy Economics* 27, 819–830.

Englama, A., Duke, O.O., Ogunleye, T.S., Ismail, F.U. 2010. Oil prices and exchange rate volatility in Nigeria: An empirical investigation. *Central Bank of Nigeria, Economic and Financial Review* 48, 31–48.

Engle, R. 1982. Autoregressive Conditional Heteroscedasticity with estimates of the variance of United Kingdom inflation. *Econometrica* 50, 987–1007.

Ferderer, J.P. 1996. Oil price volatility and the macroeconomy. *Journal of Macroeconomics* 18, 1–26.

Fong, W.M., See, K.H. 2002. A Markov switching model of the conditional volatility of crude oil futures prices. *Energy Economics* 24, 71–95.

Frankel, J., 2010. The natural resource curse: A survey. Harvard Kennedy School Faculty Research, Working Paper Series, No. 10-005.

Ghosh, S. 2011. Examining the crude oil price-exchange rate nexus for India during the period of extreme oil price volatility. *Applied Energy* 88, 1886–1889.

Gomez, M., Chaibi, A. 2014. Volatility spillovers between oil prices and stock returns: A focus on frontier markets. *The Journal of Applied Business Research* 30, 509–526.

Güntner, J.H. 2013. How do international stock markets respond to oil demand and supply shocks? *Macroeconomic Dynamics* 18, 1657–1682.

Guo, H., Kliesen, K.L. 2005. Oil price volatility and US macroeconomic activity. *Review, Federal Reserve Bank of St. Louis* 57, 669–683.

Gylfason, T., Herbertsson, T.T., Zoega, G. 1999. A mixed blessing. *Macroeconomic Dynamics* 3, 204–225.

Hammaa, W., Jarbouib, A., Ghorbel, A. 2014. The effect of oil price volatility on the Tunisian stock market at sector-level and the effectiveness of hedging strategy. *Procedia in Economics and Finance* 13, 109–127.

Hasan, M.Z., Akhter, S., Rabbi, F. 2013. Asymmetry and persistence of energy price volatility. *International Journal of Finance and Accounting* 2, 373–378.

Hooker, M.A. 1996. What happened to the oil price-macroeconomy relationship? *Journal of Monetary Economics* 38, 195–213.

Hou, A., Suardi, S. 2012. A nonparametric GARCH model of crude oil price return volatility. *Energy Economics* 34, 618–626.

Huang, B.N., Hwang, M.J., Peng, H.P. 2005. The asymmetry of the impact of oil price shocks on economic activities: An application of the multivariate threshold model. *Energy Economics* 27, 455–476.

Hwang, M., Yang, C., Huang, B., Ohta, H. 2004. Oil price volatility. *Encyclopedia of Energy* 4, 691–699.

International Monetary Fund. 2008. The role of fiscal institution in managing oil revenue boom. URL: www.imf.org/external/np/pp/2007/eng/030507.pdf.

Jiménez-Rodríguez, R., Sánchez, M. 2004. Oil price shocks: Empirical evidence for some OECD countries. European Central Bank, Working Paper, No. 363.

Kang, S.H., Kang, S.M., Yoon, S.M. 2009. Forecasting volatility of crude oil markets. *Energy Economics* 31, 119–125.

Kellogg, R. 2010. The effect of uncertainty on investment: Evidence from Texas oil drilling. NBER Working Paper, No. 11.

Kilian, L. 2009. Not all oil price shocks are alike: Disentangling demand and supply shocks in the crude oil market. *American Economic Review* 99, 1053–1069.

Kilian, L., Park, C. 2009. The impact of oil price shocks on the US stock market. *International Economic Review* 50, 1267–1287.

Krugman, P. 1987. The narrow moving band, the Dutch disease, and the competitive consequences of Mrs. Thatcher: Notes on trade in the presence of dynamic scale economies. *Journal of Development Economics* 27, 41–55.

Kuper, G.H., Soest, D.P. 2006. Does oil price uncertainty affect economic use? *Energy Journal* 27, 55–78.

Lane, P.R., Tornell, A. 1996. Power, growth, and the voracity effect. *Journal of Economic Growth* 1, 213–241.

Lee, K., 1998. Oil price changes and volatility: A correlation analysis on the economy of china. *Scholarly Writers Publications* 15(4), 44–49.

Lee, K., Ni, S., Ratti, R.A. 1995. Oil shocks and the macroeconomy: The role of price variability. *The Energy Journal* 16, 39–56.

Leite, C., Weidmann, M. 1999. Does mother nature corrupt? Natural resources, corruption and economic growth. IMF Working Paper, No. 99/85.

Leong, W., Mohaddes, K. 2011. Institutions and the volatility curse. Cambridge Working Paper in Economics, No. 1145.

Levine, R. 1997. Financial development and economic growth: Views and agenda. *Journal of Economic Literature* 35, 688–726.

Lorde, T., Jackman, M., Thomas, C. 2009. The macroeconomic effects of oil price fluctuations on a small open oil-producing country: The case of Trinidad and Tobago. *Energy Policy* 37, 2708–2716.

Malik, F., Ewing, B.T. 2009. Volatility transmission between oil prices and equity sector returns. *International Review of Financial Analysis* 18, 95–100.

Masih, R., Perters, S., Mello, L. 2010. Oil price volatility and stock price fluctuations in an emerging market: Evidence from South Korea. *Energy Economics* 33, 975–986.

Mauro, P. 1995. Corruption and growth. *The Quarterly Journal of Economics* 110, 681–712.

Mehlum, H., Moene, K., Torvik, R. 2006. Institutions and the resource curse. *Economic Journal* 116, 1–20.

Morana, C. 2001. A semiparametric approach to short-term oil price forecasting. *Energy Economics* 23, 325–338.

Mork, K.A., Olsen, O., Mysen, H.T. 1994. Macroeconomic responses to oil price increases and decreases in seven OECD countries. *Energy Journal* 15, 19–35.

Naifar, N., Al Dohaiman, M.S. 2013. Nonlinear analysis among crude oil prices, stock markets' return and macroeconomic variables. *International Review of Economics and Finance* 27, 416–431.

Narayan, P., Narayan, S. 2007. Modelling oil price volatility. *Energy Policy* 35, 6549–6553.

Neary, J.P., van Wijnbergen, S.J.G. 1986. *Natural resources and the macroeconomy*. MIT Press, Cambridge, MA.

Oberndorfer, U. 2009. Energy prices, volatility and the stock market: Evidence from the Eurozone. *Energy Policy* 37, 5787–5795.

Park, J., Ratti, R.A. 2008. Oil price shocks and stock markets in the US and 13 European countries. *Energy Economics* 30, 2587–2608.

Pindyck, R. 1991. Irreversibility, uncertainty and investment. *Journal of Economic Literature* 29, 1110–1148.

Rafiq, S., Bloch, H., Salim, R. 2009. Impact of crude oil price volatility on economic activities: An empirical investigation in the Thai economy. *Resources Policy* 34, 121–132.

Rahman, S., Serletis, A. 2012. Oil price uncertainty and the Canadian economy: Evidence from a VARMA, GARCH-in-Mean, asymmetric BEKK model. *Energy Economics* 34, 603–610.

Ramos, S.B., Veiga, H. 2013. Asymmetric effects of oil price fluctuations in international stock markets. University Carlos III De Madrid, Statistics and Econometrics Series, Working Paper, No. 10-09.

Rickne, J.K. 2009. Oil prices and real exchange rate movements in oil-exporting countries: The role of institution. IFN Working Paper, No. 810.

Rodriguez, F., Sachs, J.D. 1999. Why do resource-abundant economies grow more slowly? *Journal of Economic Growth* 4, 277–303.

Rutten, L., 2001. Risk management strategies for mineral importers. Presentation for the World Bank Managing Volatility Thematic Group, 20 March, Washington, DC.

Sachs, J.D., Warner, A.M. 1995. Natural resource abundance and economic growth. National Bureau of Economic Research, Working Paper, No. 5398.

Sadorsky, P. 1999. Oil price shocks and stock market activity. *Energy Economics* 21, 449–469.

Sadorsky, P. 2006. Modelling and forecasting petroleum futures volatility. *Energy Economics* 28, 467–488.

Sturm, M., Gurtner, F., Alegre, J.G. 2009. Fiscal policy challenges in oil exporting countries: A review of key issues. European Central Bank, Occasional Paper, No. 104.

Tornell, A., Lane, P.R. 1999. The voracity effect. *The American Economic Review* 89, 22–46.

Vo, M.T. 2009. Regime-switching stochastic volatility: Evidence from the crude oil market. *Energy Economics* 31, 779–788.

Yang, C., Hwang, M., Huang, B. 2002. An analysis of factors affecting price volatility of the US oil market. *Energy Economics* 24, 107–119.

Yaziz, S., Ahmad, M., Nian, L., Muhammad, N. 2011. A comparative study on Box-Jenkins and GARCH models in forecasting crude oil prices. *Journal of Applied Sciences* 11, 1129–1135.

24

Mutual funds and the energy sector

Alper Gormus

1   Introduction

Regardless of their skill level, one of the popular ways for investors to participate in the markets is via mutual funds. Mutual funds are essentially entities that hold a variety of assets (stocks, bonds, commodities, etc.) and offer proportional exposure of their assets (referred to as their portfolios) to investors who are willing to buy shares of those funds. In other words, if an investor buys a share of a mutual fund, they own a proportional interest in all of the assets under that fund's management.

Mutual funds hold an increasingly larger space in the financial markets. As of 2017, the total net assets (TNA) of mutual funds in the United States was USD 18.75 trillion.[1] This was an approximately 95% increase in TNA since 2008 and a 340% increase since 1998. There is an abundance of academic research which look at the relationship between energy markets and the financial markets. However, the relationship between mutual funds – which represent the whole or part of the markets – and the energy markets is not well understood. Mutual funds come in a variety of formats and categories. While diversified mutual funds have historically catered to a larger investor base, specialized mutual funds have been significantly increasing in popularity. These actively managed funds have managers that buy and sell assets which represent a particular sector and attempt to beat market benchmarks through specialized skill and knowledge. Energy sector mutual funds, in particular, have experienced a significant increase in numbers and interest in recent years. The number of energy mutual funds listed on the Morningstar database increased by 51% in the last five years (as of 2018). Furthermore, the number of energy limited partnership mutual funds increased by 81% in the same time frame. It is well understood that energy companies are directly/indirectly impacted by fluctuations in the energy markets. However, due to the unique diversification/specialization dynamics associated with energy sector mutual funds, inferring similar relationships with the energy markets would be an incomplete/inaccurate conclusion. Furthermore, any identified relationship could be an implication of fund characteristics as well as the assets in the funds' portfolios.

In the following sections, we provide a brief summary of literature related to energy markets, financial markets, and sector mutual funds. Due to the scope of this chapter, we do not provide a detailed literature review regarding the vast academic research in mutual funds. Our aim is to concentrate more on the importance of specialized mutual funds and the need to further explore their relationships with the energy markets.

2 Literature review

2.1 Energy and the financial markets

As energy markets are increasingly more influential on the financial markets around the world, the amount of academic research investigating these relationship dynamics increase as well. Although the suggested inferences from literature can vary, oil prices, in particular, has been shown to be impactful on equity markets, bond markets, and commodity markets. For example, Miller and Ratti (2009) suggest that an increase in oil prices in the short run will yield a similar increase in the stock markets, however, they also argue that this relationship reverses in the long run. On the other hand, other studies, such as the one by Sim and Zhou (2015), suggest that bullish stock markets will be positively affected by negative oil-price shocks.

Although each company's unique business model will yield different responses to oil market shocks, these shocks can significantly change the direction (expansion and contraction) of the stock market as a whole (Jammazi and Aloui 2010). In addition to the prices themselves, oil-price volatility is also shown to significantly interact with financial markets. In their 2013 study, Mensi et al. showed that volatility interaction between the US stock market and oil prices is very strong. On the other hand, Mollick and Assefa argued that, while the oil prices interact heavily with the stock markets, the interaction varies over time. Further investigating the phenomenon, Du and He (2015) not only confirmed the volatility interaction between oil prices and the stock market, but also showed the interaction to be stronger after the 2008 financial crisis. Although oil prices continue to interact with the entire stock market, energy companies have a more intimate relationship with the energy prices and price volatility. Due to a direct dependence relationship, oil price fluctuations can impact and lead energy firms (Ordu and Soytaş 2015). The specifics of the impact of oil prices on energy companies can also depend on how energy companies utilize the commodity. For example, while companies which sell oil products positively react to oil price hikes, oil refineries, which use crude oil as their input, will be negatively impacted (Hammoudeh et al. 2004).

In addition to research about traditional equity markets, some studies showed the oil market to impact other financial markets as well. For example, Nazlioglu et al. (2016) found that oil volatility has a significant influence on real estate investment trusts (REITs). In particular, the results showed a uni-directional price transmission from the oil market to all REIT categories expect mortgage REITs. From the bond market's perspective, Kang et al. (2014) showed that a significant increase in oil demand decreases the aggregate US Bond Index returns. Specifically looking at high-yield bonds, the results of Gormus et al. (2018) study suggested unidirectional volatility relationship between oil prices and the high-yield bond market.

2.2 Sector mutual funds

Mutual funds can be actively or passively managed. If the fund is actively managed, the manager makes all of the asset purchase and sale decisions as well as the overall concentration of the portfolio. These funds usually impose higher investor fees to pay for the "active management". A passive mutual fund typically represents a form of an index and mimics the asset composition and weights of that index. In theory, actively managed mutual funds promise investors access to managers' expertise, minimization of transaction costs (compared to the investor buying all individual assets separately), diversification and efficiency. Although it is still debated whether mutual funds add value to an investor's outlook, the investor expects the fund manager's knowledge, experience and skill to provide consistently abnormal positive returns.[2] More precisely, investors expect and depend on the manager's ability to acquire, process, and capitalize on relevant information towards increasing the fund's performance.

Although literature has an abundance of studies suggesting the inferior performance of actively managed funds relative to their passive counterparts (Jensen 1968; Elton et al. 1993; Brown and Goetzmann 1995; Daniel et al. 1997; Carhart et al. 2002; Cohen et al. 2005; Kosowski et al. 2006 and others), there is also significant evidence of fund managers' ability to outperform passive funds if they specialize/concentrate in certain asset characteristics (Kacperczyk et al. 2005; Keswani and Stolin 2006; Nanda et al. 2004 and others). Given that fund managers are human beings with a finite mental capacity/attention, it is not outrageous to expect managers concentrating on certain asset classes to be more efficient and successful in their portfolio decisions (Kacperczyk et al. 2016). When a fund manager concentrates on a specific category of assets, this allows them to be more precise in information gathering, processing and implementation. More importantly, a manager with superior information regarding a specific asset group/category should capitalize on that information and hold a concentrated portfolio (Levy and Livingston 1995). Specialized funds come in many shapes and sizes. They can convey a particular style of investment such as putting more weight on the size of the assets or specialize in a particular class of assets (debt, equity, commodity, etc.). As another dimension, these specializations might convey a geographical location or economic classification. One type of specialization that has been increasingly interesting to investors is related to industry concentration. These so-called sector funds put self-imposed restrictions on their portfolio diversification and heavily weigh towards (or exclusively compromise) a particular sector. Recently there has been an increase in the number of mutual funds which specialize in the energy sector. Although literature related to energy sector mutual funds is limited (and will be discussed later in the chapter), there is significant research which suggest interesting inferences regarding the performance of sector funds in general.

In their 1997 study, Khorana and Nelling evaluated 147 sector funds from 1976 to 1992 and compared them with the management and performance of 983 other domestic equity funds. The broadly defined sectors included finance, health, metals, natural resources, technology, utilities and the "unaligned" specialty sector.[3] The dataset showed that sector funds typically have higher expense ratios and consist of higher front-end loads compared to diversified funds. Authors argued that sector funds tend to be smaller in size (diversified domestic equity funds are found to be twice as large as sector funds) and their expense/load characteristics are indicative of those funds' inability to take full advantage of economies of scale.

When Khorana and Nelling (1997) evaluated the performance of sector funds over a three-year window (1989 to 1992), they found that sector funds underperform compared to the broader S&P 500 index. However, the same sector funds were observed to overperform sector-specific benchmarks. In other words, performance evaluation of sector funds is sensitive to the sector benchmarks used. In addition to performance in general, authors evaluated the performance persistence of sector funds. Their findings showed no evidence that sector funds had any persistence in performance relative to their peers. More precisely, only about 10% of the sector funds exhibited persistence. Furthermore, while total risk (as measured by standard deviation of returns) was found to be slightly higher for sector funds, the "beta" risk was found to be lower; suggesting these funds to be possibly useful in decreasing the overall risk of a diversified portfolio. In other words, while sector funds are typically less diversified, they do not represent a higher systematic risk for the investor.

In the United States, multiple sector definitions exist and they are not monitored or clearly defined. Therefore, fund managers can take advantage of these fluid definitions and game their sector/industry affiliations (Cooper et al. 2005). While Khorana and Nelling (1997) used self-identified industry categories in their study, Kacperczyk et al. (2005) chose to look at the individual assets in a given fund to measure the specialization intensity of that fund. Using domestic mutual funds and a date span from 1984 to 1999, authors constructed a measure called Industry Concentration Index (ICI). ICI essentially measures the deviation of a fund from the market portfolio in terms of industry diversification. Since the CRSP database does not provide detailed information about funds' holdings, the authors utilized the mutual funds stockholdings database published by CDA Investments Technologies. The CDA database concentrates on US mutual funds and collects data from SEC filings as well as voluntary disclosures by those funds. For this study, it is important to note that the authors intentionally excluded sector funds (as well as bond, index, and international funds) and focused on actively managed diversified funds. They created ten broadly defined industry classifications including consumer non-durable, consumer durable, healthcare, manufacturing, energy, utilities, telecom, business equities and services, wholesale/retail, and finance. One of the key goals of the study was to specifically see how the performance of funds change/compare as they concentrate more on one or more sectors. In order to establish robustness in their results, the authors evaluated the risk adjusted performance of industry concentrated funds using multiple models such as the Carhart (1997) four-factor model, the Ferson and Schadt (1996) conditional factor model, and the Daniel et al. (1997) holding-based performance measure.

The findings of Kacperczyk et al. (2005) study were interesting and revealed several key characteristics of mutual funds. First, authors observed that mutual funds substantially differ in their industry concentrations and have distinct investment styles. The funds that have more industry concentrations were seen to be overweight in growth and small-cap stocks. On the other hand, less concentrated (more diversified) funds were observed to mimic the market portfolio. From the perspective of performance, the results showed the concentrated funds to be superior compared to diversified funds. Furthermore, funds that concentrate on one or more industries were observed to have better stock picking abilities even after controlling for average industry performance. Last but not least, the authors also presented evidence of the increased value of trades for concentrated funds when they analyzed their buy and sell decisions. These results supported the previous findings of Nanda et al. (2004) which suggested that funds with focused investment strategies outperform others due to possible informational advantages.

The phenomenon of concentrated funds outperforming diversified funds was further investigated by Keswani and Stolin (2006) using UK mutual funds. These funds are ideal for studying the impacts of sector concentrations because, unlike the US system, the UK system has clearly defined and monitored sector definitions. Compiling a data set which spans from 1991 to 2001, authors used sector definitions officially identified by the Association of Unit Trust and Investment Funds (and its successor, the Investment Management Association). The key metric Keswani and Stolin (2006) wanted to evaluate was persistence in performance. In other words, they wanted to see whether funds which choose to concentrate on a sector had any recognizable performance persistence that can be associated with their industry concentration. The time window used to investigate this question was yearly[4] and the results were measured as relative performance. Authors also used variables such as number of funds in the sector, the concentration of fund family assets under management in the sector and the proportion of mature funds in the sector in order to capture competition in a given sector. Furthermore, authors controlled for the asset types in which the funds were invested. The results confirmed what previous research had suggested. Funds that concentrate on specific sectors not only have informational advantages but also portray persistence in their performance. In other words, as the industry concentration of a fund goes up, the future performance of that fund becomes more predictable.

2.3   Energy markets and specialized mutual funds

Although sector funds as a group has been studied in literature, the dynamics of individual sector categories and their place in the overall market has been less explored. For example, while numerous studies show macro shocks to be impactful on the overall stock market, the question of whether sector funds react any differently has not been clearly answered. Energy markets are abundantly shown to impact a variety of markets around the world. However, do they have similar effects on concentrated/specialized funds? One of the attempts to answer this question was the study by Ewing et al. (2018). In their analysis, the authors evaluated the impacts of energy markets (natural gas and oil) on the emerging market mutual funds (EMMFs). These types of specialized funds increased in popularity because in addition to the promise of providing conventionally anticipated benefits of investing in mutual funds (lower overall transaction costs, manager's expertise, etc.), it allows many domestic investors the opportunity to diversify in global markets without having to invest in significant amounts of research time. Although a large portion of these funds were shown to perform better than domestic funds, there can still be a large variety in performance among them (Huij and Post 2011).

In their study, Ewing et al. (2018) collected all diversified EMMFs listed in the Morningstar Database (Morningstar) and matched them with corresponding returns in the CRSP database. With a total of 518 EMMFs, authors used oil price and natural gas price futures (one-month contracts) and tested whether volatility from the energy markets interacted with the volatility of EMMFs. Their results showed that the 2008 financial crisis was important in defining the strength and direction of volatility interactions. For example, authors showed that while the volatility transmission of oil prices to EMMFs increased after 2008, transmission from natural gas volatility decreased. More interestingly, the results showed a significant volatility transmission from EMMFs to oil and natural gas prices before 2008 (much stronger than the transmission from the same energy prices to EMMFs). Although this interaction decreased with oil price volatility after 2008, it did not change much in the case of natural gas. Authors concluded that not only these funds and the energy prices were very closely interacting, they also suggested a decreased diversification benefit of combining EMMFs with energy commodities in the same portfolio.

Another type of sector funds that gained significant popularity in the last decade has been energy sector funds (EMFs). Similar to all other sector funds, there are inside and outside factors that impact the overall success and sustainability of EMFs. While some outside shocks can be influential on the entire stock market, other shocks can have more specialized effects on these funds. Oil prices, for example, are shown in literature to impact energy companies as well as the entire stock market (Gormus and Atinc 2016).

Mutual funds which concentrate/specialize in energy companies portray a unique risk profile for both managers and investors. Fund managers are not only tasked with accurately picking assets but also watch for micro and macro shocks which might impact the market as well as the sector itself. More interestingly, while an external shock can have a positive impact on one aspect of the portfolio, the same shock can have a negative impact on another aspect. Oil prices, which can impact the entire market as well as the energy sector itself, become an extremely important information source for EMF managers. However, as of publication of this chapter, the only study we could identify which evaluated the relationships between oil prices and EMFs was the study by Gormus et al. (2018).

In their study, the Gormus et al. (2018) not only evaluated the price level and the volatility impacts of oil prices on EMFs, but also investigated the mutual fund characteristics which impacted those relationships. Using the Morningstar sector categories, authors identified 91 unique EMFs. From the same database, authors collected fund characteristics information such as market capitalizations, manager tenure, fund size (total assets), management fees, number of holdings, Morningstar rating, expense ratio, return profile, risk profile and turnover ratio. Utilizing the CRSP database for daily fund prices and US Energy Information Association for oil prices, authors constructed several econometric models and tested the interactions between the variables.

In the first part of their study, Gormus et al. (2018) tested for price transmissions (at level) between the oil market and the EMFs in their dataset. Using a modified vector autoregression framework, the authors found that the majority of the EMFs were directly impacted by oil prices. In particular, 61 of the 91 EMFs were observed to be led by oil prices. In order to see whether the volatility of oil prices had any impact on the EMFs, authors utilized a volatility transmission model developed by Hafner and Herwartz (2006). This approach uses a Lagrange multiplier framework and has several advantages over previously developed volatility transmission models.[5] The results showed that even more EMFs (66 compared to the 61 from previous test) were impacted by oil price volatility and many of those relationships were bidirectional.

Although the direct/indirect impacts of oil prices on the EMFs were interesting results, they were still somewhat expected. As previously mentioned, oil prices not only have a macro impact on the entire stock market but also are intimately related to the business models of energy companies. What was an even more interesting outcome of the Gormus et al. (2018) study was the specific mutual fund characteristics authors identified which increased the probability of oil price sensitivity. Morningstar does not rate all funds. So authors first evaluated whether having a Morningstar rating had any impact on the EMFs interaction with oil prices. Using a logit regression framework, authors showed that having a Morningstar rating did increase the probability of oil prices impacting EMFs. Furthermore, authors found that market capitalization, manager's tenure and fees also increased the probability of an interaction with oil prices.

As for the fund characteristics which impacted the probability of a volatility transmission between the oil market and EMFs, authors showed that having a Morningstar rating, market capitalization, and manager's tenure to be significant. Authors explained that as a fund holds larger companies, the probability of a volatility interaction goes up. As for the manager's tenure, the results were the opposite. As the manager becomes more experienced in that particular fund, oil price volatility has a lower chance of impacting the fund. In other words, as the manager is more tenured, they do a better job in diversification.

As the last part of their analysis, authors concentrated only on Morningstar-rated EMFs. The results showed that in addition to the specific rating given by Morningstar to be an important factor, the return profile identified by Morningstar to also be important in increasing the chances of an interaction with oil price volatility. More interestingly, the results showed an unexpected relationship between the number of holdings in an EMF and its probability of interaction. As the number of holdings went up in an EMF, the probability of interaction with oil prices also went up. Although conventional wisdom states that an increase in number of assets should, in theory, decrease risk exposure, authors suggest that this result could be due to systematic effects of oil prices. In other words, as the number of assets in a portfolio goes up, that portfolio gets closer to a market portfolio and should be more prone to macro shocks that impact the entire market. So, maybe not only the specialization/concentration of a fund in terms of a sector is important, but also the number of specialized assets in a given portfolio are crucial as well. This argument could further support the suggestions of Kacperczyk et al. (2016) which state that managers are limited in their capabilities and attention. Fewer moving parts could mean the manager is being more efficient in terms of processing and acting on information per asset in the portfolio.

3 Conclusion

The literature covered in this chapter not only show the unique characteristics and importance of specialized mutual funds, but also underlines the importance of paying specific attention to EMFs. As the investment space that mutual funds occupy continues to grow, EMFs are expected to play an even more significant role in the future. In addition to studying the energy sector and energy companies, research which pays close attention to EMFs should provide further insight into the ever-changing dynamics of the stock and energy markets. Future studies which concentrate on how various investment strategies fare when they include EMFs as well as how EMFs compare/contrast with other types of specialized mutual funds would be very fruitful and revealing. Furthermore, one of the mainstream tracks of general mutual fund research which concentrate on herding behavior could be extended into specialized mutual funds in light of macro shocks.

Notes

1 https://www.statista.com/topics/1441/mutual-funds/
2 The advantages and disadvantages of investing in mutual funds is still highly debated. Although the scope of this chapter is not to add to that debate, interested readers can refer to studies such as Wermers (2000), Guercio and Reuter (2014), and Kacperczyk et al. (2016) and others for further information.
3 The authors define unaligned funds as specialty funds which concentrate on an economic sector that is different than the other six sectors used in the study.
4 Keswani and Stolin (2006) give a detailed explanation of why using time horizons of less or more than one year are not as viable as their version. Please refer to their study for further information.
5 Please see Gormus et al. (2018) for a thorough explanation of the model and its advantages over other conventional tests.

References

Brown, S. J., & Goetzmann, W. N. (1995). Performance persistence. *The Journal of Finance*, *50*(2), 679–698.
Carhart, M. M. (1997). On persistence in mutual fund performance. *The Journal of Finance*, *52*(1), 57–82.
Carhart, M. M., Carpenter, J. N., Lynch, A. W., & Musto, D. K. (2002). Mutual fund survivorship. *The Review of Financial Studies*, *15*(5), 1439–1463.
Cohen, R. B., Coval, J. D., & Pástor, Ľ. (2005). Judging fund managers by the company they keep. *The Journal of Finance*, *60*(3), 1057–1096.
Cooper, M. J., Gulen, H., & Rau, P. R. (2005). Changing names with style: Mutual fund name changes and their effects on fund flows. *The Journal of Finance*, *60*(6), 2825–2858.
Daniel, K., Grinblatt, M., Titman, S., & Wermers, R. (1997). Measuring mutual fund performance with characteristic-based benchmarks. *The Journal of Finance*, *52*(3), 1035–1058.
Du, L., & He, Y. (2015). Extreme risk spillovers between crude oil and stock markets. *Energy Economics*, 51, 455–465.
Elton, E. J., Gruber, M. J., Das, S., & Hlavka, M. (1993). Efficiency with costly information: A reinterpretation of evidence from managed portfolios. *The Review of Financial Studies*, *6*(1), 1–22.
Ewing, B. T., Gormus, A., & Soytaş, U. (2018). Risk transmission from oil and natural gas futures to emerging market mutual funds. *Emerging Markets Finance and Trade*, *54*(8), 1828–1837.
Ferson, W. E., & Schadt, R. W. (1996). Measuring fund strategy and performance in changing economic conditions. *The Journal of Finance*, *51*(2), 425–461.
Gormus, A., Diltz, J. D., & Soytaş, U. (2018). Energy mutual funds and oil prices. *Managerial Finance*, *44*(3), 374–388.
Gormus, A., Nazlioglu, S., & Soytaş, U. (2018). High-yield bond and energy markets. *Energy Economics*, 69, 101–110.
Gormus, N. A., & Atinc, G. (2016). Volatile oil and the US economy. *Economic Analysis and Policy*, 50, 62–73.
Guercio, D. D., & Reuter, J. (2014). Mutual fund performance and the incentive to generate alpha. *The Journal of Finance*, *69*(4), 1673–1704.

Hafner, C. M., & Herwartz, H. (2006). A Lagrange multiplier test for causality in variance. *Economics Letters*, *93*(1), 137–141.

Hammoudeh, S., Dibooglu, S., & Aleisa, E. (2004). Relationships among US oil prices and oil industry equity indices. *International Review of Economics & Finance*, *13*(4), 427–453.

Huij, J., & Post, T. 2011. On the performance of emerging market equity mutual funds. *Emerging Markets Reviews*, *12*, 238–249.

Jammazi, R., and Aloui, C. (2010). Wavelet decomposition and regime shifts: Assessing the effects of crude oil shocks on stock market returns. *Energy Policy*, *38*(3), 1415–1435.

Jensen, M. C. (1968). The performance of mutual funds in the period 1945–1964. *The Journal of Finance*, *23*(2), 389–416.

Kang, W., Ronald A. Ratti, and Kyung, H. Y. (2014). The impact of oil price shocks on US bond market returns. *Energy Economics*, *44*, 248–258.

Kacperczyk, M., Sialm, C., & Zheng, L. (2005). On the industry concentration of actively managed equity mutual funds. *The Journal of Finance*, *60*(4), 1983–2011.

Kacperczyk, M., Van Nieuwerburgh, S., & Veldkamp, L. (2016). A rational theory of mutual funds' attention allocation. *Econometrica*, *84*(2), 571–626.

Keswani, A., & Stolin, D. (2006). Mutual fund performance persistence and competition: A cross-sector analysis. *Journal of Financial Research*, *29*(3), 349–366.

Khorana, A., & Nelling, E. (1997). The performance, risk, and diversification of sector funds. *Financial Analysts Journal*, 62–74.

Kosowski, R., Timmermann, A., Wermers, R., & White, H. (2006). Can mutual fund "stars" really pick stocks? New evidence from a bootstrap analysis. *The Journal of Finance*, *61*(6), 2551–2595.

Levy, A., & Livingston, M. (1995). *Financial Markets, Institutions & Instruments: The Gains from Diversification Reconsidered: Transaction Costs and Superior Information*. Cambridge, MA: Blackwell Publishers.

Miller, J. I., & Ratti, R. A. (2009). Crude oil and stock markets: Stability, instability, and bubbles. *Energy Economics*, *31*(4), 559–568.

Mollick, A. V., & Assefa, T. A. (2013). US stock returns and oil prices: The tale from daily data and the 2008–2009 financial crisis. *Energy Economics*, *36*, 1–18.

Nanda, V., Wang, Z. J., & Zheng, L. (2004). Family values and the star phenomenon: Strategies of mutual fund families. *The Review of Financial Studies*, *17*(3), 667–698.

Nazlioglu, S., Gormus, N. A., & Soytaş, U. (2016). Oil prices and real estate investment trusts (REITs): Gradual-shift causality and volatility transmission analysis. *Energy Economics*, *60*, 168–175.

Ordu, B. M., & Soytaş, U. (2015). The relationship between energy commodity prices and electricity and market index performances: Evidence from an emerging market. *Emerging Markets Finance and Trade*, 1–16.

Sim, N., & Zhou, H. (2015). Oil prices, US stock return, and the dependence between their quantiles. *Journal of Banking and Finance*, *55*, 1–8.

Wermers, R. (2000). Mutual fund performance: An empirical decomposition into stock-picking talent, style, transactions costs, and expenses. *The Journal of Finance*, *55*(4), 1655–1703.

25

Oil prices and other energy commodities

Syed Abul Basher

1 Introduction

Coal, oil, and gas have been the primary fuels of the modern industrial economy for the past 250 years. "If coal drove the industrial revolution, oil fueled the internal-combustion engine, aviation",[1] and every realm of modern life. Natural gas, due to its availability, affordability, and environmental acceptability, is likely to be the most preferred fuel of the 21st century.

In recent years, prices of natural gas and coal are exhibiting similar volatility that is usually seen in crude oil prices. The main reasons behind the increased price volatility are market liberalization and greater international trade of these primary energy fuels. In that process, both natural gas and coal are increasingly exposed to the same common factors affecting crude oil prices. It's no wonder that the behavior of natural gas and coal prices are getting more like that of crude oil prices (Figures 25.1 and 25.2).

Historically, a simple 10-to-1 and 6-to-1 rule of thumb have been used to relate natural gas prices to those for crude oil (Brown and Yücel 2008). According to this rule, a $50 WTI crude oil per barrel would mean a natural gas price of $5 per million BTU at Henry Hub. In practice, the relative price relationship is more complex is determined by a variety of demand- and supply-side factors.[2]

Despite being a highly polluting fuel (relative to natural gas), coal still accounts for roughly one-third of global energy and makes up 40% of electricity generation. The price of coal follows a cycle like oil even though their demand and supply are affected by different dynamics. Since 2010, both coal and oil prices have been falling roughly in tandem and the common factor behind this price decline is a massive production of US shale gas.

Regardless of all the environmental concerns with using fossil fuels, the world has been consuming more fossil fuels and global energy appetite is projected to grow by 28% between 2015 and 2040 (Figure 25.3). Driven by strong economic growth, most of the demand for fossil fuel is expected to come from Asia, especially China and India.

While direct competition and substitution between these primary fuels are somewhat limited in the short term, depending on their respective costs of conversion technologies, they may become a much closer economic substitute in the long term (Bachmeier and Griffin 2006). Oil can always replace gas, if we accept a higher CO_2 emission factor. Both oil and coal are easy to transport and store, compared to gas which has the lowest energy density.

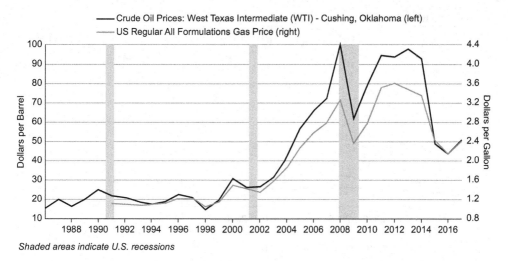

Figure 25.1   Oil and gas prices

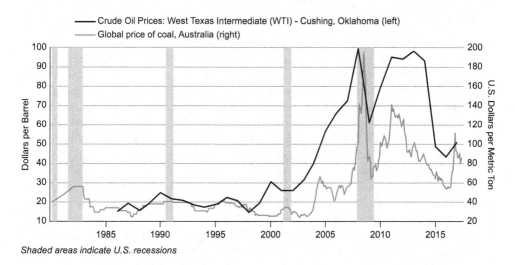

Figure 25.2   Oil and coal prices

Recognizing the crucial importance of the three fossil fuels to the economy, over the past decades a large number of papers have been written on oil prices and other energy commodities. The goal of this chapter is to summarize the recent empirical literature on the relationship between oil price and other energy commodities. These studies are categorized into three groups. The first group of studies examines market integration among fossil fuels, primarily in the context of the United States. The second group of studies examines the predictive content of futures energy prices in forecasting spot prices, while the final set of studies looks at the role of tail risk in energy commodities.

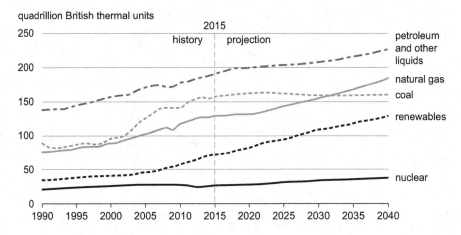

quadrillion British thermal units

Figure 25.3 World energy consumption by energy source

Source: US Energy Information Administration, International Energy Outlook 2017.

2 The interaction between crude oil and other energy commodity prices

There is no better way to understand the complex interaction among crude oil, natural gas, and coal prices than to analyze the power generation industry, which simultaneously uses all three fuels to generate electricity. And nowhere the story gets more interesting than the United States where the forces of regulation, technology, and market forces provide an intriguing narrative.

Unlike industrial use, consumers' relationship with these primary fossil fuels is rather inflexible. Consumers drive cars that run on petroleum and heat their houses with natural gas. No matter how volatile prices are, fuel switching between oil and gas is not a practical option for the consumer because of high adjustment costs, whereas direct use of coal as a fuel is limited to cooking and heating in some parts of the world.

During the late 1960s, there was a sign of growing concerns about emissions from coal-fired power plants in the United States. On 25 November 1966, the front page of the *New York Times* featured an image of New York City engulfed in high levels of smoke and haze. In fact, the air was so filthy that one resident of New York City quipped: "I not only saw the pollution, I wiped it off my windowsills" (Dwyer 2017). Meanwhile, increasing oil production along with low and stable crude oil prices during the 1960s was the catalyst for many to shift from coal- to petroleum-fired power plants. By the early 1970s, the share of oil in electric power generation culminated to around 20% – the highest share ever (Figure 25.4). However, the two great oil shocks in 1973–1974 and 1979 eliminated the cost advantage and oil was virtually banished from power production (Figure 25.4). Furthermore, the Powerplant and Industrial Fuel Use Act of 1978 (PIFUA) had simultaneously restricted the construction of new petroleum and gas power plants and encouraged the construction of new coal-based power plants. As a result, during the 1980s – when global crude oil prices were on a downhill slope, especially in the second half of 1980s – coal's share in power generation expanded (Figure 25.4).

A combination of factors has led to a sudden and welcome change in the power sector. First, the PIFUA was repealed in 1987 by President Ronald Regan to pave the way for America's energy independence and energy security. Second, by the early 1990s, the natural gas market in the United States (as well as the United Kingdom) was fully deregulated, allowing fuel substitution

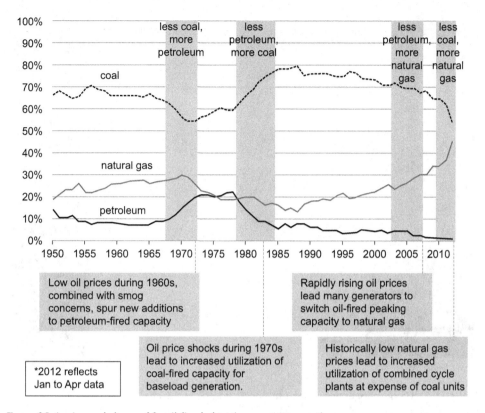

Figure 25.4 Annual share of fossil-fired electric power generation

between petroleum and natural gas as a fuel for peak generation. Higher profit margin driven by the availability of tax credits, in conjunction with the increased use of efficient combined cycle technology for power production, was responsible for much of the growth of the natural gas produced in the United States during the 1990s. Fast-forward to the 2000s, and the rapid rise of domestic shale gas production has not only contributed to a relatively sustained period of low natural gas prices, but it has also further encouraged power plant operators to use more combined-cycle units by gradually displacing coal generation (Figure 25.4).

The basic mechanism underlying the interaction between oil and gas can be traced through both demand- and supply-side channels.[3] The demand side channel concerns to what extent (or how easily) energy consumers can switch to natural gas when, say, the price of oil increases. One way to examine this is by estimating the value of elasticity of substitution. For the United States, the EIA's (2012) estimate of oil-gas elasticity is 1.89, which reflects plant operators' flexibility to choose the most economic fuel and the fact that some combustion turbine and combined-cycle units are designed to run on either petroleum or natural gas. In contrast, the estimated oil-coal elasticity is −0.63, indicating that the two fuels are complements rather than substitutes. Based on a meta-analysis of 47 studies, Stern (2012) finds that compared to the United States the extent of interfuel substitution is higher in India, Korea, Italy, the Netherlands, and Germany. Particularly, for the industrial sector, the estimated elasticities for coal-oil, oil-gas, oil-electricity,[4] and gas-electricity are significantly greater than unity, which Stern (2012) considers as good news for climate mitigation policies concerning replacing dirty fuels (e.g. coal) with relatively cleaner fuels (e.g. gas).

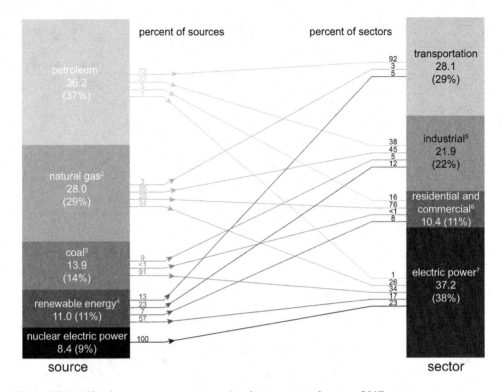

Figure 25.5 US primary energy consumption by source and sector, 2017

Source: EIA. Total = 97.7 quadrillion British thermal units (BTU).

On the supply side, a higher price, say, encourages more drilling which in turn increases production of associated or dissolved gas, that comes along as a basically free by-product when petroleum is produced. In fact, the production of associated gas has become so prominent in the United States in recent years that it triggered an inverse relationship between oil and natural gas prices (Clemente 2018).[5] Furthermore, a higher oil price may lead to a competition for the resource in the sense that skilled labors and drilling equipment are redirected from gas to oil sector due to price differential and increased level of activity.

A better way to understand substitutability or complementariness among fuels is by looking at the sources and usage of fuels. Figure 25.5 shows the primary energy sources and their consuming sectors in 2017 in the United States. As can be seen, in both the transportation and residential sectors, the extent of fuel overlapping is marginal. Only in the industrial and electric power sectors is there an opportunity for fuel substitutability.

3 Empirical evidence

3.1 Market integration

In empirical research, due to the nonstationarity of energy prices, the most common and preferred way to study the integration among oil, gas, and coal markets is by means of time series methods. Thanks to the availability of energy prices at a higher frequency, several studies have used cointegration and error correction techniques to quantify the short- and long-run relationships among prices of fossil fuels. Particularly, cointegration is widely used as a method for testing market integration.

Bachmeier and Griffin (2006) apply error correction model to test market integration both within and between crude oil, coal and natural gas markets. The within market integration in crude oil and coal is quite strong, but market integration between the three primary energy fuels is rather weak. Villar and Joutz (2006) find that the WTI oil price and Henry Hub gas price are cointegrated around a time trend over the period 1989–2005. The statistical significance of the coefficient of time trend suggests that, following a shock, natural gas price grows faster to narrow the gap with crude oil prices. Baffes (2007) finds that out of 35 internationally traded primary commodities, the pass-through of crude oil prices to natural gas was highest with an estimated elasticity of 0.64.

Hartley et al. (2008) derive several interesting results from their empirical study. Unlike previous studies that document a direct relationship between crude oil and natural gas prices, Hartley et al. find that oil prices affect natural gas prices via an indirect route, the residual fuel oil (or heavy fuel oil). This is not surprising since for many years industries and electric power plants in the United States have treated natural gas and residual fuel oil as close substitutes, using whichever fuel was less expensive (Brown and Yücel 2008). Another way of interpreting this result is that both the US natural gas and residual oil prices respond to the changes in international crude oil price, but not the other way around.

Brown and Yücel (2008) fill a gap in the literature by examining how the relationship between natural gas and crude oil change when external factors such as weather, inventories, and disruptions to production are considered. Despite the strong relationship between crude oil and natural gas, both energy prices have considerable independent movement. They find that the prices of both natural gas and crude oil are cointegrated and the causality is running from oil to natural gas prices. The results of the error correction models reveal that when natural gas prices deviate from the long-run equilibrium relationship with crude oil, natural gas prices adjust by roughly 6% a week to close the gap between the two. The rate of adjustment is doubled (12% per week) when the external factors are included in the analysis. The short-term dynamics of natural gas prices are driven by a variety of transitory and other exogenous factors, while in the long term the history of natural gas prices contributes to its motion.

However, Ramberg and Parsons (2012) have shown that the cointegrating relationship between crude oil and natural gas prices has changed over time. Put another way, the historical relationship documented in earlier studies cannot be used as a reliable predictor of the natural gas prices, at least in the longer horizon. One possible explanation for the shifting long-run equilibrium relationships between crude oil and natural gas prices is the improvement of technology in horizontal drilling and hydraulic fracturing to makes it possible to extract shale gas at a relatively low cost.

In conventional time series methods such as cointegration, the frequency and time components of economic series are analyzed separately. Time-frequency techniques such as wavelet analysis study overcome this limitation by studying the frequency components of time series without losing the time information. Vacha and Barunik (2012) apply the wavelet method to analyze co-movement among four energy variables (crude oil, gasoline, heating oil, and natural gas). Their results suggest that while heating oil, gasoline, and crude oil strongly comove, natural gas is unrelated to the three commodities. From the investment perspective, this finding implies incorporating natural gas in a well-diversified commodity portfolio.

3.2 The predictive content of energy futures

Energy prices, especially oil price, have a historical relationship with macroeconomic fluctuations. Hamilton (2011) pointed out that 10 of the 11 postwar recessions in the United States have been preceded by a sharp increase in oil price. Recognizing this relationship, Chinn et al. (2005) examine whether futures prices are unbiased and/or accurate predictors of subsequent spot prices in the markets for crude oil, natural gas, gasoline, and heating oil. In so doing, Chinn et al. consider the following regression specification:

$$s_t - s_{t-1} = \alpha + \beta\left(f_{t,t-k} - s_{t-k}\right) + \varepsilon_t \tag{25.1}$$

where the left-hand side of Equation (25.1) is the change in the spot rate and the term in parentheses on the right-hand side is called the "basis" in the commodity futures literature. The composite null hypothesis is $\alpha = 0$ and $\beta = 1$, where a rejection implies the rejection of the joint hypothesis of market efficiency and unbiased expectations.

Chinn et al. find that only for natural gas, futures prices have some ability to predict future spot prices, especially at the longer horizon (12 months). This result seems a bit surprising given the very high comovement among the prices of different energy products. In a subsequent study, Chinn and Coibion (2013) use a regression like Equation (25.1) and find that by exploiting information from heating oil and natural gas, one can anticipate a larger fraction of ex post oil price changes. Their results suggest that oil futures prices do not only fail to predict its own ex post price changes but also prices of other commodities. Moreover, since the mid-2000s the effectiveness of the predictive content of energy (and commodity) futures has sharply reduced.

In a recent paper, Jin (2016) proposed a future-based unobserved components forecasting model of crude oil price that utilizes the term structure of the future prices as additional regressors. Compared to Chinn and Coibion (2013), Jin's (2016) model provides better forecasts of oil price due to the latter's more granular assessment of the changing short-term component volatility or the changing market conditions.

3.3   Tail risk

Since the 2007–2008 global financial crisis, "tail risk" has become a buzzword among commodity traders and investors in energy markets. Tail risk is a low probability event that has an outsize impact on prices. Event such as the Eurozone sovereign debt crisis, tsunami in Japan, the Federal Reserve's possible tapering of asset purchases, and unrest in the Middle East caught many investors by surprise and the belated realization that safeguarding their portfolios against such events (both large and small) must become a more integral part of their investment strategy (*TheEconomist 2012*). Indeed, the survey of institutional investors shows that not only they routinely underestimate tail risk events, but the commonly used volatility-based risk management tools such as value-at-risk (VaR) also produce artificially depressed volatilities (*The Economist* 2012; Grepin et al. 2010).[6]

There is a growing body of empirical work[7] analyzing the impact of tail risk on asset market, but relatively few studies on the role of tail risk in explaining oil price volatility. The main reason for focusing on tail risk is to gauge the forecasting power of future asset returns that is not contained in traditional asset price predictors. Ellwanger (2017) finds that the tail risk measures have strong predictability for crude oil futures and spot returns. Furthermore, the option–implied tail risk premia convey important information on price dynamics of crude oil than traditional macroeconomic and oil market uncertainty measures.

Ewing et al. (2002) find that volatility in the natural gas market is indirectly affected by events originating in the oil sector. However, their results also show that a change in volatility in natural gas returns affects the volatility in oil returns (with a lag), implying that options traders in oil market may benefit by keeping a close eye on events in the natural gas market. On the other hand, based on daily natural gas and crude oil futures price data, Pindyck (2004) found that crude oil volatility has significant predictive power with respect to natural gas volatility but not the other way around. Unlike Ewing et al. (2002), Pindyck found volatility persistent to be short-lived, implying that fluctuations in volatility are unlikely to impact the value of real options in oil- or gas-related investment.

Besides exerting a direct effect in the form of higher gasoline prices, unanticipated oil price shocks affect expectations about the future path of the price of oil which in turn feed into the calculations of the net present value of investment decision (Baumeister and Kilian 2016). A case in point is shale gas production in the United States, which requires a crude oil price of $60 a barrel for shale gas to be economically viable. Hence, when oil price is rising, the shale gas sector attracts more investment than expected, whereas the momentum quickly turns reverse when oil price collapses.

The 2018 US-China trade war is yet another sign of how a dramatic shock in oil market could spillover into other energy commodities. Following the US duties on Chinese imports, China is contemplating to impose a 25% tariff on crude oil and other energy commodities (Kumon 2018). However, China is not banning import of US LNG, which is seen vital to the country's shift away from coal as it fights deteriorating air pollution. At the same time, China is considering importing more gas from the Middle East.

4 Discussion and conclusions

Oil shaped the 20th century through wars and prosperity. Against many predictions that the influence of crude oil would wane as new supplies and sources of energy become abundant, oil's dominance remains entrenched at least in the first half of the 21st century. A primary reason for this is the extremely slow process of changing the global fuel mix toward more cleaner energy sources. The most likely outcome for oil in the coming decades is a long plateau rather than a sharp decline.

Despite the vast literature on the nexus between oil prices and other energy commodities, there is much room for future research. First, as the supply of natural gas becomes abundant and stable, will gas follow oil to become a liquid global market with growing disconnection from oil production and prices? Second, what if citizens of richer countries decide to stop buying oil from countries with highly repressive governments, such as Saudi Arabia and Venezuela? What would be the potential impacts of such a low probability event on oil price and the resulting spillover into other energy commodities? Third, compared to about 40 years in the United States, the average age of the coal plants in Asia is only 11 years.[8] Given a lifetime of 50 years, there is still plenty of coal to be burnt in Asia. As gas price is rising in response to increasing demand in Asia, how China and India will trade off the use of coal and gas in their energy mix will be a very important topic of discussing in the decades ahead. Finally, it is still not clear why the predictive content of futures prices has become less important for subsequent price changes of energy products, and whether incorporating a richer dynamic specification of the spot and futures prices would yield superior forecasts.

As public policymakers and business professionals closely track the commodity prices, the erosion of the predictive content of future prices is a matter of serious concern across all policy areas. Furthermore, the weakening and changing equilibrium relationship between crude oil and natural gas prices, as documented by numerous time series studies, is potentially making the task of managing energy price volatility even more difficult.

Notes

1 *Economist*, "Special Report: Oil", 26 November 2016.
2 For instance, the price ratio of natural gas to crude oil fluctuated from almost 6 in December 2008 to 36 in September 2009 before falling to 21 by the end of 2010 (Ramberg and Parsons 2012).

3 See Villar and Joutz (2006) for a discussion of demand and supply side factors linking crude oil and natural gas prices.
4 Electricity is considered an alternative fuel and can be produced from a variety of energy sources including oil, coal, natural gas, nuclear energy, hydropower, wind energy, solar energy, and stored hydrogen.
5 In addition, the increasing availability of liquefied natural gas (LNG), in conjunction with growing spot gas trading, has contributed to the recent decoupling of gas price from oil price.
6 Some estimates reckon that if Israel attacks Iran – a rather low probability event – it could push oil prices temporarily towards $250 a barrel (Blas 2011). A crisis like that would not only affect oil prices, but also natural gas and coal prices, and even the cost of agriculture raw materials where oil is used as an input.
7 See Kelly and Jiang (2014) and the references cited therein.
8 Birol (2018).

References

Bachmeier, L.J. and Griffin, J.M. (2006) Testing for market integration crude oil, coal, and natural gas. *Energy Journal* 27, 55–71.

Baffes, J. (2007) Oil spills on other commodities. Policy Research Working Paper 4333, The World Bank.

Baumeister, C. and Kilian, L. (2016) Forty years of oil price fluctuations: Why the price of oil may still surprise us. *Journal of Economic Perspectives* 30, 139–160.

Birol, F. (2018) *The global energy outlook.* Podcast, Columbia Energy Exchange, Center on Global Energy Policy, Columbia University, New York.

Blas, J. (2011) Oil investors brace for rough ride. *Financial Times*, December 13.

Brown, S. and Yücel, M. (2008) What drives natural gas prices? *Energy Journal* 29, 45–60.

Chinn, M.D. and Coibion, O. (2013) The predictive content of commodity futures. *Journal of Futures Markets* 34, 607–636.

Chinn, M.D., LeBlanc, M. and Coibion, O. (2005) The predictive content of energy futures: An update on petroleum, natural gas, heating oil and gasoline. NBER Working Paper No. 11033, Cambridge, MA.

Clemente, J. (2018) The rise of U.S. associated natural gas. *Forbes*, June 3.

Dwyer, J. (2017) Remembering a city where the smog could kill. *New York Times*, February 28.

EIA (2012) Fuel competition in power generation and elasticities of substitution. *Independent Statistics & Analysis, U.S. Energy Information Administration*, June 2012, Washington DC.

The Economist (2012) *Managing investments in volatile markets: How institutional investors are guarding against tail risk events.* Economist Intelligence Unit, London.

Ellwanger, R. (2017) On the tail risk premium in the oil market. Bank of Canada Staff Working Paper 2017-46, Ottawa.

Ewing, B.T., Malik, F. and Ozfidan, O. (2002) Volatility transmission in the oil and natural gas markets. *Energy Economics* 24, 525–538.

Grepin, L., Tetrault, J. and Vainberg, G. (2010) *After black swans and red ink: How institutional investors can rethink risk management.* McKinsey & Company, New York, April.

Hamilton, J.D. (2011) Nonlinearities and the macroeconomic effects of oil prices. *Macroeconomic Dynamics* 15, 364–378.

Hartley, P.R., Medlock III, K.B. and Rosthal, J.E. (2008) The relationship of natural gas to oil prices. *Energy Journal* 29, 47–65.

Jin, X. (2016) Does the future price help forecast the spot price? Discussion Paper in Economics No. 16-8, Department of Economics, University of Aberdeen.

Kelly, B. and Jiang, B. (2014) Tail risk and asset prices. *Review of Financial Studies* 27, 2841–2871.

Kumon, T. (2018) Global commodities in for a bumpy ride from US-China trade war. *Nikkei Asian Review*, July 8.

Pindyck, R.S. (2004) Volatility in natural gas and oil markets. *Journal of Energy and Development* 30, 1–19.

Ramberg, D.J. and Parsons, J.E. (2012) The weak tie between natural gas and oil prices. *Energy* 33, 13–35.

Stern, D.I. (2012) Interfuel substitution: A meta-analysis. *Journal of Economic Surveys* 26, 307–331.

Vacha, L. and Barunik, J. (2012) Co-movement of energy commodities revisited: Evidence from wavelet coherence analysis. *Energy Economics* 34, 241–247.

Villar, J. and Joutz, F. (2006) The relationship between crude oil and natural gas prices. *Contemporary Economic Policy* 12, 33–41.

26

Oil and agricultural commodity prices

Saban Nazlioğlu[1]

1 Introduction

Recent dynamics (fluctuations and volatility) of global commodity prices have attracted an interest in examining what are the drivers and consequences of price booms and drops. The literature has focused on energy market linkages, financialization of commodities, macro variables context, and demand-supply equilibrium. This chapter is related to the literature on energy (oil) and agricultural commodity markets linkages and reviews the papers which have new perspectives and documented fresh information to better understand the interrelations between energy and agricultural commodity prices.

The rest of the chapter is organized as follows. The next section is devoted to discuss the drivers of agricultural prices followed by describing a framework for oil and agricultural price linkage in Section 3. Section 4 tries to summarize the empirical literature by focusing on referring to the papers which have employed different econometric methods and documented a fresh information. Finally, in Section 5, the concluding remarks are presented within the context of policy discussion and future directions.

2 Drivers of agricultural prices

In order to better understand what drives agricultural prices, several factors are discussed. Based on the micro economic theory, a price of a commodity is driven by demand- and supply-side conditions. Figure 26.1 describes the demand- and supply-side factors which play a role in the fluctuations of agricultural commodity prices.

2.1 Demand-side factors

The population growth is the primer determinant of demand for agricultural products. No doubt that increase in *population* stimulates demand for agricultural commodities, in particular, for food products. In addition to population growth, economic growth is one of crucial drivers of agricultural prices. The linkage between *economic growth/income increase* and agricultural commodity/food prices is twofold. First, rapid economic growth (especially after 2000 in China and

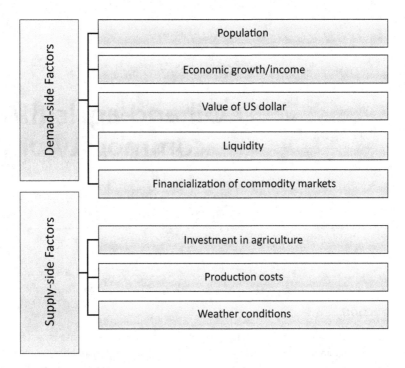

Figure 26.1 The factors driving agricultural commodity prices

India that are emerging market economies) seems to be one of key factors effecting agricultural prices because income increases leads to increase in demand for commodities. Second, as income increases food consumption increases more slowly than other goods and services (Engel's law) and hence the terms of trade between food and manufactured goods prices has declining trends (Prebisch–Singer hypothesis).

The interconnection between *value of the US dollar* and (agricultural) commodity prices is expected to be in a reverse direction. More specifically, global weakness (strength) of the dollar leads to higher (lower) agricultural prices. One reason for this relation is that the dollar is the benchmark currency for pricing agricultural commodities in global markets and thereby agricultural commodity contracts are issued in terms of the dollar. Drops in the value of the dollar requires to pay more dollar for buying commodities, which means higher commodity prices. Weaker dollar also keeps financial investors and speculators in countenance to hold more commodities because of increasing purchasing power by paying less domestic currency, and this tendency increases demand for agricultural commodities in derivatives markets. A fall in the value of the dollar directly drops price of agricultural products in terms of domestic currencies which in turn changes domestic demand for and supply of agricultural commodities.

The relationship between *liquidity* and commodity prices can be clarified within the context of overshooting model of agricultural prices. Frankel (1986) considers how agricultural prices respond to money supply changes and proposes the overshooting model under the closed-economy assumption. A decline in the money supply level in the short run leads to an increase in real interest rates. High interest rates reduce demand for storable commodities and lead speculators to shift out of commodity contracts (Frankel, 2006) and depresses commodity prices which proportionally will fall more than to the change in money supply and thereby overshoot a new long-run equilibrium for generating an expectation of sufficient future appreciation to offset higher interest rates. All these real effects will consequently vanish because the decrease in real interest rate and commodity prices as a result of the reduction in money supply disappears from short run to long run as the general price levels adjust to the money supply changes. Saghaian et al. (2002) relax the closed-economy assumption and develop the overshooting model of agricultural prices by allowing for international trade of agricultural commodities, under the assumption that agriculture and services are the flexible-prices sectors and manufacturing sector is the sticky-prices sector. The model implies that agricultural prices – as a response to money supply changes in the economy – overshoot in the short run and then turn back to their long run levels. The overshooting theory clearly implies that agricultural commodity prices are not only driven by traditional sector-specific microeconomic variables but also are closely related to macroeconomic policy which may have an important role behind agricultural price fluctuations.

After the mid-2000s, it has been observed that there has been substantial increase in capital investment to commodity futures markets, and this process is referred to as the *financialization of commodities*. It leads commodity futures to be popular as much as other classes of assets like stocks and bonds. The energy and agricultural markets which have appreciated large investment inflows of capital move in tandem as a result of the financialization. No doubt that the financialization of commodities is not a phenomenon anymore, there is a growing concentration on whether the financialization creates any distortion on commodity prices. Cheng and Xiong (2014) determine two different views in that respect which are "bubble view" and "business-as-usual view". The proponents of the bubble view argue that speculative behavior of portfolio investors causes price booms in commodity markets by adducing evidence to the 2007–2008 and 2011 bubbles in oil and grain commodities. The business-as-usual view on the other hand propounds that there is a weak evidence in favor of price booms in commodity markets as a result of speculation and commodity markets' speculations do not lead to price distortions. Even though the debate between two different views appears to be still going on, the financialization seems to substantially change behavior of commodity markets through its effects on risk sharing and information discovery (Cheng and Xiong, 2014).

2.2 Supply-side factors

Agricultural growth rate and productivity growth in agriculture have steadily slowed from 1970s which constraint global supply of agricultural commodities. Agricultural production growth on the average was 2.2% per year between 1970 and 1990 and it has declined to about 1.3% since 1990. Agricultural productivity growth contributes much more to global stock levels of agricultural commodities than agricultural production growth. Global average aggregate yield was 2.0% per year between 1970 and 1990, but declined to 1.1% between 1990 and 2007 and it is projected to decline less than 1.0% per year up to 2020 (Trostle, 2008).[2]

The key factor which determines growth in agricultural production and productivity is investment in agriculture. Not only governments but also international institutions have reduced agricultural research and development (R&D), although investment in agriculture from private sector has increased. Nonetheless, private sector investments generally focus on reducing production costs rather than technological development which is the key driver of yield improvements. On the farmers side, farmers solely are unable to invest in agricultural R&D and to pay for yield-enhancing technology to a large extent (Trostle, 2008).

The total cost of production consists of variable costs and fixed costs. The variable costs have two dimensions: cash costs (seeds, fertilizers, pesticides, energy, paid-labor, custom services, etc.) and non-cash costs (unpaid-labor, own-produced inputs, owned-machinery, etc.). The fixed costs on the other hand can be classified into capital costs (depreciation of machinery, equipment), farm overhead costs, and land costs (FAO, 2015). The cost structure is not same for all agricultural commodity prices and it clearly differs for different commodity groups such as beverages, food, and raw materials. Even though there are differences in the structure of production costs for different groups of agricultural commodities, fluctuations in the components of variable costs, in particular cash costs, play a crucial role for commodity price fluctuations.

Last but not least, weather conditions are one of main drivers of agricultural production. Adverse weather conditions result in poor harvest which in turn tightens stock-to-use levels of agricultural products.

3 Oil and agricultural price linkage: a framework

The link between oil and agricultural commodity prices in fact has an historical consideration. Oil prices effect agricultural prices through direct (supply and demand) and indirect (finance) channels (see Figure 26.2). It is a well-known fact that agriculture is an energy-intensive sector and therefore there is a direct *supply-channel* from oil prices to agricultural commodity prices. An increase in oil prices leads to an increase in input and transport costs which in turn causes agricultural prices to rise (Hanson et al., 1993). Some chemicals and fertilizers are also by-products of oil, which increase energy-intensity of agricultural prices to energy markets.

Energy market shocks which lead to oil price booms encourage incentives for production of biofuels (biodiesel and bioethanol) and hence trigger demand for biofuels. Different crops (wheat, corn, soybeans, barley, sugar cane, and sugar beet, as well as other substitute and complementary crops) are used as raw materials in biofuel production. An increase in production of biofuels increases demand for agricultural commodities and in turn leads to rise of agricultural commodity prices. This demand channel hence creates a closer link between energy and agricultural prices. It also affects other agricultural commodity prices because crops used in biofuel production – especially wheat, corn and soybeans – are the key commodities for food in the world. They not only compete with each other but also with other crops for arable land allocation. During the last decade, biofuels are the largest source of demand growth for crops and oilseeds due to the fact that 3% of global area allocated to agricultural raw materials is devoted to biofuels as of 2016 (Baffes, 2016).

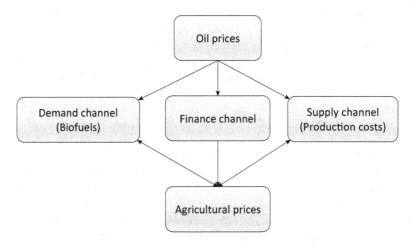

Figure 26.2 Oil and agricultural commodity prices connection

Even though historically neglected, the third link from oil prices to agricultural commodity prices is through the finance channel. The literature on the relationship between oil prices and financial sector documents that changes in oil prices affect stock market returns. This affect influences the financialization of agricultural commodities and agricultural trade. Although the co-movement between stock prices and agricultural commodity prices is found to be weak up to the mid-2000s, it has been getting stronger after the 2007–2008 food price crisis in association with the 2008 financial crisis, due to the fact that the 2008 financial crisis has led financial investors and speculators to flee from mortgage funds to agricultural commodity futures, causing a positive demand shock for agricultural commodities. Oil prices also influence the value of the dollar because oil is mainly traded in terms of the dollar in global markets similar to many commodities. High oil prices increase the dollar revenue of oil exporting countries, resulting in weak dollar in global markets. High oil prices, on the other hand, increase requirements for dollar of oil importing countries, resulting in strong dollar in global markets. Changes in oil prices hence have indirect impact on agricultural commodity prices through its direct impact on the value of dollar. The appreciation/depreciation of local currency, in return, influences local prices of agricultural commodities which would change demand and supply conditions in international markets.

4 Research questions and modeling strategies

Increasing interconnection between oil and agricultural markets has led to a huge and still growing empirical literature. Researches have focused on various kinds of research questions (co-integration, causality, volatility spillover, etc.). Even though it is unfortunately not possible to review all the papers, it is fortunately possible to draw a picture which mirrors the differences in research questions and modeling strategies.[3]

An early attempt goes back to Hanson et al. (1993), who apply an economy-wide environment computable general equilibrium (CGE) model to analyze the effects of a world oil price shocks on US agriculture and indicate that the impacts of oil price shocks vary among agricultural commodities. The study finds out that oil prices affect agriculture not only through direct and indirect input costs but also through exchange rate and foreign borrowing. CGE models suffer from arbitrary determined or calibrated price elasticities for simulating long-run sensitivity of agricultural commodity prices to oil price shocks. Since CGE framework is based on a long-run perspective, it is not able to examine interdependence between oil and agricultural prices within the context of short- to long-run perspective. If the question is to focus on modeling short-run dynamics and long-run structural behavior, one can utilize from the co-integration framework. Campiche et al. (2007) by employing co-integration analysis examine the co-movements between world crude oil and corn, sorghum, sugar, soybeans, soybean oil, and palm oil prices. The results show that while there is no co-integrating relation between oil and agricultural prices for the period 2003–2005, corn and soybean prices are co-integrated with crude oil prices during the 2006–2007 period.

Another aspect of empirical research question is to examine causal linkages between energy (specifically oil) and agricultural commodity prices. The widely used common approach is standard Granger causality analysis (Granger, 1969), which is based on estimation of VAR (vector auto regressions) or VEC (vector error correction) models. Zhang et al. (2010) estimate VEC models to distinguish short and long-run causal linkages between energy (oil, ethanol, gasoline) and agricultural commodity (corn, rice, soybeans, sugar, and wheat) prices. Authors not only find out that the agricultural commodity prices are neutral to the energy prices in the long run but also there is a weak evidence for the short-run interconnections.

The standard Granger causality analysis is sensitive to unit root and co-integration properties of VAR system and requires a careful pretesting procedure because the distribution of Wald statistic for testing causality hypothesis depends on integration order (degree of unit root) and nuisance parameters. The causality approach proposed by Toda and Yamamoto (1995) overcomes these problems and is widely used for causality analysis during last two decades. Kwon and Koo (2009) explore causal relationships among energy prices, exchange rate, and food prices for the US economy by means of the Toda and Yamamoto approach and find out that the exchange rate and energy prices affect food prices thorough various channels. Nazlioglu and Soytaş (2011), for an emerging market economy (Turkey), examine short- and long-run interdependence between world oil prices, lira-dollar exchange rate, and individual agricultural commodity prices (wheat, corn, cotton, soybeans, and sunflower). The long-run causality analysis reveals that the changes in oil prices and appreciation/depreciation of the Turkish lira are not transmitted to agricultural commodity prices in Turkey.

The causality analysis is based on Granger (1969) and Toda and Yamamoto (1995) is not able to capture regime/structural changes in causal linkages. In the presence of regime shifts, nonlinear models work better than linear models to obtain information for forecast (Baek and Brock, 1992; Chiou-Wei et al., 2008). The recent studies (Bekiros and Diks, 2008; Cheng-Lang et al., 2010; Kim et al., 2010) in the energy literature call an attention to investigate nonlinear causal linkages between oil and agricultural commodity prices due to the fact that commodity prices seem to be higher than their historical levels, signaling new price regimes.[4] Nazlioglu (2011) extends the literature on the oil-agricultural commodity prices nexus by particularly concentrating on nonlinear causal relationships between the world oil and agricultural commodity prices (corn, soybeans, and wheat) by employing the nonparametric causality method of Diks and Panchenko (2006). He finds out that while the linear causality analysis supports evidence on the neutrality, the nonlinear causality analysis shows an evidence on nonlinear feedbacks between the oil and the agricultural prices.

Either ignoring structural breaks in VAR models or incorrect specifications of them could falsely result in rejecting the null hypothesis of non-causality (Enders and Jones, 2016; Nazlioglu et al., 2016). It is therefore important to not only account for any structural shifts but also measure structural changes with a careful treatment. In a VAR specification, controlling for structural breaks and determining their sources are challenging because a break in one variable potentially causes shifts in other variables (Enders and Jones, 2016). One simple way to accommodate structural changes is to estimate rolling regressions and conduct causality analysis in each step. Cooke (2009) carries out rolling Granger causality tests to examine whether causal linkages between oil and agricultural (wheat, corn, soybean, and rice) prices are subject to any structural changes. The results present that there is an information flow from oil to corn prices in the second half of 2004.

Rolling window regressions approach to Granger causality may not be practical and also have an inference problem when sample size increases and data frequency becomes small because it requires estimating so many regressions and calculating the test statistics. Enders and Jones (2016) propose a simple and flexible method to accommodate structural changes in a causality analysis which simplifies the determination of form, number, and dates of breaks. They first extend VAR models with a Fourier approximation[5] and then examine causal linkages between oil and corn prices. Similar to Nazlioglu (2011), authors indicate that while Granger causality test based on conventional VAR estimations does not support any causal linkage between oil and corn prices, the causality analysis based on the VAR estimates with structural changes supports evidence on the direction of causation form oil to corn prices.

The methods based on estimating VAR models with either rolling window regressions or a Fourier approximation are able to test for Granger causality in the conditional mean. The conditional mean is a disputable tool if variables have non-elliptic or fat-tailed distributions such as return series and includes an overall information for the conditional distribution. Jeong et al.

(2012) develops a nonparametric test for Granger causality in quantile by imposing restrictions on conditional quantiles. This approach is also able accounts for structural breaks and nonlinear dependence of variables. Balcilar et al. (2016) focus on the interrelationships between world oil and South African agricultural commodity prices (wheat, corn, soybeans, and sunflower) within the context of Granger causality in quantiles. Although the standard Granger causality test does not indicate any causal linkage from oil to agricultural prices, the causality in quantiles in contrast shows that causation from oil prices to agricultural commodity prices vary across different quantiles of the conditional distribution.

Structural breaks and nonlinearity in prices may result in asymmetric relations between oil and agricultural prices. Effects of negative and positive oil price shocks on agricultural price dynamics appear to be a fruitful area to explore. Rafiq and Bloch (2016) focus on exploring the dynamics of commodity prices through asymmetric oil shocks for a large set of commodity prices by employing Shin et al. (2014) non-linear ARDL approach and Hatemi-J (2012) asymmetric causality test. An elaborated analysis in summary supports a long-run positive impact of oil price for 20 commodities and short-run negative impact for 13 commodity prices.

In addition to information for causal linkages, VAR models also give information for dynamic interrelationships among variables through impulse response functions and forecast error variance decompositions. VAR models however are not suitable to distinguish (demand- and supply-side) shocks and are failure to impose restrictions according to an economic theory. Structural vector auto regression (SVAR) models mitigate these shortcoming of VAR models and are suitable to identify innovations. SVAR models can decompose unpredictable changes in prices and demand and supply into mutually orthogonal components with restrictions based on economic theory. Qiu et al. (2012) by estimating a SVAR model decompose supply and demand shocks to corn prices by concentrating on the role of energy (oil, ethanol, and gasoline) markets. The results reveal that energy market shocks do not transmit to corn market; corn prices are driven by the demand shocks in the short run, and there is a steady-state equilibrium in the long run.

Another dimension of empirical research questions is of whether there is a risk transfer/volatility spillover between energy and agricultural markets because these markets have more volatile dynamics after the mid-2000s. The causality in variance tests are getting popular in order to conduct a volatility spillover analysis. To investigate volatility spillover between two series, Cheung and Ng (1996) and Hong (2001) propose the causality-in-variance tests based on cross-correlation functions (CCF) of standardized residuals from univariate GARCH (general autoregressive conditional heteroscedasticity) models. Harri and Hudson (2009) by employing the CCF approach find a causal linkage from variance of oil prices to variance of corn prices after the 2007–2008 food price crisis, implying a volatility spillover from oil to corn markets.

The CCF approach is sensitive to order of leads and lags of the standardized residuals and shows an oversize problem in small and medium samples when the volatility process is leptokurtic. Monte Carlo simulations designed by Hafner and Herwartz (2006) show that an inappropriate lead and lag order choice distorts small sample properties of the CCF-based test and thereby leads to a risk of selecting a wrong order of the CCF-based statistic. A simple Lagrange multiplier (LM) causality-in-variance test proposed by Hafner and Herwartz (2006) overcomes these shortfalls and is more robust against leptokurtic innovations in small samples. Nazlioglu et al. (2013) by employing the LM test examine volatility spillover between oil and agricultural commodity (wheat, corn, soybeans, and sugar) prices. The causality-in-variance test shows that while there is no risk transmission before the 2006 food price crisis, oil price volatility spills on agricultural prices after the crisis.

Time series studies widely focuses on small subsets of agricultural commodities such as grains (wheat, corn, soybeans, etc.) or oils (palm oil, soybean oil, sunflower oil, etc.) that are used in ethanol and/or biodiesel production. Agricultural markets are highly integrated and thereby a shock in one market is transmitted to other market(s). Since time series analysis is able to examine the impact of oil prices on agricultural commodity prices one by one, panel data framework seems to be an appropriate tool to account for the impact of such common factors on agricultural commodities. Besides, panel data methods have higher statistical power than time series analysis because they combine information from cross-sectional dimension in addition to time period. Nazlioglu and Soytaş (2012) extends the empirical literature on oil and agricultural commodity price nexus from time series analysis to the panel data context. The study covers data for not only grain and oils prices but also beverage, meat, and fresh fruit prices and employs panel co-integration and causality frameworks. The panel co-integration analysis provides a strong evidence on the positive effects of oil prices changes and the negative effect of the weak value of the US dollar on agricultural commodity prices. The panel causality analysis indicates both short- and long-run causality from oil prices and the US dollar to agricultural commodity prices.

5 Concluding remarks: policy implications and future directions

The empirical literature shows that (1) agricultural commodity prices are either neutral or non-neutral to oil price movements, (2) structural shifts in commodity prices effect the nature of relationship between commodity markets, and (3) the nature of the relationship provides us with essential information for policy analysis within the context of different perspectives.

The existence of neutrality indicates that oil prices do not have a significant impact on agricultural commodity prices. The agricultural price stabilization polices therefore may not need to account for world oil market and policy makers to manage agricultural price booms and drops may focus on supply and demand conditions of agricultural markets. Even though the neutrality implies that agricultural markets seem to be protected from oil price shocks, it does not mean that they are disintegrated from energy markets. Provided that agricultural production preferences are in tandem with energy (biofuel) policies, a tendency for increasing biofuel production (due to higher oil prices and environmental concerns) leads to increasing sensitivity of agricultural prices to oil shocks. A closer link from higher biofuels production to higher corn and soybeans (that are the main crops used in the production of ethanol and biofuels) prices have led farmers to increase production of these commodities at the expense of other crops such as wheat which in turn likely to boost the crop prices. It is well known that agricultural markets are highly integrated with each other and hence a shock in one market transmits to other markets. As the linkage between energy and agricultural markets becomes stronger, agricultural commodity prices would be more related to energy prices. Since price stabilization policies are not able to fully break off the dependence between local and global agricultural markets, policy makers should take into account energy markets in designing sound agricultural price support/stabilization policies whose costs and effectiveness increasingly depends on the dynamics of international energy and agricultural markets.

As a result of the expansion in biofuels, agricultural producers are challenged whether to produce for people or for fuel. Increasing importance of biofuels has motivated them to produce for fuels. For both the least developed and developing countries, the agricultural sector still keeps its importance in the structure of economy and a large portion of the population thereby are affected by agricultural price fluctuations. Agricultural price surges harm poor people more than others because they need to allocate the large share of their incomes on food. The food versus fuel trade-off, moving in favor of fuel after the 2000s, calls attention to invest more in agriculture in a long-run perspective to alleviate world hunger and poverty.

The neutrality and non-neutrality have also different policy implications for global investors. If agricultural prices are neutral to oil prices, then agricultural commodity markets can be viewed as an alternative to oil markets for portfolio diversification and risk sharing. The neutrality also implies that investors cannot have predictive power for spot and future prices of agricultural commodities by following past prices of oil. On the other hand, the non-neutrality shows that the dynamics of oil prices can help investors to forecast agricultural commodity prices which provides information for investment strategies. If investors expect an increase or a decrease in oil prices, they can gain revenues by investing or speculating in agricultural markets.

The recent dynamics of agricultural commodity prices are complicated and different factors may affect agricultural markets. In addition to the energy-agriculture linkage, the macro economic factors and the financialization of the commodities may play a role on the recent dynamics of agricultural prices. Analyzing agricultural price dynamics by jointly identifying the impacts of various factors may have merits to extend the literature. Researches can benefit from the developments in multivariate modeling frameworks in both time series and panel data analyses to discover price and volatility transmission between energy and agricultural markets. Domestic agricultural prices may show different degrees of dependence to world energy prices at different stages of development and this fact opens a door to focus on different samples including developed, emerging, developing, and underdeveloped countries as well as employing threshold models by controlling the level of development. The empirical literature shows a clear evidence on the importance of structural breaks in prices to examine price transmission and volatility spillover. Researchers can handle the research question within the context of developments in structural change and nonlinear models. It is worthy to emphasize as a final sentence that the motivation of re-examination of the research question might be constructed on fresh evidence to better understand the dynamics between energy and agricultural markets rather than only employing new tests which reproduce the previous findings.

Notes

1 I gratefully acknowledge that this study is carried out under the Outstanding Young Scientists Award Program 2015 of the Turkish Academy of Sciences (TÜBA-GEBİP 2015) and is a part of the project supported by The Scientific and Technological Research Council of Turkey (TUBITAK) under grant number 215K086.
2 See Trostle (2008) for much more descriptive analysis of agricultural supply statistics.
3 See Serra and Zilberman (2013) for a detailed survey (data, methods, main findings) on biofuel related price transmission literature.
4 See Nazlioglu (2011) for a discussion on the sources of non-linear behavior of agricultural commodity prices.
5 A Fourier approximation captures the dynamics of series with structural break(s) by using a small number of low-frequency components and does not require prior knowledge of the number and/or dates of the breaks.

References

Baek, E., & Brock, W. A. (1992). General test for nonlinear Granger causality: Bivariate model, Working Paper, Iowa State University and University of Wisconsin-Madison.

Baffes, J., & Haniotis, T. (2016). What explains agricultural price movements? *Journal of Agricultural Economics*, 67(3), 706–721.

Balcilar, M., Chang, S., Gupta, R., Kasongo, V., & Kyei, C. (2016). The relationship between oil and agricultural commodity prices in South Africa: A quantile causality approach. *The Journal of Developing Areas*, 50(3), 93–107.

Bekiros, S. D., & Diks, C.G.H. (2008). The relationship between crude oil spot and futures prices: Cointegration, linear and nonlinear causality. *Energy Economics*, 30, 2673–2685.

Campiche, J. L., Bryant, H. L., Richardson, J. W., & Outlaw, J. L. (2007, July). Examining the evolving correspondence between petroleum prices and agricultural commodity prices. In The American Agricultural Economics Association Annual Meeting, Portland, OR (Vol. 29, pp. 1–15).

Cheng, I., & Xiong, W. (2014). Financialization of commodity carkets. Annual Review of Financial Economics, 6, 419–441.

Cheng-Lang, Y., Lin, H., & Chang, C. (2010). Linear and nonlinear causality between sectoral electricity consumption and economic growth: Evidence from Taiwan. Energy Policy, 38(11), 6570–6573.

Cheung, Y. W., & Ng, L. K. (1996). A causality-in-variance test and its application to financial market prices. Journal of Econometrics, 72(1–2), 33–48.

Chiou-Wei, S. Z., Chen, C., & Zhu, Z. (2008). Economic growth and energy consumption revisited-evidence from linear and nonlinear Granger causality. Energy Economics, 30, 3063–3076.

Cooke, B. (2009). Recent food prices movements: A time series analysis (Vol. 942). International Food Policy Research Institute. Washington, USA.

Diks, C.G.H., & Panchenko, V. (2006). A new statistic and practical guidelines for nonparametric Granger causality testing. Journal of Economic Dynamics and Control, 30, 1647–1669.

Enders, W., & Jones, P. (2016). Grain prices, oil prices, and multiple smooth breaks in a VAR. Studies in Nonlinear Dynamics & Econometrics, 20(4), 399–419.

FAO (2015). Handbook on agricultural cost of production statistics: Guidelines for Data Collection, Compilation. Food and Agriculture Organization of the United Nations. Rome, Italy.

Frankel, J. A. (1986). Expectations and commodity price dynamics: The overshooting model. American Journal of Agricultural Economics, 68(2), 344–348.

Frankel, J. A. (2006). The effect of monetary policy on real commodity prices (No. w12713). National Bureau of Economic Research.

Granger, C. W. (1969). Investigating causal relations by econometric models and cross-spectral methods. Econometrica: Journal of the Econometric Society, 424–438.

Hafner, C. M., & Herwartz, H. (2006). A Lagrange multiplier test for causality in variance. Economics Letters, 93(1), 137–141.

Hanson, K., Robinson, S., & Schluter, G. (1993). Sectoral effects of a world oil price shock: Economy wide linkages to the agricultural sector. Journal of Agricultural and Resource Economics, 18(1), 96–116.

Harri, A., & Hudson, D. (2009, November). Mean and variance dynamics between agricultural commodity prices and crude oil prices. In Presentation at the Economics of Alternative Energy Sources and Globalization: The Road Ahead Meeting, Orlando, FL (pp. 15–17).

Hatemi-J, A. (2012). Asymmetric causality tests with an application. Empirical Economics, 43(1), 447–456.

Hong, Y. (2001). A test for volatility spillover with application to exchange rates. Journal of Econometrics, 103(1–2), 183–224.

Jeong, K., Härdle, W. K., & Song, S. (2012). A consistent nonparametric test for causality in quantile. Econometric Theory, 28(4), 861–887.

Kim, S., Lee, L., & Nam, K. (2010). The relationship between CO2 emissions and economic growth: The case of Korea with nonlinear evidence. Energy Policy, 38(10), 5938–5946.

Kwon, D. H., & Koo, W. W. (2009, July). Price transmission channels of energy and exchange rate on food sector: A disaggregated approach based on stage of process. In Agricultural and Applied Economics Association 2009 AAEA and ACCI Joint Annual Meeting, Milwaukee, Wisconsin.

Nazlioglu, S. (2011). World oil and agricultural commodity prices: Evidence from nonlinear causality. Energy Policy, 39(5), 2935–2943.

Nazlioglu, S., Erdem, C., & Soytaş, U. (2013). Volatility spillover between oil and agricultural commodity markets. Energy Economics, 36, 658–665.

Nazlioglu, S., Gormus, N. A., & Soytaş, U. (2016). Oil prices and real estate investment trusts (REITs): Gradual-shift causality and volatility transmission analysis. Energy Economics, 60, 168–175.

Nazlioglu, S., & Soytaş, U. (2011). World oil prices and agricultural commodity prices: Evidence from an emerging market. Energy Economics, 33(3), 488–496.

Nazlioglu, S., & Soytaş, U. (2012). Oil price, agricultural commodity prices, and the dollar: A panel cointegration and causality analysis. Energy Economics, 34(4), 1098–1104.

Qiu, C., Colson, G., Escalante, C., & Wetzstein, M. (2012). Considering macroeconomic indicators in the food before fuel nexus. Energy Economics, 34(6), 2021–2028.

Rafiq, S., & Bloch, H. (2016). Explaining commodity prices through asymmetric oil shocks: Evidence from nonlinear models. Resources Policy, 50, 34–48.

Saghaian, S. H., Reed, M. R., & Marchant, M. A. (2002). Monetary impacts and overshooting of agricultural prices in an open economy. *American Journal of Agricultural Economics*, 84(1), 90–103.

Serra, T., & Zilberman, D. (2013). Biofuel-related price transmission literature: A review. *Energy Economics*, 37, 141–151.

Shin, Y., Yu, B., & Greenwood-Nimmo, M. (2014). Modelling asymmetric cointegration and dynamic multipliers in a nonlinear ARDL framework. In *Festschrift in Honor of Peter Schmidt* (pp. 281–314). Springer, New York, NY.

Toda, H. Y., & Yamamoto, T. (1995). Statistical inference in vector autoregressions with possibly integrated processes. *Journal of Econometrics*, 66(1–2), 225–250.

Trostle, R. (2008). Global agricultural supply and demand: Factors contributing to the recent increase in food commodity prices. Report from the Economic Research Service, United States Department of Agriculture, WRS-0801.

Zhang, Z., Lohr, L., Escalante, C., & Wetzstein, M. (2010). Food versus fuel: What do prices tell us?. *Energy policy*, *38*(1), 445–451.

27

Oil prices and exchange rates

Hassan Anjum and Farooq Malik

1 Introduction

The relationship between oil prices and exchange rates has been an important topic of interest especially in light of the recently observed volatility in the two variables. Some studies show that a nominal appreciation of the US dollar triggers a decrease in the oil price, while other show that an increase in the oil price actually results in a depreciation of the US dollar. Figure 27.1 plots the daily nominal crude oil price (West Texas Intermediate) and the US effective dollar exchange rate index (relative to its main trading partners) from January 2000 to March 2018.

Clearly we can notice that they move in opposite directions over time. As a matter of fact, the correlation between the two variables in the level form is −0.87 for this daily series. An interesting question is, which variable drives the other variable? Although the direction of causation is widely debated in different empirical studies, the general consensus is that it is bidirectional.

This chapter takes a closer look at the research studying the relationship between oil prices and exchange rates. We start with a brief review of major theoretical transmission channels proposed in the literature, followed by a comprehensive literature review of various studies which explore the relationship between oil prices and exchanges rates. We provide important policy implications, list a few avenues of future research, and finish with a conclusion.

2 Theoretical reasoning behind the relationship between oil prices and exchange rates

Before we turn to the empirical evidence, it is important to identify the different theoretical links between oil prices and exchange rates given in the literature. There are essentially three pillars. The first establishes the impact of changes in oil prices on exchange rates; the second establishes the impact of changes in exchange rates on oil prices; and the third outlines the common factors driving the relationship between oil prices and exchange rates.

The seminal work in establishing the impact of changes in oil prices on exchange rates was done by Krugman (1983) and Golub (1983) as they give theoretical models which form the

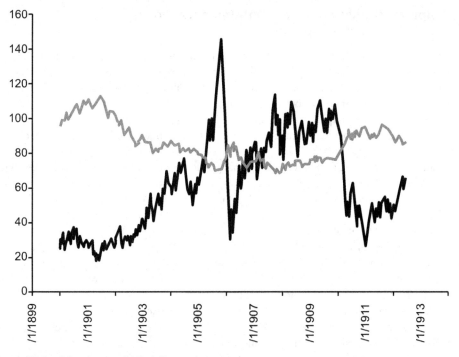

Figure 27.1   Oil prices and US dollar exchange rate

Notes: Price of crude oil (West Texas Intermediate) is measured by the black line, while the gray line shows the US dollar exchange rate against seven major trading partners.

basis of later empirical results. They argue that oil-exporting countries experience an increase in wealth in the short run if the oil price rises as wealth is transferred to oil-exporting countries and results in improvement of the current account balance in domestic currency terms. For this reason, they expect currencies of oil-exporting countries to appreciate and currencies of oil-importers to depreciate after a rise in oil prices. The relationship we see between oil prices and exchange rate in Figure 27.1 is consistent with this reasoning, as the United States was a net oil exporter during the sample period. They also argue that in the medium term, the impact of changes in oil prices on exchange rates will be determined by where the money from increased revenues of the oil-exporting countries will be invested.

The second pillar establishes the theoretical link of the impact of exchange rates on oil prices. This argument was given by Bloomberg and Harris (1995) and is based on the law of one price for tradable goods. They argue that since oil is a homogeneous commodity and is internationally traded commodity priced in US dollars; depreciation in the US dollar will reduce the oil price for foreigners, which will increase the price of crude oil in US dollars.

The third pillar documents the common factors driving oil prices and exchange rates. In other words, this provides a reasoning which establishes an indirect relationship between oil prices and exchange rates driven by common factors. These could include GDP, overall price level, interest rates, or stock prices, as all these factors simultaneously affect exchange rates and oil prices. For example, an increase in GDP typically results in an increase in oil price and interest rates, but increase in interest rates can impact exchange rates.

3   Empirical studies on the relationship between oil prices and exchange rates

In this section, we survey major studies examining the relationship between oil prices and exchange rates. Some studies consider if the oil price affects the exchange rate while others examine if exchange rate affects the oil prices. There is another related strand of literature which studies the dependence structure between oil prices and exchange rates using dynamic copula-based models and wavelet approaches.

Following studies provide evidence that suggests that changes in oil prices affect exchange rates. Using co-integration and causality tests, Chaudhuri and Daniel (1998) document that the non-stationary behavior of US dollar real exchange rates is due to the non-stationary behavior of real oil prices. Akram (2004) explores the possibility of a non-linear relationship between oil prices and the Norwegian exchange rate. He finds a negative relationship between oil prices and the value of the Norwegian exchange rate. He documents a non-linear relationship and argues that this substantially improves the forecasts compared with those from a similar model but with a linear oil price effects. Amano and Norden (1998) examine the relationship between oil price shocks and the US real effective exchange rate. They show that the two variables appear to be co-integrated and that causality runs from oil prices to the exchange rate and not vice versa. They show that the error-correction model has significant out-of-sample predictive ability for both the size and sign changes in the real effective exchange rate, which suggests that oil prices may have been the dominant source of persistent real exchange rate shocks over the post–Bretton Woods period. Huang and Guo (2007) show that real oil price shocks would lead to a minor appreciation of the long-term real exchange rate due to China's lesser dependence on imported oil than its trading partners. Chen and Chen (2007) investigate the long-run relationship between real oil prices and real exchange rates using a monthly panel of G7 countries from 1972 to 2005. They show that real oil prices may have been the dominant source of real exchange rate movements and that there is a link between real oil prices and real exchange rates as they are co-integrated. Their predictive regression estimates suggest that real oil prices have significant forecasting power. Their out-of-sample prediction estimates show greater predictability over longer horizons. Using data from 1975 to 2008, Lizardo and Mollick (2010) show that by adding oil prices to the monetary model of exchange rates, they find that oil prices significantly explain movements in the value of the US dollar against major currencies. They report that increases in real oil prices lead to a significant depreciation of the US dollar against net oil exporter currencies of Canada, Mexico, and Russia. Using linear and nonlinear causality tests, Wang and Wu (2012) study the relationship between energy prices and the US dollar exchange rates. They show evidence of significant unidirectional linear causality (bidirectional nonlinear causality) running from petroleum prices to exchange rates before (after) the recent financial crisis. They provide evidence that indicates that both volatility spillover and regime shift contribute to non-linear causality, but the former effect is much stronger. Bouoiyour et al. (2015) study the relationship between oil price and Russia's real exchange rate conditioning upon potential control variables. They find causality from oil price changes to the real exchange rate in the case of Russia.

Empirical evidence on the effect of a weak dollar on the rise in oil prices has been reported by many studies. Following studies show evidence that changes in exchange rates affect oil prices. Bloomberg and Harris (1995), using the law of one price, argue how exchange rate movements can affect oil prices. The law of one price would imply that as the US dollar weakens relative to other currencies, international buyers of oil are willing to pay higher prices for oil in US dollars. Bloomberg and Harris (1995) empirically report negative correlation between commodity prices and the US dollar. Sadorsky (2000) investigates the interaction between energy futures prices and exchange rates. He shows that futures prices for crude oil are co-integrated with a trade-weighted index of exchange rates, which means that there exists a long-run equilibrium relationship between the two variables. He further presents Granger causality results for both the long-run and short-run horizon. He presents evidence that suggests that exchange rates transmit exogenous shocks to prices of oil futures. Yousefi and Wirjanto (2004) study the impact of changes in US dollar on the formation of OPEC oil prices, using the general method of moments and report evidence of a negative correlation between US dollar exchange rate fluctuations and the formation of OPEC oil prices. Zhang et al. (2008) find a significant influence of the US dollar exchange rate on international oil prices in the long run, but report limited effects in the short run. Akram (2009) provides evidence that suggests that a decline in the US dollar leads to an increase international crude oil price and shocks to the US dollar are found to account for substantial share of fluctuations in the oil prices. Jawadi et al. (2016) find a negative relationship between the US dollar (versus euro) and oil returns, indicating that a US dollar appreciation decreases the oil price.

There is another related strand of literature which studies the dependence structure between oil prices and exchange rates using dynamic copula-based GARCH models and wavelet approaches. Salisu and Mobolaji (2013) show a bidirectional returns and spillover transmission between oil prices and the US-Nigeria exchange rate. Aloui, Aissa and Nguyen (2013) using a static copula-GARCH approach, find a statistically significant conditional dependence between oil prices and US dollar exchange rate. Using a dynamic copula-based GARCH models, Wu, Chung and Chang (2012) explore the dependence structure between the oil price and the US dollar exchange rate. They document the efficiency of the copula-based GARCH models in evaluating economic value of an asset allocation strategy. Reboredo (2012) documents a weak dependency between oil prices and the US dollar exchange rate and show that this dependency has substantially increased after the recent global financial crisis.

4 An empirical application

Since widespread studies have reported a relationship between exchange rate and oil prices, a natural question arises as to what is the nature of causality? In this section, we perform a simple Granger causality test to answer this question.

For oil price, we use the daily nominal crude oil price (West Texas Intermediate). The data was obtained from US Department of Energy. The exchange rate series used is the US effective dollar exchange rate index relative to its seven main trading partners. The data was obtained from the US Federal Reserve Bank. Daily observations were used and the sample period is from January 2000 to March 2018. If there were no trading in any one market, then those days were excluded from the sample. The data is plotted as shown in Figure 27.1 and descriptive statistics are provided in Table 27.1.

An interesting aspect is that there is a correlation of −0.225 between the returns of oil series and returns of exchange rate series. As earlier reported, the correlation between the two series in level form is −0.87. Clearly they move in opposite direction (in level form and their corresponding returns as well). Since the direction of causation has many important implications, we conduct a Granger causality test to explore the direction of causation.

Table 27.1 Descriptive statistics

	Exchange rate returns	Oil returns
Mean	−2.1E-05	0.0002
Median	1.2E-05	0.0008
Maximum	0.0248	0.1847
Minimum	−0.0410	−0.1709
Std. Dev.	0.0046	0.0246
Skewness	−0.2135	−0.0912
Kurtosis	6.5382	7.8581
Jarque-Bera	2409.53	4483.70
Probability	0.000000	0.000000
Correlation	−0.225	

Notes: The sample of daily returns covers from 1 January 2000 to 30 March 2018. The number of usable observations is 4,553. The Jarque-Bera statistic is used to test whether or not the series resembles a normal distribution.

Table 27.2 Granger causality tests

Number of Lags Used: 1

Null Hypothesis:	F-Statistic	Probability
Exchange rate returns does not Granger cause oil return	1.857	0.1729
Oil returns does not Granger cause exchange rate returns	18.372	1.9E-05

Number of Lags used: 2

Null Hypothesis:	F-Statistic	Probability
Exchange rate returns does not Granger cause oil return	1.046	0.3513
Oil returns does not Granger cause exchange rate returns	9.599	6.9E-05

Notes: The sample of daily returns covers from 1 January 2000 to 30 March 2018. The number of usable observations is 4,553.

Table 27.2 provides results from the Granger causality tests. Results show that changes in oil returns (Granger) cause returns in US dollar exchange rate (at both lag 1 and 2), while there is no evidence to suggest that causation works in the other direction.

Reboredo, Rivera-Castro and Zebende (2014) report an increased negative dependence between oil and the US dollar exchange rate after the onset of the US financial crisis (July 2008). They attribute this evidence to both contagion and interdependence. We know that our total sample (January 2000 to March 2018) yields a correlation of −0.225. We find that there is a correlation of −0.308 between the returns of oil series and exchange rates if you only look at the sample from July 2008 to March 2018. The corresponding correlation is only −0.108

from January 2000 to July 2008. Clearly the negative correlation has increased three times after the US financial crisis. Our results are consistent with Fan and Xu (2011), who show that the link between US dollar exchange rates and oil price has intensified over time. Using wavelet approach, they find that the price of oil has become more closely related to macroeconomic fundamentals and financial markets over time. Fratzscher, Schneider and Robays (2014) examine the relationship between oil prices, US dollar, and asset prices. They find bidirectional causality between the US dollar and oil prices since 2001. They argue that this is due the increased use of oil as a financial asset over the past decade. Beckmann, Berger and Czudaj (2016) also show that the intensity of relationship between oil prices and exchange rates has increased over time using daily data from 2003 to 2013 from 12 oil exporting and oil importing countries.

5 Avenues of future research

Some of the exciting recent research has examined the volatility spillover effects between oil prices and exchange rates. We investigate this by estimating a bivariate GARCH model (BEKK specification) using the daily returns computed from oil prices and exchange rates from January 2000 to March 2018. The results are presented in Table 27.3. We clearly find a statistically significant volatility and shock transmission across both markets. This clearly has important economic implications as documented in the next section.

Mensi, Hammoudeh and Yoon (2015) investigates the influence of structural changes on the asymmetry of volatility spillovers, asset allocation, and portfolio diversification between the US dollar (against euro) exchange market and oil prices. Using the bivariate DCC-EGARCH model

Table 27.3 Bivariate GARCH model

Variable	Coefficient	Std Error	T-Stat	P-value
C(1,1)	0.001632	0.000259	6.311	0.000
C(2,1)	0.000327	3.95E-05	8.287	0.000
C(2,2)	2.2E-06	0.000568	0.003	0.996
A(1,1)	0.245786	0.011594	21.199	0.000
A(1,2)	−0.00412	0.001417	−2.905	0.003
A(2,1)	0.137409	0.055092	2.494	0.012
A(2,2)	0.13819	0.009903	13.954	0.000
B(1,1)	0.872774	0.004649	187.74	0.000
B(1,2)	0.052275	7.26E-05	720.44	0.000
B(2,1)	3.370622	0.105774	31.866	0.000
B(2,2)	−0.89203	0.003444	−259.02	0.000

Notes: The sample of daily returns covers from 1 January 2000 to 30 March 2018. The number of usable observations is 4,553. Variable 1 is oil returns and variable 2 is exchange rate returns. The estimated bivariate GARCH model (BEKK) proposed by Engle and Kroner (1995) is given as

$$H_{t+1} = C'C + B'H_t B + A'\varepsilon_t \varepsilon_t' A$$

where, in our bivariate case, C is a 2×2 lower triangular matrix with three parameters, and B is a 2×2 square matrix of parameters. The latter matrix shows the extent to which current levels of conditional variances are related to past conditional variances. A is a 2×2 square matrix of parameters and measures the extent to which conditional variances are correlated with past squared errors. The elements of A capture the effects of shocks or events on volatility (conditional variance). In our case, the total number of estimated parameters is 11.

with and without structural breaks, they provide evidence of significant asymmetric volatility spillovers between the US dollar exchange rate and oil prices. They find that the model with structural breaks reduces the degree of volatility persistence and leads to more appropriate hedging and asset allocation strategies. Jawadi et al. (2016) use recent intraday data to measure realized volatility and investigate the intraday linkages between oil price and US dollar (against euro) volatilities. They find a negative relationship between the exchange rate and oil returns. They note the presence of a volatility spillover from the exchange rate market to the oil market. A promising avenue of future research would be to explore the volatility spillover across the exchange rate returns and oil returns. Since markets are more interdependent and volatility is transmitted more quickly across markets, it is important to correctly model this volatility transmission process. This has important implications for financial risk management, as there is more sharing of common information and cross market hedging.

Most studies analyze the relationship between the oil price and exchange rate without separating the underlying demand and supply factors which are responsible for the changes in oil prices. However, Kilian (2009) argue that shocks to the real price of oil may reflect oil supply shocks, shocks to the global demand for all industrial commodities, or demand shocks that are specific to the crude oil market. He shows that each shock has different effects on the real price of oil and on US macroeconomic aggregates. Kilian and Park (2009) show that the reaction of US real stock returns to an oil price shock differs greatly depending on whether the change in the price of oil is driven by demand or supply shocks. It would be really interesting to see extension of their work in the area of exchange rate market versus the oil market. Specifically, to study if the underlying cause of the oil shock (demand or supply) has a differential impact on the exchange rate dynamics.

As mentioned before, Akram (2004) documents a non-linear relationship between oil prices and the Norwegian exchange rate. Hamilton (2003) provides comprehensive and robust evidence in favor of a non-linear relationship between oil prices and real GDP growth. Malik and Nasereddin (2006), using a cascaded neural network approach, show incorporating oil prices can help improve US GDP forecasts. Thus there is evidence to suggest that oil prices have a non-linear direct and indirect impact (via GDP) on exchange rates. The empirical findings on the relationship between oil prices and exchange rates in the literature differ depending upon the sample period which further suggests the possibility of structural changes in the relationship possibly due to changes in geopolitical, economics or political factors. Given the complexities involved in modeling such a behavior, it would be interesting to model this relationship using artificial neural networks techniques since there is no consensus in the literature on the complex unknown functional form. The results could prove to be important in improving forecasts of oil prices and exchange rates.

6 Policy implications

One clear policy implication is in terms of forecasting one of the variables (oil or exchange rate) using the other. Alquist, Kilian and Vigfusson (2013) provides a comprehensive overview on predictability oil prices using macroeconomic aggregates and conclude that trade-weighted exchange rates do not have significant predictive power for the nominal price of oil in terms of point forecasts. However, Drachal (2016) using the dynamic model averaging framework shows that exchange rate is helpful in predicting spot price of oil, although its importance varies over time. If the in-sample correlation between oil prices and exchange rates is strong as we document in the empirical application, one can potentially benefit from using one of the variable to predict the other in an out-of-sample forecasts. Also, as shown earlier, given the correlation between oil prices and exchange rate is increasing over time, the potential of forecasting benefits can be substantial for financial markets participants as well as policy makers.

As documented before, there is clear evidence to suggest that there is a significant transmission of shocks and volatility across the oil prices and exchange rates series. We also document a negative correlation between the oil prices and exchanges rates (at both level and return form). Given these two stylized facts, investors and companies should account for this relationship when they compute dynamic hedging strategies and optimal portfolio weights. Thus financial market participants can improve their asset allocation and hedging strategies by taking into account the origins, direction, and volatility transmission mechanism across these markets. Also, governments should be mindful of this relationship as this means risk will spillover across the foreign exchange and energy markets. Governments can take appropriate risk mitigating steps in this regard.

Finally, the return and volatility relationship between oil prices and exchange rate have implications for increase in import prices and the overall price level in the country, which will directly affect the value of imports and the balance of payments of a country. Thus monetary policy has to be carefully designed to account for of this intricate relationship and to the fact if it is an oil-exporting country or oil-importing country.

7 Conclusion

This chapter provides a comprehensive survey on the relationship between oil prices and exchange rates. Using daily data from January 2000 to March 2018, we find that the correlation between oil price and exchange in the level form (returns) is −0.87 (−0.22). We also find that this correlation is increasing over time, possibly due to sharing of common information and cross-market hedging. We then provide different theoretical reasoning given in the literature which explains the relationship between oil prices and exchange rates. We provide a comprehensive survey of the literature showing the relationship between oil prices and exchange rates. The general consensus in the literature is that such a relationship exists although the direction of causality is still debated.

Our empirical application shows that not only negative correlation exists between returns of oil prices and exchange rates but there is a significant shock and volatility transmission between them as well. Some promising avenues of future research are listed and discussed. We also discuss important policy implications for government regarding monetary policy and discuss practical implications for financial market participants in terms of dynamic hedging and portfolio allocation.

References

Akram, Q. Farooq. 2004. "Oil prices and exchange rates: Norwegian evidence," *Econometrics Journal*, Vol. 7, 476–504.

Akram, Q. Farooq. 2009. "Commodity prices, interest rates and the dollar," *Energy Economics*, Vol. 31, 838–851.

Aloui, Riadh, Mohamed Safouane Ben Aïssa, and Duc Khuong Nguyen. 2013. "Conditional dependence structure between oil prices and exchange rates: A copula-GARCH approach," *Journal of International Money and Finance*, Vol. 32, 719–738.

Alquist, Ron, Lutz Kilian, and Robert J. Vigfusson. 2013. "Forecasting the price of oil," *Handbook of Economic Forecasting*. Elsevier, Vol. 2, 427–507.

Amano, Robert A., and Simon Van Norden. 1998. "Oil prices and the rise and fall of the US real exchange rate," *Journal of International Money and Finance*, Vol. 17, 299–316.

Beckmann, Joscha, Theo Berger, and Robert Czudaj. 2016. "Oil price and FX-rates dependency," *Quantitative Finance*, Vol. 16, 477–488.

Blomberg, S. Brock, and Ethan S. Harris. 1995. "The commodity-consumer price connection: Fact or fable? Federal Reserve Board of New York," *Economic Policy Review*, Vol. 1, 21–38.

Bouoiyour, Jamal, Refk Selmi, Aviral Kumar Tiwari, and Muhammad Shahbaz. 2015. "The nexus between oil price and Russia's real exchange rate: Better paths via unconditional vs conditional analysis," *Energy Economics*, Vol. 51, 54–66.

Chaudhuri, Kausik, and Betty C. Daniel. 1998. "Long-run equilibrium real exchange rates and oil prices," *Economics Letters*, Vol. 58, 231–238.

Chen, Shiu-Sheng, and Hung-Chyn Chen. 2007. "Oil prices and real exchange rates," *Energy Economics*, Vol. 29, 390–404.

Drachal, Krzysztof. 2016. "Forecasting spot oil price in a dynamic model averaging framework-Have the determinants changed over time?" *Energy Economics*, Vol. 60, 35–46.

Engle, Robert F., and Kenneth F. Kroner. 1995. "Multivariate simultaneous generalized ARCH," *Econometric Theory*, Vol. 11, 122–150.

Fan, Ying, and Jin-Hua Xu. 2011. "What has driven oil prices since 2000? A structural change perspective," *Energy Economics*, Vol. 33, 1082–1094.

Fratzscher, Marcel, Daniel Schneider, and Ine Van Robays. 2014. "Oil prices, exchange rates and asset prices," *Working Paper Series No 1689*, European Central Bank.

Golub, Stephen S. 1983. "Oil prices and exchange rates," *Economic Journal*, Vol. 93, 576–593.

Hamilton, James D. 2003. "What is an oil shock?," *Journal of Econometrics*, Vol. 113, 363–398.

Huang, Ying, and Feng Guo. 2007. "The role of oil price shocks on China's real exchange rate," *China Economic Review*, Vol. 18, 403–416.

Jawadi, F., Louhichi, W., Ameur, H. B. and Cheffou, A. I. 2016. "On oil-US exchange rate volatility relationships: An intraday analysis," *Economic Modelling*, Vol. 59, 329–334.

Kilian, Lutz. 2009. "Not all oil price shocks are alike: Disentangling demand and supply shocks in the crude oil market," *American Economic Review*, Vol. 99, 1053–1069.

Kilian, Lutz, and Cheolbeom Park. 2009. "The impact of oil price shocks on the US stock market," *International Economic Review*, Vol. 50, 1267–1287.

Krugman, Paul. 1983. "Oil shocks and exchange rate dynamics," In: Frenkel, J. A. (Ed.), *Exchange Rates and International Macroeconomics*. University of Chicago Press, Chicago.

Lizardo, Radhames A., and Andre V. Mollick. 2010. "Oil price fluctuations and US dollar exchange rates," *Energy Economics*, Vol. 32, 399–408.

Malik, Farooq, and Mahdi Nasereddin. 2006. "Forecasting output using oil prices: A cascaded artificial neural network approach," *Journal of Economics and Business*, Vol. 58, 168–180.

Mensi, Walid, Shawkat Hammoudeh, and Seong-Min Yoon. 2015. "Structural breaks, dynamic correlations, asymmetric volatility transmission, and hedging strategies for petroleum prices and USD exchange rate," *Energy Economics*, Vol. 48, 46–60.

Reboredo, Juan Carlos. 2012. "Modelling oil price and exchange rate co-movements," *Journal of Policy Modeling*, Vol. 34, 419–440.

Reboredo, Juan Carlos, Miguel A. Rivera-Castro, and Gilney F. Zebende. 2014. "Oil and US dollar exchange rate dependence: A detrended cross-correlation approach," *Energy Economics*, Vol. 42, 132–139.

Sadorsky, Perry. 2000. "The empirical relationship between energy futures prices and exchange rates," *Energy Economics*, Vol. 22, 253–266.

Salisu, Afees A., and Hakeem Mobolaji. 2013. "Modeling returns and volatility transmission between oil price and US-Nigeria exchange rate," *Energy Economics*, Vol. 39, 169–176.

Wang, Yudong, and Chongfeng Wu. 2012. "Energy prices and exchange rates of the U.S. dollar: Further evidence from linear and nonlinear causality analysis," *Economic Modelling*, Vol. 29, 2289–2297.

Wu, Chih-Chiang, Huimin Chung, and Yu-Hsien Chang. 2012. "The economic value of co-movement between oil price and exchange rate using copula-based GARCH models," *Energy Economics*, Vol. 34, 270–282.

Yousefi, Ayoub, and Tony S. Wirjanto. 2004. "The empirical role of the exchange rate on the crude-oil price formation," *Energy Economics*, Vol. 26, 783–799.

Zhang, Yue-Jun, Ying Fan, Hsien-Tang Tsai, and Yi-Ming Wei. 2008. "Spillover effect of US dollar exchange rate on oil prices," *Journal of Policy Modeling*, Vol. 30, 973–991.

28

Volatility spillovers on oil and forex markets

Jozef Baruník and Evžen Kočenda

1   Introduction

Volatility connectedness quantifies the dynamic and directional characterization of volatility spillovers among various assets or across markets (Diebold and Yilmaz, 2015).[1] The connectedness on financial markets is important to many areas of research, including risk management, portfolio allocation, and business cycle analysis. In this chapter we analyze connectedness between oil and forex markets. The reason for doing so is straightforward. Most of the crude oil production and sales is quoted and invoiced in US dollars. The massive amount of financial flows enters the forex market as the oil and oil-based commodities reach their destinations. Additional discussion on the channels through which the energy and foreign exchange markets may be linked was provided in Chapter 27. Hence, we hypothesize that volatility in oil prices transfers into the volatility of foreign currencies on the forex market and we analyze the extent of the associated connectedness.

Further, we extend our analysis to account for potential asymmetries in connectedness between the two markets. The asymmetries may materialize from a set of reasons. Oil is an asset where spillovers historically play a prominent role (Haigh and Holt, 2002). From the financial perspective, oil prices might be linked to large speculative trades (Hamilton, 2009; Caballero et al., 2008) and short run destabilization in oil prices may be caused by financial investors (Lombardi and Van Robays, 2011) due to oil's increasing financialization after 2001 (Fratzscher et al., 2013). Hence, asymmetries in connectedness might be a natural outcome. In this respect, currencies on the forex market would be able to continuously absorb or transfer those asymmetries because of the 24-hour operation of the global forex market with a huge information flow in terms of exchange rate quotes. Moreover, currencies are shown to exhibit asymmetric connectedness on its own (Baruník et al., 2017), which might be potentially transferred via the US dollar or other key currencies as the forex market exhibits a very high degree of integration, especially for key currencies (Kitamura, 2010).

Finally, we augment our analysis with studying the frequency dynamics of the connectedness. Baruník and Křehlík (2018) argue that shocks to economic activity impact variables at various frequencies with various strengths, and to understand the sources of connectedness in an economic system it is crucial to understand the frequency dynamics of the connectedness. The key reason rests in that agents operate on different investment horizons, represented by shorter or longer frequencies, because of the frequency-dependent formation of their preferences as shown in modeling strategies of Bandi and Tamoni (2017), Bansal and Yaron (2004), Cogley (2001), Ortu et al. (2013). In our analysis we consider the long-, medium-, and short-term frequency responses to shocks and analyze the financial connectedness at a desired frequency band.

In our analysis we proceed in the following way. We analyze connectedness between the two markets with the volatility spillover index (the DY index) of Diebold and Yilmaz (2009) that is based on forecast error variance decompositions from vector autoregressions (VARs). The methodology has been further improved in Diebold and Yilmaz (2012), who used a generalized VAR framework in which forecast-error variance decompositions are invariant to variable ordering. The DY index is a versatile measure allowing dynamic quantification of numerous aspects of volatility spillovers. In order to account for asymmetric sources of volatility we further compute the DY index with the realized semivariances introduced by Barndorff-Nielsen et al. (2010). The realized semivariances enable one to isolate and capture negative and positive shocks to volatility and thus are ideally suited to interpreting qualitative differences in volatility spillovers.[2]

Combination of the DY index and realized semivariances was introduced by Baruník et al. (2016) to measure asymmetries in volatility spillovers that are due to qualitatively different positive or negative returns. They produced a flexible measure allowing dynamic quantification of asymmetric connectedness. For a verbal interpretation of asymmetries we adopt the terminology established in the literature (Patton and Sheppard, 2015; Segal et al., 2015) that distinguishes asymmetries in spillovers originating due to qualitatively different uncertainty. Hence, we label spillovers as bad or good volatility spillovers (or negative or positive spillovers).

In addition to the total connectedness and asymmetric connectedness we also compute the frequency connectedness based on the approach of Baruník and Křehlík (2018). The frequency connectedness allows distinguishing extent of volatility spillovers among assets at various horizons. As such it allows to distinguish whether the connectedness is formed at shorter or longer frequencies.

The rest of the chapter is organized in the following way. In Section 2 we provide an overview of the literature related to volatility spillovers on the oil and forex markets. In Section 3 we formally introduce the methodological approach and formulate testable hypotheses. The data are described in Section 4. In three separate subsections of the Section 5 we present our results for total, asymmetric, and frequency connectedness. Finally, conclusions are offered in Section 6.

2 Literature review

Analyses of forex volatility spillovers based on the DY index are still infrequent. Diebold and Yilmaz (2015, Chapter 6), analyze the exchange rates of nine major currencies with respect to the US dollar from 1999 to mid-2013. They show that forex market connectedness increased only mildly after the 2007 financial crisis and the euro/US dollar exchange rate exhibits the highest volatility connectedness among all analyzed currencies. Greenwood-Nimmo et al. (2016) generalize the connectedness framework and analyze risk-return spillovers among the G10 currencies between 1999 and 2014. They find that spillover intensity is countercyclical and volatility spillovers across currencies increase during crisis times. Similarly, Bubák et al. (2011) document statistically significant intra-regional volatility spillovers among the European emerging foreign exchange markets and show that volatility spillovers tend to increase in periods characterized by market uncertainty, especially during the 2007–2008 financial crisis. Further, McMillan and Speight (2010) document the existence of volatility spillovers among the exchange rates of the US dollar, British pound, and Japanese yen with respect to the euro and show dominating effects coming from the US dollar. In addition, Antonakakis (2012) analyzes volatility spillovers among major currencies before and after the introduction of the euro and shows that the euro (Deutsch-mark) is the dominant net transmitter of volatility, while the British pound is the dominant net receiver of volatility in both periods. Finally, Baruník et al. (2017) document sizable volatility spillovers among the most actively traded currencies on the forex market. They also show that negative spillovers are chiefly tied to the dragging sovereign debt crisis in Europe while positive spillovers are correlated with the subprime crisis, different monetary policies among key world central banks, and developments on commodities markets.

There is also a segment of the literature that combines the assessment of volatility spillovers between the forex and stock markets. Grobys (2015) employ the DY index and finds very little evidence of volatility spillovers when markets are calm but a high level of total volatility spillovers following periods of economic turbulence. A similar conclusion is found by Do et al. (2015), who also emphasize that it is important to account for the volatility spillover information trans-mission especially during turbulent periods. Further, significant directional spillovers are identi-fied between the forex and stock markets in several studies targeting developed and emerging markets (Do et al., 2016; Andreou et al., 2013; Kumar, 2013; Kanas, 2001) or specific countries or regions including the United States (Ito and Yamada, 2015), Japan (Jayasinghe and Tsui, 2008), China (Zhao, 2010), the Middle East, and North Africa (Arfaoui and Ben Rejeb, 2015). In addi-tion, some studies analyze more complex interactions and volatility spillovers between the forex market and (1) stocks and bonds (Clements et al., 2015), (2) commodities (Salisu and Mobolaji, 2013), or (3) stocks, bonds, and commodities (Diebold and Yilmaz, 2009; Duncan and Kabundi, 2013; Aboura and Chevallier, 2014; Ghosh, 2014).

The research related to volatility spillovers among oil-based commodities is surprisingly limited. On weekly data, Haigh and Holt (2002) analyze the effectiveness of crude oil, heating oil, and unleaded gasoline futures in reducing price volatility for an energy trader: uncertainty is reduced significantly when volatility spillovers are considered in the hedging strategy. Using daily data for the period 1986–2001, Hammoudeh et al. (2003) analyzed the volatility spillovers of three major oil commodities (West Texas Intermediate, heating oil, and gasoline) along with the impact of dif-ferent trading centers. Spillovers among various trading centers were also analyzed by Awartani and Maghyereh (2012), who investigated the dynamics of the return and volatility spillovers between oil and equities in the Gulf region. The spillover effect between the two major markets for crude oil (NYMEX and London's International Petroleum Exchange) has been studied by Lin and Tam-vakis (2001), who found substantial spillover effects when both markets are trading simultaneously. More recently, Chang et al. (2010) have found volatility spillovers and asymmetric effects across four major oil markets: West Texas Intermediate (USA), Brent (North Sea), Dubai/Oman (Middle East), and Tapis (Asia-Pacific). Finally, Baruník et al. (2015) detect and quantify volatility spillovers among oil-based commodities: crude oil, gasoline, and heating oil. They also show asymmetries in that overall volatility spillovers due to negative (price) returns materialize to a greater degree than those due to positive returns and their occurrence correlates with low levels of crude oil inventories in the United States and often with world events that hamper crude oil supply. Negative spillovers thus frequently indicate the extent of real or potential crude oil unavailability.

To the best of our knowledge, there is no analysis of the connectedness between oil and forex markets, though.

3 Measuring asymmetric and frequency connectedness

Seminal papers by Diebold and Yilmaz (2009, 2012), along with other related studies, estimate volatility spillovers on daily (or weekly) high, low, opening, and closing prices. Estimators based on daily data offer, in general, good approximations of volatility. However, the low sampling frequency imposes some limitations. Having high-frequency data, we estimate volatility with convenient realized volatility estimators. Furthermore, to account for volatility spillover asymmetries, we follow Baruník et al. (2015, 2016), who use the realized semivariance framework of Barndorff-Nielsen et al. (2010), which offers an interesting possibility to decompose volatility spillovers due to negative and positive returns. The quantification of asymmetric volatility spillovers with realized semivariances was first employed in Baruník et al. (2015), where the authors define measures using two separate VAR systems for negative and positive semi-variances.

A natural way to describe the frequency dynamics (the long term, medium term, or short term) of the connectedness is to consider the spectral representation of variance decompositions based on frequency responses to shocks. Baruník and Křehlík (2018) introduced the general spectral representation of variance decompositions, and they show how we can use it to define the frequency-dependent connectedness measures.

In this section, we first introduce the two existing concepts of total and directional spillovers from Diebold and Yilmaz (2012), and then we describe a simple way to use realized semivariances in order to capture asymmetric volatility spillovers as well as frequency decomposition of the spillovers. In order to keep our description on a general level, we will label variables as assets.

3.1 Measuring volatility spillovers

The volatility spillover measure introduced by Diebold and Yilmaz (2009) is based on a forecast error variance decomposition from vector auto regressions (VARs). The forecast error variance decomposition traces how much of the H-step-ahead forecast error variance of a variable i is due to innovations in another variable j, thus it provides an intuitive way to measure volatility spillovers. For N assets, we consider an N-dimensional vector of realized volatilities, $\mathbf{RV_t} = (RV_{1t}, \ldots, RV_{Nt})'$, to measure total volatility spillovers. In order to measure asymmetric volatility spillovers, we decompose daily volatility into negative (and positive) semivariances that provides a proxy for downside (and upside) risk. Using semivariances allows us to measure the spillovers from bad and good volatility and test whether they are transmitted in the same magnitude (Baruník et al., 2016). Thus, we consider $\mathbf{RV_t} = (RV_{1t}, \ldots, RV_{nt})'$ to measure total volatility spillovers, and $\mathbf{RS_t^-} = \left(RS_{1t}^-, \ldots, RS_{nt}^-\right)'$ and $\mathbf{RS_t^+} = \left(RS_{1t}^+, \ldots, RS_{nt}^+\right)'$ to measure volatility spillovers due to negative and positive returns, respectively.

We start describing the procedure for the N-dimensional vector $\mathbf{RV_t} = (RV_{1t}, \ldots, RV_{Nt})'$ and later extend the framework to accommodate realized semivariance. Let us model the N-dimensional vector $\mathbf{RV_t}$ by a weakly stationary vector autoregression VAR(p) as:

$$\mathbf{RV_t} = \sum_{i=1}^{p} \Phi_i \mathbf{RV}_{t-i} + \varepsilon_t, \tag{28.1}$$

where $\varepsilon_t \sim N(0, \Sigma_\varepsilon)$ is a vector of *iid* disturbances and Φ_i denotes p coefficient matrices. For the invertible VAR process, the moving average representation has the following form:

$$\mathbf{RV_t} = \sum_{i=0}^{\infty} \Psi_i \varepsilon_{t-i}. \tag{28.2}$$

The $N \times N$ matrices holding coefficients Ψ_i are obtained from the recursion $\Psi_i = \sum_{j=1}^{p} \Phi_j \Psi_{i-j}$, where $\Psi_0 = \mathbf{I}_N$ and $\Psi_i = 0$ for $i < 0$. The moving average representation is convenient for describing the VAR system's dynamics since it allows disentangling the forecast errors. These are further used for the computation of the forecast error variances of each variable in the system, which are attributable to various system shocks. However, the methodology has its limitations as it relies on the Cholesky factor identification of VARs. Thus, the resulting forecast variance decompositions can be dependent on variable ordering. Another important shortcoming is that it allows measuring total spillovers only. Therefore, Diebold and Yilmaz (2012) use the generalized VAR of Koop et al. (1996) and Pesaran and Shin (1998) to obtain forecast error variance decompositions that are invariant to variable ordering in the VAR model and it also explicitly includes the possibility to measure directional volatility spillovers.[3]

Total spillovers

In order to define the total spillover index of Diebold and Yilmaz (2012), we consider (1) the assets' own variance shares as fractions of the H-step-ahead error variances in forecasting the ith variable that are due to the assets' own shocks to i for $i = 1, \ldots, N$ and (2) the cross variance shares, or spillovers, as fractions of the H-step-ahead error variances in forecasting the ith variable that are due to shocks to the jth variable, for $i, j = 1, \ldots, N, i \neq j$. Then, the H-step-ahead generalized forecast error variance decomposition matrix Ω has the following elements for $H = 1, 2, \ldots$.

$$\omega_{ij}^{H} = \frac{\sigma_{jj}^{-1} \sum_{h=0}^{H-1} \left(\mathbf{e}_i' \Psi_h \Sigma_\varepsilon \mathbf{e}_j \right)^2}{\sum_{h=0}^{H-1} \left(\mathbf{e}_i' \Psi_h \Sigma_\varepsilon \Psi_h' \mathbf{e}_i \right)}, \quad i, j = 1, \ldots, N, \tag{28.3}$$

where Ψ_h are moving average coefficients from the forecast at time t; Σ_ε denotes the variance matrix for the error vector, ε_t; σ_{jj} is the jth diagonal element of Σ_ε; $\mathbf{e}_i$ and $\mathbf{e}_j$ are the selection vectors, with one as the ith or jth element and zero otherwise.

As the shocks are not necessarily orthogonal in the generalized VAR framework, the sum of the elements in each row of the variance decomposition table is not equal to one. Thus, we need to normalize each element by the row sum as:

$$\tilde{\omega}_{ij}^{H} = \frac{\omega_{ij}^{H}}{\sum_{j=1}^{N} \omega_{ij}^{H}}. \tag{28.4}$$

Diebold and Yilmaz (2012) then define the total spillover index as the contribution of spillovers from volatility shocks across variables in the system to the total forecast error variance, hence:

$$S^{H} = 100 \times \frac{1}{N} \sum_{\substack{i,j=1 \\ i \neq j}}^{N} \tilde{\omega}_{ij}^{H}. \tag{28.5}$$

Note that $\sum_{j=1}^{N} \tilde{\omega}_{ij}^{H} = 1$ and $\sum_{i,j=1}^{N} \tilde{\omega}_{ij}^{H} = N$. Hence, the contributions of spillovers from volatility shocks are normalized by the total forecast error variance. To capture the spillover dynamics, we use a 200-day rolling window running from point $t - 199$ to point t. Further, we set a forecast horizon $H = 10$ and a VAR lag length of 2.[4]

Directional spillovers

The total volatility spillover index indicates how shocks to volatility spill over all the assets. However, with the generalized VAR framework, we are able to identify directional spillovers using the normalized elements of the generalized variance decomposition matrix (Diebold and

Yilmaz, 2012). The directional spillovers are important, as they allow us to uncover the spillover transmission mechanism disentangling the total spillovers to those coming from or to a particular asset in the system.

Following Diebold and Yilmaz (2012) we measure the directional spillovers received by asset i from all other assets j:

$$S^H_{N,i\leftarrow\bullet} = 100 \times \frac{1}{N} \sum_{\substack{j=1 \\ i\neq j}}^{N} \tilde{\omega}^H_{ij},$$

(28.6)

that is, we sum all numbers in rows i, except the terms on a diagonal that correspond to the impact of asset i on itself. The N in the subscript denotes the use of an N-dimensional VAR. Conversely, the directional spillovers transmitted by asset i to all other assets j can be measured as the sum of the numbers in the column for the specific asset, again except the diagonal term:

$$S^H_{N,i\rightarrow\bullet} = 100 \times \frac{1}{N} \sum_{\substack{j=1 \\ i\neq j}}^{N} \tilde{\omega}^H_{ij}.$$

(28.7)

As we now have complete quantification of how much an asset receives (transmits), denoted as the direction from (to), we can compute how much each asset contributes to the volatility in other assets in net terms. The net directional volatility spillover from asset i to all other assets j is defined as the difference between gross volatility shocks transmitted to and received from all other assets:

$$S^H_{N,i} = S^H_{N,i\rightarrow\bullet} - S^H_{N,i\leftarrow\bullet}.$$

(28.8)

3.2 Measuring asymmetric spillovers

We now describe how to capture and measure asymmetries in volatility spillovers. Specifically, we are able to account for spillovers from volatility due to negative returns $\left(\mathcal{S}^-\right)$ and positive returns $\left(\mathcal{S}^+\right)$, as well as directional spillovers from volatility due to negative returns $\left(\mathcal{S}^-_{i\leftarrow\bullet},\mathcal{S}^-_{i\rightarrow\bullet}\right)$, and positive returns $\left(\mathcal{S}^+_{i\leftarrow\bullet},\mathcal{S}^+_{i\rightarrow\bullet}\right)$. Based on the previous exposition, to isolate asymmetric volatility spillovers we need to replace the vector of volatilities $\mathbf{RV_t} = (RV_{1t}, \dots, RV_{nt})'$ defined in Equation (28.1) with the vector of negative semivariances $\mathbf{RV_t} = \left(RV_{1t},\dots,RV_{nt}\right)'$ or the vector of positive semivariances $\mathbf{RS_t^-} = \left(RS^-_{1t},\dots,RS^-_{nt}\right)$. Note that in the above definitions we dropped the H index to ease the notational burden, but it remains a valid parameter for the estimation of spillover indices.

For the ease of exposition, we might also call the spillovers from bad and good volatility as negative and positive spillovers. Their quantification now enables testing several hypotheses. A comparison of the spillover values opens the following possibilities. If the contributions of RS^- and RS^+ are equal, the spillovers are symmetric, and we expect the spillovers to be of the same magnitude as spillovers from RV. On the other hand, the differences in the realized semivariances result in asymmetric spillovers. These properties enable us to test the following hypotheses.

$$\mathcal{H}^1_0: \quad \mathcal{S}^- = \mathcal{S}^+ \quad \text{against} \quad H_A: \quad \mathcal{S}^- \neq \mathcal{S}^+.$$
$$\mathcal{H}^2_0: \quad \mathcal{S}^-_{i\leftarrow\bullet} = \mathcal{S}^+_{i\leftarrow\bullet} \quad \text{against} \quad H_A: \quad \mathcal{S}^-_{i\leftarrow\bullet} \neq \mathcal{S}^-_{i\leftarrow\bullet}.$$
$$\mathcal{H}^2_0: \quad \mathcal{S}^-_{i\rightarrow\bullet} = \mathcal{S}^+_{i\rightarrow\bullet} \quad \text{against} \quad H_A: \quad \mathcal{S}^-_{i\rightarrow\bullet} \neq \mathcal{S}^-_{i\rightarrow\bullet}.$$

Rejecting a null hypothesis means that bad and good volatility does matter for spillover transmission in terms of magnitude as well as direction. Moreover, we assume that the values of the volatility spillover indices differ over time. To capture the time-varying nature, we compute the indices using a 200-day moving window that runs from point $t - 199$ to point t; more details are provided in Section 5.

Spillover asymmetry measure

In order to better quantify the extent of volatility spillovers, we introduce a spillover asymmetry measure. In case the negative and positive realized semivariance contribute to the total variation of returns in the same magnitudes, the spillovers from volatility due to negative returns $\left(S^-\right)$ and positive returns (S^+) will be equal to the spillovers from RV, and the null hypothesis $H_0^1 : S^- = S^+$ would not be rejected. This motivates a definition of the spillover asymmetry measure (SAM) simply as the difference between positive and negative spillovers:

$$SAM = S^+ - S^-, \tag{28.9}$$

where S^+ and S^- are volatility spillover indices due to positive and negative semivariances, RS^+ and RS^-, respectively, with an H-step-ahead forecast at time t. SAM defines and illustrates the extent of asymmetry in spillovers due to RS^- and RS^+. When SAM takes the value of zero, spillovers coming from RS^- and RS^+ are equal. When SAM is positive, spillovers coming from RS^+ are larger than those from RS^- and the opposite is true when SAM is negative.

3.3 Frequency decompositions of connectedness measures

A natural way to describe the frequency dynamics (the long-term, medium-term, or short-term) of the connectedness is to consider the spectral representation of variance decompositions based on frequency responses to shocks instead of impulse responses to shocks. As a building block of the presented theory, we consider a frequency response function, $\mathbf{\Psi}(e^{-i\omega}) = \sum_h e^{-i\omega h} \mathbf{\Psi}_h$, which can be obtained as a Fourier transform of the coefficients $\mathbf{\Psi}_h$, with $i = \sqrt{-1}$. The spectral density of $\mathbf{RV}_t$ at frequency ω can then be conveniently defined as a Fourier transform of $MA(\infty)$ filtered series as

$$S_{\mathbf{RV}}(\omega) = \sum_{h=-\infty}^{\infty} E\left(\mathbf{RV}_t \mathbf{RV}_{t-h}'\right)e^{-i\omega h} = \mathbf{\Psi}\left(e^{-i\omega}\right)\Sigma\mathbf{\Psi}'\left(e^{+i\omega}\right)$$

The power spectrum $S_{\mathbf{RV}}(\omega)$ is a key quantity for understanding frequency dynamics, since it describes how the variance of the $\mathbf{RV}_t$ is distributed over the frequency components ω. Using the spectral representation for covariance, i.e. $E\left(\mathbf{RV}_t \mathbf{RV}_{t-h}'\right) = \int_{-\pi}^{\pi} S_x(\omega)e^{i\omega h}d\omega$, the following definition naturally introduces the frequency domain counterparts of variance decomposition.

While Baruník and Křehlík (2018) provide detailed derivation of the quantities, here we describe how to estimate the connectedness measures at different frequencies. The spectral quantities are estimated using standard discrete Fourier transforms. The cross-spectral density on the interval $d = (a, b) : a,b \in (-\pi, \pi), a < b$ is estimated as

$$\sum_\omega \hat{\mathbf{\Psi}}(\omega)\hat{\Sigma}\hat{\mathbf{\Psi}}'(\omega),$$

For $\omega \in \left\{\left[\frac{aH}{2\pi}\right],\ldots,\left[\frac{bH}{2\pi}\right]\right\}$ where

$$\hat{\mathbf{\Psi}}(\omega) = \sum_{h=0}^{H-1} \hat{\mathbf{\Psi}}_h e^{-2i\pi\omega/H},$$

and $\hat{\Sigma} = \hat{\varepsilon}'\hat{\varepsilon} / (T - z)$, where z is a correction for a loss of degrees of freedom, and it depends on the VAR specification.

The decomposition of the impulse response function at the given frequency band is then estimated as $\hat{\Psi}(d) = \sum_{\omega} \hat{\Psi}(\omega)$. Finally, the generalized variance decompositions at a desired frequency band are estimated as

$$\left(\hat{\theta}_d\right)_{j,k} = \sum_{\omega} \hat{\Gamma}_j(\omega)(\hat{\mathbf{f}}(\omega))_{j,k},$$

where

$$(\hat{f}(\omega))_{j,k} \equiv \frac{\hat{\sigma}_{kk}^{-1}\left((\hat{\Psi}(\omega)\hat{\Sigma})_{j,k}\right)^2}{\left(\hat{\Psi}(\omega)\hat{\Sigma}\hat{\Psi}'(\omega)\right)_{j,j}}$$

is estimated generalized causation spectrum, and

$$\hat{\Gamma}_j(\omega) = \frac{\left(\hat{\Psi}(\omega)\hat{\Sigma}\hat{\Psi}'(\omega)\right)_{j,j}}{(\Omega)_{j,j}},$$

is estimate of the weighting function, where $\Omega = \sum_{\omega} \hat{\Psi}(\omega)\hat{\Sigma}\hat{\Psi}'(\omega)$.

Then, the connectedness measures at a given frequency band of interest can be readily derived by plugging the $\left(\hat{\theta}_d\right)_{j,k}$ estimate into the traditional measures outlined above.[5]

4 Data

In this paper we compute volatility spillover measures on the foreign exchange futures contracts of six currencies and crude oil over the period 2 January 2007 to 12 February 2014. We use five-minute intraday prices of futures contracts that are automatically rolled over to provide continuous price records. The intraday returns are computed from log prices. The currencies are the Australian dollar (AUD), Canadian dollar (CAD), British pound (GBP), euro (EUR), Japanese yen (JPY), and Swiss franc (CHF).[6] All these currency contracts are quoted against the US dollar (i.e. one unit of a currency in terms of the US dollar). This is a typical approach in the forex literature (any potential domestic (US) shocks are integrated into all currency contracts). The currencies under research constitute a group of the most actively traded currencies globally (BIS, 2013; Antonakakis, 2012) and this is the reason for our choice: we aim to analyze asymmetric connectedness among the currencies that constitute two-thirds of the global forex turnover by currency pair (BIS, 2013); we do not pursue assessment of less traded currencies at the moment.

The foreign exchange, and crude oil futures contracts are traded on the Chicago Mercantile Exchange (CME) on a nearly 24-hour basis and transactions are recorded in Chicago time (CST). Trading activity starts at 5:00 p.m. CST and ends at 4:00 p.m. CST. To exclude potential jumps due to the one-hour gap in trading, we redefine the day in accordance with the electronic trading system. Furthermore, we eliminate transactions executed on Saturdays, Sundays, US federal holidays, 24–26 December and 31 December–2 January, because of the low activity on these days, which could lead to estimation bias. The data are available from Tick Data, Inc.[7]

5   Results: total, asymmetric, and frequency connectedness

5.1   Total connectedness

In Figure 28.1, we present the total connectedness among the six currencies (solid line) along with the total connectedness among the currencies and the oil (solid bold line). The total volatility spillovers measure is calculated based on Diebold and Yilmaz (2012). First we examine the connectedness on the forex market (solid line): the connectedness is quite high during the GFC period until 2010 and then in 2012 and early 2014. The total connectedness values of 65% and above during the 2008–2010 period are comparable to those found in Diebold and Yilmaz (2015). The plot exhibits a distinctive structural change in total connectedness among the six currencies under research: an initial high connectedness is interrupted by a short drop during 2009 and decreases gradually after 2010 but then in 2013 begins to rise. The period is marked by two distinctive phenomena. One is the difference between monetary policies among the Fed, ECB, and Bank of Japan. While the Fed stopped the quantitative easing (QE) policy in 2014, the ECB was beginning to pursue it and the Bank of Japan was already active in pursuing this policy. From 2013 the policy differences affected the capital flows and carry-trade operations so that the US dollar began to appreciate against the euro and yen. At the same time, falling commodity prices exerted downward pressure on inflation and interest rates. This course affects most of the currencies in our sample as commodities are quoted in vehicle currencies (USD, EUR, JPY) and interest rate cuts occurred for commodity currencies (AUD, CAD), diminishing their appeal for carry-trade activities. Hence, the increased volatility and spillovers among currencies from 2013 on are to be found in combined effects chiefly rooted in monetary steps.

Second, from Figure 28.1 we can further gauge information on the total connectedness among the currencies and the crude oil (solid bold line). By adding crude oil into the set of

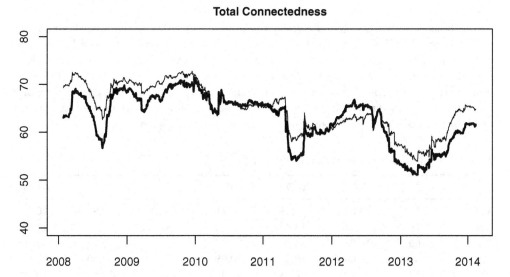

Figure 28.1   The total volatility spillovers of six currencies (solid line), the total volatility spillovers of six currencies and crude oil (bold solid line)

currencies we can imagine that we create a forex portfolio into which a crude oil is added. Gradual financialization of the crude oil makes the computation of the total connectedness a realistic exercise. A general observation is that by combining crude oil with the set of currencies a total connectedness of a hypothetical portfolio is lower over the observed time span than the total connectedness of the portfolio composed solely from the currencies. The only exception is a period in 2012 when average crude oil prices were at historically high levels. Such crude oil price development is behind the increase in the total volatility spillovers in a hypothetical portfolio.

We can further enrich our observations from the Figure 28.1 by quantifying directional spillovers among the analyzed assets. Following Diebold and Yilmaz (2012), we compute directional spillovers and show how volatility from a specific currency transmits to other currencies in our sample ("contribution TO"). Similarly we are also able to show the opposite link of the extent of spillovers going from other currencies to a specific currency ("contribution FROM"). The condensed information on the extent of such directional spillovers is presented in Table 28.1 – in aggregate form we show how specific currencies transmit and receive spillovers, or in other words how the shocks into one currency impact other currencies. The highest values lie on a diagonal and they represent the extent of how own volatility of a specific currency affects its own subsequent volatility. Other values in the matrix show the volatility spillover impact between currency pairs. An interesting and intuitive observation is that shocks to each of the two commodity currencies (AUD and CAD) impact these currencies to larger extent that the rest of currencies. Similarly, the euro and British pound do spill a great portion of their volatilities between each other. Finally, the Swiss franc and Japanese yen seem to be the calmest currencies in the portfolio as their volatility impact on each other as well as with respect to other currencies is rather low and indirectly supports their status of safe havens.

In Table 28.2 we add the crude oil to the portfolio and present the bilateral volatility impacts among the assets in a similar manner as in Table 28.1. By looking at the matrix, we observe that crude oil's own volatility dominates this asset and that pattern of volatility spillovers among the currencies remains same as that observed in Table 28.1. However, we obtain additional insights on volatility spillovers between crude oil and currencies. An important general observation is that shocks to the crude oil transfer to currencies in lesser extent than how the shocks to currencies spill over to the crude oil. And of course, there are some interesting details. First, volatility transfer from crude oil to the Japanese yen and Swiss franc seems to be quite balanced as it travels other way around. The two safe haven currencies seem to be resistant to the shocks into the crude oil and reluctant to transfer their volatilities to the oil as well. Second, shocks from the two commodity currencies (AUD and CAD) affect the crude oil to much greater extent than those from the rest of currencies. We conjecture that, despite its ongoing financialization, the crude oil is primarily a commodity and its link to other commodities that Australia and Canada export might be the reason for such degree of mutual extent of volatility spillovers.

Table 28.1 Volatility connectedness table without crude oil

	AUD	GBP	CAD	EUR	JPY	CHF	FROM
AUD	35.16	16.62	16.48	13.71	9.10	8.93	10.81
GBP	17.16	32.38	13.42	18.02	8.07	10.95	11.27
CAD	21.00	16.95	34.03	12.06	7.25	8.71	11.00
EUR	15.04	20.00	10.55	30.95	6.05	17.40	11.51
JPY	14.92	16.89	8.75	10.97	37.67	10.80	10.39
CHF	13.21	15.82	10.57	22.88	7.86	29.66	11.72
TO	13.56	14.38	9.96	12.94	6.39	9.47	66.69

Table 28.2 Volatility connectedness table with crude oil

	Crude Oil	AUD	GBP	CAD	EUR	JPY	CHF	FROM
Crude Oil	48.43	12.07	11.02	13.24	7.12	3.81	4.31	7.37
AUD	6.50	33.45	15.36	15.17	12.76	8.60	8.16	9.51
GBP	6.64	16.18	30.60	12.07	16.88	7.64	9.99	9.91
CAD	9.00	19.58	15.07	31.25	10.84	6.72	7.54	9.82
EUR	4.91	14.36	18.90	9.72	29.82	5.80	16.49	10.03
JPY	3.89	14.34	16.05	8.17	10.46	36.83	10.26	9.02
CHF	4.89	12.58	14.80	9.61	21.93	7.59	28.61	10.20
TO	5.12	12.73	13.03	9.71	11.43	5.74	8.11	65.86

5.2 Asymmetric connectedness

So far we have shown evidence based on spillovers that did not account for asymmetries. Now, we will employ the realized semivariances to separate qualitatively different shocks to volatility. Realized measures are defined on a continuous-time stochastic process of log-prices, p_t, evolving over a time horizon $(0 \leq t \leq T)$. The process consists of a continuous component and a pure jump component,

$$p_t = \int_0^t \mu_s ds + \int_0^t \sigma_s dW_s + J_t \,, \tag{28.10}$$

where μ denotes a locally bounded predictable drift process, σ is a strictly positive volatility process, and J_t is the jump part, and all is adapted to some common filtration F. The quadratic variation of the log prices p_t is:

$$[p_t, p_t] = \int_0^t \sigma_s^2 ds + \sum_{0 < s \leq t} (\Delta p_s)^2 \,, \tag{28.11}$$

where $\Delta p_s = p_s - p_{s-}$ are jumps, if present. The first component of Equation (28.11) is integrated variance, whereas the second term denotes jump variation. Andersen and Bollerslev (1998) proposed estimating quadratic variation as the sum of squared returns and coined the name "realized variance" (*RV*). The estimator is consistent under the assumption of zero noise contamination in the price process.

Let us denote the intraday returns $r_k = p_k - p_{k-1}$, defined as a difference between intraday equally spaced log prices $p_0, \ldots, p_n$ over the interval $[0, t]$, then

$$RV = \sum_{k=1}^n r_k^2 \tag{28.12}$$

converges in probability to $[p_t, p_t]$ with $n \to \infty$.

Barndorff-Nielsen et al. (2010) decomposed the realized variance into realized semivariances (*RS*) that capture the variation due to negative (*RS$^-$*) or positive (*RS$^+$*) price movements (e.g. bad and good volatility). The realized semivariances are defined as:

$$RS^- = \sum_{k=1}^n \mathbb{I}(r_k < 0) r_k^2, \tag{28.13}$$

$$RS^+ = \sum_{k=1}^n \mathbb{I}(r_k \geq 0) r_k^2. \tag{28.14}$$

Realized semivariance provides a complete decomposition of the realized variance, hence:

$$RV = RS^- + RS^+. \tag{28.15}$$

The limiting behavior of realized semivariance converges to $1/2 \int_0^t \sigma_s^2 ds$ plus the sum of the jumps due to negative and positive returns (Barndorff-Nielsen et al., 2010). The negative and positive semivariance can serve as a measure of downside and upside risk as it provides information about variation associated with movements in the tails of the underlying variable.

In short, negative realized semivariance (RS^-) isolates negative shocks to volatility or, in other words, RS^- allows capturing volatility due to negative changes (returns) in exchange rates and the crude oil. The opposite is true for positive realized semivariance (RS^+).

In Figure 28.2 we plot the dynamics of the spillover asymmetry measure (SAM) computed as the difference between the spillover indices for all six currencies (solid line) plus six currencies and the crude oil (solid bold line) where inputs are realized semivariances. The volatility associated with negative (positive) innovations to returns has been termed as bad (good) volatility (Patton and Sheppard, 2015; Segal et al., 2015). We follow this terminology and label spillovers in Figure 28.2 as bad and good volatility spillovers (or simply negative and positive spillovers).

The plot of SAM in Figure 28.2 exhibits a different pattern than that of the total connectedness measure in Figure 28.1. It provides a qualitatively new picture. When a solid line lies in a positive domain, it is a sign that asymmetries due to positive shocks measured with RS^+ dominate asymmetries due to the negative shocks. On the other hand, asymmetries due to negative shocks measured with the RS^- dominate when solid lines is situated in the negative domain.

A general observation from Figure 28.2 is that inclusion of the crude oil into the forex portfolio tends to increase dominance of the asymmetries due to positive spillovers. The pattern is most clearly visible over the time span from 2010 onwards. There is an exception, though. Shortly after the global financial crisis in 2009, inclusion of the crude oil correlates with non-negligible

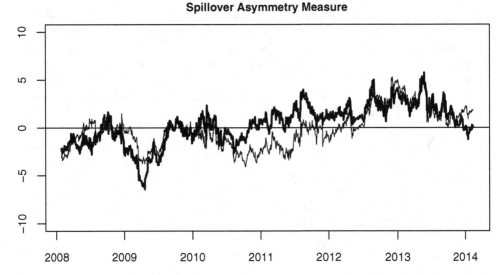

Spillover Asymmetry Measure

Figure 28.2 Spillover asymmetry measure (SAM). Solid line represents the SAM for the forex market only, while the solid bold line represents the SAM for the forex market with crude oil.

increase of the negative spillovers. This excess is underlined by an intuitive explanation. Plummeting oil prices at the end of 2008 and beginning of 2009 represent strong negative shocks that are behind the sharp increase of negative spillovers. Further developments from the end of 2009 onwards reflect rising prices and the progressive financialization of commodities (Cheng and Xiong, 2013).

Based on the plot of the SAM in Figure 28.2 we conclude that bad volatility spillovers dominate good volatility spillovers for the forex portfolio during much of the analyzed period. However, when crude oil is added into the hypothetical portfolio the dominance reverses in favor of the positive spillovers.

5.3 Frequency connectedness

In Figure 28.3 we present plots of the frequency connectedness that are computed based on Baruník and Křehlík (2018). The frequency connectedness is computed for the complete portfolio of six currencies and the crude oil. Three lines represent extent of connectedness at three horizons. Short-term horizon is represented by a simple solid line, while the medium bold line captures the medium-term horizon. Long-run connectedness is portrayed with the bold line. Short-term and medium-term connectedness share relatively similar dynamic path that begins to diverge only in 2013. Short-term and medium-term connectedness is also quite low. On the other hand long-run connectedness is rather detached from the other two frequencies. Long-run connectedness is also somewhat higher most of the time. The pattern indicates that connectedness is formed predominantly at long frequencies. This means that shocks have long-term impact and that short- and medium-term impact is rather limited.

The long-term connectedness reaches highest values during the global financial crisis and well into 2010. The long-term connectedness can be seen rising again in 2012. The outburst of

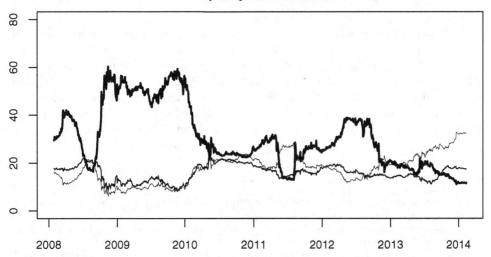

Frequency Connectedness

Figure 28.3 Dynamic frequency connectedness. The frequency connectedness at short-term horizon defined at $d_1 \in [1, 5]$ days in solid line, medium-term horizon defined at $d_2 \in (5, 20]$ days medium bold line, and long-term horizon defined at $d_3 \in (20, 300]$ days in bold line. Note that all lines through the frequency bands d_s sum to the total connectedness.

the long-term connectedness are related to financial crisis and then to the European sovereign debt crisis in 2012. Unlike short- and medium-term connectedness, the long-run connectedness seems to be quite sensitive to heightened uncertainty on the market. The sharp differences in the long-term and shorter-term connectedness should be attributed to the differences in how investors perceive the stability of the economic and financial system. High uncertainty on the market and the belief that the economic situation reflects deeper and systemic imbalances is mirrored in high long-term connectedness during the periods in which the shocks are transmitted through the system with high persistence. Finally, one should also note that a simple sum of the three lines provides the total connectedness plotted earlier in Figure 28.1.

6   Conclusion

We analyze total, asymmetric, and frequency connectedness on the oil and forex markets using high-frequency intraday data over 2007–2015. Methodologically, we compute the volatility spillover index of Diebold and Yilmaz (2012) to analyze total connectedness. Further, we use the procedure of Baruník et al. (2016) to quantify asymmetric connectedness that is due to bad and good volatility (proxied by negative and positive returns). Finally, we assess the extent of the frequency connectedness based on the approach of Baruník and Křehlík (2018). Our key results can be summarized as follows.

First, a general observation is that by combining crude oil with the set of currencies a total connectedness of the oil and forex markets over the researched period is lower than the total connectedness of the forex market itself. The year 2012 represents a single exception because of historically high oil prices associated with their higher volatility.

Second, in terms of asymmetries we show that bad volatility dominates connectedness on the forex market during much of the analyzed period. However, when we measure connectedness on both oil and forex markets the dominance reverses in favor of the good volatility.

Third, the frequency connectedness analysis reveals that dynamic of the shorter and longer term connectedness dramatically differs. While shorter-term connectedness is usually low over the whole researched period, the long-term connectedness sharply rises during the global financial crisis and European debt crisis.

Our approach brings qualitatively new insights as it provides the detailed and multifaceted evidence on the dynamics of the connectedness on two important markets. Our analysis also provides some direct implications. Specifically, we show that extent of volatility spillovers dampens when both oil and forex markets are assessed jointly. Further, our results imply that adding oil into a hypothetical portfolio of oil and foreign currencies alters asymmetry in connectedness between the two classes of assets. Finally, we show that the long-term connectedness reflects worrisome beliefs of investors and can serve as a sensitive indication of the heightened market uncertainty.

Notes

1 In the text, we use the terms "connectedness" and "spillovers" interchangeably, as both terms have been used in the literature to describe the same phenomenon.
2 The realized semivariances were quickly adopted in several recent contributions, see e.g. Feunou et al. (2013), Patton and Sheppard (2015), and Segal et al. (2015).
3 The generalized VAR allows for correlated shocks, hence the shocks to each variable are not orthogonalized.
4 In addition, we constructed the spillover index with rolling windows of 150 and 100 days to check the robustness of our results. We have also experimented with different H values and we find that the results do not materially change and are robust with respect to the window and horizon selection. The VAR lag length was chosen based on AIC to produce the most parsimonious model.

5 The entire estimation is done using the package frequencyConnectedness in R software. The package is available on CRAN or on https://github.com/tomaskrehlik/frequencyConnectedness.
6 The Australian dollar and Canadian dollar are two commodity currencies in our sample. A commodity currency refers to some currencies that co-move with the world prices of primary commodity products as the specific raw materials constitute a non-negligible part of the GDP in countries where the commodity currency is used as a legal tender. Most of these countries are typically developing countries. However, the group also includes developed countries like Canada and Australia. In the foreign exchange market, commodity currencies generally refer not only to the Australian dollar, Canadian dollar, and New Zealand dollar (see Chen and Rogoff (2003) for a detailed analysis), but also to the Norwegian krone, South African rand, Brazilian real, Russian ruble, and Chilean peso.
7 www.tickdata.com/.

References

Aboura, S. and J. Chevallier (2014). Cross-market spillovers with 'volatility surprise'. *Review of Financial Economics 23*(4), 194–207.

Andersen, T. G. and T. Bollerslev (1998). Answering the skeptics: Yes, standard volatility models do provide accurate forecasts. *International Economic Review*, 885–905.

Andreou, E., M. Matsi, and A. Savvides (2013). Stock and foreign exchange market linkages in emerging economies. *Journal of International Financial Markets, Institutions and Money 27*, 248–268.

Antonakakis, N. (2012). Exchange return co-movements and volatility spillovers before and after the introduction of euro. *Journal of International Financial Markets, Institutions and Money 22*(5), 1091–1109.

Arfaoui, M. and A. Ben Rejeb (2015). Return dynamics and volatility spillovers between FOREX and stock markets in MENA countries: What to remember for portfolio choice? *International Journal of Management and Economics 46*(1), 72–100.

Awartani, B. and A. I. Maghyereh (2012). Dynamic spillovers between oil and stock markets in the gulf cooperation council countries. *Energy Economics 36*, 28–42.

Bandi, F. M. and A. Tamoni (2017). *The horizon of systematic risk: A new beta representation*, unpublished manuscript.

Bansal, R. and A. Yaron (2004). Risks for the long run: A potential resolution of asset pricing puzzles. *The Journal of Finance 59*(4), 1481–1509.

Barndorff-Nielsen, O., S. Kinnebrock, and N. Shephard (2010). *Volatility and Time Series Econometrics: Essays in Honor of Robert F. Engle*, Chapter Measuring Downside Risk-Realised Semivariance. Oxford: Oxford University Press.

Baruník, J., E. Kočenda, and L. Vácha (2015). Volatility spillovers across petroleum markets. *Energy Journal 36*(3), 309–329.

Baruník, J., E. Kočenda, and L. Vácha (2016). Asymmetric connectedness on the US stock market: Bad and good volatility spillovers. *Journal of Financial Markets 27*, 55–78.

Baruník, J., E. Kočenda, and L. Vácha (2017). Asymmetric volatility connectedness on the forex market. *Journal of International Money and Finance 77*, 39–56.

Baruník, J. and T. Křehlík (2018). Measuring the frequency dynamics of financial connectedness and systemic risk. *Journal of Financial Econometrics forthcoming*.

BIS (2013). Triennial central bank survey foreign exchange turnover in April 2013: Preliminary global results. Technical report, Monetary and Economic Department, Bank for International Settlements.

Bubák, V., E. Kočenda, and F. Žikeš (2011). Volatility transmission in emerging European foreign exchange markets. *Journal of Banking & Finance 35*(11), 2829–2841.

Caballero, R. J., E. Farhi, and P.-O. Gourinchas (2008). Financial crash, commodity prices and global imbalances. Technical report, National Bureau of Economic Research.

Chang, C.-L., M. McAleer, and R. Tansuchat (2010). Analyzing and forecasting volatility spillovers, asymmetries and hedging in major oil markets. *Energy Economics 32*(6), 1445–1455.

Chen, Y.-C. and K. Rogoff (2003). Commodity currencies. *Journal of International Economics 60*(1), 133–160.

Cheng, I.-H. and W. Xiong (2013). The financialization of commodity markets. *Annual Review of Financial Economics (First published online as a review in advance on October 09, 2014 DOI: 10.1146/annurev-financial-110613-034432) 6*, 419–441.

Clements, A. E., A. S. Hurn, and V. V. Volkov (2015). Volatility transmission in global financial markets. *Journal of Empirical Finance 32*, 3–18.

Cogley, T. (2001). A frequency decomposition of approximation errors in stochastic discount factor models. *International Economic Review 42*(2), 473–503.

Diebold, F. X. and K. Yilmaz (2009). Measuring financial asset return and volatility spillovers, with application to global equity markets. *The Economic Journal 119*(534), 158–171.

Diebold, F. X. and K. Yilmaz (2012). Better to give than to receive: Predictive directional measurement of volatility spillovers. *International Journal of Forecasting 28*(1), 57–66.

Diebold, F. X. and K. Yilmaz (2015). *Financial and Macroeconomic Connectedness: A Network Approach to Measurement and Monitoring*. Oxford: Oxford University Press.

Do, H. X., R. Brooks, and S. Treepongkaruna (2015). Realized spill-over effects between stock and foreign exchange market: Evidence from regional analysis. *Global Finance Journal 28*, 24–37.

Do, H. X., R. Brooks, S. Treepongkaruna, and E. Wu (2016). Stock and currency market linkages: New evidence from realized spillovers in higher moments. *International Review of Economics & Finance 42*, 167–185.

Duncan, A. S. and A. Kabundi (2013). Domestic and foreign sources of volatility spillover to South African asset classes. *Economic Modelling 31*, 566–573.

Feunou, B., M. R. Jahan-Parvar, and R. Tédongap (2013). Modeling market downside volatility. *Review of Finance 17*(1), 443–481.

Fratzscher, M., D. Schneider, and I. Van Robays (2013). Oil prices, exchange rates and asset prices. (no. 1302). Technical report, Discussion Papers, DIW Berlin.

Ghosh, S. (2014). Volatility spillover in the foreign exchange market: The Indian experience. *Macroeconomics and Finance in Emerging Market Economies 7*(1), 175–194.

Greenwood-Nimmo, M. J., V. H. Nguyen, and B. Rafferty (2016). Risk and return spillovers among the G10 currencies. *Journal of Financial Markets forthcoming*.

Grobys, K. (2015). Are volatility spillovers between currency and equity market driven by economic states? Evidence from the US economy. *Economics Letters 127*, 72–75.

Haigh, M. S. and M. T. Holt (2002). Crack spread hedging: Accounting for timevarying volatility spillovers in the energy futures markets. *Journal of Applied Econometrics 17*(3), 269–289.

Hamilton, J. D. (2009). Understanding crude oil prices. *The Energy Journal 30*(2), 179–206.

Hammoudeh, S., H. Li, and B. Jeon (2003). Causality and volatility spillovers among petroleum prices of WTI, gasoline and heating oil in different locations. *The North American Journal of Economics and Finance 14*(1), 89–114.

Ito, T. and M. Yamada (2015). High-frequency, algorithmic spillovers between nasdaq and forex. Technical report, National Bureau of Economic Research.

Jayasinghe, P. and A. K. Tsui (2008). Exchange rate exposure of sectoral returns and volatilities: Evidence from Japanese industrial sectors. *Japan and the World Economy 20*(4), 639–660.

Kanas, A. (2001). Volatility spillovers between stock returns and exchange rate changes: International evidence. *Journal of Business Finance & Accounting 27*(3), 447–465.

Kitamura, Y. (2010). Testing for intraday interdependence and volatility spillover among the Euro, the pound and the Swiss franc markets. *Research in International Business and Finance 24*(2), 158–171.

Koop, G., M. H. Pesaran, and S. M. Potter (1996). Impulse response analysis in nonlinear multivariate models. *Journal of Econometrics 74*(1), 119–147.

Kumar, M. (2013). Returns and volatility spillover between stock prices and exchange rates: Empirical evidence from IBSA countries. *International Journal of Emerging Markets 8*(2), 108–128.

Lin, S. X. and M. N. Tamvakis (2001). Spillover effects in energy futures markets. *Energy Economics 23*(1), 43–56.

Lombardi, M. J. and I. Van Robays (2011). Do financial investors destabilize the oil price? European Central Bank, Working Paper No. 1346.

McMillan, D. G. and A. E. Speight (2010). Return and volatility spillovers in three euro exchange rates. *Journal of Economics and Business 62*(2), 79–93.

Ortu, F., A. Tamoni, and C. Tebaldi (2013). Long-run risk and the persistence of consumption shocks. *Review of Financial Studies 26*(11), 2876–2915.

Patton, A. J. and K. Sheppard (2015). Good volatility, bad volatility: Signed jumps and the persistence of volatility. *The Review of Economics and Statistics 97*(3), 683–697.

Pesaran, H. H. and Y. Shin (1998). Generalized impulse response analysis in linear multivariate models. *Economics Letters 58*(1), 17–29.

Salisu, A. A. and H. Mobolaji (2013). Modeling returns and volatility transmission between oil price and US-Nigeria exchange rate. *Energy Economics 39*, 169–176.

Segal, G., I. Shaliastovich, and A. Yaron (2015). Good and bad uncertainty: Macroeconomic and financial market implications. *Journal of Financial Economics 117*(2), 369–397.

Zhao, H. (2010). Dynamic relationship between exchange rate and stock price: Evidence from China. *Research in International Business and Finance 24*(2), 103–112.

29

Economic and social challenges of smart grids

Daniela Velte and Guillermo Gil Aguirrebeitia

1 Introduction

1.1 What makes an electricity grid smart?

The main difference between the conventional and the smart electricity grid consists in the flexible orchestration capacity of the latter. Smart grids create the conditions for intelligent operation, communication and data flows between grid components and between the different actors involved in grid operation, including the end user. They enable bidirectional flows of electricity and therefore the participation of the demand side both in the form of decentralized production and in the form of demand-side management (i.e. load and peak control, storage and more).

Transmission grids in Europe have already been equipped with intelligence and control devices and utilities are now in the process of modernizing the medium- and low-voltage networks.[1] The reasons for these investments by the grid operators are multi-fold, being the main benefits of smartening the grid on all network levels the following:

1   A better monitoring of electricity flows, including theft detection.
2   Reduced operational costs, due to remote control and monitoring of the grid components, early fault detection and quick repair, which leads to greater resilience, reduced outage times and better service.
3   An increased capacity and flexibility for operating the production from renewable and distributed energy sources in the grid, maximizing the output of these installations.
4   Support for "sector coupling", meaning the increasing use of electricity for transport and heating purposes (electric plug-in vehicles and heat pumps), and the optimized management of the different energy grids (electricity and gas networks, district heating and cooling etc.).

The benefits of investments in smartening the grid cannot easily be quantified, as a series of cost-benefit analyses (CBA) have shown over the years. Although the Joint Research Centre (JRC) keeps close track of developments in smart grids[2] and cooperates with relevant international bodies in the definition of a joint methodology for CBA[3] (US CHINA, 2016), the analysis needs to be done on a project-by-project basis and is very much influenced by the system boundaries chosen for the analysis (for further information see GIORDANO et al., 2012). The SG impact that is the hardest to measure in monetary terms is at the same time the most interesting for progress in the energy transition: the enabling effect in terms of market participation and generation of new business opportunities.

The developments both within the electricity grid, also called the "smart grid value chain" and the enabling effects of SG (smartness beyond the grid) are now described in more detail.

1.2 Smartness at grid level (SG value chain)

The electricity system we rely upon is undergoing a process of accelerated change towards a decentralized and decarbonized system. The final vision is an energy system that provides affordable, clean electricity worldwide. This implies a broad set of technical, regulatory, economic, and social challenges for the different agents operating along the value chain of the energy sector (Figure 29.1). Those interrelated forces drive and modulate the speed of smart grid deployment. At the same time, it is necessary to find a balance between the necessary investment in system modernization (that may lead to increased capital expenditure, CAPEX), the complexity of operation (that may lead to increased operational expenditure, OPEX), and the options for sharing benefits with the users in the form of lower electricity consumption and bills. The smart grid must create value for all actors involved. Otherwise, there is a high risk of leaving the households with the lowest investment capacity and no opportunities for self-production and consumption to pay the bill of the energy transition.

In this challenging context, digital technologies are driving the metamorphosis towards a smarter and more efficient electricity system, giving the user a more active role. The impact of digitization will affect all components of the electricity network, from generation to usage, and beyond.

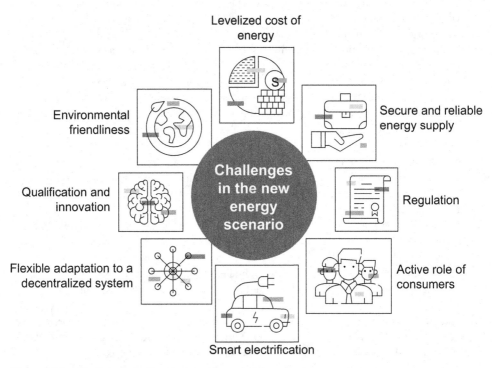

Figure 29.1 Challenges in the new energy scenario

Source: TECNALIA.

The most obvious impact is that digitization adds *smartness* to the system, creating a system that is more information-centric, intelligent and flexible. Sensors, actuators, smart meters, and many other IoT-like[4] devices are providing almost in real time precise information about system behavior and external factors, such as wind, weather, economic, or social restraints that may affect the whole system performance. Big data, analytics and the novel artificial intelligence (AI) techniques applied to the smart grid can manage the vast amount of the information produced from all these sources. They can give accurate predictions on power generation, network capacity, market conditions, and demand requirements, thus supporting the complex management and decision-making process, even in real time. At the same time, the intelligent orchestration and the smart operation of specific network elements in generation, transmission, storage, distribution, and eventually, customer management, allow for a fast reconfiguration of energy flows. It is a system that responds to sudden variations in generation conditions or demand patterns. As a result, electricity companies with smart agents can adopt new measures, such as price signals, when their own supply and demand requirements are not balanced to adjust the demand. As the smart grid turns into a dense, interconnected system of systems, in which millions or billions of actors interact, the complexity increases exponentially. Meeting all management needs without the smart-enabler technology is simply unthinkable.

Secondly, digital technologies also allow for a more *responsible* electricity system: one that is more efficient, that meets environmental and social objectives and that secures electricity provision. Efficiency is the primary goal of smart grids. This objective must be met to compensate for the additional electricity demand created by digitization itself in the form of data centers and new appliances.

Examples of more efficient grid management due to digitization already exist. For instance, in the production and transmission side, the introduction of the digital twin paradigm is leading to better operation and maintenance (O&M) strategies that improve energy production and lower overall maintenance costs. A digital twin is the software version of a physical asset to which it is interconnected via sensor and IoT-like devices. By accumulating data over time from the real asset and by applying physical dynamics modeling to the software version, it is possible to have a replica of the physical asset in the virtual world. Then, in this virtual world, it is possible to test different operation strategies much cheaper and faster than in the real world and to simulate the asset behavior under different operation conditions. The best strategies can then be deployed in the real environment with a clear O&M impact, for instance by lowering asset downtimes and by extending the asset life duration. By linking digital twins, larger parts of the entire smart grid system can be modeled and their complex interactions simulated in the virtual environment, giving precise insights and predictions about their future performance.

Yet, to reach the EU's emission reduction targets, energy efficiency must be increased at all stages of the energy chain, from generation to final consumption. The consumption part, such as in buildings and industry, have the greatest potential for energy savings, and because of that, European measures in energy efficiency focus on those sectors.[5] Building heating, cooling, and lighting is a focus of digital innovation with smart sensor, smart control, and smart operation systems to guarantee the desired comfort with lower energy bills.

The potential of these types of smart systems to monitor comfort and to provide personalized, accurate energy services is not yet fully harvested. Innovation and market reforms are still needed to ensure that the savings in energy consumption make up for the required investment. One of the most promising cases for savings through demand response (DR) participation and controllable load are advanced electric heat pumps, for which Bang et al. (2014) found that

> in a typical Danish house, the annual savings associated with intelligent control in accordance with hourly spot prices was roughly 300 DKK (EUR 40). By participating in the

regulation of the power market, the annual savings are considerably higher, but also more uncertain. Even if the heat pump only contributes with down regulation, the increase in annual savings can easily be 500 DKK (EUR 67).

In this context the European Economic and Social Committee (EESC, 2017) remarked that it is necessary to "clarify the value of user interaction with the electricity system for operators and consumers". Studies on user motivation[6] have found additional barriers, beyond economics, for example the unwillingness of consumers to hand control of certain appliances over to third parties or the lack of user-friendly interfaces and feedback to the consumer. At the same time, industry reports indicate that the market for home energy management (HEM) systems is on the rise and expected to continue to grow in the coming years.[7]

Beyond the lowering of energy bills, energy efficiency policies and innovation offer a massive potential to reduce the reliance on fossil fuels and to meet environmental objectives.

Another important topic for a responsible electricity system is to secure service provision. The assurance of electricity supply is an obligation established by the EU.[8] Due to the digitization level of the smart grid value chain, cybersecurity innovation has started to play a vital role to protect the system against vulnerabilities and attacks, and to ensure reliability and security of supply. Such attacks already occur: in December 2015, in what is considered the first successful attack to a smart grid, hackers could manipulate information systems of three energy distribution companies in Ukraine and temporarily disrupt electricity supply to more than 225,000 end consumers.[9] Apart from stealing or modifying customer data from smart meters, a devastating scenario can be imagined in which hackers, could manipulate the joint information and control systems to provoke a complete collapse of the service once the smart meters are widely deployed.

Finally, the digitization of the electricity network, along with market and regulatory factors, has a decisive impact in the *dynamism* of the system. By getting more precise information, by accessing a larger variety of contractual mechanisms, or by allowing network operators to manage some appliances remotely, users are, slowly but steadily, adopting a more active role in the smart grid value chain. In some cases, for instance when users produce energy (this is, they are prosumers) or have storage capacities (such as batteries or electric vehicles), this energy can eventually be marketed to electricity companies to meet supply and balancing requirements.

On the user side, the progressive digitization and *smartization* of systems and appliances merge with other trends, such as the prosumer role of users and electrification of the consumption. This is a breeding ground of opportunities for new entrants willing to develop new business models in a field that used to be the exclusive domain of traditional utilities. Smart grids offer opportunities for emerging actors along the entire value chain (for example, related to cybersecurity, energy marketplace platforms, or virtual power plants (VPP)), but the user interaction beyond the grid is an especially fertile field for new entrants.

1.3   Smartness beyond the grid

An obvious consequence of the development of the smart grid is that the stakeholders taking part of this development start to engage in a process of digital transformation. The grid evolves with energy-based technologies and with computing, communication and information technologies. The energy grid is overlapped with a "digital grid". The different actors need to transform themselves to manage the new situation, in which the digital transformation affects different levels in each organization. One of the most relevant implications for an organization engaged in this digital transformation process is its progressive shift towards a more customer-or user-centric paradigm. This turn from system-centric to user-centric opens the door to new opportunities beyond the grid, in the user area. By managing the consumption of appliances in the user environment, the electricity suppliers can increase flexibility and instantaneous adaptation to energy needs. If traditional energy suppliers are reluctant or fail to activate consumers, there is an opportunity for new entrants and intermediaries for accessing this potential market. However, competition in the front-end field, in this customer interface, is enormous, coming particularly from native digital players who are already occupying this interface in other domains (such as communication, entertainment or social domains) and are quickly tapping into other industries. Also, due to its dynamism, this space is very attractive for new and emerging businesses with lower overheads (e.g. no capital investments) and agile adaptation to market needs. For a company operating on the smart grid value chain, the gradual shift to a more customer-centric paradigm means to develop a better understanding of consumers, to offer a more personalized portfolio of services and to deploy a wider set of engaging mechanisms. The established utilities can take advantage of the physical and digital channels already available between providers and consumers, and this constitutes an entry barrier for new service providers, such as aggregators, who need to build their customer base from scratch. Existing IoT service providers, however, do not face this hurdle since they can easily broaden their service offer to their massive customer base.

On the user side of the smart grid, another element to consider is the prosumer role of users, those that both consume and produce energy. By using solar panels, smart control systems, batteries, and eventually electric vehicles, prosumers could integrate their systems and energy production into the smart grid system and become a more active actor in the electricity market. Apart from the direct prosumer-to-grid commercialization, new models are possible, such as peer-to-peer commercialization and prosumer community management. For instance, ENECO, a Dutch utility company, announced in 2016 CrowdNett, a plan directed to homeowners, who already have rooftop solar systems, to offer a battery system, in cooperation with TESLA, and to create with all of them a virtual power plant by tapping into a percentage of each user's storage capacity. They offer a discount on the price of the system for customers willing to participate, as well as a yearly fee if they permit CrowdNett to "borrow" up to 30% of the battery's capacity when needed. Audi, in conjunction with other partners, is carrying out a pilot project in 2018, Audi Smart Energy Network, to test the combined automobile, home, and power supply in an intelligent energy network that also interacts with the power grid. Also in this case, the systems are interconnected to form a virtual power plant. The goal is to optimize the power consumption, with renewable sources providing a greater proportion of energy and the power grid providing less.

Even though it is unlikely that a strong demand of new services from the consumer side will drive the development of new opportunities by its own, it is expected that the market developments will be the result of a collective, competitive action on the supply part, both with existing players and with new entrants, and much enhanced intervention capacity of the user on the demand-side. The big question that remains open presently is how quickly these changes can be implemented to support the successful governance of the energy transition.

2 Challenges and opportunities of smart grids in the energy transition

2.1 Technical

Progress in the implementation of SG depends in part on the technology diffusion rate of IoT for energy management in companies, administration and households, but also on the speed of deployment of high-speed communication networks. Technology diffusion has gained momentum in recent decades and digitization has become an important driver in this field, whereas new

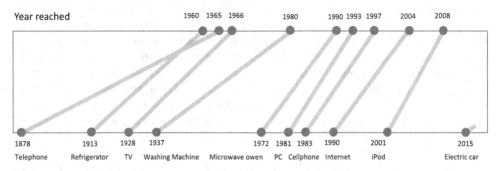

Figure 29.2 Adoption rates of new technologies (data for US households)

technology developments in the energy sector have traditionally been much slower (Figure 29.2), with longer lead times.

Technology diffusion can be slowed down by different types of barriers; among them cost, managerial complexity of data interoperability, lack of business models, and the "collective action dilemma", meaning the need for standards to facilitate cooperation between different types of actors and devices (Schwister and Fiedler, 2015). Velte et al. (2017) furthermore inform about SG experts pointing to possibly insufficient data transfer capacity to allow millions of devices to communicate with each other.

The speed of deployment of smart grids and of the devices capable of interacting with the grids will be essential to cope with additional demand derived from the "electrification" of the transport and the heating sector. In a scenario of high penetration of electric vehicles (80% of all vehicles in 2050), Europe would have to add 150 GW of new capacity (Kasten et al., 2016, p. 49) only for transport purposes, to which another 111 GW (or 223 TWh) would have to be added, by 2030, for electric heat pumps (Wind Europe, 2017, p. 12). Highly efficient and advanced applications will be able to make a substantial contribution to grid management, but not all the technologies that are presently being deployed fulfill the criterion of grid interaction capability.

In the race for decarbonizing the European transport system, electricity has the advantage of being the most flexible energy carrier offering universal access in basically all parts of Europe. These facts, together with the advancements in battery technologies and their decreasing costs, offer a reasonable perspective of progressive penetration of electric vehicles, rather than a wider uptake of alternative fuels, at least in road transport.

Transport and heating are, however, not the only sectors putting pressure on electricity demand. The deployment of more and more electrical appliances that serve users at residential, business, or public spaces also contributes to demand increase, even if the smartness of these appliances provides certain flexibility in use and charging patterns. This trend is reflected in the rising electricity consumption of data centers. Recent data on this part of electricity consumption is not available for Europe, but Avgerinou et al. (2017) point to the global developments: "information technology (IT) sector nowadays consumes approximately 7% of the global electricity, and it is forecasted that the share will rise up to 13% by 2030". For Europe, IT electricity consumption could reach 104 TWh in 2020.[10]

Self-production and self-consumption of electricity from renewable sources could help to solve these challenges if decentralization of production receives decisive support from policy and market. Wind and biomass can contribute to this, but solar technologies have the additional advantage of scalability and capability of product integration. Again, smart solutions, in this case smart inverters, play a decisive role in this context. Field trials have shown that intelligent control of PV inverters by DSOs can increase the capacity of the network for hosting distributed generation by 50% (MetaPV, 2014), and therefore maximize the contribution that solar can make to the electricity system. At the same time, the smart inverters provide feedback on energy use and production to the system owner, which can trigger investments in energy efficiency measures and change of behavior (Klöckner et al., 2018). What has been little explored so far is the potential impact of photovoltaic integration in buildings, vehicles and products on overall electricity demand, especially when combined with energy-harvesting techniques.

2.2 Market

The increasing importance of digital technologies and the associated management of large quantity of data constitutes the entrance points for new actors in the energy sector, among them aggregators, for example Actility,[11] and/or DR providers, for example Voltalis[12] in France. Blockchain-based green energy trading platforms, such as WePower,[13] are creating new access routes to financing of renewable energy projects. Virtual energy markets are starting to blossom but only in those countries in which regulation has been adapted to the new rules by opening the market up to DR and aggregation, among them France, the United Kingdom, and Belgium, as well as some regional markets in the United States.[14] It can be expected that other national energy markets follow up as soon as the newcomers have demonstrated that they have a viable business case and reliable technology. For the still lagging German market, Loßner et al. (2017) estimate that revenue for VPPs could increase between 11% and 30% by 2030, depending on the market setting and the characteristics of the distributed energy resources that are present in the system. If the distributed renewable energy resources continue to be intermittent and baseload provided by fossil-fuel power plants and nuclear continue to lose market share, the value of flexibility services to balance the market (i.e. smart grid solutions), is likely to increase, especially in a scenario of strong demand increase for electricity. There are, however, alternative solutions available for dealing with the intermittency of renewable energy generation, not least electricity storage, which are also likely to influence developments in the market. The complexity of developments makes it difficult to elaborate trustworthy forecasts of the value and price of flexibility services, and several scenarios are plausible. One can even imagine that the role of aggregators is provisional and will become less relevant when the digitization of grids, devices, building, and infrastructure reaches a higher stage of automatization.

The business case of aggregators is intrinsically linked to the fate of decentralized production, and, particularly, the possibility to implement shared solutions. However, the lack of appropriate regulatory settings for shared self-production and consumption schemes is hindering the adoption of innovative solutions in most member states presently. Even where such schemes are supported by the legal framework, technical and administrative hurdles remain that make the business case unviable for the time being.[15] This is not only due to interventions of the incumbents of the energy system to combat "load defection",[16] but also to genuine concerns on the policy side about the sharing of burdens and benefits in the energy transition. Rising electricity prices in a world that depends increasingly on a secure and affordable supply and distribution system will aggravate the problem of energy poverty in Europe, as it will affect primarily those households that are "hooked" to the grid and this could trigger political action in the population, as has already occurred in Bulgaria.[17]

3 Longer-term outlook

Longer-term scenarios on the role of smart grids in the energy transition are often strongly technology driven, since technological progress is a strong driving force within the energy transition. However, as pointed out before, the speed of deployment and market uptake of new technologies is moderated by a complex combination of legal, market and social factors that deserve due consideration. Velte et al. (2017) propose two possible scenarios for smart grid development that are not technology but policy driven. The main difference between the more conservative "networks in control" and the more ambitious "people have the power" scenarios, which were both developed with vast expert support, resides in the celerity of opening the distribution networks to service offers from new actors, including prosumers, industrial and residential DR programs, and mobility service providers. Active market participation and interaction with the distribution network is essential to create a successful and stable business case for aggregators during the transition period, to support the viability of combined heat and power (CHP) plants, to achieve a more efficient management of heat and electricity and to assure benefits from the self-production of energy. If SG implementation remains limited to the transmission and distribution system, as described in the "networks in control" scenario, efficiency gains will mainly benefit the system operators through improved prediction and self-healing capacity, but the efficiency potential of demand-side management will be exploited to a much lower degree.

The EU has just agreed to raise renewable contribution to the energy mix 32% by 2030 and has set a separate target for transport (14%).[18] The agreement also clarifies the rules for self-production, consumption, storage, and sale of self-produced energy for installations up to 25 kW. These recent decisions are especially relevant for the main driving force behind the energy transition: the citizens, who are making a major financial contribution by investing in small-scale renewable projects either individually or collectively. The member states have 18 months to transpose these decisions into national law, but many governance aspects of the transition are still under negotiation at EU level, and these aspects have a strong impact on the effectiveness of policy implementation on national level. What Europe is still lacking is an efficient tool to track progress and efficiency gains in the final use of energy, and the contribution that smart grids make to this.

4 Conclusions

The energy system, essentially unchanged for many decades, is recently evolving towards a decarbonized and decentralized system with a deep impact on the existing electricity infrastructures. The share of renewable low-carbon and fossil-fuel-free energy from distributed sources across the electricity network will increase, due to social, environmental, and economic factors. At the same time, electricity demand is expected to grow due to the digitization of the society and the general electrification trend in sectors with high energy demand, such as in transport or heating. These factors create major technical and economic challenges for the efficiency and governance of the electricity system. In response to these challenges, smart grids are a critical pillar to ensure the provision of the affordable and clean electricity that our society and environment need.

The transition towards the full vision of the SG creates multiple challenges that require an interdisciplinary approach of future research directions, combining technical, economic, and social requirements.

The digitization of the grid, together with new energy-based technologies – such as batteries – is changing the approaches for electricity system management and its flexible adaptation to oscillations in production or demand. This digitization process of the network with new digital enablers, such as sensors, actuators, or AI-based agents, is still in its initial stages. The grid's current capacity to cope effectively with all the new requirements related to intermittent generation, on-site production, and secure supply is limited, especially when considering the changes that are under way in the electricity system itself. Beyond the grid, smart appliances for users and energy-related applications, such as solar panels, batteries, or electric vehicles, are progressively becoming part of the system. This leads to millions of electrical and digitally connected installations, which will play an increased role for the real-time adaptation of the smart grid once they are fully integrated through intelligent decision and control systems. A holistic planning and management approach involving all actors is needed to ensure the secure delivery of energy services in the next decades.

At the same time, the willingness for the user to participate in the game depends on how clearly the benefits are transferred to them. In this sense, the smart grid is changing the energy business concept and providing a fertile ground for new, customer-centered business models for both existing and new actors of the electricity value chain.

Notes

1 Information obtained during interviews with DSOs carried out in the EASME study on smart grids (VELTE et al., 2017).
2 Smart Grid Projects Outlook 2017, (available on url:at http://ses.jrc.ec.europa.eu/smart-grids-observatory).
3 Chris MARNAY, Berkeley Lab; Liping LIU, China Southern Grid; JianCheng YU, State Grid Co. of China; Tianjin Eco-city: Dong Zhang, State Grid Co. of China; Josh MAUZY, Southern California Edison; Brendan SHAFFER, University of California, Irvine; XuZhu DONG, China Southern Grid; Will AGATE, Philadelphia Industrial Development Corp; Silvia VITIELLO, Joint Research Centre, European Commission; "White Paper on Benefit Analysis of Smart Grid Projects", (available on url:at https://eta.lbl.gov/sites/default/files/publications/ccwg_benefits_wp_v28-0_20161027_v3-0.pdf).
4 Internet of Things.
5 Energy Efficiency Directive, (available on url:at https://ec.europa.eu/energy/en/topics/energy-efficiency/energy-efficiency-directive).
6 See, for example, ADVANCED Consortium (2014), "Consolidated Report on the Key ADVANCED Conclusions".
7 For more information on HEMS and their cost and electricity saving potential see New York State Energy Research and Development Authority (2017), "Home Energy Management System Savings Validation Pilot, Report Number 17–16", (available on url:at https://www.nyserda.ny.gov/-/media/Files/Publications/Energy-Analysis/Home-Energy-Management-System-Savings-Validation-Pilot.pdf).
8 Security of supply of electricity, summary of Directive 2005/89/EC — measures to safeguard security of electricity supply and infrastructure investment, (available on url:at https://eur-lex.europa.eu/legal-content/EN/TXT/?uri=LEGISSUM%3Al27016).
9 Wikipedia, "December 2015 Ukraine power grid cyberattack", (available on url:at https://en.wikipedia.org/wiki/December_2015_Ukraine_power_grid_cyberattack).
10 Avgerinou et al., citing Bertoldi, P., Hirl, B., Labanca, N., Energy Efficiency Status Report (2012), "Electricity Consumption and Efficiency Trends in the EU-27. European Commission", *Joint Research Centre*, (available on url:at http://publications.jrc.ec.europa.eu/repository/handle/JRC69638).
11 Actility, S.A.; www.actility.com/.
12 Voltalis; www.voltalis.com/.
13 WePower UAB; https://wepower.network/#.
14 For a recent overview of aggregators in these countries, see www.adlittle.com/en/node/22770.
15 For more information on the situation in the member states, see the PVP4Grid project at www.pvp4grid.eu/.
16 RMI (2015), "The Economics of Load Defection", (available on url:at www.rmi.org/wpcontent/uploads/2017/04/2015-05_RMI-TheEconomicsOfLoadDefection-FullReport-1.pdf).
17 See, for example: Cage, Sam; Tsolova, Tsvetelia; "Bulgarian government resigns amid growing protests", Reuters, 2013, (available on url:at www.reuters.com/article/us-bulgaria-government/bulgarian-government-resigns-amid-growing-protests-idUSBRE91J09J20130220).
18 European Commission – Statement: "Europe leads the global clean energy transition: Commission welcomes ambitious agreement on further renewable energy development in the EU", 2018, (available on url:at http://europa.eu/rapid/press-release_STATEMENT-18-4155_en.htm).

References

Avgerinou, M., Bertoldi, P., and Castellazzi, L. (2017), "Trends in Data Centre Energy Consumption under the European Code of Conduct for Data Centre Energy Efficiency", *Energies*. doi: 10.3390/en10101470

Bang, C., Togeby, M. and Holmberg Rasmussen, L. (2014), "Ready project. Summary of Main Findings–With a Focus on Market Aspects and Local Grid Constraints", EA Energy Analyses.

Barnard, M. (2015), "What exactly is the difference between grid parity and socket parity?", (available on url:at https://www.quora.com/What-exactly-is-the-difference-between-gridparity-and-socket-parity).

EESC (2017), European Economic and Social Committee, "Energy Union Governance", 26 Apr 2017, adopted references: TEN/617 EESC-2016

Giordano, V., Onyeji, I., Fulli, G., Sánchez Jiménez, M., and Filiou, C. (2012), "Guidelines for conducting a cost-benefit analysis of Smart Grid projects", Joint Research Centre, Report EUR 25246 EN, ISBN 978-92-79-23339-5.

Kasten, P., Bracker, J., Haller, M., and Purwanto, J. (2016), "Assessing the status of electrification of the road transport passenger vehicles and potential future implications for the environment and European energy system", Öko-Institut e.V. and Transport & Mobility Leuven (TML), Framework Service Contract No EEA/ACC/13/003/LOT.

Klöckner, C., Andres, J., Chebaeva, N., Dimitrova, E., Frieden, D., Koksvik, G., Koljonen, T., Löfström, E., Qiu, X., Røyrvik, J., Tzanev, D., and Velte, D. (2018), "ECHOES report: An analysis of the potential of advanced social science knowledge in policymaking", in print.

Loßner, M., Böttger, D., and Bruckner, T. (2017), "Economic Assessment of Virtual Power Plants in the German Energy Market: A Scenario-Based and Model-Supported Analysis", *Energy Economics* 62: 125–138.

MetaPV Study (2014), 3E (coordinator); "Cost-effective integration of photovoltaics in existing distribution grids: Results and Recommendations".

Schwister, F. and Fiedler, M. (2015), "What Are the Main Barriers to Smart Energy Information Systems Diffusion?", *M. Electron Markets* 25: 31. (available on url:at https://doi.org/10.1007/s12525-014-0162-x).

US China Climate Change Working Group, Smart Grid (2016); Chris MARNAY, Berkeley Lab; Liping LIU, China Southern Grid; JianCheng YU, State Grid Co. of China; Tianjin Eco-city: Dong Zhang, State Grid Co. of China; Josh MAUZY, Southern California Edison; Brendan SHAFFER, University of California, Irvine; XuZhu DONG, China Southern Grid; Will AGATE, Philadelphia Industrial Development Corp; Silvia VITIELLO, Joint Research Centre, European Commission; "White paper on benefit analysis of smart grid projects", (available on url:at https://eta.lbl.gov/sites/default/files/publications/ccwg_benefits_wp_v28-0_20161027_v3-0.pdf).

Velte, D., Zaldua, M., Von Jagwitz, A., Delnooz, A., Daan, S., García, E., Laes, E., Urcola, I., Vingerhoets, P., Baiocco, S., and Faberi, S. (2017), "Study on barriers and opportunities for Smart Grid deployment: Final report EASME studies on smart grids, lot 2", EASME/COSME/2015/16 – Study on Smart Grids Draft Final Report.

Wind Europe (2017), "Renewable Power for All: a call for an environmentally beneficial electrification and multi-sectoral integration", Windeurope.org.

Part V
Energy modeling

30

CGE models in energy economics

Ken'ichi Matsumoto and Shinichiro Fujimori

1 Introduction

Energy is one of the most important drivers for the modern economy and its role has become even more important in the last couple of decades. The sufficient energy supply is essential particularly for the industrialized economy. Energy supply and demand structures are complex. Supply side is related to fossil fuel resource reservoir and depletion, renewable potential, and geographical location. The energy conversion technology such as power generation technologies and fuel refineries determines the efficiency and also the environmental aspects (greenhouse gas (GHG) and air pollutants emissions). Demand side is determined by energy end-use technology, activity level (e.g. passenger transport), human behavior responding to the price changes, and so on. Those things are interacting with each other in conjunction with costs, energy prices, and relevant policies. Because of such close relationship between energy and economy, energy issues have been major topics in economics.

In economic analysis, energy issues (e.g. prices, resource depletion, and environment) have been analyzed by various economic methodology (see also other chapters in this book). A computable general equilibrium (CGE) model is one of them and has played significant roles in the economic research in order to better understand entire economic response to particular policy intervention or other relevant shocks to the economy. This chapter introduces CGE modeling studies in energy economics.

Section 2 of the chapter describes the overview of CGE models, including basics of the models. In Section 3, we show the reviews of research articles in energy economics with various CGE models, although we can only introduce a limited number of articles because a huge number of studies exist. Section 4 concludes this chapter with insights for future works.

2 Overview of CGE models

2.1 Brief explanation of CGE models

CGE models are a type of economic models that use actual economic data to simulate how economic conditions are affected by changes in policy, technology, or other external factors (external shocks). CGE models are also called applied general equilibrium (AGE) models.

A CGE model consists of equations describing model variables and a database consistent with the equations. The formulation is based on neo-classical theory, assuming optimization behavior of economic agents where producers and consumers are supposed to maximize profit and welfare respectively. CGE models are numerical models based on general equilibrium theory pioneered by Herbert Scarf in 1967 [1,2]. This method was first used by Shoven and Whalley [3,4].

CGE models target whole economy of a country, region, or the world. This means that unlike partial equilibrium analysis, which focuses on a market of a specific goods or service, CGE models describe economic activities of all sectors including industrial sectors, household, and government. Industrial sectors are usually aggregated and the level of aggregation depends on the model targets (e.g., global or national model) and aims of the studies (e.g., power generation sectors are highly disaggregated if the energy is the focus). Thus, CGE models estimate the impact of changes in one part of the economy not only to that part but also to the other part of the economy. For example, a gasoline tax might affect energy prices and energy demand for vehicles, thus might also affect demand for other transportation, transportation equipment manufacture, and whole economic activities. CGE models are similar to input-output (IO) models (Chapter 31 in this book) in the sense that both of them use IO database, but prices have a more important role in CGE, where substitutions among inputs via price changes are represented, whereas IO models freeze the input coefficient.

CGE models are basically a type of economic models. Thus, they were originally applied for economic policies, including trade policy and taxes. However, as energy and climate change issues have been highly demanded recently, they have been used for analysis of energy efficiency improvement and GHG emission reduction.

2.2 Models and data

In order to conduct CGE analysis, the model itself (model equations) and databases are required. CGE models are often developed using nested CES (constant elasticity of substitution) production and utility functions, but other forms of functions such as linear expenditure system are also applied. Early CGE models were developed by using programing language such as C and FORTRAN, which was expensive for development. However, in recent years models are developed by numerical software such as the GAMS (General Algebraic Modeling System)[1] and GEMPACK (General Equilibrium Modelling PACKage).[2] Therefore, the cost for modeling is lowered.

Databases used in CGE models usually consist of economic activities and elasticities. Because CGE models usually need data of a single period (i.e., no time series data are necessary), no historical time series data are often unnecessary.

Economic activities of individual sectors (i.e., industry, household, and government) in monetary terms (e.g., input and output of production, consumption, trade, labor supply, and investment) are supplied as a form of IO table or social accounting matrix (SAM). It covers the whole economy of a country or the whole world. Sectoral coverage depends on the models from relatively simple to highly detailed such as by disaggregating technology of power sectors.

Elasticities are parameters that capture the response of the economy (e.g., 1% of change in relative price of A and B changes the ratio of the consumption of A and B) in CES functions. These elasticities usually include elasticities of substitution, elasticities of transformation, Armington elasticities for imports, and income elasticities of demand. For example, elasticities of substitution indicate how easy inputs to production may be substituted for another input.

Furthermore, additional data such as energy (including power generation by technology) and GHG emissions are necessary for analysis of energy and environmental analyses. Because the recent Global Trade Analysis Project (GTAP) databases also cover energy and GHG emissions, the barrier to develop CGE models for these fields is lowered.

2.3 Types of CGE models

CGE models can be classified into multiple categories. The important aspects of the models are how to handle geographical regions and time scale. From the geographical perspective, the models can be classified into "country" and "global" models.[3]

- *Country models*: Country models focus on economy of a specific country. This type of model is often used in policy analysis of a country of interest. The models can be classified into single country and multi-region models. Single country models, which handle the country as an only region in the model, is the most orthodox type of the country models. On the other hand, multi-region models disaggregate the country into multiple regions such as states, provinces, prefectures, or other defined regions in the country, thus interaction among the regions are taken into account. Compared with global models, they have advantages on data and sectoral details, particularly for the single country models. Because the model targets one country, only SAM or IO table (and energy and CO_2 emissions if necessary) of the country is needed. These data are usually available at the statistical bureau of the country. From the viewpoint of sectoral details, because of the data availability in detailed sectors for country data and less computational costs (due to the less number of geographical regions), the models can handle higher resolution of the sectors. On the other hand, their disadvantages are as follows. Because the rest of the world is usually out of the scope in country models, international trade and impact of external shocks of the country to other counties are weak.
- *Global models*: Global CGE models cover the whole world. Therefore, impact of sector(s) of one country to the other countries can be analyzed. The most difficult aspect of this type of models is data, because consistent data (not only domestic economic activities but also international trade) for all countries in the world are necessary. However, thanks to the GTAP of Purdue University,[4] global IO tables for CGE analysis have been available since 1992. However, sectoral coverage of global CGE models is still less detailed than country models. The resolution of global CGE models are thus usually around 20 for both industrial sectors and geographical regions.

From the temporal perspective, the models can be classified into "static" and "dynamic" models. CGE models of early years were static (also called comparative static). However, in recent year, particularly in energy economics, dynamic models have frequently been used.

- *Static models*: Static models are the basic type of the model and are also called comparative static. The static type considers economy at one time point. Thus, the model analyzes, for example for policy analysis such as carbon tax, how economy reacts to external shocks or introduction of policies. The results of the analysis show how economy changes after achieving new equilibrium conditions due to the shocks or policies (i.e. economy is adjusted to a new equilibrium). Therefore, it can be either short-term or long-term equilibrium depending on the modeling, although time-scale is not explicitly considered in this type.

- *Dynamic models:* In contrast, dynamic CGE models explicitly considers "time" in the future, which is often at annual, five-year, or ten-year intervals. Dynamic models can be classified into two types: recursive dynamic and forward looking (or optimization). Recursive-dynamic models are accumulation of static CGE models. This means that models are solved sequentially along with time (time t, $t + 1$, $t + 2$, . . .). They assume that behavior of economic agents depends only on current and past states of the economy, thus myopic agents. On the other hand, forward-looking models are that behavior of agents depend not only on current and past economic states but also on future economic states. Therefore, different from recursive-dynamic models, the models are solved the whole periods considered simultaneously, thus more computational power is required. Comparing with static CGE models, development of dynamic models is more challenging because it needs assumptions for the future, such as economic growth and population change. In particular, to model long-time future (e.g., 100 years) in energy economics, further assumptions such as energy efficiency improvement and new energy technologies are required. Despite such huge challenges, this type of model (either recursive dynamic or forward looking) is more frequently used than the static type in recent energy economic studies.

2.4 Strengths and weaknesses of CGE models

The most noticeable strength of the CGE modeling approach is that it handles the whole economic activities of the world (or a country or regions). This means that unlike a partial equilibrium approach the models can analyze an exogenous shock (or impact or change) in one sector to the whole economy. For example, this approach is useful to evaluate the impact of increase in oil price not only on oil and energy demand but also on the other sectors such as the prices of and demand for other goods and services and final demand that would help to understand macroeconomic response (e.g., GDP and welfare).

However, CGE is not of course the perfect tool, but it has its weaknesses. From the economic aspect, validation of model accuracy and parameter estimations are the issues. In CGE models, most of the parameters in the models are calibrated with single year data (SAM) and the other parameters (elasticities) are often taken from literature or existing models. Thus, accuracy of models from time series perspective is an issue of CGE. This also means that the parameter calibration strongly relies on single year snapshot that could have extreme condition. The obvious example is that if the parameters are calibrated on the SAM in year 2008, the parameters could involve more or less characteristics of financial crisis of 2007–2008. This kind of disadvantage could lead a bias in the CGE simulation.

From the energy aspect, top-down models like CGE models usually do not have details in energy technology compared to bottom-up approaches such as energy technology models. Considering detailed technology is essential particularly when the models consider long-term future such as the analysis of climate policy. Recently, there exist studies that couple CGE and energy technology models [5,6], but such studies are still rare (Chapter 32 in this book).

3 CGE modeling research in energy economics

3.1 Features of CGE models in energy economics

CGE models used in the field of energy economics are usually much more complicated than those used in pure economic analysis. In pure economic CGE models, the models are developed based only on economic data, usually IO tables or system of national account.

However, for the CGE models in energy economics, further components are indispensable to analyze energy and the related issues. The most important sectors are energy sectors, particularly power generation. In usual CGE models, power generation is often represented by a single electricity sector. However, to adequately analyze energy related topics and policy, understanding substitution among power sources is an important factor, particularly when analyzing future scenarios of climate mitigation policy. Furthermore, with regard to power sector in the long-term analysis, technologies such as biomass and carbon capture and storage will also play important roles. Thus, incorporating these components or factors into CGE models are essential.

One more important aspect for the CGE models in energy economics is the treatment of land use [7]. Land-use is important in terms of energy studies from two points: CO_2 emissions from land use and land-use change [8]; and competition of agricultural areas between food production and energy crop. Recent climate mitigation studies have shifted towards more radical emissions reduction scenarios (e.g., 2 °C goal) which requires zero or negative emissions in the latter half of this century. That would essentially mean that land-related CO_2 emissions play an critically important role as well as energy related emissions. In other words, if emissions from land use or land-use change changed, possible emissions from energy use should be simultaneously changed if allowable CO_2 emissions are fixed.

The second point is directly related to energy use. It is considered that biomass energy plays an important role in climate mitigation, particularly for a large emission reduction [9–11]. The biomass energy will be produced as energy crops; thus they will compete with agricultural (food) production. This leads a question if sufficient agricultural and energy crops can be produced subject to the limited land areas under climate mitigation policy and Hasegawa et al. [12] pointed out that mitigation policy could worsen food security. Therefore, in order to consistently analyze these points, considering land use and land-use change in CGE models in energy economics, particularly in climate mitigation analysis, is significant.

There are a huge number of CGE models used in the literature.[5] The selected key models (all the models are a global type) are the AIM/CGE model (National Institute of Environmental Studies, Japan) [13,14], the EPPA model (Massachusetts Institute of Technology, the United States) [15,16], the ENV-Linkages model (Organisation for Economic Co-operation and Development) [17], the IMACLIM model (International Research Center on Environment and Development, France) [18,19], the GEM-E3 model (European Commission) [20,21], WorldScan (Netherlands Bureau for Economic Policy Analysis, the Netherlands) [22,23], and the PET model (National Center for Atmospheric Research, the United States) [24,25].

3.2 Review of CGE modeling research

CGE models have been used in energy economic research for more than 30 years, and more and more research articles are published in recent years, particularly in relation with climate change.

By searching research articles on energy research of CGE models,[6] we found 517 documents (as of 16 May 2017). Figure 30.1 shows the number of articles found in three well-known databases. As it shows, the first article was published in the early 1980s. The number of articles related to energy research using CGE models published is increasing from just double digits in 1980s to more than thousand in 2010s.

The first article found in Scopus was published in 1984 [26].[7] Dick et al. [26] use multiple static national CGE models to analyze economic impact of oil-price increases in developing countries. Similar to this study, CGE studies in the early period mainly focuses on economic

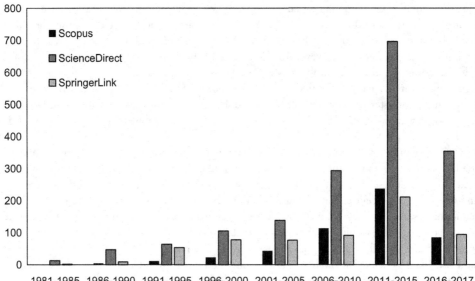

Figure 30.1 The number of articles found in three well-known databases. Scopus includes title, keywords, and abstract of journals from broader publishers, although full papers are not searchable. In contrast, the articles found in ScienceDirect and SpringerLink are limited to specific publishers, but the full papers are searchable.

Source: www.scopus.com/home.uri,www.sciencedirect.com/, and link.springer.com/.

Table 30.1 Features of selected papers of CGE models in energy economics

No.	Article	Main topic	Global or country	Geographical coverage	Time scale
1	Bergman [34]	Nuclear power	Country (Sweden)	Single	Static
2	Dick et al. [26]	Oil price	Country (four developing countries)	Four single	Static
3	Despotakis and Fisher [27]	Oil price	Local (California)	Single	Static
4	Fisher and Despotakis [28]	Energy tax	Local (California)	Single	Static
5	Boyd and Uri [29]	Energy tax	Country (US)	Single	Static
6	Uri and Boyd [30]	Gasoline tax	Country (US)	Single	Static
7	Uri and Boyd [31]	Tax on refined petroleum products (elimination)	Country (Philippines)	Single	Static
8	Semboja [32]	Energy tax	Country (Kenya)	Single	Static
9	Semboja [33]	Energy efficiency	Country (Kenya)	Single	Static
10	Li and Rose [35]	Carbon tax	Local (Pennsylvania)	Single	Static

No.	Article	Main topic	Global or country	Geographical coverage	Time scale
11	Welsch [36]	Carbon/energy tax	Region (EU)	Two regions	Dynamic
12	Uri and Boyd [37]	Motor fuels excise tax	Country (USA)	Single	Static
13	Naqvi [38]	Energy, economy, and equity	Country (Pakistan)	Single	Static
14	Galinis and van Leeuwen [39]	Nuclear power	Country (Lithuania)	Single	Static
15	Bach [40]	Environmental fiscal reform	Country (Germany)	Single	Dynamic
16	Steininger and Voraberger [41]	Biomass energy	Country (Austria)	Single	Static
17	Hanley et al. [42]	Energy efficiency	Local (Scotland)	Single	Dynamic
18	Kiuila et al. [43]	Ecological tax reform	Country (Poland)	Single	Static
19	Müller-Fürstenberger and Stephan [44]	Climate change and technological innovation	Global	Two regions	Dynamic
20	Otto et al. [45]	Energy and technology	Illustrative data	Single	Dynamic
21	Otto et al. [46]	Climate mitigation	Country (Netherlands)	Single	Dynamic
22	Löschel and Otto [47]	Climate mitigation	Country (Netherlands)	Single	Dynamic
23	Wang et al. [48]	Climate mitigation	Country (China)	Single	Dynamic
24	Matsumoto [49]	Climate mitigation	Country (Japan)	Single	Dynamic
25	Timilsina et al. [50]	Oil price and biomass	Global	25 regions	Dynamic
26	O'Neill et al. [25]	Urbanization	Global	Nine regions	Dynamic
27	Solaymani and Kari [51]	Energy subsidy reform	Country (Malaysia)	Single	Static
28	Broberg et al. [52]	Energy efficiency and rebound effect	Country (Sweden)	Single	Static

impact of energy-related taxes, energy price increases, and energy efficiency [27–33]. Furthermore, because of the computational power in those days, the models were much simpler (in terms of types of energy, geographical coverage, and time scale) than those used in recent years.

From the mid-1990s, energy research in terms of climate change has been increasing because of the United Nations Framework Convention on Climate Change entered into force in 1992 and the Kyoto Protocol adopted in 1997. For example, Li and Rose [35] analyzed the impact of carbon tax on economy and energy in Pennsylvania. Similarly, Welsch [36] analyzed the impact of carbon tax on European economy, particularly focusing on different tax recycling methods. There are a lot of other studies on climate change analyses (the main topic in energy economics), but they are reviewed in Section 3.3.

Other types of studies after the mid-1990s include price (including) aspects (motor fuels excise tax [37]; environmental fiscal reform [40]; ecological tax reform [43]; oil price and biomass [50]; energy subsidy reform [51]), specific energy sources (nuclear power [39]; biomass [41]), and others (energy, economy, and equity [38]; energy efficiency [42]; urbanization [25]; energy efficiency and rebound effect [52]).

When energy efficiency is handled in CGE models (as a research topic to analyze the effect of energy efficiency or as an assumption for the future), autonomous energy efficiency improvement (AEEI), which exogenously handles energy efficiency improvement (e.g., 2% per annum), is frequently used. However, this approach does not take into account the source of energy efficiency improvement, meaning that energy efficiency improves without explicit costs for the improvement. To address such an issue, the models that consider endogenous technological change have been developed [44–49]. There are two ways to express endogenous technological change in the literature: research and technology (R&D) investment and learning by doing (LbD). The R&D approach, which essentially is based on the growth theory [53], views innovation as a function of expenditure in R&D. This means that technological knowledge can be produced by investing resources into R&D activities [44]. The LbD approach assumes that the accumulation of technological knowledge is a side-product of applying certain technologies [44]. As far as the authors searched articles, most of the studies of CGE models with endogenous technological change in energy economics have been implemented in terms of climate change (see also the special issue on endogenous technological change from the Energy Journal published in 2006). Otto et al. [45] were one exception, which analyzed the relationship between energy and technological change focusing on energy biased technological change.

3.3   Global CGE modeling and its role in climate change mitigation analysis

A number of CGE models have been developed and applied to the global mitigation analysis which has been a major application filed for the CGE models which focus on energy markets last a couple of decades. Integrated assessment models (IAMs) community have been made tens of model inter-comparison exercises and CGE models were involved in. The most well-known exercise is energy modeling forum (EMF),[8] which deals with various relevant and timely topics (mostly related to climate policy). For example, EMF27 presents the technological uncertainty and its implications for the long-term climate mitigation [54]. The other series of model inter-comparison recently taken is led by EU: AMPERE [55], LIMITS [56], and ADVANCE [57,58]. Here we list the global CGE models recently joining these exercises.

In the context of climate mitigation studies, power generation is one of the major CO_2 emissions sources and therefore, most models represent electricity sector in detailed. Until the early 2000s, IAMs were required to represent energy related CO_2. Since non-energy related CO_2 emissions and non-CO_2 emissions along with biomass energy have been focused [59,60], IAMs have been required to represent those things and the involved CGEs are not the exception. Such modeling trend is reflected in the recent CGE model features where land, agricultural and other emissions species are more or less implemented. Furthermore, more interactions with other models (e.g., Earth system models) have been carried out so that the weakness of CGE model is complemented.

Other than the above, there are several topics that have been dealt with by global CGE models within the context of climate mitigation analysis. First, the assessment of emission trading is one of the research area where CGE models are good at. The most recent article would be Fujimori et al. [61], but many articles are accumulated [62–65]. Unemployment is always the concern for the social security and some models have tried to represent it [66,67].

Table 30.2 List of global CGE models in recent IAM model inter-comparison exercises

Model name	Article	Interaction with other model	Number of regions	Agriculture/ Land	Power sector	Emissions	Other features
AIM/CGE	Fujimori et al.[a]	Climate, land allocation, agriculture, water models	17	9 sectors/ 9 AEZs	12 sectors	GHGs[b], APs[c]	Recursive dynamic
EPPA	Paltsev et al.[d]	Earth System model	16	2 sectors/ single	10 sectors	GHGs, APs,	Recursive dynamic
ENV-LINKAGE	Château et al.[e]	–	15	?	7 sectors	GHGs, APs	Recursive dynamic
FARM	Sands et al.[f]	–	15	11 sectors/ 18 AEZs	9 sectors	CO_2	Recursive dynamic
IMACLIM	Waisman et al.[g]	Land use and energy models	12	2 sectors/ single	13 sectors	CO_2	Recursive dynamic
iPETS	Ren et al.[h]	Land use and land surface models	9	2 sectors/ single	1 sector	CO_2	Intertemporal optimization
GEM-E3	Capros et al.[i]	Energy model	38	1 sector/ No	10 sectors	GHGs, SOx and NOx	Recursive dynamic

a: www.nies.go.jp/social/dp/pdf/2012-01.pdf.
b: CO_2, CH_4, N_2O, SF_6, HFCs, and PFCs.
c: BC, OC, CO, VOC, NO_X, SO_2, and NH_3.
d: web.mit.edu/globalchange/www/MITJPSPGC_Rpt125.pdf.
e: Château et al. [17].
f: Sand et al. [68].
g: Waisman et al. [6] and www2.centre-cired.fr/IMACLIM/?lang=en.
h: Ren et al. [69].
i: Capros et al. [70].

4 Conclusions: insights for future works

In this chapter, after briefly introduced CGE models and those used in energy economics, we reviewed research articles' CGE modeling research in the field. In the early phase (1980s to early 1990s), energy prices and tax and energy efficiency were the main topic. In that period, the number of the related studies was limited. After 1990s, because climate change has been a vital issue, research on energy issues in terms of climate mitigation has been the most popular topic in energy economics. In addition, large-scale dynamic global CGE models have been frequently used in such studies. For future studies in this field, it is expected that models and data will be more advanced. The important points will be as follows.

- *Resolution of sectors and geographical regions*: In country models, which mainly relies on IO table or SAM of the country, the resolution of industrial sector is usually high enough for desired analyses. For global model, with the development of GTAP model and database, the resolution of both industrial sectors and geographical regions has been improved (57 sectors and 140 regions in GTAP 9). However, its resolution may not be enough for analyzing specific areas. The models with higher resolution need huge computational power. Because of rapid evolution of computers, this will be a less significant issue in the near future.

- *Coupling a CGE model with other types of model*: CGE models in energy economics have various modules in them such as energy, environment (GHG emissions), and land use. However, these modules need to be more or less a simplified form when directly modeling such modules in CGE models. As the choice of energy sources and technologies is diversified and analysis assuming large-scale changes in energy system is required particularly in the context of climate mitigation, it is required to detailed information of energy system, which is not possible only with CGE models. Thus, a CGE model combined with a bottom-up energy technology model is an urgent requirement. In addition, for long-term analysis, it is required to improve estimation of for example materials, transportation, and agricultural products, which are closely related to climate change and energy. Therefore, coupling physical models (i.e., non-economic models) into a CGE model is an important point to evolve the models.
- *Validation of CGE accuracy and parameter estimations*: Since parameters are calibrated by single year data SAM, CGE is rarely validated with the time series data. Although a few attempts exist [71,72], the validation is still the remained tasks for the CGE model.

These issues will help promoting CGE models not only in energy economics but also in the broader field in economics.

Acknowledgments

This study was supported by JSPS KAKENHI Grant Number 15K16161, 15K00669, and 19H02273, MEXT KAKENHI Grant Number 16H01799, and the Global Environment Research Fund of the Ministry of the Environment of Japan S-14 and 2-1908.

Notes

1 GAMS Development Corporation, GAMS, www.gams.com/.
2 Centre of Policy Studies, GEMPACK General Equilibrium Modelling Software, www.copsmodels.com/gempack.htm.
3 In between the two categories, there exist regional models, such as that of the European Union [36].
4 Center for Global Trade Analysis, GTAP: Global Trade Analysis Project www.gtap.agecon.purdue.edu/.
5 These models are explained in detail in Section 3.3.
6 Here, we searched articles using "computable general equilibrium" AND "energy" for searching phrases in article title, abstract, or keywords (www.scopus.com/home.uri). By using ScienceDirect provided by Elsevier (www.sciencedirect.com/), we can find 1,704 articles (only full research articles and review articles). Similarly, from SpringerLink provided by Springer (link.springer.com/), we could find 614 documents (only English articles). We did not include "CGE" as a phrase for this search because CGE was also used for the abbreviation of different phrases. The number of searched results include articles irrelevant to CGE research or energy research.
7 By searching ScienceDirect, we can find a few more older articles on energy with CGE models. The oldest one in the database is Bergman [34], which analyzed the impact of discontinuation of nuclear power in Sweden.
8 Energy Modeling Forum, emf.stanford.edu/.

References

[1] Scarf, HE. The Approximation of fixed points of a continuous mapping. *SIAM Journal on Applied Mathematics* 1967;15:1328–1343. doi:10.1137/0115116.
[2] Scarf, HE. On the computation of equilibrium prices. *Cowles Foundation Discussion Papers* 1967;232.
[3] Shoven, JB, Whalley, J. A general equilibrium calculation of the effects of differential taxation of income from capital in the U.S. *Journal of Public Economics* 1972;1:281–321.

[4] Shoven, JB, Whalley, J. General equilibrium with taxes: A computational procedure and an existence proof. *The Review of Economic Studies* 1973;40:475–489. doi:10.2307/2296582.

[5] Fujimori, S, Masui, T, Matsuoka, Y. Development of a global computable general equilibrium model coupled with detailed energy end-use technology. *Applied Energy* 2014;128:296–306. doi:10.1016/j.apenergy.2014.04.074.

[6] Waisman, H, Guivarch, C, Grazi, F, Hourcade, JC. The Imaclim-R model: Infrastructures, technical inertia and the costs of low carbon futures under imperfect foresight. *Climatic Change* 2012;114:101–120. doi:10.1007/s10584-011-0387-z.

[7] Fujimori, S, Hasegawa, T, Masui, T, Takahashi, K. Land use representation in a global CGE model for long-term simulation: CET vs. logit functions. *Food Security* 2014;6:685–699. doi:10.1007/s12571-014-0375-z.

[8] Popp, A, Calvin, K, Fujimori, S, Havlik, P, Humpenöder, F, Stehfest, E, et al. Land-use futures in the shared socio-economic pathways. *Global Environmental Change* 2017;42:331–345. doi:10.1016/j.gloenvcha.2016.10.002.

[9] Matsumoto, K, Tachiiri, K, Kawamiya, M. Evaluating multiple emission pathways for fixed cumulative carbon dioxide emissions from global-scale socioeconomic perspectives. *Mitigation and Adaptation Strategies for Global Change* 2016:1–26. doi:10.1007/s11027-016-9726-8.

[10] Fujimori, S, Su, X, Liu, J-Y, Hasegawa, T, Takahashi, K, Masui, T, et al. Implication of Paris Agreement in the context of long-term climate mitigation goals. *Springerplus* 2016;5. doi:10.1186/s40064-016-3235-9.

[11] Winchester, N, Reilly, JM. The feasibility, costs, and environmental implications of large-scale biomass energy. *Energy Economics* 2015;51:188–203. doi:10.1016/j.eneco.2015.06.016.

[12] Hasegawa, T, Fujimori, S, Shin, Y, Tanaka, A, Takahashi, K, Masui, T. Consequence of climate mitigation on the risk of hunger. *Environmental Science & Technology* 2015;49:7245–7253. doi:10.1021/es5051748.

[13] Masui, T, Matsumoto, K, Hijioka, Y, Kinoshita, T, Nozawa, T, Ishiwatari, S, et al. An emission pathway for stabilization at 6 Wm-2 radiative forcing. *Climatic Change* 2011;109:59–76. doi:10.1007/s10584-011-0150-5.

[14] Fujimori, S, Hasegawa, T, Masui, T, Takahashi, K, Herran, DS, Dai, H, et al. SSP3: AIM implementation of Shared Socioeconomic Pathways. *Global Environmental Change* 2017;42:268–283. doi:10.1016/j.gloenvcha.2016.06.009.

[15] Jacoby, HD, Reilly, JM, McFarland, JR, Paltsev, S. Technology and technical change in the MIT EPPA model. *Energy Economics* 2006;28:610–631. doi:10.1016/j.eneco.2006.05.014.

[16] Octaviano, C, Paltsev, S, Gurgel, AC. Climate change policy in Brazil and Mexico: Results from the MIT EPPA model. *Energy Economics* 2016;56:600–614. doi:10.1016/j.eneco.2015.04.007.

[17] Château, J, Dellink, R, Lanzi, E. An overview of the OECD ENV-Linkages model. *Version* n.d.;3. doi:10.1787/5jz2qck2b2vd-en.

[18] Crassous, R, Hourcade, J-C, Sassi, O. Endogenous structural change and climate targets modeling experiments with Imaclim-R. *The Energy Journal* 2006;SI2006. doi:10.5547/ISSN0195-6574-EJ-VolSI2006-NoSI1-13.

[19] Bibas, R, Méjean, A, Hamdi-Cherif, M. Energy efficiency policies and the timing of action: An assessment of climate mitigation costs. *Technological Forecasting and Social Change* 2015;90:137–152. doi:10.1016/j.techfore.2014.05.003.

[20] Pan, H. The cost efficiency of Kyoto flexible mechanisms: A top-down study with the GEM-E3 world model. *Environmental Modelling & Software* 2005;20:1401–1411. doi:10.1016/j.envsoft.2004.09.020.

[21] Karkatsoulis, P, Siskos, P, Paroussos, L, Capros, P. Simulating deep CO2 emission reduction in transport in a general equilibrium framework: The GEM-E3T model. *Transportation Research Part D: Transport and Environment* 2016. doi:10.1016/j.trd.2016.11.026.

[22] van den Broek, M, Veenendaal, P, Koutstaal, P, Turkenburg, W, Faaij, A. Impact of international climate policies on CO2 capture and storage deployment: Illustrated in the Dutch energy system. *Energy Policy* 2011;39:2000–2019. doi:10.1016/j.enpol.2011.01.036.

[23] Bollen, J. The value of air pollution co-benefits of climate policies: Analysis with a global sector-trade CGE model called WorldScan. *Technological Forecasting and Social Change* 2015;90:178–191. doi:10.1016/j.techfore.2014.10.008.

[24] Dalton, M, O'Neill, B, Prskawetz, A, Jiang, L, Pitkin, J. Population aging and future carbon emissions in the United States. *Energy Economics* 2008;30:642–675. doi:10.1016/j.eneco.2006.07.002.

[25] O'Neill, BC, Ren, X, Jiang, L, Dalton, M. The effect of urbanization on energy use in India and China in the iPETS model. *Energy Economics* 2012;34:S339–S345. doi:10.1016/j.eneco.2012.04.004.

[26] Dick, H, Gupta, S, Vincent, D, Voigt, H. The effect of oil price increases on four oil-poor developing countries. *Energy Economics* 1984;6:59–70. doi:10.1016/0140-9883(84)90045-8.

[27] Despotakis, KA, Fisher, AC. Energy in a regional economy: A computable general equilibrium model for California. *Journal of Environmental Economics and Management* 1988;15:313–330. doi:10.1016/0095-0696(88)90005-8.

[28] Fisher, AC, Despotakis, KA. Energy taxes and Economic performance. *Energy Economics* 1989;11:153–157. doi:10.1016/0140-9883(89)90009-1.

[29] Boyd, R, Uri, ND. An analysis of the proposed Btu tax on the US economy. *International Journal of Energy Research* 1993;17:727–746. doi:10.1002/er.4440170807.

[30] Uri, ND, Boyd, R. Using the gasoline tax to reduce the US federal government's budget deficit. *Applied Energy* 1993;46:215–239. doi:10.1016/0306-2619(93)90073-X.

[31] Uri, ND, Boyd, R. An evaluation of the effects of the tax on refined petroleum products in the Philippines. *Energy Economics* 1993;15:154–165. doi:10.1016/0140-9883(93)90001-8.

[32] Semboja, HHH. The effects of energy taxes on the Kenyan economy. *Energy Economics* 1994;16:205–215. doi:10.1016/0140-9883(94)90034-5.

[33] Semboja, HHH. The effects of an increase in energy efficiency on the Kenya economy. *Energy Policy* 1994;22:217–225. doi:10.1016/0301-4215(94)90160-0.

[34] Bergman, L. The impact of nuclear power discontinuation in Sweden. *Regional Science and Urban Economics* 1981;11:269–286. doi:10.1016/0166-0462(81)90010-7.

[35] Li, P-C, Rose, A. Global warming policy and the Pennsylvania economy: A computable general equilibrium analysis. *Economic Systems Research* 1995;7:151–172. doi:10.1080/09535319500000018.

[36] Welsch, H. The carbon tax game: Differential tax recycling in a two-region general equilibrium model of the European community. *Weltwirtschaftliches Archiv* 1996;132:356–377. doi:10.1007/BF02707811.

[37] Uri, ND, Boyd, R. Aggregate impacts of the proposed reduction in the motor fuels excise tax in the United States. *Energy Economics* 1998;20:309–323. doi:10.1016/S0140-9883(97)00022-4.

[38] Naqvi, F. A computable general equilibrium model of energy, economy and equity interactions in Pakistan. *Energy Economics* 1998;20:347–373. doi:10.1016/S0140-9883(97)00027-3.

[39] Galinis, A, van Leeuwen, MJ. A CGE model for Lithuania: The future of nuclear energy. *Journal of Policy Modeling* 2000;22:691–718. doi:10.1016/S0161-8938(98)00028-3.

[40] Bach, S, Kohlhaas, M, Meyer, B, Praetorius, B, Welsch, H. The effects of environmental fiscal reform in Germany: A simulation study. *Energy Policy* 2002;30:803–811. doi:10.1016/S0301-4215(02)00005-8.

[41] Steininger, KW, Voraberger, H. Exploiting the medium term biomass energy potentials in Austria: A comparison of costs and macroEconomic impact. *Environmental and Resource Economics* 2003;24:359–377. doi:10.1023/A:1023680125027.

[42] Hanley, ND, McGregor, PG, Swales, JK, Turner, K. The impact of a stimulus to energy efficiency on the economy and the environment: A regional computable general equilibrium analysis. *Renewable Energy* 2006;31:161–171. doi:10.1016/j.renene.2005.08.023.

[43] Kiuila, O, Wójtowicz, K, Żylicz, T, Kasek, L. Economic and environmental effects of unilateral climate actions. *Mitigation and Adaptation Strategies for Global Change* 2014:263–278. doi:10.1007/s11027-014-9597-9.

[44] Müller-Fürstenberger, G, Stephan, G. Integrated assessment of global climate change with learning-by-doing and energy-related research and development. *Energy Policy* 2007;35:5298–5309. doi:10.1016/j.enpol.2006.01.038.

[45] Otto, VM, Löschel, A, Dellink, R. Energy biased technical change: A CGE analysis. *Resource and Energy Economics* 2007;29:137–158. doi:10.1016/j.reseneeco.2006.03.004.

[46] Otto, VM, Löschel, A, Reilly, J. Directed technical change and differentiation of climate policy. *Energy Economics* 2008;30:2855–2878. doi:10.1016/j.eneco.2008.03.005.

[47] Löschel, A, Otto, VM. Technological uncertainty and cost effectiveness of CO2 emission reduction. *Energy Economics* 2009;31:S4–S17. doi:10.1016/j.eneco.2008.11.008.

[48] Wang, K, Wang, C, Chen, J. Analysis of the economic impact of different Chinese climate policy options based on a CGE model incorporating endogenous technological change. *Energy Policy* 2009;37:2930–2940. doi:10.1016/j.enpol.2009.03.023.

[49] Matsumoto, K. Analyzing economic impacts of CO2 abatement and R&D promotion in Japan applying a dynamic CGE model with technological change. *Journal of Global Environment Engineering* 2011;16:25–33.

[50] Timilsina, GR, Mevel, S, Shrestha, A. Oil price, biofuels and food supply. *Energy Policy* 2011;39:8098–8105. doi:10.1016/j.enpol.2011.10.004.

[51] Solaymani, S, Kari, F. Impacts of energy subsidy reform on the Malaysian economy and transportation sector. *Energy Policy* 2014;70:115–125. doi:10.1016/j.enpol.2014.03.035.

[52] Broberg, T, Berg, C, Samakovlis, E. The economy-wide rebound effect from improved energy efficiency in Swedish industries: A general equilibrium analysis. *Energy Policy* 2015;83:26–37. doi:10.1016/j. enpol.2015.03.026.

[53] Romer, PM. Endogenous technological change. *Journal of Political Economy* 1990;98:71–102.

[54] Kriegler, E, Weyant, JP, Blanford, GJ, Krey, V, Clarke, L, Edmonds, J, et al. The role of technology for achieving climate policy objectives: Overview of the EMF 27 study on global technology and climate policy strategies. *Climatic Change* 2014;123:353–367. doi:10.1007/s10584-013-0953-7.

[55] Kriegler, E, Riahi, K, Bosetti, V, Capros, P, Petermann, N, van Vuuren, DP, et al. Introduction to the AMPERE model intercomparison studies on the economics of climate stabilization. *Technological Forecasting and Social Change* 2015;90:1–7. doi:10.1016/j.techfore.2014.10.012.

[56] Kriegler, E, Tavoni, M, Riahi, K, van Vuuren, DP. Introducing the LIMITS special issue. *Climate Change Economics* 2013;4:1302002. doi:10.1142/S2010007813020028.

[57] Luderer, G, Pietzcker, RC, Carrara, S, de Boer, HS, Fujimori, S, Johnson, N, et al. Assessment of wind and solar power in global low-carbon energy scenarios: An introduction. *Energy Economics* 2017;64:542–551. doi:10.1016/j.eneco.2017.03.027.

[58] van Vuuren, DP, Edelenbosch, OY, McCollum, DL, Riahi, K. A special issue on model-based long-term transport scenarios: Model comparison and new methodological developments to improve energy and climate policy analysis. *Transportation Research Part D: Transport and Environment* 2017. doi:10.1016/j. trd.2017.05.003.

[59] Weyant, JP, Chesnaye, FC de la, Blanford, GJ. Overview of EMF-21: Multigas mitigation and climate policy. *The Energy Journal* 2006;SI2006. doi:10.5547/ISSN0195-6574-EJ-VolSI2006-NoSI3-1.

[60] Wise, M, Calvin, K, Thomson, A, Clarke, L, Bond-Lamberty, B, Sands, R, et al. Implications of limiting CO2 concentrations for land use and energy. *Science (80-)* 2009;324.

[61] Fujimori, S, Kubota, I, Dai, H, Takahashi, K, Hasegawa, T, Liu, J-Y, et al. Will international emissions trading help achieve the objectives of the Paris Agreement? *Environmental Research Letters* 2016;11:104001. doi:10.1088/1748-9326/11/10/104001.

[62] Fujimori, S, Masui, T, Matsuoka, Y. Gains from emission trading under multiple stabilization targets and technological constraints. *Energy Economics* 2015;48:306–315. doi:10.1016/j.eneco.2014.12.011.

[63] Böhringer, C, Löschel, A, Moslener, U, Rutherford, TF. EU climate policy up to 2020: An economic impact assessment. *Energy Economics* 2009;31:S295–S305. doi:10.1016/j.eneco.2009.09.009.

[64] Carbone, JC, Helm, C, Rutherford, TF. The case for international emission trade in the absence of cooperative climate policy. *Journal of Environmental Economics and Management* 2009;58:266–280. doi:10.1016/j.jeem.2009.01.001.

[65] Böhringer, C, Welsch, H. Contraction and convergence of carbon emissions: An intertemporal multi-region CGE analysis. *Journal of Policy Modeling* 2004;26:21–39. doi:10.1016/j.jpolmod.2003.11.004.

[66] Guivarch, C, Monjon, S. Identifying the main uncertainty drivers of energy security in a low-carbon world: The case of Europe. *Energy Economics* 2016. doi:10.1016/j.eneco.2016.04.007.

[67] Vandyck, T, Keramidas, K, Saveyn, B, Kitous, A, Vrontisi, Z. A global stocktake of the Paris pledges: Implications for energy systems and economy. *Global Environmental Change* 2016;41:46–63. doi:10.1016/j.gloenvcha.2016.08.006.

[68] Sands, RD, Förster, H, Jones, CA, Schumacher, K. Bio-electricity and land use in the Future Agricultural Resources Model (FARM). *Climatic Change* 2014;123:719–730. doi:10.1007/s10584-013-0943-9.

[69] Ren, X, Weitzel, M, O'Neill, BC, Lawrence, P, Meiyappan, P, Levis, S, et al. Avoided economic impacts of climate change on agriculture: Integrating a land surface model (CLM) with a global economic model (iPETS). *Climatic Change* 2016:1–15. doi:10.1007/s10584-016-1791-1.

[70] Capros, P, van Regemorter, D, Paroussos, L, Karkatsoulis, P, Perry, M, Abrell, J, et al. GEM-E3 model documentation. *Publications Office of the European Union* 2013. doi: 10.2788/47872

[71] Fujimori, S, Dai, H, Masui, T, Matsuoka, Y. Global energy model hindcasting. *Energy* 2016;114:293–301. doi:10.1016/j.energy.2016.08.008.

[72] Jorgenson, DW. Econometric methods for modeling producer behavior. In: Griliches, Z, Intriligator, MD, editors. *Handbook of Econometrics*, Amsterdam: North Holland; 1986, pp. 1841–915. doi:10.1016/ S1573-4412(86)03011-8.

31

A methodological framework for assessing macroeconomic impacts of energy security improvements in Asia

Deepak Sharma, Suwin Sandu, and Muyi Yang

1   Introduction

The Asian countries have experienced significant economic growth since the late 20th century, and these trends are expected to continue in the years to come (OECD 2018). This growth will however bring with it an unprecedented demand for energy. According to the International Energy Agency (IEA), energy demand in the Asia-Pacific region is projected to increase by 1.8% per year over the period 2016–2040 – faster than the projected world average annual growth rate of 1.4% over the period. This will make the Asia-Pacific region the world's largest energy consumer by 2040, accounting for approximately 60% of total energy consumption (IEA 2017).

Such rapid growth in energy demand could lead to a tightening of energy markets, growing import dependence, and rising price volatility, thus threatening the security of energy supply and socioeconomic prosperity of the region. The intensity of this threat could be further exacerbated by the impending threat of climate change, caused by ever-increasing rates of greenhouse gases (GHG) emissions from excessive use of fossil fuels. Search is therefore on for ways to redress the energy security challenge in the region. Among various policy options under consideration to redress the challenge, a broad consensus seems to have emerged on two options, namely, diversification of fuel-mix, with reduced reliance on fossil fuels and their replacement with low-emission sources (such as, wind, solar and nuclear); and energy efficiency improvements.

Several studies have been conducted to analyse the impacts of these policy options. Most of these studies have however tended to be micro-assessments, focusing on the immediate impact of specific policy measures on energy security. For example, some studies analyze measures (such as feed-in tariffs, tax exemptions, and public grants) to promote renewable energy and its impacts on fossil fuel consumption, energy prices, and emissions (Kumar 2016; Kumar, Shrestha & Abdul Salam 2013; Mofijur et al. 2015; Tongsopit et al. 2016). Other studies estimate the potential for energy savings and emission reduction from higher energy efficiency standards in households (Lu 2006; Mahlia, Masjuki & Amalina 2004; Shi 2015), transport (Karali & Gopal 2017), and industrial processes (Worrell et al. 2009).

While useful, such foci do not provide insights into the broader macroeconomic, and hence policy-significant, impacts of policy measures to improve energy security. For example, promotion of biofuels may be an attractive option to reduce fossil fuel dependence, but it may be less attractive from a broader macroeconomic perspective, due to the potential impacts of biofuel production on land use, water supply, and food prices, which may in turn affect economic growth, employment, and social welfare.

Against this backdrop, the primary objective of this (and the following) chapter is to examine the macroeconomic impacts of energy security improvements, especially identifying the trade-offs that policy makers may like to consider while designing policies to redress the energy security challenge in the region. This chapter outlines the methodological framework to analyse the macroeconomic impacts of energy security improvements. The next chapter analyses the macroeconomic impacts of energy security improvements for seven major Asian countries (China, India, Indonesia, Japan, Korea, Malaysia, and Thailand), for the period 2015–2050. These countries collectively account for 44% of the world population, 30% of economic output, 35% of primary energy consumption, and 41% of GHG emissions in 2015 (World Bank 2018).

2   Methodological framework

The methodological framework for analyzing macroeconomic impacts of alternative energy security improvements scenarios is shown in Figure 31.1. This framework comprises five key elements: identification of attributes in terms of which the socioeconomic and energy security outcomes of alternative scenarios are assessed (Section 2.1); procedures for integrating socioeconomic and energy security domains into a single platform (Section 2.2); development of alternative future scenarios and underlying policy drivers and assumptions for each scenario (Section

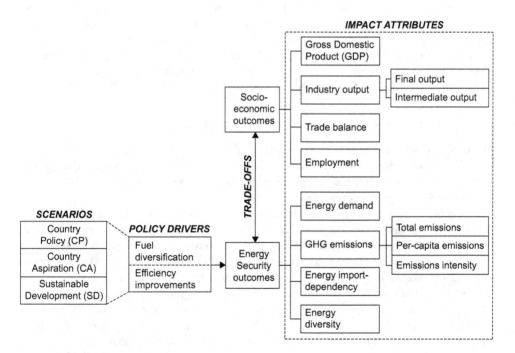

Figure 31.1   Methodological framework

2.3); development of an analytical model to determine the impact (in terms of selected attributes) of alternative scenarios (Section 2.4); and development of composite socioeconomic and energy security indices to enable analyses of policy trade-offs (Section 2.5).

2.1 Impact attributes

There are a range of attributes that can be used in order to assess the impact of policies. The selection of impact attributes used in this chapter is broadly based on the guidelines suggested by OECD (2011). The essence of these guidelines is that the attributes should appropriately reflect the country context; they should be analytically sound; they should be measurable; they should be temporally consistent and comparable across countries, regions, sectors; and, most importantly, they should be of policy significance.

Guided by these requirements, eight attributes are selected in this chapter; four for measuring socioeconomic outcomes and four for measuring energy security outcomes. The socioeconomic outcomes are measured in terms of economic growth (GDP), industry output (both final and intermediate demand), trade balance (including trade with different countries and trade-dependency of the country), and employment.

The measures of energy security outcomes are not straightforward. Energy security has traditionally been referred to as assured and affordable access to domestic energy resources such as oil, gas, and coal. This construct has however become less useful to policy makers as energy sector becomes increasingly globalized, both in terms of its integration with international markets and in terms of emerging global issues such as climate change (von Hippel et al. 2011). In this chapter, energy security is therefore measured in terms of energy demand, energy-related environmental emissions, energy import dependency, and energy diversity.

The energy demand attributes include both primary and final energy demand. The environmental attributes include: total and per-capita greenhouse-gas (GHG) emissions, and greenhouse-gas intensity of the economy. Energy import-dependency is expressed in terms of the ratio of net energy imports to total primary energy demand. Energy diversity measures the degree of diversification of primary and final energy sources in the economy. It is measured by Herfindahl index, with a low value of the index suggesting greater diversity.

2.2 Integration of socioeconomic and energy security domains

The socioeconomic and energy security domains are integrated in this chapter with the view to identify trade-offs between different policy objectives, for example, trade-offs between energy security and economic prosperity; energy security and country's trade balance; and environmental sustainability and job opportunities.

The core platform to integrate these domains is a Multi-Country Input-Output (MCIO) table, developed specifically for this purpose. The IO table for a country portrays its economy as a system of interrelated goods and services, at disaggregated levels. The Global Trade Analysis Project (GTAP) databases are used as the bases to develop national IO tables as they are available in consistent (industry-classification) formats (Aguiar, Narayanan & McDougall 2016). The bilateral trade data in GTAP databases are, however, not available at disaggregated levels; exports are presented as aggregate sectoral exports to the destination country (i.e. not to the consuming sectors), while imports are presented as sectoral total imports by the consuming sectors with no detail about the country of origin. The national IO tables developed from GTAP databases are accordingly extended in this chapter to represent trade (i.e. exports and imports) at disaggregated levels. For this purpose, the method proposed by Peters, Andrew & Lennox (2011) for developing MCIO tables from GTAP databases is followed; it distributes bilateral exports (in terms of the prices of the producing country) in the same proportion as sectoral consumption patterns of the importing country (in terms of the prices of the consuming country). The difference between the prices received by the exporters and prices paid by the importers are considered as trade margins, and are added to the value added component of the national IO tables in order to retain input-output balance across all sectors. Further, since the current GTAP databases are available for the 2011 base year, the MCIO tables are rebased to 2015, using the most recent macroeconomic indicators (such as, total household consumption, government expenditure, and total investment) available from the World Bank (World Bank 2018).

The MCIO tables are then extended by incorporating data from the International Energy Agency (IEA 2018), to provide a disaggregated representation of energy production and consumption by sector as well as electricity generation using different technologies. Further, greenhouse gas emission factors are used to develop environmental accounts associated with the MCIO tables. Such integration of multi-country economic accounts with energy and environmental accounts enables an assessment to be made of the macroeconomic impacts of energy policies, not only on the domestic economy but also on regional trade and the environment. Table 31.1 presents the list of countries/regions, sectors, commodities, primary production factors, final demand categories, and greenhouse gas emissions included for the analysis in this chapter.

2.3 Scenario descriptions and assumptions

This chapter develops three energy policy scenarios up to the year 2050, namely, Country Policy (CP), Country Aspiration (CA), and Sustainable Development (SD) scenarios.

These scenarios broadly align with the recent IEA's World Energy Outlook (2017), which considers three scenarios: Country Policy, New Policy, and Sustainable Development. The CP scenario in this chapter represent a continuation of existing energy plans and policies that have already been put in place in the form of legislation or national and global agreements. The CA scenario assumes a heightened emphasis on promoting energy security. In particular, it incorporates, in addition to policies and measures of the CP scenario, more ambitious targets for energy security improvement. The SD scenario goes even further; while assuming more aggressive energy policies, it sets achievement of the Paris Agreement and the UN's Sustainable Development Goals (SDGs), especially those related to energy sector, as its main goals. Specifically, it assumes universal access to modern energy by 2030, as well as energy efficiency targets and electricity supply options that will significantly reduce greenhouse gas emissions from the current levels.

The salient features of the three scenarios are summarized in Table 31.2. The scenarios differ from each other in terms of the depth of the two key energy policy drivers, namely, energy efficiency improvements and fuel diversification. Fuel diversification is further divided into three variables: (1) electricity supply options; (2) transportation fuel-use options; and (3) access to modern energy services (mainly electricity and cooking fuels).

The targets for energy efficiency improvements are derived from various sources, as informed by the assumptions about future growth rates of GDP per unit final energy ratios for various sectors of the economy (including industry, transport, commercial, agriculture, and households). For China and India, this ratio is estimated from IEA (2017) for all scenarios. For other countries (Japan, Korea, Indonesia, Malaysia, and Thailand), estimates are based on country reports in the case of CP and CA scenarios (ACE 2017; METI 2015; MTIE 2014). For the SD scenario, GDP per unit final demand for these five countries is assumed to follow the trends in IEA (2017).

Table 31.1 Coverage of socioeconomic and energy security domains

COUNTRIES	SECTORS	COMMODITIES	PRIMARY FACTORS
China	**Energy sectors**	**Energy commodities**	Capital
India	Coal mining	Coal	Unskilled labor
Indonesia	Crude oil exploration	Crude oil	Skilled labor
Japan	Natural gas production	Refined oil	Natural resources
Korea	Uranium mining	Natural gas	**FINAL DEMAND**
Malaysia	Combustible renewable energy	Uranium	Household
Thailand	Non-combustible renewable energy	Bioenergy	consumption
REGIONS	Petroleum refining	Heat	Government
Rest of Asia	Heat production	Electricity	expenditure
Rest of the world	Electricity generation	**Non-energy**	Investment
	Traditional coal-fired power	**commodities**	**TRADE**
	Advanced coal-fired power	Paper products	Exports
	Traditional gas-fired power	Chemical products	Imports
	Advanced gas-fired power	Iron and steel	**EMISSIONS**
	Oil-fired power	Non-ferrous metals	Carbon dioxide
	Nuclear power	Non-metal minerals	Methane
	Hydropower	Other manufactured	Nitrogen dioxide
	Noncombustible renewable power	products	
	Combustible renewable power	Mining products	
	Non-energy sectors	Agriculture products	
	Industrial	Commercial services	
	Paper manufacturing	Land transport	
	Chemical manufacturing	Water transport	
	Iron and steel manufacturing	Air transport	
	Non-ferrous metals manufacturing		
	Non-metallic minerals manufacturing		
	Non-intensive manufacturing		
	Non-energy mining		
	Agriculture		
	Commercial services		
	Transport services		
	Land		
	Water		
	Air		

The assumptions for electricity supply options, and access to modern energy services, are taken directly from IEA (2017) for China, India, and Japan. IEA (2017) has also published forecasts for the Southeast Asia region as a whole; this information is used to develop forecasts for Indonesia, Malaysia, and Thailand. For Korea, the values are estimated based on the assumptions for Japan, based on trends observed in the recent past.

The assumptions about transportation fuel-use options are based on WEC (2016), with CP, CA and SD scenarios broadly corresponding with the three WEC scenarios: Hard Rock, Modern Jazz, and Unfinished Symphony. Further, the three energy policy scenarios (CP, CA, and SD) are in accord with the medium population growth scenario of the United Nations, and the long-term historic trends in labor productivity growth (UN 2017).

Table 31.2 Scenario assumptions

	CHINA			JAPAN			KOREA			INDIA			INDONESIA			MALAYSIA			THAILAND		
	CP	CA	SD	CP	CA	SD	CP	CA	SD	CP	CA	SD	CP	CA	SD	CP	CA	SD	CP	CA	SD
SOCIOECONOMIC DRIVERS																					
Population growth (% pa)	−0.1			−0.5			0.0			0.7			0.6			0.9			−0.1		
Labor productivity growth (% pa)	1.4			1.0			1.3			1.6			1.4			1.3			1.6		
ENERGY POLICY DRIVERS																					
Energy efficiency — Energy productivity growth (% per year)																					
Industry	3.1	4.1	6.9	0.1	0.9	1.5	1.9	2.8	2.6	3.2	5.4	8.1	1.3	2.8	4.0	2.9	2.9	4.1	2.0	2.9	3.6
Transport services	0.6	2.7	4.9	0.1	0.8	1.6	1.4	3.3	2.6	1.1	3.8	6.7	1.1	3.9	6.0	2.6	4.0	6.1	2.1	3.0	5.4
Commercial services	1.9	3.2	4.6	0.1	0.8	1.6	0.3	0.3	2.6	4.8	6.8	8.3	1.7	4.5	5.9	2.6	4.6	6.0	0.6	1.1	5.4
Agriculture	1.5	2.1	3.6	0.1	0.8	1.6	0.1	2.0	2.6	4.8	8.8	9.2	1.7	4.6	4.6	2.6	9.9	10.4	3.4	4.2	4.9
Residential	1.0	3.3	4.7	0.1	0.8	1.6	1.3	1.4	3.1	4.8	8.9	9.7	1.7	4.5	5.9	2.6	4.6	6.0	2.4	3.5	5.4
Fuel diversification — Electricity generation mix (% 2050)																					
Coal	75.0	39.2	12.6	32.7	21.9	2.1	42.7	31.5	0.4	71.2	47.2	9.8	46.5	85.7	11.2	32.4	52.3	13.0	20.4	24.4	3.9
Gas	2.3	8.1	10.1	36.7	28.1	9.4	20.1	17.6	6.7	9.1	8.3	17.3	23.0	21.8	16.9	59.0	32.4	48.0	71.6	50.5	48.0
Oil	0.1	0.0	0.0	1.3	1.0	0.3	2.9	0.2	0.1	2.5	0.5	0.5	18.0	2.2	1.3	1.0	0.2	0.3	1.6	0.1	0.1
Nuclear	2.4	10.8	16.9	20.7	21.6	32.3	32.9	46.5	79.3	2.6	6.2	10.9	0.0	0.0	0.0	0.0	0.0	0.0	0.0	0.0	0.0
Hydro	16.8	14.8	18.2	4.4	9.6	16.1	0.6	0.9	1.7	10.9	8.3	11.0	7.4	9.9	12.8	7.4	12.6	31.1	3.7	3.7	5.8
Non-combustible Renewable	0.9	3.0	4.1	2.5	4.5	6.9	0.3	0.5	0.9	1.4	2.8	4.5	0.1	2.1	2.5	0.4	1.8	3.9	2.4	15.7	22.4
Combustible Renewable	2.5	24.1	38.2	1.6	13.4	33.0	0.4	2.8	7.9	2.2	26.7	46.0	5.0	19.4	55.4	0.1	0.7	3.6	0.4	5.6	19.7
Transport fuel-mix (% 2050)																					
Oil	65.9	50.4	42.0	89.1	81.6	78.0	85.8	82.6	77.6	88.4	83.4	80.1	91.5	73.0	71.9	87.0	71.3	60.0	51.1	51.1	51.1
Gas	9.3	8.2	6.9	0.5	0.4	0.4	4.5	4.0	3.3	3.0	2.6	2.2	0.1	0.1	0.1	1.6	1.4	1.2	11.6	10.2	8.6
Biofuels	2.8	3.5	5.4	0.0	0.0	0.0	7.1	9.1	13.8	2.0	2.5	3.8	8.4	10.6	16.1	11.1	14.2	21.4	37.2	21.1	15.7
Electricity	22.0	37.9	45.8	10.4	17.9	21.7	2.5	4.4	5.3	6.7	11.4	13.8	0.0	16.3	12.0	0.3	13.1	17.5	0.1	17.6	24.6
Access to modern energy services (100% by year)																					
Electricity	F.A.	F.A.	F.A.	F.A.	F.A.	F.A.	F.A.	F.A.	F.A.	2043	2043	2030	2020	2020	2020	2020	2020	2020	F.A.	F.A.	F.A.
Cooking fuels	2060	2050	2030	F.A.	F.A.	F.A.	F.A.	F.A.	F.A.	2060	2050	2030	2060	2050	2030	2030	2030	2030	2060	2030	2030

Notes: Data in this table is developed based on information contained in ACE (2017), IEA (2017), METI (2015), MTIE (2014), UN (2017) and WEC (2016).
CP – Country Policy scenario; CA – Country Aspiration scenario; SD – Sustainable Development scenario.
F.A. – Full access to modern energy services.

2.4 Modeling approach

The two key modeling approaches that can be used to assess macroeconomic impacts of policies are computable general equilibrium (CGE) and input-output (IO).

The CGE modeling represents the economy as a system of interrelated elements, where the balancing between demand and supply is achieved through competitive-market-clearing principles. While it is a useful representation of an economy, its value for analysing the policy impacts is questionable on the following grounds: its underlying assumption of perfectly competitive markets; existence of a perpetual balance between demand and supply; role of prices in ensuring demand-supply balances; applicability for markets typified by varying degrees of regulated control and countries at various stages of economic development; and assessment of sub-macro level trade-offs, which are useful for engendering policy support. Moreover, the computational approach embedded in CGE models is less transparent for modeling the policy impacts of alternative scenarios.

While the IO model also portrays the national economy as a system of interrelated goods and services as does the CGE, its underlying analytics allows significant flexibility in terms of representing the structure and dynamics of an economy at disaggregated levels. It also provides a sound basis to represent market and non-market elements of the economy in a balanced manner. Additionally, it enables market-based clearance for those segments of the economy where price mechanisms work (by introducing flexible production functions instead of traditional fixed-coefficient Leontief function). Moreover, it is relatively more transparent in terms of both assumptions and computation approaches.

In view of the above noted advantages of the IO model, particularly its appropriateness for capturing features that are specific to the Asian countries (e.g. mixed market/non-market, and rapidly urbanizing and industrializing, economies), the core framework employed in this chapter centers on the application of energy-oriented MCIO platform. The base MCIO table (Section 2.3) can be transformed into MCIO coefficient matrices that underpin the model. In this base MCIO coefficient structure, the technology structure of a particular sector j in country r is presented under columns of the matrix, which comprises technical coefficients of an input from domestic sector i (a_{ij}^{rr}), coefficients showing imports of outputs from sector i in a foreign country s (a_{ij}^{sr}), and coefficients of primary factor v (c_{vj}). These coefficients represent the proportions of inputs required (from domestic sector, foreign country, and primary factors of production, respectively) for each unit of production of a particular sector. The MCIO coefficient structure also contains final demand sector k as a column in the matrix, which comprises output coefficients from both domestic and foreign sectors i. These output coefficients represent proportions of output required from sector i (from both domestic and foreign sectors) to fulfill final demand k (b_{ik}). An outline of the modeling structure is shown in Figure 31.2.

The modeling begins by asking the question, how will a technological change in one sector affect the rest of the economy? To introduce this in the model, the MCIO coefficients are exogenously changed, according to the assumptions underpinning alternative energy policy scenarios (Table 31.2). For example, energy efficiency improvements in a particular economic sector imply a relative reduction in the use of energy input to produce the same amount of output from that sector. The technical coefficients, representing energy inputs, are therefore assumed to be exogenously reduced over the time frame.

Another example: a switch from conventional, relatively inefficient, fossil-fuel power generation plants to renewable-based power generation plants will entail adjustments in the values of technical coefficients in the MCIO matrix; the technical coefficients representing electricity generation from fossil-fuel power plants are reduced, while those of renewable-based power plants

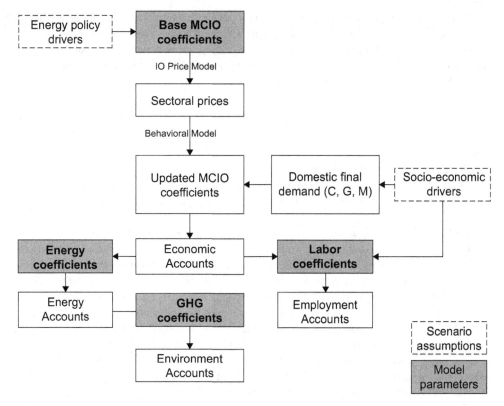

Figure 31.2 Model structure

are increased in the same proportion. This technique of adjusting technical coefficients is well established, and has long been used to examine the impacts of changes in energy technologies in the IO framework (see e.g. Faber, Idenburg & Wilting 2007; Gowdy & Miller 1968; Just 1974). The CGE modeling also applies the same principles for introducing technology shocks (see e.g. Burfisher 2011; Fatai, Oxley & Scrimgeour 2003).

Alternatively, the MCIO coefficients can be endogenously determined within the model, by using price mechanisms. This is common in studies that examine the impact of carbon tax where the tax are assumed to be imposed on each sector i; this will translate into equivalent indirect taxes. The increased tax is then assumed to be fully transferred through energy and material prices (Creedy & Martin 2000), thus increasing the prices of factor inputs in proportion to sectors' carbon emissions. Such increases in relative prices of various sectors, where sectoral outputs are used by consuming sectors in the economy, will force a change in IO coefficients. This approach however becomes less attractive in the context of this chapter, as this chapter focuses on assessing the impacts of various energy technology options. In such a technology-driven assessment, sectoral prices will be endogenously determined by the adoption of various technology options, which can be achieved by exogenously changing the technical coefficients, based on scenario assumptions. As a result, the former approach of exogenously changing the technical coefficients is employed in this chapter.

A change in technology will induce changes in the input-mix of various production sectors. As a result, the prices of sectoral outputs would change. In the case of energy efficiency improvements in a particular economic sector, for example, this would imply a change in output price of that sector relative to other sectors. Similarly, a switch from conventional technology to advanced technology in a particular sector would result in increased output prices of that sector, compared with output prices of other sectors. These price effects are estimated using the standard *Leontief* IO price model, as shown in Equation 31.1:

$$P_i = [I-A']^{-1} \, C'_j \tag{31.1}$$

where

P_i: vector of sectoral price index;
A: matrix of IO technical coefficients, adjusted for new energy technology; and
C_j: vector of total primary factor coefficients for each sector j.

It should be noted that the sectoral prices calculated from equation 1 will be in terms of an index change (i.e. a deviation from the base price of 'one'). This is because of normalization of prices in this approach. The base IO table presents value (price × quantity) flows. The use of price normalization approach translates value data into price and quantity data, by normalizing the initial (base) prices in the model into 'one'. If the base IO coefficient matrix is used to calculate sectoral prices from Equation 31.1 (instead of using an updated IO coefficient matrix with changed technology), the result will be equal to 'one' for all sectors. The coefficients for each column in the IO model are thus interpreted as the quantity of input per $1 of produced output, instead of value of input. This is the same approach that is also applied in CGE models, as it considerably reduces the information required to develop model database, without reducing the capability of the model to generate meaningful results (Burfisher 2011). Thus the estimated prices from Equation 31.1 are presented in terms of index of changes in sectoral prices.

Such changes in relative sectoral prices will induce substitution among sectoral factor inputs. However, factor substitution effects cannot be estimated using standard IO quantity model, because of the underlying assumption of fixed proportionality of factor inputs (i.e. no substitution) – *Leontief* production function. This limitation is overcome by introducing flexible neo-classical production functions in the IO model (Rose 1984). In essence, the Leontief IO coefficients (Equation 31.2) are replaced with the IO variables (Equation 31.3):

$$a_{ij}^{Leontief} = \frac{z_{ij}}{X_j} \tag{31.2}$$

$$a_{ij}^{CES} = \gamma^{\sigma-1} a_{ij}^{Leontief} \left(\frac{P_j}{P_i}\right)^{\sigma} \tag{31.3}$$

where

z_{ij}: output of sector i used in sector j;
X_j: total output of sector j;
γ: scale parameter; and
σ: substitution elasticity.

In the behavioral Equation (31.3), the input-output relationships will not stay fixed, but will change in response to changes in relative sectoral prices. The updated final demand coefficients

(b_{ik}^{CES}) are also determined in the same way. This equation is derived from CES (constant elasticity of substitution) input demand function. In this way, the substitution possibilities can be accounted for within the IO framework.

The updated MCIO coefficients form the basis to calculate economic accounts in the same way as the standard IO model. The main driver is population growth, which is used to determine domestic final demand for the future year t (F_k^t), where k includes total household consumption (C), total government expenditure (G), and total investment demand (M). Sectoral final demand is accordingly determined by:

$$F_i^t = \bar{B} F_k^t \tag{31.4}$$

where $\bar{B}$ is the coefficient matrix of individual elements b_{ik}^{CES}. The outcome of Equation (31.4) is then used to determine sectoral outputs for year t by using the following IO identity:

$$X_i^t = \left[I - \bar{A}^{rs} \right]^{-1} F_i^t \tag{31.5}$$

This equation forms the basis to estimate individual elements of the MCIO table, which form the economic accounts. In addition to these economic accounts, 'satellite' accounts (such as energy, emissions, and employment, expressed in physical units) are also developed in correspondence with the sectoral outputs in Equation (31.5) (see Miller & Blair 2009 for further details). In essence, the coefficient matrices of the satellite accounts are developed for the base year, where information on physical units of these accounts are divided by sectoral outputs. In the case of energy, for example, the matrix of energy coefficients are developed by dividing sectoral energy use (in toe) with sectoral output (in $). These 'satellite' coefficient matrices are then multiplied with Equation (31.5) to obtain values for satellite accounts.

To summarize, this model portrays economies as systems of interrelated goods and services, captures the interdependencies between different economies across regions through trade linkages, and can easily integrate other domains (energy, environment and social) within a single framework. It therefore constitutes an extremely useful analytical tool for examining the macroeconomic impacts of policies and strategies aimed at redressing energy security challenge.

2.5 Composite indices

To enable an assessment to be made of the trade-offs between energy security and socioeconomic outcomes, in terms of selected impact attributes (as shown in Figure 31.1), each of these outcomes (i.e. socioeconomic and energy security) is combined into a composite index. For example, composite socioeconomic index is calculated as a weighted mean of individual attributes, namely, GDP, industry output, trade balance, and employment. Similarly, composite energy security index represents a weighted mean of energy-import dependency, energy diversity, per-capita GHG emissions, and GHG intensity. The analysis in the following chapter employs an equal-weight index, where individual attributes are treated as equally important. Differential weight can however assign to different attributes if policy makers wish to give higher importance to specific attributes (employment, for example), relative to, for example, economic growth.

Given that all attributes are expressed in different units of measurement, they need to be first normalized into a dimensionless index, and then scaled from 0 to 100, where 100 represents most favorable outcome, and zero, least favorable. Attributes where a higher value indicates a more favorable outcome (such as, employment) are normalized as follows:

$$x_i = \frac{\left[x_i - \min\left(x_i\right)\right]}{\left[\max\left(x_i\right) - \min\left(x_i\right)\right]} \tag{31.6}$$

where $\min\left(x_i\right)$ and $\max\left(x_i\right)$ are the lowest and highest values for any given attribute i. For attributes where a high value indicates an unfavorable outcome (such as, energy-import dependency), the normalization function takes the form:

$$x_i = \frac{\left[\max\left(x_i\right) - x_i\right]}{\left[\max\left(x_i\right) - \min\left(x_i\right)\right]} \tag{31.7}$$

Once all attributes are normalized, they can be combined into a composite index to allow an examination of trade-offs between different composite indices.

3 Conclusions

This chapter outlines the methodological framework that can be used to examine the macroeconomic impacts of energy security improvements. It comprises five key elements: identification of attributes, in terms of which the socioeconomic and energy security outcomes of alternative scenarios are assessed; procedures for integrating socioeconomic and energy security domains into a single platform; development of alternative future scenarios and underlying policy drivers and assumptions for each scenario; development of the analytical model to delineate the impact (in terms of selected attributes) of alternative scenarios; and development of composite socioeconomic and energy security indices to enable the analyses of policy trade-offs. It is contended that this framework is suitable to examine the macroeconomic impacts of and strategies aimed at redressing energy security challenge as it portrays economies as systems of interrelated goods and services at disaggregated levels, captures the interdependencies between different economies across the region through trade linkages, can easily integrate other domains (energy, environment and social) within a single framework, and can combine different attributes into a composite index, to enable assessments of trade-offs between the outcomes of different domains. Chapter 8 will demonstrate the application of this framework for major Asian countries.

References

ACE 2017, *The 5th ASEAN Energy Outlook 2015–2040*, ASEAN Centre for Energy, Indonesia.

Aguiar, A., Narayanan, B. & McDougall, R. 2016, 'An Overview of the GTAP 9 Data Base', *Journal of Global Economic Analysis*, vol. 1, pp. 181–208.

Burfisher, M.E. 2011, *Introduction to Computable General Equilibrium Models*, Cambridge University Press, New York.

Creedy, J. & Martin, C. 2000, 'Carbon Taxation, Fuel Substitution and Welfare in Australia', *The Australian Economic Review*, vol. 33, pp. 32–48.

Faber, A., Idenburg, A.M. & Wilting, H.C. 2007, 'Exploring Techno-Economic Scenarios in an Output-Input Model', *Futures*, vol. 39, pp. 16–37.

Fatai, K., Oxley, L. & Scrimgeour, F.G. 2003, 'Energy Efficiency and the New Zealand Economy', paper presented to the *International Congress on Modelling and Simulation (MODSIM)*, Townsville, Australia.

Gowdy, J.M. & Miller, J.L. 1968, 'An Input-Output Approach to Energy Efficiency in the USA and Japan (1960–1980)', *Energy*, vol. 16, pp. 897–902.

IEA 2017, *World Energy Outlook 2017*, International Energy Agency, Paris.

IEA 2018, *World Energy Statistics and Balances*, International Energy Agency, Paris.

Just, J. 1974, 'Impacts of New Energy Technology Using Generalised Input-Output Analysis', *Computers & Operations Research*, vol. 1, pp. 97–109.

Karali, N. & Gopal, A.R. 2017, *Improved Heavy-Duty Vehicle Fuel Efficiency in India*, The International Council on Clean Transportation, Washington DC.

Kumar, S. 2016, 'Assessment of Renewables for Energy Security and Carbon Mitigation in Southeast Asia: The Case of Indonesia and Thailand', *Applied Energy*, vol. 163, pp. 63–70.

Kumar, S., Shrestha, P. & Abdul Salam, P. 2013, 'A Review of Biofuel Policies in the Major Biofuel Producing Countries of ASEAN: Production, Targets, Policy Drivers and Impacts', *Renewable and Sustainable Energy Reviews*, vol. 26, pp. 822–36.

Lu, W. 2006, 'Potential Energy Savings and Environmental Impact By Implementing Energy Efficiency Standard for Household Refrigerator in China', *Energy Policy*, vol. 34, pp. 1583–9.

Mahlia, T.M.I., Masjuki, H.H. & Amalina, M.A. 2004, 'Cost-Benefit Analysis of Implementing Minimum Energy Efficiency Standards for Household Refrigerator-Freezers in Malaysia', *Energy Policy*, vol. 32, pp. 1819–24.

METI 2015, *Long-Term Energy Supply and Demand Outlook*, Ministry of Economy, Trade and Industry (Japan), Tokyo.

Miller, R.E. & Blair, P.D. 2009, *Input-Output Analysis: Foundations and Extensions*, 2nd edn., Cambridge University Press, Cambridge.

Mofijur, M., Masjuki, H.H., Kalam, M.A., Ashrafur Rahman, S.M. & Mahmudul, H.M. 2015, 'Energy Scenario and Biofuel Policies and Targets in ASEAN Countries', *Renewable and Sustainable Energy Reviews*, vol. 46, pp. 51–61.

MTIE 2014, *Korea Energy Master Plan: Outlook & Policies to 2035*, Ministry of Trade, Industry and Energy (Korea), Seoul.

OECD 2011, *Towards Green Growth: Monitoring Progress, OECD Indicators*, Organisation for Economic Co-operation and Development, Paris.

OECD 2018, *Economic Outlook for Southeast Asia, China and India 2018: Fostering Growth Through Digitalisation*, OECD Publishing, Paris.

Peters, G., Andrew, R. & Lennox, J. 2011, 'Constructing an Environmentally-Extended Multi-Regional Input-Output Table Using the GTAP Database', *Economic Systems Research*, vol. 23, pp. 131–52.

Rose, A. 1984, 'Technological Change and Input-Output Analysis: An Appraisal', *Socio-Economic Planning Sciences*, vol. 18, pp. 305–18.

Shi, X. 2015, 'Application of Best Practice for Setting Minimum Energy Efficiency Standards in Technically Disadvantaged Countries: Case Study of Air Conditoners in Brunei Darussalam', *Applied Energy*, vol. 157, pp. 1–12.

Tongsopit, S., Kittner, N., Chang, Y., Aksornkij, A. & Wangjiraniran, W. 2016, 'Energy Security in ASEAN: A Quantitative Approach for Sustainable Energy Policy', *Energy Policy*, vol. 90, pp. 60–72.

UN 2017, *World Population Prospects: The 2017 Revision*, Department of Economic and Social Affairs, the United Nations, New York.

von Hippel, D., Suzuki, T., Williams, J.H., Savage, T. & Hayes, P. 2011, 'Energy Security and Sustainability in in Northeast Asia', *Energy Policy*, vol. 39, pp. 6719–30.

WEC 2016, *World Energy Scenarios: The Grand Transition*, World Energy Council, London.

World Bank 2018, 'World Development Indicators'. World Bank Open Data. https://datacatalog.worldbank.org/dataset/world-development-indicators

Worrell, E., Bernstein, L., Roy, J., Price, L. & Harnisch, J. 2009, 'Industrial Energy Efficiency and Climate Change Mitigation', *Energy Efficiency*, vol. 2, pp. 109–23.

32

Top-down and bottom-up models

Bora Kat

Energy is a crucial intermediate input in production activities as well as a final consumption good that has progressively gained considerable importance in recent times more than ever before. Energy has come into prominence not only because the demand for energy has remarkably increased and it has been an integral part of economic activities, but also due to the scarcity of natural energy resources as well as the environmental problems that accompany increased energy use. As a result, the need has emerged for economic models that embody energy as an explicit input and are also capable of addressing environmental concerns. Although the literature on energy modeling has a long history, it began proliferating in the 1970s with the sharp increases in energy prices due to the first oil crisis in 1973. The impacts of energy prices on economies revealed the need for modeling approaches in which the link between economic activities and energy use is represented. Thereafter, great progress occurred in the efforts to create such links, from basic relationships to sophisticated procedures and theoretically consistent frameworks over the course of time. This chapter scrutinizes these linking efforts on the basis of two broad modeling paradigms: top-down (TD) and bottom-up (BU) modeling. First, brief descriptions of these modeling paradigms are given with their general characteristics, advantages, and drawbacks. Attempts at linking the two models are then presented. Finally, the chapter ends with concluding remarks.

1 Two modeling paradigms: bottom-up (BU) and top-down (TD)

There are various ways to classify the models representing the interaction between energy and the economy since these models are very diverse in their characteristics. These classifications may be based on the spatial coverage, assumptions, planning horizon, degree of endogenization, underlying methodology, sectoral coverage, mathematical approach, and so on. However, over the course of time, researchers have come to agree that there are two broad and widespread modeling approaches, TD and BU (Grubb et al., 1993), categorized according to the perspective from which the models are created. The two modeling approaches differ mainly with respect to the emphasis attributed to technological details of the energy system and to the consistency of the models in terms of economic theory. Conventional BU models treat energy systems starting from primary energy extraction activities including conversion, refining, transport, and distribution processes to the end-use of the energy commodity without paying much attention to interactions with the rest of the economy. Conventional TD models, on the other hand, provide an extensive representation of the overall economy along with interactions between sectors. Moreover, these models reflect the microeconomic decision-making rationale of the agents in the economy or macroeconomic feedback relating the energy sector to other sectors in the economy, but they have a limited representation of the current practices and lack in the application of new technologies. The rest of this section is devoted to a detailed description of these two approaches.

1.1   BU models

Conventional BU models mainly seek a plan that matches the intertemporal energy supply with the demand, where the energy sector is represented in technological detail, especially on the supply side. These models portray the energy sector from an engineer's point of view, which is why they are also called engineering models. Optimization tools, especially linear and nonlinear programming, are widely used in order to find solutions in BU models where the objective is considered to be the minimum cost or the maximum profit plan. However, there is a wide range of studies employing other objectives (e.g. maximizing social welfare) or multiple objectives (e.g. joint optimization of cost and emissions) (Antunes & Henriques, 2016), as well as studies in which side constraints (e.g. supply security, reliability or emission constraints, import restrictions), considering the concerns of the decision-makers, are embedded.

Although there exist BU models that include a high level of detail in technological options, exhaustive regional disaggregation, or high temporal resolution, here it is preferred to follow the notation of (Böhringer & Rutherford, 2009) to describe the conceptual BU model for the sake of simplicity and to help the reader better grasp the linking concepts that will be presented in the following sections.

$$max \ p^{T}\left[e - x\right] \tag{32.1}$$

subject to

$$Ax + Bz \leq Ce \tag{32.2}$$
$$e, x \geq 0 \tag{32.3}$$
$$l \leq z \leq u \tag{32.4}$$

Here, p^{T} is the price vector, while e and x are energy sector supplies and demands, respectively. $A, C \in R^{Mxn}$ and $B \in R^{MxN}$ denote technical constraints and $z \in R^{N}$ stands for energy system variables, while l and u are lower and upper limits on z, respectively. The objective (Equation (32.1)) is to maximize the total profit in the energy sector subject to technical constraints (Equation 32.2)) as well as non-negativity inequalities for e and x (Equation 32.3)) and lower and upper bounds on z (Equation 32.4)).

BU models are also classified as partial equilibrium models since they focus on a specific sector (i.e. they do not employ an endogenous mechanism to represent the macroeconomic feedbacks from the rest of the economy). The energy demand in BU models is usually exogenous or represented via a simple relationship depending on several exogenous factors, such as GDP growth, population growth, primary energy prices, and so forth, that trigger the change in sectoral or overall energy demand. These models, on the other hand, give the description of current and prospective supply technologies in detail where these technologies compete with each other based on their financial and technical characteristics such as initial investment, fixed and variable overhead and maintenance costs, the duration for which they can operate, fuel costs, decommissioning costs, technical efficiency, and so forth. Moreover, BU models might consider not only the supply of final energy but also the extraction and conversion activities as well as reserve availabilities. Environmental characteristics (emission or pollution coefficients) of the technological options are also taken into account for BU models with an environmental component.

As noted for energy models in general, there are also numerous BU models differing from each other by their spatial coverage, planning horizon, sectoral coverage, and so forth. However, there are two modeling families, MARKAL (an acronym for MARKet ALlocation; Loulou et al., 2004a) and MESSAGE (Schrattenholzer, 1981), which have come to the forefront with their extensive ability to represent energy systems comprehensively. Moreover, their flexibility enables them to be used for a wide range of purposes in different regions. These models draw their strength mainly from ongoing improvement efforts that have been continuing for years. The term "family" is used for these models since not only have various extensions of them been developed, in which stochastic or dynamic features are incorporated, but also these models are integrated into several other models that focus on other sectors as well as the overall economy or address policy issues such as greenhouse gas (GHG) mitigation or land use.

1.2   TD models

Conventional TD models deal with the whole economy in an aggregated fashion. The energy sector in these models is either just one of those sectors in the overall economy without a specific treatment or it is a differentiated sector with limited specification. Contrary to BU models, these models put more emphasis on economy-wide market interactions and represent the flow of factors of production, commodities, and income across the whole economy in a certain region or at a national or global scale. Although Ramsey growth models (e.g. DICE and RICE; Nordhaus & Boyer, 2000), macroeconometric models (e.g. Danmarks Statistik, 1996; Chapter 33 in this handbook), or input-output models (e.g. Fathurrahman et al., 2015; Chapter 8 in this handbook) are also employed as TD energy models, this section focuses on computable general equilibrium (CGE) models in line with the predominant trend in the literature. The reader is referred to Chapter 30 in this handbook for a general comparative discussion of CGE models.

CGE models represent the interaction of agents in a Walrasian economic equilibrium system, which was formalized by Arrow and Debreu (1954), and provide a portrayal of the circular flow in an economy. Households own the factors of production and consume the end goods, and firms produce goods and services by using the factors of production that they rent from the households. The government is usually described as a passive agent that collects taxes from activities or institutions and distributes them through transfer payments. CGE models have become the main tool in addressing the real-world consequences of policies on employment, taxation, public finance, international trade, and climate change as well as energy-related issues, where impacts of different policy alternatives on welfare, income, sectoral/overall output, and relative prices can be assessed. It was not only the developments in computing technology but also the availability of software packages as well as data that fit the modeling requirements that led this approach to become prevalent among policy analysts.

CGE models use simplified and stylized functional forms to define smooth continuous production and utility functions where the parameters are estimated based on historically derived relationships. The profit-maximizing behavior of producers and utility-maximizing behavior of consumers based on neoclassical economic theory are then completely defined within the framework of these functional forms. Given that a CGE model is a system of nonlinear equations where the number of equations is equal to the number of variables, the model can be formulated as a nonlinear optimization problem with a dummy objective or as a mixed complementarity problem (MCP) (Mathiesen, 1985; Rutherford, 1995). The activities of different agents in the economy are described by three types of conditions in a CGE model (Paltsev, 2004):

- *Zero-profit conditions*: These conditions require that the value of inputs be equal to or greater than the value of outputs (i.e. any activity operated at a positive level must earn zero profit). Such a condition can be described as follows:

$$-profit \geq 0; output \geq 0; output^T\left(-profit\right) = 0$$

- *Market-clearing conditions*: These conditions imply that supply must be equal to demand for each commodity with a positive price. Such a condition can be described with the following expression:

$$supply - demand \geq 0; p \geq 0; p^T\left(supply - demand\right) = 0$$

- *Income-balance conditions*: For each agent, including the government, expenditures must exhaust the total income (value of factor endowments and tax revenue):

$$income = endowment + tax\ revenue$$

CGE models are calibrated, that is, parameters for utility and production functions are estimated, based on a social accounting matrix (SAM), which is a matrix representation of national accounting balances. A schematic representation of a SAM can be seen in Figure 1.1 (Sue Wing, 2004)

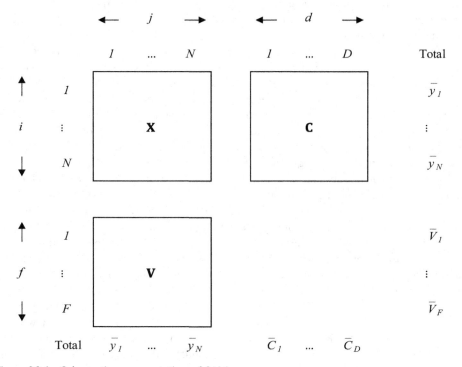

Figure 32.1 Schematic representation of SAM

where X, C, and V represent the intersectoral flows, final demand, and value-added activities, respectively. Each account is represented by a row and a column, and the cell entries denote a payment from the account of a column to the account of a row. Note that the balance of row and column sums together with the balance of the sum of entries in C and V ensure that the aforementioned equilibrium conditions (zero-profit, market-clearance, and income-balance) are satisfied.

In TD models, energy is generally treated as an explicit factor of production together with conventional ones. Representing the energy sector and specifically the power sector through aggregate production functions simplifies the activities in these sectors when the discrete nature of the technologies in these sectors is taken into account. Thus, this representation is too elementary to capture technology choices in the energy sector. As noted earlier in this section, CGE models have become the main tool in analyzing the real-world consequences of a wide range of policies not limited to energy or climate change issues. There are several CGE models that are specifically well suited to address energy-related policies, such as the MIT Emissions Predictions and Policy Analysis (EPPA) model (Babiker et al., 2001; Chen et al., 2015; Paltsev et al., 2005); GEM-E3 (Capros et al., 2013), used by the European Commission; the Phoenix Model (Sue Wing et al., 2011), developed by the Joint Global Change Research Institute at the University of Maryland; GEMINI-E3, developed jointly by the French Ministry of Equipment and the French Atomic Energy Agency with the collaboration of the Swiss Federal Institute of Technology (Bernard & Vielle, 2008); and the OECD's ENV-Linkages model (the successor of GREEN) (Château et al., 2014).

2   Integration of top-down and bottom-up models

TD and BU approaches originated from different fields with different purposes. The energy sector in conventional TD models is usually represented in an aggregate manner via smooth production functions as noted in the previous section; thus, these models lack in representing the current discrete energy technologies and costs, and in their time-varying behavior, as well. Moreover, the conservation of matter and energy may be violated in TD models. Conventional BU models, on the other hand, describe current and backstop technologies in detail while they lack in the ability to capture price distortions, economy-wide interactions, and income effects (Böhringer & Rutherford, 2006). These key differences between the two modeling approaches lead to inconsistent outcomes (Grubb et al., 1993; Wilson & Swisher, 1993). More clearly, TD models show a higher use of energy due to the assumption of significant unexploited opportunities in BU models for cost-effective investments in energy efficiency (Koopmans & te Velde, 2001).

The two approaches substantially complement each other rather than opposing each other. Thus, given the shortcomings of both paradigms, there have been considerable attempts of proposing a model that combines the BU and TD approaches since a complete analysis of policies related to energy production and consumption needs to incorporate the strengths of each paradigm. As indicated in Section 1.2, the two modeling approaches differ mainly with respect to the emphasis attributed to technological details of the energy system and consistency in terms of economic theory. Accordingly, as discussed by Hourcade et al. (2006), there are three main dimensions that characterize an energy-economy model: technological explicitness, macroeconomic completeness, and microeconomic realism. Conventional BU models lie on the technological explicitness-macroeconomic completeness layer, whereas conventional TD models lie on the macroeconomic completeness-microeconomic realism layer while researchers in this field pursue an ideal model with a representation of all dimensions to some reasonable extent.

The efforts to integrate BU and TD models (i.e. to create hybrid models) achieve a certain level of success in each of the three dimensions in various ways. Before an in-depth analysis of these efforts, it would be helpful to touch on two crucial paradigms in coupling BU and TD models: the "soft link" and the "hard link". The definitions of "soft link" and "hard link" (also called "informal" and "formal" linking; Wene, 1996) in the literature differ with slight nuances; in other words, there is not a consensus among researchers on the definition of or the distinction between soft and hard links (Helgesen, 2013). For example, Wene (1996) explained the difference between the two linking approaches based on whether the information transfer between the models is directly controlled by the user via judgments or by computer programs via formalized procedures. Bauer et al. (2008), on the other hand, used these paradigms only for the integration of a BU model (an energy system model) and a macroeconomic growth model while putting the integrated models of the CGE modeling framework in another class.

Jacobsen (1998) defined "hard-linking" as integrating the models with interactions in an iterative procedure. However, a more common classification applied in various other studies (Böhringer & Rutherford, 2008, 2009; Lanz & Rausch, 2011a) is to define "soft-linking" as integrating the existing separate large-scale BU and TD models in an iterative manner until convergence in key parameters is satisfied while referring to "hard-linking" as the complete integration of the models. In these studies, besides the soft-linked and hard-linked models, a third approach is identified in which a reduced form of one model, either TD or BU, is integrated or embedded into the other. The classification scheme in this chapter is closest to this approach, with a slight difference: the last category (integration of a core and a reduced form model) is also accepted as a "hard link" in line with the work of Riekkola et al. (2013). Hybrid modeling efforts are discussed in the remainder of this section based on this classification scheme. First, the models with a "soft link" are explained. Subsequently, models with a "hard link" are presented within two subsections: integration of a core model with a reduced form model, and completely integrated models.

2.1 Soft-linked models

In soft-linked models, existing models are coupled in such a way that the information between the models is transferred until a predetermined convergence criterion is satisfied. However, there exist several complications in this approach since the two modeling paradigms of BU and TD are introduced to serve for different purposes and analyses to answer different research and policy questions (Jacobsen, 1998). Moreover, the models significantly differ in their behavioral assumptions and accounting systems (Böhringer & Rutherford, 2008). Thus, achieving overall consistency between these models is not straightforward.

Attempts to develop soft-linked models date back to the end of the 1970s. Hoffman and Jorgenson (1977) combined an econometric model of interindustry transactions for the US economy with a process analysis model of the energy sector (the Brookhaven Energy System Optimization Model (BESOM)), where the former transfers demand for energy outputs while the latter provides resources, technologies, prices (some of them dual prices obtained from BESOM), and capital requirements as well as environmental information. Another attempt at a soft-linked model is HYBRIS (Jacobsen, 1998), in which three BU modules (energy supply, electricity demand in households, and heat demand in households) and a national TD model of Denmark are linked where the TD model is used as it is while the BU modules are reorganized for integration. This study also provided an insight into linking problems such as different responses to impacts of energy price changes or income developments. Messner and Schrattenholzer (2000), on the other hand, integrated a TD model, MESSAGE, with a BU model, MACRO, via a fully automated link, emphasizing that the integrated model demonstrates more transparency compared to hard-linked models including similar TD and BU components. The integrated model iterates for each period until the supply curves (transferred from MESSAGE to MACRO) and demand curves (transferred from MACRO to MESSAGE) are matched in 11 world regions, where the iteration process is triggered by exogenous growth rates of GDP and energy intensity reduction that comes from a separate scenario generator module. Martinsen (2011) proposed the integration of the national macroeconomic model MSG6 and the MARKAL Norway model with the introduction of technology learning from a third model, a global technology-rich energy systems model, ETP. The calibration and consistency check phases are carried out over electricity generation and associated cost figures.

Drouet et al. (2005) developed a soft-linked model for Switzerland by using reduced forms of the dynamic-recursive CGE model GEMINI-E3 and the BU model ETEM-SWI, which they called GEMINI-E3S and ETEM-RES. The integration focuses on the residential sector; thus, the sector is removed from the TD model and the BU model is designed only for the residential sector. The model iterates until the convergence criterion on the level of carbon prices is satisfied while the carbon taxes, energy prices, and useful energy demands are transferred from the TD to the BU model and final energy demands and carbon emissions flow in the opposite direction. The GEMINI-E3 model was coupled with TIAM-WORLD in another study by Labriet et al. (2015), which differs from the other soft-linked models as TIAM-WORLD itself is an integrated model with price-elastic final energy service demands. The coupling requires a detailed mapping between the two models in terms of the regions, the activity sectors, and the energy goods. Another sectoral integration attempt is that of Schäfer and Jacoby (2006), which couples the MIT EPPA model with the MARKAL model of transport technology. However, since the transportation sector in EPPA is aggregated, a third model, a model of modal splits, is employed to satisfy consistency with the disaggregated BU representation. The iterative process between the models takes place over the energy use in the models. Labandeira et al. (2009) analyzed the impacts of the European Union Emissions Trading Scheme (ETS) on the Spanish economy by using an integrated model in a similar setting where the BU model is formulated as an MCP. The work of Fortes et al. (2014) differs from these studies with its coverage in linking, which they call "full-link", not focusing on integration over a single sector but rather over all sectors. The proposed model, HYBTEP, integrates the national TD model GEM-E3_PT with the national BU model TIMES_PT for Portugal. There are also two linking modules, a demand generator and an energy link, between the models. The models are run independently for the whole planning horizon and iterations are carried out by checking whether the maximum deviation between the two models over all sectors is below the predetermined threshold level.

2.2 Hard-linked models

Integration of a core model with a reduced form model

Unlike the iterative process employed in soft-linked models, hard-linked models are integrated in a single framework in which the solution is obtained via simultaneous optimization. Almost all the models presented in this section couple a core BU model with a reduced form of the TD model, where the non-energy sectors are represented in an aggregated fashion (i.e. a one-sector economy without sectoral disaggregation). The models, in other words, link the physical process analysis with a long-term macroeconomic growth model. The pioneering study in this genre of modeling is ETA-MACRO (Manne, 1977), which is the predecessor of GLOBAL 2100 (Manne & Richels, 1990), MARKAL-MACRO (Manne & Wene, 1992), and the MERGE model (Manne et al., 1995). Moreover, there are further extensions of MARKAL-MACRO models (Bahn et al.,

1999; Kypreos, 1996; Loulou et al., 2004b; Strachan & Kannan, 2008). In the rest of this section, this modeling framework is summarized, employing the notations used in these studies.

The models in this class propose economy-wide solutions by maximizing the sum of discounted utility of consumption (*UTIL*) on the part of a representative household over all periods with a utility discount factor of *udf* (Equation (32.5)), while the aggregate economic output (Y_t) in the economy is calculated using a constant elasticity of substitution (CES) production function (Equation (32.6)), where subscript *t* refers to the year or period. The key feature in this modeling avenue is the links between the energy sector and the rest of the economy via the economy-wide production function as well as the relationship between energy costs (EC_t) and other macroeconomic variables (Equation 32.7)), as shown below:

$$UTIL = \sum_{t=1}^{T} \frac{U(C_t)}{(1+udf)^t} \tag{32.5}$$

$$Y_t = \left[a\left(K_t^\alpha L_t^{1-\alpha}\right)^\rho + \sum_{dm} b_{dm} D_{dm,t}^\rho \right]^{\frac{1}{\rho}} \tag{32.6}$$

$$Y_t = C_t + I_t + EC_t \tag{32.7}$$

Here, $\rho = \left(\frac{\sigma-1}{\sigma}\right)$, σ denoting elasticity of substitution; *a*, *b* denote scaling factors and α denotes the value share of capital. K_t and L_t represent capital and labor, and $D_{dm,t}$ is the demand for energy services of type *dm* in year *t*. C_t and I_t represent consumption and investments. (C_t) represents the utility of consumption, which is generally assumed to be the logarithm of the consumption. Note that there are various extensions of the standard version in which the disaggregation of the second aggregate in the production function as well as the nesting structure between capital, labor, and energy inputs or sectoral disaggregation differ (e.g. Kat, 2011; Kumbaroğlu, 1997). Güven (1994) also reformulated the ETA-MACRO model for Turkey to include foreign trade and currency restrictions, where the inclusion of foreign trade enhances the representativeness of the model for countries in which growth is highly dependent on foreign capital inflows.

WITCH, developed by Bosetti et al. (2006), represents another type in this modeling genre, where the core model is a TD model and the BU model is the reduced party. It is a multiregion Ramsey-type neoclassical optimal growth model with a relatively detailed representation for the energy sector (and especially for the power sector). WITCH is a forward-looking model that incorporates a description of endogenous and induced technical change in a game theoretical structure. The works of Edenhofer et al. (2005) and Bauer et al. (2008) are two studies in a similar setting; the former introduces a hard-linked model, MIND, while the latter presents a comparison of soft-and hard-linking approaches with the inference that the simultaneous equilibrium of the energy and capital market is not ensured via the soft-link approach.

Completely integrated models

The other type of hard-linked models originated from several pedagogic studies (Böhringer, 1998; Böhringer & Löschel, 2006; Böhringer & Rutherford, 2005, 2008). The idea in this approach is to cast both models, the TD economic equilibrium model and the BU activity analysis, as MCPs and solve them in a single consistent framework. In other words, a set of discrete BU technologies, mostly related to the power sector, are directly embedded into a top-down CGE model.

As noted in Section 1.2, a competitive market equilibrium problem can be formulated as an MCP (Mathiesen, 1985; Rutherford, 1995). The BU formulation presented in Section 1.1 can also be reformulated as an MCP using Kuhn-Tucker conditions of the problem (Böhringer & Rutherford, 2009) as follows:

$$C^T \pi \geq p; \; e \geq 0; \; e^T (C^T \pi - p) = 0 \tag{32.8}$$

$$p \geq A^T \pi; \; x \geq 0; \; x^T (p - A^T \pi) = 0 \tag{32.9}$$

$$Ax + Bz \geq Ce; \; \pi \geq 0; \; \pi^T (Ax + Bz - Ce) = 0 \tag{32.10}$$

$$l \leq z \leq u; \; \lambda, \mu \geq 0; \; \lambda^T (z - l) = 0; \; \mu^T (u - z) = 0 \tag{32.11}$$

$$\lambda + B^T \pi = \mu \tag{32.12}$$

Note that π is the dual variable of Equation (32.2), whereas λ and μ are dual variables of lower and upper bounds on z. Thus, in fact, Equations (32.8)–(32.12) define all complementarity relations between the primal BU equations and their dual variables and vice versa for the dual BU problem. These equations and the equilibrium conditions put forward in Section 1.2 along with the following equation define the integrated hybrid model.

$$p^T [e - x] = \mu^T u - \lambda^T l \tag{32.13}$$

Equation (32.13) is a result of the equivalence relation between primal and dual objective values in the optimal solution.

This modeling framework was employed in several studies. For example, Frei et al. (2003) extended the model as a dynamic hybrid model by incorporating the endogenous formulation of investment decisions. Kumbaroğlu and Madlener (2003) developed a backward-looking dynamic CGE model, SCREEN, and demonstrated it for the case of Switzerland. Sue Wing (2006) and Proença and St. Aubyn (2013) developed similar hybrid models for assessing the cost of limiting CO_2 emissions in the United States and the effects of feed-in tariffs to promote renewable energy in Portugal, respectively. The work of Böhringer et al. (2003) differs from these studies in that the agents have forward-looking behavior, unlike the backward-looking, static, or dynamic-recursive models.

An important challenge in merging TD and BU models in a single consistent framework is the compatibility of the data. In other words, the data resources as well as the way they are used in the corresponding models differ significantly from each other. For instance, to achieve a consistent integration between the models, factors of production in TD models should be compatible with not only inputs of BU models but also with the fixed and variable costs of operations or maintenance. Therefore, data reconciliation and use of BU information in a TD model are challenging but essential research avenues in hybrid modeling (Kiuila & Rutherford, 2013; Koopmans & te Velde, 2001; McFarland & Herzog, 2006; McFarland et al., 2004; Peters, 2016; Rodrigues & Linares, 2014, 2015; Sue Wing, 2008).

Instead of employing the ad hoc methods used to disaggregate the energy sector and specifically the power sector in the CGE modeling framework, Sue Wing (2008) proposed a robust and transparent mathematical scheme to reconcile and integrate BU engineering information with TD macroeconomic data. This procedure was then used by Eskeland et al. (2012), whereby a CGE model, GRACE, was extended to include power sector disaggregation and called GRACE-EL. Rodrigues and Linares used a similar routine for extending the power sector disaggregation, but with high temporal resolution (2014, 2015). Peters (2016), on the other hand, developed the GTAP-Power Data Base, an electricity-detailed extension of the GTAP 9 Data Base, by using matrix balancing methods where the GTAP-Power Data Base not only includes technological detail in power generation technologies but also has base/peak load disaggregation.

Although the integrated MCP formulation, with its overall consistency, aroused interest among researchers and was implemented in numerous studies as summarized above, it was realized in practice that the approach has severe limitations due to the complexity and dimensionality that the BU model brings with it (i.e. upper and lower bounds on decision variables with concomitant income effects). A block decomposition algorithm and an iterative solution procedure were then proposed to make this consistent framework practically applicable (Böhringer & Rutherford, 2006, 2009). The decomposition of the integrated model, in fact, implies that these models are not hard-linked anymore, but are soft-linked. Nevertheless, it is preferred to keep them under this heading due to the submodels' close link with the corresponding integrated framework as well as to stick to the theoretical consistency in the decomposition algorithm. Moreover, this approach is also referred to as "hard-linked" in several studies (e.g. Villasana, 2015; Tapia-Ahumada et al., 2015).

A schematic representation of the decomposition algorithm and the iterative solution procedure can be seen in Figure 32.1, in which a TD economic model and a BU electricity model are coupled. It is crucial to have the submodels initially set to a consistent benchmark, which is referred to as data reconciliation and model calibration. After ensuring that the two submodels are consistent, or in other words that the BU power sector input-output figures are consistent with the corresponding figures for aggregated power sector in the SAM, the models are solved iteratively based on the exogenous variables transferred from the other submodel. In each iteration, a convergence check is carried out after the solution of the BU electricity model and the

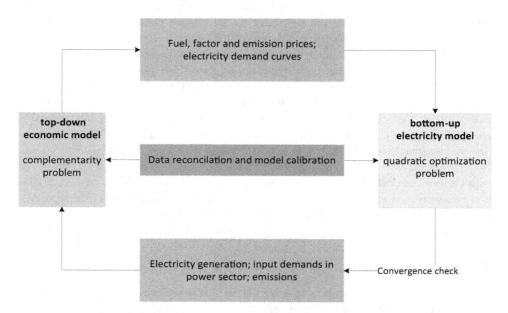

Figure 32.2 Iterative decomposition algorithm based on several previous studies (Böhringer & Rutherford, 2006, 2008; Lanz & Rausch, 2011b; Rausch & Mowers, 2012; Ross, 2014b)

procedure terminates when the maximum deviation in decision variables is under a predetermined threshold between two successive iterations.

One of the key points in the block decomposition algorithm is the need for revision in the objective function of the BU model (i.e. cost minimization/profit maximization) to incorporate the demand response. This is achieved by redefining the objective function as the maximization of total surplus, namely the sum of consumer and producer surplus, which creates a quadratic programming problem (Böhringer & Rutherford, 2009). Moreover, as proposed by Böhringer and Rutherford (2009), "a Marshallian demand approximation in the energy sector provides a precise local representation of general equilibrium demand" and rapid convergence is observed as the energy sector (or specifically the electricity sector) is small relative to the rest of the economy (remember the elephant and rabbit stew metaphor of Hogan & Manne, 1977). However, there are also studies (Villasana, 2015; Tapia-Ahumada et al., 2015) in which the demand response is reflected via an additional iteration procedure only within the BU model while keeping cost minimization as the objective.

The block decomposition algorithm has been implemented in various studies to integrate existing models of BU electricity models and TD CGE models (Hwang & Lee, 2015; Labandeira et al., 2009; Lanz & Rausch, 2011a, 2011b; Villasana, 2015; Rausch & Mowers, 2014; Ross, 2014b; Tapia-Ahumada et al., 2014, 2015; Tuladhar et al., 2009). Tuladhar et al. (2009) proposed the integrated model MRN-NEEM, which couples the TD model MRN (Multi-Region National Model) and the BU model NEEM (North American Electricity and Environment Model). Ross demonstrated the integration of two versions of the Dynamic Integrated Economy/Energy/Emissions Model (DIEM), the DIEM-CGE and DIEM-Electricity models (2014a), in which the block decomposition algorithm is employed (2014b). Hwang and Lee (2015) employed a block decomposition algorithm to analyze policies related to Korean electricity industry reform. The study by Labandeira et al. (2009), which was classified among the soft-linked models, can also be referred to in this section since the BU model is formulated as an MCP in which a price-responsive demand function is incorporated. Lanz and Rausch (2011a) coupled the MIT U.S. Regional Energy Policy (USREP) model with a BU formulation of the electric sector. Rausch and Mowers (2012), on the other hand, coupled USREP with the ReEDS (Renewable Energy Deployment System) model (Short et al., 2011), a recursive-dynamic power generation and transmission expansion planning model focusing on renewable technologies. Tapia-Ahumada et al. (2014, 2015) again used the MIT USREP model as the TD component and developed an integrated benchmark model by linking the USREP to the BU electricity model EleMod to examine the performance of the TD-only approach in terms of modeling intermittent renewable energy. The TD-only approach in that study is exemplified by the EPPA and the USREP, and the results suggest that the TD-only approach is not robust with respect to key parameters (those are a priori unknown and highly uncertain). Villasana (2015) coupled the MIT EPPA model with the new Renewables Integration and Storage Assessment (RISA) model, a power generation expansion planning model for Mexico in which the hourly load profiles are incorporated, in order to analyze the value of storage under large-scale penetration of renewable energy in regards to climate policy.

3   Concluding remarks

Energy-economy modeling has been arousing interest among researchers and policy makers for nearly half a century. This chapter focuses on energy-economy modeling efforts with a specific emphasis on the decades-long debate about two main approaches in this field, top-down and bottom-up, and scrutinizes their characteristics, advantages, and shortcomings while referring to the seminal efforts as well as significant studies for each modeling framework. More importantly, hybrid modeling approaches, which couple the two modeling frameworks to benefit from the strengths of each, are elaborated with particular attention to the existing state-of-the-art models. Energy policies and critical issues related to the latest developments in advanced energy technologies (e.g. energy storage, renewable energy generation, intermittency of renewable resources), environmental impacts of increasing energy use such as global warming, penetration of new technologies such as electric vehicles into the market, and changes in consumer behaviors in line with the developments in information and communication technologies need to be analyzed in a consistent framework that is able to capture the details of the discrete nature of technologies as well as economic theory. Thus, efforts towards hybrid modeling become even more important on top of the theoretical and practical efforts summarized in this chapter.

References

Antunes, C. H., & Henriques, C. O. (2016). *Multi-Objective Optimization and Multi-Criteria Analysis Models and Methods for Problems in the Energy Sector* (pp. 1067–1165). https://doi.org/10.1007/978-1-4939-3094-4_25

Arrow, K. J., & Debreu, G. (1954). Existence of an equilibrium for a competitive economy. *Econometrica, 22*(3), 265. https://doi.org/10.2307/1907353

Babiker, M. H., Reilly, J. M., Mayer, M., Eckaus, R. S., Sue Wing, I., & Hyman, R. C. (2001). *The MIT Emissions Prediction and Policy Analysis (EPPA) Model: Revisions, Sensitivities, and Comparisons of Results* (MIT Joint Program on the Science and Policy of Global Change Report Series). Retrieved from https://globalchange.mit.edu/sites/default/files/MITJPSPGC_Rpt71.pdf

Bahn, O., Kypreos, S., Bueler, B., & Luthi, H. J. (1999). Modelling an international market of CO2 emission permits. *International Journal of Global Energy Issues, 12*(1/2/3/4/5/6), 283–291. https://doi.org/10.1504/IJGEI.1999.000825

Bauer, N., Edenhofer, O., & Kypreos, S. (2008). Linking energy system and macroeconomic growth models. *Computational Management Science, 5*(1–2), 95–117. https://doi.org/10.1007/s10287-007-0042-3

Bernard, A., & Vielle, M. (2008). GEMINI-E3, a general equilibrium model of international–national interactions between economy, energy and the environment. *Computational Management Science, 5*(3), 173–206. https://doi.org/10.1007/s10287-007-0047-y

Böhringer, C. (1998). The synthesis of bottom-up and top-down in energy policy modeling. *Energy Economics, 20*(3), 233–248. https://doi.org/10.1016/S0140-9883(97)00015-7

Böhringer, C., & Löschel, A. (2006). Promoting renewable energy in Europe: A hybrid computable general equilibrium approach. *The Energy Journal, 27*(Special Issue), 135–150. Retrieved from www.jstor.org/stable/pdf/23297049.pdf?casa_token=w8XEvUlSuHQAAAAA:PXe2gi8-ZBuhMoKHoid_9c_qSGUweto-LPIEWgmTYU-98TpnqhiX9-jTFqThD9_nzm6VDpVM0F8_wwc2LbnC41k7tGissw GR21qc3ZRkil6hQtcQgtWy

Böhringer, C., Müller, A., & Wickart, M. (2003). Economie impacts of a premature nuclear phase-out in Switzerland: An applied general equilibrium analysis. *Swiss Journal of Economics and Statistics, 139*(IV), 461–505. Retrieved from www.sjes.ch/papers/2003-IV-2.pdf

Böhringer, C., & Rutherford, T. F. (2005). *Integrating Bottom-Up into Top-Down: A Mixed Complementarity Approach* (ZEW Discussion Paper). *ZEW Discussion Paper*. Retrieved from ftp://ftp.zew.de/pub/zew-docs/dp/dp0528.pdf

Böhringer, C., & Rutherford, T. F. (2006). *Combining Top-Down and Bottom-Up in Energy Policy Analysis: A Decomposition Approach* (ZEW Discussion Paper). *ZEW Discussion Paper*. Retrieved from ftp://ftp.zew.de/pub/zew-docs/dp/dp06007.pdf

Böhringer, C., & Rutherford, T. F. (2008). Combining bottom-up and top-down. *Energy Economics, 30*(2), 574–596. https://doi.org/10.1016/j.eneco.2007.03.004

Böhringer, C., & Rutherford, T. F. (2009). Integrated assessment of energy policies: Decomposing top-down and bottom-up. *Journal of Economic Dynamics and Control, 33*(9), 1648–1661. https://doi.org/10.1016/j.jedc.2008.12.007

Bosetti, V., Carraro, C., Galeotti, M., Massetti, E., & Tavoni, M. (2006). WITCH a world induced technical change hybrid model. *The Energy Journal, 27*, 13–37. https://doi.org/10.2307/23297044

Capros, P., Paroussos, D., Van Regemorter, L., Karkatsoulis, P., Fragkiadakis, C., Tsani, S., Charalampidis, I., & Revesz, T. (2013). *GEM-E3 Model Documentation* (JRC Technical Reports).

Château, J., Dellink, R., & Lanzi, E. (2014). *An Overview of the OECD ENV-Linkages Model:Version 3* (OECD Environment Working Papers No. 65). Paris. Retrieved from https://doi.org/10.1787/5jz2qck2b2vd-en

Chen, Y.-H. H., Paltsev, S., Reilly, J. M., Morris, J. F., Babiker, M. H., & Prinn, R. G. (2015). *The MIT EPPA6 Model: Economic Growth, Energy Use, and Food Consumption. MIT Joint Program on the Science and Policy of Global Change Report Series.* Cambridge. Retrieved from http://globalchange.mit.edu/

Danmarks Statistik. (1996). *ADAM: A Model of the Danish Economy.* Retrieved from https://scholar.google.com.tr/scholar?hl=en&as_sdt=0%2C5&q=Danmarks+Statistik%2C+1996.+ADAM%7DA+Model+of+the+Danish+Economy%2C+March+1995+in+Danish+&btnG=

Drouet, L., Haurie, A., Labriet, M., Thalmann, P., Vielle, M., & Viguier, L. (2005). A coupled bottom-up/top-down model for GHG abatement scenarios in the Swiss housing sector. *Energy and Environment*, 27–61. https://doi.org/10.1007/0-387-25352-1_2

Edenhofer, O., Bauer, N., & Kriegler, E. (2005). The impact of technological change on climate protection and welfare: Insights from the model MIND. *Ecological Economics*, *54*(2–3), 277–292. https://doi.org/10.1016/J.ECOLECON.2004.12.030

Eskeland, G. S., Rive, N. A., & Mideksa, T. K. (2012). Europe's climate goals and the electricity sector. *Energy Policy*, *41*, 200–211. https://doi.org/10.1016/J.ENPOL.2011.10.038

Fathurrahman, F., Kat, B., & Soytaş, U. (2015). Simulating Indonesian fuel subsidy reform: A social accounting matrix analysis. *Annals of Operations Research*. https://doi.org/10.1007/s10479-015-1954-x

Fortes, P., Pereira, R., Pereira, A., & Seixas, J. (2014). Integrated technological-economic modeling platform for energy and climate policy analysis. *Energy*, *73*, 716–730. https://doi.org/10.1016/J.ENERGY.2014.06.075

Frei, C. W., Haldi, P.-A., & Sarlos, G. (2003). Dynamic formulation of a top-down and bottom-up merging energy policy model. *Energy Policy*, *31*(10), 1017–1031. https://doi.org/10.1016/S0301-4215(02)00170-2

Grubb, M., Edmonds, J., ten Brink, P., & Morrison, M. (1993). The costs of limiting Fossil-Fuel CO2 emissions: A survey and analysis. *Annual Review of Energy and the Environment*, *18*(1), 397–478. https://doi.org/10.1146/annurev.eg.18.110193.002145

Güven, Ç. (1994). Energy planning under import restrictions. *European Journal of Operational Research*, *72*(3), 518–528. https://doi.org/10.1016/0377-2217(94)90420-0

Helgesen, P. I. (2013). *Top-Down and Bottom-Up: Combining Energy System Models and Macroeconomic General Equilibrium Models* (No. 1). Retrieved from www.ntnu.no/documents/7414984/202064323/2013-12-11+Linking+models_444.pdf/4252b320-d68d-43df-81b8-e8c72ea1bfe1

Hoffman, K. C., & Jorgenson, D. W. (1977). Economic and technological models for evaluation of energy policy. *The Bell Journal of Economics*, *8*(2), 444. https://doi.org/10.2307/3003296

Hogan, W. W., & Manne, A. S. (1977). Energy economy interactions: the fable of the elephant and the rabbit? In C. J. Hitch (Ed.), *Modeling energy – economy interactions: Five approaches: Resources for the Future* (pp. 247–277). Washington, DC.

Hourcade, J.-C., Jaccard, M., Bataille, C., & Ghersi, F. (2006). Hybrid modeling: New answers to old challenges to cite this version: Hybrid modeling: New answers to old challenges. *The Energy Journal*, *2006*(2 [Special Issue]), 1–12.

Hwang, W.-S., & Lee, J.-D. (2015). A CGE analysis for quantitative evaluation of electricity market changes. *Energy Policy*, *83*, 69–81. https://doi.org/10.1016/J.ENPOL.2015.04.006

Jacobsen, H. K. (1998). Integrating the bottom-up and top-down approach to energy–economy modelling: The case of Denmark. *Energy Economics*, *20*(4), 443–461. https://doi.org/10.1016/S0140-9883(98)00002-4

Kat, B. (2011). *Mathematical modeling for energy policy analysis.* Ankara, Turkey: Middle East Technical University. Retrieved from http://etd.lib.metu.edu.tr/upload/12613762/index.pdf

Kiuila, O., & Rutherford, T. F. (2013). Piecewise smooth approximation of bottom–up abatement cost curves. *Energy Economics*, *40*, 734–742. https://doi.org/10.1016/J.ENECO.2013.07.016

Koopmans, C. C., & te Velde, D. W. (2001). Bridging the energy efficiency gap: using bottom-up information in a top-down energy demand model. *Energy Economics*, *23*(1), 57–75. https://doi.org/10.1016/S0140-9883(00)00054-2

Kumbaroğlu, G. S. (1997). A model for long-term global air quality prediction and development of efficient control strategies in Turkey. *European Journal of Operational Research*, *102*(2), 380–392. https://doi.org/10.1016/S0377-2217(97)00116-1

Kumbaroğlu, G.S., & Madlener, R. (2003). Energy and climate policy analysis with the hybrid bottom-up computable general equilibrium model SCREEN: The case of the Swiss CO2 act. *Annals of Operations Research*, *121*(1/4), 181–203. https://doi.org/10.1023/A:1023311420542

Kypreos, S. (1996). *The MARKAL-MACRO Model and the Climate Change*. Retrieved from www.iaea.org/inis/collection/NCLCollectionStore/_Public/27/063/27063507.pdf

Labandeira, X., Linares, P., & Rodríguez, M. (2009). An integrated approach to simulate the impacts of carbon emissions trading schemes. *The Energy Journal, 30*(Special Issue 2: Climate Change Policies after 2012), 217–237. https://doi.org/10.2307/41323217

Labriet, M., Drouet, L., Vielle, M., Loulou, R., & Kanudia, A. (2015). *Assessment of the Effectiveness of Global Climate Policies Using Coupled Bottom-Up and Top-Down Models* (No. 023.2015). Retrieved from https://papers.ssrn.com/sol3/papers.cfm?abstract_id=2580216

Lanz, B., & Rausch, S. (2011a). General equilibrium, electricity generation technologies and the cost of carbon abatement. *Energy Economics, 33*(5), 1035–1047. https://doi.org/10.1016/j.enpol.2004.04.012

Lanz, B., & Rausch, S. (2011b). *General Equilibrium, Electricity Generation Technologies and the Cost of Carbon Abatement*. MIT Joint Program Report Series, Report 194, Cambridge. (http://globalchange.mit.edu/publication/14010)

Loulou, R., Goldstein, G., & Noble, K. (2004a). *Documentation for the MARKAL Family of Models–Part I: Standard MARKAL. iea-etsap.org*. Retrieved from http://iea-etsap.org/MrklDoc-I_StdMARKAL.pdf

Loulou, R., Goldstein, G., & Noble, K. (2004b). *Documentation for the MARKAL Family of Models–Part II: MARKAL-MACRO*. Retrieved from www.etsap.org/tools.htm

Manne, A. S. (1977). ETA-MACRO: A model of energy-economy interactions. *Adsabs.Harvard.Edu*. Palo Alto, CA. Retrieved from http://adsabs.harvard.edu/abs/1977STIN . . . 7826612M

Manne, A. S., Mendelsohn, R., & Richels, R. (1995). MERGE: A model for evaluating regional and global effects of GHG reduction policies. *Energy Policy, 23*(1), 17–34. https://doi.org/10.1016/0301-4215(95)90763-W

Manne, A. S., & Richels, R. G. (1990). CO2 emission limits: An economic cost analysis for the USA. *The Energy Journal, 11*, 51–74. https://doi.org/10.2307/41322654

Manne, A. S., & Wene, C. O. (1992). *MARKAL-MACRO: A Linked Model for Energy-Economy Analysis*. Upton, NY: Brookhaven National Lab. Retrieved from https://inis.iaea.org/search/search.aspx?orig_q=RN:23055026

Martinsen, T. (2011). Introducing technology learning for energy technologies in a national CGE model through soft links to global and national energy models. *Energy Policy, 39*(6), 3327–3336. https://doi.org/10.1016/J.ENPOL.2011.03.025

Mathiesen, L. (1985). Computational experience in solving equilibrium models by a sequence of linear complementarity problems. *Operations Research, 33*(6), 1225–1250.

McFarland, J. R., & Herzog, H. J. (2006). Incorporating carbon capture and storage technologies in integrated assessment models. *Energy Economics, 28*(5–6), 632–652. https://doi.org/10.1016/J.ENECO.2006.05.016

McFarland, J. R., Reilly, J. M., & Herzog, H. J. (2004). Representing energy technologies in top-down economic models using bottom-up information. *Energy Economics, 26*(4), 685–707. https://doi.org/10.1016/j.eneco.2004.04.026

Messner, S., & Schrattenholzer, L. (2000). MESSAGE–MACRO: Linking an energy supply model with a macroeconomic module and solving it iteratively. *Energy, 25*(3), 267–282. https://doi.org/10.1016/S0360-5442(99)00063-8

Nordhaus, W., & Boyer, J. (2000). *Warming the world: Economic models of global warming*. Cambridge: MIT Press. Retrieved from https://books.google.com/books?hl=en&lr=&id=GbcCZHGQliwC&oi=fnd&pg=PP15&dq=Warming+the+World++Economic+Models+of+Global+Warming&ots=GzjQ6vdWjg&sig=4RrgqV-Pf6RhO4KfLui4sGx8yz4

Paltsev, S. (2004). *Moving from static to dynamic general equilibrium economic models*. MIT Joint Program on the Science and Policy of Global Change Report Series. Cambridge. Retrieved from http://globalchange.mit.edu/files/document/MITJPSPGC_TechNote4.pdf

Paltsev, S., Reilly, J. M., Jacoby, H. D., Eckaus, R. S., Mcfarland, J. R., Sarofim, M., . . . Babiker, M. H. (2005). *The MIT Emissions Prediction and Policy Analysis (EPPA) model: Version 4*. MIT Joint Program on the Science and Policy of Global Change Report Series. Cambridge.

Peters, J. C. (2016). The GTAP-power data base: Disaggregating the electricity sector in the GTAP data base. *Journal of Global Economic Analysis, 1*(1), 209–250.

Proença, S., & St. Aubyn, M. (2013). Hybrid modeling to support energy-climate policy: Effects of feed-in tariffs to promote renewable energy in Portugal. *Energy Economics, 38*, 176–185. https://doi.org/10.1016/J.ENECO.2013.02.013

Rausch, S., & Mowers, M. (2012). *Distributional and Efficiency Impacts of Clean and Renewable Energy Standards for Electricity*. MIT Joint Program on the Science and Policy of Global Change Report Series. Cambridge. Retrieved from http://globalchange.mit.edu/

Rausch, S., & Mowers, M. (2014). Distributional and efficiency impacts of clean and renewable energy standards for electricity. *Resource and Energy Economics*, *36*(2), 556–585. https://doi.org/10.1016/j. reseneeco.2013.09.001

Riekkola, A. K., Berg, C., Ahlgren, E. O., & Söderholm, P. (2013). *Challenges in Soft-Linking: The Case of EMEC and TIMES-Sweden* (No. 133). *Working Papers*. National Institute of Economic Research. Retrieved from https://ideas.repec.org/p/hhs/nierwp/0133.html

Rodrigues, R., & Linares, P. (2014). Electricity load level detail in computational general equilibrium–part I–data and calibration. *Energy Economics*, *46*, 258–266. https://doi.org/10.1016/j.eneco.2014.09.016

Rodrigues, R., & Linares, P. (2015). Electricity load level detail in computational general equilibrium–part II–welfare impacts of a demand response program. *Energy Economics*, *47*, 52–67. https://doi.org/10.1016/J.ENECO.2014.10.015

Ross, M. T. (2014a). *Structure of the Dynamic Integrated Economy/Energy/Emissions Model: Electricity Component, DIEM-Electricity*. NI WP 14-11. Durham, NC: Duke University.

Ross, M. T. (2014b). *Structure of the Dynamic Integrated Economy/Energy/Emissions Model: Computable General Equilibrium Component, DIEM-CGE*. NI WP 14-12. Durham, NC: Duke University.

Rutherford, T. F. (1995). Extension of GAMS for complementarity problems arising in applied economic analysis. Journal of Economic Dynamics and control, 19(8), 1299-1324.

Schäfer, A., & Jacoby, H. D. (2006). Experiments with a hybrid CGE-MARKAL model. *The Energy Journal*, *27*, 171–177. https://doi.org/10.2307/23297051

Schrattenholzer, L. (1981). *The Energy Supply Model MESSAGE*. RR-81-031. Retrieved from http://pure. iiasa.ac.at/id/eprint/1542/

Short, W., Sullivan, P., Mai, T., Mowers, M., Uriarte, C., Blair, N., Heimiller, D. and Martinez, A., (2011). Regional energy deployment system (ReEDS) (No. NREL/TP-6A20-46534). National Renewable Energy Lab.(NREL), Golden, CO (United States).

Strachan, N., & Kannan, R. (2008). Hybrid modelling of long-term carbon reduction scenarios for the UK. *Energy Economics*, *30*(6), 2947–2963. https://doi.org/10.1016/J.ENECO.2008.04.009

Sue Wing, I. (2004). *Computable General Equilibrium Models and Their Use in Economy-Wide Policy Analysis*. MIT Joint Program on the Science and Policy of Global Change Report Series. Cambridge. Retrieved from http://web.mit.edu/globalchange/www/MITJPSPGC_TechNote6.pdf

Sue Wing, I. (2006). The synthesis of bottom-up and top-down approaches to climate policy modeling: Electric power technologies and the cost of limiting US CO2 emissions. *Energy Policy*, *34*(18), 3847–3869. https://doi.org/10.1016/j.enpol.2005.08.027

Sue Wing, I. (2008). The synthesis of bottom-up and top-down approaches to climate policy modeling: Electric power technology detail in a social accounting framework. *Energy Economics*, *30*(2), 547–573. https://doi.org/10.1016/j.eneco.2006.06.004

Sue Wing, I., Daenzer, K., Fischer-Vanden, K., & Calvin, K. (2011). *Phoenix Model Documentation*. Joint Global Change Research Institute, Maryland.

Tapia-Ahumada, K., Octaviano, C., Rausch, S., & Pérez-Arriaga, I. (2014). *Modeling Intermittent Renewable Energy: Can We Trust Top-Down Equilibrium Approaches?* In *CEEPR Working Paper Series, WP-2014-004*. Massachusetts Institute of Technology.

Tapia-Ahumada, K., Octaviano, C., Rausch, S., & Pérez-Arriaga, I. (2015). Modeling intermittent renewable electricity technologies in general equilibrium models. *Economic Modelling*, *51*, 242–262. https://doi. org/10.1016/j.econmod.2015.08.004

Tuladhar, S. D., Yuan, M., Bernstein, P., Montgomery, W. D., & Smith, A. (2009). A top-down bottom-up modeling approach to climate change policy analysis. *Energy Economics*, *31*(Suppl. 2), S223–S234. https://doi.org/10.1016/j.eneco.2009.07.007

Wene, C. O. (1996). Energy-economy analysis: Linking the macroeconomic and systems engineering approaches. *Energy*, *21*(9), 809–824. https://doi.org/10.1016/0360-5442(96)00017-5

Villasana, C. A. O. (2015). *The value of electricity storage under large-scale penetration of renewable energy: A hybrid modeling approach* (Doctoral dissertation, Massachusetts Institute of Technology, Engineering Systems Division).

Wilson, D., & Swisher, J. (1993). Exploring the gap: Top-down versus bottom-up analyses of the cost of mitigating global warming. *Energy Policy*, *21*(3), 249–263. https://doi.org/10.1016/0301-4215(93)90247-D

33

Macro-econometric and structural models

Ulrike Lehr and Christian Lutz

1 Introduction and background

Energy is at the core of many economic activities. It literally drives growth, production, and transport and contributes to the most basic needs of people. Changes in energy prices have caused economic downturns and upswings, the perspectives of sustainable future energy use give rise to technological changes, new opportunities and players, and energy exports contribute 13% to total global trade (WTO, 2017).

Despite the pertaining neoclassical economists' view that resources are used efficiently, and nothing is to be wasted, energy use and consumption in reality tell us differently. Most energy economic models thus try to incorporate inefficiencies and rigidities, often despite their theoretical foundations (for examples of modeling energy efficiency and rebound effects with a CGE; see Figus et al., 2017 and the works cited therein). Model types, which link energy and economy, vary with the theoretical approach (neoclassical, institutional, and evolutionary), the regional scale (global, national, and regional) and the level of disaggregation (industries, companies, aggregates, agents). For instance, sector models focus on a single energy consuming sector (e.g. the electricity industry, the steel industry, or transport), which is then modeled in detail with the respective (market) logic. In the case of a bottom-up model, feedbacks to the overall economy are not analyzed. In the other case (macroeconomic model or top-down model), the focus is on linking all sectors or industries and their feedback on overall economic development. Depending on the respective policy question to be answered, these models are developed for individual countries, regions or the world. Globally, the advantage of including international feedback is juxtaposed with the use of international data sets (usually less up-to-date and less detailed than national data) and the high complexity of the model relationships. One way of combining the advantages of both approaches is the mostly "soft" link through the exchange of data via selected interfaces. Overviews of model approaches can be found, inter alia in West (1996), IEA (2014a, p. 56ff) and Lutz & Breitschopf (2016).

Energy consumption is characterized by various rigidities. Commuters cannot react to price changes instantaneously, except for staying home. Households' demand for fuel used in transport is often as price inelastic as their demand for residential heating fuels. The latter responds rather to temperature changes than to the price for heating oil. Low price periods lead to storage, but

473

consumption follows different pattern. The same holds for energy-intensive industries such as iron and steel, paper or basic chemicals. In the short run, energy use mainly depends on output (i.e. energy efficiency is fixed and can only be improved by investing in more energy-efficient capital). Such short-term inelasticity can be observed in almost any energy consuming activity. To understand the impact of energy consumption, energy price changes and changes in the fuel mix or in transport modes on the economy, it pays to look at energy consuming sectors in detail and analyze their consumption behavior and energy demand over time. The development of capital stocks over time is crucial, to implicitly consider the higher long-term price elasticities and the rigidities in the short run. Macro-econometric energy models, often called structural models or integrated models have been developed for this purpose. Different industries and consumption purposes are modeled separately and their interrelations including the energy content are taken into account.

The remainder of this contribution is organized as follows. The next section will give an overview of the most prominent macro-econometric models currently used for environmental and energy policy analysis in EU (United Kingdom, Germany) and the United States (so-called e3 models). Section 3 will give an overview of selected results from modeling exercises, and Section 4 concludes and gives an outlook.

2 Macro-econometric models in the environment-energy-economy nexus

The most prominent macroeconomic models used in energy policy analysis are falling into one of the following three categories: general equilibrium models (CGE) (see Chapter 30 in this handbook), agent based models (see Chapter 36 in this handbook) and (macro) econometric input-output models (IOE – Econometric Input Output Models, according to Máñez Costa et al., 2016) West (1996) mainly differentiates between CGE and IOE models, which are referred to as macro-econometric structural models in the following. For climate change analyses Integrated Assessment Models (IAM) are applied. They link climate models with CGEs and have gained prominence and visibility, but are often highly aggregated regarding regions and industries and of lesser importance in purely energy economic questions.

All models fall short of reality. However, models can contribute meaningful results to the discussion on future energy systems, the economic impacts of a transition towards a more sustainable use of energy and the economic implications of climate change mitigation from a fuels switch. To be able to do so, the models have to be capable of representing the transformation to a low-GHG economy by addressing (Barker, 2013):

- GHG emissions by source
- Long time scales, 2050 for transition to a low-carbon economy
- National and international policies
- Different fossil fuels and different user characteristics
- Details for critical low-carbon technologies.

These characteristics suggest that suitable models will project to 2050 or further, show policies at least by large GHG-emitting countries (in a global model), include a detailed energy system in these countries, allow for the representation of technological change and allow for radical (non-marginal) changes in technology and behavior (Barker, 2013). IOE or macro-econometric structural models meet these criteria. Moreover, they are based on statistical data sets from either UN, OECD, international datasets such as EXIOBASE, EORA and WIOD or national accounts and national statistics. They are "structural", which means that variables are disaggregated to different economic sectors, different consumption goods or purposes and different fuels. Finally, dynamic behavioral equations are econometrically estimated from effects from previous outcomes: that is, history matters in a sense that historical elasticities of demand are supposed to remain constant and capital stocks as power plants, factories, buildings, and vehicles will only change slowly over time.

Figure 33.1 shows the typical elements of this modeling approach. Starting from national accounts, which represent the activities of the state, enterprises, private households and the rest of the world as well as their linkages for each year, a consistent framework is given. In addition, the interdependence of different economic sectors is modeled with input-output tables for each year, too. The energy system is based upon energy balances, providing a consistent calculation framework for the use of energy from production to primary energy supply and final energy

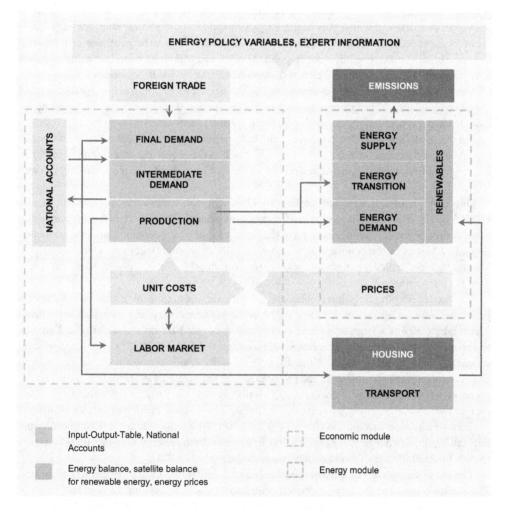

Figure 33.1 Basic elements of macro-econometric e3 models

Source: GWS, own graph.

consumption by fuel and by sector. The economic core and the energy and environment modules in these models are interlinked. Energy prices affect unit costs of production and profits, as well as households' and public budgets, increases in production affect energy consumption, GHG emissions and fossil fuel imports. A transformation towards sustainable energy systems comes with various economic effects, depending on the respective production structure, the international competitiveness of the respective economy and its advantages in resource endowment, be it natural resources, knowledge, or human capital.

One group of models is based on the INFORUM[1] philosophy (Almon, 1991). INFORUM stands for INterindustry FORcasting Project at the University of Maryland (USA), which was founded by Clopper Almon in 1967. The philosophy is dedicated to research and consulting activities regarding policy analysis and business planning based on quantitative, macroeconomic modeling. The group can be considered a pioneer in construction of dynamic models which use a "bottom-up" approach for top-down models. Today, there exists a worldwide network of research associates (INFORUM Group). The core instrument of all INFORUM Group members is bottom-up macroeconomic modeling at different scope and depth, which serve as tools to analyze ex post development(s) plus ex ante projections and forecasts. These interindustry macro-econometric models combine input-output-structure with econometric equations in a dynamic framework, are characterized by disaggregated, detailed data input and provide capable tools not only for projections but also for scenario analyses answering "what if" questions.

Most INFORUM models are characterized by the principles of construction bottom-up and complete integration. The bottom-up design principle implies that all sectors of the economy are modeled in great detail, and the overall economic variables are formed through explicit aggregation in the model context. The principle of full integration includes a complex and simultaneous modeling that describes the inter-industrial link as well as the origin and distribution of incomes, the redistributive activity of the state and the income of households for the various goods and services.

One example of this modeling philosophy is the German environmental economic model PANTA RHEI. The name speaks for itself: it cites the Greek philosopher Heraclitus ("everything flows"), and the model captures long-term structural change in the economy and environmental flows. In addition to the comprehensive economic modeling, energy consumption and air pollutants, transport, buildings, and household energy consumption are recorded in detail. All model parts are interconnected.

The model is completely interdependent (as outlined above), meaning that the effects of a policy measure on all model variables are recorded simultaneously and no effects are "lost". The model contains a large set of macroeconomic data based on official statistics and enables sector-specific statements in 63 economic sectors. Basically, PANTA RHEI can be coupled with an international model system, for a global policies and questions. It was used, for example, to evaluate the employment effects of the promotion of renewable energy (Lehr et al., 2012) or the economic effects of a series of energy scenarios that formed the basis for the 2010 energy concept in Germany (Lindenberger et al., 2010). Recent applications include economic evaluation of climate protection measures in Germany (Lutz et al., 2014; Lehr & Lutz, 2016) and economic impacts of climate change (Lehr et al., 2016). In addition to the energy modules, PANTA RHEI records in detail the use of land and raw materials (Meyer et al., 2012).

The individual model components are closely and consistently linked by prices and quantities. The transport module, for example, contains information on the consumption of fuel in liters, which – multiplied by fuel prices – is part of the final demand of households and the wholesale demand of the economic sectors. Changes in the level of taxes or international oil prices lead to a change in demand for fuels and the related economic behavior in Germany (Lutz, 2011).

The economic core called INFORGE consists essentially of a macro-econometric structural model with a time series of input-output tables in the center, the system of national accounts and the labor market. It is described in detail in Maier et al. (2015).

The energy model describes the relation between economic development, energy consumption and CO_2 emissions. It includes primary energy supply, transformation and final energy consumption. It distinguishes 20 final energy consumers and 30 energy sources (Lutz et al., 2014). The transport module describes the stock of vehicles and average consumption plus consumption of newly registered cars, while the housing module projects the demand for heating in the housing stock (Lehr et al., 2011). Again, new buildings have to meet much more stringent regulation, but insulation of old buildings is key to reduce energy consumption over time. By varying the parameters of important influencing factors, effects on energy prices, gross domestic product, employment, price level and a multitude of other monetary variables in the PANTA RHEI model can be determined. Scenario analyses compare alternative developments (scenarios) with a reference development or each other. The scenarios deviate from the reference scenario in one or a few parameter settings (e.g. energy tax rates). Differences in the model results can then be attributed to the changed parameter settings. To understand the model, the concept of simultaneous solutions is helpful. PANTA RHEI does not use a block-recursive solution method that contains the result of an equation or a defined equation block in the next equation block. Rather, the solution method is iterative, so that each result of the equation affects the results of all other equations, no matter where an equation was placed in the program code.

The SNA balance at the model's core enforces double entry accounting for the whole economy. This results in strict requirements for the consistency of the system: no cash flow has to be disregarded and requires an offsetting entry. As a result, gross domestic product is always identical to the sum of its components (consumption, investment and foreign trade). However, this consistency requirement applies not only to macroeconomic aggregates, but also to all sectors of the economy: here, too, revenue and expenditure must be properly accounted for. The model PANTA RHEI ensures that every euro is spent only once.

The Long-term Interindustry Forecasting Tool (LIFT) is a dynamic model of the US national economy (IEC, 2015). It combines an interindustry input-output formulation with extensive use of regression analysis to employ a "bottom-up" approach to macroeconomic modeling. In this way, as the authors describe in IEC (2015), the model works like the actual economy, building the macroeconomic aggregates from details of industry activity, rather than by distributing predetermined macroeconomic quantities among industries. LIFT contains full demand and supply accounting for 110 productive sectors.

An alternative route to similar results has been taken by the Cambridge Econometrics (CE) in the development of the E3ME model. Barker et al. (2011) compare E3ME with the INFORUM type model GINFORS. The model E3ME was developed over the last 20 years and is characterized by Pollitt (2014) as follows:

A high level of disaggregation, enabling detailed analysis of sectoral and country-level effects from a wide range of scenarios. Social impacts (including unemployment levels and distributional effects) are important model outcomes. Its econometric specification addresses concerns about conventional macroeconomic models and provides a strong empirical basis for analysis. It can fully assess both short and long-term impacts and is not limited by many of the restrictive assumptions common to CGE models. It allows for integrated treatment of the world's economies, energy systems, emissions and material demands. This enables it to capture two-way linkages and feedbacks between these components. E3ME covers 59 global regions, with a detailed sectoral disaggregation in each one – 69 for EU and 43 for non-EU

– and projects forwards annually up to 2050. It is frequently applied at national level, in Europe and beyond, as well as for wider (European and global) policy analysis.

3 Scenario analyses and typical results

The models described above have been developed and used as tools in policy analysis for a wide range of applications (see Chapter 38 in this handbook for use in energy policy). A typical set of questions asked to the researcher and answered by model results and their interpretation is "what are the economic effects of a certain policy or strategy or a price change on global energy markets? Who will win and who will lose, i.e. who will support the policy and who will oppose it?" Answers involve scenario analyses most of the time and compare the results of a model "run" which includes the policy in question to the set of results from a model run without the respective policy. A scenario without the measure is often called a reference scenario and, in many cases, describes a business as usual development. If all other things stay equal (ceteris paribus hypothesis), the differences in the model output will be directly related and "caused" by the policy measure.

Key macroeconomic impacts include economic development measured as GDP, employment, price and trade effects. Changes in energy consumption and their monetary implications are also very important. Models are also able to calculate environmental effects, some of the additional benefits of a clean energy transition (IEA, 2014a).

For German ministries, employment effects of the expansion of renewable energies in Germany have been calculated using the model PANTA RHEI described above (Lehr et al., 2012,). A zero scenario without the development of renewable energy since 1995 is the reference. The expansion of renewable energy essentially follows the scenario of the official strategy (Nitsch et al., 2012). In the short term, the effects are strongly influenced by the assumptions regarding the exports of German renewable energy equipment. In an unfavorable but unlikely scenario with zero exports, negative macroeconomic effects occur over a number of years. In the long term from the year 2030, the macroeconomic effects of the expansion of renewable energy will in any case be clearly positive and will increase with decreasing fossil energy imports and increasing profitability of renewable energy. For mild export assumptions, the positive effects of expansion in 2030 are 1.4% for GDP and 0.3% for employment compared to the zero scenario.

Using the global macroeconomic model E3ME, Cambridge Econometrics examined the macroeconomic effects of increased global renewable energy expansion by 2030 for IRENA (2016). The IEA's New Policies Scenario (IEA, 2014b), which contains implemented and future-oriented policy measures in 2014, serves as a reference. This business-as-usual mirrors IRENA's REmap scenario, which aims to double the share of renewable energy in global energy use from 2010 to 2030 according to the IRENA roadmap. The net effects in the REmap scenario in the year 2030 are 0.6% higher global GDP and 0.14% higher global employment than in the reference. However, negative effects also occur in individual countries and economic sectors. The positive macroeconomic effects of the expansion of renewable energies are fueled by further welfare-enhancing benefits in the form of lower GHG emissions and improved health.

Economic impacts of increased energy efficiency worldwide have been determined by the OECD (Château et al., 2014) with a CGE model for the year 2035. Based on the New Policies Scenario of the World Energy Outlook as a reference, an "Efficient World" scenario was identified (IEA, 2012). It is characterized by the fact that investments with short pay-off periods are made in energy efficiency, which do currently not take place due to specific barriers. Put simply, it is assumed that the "economic potential" for energy saving is exhausted. As a result, global GDP in 2035 is 1.1% higher than in the reference. The overall positive effects are offset by losses in individual countries and sectors, which are heavily dependent on existing fossil energy sources and which largely export or use them.

At the EU level, comparable calculations for the EU Commission have been making use of two different models: the macroeconomic model E3ME and the CGE model GEM-E3 (Cambridge Econometrics et al., 2015). Compared to a reference calculated for the EU, additional measures to increase energy efficiency were put under the spot. In the scenarios, primary energy supply in 2030 will be 25% to 40% lower than in the reference. Interestingly, both models come to slightly different conclusions about the macroeconomic advantages of increased energy efficiency. While in the macroeconomic model the positive effects on GDP and employment increase with increased energy efficiency, in the CGE model the positive employment effect is significantly greater, while the impact on GDP is slightly negative. Improving energy efficiency by 30% leads to a higher GDP of 1.1% for the macroeconomic model, while GDP is 0.22% lower for the CGE model. In terms of employment, the effects in both models are clearly positive: 1.9% more in GEM-E3 and 0.3% more in E3ME. In GEM-E3 the substitution between labor and capital is more pronounced than in E3ME. In this context, assumptions about the possible displacement of other investments by energy efficiency investments are the important model difference: GEM-E3 assumes full crowding out, E3ME full additionality of efficiency investments.

Pollitt et al. (2017) show significantly positive macroeconomic effects in a recent study for DG Energy about economy-wide impacts of additional energy efficiency measures in the EU until 2030. An energy efficiency increase by 40% until 2030 will increase GDP by about 4% against a reference without assuming crowding out. In case of partial crowding out, GDP impacts will be 2.2% in 2030. Employment effects in percent reach about half of the GDP impacts.

With the LIFT model, an economy-wide assessment of the employment impacts associated with the US Environmental Protection Agency's (EPA's) proposed Clean Power Plan has been conducted (IEC, 2015). This analysis expands according to the authors upon the employment analysis included in EPA's regulatory impact analysis (RIA) for the proposed plan, as it captures several indirect effects not included in the EPA analysis. These include the employment impacts associated with changes in electricity and other energy prices (both positive and negative, depending on the year), the productivity impacts associated with heat rate improvements at power plants, households and businesses re-directing expenditures to other uses because of increased demand-side energy efficiency, expenditures crowded out by energy efficiency expenditures, and changes in investments for air pollution control devices. Based on these effects and those captured in EPA's RIA for the proposed rule, this analysis estimates a net gain of 74,000 jobs in 2020, and projects that these annual employment gains will increase to 196,000 to 273,000 jobs between 2025 and 2040.

4 Summary and outlook

As outlined in the introduction of this handbook, "The need for integrated assessment of the relationship between energy, economy, environment, and societal concerns is apparent. Energy policy makers face the challenge of meeting a diverse set of criteria in these four dimensions". Global agreements and targets as the Sustainable Development Goals for 2030 call for integrated modeling of policies to reach these targets, evaluate different options and assessment process. They are particularly prone to answer questions on energy consumption, to show trade-offs and solutions. Macro-econometric or structural models provide valuable insights for this, policy instruments and their impacts and shifts in the energy system. Socioeconomic impacts of policies can be considered, which are important for successful policy implementation in the short and medium term. This is a major advantage against CGE models, which have a longer time horizon and just compare two states of equilibrium assuming fully functioning markets and abstracting from time. Macro-econometric models have been developed to model inefficient allocations and rigidities deviating from (neo)classical economic theory. A report for the EU Commission has identified better inclusion of endogenous technical change and the role of financing as major shortcomings of recent modeling efforts (Mercure et al., 2016).

In times of big data and open access to statistical data macro-econometric model building is facing different opportunities and challenges. On the one hand, availability of time series of structural information such as input-output tables, bilateral trade data, SNA and energy and emission balances opens new ways to estimate behavioral parameters and to more sophisticated modeling. More detailed information on different agents offers the option to integrate agent-based modeling, among others to depict policies more realistically and take distributional issues into account. Results of energy policies in macro-econometric models can be related to personal income distribution data or respective models to make social concerns visible. Chapter 39 in this handbook discusses quantifying these concerns and including them as a criterion in MCDM models for energy policy.

International data have to be used to consider global deployment of energy technologies and policy implications on international competitiveness. On the other hand, a major argument against large-scale structural models is their black box character. Transparency and accountability will be even more challenging with higher data availability. This is however no exclusive problem of macro-econometric models. Data complexity and number of equations are often much higher in natural sciences and engineering. Comprehensive documentation of models and model results, open source modeling, and detailed model comparisons are needed to further improve macro-econometric models, their real world application and acceptance. Big data can be used to test parts of the models to improve their micro-foundation. Models have to be tailor-made to meet specific application needs.

Note

1 For more information on the INFORUM group, see www.inforum.umd.edu/index.html.

References

Almon, C. (1991): The INFORUM Approach to Interindustry Modelling. *Economic Systems Research*, 3, 1–7.

Barker, T. (2013): Doing macroeconomic research on climate-change mitigation for national and international policymakers. Terry Barker Inaugural lecture as Honorary Professor, School of Environmental Sciences, University of East Anglia, 13 September, University of East Anglia, Norwich, UK.

Barker, T., Lutz, C., Meyer, B. & Pollitt, H. (2011): Models for Projecting the Impacts of ETR. In: Ekins, P. & Speck, S. (eds.): *Environmental Tax Reform (ETR): A Policy for Green Growth*, pp. 175–203. Oxford University Press, New York.

Cambridge Econometrics, E3M-Lab, Warwick Institute for Employment Research IER & ICF International (2015): Assessing the Employment and Social Impact of Energy Efficiency, Final Report Volume 1: Main Report, Cambridge.

Château, J., Magné, B. & Cozzi, L. (2014): Economic Implications of the IEA Efficient World Scenario, OECD Environment Working Papers, No. 64, OECD Publishing. http://dx.doi.org/10.1787/5jz2qcn29lbw-en.IEA 2012.

Figus, G., Turner, K., McGregor, P. & Katris, A. (2017): Making the Case for Supporting Broad Energy Efficiency Programmes: Impacts on Household Incomes and Other Economic Benefits. *Energy Policy*, 111, 157–165. DOI: 10.1016/j.enpol.2017.09.028

IEA (2012): *World Energy Outlook 2012*. IEA Publications, Paris.

IEA (2014a): *Capturing the Multiple Benefits of Energy Efficiency*. IEA Publications, Paris.

IEA (2014b): *World Energy Outlook 2014*. IEA Publications, Paris.

Industrial Economics Incorporated (IEC) (2015): *Assessment of the Economy-Wide Employment Impacts of EPA's Proposed Clean Power Plan.* Cambridge MA. www.inforum.umd.edu/papers/otherstudies/2015/iec_inforum_report_041415.pdf

IRENA (2016): *Renewable Energy Benefits: Measuring the Economics.* IRENA, Abu Dhabi.

Lehr, U. & Lutz, C. (2016): German Energiewende – quo vadis? In: Bardazzi, R., Pazienza, M. G., Tonini, A. (eds.): *European Energy and Climate Security: Public Policies, Energy Sources, and Eastern Partners,* pp. 203–232. Springer, Heidelberg.

Lehr, U., Lutz, C. & Edler, D. (2012): Green Jobs? Economic Impacts of Renewable Energy in Germany. *Energy Policy,* 47, 358–364. DOI: 10.1016/j.enpol.2012.04.076

Lehr, U., Mönnig, A., Wolter, M. I., Lutz, C., Schade, W. & Krail, M. (2011): Die Modelle ASTRA und PANTA RHEI zur Abschätzung gesamtwirtschaftlicher Wirkungen umweltpolitischer Instrumente – ein Vergleich. GWS Discussion Paper 11/4, Osnabrück.

Lehr, U., Nieters, A. & Drosdowski, T. (2016): Extreme Weather Events and the German Economy: The Potential for Climate Change Adaptation. In: Leal Filho, W., Musa, H., Cavan, G., O'Hare, P., & Seixas, J. (eds.): *Climate Change, Adaptation, Resilience and Hazards,* pp. 125–141. Springer, Heidelberg.

Lindenberger, D., Lutz, C. & Schlesinger, M. (2010): Szenarien für ein Energiekonzept der Bundesregierung. *Energiewirtschaftliche Tagesfragen,* 60–11, 32–35.

Lutz, C. (2011): Energy Scenarios for Germany: Simulations with the model PANTA RHEI, 19th INFORUM World Conference, South Africa. URL: www.gws-os.com/discussionpapers/documentation/PantaRhei_19thInforumConferencePublication.pdf

Lutz, C. & Breitschopf, B. (2016): Systematisierung der gesamtwirtschaftlichen Effekte und Verteilungswirkungen der Energiewende. GWS Research Report 2016/1, Osnabrück.

Lutz, C., Tode, C., Lindenberger, D. & Schlesinger, M. (2014): Energy Reference Forecast and Energy Policy Targets for Germany. *Die Unternehmung,* 3, 154–163.

Maier, T., Mönnig, A., Zika, G. (2015): Labour demand in Germany by industrial sector, occupational field and qualification until 2025 – Model calculations using the IAB/INFORGE model. *Economic Systems Research,* 27, 19–42.

Máñez Costa, M., Rechid, D., Bieritz, L., Lutz, C., Nieters, A., Stöver, B., Jahn, M., Rische, M.-C., Schulze, S., Yadegar, E., Hirschfeld, J., Schröder, A., Hirte, G., Langer, S. & Tscharaktschiew, S. (2016): Synthesis of Existing Regional and Sectoral Economic Modelling and Its Possible Integration with Regional Earth System Models in the Context of Climate Modelling, Report 27, Climate Service Center, Hamburg.

Mercure, J. F., Knobloch, F., Pollitt, H., Lewney, R., Rademakers, K., Eichler, L., van der Laan, J. & Paroussos, L. (2016): *Policy-Induced Energy Technological Innovation and Finance for Low Carbon Economic Growth.* European Commission, Brussels.

Meyer, B., Meyer, M. & Distelkamp, M. (2012): Modeling Green Growth and Resource Efficiency: New Results. *Mineral Economics,* 24–2, 145–154.

Nitsch, J., Pregger, T., Naegler, T., Gerhardt, N. & Wenzel, B. (2012): Langfristszenarien und Strategien für den Ausbau der erneuerbaren Energien in Deutschland. DLR Stuttgart, Fraunhofer-IWES, Kassel, IfnE Teltow; Studie im Auftrag des BMU, März.

Pollitt, H. (2014): *E3ME Technical Manual,* Version 6. Cambridge Econometrics, Cambridge.

Pollitt, H., Alexandri, E., Anagnostopoulos, F., De Rose, A., Farhangi, C., Hoste, T., Markkanen, S., Theillard, P., Vergez, C. & Boogt, M. (2017): The Macro-Level and Sectoral Impacts of Energy Efficiency Policies, Final Report, European Union, July.

West, G. R. (1996): Comparison of Input-Output, IO-Econometric and CGE Impact Models at the Regional Level. *Economic Systems Research,* 7, 209–227.

WTO (2017): Data on Exports by Region. Updated Yearly in October. URL: www.wto.org/english/res_e/statis_e/merch_trade_stat_e.htm

34

Index decomposition analysis
Models and applications

Tian Goh and B. W. Ang

1 Introduction

In the face of greater oil price volatility, increasing pressures to address climate change and the growing global demand for energy, an understanding of the factors that contribute to changes in energy consumption has become a key priority for energy policymakers. Energy policies are now required to fulfill the twin goals of energy security and climate mitigation. A credible, robust, and transparent energy accounting system is thus necessary to help governments and international organizations track changes in energy consumption and gain a better understanding of the energy system. Index decomposition analysis (IDA)[1] is one such tool given that it quantifies the factors driving energy consumption. In other words, IDA breaks down the change in energy consumption into contributions from predefined factors such as population growth, economic development, economic structural changes, and improvements to energy efficiency. Based on these results, policymakers can understand major trends driving energy demand, quantify energy savings from energy efficiency, and project future energy demand, allowing for the integrated assessment of energy, environment and economic concerns.

This chapter introduces IDA with a focus on its latest developments in energy and emission analyses. Discussions in the earlier publications are consolidated and new methodological advancements and application areas are introduced.[2] The chapter begins with an overview of the key developments in IDA since the late 1970s, when the approach was first developed. More popular IDA methods, including their formulae, are then presented. A specific application area, energy-related CO_2 emission studies, is introduced and a case study is presented to show how IDA can be applied in practice to CO_2 emissions accounting. Key application areas are further discussed and finally a summary of the methodological issues that have emerged in recent years is presented.

2 Key developments in IDA

Following the world oil crisis in 1973 and 1974, energy security and energy costs became key national issues in many oil importing countries. Policymakers and analysts sought to understand the factors shaping changes in energy consumption and energy efficiency. IDA was developed as a tool in the late 1970s to quantify these factors for the industry sector. Since the 1980s, it has been widely applied to industrial energy demand analysis where effects such as structural change and energy intensity are quantified. It was later extended to other energy-consuming sectors such as transportation, residential and service, and to economy-wide studies which cover all energy end-use sectors.

The first studies analyzed the contribution of each factor to the total change in energy consumption over a particular time period. A typical decomposition analysis took the following form. First, a reference year (or base year) is defined. Next, the hypothetical energy consumption values in a target year had all the other factors, besides the factor of interest, remained unchanged in comparison to the reference year, is computed. The difference between the hypothetical energy consumption level and the actual energy consumption level is then assigned as the contribution of the factor to the overall change in energy consumption. It was later discovered that this approach is very similar to the Laspeyres index. In fact, although IDA was developed independent of index number theory, it later emerged that the method is similar to index number problems in economics (Boyd et al., 1988). However, unlike the conventional index number problems which deal primarily with two factors, namely quantity and price, IDA often involves more than two factors. Studies that involve more than five factors are relatively common in recent years.

In the 1990s, researchers as well as national and international agencies began adopting IDA for energy policy analysis. The wide variety of decomposition methods available made the choice of method arbitrary. Hence, researchers sought to compare these methods and consolidated them under a unified decomposition framework with the development of two general parametric Divisia index methods in 1992 (Liu et al., 1992). By treating the weights as variables, the two general methods were capable of representing an infinite number of decomposition models. The Laspeyres index approach and Divisia index approach, which most existing IDA methods are associated with, could thus be classified under this framework as two special cases.

The quest to improve IDA as an analytical tool was further energized by the development of the first perfect decomposition method, which is independent of the number of factors included in the formulation, in 1997 (Ang & Choi, 1997). This method later came to be known as the logarithmic mean Divisia index II (LMDI-II).[3] Based on the terminology in index number theory, IDA methods that are perfect (or complete) in decomposition pass the factor-reversal test. A simpler method based on the Divisia index which also passes this test was developed later, and named LMDI-I. The desire to achieve perfect decomposition arose from the difficulty policymakers faced in interpreting the decomposition results when an unexplainable residual term could not be allocated to any factor. Subsequently, Sun (1998) developed a perfect decomposition method based on the additive Laspeyres index which was later found to be similar to the Shapley value in concept (Ang et al., 2003). This was later termed the Shapley/Sun method or the refined Laspeyres method. A third method that is perfect in decomposition was developed in 2002: the generalized Fisher ideal index method (Ang et al., 2004). It is an extension of the two-factor Fisher ideal index number. Researchers and analysts have placed considerable emphasis on the property of perfect decomposition. In recent years, only IDA methods that satisfy this property are normally used.

With a set of unique features of its own and the similarity to index number problems, the approach was named "index decomposition analysis" in 2000 (Ang & Zhang, 2000). IDA has since been widely accepted as what had earlier been known as decomposition analysis or factorization analysis. Growing international concern regarding climate change peaked in the 21st century. This encouraged rapid growth in the use of IDA to study drivers of energy consumption, energy efficiency and CO_2 emissions. IDA emerged as a well-established energy accounting tool, with LMDI as the most popular method for the analysis. In 2004, a study classified the IDA methods and recommended LMDI as the method of choice (Ang, 2004b). Since then, there has been an exponential growth in the use of IDA and LMDI in energy and emission studies (Ang, 2015). In recent years, interest in the use of IDA has been catalyzed by the signing of the Paris Climate Agreement in 2015 and the need for countries to assess their performance towards their emission reduction targets. The use of IDA has since expanded to include emissions accounting, multi-level and spatial comparisons, prospective analyses, and application areas other than energy and emissions.

3   IDA methods

3.1   Basic identities

An IDA study begins by defining factors that contribute to changes in an aggregate indicator of interest such as energy consumption or energy intensity. The relationship between the indicator and the factors is captured in a formula known as the IDA identity. IDA methods can be classified into dimensions based on (1) type of indicator, either quantity or intensity indicator, (2) decomposition method, (3) decomposition procedure, either additive or multiplicative, and (4) decomposition identity.

Quantity indicators refer to energy consumption or emissions, while intensity indicators refer to a ratio of the quantity with respect to another quantity of interest, such as energy per GDP, otherwise known as energy intensity. After choosing the indicator, one needs to select a decomposition method. Decomposition methods can be classified into two major groups: methods linked to the Laspeyres index and methods linked to the Divisia index. This classification is shown in Figure 34.1. Finally, the decomposition can be conducted additively or multiplicatively. For additive decomposition, the total change in an indicator is the sum of the contribution of each factor, while for multiplicative decomposition, the total change is a product of the contribution of each factor.

The simplest IDA identity is the two-factor identity. It is used in a decomposition of energy intensity. This is also the form used in most studies in the late 1970s and early 1980s. The industry sector is used as an example with energy consumption measured in an energy unit and industrial output measured in a monetary unit. Let the total energy consumption in the industry sector of a country be the sum of the consumption from n industry sub-sectors and define the following variables for time t.

E = Total energy consumption the industry sector
$E_{i,t}$ = Energy consumption in sub-sector i
Y_t = Total industrial output
$Y_{i,t}$ = Total industrial output of sub-sector i
$S_{i,t}$ = Share of output of sub-sector i
$I_{i,t}$ = Energy intensity of sub-sector i
I_t = Energy intensity of the industry sector.

The aggregate energy intensity is then given by

$$I_t = \frac{E_t}{Y_t} = \sum_i \frac{Y_{i,t}}{Y_t} \frac{E_{i,t}}{Y_{i,t}} = \sum_i S_{i,t} I_{i,t}$$

$$(34.1)$$

The summation is taken over n sub-sectors. We can see from Equation (34.1) that energy intensity is expressed in terms of share of sub-sector output and sub-sector energy intensity.

A change in energy intensity between year 0, the reference year, and year T, the target year, can then be expressed as a ratio (i.e. $D_{tot} = I_T/I_0$) or a difference (i.e. $\Delta I_{tot} = I_T - I_0$); they correspond to multiplicative and additive decomposition respectively and can be expressed as a product of the structural and intensity effects:

$$D_{tot} = D_{str}D_{int}$$

(34.2)

or as a sum of the structural and intensity effects:

$$\Delta I_{tot} = \Delta I_{str} + \Delta I_{int}$$

(34.3)

In the multiplicative procedure, all terms are given in indices while in the additive procedure, all terms have the same unit of measure as the aggregate indicator (i.e. energy intensity). If there is no contribution from an effect, the effect obtained via multiplicative decomposition will be unity while the effect obtained via additive decomposition will be zero. The structural effect represents the contribution of changes in industrial structure to the change in total energy intensity, while the energy intensity effect represents the contribution of changes in sub-sectoral energy intensity to the total change in energy intensity. The decomposition is thus able to separate changes in industrial structure from changes in energy intensity. Hence, it provides a more accurate quantification of changes in industrial energy efficiency.

If one wishes to examine changes in energy consumption (quantity indicator) instead, the identity can be transformed to a three-factor identity:

$$E_t = \sum_i Y_t \frac{Y_{i,t}}{Y_t} \frac{E_{i,t}}{Y_{i,t}} = \sum_i Y_t S_{i,t} I_{i,t}$$

(34.4)

In this case, the multiplicative decomposition is a product of three factors, the activity effect, the structural effect and the intensity effect:

$$D_{tot} = D_{act}D_{str}D_{int}$$

(34.5)

while the additive decomposition is a sum of the three factors:

$$\Delta E_{tot} = \Delta E_{act} + \Delta E_{str} + \Delta E_{int}$$

(34.6)

3.2   IDA formulae

As shown in Figure 34.1, decomposition methods can be classified into two groups, methods linked to the Laspeyres index and methods linked to the Divisia index. A list of the methods in each group are shown in the figure. The Laspeyres, Paasche, Marshall-Edgeworth, Generalized

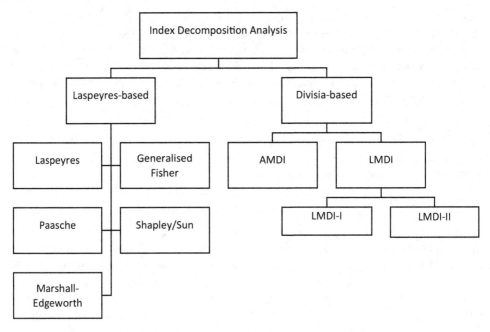

Figure 34.1   Summary of index decomposition methods

Fisher and Shapley/Sun methods are those linked to the Laspeyres index, while the arithmetic mean Divisia index (AMDI), LMDI-I and LMDI-II are methods linked to the Divisia index. The formulae for the decomposition problems presented in Section 3.1 are shown in Table 34.1.[4] Each of these methods possesses certain unique properties.[5]

The Laspeyres index method was the first method to be used in the 1980s. It is intuitive, easy to use and easy to interpret. However, it is not perfect in decomposition; it leaves an unexplainable residual term that cannot be allocated to any predefined factors. At times, the residual is large and complicates the interpretation of results. The Laspeyres index is also not symmetric as the weights are assigned to the reference year. In the Paasche index, on the other hand, the weights are assigned to the target year. It is intuitive and easy to use, and shares most of the properties of the Laspeyres index.

The Marshall-Edgeworth index method, which contains two factors, improved on this shortcoming by allocating the weights equally between the reference and target year. The arithmetic average of the factor in the reference year and target year is used. While the additive Marshall-Edgeworth method is based on the arithmetic mean of the Laspeyres and Paasche indices, the Fisher ideal index method is based on the geometric mean of the two indices and can only be used in the multiplicative form. The Marshall-Edgeworth index can be used in the additive and multiplicative forms. Although the Marshall-Edgeworth method and Fisher ideal method are symmetric and perfect in decomposition, they are by definition, methods with only two factors. This limits their applicability to decompositions with multiple factors.

Further improvements were made to the methods linked to the Laspeyres index, culminating in the development of two methods which are perfect in decomposition and can handle multiple factors. The additive method is the Shapley/Sun method while the multiplicative method is the generalized Fisher ideal index method. The Shapley/Sun method distributes the residual term to

Table 34.1 Formulae of commonly used IDA methods

Method		Formulae for energy consumption		Formulae for energy intensity	
		Additive $\Delta E_{tot} = \Delta E_{act} + \Delta E_{str} + \Delta E_{int}$	Multiplicative $D_{tot} = D_{act} D_{str} D_{int}$	Additive $\Delta I_{tot} = \Delta I_{str} + \Delta I_{int}$	Multiplicative $D_{tot} = D_{str} D_{int}$
Laspeyres	Activity	$\sum_i Y_T S_{i,0} I_{i,0} - E_0$	$\left(\sum_i Y_T S_{i,0} I_{i,0}\right)/E_0$	N.A.	N.A.
	Structure	$\sum_i Y_0 S_{i,T} I_{i,0} - E_0$	$\left(\sum_i Y_0 S_{i,T} I_{i,0}\right)/E_0$	$\sum_i S_{i,T} I_{i,0}^* - I_0$	$\left(\sum_i S_{i,T} I_{i,0}\right)/I_0$
	Intensity	$\sum_i Y_0 S_{i,0} I_{i,T} - E_0$	$\left(\sum_i Y_0 S_{i,0} I_{i,T}\right)/E_0$	$\sum_i S_{i,0} I_{i,T} - I_0$	$\left(\sum_i S_{i,0} I_{i,T}\right)/I_0$
Paasche	Activity	$E_T - \sum_i Y_0 S_{i,T} I_{i,T}$	$E_T /\left(\sum_i Y_0 S_{i,T} I_{i,T}\right)$	N.A.	N.A.
	Structure	$E_T - \sum_i Y_T S_{i,0} I_{i,T}$	$E_T /\left(\sum_i Y_0 S_{i,0} I_{i,T}\right)$	$I_T - \sum_i S_{i,0} I_{i,T}$	$I_T /\left(\sum_i S_{i,0} I_{i,T}\right)$
	Intensity	$E_T - \sum_i Y_T S_{i,T} I_{i,0}$	$E_T /\left(\sum_i Y_0 S_{i,T} I_{i,0}\right)$	$I_T - \sum_i S_{i,T} I_{i,0}$	$I_T /\left(\sum_i S_{i,T} I_{i,0}\right)$
Marshall-Edgeworth	Activity	N.A.		N.A.	N.A.
	Structure	N.A.	N.A.	$\left(\Delta I_{str}^L + \Delta I_{str}^P\right)/2$	$\dfrac{\sum_i (S_{i,T} I_{i,0} + S_{i,T} I_{i,T})}{\sum_i (S_{i,0} I_{i,0} + S_{i,0} I_{i,T})}$
	Intensity	N.A.	N.A.	$\left(\Delta I_{int}^L + \Delta I_{int}^P\right)/2$	$\dfrac{\sum_i (S_{i,0} I_{i,T} + S_{i,T} I_{i,T})}{\sum_i (S_{i,0} I_{i,0} + S_{i,T} I_{i,0})}$
Shapley / Sun	Activity	$\Delta E_{act}^L + \frac{1}{2}\sum_i \Delta Y\left(\Delta S_i I_{i,0} + S_{i,0}\Delta I_i\right) + \frac{1}{3}\sum_i \Delta Y \Delta S_i \Delta I_i$	N.A.	N.A.	N.A.
	Structure	$\Delta E_{str}^L + \frac{1}{2}\sum_i \Delta S_i\left(\Delta Y I_{i,0} + E_0\Delta I_i\right) + \frac{1}{3}\sum_i \Delta Y \Delta S_i \Delta I_i$	N.A.	$\left(\Delta I_{str}^L + \Delta I_{str}^P\right)/2$	N.A.
	Intensity	$\Delta E_{int}^L + \frac{1}{2}\sum_i \Delta I_i\left(\Delta Y S_{i,0} + E_0\Delta S_i\right) + \frac{1}{3}\sum_i \Delta Y \Delta S_i \Delta I_i$	N.A.	$\left(\Delta I_{int}^L + \Delta I_{int}^P\right)/2$	N.A.
Generalized Fisher	Activity	N.A.	$\left(D_{act}^L D_{act}^P\right)^{1/3}\left(\dfrac{\sum_i Y_T S_{i,0} I_{i,T}\sum_i Y_T S_{i,T} I_{i,0}}{\sum_i Y_0 S_{i,0} I_{i,T}\sum_i Y_0 S_{i,T} I_{i,0}}\right)^{1/6}$	N.A.	N.A.

(Continued)

Table 34.1 (Continued)

Method		Formulae for energy consumption	Formulae for energy intensity	
	Structure	N.A.	$\left(D_{str}^L D_{str}^P\right)^{1/3}\left[\dfrac{\sum_i Y_0 S_{i,T} I_{i,T}}{\sum_i Y_0 S_{i,0} I_{i,T}}\dfrac{\sum_i Y_T S_{i,T} I_{i,0}}{\sum_i Y_T S_{i,0} I_{i,0}}\right]^{1/6}$	$\sqrt{D_{str}^L D_{str}^P}$
	Intensity	N.A.	$\left(D_{int}^L D_{int}^P\right)^{1/3}\left[\dfrac{\sum_i Y_0 S_{i,T} I_{i,T}}{\sum_i Y_T S_{i,0} I_{i,T}}\dfrac{\sum_i Y_T S_{i,0} I_{i,T}}{\sum_i Y_T S_{i,0} I_{i,0}}\right]^{1/6}$	$\sqrt{D_{int}^L D_{int}^P}$
LMDI-I	Activity	$\sum_i L\!\left(E_{i,T},E_{i,0}\right)\ln\!\left(\dfrac{Y_T}{Y_0}\right)$	N.A.	N.A.
	Structure	$\sum_i L\!\left(E_{i,T},E_{i,0}\right)\ln\!\left(\dfrac{S_{i,T}}{S_{i,0}}\right)$	$\exp\left[\sum_i \dfrac{L\!\left(E_{i,T},E_{i,0}\right)}{L\!\left(E_T,E_0\right)}\ln\!\left(\dfrac{S_{i,T}}{S_{i,0}}\right)\right]$	$\exp\left[\sum_i \dfrac{L\!\left(\frac{E_{i,T}}{Y_T},\frac{E_{i,0}}{Y_0}\right)}{L\!\left(I_T,I_0\right)}\ln\!\left(\dfrac{S_{i,T}}{S_{i,0}}\right)\right]$
	Intensity	$\sum_i L\!\left(E_{i,T},E_{i,0}\right)\ln\!\left(\dfrac{I_{i,T}}{I_{i,0}}\right)$	$\exp\left[\sum_i \dfrac{L\!\left(E_{i,T},E_{i,0}\right)}{L\!\left(E_T,E_0\right)}\ln\!\left(\dfrac{I_{i,T}}{I_{i,0}}\right)\right]$	$\exp\left[\sum_i \dfrac{L\!\left(\frac{E_{i,T}}{Y_T},\frac{E_{i,0}}{Y_0}\right)}{L\!\left(I_T,I_0\right)}\ln\!\left(\dfrac{I_{i,T}}{I_{i,0}}\right)\right]$
LMDI-II	Activity	$\sum_i \dfrac{L\!\left(\frac{E_{i,T}}{E_T},\frac{E_{i,0}}{E_0}\right)}{\sum_i L\!\left(\frac{E_{i,T}}{E_T},\frac{E_{i,0}}{E_0}\right)}L\!\left(E_T,E_0\right)\ln\!\left(\dfrac{Y_T}{Y_0}\right)$	N.A.	N.A.
	Structure	$\sum_i \dfrac{L\!\left(\frac{E_{i,T}}{E_T},\frac{E_{i,0}}{E_0}\right)}{\sum_i L\!\left(\frac{E_{i,T}}{E_T},\frac{E_{i,0}}{E_0}\right)}L\!\left(E_T,E_0\right)\ln\!\left(\dfrac{S_{i,T}}{S_{i,0}}\right)$	$\exp\left[\sum_i \dfrac{L\!\left(\frac{E_{i,T}}{E_T},\frac{E_{i,0}}{E_0}\right)}{\sum_i L\!\left(\frac{E_{i,T}}{E_T},\frac{E_{i,0}}{E_0}\right)}L\!\left(I_T,I_0\right)\ln\!\left(\dfrac{S_{i,T}}{S_{i,0}}\right)\right]$	$\exp\left[\sum_i \dfrac{L\!\left(\frac{E_{i,T}}{E_T},\frac{E_{i,0}}{E_0}\right)}{\sum_i L\!\left(\frac{E_{i,T}}{E_T},\frac{E_{i,0}}{E_0}\right)}\ln\!\left(\dfrac{S_{i,T}}{S_{i,0}}\right)\right]$
	Intensity	$\sum_i \dfrac{L\!\left(\frac{E_{i,T}}{E_T},\frac{E_{i,0}}{E_0}\right)}{\sum_i L\!\left(\frac{E_{i,T}}{E_T},\frac{E_{i,0}}{E_0}\right)}L\!\left(I_T,I_0\right)\ln\!\left(\dfrac{I_{i,T}}{I_{i,0}}\right)$	$\exp\left[\sum_i \dfrac{L\!\left(\frac{E_{i,T}}{E_T},\frac{E_{i,0}}{E_0}\right)}{\sum_i L\!\left(\frac{E_{i,T}}{E_T},\frac{E_{i,0}}{E_0}\right)}L\!\left(I_T,I_0\right)\ln\!\left(\dfrac{I_{i,T}}{I_{i,0}}\right)\right]$	$\exp\left[\sum_i \dfrac{L\!\left(\frac{E_{i,T}}{E_T},\frac{E_{i,0}}{E_0}\right)}{\sum_i L\!\left(\frac{E_{i,T}}{E_T},\frac{E_{i,0}}{E_0}\right)}\ln\!\left(\dfrac{I_{i,T}}{I_{i,0}}\right)\right]$

Note: $L(x,y)$ is the logarithmic mean of two positive numbers x and y, and is given by $L(x,y) = \dfrac{x-y}{\ln x - \ln y}$, for $x \neq y$, $L(x,y) = x$ for $x = y$.

the predefined factors based on the principle of "jointly created and equally distributed" (Sun, 1998). This means that in a two-factor decomposition half the residual is allocated to each factor while in a three-factor decomposition, the residual generated by altering two factors is allocated in two equal parts while the residual generated by three factors is allocated in three equal parts. Based on this logic, it can be observed that the number of terms needed to allocate the residual increases exponentially with the number of factors in the identity. On the other hand, the generalized Fisher ideal index method utilizes the geometric average of all combinations of the Laspeyres and Paasche indices and is perfect in decomposition. However, it suffers from the same problem as the Shapley/Sun method, where the number of terms required to allocate the residual increases exponentially. When only two factors are used, the Shapley/Sun method is equivalent to the Marshall-Edgeworth method, while the generalized Fisher ideal index method is equivalent to the Fisher ideal index method.

Another class of methods are based on the Divisia index. The first method that is perfect in decomposition emerged from this class; LMDI is based on logarithmic change and its weight function is based on the logarithmic mean. In comparison to other perfect decomposition methods, LMDI is simpler as the formulae does not increase in complexity as the number of factors increases. It is also symmetric. Additionally, the multiplicative and additive decomposition results are linked by a simple formula, meaning that the choice of decomposition procedure is inconsequential. No such relationship was found for the methods linked to the Laspeyres index. Ang (2015) provides detailed discussions of the origin, development, and properties of various LMDI methods.

The first LMDI method that was developed is LMDI-II. It uses a more complicated weighting function compared to LMDI-I, which was developed later. The weights in LMDI-II in the multiplicative form sum to unity. This enables it to give consistent results regardless of whether the quantity or intensity indicator is selected for the decomposition. However, it is neither consistent in aggregation nor perfect in decomposition at the subcategory level. Consistency in aggregation allows for the aggregation of results in a subcategory to obtain results at the category level. These properties are important in multilevel analysis where aggregation from the sub-sectoral to the sectoral level is necessary and the decomposition results at the sub-sectoral level are of interest. In addition, by applying the principle of "proportionally distributed by sub-category" to achieve perfect decomposition at the subcategory level, methods linked to the Divisia index collapse to LMDI-I. Due to these desirable properties, Ang (2004b, 2015) recommends the use of LMDI-I. There are however specific situations where LMDI-II may be preferred to LMDI-I, such as in multiplicative decomposition analysis where the aggregate is an intensity indicator.

4 Decomposing CO_2 emissions from electricity generation

4.1 Basic IDA identities

While IDA was initially developed as an energy accounting tool, it can be extended to other application areas. One simple extension is to energy-related CO_2 emission studies. Interest in analysing CO_2 emissions has grown in tandem with mounting international pressure to address climate change. Emissions accounting can help policymakers to track progress in climate mitigation and quantify the drivers of changes in CO_2 emissions. Ang (2015) points out that since 2000 there have been more IDA studies on CO_2 emissions than on energy consumption. This section provides details on how this extension can be made and illustrates this with a case study based on the electricity generation sector.[6]

An extension to CO_2 emissions studies requires the breaking down of energy consumption into various fossil fuel types. This allows one to consider the different fossil fuel emission factors associated with each fuel type. In addition, non-fossil-based energy sources are also included in the decomposition identity to take into account the contribution of renewables and nuclear energy. Let the total CO_2 emissions from electricity generation in a country be the sum of the emissions from n fossil fuels and define the following variables for time t.

C = Total CO_2 emissions from electricity generation
$C_{i,t}$ = CO_2 emissions from fossil fuel i
G_t = Total electricity output
Q_t = Total electricity output from fossil fuels
$Q_{i,t}$ = Total electricity output from fossil fuel i
$F_{i,t}$ = Total energy input from fossil fuel i
P_t = Share of fossil fuels in total electricity output given by Q_t / G_t
$m_{i,t}$ = Share of fossil fuel i in total electricity output from fossil fuels given by $Q_{i,t} / Q_t$
$u_{i,t}$ = Power generation efficiency of fossil fuel i given by $F_{i,t} / Q_{i,t}$
$e_{i,t}$ = Emission factor of fossil fuel i given by $C_{i,t} / F_{i,t}$.

The basic identity for CO_2 emissions from electricity generation is then given by

$$C_t = \sum_i G_t \frac{Q_t}{G_t} \frac{Q_{i,t}}{Q_t} \frac{F_{i,t}}{Q_{i,t}} \frac{C_{i,t}}{F_{i,t}} = \sum_i G_t p_t m_{i,t} u_{i,t} e_{i,t} \tag{34.7}$$

The summation is taken over n fossil fuels used. As with energy consumption, a change in CO_2 emissions between year 0, the reference year, and year T, the target year, can then be expressed as a ratio (i.e. $D_{tot} = C_T / C_0$) or a difference (i.e. $\Delta I_{tot} = C_T - C_0$). They correspond to multiplicative and additive decomposition respectively and can be expressed as a product of the activity effect, fossil share effect, fossil fuel mix effect, power generation efficiency effect and emission factor, as

$$D_{tot} = D_{act} D_{shr} D_{mix} D_{eff} D_{emf} \tag{34.8}$$

or as a sum of the effects as

$$\Delta C_{tot} = \Delta C_{act} + \Delta C_{shr} + \Delta C_{mix} + \Delta C_{eff} + \Delta C_{emf} \tag{34.9}$$

Another way of analysing the performance of the electricity generation sector is to compare the change in the "aggregate carbon intensity" (ACI) of electricity. The ACI is defined as the average level of CO_2 emissions per unit of electricity produced in a country and is measured as an aggregate at that level (Ang et al., 2011). It is normally expressed in kilograms of CO_2 emissions per kilowatt-hours (kgCO$_2$/kWh). It is a better measure of performance compared to CO_2 emissions as it eliminates the activity effect. The identity for the ACI is

$$V_t = \sum_i \frac{Q_t}{G_t} \frac{Q_{i,t}}{Q_t} \frac{F_{i,t}}{Q_{i,t}} \frac{C_{i,t}}{F_{i,t}} = \sum_i p_t m_{i,t} u_{i,t} e_{i,t} \tag{34.10}$$

Much like its counterpart, the energy intensity, its corresponding multiplicative and additive decomposition formulae do not include the activity effect. They are shown below.

$$D_{tot} = D_{shr} D_{mix} D_{eff} D_{emf}$$

(34.11)

$$\Delta V_{tot} = \Delta V_{shr} + \Delta V_{mix} + \Delta V_{eff} + \Delta V_{emf}$$

(34.12)

4.2 A case study

A case study comparing the performance of OECD countries and non-OECD countries between 1990 and 2014 is presented.[7] Given their popularity, LMDI-I and LMDI-II are used in this case study for illustration purposes. The formulae used are summarized in Table 34.2. Additive and multiplicative LMDI-I are used to decompose changes in CO_2 emissions, the quantity indicator, while additive LMDI-I and multiplicative LMDI-II are used to decompose changes in the ACI, the intensity indicator. LMDI-I is preferred for its simpler formulae while multiplicative LMDI-II produces the same results regardless of whether one decomposes a quantity or intensity indicator (Ang, 2015). Other methods can also be used for the decomposition. Considerations relating to the choice of method are discussed in Section 6.1.

Global CO_2 emissions from electricity generation increased from 6.44 gigatonnes (Gt) of CO_2 in 1990 to 12.20 GtCO_2 in 2014, nearly doubling in value. Due to economic development and greater electrification, non-OECD countries saw a larger increase compared to OECD countries. CO_2 emissions from electricity generation increased by 194% in non-OECD countries compared to 16% in OECD countries. Non-OECD countries also overtook OECD countries in total CO_2 emissions and accounted for a larger share of global CO_2 emissions from electricity generation in 2014 compared to OECD countries. In terms of ACI, both OECD and non-OECD countries saw a decrease between 1990 and 2014, from 0.497 to 0.409 kgCO_2/kWh for OECD countries, and from 0.631 to 0.598 kgCO_2/kWh for non-OECD countries. A clearer picture of the contribution of each factor to these changes can be obtained via decomposition analysis. The data used for decomposition is provided in Table 34.3.

First, we begin with a simple decomposition of CO_2 emissions using the additive LMDI-I. This is the most popular approach as the contribution of each effect to the total change is given in the same units as the indicator, making results interpretation straightforward. The decomposition results are shown in Table 34.4a and Figure 34.2. An increase in electricity consumption worldwide, which is reflected in the activity effect, was the main driver of CO_2 emissions in both OECD and non-OECD countries. In contrast, power generation efficiency consistently led to a reduction in CO_2 emissions. On the other hand, the fossil share effect and fossil fuel mix effect led to increases in CO_2 emissions in non-OECD countries but had the inverse effect in OECD countries. This represents a shift away from cleaner energy sources in non-OECD countries. Specifically, the share of non-fossil based energy sources (fossil share effect) decreased and the usage of coal (fossil fuel mix effect) increased in non-OECD countries. For OECD countries, the fossil share effect did not contribute significantly to the reduction in emissions, highlighting the lack of progress in a shift to non-fossil based energy since 1990. The reduction in CO_2 emissions was driven by a shift to natural gas (fossil fuel mix effect) and improvements to power generation efficiency of coal and natural gas plants. Lastly, the emission factor effect is zero as this study uses constant emission factors.[8]

By quantifying the contribution of each factor to the total change in emissions, one can get a better picture of the factors driving CO_2 emissions and make more informed policy decisions on actions that can be taken at the national and international levels. For instance, the lacklustre

Table 34.2 Summary of formulae used for LMDI-I and LMDI-II

Indicator	Effect	LMDI-I		LMDI-II
		Additive	Multiplicative	Multiplicative
		$\Delta C_{tot} = \Delta C_{act} + \Delta C_{shr}$ $+ \Delta C_{mix} + \Delta C_{eff} + \Delta C_{emf}$	$D_{tot} = D_{act} D_{shr} D_{mix} D_{eff} D_{emf}$	$D_{tot} = D_{act} D_{shr} D_{mix} D_{eff} D_{emf}$
CO_2 emissions	Activity	$\sum_i L(C_i^T, C_i^0) \ln\left(\dfrac{G^T}{G^0}\right)$	$\exp\left[\sum_i \dfrac{L(C_i^T, C_i^0)}{L(C^T, C^0)} \ln\left(\dfrac{G^T}{G^0}\right)\right]$	$\dfrac{G_T}{G_0}$
	Fossil share	$\sum_i L(C_i^T, C_i^0) \ln\left(\dfrac{p^T}{p^0}\right)$	$\exp\left[\sum_i \dfrac{L(C_i^T, C_i^0)}{L(C^T, C^0)} \ln\left(\dfrac{p^T}{p^0}\right)\right]$	$\dfrac{p_T}{p_0}$
	Fossil Mix	$\sum_i L(C_i^T, C_i^0) \ln\left(\dfrac{m_i^T}{m_i^0}\right)$	$\exp\left[\sum_i \dfrac{L(C_i^T, C_i^0)}{L(C^T, C^0)} \ln\left(\dfrac{m_i^T}{m_i^0}\right)\right]$	$\exp\left[\sum_i \dfrac{L\left(\frac{C_i^T}{C^T}, \frac{C_i^0}{C^0}\right)}{\sum_i L\left(\frac{C_i^T}{C^T}, \frac{C_i^0}{C^0}\right)} \ln\left(\dfrac{m_i^T}{m_i^0}\right)\right]$
	Generation Efficiency	$\sum_i L(C_i^T, C_i^0) \ln\left(\dfrac{u_i^T}{u_i^0}\right)$	$\exp\left[\sum_i \dfrac{L(C_i^T, C_i^0)}{L(C^T, C^0)} \ln\left(\dfrac{u_i^T}{u_i^0}\right)\right]$	$\exp\left[\sum_i \dfrac{L\left(\frac{C_i^T}{C^T}, \frac{C_i^0}{C^0}\right)}{\sum_i L\left(\frac{C_i^T}{C^T}, \frac{C_i^0}{C^0}\right)} \ln\left(\dfrac{u_i^T}{u_i^0}\right)\right]$
	Emission factor	$\sum_i L(C_i^T, C_i^0) \ln\left(\dfrac{e_i^T}{e_i^0}\right)$	$\exp\left[\sum_i \dfrac{L(C_i^T, C_i^0)}{L(C^T, C^0)} \ln\left(\dfrac{e_i^T}{e_i^0}\right)\right]$	$\exp\left[\sum_i \dfrac{L\left(\frac{C_i^T}{C^T}, \frac{C_i^0}{C^0}\right)}{\sum_i L\left(\frac{C_i^T}{C^T}, \frac{C_i^0}{C^0}\right)} \ln\left(\dfrac{e_i^T}{e_i^0}\right)\right]$
ACI		$\Delta V_{tot} = \Delta V_{shr} + \Delta V_{mix}$ $+ \Delta V_{eff} + \Delta V_{emf}$	$D_{tot} = D_{shr} D_{mix} D_{eff} D_{emf}$	$D_{tot} = D_{shr} D_{mix} D_{eff} D_{emf}$
	Fossil share	$\sum_i L\left(\dfrac{C_i^T}{G^T}, \dfrac{C_i^0}{G^0}\right) \ln\left(\dfrac{p^T}{p^0}\right)$	$\exp\left[\sum_i \dfrac{L\left(\frac{C_i^T}{G^T}, \frac{C_i^0}{G^0}\right)}{L(C^T/G^T, C^0/G^0)} \ln\left(\dfrac{p^T}{p^0}\right)\right]$	$\dfrac{p_T}{p_0}$
	Fossil Mix	$\sum_i L\left(\dfrac{C_i^T}{G^T}, \dfrac{C_i^0}{G^0}\right) \ln\left(\dfrac{m_i^T}{m_i^0}\right)$	$\exp\left[\sum_i \dfrac{L\left(\frac{C_i^T}{G^T}, \frac{C_i^0}{G^0}\right)}{L(C^T/G^T, C^0/G^0)} \ln\left(\dfrac{m_i^T}{m_i^0}\right)\right]$	$\exp\left[\sum_i \dfrac{L\left(\frac{C_i^T}{C^T}, \frac{C_i^0}{C^0}\right)}{\sum_i L\left(\frac{C_i^T}{C^T}, \frac{C_i^0}{C^0}\right)} \ln\left(\dfrac{m_i^T}{m_i^0}\right)\right]$
	Generation Efficiency	$\sum_i L\left(\dfrac{C_i^T}{G^T}, \dfrac{C_i^0}{G^0}\right) \ln\left(\dfrac{u_i^T}{u_i^0}\right)$	$\exp\left[\sum_i \dfrac{L\left(\frac{C_i^T}{G^T}, \frac{C_i^0}{G^0}\right)}{L(C^T/G^T, C^0/G^0)} \ln\left(\dfrac{u_i^T}{u_i^0}\right)\right]$	$\exp\left[\sum_i \dfrac{L\left(\frac{C_i^T}{C^T}, \frac{C_i^0}{C^0}\right)}{\sum_i L\left(\frac{C_i^T}{C^T}, \frac{C_i^0}{C^0}\right)} \ln\left(\dfrac{u_i^T}{u_i^0}\right)\right]$
	Emission factor	$\sum_i L\left(\dfrac{C_i^T}{G^T}, \dfrac{C_i^0}{G^0}\right) \ln\left(\dfrac{e_i^T}{e_i^0}\right)$	$\exp\left[\sum_i \dfrac{L\left(\frac{C_i^T}{G^T}, \frac{C_i^0}{G^0}\right)}{L(C^T/G^T, C^0/G^0)} \ln\left(\dfrac{e_i^T}{e_i^0}\right)\right]$	$\exp\left[\sum_i \dfrac{L\left(\frac{C_i^T}{C^T}, \frac{C_i^0}{C^0}\right)}{\sum_i L\left(\frac{C_i^T}{C^T}, \frac{C_i^0}{C^0}\right)} \ln\left(\dfrac{e_i^T}{e_i^0}\right)\right]$

Table 34.3 Illustrative example based on OECD and non-OECD countries[1]

		1990					2014				
		Coal	Oil	Gas	Non-fossil	Total	Coal	Oil	Gas	Non-fossil	Total
OECD	Electricity output (TWh)	3,093	697	770	3,069	7,629	3,467	277	2,615	4,425	10,784
	CO_2 emissions (GtCO$_2$)	2.93	0.46	0.40	0	3.79	3.15	0.19	1.07	0	4.40
Non-OECD	Electricity output (TWh)	1,333	639	957	1,261	1,261	6,230	746	2,540	3,516	13,031
	CO_2 emissions (GtCO$_2$)	1.53	0.53	0.59	0	2.65	5.85	0.61	1.34	0	7.80

1 Data from IEA World Energy Balance Database.

Table 34.4a Additive decomposition results of change in CO_2 emissions (GtCO$_2$)

	Effect	ΔC_{tot}	ΔC_{act}	ΔC_{shr}	ΔC_{mix}	ΔC_{eff}	ΔC_{emf}
OECD	LMDI-I	0.61	1.39	−0.05	−0.44	−0.29	0.00
Non-OECD	LMDI-I	5.15	5.33	0.20	0.41	−0.79	0.00

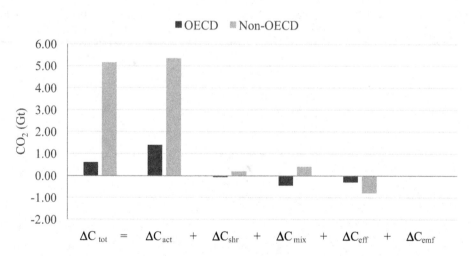

Figure 34.2 Decomposition results of change in CO_2 emissions from electricity generation from 1990 to 2014 in OECD and non-OECD countries based on additive LMDI-I

progress in enhancing the share of non-fossil-based energy points towards the need for drastic changes to market conditions, regulatory frameworks and political conditions to create a more conducive environment for the widespread deployment of renewables. In terms of climate mitigation, the decomposition results also show that improvements to power generation efficiency are the low-hanging fruit and should be strongly supported, especially in rapidly developing economies.

Multiplicative decomposition can also be used to identify drivers of CO_2 emissions. If an effect does not contribute to changes in CO_2 emissions, such as the constant emission factor in this example, it will be unity. A value above 1 represents a contribution to an increase in emissions while a value between 0 and 1 represents a contribution to a decrease in emissions. The results are shown in Table 34.4b and Figure 34.3. They are consistent with the findings from the additive decomposition. In fact, there is a simple relationship between additive and multiplicative decomposition. The relationship is as follows.

$$\frac{\Delta C_{tot}}{lnD_{tot}} = \frac{\Delta C_{act}}{lnD_{act}} = \frac{\Delta C_{shr}}{lnD_{shr}} = \frac{\Delta C_{mix}}{lnD_{mix}} = \frac{\Delta C_{eff}}{lnD_{eff}} = \frac{\Delta C_{emf}}{lnD_{emf}} \tag{34.13}$$

This is a unique property of LMDI and it makes the choice between additive and multiplicative decompositions inconsequential as one can be easily derived from the other.

The activity effect is often large, as can be observed in Figures 34.2 and 34.3, and it often overshadows the other factors. By using CO_2 emissions per unit of electricity produced (ACI)

Table 34.4b Multiplicative decomposition results of change in CO_2 emissions

	Effect	D_{tot}	D_{act}	D_{shr}	D_{mix}	D_{eff}	D_{emf}
OECD	LMDI-I	1.161	1.405	0.987	0.898	0.932	1.000
	LMDI-II	1.161	1.414	0.986	0.894	0.931	1.000
Non-OECD	LMDI-I	2.948	3.063	1.044	1.089	0.847	1.000
	LMDI-II	2.948	3.110	1.045	1.072	0.847	1.000

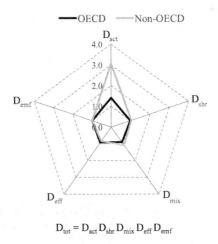

$$D_{tot} = D_{act} D_{shr} D_{mix} D_{eff} D_{emf}$$

Figure 34.3 Decomposition results of change in CO_2 emissions from electricity generation from 1990 to 2014 in OECD and non-OECD countries based on multiplicative LMDI-I

Table 34.5a Additive decomposition results of change in ACI (kgCO₂/kWh)

	Effect	ΔV_{tot}	ΔV_{shr}	ΔV_{mix}	ΔV_{eff}	ΔV_{emf}
OECD	LMDI-I	−0.089	−0.006	−0.052	−0.031	0.000
Non-OECD	LMDI-I	−0.033	0.026	0.041	−0.101	0.000

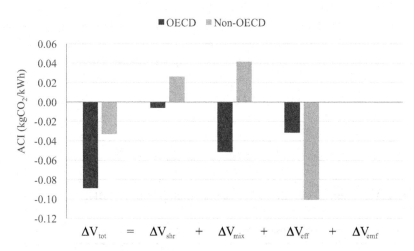

Figure 34.4 Decomposition results of change in ACI of electricity generation from 1990 to 2014 in OECD and non-OECD countries based on additive LMDI-I

as a measure of performance, the activity effect can be eliminated from the decomposition. We decompose changes in the ACI into contributing factors. Additive LMDI-I is used first. The results are shown in Table 34.5a and Figure 34.4. By eliminating the activity effect, the contributions of each factor become more pronounced. The unit of measure is kgCO₂/kWh, in contrast to Gt of CO₂ used previously. Power generation efficiency was the main contributor to the reduction in ACI in non-OECD countries while the fossil fuel mix effect was the main contributor in OECD countries due to a switch to natural gas. The fossil share effect led to a slight decrease in ACI in OECD countries and an increase in non-OECD countries. This underscores the need to address the underlying issues causing the difference in uptake of cleaner energy sources between developed and developing countries.

Multiplicative decomposition can also be used to decompose the ACI. As mentioned previously, there is a simple relationship between additive and multiplicative decompositions and hence the results for LMDI-I are trivial and will not be presented. Instead, the results for LMDI-II are presented (see Figure 34.5). Multiplicative LMDI-II is selected to highlight an important property – the decomposition results are independent of the choice of indicator. The results for LMDI-II in Tables 34.4b and 34.5b are the same for all effects, with the exception of the activity effect which does not exist when the ACI is decomposed. This property is unique to multiplicative LMDI-II and is due to the fact that its weights sum to unity and the change is measured as a ratio. However, ratio changes are often harder to interpret. There are also challenges in attributing the contribution of each factor to individual fuel types, unlike in additive decomposition, where the attribution to each fuel type can be derived directly from the decomposition.

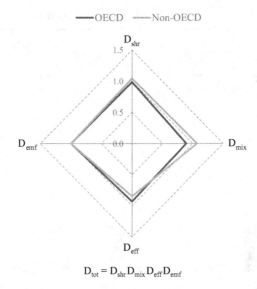

$$D_{tot} = D_{shr} D_{mix} D_{eff} D_{emf}$$

Figure 34.5 Decomposition results of change in ACI of electricity generation from 1990 to 2014 in OECD and non-OECD countries based on multiplicative LMDI-II

Table 34.5b Multiplicative decomposition results of change in ACI

	Effect	D_{tot}	D_{shr}	D_{mix}	D_{eff}	D_{emf}
OECD	LMDI-II	0.821	0.986	0.894	0.931	1.000
Non-OECD	LMDI-II	0.948	1.045	1.072	0.847	1.000

5   Application areas

Following the initial use of IDA to study industrial energy consumption trends, there has been a rapid growth in studies on energy consumption and energy efficiency, as well as the expansion of IDA's application areas. New areas include energy-related CO_2 emissions, cross-country comparisons, prospective analyses, and areas beyond energy and emissions. This section provides an overview of the developments in these application areas and how one can apply IDA to these areas. A salient feature that emerges is the flexibility of IDA in terms of its application which in turn makes it a popular tool in energy and emission analyses.

5.1   Understanding drivers of energy consumption

While IDA began with studies on energy use in the industry sector, the scope has gradually broadened to cover other major sectors of energy use and the entire economy. The aim is to understand overall trends in energy consumption – how energy consumption evolves in the economy. Studies decomposing changes in energy consumption typically use the three-factor IDA identity which comprises an activity effect, a structural effect and an intensity effect. An equal focus is given to all these drivers of energy consumption and the aim is to understand which drivers shape the trend in energy consumption over time. The main activity that drives energy consumption varies from one energy consuming sector to another. As a result, the most appropriate activity indicator chosen may also vary from one sector to another. In some cases, the choice of the activity indicator will depend on data availability and quality. Irrespective of the activity indicator used, the basic structure of the IDA identity as well as how the decomposition analysis is performed and the results obtained are interpreted generally remain the same for all the sectors.

In studies on the industrial sector and the service sector, activity is usually given by economic output and measured in monetary terms. The structural effect is defined as the impact of a shift in economic activity among different sub-sectors. The intensity effect measures the effect of changes in energy intensity of individual sub-sectors. For such cases, monetary activity is usually used as the denominator of energy intensity. Some sectors, such as the residential sector and a large part of the passenger transport sector, do not generate economic output. Hence, the use of physical units of measures was introduced. For example, in passenger transportation, passenger-kilometre is an activity indicator that is commonly used. The corresponding structural effect will be the transport modal shift which measures changes in shares of different modes of transportation in terms of passenger-kilometers, and the intensity effect measured in energy use per passenger-kilometer. Similarly, for freight transportation, the activity indicator can be given by the freight transported in tonne-kilometers. Another example is the electricity generation sector where energy intensity is measured as power generation efficiency and the structural effect is the contribution of a change in fuel mix of electricity generation to the total change in electricity output.

The developments mentioned above highlight IDA's versatility, an important property that enhances its usability. It can accommodate different measures for each factor and the decomposition identity can be tailored to suit different needs. At the same time, the consistency in the analysis framework which allows for easy comparisons among sectors with regard to key drivers of energy use is also a unique feature of IDA in energy analysis.

5.2 Tracking energy efficiency trends

Energy efficiency is the most popular application area of decomposition analysis among national and international agencies. Energy efficiency is of interest to policymakers as an improvement to energy efficiency is one of the simplest ways to address the energy trilemma; energy efficiency can help to address energy security concerns, enhance economic competitiveness and contribute to climate mitigation. It is often seen as the "hidden" fuel as improvements to energy efficiency can reduce energy consumption and improve energy security. IDA allows policymakers to quantify energy efficiency in terms of its contribution to the change in total energy consumption. This makes the effect of the "hidden" fuel visible and an indicator of performance in energy efficiency policies.

When IDA is used to track performance in energy efficiency, less attention is paid to the activity and structural effects. In fact, government energy agencies have little control over activity and structural effects which are largely influenced by the global economic climate and national policies which are not directly related to energy. On the other hand, they are able to implement policies to encourage greater energy efficiency in various energy consuming sectors. The isolation of the structural effect from improvements in energy efficiency allows IDA to give a more accurate evaluation of performance of energy efficiency policies. As the key interest is the energy intensity effect, which is often used as a proxy for energy efficiency, the two-factor identity is commonly used for this purpose.

Energy efficiency can be quantified in two ways: by an energy efficiency index or by energy savings (Ang et al., 2010). In the first case, energy efficiency can be tracked by sectors, for example IEA (2015a) compared the power generation efficiency effect of electricity production across countries using IDA. It can also be tracked by aggregating intensity effects at the sector level to form a composite energy efficiency indicator at the national level. This is often used to generate a national energy efficiency index. The second case presents energy efficiency improvements as the "energy savings" had the energy efficiency improvements not taken place (Che & Pham, 2012; Office of Energy Efficiency, 2013; Belzer, 2014; IEA, 2015b). This is done by computing the contribution of the intensity effect to total change in energy consumption and adding this contribution to the actual energy consumption trend to obtain a business-as-usual energy consumption level. Policymakers can then visualize how much a country has saved in terms of energy consumption due to gains in energy efficiency. In this way, the "hidden" fuel is revealed. More recently, researchers have combined IDA with econometric modeling to understand the impact of prices on energy efficiency. IDA is first conducted to quantify the impact of energy intensity and regression techniques are then used to analyze the impact of prices on the energy intensity effect (Mulder & de Groot, 2012; Parker & Liddle, 2016).

5.3 Understanding drivers of GHG emissions

Since the United Nations Framework Convention on Climate Change entered into force in 1994, there has been growing international pressure for all countries to participate in climate mitigation efforts. This has catalyzed the growth in studies using decomposition analyses to understand the drivers of CO_2 emissions from energy use to support the development of climate policies. IDA has transformed from an energy accounting tool to an emissions accounting tool. A large number of journal articles have been published on the decomposition of CO_2 emissions, and numerous national and regional agencies have used IDA to decompose drivers of emissions. The growth in this application area has in fact surpassed that of studies on energy in recent years (Ang, 2015). A literature review on the application of IDA to CO_2 emission studies can be found in Xu and Ang (2013).

Decomposition of CO_2 emissions requires a simple and straightforward extension from the well-established three-factor identity. This is done by computing emissions using the fuel emission factor of each fuel type, as mentioned in Section 4. The carbon intensity effect or carbon emission coefficient is the fourth term in the identity. The other terms remain the same as before. The simplest identity is the Kaya identity. It does not require sectoral data as changes in economic structure are not quantified. The Kaya identity was used in the International Panel on Climate Change (2014) 5th Assessment Report to decompose national emissions. It consists of four factors, the population effect, GDP per capita effect, energy intensity effect, and carbon intensity effect. The carbon intensity effect measures the amount of emissions for every unit of energy consumed. It can be further broken down into two factors – the fossil fuel mix effect and CO_2 emission coefficient. The fuel mix effect is sometimes referred to as the structural effect and should not be confused with the structural effect in the three-factor identity which measures the effect of changes in the structure of the economy.

Another common way of analysing CO_2 emissions is to decompose the emissions intensity – the emissions per unit of GDP. A decreasing emissions intensity is preferred, much like a decreasing energy intensity. As discussed earlier, an additional factor, the carbon intensity, is included in the decomposition identity. The carbon intensity can be further broken down into more effects for specific sectors such as the power generation sector. In this way, effects such as the generation efficiency effect and fossil share effect can be quantified and their corresponding contribution to emission reduction potentials can be estimated (Ang et al., 2011). IDA has also been used to decompose other undesirable emissions such as sulphur dioxide and nitrogen oxides (see for example Lin & Chang, 1996; Lu et al., 2012). However, international focus on climate change has made studies on CO_2 emissions far more prevalent.

5.4   Cross-country comparisons of energy and emissions

While IDA was initially developed for studying changes in energy consumption over time in a country (i.e. temporal decomposition analysis), it has since been extended to cross-country comparisons (i.e. spatial decomposition analysis). Examples of early studies are Ang and Zhang (1999), Schipper et al. (2001) and Bataille et al. (2007). A recent literature review of spatial IDA by Ang et al. (2016) lists 11 such studies. Cross-country or regional comparisons allow for benchmarking of energy efficiency performance and comparison of drivers. In spatial decomposition, the reference and target years are replaced by two countries or regions. The identities and decomposition formulae are exactly the same as described in Section 3. As an example, the comparison of country 1 and country 2 will yield the following additive decomposition results

$$\Delta E = E_1 - E_2 = \Delta E_{act} + \Delta E_{str} + \Delta E_{int}$$

(34.14)

Symmetry is an important property in spatial decomposition as the choice of either country 1 or country 2 as the base country should not affect the decomposition results. Spatial decomposition analysis is also more dependent on the IDA method chosen than temporal decomposition analysis as the data tend to cover a wider range, especially if two very different countries, such as in terms of economic or population size, are compared (Ang et al., 2015). The choice between intensity and quantity indicators is also important in spatial comparisons. A quantity indicator is scale-dependent and hence if a large energy consumer is compared against a small energy consumer, the activity effect will dominate the decomposition. The resulting activity effect is nearly meaningless. In this case, an intensity indicator is more appropriate as only the structure and intensity effects are of interest.

When comparisons are made for a group of countries, it is preferable that each country is compared with the mean of all the countries in the group. This ensures that the reference entity is the same and allows the regions to be ranked for benchmarking purposes. The decomposition results between country 1 and 2 can also be easily derived as the difference between the effect obtained from country 1 and the mean, and country 2 and the mean. In addition, this method satisfies the circularity property in index number theory. More details on spatial decomposition analyses can be found in Ang et al. (2015). A further extension of the traditional temporal decomposition is its integration with spatial temporal decomposition to give an integrated spatial-temporal decomposition approach. A recent study of this extension can be found in Ang et al. (2016).

5.5   Prospective analyses

A new application area of IDA that has emerged after 2010 is prospective analysis. Until then IDA was mainly used in retrospective analyses where developments of an aggregate indicator in the past are analyzed. In contrast, in prospective analyses, developments of an aggregate indicator in the future are studied. Ang (2015) lists three specific applications in prospective analyses and they can be briefly described as follows.

The first application is to make future forecasts of an aggregate indicator on the basis of the decomposed effects obtained in a retrospective analysis. The prospective analysis conducted therefore follows a conventional decomposition analysis using historical time series data. The rationale of using such an approach is that, having known their past developments, it is deemed more meaningful to make forecasts of the individual decomposed components (e.g. activity, structure, and intensity effects) and then combine the results for the components to give the future forecasts of the aggregate indicator than to simply make forecasts based directly on the aggregate indicator itself. Furthermore, future developments of the aggregate indicator can be better understood since they are dependent on the underlying developments of the individual decomposed components. Studies using such a prospective IDA approach include Lescaroux (2013) and O'Mahony et al. (2013).

The second application in prospective analyses is to harmonize and compare projection results across different models or scenarios through quantifying the underlying drivers or effects which provide a common basis for comparisons. For instance, in long-term decarbonization studies, different models and scenarios generally lead to a diversity of projected emission paths which are often difficult to understand and decipher. Studies have been reported to try to harmonise the results to enhance their reading through a post-treatment analysis using IDA, which helps reveal the contribution of a set of common drivers to total emission changes for different models or scenarios (Förster et al., 2013; Park et al., 2013). IEA (2015c), for example, uses IDA to compare two scenarios to understand the contribution of different policies to total emission reduction. The advantage of using IDA to compare models or scenarios is that contributions from a common set of factors for each of the models or scenarios can be easily obtained so that comparisons can be readily made between models or scenarios in terms of the contributions of these factors.

The third application is to unravel projected energy savings or reduced emissions for a future year by effect through decomposing the differences between the projected energy consumption or emission levels for the year for two different scenarios. In general, one of the scenarios in the comparison is often the business-as-usual case or the reference case (Gambhir et al., 2015; Kesicki, 2013). There is a strong similarity between this application of prospective analyses and spatial decomposition analyses, where country 1 and 2 are replaced by two scenarios which are to be compared against each other in a specific future year, and the identities and decomposition formulae are exactly the same as that described in Section 3.

5.6 Areas other than energy and emissions

The development and application of IDA have been strongly associated with energy consumption and emissions. Its simplicity and versatility, however, have motivated other areas of study. These areas cover a fairly wide spectrum and they include, for example, wind power deployment (Lu et al., 2015), agriculture (Sands et al., 2014), land use (Gingrich et al., 2015), water use (Zhao & Chen, 2014), toxic chemical management (Fujii & Managi, 2013), material use (Pothen & Schymura, 2015), investment (Knetsch & Nagengast, 2016), and natural capital (World Bank, 2010). Some of these areas, such as water use and material use, are similar to energy consumption in concept as they involve the consumption of natural resources. An extension of IDA to study the specific problem, such as how changes in industrial water consumption is affected by total industrial production, the mix of industrial sub-sectors and water intensities of sub-sectors, is therefore a straightforward and logical one. The IDA formulation and application are generally similar to those in energy and emission studies, and the decomposition results obtained can be interpreted in the same manner. Other application areas, such as agriculture, investment, and land use are not as well-established and commonly adopted. An issue that may arise is the interpretability of drivers chosen. The key drivers for these new application areas may not be as well accepted as in the case of energy and emission studies and hence may not be easily understood across policy studies.

6 Methodological and application issues

A number of methodological issues concerning the use of IDA have emerged over the years. Some issues that were studied in the earlier years include the problem of the unexplainable residual, time-reversal method selection, chaining versus non-chaining decomposition, and the zero value problem. This section covers a number of more recent methodological developments in IDA. They include new developments in issues that have been addressed previously as well as new methodological issues that have already been brought up in more recent IDA literature.

6.1 Method selection

Ang (2004b) classified various IDA methods, evaluated them based on theoretical foundation, adaptability, ease of use, and ease of understanding and results presentation, and recommended LMDI-I. Since then, there has been a general consensus that this is the preferred IDA method and most IDA studies have adopted LMDI, in particular LMDI-I. Specifically, it is perfect in decomposition at the sub-category level and is consistent in aggregation. It is thus the only method that fulfills the conditions required for multidimensional decomposition when results at the subcategory are of interest. LMDI-II, on the other hand, is preferred when it is important for the weights to sum to unity. A recent guide to method selection in LMDI is given in Ang (2015). Although LMDI is perfect in decomposition and can handle multiple factors easily, it faces some challenges when the dataset contains zero or negative values. In such cases, methods linked to the Laspeyres index may be easier to use. In addition, when there are only two factors in the decomposition, the Marshall-Edgeworth index or the Fisher ideal index may be adopted. As in the case of LMDI, these two methods are perfect in decomposition.

6.2 Zero and negative values

Zero and negative values are another issue that complicates the decomposition. Zero values occur more frequently when different fuel types are considered while negative values are rare in IDA. Zero values become a problem when a fuel type is used in either the reference or target year, but not the other. This means that the quantity of a specific fuel used in that year is zero. When LMDI is used, the logarithmic term cannot take a zero value. Ang and Liu (2007a) show that by replacing the zero value with a small value (e.g. 10^{-20}), the results converge to the analytical limit, hence providing a solution to the zero value problem. The negative value problem was also addressed by Ang and Liu (2007b). There are three types of negative value changes. The first concerns a change from a negative value to another negative value. In this case, the LMDI formulae can be applied without any transformations. The second form involves a change from a negative value to zero or vice versa. In this case, the zero value can be replaced by a small negative value (e.g. -10^{-20}). The final type of change is a change from a negative to positive value or vice versa. Here, Ang and Liu (2007b) show that in the analytical limit, the factor with a negative value accounts for the change of the entire sector while the other factors do not contribute at all. When zero or negative values prevail in the dataset, Laspeyres-based methods instead of LMDI may be adopted.

6.3 Multidimensional and multilevel studies

In the last few years, due to greater availability of data, a growing number of multidimensional and multilevel decomposition studies to obtain more information through IDA have been reported. These studies include multiple attributes such as sectoral disaggregation, disaggregation by fuel type and geographical region in the decomposition. They can be seen as extensions of the conventional single-level IDA which is unable to meet certain needs in policy analysis (Xu & Ang, 2014). For example, sectoral disaggregation is the breaking down of factors by economic or industrial sector. Disaggregation can be performed by sector, subsector, firm or fuel type. The choice of level of disaggregation affects the results and hence results need to be interpreted based on the level of disaggregation used. When the decomposition at intermediate levels, for example at the economic sector level or regional level, are of interest, the decomposition should preferably be perfect at the subcategory level and be consistent in aggregation (Ang & Wang, 2015). LMDI-I is the only method that fulfills these criteria. In addition, by distributing the residual terms at the subcategory levels, all other methods collapse to LMDI-I. Hence, for multidimensional and multilevel studies, LMDI-I is the recommended approach.

6.4   Linking physical and monetary based indicators

Another complication that arises from sectoral disaggregation is the need for a uniform activity indicator in order for the structural effect to be clearly and meaningfully defined. When applying IDA to study industry energy consumption, monetary activity is usually the default activity measure but physical measures are usually more representative of technical efficiency change. In tracking energy efficiency trends, physical measures are generally preferred to monetary measures. However, different industrial subsectors which produce distinct outputs and use different processes will inevitably have differing physical measures of activity. The issue is how the decomposition can be conducted at the subsector level by physical measures and later aggregated at the sectoral level based on monetary activity. Ang and Xu (2013) refine an approach known as the activity revaluation approach to address this issue. The revaluated monetary value is analogous to physical production and hence the resulting energy intensity effect derived is independent of price fluctuations. The refined approach also presents consistent results as that of other sectors such as transport and residential sectors. The consistency means that the aggregation at the economy-wide level is straightforward. One drawback of the approach is that it can only be used for quantity indicators. How it can be extended to intensity indicators is an area for further research.

6.5   Attribution analysis in multiplicative decomposition

The greater interest in multidimensional studies has also fuelled a desire to quantify the contribution of factors at the subcategory level to various attributes. In additive decomposition, this is simply obtained directly from the decomposition results. The results at the subcategory level can then be summed to obtain the results at the category level. This is not the case for multiplicative decomposition, where results are obtained as the product of factors. Instead, an additional step is needed to distribute the contribution of a factor to each subcategory. This is known as attribution analysis and a procedure was proposed by Choi and Ang (2012). The technique allocates the percentage change in an aggregate, such as the energy intensity effect, to various subcategories such as economic sectors. It is based on the attribution analysis used in national accounts and involves a transformation between the geometric and arithmetic mean. The introduction of the attribution analysis technique put multiplicative IDA on equal footing as additive IDA, where the contribution of factors at the subcategory level to various attributes can be similarly quantified. The technique has since been adopted in a number of IDA studies.

6.6   Spatial and temporal IDA

An extension of multidimensional studies is the integration of spatial and temporal decompositions within a single analysis framework. This allows analysts to compare the performance of countries across time and with respect to each other at any point in time. Ang et al. (2016) present such a framework. Spatial decomposition is first conducted with respect to a fixed benchmark over all the years and countries involved. Next, indirect spatial comparisons of two countries follow the method described in Section 5.4. Thereafter, temporal decomposition results are obtained by taking the difference between the effect arising from country 1 and the benchmark in the target year, and the effect arising from country 1 and the benchmark in the base year. As the benchmark is constant over time, the spatial decomposition results for different time periods can be compared. A two-dimensional plot may be used to integrate the temporal and spatial decomposition results. Two effects (e.g. the structural and intensity effects) can be presented on the horizontal and vertical axes and the position of countries are plotted with respect to their coordinates. Each time period is represented by one point on the plot and an arrow joins these points to indicate the path taken by the country over time. A contour plot may be used to represent the indicator value and the origin of the contour plot represents the benchmark value. The plot allows for the mapping of a country's progress over time, as well as the classification of countries by quadrants, which indicates levels of performance with respect to each driver.

7 Conclusion

Since its introduction in the late 1970s, researchers have made extensions to IDA, worked to tackle its limitations and improved its applicability. With these developments and improvements, IDA has become a well-established methodology for energy and emissions accounting. A large number of application studies in the form of archival journal articles have been reported. In addition, many studies with a strong policy focus have been conducted by research institutes, national agencies, and international organizations. Studies to refine the technique have also continued to enhance its applicability and usefulness. From its initial application as a tool to understand industrial energy use, IDA has branched into emissions and new application areas such as spatial comparisons and prospective analyses. LMDI has also become the mainstream method for IDA and there are clear guidelines on the choice of indicator, method, procedure and identity.

In this chapter, we give an overview of the problems researchers have faced over the years and their resolution, following which we provide guidelines on how IDA can be used. The main application areas and developments in this field of study are also summarized. In the near future, the use of IDA for tracking economy-wide energy efficiency trends and CO_2 emission studies is likely to continue to grow as international pressure for countries to participate in climate mitigation efforts increases. In addition, IDA will increasingly be used in areas such as benchmarking and forecasting. As we continue to improve the methods in order to unravel the complexities surrounding the use of energy and its impact on the environment, the economy and society, new methodological issues and application areas requiring further research will emerge.

Notes

1 Index decomposition analysis is one of several decomposition models that are used to quantify factors. Other decomposition models include the input–output based structural decomposition analysis (SDA) and production theoretical analysis (PDA). See Rose and Casler (1996) and Zhou and Ang (2008), respectively.
2 Three related articles published in two handbooks and an encyclopedia are Ang (1999), Ang (2004a), and Zhou and Ang (2015).
3 The Marshall-Edgeworth index method and the Fisher ideal index method are perfect in decomposition but they apply only to the two-factor case.
4 For conciseness, the formulae of AMDI are not shown in Table 1. The formulae of AMDI are similar to those of LMDI except that the logarithmic mean $L(x,y)$ in LMDI is replaced by the arithmetic mean $(x + y)/2$. The AMDI method passes the time-reversal test but fails the factor-reversal test. When it was first proposed, the LMDI method was taken as a refined version of the AMDI (Ang & Choi, 1997).
5 The list of methods included in Figure 34.1 is not exhaustive. The list contains only methods which are often used or referred to in the IDA literature.
6 The electricity generation sector is selected as it is more homogenous. In contrast, economy-wide emissions include various sectors such as transport which have different activity indicators compared to other sectors such as industry. The electricity generation sector also encompasses most of the non-fossil-based electricity sources and hence can provide details on a country's switch to cleaner energy sources.

7 Data was obtained from the IEA world energy balance database.
8 The emission factors for computing CO_2 emissions from fuel consumption, measured in tonnes of CO_2 per tonne of oil equivalent, are taken as 3.99 for coal, 3.08 for oil, and 2.33 for natural gas.

References

Ang, B. W. (1999). Decomposition methodology in energy demand and environmental analysis. In van den Bergh, J.C.J.M. (Ed.) *Handbook of Environmental and Resource Economics* (pp. 1146–1163). Gloucester, GL: Edward Elgar Publishing Limited.

Ang, B. W. (2004a). Decomposition analysis applied to energy. In Cleveland, C. J. (Ed.) *Encyclopedia of Energy Volume 1* (pp. 761–769). Amsterdam: Elsevier.

Ang, B. W. (2004b). Decomposition analysis for policymaking in energy: Which is the preferred method? *Energy Policy*, 32(9), 1131–1139.

Ang, B. W. (2015). LMDI decomposition approach: A guide for implementation. *Energy Policy*, 86, 233–238.

Ang, B. W., & Choi, K. H. (1997). Decomposition of aggregate energy and gas emission intensities for industry: A refined Divisia index method. *The Energy Journal*, 18(3), 59–73.

Ang, B. W., Liu, F. L., & Chew, E. P. (2003). Perfect decomposition techniques in energy and environmental analysis. *Energy Policy*, 31(14), 1561–1566.

Ang, B. W., Liu, F. L., & Chung, H.-S. (2004). A generalized Fisher index approach to energy decomposition analysis. *Energy Economics*, 26, 757–763.

Ang, B. W., & Liu, N. (2007a). Handling zero values in the logarithmic mean Divisia index decomposition approach. *Energy Policy*, 35(1), 238–246.

Ang, B. W., & Liu, N. (2007b). Negative-value problems of the logarithmic mean Divisia index decomposition approach. *Energy Policy*, 35(1), 739–742.

Ang, B. W., Mu, A. R., & Zhou, P. (2010). Accounting frameworks for tracking energy efficiency trends. *Energy Economics*, 32(5), 1209–1219.

Ang, B. W., Su, B., & Wang, H. (2016). A spatial-temporal decomposition approach to performance assessment in energy and emissions. *Energy Economics*, 60, 112–121.

Ang, B. W., & Wang, H. (2015). Index decomposition analysis with multidimenstional and multilevel energy data. *Energy Economics*, 51, 67–76.

Ang, B. W., & Xu, X. Y. (2013). Tracking industrial energy efficiency trends using index decomposition analysis. *Energy Economics*, 40, 1014–1021.

Ang, B. W., Xu, X. Y., & Su, B. (2015). Multi-country comparisons of energy performance: The index decomposition analysis approach. *Energy Economics*, 47, 68–76.

Ang, B. W., & Zhang, F. Q. (1999). Inter-regional comparisons of energy-related CO_2 emissions using the decomposition technique. *Energy*, 24(4), 297–305.

Ang, B. W., & Zhang, F. Q. (2000). A survey of index decomposition analysis in energy and environmental studies. *Energy*, 25(12), 1149–1176.

Ang, B. W., Zhou, P., & Tay, L. P. (2011) Potential for reducing global carbon emissions from electricity production: A benchmarking analysis. *Energy Policy*, 39(5), 2482–2489.

Bataille, C., Rivers, N., Mau, P., Joseph, C., & Tu, J. J. (2007). How malleable are the greenhouse gas emission intensities of the G7 nations? *The Energy Journal*, 28(1), 145–169.

Belzer, D. B. (2014). A Comprehensive System of Energy Intensity Indicators for the US: Methods, Data and Key Trends. *PNNL-22267*. Richland, WA: Pacific Northwest National Laboratory.

Boyd, G., Hanson, D. A., & Sterner, T. (1988). Decomposition of changes in energy intensity: A comparison of the Divisia index and other methods. *Energy Economics*, 10(4), 309–312.

Che, N., & Pham, P. (2012). *Economic Analysis of End-Use Energy Intensity in Australia*. Canberra: Australian Government, Bureau of Resources and Energy Economics.

Choi, K. H., & Ang, B. W. (2012). Attribution of changes in Divisia real energy intensity index: An extension to index decomposition analysis. *Energy Economics*, 34(1), 171–176.

Förster, H., Schumacher, K., De Cian, E., Hübler, M., Keppo, I., Mima, S., & Sands, R. (2013). European energy efficiency and decarbonisation strategies beyond 2030: A sectoral multi-model decomposition. *Climate Change Economics*, 4(1), 1340004-1–1340004-29.

Fujii, H., & Managi, S. (2013). Decomposition of toxic chemical substance management in three US manufacturing sectors from 1991–2008. *Journal of Industrial Ecology*, 17, 461–471.

Gambhir, A., Tse, L.K.C., Tong, D., & Martinez-Botas, R. (2015). Reducing China's road transport sector CO_2 emissions to 2050: Technologies, costs and decomposition analysis. *Applied Energy*, 157, 905–917.

Gingrich, S., Niedertscheidera, M., Kastnera, T., Haberla, H., Cosorc, G., Krausmanna, . . . Reith-Musela, A. (2015). Exploring long-term trends in land use change and aboveground human appropriation of net primary production in nine European countries. *Land Use Policy*, 47, 426–438.

IEA (2015a). *CO₂ Emissions from Fuel Combustion*. Paris: OECD/IEA.

IEA (2015b). *Energy Efficiency Market Report 2015*. Paris: OECD/IEA.

IEA (2015c). *Energy and Climate Change: World Energy Outlook Special Report*. Paris: OECD/IEA.

IPCC (2014). Summary for policymakers. In: Edenhofer, O., Pichs-Madruga, R., Sokona, Y., Farahani, E., Kadner, S., Seyboth, K., Adler, A., Baum, I., Brunner, S., Eickemeier, P., Kriemann, B., Savolainen, J., Schlomer, S., von Stechow, C., Zwickel, T., & Minx, J.C. (Eds.), *Climate Change 2014, Mitigation of Climate Change: Contribution of Working Group III to the Fifth Assessment Report of the Intergovernmental Panel on Climate Change*. Cambridge and New York, NY: Cambridge University Press.

Kesicki, F. (2013). Marginal abatement cost curves: Combining energy system modelling and decomposition analysis. *Environmental Modeling & Assessment*, 18, 27–37.

Knetsch, T. A., & Nagengast, A. J. (2016). On the Dynamics of the Investment Income Balance. *Discussion Paper No 21*. Frankfurt: Deutsche Bundesbank

Lescaroux, F. (2013). Industrial energy demand, a forecasting model based on an index decomposition of structural and efficiency effects. *OPEC Energy Review*, 477–502.

Lin, S. J., & Chang, T. C. (1996). Decomposition of SO₂, NOₓ and CO₂ emissions from energy use of major economic sectors in Taiwan. *The Energy Journal*, 17, 1–17.

Liu, X. Q., Ang, B. W., & Ong, H. L. (1992). The application of the Divisia index to the decomposition of changes in industrial energy consumption. *The Energy Journal*, 13(4), 161–177.

Lu, X., McElroy, M. B., Peng, W., Liu, S., Nielsen, C. P., & Wang, H. (2015). Challenges faced by China compared with the US in developing wind power. *Nature Energy*, 1, 1–6.

Lu, X., McElroy, M. B., Wu, G., & Nielsen, C. P. (2012). Accelerated reduction in SO₂ emissions from the U.S. power sector triggered by changing prices of natural gas. *Environmental Science and Technology*, 46, 7882–7889.

Mulder, P., & de Groot, H.L.F. (2012). Structural change and convergence of energy intensity acrosss OECD countries, 1970–2005. *Energy Economics*, 34, 1910–1921.

Office of Energy Efficiency (2013). *Energy Efficiency Trends in Canada*. Ottawa: Natural Resources Canada.

O'Mahony, T., Zhou, P., & Sweeney, J. (2013). Integrated scenarios of energy-related CO₂ emissions in Ireland: A multi-sectoral analysis to 2020. *Ecological Economics*, 93, 385–397.

Park, N.B., Yun, S. J., & Jeon, E. C. (2013). An analysis of long-term scenarios for the transition to renewable energy in the Korean electricity sector. *Energy Policy*, 52, 288–296.

Parker, S., & Liddle, B. (2016). Energy efficiency in the manufacturing sector of the OECD: Analysis of price elasticities. *Energy Economics*, 38–45.

Pothen, F., & Schymura, M. (2015). Bigger cakes with fewer ingredients? A comparison of material use of the world economy. *Ecological Economics*, 109, 109–121.

Rose, A., & Casler, S. (1996). Input-output structural decomposition analysis: A critical appraisal. *Economic Systems Research*, 8(1), 33–62.

Sands, R. D., Jones, C. A., & Marshall, E. (2014). *Global Drivers of Agricultural Demand and Supply*. Washington, DC: U.S. Department of Agriculture, Economic Research Service.

Schipper, L., Murtishaw, S., & Unander. F. (2001). International comparisons of sectoral carbon dioxide emissions using a cross-country decomposition technique. *The Energy Journal*, 22(2), 35–75.

Sun, J. W. (1998). Changes in energy consumption and energy intensity: A complete decomposition model. *Energy Economics*, 20(1), 85–100.

World Bank (2010). *The Changing Wealth of Nations: Measuring Sustainable Development in the New Millennium*. Washington, DC: World Bank.

Xu, X. Y., & Ang, B. W. (2013). Index decomposition analysis applied to CO₂ emission studies. *Ecological Economics*, 93, 313–329.

Xu, X. Y., & Ang, B. W. (2014). Multilevel index decomposition analysis: Approaches and application. *Energy Economics*, 44, 375–382.

Zhao, C., & Chen, B. (2014). Driving force analysis of the agricultural water footprint in China based on the LMDI method. *Environmental Science & Technology*, 48, 12723–12731.

Zhou, P., & Ang, B. W. (2008). Decomposition of aggregate CO₂ emissions: A production-theoretical approach. *Energy Economics*, 30, 1054–1067.

Zhou, P., & Ang, B. W. (2015). Index decomposition analysis for tracking of energy efficiency trends. In: Managi, S. (Ed.), *The Routledge Handbook of Environmental Economics in Asia* (pp. 83–97). New York, NY: Routledge.

35

Electricity price forecasting

Rafał Weron and Florian Ziel

1 Introduction

The beginnings of *electricity price forecasting* (EPF) can be traced back to the early 1990s, when power sector deregulation led to the introduction of competitive markets in the UK and Scandinavia. The changes quickly spread throughout Europe and North America, and nowadays – in many countries worldwide – electricity is traded under market rules using spot and derivative contracts (Joskow, 2008; Mayer and Trück, 2018).

When modeling and forecasting electricity prices we have to bear in mind that electricity is a very special commodity – it is economically non-storable (hence requires a constant balance between production and consumption) and is dependent on weather (both on the demand and supply sides) and the intensity of business activities (on-peak vs. off-peak hours). The resulting spot price dynamics exhibits seasonality at the daily, weekly, and annual levels, and abrupt, short-lived, and generally unanticipated price spikes. The forward prices are less volatile due to averaging over weekly, monthly, quarterly, or even annual delivery periods.

Over the last 25 years, a variety of methods and ideas have been tried for EPF, with varying degrees of success (Gürtler and Paulsen, 2018; Nowotarski and Weron, 2018; Weron, 2014; Ziel and Steinert, 2018). In this chapter we first briefly discuss the forecasting horizons (Section 2) and the types of forecasts (Section 3), then review the forecasting tools (Section 4) and the evaluation techniques (Section 5) used in the EPF literature. Note that we use EPF as the abbreviation for both *electricity price forecasting* and *electricity price forecast*. The plural form (i.e. forecasts) is abbreviated EPFs.

2 Horizons

In the EPF literature, it is customary to talk about short-, medium-, and long-term predictions, even though there are no strict or even commonly accepted definitions. *Short-term* horizons range from minutes to days; sometimes horizons of less than an hour are referred to as *very short-term*. As a thumb rule, short-term corresponds to horizons for which reliable meteorological forecasts for temperature, wind speed, cloud cover, and so forth are available. Short-term predictions are mainly relevant for market operations and system stability Weron (2014).

Medium-term forecasting covers horizons beyond reliable meteorological predictions, but without major impact of political and technological uncertainty, with lead times measured in weeks, months, quarters, or even years. The practical relevance arises mainly from maintenance scheduling, resources reallocation, bilateral contracting, derivatives valuation, risk management, and budgeting. Finally, *long-term* horizons refer to everything from a few years up to several decades. Such far-reaching forecasts are performed to answer questions about investment planning and policy making (Ziel and Steinert, 2018).

2.1 Intraday and day-ahead

Unlike most other commodity or financial markets, the electricity 'spot market' is typically a *day-ahead* market that does not allow for continuous trading. Agents submit their bids and offers for delivery of electricity during each hour (or blocks of hours) of the next day before a certain market closing time (often called *gate closure*). Then, prices for all *load periods* of the next day are determined at the same time during a uniform-price auction (Weron, 2014).

In electricity markets with zonal pricing (as in Europe), next to the day-ahead markets, so-called *intraday* markets exist. These markets start operating more or less after the day-ahead auction results are announced and run until a few minutes before delivery. Their main purpose is to balance deviations resulting from positions in day-ahead contracts and unexpected changes in demand or generation (Gianfreda et al., 2016; Zaleski and Klimczak, 2015). In most European countries intraday markets operate as continuous trading sessions (e.g. Germany, France, Poland, UK; see Kiesel and Paraschiv, 2017; Wolff and Feuerriegel, 2017), but in some they are organized in the form of multiple consecutive auctions (e.g. Italy, Spain; see Monteiro et al., 2016). However, in the very few intraday EPF publications that exist (Andrade et al., 2017; Maciejowska et al., 2019; Narajewski and Ziel, 2018; Uniejewski et al., 2019), even when markets with continuous trading are considered only an aggregate characteristic, such as the volume weighted intraday price over a certain trading period, is predicted.

Finally, in basically all electricty markets there exist so-called *balancing* (or *realtime*) markets, which are operated by *transmission system operators* (TSOs). These technical markets operate from a few hours before delivery until the delivery itself. Their only purpose is to guarantee system stability Weron (2006). Usually these markets exhibit high price fluctuations, which results in the demand for sophisticated forecasting models. As a consequence, the literature on predicting balancing prices is rather sparse (Klæboe et al., 2015).

2.2 Medium term

For medium-term horizons, the value of meteorological predictions as well as their impact on EPFs disappears. Still, deterministic demand patterns (e.g. reduced electricity consumption during holiday periods) impact the price dynamics as in the short-term (Ziel et al., 2015). On the other hand, structural variables become important, most notably prices of fuels used for conventional power generation (Maciejowska and Weron, 2016; Mohamed and El-Hawary, 2016). These mainly include natural gas, oil, coal, lignite, and uranium, but also CO_2 permits in markets with carbon pricing schemes (like the European Union). Moreover, plans for changes in the power plant portfolio, e.g. maintenance periods, retirement of old power plants or installation of new capacity, become relevant and can be incorporated into mid-term models. The same holds for grid expansions. For instance, when interconnectors between small market zones are implemented, they can have a drastic influence on price dynamics (Ries et al., 2016). Also, prices or complete order books of electricity derivatives can help to forecast spot prices (Steinert and Ziel, 2018).

The EPF literature suggests that a suitable forecasting setup should either be based on statistical models with a substantial amount of exogenous variables, see Section 4.1, or on structural models, see Section 4.4 (Bello et al., 2016; Weron, 2014; Ziel and Steinert, 2018). Among experts in this field, there is a clear majority opinion that the longer the forecasting horizon the better the performance of structural models compared to statistical approaches. Unfortunately, so far there is no research study available which would support this point of view.

2.3 Long term

For long-term forecasting horizons political/regulatory, technological, economical, and social risks come into play. All these components are hard to predict on their own, which makes incorporating them into electricity price models a laborious and an almost impossible task. Complex models must be developed, large teams of experts from different disciplines may be needed and the evaluation becomes tricky, as we require decades of data (not only for electricity prices, but also for all exogenous variables). Consequently, the literature on long-term EPF is almost non-existent (Ziel and Steinert, 2018). Yet, there are papers which look at electricity prices far into the future (e.g. Lund et al., 2018). These studies consider usually only scenarios or projections, in the sense that they describe future paths conditioned on certain external factors, like political decisions. However, the paths are not associated with probabilities, which would be required for referring to them as forecasts.

3 Types of forecasts

The vast majority of EPF papers are concerned only with point forecasts (Weron, 2014). Yet, the increased market competition, aging infrastructure, (see Chapters 14 and 29) have had the effect of probabilistic forecasting becoming more and more important to energy systems planning and operations (Nowotarski and Weron, 2018). After a decade of limited interest, probabilistic EPF gained momentum with the Global Energy Forecasting Competition (GEFCom2014; Hong et al., 2016), which focused solely on probabilistic energy (load, price, wind, and solar) forecasting and used the pinball loss (Equation 35.7) as the only evaluation criterion. Still, probabilistic EPF is not that common. In the last three years only about 15% of Scopus-indexed EPF articles concerned interval or distributional predictions (Ziel and Steinert, 2018). Ensemble forecasts, which in contrast to point and probabilistic predictions do not focus on only one point at a time, are even less popular. This is surprising, given that path-dependency is crucial for many optimization problems arising in power plant scheduling, energy storage and trading. But we expect more ensemble EPF papers to be published in the coming years.

3.1 Point

The day-ahead price series typically is a result of a conducted once per day (usually around noon) auction, during which all hourly prices for the next day are disclosed at once (Weron, 2014). In the intraday markets that nowadays operate in quite a few countries worldwide, the load periods can be shorter than one hour, e.g. the European Power Exchange (EPEX) also trades half- and quarter-hourly products (Kiesel and Paraschiv, 2017). In either case the day can be divided into a finite number of load periods $h = 1, \ldots, H$. Hence it is natural to denote by $P_{d,h}$ the price for day d and load period h. A point forecast of $P_{d,h}$, denoted by $\hat{P}_{d,h}$, is usually understood in the EPF literature – without explicitly saying it – as the expected value (or mean) of the price random variable, i.e. $\mathbb{E}\left(P_{d,h}\right)$, see the top left panel in Figure 35.1. This notion can be easily extended

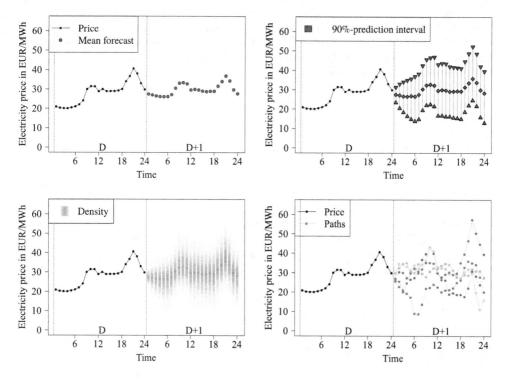

Figure 35.1   Illustration of the three types of forecasts discussed in Section 3: the mean as the most commonly used *point* prediction (top left), 90% prediction interval (top right) and a density forecast (bottom left) as examples of *probabilistic* forecasts, and five simulated trajectories that form an *ensemble* forecast (bottom right)

to *quantile* forecasts, which are the building blocks for probabilistic predictions. For instance, $\hat{q}_{0.5,P}$ could be a point forecast for the median $q_{0.5,P}$ of $P_{d,h}$ (recall that the median is the 50% or 0.5-quantile), while the pair $[\hat{q}_{0.05,P}, \hat{q}_{0.95,P}]$ yields a symmetric 90% prediction interval, illustrated in the top right panel of Figure 35.1.

3.2   Probabilistic

There are two main approaches to probabilistic forecasting. The more popular one builds on the point forecast and the distribution of errors associated with it. The other directly considers the distribution of the spot price and is, for instance, utilized in quantile regression averaging (QRA; see Nowotarski and Weron, 2015). In both cases the focus can be on prediction intervals (as in the top right panel in Figure 35.1), selected quantiles – quartiles, deciles, percentiles – or the whole predictive distribution (as in the bottom left panel in Figure 35.1).

If we consider the mean price at a future date, i.e, $\hat{P}_{d,h} = \mathbb{E}\left(P_{d,h}\right)$, as the 'point forecast' then we can write: $P_{d,h} = \hat{P}_{d,h} + \varepsilon_{d,h}$, which implies:

$$F_P(x) = F_\varepsilon\left(x - \hat{P}_{d,h}\right),$$

(35.1)

where F_ε is the distribution of errors associated with $\hat{P}_{d,h}$. This means that the distribution of errors has an identical shape to the distribution of prices, only is shifted by $\hat{P}_{d,h}$ to the left on the horizontal axis. The corresponding quantile function $\hat{q}_{\alpha,\varepsilon}$ is also shifted with respect to $\hat{q}_{\alpha,P}$, but now on the vertical axis and down:

$$\hat{q}_{\alpha,P} - \hat{P}_{d,h} = \hat{q}_{\alpha,\varepsilon}, \tag{35.2}$$

Equivalently in terms of the inverse empirical *cumulative distribution function* (CDF) we can write:

$$\hat{F}_P^{-1}(\alpha) = \hat{P}_{d,h} + \hat{F}_\varepsilon^{-1}(\alpha). \tag{35.3}$$

The latter two relationships follow directly from the definition of the inverse empirical CDF and Equation (35.1). They also provide the basic framework for constructing probabilistic forecasts from distributions of prediction errors. Thus, if a dense grid of quantiles is considered (e.g. 99 percentiles: $\alpha_1 = 0.01, \alpha_2 = 0.02, \ldots, \alpha_{99} = 0.99$) then $\hat{q}_{\alpha_1,P}, \ldots, \hat{q}_{\alpha_L,P}$ approximate $\hat{F}_P$ pretty well. If we assume that F_P has a density f_P, i.e. $F_P(x) = \int_{-\infty}^{x} f_P(z)dz$, then a density forecast $\hat{f}_P$ can be provided as well.

3.3 Ensemble

The probabilistic forecasting concept discussed in Section 3.2 seems to be very general. Still, it is not sufficient to answer many problems in energy forecasting. The reason is that $\hat{P}_{d,h}$ is considered on its own, independently of the forecasts for the neighboring hours. However, instead of looking at the H univariate price distributions $F_{P_{d,1}}, \ldots, F_{P_{d,H}}$, we should be focusing on the H-*dimensional distribution* $\boldsymbol{F}_P$ of the H-dimensional price vector $\boldsymbol{P}_d = (P_{d,1}, \ldots, P_{d,H})'$. Thus, we require a forecast $\hat{\boldsymbol{F}}_{\boldsymbol{P}_d}$ for the multivariate distribution of $\boldsymbol{P}_d$. Unfortunately, many models cannot provide such a direct distributional forecast.

The solution to the latter problem is to compute an *ensemble forecast*. An ensemble is a collection of M paths $\mathcal{E}_M(\hat{\boldsymbol{P}}_d) = (\hat{\boldsymbol{P}}_d^{(1)}, \ldots, \hat{\boldsymbol{P}}_d^{(M)})$ simulated from a forecasting model, typically using Monte-Carlo. These *paths*, visualized in the bottom right panel of Figure 35.1, are also called *trajectories* or *scenarios*. The Glivenko-Cantelli theorem implies that for large M the ensemble approximates the underlying distribution $\boldsymbol{F}_P$ arbitrarily well. For practical applications it is important to remember that M should be chosen as large as possible (i.e. the ensemble should be composed of thousands or millions of paths). Finally, note that although new to EPF, the same or similar concepts have been used in different disciplines under different names: *simultaneous prediction intervals* (SPIs; as opposed to marginal PIs), *prediction bands*, *spatio-temporal trajectories* or *scenarios*, and *numerical weather prediction ensembles* (NWP).

4 Models

Nearly all review and survey publications introduce their own classifications of the techniques used for EPF. Some are better, some are worse, but most have many things in common. Here we review the classification of Weron (2014) with five groups of models, starting from the two most popular classes. Of course, many approaches considered in the literature are hybrid solutions, combining techniques from two or more classes.

4.1   Statistical

Statistical (also called *econometric*) approaches forecast the current price by a weighted combination of the past prices and/or past or current values of exogenous variables (e.g. demand or weather forecasts), typically in a linear regression setting. Autoregressive terms are often used to account for the dependencies between today's prices and those of the previous days, like in the ARX model proposed by Misiorek et al. (2006) and later used in a number of EPF studies (Gaillard et al., 2016; Kristiansen, 2012; Maciejowska et al., 2016; Marcjasz et al., 2019; Nowotarski et al., 2014; Uniejewski et al., 2016; Weron, 2006):

$$P_{d,h} = \beta_{h,0} + \underbrace{\beta_{h,1}P_{d-1,h} + \beta_{h,2}P_{d-2,h} + \beta_{h,3}P_{d-7,h}}_{\text{autoregressive effects}} + \underbrace{\beta_{h,4}P_{d-1,min}}_{\text{non-linear effect}}$$

$$+ \underbrace{\beta_{h,5}L_{d,h}}_{\text{load forecast}} + \underbrace{\beta_{h,6}D_{Sat} + \beta_{h,7}D_{Sun} + \beta_{h,8}D_{Mon}}_{\text{weekday dummies}} + \varepsilon_{d,h}, \tag{35.4}$$

where $P_{d,h}$ is the price for day d and hour h, $P_{d-1,min}$ is the minimum of the previous day's 24 hourly prices, $L_{d,h}$ refers to the load forecast for day d and hour h (known on day $d-1$), and the three dummies ($D_{Sat}, D_{Sun}, D_{Mon}$) model the weekly seasonality. Following Ziel (2016), some authors refer to such parsimonious structures as *expert* models, since they are built on some prior knowledge of experts.

The standard approach to estimate model (35.4) is ordinary least squares (OLS). The procedure uses electricity prices from the past $\mathcal{D}$ days, i.e. $P_{1,h},\ldots,P_{\mathcal{D},h}$, to predict the prices for the following day(s), i.e. $P_{\mathcal{D}+1,h},P_{\mathcal{D}+2,h}$, etc. The value of $\mathcal{D}$ should be chosen with care, so that the estimation sample is 'long enough' to be able to extract patterns, but not 'too long' to give too much weight to distant past. Some authors also argue that $\mathcal{D}$ should be a multiple of the weekly cycle. Overall, there is no industry standard. Many studies consider a 'year' ($\mathcal{D} = 360, 7 \times 52 = 364$ or 365 days) or 'two years' ($D = 2 \times 364 = 728$ or $2 \times 365 = 730$) of hourly prices, but some use as short windows as 10–13 days, while other as long as four years (see Marcjasz et al., 2018, for a review). The problem of optimal window length has been apparently overlooked in the EPF literature. Only very recently a few authors tackle it in a systematic way. Hubicka et al. (2019) propose a novel concept in energy forecasting that combines day-ahead predictions across different calibration windows (from 28 to 728 days) and show that this kind of averaging yields better results than selecting ex ante only one 'optimal' window length. Marcjasz et al. (2018) go one step further and introduce a new, well-performing weighting scheme for averaging these forecasts.

While (auto)regression models constitute the largest subset of statistical models, this class also includes:

- Similar-day methods, like the *naive* method used by Contreras et al. (2003) and Conejo et al. (2005), which sets $\hat{P}_{d,h} = P_{d-7,h}$ for Monday, Saturday or Sunday, and $\hat{P}_{d,h} = P_{d-1,h}$ otherwise;
- Exponential smoothing (Cruz et al., 2011; Jonsson et al., 2013);
- Threshold models, like Markov regime-switching (MRS; Misiorek et al., 2006), threshold AR (TAR; Misiorek et al., 2006; Weron and Misiorek, 2008) or logistic smooth transition regression (LSTR; Gonzalez et al., 2012);
- Models with GARCH innovations, typically in the context of volatility forecasting (Huurman et al., 2012; Koopman et al., 2007);
- Shrinkage techniques, primarily LASSO (Ludwig et al., 2015; Ziel, 2016; Ziel and Weron, 2018), but also ridge regression and elastic nets (Uniejewski et al., 2016).

Statistical models are attractive because physical interpretation may be attached to the regressors, thus allowing engineers and system operators to better understand their behavior. The drawback is that – when used on their own – statistical models have problems with representing nonlinear phenomena, even though nonlinear models can be approximated pretty well by linear ones (under some regularity conditions). Nevertheless, nonlinear dependencies can be explicitly included via nonlinear variables, like $P_{d-1,min}$ in Equation (35.4). Alternatively, electricity spot prices (as well as exogenous variables) can be transformed using nonlinear functions, e.g. the area hyperbolic sine or the PIT defined in Equation (35.6), prior to fitting a statistical model. As Marcjasz et al. (2018) and Uniejewski et al. (2018) report, this usually leads to significantly lower prediction errors.

4.2   Computational intelligence

The second, much more popular in the engineering literature, class of models is that of *computational* (CI) or *artificial intelligence* (AI). It is a very diverse group of nature-inspired tools developed to solve problems which (linear) statistical methods cannot handle efficiently. They combine elements of learning, evolution and fuzziness to create approaches that are capable of adapting to complex dynamic systems (in this sense they may be regarded as 'intelligent'). Artificial neural networks (ANNs), fuzzy systems and evolutionary computation (genetic algorithms, evolutionary programming, swarm intelligence) are unquestionably the main classes of CI (Keller et al., 2016). Some authors additionally include probabilistic reasoning and belief networks (at the intersection with traditional AI), artificial life techniques (at the intersection with biochemistry) and wavelets (at the intersection with digital signal processing), while others associate CI with machine learning, soft computing and data mining (see Weron 2014 for a discussion).

CI models are flexible and can handle several types of nonlinearity, but at the cost of high computational complexity. Still, they are popular for short-term predictions. Like in load forecasting, ANNs have probably received the most attention (Abedinia et al., 2017; Amjady, 2006; Catalão et al., 2007; Dudek, 2016; Keles et al., 2016). Other techniques – like fuzzy logic, support vector machines (SVM), and evolutionary computation (genetic algorithms, evolutionary programming, swarm intelligence) – have been also applied, but typically in hybrid constructions (see Aggarwal et al., 2009; Weron, 2014, for reviews). Note, however, that the calibration of CI models is sensitive to initial parameters (starting values). A possible remedy is to use committee machines, i.e. averaging forecasts coming from different models or runs of the same model (Marcjasz et al., 2019), though this increases the computational burden even more.

4.3   Reduced form

The third class of *reduced-form* (also called *quantitative* or *stochastic*) approaches is not as universal as the previous two. As Weron (2014) argues, these models are not built to provide accurate hourly spot price forecasts, but rather to replicate the main characteristics of electricity prices at the daily time scale. Such models provide a simplified, hence the term 'reduced-form', yet realistic to some extent price dynamics and are commonly used for computationally intensive derivatives pricing (e.g. of electricity futures and options) and value-at-risk calculations. The two most popular model classes for the spot price dynamics include:

*   *Jump-diffusions*, which are a combination of Brownian dynamics and Poisson-type point (jump) processes (Benth et al., 2012; Cartea and Figueroa, 2005; Geman and Roncoroni, 2006; Weron, 2008).

- *Regime-switching* models, typically involving a latent process describing the current state of the spot price (e.g. base regime vs. spike regime) and Brownian dynamics in one or more regime (Chen and Bunn, 2014; De Jong, 2006; Janczura et al., 2013; Janczura and Weron, 2010).

The reduced-form models can be either build for the spot or forward prices (Benth et al., 2008; Eydeland and Wolyniec, 2003; Weron, 2006). The main drawback of the former is the difficulty encountered when pricing derivatives, i.e. the identification of the risk premium linking spot and forward prices (Weron and Zator, 2014). On the other hand, forward price models allow for pricing of derivatives in a straightforward manner (but only those written on the forward price of electricity). However, they too have their limitations – scarcity of data for calibration and problems with deriving the properties of spot prices from the predicted forward curves (which include the risk premium).

4.4   Fundamental

Fundamental (also called *structural*) methods constitute the fourth class and include models that try to capture the basic physical and economic factors affecting the production and trading of electricity via a system of functional relationships. The latter are first postulated, then modeled and predicted independently (often via statistical, CI or reduced-form techniques) and aggregated to yield the equilibrium spot price. In general, two subclasses of fundamental models can be identified:

- *Parameter-rich* fundamental models, often developed as in-house products that use proprietary information (Eydeland and Wolyniec, 2003; Vehviläinen and Pyykkönen, 2005).
- *Parsimonious structural* models of supply and demand that are built on publicly available information (Carmona and Coulon, 2014; Kanamura and Ohashi, 2007; Ziel and Steinert, 2016, 2018).

Because of the nature of fundamental data – which is often available only at the weekly or monthly resolution – parameter rich models are better suited for medium-term rather than short-term predictions. Also the parsimonious structural models are rarely used for short-term horizons. They are typically calibrated to daily data and, like reduced-form models, used for derivatives pricing and risk management; the X-model of Ziel and Steinert (2016) is one of the few exceptions. Compared to reduced-form models, they allow for a better description of the market fundamentals and price nonlinearities, in particular price spikes, mainly due to direct modeling of the nonlinear supply curve. This comes, however, at the cost of increasing the computational complexity.

4.5   Multi-agent

Multi-agent models simulate the operation of a system of interacting with each other heterogeneous agents, e.g. generating units, traders. Like fundamental models, they yield the equilibrium spot price by matching the demand and supply in the market. But unlike them, they construct the supply (and sometimes the demand) curve from the bids of the individual agents, not model it at the aggregate level (for a review, see Ventosa et al., 2005).

Historically, *cost-based* or *production-cost* models (PCM) were the first members of this class. They were used in the pre-deregulation era with little price uncertainty to predict prices on an hour-by-hour, bus-by-bus level by matching demand forecasts to the supply, obtained by stacking up existing and planned generation units in order of their operating costs. *Equilibrium* (also called *game theoretic*) approaches, including the Nash-Cournot framework, supply function equilibrium and strategic PCMs, may be viewed as generalizations of PCMs that admit strategic bidding. This framework has been used extensively for the analysis of bidding strategies (Borgosz-Koczwara et al., 2009) or market power and market design (Holmberg et al., 2013), but EPF applications are very limited (Ruibal and Mazumdar, 2008). Finally, the increasingly popular adaptive *agent-based simulation* techniques can address features of electricity markets that static equilibrium models ignore, but again, their use for EPF is scarce (Young et al., 2014).

5 Forecast evaluation

All forecasting methods – point, probabilistic, or ensemble – require evaluation with respect to the actual price $P_{d,h}$. While for point predictions it is relatively straightforward, for probabilistic and ensemble forecasts this becomes tricky. Therefore, the concept of a *score* (*scoring rule* or *loss*) comes in handy. In general, this is a function of the forecast and the actual price: $S(\text{'forecast'}, \hat{P}_{d,h})$. A score is called *strictly proper* with respect to the forecasting target (e.g. the mean or the median) if only the true model optimizes the score; in this case the true model can be identified (Gneiting and Raftery, 2007).

5.1 Point forecasts

In point forecasting, scores are usually based on the so-called *forecast* or *prediction error*, defined as the difference between an observed value and its forecast, i.e. $e_{d,h} \equiv P_{d,h} - \hat{P}_{d,h}$. The sign does not matter since the most widely used scores of forecast accuracy:

- The *absolute error* defined by $AE\left(\hat{P}_{d,h}, P_{d,h}\right) = \left|P_{d,h} - \hat{P}_{d,h}\right| = \left|e_{d,h}\right|$
- The *square error* defined by $SE\left(\hat{P}_{d,h}, P_{d,h}\right) = \left(P_{d,h} - \hat{P}_{d,h}\right)^2 = e_{d,h}^2$

are symmetric. Averaging across the test sample yields the two most popular measures – the *mean absolute error* (MAE) and the *root mean square error* (RMSE):

$$\text{MAE} \equiv \frac{1}{\mathcal{D}\mathcal{H}}\sum_{d=1}^{\mathcal{D}}\sum_{h=1}^{\mathcal{H}}\left|e_{d,h}\right| \quad \text{and} \quad \text{RMSE} \equiv \sqrt{\frac{1}{\mathcal{D}\mathcal{H}}\sum_{d=1}^{\mathcal{D}}\sum_{h=1}^{\mathcal{H}}e_{d,h}^2}, \tag{35.5}$$

where $\mathcal{D}$ is the number of days in the test sample and $\mathcal{H}$ the number of load periods per day, i.e. $\mathcal{H} = 24$ for hourly periods. The absolute error is a strictly proper score for the median and the square error for the mean. Thus, the MAE is recommended for evaluating median and the RMSE for mean forecasts. However, both measures are commonly used in practice, despite the fact that the vast majority of point forecasts are mean predictions.

Since absolute and square errors are scale-dependent and hence hard to compare between different datasets, many authors use measures based on *percentage errors*, i.e. $e_{d,h}/P_{d,h}$. By far the most popular is the *mean absolute percentage error* (MAPE), which is computed as the mean of $|e_{d,h}|/P_{d,h}$ in the test sample. The MAPE measure works well in load forecasting, but for electricity price trajectories with close to zero or even negative values it may lead to absurd results and other more robust measures are preferred. So-called *scaled errors* were proposed by Hyndman and Koehler (2006) as a robust alternative to percentage errors. The idea is to divide $e_{d,h}$ by the MAE of a naïve forecast in the calibration window (instead of the actual price) and compute the *mean absolute scaled error* (MASE) as the mean of $|e_{d,h}|/\text{MAE}_{\text{naïve}}$ in the test sample. A scaled error is less than one if it arises from a better forecast than the average naïve forecast computed on the training data, and is greater than one if the forecast is worse.

Despite obvious advantages, scaled errors have not been used extensively in energy forecasting, one of the few examples is Jonsson et al. (2013). Alternative normalizations have been proposed instead, e.g. dividing $|e_{d,h}|$ by the average price attained in a given week. This yields the *weekly-weighted* MAE (WMAE; Weron and Misiorek, 2008), also called the *mean weekly error* (MWE; Conejo et al., 2005). As there is no 'industry standard', the error benchmarks used in the EPF literature vary a lot and – what is worse – are not used consistently, e.g. compare the two different definitions of MWE in Contreras et al. (2003) and Conejo et al. (2005).

5.2 Probabilistic forecasts

The main challenge with evaluating probabilistic forecasts is that we never observe the true distribution F_P of the underlying process and hence cannot compare the predictive distribution $\hat{F}_P$ with the actual one. All we can do is compare $\hat{F}_P$ with observed past prices. Over the years, a number of ways have been developed to evaluate probabilistic forecasts. The chosen approach will depend on the forecasting target – a quantile forecast requires a different evaluation than a predictive distribution, but sometimes it may also depend on the preference of the forecaster (see Nowotarski and Weron, 2018, for a recent review).

Gneiting and Katzfuss (2014) argue that 'probabilistic forecasting aims to maximize the sharpness of the predictive distributions, subject to reliability', where *reliability* (also called *calibration* or *unbiasedness*) refers to the statistical consistency between the distributional forecasts and the observations, while *sharpness* to how tightly the predicted distribution covers the actual one, i.e. to the concentration of the predictive distributions. For instance, if a 90% prediction interval (PI) covers 90% of the observed prices, then this PI is said to be reliable (Pinson et al., 2007), well calibrated (Gneiting et al., 2007) or unbiased (Taylor, 1999). To obtain the empirical coverage we typically focus on the indicator series of 'hits and misses': $I_{d,h} = 1$ if $P_{d,h} \in \left[\hat{L}_{d,h}, \hat{U}_{d,h}\right]$ and zero otherwise. Some authors simply report the empirical coverage itself (*PI coverage probability*, PICP), while others subtract it from the nominal level (*PI nominal coverage*, PINC) to obtain the *average coverage error*: ACE = PICP − PINC. Generally, the closer is ACE to zero the better. However, to formally check *unconditional coverage* (UC), i.e. whether $\mathbb{P}\left(I_{d,h} = 1\right) = (1 - \alpha)$, we can use the approach of Kupiec (1995), which tests if $I_{d,h}$ is i.i.d. Bernoulli with mean $(1 - \alpha)$.

Since the Kupiec test does not have any power against the alternative that the ones and zeros come clustered together in $I_{d,h}$, Christoffersen (1998) introduced the *independence* and *conditional coverage* (CC) tests. Independence is tested against an explicit first-order Markov alternative and the latter is simply a joint test for independence and UC. In order to capture more than just the first-order dependency, we can conduct the independence test (and consequently the CC test) for any time lag or use the Ljung-Box statistics for a joint test of independence for several lags (Berkowitz et al., 2011).

Testing for the goodness-of-fit of a predictive distribution is, in general, more challenging than evaluating the reliability of a PI. The most common approach is to use the *Probability Integral Transform*:

$$\text{PIT}_{d,h} = \hat{F}_P\left(P_{d,h}\right). \tag{35.6}$$

If the distributional forecast is perfect, then $\text{PIT}_{d,h}$ is independent and uniformly distributed, which can be assessed using a formal statistical test or graphically (Gneiting and Katzfuss, 2014).

Alternatively, we can first apply the inverse of the standard normal CDF to $\text{PIT}_{d,h}$ to yield a Gaussian random variable, then jointly test for independence and normality (i.e. for conditional coverage) using the approach of Berkowitz (2001). The argument behind this is that in finite samples, tests based on the Gaussian likelihood are more convenient and flexible than tests of uniformity.

The definition of *sharpness*, on the other hand, derives from the idea that reliable predictive distributions of null width would correspond to perfect point predictions (Gneiting and Raftery, 2007). Unlike reliability, which is a joint property of the predictions and the observations, sharpness is a property of the forecasts only. Sharpness is closely related to the concept of the proper scoring rules. In fact, scoring rules assess reliability and sharpness simultaneously (Gneiting and Katzfuss, 2014).

The *pinball loss* for quantile forecasts and the *continuous ranked probability score* (CRPS) for distributional forecasts are the two most popular proper scoring rules in energy forecasting. The pinball loss is a special case of an *asymmetric piecewise linear loss* function:

$$PL\left(\hat{q}_{\alpha,P}, P_{d,h}, \alpha\right) = \begin{cases} (1-\alpha)\left(\hat{q}_{\alpha,P} - P_{d,h}\right), & \text{for } P_{d,h} < \hat{q}_{\alpha,P}, \\ \alpha\left(P_{d,h} - \hat{q}_{\alpha,P}\right), & \text{for } P_{d,h} \geq \hat{q}_{\alpha,P}, \end{cases} \tag{35.7}$$

where $\hat{q}_{\alpha,P}$ is the quantile function and $P_{d,h}$ is the actually observed price. The pinball loss (also known as the *linlin, bilinear*, or *newsboy* loss; Elliott and Timmermann, 2016) is a strictly proper score for the α-th quantile. To provide an aggregate score, the pinball loss can be averaged across different quantiles, e.g. 99 percentiles (but also across the 24 hours of the target day, as in the GEFCom2014 competition; see, e.g. Dudek, 2016; Maciejowska and Nowotarski, 2016). If the α-grid is arbitrarily dense, then this average converges to:

$$CRPS\left(\hat{F}_P, P_{d,h}\right) = \int_{-\infty}^{\infty} F(z) - \mathbb{I}_{\{z \geq P_{d,h}\}} dz = \mathbb{E}\left|\hat{P}_{d,h} - P_{d,h}\right| - \frac{1}{2}\mathbb{E}\left|\hat{P}_{d,h} - \hat{P}'_{d,h}\right|, \tag{35.8}$$

where random variables $\hat{P}_{d,h}$ and $\hat{P}'_{d,h}$ are two independent copies distributed as $\hat{F}_P$; the CRPS is a strictly proper score for the true distribution F_P. The latter representation reflects the reliability in the first term and the lack of sharpness in the second. Naturally, a lower pinball or CRPS score indicates a better forecast. Scores for two probabilistic forecasts can be tested for equal predictive performance using one of the methods discussed in Section 5.4.

5.3 Ensemble forecasts

When evaluating ensemble forecasts we consider $\mathcal{E}_M(\hat{P}_d) = (\hat{P}_d^{(1)}, \ldots, \hat{P}_d^{(M)})$, i.e. the ensemble that approximates the multivariate distributional forecast $\hat{F}_P$ of $\mathbf{P}_d$, and a scoring rule for multivariate distributions. Out of the rules defined in the literature (Gneiting and Raftery, 2007; Scheuerer and Hamill, 2015), the *Dawid-Sebastiani* and *variogram scores* are not strictly proper for multivariate distributions, while the *log-score* requires forecasts of a multivariate density, which for many models is not available. Only the *energy score* introduced by Gneiting and Raftery (2007) satisfies our criteria and hence is recommended for evaluating ensemble forecasts. It can be regarded as a multivariate version of the CRPS:

$$ES\left(\hat{F}_P, \mathbf{P}_d\right) = \mathbb{E}\|\hat{P}_d - \mathbf{P}_d\|_2 - \frac{1}{2}\mathbb{E}\|\hat{P}_d - \hat{P}'_d\|_2 \tag{35.9}$$

where $\hat{P}_d$ and $\hat{P}_d'$ are two independent copies distributed as $\hat{F}_p$ and $\| \cdot \|_2$ denotes the Euclidean norm. The energy score can be estimated using the ensemble $\mathcal{E}_M\left(\hat{P}_d\right)$ by replacing the expected values in Eqn. (9) by the sample means across the ensemble. The energy score is based on the energy distance, which is an extremely powerful tool in multivariate statistics (Székely and Rizzo, 2013). For instance, it allows to construct tests for multivariate independence or tests for the equality of two multivariate distributions.

5.4 Testing for equal predictive performance

The methods discussed in Sections 5.1–5.3 can be used to rank the forecasts, but not to draw statistically significant conclusions on the outperformance of the forecasts of one model by those of another. The extremely simple Diebold and Mariano (1995) test can be used for exactly this purpose. It is an asymptotic z-test of the hypothesis that the mean of the *loss differential* series:

$$\delta_{d,h} = S_1\left(\hat{F}_p, \hat{P}_{d,h}\right) - S_2\left(F_p, P_{d,h}\right) \tag{35.10}$$

is zero, where $S_i(\cdot, \cdot)$ is the score of the forecasts of model i. Although the DM test is much more popular in the point forecasting literature, it is readily applicable to probabilistic and ensemble forecasts (Nowotarski and Weron, 2018). In the point forecasting context, $S_i(\cdot, \cdot)$ will usually be the absolute $|e_{d,h}|$ or squared $e^2_{d,h}$ error, and in the probabilistic or ensemble forecasting context, it may be any strictly proper scoring rule, in particular the pinball loss, the CRPS or the energy score. Given the loss differential series, we compute the statistic:

$$\mathrm{DM} = \sqrt{\mathcal{D}\mathcal{H}}\,\frac{\hat{\mu}\left(\delta_{d,h}\right)}{\hat{\sigma}\left(\delta_{d,h}\right)}, \tag{35.11}$$

where $\hat{\mu}\left(\delta_{d,h}\right)$ and $\hat{\sigma}\left(\delta_{d,h}\right)$ are the sample mean and standard deviation of $\delta_{d,h}$, respectively, and $\mathcal{D}\mathcal{H}$ is the length of the out-of-sample test period. The key hypothesis of equal predictive accuracy (i.e. equal expected loss) corresponds to $\mathbb{E}(\delta_{d,h}) = 0$, in which case, under the assumption of covariance stationarity of $\delta_{d,h}$, the DM statistic is asymptotically standard normal, and one- or two-sided asymptotic tail probabilities are readily calculated. To avoid a common mistake, we should remember that the DM test compares forecasts of two models, not the models themselves (Diebold, 2015).

Since in day-ahead electricity markets the predictions for all 24 hours of the next day are usually made at the same time using the same information set, forecast errors for a particular day will typically exhibit high serial correlation. Therefore, it is advisable to separately conduct the DM tests for each load period $h = 1,\ldots,\mathcal{H}$ (as in Bordignon et al., 2013; Nowotarski et al., 2014; Uniejewski et al., 2016) or jointly for all load periods (as suggested by Ziel and Weron, 2018). Obviously, in both approaches the out-of-sample length $\mathcal{D}\mathcal{H}$ in Equation (35.11) is reduced to $\mathcal{D}$. Note, that for ensemble forecasting only the latter approach is feasible, so that only one statistic for each pair of models is computed based on the $\mathcal{H}$-dimensional vector of errors for each day.

Alternative forecast comparison test procedures include the *model confidence set* (MCS) approach of Hansen et al. (2011), a test of *forecast encompassing* (Harvey et al., 1998) and the Giacomini and White (2006) test for *conditional predictive ability* (CPA). For two models, the MCS approach is similar to the DM test but estimates the distribution of the test statistic by a bootstrap procedure. In the test of *forecast encompassing*, the null hypothesis is that model 2 encompasses model 1, i.e.

that predictions of model 1 do not contain additional information with respect to those of model 2. Finally, in the CPA test the null hypothesis is H_0: $\phi = 0$ in the regression:

$$\delta_{d,h} = \phi' \mathbb{X}_{d-1,h} + \varepsilon_{d,h}, \tag{35.12}$$

where $\mathbb{X}_{d-1,h}$ contains elements from the information set on day $d-1$ and load period h (or all load periods for a joint score), i.e. a constant and lags of $\delta_{d,h}$. While both the CPA and DM tests can be used for nested and non-nested models – as long as the calibration window does not grow with the sample size (Giacomini and Rossi, 2013) – only the CPA test accounts for parameter estimation uncertainty (through 'conditioning') and hence is the preferred option.

6 Conclusions

We have presented an overview and guidelines for the rigorous use of methods, evaluation measures and tests for EPFs. However, this chapter has a much broader reach. Most of the presented approaches are universal enough to be used for energy forecasting in general, for instance, very short-term load forecasting for smart grid applications (see Chapters 14 and 29) or wind and solar power forecasting. Moreover, with the increasing role of probabilistic and ensemble predictions in general, we hope that this review will propel those working in other areas of forecasting to move into the continuously evolving (see Chapter 7) and still largely unexplored world of wholesale electricity markets.

Acknowledgments

This work was partially supported by the German Research Foundation (DFG, Germany) and the National Science Center (NCN, Poland) through grant IMMORTAL (DFG 379008354; NCN 2016/23/G/HS4/01005).

References

Abedinia, O., Amjady, N., and Zareipour, H. (2017). A new feature selection technique for load and price forecast of electrical power systems. *IEEE Transactions on Power Systems*, 32(1):62–74.

Aggarwal, S., Saini, L., and Kumar, A. (2009). Electricity price forecasting in deregulated markets: A review and evaluation. *International Journal of Electrical Power and Energy Systems*, 31:13–22.

Amjady, N. (2006). Day-ahead price forecasting of electricity markets by a new fuzzy neural network. *IEEE Transactions on Power Systems*, 21(2):887–896.

Andrade, J., Filipe, J., Reis, M., & Bessa, R. (2017). Probabilistic price forecasting for day-ahead and intraday markets: Beyond the statistical model. *Sustainability*, 9(11), 1990.

Bello, A., Bunn, D., Reneses, J., and Muñoz, A. (2016). Parametric density recalibration of a fundamental market model to forecast electricity prices. *Energies*, 9(11):959.

Benth, F., Kiesel, R., and Nazarova, A. (2012). A critical empirical study of three electricity spot price models. *Energy Economics*, 34(5):1589–1616.

Benth, F. E., Benth, J. S., and Koekebakker, S. (2008). *Stochastic Modeling of Electricity and Related Markets*. World Scientific, Singapore.

Berkowitz, J. (2001). Testing density forecasts, with applications to risk management. *Journal of Business & Economic Statistics*, 19(4):465–474.

Berkowitz, J., Christoffersen, P., and Pelletier, D. (2011). Evaluating value-at-risk models with desk-level data. *Management Science*, 57(12):2213–2227.

Bordignon, S., Bunn, D. W., Lisi, F., and Nan, F. (2013). Combining day-ahead forecasts for British electricity prices. *Energy Economics*, 35:88–103.

Borgosz-Koczwara, M., Weron, A., and Wyłomańska, A. (2009). Stochastic models for bidding strategies on oligopoly electricity market. *Mathematical Methods of Operations Research*, 69(3):579–592.

Carmona, R. and Coulon, M. (2014). A survey of commodity markets and structural models for electricity prices. In Benth, F., Kholodnyi, V., and Laurence, P., editors, *Quantitative Energy Finance: Modeling, Pricing, and Hedging in Energy and Commodity Markets*, pages 41–83. Springer, New York.

Cartea, A. and Figueroa, M. (2005). Pricing in electricity markets: A mean reverting jump diffusion model with seasonality. *Applied Mathematical Finance*, 12(4):313–335.

Catalão, J.P.S., Mariano, S.J.P.S., Mendes, V.M.F., and Ferreira, L.A.F.M. (2007). Short-term electricity prices forecasting in a competitive market: A neural network approach. *Electric Power Systems Research*, 77(10):1297–1304.

Chen, D. and Bunn, D. (2014). The forecasting performance of a finite mixture regime-switching model for daily electricity prices. *Journal of Forecasting*, 33(5):364–375.

Christoffersen, P. (1998). Evaluating interval forecasts. *International Economic Review*, 39(4):841–862.

Conejo, A. J., Contreras, J., Espínola, R., and Plazas, M. A. (2005). Forecasting electricity prices for a day-ahead pool-based electric energy market. *International Journal of Forecasting*, 21:435–462.

Contreras, J., Espínola, R., Nogales, F., and Conejo, A. (2003). ARIMA models to predict next-day electricity prices. *IEEE Transactions on Power Systems*, 18(3):1014–1020.

Cruz, A., Muñoz, A., Zamora, J., and Espinola, R. (2011). The effect of wind generation and weekday on Spanish electricity spot price forecasting. *Electric Power Systems Research*, 81(10):1924–1935.

De Jong, C. (2006). The nature of power spikes: A regime-switch approach. *Studies in Nonlinear Dynamics & Econometrics*, 10(3):Article 3.

Diebold, F. X. (2015). Comparing predictive accuracy, twenty years later: A personal perspective on the use and abuse of Diebold-Mariano tests. *Journal of Business and Economic Statistics*, 33(1):1–9.

Diebold, F. X. and Mariano, R. S. (1995). Comparing predictive accuracy. *Journal of Business and Economic Statistics*, 13:253–263.

Dudek, G. (2016). Multilayer perceptron for GEFCom2014 probabilistic electricity price forecasting. *International Journal of Forecasting*, 32:1057–1060.

Elliott, G. and Timmermann, A. (2016). *Economic Forecasting*. Princeton University Press, Princeton, NJ.

Eydeland, A. and Wolyniec, K. (2003). *Energy and Power Risk Management: New Developments in Modeling, Pricing, and Hedging*. John Wiley & Sons, Hoboken, NJ.

Gaillard, P., Goude, Y., and Nedellec, R. (2016). Additive models and robust aggregation for GEFCom2014 probabilistic electric load and electricity price forecasting. *International Journal of Forecasting*, 32(3):1038–1050.

Geman, H. and Roncoroni, A. (2006). Understanding the fine structure of electricity prices. *Journal of Business*, 79:1225–1261.

Giacomini, R. and Rossi, B. (2013). Forecasting in macroeconomics. In Hashimzade, N. and Thornton, M., editors, *Handbook of Research Methods and Applications on Empirical Macroeconomics*, pages 381–407. Edward Elgar, Cheltenham.

Giacomini, R. and White, H. (2006). Tests of conditional predictive ability. *Econometrica*, 74(6):1545–1578.

Gianfreda, A., Parisio, L., and Pelagatti, M. (2016). The impact of RES in the Italian day-ahead and balancing markets. *Energy Journal*, 37:161–184.

Gneiting, T., Balabdaoui, F., and Raftery, A. (2007). Probabilistic forecasts, calibration and sharpness. *Journal of the Royal Statistical Society B*, 69:243–268.

Gneiting, T. and Katzfuss, M. (2014). Probabilistic forecasting. *The Annual Review of Statistics and Its Application*, 1:125–151.

Gneiting, T. and Raftery, A. (2007). Strictly proper scoring rules, prediction, and estimation. *Journal of the American Statistical Association*, 102(477):359–378.

Gonzalez, V., Contreras, J., and Bunn, D. (2012). Forecasting power prices using a hybrid fundamental-econometric model. *IEEE Transactions on Power Systems*, 27(1):363–372.

Gürtler, M. and Paulsen, T. (2018). Forecasting performance of time series models on electricity spot markets: A quasi-meta-analysis. *International Journal of Energy Sector Management*, 12(1):103–129.

Hansen, P. R., Lunde, A., and Nason, J. M. (2011). The model confidence set. *Econometrica*, 79:453–497.

Harvey, D., Leybourne, S., and Newbold, P. (1998). Tests for forecast encompassing. *Journal of Business and Economic Statistics*, 16:254–259.

Holmberg, P., Newbery, D., and Ralph, D. (2013). Supply function equilibria: Step functions and continuous representations. *Journal of Economic Theory*, 148(4):1509–1551.

Hong, T., Pinson, P., Fan, S., Zareipour, H., Troccoli, A., and Hyndman, R. J. (2016). Probabilistic energy forecasting: Global Energy Forecasting Competition 2014 and beyond. *International Journal of Forecasting*, 32(3):896–913.

Hubicka, K., Marcjasz, G., and Weron, R. (2019). A note on averaging day-ahead electricity price forecasts across calibration windows. *IEEE Transactions on Sustainable Energy*, 10:321–323.

Huurman, C., Ravazzolo, F., and Zhou, C. (2012). The power of weather. *Computational Statistics and Data Analysis*, 56(11):3793–3807.

Hyndman, R. and Koehler, A. (2006). Another look at measures of forecast accuracy. *International Journal of Forecasting*, 22(4):679–688.

Janczura, J., Trück, S., Weron, R., and Wolff, R. (2013). Identifying spikes and seasonal components in electricity spot price data: A guide to robust modeling. *Energy Economics*, 38:96–110.

Janczura, J. and Weron, R. (2010). An empirical comparison of alternate regime-switching models for electricity spot prices. *Energy Economics*, 32(5):1059–1073.

Jonsson, T., Pinson, P., Nielsen, H. A., Madsen, H., and Nielsen, T. (2013). Forecasting electricity spot prices accounting for wind power predictions. *IEEE Transactions on Sustainable Energy*, 4(1):210–218.

Joskow, P. (2008). Lessons learned from electricity market liberalization. *Energy Journal*, 29:9–42.

Kanamura, T. and Ohashi, K. (2007). A structural model for electricity prices with spikes: Measurement of spike risk and optimal policies for hydropower plant operation. *Energy Economics*, 29(5):1010–1032.

Keles, D., Scelle, J., Paraschiv, F., and Fichtner, W. (2016). Extended forecast methods for day-ahead electricity spot prices applying artificial neural networks. *Applied Energy*, 162:218–230.

Keller, J., Liu, D., and Fogel, D. (2016). *Fundamentals of Computational Intelligence: Neural Networks, Fuzzy Systems, and Evolutionary Computation*. Hoboken, NJ: Wiley.

Kiesel, R. and Paraschiv, F. (2017). Econometric analysis of 15-minute intraday electricity prices. *Energy Economics*, 64:77–90.

Klæboe, G., Eriksrud, A. L., and Fleten, S.-E. (2015). Benchmarking time series based forecasting models for electricity balancing market prices. *Energy Systems*, 6(1):43–61.

Koopman, S., Ooms, M., and Carnero, A. (2007). Periodic seasonal Reg-ARFIMA-GARCH models for daily electricity spot prices. *Journal of the American Statistical Association*, 102:16–27.

Kristiansen, T. (2012). Forecasting Nord Pool day-ahead prices with an autoregressive model. *Energy Policy*, 49:328–332.

Kupiec, P. H. (1995). Techniques for verifying the accuracy of risk measurement models. *The Journal of Derivatives*, 3(2):73–84.

Ludwig, N., Feuerriegel, S., and Neumann, D. (2015). Putting big data analytics to work: Feature selection for forecasting electricity prices using the LASSO and random forests. *Journal of Decision Systems*, 24(1):19–36.

Lund, H., Sorknæs, P., Mathiesen, B. V., and Hansen, K. (2018). Beyond sensitivity analysis: A methodology to handle fuel and electricity prices when designing energy scenarios. *Energy Research & Social Science*, 39:108–116.

Maciejowska, K.; Nitka, W.; Weron, T. (2019). Day-ahead vs. intraday – Forecasting the price spread to maximize economic benefits. *Energies*, 12:631.

Maciejowska, K. and Nowotarski, J. (2016). A hybrid model for GEFCom2014 probabilistic electricity price forecasting. *International Journal of Forecasting*, 32(3):1051–1056.

Maciejowska, K., Nowotarski, J., and Weron, R. (2016). Probabilistic forecasting of electricity spot prices using Factor Quantile Regression Averaging. *International Journal of Forecasting*, 32(3):957–965.

Maciejowska, K. and Weron, R. (2016). Short- and mid-term forecasting of baseload electricity prices in the U.K.: The impact of intra-day price relationships and market fundamentals. *IEEE Transactions on Power Systems*, 31(2):994–1005.

Marcjasz, G., Serafin, T., and Weron, R. (2018). Selection of calibration windows for day-ahead electricity price forecasting. *Energies*, 11(9):2364.

Marcjasz, G., Uniejewski, B., and Weron, R. (2019). On the importance of the long-term seasonal component in day-ahead electricity price forecasting with NARX neural networks. *International Journal of Forecasting*. DOI: 10.1016/j.ijforecast.2017.11.009.

Mayer, K. and Trück, S. (2018). Electricity markets around the world. *Journal of Commodity Markets*, 9:77–100.

Misiorek, A., Trück, S., and Weron, R. (2006). Point and interval forecasting of spot electricity prices: Linear vs. non-linear time series models. *Studies in Nonlinear Dynamics & Econometrics*, 10(3):Article 2.

Mohamed, A. and El-Hawary, M. (2016). 2016 IEEE Canadian Conference on Electrical and Computer Engineering (CCECE), Vancouver, BC, Canada, DOI: 10.1109/CCECE.2016.7726765.

Monteiro, C., Ramirez-Rosado, I., Fernandez-Jimenez, L., & Conde, P. (2016). Short-term price forecasting models based on artificial neural networks for intraday sessions in the Iberian electricity market. *Energies*, 9(9), 721.

Narajewski, M., Ziel, F. (2018) Econometric modelling and forecasting of intraday electricity prices. Working Paper, arXiv:1812.09081.

Nowotarski, J., Raviv, E., Trück, S., and Weron, R. (2014). An empirical comparison of alternate schemes for combining electricity spot price forecasts. *Energy Economics*, 46:395–412.

Nowotarski, J. and Weron, R. (2015). Computing electricity spot price prediction intervals using quantile regression and forecast averaging. *Computational Statistics*, 30(3):791–803.

Nowotarski, J. and Weron, R. (2018). Recent advances in electricity price forecasting: A review of probabilistic forecasting. *Renewable and Sustainable Energy Reviews*, 81:1548–1568.

Pinson, P., Nielsen, H., Moller, J., Madsen, H., and Kariniotakis, G. (2007). Non-parametric probabilistic forecasts of wind power: Required properties and evaluation. *Wind Energy*, 10(6):497–516.

Ries, J., Gaudard, L., and Romerio, F. (2016). Interconnecting an isolated electricity system to the European market: The case of Malta. *Utilities Policy*, 40:1–14.

Ruibal, C. and Mazumdar, M. (2008). Forecasting the mean and the variance of electricity prices in deregulated markets. *IEEE Transactions on Power Systems*, 23(1):25–32.

Scheuerer, M. and Hamill, T. M. (2015). Variogram-based proper scoring rules for probabilistic forecasts of multivariate quantities. *Monthly Weather Review*, 143(4):1321–1334.

Steinert, R. and Ziel, F. (2019). Short-to mid-term day-ahead electricity price forecasting using futures. Working Paper, arXiv:1801.10583. To appear in: *The Energy Journal*, 40(1): 105–127.

Székely, G. J. and Rizzo, M. L. (2013). Energy statistics: A class of statistics based on distances. *Journal of Statistical Planning and Inference*, 143(8):1249–1272.

Taylor, J. W. (1999). Evaluating volatility and interval forecasts. *Journal of Forecasting*, 18:111–128.

Uniejewski, B., Marcjasz, G., Weron, R. (2019) Understanding intraday electricity markets: Variable selection and very short-term price forecasting using LASSO, *International Journal of Forecasting* (doi: 10.1016/j.ijforecast.2019.02.001)

Uniejewski, B., Nowotarski, J., and Weron, R. (2016). Automated variable selection and shrinkage for day-ahead electricity price forecasting. *Energies*, 9:621.

Uniejewski, B., Weron, R., and Ziel, F. (2018). Variance stabilizing transformations for electricity spot price forecasting. *IEEE Transactions on Power Systems*, 33(2):2219–2229.

Vehviläinen, I. and Pyykkönen, T. (2005). Stochastic factor model for electricity spot price: The case of the Nordic market. *Energy Economics*, 27(2):351–367.

Ventosa, M., Baillo, A., Ramos, A., and Rivier, M. (2005). Electricity market modeling trends. *Energy Policy*, 33(7):897–913.

Weron, R. (2006). *Modeling and Forecasting Electricity Loads and Prices: A Statistical Approach*. John Wiley & Sons, Chichester.

Weron, R. (2008). Market price of risk implied by Asian-style electricity options and futures. *Energy Economics*, 30:1098–1115.

Weron, R. (2014). Electricity price forecasting: A review of the state-of-the-art with a look into the future. *International Journal of Forecasting*, 30(4):1030–1081.

Weron, R. and Misiorek, A. (2008). Forecasting spot electricity prices: A comparison of parametric and semiparametric time series models. *International Journal of Forecasting*, 24:744–763.

Weron, R. and Zator, M. (2014). Revisiting the relationship between spot and futures prices in the Nord Pool electricity market. *Energy Economics*, 44:178–190.

Wolff, G. and Feuerriegel, S. (2017). Short-term dynamics of day-ahead and intraday electricity prices. *International Journal of Energy Sector Management*, 11(4):557–573.

Young, D., Poletti, S., and Browne, O. (2014). Can agent-based models forecast spot prices in electricity markets? Evidence from the New Zealand electricity market. *Energy Economics*, 45:419–434.

Zaleski, P. and Klimczak, D. (2015). Prospects for the rise of renewable sources of energy in Poland: Balancing renewables on the intra-day market. In Zamasz, K., editor, *Capacity Market in Contemporary Economic Policy*, 124–138. Difin, Warsaw.

Ziel, F. (2016). Forecasting electricity spot prices using LASSO: On capturing the autoregressive intraday structure. *IEEE Transactions on Power Systems*, 31(6):4977–4987.

Ziel, F. and Steinert, R. (2016). Electricity price forecasting using sale and purchase curves: The X-model. *Energy Economics*, 59:435–454.

Ziel, F. and Steinert, R. (2018). Probabilistic mid- and long-term electricity price forecasting. *Renewable and Sustainable Energy Reviews*, 94:251–266.

Ziel, F., Steinert, R., and Husmann, S. (2015). Efficient modeling and forecasting of electricity spot prices. *Energy Economics*, 47:89–111.

Ziel, F. and Weron, R. (2018). Day-ahead electricity price forecasting with high-dimensional structures: Univariate vs. multivariate modeling frameworks. *Energy Economics*, 70:396–420.

36

Paths and processes in complex electricity markets

The agent-based perspective

*Alessandro Sciullo, Elena Vallino,
Martina Iori, and Magda Fontana*

1 Electricity systems as complex systems

1.1 The complexification of electricity systems

An electricity market emerges from the interaction of several heterogeneous actors. On the one hand, generators, transmission system operators, distribution system operators, and retailers are engaged in producing and delivering a good with distinctive features: electricity is not storable, demand is subject to stochastic and temporal variations, and provision takes place via a physical network in which supply needs always to be equal to demand (Bollinger et al. 2016). On the other hand, households by virtues of policies aiming at discarding the traditional natural monopoly structure and at favoring generalized access and efficient economic conditions have assumed an unprecedented active role. Households can switch retailers and tariffs acting as a driver for competition and, by becoming prosumers, can participate in energy production and distribution. This interplay blurs the boundaries of the economic categories of demand and supply and casts doubts on the explanatory and predictive power of market models based on equilibrium.

The understanding of the electricity market behaviors requires the joint investigation of different processes like technology diffusion (i.e. smart grid), service innovation and the widening set of motivations for individual behaviors. Objectives like profit and utility maximization need to be complemented as the awareness of the consequences of climate change and the need for sustainable energy production and consumption increases.

This chapter aims to set out the ways in which complex systems thinking and modeling could be useful in understanding the functioning and evolution of the electricity markets. The final objective is to provide useful insights in order to address current and future policy challenges that is "to design appropriate economic and control mechanisms to handle demand and supply transactions among the increasingly heterogeneous and dispersed collection of participants in modern electric power systems" (Tesfatsion 2018).

1.2 Complex systems: a general outline

The study of social phenomena as complex systems has become a fruitful area of research and application over the last 30 years, particularly since the founding of the Santa Fe Institute in 1984. However, the application of the concepts developed in the complexity domain to the understanding of energy systems is relatively recent (Tesfatsion 2018; Vasiljevka et al. 2017; Bale et al. 2015; Moglia et al. 2018).

In biological and physical sciences and in engineering systems theory is widely used, exploiting the powerful representation of a system as a collection of its parts which are interacting among themselves. The branch of systems dynamics acknowledges the role of positive and negative feedback, that produces systems running out of control, and the role of virtuous and vicious cycles, in which systems can be kept on the same track for a long time. Starting from this background, scholars of the Santa Fe Institute investigated the common features of a range of systems exhibiting complexity, such as emergence, non-linearity, self-organization, co-evolution, adaptation (Holland 1995). Complexity studies analyze how processes which are different in nature and domain, such as physical, social and political phenomena, interact with each other, and, most importantly, influence each other, leading to the development of emergent properties at the system level (Fontana 2010, De Marchi and Page 2014). The core aim of this research stream is of course linked to the possibility to improve the management of complex systems thanks to the understanding of these features and principles.

Complexity science is presently an established domain of research, characterized by multi-disciplinarity, including an increasing body of scholars in different disciplines (Squazzoni 2010), such as economics (Farmer and Foley 2009; Arthur 1999; Foxon et al. 2013; Fontana 2010), innovation (Bonifati 2010), and private and public management (Secchi and Neumann 2016; Anderson 1999; Teisman and Klijn 2008). The advocacy for the application of a broader range of complexity tools and approaches to economic issues is constantly increasing. Figure 36.1

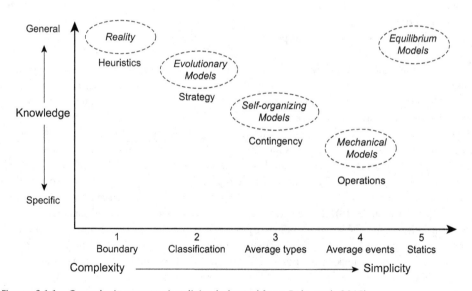

Figure. 36.1   Complexity versus simplicity (adapted from Bale et al. 2015)

illustrates the relation of modeling techniques in the field of complexity studies with the more conventional and simplistic ones, such as the calculation of an equilibrium given by the interplay between supply and demand. In the following paragraphs we focus on the features of energy systems that qualify these structures as suitable for a complexity oriented analysis.

1.3 Characteristics of complexity science and relevance for energy systems

One area where complexity methods can add value over other modeling methods is in addressing questions at the technology-policy-behavior interface by incorporating social and institutional elements in the study of energy systems.

Electricity is a peculiar commodity, in fact it is a homogeneous good produced by heterogeneous sources with different costs of production (Domanico 2007). It cannot be stored in large quantity, and it demands a continuous balance between demand and supply. For this reason a comprehensive simulation of electricity market should consider all the aspects and actors in the system and their interaction. Each of these entities cannot be imagined as independent and cannot be imagined as ordinary boundary condition (Chassin et al. 2014).

Energy systems thus can be understood as complex adaptive systems in that they are composed by interrelated, heterogeneous elements (agents and objects). In addition, there is no autonomous control over the whole system, and, in that sense, self-organized emergent behavior arises and it cannot be predicted by understanding each of the component elements separately. For example, the introduction of a new technology (an object) will influence the behavior of one or more individuals (agents), which leads to direct and indirect effects (such as resilience, security) on other parts of the system.

Energy systems exhibit both complex social and technological dynamics. Existing modeling approaches focus only on some of the aspects of this complexity (Bale et al. 2015). From a complexity perspective, energy systems are composed by (1) agents that interact through networks under the rules given by institutions, which leads to the development of emergent properties and co-evolutionary dynamics, (2) objects, such as technologies and infrastructures whose adoption is dynamic and fluctuating, and (3) the environment, which provides both the resources and also the social and political framework in which the dynamics of the energy system occur (Ibid.).

The crucial agents in energy systems are households and enterprises as energy consumers, energy conversion and supply companies, economic and environmental regulators, and local and central governments. These agents adapt and react to other agents' actions and to objects, and are heterogeneous in features, objectives and processes of decision-making. They interact through physical and social networks, by sharing information or learning from one another, influenced by social norms and institutional rules (Tesfatsion 2018; Vasiljevka et al. 2017). In this sense they do not own the perfect rationality that characterizes the entities of standard economic models (De Marchi and Page 2014). This may lead to self-organization and emergent properties, such as shared practices for energy use or given institutional arrangements for markets governing energy supply (Moglia et al. 2018). These interactions are dynamics over time and change following the availability of new objects and policies. However, as both technologies and institutions are embedded in positive feedbacks in the adoption process, change is subject to path dependency and systems experience lock-in phenomena (Unruh 2000). This implies that potentially advantageous innovations may not be adopted if they are not compatible with the current system, or if virtuous circles are not triggered (Bale et al. 2015).

Due to the heterogeneity of objects, agents, interactions and processes involved in energy systems, the application of complexity science in this domain calls for a methodology that should be able to promote a deep collaboration across disciplines, embracing the perspectives of mathematics, engineering, economics and the social sciences, as well as engagement with practitioners in the field.

2 Concepts and tools for dealing with complexity: agent-based modeling (ABM)

2.1 ABM, the right modeling for social sciences

Dynamics and properties of energy systems are thus inherently complex. As well as other social processes, they 'emerge' in an unpredictable way from many non – linear interactions among many heterogeneous elementary agents and they are not decomposable into separate sub-processes – economic, demographic, cultural – whose isolated analysis can be aggregated to give adequate analysis of the social process as a whole (Epstein and Axtell 1996; Gilbert 2004).

The challenge for social scientists is to find a way to deal with three main properties that characterize complex social systems (CSS): *heterogeneity* of agents and interactions; *emergence* as a non-linear process that link different levels of the system; *path-dependency* as the influence that the initial conditions may have on the dynamics of the system. In consideration of these complex properties it has been said that social science is often the actual hard science.[1]

As mentioned in paragraph 1, in order to explore this complexity, a modeling approach is needed to replace "the part of the universe under consideration by a model of similar but simpler structure [as] no substantial part of the universe is so simple that it can be grasped and controlled without abstraction" (Rosenblueth and Wiener 1945).

The best candidate to implement this modeling approach in social science is Agent Based Modeling. Through statistical models in fact it is not feasible to grasp heterogeneity and non-linearity. Other simulation techniques (Table 36.1), based on parameterized systems of differential equations are not able to capture physical, institutional and behavioral aspects and to combine empirical accuracy and analytical tractability (Borrill and Tesfatsion 2011). Some computational and computer-based simulations are efficient in grasping some emergent processes and dynamics aspects but are only partially suitable to represent and analyze heterogeneity and interaction. ABM is the only approach that allows representing many heterogeneous agents acting and interacting in an evolving multi-level environment following evolutionary rules of behaviors based on their learning processes.

Table 36.1 Social science simulation techniques (adapted from Gilbert and Troitzsch 2005)

Simulation technique		No. of Levels	Interaction among agents	Complexity of agents	Number agents
System dynamics		1	No	Low	1
Microsimulation		2	No	High	Many
Queuing models		1	No	Low	Many
Multilevel simulation		2+	Maybe	Low	Many
Cellular automata		2	Yes	Low	Many
ABM	Multi-agents	2+	Yes	High	Few
	Learning models	2+	Maybe	High	Many

ABM is a relatively young methodology that has been going through a fast development over the last two decades. In ABM social systems are modeled following a bottom-up approach as collections of autonomous interacting agents that operate within a computational world and adapt their behavior through learning procedures. Non-trivial properties at the macro-global level may arise from adaptation, learning and interaction mechanisms at the micro-individual level (Epstein 1999). In comparison to traditional equation-based modeling, ABM permits a more realistic representation of real-world systems composed of interacting distributed entities with limited information, limited possible responses, limited material resources and limited computational capabilities. The modeled systems are implicitly evolutionary as agents, like real people, can only acquire new data about their world locally and constructively, through interactions, and can have incomputable beliefs about their world that drive their behaviors and interactions (Borrill and Tesfatsion 2011).

Roughly speaking, an agent-based model is composed of three main ingredients (Epstein and Axtell 1996): *agents*, which are the people of artificial societies; *environment*, which is the natural or artificial landscape over which agents act and interact; *rules*, which define behaviors and interactions of agents and environment. Agents and environment should be clearly distinguishable in terms of *agency*, intended as the capability to autonomously act that is definitely what defines an agent (Gilbert and Troitzsch 2005).

Some principles should be considered in modeling ABM (Tesfatsion 2018):

1   *Agent scope*, that is, what agents represent (social, biological and/or physical entities).
2   *Agent definition and autonomy*. Agents are entities capable of acting over time on the basis of their own state (properties and rules) and their interactions are driven by rules embodied within agent states and not determined by the exterior.
3   *Constructivity (local and system)* that at any given time determines the action of an agent as a function of the agent's own state and the state of the modeled system as the ensemble of agent states.
4   *Historicity* or *path-dependency* that strongly connects all subsequent events in the modeled system to the given initial agent states.

In this framework, the modeler is an observer with a role that is limited to the initial settings and to the non-perturbational observation and analysis.

ABM definitely offer to social scientists a virtual laboratory where experiments can be carried out to develop and explore theories and dynamic aspects of change and to observe relations between different levels of the social systems (Gilbert and Troitzsch 2005).

2.2   How to design and implement an ABM in practice: toward a standardization

In order to build an ABM two main requirements have to be satisfied: a good conceptual design and formalization and a proper performing software implementation. One of the main criticalities for ABMs exploitation has been the lack of standardization with regard to both these aspects, a condition that hampered the starting of a cumulative knowledge process and the establishment of a robust community of scientists in the field. In the last decade two promising tools for ABM standardization have been gaining relevance: Netlogo as the programming language and the ODD protocol as a standardized conceptual framework.

Modeling cycle and ODD protocol

Autonomous processes that derive from agents' behaviors and decisions could make ABMs unpredictable. ABM modeling activity should be intended as a circular process that drives continuous

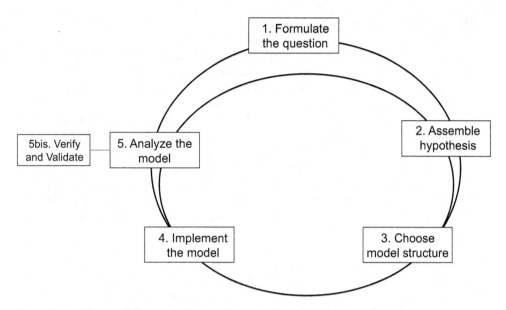

Figure 36.2   The modeling cycle (adapted from Railsback and Grimm 2012)

refinements and growing complexity of the model on the basis of the results produced by the model itself, as it is shown in Figure 36.2.[2]

1   *Formulate the question.* It is the primary filter for designing a model even if the question itself can be reformulated and refined along the modeling activity.
2   *Assemble hypotheses for essential processes and structures* that are explanatory hypotheses about the main components of the system under observation and their behaviors and interactions. They have to be simple in order to develop a first understanding of the system behavior and then they should be gradually specified and detailed so that model grows in complexity at each cycle.
3   *Choose scales, entities, state variables, procedures and parameters,* that is the (written) formulation of the model aimed at mathematically formalizing and operationalizing the hypotheses.
4   *Implement the model* through coding. Although it may seem a mere technical part of the cycle it is relevant to explore, in the logical way provided by programming languages, the rigor and consequences of hypotheses and assumptions.
5   *Analyze, test, and revise the model.* This is the actual scientific task aimed at assessing the robustness of the hypotheses and of the model itself. The *validation* activity (5bis in the figure) deserves particular attention as it is aimed at verifying, beyond the logic of the model, if the simulated outcomes reproduce, at least in stylized forms, the distribution of the phenomena in the real world that the model has been designed to describe.

Standardizing ABMs' designing process is crucial in order to force modelers in clearly formulating and formalizing their hypothesis and to make it possible to re-implement the models and, to the extent it is feasible, replicate their results.[3]

To bring the benefits of standardization to ABMs, a large group of experienced modelers developed the *Overview, Design concepts, and Details Protocol (ODD)* (Grimm et al. 2010).

The protocol is structured in three sections:

- *Overview*, aimed at providing a general description of what the model is about and how it is designed. The overview is divided in three subsections: purpose (i.e. scope and objective); entities, state variables and scales (i.e. agents, environment and properties); and process overview and scheduling (i.e. dynamics of the simulated system).
- *Design concepts*, aimed at depicting the model's essential components that characterize in details agents, environment and rules in order to deal with heterogeneity, emergence and path-dependency. It is divided into ten subsections: basic principles, emergence, adaptation, objectives, learning prediction, sensing, interaction, stochasticity, collectives, and observation.
- *Details*, which provide all the information needed to make the model implementation clear and repeatable. It is divided in three sections: initialization (i.e. initial conditions of simulation), input data (i.e. how the model is fed), and submodels (i.e. modeling of sub-systems and processes).

Object-oriented programming and Netlogo

After having defined it conceptually, making an ABM a working simulation is above all a matter of computation and for this reason ABM has been developing in the last two decades jointly with the development of IT sciences. Among the different programming languages, object-oriented programming (OOP) is the most suitable as the main element of an OOP are objects, virtual structures that hold both data (variables) and procedures (algorithms). Agents and environment are thus naturally implemented in OOP as objects. The agent's internal states (stable and variable properties) are implemented as the object data while the agent's behaviors are implemented as objects' procedures.

A recent review listed approximately 80 specific software tools for building ABMs that differentiate in their suitability to different fields of application, in their performance in terms of computational power and in the required programming skills (Abar et al. 2017).

Among these platforms, Netlogo[4] has been growing in diffusion among modelers for the last decade and today is considered as the standard for building ABMs of social phenomena.

Netlogo is developed in Java and it has been designed as an exploitation of the Logo language (a language created to teach programming to young students). It is a semi-natural programming language perfectly suitable to develop ABM as its main programming elements are agents ("turtles", patches and links) and it provides a huge library of primitives (both variables and methods) to model their properties, interactions and behaviors. These ABM-friendly features stand behind the worldwide success of Netlogo in modeling community even if it is not the most performing software tool. In fact, while on the one hand Netlogo makes it possible to "play" with models also for researchers without any (or very few) skills in programming, on the other hand, even in the case of experts programmers dealing with the designing of models that require large amount of computational power, Netlogo still provides a powerful environment to assess at a small scale the overall functioning of the model.

3 Energy-complexity models: some examples

3.1 Two generations of models

Looking at the electricity systems as paradigmatic example of socio-technical systems (Bollinger et al. 2016), here some agent-based simulations are proposed as examples of their potential in investigating electricity systems. By representing the behavior of real actors of the systems (whose importance is highlighted in Chapter 17), ABMs allow us to observe how the technical and social subsystems of an infrastructure co-evolve, and which overall system behavior might emerge from their ongoing interactions, at multiple system levels and time scales

It is clear that the worldwide process of liberalization and the recent technological advances have shaped the evolution of ABM in electricity markets. The introduction in the market of new autonomous actors and the transition from a monopolistic centralized structure to a system in which heterogeneous distributed agents strategically act favors the use of ABM as a crucial tool in electricity market simulation. In the electricity market context, agents' behavior should respect some real, physical and economic, constraints. Moreover, these entities have an imperfect local information about the environment and the purposes of other agents. They aim at satisfying some own specific goals, adapting their behaviors during the simulation and making decisions in a very uncertain environment, with few information about future events. The ABM paradigm can reproduce all these key features of the electricity market in several conditions, considering also out-of-equilibrium situations or states in which multiple equilibria are present.

In the following a brief literature review of ABM application in the field of electricity systems is presented.[5] In the early 2000s, shortly after the beginning of the deregulation process, the first agent-based studies (among which Bower and Bunn 2000) started appearing, focusing on the challenges that decentralized open markets were facing. At the beginning they mainly dealt with the design of wholesale markets, the price forecasting and the bidding strategies (Guerci and Rastegar 2009). Furthermore, some large-scale simulations have been designed to catch all these aspects of the market (Praça et al. 2003; Conzelmann et al. 2005; Grozev et al. 2005; Sun and Tesfatsion 2007). This part of literature is constantly updated and, during the years, models have been improved with the introduction of network constraints (Veit et al. 2009) and statistical validation (Young et al. 2014). It is important to emphasise that in these early simulations the main agents are generator companies, whereas demand is mainly considered as completely inelastic and consumers do not have an active role in the market.

One may think that a new stream of ABM literature about electricity market arose with the growing use of renewable sources in the process of energy generation, occurred during the first decade of 2000s. Several simulations, adding this new element of investigation, tried to respond to some rising concerns about reliability of supply, network balancing and prediction of wholesale prices (Sensfuss et al. 2008; Cai et al. 2011; Bublitz et al. 2014). As in the previous analyses, the main entities described in these simulations are production companies.

Finally, analysing the literature is evident that the advancement of technology in the last few years and the institutional interest on smart grids moved the scholars' attention toward the implementation of ABM simulations able to describe the future restructured electricity market. These investigations are connected to the previous branch of literature, since the future electricity market will make the demand side more flexible, leading to a successful integration of renewable sources. However, they represent an additional challenge in this already complex system. Smart technologies brought out new participants in the market: consumers will have an active role and retailers will become essential actors in the future electricity market. It may be supposed that these considerations lead to the introduction of retailers (Yousefi et al. 2011) and consumers (Thimmapuram and Kim 2013; Kowalska-Pyzalska et al. 2014) as dynamic agents in the new simulations. In the literature, the main branches of investigation about smart grids concern its effects on the wholesale market (Lupo and Kiprakis 2015; Pinto et al. 2015), the analysis of future scenarios in which there are high penetration of smart appliances and of distributed generators (Kahrobaee et al. 2014), and some largescale simulations able to describe several aspects both of retail and wholesale markets (Aliprantis et al. 2010; Rylatt et al. 2013). Despite that, the number of studies about retail market is still restricted and mainly concentrated on the supply side or the demand one, instead of considering both these parts of the market (a first attempt is represented by Bompard et al. 2007). However, supply and demand are deeply interconnected, influencing each other, and both are fundamental aspects in the implementation of a well-functioning retail market.

3.2 Three energy-complexity models in details

In this section we report some examples of researches in this domain that have been performed in the UK.

In the Future Energy Decision Making for Cities project a dynamical network model has been developed to analyse the influence of social networks on the adoption of domestic energy technologies. Unexpected system-level behaviors emerge by the interaction of households within the network. This work has the advantage to integrate social aspects with technological and economic dimensions in a quantitative model which can be useful for the assessment of local authority interventions (Bale et al. 2014).

The Complex Adaptive Systems, Cognitive Agents and Distributed Energy (CASCADE) project developed an agent-based model on energy infrastructure (Rylatt et al. 2013). The aim is to gain policy- and industry-relevant insights into the smart grid concept. It includes heterogeneity of behaviors among different social, economic and technical actors, and agents learning capacity. Three models are integrated: electricity supply and demand, the electricity market and power flow. Weather data is used to inform the variation of the renewable energy generation: this allows to deal with the issue of intermittency, which is crucial for grid balancing and for the profitability of energy suppliers. The CASCADE models have found that an aggregator can stabilize the demand across groups of domestic households together with smart energy control and communication devices. This result contrasts with alternative methods that use wholesale price signals, which produce instability. Furthermore, the project Preventing Wide-Area Blackouts Through Adaptive Islanding of Transmission Networks utilized graph theory to analyse how local behavior of elements of an electrical grid influences the resilience of the grid as a whole (Bialek 2012). Foxon (2011) analyses the transition to sustainable low carbon energy system, focusing in his framework on five key coevolving systems: technologies, institutions, business strategies, user practices and ecosystems. Bale et al. (2015) provide further examples of applications of complexity studies to energy systems, with some highlights on works that addresses environmental sustainability and long-term changes in the energy domain.

4 The relevance of ABM for energy systems: potential for policy design and the way forward

The nonlinearities that ground the functioning of complex systems make policy design and evaluation particularly difficult. Complex systems are not governed by the traditional causality: feedback mechanisms generated by adaptation to policy intervention and heterogeneity in agents and in their response require methods that go beyond the traditional statistical approaches.

Agent-based models meet the challenge of exploring complexity from a number of perspectives. Their ability of capturing the heterogeneity in behaviors and features of the actors and to explicitly model the interaction cuts down the most important modeling barriers faced by the traditional approaches. The possibility of including geo-localized data also ensures maximum precision in defining the relationship between the simulated scenarios and the relevant environment.

In addition, the output of the simulation embraces all the possible levels of analysis since micro, meso and macro layers can be investigated simultaneously in a temporal dimension. With respect to other approaches, the observed system can be explored in terms of structure and processes. That is to say, that the typical output of an agent-based model includes rates, levels, time series, and equilibrium values (if any).

Important limitations of agent-based models, such as the high number of parameters and the crucial role of stochasticity in determining the dynamics of the simulated system, have recently been overcome by the advances in the techniques of parametrization, calibration, and in robustness analyses.

These properties make agent-based simulation an ideal candidate to model the energy market. The interplay between the physical infrastructures, the market actors and the social environment can be easily modeled by coupling agent-based simulation with network analysis. At the same time the increasing richness of available data allows for correct parametrization and for a safe simulation of evolutionary scenarios (see in this sense Bale et al. 2015; Tesfatsion 2018). The awareness of the potentiality of agent-based model is spreading beyond the academic arena towards government and policy advisors as witnessed by the design of European simulation platforms for electricity systems that include technical, economic and social factor (Covrig et al. 2016).

However, there is room for improvements. ABMs have been used so far mainly to model Transmission/Distribution dynamics and their application should be extended to the analysis of consumer behavior (Vasiljevka et al. 2017). The liberalization of electricity markets and the drive towards renewables-based generation are inciting a shift towards a more bottom up structure of electricity systems. This means that electricity production is increasingly determined by the distributed decisions of numerous actors to invest in and deploy (distributed) generation technologies. The interactions of these actors with one another – in social networks, markets and organizations – will influence, and be influenced by, the physical infrastructure. Insofar as electricity networks act as essential mediators of and constraints on electricity supply and demand, understanding their technical functionality is essential to shape more sustainable, reliable and resilient electric power systems.

Acknowledgments

The chapter was supported by the European Energy Research Alliance (EERA) Joint Programme on Economic, Environmental and Social Impacts (JP e3s).

Notes

1 Simon, H. (1987) *Giving the Soft Science a Hard Sell*, Boston Globe, May 3rd, Boston.
2 In Figure 36.2 the black line is the original proposed by the authors. We proposed the grey circle as the actual need of reformulating the questions is unlikely to emerge at each iteration of the cycle.
3 ABMs are not deterministic by definition. The results produced by the procedures implemented to simulate nonlinearity of the simulated processes are unlikely to be the same even when simulations start from the same initial conditions.
4 NetLogo is a multi-agent programmable modeling environment. It is authored by Uri Wilensky and developed at the CCL. It can be downloaded from Northwestern Netlogo.
5 A complete review of the literature falls beyond the scope of this paper. For a more detailed survey, see Ringler et al. (2016), Sensfuss et al. (2007), and Zhou et al. (2007).

References

Abar, S., Theodoropoulos, G.K., Lemarinier, P., O'Hare, G.M.P. (2017) Agent based modelling and simulation tools: A review of the state-of-art software. *Computer Science Review*, 24: 13–33.

Aliprantis, D., Penick, S., Tesfatsion, L., Zhao, H. (2010) Integrated retail and wholesale power system operation with smart-grid functionality. In: Power and Energy Society General Meeting.

Anderson, P. (1999) Perspective: Complexity theory and organization science. *Organization Science*, 10(3): 216–232.

Arthur, W.B. (1999) Complexity and the economy. *Science*, 284: 107–109.

Bale, C.S., McCullen, N.J., Foxon, T.J., Rucklidge, A.M., Gale, W.F. (2014) Modeling diffusion of energy innovations on a heterogeneous social network and approaches to integration of real-world data. *Complexity*, 19: 83–94.

Bale, C.S., Varga, L., Foxon, T.J. (2015) Energy and complexity: New ways forward. *Applied Energy*, 138: 150–159.

Bialek, J. (2012) Preventing wide-area blackouts through adaptive islanding of transmission networks. UKERC The Meeting Place.

Bollinger, L.A., van Blijswijkb, M.J., Dijkemac, G.P.J., Nikolicb, I. (2016) An energy systems modelling tool for the social simulation community, *Journal of Artificial Societies and Social Simulation*, 19(1): 1.

Bompard, E.F., Abrate, G., Napoli, R., Wan, B. (2007) Multiagent models for consumer choice and retailer strategies in the competitive electricity market. *International Journal of Emerging Electric Power Systems* 8(2).

Bonifati, G. (2010) 'More is different', exaptation and uncertainty: Three foundational concepts for a complexity theory of innovation. *Economics of Innovation and New Technology*, 19(8): 743–760.

Borrill, P.L., Tesfatsion, L. (2011) Agent-based modeling: The right mathematics for the social sciences? The Elgar companion to recent economic methodology, Edward Elgar Publishing.

Bower, J., Bunn, D. W. (2000) Model-based comparisons of pool and bilateral markets for electricity. *The Energy Journal*, 21(3).

Bublitz, A., Genoese, M., Fichtner, W. (2014) An agent-based model of the German electricity market with short-time uncertainty factors. In: 11th International Conference on the European Energy Market.

Cai, C., Jahangiri, P., Thomas, A. G., Zhao, H., Aliprantis, D. C., Tesfatsion, L. (2011) Agent-based simulation of distribution systems with high penetration of photovoltaic generation. In: IEEE Power and Energy Society General Meeting.

Chassin, D.P., Fuller, J.C., Djilali, N. (2014) An agent-based simulation framework for smart grids. *Journal of Applied Mathematics*, 2014: 12.

Conzelmann, G., Boyd, G., Koritarov, V., Veselka, T. (2005) Multi-agent power market simulation using EMCAS. In: IEEE Power Engineering Society General Meeting. 3.

Covrig, C., De Santi, G., Fulli, G., Masera, M., Olariaga, M. Bompard, E., Chicco, G., Estebsari, A., Huang, T., Pons, E., Profumo, F., Tenconi, A., De Doncker, R., Grigull, M., Monti, A., Stevic, M., Vogel, S. (2016) A European platform for distributed real time modelling & simulation of emerging electricity systems, Technical Report, Publications Office of the European Union, Bruxelles. DOI: 10.2790/24617

De Marchi, S., Page, S.E. (2014) Agent-based models. *Annual Review of Political Science*, 17: 1–20.

Domanico, F. (2007) Concentration in the European electricity industry: The internal market as solution? *Energy Policy*, 35(10): 5064–5076.

Epstein, J.M. (1999) Agent-based computational models and generative social science. *Complexity*, 4(5): 41–60.

Epstein, J.M., Axtell, R. (1996) Growing artificial societies. Social Science from the Bottom Up. Brookings Institution Press, Washington, DC.

Farmer, J.D., Foley, D. (2009) The economy needs agent-based modelling. *Nature*, 460: 685–686.

Fontana, M. (2010) Can neoclassical economics handle complexity? The fallacy of the oil spot dynamic. *Journal of Economic Behavior & Organization*, 76(3): 584–596.

Foxon, T.J. (2011) A coevolutionary framework for analysing a transition to a sustainable low carbon economy. *Ecological Economics*, 70: 2258–2267.

Foxon, T.J., Köhler, J., Michie, J., Oughton, C. (2013) Towards a new complexity economics for sustainability. *Cambridge Journal of Economics*, 37: 187–208.

Gilbert, N. (2004) Agent-based social simulation: Dealing with complexity. *The Complex Systems Network of Excellence*, 9(25), 1–14.

Gilbert, N., Troitzsch, K. (2005) *Simulation for the Social Scientist*. Oxford University Press, Oxford, UK.

Grimm, V., Berger, U., DeAngelis, D., Polhill, J.G., Giske, J. (2010) The ODD protocol: A review and a first update. *Ecological Modelling*, 221: 2760–2768.

Grozev, G., Thatcher, M., De Silva, P., Chan, W.Y. (2005) NEMSIM: Agent-based simulator for Australia's national electricity market. In: SimTecT 2005 Conference Proceedings.

Guerci, E., Rastegar, M.A. (2009) From uniform auction to discriminatory auction: Assessment of the restructuring proposal for the Italian electricity day-ahead market. EUI Working Paper RSCAS 2009/69, European University Institute, Robert Schuman Centre for Advanced Studies.

Holland, J.H. (1995) *Hidden Order: How Adaptation Builds Complexity*. Addison-Wesley, New York, NY.

Kahrobaee, S., Rajabzadeh, R.A., Soh, L.K., Asgarpoor, S. (2014) Multiagent study of smart grid customers with neighbourhood electricity trading. *Electric Power Systems Research*, 111.

Kowalska-Pyzalska, A., Maciejowska, K., Suszczynski, K., Sznajd-Weron, K., Weron, R. (2014) Turning green: Agent-based modelling of the adoption of dynamic electricity tariffs. *Energy Policy*, 72.

Lupo, S., Kiprakis, A. (2015) Agent-based models for electricity markets accounting for smart grid participation. In International Conference on Wireless and Satellite Systems (pp. 48–57). Springer, Cham.

Moglia, M., Podkalicka, A., McGregor, J. (2018) An agent-based model of residential energy efficiency adoption. *Journal of Artificial Societies and Social Simulation*, 21(3).

Pinto, T., et al. (2015) Smart grid and electricity market joint simulation using complementary multi-agent platforms. In: PowerTech.

Praça, I., Ramos, C., Vale, Z., Cordeiro, M. (2003) MASCEM: A multiagent system that simulates competitive electricity markets. *Intelligent Systems*, 18(6).

Railsback, S., Grimm, V. (2012) *Agent-Based and Individual-Based Modeling: A Practical Introduction*. Princeton University Press, Princeton, NJ, US.

Ringler, P., Keles, D., Fichtner, W. (2016) Agent-based modelling and simulation of smart electricity grids and markets: A literature review. *Renewable and Sustainable Energy Review*, 57.

Rosenblueth, A., Wiener, N. (1945) The role of models in science. *Philosophy of Science*, 12(4): 316–321.

Rylatt, M., et al. (2013) CASCADE: An agent based framework for modeling the dynamics of smart electricity systems. *Emergence: Complexity and Organization*, 15(2).

Secchi, D., Neumann, M. (2016) *Agent-Based Simulation of Organizational Behavior*. Springer, Cham.

Sensfuss, F., Ragwitz, M., Genoese, M. (2008) The merit-order effect: A detailed analysis of the price effect of renewable electricity generation on spot market prices in Germany. *Energy Policy*, 36(8).

Sensfuss, F., Ragwitz, M., Genoese, M., Möst, D. (2007) Agent-based simulation of electricity markets: A literature review. *Working Paper Sustainability and Innovation S5/2007*. Fraunhofer ISI.

Squazzoni, F. (2010) The impact of agent-based models in the social sciences after 15 years of incursions. *History of Economic Ideas*, 197–233.

Sun, J., Tesfatsion, L. (2007) Dynamic testing of wholesale power market designs: An open-source agent-based framework. *Computational Economics*, 30(3).

Teisman, G. R., Klijn, E. H. (2008) Complexity theory and public management: An introduction. *Public Management Review*, 10(3): 287–297.

Tesfatsion, L. (2018) Electric power markets in transition: Agent-based modeling tools for transactive energy support. In Hommes, C., LeBaron, B. (eds.) *Handbook of Computational Economics*, volume 4. Elsevier, Amsterdam.

Thimmapuram, P.R., Kim, J. (2013) Consumers' price elasticity of demand modeling with economic effects on electricity markets using an agent-based model. *Transactions on Smart Grid*, 4(1).

Unruh, G.C. (2000) Understanding carbon lock-in. *Energy Policy*, 28(12), 817–830.

Vasiljevka J., Douwb, J., Mengolini, A., Nikolic, I. (2017) An agent-based model of electricity consumer: Smart metering policy implications in Europe download. *Journal of Artificial Societies and Social Simulation*, 20(1): 12.

Veit, D.J., Weidlich, A., Krat, J.A. (2009) An agent-based analysis of the German electricity market with transmission capacity constraints. *Energy Policy*, 37(10). 4132-4144.

Young, D., Poletti, S., Browne, O. (2014) Can agent-based models forecast spot prices in electricity markets? Evidence from the New Zealand electricity market. *Energy Economics*, (45).

Yousefi, S., Moghaddam, M.P., Majd, V.J. (2011) Optimal real time pricing in an agent-based retail market using a comprehensive demand response model. *Energy*, 36(9).

Zhou, Z., Chan, W.K.V., Chow, J.H. (2007) Agent-based simulation of electricity markets: A survey of tools. *Artificial Intelligence Review*, 28(4).

37

Behavioral economics and energy market

Özlem Özdemir

1 Introduction

In neoclassical economics, individuals are assumed to be rational, to have full information and to be transitive in their preferences. Most policy suggestions are based on the analyses and models with respect to these assumptions. However, according to the empirical findings of the behavioral economics field, mostly because of the careful design of laboratory experiments (Bull, 2012), individuals are not rational and they do not optimize the cost/utility or benefit when they make decisions such as energy conservation or saving. "Behavioral economics is about formalizing and demonstrating consistent deviations from the rational economic model" (EIA Staff Meeting, 2013). More specifically, "it has taken up the difficult task of working out how cognitive biases, mental rules of thumb, interpersonal relations and social networks and norms can cause real-life economic decisions to deviate from the standards of rational, self-interested maximization" (Russell Sage Foundation; Kahneman and Tversky, 1982; Thaler and Sunstein, 2008; DellaVigna, 2009).

There are mainly three cognitive biases that may cause these behaviors that are contradictory to the classical theoretical results (Mullainathan and Thaler, 2000). The first bias is called bounded rationality, that "reflects the cognitive abilities that constrain human problem solving" which, for example, states that a person can perceive the same information differently when the information is framed differently (framing effect). In addition, an individual may perceive losing something more costly than gaining it (loss aversion). The second bias is the bounded willpower that "captures the act that people sometimes make choices that are not in their long-run interest" and thus, describes the gap between what a person believes and how he/she behaves. "Bounded self-interest incorporates the comforting fact that humans are often willing to sacrifice their own interests to help others". It is defined as the motives that individual take into account when they make decisions such as social norms, altruism, thinking of others rather than optimizing their own interest, self-utility.

With respect to these biases, behavioral economics, while trying to explain the decision-making processes of individuals, aims to model the decisions of economic actors; the consumers, the producers, the distributers, the policy makers of different sectors. This approach complements the classical economics theoretical and empirical claims about how the price, quantity, demand, supply, strategies are determined in the market through investigating different market mechanisms, mostly in experimental settings. An economic experiment allows to test the findings of theories, different policies (existing and/or suggested policies), and tries to explain the facts in a controlled environment.

Behavioral themes are categorized as four: limited consumer capacity (bounded rationality as explained above), status quo, loss aversion, and time inconsistency. Table 37.1 describes these themes taking into account the stages of the decision-making process:

Table 37.1 Consumer biases and effects on the decision-making process

Bias	What does it mean	How does it affect the decision?		
		Access	Assess	Act
Limited consumer capacity	Consumers have difficulties assessing many different options and large amounts of information about them	Consumers' awareness of the challenges they face means that they do not search at all	Consumers adopt filters or shortcuts to navigate the information (e.g. rules of thumb, reference points)	Consumers switch to an option that is better instead of the best one for them
Status quo bias	Consumers prefer the current option	Consumers do not search for alternatives deals beyond their current package and or provider	Consumers over emphasize knowledge of existing package and or provider	Consumers do not switch away from current package and or provider
Loss aversion	Consumers attach more weight to monetary losses than to monetary gains and avoid risk taking behavior	Consumers search less when energy prices fall than when they rise	Consumers give too much weight to possible losses relative to potential gains	Consumers postpone making decisions
Time inconsistency	Their preference for immediate gains means that they place too much weight on costs incurred now compared to future savings	Consumers do not search for new or alternative energy	Consumers over emphasize short term discounts	Consumers do not make a decision

Source: EON Energy Research Center Series, 2011.

"access (consumers find information about their tariff and other variable; assess (consumer evaluate the information and decide which deal is best for them; act (consumers choose the best deal).

2 Key principles of behavioral economics applied to energy market

We can categorize the key principals of behavioral economics as framing and psychological cues, bounded rationality, choice architecture and heuristics, prosocial behavior, commitment mechanisms, goalsetting, time inconsistency, incentives (Todd, Annika and Sebastien Houde; Mont, Lehner, and Heiskanen, 2014). Key types of behaviors that are related to these principles in energy market are energy consumption, both at home and at work, based on routine, automatic behavior; investing in energy efficiency improvements such as energy efficient appliances building insulation; and switching energy contract or provider.

Framing of information about a certain energy efficient products attributes, energy consumption (e.g. how much electricity a household consumes monthly) or applied/planned energy policy programs is very important for the consumers to understand the provided information correctly and effectively when they make choices. Energy labeling/rating is one of the examples that clarifies the energy efficiency gap for electrical appliances. Supplementing the information about running costs and emissions regularly is another. In addition, consumers are found to be loss averse, they can take any precaution to avoid loss. In particular, the adoption of home insulation is found to increase by presenting bill reductions as avoided extra costs rather than savings. Moreover, if appliances with energy conservations is set as a default, there will be higher energy savings. Finally, consumers value energy-efficiency more highly when running cost information is provided for the operational life rather than for a shorter time period.

In terms of the choices, people act as bounded rational. In fact, they do not buy the cheapest or the most expensive appliance, instead they tend to choose the one that represents a compromise (extremeness aversion). In addition, in terms of energy usage, the in-home energy consumption displays play an important role to decrease the energy consumption (information feedback effect). Social approval is one of the most significant principal that can be applied to the energy efficiency programs. Households are found to reduce energy consumption when they know that their community is saving, they do not care about the absolute levels of performance, and rather they look at the relative performance and participation level. Consumers tend to procrastinate when the products or equipment's are expensive such as insulation. Small actions and immediate (rather than long run) rewards are found to be effective in overcoming procrastination. In fact, the nudge-inducing policies, mostly in the form of particular taxes, subsidies, or other regulations can improve the choices of the consumers in terms of efficient energy usage and "green" behavior. Finally, by considering solely the energy efficiency rating, consumers may end up purchasing appliances which are very energy efficient with respect to other goods in their class, yet energy intensive in absolute terms (Wells et al., 2016)

Loss aversion bias is one the most important behavioral action that arises when the cost associated with giving up something is perceived as greater than the benefit that would accrue to the acquisition of the same thing (Kahneman, 2003; Gsottbauer and van den Bergh, 2011). Individuals tend to keep their status (the status-quo bias), try not to lose something they own and value it more than when the same is good is evaluated as a gain (endowment effect).

Behavioral insights can be used as a tool to policy makers. "Behaviorally tested interventions are defined as initiatives based on an ad-hoc test, or scaled out after an initial experiment";

whereas, "behaviorally informed interventions as initiatives designed explicitly on previously existing behavioral evidence", and "behaviorally aligned interventions as initiatives that, at least a posteriori, can be found to be aligned to behavioral evidence" (Sousa Lourenço et al., 2016). These insights can be used to diagnose a problem, design and implement or evaluate a policy. Further, the behavioral interventions tackling environmental problems aim to encourage energy conservation through smart meters that provide real-time feedback to consumers or social comparisons that benchmark a household against that of relevant social group in terms of energy consumption. They also incentivize environmentally sustainable consumption patterns through informing about for example CO_2 emissions from cars (OECD, 2017a, 2017b)

3   Literature review and sample cases that use behavioral economics in energy markets

In energy market, the existing literature shows that preference orders are different among consumers that makes modeling of energy consumption difficult. Further, the value that an individual give to the energy saving or energy efficient products is not the same as the value that the policy makers give to them. Yet, these kinds of energy issues are far behind the consumer expenditure for work, health, family, and education in terms of their priorities when they decide where to spend their budget. Economists mainly focus on equipment cost, energy prices, and personal electricity consumption topics when they try to model the energy market. However, behavioral economics research on energy show that consumers fail to purchase energy efficient vehicles, appliances, and lighting, hence they perceive energy efficiency as a "shrouded attribute". Energy efficiency is not a prior idea on the top of the mind. Individuals also perceive the energy efficient product purchases or energy saving types of decisions as procrastinate. They delay and often look at these as long-run. the non-priced based behaviors should be investigated in order to understand the reasons behind the consumer perception of energy efficiency. The non-priced concepts are social approval, consumption feedback, goal setting (Allcott and Mullainathan).

Many of the empirical studies related to energy attempt to reduce energy demand; though energy conservation and efficiency. Energy conservation "is used to mean reductions in energy use, holding the energy use per unit of output constant. Energy efficiency "measures energy use per unit of output. Literature implies that individual responsiveness to energy price changes, consistent with the law of demand, yet vary a lot in different contexts. Informing consumers about their energy use works but may not be cost-effective all the time. Finally, the use of social norms can decrease energy consumption in many contexts (Hahn and Metcalfie, 2016). The objective of the price related experiments was to increase the price of energy for consumers during high demand periods.

Most of the studies investigating the applications of behavioral economics through field or laboratory experiments have been done in developing countries, mainly in the United States (Parker, Hoak, Meier, Brown, 2006; Schweiker and Shukuya, 2010). The energy consumption of ten identical all-electric homes in the United States shows that households with similar demographics exhibit very diversified electricity consumption with a range of two to three times. According to the Logica Survey (2007) conducted to 10,048 Europeans in ten countries, 80% of the respondents are found to care about climate change and 45% do not know how much energy they use at any one moment, while more than half of them believe they have done enough to save energy.

Many field studies designed experiments for two groups of households, one paying standard price for electricity all day (control group), the other (treatment group) pays different prices for peak and off peak times (e.g. Caves and Christensen, 1980; Caves, Christensen, and Herriges,

1984; Faruqui and George, 2005; Wolak, 2006). Results indicate peak period electricity usage reductions. Allcott (2011a) conducted a field experiment to 700 households in Chicago, setting hourly electricity rates for the treatment group each day based on the supply costs of energy. Consumers are found to reduce electricity consumption, mainly during peak times, and welfare increased by hundreds of millions of dollars, yet this was a small portion of households' total electricity expenditures. Jessoe and Rapson (2014) investigated the effect of price increases and real-time information on energy consumption and concluded that price increase alone decreased electricity usage by 0% to 7%, adding information feedback decreased usage by 8% to 22%. LaRiviere et al. (2014) used the price and nudge on investments in energy efficiency (ads for an in home energy audit). They stated that nudge was effective, yet less than installing an equipment.

Most of the studies examining the energy efficiency and saving through experiments (mainly field experiments) have been done in the United States. In Ito, Ida, and Tanaka (2015), moral suasion and price increase were taken as the treatment to 700 households in Kyoto, Japan. Moral suasion is found to have an effect on electricity usage only a few days, the price increase reduce the usage by 14% to 17% during peak periods more sustainably. Pellerano et al. (2015) conducted a natural field experiment in Quito, Ecuador, to 28,000 households and concluded that social comparison among households' energy consumption was effective only by 1%, however, adding financial incentives may be counterproductive.

In sum, the literature on experiments related to the effects of pricing of energy usage has mainly been done for residential customers in the United States and for electricity. Hence, experiments for the other forms of energy such as gasoline, heating oil, and natural gas and in other countries need further research.

Few studies have been done on the impact of providing additional information about an energy conservation and energy efficiency products. Ivanov et al. (2013) conducted a field experiment in Minnesota, putting smart meter (programmable thermostat), The treatment group was found to use 15% less energy on peak days. Similarly, Gans, Alberini, and Longo (2013), in their experiment in Northern Ireland, found the reduction to be 11% to 17% with smart meter. Additionally, informing households about energy consumption, this time not through an installation of an equipment, rather mentioning that they are being monitored for a study, decreased usage by 2.7%. In Allcott and Taubinsky (2015), customers were asked to choose between energy-efficient light bulbs and conventional bulbs. Having information about relative electricity use and replacement costs increased market share of energy-efficient bulbs by about 12%. However, the information about products with Energy Star labels, such as water heaters, did not change consumer purchasing behaviors (Allcott and Sweeney, 2014). In that case, the financial incentives like a USD 100 customer rebate increased the buying rate of Energy Star products by 22%. In 2014 study of European Commission, London Economics and IPSOS, for nine European countries (Czech Republic, France, Italy, Norway, Poland, Portugal, Romania, Slovenia, and United Kingdom), alphabetic labels are found to be more intuitive and better understood than labels with numeric scales for energy efficient products. In sum, proving information about the energy efficiency of a product has been found to be effective to increase the purchasing most of the time, depending on the context. The most successful treatment that reduces the electricity usage is the combination of smart meters with the installation of real time information display.

As about the use of social norms to increase the energy conservation and the adoption of energy efficient technologies, very few studies exist and the definition of social norm changes in different disciplines. It is generally defined as an expected type of behavior in a particular situation (Cialdini and Trost, 1998). "Economists and psychologists doing field experiments often use a descriptive social norm (e.g. describing how a subject's energy consumption compares with her neighbors) or an injunctive social norm (e.g. describing how other people think about the subject's energy consumption). In the energy World, the norm is typically assumed to be average behavior of people in similar markets" (Hahn and Metcalfe, 2016).

In the recent work, OPOWER sends home electricity and gas use reports to consumers and compares it with that of similar households and as a result the electricity consumption in average household reduce by over 2%. If scaled nationwide, this program may reduce carbon emissions in the United States by 0.5% saving $165 per metric ton of reductions (Allcott, 2011b). Dolan and Metcalfe (2013), however, investigated the effect of social norm separately from information on energy efficiency. As a result of their natural field experiment to 600 households in London, they found that social norms reduce the energy consumption. In their extended study, they combined social norms with financial incentives, concluded that these two mechanisms when applied together did not work effectively. In fact, in Herberich, Price, and List (2011) studied the effects of subsidy to lower the price of lightbulbs and a social norm statement mentioning the number of households in a specific neighborhood that have adopted the lightbulbs on electricity usage, and they found social norms being effective on the adoption margin but not on the number of lightbulbs purchased. However, subsidies were found to affect both behaviors. Moreover, LaRiviere et al. (2014) informed households on how their electricity usage related to other households, then they offered them an in home energy audit; they provide the usage information as (1) the relative use in KWh, (2) the relative use in monthly expenditure, (3) the relative use in CO2 emissions, (4) their absolute use in KWh. Only the KWh comparison increased the likelihood of audits. In recent work, the Social and Behavioral Sciences Team with the White House paired with US Department of Energy to design and assess the Home Energy Score, residential buildings' energy efficiency profiles and provides recommendation for improving them (2016).

Behavioral nudges can change behavior. It is difficult to determine the effects of policies without randomized, controlled field experiments. Governments can fund behavioral programs among the other type of energy innovation programs; they can encourage private sector to nudge consumers to make more energy saving, efficient choices through behavioral incentives; finally, it is possible to provide information disclosures such as vehicle and appliance energy efficiency ratings to demonstrate the financial value of energy efficiency to consumers (Allcott and Mullainathan, 2010).

There are so many further research needed to be done on energy use behavior: still very little has been known about the effects of behavioral insights on energy consumption in developing countries, very few studies have looked at the loss aversion and its impact on energy demand, more research is necessary on how technology adoption affects energy consumption and economic efficiency. Another area that needs to be investigated is the subsidies in the commercial and industrial sector for energy efficiency. Two studies by Bloom et al. (2010) and Gosnell et al. (2016) suggest that productive efficiency can improve energy efficiency. The first study examined the effect of management practices in over 300 manufacturing firms in the UK and they found that better managed firms are more productive and use less energy per unit of output. Second study showed that lowering energy use in the aviation sector is beneficial for workers, shareholders and the environment. "A key motivation for doing behavioral science experimentation on energy use is to generate new insights for the purpose of changing policy" (Hahn and Metcalfe, 2016). Tables 37.2 and 37.3 summarize the behavioral studies about households' and workplaces' energy saving, respectively (e.g., Xu and Binyet, 2018; Park and Kwon, 2017; Iwata et al., 2015).

4 Behavioral studies about households' energy saving

Table 37.2 Behavioral studies about households' energy saving

Year	Author	Name of the Article	Research Question	Theoretical Framework	Survey Area	Sample Size	Method	Influencing Factors			Behavior
								Demographic Variables	Individual Subjective characteristic Factors	External Factors	
2010	Ek and Söderholm	The devil is in the details: Household electricity saving behavior and the role of information	The purpose of this paper is to analyze Swedish households' willingness to increase their daily efforts to save electricity.		Sweden	1200	ordered probit model	X	X	X	Electricity Saving Behavior
2011	Gadenne et al.	The influence of consumers' environmental beliefs and attitudes on energy saving behaviours	In this article, a conceptual framework of consumer environmental behaviour and its antecedents is developed.	Theory of Planned Behavior	Australia	218	MANOVA, Multiple Regression Analysis	X	X	X	Environmental behavior
2011	Feng and Reisner	Factors influencing private and public environmental protection behaviors: results from a survey of residents in Shaanxi, China	"What demographic variables differentiate between high and low levels of private (shallow environmentalism) and public (deep environmentalism) attitudes and behaviors?"		Shaanxi	347	Multiple Linear Regression Analysis	X	X		Individual Behaviors; Public Behaviors

Year	Author	Title	Description	Theory	Location	Sample	Method				Dependent Variable
2011	Wang et al.	Determinants and policy implications for household electricity-saving behaviour: Evidence from Beijing, China	The current paper attempts to address three issues: What is the present situation of household electricity conservation in Beijing? What are the major determinants that influence the household electricity saving behaviour in China? Does policy direction exert any impact in encouraging household electricity saving behaviour?	Theory of Planned Behavior	Beijing	816	Logistic Regression Analysis	X	X	X	Electricity Saving Behavior
2011	Sütterlin et al.	Who puts the most energy into energy conservation? A segmentation of energy consumers based on energy-related behavioral characteristics	The present paper aims to identify and describe different types of energy consumers in a more comprehensive way than previous segmentation studies using cluster analysis.		Swiss	1506	Cluster Analysis	X	X	X	Energy saving actions

(Continued)

Table 37.2 (Continued)

Year	Author	Name of the Article	Research Question	Theoretical Framework	Survey Area	Sample Size	Method	Influencing Factors			Behavior
								Demographic Variables	Individual Subjective characteristic Factors	External Factors	
2011	Martinsson et al.	Energy saving in Swedish households. The (relative) importance of environmental attitudes	The aim of this study is to figure out what more exactly makes which households save or not save energy. It examines the main determinants of household energy saving and the relative importance of various factors by using a large survey data set on Swedish inhabitants and their environmental attitudes and energy-related behaviours.		Sweden	data from the period of 2004–2007 of an institute	Regression Analysis	X		X	Energy Saving Behavior_heating and hot water usage

Year	Author	Title	Description	Theory	Location	Sample	Analysis			Behavior
2012	Liu et al.	Sustainable consumption: Green purchasing behaviours of urban residents in China	This paper develops an overall analytical framework based on the reasoned action theory and discusses three major topics which are current level of urban residential involvment of green purchasing (GP) practices, the variables affecting the individual's GP behaviors and the relationship between the predicting variables and the level of actual GP behaviors.	Theory of Reasoned Action	Suzhou	336	Path analysis_ multiple regression	X	X	Green Purchasing Behavior
2012	Kang et al.	The Energy-Saving Effects of Apartment Residents' Awareness and Behavior	This study aims to raise awareness about the need for promoting energy-conservation and distributing relevant information, and to seek additional roles for apartment residents' in their energy-saving efforts.		The subjects were selected from among those living in the "Best Energy-Saving Apartments," designated by the Busan Metropolitan Government and Korea Energy Management Corporation, and other apartments	First test: 197 Second test: 78	T-test	X		Energy Saving Behavior

(Continued)

Table 37.2 (Continued)

Year	Author	Name of the Article	Research Question	Theoretical Framework	Survey Area	Sample Size	Method	Influencing Factors			Behavior
								Demographic Variables	Individual Subjective characteristic Factors	External Factors	
2013	Yue et al.	Factors influencing energy-saving behavior of urban households in Jiangsu Province	In this research, the willingness of households to adopt different energy-saving behavior has been analyzed, and factors influencing energy-saving behavior in Jiangsu Province, China, have been examined.		Jiangsu	638	Regression Analysis	X	X	X	Energy Saving Behavior
2013	Webb et al.	Self-determination theory and consumer behavioural change: Evidence from a household energy-saving behaviour study	The present study tests a simplified model combining constructs from the Model of goal directed behavior with self-determination theory to explain consumers' energy conservation intentions and behaviour.	Self determination theory and modified version of model of goal-directed behavior	Australia	200	Structural Equation Model		X		Energy Saving Behavior
2013	Hori et al.	The determinants of household energy-saving behavior: Survey and comparison in five major Asian cities	This study aims to clarify the differences among factors influencing energy-saving behavior across five major Asian cities		Dalian, Chongqing, Fukuoka, Bangkok and Ho Chi Minch	2302 + 386 + 215 + 422 + 745	Tukey–Kramer method, OLS Regression	X	X	X	Energy Saving Behavior; Environmental Behavior

Year	Author	Title	Description	Extra	Location	Sample	Method	Variables				Category
2013	Ma et al.	Chinese consumer attitudes towards energy saving: The case of household electrical appliances in Chongqing	This paper reports the findings of a survey carried out in 2009 and 2010 in order to reveal information about attitudes towards energy and energy saving in the context of household electrical appliances		Chongqing	246	Correlation analysis		X	X	X	Energy Saving
2013	Mizobuchi and Takeuchi	The influences of financial and non-financial factors on energy-saving behaviour: A field experiment in Japan	This study integrates both financial and non-financial factors to identify key internal and external variables that determine household electricity-saving behaviour.		Japan	236	Econometric model	Financial variables consist of reward, household income and standard socio-demographic elements. Non-financial variables consist of comparative feedback, social norms				Electricity Consumption
2013	Yu et al.	Evaluating the direct and indirect rebound effects in household energy consumption behavior: A case study of Beijing	This paper examines whether increases in energy efficiency of major household items cause additional short-run utilization of these end uses and other end uses for households in Beijing.	Direct and Indirect Rebound Effect	Beijing	775	An Integrated Model (by combining logit model and resource allocation model)	Energy efficiency, Accessibility, Employment, Income, Household size, Children presence				Household Energy Consumption

(Continued)

Table 37.2 (Continued)

Year	Author	Name of the Article	Research Question	Theoretical Framework	Survey Area	Sample Size	Method	Influencing Factors			Behavior Factors
								Demographic Variables	Individual Subjective characteristic Factors	External Factors	
2014	Wang et al.	Factors influencing sustainable consumption behaviors: A study of rural residents in China	This study develops the scales of rural residents' sustainable consumption behavior (SCB) and their antecedents and tries to bring forward a multifactor model for the first time to analyze whether there is significant influencing path existing from the antecedents to the rural resident's SCB.	Sustainable Consumption Behaviors	50 villages among 35 selected regions in China	1403	K-means cluster analysis, path analysis_ stepwise regression	X	X	X	Sustainable Consumption Behavior
2014	Wang et al.	Determinants of energy-saving behavioral intention among residents in Beijing: Extending the theory of planned behavior	This paper provides an empirical analysis that identifies and explores the determinants of an energy-saving behavioral intention among residents from the perspective of the theory of planned behavior.	Theory of Planned Behavior	Beijing	276	Structural Equation Model	X	X	X	Energy Saving Behavior

Year	Author	Title	Description		Location	Sample	Method			Outcome
2014	Arikawa et al.	Attitudes toward nuclear power and energy-saving behavior among Japanese households	It evaluates Japanese attitudes toward nuclear power and energy-saving behavior after the Fukushima Daiichi Nuclear Disaster . In the first part of the paper, it is examined the relationship between socioeconomic characteristics and acceptance of nuclear power in light of global warming. In the second part of the paper, it is examined the relationship between electricity demand and acceptance of nuclear power.		Japan	830 + 503	Ordered probit model	X	X	Intensity of use of electrical appliances, energy saving behavior
2015	Iwada et al.	Do households misperceive the benefits of energy-saving actions? Evidence from a Japanese household survey	This study attempts to provide further evidence on whether and the extent to which individuals misperceive the potential energy savings (mone-tary benefits) of energy-saving actions.		Tokyo	1200	Bivariate regression	X	Perceived benefit	Energy Saving Actions (18 energy-saving actions)
2015	Jridi et al.	Household preferences for energy saving measures: Approach of discrete choice models	The aim of this paper is crystallized around the research of the energy saving measures adoption's determinants in the residential sector.	Economic Theory	Tunisia	3000	Discrete choice model	X		X → Energy Saving Adoption

(*Continued*)

Table 37.2 (Continued)

Year	Author	Name of the Article	Research Question	Theoretical Framework	Survey Area	Sample Size	Method	Influencing Factors			Behavior
								Demographic Variables	Individual Subjective characteristic Factors	External Factors	
2016	Yang et al.	Who exhibits more energy-saving behavior in direct and indirect ways in china? The role of psychological factors and socio-demographics	It examines how people's demographic characteristics and psychological factors affect their direct and indirect energy curtailment behaviors at home as well as the different effects of these antecedents.		Hefei, anyang, Beijing	526	T-test, ANOVA, SEM, OLS regression	X	X		Energy Curtailment behavior
2016	Boudet et al.	Clustering household energy-saving behaviours by behavioural attribute	The aim of the study is to cluster behaviours according to nine different attributes		All collected data between April 2010 and June 2013.	261 energy saving behavior	Content Analysis and categorization	Clustering based on 9 attributes which are energy savings, cost, frequency of performance, required skill level, observability, locus of decision, household function, home topography, and appliance topography			Energy Saving Behavior

Year	Author	Title	Description	Country	Sample	Method				Category
2016	Pothitou et al.	Environmental knowledge, pro-environmental behaviour and energy savings in households: An empirical study	The aim of this study is to test the relationship between house-hold occupants' environmental predisposition and knowledge versus their energy behaviour, attitudes, habits; and ownership and frequency of use of household appliances.	England	249	Correlation analysis and PCA	X	X	X	Energy Behaviours, Attitudes and Habits
2017	Ding et al.	Research on differences in the factors influencing the energy-saving behavior of urban and rural residents in China—A case study of Jiangsu Province	This paper conducts a comparative study of urban-rural differences in energy consumption activities and the influencing factors in Jiangsu Province to develop findings that can help guide China's low-carbon energy consumption policy.	Jiangsu	187	correlation analysis, multiple regression analysis	X	X	X	Electricity Saving Behavior
2017	Hasan and Mozumber	Income and energy use in Bangladesh: A household level analysis	It examines how energy use at the household level moves with income in Bangladesh	Bangladesh	12240	quantile regression, nonparametric and semiparametric regression	X	Expenditure per capita, imcome per capita/ rural or urban		Electricity Use and Other Types of Energy Use

(Continued)

Table 37.2 (Continued)

Year	Author	Name of the Article	Research Question	Theoretical Framework	Survey Area	Sample Size	Method	Influencing Factors			Behavior
								Demographic Variables	Individual Subjective characteristic Factors	External Factors	
2017	Hu et al.	A survey on energy consumption and energy usage behavior of households and residential building in urban China	One of the objectives of the paper is to understand the characteristics and trends of urban residential building energy consumption. Moreover, it explores a full picture of the urban residential building energy usage behaviors and understand the distribution of typical behaviors of urban households. Finally, the study investigates the effect and reactions of current energy efficiency policies and behaviors driven policies in urban residential building sector.		China	4964	Descriptive Analysis	X	X	X	Energy Consumption & Energy Use Behavior
2017	James and Ambrosse	Retrofit or behaviour change? Which has the greater impact on energy consumption in low income households?	This study evaluated the efficacy of three programmes-retrofit, behavior change, retrofit & behavior change, designed to help low income households become more energy efficient		Australia	320	T-test	saving in energy consumtion, saving in energy bills, saving in greeenhouse gas emission, increased thermal comfort in hh			Energy Consumption

Year	Author	Title	Objective	Theory	Country	Sample	Method	Variables	Household Energy Consumption	Energy-Saving Habits and Behavioral Changes	Electricity Saving Behavior
2017	Jareemit & Limmee-chokchai	Influence of Changing Behavior and High Efficient Appliances on Household Energy Consumption in Thailand	This paper presents the investigation of significant parameters regarding behavior changes and high energy efficient home appliances which could decrease energy consumption in Thai households.		Bangkok		Multiple Regression Analysis	two hundred combinations of forty-eight variables covering occupancy schedules and energy efficient home appliances	X		
2017	Jareemit & Limmee-chokchai	Understanding residents perception of energy saving habits in Households in bangkok	This paper investigates the existing residents' behavior and their interest in behavior change for reducing home energy consumption.		Bangkok	400	Descriptive Analysis	Existing saving habits, Number of home appliances and usage patterns, Perception of Thailand energy conservation plan and the government's campaigns	X	X	
2017	Park and Kwan	What motivations drive sustainable energy-saving behavior?: An examination in South Korea	The current study thus explores the motivations influencing users' energy-saving behavior by examining their purchasing activities.	Theory of Planned Behavior & General Model of Perceivedf Value	South Korea	1050	Structural Equation Model		X	X	X

(Continued)

Table 37.2 (Continued)

| Year | Author | Name of the Article | Research Question | Theoretical Framework | Survey Area | Sample Size | Method | Influencing Factors | | | Behavior |
								Demographic Variables	Individual Subjective characteristic Factors	External Factors	
2017	Sun et al.	Environmental Ideology and Household Energy Conservation in Beijing	The study figures out whether Chinese urbanites who label themselves as environmentalists consume fewer resources than the average urbanite.		China	1000	Econometric model	Choice of appliances, Expenditures for energy consumption, Choice of cars and gasoline consumption.			Energy Consumption
2017	Trombley ad Hawala	Can further energy reductions be achieved through behaviour changes in low income households?	This work is based on a project which tries to see how education can initiate behaviour changes in participants to reduce their electricity usage.		Australia	476	Descriptive Analysis	Treatment			Energy Saving
2018	Zhang et al.		This paper aims to explore the mechanisms of factors affecting urban household energy-saving behavior including the habitual energy-saving behaviors and purchasing energy-saving behaviors		Shandong	297	SEM	X	X	X	Energy Saving Behavior

Year	Author	Title	Description	Location	Sample	Method	Socio-economic variables		Energy Consumption
2018	Borozan	Regional-level household energy consumption determinants: The european perspective	Starting from the assumption that household energy use is manifold and intertwined, shaped by many factors which overlap not only at the individual level, but also at a higher level of scales, the paper developed a more integrated approach to its determinants.	12 EU Member states_64 european regions	-	Panel Data Analysis	Socio-economic variables as Human capital, Economic dimension, Labor market, Poverty and Contextual variables as Weather and location, Level of development		Energy Consumption
2018	Baldini et al.	The impact of socioeconomic and behavioural factors for purchasing energy efficient household appliances: A case study for Denmark	This study aims to model influential factors behind Danish consumer choice of energy efficient appliances.	Denmark	1716	Logistic Regression Analysis	X	X	Propensity to purchase energy efficient appliances
2018	Camara et al.	Enhancing household energy consumption: How should it be done?	The first objective of this article is to examine how the actors –that influence household energy use through information campaigns on various energy-savings behaviours (e.g., use of public transportation, washing clothes with full machines, and use low-energy bulbs)- try to affect everyday life choices	Guinea-Conakry	11 Guinean websites and energy companies and 20 respondents	Discourse analysis	Consumer's knowledge on energy efficiency, effects of linking actors such as websites, newspapers and etc.		Household energy behavior

(Continued)

Table 37.2 (Continued)

Year	Author	Name of the Article	Research Question	Theoretical Framework	Survey Area	Sample Size	Method	Influencing Factors			Behavior
								Demographic Variables	Individual Subjective characteristic Factors	External Factors	
2018	Li and Just	Modeling Household Energy Consumption and Adoption of Energy Efficient Technology	In this study, the authors develop a unified structural model of household discrete technology choice and continuous energy consumption using a second-order translog flexible form for indirect utility to derive compatible household specifications for multiple types of short-run fuel demand and multiple types of long-run technology choice.		California	2408	Model Construction	Socio-economic characteristics, housing characteristics, appliance holdings by energy use, and annual consumption of electricity and natural gas.			Short run household demand for electricity and natural gas / long-run technology choices
2018	Prasanna et al.	Recent experiences with tariffs for saving electricity in households	In this paper, two simple tariffs are reviewed: progressive tariffs (PTs), which penalise high consumption of electricity, and electricity saving feed-in tariffs (ESFITs), which provide incentives to reduce consumption of electricity.	Prospect Theory, Loss Aversion	PT data is gathered from California, Canada, Japan, China, Germany, Switzerland. ESFIT data is obtained from Canada, US, Japan, Germany, Switzerland		Descriptive Analysis	Price elasticity for PT, incentive elasticity for ESFIT			Electricity Consumption

Year	Author	Title	Description	Theory/Framework	Country	Sample	Method			Dependent Variable
2018	Ru et al.	Exploring the effects of normative factors and perceived behavioral control, on individual's energy-saving intention: An empirical study in eastern China	The aim of the paper is to develop a more through understanding of what motives Chinese individual's energy saving behavior, which has a significant implicatioon to deal with the increasingly serious energy overuse problems in China.	Theory of Planned Behavior	China	450	Structural Equation Model	X	X	Energy Saving Intention
2018	Thogersen	Frugal or green? Basic drivers of energy saving in European households	This paper examines how energy saving at home relates to two of people's multiple self-identities as an environmentally friendly and a frugal person.		10 european countires	320 for each country	Structural Equation Model	X		Energy Saving Behavior
2018	Trotta	Factors affecting energy-saving behaviours and energy efficiency investments in British households	The objective of this paper is to identify the socio-demographic, dwelling, and environmental factors that have the strongest influence on the daily energy-saving behaviours, the adoption of energy efficient appliances and the energy efficient retrofit investments made by British households.		England	2009	OLS and AMEs Probit X	Dwelling type X		Energy Saving Behavior

(Continued)

Table 37.2 (Continued)

| Year | Author | Name of the Article | Research Question | Theoretical Framework | Survey Area | Sample Size | Method | Influencing Factors | | | Behavior |
								Demographic Variables	Individual Subjective characteristic Factors	External Factors	
2018	Tumbaz and Moğulkoç	Profiling energy efficiency tendency: A case for Turkish households	This study investigates the behaviors and attitudes of Turkish households regarding energy efficiency.		Turkey	526	Two step cluster analysis	Currrent behavior and attitude		X	Energy Efficiency
2018	Wang et al.	Analysis of factors influencing residents' habitual energy-saving behaviour based on NAM and TPB models: Egoism or altruism?	This research takes the motivation of energy saving as the starting point, through the analysis of the impact of the daily energy- saving behaviour of residents, to explore the daily energy-saving behaviour of Chinese urban residents is out of "egoism" or "altruism".	Normative Activation Theory and Theory of Planned Behavior	China	561	Structural Equation Model	X	X	X	Energy Saving Behavior
2018	Wang et al.	Exploring the effects of non-cognitive and emotional factors on household electricity saving behavior	The main purpose of this research is to analyze the effects of non-cognitive (personal moral norm and habit) and emotional factors (positive anticipated emotion) on household electricity saving behavior.	Theory of Interpersonal Behavior and Theory of planned behavior	China	320	Structural Equation Model	Personal moral norm and habit and positive anticipated emotion			Electricity Saving Behavior

5 Behavioral studies about workplaces' energy saving

Table 37.3 Behavioral studies about workplaces' energy saving

Year	Author	Name of the Article	Research Question	Theoretical Framework	Survey Area	Sample Size	Method	Inflencing Factors	Behavior
2015	Dixon et al.	Saving energy at the workplace: The salience of behavioral antecedents and sense of community	The study investigates the role of organizational sense of community and its moderating role on the effect of subjective norms on energy conservation intentions and self-reported behavior.	Theory of Planned Behavior	US	2919	Multiple Linear Regression, Hierarchical Regression Model	Attitude, social norms, perceived behavioral control, sense of community	Energy Conservation Behavior
2017	Gao et al.	Application of the extended theory of planned behavior to understand individual's energy saving behavior in workplaces	The main idea of this research is to explore the determinants of individual's energy saving behavior in workplaces.	Theory of Planned Behavior	China	468	Structural Equation Model	Attitude, social norms, perceived behavioral control, descriptive norm, personal moral norm	Energy Saving Behavior
2017	Leygue et al.	Saving energy in the workplace: Why, and for whom?	The aim of the present research is to investigate what motives employees to reduce their energy use at work when their job specifications do not include it.		United Kingdom	Study 1=293 Study 2=94	Explatory Factor Analysis, OLS Regression	Motivation, intention, attitude	Save Energy

(Continued)

Table 37.3 (Continued)

Year	Author	Name of the Article	Research Question	Theoretical Framework	Survey Area	Sample Size	Method	Inflencing Factors	Behavior
2012	Nisifrou et al.	Behaviour, attitudes and opinion of large enterprise employees with regard to their energy usage habits and adoption of energy saving measures	The present study aims in investigating energy usage habits of a large enterprise employees in Cyprus, in evaluating their perception on consumption on various energy saving measures and finally, in statistically analyzing their behaviour, attitudes and opinion on energy usage and energy saving measures.		Cyprus	303	Descriptive Statistics, Mann–Whitney analysis, Kruskal–Wallis one-way test, Correlation tests	Demograpics, behavior, attitude	Energy Saving Measures, Energy Usage
2016	Wells et al.	The role of generativity and attitudes on employees home and workplace water and energy saving behaviours	this paper seeks to examine the links between home and workplace energy and water saving behaviours, within the under-researched tourism context, and to examine the influence of generativity on these relationships		Iran	447	Partial Least Square Regression	Generativity, attitude	Energy and Water Saving Behavior at home and at work
2017	Xu et al.	Investigating willingness to save energy and communication about energy use in the American workplace with the attitude-behavior-context model	This study examines how attitudinal factors (energy saving belief and belief about the link between comfort and productivity) and contextual factors (group norms and organizational support) were associated with employees' willingness to save energy in the workplace at some cost of comfort and the perceived ease of communicating to co-workers about saving energy.	Attitude-behavior-context model	USA	245	Logistic Regression	Attitude, group norms, organizational support	Save Energy

Year	Author	Name of the Article	Research Question	Theoretical Framework	Survey Area	Sample Size	Method	Inflencing Factors	Behavior
2018	Zhang et al.	Promoting firms' energy-saving behavior: The role of institutional pressures, top management support and financial slack	The study builds a model integrating external pressures, top management support and financial slack.	Instutional Theory	Beijing	135	Partial Least Square Regression	Finacial slack, Top management support	Firm's Energy Saving Behavior
2018	Endrejat and Kauffeld	Can't get no satisfaction? Motivating organisational energy efficiency efforts in Germany	The paper argues that satisfaction with a PI(participatory interventions) triggers a positive affect towards energy-savings, and thereby, helps participants to internalize energy-saving motivation	Self-Determination Theory	Germany	219	t-test, stepwise regression	Participation Intervention(PI), satisfaction with PI	Energy Saving Motivation
2013	Greaves et al.	Using the theory of planned behavior to explore environmental behavioral intentions in the workplace	The objective of the present study is to explore environmental behavioral intentions in a workplace setting.	Theory of Planned Behavior	UK	875	Path analysis	Attitude, social norms, perceived behavioral control	Behavioral intention to save energy

(Continued)

Table 37.3 (Continued)

Year	Author	Name of the Article	Research Question	Theoretical Framework	Survey Area	Sample Size	Method	Inflencing Factors	Behavior
2017	Zierler et al.	The energy efficiency behaviour of individuals in large organisations: A case study of a major UK infrastructure operator	This paper addresses individuals' energy-use behaviours in organisations in three main stages, based on a survey among mid-level managers at a major infrastructure operator in Great Britain. First, a principal components analysis is performed to identify key determinant constructs driving energy-efficient behaviours in organisations; then clusteranalysis is undertaken, in an effort to identify differences in behavioural influences between demographicgroups and finally, astructural equation model of individuals' energy use intentions and behaviours using the newly-identifiedconstructs is developed	Theory of Planned Behavior, The Theory of Interpersonal Behavior	UK	628	Cluster analysis, Structural Equation Model	Technology adoption norms, personal evaluations of the economic and environmental benefits to the organisation of energy efficiency, stated intention to save energy, perceived flexibility of performance goals, awareness of energy-saving information, and perceived efficacy of small-scale energy conservation actions	Energy Consumption Behavior
2011	Carrico and Riemel	Motivating energy conservation in the workplace: An evaluation of the use of group-level feedback and peer education	The primary aim of this study is to evaluate the effectiveness of the interventions which are group-level feedback and peer education in a real-world organizational setting		Canada	609	Factorial design, HLM	peer education, group-level feedback	Energy Conservation Behavior

References

Allcott, H. (2011a). Rethinking real-time electricity pricing. *Resource and Energy Economics, 33*(4), 820–842.

Allcott, H. (2011b). Social norms and energy conservation. *Journal of Public Economics, 95*(9–10), 1082–1095.

Allcott, H., & Taubinsky, D. (2015). Evaluating behaviorally motivated policy: Experimental evidence from the lightbulb market. Working paper, New York University, pp. 1–80.

Allcott, H., & Mullainathan, S. (2010). Behavior and energy policy. *Science, 327.*

Allcott, H., & Sweeney, R. (2014). Can retailers inform consumers about energy costs? Evidence from a field experiment. Working Paper, New York University, pp. 1–52.

Arikawa, H., Cao, Y., & Matsumoto, S. (2014). Attitudes toward nuclear power and energy-saving behavior among Japanese households. *Energy Research & Social Science, 2,* 12–20.

Baldini, M., Trivella, A., & Wente, J.W. (2018). The impact of socioeconomic and behavioural factors for purchasing energy efficient household appliances: A case study for Denmark. *Energy Policy, 120,* 503–513.

Bloom, N., Genakos, C., Martin, R., & Sadun, R. (2010). Modern management good for the environment of just hot air? *Economic Journal, 120,* 551–572.

Borozan, D. (2018). Regional-level household energy consumption determinants: The European perspective. *Renewable and Sustainable Energy Reviews, 90,* 347–355.

Boudet, H.S., Flora, J.A., & Armel, K.C. (2016). Clustering household energy-saving behaviours by behavioural attribute. *Energy Policy, 92,* 444–454.

Bull. J. (2012). Loads of green washing—can behavioural economics increase willingness-to-pay for efficient washing machines in the UK?. *Energy Policy, 50,* 242–252.

Carrico, A.R., & Riemer, M. (2011). Motivating energy conservation in the workplace: An evaluation of the use of group-level feedback and peer education. *Journal of Environmental Psychology, 31*(1), 1–13.

Caves, D., & Christensen, L. (1980). Econometric analysis of time-of-use electricity pricing experiments. *Journal of Econometrics, 14*(3), 287–306.

Caves, D., Christensen, L., & Herriges, J. (1984). Consistency of residential customer response in time-of-use electricity pricing experiments. *Journal of Econometrics, 26*(1–2), 179–203.

Cialdini, R. & Trost, T. (1998). Social influence: Social norms, conformity and compliance. In D. Girbert, S. Fiske, & G. Lindzey (Eds.), *The handbook of social psychology* (pp. 151–192).

DellaVigna, S. (2009). Psychology and economics: Evidence from the field. *Journal of Economic Literature, 47*(2), 315–372.

Ding, Z., Wang, G., Liu, Z., & Long, R. (2017). Research on differences in the factors influencing the energy-saving behavior of urban and rural residents in China: A case study of Jiangsu Province. *Energy Policy, 100,* 252–259.

Dixon, G.N., Deline, M.B., McComas, K., Chambliss, L., & Hoffmann, M. (2015). Saving energy at the workplace: The salience of behavioral antecedents and sense of community. *Energy Research & Social Science, 6,* 121–127.

Dolan, P., & Metcalfe, R. (2013). Neighbors, knowledge, and nuggets: Two natural field experiments on the role of incentives on energy conservation. *LSE CEP Discussion Paper, 33*(1), 264–277.

EIA Office of Energy Consumption and Efficiency Analysis, July 17, 2013, Washington, DC.

Ek, K., & Söderholm, P. (2010). The devil is in the details: Household electricity saving behavior and the role of information. *Energy Policy, 38*(3), 1578–1587.

Endrejat, P.C., & Kauffeld, S. (2018). Can't get no satisfaction? Motivating organisational energy efficiency efforts in Germany. *Energy Research & Social Science, 44,* 146–151.

Faruqui, A., & George, S. (2005). Quantifying customer response to dynamic pricing. *The electricity Journal, 18*(4), 53–63.

Feng, W., & Reisner, A. (2011). Factors influencing private and public environmental protection behaviors: Results from a survey of residents in Shaanxi, China. *Journal of Environmental Management, 92*(3), 429–436.

Gadenne, D., Sharma, B., Kerr, D., & Smith, T. (2011). The influence of consumers' environmental beliefs and attitudes on energy saving behaviours. *Energy Policy, 39*(12), 7684–7694.

Gans, W., Alberini, A., & Longo, A. (2013). Smart meter devices and the effect of feedback on residential electricity consumption: Evidence from natural experiment in Northern Island. *Energy Economics, 36,* 729–743.

Gao, L., Wang, S., Li, J., & Li, H. (2017). Application of the extended theory of planned behavior to understand individual's energy saving behavior in workplaces. *Resources, Conservation and Recycling, 127,* 107–113.

Gosnell, G.K., List, J.A., & Metcalfe, R.D. (2016). A new approach to and age-Old problem: Solving externalities by incenting workers directly. Working paper.

Greaves, M., Zibarras, L.D., & Stride, C. (2013). Using the theory of planned behavior to explore environmental behavioral intentions in the workplace. *Journal of Environmental Psychology*, *34*, 109–120.

Gsottbauer, E., & van den Bergh, J.C.J.M. (2011). Environmental policy theory given bounded rationality and other-regarding preferences. *Environmental and Resource Economics*, *49*(4), 263–304.

Hahn, R., & Metcalfie, R. (2016). The impact of behavioral science experiments on energy policy. http://cbpp.georgetown.edu/sites/cbpp.georgetown.edu/files/Hahn-Metcalfe%20Working%20Paper%202016.pdf

Hasan, S.A., & Mozumder, P. (2017). Income and energy use in Bangladesh: A household level analysis. *Energy Economics*, *65*, 115–126.

Herberich, D.H., Price, M., & List, J.A. (2011). How many eonomists does it take to change a light bulb? A natural field experiment on technology adoption. Working paper.

Hori, S., Kondo, K., Nogata, D., & Ben, H. (2013). The determinants of household energy-saving behavior: Survey and comparison in five major Asian cities. *Energy Policy*, *52*, 354–362.

Hu, S., Yan, D., Guo, S., Cui, Y., & Dong, B. (2017). A survey on energy consumption and energy usage behavior of households and residential building in urban China. *Energy and Buildings*, *148*, 366–378e.

Ito, K., Ida, T., & Tanaka, M. (2015). The persistence of moral and economic incentives: Field experimental evidence from energy demand. NBER working paper 20910.

Ivanov, C., Getachew, L., Fenrick, S., & Vittetoe, B. (2013). Enabling technologies and energy savings: The case of energywise smart meter pilot connexus energy. *Utilities Policy*, *28*, 76–84.

Iwata, K., Katayama, H., & Arimura, T.H. (2015). Do households misperceive the benefits of energy-saving actions? Evidence from a Japanese household survey. *Energy for Sustainable Development*, *25*, 27–33.

James, M., & Ambrose, M. (2017). Retrofit or behaviour change? Which has the greater impact on energy consumption in low income households? *Procedia Engineering*, *180*, 1558–1567.

Jareemit, D., & Limmeechokchai, B. (2017a). Influence of changing behavior and high efficient appliances on household energy consumption in Thailand. *Energy Procedia*, *138*, 241–246.

Jareemit, D., & Limmeechokchai, B. (2017b). Understanding resident's perception of energy saving habits in households in Bangkok. *Energy Procedia*, *138*, 247–252.

Jessoe, K., & Rapson, D. (2014). Knowledge is less power: Experimental evidence from residential energy use. *American Economic Review*, *104*(4), 1–42.

Jridi, O., Bargaoui, S.A., & Nouri, F.Z. (2015). Household preferences for energy saving measures: Approach of discrete choice models. *Energy and Buildings*, *103*, 38–47.

Kahneman, D. (2003). Maps of bounded rationality: Psychology for behavioral economics. *The American Economic Review*, *93*(5), 1449–1475.

Kahneman, D., Slovic, P., & Tversky, A. (Eds.) (1982). Judgment under uncertainty: Heuristics and biases. Cambridge University Press.

Kang, N.N., Cho, S.H., & Kim, J.T. (2012). The energy-saving effects of apartment residents' awareness and behavior. *Energy and Buildings*, *46*, 112–122.

LaRiviere, L., Holladay, S., Novgorodsky, D., & Price, M.K. (2014). Prices vs Nudges: A large field experiment on energy efficiency fixed cost investments. Working paper University of Tennessee, pp. 1–48.

Leygue, C., Ferguson, E., & Spence, A. (2017). Saving energy in the workplace: Why, and for whom? *Journal of Environmental Psychology*, *53*, 50–62.

Li, J., & Just, R. E. (2018). Modeling household energy consumption and adoption of energy efficient technology. *Energy Economics*, *72*, 404–415.

Liu, X., Wang, C., Shishime, T., & Fujitsuka, T. (2012). Sustainable consumption: Green purchasing behaviours of urban residents in China. *Sustainable Development*, *20*(4), 293–308.

Ma, G., Andrews-Speed, P., & Zhang, J. (2013). Chinese consumer attitudes towards energy saving: The case of household electrical appliances in Chongqing. *Energy Policy*, *56*, 591–602.

Martinsson, J., Lundqvist, L. J., & Sundström, A. (2011). Energy saving in Swedish households: The (relative) importance of environmental attitudes. *Energy policy*, *39*(9), 5182–5191.

Mizobuchi, K., & Takeuchi, K. (2013). The influences of financial and non-financial factors on energy-saving behaviour: A field experiment in Japan. *Energy Policy*, *63*, 775–787.

Mullainathan, S., & Thaler, R. (2000). "Behavioral economics" NBER. Working Paper series.

Mont, O., Lehner, M., & Heiskanen, E. (2014). Nudging- a tool of sustainable behavior? *Swedish Environmental Economics and Policy*, *10*(2), 206–225.

Nisiforou, O.A., Poullis, S., & Charalambides, A.G. (2012). Behaviour, attitudes and opinion of large enterprise employees with regard to their energy usage habits and adoption of energy saving measures. *Energy and Buildings*, *55*, 299–311.

OECD (2017a) Use of behavioral insights in consumer theory. OECD Science, Technology and Industry Policy Papers No 36 OECD Publishing, Paris.

OECD (2017b). *Behavioral insights and public policy: Lessons from around the world.* Paris: OECD Publishing.

Park, E., & Kwon, S. J. (2017). What motivations drive sustainable energy-saving behavior? An examination in South Korea. *Renewable and Sustainable Energy Reviews, 79,* 494–502.

Parker, D., Hoak, D., Meier, A., Brown, R. (2006). http://fsec.ucf.edu/en/publications/pdf/fsec-cr-1665-06.pdf

Pellerano, J., Price, M.K., Puller, S.L., & Sanchez, G.E. (2015). Do extrinsic incentives undermine social norms? Evidence from a field experiment in energy conservation. Working paper. Universidad Iberoamericana, pp. 1–24.

Pothitou, M., Hanna, R.F., & Chalvatzis, K.J. (2016). Environmental knowledge, pro-environmental behaviour and energy savings in households: An empirical study. *Applied Energy, 184,* 1217–1229.

Prasanna, A., Patel, M.K., Mahmoodi, J., & Brosch, T. (2018). Recent experiences with tariffs for saving electricity in households. *Energy Policy, 115,* 514–522.

Ru, X., Wang, S., & Yan, S. (2018). Exploring the effects of normative factors and perceived behavioral control on individual's energy-saving intention: An empirical study in eastern China. *Resources, Conservation and Recycling, 134,* 91–99.

Schweiker, M., & Shukuya, M. (2010). Comparative effects of building envelope improvements and occupant behavioural changes on the exergy consumption for heating and cooling. *Energy Policy, 38,* 6, 2976–2986.

Sousa Lourenço, J., et al. (2016). Behavioral insights applied to policy, European report 2016, Science for Policy report, Joint Research center, European Commission, Brussels.

Sun, W., Zhang, X., Li, H., Wu, J., & Zheng, S. (2018). Environmental ideology and household energy conservation in Beijing. *Journal of Cleaner Production, 195,* 1600–1608.

Sütterlin, B., Brunner, T.A., & Siegrist, M. (2011). Who puts the most energy into energy conservation? A segmentation of energy consumers based on energy-related behavioral characteristics. *Energy Policy, 39*(12), 8137–8152.

Thaler, R., & Sunstein, C. (2008). *Nudge.* New Haven, CT: Yale University Press.

Thøgersen, J. (2018). Frugal or green? Basic drivers of energy saving in European households. *Journal of Cleaner Production, 197,* 1521–1530.

Trombley, J., & Halawa, E. (2017). Can further energy reductions be achieved through behaviour changes in low income households? *Energy Procedia, 121,* 230–237.

Trotta, G. (2018). Factors affecting energy-saving behaviours and energy efficiency investments in British households. *Energy Policy, 114,* 529–539.

Tumbaz, M.N.M., & Mo ulkoç, H.T. (2018). Profiling energy efficiency tendency: A case for Turkish households. *Energy Policy, 119,* 441–448.

Wang, B., Wang, X., Guo, D., Zhang, B., & Wang, Z. (2018). Analysis of factors influencing residents' habitual energy-saving behaviour based on NAM and TPB models: Egoism or altruism? *Energy Policy, 116*(C), 68–77.

Wang, P., Liu, Q., & Qi, Y. (2014). Factors influencing sustainable consumption behaviors: A survey of the rural residents in China. *Journal of Cleaner Production, 63,* 152–165.

Wang, S., Lin, S., & Li, J. (2018). Exploring the effects of non-cognitive and emotional factors on household electricity saving behavior. *Energy Policy, 115,* 171–180.

Wang, Z., Zhang, B., & Li, G. (2014). Determinants of energy-saving behavioral intention among residents in Beijing: Extending the theory of planned behavior. *Journal of Renewable and Sustainable Energy, 6*(5), 053127.

Wang, Z., Zhang, B., Yin, J., & Zhang, Y. (2011). Determinants and policy implications for household electricity-saving behaviour: Evidence from Beijing, China. *Energy Policy, 39*(6), 3550–3557.

Webb, D., Soutar, G.N., Mazzarol, T., & Saldaris, P. (2013). Self-determination theory and consumer behavioural change: Evidence from a household energy-saving behaviour study. *Journal of Environmental Psychology, 35,* 59–66.

Wells, V.K., Taheri, B., Gregory-Smith, D., & Manika, D. (2016). The role of generativity and attitudes on employees home and workplace water and energy saving behaviours. *Tourism Management, 56,* 63–74.

Wolak, F. (2006). *Residential customer response to real-time pricing: The anaheim critical peak pricing experiment.* Berkeley: Centre for the study Energy Markets, UC.

Xu, D., & Binyet, E. (2018). Enhancing household energy consumption: How should it be done? *Renewable and Sustainable Energy Reviews, 81,* 669–681.

Xu, X., Maki, A., Chen, C. F., Dong, B., & Day, J. K. (2017). Investigating willingness to save energy and communication about energy use in the American workplace with the attitude-behavior-context model. *Energy Research & Social Science, 32,* 13–22.

Yang, S., Zhang, Y., & Zhao, D. (2016). Who exhibits more energy-saving behavior in direct and indirect ways in china? The role of psychological factors and socio-demographics. *Energy Policy*, *93*, 196–205.

Yu, B., Zhang, J., & Fujiwara, A. (2013). Evaluating the direct and indirect rebound effects in household energy consumption behavior: A case study of Beijing. *Energy Policy*, *57*, 441–453.

Yue, T., Long, R., & Chen, H. (2013). Factors influencing energy-saving behavior of urban households in Jiangsu Province. *Energy Policy*, *62*, 665–675.

Zhang, C.Y., Wei,Y., & Zhou, G. (2018). Promoting firms' energy-saving behavior: The role of institutional pressures, top management support and financial slack. *Energy Policy*, *115*, 230–238.

Zhang, C.Y.,Yu, B., Wang, J. W., & Wei,Y. M. (2018). Impact factors of household energy-saving behavior: An empirical study of Shandong Province in China. *Journal of Cleaner Production*, *185*, 285–298.

Zierler, R., Wehrmeyer, W., & Murphy, R. (2017). The energy efficiency behaviour of individuals in large organisations: A case study of a major UK infrastructure operator. *Energy Policy*, *104*, 38–49.

38

The use of foresight
in energy policy

Erik Laes

1 Introduction

In view of long-term energy or climate mitigation goals, energy policy frequently makes use of technical-economic programming models of energy systems and to compile energy/environment scenario evaluation, in order to evaluate costs and benefits of different strategic options. It is certainly no easy task to make such long-term (frequently 30 years or more) evaluations in an environment determined by complex interactions between technological, economic, social, cultural and institutional spheres. Evaluation nevertheless presupposes that these evolutions can be understood, described and integrated in a scientific way. Numerous techniques and approaches are in use, drawing on different scientific disciplines (e.g. statistics, economics, psychology, marketing, organizational theory, etc.). Broadly, these are referred to as methods of scientific foresight (sometimes also referred to as 'future studies'), defined by Rotmans (2001) as 'a multi- or interdisciplinary process of structuring knowledge elements from various scientific disciplines in such a manner that all relevant aspects of a complex problem are considered in their mutual coherence for the benefit of decision making'. The methodological guidance provided in this chapter is timely in view of the growing interest in building ever more complex and integrated energy models (e.g. the POTENCIA model built and operated by the European Commission's Joint Research Centre)[1] (Mantzos et al. 2017) and/or combining quantitative (i.e. model-based) and qualitative (i.e. narrative) methodologies to support the long-term energy transition (Holtz et al. 2015; Guivarch et al. 2017; McDowall and Geels 2017).

It will come as no surprise that scientific foresight is fraught with difficulties. In contrast with the clear success stories of foresight in domains such as classical mechanics, foresight in a complex domain such as energy policy is typically characterized by causal processes which are not (yet) captured and which take some time (sometimes even several decades) to be fully understood (Aligica 2003). And in the meantime, there is always the possibility of 'surprising events' or the added difficulty of free choice as a confounding factor for pure causality. Several authors have already tried to capture the transformation of science (in terms of its production, function and use) in such 'complex' environments under different denominators: 'trans-science' (Weinberg 1972), 'regulatory science' (Jasanoff 1990), 'post-normal science' (Funtowicz and Ravetz 1993) or 'mode-2 science' (Gibbons et al. 1994). Despite often significant differences, all these concepts use 'classical science' (i.e. mode-1 science, to adopt Gibbons's nomenclature) as a baseline against which changes are portrayed. Following these authors, the results of foresight exercises can no longer simply be communicated to decision-makers or wider audiences under the banner of 'scientific truth', or as a 'scientific fact'. The core problem of scientific foresight lies in assessing the solidity of the insights it provides for decision-making (Harries 2003). If foresight cannot rely on 'traditional science' and the strength attributed to its argumentation (based on empirical testing), how then can it assert its value? How can we distinguish a 'good' foresight exercise from a 'bad' one? And what exactly is the meaning of 'good' – rigorous, credible, useful, successful, anything else? Furthermore, which aspect of a foresight exercise should be judged: the data on which the exercise is based, the methodology used (e.g. is a particular method applied correctly), the results (e.g. in terms of correspondence with other foresight exercises, or coherence of the scenario storylines) or the outcomes (e.g. in terms of influence on decision-making, trust-building, building communication channels, etc.)? Who is authorized to make such judgments? The decision-makers who are supposed to make use of foresight results? Or the research community involved in producing scientific foresights? Or a wider group of stakeholders with a legitimate interest in the issue at stake?

Drawing on this background of 'mode 2-science', this chapter aims to provide some guidance on what we believe to be the most important factors to be taken into account when setting up scenario and modeling exercises as a platform for open discussion with other stakeholders and decision-makers on (long-term) energy policy in order to arrive at 'rational' energy policy decisions. This chapter is structured as follows. In Section 2, we will introduce a (probably somewhat unfamiliar) philosophical framework called 'constructivism'. In Section 3, we will give a constructivist reading of scientific foresight as a combined scientific-political practice and point out some of the main points of interest. Section 4 will give some practical recommendations on using scientific foresight as a deliberative platform. Section 5 concludes.

2   Theoretical background: constructivism

Constructivism as a theory of knowledge has a quite unfamiliar outlook on concepts such as 'reason' or 'rationality' (Heyligen 1997). Based on a pragmatic reconstruction of the use of the concept of rationality in language, some constructivists show that it represents a category for the assessment of actions and decisions (ex post or ex ante) (Rescher 1988; Batens 1992). Three types of rationality can be distinguished: the (cognitive) rationality of propositions, the practical rationality of the suitability of actions to reach aims (means/end rationality) and the evaluative rationality of the aims and purposes themselves. Any form of action (intended, proposed or actually carried out) is implicitly or explicitly supported by rationality claims in these three domains. Ideally, rational procedures would lead to conclusions or actions that everyone else would take in the given situation – at least, such a claim is often implied by a commonsense understanding of science. Rational procedures should allow us to arrive at non-arbitrary answers. As such, the concept is used to designate the invariance with respect to individual persons. But one big caveat is necessary here: the invariance with respect to individual persons does not extend to the pragmatically necessary considerations for contextual dependencies. It does not follow that the invariance also holds with respect to situations or contexts. Constructivist rationality claims therefore do not allow for contextualization but postulate it.

What do we mean by contexts? A context is any situation in which we are faced with a problem. Applied to the specific context of scientific research, this means that even if a research problem would be formulated relatively generically it would have to be answered through some form of contextual judgment. Constructivism asserts that scientific knowledge is not simply 'a mirror of nature'. Scientific knowledge is knowledge which is produced following a certain ingenious methodology (referred to as 'the scientific method'), but is nevertheless applied to a concrete problem and within a concrete context. In an actual situation, only a limited number of scientists will work on the problem, with limited resources (in terms of time and money) and limited knowledge. Nevertheless, they try to make these results 'universally acceptable' (at least to the scientific community) by some in-built characteristics. They do so by an implicit or explicit negotiation of objective, subjective and intersubjective selection criteria on which the acceptance or rejection of scientific knowledge depends (Heyligen 1997). Objective criteria reflect on the suitability of knowledge to represent the object of interest as an object (i.e. something that will not change its qualities from one context to another): one can think of criteria such as controllability, reproducibility and non-ambiguity of research (in other words, the standard criteria of empirical research). Subjective criteria reflect on the suitability of knowledge to be assimilated or internalized by an individual: utility, simplicity, and coherence with existing knowledge can all be relevant knowledge selectors. Intersubjective criteria point at the degree of acceptance of an idea within a group of subjects (e.g. peers): collective utility, expressiveness, degree of formalization, conformity with existing beliefs and authority all belong to this category.

One of the most influential constructivist theories in the field of science and technology studies is the so-called 'actor-network theory' (ANT) which evolved from the work of Michel Callon and Bruno Latour (see e.g. Callon 1987; Latour 1993). They describe the action of science and technology as the progressive constitution of a 'network'. The concept 'network' should not be considered in the classical sense of the word. A network is a system in which both human and non-human actors (Latour uses the overlapping notion of an 'actant' for describing both) assume identities according to prevailing strategies of interaction. This is in line with what we wrote about contextual rationality in the above section. Scientific and technological facts do not exist separated from society and the scientific community. They only get their original meaning in a network (a context), and retain the traces of this original construction work. From one context to another, they can be 're-presented' (in a literal sense of 'being made present again') by a 'representative'. With this notion of 'representation', the 'sphere of science' is opened up to the 'sphere of politics' – i.e. both can be analyzed with the same conceptual apparatus (delegation, democracy, etc.). Latour (2004) cleverly points out the parallels between a political representative claiming to speak for 'the public' and an expert claiming to speak for an 'environmental asset': both need consultation mechanisms, negotiations and have to put 'work' into assuring that they faithfully represent their constituency (in the case of the politician, by organizing meetings, listening to trusted intermediaries, etc.; in the case of the expert, by attending scientific meetings, doing laboratory work, etc.); and one is certainly not more mysterious or unproblematic than the other. In ANT, the most important of these negotiations is translation, a multifaceted interaction in which actors (1) create common definitions and meanings, (2) define representations, and (3) try to persuade each other in the pursuit of individual and collective objectives. Actors share the scene in the reconstruction of the network of interactions leading to the stabilization of the system. This closure of the debate creates 'facts', statements that are not questioned any more.

Summing up, in a constructivist reading of 'rationality' this concept appears as a normative concept which can only be legitimized and renewed through contextual action. Rationality is always 'ours', the concept of and the criteria for rationality are constructed by and in society – without reference to some stable, ideal, non-temporal instance outside of society. However, a constructivist understanding of science does not have to lead to relativism. The pursuit of intersubjective accordance still implies a continuous touchstone and a steering mechanism for scientific knowledge. It does imply a greater sense of open-mindedness towards diverging insights.

As such, constructivism provides us with a very versatile language for describing combined scientific-political undertakings such as scientific foresight activities. In the following section, we will explore this statement further.

3 A constructivist reading of energy foresight

A constructivist reading of scientific foresight practice presents a possibly challenging perspective on the 'conventional wisdom' of scenario-based foresight and decision-making (Chermack and van der Merwe, 2003). Latour (2004) describes 'scenarization' as one step in a combined political-epistemological process. He uses the analogy of a 'parliament of things'. First, we have to select the 'actants' which will be represented at the table (in the case of energy scenarios, this could be different power plants, future consumption patterns, different resources, etc.). Then, we have to decide how these actants will be represented (a power plant could be represented by technical and economic data, consumers could be represented by a model of rational economic behavior, etc.). Next, we have to bring all of these represented actants together in a hierarchy (i.e. we have to decide to which representative we are going to trust most). This process is called a 'scenarization' in Latourian terms. Keulartz et al. (2004) have called this the task of dramatic rehearsal – i.e. the imagining of a plurality of possible futures and the way that leads to their realization. 'Dramatic' should be understood in three senses: in a concern with the interaction of personalities, a concern with a plot (e.g. creative redescriptions, new narratives), and a concern for open-endedness. Most important for our purposes is also that scenarios have to fulfill their role as 'boundary objects', spanning the domains of 'science' and 'decision-making'. The concept of a 'boundary object' was introduced in social studies of science to describe how members of different 'social worlds' manage to cooperate successfully despite their very different viewpoints and interests (Gieryn, 1995). Broadly speaking, a boundary object should be both plastic enough to adapt to the needs and constraints as experienced by the different parties involved in negotiating energy policy, while still being robust enough to maintain a common identity. Boundary objects thus acquire different meanings in different social worlds, but their structure is still common enough to more than one world in order to make them recognisable – in other words, there are a means of translation. For instance, one important function of scientific foresight exercises would be to protect scientists on one side from accusation of bias or illegitimacy (because the exercises are situated clearly as 'official' objects of advisory science, and hence no confusion with 'pure' research science is possible), while protecting policy makers on the other hand from accusations of allowing technocratic intrusions into their domain of competency. This means indicators have to fulfill conditions of both scientific and political legitimacy. Scenarios should be relevant to the concerns of decision-makers (i.e. they show possibilities for practical intervention and are politically legitimate), and if they are able to withstand scrutiny by scientists (i.e. they have to be based on an adequate analysis of the present situation and the range of possible futures implied by this present situation). In this section, we will investigate the different ways in which such 'scenarizations' can be drawn up, based on an overview of 50 years of scenario-building practice (van Notten et al. 2003) (Section 3.1), before turning to an overview of the most commonly used methods (Section 3.2) and models (Section 3.3).

3.1 A typology of foresight exercises

Within the broad confines of scenario-building practices, some family resemblances can be discerned. For instance, the difference between quantitative (modeling) and qualitative (narrative) traditions of scenario building can be underscored (the former approach prevails in the field of energy). Hybrid scenarios combine both approaches. Earlier attempts at forecasting (prediction) have proven to be largely unsuccessful (particularly in the case of long-term scenarios) and are increasingly being abandoned by scenario builders – although there still appear to exist some expectations of correct prediction on the part of policy makers. But for our present purposes, the most relevant distinction to be made is the one between primarily descriptive or exploratory scenarios – i.e. scenarios describing possible developments starting from what we know about current conditions and trends, and primarily normative, anticipatory or backcasting scenarios – i.e. scenarios which are constructed to lead to a future that is afforded a specific subjective value by the scenario developers. Neither of these two types is 'value free', since both embody extra-scientific judgments, for example about 'reasonable' assumptions. However, they differ in terms of overall purpose. That is, the choice between exploratory and anticipatory approaches depends on the objectives of the scenario development exercise. Anticipatory scenarios represent organized attempts at evaluating the feasibility and consequences of trying to achieve certain desired outcomes (or avoid the risks of undesirable ones). Exploratory (or 'what-if' analysis), on the other hand, tries to articulate different plausible future outcomes, and explore their consequences. The accent is mostly on prioritizing technological choices, the analysis is performed in a relatively closed process by technically or economically schooled experts, and the government (or administrative bodies) mostly assumes the role of client (they 'place an order' for the analysis). Finally, a distinction can be made between trend scenarios, based on the extrapolation of (perceived) dominant trends, and peripheral scenarios, which focus on unexpected developments and genuine 'surprising events'. Other common characteristics include the time scale covered (long vs. short term), the spatial scale (global, regional, local), and the subject (issue-based, area-based or institution-based). All in all, a wide variety of choices can (and have!) to be negotiated, thus opening up the necessary space for 'contextual (constructivist) wisdom' to prevail.

3.2   Foresight methods

Are scientific foresight exercises methodical, and how can we discern a 'good' method from a 'bad' one? Before answering this question, it is good to be clear about what we mean when we say we are working in a 'methodical' way. Working in a 'methodical' way implies applying a set of rules or methods to the 'object' under study. An important aspect of 'methodical' research is that the rules or methods should be applicable in more than one context. Thus, a method has an external relationship to the study object: the method has shown its use in other contexts and derives from this a certain authority. If we interpret this external relationship very strictly, this clearly conflicts with core constructivist insights (there is no knowledge other than contextual knowledge). However, if we see the development of scientific foresight methodology as an ongoing process which cannot be bounded by limitations of strict rigour and remain attentive to contextual variations (as Blass (2003) proposes to do), we see no reason to reject a methodical approach to future studies. The lack of one unified scientific foresight method is not a problem. Rather, the problem is that scientific foresight draws upon a number of methods stemming from different research traditions and disciplines without always being very candid about the inherent limitations of these methods. Therefore, we will try to address this aspect in the next few sections.

The participative approach

The participative approach includes all methods which involve people (experts, decision-makers, stakeholders, or laypeople) outside of the core research group developing the scenarios, either in the fact-finding or the evaluations stages of scenario development. According to van Notten et al. (2003), expert input is more and more complemented by stakeholder input in today's scenario development projects. Numerous participatory techniques exist: focus groups, citizen juries, envisioning workshops, etc. (see e.g. Joss and Bellucci (2002)). The advantage of participative approaches is of course that qualitative information can be integrated into the scenario exercise. They also enable imagining structural changes in the issue under study, whereas models (cf. *infra*) only allow a logic of 'smooth development'. On the downside however, participative approaches suffer from a lack of theoretical foundations (or, for that matter, a lack of a common vocabulary) enabling a judgment concerning the quality of a particular participative project or the choice of the right participatory tool adapted to a specific context (Rowe and Frewer 2004). One particular participative (expert) approach which has been applied frequently in future studies is the 'Delphi method' (and one of the case studies discussed in section 4 makes use of it). Therefore, we will discuss this particular method in more detail.

Delphi method

The Delphi method was developed from the hypothesis that, in view of the many factors that might influence the future in unpredictable ways, it is best to draw upon a large group of experts for offering insights. Thus, the Delphi method consists of a formal methodology in which a large group of experts can combine their knowledge systematically and create narratives of the future. The Delphi method has a long history of application and testing (it was developed in the 1950s by the RAND Corporation). Put very briefly, the method involves an iterative questioning of experts. In successive rounds, a group of experts is asked to supply responses to a list of questions involving the future. At the conclusion of every round, the participants are given a statistical representation of all answers and may then change their views in light of what other experts believe. 'Outliers' are asked for the reasons for their 'deviant' answer. The answers are presented anonymously to eliminate the possibility of placing undue weight on the responses of persons who hold a high status within the group of peers. This process is repeated until a sufficient degree of consensus is reached among the experts.

The main advantage (compared to models which are also capable of dealing with large amounts of data – cf. *infra*) is that the Delphi method is able to draw upon 'background' or 'tacit' knowledge that is able to make sense of statistical regularities. The use of background knowledge (stemming from different contexts) is crucial in domains such as technological developments, public policy and management, where 'successful' foresight depends less on observing statistical regularities than on knowledge of behavioral regularities, institutional arrangements, intentions and preferences of relevant people, traditions, customs, fashions, national attitudes and climates of opinion, etc. (Aligica 2003). Certain 'privileged witnesses' – be they certified experts or social actors that happen to move in relevant contexts or institutional structures – are considered to be 'repositories' of this background knowledge. The purpose of the Delphi exercise is then to transform this somewhat unstructured repository of background knowledge (which likely consists of rules of thumb, analogies, metaphors, intuitive correlations, etc.) into a structured set of reliable statements about the future. Two generic questions emerge: 'How can we assure that we have drawn upon the 'right' repository (i.e. which experts should be selected for the Delphi exercise, and how should we evaluate their knowledge)?'; and 'How can we assure that the unstructured 'background' knowledge is translated into 'structured' statements about the future without losing vital knowledge in the process?'. These questions also point out the limitations of the Delphi method.

On the first question, expert bias is a well-reported issue in literature (see e.g. Tichy 2004). Expert bias may arise from various sources:

- *Availability*: experts tend to give greater weight to readily available data or recent experience, while losing sight of long-term developments;

- *Involvement*: the value orientations of an expert, often depending on the institute in which he/she is working, or the discipline he/she masters, can shape the way in which assessments are made;
- *Motivation*: experts might have a desire to influence the results of the Delphi exercise, might have a desire to appear knowledgeable, or might experience a desire not to contradict a position taken earlier, etc.;
- *Desirability of future events*: experiments clearly show that experts perceive generally desirable events (not necessarily related to their own discipline or institute) as more likely to occur;
- *Optimism*: experts tend to be over-optimistic with regard to the realization of the innovations that they are working on (e.g. with regard to diffusion time of the innovation, the competitiveness of competitors, etc.);
- *Satisficing*: experts tend to reduce complexity by closing their eyes to the fact that the introduction of a new technology entails a complex of innovations rather than one technical innovation. In particular, organizational innovations (crucial to the diffusion of new technologies) tend to be overlooked;
- *Overconfidence*: experts tend to be over-confident about their ability to make quantitative judgments.

These different types of bias do not invalidate the Delphi approach as such, but do underscore the importance of a careful selection of experts. For instance, Tichy (2004) proposes to not only use the assessments and prediction of top-experts (since these tend to be most vulnerable to optimism biases), but to use mixed panels of experts of different grades, with different types of knowledge and affiliation (business, academia, administration, lobby groups, etc.). Even then, discussion of the results should take into account the over-optimism of top-experts, since this will tend to influence the outcomes in a certain direction.

On the second question, an important limitation of the Delphi method is that it is designed to bring a disparate group of 'informed opinion holders' to a consensus about the future,[2] if only on a range of probabilities. To us, it seems impossible that any panel of experts correctly identifies the 'winners' and 'losers' (e.g. with regard to energy technologies) of the future. Even if a Delphi exercise 'officially' claims not to do so, it is clear that the set-up (involving a panel of top-experts) serves to influence decision-makers in precisely that way. Rather than seeking consensus, we believe it would be more valuable to trace different paths and fully articulate the differences of opinion. People known for their different ways of thinking should be granted the possibility to provide challenges to existing assumptions and provide novel insights. By inviting these people to comment on the results of a Delphi consensus and on how they believe current perceptions shape scenario stories and the supporting set of assumptions, one could learn valuable lessons. These insights should push the taken-for-granted views.

3.3   Foresight models

Models can be classified according to different criteria.[3] The following terminologies are very often used (Boulanger and Bréchet, 2003):

- 'Top-down' and 'bottom-up' models
- Neo-Keynesian models and neo-classical models
- Econometric models
- Partial equilibrium and general equilibrium models
- Simulation and optimization models.

Any model is a simplified abstraction of the real world. In constructivist terms, it will only allow the entry and representation of 'actants' on very strict conditions. A model determines a process of making entirely by the categories of means and ends. A tool or instrument (e.g. a mathematical code) is the realization of the model. The model not only precedes the construction process, it also survives it.[4] For people who are not familiar with models they look as black boxes. In this section we will try to explain some basic principles of different types of models and identify the limitations of different modeling approaches. We will focus on bottom-up (technical) models and top-down macro-economic approaches (in view of the cases we will discuss).

Technical bottom-up models: simulation and optimization

A bottom-up approach is easily understood as details of individuals/firms/technologies are simply aggregated in a similar way as an accounting system. Usually, bottom-up models are not dealing with the whole economy, but only with some particular aspects which are modeled in great detail like: the energy system, the transport system, etc. Bottom-up models usually put a strong emphasis on the representation of different technologies. Economic aspects are modeled in three possible ways:

1   Either they are *completely ignored* (hence, only technical engineering parameters are taken into account);
2   *Basic cost accounting* aspects are considered. Investment and operational costs of technological options are taken into account, usually in a cost-minimizing framework;
3   The model operates as a *partial equilibrium* model. Partial equilibrium models compute an economic equilibrium between quantities offered and prices charged for commodities and services of the part of the economy within the scope of the model (therefore the term "partial"). These models assume that the link to other parts of the economy which are not explicitly covered is weak enough, such that feedbacks from these other parts can be neglected in the first place. Partial equilibrium models also incorporate demand price elasticities. This means that for instance increases in costs by environmental regulations do not only provoke shifts in the choice of technologies, but also shifts in the demand for products.

Bottom-up models can be used for *simulation* and *optimization* purposes. Simulation models can be represented by flowcharts, linking various processes by material and energy flows (an exogenously determined demand for steel is linked to different steel manufacturing processes, each with their own technical characteristics, emission coefficients, etc.). Optimization models also use the same type of information as simulation models and have similar structures that can be represented by flowcharts. Additional information in optimization models relates to the price of purchased energies and materials, investment and operational costs of different technologies. Alternative processes to fulfill the same demand requirements are represented as well. The total system cost is defined as the sum of all cost components in the system: cost of raw materials and primary energies, operational costs for the processes, investment cost for new capacities and possibly environmental taxes. The values for the variables (determining the processes) are determined by minimizing the total system cost. This means that, from all possible solutions to fulfill the final demand requirements, the combination is chosen that minimises the systems cost. The basic difference with simulation models is the determination of the value of process variables. In simulation models these values are determined from historical observations or based on *ad hoc* analysis, in optimization models these are determined by the optimization process. To illustrate the difference we consider the determination of primary energy consumption per energy carrier in the electricity sector. In optimization models, this will be determined by the characteristics of different technologies and the energy prices. In simulation models this will be based on historical information or on *ad hoc* analysis.

It should be clear that optimization is a *normative* approach (and this should clearly be communicated!), rather than explorative. The model tells us what should be done rather than what will be done. Further advantages and disadvantage of the optimization approach include:

Advantages

- *Transparent and univocally defined solutions*: in developing long-term scenarios (i.e. horizon 2050–2100), hundreds of parameters relating to the choice of technologies will have to be defined. Thousands of possible solutions exist to fulfill the demand requirements. Optimization will select only one without any arbitrary rules. This is particularly useful in comparing scenarios being developed under different external conditions;
- *Rational and consistent with economic theory*: the behavior of people is conditioned by social and cultural values and therefore they maybe not fully rational in the economic sense, but the rationality hypothesis is fully consistent with the economic theory. Minimization of the system costs corresponds to the solution of a free market under the hypothesis of perfect competition (although market imperfections can to a certain extent be introduced to these models, e.g. taxes, subsidies). However, the solution does not correspond to solutions when market imperfections are considered, like oligopoly and monopoly;
- *Endogenous investment decisions*: optimization allows for endogenous technology choices (i.e. the choices are determined by the model itself) in a consistent framework. This becomes very relevant in establishing long term scenarios as all existing capacities are replaced.
- *Development of conditional scenarios*: optimization models are very well suited to develop conditional scenarios. Other constraints such as environmental regulation for other pollutants or limiting primary energy supply for some energy carriers can be easily handled.

Drawbacks

- *Flip-flap behavior*: optimization will always select the cheapest technology to fulfill the full capacity needs, unless it is constrained by the user (e.g. in terms of resource constraints, imposed limits to the speed of diffusion of certain technologies, etc.). The result is that small deviations in prices can have a very strong impact on model result, especially in the choice of fuels and technologies. In reality these shifts will only occur from a certain threshold. This phenomenon is known as the flip-flap behavior in optimization models;
- *No guaranteed coherence*: bottom-up models usually ignore feedback effects of the economy (apart from price elasticities in partial equilibrium approaches). Thus, one major disadvantage of this type of models is that they do not cover the full economy, but only concentrate on particular aspects, like energy production and consumption. For this reason, the use of engineering bottom-up models does not guarantee the coherence of scenarios (but some of them can be connected to macro-economic models);
- *Temporal disaggregation level*: energy prices fluctuate over time (day by day, month by month, and year by year). When working with low temporal disaggregation (for instance five-year period) the average prices over the period is used in the model, but this will not necessarily correspond to the results obtained by introducing the price fluctuations in a model with a high temporal disaggregation level;
- *Inapplicability of the maximum penetration of the cheapest technology*: the maximum penetration of the cheapest technology (which cost optimization implies) is not applicable when relative

costs between technologies are site dependent or linked to parameters not taken into account in the optimization, which is often the case with energy demand technologies. In such cases, simulation is used rather than optimization. An advantage of simulation is also that it allows taking into account a dispersion in the cost values;

- *The 'complexity paradox'*: developed by Oreskes (2003, pp. 19–20), we can reformulate the paradox as follows: 'The more we strive for realism by incorporating as many as possible of the different processes and parameters that we believe to be relevant to the operation of the modeled system, the more difficult it is for us to know if our tests of the model are meaning-ful'. This leads to the ironic situation that as we add more factors to a model, its value as a heuristic instrument may decrease even as our intuitive faith in the model increases.

Economic top-down models: macro-economic and general equilibrium models

These models can be considered as *top-down* models. CGE models and macro-econometric models are covered in Chapters 30 and 33 of this handbook. For a discussion on integration of top-down and bottom-up models please see Chapter 32. They represent the whole economy as a closed system. They differentiate the behavior of different types of economic agents (consumers, producers, and government) in a consistent framework. Macro-economic (econometric) models and general equilibrium models are different in some aspects, such as the economic background, the scientific methodology, model specification and empirical verification and calibration.

A basic entry point for understanding the differences between macro-economic and general equilibrium models is the *equilibrium* concept in economics. The equilibrium concept applies for goods, services, and labor. If all markets for goods, services and labor are in equilibrium, one speaks about a general equilibrium. A general equilibrium is a very interesting concept, as well for economists as for policy makers, because general equilibrium corresponds to a situation of maximum welfare. However, the equilibrium concept is a rather static view on the world. Technological and scientific evolution are constantly moving the production constraints, thus changing the optimal quantity of labor at given price. Consumer preferences might depend on several factors such as social and cultural values which are independent of the economic context. So the real world is rather complex, and the equilibrium conditions are probably never realized, but the market clearing mechanism is constantly working thus moving the world towards a new equilibrium. From this discussion the following questions arise: 'What is the speed of adjustment towards the new equilibrium?'; 'What is moving faster, the move towards the new equilibrium or the new equilibrium itself?'; and 'Do the markets need government intervention?'

A basic difference between econometric models and general equilibrium models is how they look at equilibrium. Macro-econometric models concentrate on the disequilibrium in different markets, frequently with a special emphasis on the labor market. General equilibrium models concentrate on the welfare aspects associated to the equilibrium position.

Macro-economic models represent the economic circle: people work and earn money which they can spend, thus generating demand for consumer goods and services. The supply of goods is represented by some type of production functions, determining the amounts of production factors (employment, capital, energy) needed to produce the desired level of goods and services, based on relative prices of the production factors. Econometric models represent the economy in a system of equations, determining simultaneously the value of the endogenous variables. Frequently, reduced form equations are used to describe the behavior of economic agents. While economic textbooks describe markets by demand and supply curves and the price and the quantity of goods as the result of the confrontation of supply and demand, econometric models use behavioral equations linking prices and quantities directly to other variables in the model, without going explicitly through the system of demand and supply. The scientific methodology applied in building econometric models is highly empirical. Historical data (on yearly, quarterly or monthly basis) or cross section data (for instance data related to different world regions) are used to determine model parameters and functional specifications. Regression techniques produce parameter values and regression statistics allowing to judge the quality of equations and the statistical significance of parameters. However, econometricians will never judge the quality of equations on regression statistics only but will use economic insights (does this result make sense?) and past experience. For simulation purposes, an econometric model needs lagged historical observations and assumptions on (a few) exogenous variables.

Advantages

- Econometrical models can be used to produce autonomous scenarios, painting a *coherent* and *accurate* picture of a whole economic system.

Drawbacks

- The *simulation horizon is limited* by the methodology (typically 5–10 years). This limitation is due to reduced form specifications and the empirical way to derive model parameters;
- Econometric models usually *do not have explicit representations of technologies and technological improvement*. Technological improvement is frequently hidden in a number of constants in behavioral equations;
- Econometric models usually face *problems in simulating structural changes and shocks*;
- Econometric models have a *strong emphasis on the demand side* of the economy, assuming supply will follow automatically. This paradigm is typical for the short or medium period.

General equilibrium models focus strongly on the welfare aspects related to the equilibrium conditions of the economy. The underlying paradigm of general equilibrium models is of a neo-classical nature. Basically micro-economic theory is implemented in the modeling structure. General equilibrium models also present the whole economy in a consistent way and differentiate the behavior of different economic agents: consumers, producers and government. Contrary to econometric models, general equilibrium models represent the economy by subsets of demand- and supply equations and use a global market clearing mechanism as simulation technique. Producers are represented in the model by production functions. Production functions express the amount of output that can be produced by given combinations of different production factors. As producers want to minimise production costs, the equilibrium quantities of production factors are determined by the relative prices. Consumers are modeled in a similar way, starting from a utility function. Utility functions express the degree of satisfaction corresponding to a basket of different quantities of goods. Under the consumers' budget constraint, the relative price of different consumption goods will determine the amounts consumed, maximizing the utility. The model uses different types of parameters. Substitution elasticities appear in the production functions. These are rarely estimated econometrically. Frequently they are taken from the literature. Scaling parameters are derived in a calibration procedure so that the model reproduces the base year data.

Advantages

- General equilibrium models are typically designed to make comparative analyses of different scenarios for *long periods*. However, they are not designed to make a forecast. Indeed these models require some type of baseline scenario which must largely be based on external assumptions for sectoral growth rates, technological progress and others;

- The *level of detail* in general equilibrium models can be very high. They can be combined with bottom-up engineering models to include a great number of sectors, processes and technologies.

Drawbacks

- The scientific methodology in general equilibrium models is *highly theoretical and deductive*. In fact, production functions and utility functions are very abstract concepts which are very difficult to observe empirically.

Conclusion on models

All models present advantages and drawbacks. It is important to be candid about this 'fact of life' in communications towards non-expert audiences. Our short review tends to show that model methodologies can become complementary to each other, depending on the type of application considered. Therefore, often a combination of methods and models becomes the best answer to quantitative modeling of long-term energy provision developments:

- *Econometric models* are *not suited for mid- (2030) or long-term (2050 and beyond) projections*, as for the mid and long term, the technical elements and structural changes can become very important;
- *Bottom-up models* are *fully disaggregated* and therefore present both the best representation of sector and region specificities for emission related variables. As they rely on detailed descriptions of the most energy intensive installations, they are totally *transparent* (at least for those who take enough time to review the often extensive databases);
- The sectoral representation of *general equilibrium models* is focused on the macro-economic variables and its *consistency* derives from the underlying economic theory;
- *Technological change* is explicitly represented in bottom-up models. General equilibrium models include some concepts of technological change in a more aggregated or general way, which is *less transparent*;
- *Direct costs* are established by *bottom-up models* for technology/reduction measures. *General equilibrium models* are better suited to analyze *indirect costs* such as effects on GDP, welfare loss, employment, government balance;
- *Bottom-up models* will provide the best operational results on the penetration of emission reduction technologies, on the impact of regulatory measures, or on the reduction potential of voluntary agreements. *General equilibrium models* will provide the best results regarding economic impacts of different types of policies, in particular on economic instruments and alternative economic assumptions such as variations in relative prices.

No modeling approach is able to overpass the very large uncertainties inherent to long-term projections. It is therefore most suitable to apply methods which clearly implement key assumptions in a transparent and coherent manner. For this task, bottom-up models, with their very fine disaggregation at the sector and/or regional levels, and sometimes at the installations level, appear as the most suitable. On the downside however, this very fine disaggregation entails building databases holding thousands of variables, which all have to be checked for validity. Moreover, it will be difficult to secure stakeholder agreement when contested parameter choices (e.g. uncertain performance data for future technologies) have to be secured. Furthermore, one should distinguish carefully between ignorance and uncertainty. Uncertainties can be usually quantified to a certain extent using probability density distributions and then be integrated in to modeling exercises by applying stochastic programming. For uncertainties you know at least the "space" of the events but it may be difficult to attach "the right number" of probability to them (but in principle it would be possible). For ignorance it is much worse: You do not even know "event space"! There is by definition nothing you can do about ignorance.

4   Methodological recommendations for energy foresight

In this section, we will set out the contours of a 'model process' for setting up a long-term (energy) foresight exercise as a communicative platform. Within the context of the present chapter, our proposal will remain largely programmatic, as further specifications will necessarily depend on the contextual needs of the moment. Therefore, our 'model process' will be set out in the form of a 'menu' of tasks or activities undertaken in a foresight exercise (see e.g. Fontela 2000), followed by a short comment on what we believe to be the essential requirements (in view of communicative purposes) of that particular task. We are not proposing that these requirements should be fulfilled in each and every case, nor that every foresight exercise should necessarily perform all the tasks outlined in the following sections. Rather, our 'menu' should be seen as a checklist, enabling the energy foresight community to reflect on the propositions and to develop a more thorough justification on the choices made in their foresight activities. Also, we are not suggesting that the tasks should be performed in a linear way – rather, we can easily imagine that scenario-building groups will oscillate back and forth between some of the tasks, in search of some kind of a 'reflexive equilibrium'.

5.1   Process architecture

Preparatory stages

The importance of the preparatory stages in setting up a foresight exercise cannot be overstressed. It is in these stages that the seeds of a common understanding are sown. Ideally, all participants in the exercise should be involved from the beginning and decide collectively on the 'rules of the game'. Leaving participants out of the preparatory stages and involving them only in the latter stages of scenario development (e.g. through 'extended peer review') could induce a perception that certain rules are imposed upon them, thus limiting the communicative outreach of the scenarios coming out of the foresight exercise. All in all, the principal aim of the preparatory stages would be to encourage the group of participants in the foresight exercise to see itself as a community whose members are committed to crafting solutions to common problems. All participants should be able to see themselves (to a maximum extent possible) as the 'owners' of the scenarios. Preparations involve:

- *Discuss the basic assumptions*: A common understanding should be reached on the basic aims of the foresight exercise (e.g. 'merely' exploring possible futures vs. making recommendations on research priorities towards policy makers; normative vs. descriptive scenarios, etc.), the intended use of the scenarios, the available foresight 'tools' (e.g. developing a common understanding on the possibilities and limitations of available mathematical models), and the management of uncertainties and surprises;

- *Discuss rules of interaction*: A common understanding should be reached on the activities that will be undertaken in the foresight exercise, the timing and sequence of steps, management of possible conflict of opinion, representation of minority points of view, etc.

Problem structuring

The problem structuring phase starts with an identification of all relevant 'actants' to the problem at hand. Such identification can be aided by drawing upon established energy system indicators, other existing scenario studies, etc. However, problem structuring should not be limited to these established 'actants'. Initially, this phase should create an opening towards a wide range of perspectives and strive to include solid trends as well as loose bits of information, perceptions, impressions, etc. Also, it is important to acknowledge the legitimacy of emotional responses. Such responses should not be dismissed *a priori* or confused with cognitive bias, motivational resistance, self-interest, rigidity, etc. Problem structuring subsequently proceeds by:

- *Structuring, selecting and summarizing perspectives for further analysis*: Participants in the foresight exercise should be encouraged to think about how the perspectives collected in a broad 'brainstorming' could be enrolled in a network (in the sense that Latour gave to this concept) (e.g. 'greenhouse gas emissions' could be an object of technical measurements, a legitimate goal of global policy-making initiatives, a factor in public opinion, etc.). In this step, one should strive for a good articulation and understanding of each of the different perspectives, so that no ambiguities will arise in the latter stages of scenario development;
- *Distinguish between 'active' and 'passive' actants*: Next, a consensus should be reached on which 'actants' will be used as 'driving forces' for scenario development, and which will be used as 'dependent' actants. In general, when defining dependent actants, common scenario practice puts too much weight on measurable values such as GDP or emissions; seemingly non-measurable values such as prevalent social habits or political movements occur – if at all – only as independent values. This phenomenon influences modeling in that we become less aware of effects on seemingly non-measurable values. Therefore, we suggest that actants which are considered to be neither very 'active' (for the time being) nor 'measurable' (i.e. these actants 'pass under the radar'), but are nevertheless deemed to be relevant, should not be excluded from further analysis. They could for instance be used to test scenario robustness against possible surprises (i.e. a 'passive' actant suddenly becoming 'active');
- If the aim of the scenario exercise is to provide 'decision joints' for policy makers, distinguish between 'steering' and 'context' variables;
- *Assessment of actants' actions*: In this step, best available knowledge concerning the different actants is sought out. Methods for assessing and measuring parameters should be explored (e.g. trend analysis), creating an awareness of different existing measurement techniques (if this is relevant), and creating an awareness for the uncertainties and limitation associated with different methods. Detailed methods for data and uncertainty management have been developed (see e.g. Craye and Funtowicz 2004). Also in this step, advice of external experts can be solicited.

Scenario building

Scenario building can then take place using the well-known technique of 'morphological analysis', which aims to explore possible futures in a systematic way by studying all the combinations resulting from the breakdown of a system. The process of 'breaking down' the system implies the definition of a set of actants, which could each influence the development of the energy system into different directions. These possible developments are formulated as 'hypotheses' or 'possible configurations'. The total number of combinations represents a 'morphological space', which must then be narrowed down to several coherent sets by formulating certain conditions ('exclusions' and 'compromises').

- *Selection of actants (driving forces, steering variables, measurement variables, etc.)*: It is likely that the problem structuring phase will yield a large number of possible actants, which would be unpractical for scenario building. Therefore, the most 'relevant' ones should be selected, if possible on a consensual basis;
- *Explore instances of 'undecidedness' governing future actants' actions*: For each of the 'relevant' actants, a number of hypotheses should be developed on its future 'behavior'. Participants should be encouraged to stretch their imagination to a maximum extent possible. From the methodological point of view it is important that the hypotheses about possible future developments are developed independently for each actant (and if possible by different persons) in order to avoid a conscious or unconscious 'predetermination' of possible constellations;
- *Develop scenarios based on several structuring principles*: The scenario foresight group could be encouraged to split into smaller subgroups, while each subgroup is given the task to devise, elaborate and defend a plausible and coherent account of how the energy system could develop as seen from the perspective of a structural principle (e.g. more energy autonomy, minimizing environmental impacts, etc.). Reasoning from particular principles, subgroups should also seek out actants from other commonwealths that would support their visions (i.e. compromises can be found by identifying actants which could 'work together'). Subsequently, each subgroup should be given the opportunity to question the other subgroup's reasoning by identifying 'exclusions' – i.e. incompatible pairs of actants;
- *Develop scenarios on the basis of compromises between different structuring principles*: Based on the 'compromises' and 'exclusions' identified in the previous step, coherent scenario narratives can be developed. The most important combinations (in view of coherence) are those which include the largest possible number of compromises. This task is preferably assigned to professionals who have not been involved in defining the input.

Comparison, evaluation, and policy recommendations

This last step involves an evaluation of scenario results and (possibly) the formulation of policy recommendations.

- *Use formal mathematical modeling tools where applicable*: Wherever possible, quantification of scenario results should be a goal. Certainly for energy systems this will normally be a requirement, since most stakeholders will also rely on technical-economic parameters and arguments to support their positions;
- *Translate scenario assumptions into policy instruments*: It could be useful to explore which policy instruments would be congruent with a particular future vision. This will help participants to commit to the legitimacy, in principle, of different policy instruments. Participants should also be encouraged of course to think about difficulties of using a certain policy instrument within the logic of the different scenarios;
- *Derive policy recommendations*: If this was set as the aim of the foresight exercise to begin with, results of the previous step can be used to formulate recommendations for policy makers. Such recommendations should however be based on common principles, which

should be defined from the outset of the foresight exercise. Like candidate principles are for instance: 'robustness' (i.e. a 'good performance' of the policy measure under different scenario assumptions), 'precaution' (i.e. avoiding possible serious impacts or irreversibilities), 'economic optimization' (i.e. selecting policy measures on the basis of welfare costs), etc.

- *Communication to wider audiences*: All findings of the foresight exercise should be summarized into an understandable format for lay audiences. This task could be assigned to communication professional – e.g. science journalists.

5 Conclusions

We have stressed the crucial role of long-term scientific foresight exercises not only in support of the development of energy strategies but also as tools of deliberation and communication. This belief is founded not only in the urgency of some of the global (energy) challenges facing us (a staggering increase in global economic output, resources under continuous pressure worldwide, rising inequalities, etc.), but also in the existence of very different and often contradictory views about how energy systems operate and interrelate with other developments, and consequently, how they could or should be managed. Nevertheless, good intentions can never be a substitute for thoughtful reflection in order to enhance the chances of successful communication. In this chapter we have provided some guidance on how scenario exercises can be designed to meet the challenges of developing sound scientific advice based on intense stakeholder deliberations in such uncertain and complex contexts. In particular, we have shown how a link can be drawn between constructivist perspectives on science and technology and scientific foresight in the hope of informing the process of scenario-based planning and communication. Our constructivist reading suggest that 'positivistic' approaches to foresight – suggesting that the 'true futures' are out there and the job of the scenario exercise is to find it – should be rejected. Instead, scenario-based foresight can be approached from a constructivist perspective and still produce results. Scenario analysis can play a major role in addressing the core question of how to scan the future in a structured, integrated and policy-relevant manner. From the review of scientific literature discussed in this chapter, we offered some guidelines of good practice for the benefit of the energy foresight community. Keeping in mind however that a real foresight exercise should be tailored more specifically to the practical needs of the problems being addressed in a particular context. There can be no 'one-size fits all' approach to the complex challenge of developing long-term energy strategies.

Notes

1 https://ec.europa.eu/jrc/en/publication/potencia-new-eu-wide-energy-sector-model.
2 We are referring here to the Delphi method in its 'purest' form, that is the classical technology Delphi. Other applications exist which do not imply any prediction of the future: the policy Delphi and the decision Delphi.
3 The following section is mainly based on ECONOTEC/VITO (2005).
4 We draw here upon the distinction introduced by Arendt (1958) between 'instruments' and 'works of art'.

References

Aligica, P. (2003), "Prediction, explanation and the epistemology of future studies", *Futures*, Vol. 35, pp. 1027–1040.
Arendt, H. (1958), *The human condition*, University of Chicago Press, Chicago/London.
Batens, D. (1992), *Menselijke kennis: Een pleidooi voor een bruikbare rationaliteit*, Garant, Leuven.

Blass, E. (2003), "Researching the future: Method or madness?", *Futures*, Vol. 35, pp. 1041–1054.

Boulanger, P. and Bréchet, T. (2003), "Analyse comparative des classes de modèles", Institut pour un Développement Durable (IDD), <http://club.euronet.be/idd>

Callon, M. (1987), "Society in the making: The study of technology as a tool for sociological analysis", in Bijker, W., Hughes, T. and Pinch, T. (Eds.), *The social construction of technological systems: New directions in the sociology and history of technology*, MIT Press, Cambridge, pp. 83–106.

Chermack, T. and van der Merwe, L. (2003), "The role of constructivist learning in scenario planning", *Futures*, Vol. 35, pp. 445–460.

Craye, M., Funtowicz, S. and van der Sluijs, J. (2004), "A reflexive approach to dealing with uncertainties in environmental health risk science and policy", *International Journal for Risk Assessment and Management*, Vol. 4, No. 2, pp. 216–236.

ECONOTEC/VITO (2005), "Characteristics of models for the calculation of GHG emissions in Belgium", final report in the framework of a study carried out for the Federal Public Service of Public Health, Food Chain Safety and Environment – DG Environment, Brussels.

Fontela, E. (2000), "Bridging the gap between scenarios and models", *Foresight*, Vol. 2, No. 10, pp. 10–14.

Funtowicz, S.O. and Ravetz, J.R. (1993), "Science for the post-normal age", *Futures*, Vol. 25, pp. 739–755.

Gibbons M., Limoges, C., Nowotny, H., Schwartzman, S., Scott, P. and Trow, M. (1994), *The new production of knowledge: The dynamics of science and research in contemporary societies*, Sage Publications, London.

Gieryn, T. (1995), "Boundaries of science", in Jasanoff, S., Markle, G., Petersen, J. and Pinch, T. (Eds.), *Handbook of science and technology studies*, Sage, Thousand Oaks, pp. 393–443.

Guivarch, C., Lempert, R. and Trutnevyte, E. (2017), Scenario techniques for energy and environmental research: An overview of recent developments to broaden the capacity to deal with complexity and uncertainty. *Environmental Modelling and Software*, Vol. 97, pp. 201–210.

Harries, C. (2003), "Correspondence to what? Coherence to what? What is good scenario-based decision making?", *Technological Forecasting & Social Change*, No. 70, pp. 797–817.

Heyligen, F. (1997), "Objective, subjective and intersubjective selectors of knowledge", <http://pespmc1.vub.ac.be/HEYL.html>

Holtz, G., Alkemade, F., de Haan, F., Köhler, J., Trutnevyte, E., Luthe, T., Halbe, J., Papachristos, G., Chappin, E., Kwakkel, J. and Ruutu, S. (2015), "Prospects of modelling societal transitions: Position paper of an emerging community", *Environmental Innovation and Societal Transition*, Vol. 17, pp. 41–58.

Jasanoff, S. (1990), *The fifth branch: Science advisers as policymakers*, Harvard University Press, Cambridge.

Joss, S. and Bellucci, S. (Eds.) (2002), *Participatory technology assessment: European perspectives*, CSD/TASwiss, London.

Kahneman, D. and Tversky, A. (1982), "The simulation heuristic", in Kahneman, D., Slovic, P. and Tversky, A. (Eds.), *Judgment under uncertainty: Heuristics and biases*, Cambridge University Press, Cambridge, pp. 201–208.

Keulartz, J., Schermer, M., Korthals, M. and Swierstra, T. (2004), "Ethics in technological culture: A programmatic proposal for a pragmatist approach", *Science, Technology and Human Values*, Vol. 29, pp. 3–29.

Latour, B. (1993), *We have never been modern*, Harvester Wheatsheaf, New York.

Latour, B. (2004), *The politics of nature*, Harvard University Press, Cambridge.

Mantzos, L., Matei, N. A., Rózsai, M., Russ, P., and Ramirez, A. S. (2017). "POTEnCIA: A New EU-Wide Energy Sector Model." In *2017 14th International Conference on the European Energy Market (EEM)*, 1–5. https://doi.org/10.1109/EEM.2017.7982028.

McDowall, W. and Geels, F.W. (2017), "Ten challenges for computer models in transitions research: Commentary on Holtz et al.", *Environmental Innovation and Societal Transition*, Vol. 22, pp. 41–49.

Oreskes, N. (2003), "The role of quantitative models in science", in Canham, C., Cole, J. and Lauenroth, W. (Eds.), *The role of models in ecosystem science*, Princeton University Press, Princeton, pp. 13–31.

Rescher, J. (1988), *Rationality*, Cambridge University Press, Cambridge.

Rotmans, J. (2001), "Integrated assessment: A bird's eye view", ICIS, Maastricht University, Maastricht.

Rowe, G. and Frewer, L. (2004), "Evaluating public participation exercises: A research agenda", *Science, Technology and Human Values*, Vol. 29, No. 4, pp. 512–557.

Tichy, G. (2004), "The over-optimism among experts in assessment and foresight", *Technological Forecasting & Social Change*, No. 71, pp. 341–363.

van Notten, P., Rotmans, J., van Asselt, M. and Rothman, D. (2003), "An updated scenario typology", *Futures*, Vol. 35, pp. 423–443.

Weinberg A. (1972), "Science and transscience", *Minerva*, Vol. 10, pp. 209–222.

39

Multi-criteria decision analysis for energy policy

*Laurence Stamford, Burcin Atilgan Türkmen,
Jasmin Cooper, and Adisa Azapagic*

1   Introduction

At its core, the concept of sustainable development aims to ensure that all people, in current and future generations, benefit from continuing prosperity (WCED, 1987). The most prominent reflection of this concept in the present day is the attempt to reconcile economic prosperity with the prevention and mitigation of climate change. The energy sector naturally underpins all other parts of the global economy and, therefore, efforts to successfully decouple economic growth from greenhouse gas (GHG) emissions have occurred in the energy sector at a scale not seen elsewhere. In 2017, for instance, the total global investment in low-carbon electricity generation amounted to USD 315 billion, while energy efficiency initiatives saw USD 236 billion in spending (IEA, 2018).

However, while decarbonization is a critical point on the path to sustainable development, it is important to retain the aforementioned vision of a broad, continuing prosperity. This involves recognition of the fact that sustainability is a highly complex, multivariate problem, involving more than GHG emissions and the usual cost considerations. Consequently, operationalizing the concept of sustainable development is far from trivial.

2   Sustainable development and the energy sector

Traditionally, the breadth of sustainability has been described with reference to a wide range of interacting aspects that can be categorized under three overarching 'pillars'(United Nations, 2005), otherwise referred to as the 'triple bottom line' (Elkington, 1997): environment, economy and society. The UN's 17 Sustainable Development Goals (SDGs) (United Nations, 2015), which came into force for member states at the start of 2016, provide a widely acknowledged set of themes around which we might further specify the aims of sustainability:

1   End poverty in all its forms everywhere
2   End hunger, achieve food security and improved nutrition and promote sustainable agriculture
3   Ensure healthy lives and promote well-being for all at all ages
4   Ensure inclusive and equitable quality education and promote lifelong learning opportunities for all

5 Achieve gender equality and empower all women and girls
6 Ensure availability and sustainable management of water and sanitation for all
7 Ensure access to affordable, reliable, sustainable and modern energy for all
8 Promote sustained, inclusive and sustainable economic growth, full and productive employment and decent work for all
9 Build resilient infrastructure, promote inclusive and sustainable industrialization and foster innovation
10 Reduce inequality within and among countries
11 Make cities and human settlements inclusive, safe, resilient and sustainable
12 Ensure sustainable consumption and production patterns
13 Take urgent action to combat climate change and its impacts
14 Conserve and sustainably use the oceans, seas and marine resources for sustainable development
15 Protect, restore and promote sustainable use of terrestrial ecosystems, sustainably manage forests, combat desertification, and halt and reverse land degradation and halt biodiversity loss
16 Promote peaceful and inclusive societies for sustainable development, provide access to justice for all and build effective, accountable and inclusive institutions at all levels
17 Strengthen the means of implementation and revitalize the Global Partnership for Sustainable Development.

In the context of this book, the SDGs illustrate two important points:

1 First, the energy sector plays a critical role in sustainable development. This occurs partly via the explicit call for affordable and sustainable energy provision in Goal 7, but also via its role in satisfying so many of the other SDGs. For instance, energy is a crucial enabler of water and sanitation (Goal 6); as an 'extractive' industry it is closely linked to the effects of mining on ecosystems and biodiversity (Goal 15); it is a major global provider of skilled employment (Goal 8) with over 10 million people working directly in the renewables sub-sector alone (IRENA, 2018); and it is the single biggest contributor to climate change (Goal 13), accounting for over a third of global GHG emissions (IPCC, 2014). Thus, decisions taken in the energy sector have a profound effect on the sustainability of the world's economy and the prosperity of its people.

2 Second, the SDGs demonstrate the wide range of key issues upon which the energy sector might have an impact. Developing policy with the intention of steering the energy sector in a sustainable direction is akin to a complex game of chess, with each move having a number of knock-on effects which will affect the outcome either directly or indirectly. As a result, sustainable decision-making in this area requires careful deliberation and rigorous analysis.

The above two points are explored further in the following section.

3 The case for multi-criteria decision analysis in energy policy

As outlined above, the energy sector has a far-reaching impact on sustainable development. The recognition of this has led to the adoption of a large number of sustainability-related policies and initiatives by governments and energy companies worldwide. Regarding climate change, following the 2015 Paris Agreement, 141 countries submitted Nationally Determined Contributions with specific emission reduction targets for their energy sectors, at a total estimated cost of approximately USD 470 billion (The World Bank, 2016). Similarly, in the corporate world, the

Science Based Targets initiative has independently approved the emissions reductions targets set by 126 companies, 14 of which are in the energy sector, while a further 343 companies (32 in the energy sector) have committed to taking action (Science Based Targets, 2018).

While the above examples deal solely with GHGs, commitment to broader sustainability targets and policies is gaining traction in the energy sector. The EU, for instance, has set sectoral targets for 2020 and 2030 covering emissions, energy efficiency and the share of renewables in the energy mix, with policies including, among others, a reformed emissions trading scheme (European Commission, 2014). Meanwhile the rise of corporate social responsibility (CSR) reporting has been notable over the past decade: the Global Reporting Initiative, for example, provides the most widely adopted framework for companies to track their progress on a variety of sustainability metrics aligned with the UN SDGs. As of mid-2018, it has received sustainability reporting data from 12,761 organizations, of which 1,118 are in the energy sector (GRI, 2018).

It is clear then that commitment to some form or aspects of sustainability in the energy sector appears high, by both governments and businesses. However, it is also notable that the majority of target-setting in policy still refers solely to climate change mitigation, while the tackling of broader sustainability issues may occur more often via the adoption of general principles and attempts to increase transparency, rather than by concrete policies and actions. This is perhaps not surprising when considering the challenge: just as life cycle thinking is recognized as a prerequisite for environmental sustainability (Azapagic, 2004), the same holistic view is needed to ensure broader sustainability (Stamford and Azapagic, 2011). Combined with the need to address a wide range of issues, this means that robust, decision-making for sustainable development requires that many criteria are accounted for simultaneously.

This is illustrated in Figure 39.1 by a hypothetical example of a natural gas power plant project. As per this example, relevant issues span climate change, air and water emissions, employment, safety and others, while varying geographically and over time throughout the life cycle.

The literature provides a wealth of attempts to assess sustainability via metrics, otherwise referred to as sustainability indicators or criteria, which span environmental, economic and social issues. A variety of journal articles are available reviewing the use of such metrics and assessment

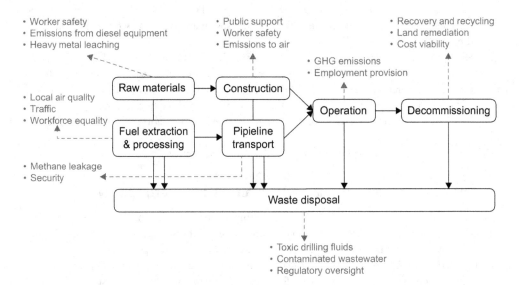

Figure 39.1 Potential sustainability issues in the life cycle of a natural gas power plant

frameworks, such as Singh et al. (2012), and interested readers are directed to these works for a more detailed overview. Specifically in the energy sector, examples of the use of sustainability indicators are found in Switzerland (Roth et al., 2009; Volkart et al., 2017), the UK (Stamford and Azapagic, 2012; Cooper et al., 2018c), Turkey (Atilgan and Azapagic, 2016b), Mexico (Santoyo-Castelazo et al., 2014), China (Ren et al., 2015) and many other countries.

However, any such sustainability assessment is typically faced with challenges in interpreting its outputs. Sustainability is often characterized by the existence of so-called 'wicked problems' (Rittel and Webber, 1973; Peterson, 2009; Azapagic and Perdan, 2014): that is, broadly speaking, that they have ill-defined goals or end points, cannot be reduced to 'true-or-false' or 'right-or-wrong' status, are defined according to the values of different stakeholders, have a very large number of potential solutions, and are fraught with contradictory or incomplete information.

Some of these characteristics are explored below using energy technologies as an example.

3.1   Complexity and contradiction

As established, sustainable development is a complex, multivariate problem. It is not uncommon for sustainability frameworks to include 40 or more criteria by which different options are evaluated (see, for example, Roth et al., 2009; Stamford and Azapagic, 2011). Often this results in contradiction between the assessment criteria, leading to the need to make trade-offs. Consider, for instance, Table 39.1, which shows a selection of sustainability criteria applied to both nuclear and natural gas power.

By reference to both competing technologies, it appears that nuclear power is comparatively 'good' in terms of carbon footprint and job creation, but 'bad' in its total cost and contribution to human health impacts. In cases where such information is to be used to formulate policies that favor one technology over the other, clearly it is non-trivial to make an objective judgment. Policies based solely on incentivizing low-carbon technologies, for example, might provide some form of financial assistance to nuclear power plant developers in order to achieve their aim, but this would come at the expense of human health and electricity costs.

Similar trade-offs are evident throughout policy making, with transport fuels providing a well-known example. Throughout Europe, tax rates on diesel fuel have historically been significantly lower than those on petrol: in 2014, for instance, the average tax on petrol in EU member states was €0.63 per litre, while that on diesel was €0.49 per litre (Transport & Environment, 2015). This situation is supported by policy goals to reduce GHG emissions, since diesel vehicles have lower emissions per kilometre than their equivalent petrol cars. However, their emissions of particulate matter and NOx are both higher than those of petrol, affecting human health. Thus, in this case, policy appears to trade short-term human health impacts for long-term climate change impacts.

Table 39.1 Illustrative sustainability attributes of nuclear and gas power (Stamford and Azapagic, 2012)

Sustainability criterion	Nuclear (pressurized water reactor)	Natural gas (combined cycle gas turbine)
Total levelized cost (£/MWh)	94.60	65.70
Carbon footprint (g CO_2 eq./kWh)	6.23	366
Human toxicity (g dichlorobenzene eq./kWh)	115	5.44
Employment provision (person-years/TWh)	80.8	62.4

Such contradictions arising from sustainability criteria often lead to the unconscious adoption of value judgments, as discussed below.

3.2 Value judgment

As contradictory results appear from sustainability assessments, trade-off decisions become necessary. In many cases it is not possible to make a decision on an objective basis, leading to the values-based decision-making, which can occur either consciously or subconsciously.

Using the example in Table 39.1 it might be possible to make an objective judgment about the rationality of a policy to assist financially nuclear power plant owners based on the lower GHG emissions of their plants. For instance, using the information available, one could estimate the cost per unit of GHG emissions saved based on the difference between the carbon footprints and costs of competing energy technologies. On such a basis, the trade-off between cost and climate impacts could be somewhat rationalized.

However, the same cannot be said of other trade-offs. For instance, is it preferable to maximize employment by choosing nuclear power, or to minimize electricity costs by selecting gas power? Low energy costs and full employment are both common, sensible aims of economic policy, meaning that a decision between the two is unlikely to be made on objective grounds. At such points, value judgments become relevant. Gainful employment is associated with personal satisfaction and contentment, while benefitting the economy and all of society; therefore, surely employment must be prioritized. On the other hand, lower energy costs benefit the poorest members of society, greatly enhancing the quality of life of the people most in need; thus, surely energy cost should be minimized. In truth, such questions cannot be resolved without the use of value judgments which, by their nature, vary between individuals. Consequently, a universally 'correct' answer cannot be found.

3.3 Uncertainty and variability

Policy decisions often deal with changeable or uncertain information. Continuing with the example in Table 39.1, it is likely that the overall costs of nuclear and gas power are contingent upon a range of other factors: the interest rates at which capital can be borrowed, the location of the plant, unforeseen events that could delay construction and many more. Therefore, many attributes of the options being assessed cannot be known with absolute certainty. Rather, the values assumed, like those in Table 39.1, will be those considered the most likely out of a range of possibilities.

Extending this to decisions with many criteria, it is likely that each criterion has a differing level of certainty. The number of employees at a power plant, for instance, may be known in advance to a high degree of certainty, perhaps within the range of ±5%. In contrast, the impact of the plant on local air quality depends on the type and quality of fuel purchased, the condition and operation of pollution control measures on-site, the local and regional weather conditions and other factors, which might lead to a level of certainty of ±50%.

This added complexity further hinders the ability of decision-makers to make decisions.

To summarize the effects of complexity, contradiction, value judgments and uncertainty, it can be said that the 'wicked' nature of sustainability problems leaves those wishing to make informed decisions at risk of so-called 'analysis paralysis': the failure to complete their assessment and make a final decision due to overwhelming complexity. Without some form of robust decision analysis, policy decisions that could be critically important might be avoided, stalled or replaced with suboptimal solutions that disregard the available information. Herein lies the case for multi-criteria decision analysis in energy policy, and in sustainability policy making in general.

4 Multi-criteria decision analysis techniques

Multi-criteria decision analysis (MCDA), also referred to as multi-criteria decision-making, is a broad field with a variety of methodological approaches, the extent of which is too great to be encompassed here. For such purposes, readers are directed to dedicated publications (such as Azapagic and Perdan, 2005a, 2005b; Department for Communities and Local Government, 2009; Cinelli et al., 2014).

As a general concept, MCDA aims to support complex decision-making situations with multiple, potentially conflicting objectives which are ascribed differing value by different stakeholders. The field consists of many different schools of thought and techniques, with intense debate between the different schools. However, regardless of the specific methodology chosen, the overarching aims of MCDA are to:

- provide a structured, numerical and transparent way of aiding decision-making;
- increase understanding of the decision-maker's values and those of others, as well as providing insight into how those values affect the decision;
- provide insight into the most influential parameters of the decision, potentially leading to targets or critical trigger points.

Before embarking on MCDA, it should be borne in mind that MCDA cannot remove subjectivity from a decision (although it can make that subjectivity more transparent and tractable). MCDA can also be pragmatically difficult and time consuming. These issues are discussed in more depth below under 'benefits, limitations and weaknesses of MCDA'.

The common principles of all forms of MCDA can be defined simply in terms of the options which are to be assessed (referred to as the '*alternatives*'), the *criteria* against which those alternatives are to be assessed, the performance of each alternative against each criterion (otherwise referred to as the '*attributes*' of the alternatives), and the *weight* applied to each criterion.

The basic process of an MCDA is outlined in Figure 39.2. As shown, the process begins by identifying the problem clearly, including contextualization and development of a common

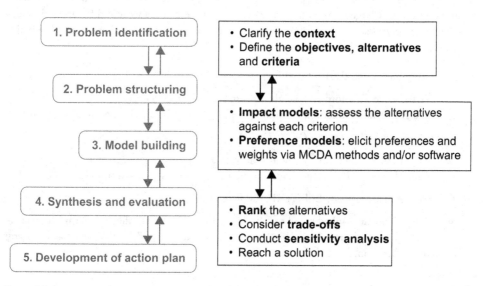

Figure 39.2 A typical MCDA process outlining the stages (left) and activities (right)

Source: Based on Catrinu-Renström et al. (2013) and Belton and Stewart (2002).

understanding between the different practitioners or involved parties. Secondly, the problem must be structured. This includes defining the objectives of the process, the alternatives that are available to choose among, and the criteria by which those alternatives will be judged.

Once the problem has been defined, model building can begin. This encompasses some form of impact assessment by which each alternative is evaluated against the identified criteria: such modeling may include, for instance, cost estimation, emissions estimation or more comprehensive methods such as life cycle assessment. The model building stage also includes elicitation of preferences in which all available stakeholders should evaluate the relative importance of each criterion according to their views. This can be achieved by a variety of MCDA methods, as outlined below.

Once the criteria, attributes and weights are established, the problem can be evaluated in a quantitative synthesis of the available information. This can be described by a decision matrix (Wang et al., 2009), as follows:

	Alternatives	A_1	A_2	...	A_m
Criteria	Weights				
C_1	w_1	x_{11}	x_{12}	...	x_{1m}
C_2	w_2	x_{21}	x_{22}	...	x_{2m}
$\vdots$	$\vdots$	$\vdots$	$\vdots$	$\ddots$	$\vdots$
C_n	w_n	x_{n1}	x_{n2}	...	x_{nm}

where n is the number of criteria, m is the number of alternatives, w_n is the weight of criterion n, and x_{nm} is the performance of alternative m against criterion n.

The overall performance of each alternative is expressed as the sum of its weighted performance for each criterion. Subsequently, the alternatives can be ranked against each other to reveal the preferred option.

It should be noted that, while Figure 39.2 outlines the MCDA process, there are many available methodologies within that process, particularly with regard to steps three and four (model building and synthesis). A large body of literature exists developing and applying different techniques in order to model impacts, elicit and model preferences, and evaluate the alternatives. The major approaches include (but are not limited to):

- Multi-attribute value theory (MAVT)

  o Partial value functions and weights are established for each criterion, enabling calculation of a global value function, V. Additive and multiplicative models are used to obtain V.

- Multi-attribute utility theory (MAUT)

  o Partial utility functions are calculated for each criterion, enabling calculation of a global utility function, U. Additive and multiplicative models are used to obtain U.

- Outranking methods (e.g. ELECTRE, PROMETHEE)

  o Alternatives are ranked based on whether they dominate another alternative in a specified number of criteria *and* are not themselves dominated by that alternative in any other criterion.

- Fuzzy set theory

  o Fuzzy logic is used to tackle uncertainty by assigning numerical values 'membership functions' to several input parameters

- Analytical hierarchy process (AHP)

  o Pairwise comparison matrices are used to establish the relative importance of criteria. The matrices are used to derive an overall rating for each alternative via the eigenvalue method.

For more information on any of the techniques outlined above, readers may wish to explore Belton and Stewart (2002) and Azapagic and Perdan (2005b).

The following section discusses the implementation of MCDA following the AHP approach, which is one of the methods used widely in sustainability-related energy decision-making (Wang et al., 2009).

5 An illustrative example using analytical hierarchy process

AHP was developed in the late 1970s, predominantly by its inventor Thomas Saaty (Saaty, 1980). Since that time, it has been used widely in the scientific literature, in business and in policy making.

5.1 Problem structuring

Like all forms of MCDA, AHP broadly follows the steps laid out in Figure 39.2, beginning with problem identification and structuring. Structuring in AHP is always hierarchical, based on the overall goal of exercise and a user-defined categorization of hierarchical issues, represented by criteria. An example of AHP problem structuring is shown in Figure 39.3 based on the hypothetical selection of a new piece of technology for installation in a plant. Note that the attributes of two alternatives are also shown for illustrative purposes, but that those attributes would be established in the next step of the assessment: model building.

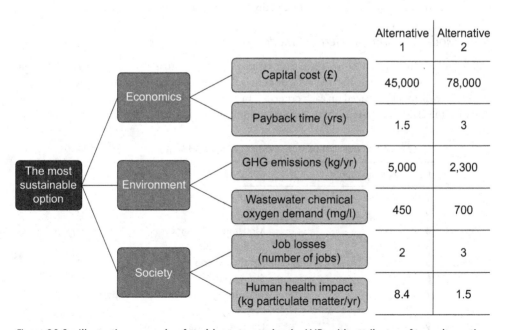

Figure 39.3 Illustrative example of problem structuring in AHP, with attributes of two alternatives

5.2 Model building – impact models

As mentioned previously, the attributes of each alternative must be established via some form of modeling which might include economic accounting methods, emissions estimation, environmental life cycle assessment, epidemiological modeling and/or others. However, the numerical form of each attribute may differ. In some cases, attributes may be binary: for instance, of several alternatives, only some may comply with a particular policy, in which case their compliance could be indicated by a value of 0 or 1. In other cases, it may be necessary to translate unmeasurable, qualitative attributes into quantitative values using a descriptive, ordinal scale.

However, typically many attributes can be expressed as the direct numerical outputs of the various modeling approaches applied. In such cases, it is likely that *scaling* will be required to express the values in equivalent ranges of magnitude: typically, this is achieved by *re-mapping* onto a scale of 0 to 1. This can be achieved using either local or global re-mapping: a local re-map sets the minimum value as '0' and the maximum as '1', while a global re-map uses scaling based on experience or judgment. In Figure 39.3, for instance, a local re-map would translate the capital costs of the two alternatives into '0' for Alternative 1 and '1' for Alternative 2, as there are only two alternatives to choose from.

In contrast, in a global re-map the practitioner might judge that the best possible outcome would be a capital cost of £0 and the highest cost acceptable might be £100,000. Based on this judgment, in the simplest form of global re-mapping, linear scaling would be applied to transform the capital cost values into (45,000 ÷ 100,000 =) 0.45 for Alternative 1 and (78,000 ÷ 100,000 =) 0.78 for Alternative 2. A more advanced re-mapping might instead take into account more complex relationships, such that the values are mapped onto the scale of 0 to 1 in a non-linear fashion. For instance, taking a linear approach, a capital cost of £78,000 is 58% 'worse' than a cost of £45,000 but, in reality, it may be the case that the potential investor can fund up to £50,000 through cash, while anything above that figure requires borrowing and, therefore, interest repayment. Consequently, £78,000 may be viewed as more than 58% 'worse' than £45,000. This type of relationship can often be accommodated by MCDA models using various value functions. For an example of the use of different value functions, see the case study in section 7.2.

5.3 Model building – preference modeling

Following structuring of the problem and estimation of the attributes of each alternative, an MCDA process must elicit the preferences of stakeholders in order to establish the weights of importance that will be placed on each criterion. In AHP, this is achieved by 'pairwise comparison' in which the criteria are rated against each other using a 1–9 ordinal scale, as shown in Table 39.2.

Table 39.2 Pairwise comparison ordinal scaling in AHP

Intensity of importance	Definition
1	Equal importance
2	Weak
3	Moderate importance
4	Moderate plus
5	Strong importance
6	Strong plus
7	Very strong or demonstrated importance
8	Very, very strong
9	Extreme importance

Often the pairwise comparison process is presented to stakeholders as a sliding scale, as follows:

Criterion 1	9 8 7 6 5 4 3 2 1 2 3 4 5 6 7 8 9	Criterion 2

Thus, the stakeholders must use their own understanding of the problem and their own value system to rate the criteria. Note that it is important that pairwise comparison proceeds in a hierarchical manner, following the structure of the problem. Thus, in the example given in Figure 39.3, the higher-level categories 'Economics', 'Environment' and 'Society' must be compared against each other, while the lower level criteria are only compared within their categories. Therefore, in this case, only one pairwise comparison would take place per category: for example, capital cost versus payback time in the Economy category.

Once complete, the pairwise comparisons must be normalized to establish the criteria weights, all of which must lie in a range of 0 to 1. This is achieved by populating a matrix of the preferences, as follows:

Criteria	C_1	C_2	$\cdots$	C_n
C_1	p_1/p_1	p_1/p_2	$\cdots$	p_1/p_n
C_2	p_2/p_1	p_2/p_2	$\cdots$	p_2/p_n
$\vdots$	$\vdots$	$\vdots$	$\ddots$	$\vdots$
C_n	p_n/p_1	p_n/p_2	$\cdots$	p_n/p_n

where n is the number of criteria and p is the preference of the stakeholder for each criterion on the aforementioned scale of 0 to 9.

Based on the matrix of preferences, the final weights of the criteria can be calculated by several methods, including the arithmetic mean method, characteristic root method and least square method. In practice, the consistency of the pairwise comparisons is an important consideration, as it is unlikely that all comparisons will agree with each other. For instance, if criterion 1 is rated as having 'very strong' importance ($p = 7$) relative to criterion 2, and criterion 2 is rated as 'very strong' ($p = 7$) relative to criterion 3, then it must be the case that criterion 1 has 'very, very strong' ($p = 8$) or 'extreme importance' ($p = 9$) relative to criterion 3. As this may not always be observed during real-world scenarios, a consistency ratio is often derived to ensure sufficient robustness.

5.4 Synthesis

After the attributes of each alternative have been estimated and re-mapped (if necessary), and the criteria weights have been established, the value of each alternative is calculated as follows:

$$V(a) = \sum_{i=1}^{n} w_i x_i (a)$$

where $V(a)$ is the total value of Alternative a, w_i is the weighting factor of criterion i, and $x_i(a)$ is the score of Alternative a on criterion i. In AHP, due to the hierarchical nature of the problem structure, the calculation of each result must proceed hierarchically. An example is provided in Figure 39.4, building on the previous example with the addition of illustrative re-mapped attributes and individual criteria weights.

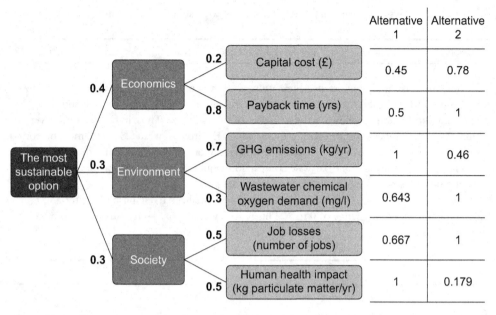

	Alternative 1	Alternative 2
Capital cost (£)	0.45	0.78
Payback time (yrs)	0.5	1
GHG emissions (kg/yr)	1	0.46
Wastewater chemical oxygen demand (mg/l)	0.643	1
Job losses (number of jobs)	0.667	1
Human health impact (kg particulate matter/yr)	1	0.179

Figure 39.4 Illustrative example of an AHP problem with re-mapped attributes (in the table on the right) and criteria weights (on top of the branching lines on the left)

In this case, the overall value of each alternative is as follows:

$$V(1) = 0.4\left((0.2\times0.45)+(0.8\times0.5)\right)+0.3\left((0.7\times1)+(0.3\times0.643)\right)$$
$$+\, 0.3\left((0.5\times0.667)+(0.5\times1)\right) = 0.714$$

$$V(2) = 0.4\left((0.2\times0.78)+(0.8\times1)\right)+0.3\left((0.7\times0.46)+(0.3\times1)\right)$$
$$+\, 0.3\left((0.5\times1)+(0.5\times0.179)\right) = 0.746$$

Since the direction of preference of each criterion in this assessment is negative – i.e. a lower value is preferred for all criteria – a lower overall value is preferred. Therefore, Alternative 1 is preferable to Alternative 2.

5.5   Other considerations

MCDA practitioners should be aware of two additional issues that are not covered in depth above, as follows:

i)   Direction of preference

It is often the case that impact models yield a range of metrics with mixed directions of prefer-ence. For instance, stakeholders may wish to minimize GHG emissions but to maximize net pres-ent value (NPV). Such metrics cannot be imported as criteria directly into MCDA as their goals are in conflict. In these cases, the scaling procedure must *invert* some of the metrics to ensure that the direction of preference is consistent.

ii) Uncertainty

In practice it is likely that some of the attributes of alternatives will be uncertain. For instance, practitioners may have actual quotes for the capital costs of new installations, but the costs of operation and maintenance may be less well established. In such cases, statistical techniques like Monte Carlo simulation can be added to MCDA to explore the consequences of this uncertainty.

6   Benefits, limitations, and weaknesses of MCDA

MCDA provides the structure needed to guide complex decisions. Moreover, in the evaluation stage of the MCDA, considerable insight can be generated into the implications of stakeholders' preferences and the attributes of the alternatives. For instance, many MCDA software packages allow users to explore the effects of altering criteria weights on the overall outcome. Real-time exploration such as this can demonstrate to users precisely how their expressed preferences would need to change in order to lead to a different outcome. In situations where stakeholders have greatly differing values, this can be an invaluable route to consensus-building and conflict resolution (Stirling, 2006).

However, MCDA has limitations that should be borne in mind. First, it revolves around the preferences of its users and, therefore, is subjective. Moreover, it is logistically difficult to involve a very large number of stakeholders in any preference elicitation process simply because of the time and resource requirements; this has led to suggestions that MCDA cannot truly be representative or democratic (Hanley, 2001). However, its proponents point out that, for many systems, no objective decision-making process can exist. Similarly, the complexity of certain decisions effectively rules out the participation of society as a whole, leaving MCDA as an imperfect but invaluable tool.

Second, like any form of decision analysis, MCDA can only be effective in leading to an optimal decision if the selected criteria describe the decision space sufficiently. In other words, the criteria must truly represent the concerns of all stakeholders without omitting or overemphasizing any particular aspect. In practice, it may be the case that the number of criteria necessary to fulfill this need render the process impractical; therefore, where potentially important issues are not captured by the assessment criteria, practitioners must bear in mind this limitation when making a final decision. It is often the case that social impacts are less easily quantified than economic or environmental impacts and, indeed, much research is ongoing in this area. Initiatives such as the Social Hotspots Database (SHDB, 2018), for instance, seek to provide quantitative metrics of social risks. Readers are directed also to Chapter 17 for an overview of quantitative measures of social acceptance, the likes of which might be incorporated into an MCDA.

Finally, the lack of standardization and consensus around MCDA methodologies is another potential weakness in its implementation, as experts are typically required to guide the process.

7   Application of MCDA: illustrative case studies

The following sections demonstrate the application of MCDA via two illustrative case studies in the context of sustainability decision-making in the energy arena: one related to the electricity sector in Turkey and another to shale gas in the UK.

7.1 The electricity sector in Turkey

This case study is set within the context of national energy policy in Turkey with a focus on electricity. It considers 14 electricity technologies and 19 environmental, economic and social sustainability criteria to estimate the impacts of 14 future electricity scenarios for the year 2050. The analysis is conducted using the software Web-HIPRE V1.22 (Mustajoki and Hämäläinen, 2000).

As outlined above (Figure 39.2), the process begins with problem identification.

7.1.1 Problem identification

Turkey is a fast developing country with the second highest growth rate in natural gas and electricity demand after China (IBP, 2015). In 2010, the national installed electrical capacity of 49,524 MW generated 211,208 GWh of electricity: four times more than in 1990 (TEIAS, 2012). Moreover, as Turkey lacks domestic gas sources, and gas provides almost half of its electricity demand (TEIAS, 2012), the country has become increasingly dependent on imports, particularly from Russia (TPAO, 2011). Given the unstable geo-political situation, improving security of energy supply is one of the main objectives of Turkish energy policy which aims to reduce the dependency on natural gas by up to 30% by 2023 (MENR, 2009a). Diversifying gas supplies, both in terms of countries and transit routes, is also an important goal for the country (MENR, 2009b, 2009a). Enhancing energy security is goal shared by a large number of countries worldwide; readers are referred to Chapter 8 of this book to gain further insight into the economics of energy security improvements.

To meet the growing energy demand and reduce gas-import dependency, Turkey also aims to expand coal power capacity by utilizing domestic coal through clean coal technologies (MENR, 2009b). There are significant domestic reserves of coal, with lignite being much more abundant than hard coal (TKI, 2012). However, most of the Turkish lignite is of poor quality with a low calorific value and high sulphur and ash content.

Despite these economic, political and environmental disadvantages, gas and coal supply 72.5% of Turkish electricity demand, as shown in Table 39.3. Attempts since the 1970s to introduce

Table 39.3 Turkey's electricity mix in 2010 (based on Atilgan and Azapagic, 2016a)

Source	Contribution to electricity mix (%)
Natural gas	**46.5**
Coal	**26.1**
Lignite	*17.0*
Hard coal	*9.1*
Hydropower	**24.5**
Large reservoir (>500 MW)	*14.5*
Small reservoir (<500 MW)	*6.5*
Run of river	*3.5*
Onshore wind	**1.4**
Liquid fuels	**1.0**
Geothermal	**0.3**
Other renewables and waste	**0.2**
Total	**100**
	(211,208 GWh)

nuclear power have not been successful, leaving hydropower to account for the bulk of Turkey's low-carbon electricity: 24.5% of total supply (MENR, 2012).

This situation exists despite the abundant renewable energy sources available to Turkey. Consequently the government has set targets for 2023 to exploit fully the economically viable hydropower potential of 140 TWh/year (DSI, 2010); to increase the installed capacity of wind power to 20 GW out of 48 GW estimated total potential (EMRA, 2014); to utilize the full geo-thermal power potential of 600 MW; and to promote electricity generation from solar energy (MENR, 2009a). On the latter point, due to its sunny climate, the potential for solar power in Turkey is estimated at 380 TWh per year (EMRA, 2014), yet it remains almost completely unexploited.

The high contribution of fossil fuels in the electricity mix, together with the increasing demand, has led to a steady increase in GHG emissions which Turkey is under pressure to mitigate. Moreover, the fact that much of the gas and coal fuel is imported has led to high electricity prices, negatively affecting the economy and society: prices in recent years have been approximately 10%–20% higher than the OECD average at USD 185/MWh (IEA, 2014).

Other social issues include the health and safety of workers in the energy sector. For instance, in 2014 alone there were over 300 deaths in two major coal mine accidents (Acar et al., 2015).

Clearly Turkey, like many countries, faces a variety of environmental, economic and social issues in developing its electricity mix; based on its current situation and the UN SDGs, Turkey must ensure that the future of the sector is much less GHG intensive, envi-ronmentally sound, socially equitable, safe, reliable and economically viable. In other words, it faces a complex, multivariate sustainability problem affecting a great variety of stakehold-ers. Thus, MCDA can be used as a tool to enable rational, transparent decision-making in this context.

7.1.2 Problem structuring

7.1.2.1 Criteria

Drawing on the 'three pillars' concept and prior work in this area (Atilgan and Azapagic, 2017), a list of decision criteria is proposed in Table 39.4. In keeping with the idea that sustainable development must be cognisant of indirect impacts and all stakeholders that could be affected by a decision, the criteria are based on a life cycle approach to account for impacts spanning raw material extraction through to electricity generation and waste management. For this reason, the environmental criteria are drawn from the field of life cycle assessment using the CML 2001 impact assessment methodology (Guinée et al., 2002). Similarly the economic and social criteria encompass the lifespan of each project.

7.1.2.2 Alternatives

As the purpose of the process is to aid sustainable development of the electricity sector, this example includes various potential future electricity mix scenarios. In an exploratory MCDA such as this, it is desirable for the alternatives considered to be either exhaustive or broad enough to encompass practically the whole range of possibilities. Otherwise, the outcomes of the MCDA will not truly reflect the decision space.

Table 39.4 Criteria for assessing the sustainability of electricity scenarios (Atilgan and Azapagic, 2017)

Criteria categories	Sustainability issues	Sustainability criteria	Units
Environmental	Resource depletion	Abiotic resource depletion potential (elements)	kg Sb eq./kWh
		Abiotic resource depletion potential (fossil fuels)	MJ/kWh
	Climate change	Global warming potential	kg CO$_2$ eq./kWh
	Emissions to air, water and soil	Acidification potential	kg SO$_2$ eq./kWh
		Eutrophication potential	kg PO$_4$ eq./kWh
		Fresh water aquatic ecotoxicity potential	kg DCB[a] eq./kWh
		Human toxicity potential	kg DCB[a] eq./kWh
		Marine aquatic ecotoxicity potential	kg DCB[a] eq./kWh
		Ozone layer depletion potential	kg CFC-11 eq./kWh
		Photochemical oxidants creation potential	kg C$_2$H$_4$ eq./kWh
		Terrestrial ecotoxicity potential	kg DCB[a] eq./kWh
Economic	Costs	Capital costs	US$
		Total annualized costs	US$/year
		Levelized costs	US$/kWh
Social	Provision of employment	Direct employment	jobs-years/TWh
		Total employment (direct + indirect)	jobs-years/TWh
	Worker safety	Injuries	no. of injuries/TWh
		Fatalities due to large accidents	no. of fatalities/TWh
	Energy security	Imported fossil fuels potentially avoided	koe[b]/kWh

[a] *DCB*: dichlorobenzene.
[b] *koe*: kilogram oil equivalent.

Therefore, as shown in Table 39.5, a total of 14 alternatives are considered in this example: four main scenarios, each with two to four sub-scenarios. This range of alternatives explores business as usual (BAU) as well as a range of GHG emission reduction targets and parameter variations.

The future scenarios shown here are predicated on an average of 3.55% per annum growth in electricity demand to 2050, resulting in a final annual demand of 852 TWh in 2050 (MENR, 2014).

In the BAU scenarios, fossil fuel power generation would continue dominating the electricity mix in 2050 without any additional energy policies, climate change policies, or incentives for carbon capture and storage (CCS). Direct GHG emissions (emitted during the operation of power plants) are up to five times higher than in 2000.

Scenarios A, B and C are driven by different targets for direct GHG emissions. In A-1 to A-4, limited action takes place to mitigate climate change and emissions double relative to the levels in 2000, growing by around 1.1% annually. Scenarios B-1 to B-4 assume that the GHG emissions from the electricity sector are equal to 2000 levels by 2050. Here, low carbon technologies gain importance to limit the increase in direct emissions to around 0.7% per year. For C-1 to C-4, the emissions are equal to 1990 levels, decreasing by 2.7% year on year up to 2050. As these

Table 39.5 Outline of the baseline electricity mix and all alternatives for the year 2050 (Atilgan and Azapagic, 2017)

Scenario	Direct emissions[a] (Mt CO_2-eq./year)	Assumptions
Baseline (2010)	99[b]	Current electricity mix. Coal and gas contribute 46.5% and 26.1%, respectively, to the total generation of 211 TWh. The next largest contribution is from hydropower (24.5%). Onshore wind contributes 1.4% and geothermal 0.3%.
BAU-1	370	The scenario was originally developed by Greenpeace and EREC (2008). There are no GHG emission targets and GHG emissions are five times greater than in 2000. A mix of fossil fuel (83.9%) and renewable (16.1%) technologies is assumed. CCS and nuclear plants are not considered.
BAU-2	297	Follows the current energy trends, policies and planned projects. There are no GHG emission targets and the emissions are four times higher than in 2000. Assumes a mix of fossil fuel technologies (69.5%), renewables (21.5%) and nuclear power (9%). The use of CCS is not considered.
A-1	150	GHG emissions are double the equivalent emissions in 2000 by 2050; limited action to reduce emissions. There is a strong support for fossil technologies. Assumes a mix of fossil fuel technologies without CCS (46%) and with CCS (29%), and renewable (25%) options. Nuclear power is not considered.
A-2	"	GHG emissions are double the equivalent emissions in 2000 by 2050; limited action is taken to reduce the emissions. There is a strong support for fossil fuel and nuclear plants. Assumes a mix of fossil fuel technologies without CCS (41%) and with CCS (19%), renewables (25%) and nuclear (15%).
A-3	"	GHG emissions are double the equivalent emissions in 2000 by 2050; limited action is taken to reduce the emissions. There is a strong support for renewable and nuclear electricity. Assumes a mix of fossil fuel technologies without CCS (39%), renewables (36%) and nuclear power (25%). The use of CCS is not considered.
A-4	"	GHG emissions are double the equivalent emissions in 2000 by 2050; limited action is taken to reduce emissions. There is a concentration of investment in renewable technologies. Assumes a mix of fossil fuel technologies without CCS (39%), renewables (56%) and nuclear (5%). The use of CCS is not considered.
B-1	75	GHG emissions are equal to 2000 levels by 2050. There is a strong support for fossil fuel technologies. Assumes a mix of fossil fuel technologies without CCS (22%) and with CCS (53%), and renewables (25%). Nuclear energy is not considered.
B-2	"	GHG emissions are equal to 2000 levels by 2050. There is a strong support for fossil fuel and nuclear electricity. Assumes a mix of fossil fuel technologies without CCS (23%) and with CCS (37%), renewables (25%) and nuclear (15%).
B-3	"	GHG emissions are equal to 2000 levels by 2050. There is a strong support for renewable and nuclear power. Assumes a mix of fossil fuel technologies without CCS (21%) and with CCS (5%), renewables (44%) and nuclear (30%).
B-4	"	GHG emissions are equal to 2000 levels by 2050. There is a concentration of investment in renewable technologies. Assumes a mix of fossil fuel technologies without CCS (21%) and with CCS (5%), renewables (69%) and nuclear (5%).

Scenario	Direct emissions[a] (Mt CO$_2$-eq./year)	Assumptions
C-1	33	GHG emissions are equal to 1990 levels by 2050. There is a strong support for fossil fuel technologies. Assumes a mix of fossil fuel technologies without CCS (5%) and with CCS (60%), and renewables (35%). Nuclear plants are not considered.
C-2	"	GHG emissions are equal to 1990 levels by 2050. There is a strong support for fossil fuel and nuclear electricity. Assumes a mix of fossil fuel technologies without CCS (8%) and with CCS (42%), renewables (35%) and nuclear (15%).
C-3	"	GHG emissions are equal to 1990 levels by 2050. There is a strong support for renewable and nuclear electricity. Assumes a mix of fossil fuel technologies without CCS (11%) and with CCS (5%), renewables (49%) and nuclear (35%).
C-4	"	GHG emissions are equal to 1990 levels by 2050. There is a concentration of investment in renewable technologies. Assumes a mix of fossil fuel technologies without CCS (11%) and with CCS (5%), renewables (79%) and nuclear (5%).

[a] Direct emissions refer to emissions from operation of power plants, as opposed to life cycle emissions which span the whole life cycle of electricity generation.
[b] Source: FutureCamp (2011). For comparison, direct emissions in 1990 were 33 Mt CO$_2$eq/year and in 2000 75 Mt CO$_2$eq/year (TUIK, 2013).

Table 39.6 Generation technologies and expected lifetimes

Technology	Lifespan (years)
Nuclear	60
Lignite	30
Lignite CCS[a]	30
Hard coal	30
Hard coal CCS[a]	30
Gas	25
Gas CCS[a]	25
Solar	25
Biomass	25
Reservoir	150
Run-of-river	80
Wind onshore	25[b]
Wind offshore	25[b]
Geothermal	25

[a] Carbon capture and storage.
[b] 40 years for fixed and 20 years for moving parts.

scenarios are more constrained than B, low carbon technologies have a leading role in electricity generation.

Each scenario is composed of a mix of generation technologies. The technologies included are those currently deployed in the electricity mix plus those expected to be available in the near future (see Table 39.6).

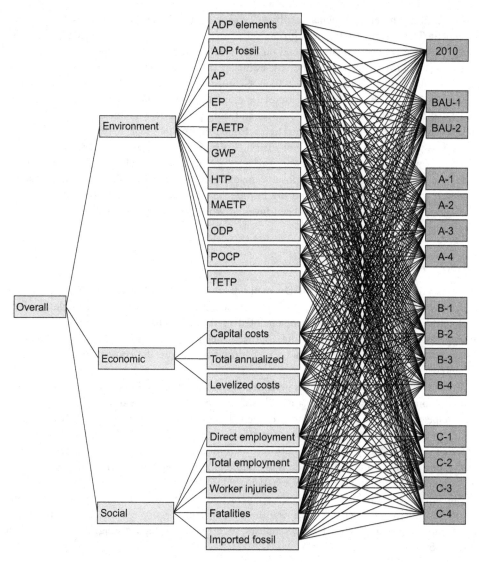

Figure 39.5 Decision tree illustrating the problem structure for electricity scenarios in Turkey

Based on the criteria and alternatives defined above, the decision tree shown in Figure 39.5 demonstrates the structure of the problem.

7.1.3   Model building

7.1.3.1   Impact modeling

Since the focus on this chapter is on MCDA as a process, this section only provides an overview of the impact modeling methods used to estimate each criterion. For more detail, readers are directed to Atilgan and Azapagic (2016b) and Atilgan and Azapagic (2017).

In summary, the environmental attributes of each alternative are calculated using life cycle assessment (LCA), supported by background inventory data from the NEEDS (2010) and Ecoinvent (2010) databases, which are based on European conditions. The economic attributes are based on discounted cash flow using cost estimates from Bauer et al. (2008), Gärtner (2008), Fürsch et al. (2011), Schröder et al. (2013), Greenpeace and EREC (2012) and Sensfuß and Pfluger (2014). Finally, the social attributes are estimated using data on employment factors in OECD countries (Rutovitz and Harris, 2012) and labor productivity (Yilmaz, 2014), plus injury and fatality rates based on the historical trends from 1996 to 2013 (SSI, 2013).

As discussed in section 5.2, scaling of attributes is typically required in MCDA. However, this function is provided in MCDA software packages: in this case Web-HIPRE V1.22 (Mustajoki and Hämäläinen, 2000). In each case, local re-mapping is conducted within the software, assuming linear scales for each attribute. Finally, in order to ensure consistent direction of preference (see section 5.5), the attributes have been inverted where necessary such that higher values are always preferred.

7.1.3.2 Preference models

As discussed in section 4, various MCDA methods are available with which to elicit stakeholder preferences and derive criteria weights. As this case study is an illustrative example, a direct, exploratory approach is used and implemented in the Web-HIPRE V1.22 software (Mustajoki and Hämäläinen, 2000). Under this approach, weights are directly applied in a hierarchical fashion using arbitrary values which are then varied to explore the consequences of different stakeholder perspectives.

In the first iteration, the MCDA is performed assuming an equal importance of the environmental, economic and social criteria categories, and equal importance of each criterion within their respective category. Thus, the environmental, economic and social categories each have a weight of 1/3 (using the nomenclature of section 5.4, $w_i = 0.33$). Given the differing number of criteria in each category and the need to maintain the hierarchy, this means that the individual weight of each environmental criterion is $w_i = 0.33/11 = 0.03$, economic criterion $w_i = 0.33/3 = 0.11$ and social criterion $w_i = 0.33/5 = 0.066$.

Subsequent iterations of the process explore a high preference for each category: environmental, economic and social. In each case the emphasized category is assumed to be five times more important than the other two categories, such that the category weights are 0.71, 0.145 and 0.145.

7.1.4 Synthesis and evaluation

Following the establishment of the alternatives, criteria and weights, the total value of each alternative can be calculated as described in section 5.4. Assuming equal importance of the environmental, economic and social categories, as shown in Figure 39.6, it is clear that all future alternatives are preferable to the baseline 2010 case.

Alternative C-3 is ranked best with a total score of 0.69, followed by B-3 and C-4 with 0.66 and 0.65, respectively. By comparison, the current electricity mix scores only 0.23. Although C-4 is the third best overall, it is the worst option in terms of economic sustainability; however, it has the best score for the social category. Alternative B-1 is the least sustainable, scoring only 0.47, but is still twice as high as today's electricity mix. A-1 and C-1 follow closely with 0.51. Even though BAU-1 is the worst option for the environmental and social aspects, it has the best economic performance among the scenarios.

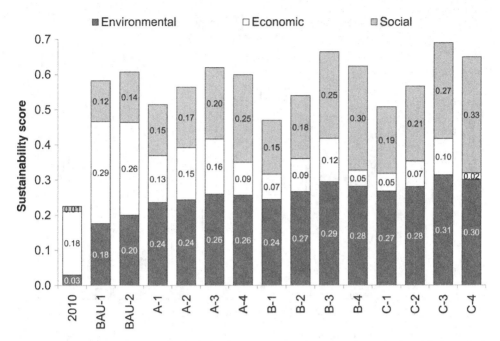

Figure 39.6 MCDA synthesis for Turkish electricity scenarios assuming equal weighting of criteria categories (Atilgan and Azapagic, 2017)

The other iterations of the MCDA, in which environmental, economic and social categories are emphasized in turn using higher weights, yield the results shown in Figure 39.7 which shows the three most preferable alternatives under each weighting regime. This analysis shows that scenarios C-3 and C-4 perform very well under severe weighting changes: whether the weighting regime is equal, environmentally biased or socially biased, they are always ranked as the top three options. The only clear potential conflict between stakeholders exists for those with strong preferences for economics: for such people, BAU-1, BAU-2 and A-3 are the most optimal alternatives.

However, deeper analysis of the results shows that alternative B-3 lies within the top four most preferable options for all weighting regimes, suggesting that B-3 represents the best compromise between divided stakeholders.

Further insight can be gained by performing sensitivity analyses on the weighting factors. As the weighting regime with emphasis on economics yields very different outcomes to the other weighting regimes, it is useful to further explore the level of economic weighting and its effects on the outcome. Figure 39.8 shows an output from the Web-HIPRE V1.22 software, demonstrating a sensitivity analysis on economic weight. The vertical line at '0.71' represents the weight placed on the economic category under the economically emphasized weighting regime (see section 7.1.3.2). The colored lines represent the 14 different alternatives considered in the assessment, with the highest value showing the preferred alternative at a given weight. The vertical line at '(0.41)' represents the weight that would need to be placed on the economic category to incur a change in the ranking of alternatives, at which point C-3 becomes the preferred alternative.

This type of analysis allows practitioners to pinpoint the conditions at which universally acceptable solutions can be found. Based on the exploration above, it becomes clear that all stakeholders are likely to converge onto a position in which alternative C-3 is a very highly

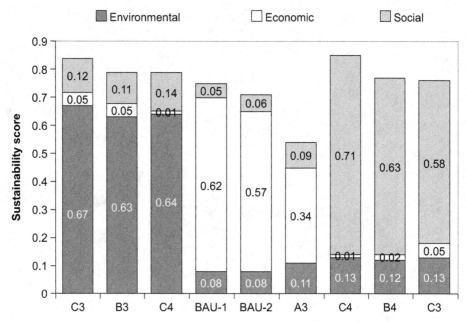

Figure 39.7 Top three Turkish electricity scenarios under different weighting regimes

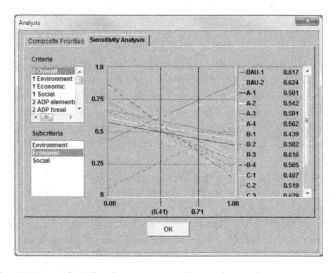

Figure 39.8 Sensitivity analysis for the economically emphasized weighting regime

ranked option, regardless of their values, provided they do not weight the economic category at more than 0.41.

Analyses like this also demonstrate how the ability to alter weighting factors and observe the outcome, in real-time, can support consensus-building and compromise within a policy context. By allowing stakeholders to see the preferred alternatives that result from their values and from the values of others, and to manipulate the decision parameters and observe the consequences, the decision space is more clearly illuminated and navigated.

7.1.5   Development of an action plan

The insights generated from the analysis above lead to starting points for policy actions. Firstly, alternative C-3 appears to be the most robust future electricity scenario, provided economics are not very strongly favored over environmental and social issues. In such cases of strong economic prioritization, B-3 appears to be a robust compromise between all stakeholders as it is always ranked in the top four alternatives. It is also clear that the electricity mixes in C-3 and B-3 are both heavily reliant on renewables and nuclear energy, with strong similarities, as shown in Figure 39.9. Based on the projected electricity demand in 2050 of 852 TWh per year, it becomes possible to devise strategies specifically tailored to this future. For instance, if solar PV must provide 6%–8% of supply in 2050, totalling 51–68 TWh per year, then a typical yield of 1500 kWh/kWp for Turkish climatic conditions (PVGIS, 2012) suggests that 34–45 GW of solar PV must be installed before then. This provides a starting point from which industry lead times can

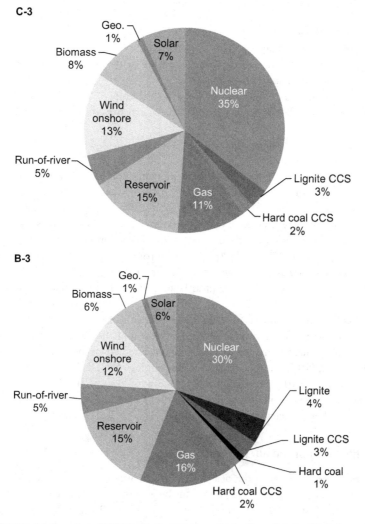

Figure 39.9   Electricity mix in 2050 in Turkey under alternatives C-3 and B-3 (based on Atilgan and Azapagic, 2017)

be estimated, preferred locations identified, workforce and regulatory requirements evaluated and, ultimately, appropriate incentive schemes developed.

7.2   Shale gas in the UK

This section demonstrates the use of MCDA at the level of technology selection to assist with policy development for shale gas exploitation. It uses 18 sustainability criteria addressing environmental, economic and social issues, and considers nine electricity generation technologies for application in the UK. The analysis is conducted using the software Web-HIPRE V1.22 (Mustajoki and Hämäläinen, 2000).

This MCDA follows the Simple Multi-Attribute Rating Technique (SMART) first proposed by Edwards (1977), and this section is structured to reflect that approach. SMART consists of six steps which closely align with the generic MCDA steps outlined in Figure 39.2 (section 4), as follows:

1   identification of the alternatives to be compared;
2   identification of the decision criteria;
3   scoring of the criteria in order of importance (a score of 10 for the least important, increasing thereafter) and estimation of their weights;
4   rating of the alternatives on a scale of 0 (worst) to 1 (best);
5   estimation of the overall scores and ranking of the alternatives on a scale from 0 (worst) to 1 (best); and
6   identification of the best alternative.

Exploitation of shale gas is a contentious topic in many countries. At present, shale gas is exploited at a large scale only in the United States, with more than 30 other nations considering its development (Cooper et al., 2016). The UK is at the cusp of starting the exploitation, with the government and industry keen to develop a shale gas industry, but with a strong opposition from numerous bodies, including non-governmental organizations, local residents and activists (Gosden, 2017; Johnston, 2017; Ward, 2017). The impacts on the environment are the main argument against the exploitation of shale gas while the supporters highlight improved national energy security and economic development as key aspects in its favor (House of Lords, 2014; Moore et al., 2014).

Existing literature on the impacts of shale gas has tended to focus on its GHG emissions, but the debate over its sustainability is much broader. Since the topic has become so widely discussed, including via social media, and has led to extremely polarized views in politics, industry and the public (Cooper et al., 2018b), policy making is challenging. MCDA is one means of bringing clarity and transparency to the decision-making process.

With this in mind, the overall goal of this process is to assess the overall sustainability of shale gas relative to the other electricity options in the UK.

7.2.1   Identification of the alternatives

Energy sources for deployment in the near-term must be well established, economically viable and already commercially deployed. Therefore, in the electricity sector, the alternatives to shale gas are found in the existing electricity mix. As shown in Figure 39.10, the UK power grid is currently dominated by natural gas (40%) and nuclear power (19%) with sizeable contributions from wind (15%) and bioenergy (8%). Coal has also been a major component of the mix historically,

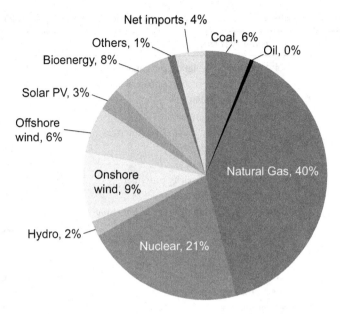

Figure 39.10 UK electricity mix in 2017 (BEIS, 2018)

while the capacity of solar PV has been growing quickly in recent years. Hydropower resources are not particularly prevalent in the UK, but nevertheless hydropower has been exploited for many decades and has some potential for further growth.

Of the natural gas consumed in the UK, less than half is extracted domestically (mostly from the North Sea), while approximately one third is imported from nearby countries such as Norway. The remainder of approximately 15% is imported in the form of LNG, and this share has been increasing (Cooper et al., 2014). Consequently, when considering shale gas it is pertinent to also consider 'conventional' natural gas and LNG.

Thus, the alternatives selected for this analysis are shale gas, conventional gas, LNG, coal, nuclear, hydro, solar PV, wind, and biomass power.

7.2.2 Identification of the decision criteria

A list of sustainability criteria is shown in Table 39.7, taken from Cooper et al. (2018c). Similarly to the previous case study, the criteria are designed to reflect the environmental, economic and social aspects of sustainability and the impacts of electricity generation on a broad range of stakeholders. The quantification methodologies for the environmental criteria are explained in Cooper et al. (2014), while the economic criteria are discussed in Cooper et al. (2018a) and the social metrics in Cooper et al. (2018b).

Based on the criteria and alternatives defined above, the decision tree shown in Figure 39.11 demonstrates the structure of the problem.

7.2.3 Scoring of the criteria and estimation of weights

Following life cycle assessment, levelized cost estimation and social sustainability assessment in the literature, the attributes of each alternative are quantified, as shown in Table 39.8.

Table 39.7 Sustainability criteria for assessing electricity generation technologies (Cooper et al., 2018c)

Criteria categories	Sustainability criteria	Units
Environmental	Abiotic resource depletion potential (elements)	kg Sb eq./kWh
	Abiotic resource depletion potential (fossil fuels)	MJ/kWh
	Acidification potential	kg SO$_2$ eq./kWh
	Eutrophication potential	kg PO$_4$ eq./kWh
	Fresh water aquatic ecotoxicity potential	kg DCB[a] eq./kWh
	Global warming potential	kg CO$_2$ eq./kWh
	Human toxicity potential	kg DCB[a] eq./kWh
	Marine aquatic ecotoxicity potential	kg DCB[a] eq./kWh
	Ozone layer depletion potential	kg CFC-11 eq./kWh
	Photochemical oxidants creation potential	kg C$_2$H$_4$ eq./kWh
	Terrestrial ecotoxicity potential	kg DCB[a] eq./kWh
Economic	Levelized cost of electricity	GBP pence/kWh
	Capital cost	GBP pence/kWh
	Fuel cost	GBP pence/kWh
Social	Direct employment	person-years/TWh
	Worker injuries	no. of injuries/TWh
	Public support index	%
	Diversity of fuel supply	no units

a *DCB*: dichlorobenzene.

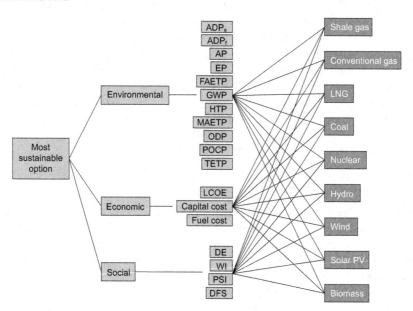

Figure 39.11 Decision tree illustrating the problem structure for sustainable electricity technologies in the UK

Notes: ADP$_e$: abiotic depletion of elements; ADP$_f$: abiotic depletion of fossil fuels; AP: acidification potential; EP: eutrophication potential; FAETP: freshwater aquatic ecotoxicity; GWP: global warming potential; HTP: human toxicity potential; MAETP: marine aquatic ecotoxicity potential; ODP: ozone depletion potential; POCP: photochemical oxidant creation potential; TETP: terrestrial ecotoxicity potential; LCOE: levelized costs of electricity; DE: direct employment; WI: worker injuries; PSI: public support index; DFS: diversity of fuel supply.

Table 39.8 Attributes of the nine alternatives based on 18 sustainability criteria (Cooper et al., 2018c)

Sustainability criteria		Alternatives								
		Shale gas	Conven'l gas	LNG	Coal	Nuclear	Hydro	Solar PV	Wind	Biomass
Environmental	ADP$_e$ (mg Sb$_{-Eq.}$/kWh)	0.68	0.24	0.26	0.04	0.07	0.01	10.91	0.22	0.14
	ADP$_f$ (MJ/kWh)	6.58	6.33	7.43	11.70	0.09	0.04	1.05	0.15	0.62
	AP (g SO$_{2-Eq.}$/kWh)	0.35	1.71	3.41	5.13	0.06	0.01	0.43	0.06	1.39
	EP (g PO$_{4-Eq.}$/kWh)	0.17	0.06	0.06	1.86	0.02	0.01	0.29	0.03	0.49
	FAETP (g DCB$_{-Eq.}$/kWh)	13.10	2.47	4.02	287.90	21.20	1.65	63.90	14.70	20.90
	GWP (g CO$_{2-Eq.}$/kWh)	455.78	420.00	490.00	1078.84	7.79	3.70	88.91	12.35	58.51
	HTP (g DCB$_{-Eq.}$/kWh)	54.30	38.00	39.50	294.86	111.43	6.15	205.47	61.81	208.50
	MAETP (kg DCB$_{-Eq.}$/kWh)	37.42	0.50	0.90	1577.32	43.66	2.70	205.69	23.08	42.48
	ODP (µg R11$_{-Eq.}$/kWh)	17.30	18.90	5.51	5.59	19.00	0.23	17.40	0.74	5.16
	POCP (mg C$_2$H$_{4-Eq.}$/kWh)	83.80	34.40	66.60	285	5.55	2.04	67.00	6.97	131
	TETP (g DCB$_{-Eq.}$/kWh)	1.70	0.15	0.22	1.75	0.74	0.19	1.12	1.81	4.26
Economic	Levelized cost of electricity (pence/kWh)	9.59	8.00	7.62	13.85	7.70	14.60	6.70	9.73	11.75
	Capital cost (pence/kWh)	0.81	0.90	0.81	4.60	7.00	11.29	5.70	7.70	4.50
	Fuel cost (pence/kWh)	6.51	4.90	4.53	3.60	0.50	0.00	0.00	0.00	5.30
Social	Direct employment (person-yr/TWh)	47.70	62.00	326.88	191.00	87.00	782.35	653.00	368.00	385.79
	Worker injuries (no. injuries/TWh)	0.53	0.54	2.10	4.50	0.59	14.59	4.84	2.30	2.98
	Public support index (%)	5.60	34.00	14.50	-7.00	9.00	72.00	75.00	59.00	57.00
	Diversity of fuel supply (no units)	1.00	1.00	0.04	0.86	0.85	1.00	1.00	1.00	0.96

Notes: ADP$_e$: abiotic depletion of elements; ADP$_f$: abiotic depletion of fossil fuels; AP: acidification potential; EP: eutrophication potential; FAETP: freshwater aquatic ecotoxicity; GWP: global warming potential; HTP: human toxicity potential; MAETP: marine aquatic ecotoxicity potential; ODP: ozone depletion potential; POCP: photochemical oxidant creation potential; TETP: terrestrial ecotoxicity potential.

Scaling of the attributes (see section 5.3) is achieved in the MCDA software package Web-HIPRE V1.22 (Mustajoki and Hämäläinen, 2000) and the attributes have been inverted where necessary to ensure that higher values are always preferred (see direction of preference in section 5.5).

Local re-mapping is conducted for each attribute, but both linear and exponential value functions are used to explore the sensitivity of the MCDA to the relationship between attribute values and preference. This is discussed in detail in the next section.

Finally, criteria weights must be derived. Similarly to the prior case study, the MCDA begins with the assumption that stakeholders have no particular preference between the environmental, economic and social categories, and that all criteria within those categories are equally important. Subsequently, sensitivity analysis is used to explore the effects of varying preferences.

7.2.4   Rating of the alternatives and estimation of their overall scores

The results in Figure 39.12 indicate that, if the environmental, economic and social categories are equally important, the best options are wind and solar PV. This is true whether the linear (LVF) or exponential value functions (EVF) are used to scale the attributes: under linear scaling, wind and solar PV achieve scores of 0.79 and 0.78, respectively, while under exponential scaling they both achieve 0.90. This provides some confidence in selecting them as the preferred options.

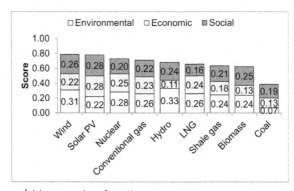

a) Linear value function

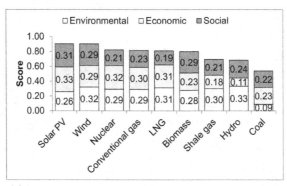

b) Exponential value function

Figure 39.12   Ranking of the electricity options assuming equal weightings for the sustainability criteria categories (Cooper et al., 2018c)

Indeed, under both value functions, the overall ranking of the alternatives does not change considerably. Coal power is always the least preferred option with 0.39 (LVF) and 0.54 (EVF). Shale gas ranks seventh out of nine options for both value functions, scoring 0.64 and 0.69, respectively. Some changes to the ranking do occur: hydroelectricity, for instance, performs better under the LVF (fifth place) than the EVF (eighth place), while biomass is the opposite, ranking eighth for the LVF but rising to sixth place for the EVF. This highlights the importance of value functions in the scaling of attributes: the exponential value function places greater emphasis on the magnitude of difference between the attributes of different alternatives. For instance, as shown in Table 39.8, biomass ranks relatively poorly for six out of 11 environmental criteria and two out of three economic criteria, but it is still much better (up to two orders of magnitude) than the worst option for each of those criteria. Thus, using the EVF, which penalizes outliers more strongly, leads to a more generous (and arguably reasonable) outcome for biomass.

As can be seen in Figure 39.12, the environmental category contributes the most to the overall score for shale gas (38% for the LVF and 43% for the EVF), followed by the social (30% and 33%) and finally the economic category (26% and 29%). Similar contributions are found for most other options.

However, sensitivity analysis demonstrates that it is possible to change the ranking of the alternatives by changing the weights placed on each criteria category, as follows.

Sensitivity to environmental weighting

Under a linear scaling value function, the ranking of alternatives does not alter until the weight placed on the environmental category is seven times greater than the economic and social categories. At that point, wind falls to second place and solar PV to seventh, while hydropower becomes the most preferred option. Under this weighting scheme, shale gas ranks sixth out of nine.

Sensitivity to economic weighting

Under the LVF, a ranking change is triggered when the weighting of the economic category is 23 times higher. Even in this case, solar PV remains the most favored alternative while wind power slides to fifth place due to its higher capital costs (see Table 39.8). At this point, shale gas ranks sixth.

Sensitivity to social weighting

The weight of the social category must be increased until it is 12.3 times more important than the other categories in order to trigger a change in ranking. At that point, LNG becomes the worst alternative while solar PV and wind remain dominant. Shale gas ranks seventh.

Therefore, it appears that major changes in the weighting of the three criteria categories are needed to change the outcome. Moreover, even under such changes, shale gas ranks in sixth or seventh place out of the nine options.

Based on its performance in different sustainability criteria (Table 39.8), and not considering any improvements in its sustainability, there are only two scenarios in which shale gas could become the top-ranking alternative. These are as follows:

1   Capital cost must be weighted 1,000–10,000 times more highly than the other economic indicators and, simultaneously, the economic category must be weighted 1,000 times higher than the other two categories.

2   The importance of worker injuries must be 1,000 times higher than that of all other social criteria and, at the same time, the importance of the social category must be 1,000 times greater than of the other two.

Clearly these are extreme weighting regimes that are unlikely to be expressed by the majority of stakeholders.

7.2.5   Identification of the best alternative

Given the exploration of value functions and weighting variation discussed above it is clear that, given the sustainability data available, wind and solar PV are the preferred technologies for UK deployment, and that this outcome is quite robust. It is also clear that shale gas remains ranked sixth or seventh out of nine alternatives under a variety of different weights and scaling value functions. This suggests that policy tools should be directed towards wind and solar power rather than shale gas.

However, by exploring the triggers necessary to make shale gas the most favorable alternative, the outputs of the MCDA can also be used to set improvement targets for shale gas which could aid policy makers. This is outlined below.

7.2.6   Setting targets

By manipulating the attributes of shale gas in the MCDA software through various iterations, it is possible to identify the environmental, economic and social improvements that would be needed for shale gas to become the most favored alternative (Cooper et al., 2018c).

For example, assuming linear value functions and equal weighting between environmental, economic and social categories, an 80% reduction in economic costs would lead to shale gas becoming the favored alternative. Alternatively, a combination of 50% cost reductions and an increase in the weight placed on economics would yield the same result.

In environmental terms, it is difficult to improve shale gas to the point where it emerges as the preferred alternative. For instance, even a 100-fold reduction in all the environmental impacts would still be insufficient without a simultaneous increase in the weighting placed on environmental importance.

Social improvements could also result in shale gas ranking in first place but these would include, for instance, 13 times higher public support or 16 times higher employment (assuming equal weighting between criteria categories).

Therefore, it appears that in this case the targets necessary for shale gas to become the preferred alternative are too ambitious to achieve. However, without the MCDA process this understanding could not have been gained. In other cases where decisions are more marginal, the potential of MCDA to assist in target-setting is clear.

8   Conclusions

Energy policy is at the heart of sustainable development, but decision-making related to energy sustainability is a complex task. Particularly in the world of policy, it is critical to consider a broad range of issues simultaneously; these might range from capital and operational costs to greenhouse gas emissions, human health impacts, employment provision and public support, among many others. Multi-criteria decision analysis (MCDA) is a quantitative method of bringing clarity and transparency to such complex, multivariate decisions in a way that accounts for the diverse views of different stakeholders.

While MCDA is a very broad topic with great diversity of methods, the general procedure and available options have been highlighted in this chapter, starting with problem identification and progressing to problem structuring, impact and preference modeling, synthesis and evaluation. Through these stages, MCDA has been highlighted as a way to provide a structured, numerical and transparent way of making decisions, as well as to increase understanding of the relationship between stakeholder values and preferred outcomes, provide insight into the most influential parameters of the decision, and aid in target setting. The availability of software allows rapid iteration of the process and can be invaluable in reaching consensus and informed compromise.

While MCDA can be time consuming and is ultimately subjective in nature, it offers a useful tool for making the 'wicked problems' of sustainable energy more tractable.

References

Acar, S., Kitson, L. and Bridle, R. (2015). "Subsidies to coal and renewable energy in Turkey." *The International Institute for Sustainable Development*, Manitoba, Canada.

Atilgan, B. and Azapagic, A. (2016a). "Assessing the environmental sustainability of electricity generation in Turkey on a life cycle basis." *Energies* **9**(1).

Atilgan, B. and Azapagic, A. (2016b). "An integrated life cycle sustainability assessment of electricity generation in Turkey." *Energy Policy* **93**: 168–186.

Atilgan, B. and Azapagic, A. (2017). "Energy challenges for Turkey: Identifying sustainable options for future electricity generation up to 2050." *Sustainable Production and Consumption* **12**: 234–254.

Azapagic, A. (2004). "Appendix: Life cycle thinking and Life Cycle Assessment (LCA)." *Sustainable Development in Practice: Case Studies for Engineers and Scientists*. Perdan, S. and Clift, R. Chichester, John Wiley & Sons.

Azapagic, A. and Perdan, S. (2005a). "An integrated sustainability decision-support framework Part I: Problem structuring." *International Journal of Sustainable Development & World Ecology* **12**(2): 98–111.

Azapagic, A. and Perdan, S. (2005b). "An integrated sustainability decision-support framework Part II: Problem analysis." *International Journal of Sustainable Development & World Ecology* **12**(2): 112–131.

Azapagic, A. and Perdan, S. (2014). "Sustainable chemical engineering: Dealing with "wicked" sustainability problems." *AIChE Journal* **60**(12): 3998–4007.

Bauer, C., Heck, T., Dones, R., Mayer-Spohn, O. and Blesl, M. (2008). "Final report on technical data, costs, and life cycle inventories of advanced fossil power generation systems, NEEDS (New Energy Externalities Development for Sustainability)."

BEIS (2018). *Energy Trends: June 2018*. London, Department for Business, Energy & Indsutrial Strategy.

Belton, V. and Stewart, T. J. (2002). *Multiple Criteria Decision Analysis*. Boston, MA, Springer.

Catrinu-Renström, M. D., Barton, D. N., Bakken, T. H., Marttunen, M., Mochet, A. M., May, R. and Hanssen, F. (2013). *Multi-Criteria Analysis Applied to Environmental Impacts of Hydropower and Water Resources Regulation Projects*. Trondheim, SINTEF Energy Research.

Cinelli, M., Coles, S. R. and Kirwan, K. (2014). "Analysis of the potentials of multi criteria decision analysis methods to conduct sustainability assessment." *Ecological Indicators* **46**: 138–148.

Cooper, J., Stamford, L. and Azapagic, A. (2014). "Environmental impacts of shale gas in the UK: Current situation and future scenarios." *Energy Technology* **2**(12): 1012–1026.

Cooper, J., Stamford, L. and Azapagic, A. (2016). "Shale gas: A review of the economic, environmental, and social sustainability." *Energy Technology* **4**(7): 772–792.

Cooper, J., Stamford, L. and Azapagic, A. (2018a). "Economic viability of UK shale gas and potential impacts on the energy market up to 2030." *Applied Energy* **215**: 577–590.

Cooper, J., Stamford, L. and Azapagic, A. (2018b). "Social sustainability assessment of shale gas in the UK." *Sustainable Production and Consumption* **14**: 1–20.

Cooper, J., Stamford, L. and Azapagic, A. (2018c). "Sustainability of UK shale gas in comparison with other electricity options: Current situation and future scenarios." *Science of the Total Environment* **619–620**: 804–814.

Department for Communities and Local Government (2009). *Multi-Criteria Analysis: A Manual*. London, Communities and Local Government Publications.

DSI. (2010). "Turkey water report 2009." Retrieved 20 March 2012, from www2.dsi.gov.tr/english/pdf_files/TurkeyWaterReport.pdf.

Ecoinvent. (2010). *Ecoinvent Database v2.2. from Swiss Centre for Life Cycle Inventories.* St Gallen, Switzerland: Ecoinvent.

Edwards, W. (1977). "How to use multi attribute utility measurement for social decision making." *IEEE Transactions on Systems, Man, and Cybernetics* **7**(5): 326–340.

Elkington, J. (1997). *Cannibals with Forks: The Triple Bottom Line of 21st Century Business.* Oxford, Capstone Publishing Ltd.

EMRA (2014). *Data on Energy Potential of Turkey.* Ankara, Republic of Turkey Energy Market Regulatory Authority. [Personel communication, 15.06.2014].

European Commission. (2014). "2030 energy strategy." Retrieved August 2018, from https://ec.europa. eu/energy/en/topics/energy-strategy-and-energy-union/2030-energy-strategy.

Fürsch, M., Hagspiel, S., Jägemann, C., Nagl, S., Lindenberger, P.D.D., Glotzbach, L., Tröster, D. E. and Ackermann, D. T. (2011). *Roadmap 2050: Cost-Efficient RES-E Penetration and the Role of Grid Extensions.* Germany, Institute of Energy Economics at the University of Cologne.

FutureCamp (2011). "Baseline emission calculations." *Verified Carbon Standard (VCS), Version 3.* Ankara, Turkey. version 3.

Gärtner, S. (2008). "Final report on technical data, costs and life cycle inventories of biomass CHP plants, NEEDS (New Energy Externalities Development for Sustainability)."

Gosden, E. (2017). "Cuadrilla starts drilling at Lancashire fracking site." *The Times.* London, UK, The Times.

Greenpeace and EREC (2008). *Global Energy [R]Evolution: A Sustainable Turkey Energy Outlook,* Greenpeace International, European Renewable Energy Council (EREC), London, UK.

Greenpeace and EREC (2012). *Global Energy [R]Evolution: A Sustainable World Energy Outlook,* Greenpeace International, European Renewable Energy Council (EREC), London, UK.

GRI. (2018). "Sustainability disclosure database." Retrieved August 2018, from Global Reporting Initiative. http://database.globalreporting.org/

Guinée, J.B., Gorrée, M., Heijungs, R., Huppes, G., Kleijn, R., Koning, A. D., Oers, L. V., Wegener Sleeswijk, A., Suh, S., Udo de Haes, H. A., Bruijn, H. D., Duin, R. V. and Huijbregts, M.A.J. (2002). *Handbook on Life Cycle Assessment: Operational Guide to the ISO Standards.* Dordrecht, Kluwer Academic Publishers,.

Hanley, N. (2001). "Cost-benefit analysis and environmental policy-making." *Environment and Planning C* 19: 103–118.

House of Lords (2014). *The Economic Impact on UK Energy Policy of Shale Gas and Oil.* London, UK, House of Lords: Economic Affairs Committee. **3**. www.publications.parliament.uk/pa/ld201314/ldselect/ldeconaf/172/172.pdf

IBP (2015). *Turkey Investment and Business Guide, Volume 1: Strategic and Practical Information.* Washington DC, USA, International Business Publications.

IEA (2014). "Electricity information 2014." Paris, International Energy Agency. www.oecd-ilibrary.org/docserver/download/6114241e.pdf?expires=1434571462&id=id&accname=ocid177243&checksum=643876DBDF4236883EBD23DDFC9665CC.

IEA. (2018). "World Energy Investment 2018." Retrieved August 2018, from https://webstore.iea.org/world-energy-investment-2018.

IPCC (2014). "Climate change 2014: Synthesis report: Contribution of working groups I, II and III to the fifth assessment report of the intergovernmental panel on climate change." *Climate Change 2014.* Pachauri, R. K. and Meyer, L. A. Geneva, Switzerland, IPCC.

IRENA (2018). *Renewable Energy and Jobs: Annual Review 2018.* Masdar City, International Renewable Energy Agency.

Johnston, I. (2017). "Election 2017: Conservatives Back Fracking 'Revolution' in the Party Manifesto." *The Independent.* London, UK.

MENR (2009a). *Electricity Energy Market and Supply Security Strategy.* Ankara, The Ministry of Energy and Natural Resources.

MENR (2009b). *The Republic of Turkey Ministry of Energy and Natural Resources Strategic Plan (2010–2014),* The Republic of Turkey Ministry of Energy and Natural Resources: 1–45.

MENR (2012). *Mavi Kitap (Blue Book).* Ankara, Ministry of Energy and Natural Resources: 20–69. www.enerji.gov.tr

MENR (2014). "Turkey 3.0 LEAP model." Last updated 21 November 2014. Retrieved 11 November 2014, from www.enerji.gov.tr/tr-TR/EIGM-Raporlari.

Moore, V., Bereford, A., Gove, B., Underhill, R., Parnham, S., Crow, H., Cunningham, R., Huyton, H., Sutton, J., Melling, T., Billings, P. and Salter, M. (2014). "Hydraulic fracturing for shale gas in the UK:

Examining the evidence for potential environmental impacts." London, UK, The Royal Society for the Protection of Birds (RSPB). www.rspb.org.uk/Images/shale_gas_report_evidence_tcm9-365779.pdf

Mustajoki, J. and Hämäläinen, R. P. (2000). "Web-HIPRE: Global decision support by value tree and AHP analysis." *INFOR* **38**(3): 208–220.

NEEDS. (2010). "New Energy Externalities Development for Sustainability (NEEDS): Life cycle inventroy database: The European reference life cycle inventory database of future electricity supply systems." Retrieved from www.needs-project.org/needswebdb/search.php.

Peterson, H. (2009). "Transformational supply chains and the 'wicked problem' of sustainability: Aligning knowledge, innovation, entrepreneurship, and leadership." *Journal on Chain and Network Science* **9**(2): 71–82.

PVGIS. (2012). "Photovoltaic geographical information system: Interactive maps." Retrieved September 2018, from http://re.jrc.ec.europa.eu/pvgis/apps4/pvest.php.

Ren, J., Manzardo, A., Mazzi, A., Zuliani, F. and Scipioni, A. (2015). "Prioritization of bioethanol production pathways in China based on life cycle sustainability assessment and multicriteria decision-making." *The International Journal of Life Cycle Assessment* **20**(6): 842–853.

Rittel, H.W.J. and Webber, M. M. (1973). "Dilemmas in a general theory of planning." *Policy Sciences* **4**: 155–169.

Roth, S., Hirschberg, S., Bauer, C., Burgherr, P., Dones, R., Heck, T. and Schenler, W. (2009). "Sustainability of electricity supply technology portfolio." *Annals of Nuclear Energy* **36**(3): 409–416.

Rutovitz, J. and Harris, S. (2012). *Calculating Global Energy Sector Jobs: 2012 Methodology*. Institute for Sustainable Futures, UTS, Sydney, Australia.

Saaty, T. L. (1980). *The Analytic Hierarchy Process: Planning Setting Priorities, Resource Allocation*. New York, McGraw-Hill International.

Santoyo-Castelazo, E., Stamford, L. and Azapagic, A. (2014). "Environmental implications of decarbonising electricity supply in large economies: The case of Mexico." *Energy Conversion and Management* **85**: 272–291.

Schröder, A., Kunz, F., Meiss, J., Mendelevitch, R. and Hirschhausen, C. V. (2013). *Current and Prospective Costs of Electricity Generation Until 2050*. Berlin, Deutsches Institut für Wirtschaftsforschung (DIW).

Science Based Targets. (2018). "Companies taking action." Retrieved August 2018, from https://sciencebasedtargets.org/companies-taking-action/.

Sensfuß, F. and Pfluger, B. (2014). "Optimized pathways towards ambitious climate protection in the European electricity system (EU Long-term scenarios 2050 II)." Fraunhofer Institute for Systems and Innovation Research ISI, Germany.

SHDB. (2018). *Social Hotspots Database*. Retrieved October 2018, from www.socialhotspot.org/.

Singh, R. K., Murty, H. R., Gupta, S. K. and Dikshit, A. K. (2012). "An overview of sustainability assessment methodologies." *Ecological Indicators* **15**(1): 281–299.

SSI. (2013). "Statistics." Retrieved 27 March 2015, from www.sgk.gov.tr/wps/portal/tr/kurumsal/istatistikler/sgk_istatistik_yilliklari.

Stamford, L. and Azapagic, A. (2011). "Sustainability indicators for the assessment of nuclear power." *Energy* **36**(10): 6037–6057.

Stamford, L. and Azapagic, A. (2012). "Life cycle sustainability assessment of electricity options for the UK." *International Journal of Energy Research* **36**(14): 1263–1290.

Stirling, A. (2006). "Analysis, participation and power: Justification and closure in participatory multi-criteria analysis." *Land Use Policy* **23**: 95–107.

TEIAS. (2012). "Electricity generation and transmission statistics of Turkey." Retrieved 2 June 2014, from www.teias.gov.tr/TurkiyeElektrikIstatistikleri.aspx.

TKI (2012). *Lignite Sector Report of Turkey 2011*. Ankara, Ministry of Energy and Natural Resources, General Directorate of Turkish Coal Enterprises: 1–61.

TPAO (2011). *The Oil and Gas Sector Report of Turkey*. Ankara, Turkish Petroleum Corporation: 1–26.

Transport & Environment (2015). *Europe's Tax Deals for Diesel*. Brussels, Transport & Environment.

TUIK (2013). *National Greenhouse Gas Inventory Report, 1990–2012*. Ankara, Turkish Statistical Institute. http://web.ogm.gov.tr/diger/iklim/Dokumanlar/RAPORLAR/2012%20TURKEY%20NIR%20Part%20I%20(wo%20LULUCF).pdf

United Nations (2005). *2005 World Summit Outcome*, United Nations.

United Nations (2015). *Transforming Our World: The 2030 Agenda for Sustainable Development*, United Nations.

Volkart, K., Weidmann, N., Bauer, C. and Hirschberg, S. (2017). "Multi-criteria decision analysis of energy system transformation pathways: A case study for Switzerland." *Energy Policy* **106**: 155–168.

Wang, J.-J., Jing, Y.-Y., Zhang, C.-F. and Zhao, J.-H. (2009). "Review on multi-criteria decision analysis aid in sustainable energy decision-making." *Renewable and Sustainable Energy Reviews* 13(9): 2263–2278.

Ward, A. (2017). Ineos wins injunction against shale protesters. *Fimamcial Times (FT)*. London, UK.

WCED (1987). *Our Common Future*, Oxford University Press, Oxford.

The World Bank. (2016). *Intended Nationally Determined Contributions (INDCs)*. Retrieved August 2018, from The World Bank http://spappssecext.worldbank.org/sites/indc/Pages/INDCHome.aspx.

Yilmaz, S. A. (2014). "Yesil Isler ve Turkiye'de Yenilenebilir Enerji Alandaki Potansiyeli." *Sosyal Sektorler ve Koordinasyon Genel Mudurlugu*. Ankara, Sosyal Sektorler ve Koordinasyon Genel Mudurlugu, Kalkinma Bakanligi, Ankara.

Index

Printed in the United States
by Baker & Taylor Publisher Services